LET'S GO

■ THE RESOURCE FOR THE INDEPENDENT TRAVELER

"The guides are aimed not only at young budget travelers but at the indepedent traveler; a sort of streetwise cookbook for traveling alone."

—*The New York Times*

"Unbeatable; good sight-seeing advice; up-to-date info on restaurants, hotels, and inns; a commitment to money-saving travel; and a wry style that brightens nearly every page."

—*The Washington Post*

"Lighthearted and sophisticated, informative and fun to read. [Let's Go] helps the novice traveler navigate like a knowledgeable old hand."

—*Atlanta Journal-Constitution*

"A world-wise traveling companion—always ready with friendly advice and helpful hints, all sprinkled with a bit of wit."

—*The Philadelphia Inquirer*

■ THE BEST TRAVEL BARGAINS IN YOUR PRICE RANGE

"All the dirt, dirt cheap."

—*People*

"Anything you need to know about budget traveling is detailed in this book."

—*The Chicago Sun-Times*

"Let's Go follows the creed that you don't have to toss your life's savings to the wind to travel—unless you want to."

—*The Salt Lake Tribune*

■ REAL ADVICE FOR REAL EXPERIENCES

"The writers seem to have experienced every rooster-packed bus and lunar-surfaced mattress about which they write."

—*The New York Times*

"Value-packed, unbeatable, accurate, and comprehensive."

—*The Los Angeles Times*

"[Let's Go's] devoted updaters really walk the walk (and thumb the ride, and trek the trail). Learn how to fish, haggle, find work—anywhere."

—*Food & Wine*

LET'S GO PUBLICATIONS

TRAVEL GUIDES

Australia 8th edition
Austria & Switzerland 12th edition
Brazil 1st edition
Britain & Ireland 2005
California 10th edition
Central America 9th edition
Chile 2nd edition
China 5th edition
Costa Rica 2nd edition
Eastern Europe 2005
Ecuador 1st edition **NEW TITLE**
Egypt 2nd edition
Europe 2005
France 2005
Germany 12th edition
Greece 2005
Hawaii 3rd edition
India & Nepal 8th edition
Ireland 2005
Israel 4th edition
Italy 2005
Japan 1st edition
Mexico 20th edition
Middle East 4th edition
Peru 1st edition **NEW TITLE**
Puerto Rico 1st edition
South Africa 5th edition
Southeast Asia 9th edition
Spain & Portugal 2005
Thailand 2nd edition
Turkey 5th edition
USA 2005
Vietnam 1st edition **NEW TITLE**
Western Europe 2005

ROADTRIP GUIDE

Roadtripping USA **NEW TITLE**

ADVENTURE GUIDES

Alaska 1st edition
New Zealand **NEW TITLE**
Pacific Northwest **NEW TITLE**
Southwest USA 3rd edition

CITY GUIDES

Amsterdam 3rd edition
Barcelona 3rd edition
Boston 4th edition
London 2005
New York City 15th edition
Paris 13th edition
Rome 12th edition
San Francisco 4th edition
Washington, D.C. 13th edition

POCKET CITY GUIDES

Amsterdam
Berlin
Boston
Chicago
London
New York City
Paris
San Francisco
Venice
Washington, D.C.

LET'S GO

CHINA

SHELLEY JIANG EDITOR
SHELLEY CHEUNG ASSOCIATE EDITOR
FANNI LI ASSOCIATE EDITOR

RESEARCHER-WRITERS

SHERRY CHEN   LUCY F. V. LINDSEY
GARY COONEY   XIAO LINDA LIU
SEAN CREEHAN   THOMAS LOWE
A. JUSTINA HIERTA   ZHENZHEN LU
MEGHAN HOWARD   DARRYL WEE
          YINGZHEN ZHANG

BRIANA CUMMINGS MANAGING EDITOR
CLIFFORD EMMANUEL MAP EDITOR

ST. MARTIN'S PRESS ✕ NEW YORK

HELPING LET'S GO. If you want to share your discoveries, suggestions, or corrections, please drop us a line. We read every piece of correspondence, whether a postcard, a 10-page email, or a coconut. **Address mail to:**

> Let's Go: China
> 67 Mount Auburn Street
> Cambridge, MA 02138
> USA

Visit Let's Go at **http://www.letsgo.com,** or send email to:

> feedback@letsgo.com
> Subject: "Let's Go: China"

In addition to the invaluable travel advice our readers share with us, many are kind enough to offer their services as researchers or editors. Unfortunately, our charter enables us to employ only currently enrolled Harvard students.

CONTENTS

DISCOVER CHINA 1
When to Go 1
Things to Do 2
Suggested Itineraries 5

ESSENTIALS 9
Planning Your Trip 9
Safety and Health 23
Getting to China 34
Getting Around China 43
Keeping in Touch 49
Accommodations 55
Specific Concerns 65
Other Resources 70

LIFE AND TIMES 73
Land 73
Flora and Fauna 73
History 74
People 84
Culture 93
Additional Resources 102

ALTERNATIVES TO TOURISM .. 104
A Philosophy for Travelers 104
Volunteering 105
Studying 112

BEIJING AND THE NORTH COAST 119
BEIJING 北京 119
Great Wall 长城 166
TIANJIN 天津 169
HEBEI 河北 176
Shijiazhuang 石家庄 177
Chengde 承德 181
Shanhaiguan 山海关 187
SHANDONG 山东 191
Ji'nan 济南 191
Tai'an 泰安 196
Qufu 曲阜 203
Qingdao 青岛 207
Yantai 烟台 216
Weihai 威海 219

THE NORTHEAST 223
HEILONGJIANG 黑龙江 223
Harbin 哈尔滨 224
Qiqihar 齐齐哈尔 232
JILIN 吉林 240
Changchun 长春 240
Jilin City 吉林市 244
Yanji 延吉 247

Changbaishan 长白山 249
LIAONING 辽宁 254
Shenyang 沈阳 254
Dandong 丹东 258
Dalian 大连 261

CENTRAL CHINA 267
SHAANXI 陕西 267
Xi'an 西安 269
Huashan 华山 279
Yan'an 延安 281
HENAN 河南 285
Zhengzhou 郑州 285
Luoyang 洛阳 290
Kaifeng 开封 296
Anyang 安阳 301
SHANXI 山西 303
Taiyuan 太原 304
Wutaishan 五台山 309
Datong 大同 311
INNER MONGOLIA 内蒙古 316
Hohhot 呼和浩特 316
Hohhot Grasslands 草原 322
Baotou 包头 323
Dongsheng 东胜 327
Manzhouli 满洲里 329

SHANGHAI AND THE YANGZI DELTA 333
SHANGHAI 上海 333
JIANGSU 江苏 357
Nanjing 南京 357
Suzhou 苏州 366
Wuxi 无锡 375
Zhenjiang 镇江 381
Yangzhou 扬州 385
ZHEJIANG 浙江 389
Hangzhou 杭州 390
Shaoxing 绍兴 398
Ningbo 宁波 402
Putuoshan 普陀山 406

YANGZI BASIN 412
ANHUI 安徽 412
Hefei 合肥 412
Tunxi 屯溪 419
Tangkou 汤口 422
Huangshan 黄山 424
Jiuhuashan 九华山 429
JIANGXI 江西 432
Nanchang 南昌 433
Jingdezhen 景德镇 436
Lushan 庐山 439

Jinggangshan 井冈山 444
HUNAN 湖南 447
Changsha 长沙 447
Zhangjiajie 张家界 456
HUBEI 湖北 459
Wuhan 武汉 459
Yichang 宜昌 465
Shennongjia 神农架 468
Xiangfan 襄樊 470
Wudangshan 武当山 471

SOUTH COAST **476**
FUJIAN 福建 476
Fuzhou 福州 477
Wuyishan 武夷山 483
Quanzhou 泉州 487
Xiamen 厦门 491
GUANGDONG 广东 498
Guangzhou 广洲 498
Zhongshan 中山 510
Zhaoqing 肇庆 512
Shaoguan 韶关 514
Zhuhai 珠海 517
Shenzhen 深圳 520
Shantou 汕头 524
Chaozhou 潮州 527
Meizhou 梅洲 529
HAINAN 海南 533
Haikou 海口 533
Sanya 三亚 537

HONG KONG AND MACAU .. **542**
HONG KONG, SAR 香港 543
Kowloon 九龙 554
Hong Kong Island 香港岛 564
New Territories 新界 575
Lantau Island 大屿山 579
MACAU 澳門 583

THE SOUTHWEST **597**
GUANGXI 广西 597
Nanning 南宁 600
Guilin 桂林 605
Yangshuo 阳朔 611
Longsheng 龙胜 616
Beihai 北海 619
GUIZHOU 贵州 623
Guiyang 贵阳 623
Anshun 安顺 627
Kaili 凯里 631
Kaili Minority Villages 634
Zunyi 遵义 638
YUNNAN 云南 640
Kunming 昆明 641
Xishuangbanna 西双版纳 652
Jinghong 景洪 653
Damenglong 大勐龙 660

Baoshan 保山 and Dehong 德宏 662
Tengchong 腾冲 664
Ruili 瑞丽 666
Dali 大理 668
Lijiang 丽江 674
Tiger Leaping Gorge 虎跳峡 679
Zhongdian 中甸 682
Deqin 德钦 686

SICHUAN AND CHONGQING ... 689
SICHUAN 四川 689
Chengdu 成都 689
Leshan 乐山 703
Emeishan 峨眉山 706
Kangding 康定 714
Jiuzhaigou 九寨沟 716
Songpan 松潘 720
CHONGQING 重庆 727
THREE GORGES 三峡 734

THE NORTHWEST **741**
NINGXIA 宁夏 741
Yinchuan 银川 744
Zhongwei 中卫 748
GANSU 甘肃 752
Lanzhou 兰州 752
Xiahe 夏河 760
Tianshui 天水 765
Zhangye 张掖 769
Jiayuguan 嘉峪关 772
Dunhuang 敦煌 777
XINJIANG 新疆 782
Ürümqi 乌鲁木齐 783
Altai Prefecture 阿勒泰地区 789
Burqin 布尔津 791
Yining 伊宁 793
Turpan 吐鲁番 796
Korla 库尔勒 802
Kuqa 库车 804
Kashgar 喀什 807
The Karakorum Highway 812
Hotan 和田 815
QINGHAI 青海 819
Xining 西宁 819
Golmud 格尔木 824

TIBET **827**
Lhasa 拉萨 837
Tsetang 泽当 851
FRIENDSHIP HIGHWAY 853
Gyantse 江孜 855
Shigatse 日喀则 858
Mt. Everest 珠穆郎玛峰 862

APPENDIX **866**
INDEX **880**
MAP INDEX **896**

HOW TO USE THIS BOOK

Welcome to *Let's Go: China!* While Mao's little red book this is not, it will guide you through your travels with sage advice and tips from the road. Keep us close, and we promise we won't purge you.

INTRODUCTION. First up is **Discover**—the best of China, short and sweet. **Suggested Itineraries** takes you through the not-to-be-missed with six different routes. Read the **Essentials** before you go, for the nitty-gritty on visas, vaccines, transportation, and more. **Life and Times** gives an overview of China's history, culture, art, and food. Finally, the **Alternatives to Tourism** chapter offers travelers the chance to take another look at China—through the eyes of a volunteer, teacher, or student.

COVERAGE. Like the recent economic progress of China itself, our coverage moves from east to west. We begin in Beijing, swing up to the northeast, curve down into central, coastal, and southern China, and end in Tibet. Each chapter is a geographical region, with further divisions by province or autonomous region. The **black tabs** in the margin help you navigate between chapters quickly and easily.

GETTING AROUND. The transportation section at the beginning of each city lists various destinations, each followed by parentheses containing the trip's duration, frequency, and price. Major cities list options to other big cities and transportation hubs throughout China; smaller towns list nearby regional destinations as well as the nearest hubs. If you don't see the city you're looking for, try looking up the transportation listings for that city as well. If only one price for train tickets is listed, this is almost always the hard seat price; if the trip is longer than 6hr., then the price is for the hard sleeper.

CHINESE, PLEASE. We provide the pinyin romanization (zhōngguó) and Chinese characters (中国) for every city, train station, major street, establishment, sight, etc. The most common phrases (Bank of China, PSB, etc.) are listed in the appendix rather than in every city. The intrepid can try pronouncing the name (consult the **Pinyin Pronunciation Guide**, p. 867), but pointing at the characters works fine as well. We've also added characters for streets and landmarks to all of our **maps**, so if you're lost, show a friendly passerby the map, and simply point and gesture.

PRICE DIVERSITY. Our researchers list establishments in order of value from best to worst. Our absolute favorites are denoted by the Let's Go thumb's up (�). Since the best value does not always mean the cheapest price, we have also incorporated a system of price ranges in the guide (p. xvi).

LAST BUT NOT LEAST. The appendix has a **glossary** of frequently encountered words, handy measurement **conversions**, a climate chart, an extensive ✎ **Mandarin phrasebook** with pinyin, English, and characters for each entry, and select phrases in Cantonese, Tibetan, and Uighur.

A NOTE TO OUR READERS. The information for this book was gathered by *Let's Go* researchers from May through August of 2004. Each listing is based on one researcher's opinion, formed during his or her visit at a particular time. Those traveling at other times may have different experiences since prices, dates, hours, and conditions are always subject to change. You are urged to check the facts presented in this book beforehand to avoid inconvenience and surprises.

RESEARCHER-WRITERS

Sherry Chen 开心果   *Northeast and Beijing*

Roaming the rustic expanses of the vast northeast, Sherry and her infectious enthusiasm never wavered, as she sent back countless tales of her quirky adventures. She hugged baby Siberian tigers in Changbaishan, galloped into the sunset in the Hulun Buir grasslands, battled uncooperative PSB officers everywhere, befriended a giant string bean, and ended her epic journey in Beijing, face to face with Chairman Mao himself. China hasn't recovered from Sherry.

Gary Cooney 孙悟空   *South and East Coasts*

After conquering Mt. Olympus for *Let's Go: Greece 2003*, Gary leapt back into the fray, hopping across no fewer than seven mountains. Along the way, our kind-hearted Irish philanthropist sang revolutionary songs with locals, fended off hungry monkeys, and even steeled himself to sample a wiggly sea worm, before finally finding peace on the beaches of Xiamen. His stories kept us laughing, and his witty writing left us with little to do and much to admire.

Sean Creehan 龙卷风   *Southwest*

Sean was nothing short of amazing, as he blazed through his route with speed, thoroughness, and fabulous insight. Meeting everything China threw at him with unflappable calm, Sean trekked the ravines of Tiger Leaping Gorge and hiked through mud and pouring rain. At the end of the day, he still found time to kick back in backpacker cafes and down a beer or two. Next year, he'll be studying at Beijing University, with a plentiful supply of Yanjing by his side.

A. Justina Hierta 大漠战士   *Central China and Inner Mongolia*

Hailing from Ann Arbor, Michigan, this ravishing Gemini planted roots far, far away from home. Justina has lived in Hong Kong, studied in Beijing, researched in Rwanda, and left footprints all over China and Southeast Asia. With a travel log that thick, there was no challenge this hardy researcher wasn't up for. From sacred mountains and rolling grasslands, to singing sand dunes and ancient tombs (and more tombs!), Justina took it all in elegant stride.

Meghan Howard 青藏女侠   *Sichuan, Qinghai, and Tibet*

With her homesteader roots in Minnesota, Meghan always kept in stride with her curiosity. She learned Sanskrit, Tibetan, and Chinese to study Buddhism more deeply, breathing in its culture along with mountain air and the zing of grazing yaks. After mock-marrying a local, she jetted off to the true love of her life, Tibet. Not even a broken ankle could keep her from visiting monastery after monastery and delivering clear, precise copy from the rugged highlands.

Lucy F. V. Lindsey 香港小姐   *Hong Kong, Macau, and the South Coast*

In the words of the amazing Lucy, "China's in my blood, and I have to go back." And we're sure glad she did. A photographer, musician, and artist, Lucy has an eye for the uncanny and the eloquence to put it into beautiful prose. Our sassy Cambridge, Massachusetts native took southern China by storm, weaving through karst in Guilin, staring down monkeys in Longsheng, picking up *dinero* in Macau, and unleashing her smooth grooves in Guangzhou and Hong Kong.

Xiao Linda Liu 四川辣妹子   *Beijing and the North Coast*

Unlike the ultra-spicy food of her hometown of Chengdu, Linda is quite possibly the sweetest girl her editors have ever met. Meticulous and with a humorous voice all her own, Linda dazzled us with her writing, hard work, and unwavering cheerfulness. She breezed through Qingdao, sampled fine food in Beijing, and scrambled up the crumbling Wild Wall. An aspiring photographer, she showered her editors with beautiful photographs and gifts from the road.

Thomas Lowe 流浪歌星   *Northwest*

Our self-proclaimed "karaoke king of China" plunged into the northwest with unflagging enthusiasm and optimism. Tom made friends everywhere he went, danced and sang at Uighur weddings, and charmed his way into the hearts of cows and monks alike. This British boy slid down giant desert dunes, rode (and made friends with) camels, and sent back copy mirroring his irrepressible glee. Wherever he goes, we're sure the world won't be able to resist Tom.

Zhenzhen Lu 璇仙   *Northern Sichuan, Yangzi River Basin*

Artist, musician, writer, archaeologist, dreamer, and now a talented RW as well—what more could Zhenzhen be? Shanghainese by birth and New Yorker by upbringing, Zhenzhen scaled mountains with monks, narrowly escaped death, and turned down an offer to study *wushu* at Wudangshan, all so she could send back beautifully written copy to her appreciative editors. Zhenzhen thanks her family (Mom, Dad, WW), relatives, and friends for all their support.

Darryl Wee 文武状元   *Guangxi and Hainan*

Darryl's friend once described him as a post-modern post-intellectual, though of course, he escapes all such categories. A master of the written word, Darryl speaks four versions of English, including "Queen's" and faux-American, along with Mandarin, Cantonese, and French. Armed with these seven dialects, and grit left over from his Singaporean military training, Darryl took his route with flourish, ending at the "End of the Earth" on the island paradise of Hainan.

Yingzhen "Nancy" Zhang 小蝴蝶   *Shanghai and the Yangzi Delta*

A researcher for *Let's Go: Italy 2004*, Nancy eagerly grabbed her backpack to return to life on the road. Instead of exotic destinations, Nancy traveled to her home, the Shanghai region, to write about what she knows best, readily sharing the beautiful (West Lake), the bustling (shopping on Nanjing Lu), and the bizarre (eyelash perms) in one of China's most cosmopolitan areas. Spirited and energetic, Nancy never failed to draw forth amazed exclamations!

CONTRIBUTING WRITERS

Victoria Drake helped plan a new national park in Yunnan in 2002.

Josh Levin is a *Let's Go* veteran and has traveled Tibet and Xinjiang.

Emma Nothmann has done just about every job possible at Let's Go, from Researcher to Editor to Publishing Director of the 2005 series.

ABOUT LET'S GO

GUIDES FOR THE INDEPENDENT TRAVELER

At Let's Go, we see every trip as the chance of a lifetime. If your dream is to grab a machete and forge through the jungles of Brazil, we can take you there. If you'd rather bask in the Riviera sun at a beachside cafe, we'll set you a table. We write for readers who know that there's more to travel than sharing double deckers with tourists and who believe that travel can change both themselves and the world—whether they plan to spend six days in London or six months in Latin America. We'll show you just how far your money can go, and prove that the greatest limitation on your adventures is not your wallet, but your imagination. After all, traveling close to the ground lets you interact more directly with the places and people you've gone to see, making for the most authentic experience.

BEYOND THE TOURIST EXPERIENCE

To help you gain a deeper connection with the places you travel, our researchers give you the heads-up on both world-renowned and off-the-beaten-track attractions, sights, and destinations. They engage with the local culture, writing features on regional cuisine, local festivals, and hot political issues. We've also opened our pages to respected writers and scholars to hear their takes on the countries and regions we cover, and asked travelers who have worked, studied, or volunteered abroad to contribute first-person accounts of their experiences. We've also increased our coverage of responsible travel and expanded each guide's Alternatives to Tourism chapter to share more ideas about how to give back to local communities and learn about the places you travel.

FORTY-FIVE YEARS OF WISDOM

Let's Go got its start in 1960, when a group of creative and well-traveled students compiled their experience and advice into a 20-page mimeographed pamphlet, which they gave to travelers on charter flights to Europe. Four and a half decades later, we've expanded to cover six continents and all kinds of travel—while retaining our founders' adventurous attitude toward the world. Our guides are still researched and written entirely by students on shoestring budgets, experienced travelers who know that train strikes, stolen luggage, food poisoning, and marriage proposals are all part of a day's work. This year, we're expanding our coverage of South America and Southeast Asia, with brand-new *Let's Go: Ecuador*, *Let's Go: Peru*, and *Let's Go: Vietnam*. Our adventure guide series is growing, too, with the addition of *Let's Go: Pacific Northwest Adventure* and *Let's Go: New Zealand Adventure*. And we're immensely excited about our new *Let's Go: Roadtripping USA*—two years, eight routes, and sixteen researchers and editors have put together a travel guide like none other.

THE LET'S GO COMMUNITY

More than just a travel guide company, Let's Go is a community. Our small staff comes together because of our shared passion for travel and our desire to help other travelers see the world. We love it when our readers become part of the Let's Go community as well—when you travel, drop us a postcard (67 Mt. Auburn St., Cambridge, MA 02138, USA) or send us an e-mail (feedback@letsgo.com) to tell us about your adventures and discoveries.

For more information, visit us online: www.letsgo.com.

ACKNOWLEDGMENTS

LET'S GO

TEAM PRC THANKS: The greatest ▨RW team *ever*—without you this book would be nothing. We heart you. Brie for gentle guidance and hyphens. Cliff for being tall and dashing (and dashing maps). Proofers for more hyphens. Jeremy for coffee and letting us menace him. Anne, Sarah, Dan, Marcel, and Leigh for late-night company and snacks. Jesse and Colin for insanity. Eastern Europe for barbarian hordes. Jackie Chan for fish.

SHELLEY THANKS: Beta and Gamma—for telling me about Huang Fei Hong, wit, and laughter. Cliff, Maria, Feng, Elizabeth, and everyone else in the "committee" who tried to pry me from the Go (and sometimes you even succeeded!). Kathy, Nancy, Liz, and Alison, my fab four. ▨ Toscanini's, for keeping me sane. My parents, 爷爷姥姥, 小姨小姨夫, 桐桐 for everything and more.

SHELLEY C. THANKS: Alpha and Gamma for communal giggling, martial arts prowess, and oh-so-much name confusion. Anne and Barb for Roswell, food, and love. ▨ Erin, Nina, and David for being fabs. Blockies and Greenough Crew plus—you know who you are. Buddy for emotional support. Jay Chou and Nic Tse for happy tunes. Julie and Annie, 'cuz I have to (wink). 媽咪 for 湯水 and always worrying.

FANNI THANKS: Alpha for introducing real caffine, Beta for sandwich-guessing, and both for *dimming* my *sum* with full out silliness. Thanks to Yaokai for translating crazy Sichuanese, Zi for movies, Natasha for jumping fences, Fat Fat and Dina for keeping mice out, and everyone in Canada for fun, mahjong and love, esp. Shirls. Finally, mum and dad for poker and ▨ restaurant quality home-cooking.

CLIFF THANKS: All of the China RWs for their ceaseless diligence amid back alleys, mountain tops, and desert basins. Adobe and Dell for providing the tools of my craft. Mom for the impromptu visits and gallons of pasta salad and pilau. Alpha, Beta, and Gamma, the proprietors of Mao's Happy Pagoda, for loving China (troublesome maps and all).

Editor Shelley "Alpha" Jiang
Associate Editors Shelley "Beta" Cheung, Fanni "Gamma" Li
Managing Editor Briana Cummings
Map Editor Clifford Emmanuel
Typesetter Melissa Rudolph

Publishing Director
Emma Nothmann
Editor-in-Chief
Teresa Elsey
Production Manager
Adam R. Perlman
Cartography Manager
Elizabeth Halbert Peterson
Design Manager
Amelia Aos Showalter
Editorial Managers
Briana Cummings, Charlotte Douglas, Ella M. Steim, Joel August Steinhaus, Lauren Truesdell, Christina Zaroulis
Financial Manager
R. Kirkie Maswoswe
Marketing and Publicity Managers
Stef Levner, Leigh Pascavage
Personnel Manager
Jeremy Todd
Low-Season Manager
Clay H. Kaminsky
Production Associate
Victoria Esquivel-Korsiak
IT Director
Matthew DePetro
Web Manager
Rob Dubbin
Associate Web Manager
Patrick Swieskowski
Web Content Manager
Tor Krever
Research and Development Consultant
Jennifer O'Brien
Office Coordinators
Stephanie Brown, Elizabeth Peterson

Director of Advertising Sales
Elizabeth S. Sabin
Senior Advertising Associates
Jesse R. Loffler, Francisco A. Robles, Zoe M. Savitsky
Advertising Graphic Designer
Christa Lee-Chuvala

President
Ryan M. Geraghty
General Manager
Robert B. Rombauer
Assistant General Manager
Anne E. Chisholm

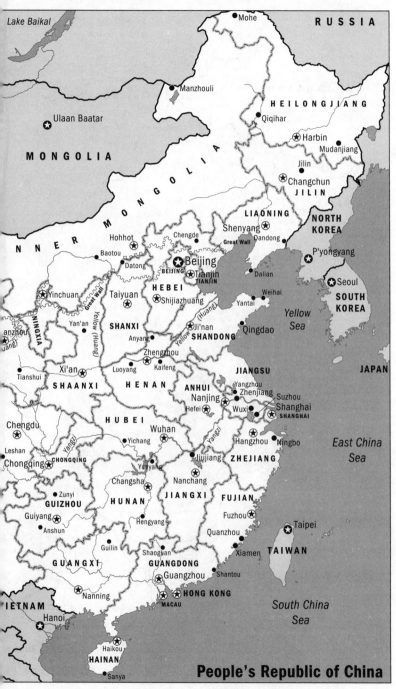

People's Republic of China

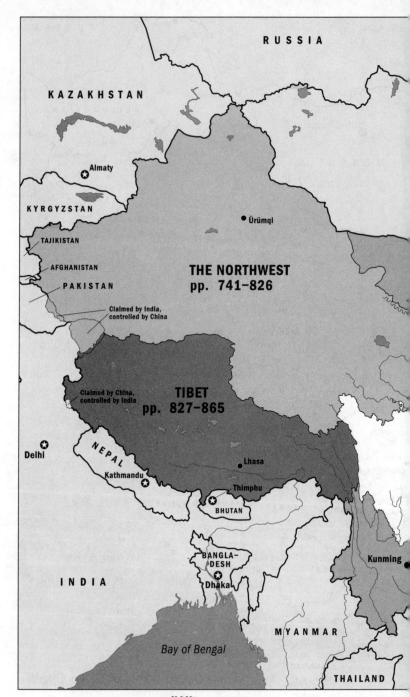

China: Chapters

THE NORTHEAST
pp. 223–266

CENTRAL CHINA
pp. 267–332

BEIJING AND
THE NORTH COAST
pp. 119–222

SICHUAN AND
CHONGQING
pp. 689–740

YANGZI BASIN
pp. 412–475

SHANGHAI AND
THE YANGZI DELTA
pp. 333–411

THE SOUTHWEST
pp. 597–688

SOUTH
COAST
pp. 476–541

HONG KONG
AND MACAU
pp. 542–596

RUSSIA

MONGOLIA

NORTH KOREA

SOUTH KOREA

JAPAN

TAIWAN

VIETNAM

LAOS

Ulaan Baatar

Harbin

Changchun

Shenyang

Great Wall

P'yongyang

Seoul

Hohhot

Beijing

Tianjin

Yinchuan

Taiyuan

Lanzhou

Qingdao

Yellow
Sea

Xi'an

Hefei

Nanjing

Shanghai

Chengdu

Wuhan

Hangzhou

Chongqing

East China
Sea

Guiyang

Guangzhou

Taipei

South China
Sea

Hanoi

Haikou

0   400 miles
0   400 kilometers

PRICE RANGES >> CHINA

Our researchers list establishments in order of value from best to worst; our favorites are denoted by the Let's Go thumbs-up (🖐). Since the best value is not always the cheapest price, however, we have also incorporated a system of price ranges, based on a rough expectation of what you will spend. For **accommodations,** we base our range on the cheapest price for which a single traveler can stay for one night. For **restaurants** and other dining establishments, we estimate the average amount a traveler will spend. The table below tells you what you will *typically* find in China at the corresponding price range; keep in mind that no system can allow for every individual establishment's quirks.

ACCOMMODATIONS	RANGE	WHAT YOU'RE *LIKELY* TO FIND
❶	under Y80	In big cities, dorm rooms or dorm-style rooms. In mid-level cities or rural areas, this may also be a no-frills hotel room, either a single or a double. Expect communal baths. Bring your own towels.
❷	Y81-180	A basic hotel room, usually with communal bath and limited amenities. Typically located near the train station. In big cities, this may be a nice room in a hostel.
❸	Y181-250	A standard room with a private bath. Should have decent amenities, such as phone, A/C, and TV. Breakfast may be included in the price of the room.
❹	Y251-350	Similar to 3, but may have more amenities or be in a more touristed area.
❺	Y351+	Large upscale hotels fully armed with luxuries, or a hotel in a heavily-touristed region. If it's a 5 and it doesn't have the perks you want, you've paid too much.

FOOD	RANGE	WHAT YOU'RE *LIKELY* TO FIND
❶	under Y8	Street vendors, cafeteria-style food courts, snack stands, night market stalls, or small dumpling and noodle shops. Cheap and quick.
❷	Y9-30	A sit-down meal in a restaurant, typically simple and family-style. Vegetable dishes run about Y6-15; meat dishes will cost more.
❸	Y31-60	Entrees are more expensive, but chances are, you're paying for decor and ambience. Or this may be an overpriced restaurant in a tourist area. Seafood, duck, and other options.
❹	Y61-100	Exotic cuisine such as seafood, snake, and other delicacies. You're probably not eating dumplings here.
❺	Y101+	Expect delicious food elaborately prepared with great service in a well-appointed, perhaps famous, restaurant; otherwise you're paying for nothing more than hype.

DISCOVER
CHINA

Travelers come to China for many things—ancient palaces, the Great Wall, cups of tea, mountains, deserts, and musing Buddhas. To say that they find what they were looking for would be an understatement. China has a thousand faces, from the extravagantly in-your-face new to the hauntingly old, and guessing what you'll see next is like trying to predict the latest fashions in Shanghai. The country won't simply meet your expectations of narrow cobblestoned *hútòng*, old men smoking a pipe over a game of *mahjong*, or even rice paddies dotted with water buffalo and workers wearing straw hats. The *mahjong* games are still there, of course, and the water buffalo still wallow, but as often as not the ivory (and plastic) chips are played out to the beat of synthesized pop, the tiny alleys have grown up to become broad paved avenues humming with traffic, and the peasant whips out a cell phone to call up her sister in the city.

Five thousand years of history haven't slowed this vast breadth of peoples and landscapes down one whit. The same fervor that led the country through revolution after revolution now propels China irrevocably into the future. Nor has China forgotten to look back: its millennia of history and tradition are as much a source of pride as the latest growth reports and gleaming new highrises. But China is not without growing pains, and part of its fascination is the neverending balancing act of past and present, with one sometimes shoved aside for the other. The twang of *er hu* strings jangles against the buzz of construction, proud red walls that once gazed out upon imperial processions now watch over neon-lit streets, and the brief respite of tranquility on a mountain top is suddenly broken by an eager crowd. No matter what you think China is, you won't find it in one place or in one single moment. China has a thousand faces, and it's going to show you all of them.

CHINA FACTS AND FIGURES

POPULATION: 1.3 billion

LAND AREA: 9.6 million km²

POP. DENSITY: 135.4 people per km²

NUMBER OF CELL PHONE USERS: 300 million

NUMBER OF SMS TEXT MESSAGES SENT PER YEAR: 220 billion

VARIETIES OF TEA GROWN: over 1200

AMOUNT OF TEA CONSUMED PER YEAR: 17.4 billion liters

AMOUNT OF BEER PRODUCED PER YEAR: 23 million tons

NUMBER OF PEOPLE PER YEAR INJURED BY EXPLODING BEER BOTTLES: 470

WHEN TO GO

There's never a wrong time to go to China. Winters may be bitterly cold in the north, but the **Chinese New Year** makes it a particularly festive, exciting time. China's peak travel season usually kicks in around early July, and not even the hot summers deter people from taking to the kilometers of rail. Hotel prices rise with

DISCOVER

the temperature, budget rooms vanish at an alarming pace, train tickets are quickly snapped up, and yellow-hatted tour groups march out in full force. Come September and cooler seasons, students return to school and peace reigns over mountains and temples, making early **autumn** and late **spring** some of the best times to begin your rambles in China.

The **rainy season** lasts from May to July, longer in southern China. The area south of the Yangzi River is affected the most, but even cities as far north as Beijing can get pelted by sudden heavy rainstorms whipping up out of the blue. In June through August, seasonal **flooding** is a serious concern, in particular along the Yangzi and Yellow Rivers. Floods and landslides due to heavy summer rains can make transportation treacherous, especially in rural areas, with their dirt roads, rickety bridges, and unreliable vehicles. Summer **monsoons** unleash deluges of rain in southern Yunnan, Guangxi, and Guangdong provinces, as well as in Hong Kong and Macau. **Typhoons,** or hurricanes, are the strongest in late summer and early autumn, lashing the south coasts with vigor. Taking all this into consideration, late-October through April may be the best time to visit China's south coasts, where winters are mild and dry.

Weather concerns aside, millions of Chinese travel or visit family and friends during **holidays** and **festivals,** resulting in price hikes, fully-booked hotels, sold-out train, bus, and plane tickets, and crowded sights. The major holidays occur in the days leading up to and after the Chinese New Year (late Jan.-Feb.), International Labor Day (May 1), People's Liberation Army Day (Aug. 1), and National Day (Oct. 1). For a complete list of the festivals in China, see p. 101.

THINGS TO DO
THE WAY OF THE BACKPACKER

Story-rich but currency-poor, backpackers flock to cheap and scenic towns in every country. The southwest of China is a mecca for footloose travelers, with distinctive natural splendor, tiny villages, colorful minority cultures, and plenty of opportunities for independent exploration and trekking. China's classic backpacker town, **Yangshuo** (p. 611) is well-known for its cafe-crowded "West Street" and the cheerful company of friendly travelers, always ready to barrel off into the wilds or down another beer or two. Its counterpart in Yunnan province, **Dali** (p. 668), breathes much of the same fresh-faced, laid-back air. Longer treks to tropical **Xishuangbanna** (p. 652) in southern Yunnan pass through rainforest, *stupas*, rice paddies, and villages of the Dai minority. North of Dali, backpackers take off to **Lijiang** (p. 674), less a city than a picturesque maze of canals and waterways. From here, the majestic snowy peaks, sapphire lakes, and gorges of northern Yunnan are only hours away. For those wanting to sample life in the big city, Shanghai's **Nanjing Xi Lu** and **French Concession** (p. 350), Beijing's **Sanlitun** (p. 159), Hong Kong's **Lan Kwai Fong** (p. 572), and much of **Guangdong province** (p. 498) welcome more permanent foreign vagabonds.

OFF (AND ON) THE BEATEN PATH

With China's considerable population, traveling inevitably becomes something of a group affair on a massive scale. Don't let the crowds faze you—popular isn't necessarily bad. In fact, China's most swarming sights are also jaw-dropping gorgeous. But there are also swathes of (relatively) unfrequented country out there, as beautiful as the well-traveled destinations. Tiny Miao, Dong, and other minority

⚑LET'S GO PICKS

BEST HIGHS: The forests and snow-capped giants above **Yining** (p. 793) or **Karakul Lake** (p. 812). The myriad skyscrapers rising above **Hong Kong Island** (p. 568). And to top them all, **Everest Base Camp** (p. 862). Enough said.

BEST LOWS: The scalding sands of **Turpan Depression,** the second-lowest point in the world. The world's lowest glacier at **Meilixueshan** (p. 687).

BEST WAYS TO START THE MORNING: Watch the sun rise above the mists from **Huangshan**'s peaks (p. 424). Mingle with tourists and PLA soldiers at the dawn flag-raising ceremony in **Tian'anmen Square** (p. 142).

BEST WAYS TO END THE DAY: Chug brandy in **Tunxi** (p. 419)—just avoid the snake at the bottom of the bottle. Guzzle Tsingtao beer at the brewery in **Qingdao** (p. 207). Join the crowds in tai chi or karaoke in the parks and plazas.

BEST WAY TO TEMPT FATE: Trekking at steeply plunging **Tiger Leaping Gorge** (p. 679). Footing it across the **Taklimakan Desert** (p. 804).

BEST PLACE TO HANG WITH BATS: **Wuyishan's** Thread of Sky (p. 487).

BEST PLACE TO CUDDLE UP: Hug a giant panda at **Wolong Nature Reserve** (p. 702).

BEST TEA: Walk through the sprawling fields of **Longjing tea plantations,** west of Hangzhou (p. 397). Sip "silver needle" tea while batting away thirsty monkeys on Yueyang's **Junshan Island** (p. 455). Inhale the pungent scent of yak-butter tea wafting through the alleys in **Lhasa** (p. 837).

BEST BARGAINS: Shop the **Hotan Bazaar** (p. 817), Lhasa's **Barkhor Market** (p. 844), Hong Kong's **Golden Mile** (p. 562), and Dali's **village markets** (p. 672).

villages scatter around the remote **Kaili** (p. 634) countryside. Raft down the **Wuyang River** (p. 637) instead of being herded down the Yangzi River. Away from the tourist- and backpacker-saturated Guilin and Yangshuo, keep company with wallowing water buffalo as you hike over **Longsheng's** terraced hills (p. 616). Nothing can quite compare to the piercing peaks of the perennially busy **Huangshan** (p. 424), but the more secluded **Wuyishan** (p. 483) is just as lovely and enchanting in its own right, with jutting cliffs and flowing streams. Avoid the sweltering crush of bodies on Badaling Great Wall; the wilder, unrestored **Simatai** (p. 168) and **Huanghuacheng** (p. 168) is worth the distance. Strike out into northwest China's stark expanse of sand and sky and explore the Silk Road towns of **Kashgar** (p. 807) and **Kuqa** (p. 804), the Tibetan-style village of **Xiahe** (p. 760), and the **Yili River** region (p. 793) in the far north. Safely tucked within a bastion of peaks and glaciers in northern Yunnan and western Sichuan, **Deqin** (p. 686), **Kangding** (p. 714), and **Moxi** (p. 712) have yet to attract hordes of visitors to their magnificent landscape.

SKYSCRAPER HIGH

Bigger, faster, glitzier—all of China's cities are on the bumpy road to modernization, egged on by the clatter of construction, the hiccup of car horns, and the beat of the latest Canto-pop hit. Where once narrow *hútòngs* and stately red-walled mansions defined the Chinese cityscape, skyscrapers now rapidly leap up to dazzle the night sky. Yet these cities are far more than your average metropolis, and a walk through the streets reveals the real city behind the hype. Join the children flying kites in Tian'anmen Square in the heart of **Beijing** (p. 119), or ascend the white marble steps that only emperors could tread in the Forbidden City. Tilt your head up to admire the fancifully crowned high-rises of **Shanghai** (p. 333), then enjoy a

TOP TEN LIST

BEST PLACES TO STAGE A MARTIAL ARTS FILM

1. Fight gripping duels with fellow martial arts masters on the treacherous edge of the cliffs of **Huashan Mountain** (p. 279).

2. Lightly leap from treetop to treetop in the **Bamboo Sea** (p. 726), without disturbing the snoozing and snacking pandas below.

3. Hightail it down the crowded streets of **Kowloon** (p. 554) a la Jackie Chan, deftly avoiding oncoming traffic.

4. Race across a vast expanse of sand upon your trusty camel, with a legion of barbarians at your back in the **Gobi Desert** (p. 798).

5. Battle your way across rushing rapids, as you balance on top of the waterfalls of **Jiuzhaigou** (p. 716)—don't slip and fall!

6. Go up against the fearless fighting monks of **Shaolin Monastery** (p. 289), the seat of southern martial prowess.

7. Recover your inner *qi* meditating in the caves above **Chimpu Hermitage** (p. 851).

8. Plot assassinations with mysterious women in a dimly lit, smoky bar of 1930s **Shanghai** (p. 333).

9. Ride with the Mongols upon the endless grasslands of **Hulun Buir** p. 331), then kick back and chug mare's milk wine by a bonfire.

10. Turn a quiet sip of tea into a table-flipping, chopstick-brandishing battle in a teahouse by the **West Lake** (p. 390).

balmy evening along the colorfully lit Bund, its concession-era buildings exuding Old World charm. Shop by day in the energetic street markets of **Hong Kong's** Kowloon (p. 554) and dance the night away at trendy Lan Kwai Fong. Beyond these spotlight cities, other urban centers tantalize visitors with more subtle pleasures: the tea gardens, parks, and spicy cuisine of **Chengdu** (p. 689); **Qingdao's** (p. 207) sandy beaches and world-famous beer; the terracotta warriors and ancient tombs of historic **Xi'an** (p. 269); flower-bedecked **Kunming** (p. 641) with its minority cultures and genuine, pleasant atmosphere; and the seaside grace, colonial architecture, and cosmopolitan flair of **Xiamen** (p. 491).

NATURAL HIGH

Adventurers and nature-lovers take note: ragged, piercing peaks, grasslands stretching horizon to horizon, pristine highland lakes, forests, glacial mountain ranges, and deserts all await your exploration. Though the independent hiker may be disappointed by the paved, well-traveled trails of some of China's most famous (and gorgeous) national parks and wildernesses, those willing to strike out on their own can find a growing number of opportunities for thrillseekers in the great outdoors. The vast sand dunes in **Dunhuang** (p. 777) and **Zhongwei** (p. 748) become impromptu playgrounds for tobogganing, parasailing, gliding, camel rides, and camping in the desert. Forget the tour groups and test your mettle against the untrammeled trails of **Zhangjiajie** (p. 456), an otherworldly wilderness of steeply plunging ravines and twisting pinnacles of stone. Few ever find their way into **Shennongjia** (p. 468), but those that do discover untamed tangles of forest and astounding ecological diversity. An adventure-seekers' wonderland, **Sichuan** province offers deep foliage, clear waters, and snow-topped peaks, reminding visitors that the lofty Tibetan Plateau is only slightly further west. Marvel at the breathtaking lakes and gullies of **Jiuzhaigou** (p. 716), then embark upon a horse trek in **Songpan** (p. 720) up mountainsides and through grasslands scattered with wildflowers. Far in the northeast, **Changbaishan** (p. 249) is a hiker's best bet for rigorous climbs up mountains and rocks to a deep volcanic lake. Clichés aside, you can always ride off into the sunset upon the wind-ruffled grasslands of **Inner Mongolia** (p. 322) and sleep under a yurt, with the stars twinkling overhead. The truly daring can venture to the jagged **Karakorum** and **Pamir Mountains** (p. 812) on the border with Pakistan, where the mountains soar impossibly high and the lakes reflect the skies.

SPIRITUAL HIGH

From holy mountains to ancient grottoes, flying-eaved pagodas and temples echoing with chanting, China has more than enough for the spirit-hungry and the soul-seeking, or even just those looking for a little beauty. There's at least one or two temples in every city and town, but a few deserve special mention: Chengde's **Eight Outer Temples** (p. 181); the **Labrang Monastery** (p. 762) surrounded by thousands of prayer wheels; the ancient **Famen Temple** in Xi'an (p. 278), sacred in the history of Buddhism; the golden *stupas* and pagodas of southern Yunnan (p. 658), with their distinctive south Asian influence; and, of course, all the monasteries in **Tibet** (p. 827). The **Mogao Grottoes** (p. 781) in Dunhuang, **Matisi Temple Grottoes** (p. 771), **Yungang Temple Grottoes** (p. 315), and the **Dazu Carvings** (p. 734) offer more examples of ancient Buddhist paintings, sculptures, and tapestries.

Perhaps the most magnificent are the four sacred **Buddhist mountains,** combining spiritual wonder, architectural intricacies, and natural beauty. Like many of the jagged peaks in China, they sit wreathed in mists and clouds, blissfully in a world of their own. **Emeishan** (p. 706) and **Jiuhuashan** (p. 429) offer intrepid climbs, mountain peace, and chattering monkeys. Devout worshippers from as far as Mongolia and Tibet brave the peaks isolating **Wutaishan** (p. 309). For a pilgrimage of a different sort, take a boat to **Putuoshan** (p. 406), a paradisiacal mountain island graced with bamboo, cliffs, and serene temples. Not to be outdone, Daoists have their own sacred **Daoist mountains,** known as Wuyue (the Five Peaks). The most prestigious, **Taishan** (p. 200), "Eastern Yue," saw centuries of imperial processions. **Huashan** (p. 279), "Western Yue," has a place in the legends thanks to the storied martial arts prowess of its disciples, as well as its mystical knife-sharp peaks and dizzyingly steep ravines. **Songshan** (p. 288), "Middle Yue," is better known for the Buddhist **Shaolin Monastery** and its contingent of ass-kicking monks. Don't confuse **Hengshan** in the north (p. 316), famed for the Hanging Monastery precariously suspended underneath a cliff, with **Hengshan** in the south (p. 453).

SUGGESTED ITINERARIES

BEST OF CHINA (5-6 WEEKS) Dive headlong into China in fast-paced, dazzling **Beijing** (p. 119), capital city and pulsing heart of the nation. See how emperors spent their summers in lavish palaces, then jump-start yours in the bars and clubs of Sanlitun. Hop a train to **Xi'an** (p. 269) to admire ancient China at its grandest in the tombs of its emperors (and one empress). Leave imperial ostentation behind for the breezy air of laid-back **Chengdu** (p. 689), a perfect springboard into the mountain wilderness beyond. Don't miss a trip north to **Jiuzhaigou** (p. 716), with its turquoise waters so pristine that you'll never want to leave. Swinging back down, search for your own Buddhist halo on the holy mountains of **Emeishan** (p. 706) before journeying south to fair **Kunming** (p. 641), city of flowers and gateway to the minority villages and wilds of Yunnan. Travel next to the story-

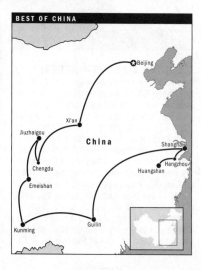

BEST OF CHINA

Beijing

Xi'an

Jiuzhaigou

China

Chengdu

Shanghai

Hangzhou

Huangshan

Emeishan

Kunming

Guilin

book scenery of **Guilin** (p. 605), nestled amid soft limestone peaks and terraced rice paddies. Then plunge into cosmopolitan **Shanghai** (p. 333), with its blend of European charm and non-stop glitz along the Bund. Seek a calmer pace by the willow-shaded shores of the West Lake in **Hangzhou** (p. 390). Finish up with a hike up **Huangshan** (p. 424), China's most famous mountain, and justifiably so. Locals will tell you that after climbing its jagged pine-strewn peaks and glimpsing a sunrise from its summit, you'll never have to visit another mountain again.

Wander the rain-misted paths of **Wuyishan** (p. 483), a realm of gurgling streams, peaks, waterfalls, and secluded trails. Haunting mosques remind **Quanzhou** (p. 487) of its ancient sea-faring days as a port on the "Silk Road of the Sea." Daydream upon **Xiamen's** island of **Guylangyu** (p. 496), with its tranquil gardens and ocean views. After all that serenity, head to cosmopolitan **Guangzhou** (p. 498), and crown your trip with a few energized days and glamorous nights in **Hong Kong** (p. 543).

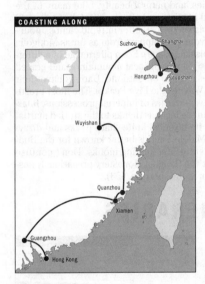

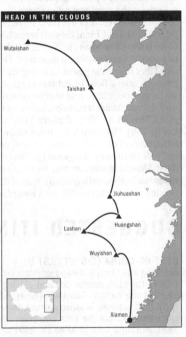

COASTING ALONG (3-4 WEEKS) Lazy and idyllic, a ramble through the coasts of southern China passes through serene scenery and comfortable urban centers. Indulge in unabashedly modern **Shanghai** (p. 333), where there's enough shopping and strolling for even the most avid urbanite. Then enter another world upon the Buddhist island of **Putuoshan** (p. 406), cooled by sea breezes and shaded by bamboo groves. Sip freshly harvested tea from the fields of Longjing near **Hangzhou** (p. 390) and relax with a cup of China's most famous tea. A ferry down the Grand Canal brings you to the classical gardens, canals, and half-moon bridges of **Suzhou** (p. 366).

HEAD IN THE CLOUDS (4 WEEKS) Lose yourself in dizzying beauty from the height of China's mist-wreathed peaks. A train from Beijing takes you to the remote mountain village of **Wutaishan** (p. 309), where Buddhist monks jostle with Mongol-speaking pilgrims. Huff and puff up the steep steps of **Taishan** (p. 196), and don't forget to say a prayer to the mountain gods once you've reached the summit. Heading south into Anhui, wander the paths of **Jiuhuashan** (p. 429), chat with friendly monks, and breathe in Buddhist incense and natural serenity. Not far from Jiuhuashan, **Huangshan** (p. 424) soars above the mists and clouds, an inspiration to poets, artists, and jaded travelers alike. Then wind your way down to **Lushan** (p. 439), where waterfalls tumble down forest-cloaked mountainsides. And there's no better way to end your tour of China's mountains than a float on a bamboo raft on the Nine Bend River of **Wuyishan** (p. 483). After all those muscle-aching climbs, bask on the sunny beaches of **Xiamen** (p. 491), or sip a fragrant cup of eight-treasures tea on the fair isle of **Gulangyu**.

Altai (p. 789), with their nearby Mongol and Kazakh villages, icy waters, summer wildflowers, birch forests, and mountains reaching to the sky. Forging on with the Silk Road, skirt the northern edge of the Tarim Basin and the Taklimakan Desert. Stop briefly in **Korla** (p. 802), then continue west to **Kuqa** (p. 804) for a fascinating glimpse into Uighur culture and more parched vistas. Finish in the clamor and excitement of **Kashgar** (p. 807), whose lively bazaars and colorful international mix make it the perfect modern-day Silk Road outpost.

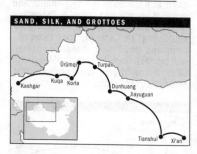

SAND, SILK, AND GROTTOES

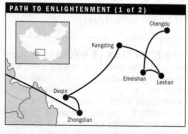

PATH TO ENLIGHTENMENT (1 of 2)

SAND, SILK, AND GROTTOES (4-5 WEEKS) Trace the ribbon of Silk Road that once crossed expanses of sun-burnt desert 2000 years ago from China to India, Central Asia, Arabia, and beyond. Begin your journey in the ancient dynastic capital of **Xi'an** (p. 269), from where camel caravans set out, laden with silk. Clamber over the rocks and cliffs of **Tianshui** (p. 765), and peek at the thousands of Buddhist sculptures tucked into the Maijishan Grottoes. Climb the Great Wall's last and most stately pass at **Jiayuguan** (p. 772), gazing west at the first hints of the stark desert and mountains. **Dunhuang** (p. 777) marked the last lonely outpost of the Han empire. Before passing into the "barbarian" lands beyond, ancient merchants stopped to pray for luck and safety at the **Mogao Grottoes**, now the world's best-preserved Buddhist cave art. Quench your thirst with refreshingly sweet melons and grapes at **Turpan** (p. 796), in the midst of fiery red mountains and ancient ruins. Plunge back into the whirl of city life in **Ürümqi**, or sleep beneath the stars by the shores of **Tianchi** (p. 788), the "Heavenly Lake." Those who have extra time can loop up to isolated **Yining** (p. 793) and

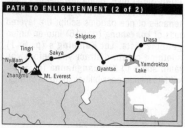

PATH TO ENLIGHTENMENT (2 of 2)

PATH TO ENLIGHTENMENT (4 WEEKS) Set out from **Chengdu** (p. 689) to the sacred Buddhist mountain of **Emeishan** (p. 706), where the misty peaks and soft chants and prayers echoing from monasteries will convince you that you're no longer on earth. After admiring the Big Buddha of **Leshan** (p. 703), trek down to the Tibetan town of **Kangding** (p. 714), tucked within icy mountain ranges and alpine grasslands. **Deqin** (p. 686) sits by the pristine Mekong River, which tumbles down from the Tibetan plateau. Meadows starred with wildflowers scatter around **Zhongdian** (p. 682), the gateway to Tibet. Make the mighty leap to the "Roof of the World," where the sky is wider, bluer, and closer

DISCOVER

than ever before. Breathe in the scent of yak-butter lamps in **Lhasa's** (p. 837) hallowed Jokhang Temple and enjoy the cool breezes by the shores of **Lake Namtso** (p. 848). Then embark upon the **Friendship Highway,** an exhilarating journey to the border of Nepal. Hike by the sapphire waters of **Lake Yamdroktso** (p. 853) and cheer on the horse racers at **Gyantse** (p. 855). Stop by **Shigatse** (p. 858) to see the Tashilhunpo Monastery, ancient home to the Panchen Lama. Brightly colored prayer flags flap in the winds at the monasteries of **Sakya** (p. 861). Watch the sunlight play upon the incomparable visage of **Mt. Everest** (p. 862) from the base camp, then careen off upon the last magnificent stretch of the Friendship Highway.

THE LONG TREK (5 WEEKS) For journeys into the wilds, free-flowing beer, and cheerful backpacking friends, break away from the tour groups to appreciate southwest China at its loveliest. The haven for wandering Westerners, **Yangshuo** (p. 611) promises friendly cafes as well as floats down the Li River along the region's limestone hills and verdant greenery. Endless terraces of rice paddies sculpt the layered hills of **Longsheng** (p. 616) into an unforgettable vista. Let **Kunming's** (p. 641) soothing charm distract you before you jaunt south to **Xishuangbanna** (p. 652), with its myriad possibilities for treks through lush rainforests, tiny Dai minority villages, and rice paddies. Swap adventurous tales with fellow backpackers in expat-friendly **Dali** (p. 668) and bargain for batik in the markets. Listen to the haunting tones of ancient Naxi music in **Lijiang** (p. 674), wander its narrow cobblestone streets, then scale the snow mountain looming over the ancient town. By far, **Tiger Leaping Gorge** (p. 679) remains an incredible and thrilling stop on any journey north, with its deep chasms and rushing river. Row across the ice-blue **Lugu Lake** (p. 681) to island monasteries, or trek along its shores, discovering Mosuo villages along the way. Greet the dawn with the early morning chants and music of russet-robed lamas in **Zhongdian** (p. 682), thought by some to be the legendary "Shangri La." After exploring its nearby lakes and mountains, challenge yourself with the Meili Snow Mountains of **Deqin** (p. 686), a tiny Tibetan town nestled amid peaks and grasslands.

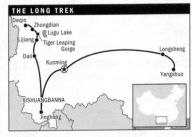

THE LONG TREK

ESSENTIALS

PLANNING YOUR TRIP

BEFORE YOU GO

Passport (p. 12). Required for all travelers to China, Hong Kong, or Macau.

Visa (p. 12). Required for all travelers to China. Required for some travelers to Hong Kong or Macau. Apply for visas at least 2-3 weeks in advance. It's also possible to apply for visas to China in Hong Kong. The regular processing time for visas is 5-10 days, depending on location.

Letter of Invitation (p. 14). Typically required to work or study in China.

Special Permits (p. 14). Travelers need special **travel permits** to visit certain "sensitive" regions in China.

Work Permit (p. 14). Required of all foreigners planning to work in China.

Driving Permit (p. 48). Required for all those planning to drive.

Recommended Vaccinations (p. 27). No vaccinations are required to enter China, unless entering from an area infected with yellow fever.

Other Health: Malaria pills are recommended for those traveling to malaria risk areas (p. 30).

EMBASSIES AND CONSULATES

CHINA'S CONSULAR SERVICES ABROAD

Australia: 15 Coronation Dr., Yarralumla, ACT 2600, Canberra (☎61 2 6273 4780, ext. 257 or ext. 218; automatic answering machine 6273 4783; www.chinaembassy.org.au). **Consulates:** 75-77 Irving Rd., Toorak, Melbourne VIC 3142 (☎3 9822 0604, visas 9804 3683; fax 9822 0606; http://melbourne.china-consulate.org); 45 Brown St., East Perth WA 6004 (☎8 9222 0333, visas 9222 0300; fax 9221 6144); 39 Dunblane St., Camperdown, Sydney NSW 2050 (☎2 8595 8002, visas 8595 8020; http://sydney.chineseconsulate.org).

Canada: 515 St. Patrick St., Ottawa, ON K1N 5H3 (☎613-789-3434; fax 789-1414; www.chinaembassy-canada.org). **Consulates:** 1011 6th Ave. SW, Ste. 100, Calgary, AB T2P OW1 (☎403-264-3322; fax 264-6656); 240 St. George St., Toronto, ON M5R 2P4 (☎416-964-7260; fax 324-6468); 3380 Granville St., Vancouver, BC V6H 3K3 (☎604-736-3910; fax 736-4343).

Ireland: 40 Ailesbury Rd., Dublin 4 (☎353 1 269 1707; fax 283 9938).

New Zealand: 2-6 Glenmore St., Kelburn, Wellington (☎64 4 472 1382; www.chinaembassy.org.nz). **Consulate:** 588 Great South Rd., Greenlane, Auckland (☎9 525 1588, visas 525 0110; fax 525 0733).

United Kingdom: 49-51 Portland Place, London W1B 4JL; visa and consular section, 31 Portland Place, London W1B 3QD (☎44 20 7299 4049, visa and consular section 7631 1430; www.chinese-embassy.org.uk). **Consulates:** Denison House, 49 Denison Rd., Rusholme, Manchester M14 5RX (☎161 248 9304; fax 257 2672); 55 Corstorphine Rd., Edinburgh EH12 5QG (☎131 337 9896, visas 316 4789; fax 337 8871).

United States: 2300 Connecticut Ave., NW, Washington, D.C. 20008; visa office, 2201 Wisconsin Ave., NW, Rm. 110, Washington, D.C. 20007 (☎202-328-2500, visas 338-6688; www.china-embassy.org). **Consulates:** 100 W. Erie St., Chicago, IL 60610 (☎312-803-0095, visas 803-0098; fax 803-0122); 3417 Montrose Blvd., Houston, TX 77006 (☎713-524-0780, visas 524-4311; www.chinahouston.org); 443 Shatto Pl., Los Angeles, CA 90020 (☎213-807-8088, visas 807-8018; www.chinaconsulatela.org); 520 12th Ave., New York, NY 10036 (☎212-736-9301, visas 868-2074; www.nyconsulate.prchina.org); 1450 Laguna St., San Francisco, CA 94115 (☎415-674-2900, visas 928-6931; www.chinaconsulatesf.org).

CONSULAR SERVICES IN CHINA

Australia: 21 Dongzhimen Wai Dajie, Sanlitun, Beijing 100600 (☎10 6532 2331, ext. 129; www.austemb.org.cn). **Consulates:** Guangdong International Hotel, 339 Huanshi Dong Lu, 15th fl., Guangzhou 510098 (☎20 8335 0909; www.austcon-guang-zhou.org); 23/F Harbour Centre, 25 Harbour Rd., Wan Chai, Hong Kong (☎852 2827 8881; www.australia.org.hk); CITIC Square, 1168 Nanjing Xi Lu, Level 22, Shanghai 200041 (☎21 5292 5500; www.aus-in-shanghai.com.cn).

Canada: 19 Dongzhimen Wai Dajie, Chaoyang District, Beijing 100600 (☎10 6532 3536; www.beijing.gc.ca). **Consulates:** Metropolitan Tower, Wuyi Lu, Room 1705, Chongqing 400010 (☎23 6373 8007; www.chongqing.gc.ca); China Hotel Office Tower, Liuhua Lu, Ste. 801, Guangzhou 510015 (☎20 8666 0569; www.guang-zhou.gc.ca); Exchange Square, Tower One, 8 Connaught Pl., 14th fl., Hong Kong (☎852 2847 7562; fax 2810 7561); Shanghai Center, West Tower, 1376 Nanjing Xi Lu, Ste. 604, Shanghai 200040 (☎21 6279 8400; www.shanghai.gc.ca).

Ireland: 3 Ritan Dong Lu, Chaoyang District, Beijing 100600 (☎10 6532 2691; fax 6532 6857). **Consulates:** Chungnam Bldg., 1 Lockhart Rd., 6th fl., Wan Chai, Hong Kong (☎852 2527 4897; fax 2520 1833); Shanghai Center, 1376 Nanjing Xi Lu, Ste. 700A, Shanghai 200040 (☎21 6279 8729; fax 6279 8739).

New Zealand: 1 Ritan Donger Jie, Chaoyang District, Beijing 100600 (☎10 6532 2731; www.nzembassy.com/china). **Consulates:** 6501 Central Plaza, 18 Harbour Rd., Wan Chai, Hong Kong (☎852 2525 5044; www.nzembassy.com); Qihua Tower, Huaihai Zhong Lu, #15A, Shanghai 200031 (☎21 6471 1108; fax 6431 0226).

United Kingdom: Kerry Center, 11 Guanghua Lu, 21st fl., Jianguomen Wai, Beijing 100600 (☎10 5192 4000, visa and consular services 8529 6600; www.uk.cn). **Consulates:** 28/F Metropolitan Tower, 68 Zourong Lu, Chongqing 400100 (☎23 6381 0321; fax 6381 0322); Guangdong Int'l Hotel, 339 Huanshi Dong Lu, 2nd fl., Guangzhou 510098 (☎20 8335 1354; fax 8332 7509); 1 Supreme Court Rd. Central, Admiralty, Hong Kong (☎852 2901 3000; fax 2901 3066; www.britishconsulate.org.hk); Shanghai Center, 1376 Nanjing Xi Lu, Ste. 301, Shanghai 200040 (☎21 6279 7650; 6279 7651).

United States: 2 Xiushui Dong Jie, Jianguomen Wai, Chaoyang, Beijing 100600 (☎10 6532 3431, after hours 6532 1910; www.usembassy-china.org.cn). **Consulates:** 4 Lingshiguan Lu, Chengdu 610041 (☎28 8558 3992; fax 8558 3520); 1 Shamian Nan Jie, Shamian Island 200S1, Guangzhou 510133 (☎20 8121 8000; fax 8121 9001); 26 Garden Rd., Central, Hong Kong (☎852 2523 9011; fax 2845 1598; www.hongkong.usconsulate.gov); 1469 Huaihai Zhong Lu, Shanghai 200031 (☎21 6433 6880, after hours 6433 3936; fax 6433 4122); 52 Shisi Wei Lu, Heping, Shenyang 110003 (☎24 8624 1198; fax 2322 2374).

OTHER CONSULATES

India: 1 Ritan Dong Lu, Jianguomen Wai, Beijing (☎10 6532 1908; fax 6532 4684). **Consulates:** 1008 Shanghai International Trade Centre, 2201 Yan'an Xi Lu, Shanghai (☎21 6275 8885 or 6275 8886; fax 6275 8881); 26A United Center, 95 Queensway, Hong Kong (☎852 2527 5724; fax 2866 4124).

Indonesia: Office Bldg. B, Sanlitun, Beijing (☎ 10 6532 5489; fax 6532 5368). **Consulates:** 127 Leighton Rd., 2nd fl., Causeway Bay, Hong Kong (☎ 852 2890 4421; fax 2895 0189); Dongfang Hotel, 120 Liuhua Lu, Guangzhou (☎ 20 8601 8772; fax 8601 8773).

Kazakhstan: 9 Dongliu Jie, Sanlitun, Beijing (☎ 10 6532 6182; fax 6532 6183).

Kyrgyzstan: Tayuan Diplomatic Bldg., 14 Liangmahe Nan Lu, Sanlitun, Beijing (☎ 10 6532 6458; fax 6532 6459).

Laos: 11 Dongsi Jie, Sanlitun, Beijing (☎ 10 6532 1224; fax 6532 6748).

Malaysia: 13 Dongzhimen Wai Dajie, Sanlitun, Chaoyang District, Beijing (☎ 10 6532 2531; fax 6532 5032). **Consulates:** CITIC Plaza, Tianhe Bei Lu, 19th fl., Guangzhou (☎ 20 3877 0766; fax 3877 0769); Malaysia Bldg., 50 Gloucester Rd., 24th fl., Wan Chai, Hong Kong (☎ 852 2527 8109; fax 2865 1628); CITIC Square, 1168 Nanjing Xi Lu, Shanghai (☎ 21 5292 5424; fax 5292 5952).

Mongolia: 2 Xiushui Bei Jie, Jianguomen Wai, Beijing, (☎ 10 6532 1203; fax 6532 5045).

Myanmar: 6 Dongzhimen Wai Dajie, Sanlitun, Beijing (☎ 10 6532 1425, visa 6532 1488; fax 6532 1344). **Consulates:** Sung Hung Kai Ctr., 30 Harbour Rd., Rm. 2401, 24th. fl., Wan Chai, Hong Kong (☎ 852 2827 7929; fax 2827 6597); Camellia Hotel, 154 Dongfeng Dong Lu, Kunming (☎ 871 317 6609; fax 317 6309).

Nepal: 1 Xiliu Jie, Sanlitun, Beijing (☎ 10 6532 1795; fax 6532 3251). **Consulate:** 13 Luobulinka (Norbulinka) Lu, Lhasa (☎ 891 682 2881; fax 683 6890).

North Korea: 3 Dongsi Jie, Sanlitun, Beijing (☎ 10 6532 1189; fax 6532 3251). **Consulate:** Int'l Trade Center, 2200 Yan'an Xi Lu, 4th fl., Shanghai (☎ 21 6219 6420; fax 6209 2056).

Pakistan: 1 Dongzhimen Wai Dajie, Beijing (☎ 10 6532 2504 or 6532 2581; fax 6532 2715).

Philippines: 23 Xiushui Bei Jie, Jianguomen Wai, Beijing (☎ 10 6532 1872 or 6532 2518; fax 6532 3761). **Consulates:** United Centre, 95 Queensway, 14th fl., Admiralty, Hong Kong (☎ 852 2823 8500; fax 2866 9885); Shanghai Center, 1376 Nanjing Xi Lu, Ste. 368, Shanghai (☎ 21 6279 8337; fax 6279 8332); Guangdong Int'l Hotel, 339 Huanshi Dong Lu, Guangzhou (☎ 20 7331 1461; fax 8333 0573).

Russia: 4 Dongzhimen Nei Beizhong Jie, Beijing (☎ 10 6532 2051, visas 6532 1267; fax 6532 4851). **Consulates:** 20 Huangpu Lu, Shanghai (☎ 21 6324 2682; fax 6306 9982); Sun Hung Kai Ctr., 30 Harbour Rd., Room 2932, Wan Chai, Hong Kong (☎ 852 2877 7188; fax 2877 7166); 31 Nan Shisanwei Lu, Shenyang (☎ 24 2322 3927; fax 2322 3907).

Singapore: 1 Xiushui Bei Jie, Jianguomen Wai, Beijing (☎ 10 8529 6256; fax 8529 6254). **Consulates:** Admiralty Centre, 18 Harcourt Rd., Tower I, 9th fl., Rm. 901, Admiralty, Hong Kong (☎ 852 2527 2212; fax 2866 1239); 89 Wanshan Lu, Shanghai (☎ 21 6278 5566; fax 6295 6038); 19 Hubin Bei Lu, United Overseas Bank Building, Xiamen (☎ 592 511 4695; fax 511 4702).

South Korea: 14 Liangmahe Nan Lu, Beijing (☎ 10 6532 6775; fax 6532 6778). **Consulate:** 8 Qinling Lu, Qingdao (☎ 532 897 6001; fax 897 6005).

Thailand: 40 Guanghua Lu, Jianguomen Wai, Beijing (☎ 10 6532 2151; fax 6532 1749). **Consulates:** Fairmont House, 8 Cotton Tree Dr., 8th fl., Central, Hong Kong (☎ 852 2521 6481; fax 2521 8629); 7 Zhongshan Dong Yi Lu, Shanghai (☎ 21 6321 9371; fax 6323 4140).

Vietnam: 32 Guanghua Lu, Jianguomen Wai, Beijing (☎ 10 6532 5414; fax 6532 5720). **Consulates:** 230 Wan Chai Rd., Wan Chai, Hong Kong (☎ 852 2591 4510); Hotel Landmark B building, Qiaoguang Lu, Haizhu Square, Guangzhou (☎ 20 8330 591; fax 8330 5915).

ESSENTIALS

CHINA NATIONAL TOURIST OFFICES

Australia: 19th fl., 44 Market St., Sydney, NSW 2000 (☎02 9299 4057; www.cnto.org.au).

Canada: 480 University Ave., Ste. 806, Toronto, ON M5G 1V2 (☎416-599-6636; fax 599-6382).

China: No. 9A, Jianguomen Nei Dajie, Beijing 100740 (☎10 6513 8866; www.cnta.com).

United Kingdom: 4 Glentworth St., London NW1 5PG (☎20 7935 9787; fax 7487 5842).

United States: 350 5th Ave., Ste. 6413, New York, NY 10118 (☎212-760 8218; fax 760 8809; www.cnto.org); 333 West Broadway, Ste. 201, Glendale, CA 91204 (☎818-545 7505; fax 545 7506).

DOCUMENTS AND FORMALITIES

PASSPORTS

REQUIREMENTS

Citizens of Australia, Canada, Ireland, New Zealand, the UK, and the US need valid passports to enter China and re-enter their home countries. China does not allow entrance if your passport expires in under six months. Returning home with an expired passport is illegal and may result in a fine.

NEW PASSPORTS

Citizens of Australia, Canada, Ireland, New Zealand, the UK, and the US can apply for a passport at any passport office and many post offices and courts of law. Any new passport or renewal applications must be filed well in advance of the departure date, although most passport offices offer rush services for a very steep fee.

PASSPORT MAINTENANCE

Photocopy the page of your passport with your photo, as well as your visas, traveler's check serial numbers, and any other important documents. Carry one set of copies in a safe place, apart from the originals, and leave another set at home. Consulates also recommend that you carry an expired passport or an official copy of your birth certificate in a part of your baggage separate from other documents.

If you lose your passport, immediately notify the local Public Security Bureau (see **Local Laws and Police,** p. 24) and the nearest embassy or consulate of your home government. To expedite its replacement, you will need to know all information previously recorded and show ID and proof of citizenship. In some cases, a replacement may take weeks to process, and it may be valid only for a limited time. Any visas stamped in your old passport will be irretrievably lost. In an emergency, ask for immediate temporary traveling papers that will permit you to re-enter your home country.

VISAS, INVITATIONS, AND WORK PERMITS

VISAS

As of August 2004, citizens of Australia, Canada, Ireland, New Zealand, the UK, and the US need a visa in addition to a valid passport for entrance into China. Visas are issued at Chinese consulates and embassies worldwide and in Hong Kong through numerous travel agencies and even some hotels and guesthouses. Getting a Chinese tourist visa in Hong Kong is both easier and cheaper than getting one abroad (see **Hong Kong: Consulates, Visas, and Immigration,** p. 551).

VISA TYPE	aka	entry	duration of stay	passport must be valid for
TOURIST	TYPE "L"	single, double	up to 30 days	6 months beyond departure date
		multiple	6-12 months	
BUSINESS	TYPE "F"	single or double	up to 6 months	6 months beyond
		multiple	up to 6 or 12 months	6 months beyond
LONG-TERM WORK	TYPE "Z"	multiple	up to 1 year	6 months beyond
STUDENT	TYPE "F"	single	up to 6 months	6 months beyond
	TYPE "X"	single	6-12 months	

Tourist visas (Type "L") are typically valid for a single- or double-entry only. Official embassy policy issues multiple-entry tourist visas only to those who have relatives in China or own land in the country. Though the stated maximum duration of stay is 30 days, the visa office will generally grant longer stays up to 90 days to those who request it. It may be safest to ask for twice the number of days you actually need. Some embassies require you to obtain a visa invitation from a Chinese tour or travel agency (or a travel itinerary and airplane tickets).

Double-check entrance requirements at the nearest embassy or consulate of China (p. 9) for up-to-date info before departure. US citizens can also consult www.pueblo.gsa.gov/cic_text/travel/foreign/foreignentryreqs.html.

When applying for a visa, make sure your passport is valid six months beyond the date of your intended return (nine months for a multiple-entry visa) and has several blank pages. You will need a completed application form, a recent passport-sized photo, a valid passport, and the appropriate visa fee.

Australia: Tourist visas single-entry AUS$30, double-entry AUS$45, 6-month multiple entry AUS$60, and 1-year multiple entry AUS$90. Mail a self-addressed stamped envelope and additional AUS$10 (cash, money order, or certified check) for mail processing (4 working days). Rush fees 2- to 3-day service AUS$30, same-day service AUS$50.

Canada: Tourist visas single-entry CDN$50, double-entry CDN$75. Business visas 6-month multiple-entry CDN$100, 1-year multiple-entry CDN$150. Mail processing costs depend on the type of visa: single-entry CDN$71; double-entry CDN$96; self-addressed stamped envelope required. Embassy only accepts applications through the **Golden Mile Travel Consultant,** 203-1390 Prince of Wales Dr., Ottawa, ON K2C 3N6 (☎613-224-6863; fax 224-7863). Cash, money order, or company check only; no personal checks. Regular processing 5 business days $21. Rush fees 2-day service CDN$78, next-day service CDN$93.

New Zealand: Tourist visas single-entry NZ$60, double-entry NZ$90. Cash and company check only. Mail processing NZ$15; self-addressed stamped envelope required. Processing takes 7-10 business days. Rush fees 2- to 3-day service NZ$40, same-day service NZ$60.

United Kingdom: Tourist visas 3-month single-entry UK£30, 3-month double-entry UK£45, 6-month multiple-entry UK£60, and 1-year multiple-entry UK£90. Mail processing additional UK£20. Cash only. Processing takes 3 business days. Rush fees next-day service UK£15, same-day service UK£20.

United States: Tourist visas single-entry US$50, double-entry US$75, 6-month multiple-entry US$100, and 1-year multiple-entry visa US$150. Cash, money order, and company check only; no personal checks. Visa applications can be obtained through a fax-back service (New York 212-868-7761, Washington 202-265-9809). Mail-in applications no longer accepted; applicants must go personally to the embassy, entrust another person, or ask a travel agency or visa service. Regular processing takes 4 business days. Rush fees 2- to 3-day service US$20, same-day service US$30.

Visa extensions are the domain of the **Foreign Affairs section** of the Public Security Bureau (PSB) in China (listed in the **Practical Information** section of every city). Depending on where you are, it is usually not a problem to get one visa extension for an additional two to four weeks. Getting a second extension, however, is more difficult. You might be better off heading to Hong Kong for a few days and getting a new tourist visa there. Whatever you decide, **do not overstay the duration of your visa**—you risk heavy fines and detainment when you depart China.

INVITATIONS

Business ("F"), work ("Z"), and student ("F" or "X") visas generally require a **letter of invitation** from the appropriate Chinese corporation, government office, or educational institution. For multiple-entry business visas, you will also need your company's license to do business in China. For student visas, you will also need to complete a JW-202 form (further confirmation that you are indeed welcome at the school you will attend) from a school or university in China, the original and a copy of the letter of acceptance, and a physical examination record form (Q-2), which must be filled out and signed by a doctor. Study abroad programs operating in China usually assist participants with getting visas and residence permits. Students enrolling directly in Chinese universities should contact the university to obtain necessary forms. For more information on study abroad programs in China, see **Alternatives to Tourism,** p. 112.

WORK PERMITS

Admission as a visitor does not include the right to work, which is authorized only by a work permit. If you're planning on (legally) working in China, you must obtain a work permit, which you'll need in order to apply for a long-term multiple-entry work visa. To obtain a work permit, you must have a valid passport, be over the age of 18, and procure a number of important documents. These include, but are not limited to, a medical report, your credentials (diploma, resume, or transcript), a letter of intention for employment, and a report of reasons for employment. Your employer will provide documents stating your accepted employment, and they will submit your documents to Chinese authorities in order to get you a work permit. So all *you* have to do is get a check-up. You could help speed up the process by having your credentials (diploma, resume, etc.) translated into Chinese, preparing a detailed trip itinerary, and making sure you get all your shots.

SPECIAL PERMITS

Only 20 years ago, much of China was off-limits to foreign travelers. These days, almost the whole country is open to foreigners, but China's policy of travel restrictions still lingers. Foreigners need special **alien travel permits** (wàiguórén lǚxíng zhèng, 外国人旅行证 ; or pīzhèng, 批证) to visit certain regions in China, while some areas remain entirely closed. In general, only border regions, especially those populated by ethnic minorities, require special permits to visit, but areas near military bases are usually closed as well. Travelers to Tibet first must obtain a **Tibet Tourism Bureau Permit,** in addition to further alien travel permits while traveling outside of Lhasa. Other areas that require special permits include Northern Xinjiang, certain wilderness areas, and other border regions. The list of areas closed to foreign travelers is in a constant state of flux, and official Beijing policy can often take considerable time to reach the hinterlands of Xinjiang. Be aware that locals may often not be aware of travel restrictions. Travel permits are issued at the discretion of the Public Security Bureau (PSB), which decides how much

ESSENTIALS

they cost and how long they take to process. The local PSB reserves the right to cancel or modify your permit at any time, so it is best to get to your destination as fast as possible once you've obtained a permit for it.

IDENTIFICATION

When you travel, always carry at least two forms of identification on your person, including one photo ID; a passport and a driver's license or birth certificate is usually adequate. Many establishments, especially banks, may require several IDs in order to cash traveler's checks. Never carry all of your IDs together. Split them up in case of theft or loss, and keep photocopies of them in your luggage and at home.

STUDENT, TEACHER, AND YOUTH IDENTIFICATION

The **International Student Identity Card (ISIC),** the most widely accepted form of student ID, provides discounts on some sights, accommodations, food, and transport; access to a 24hr. emergency helpline; and insurance benefits for US cardholders (see **Insurance,** p. 27). Applicants must be full-time secondary or post-secondary school students at least 12 years of age. Because of the proliferation of fake ISICs, some services (particularly airlines) require additional proof of student identity. The **International Teacher Identity Card (ITIC)** offers teachers the same insurance coverage as the ISIC and similar but limited discounts. For travelers who are 25 years old or under but are not students, the **International Youth Travel Card (IYTC)** also offers many of the same benefits as the ISIC.

ESSENTIALS

Each of these identity cards costs US$22. ISICs and ITICs are valid through the academic year in which they are issued; IYTCs are valid for one year from the date of issue. Many student travel agencies (p. 34) issue the cards. For a list of issuing agencies or more information, see the **International Student Travel Confederation (ISTC)** website (www.istc.org).

Most places in China that offer student admissions may not immediately recognize the ISIC, but will accept it as long as you explain to them what it is. This may require a bit of Chinese language skills, time, and persistence. In Hong Kong and Macau, ISICs are widely recognized. If you can get a **Chinese student card,** you will generally fare better, especially in places that only sell student tickets to Chinese students. Some places in backpacker cities like Yangshuo will provide a Chinese student card to those who nominally sign up to take Chinese classes with them. Anyone studying legitimately on the mainland, for no matter how short a time, can get one of these red plastic-covered wallet-sized booklets. Forged Chinese student IDs do exist in popular destinations, but the government is clued in to the proliferation of counterfeits among foreigners: charlatans are almost always exposed.

CUSTOMS

Upon entering China, you must complete a form declaring certain items from abroad and pay a duty on the value of those articles that exceeds the allowance established by China's customs service. One copy must be given to customs, while the carbon copy should be kept for inspection upon exit. Tourists are allowed to bring into China no more than 50g of gold or silver jewelry, perfume (a "reasonable quantity" of perfume), and one of each of the following electronic appliances: camera, portable tape-recorder, portable video camera, or computer. Electronic goods cannot be sold if they were imported duty-free for personal use. The customs officer may check your forms when you leave China to make sure you still have everything you originally declared. Tourists staying less than six months can bring 400 cigarettes and two bottles of wine or spirits. Stay over six months and you can bring 600 cigarettes and four bottles of your favorite alcoholic beverage. All gifts and items imported on behalf of others must be declared and may be charged duty. Foreigners are not allowed to bring in Chinese currency in cash, so it's best to exchange your money in China. Unlimited amounts of foreign currencies and traveler's checks can be brought into the country, however.

What souvenirs are you allowed to take out of China? Y300 per person and 4 cartons of tobacco products. Exporting jewelry will require special invoices issued by China. For cultural relics, you'll need to get an invoice permit or export license from the cultural administrative department. Antiques (real and imitation) need to be marked with a red wax seal. For both import and export, Chinese customs has a long list of prohibited items: fire arms and explosives, pornographic or political literature, narcotics, infected plants, animals, or foodstuffs, and radio transmitters, to name a few. Furthermore, the government prohibits the export of valuable cultural relics, rare animals and plants, and precious metals and gems. It is wise to make a list, including serial numbers, of any valuables that you carry with you from home. If you register this list with customs before your departure and have an official stamp it, you will avoid import duty charges and ensure an easy passage upon your return. Be especially careful to document items manufactured abroad.

All of this sounds very complicated, but in fact most travelers report little difficulty with customs when entering and exiting China. Note that goods and gifts purchased at **duty-free** shops abroad are not exempt from duty or sales tax at your point of return and thus must be declared as well. "Duty-free" merely means that you need not pay a tax in the country of purchase. Upon returning home, you must similarly declare all articles acquired abroad and pay a duty on the value of articles in excess of your home country's allowance. Be sure to keep receipts for all goods acquired abroad. For more information, contact your local customs office or visit the website www.customs.ustreas.gov.

MONEY

CURRENCY AND EXCHANGE

The standard unit of Chinese currency is the **rénmínbì** (RMB; 人民币; "people's currency"), commonly referred to as the **yuán** (元). The *yuán* is divided into 10 units of *jiǎo* (角) and 100 units of *fēn* (分); 10 *fēn* equals 1 *jiǎo*. Be aware that the size of coins and bills increases with value. Some vendors try to trick foreign tourists by giving change in the smaller *jiǎo* rather than the bigger *yuán*. Almost all prices in China, as well as those in this book, are posted in *yuán* (RMB) decimal form. When referring to prices orally, the Chinese usually substitute the colloquial *kuài* for *yuán* and *máo* for *jiǎo*.

The RMB is not traded on international markets and can only be purchased and exchanged in China. The exchange rate of the RMB is pegged to the dollar at 8.282. Occasionally, American Express Travel Service Outlets have been known to exchange RMB for US dollars. The first place where currency exchange is available is in the airport of arrival. In China, you can exchange currency at many of Bank of China's 30,000 branches, not to mention airports, upscale hotels, and tourist stores where Bank of China has set up shop. State administration controls the exchange rate, and the fee for each exchange is also standardized at 7.75% of the transaction. You can also obtain RMB by using an ATM card or a credit card (p. 18), although ATM access and credit card acceptance is limited to cities and major tourist destinations. As you lose money with every transaction, **convert large sums** (unless the currency is depreciating rapidly), but no more than you'll need.

No matter where you exchange money in China, there's always the possibility that you'll end up with a few counterfeit bills, but the chances are probably slightly greater on the street than in a bank. **Keep all receipts from financial transactions.** You will not be allowed to exchange RMB back into foreign currency unless you have proof of how you got the RMB in the first place.

If you use traveler's checks or bills, carry some in small denominations (the equivalent of US$50 or less) for times when you are forced to exchange money at disadvantageous rates. Also bring some in large denominations since charges may be levied per check cashed. Store your money in a variety of forms: always carry with you some cash, some traveler's checks, and an ATM and/or credit card. All travelers should also consider carrying some US dollars (about US$50 worth), which are often preferred by local tellers. In Hong Kong and Macau, it is possible to exchange most major currencies, but in China, bank tellers are more likely to exchange US dollars than other currencies.

THE YUÁN (Y)		
AUS$1 = Y5.99		Y1 = AUS$0.17
CDN$1 = Y6.28		Y1 = CDN$0.16
NZ$1 = Y5.44		Y1 = NZ$0.18
UK£1 = Y15.38		Y1 = UK£0.07
US$1 = Y8.28		Y1 = US$0.12
EUR€1 = Y10.26		Y1 = EUR€0.09
HK$1 = Y1.06		Y1 = HK$0.94

ESSENTIALS

ESSENTIALS

TRAVELER'S CHECKS

Traveler's checks are one of the safest and least troublesome means of carrying funds. American Express and Visa are the most recognized brands in China. Many banks and agencies sell them for a small commission. Check issuers provide refunds if the checks are lost or stolen, and many offer additional services, such as toll-free refund hotlines abroad, emergency message services, and stolen credit card assistance. The Bank of China is the most ubiquitous place to cash your checks. Other places include the Industrial & Commercial Bank of China and high-end hotels. Ask about toll-free refund hotlines and the location of refund centers when purchasing checks, and always carry emergency cash.

American Express: Checks available with commission at select banks, at all AmEx offices, and online (www.americanexpress.com; US residents only). American Express cardholders can also purchase checks by phone (☎800-721-9768). Checks available in Australian, Canadian, European, Japanese, British, and US currencies. For purchase locations or more information contact AmEx's service centers: in Australia ☎800 68 80 22; in New Zealand 0508 555 358; in the UK 0800 587 6023; in the US and Canada 800-221-7282; elsewhere, call the US collect at 1 801-964-6665. In Beijing, Tianjin, Hebei, Henan, Shandong, Shanxi, Inner Mongolia, and the northeastern provinces, call ☎10 800 7 44 0106; in the rest of China 10 800 44 0106.

Visa: Checks available (generally with commission) at banks worldwide. AAA offers commission-free checks to its members. For the location of the nearest office, call Visa's service centers: in the UK ☎0800 89 5078; in the US 800-227-6811; elsewhere, call the UK collect at 44 173 331 8949. In China, call ☎1 0800 440 0027. Checks available in Canadian, Japanese, European, British, and US currencies.

Travelex/Thomas Cook: Issues Visa traveler's checks. Members of AAA and affiliated automobile associations receive a 25% commission discount on check purchases. In the US and Canada call ☎800-287-7362; in the UK call 0800 62 21 01; elsewhere in the world call collect 44 1733 31 89 50.

Exchange rates for traveler's checks are actually more favorable than those for cash in China, making traveler's checks the preferred way to carry money on the mainland. A 0.75% commission fee is charged per transaction, and a proof of purchase may be required. There is only one drawback: although traveler's checks are easily exchanged at most banks and upscale hotels, they are not generally accepted at budget hotels and guesthouses, restaurants, or sights.

CREDIT, DEBIT, AND ATM CARDS

Budget travelers in China will probably find that few of the establishments they frequent will accept credit cards. Aside from the occasional splurge or big hotel, you will probably reserve use of your credit card for financial emergencies. Credit card and debit card acceptance may also be more common in heavily touristed destinations. **Mastercard** and **Visa** are the most welcomed; **American Express** cards work at some ATMs and at AmEx offices and major airports.

ATMs get the same wholesale exchange rate as credit cards, but there is often a limit on the amount of money you can withdraw per day (usually around US$500). There is typically also a surcharge of US$1-5 per withdrawal. The two major international money networks are **Cirrus** (US ☎800-424-7787; www.mastercard.com) and **Visa/PLUS** (US ☎800-843-7587; www.visa.com). The number of **ATMS** in China linked to these networks is on the rise, especially on the eastern seaboard and in cities. However, ATMs are practically non-existent in the far northeast, Inner Mongolia, parts of Central China, the western provinces, and the rural southwest. Tibet has one ATM in Lhasa, while Xinjiang has not a single ATM. Travelers planning extended stays in China might wish to open a local account at a Chinese bank and get a domestic ATM card to minimize the amount of cash carried.

GETTING MONEY FROM HOME

If you run out of money while traveling, the easiest and cheapest solution is to have someone back home make a deposit to the bank account linked to your credit card or cash (ATM) card. Failing that, some people choose to send money abroad in cash via FedEx or DHL Worldwide Express to avoid fees and taxes. Note that this method is illegal. Consider one of the following other options.

WIRING MONEY. It is possible to arrange a **bank money transfer,** which means asking a bank back home to wire money to a bank in China. Travelers from the US, Canada, and the UK can wire money abroad through Western Union's international money transfer services. In the US, call ☎ 800-325-6000; in Canada 800-235-0000; in the UK 0800 83 38 33; in China 021 3312 4699. To wire US$500 from New York to China, Western Union charges $43 to complete the transaction within minutes, and $36 for a 5-business-day service. There are thousands of Western Union locations throughout China. To find the nearest Western Union location, consult www.westernunion.com. Except in Hong Kong, where a variety of money changers and travel services can receive the wire, the service is usually handled by the post office or local bank. Look for foreign remittance windows in the main post offices and Agricultural Banks of these cities. Western Union only transfers US dollars and RMB. **American Express** offices also provide money transfer services.

US STATE DEPARTMENT (US CITIZENS ONLY). In emergency situations, the US State Department can set up a trust account to forward money to the nearest consular office, which will then disburse it according to instructions for a US$30 fee. This process can take 3-10 business days depending on the method used to transfer funds; it is advisable to use Western Union directly when possible. If you wish to use this service, you must contact the Overseas Citizens Service division of the US State Department (☎ 202-647-5225; nights, Sundays, and holidays ☎ 647-4000). In the event that no one is able to provide financial assistance, the US consulate may be able to provide a loan to help destitute Americans return home, but the criteria are extremely strict.

COSTS

The cost of your trip will vary considerably, depending on where you go, how you travel, and where you stay. The most significant expenses will probably be your round-trip (return) airfare to China (see **Getting to China: By Plane,** p. 34). Before you go, spend some time calculating a reasonable daily budget.

TIERED PRICING SYSTEM. For the most part, China has eliminated the officially-sanctioned **tiered pricing system** that charges foreigners more than overseas Chinese and overseas Chinese more than mainlanders. Admissions to sights and tickets for air and train travel are now charged equally. However, some hotel owners may overcharge foreigners or pretend that cheaper rooms are unavailable. Taxi drivers and other services with independently negotiated costs may see foreigners as easy to swindle (like all tourists) and up their prices. Your best defense is bargaining.

STAYING ON A BUDGET

The average income and cost of living in China are much lower than in the West, but this doesn't always translate into cheap accommodations and transportation for travelers. A dorm bed in Yangshuo runs a mere US$2 a night, but the cheapest hotels in Tianjin (and other booming cities) start at US$15-20. Some hotels or hostels also may not accept foreigners. To give you a general idea, a bare-bones day in China (basic dorms, hostels, or spartan rooms in a rural area; food from street stalls or noodle and dumpling joints) would cost about US$6-8 (Y50-60) in the rural areas out west (Yunnan, Guangxi, Tibet, Sichuan, Gansu, Xinjiang) and about US$12-18 (Y100-150) in the densely populated south and east. A slightly more comfortable day (sleeping in a private room or a nicer room, eating one meal a day at a restaurant, going out at night) would run US$20-40 (Y160-300), again depending on location. For a luxurious day, the sky's the limit (especially in Beijing, Shanghai, and Hong Kong). Don't forget to factor in emergency funds (at least US$200) when planning how much money you'll need.

TIPS FOR SAVING MONEY

Some simple ways include opportunities for free entertainment, splitting accommodation and food costs with trustworthy fellow travelers, taking night trains to save on a night's accommodations, and buying food from street vendors and at nightmarkets. Do your laundry in the sink (unless you're explicitly prohibited from doing so). That said, don't go overboard. Though staying within a budget is important, don't do so at the expense of your health or a great travel experience.

TIPPING AND BARGAINING

Tipping and especially bargaining in the developing world are quite different from than what you may be accustomed to. **Tipping** is very uncommon in Asia. In China, don't feel obligated to tip anyone; they shouldn't expect you to. The same thing goes in Hong Kong and Macau, except in the fanciest of hotels. **Bargaining,** however, is a must. Travelers to China should make an attempt to learn the basics of bargaining etiquette, both in order to conduct themselves courteously in a foreign culture and to prevent unwittingly paying too much. As a rule of thumb, if there is no set price given, it is almost certainly negotiable, and even if there is a set price, it may well be negotiable too. This is true whether you're buying souvenirs, ordering dumplings at a food stall, checking into a guesthouse, or hiring a guide to take you sightseeing.

PACKING

Pack lightly: Lay out only what you absolutely need, then take half the clothes and twice the money. The Travelite FAQ (www.travelite.org) is a good resource for tips on traveling light. The online **Universal Packing List** (http://upl.codeq.info) will generate a customized list of suggested items based on your trip length, the expected climate, your planned activities, and other factors. If you plan to do a lot of hiking, also consult **Camping and the Outdoors,** p. 60.

> **Luggage:** If you plan to cover most of your itinerary by foot, a sturdy **frame backpack** is unbeatable. For the basics on buying a pack, see p. 62. Toting a **suitcase** or **trunk** is fine if you plan to live in 1 or 2 cities and explore from there, but not a great idea if you plan to move around frequently. In addition to your main piece of luggage, a **daypack** (a small backpack or courier bag) is useful. You may want to bring a lock to secure your pack, as pickpockets and thieves are common in train and bus stations.

> **Clothing:** No matter when you're traveling, it's a good idea to bring a warm jacket or wool sweater, a rain jacket (Gore-Tex® is both waterproof and breathable), sturdy shoes or hiking boots, and thick socks. Flip-flops or waterproof sandals are must-haves for

ESSENTIALS

THE ART OF THE DEAL. Bargaining in China is a must: no price is set in stone, and vendors will skyrocket prices at the mere scent of a *lǎowài*. It's up to you to get them down to a reasonable rate. With the following tips and some finesse, you might be able to impress even the most hardened hawkers:

1. **Bargaining needn't be a fierce struggle laced with barbs.** Quite the opposite: good-natured wrangling with a cheerful face may prove your best weapon.

2. **Use your poker face.** The less you betray your interest in the item the better. If you touch an item to inspect it, the vendor will be sure to "encourage" you to name a price or make a purchase. Coming back again and again is a good way of ensuring that you pay a ridiculously high price. Never get too enthusiastic about the object. Point out flaws in workmanship and design. Be cool.

3. **Overcome the language barrier:** Although body language and a big, smiling face can be one of your greatest weapons, merchants will immediately drop the price if you throw out a few words of Chinese. Some useful phrases:
Duōshǎo qián? (How much is it?)
Tài guì le! (That's too expensive!)
Duì wǒ kànlái, zhōngguó shì shìjiè shàng zuì piàoliàng de guójiā. (In my opinion, China is the most beautiful country in the world.)
Be careful, though—in minority areas, where Han Chinese aren't necessarily beloved, using Chinese might just annoy the merchant. In this case, act stupid and lovable and do your best.

4. **Know when to bargain.** In most cases, it's quite clear when it's appropriate to bargain. Except when in large department and grocery stores, expensive boutiques, restaurants, and foreign shops, you can expect to bargain for what you buy. When in doubt, ask tactfully, "Can you lower the price" (*Nǐ néng piányi yìdiǎn ma?*) or whether discounts (*zhékòu*) are given.

5. **Never underestimate the power of peer pressure.** Bargaining with more than one person at a time always leads to higher prices. Alternately, try having a friend discourage you from your purchase—if you seem to be reluctant, the merchant will want to drop the price to interest you again.

6. **Know when to turn away.** Feel free to refuse any vendor or driver who bargains rudely, and don't hesitate to move on to another vendor if one will not be reasonable about the final price he offers. However, to start bargaining without an intention to buy is a major *faux pas*. Agreeing on a price and declining it is also poor form. Turn away slowly with a smile and "thank you" upon hearing a ridiculous price: the price may plummet.

7. **Start low.** Never feel guilty offering a ridiculously low price. Your starting price should be no more than one-third to one-half the asking price. Chances are, even after bargaining hard, you'll still pay twice what a local would.

grubby hostel showers. You may also want one outfit for going out, and maybe a nicer pair of shoes. If you plan to visit religious or cultural sites, remember that you will need modest and respectful dress. Travelers to deserts, mountains, and highlands should be aware that temperatures drop drastically at night, even though it may be a sweltering 44°C by day. However, clothing in China is inexpensive and easy to find, though backpacking and outdoors gear is likely to be unavailable.

Converters and Adapters: In China, electricity is 220 volts AC, enough to fry any 120V North American appliance. Americans and Canadians should buy an adapter, which changes the shape of the plug (US$5), and a converter, which changes the voltage (US$20-30). Don't make the mistake of using only an adapter unless appliance instructions explicitly state otherwise. Residents of Australia, Ireland, New Zealand, and the UK won't need a converter. China uses a variety of plug outlets, the most common of which are two-pronged, similar to those in the US and Canada, though not polarized. These can be found in many mid-ranged hotels. China also uses a three-pronged rectangular blade plug, similar to those in the UK, and an oblique three-pronged plug like those in Australia. Residents of all other countries who want to use appliances outside the bathroom will have to buy an adapter. The electricity in rural China is not especially stable, so if your trip takes you out of city areas, pack light on appliances and heavy on battery power. For more on all things adaptable, check out http://kropla.com/electric.htm.

Toiletries: Toothbrushes, towels, cold-water soap, talcum powder (to keep feet dry), deodorant, razors, tampons and condoms are often available, but may be difficult to find; bring extras. Contact lenses, though inexpensive, may be difficult to find, so bring enough extra pairs and solution for your entire trip. Bring your glasses and a copy of your prescription in case you need emergency replacements. If you use heat-disinfection, either switch temporarily to a chemical disinfection system (check first to make sure it's safe with your brand of lenses), or buy a converter to 220V.

First-Aid Kit: For a basic first-aid kit, pack bandages, a pain reliever, antibiotic cream, a thermometer, a Swiss Army knife, tweezers, moleskin, decongestant, motion-sickness remedy, diarrhea or upset-stomach medication (Pepto Bismol or Imodium), an antihistamine, sunscreen, insect repellent, burn ointment, and a syringe for emergencies (get an explanatory letter from your doctor).

Film: Chinese brands of film are widely available and inexpensive. Most imported brands are easy to find as well, but they are not as cheap as Chinese brands. Slide or black-and-white film can be impossible to purchase outside of major cities. Less serious photographers may want to bring a disposable camera or two. Despite disclaimers, airport security X-rays can fog film, so buy a lead-lined pouch at a camera store or ask security to hand-inspect it. Always pack film in your carry-on luggage, since higher-intensity X-rays are used on checked luggage.

Other Useful Items: For safety purposes, you should bring a **money belt** and small **padlock.** Basic **outdoors equipment** (plastic water bottle, compass, waterproof matches, pocketknife, sunglasses, sunscreen, hat) may also prove useful. Quick repairs of torn garments can be done on the road with a **needle and thread;** also consider bringing electrical tape for patching tears. If you want to do laundry by hand, bring **detergent,** a small rubber ball to stop up the sink, and string for a makeshift clothes line. Travelers to southern China may consider bringing **mosquito netting.** Other things you're liable to forget are an **umbrella;** sealable **plastic bags** (for damp clothes, soap, food, shampoo, and other spillables); an **alarm clock;** safety pins; rubber bands; a flashlight; earplugs; garbage bags; and a small **calculator.**

Important Documents: Don't forget your passport, traveler's checks, ATM and/or credit cards, ID, and photocopies of all of the aforementioned in case these documents are lost or stolen (p. 15). Also check that you have any of the following that might apply to you: driver's license (see p. 15); travel insurance forms; and ISIC (p. 15).

SAFETY AND HEALTH

GENERAL ADVICE

In any type of crisis situation, the most important thing to do is **stay calm.** Your country's embassy abroad (p. 10) is usually your best resource when things go wrong: registering with that embassy upon arrival in the country is often a good idea. The government offices listed in the **Travel Advisories** box (p. 26) can provide information on the services they offer their citizens in case of emergencies abroad.

LOCAL LAWS AND POLICE

Remember that you are subject to the laws (and the penalties) of the country in which you travel, not to those of your home country, and it is your responsibility to familiarize yourself with these laws before leaving. Foreigners who break the law in China are prosecuted according to Chinese law and tried in Chinese courts. The local law enforcement agency is the **Public Safety Bureau** (gōng ān jú; 公安局, PSB). They have offices in nearly every town and city in China and take care of everything from traffic control to residence permits to crime to politically sensitive gatherings and dissidents. A special subdivision, the **Foreign Affairs Office** (waì shì chù; 外事处), deals with all matters related to foreigners. They handle visa extensions and issue alien travel permits to regions of China closed to foreigners (see **Special Permits,** p. 14). Along the same lines, they also enforce these same permits. If you are found in a closed-off area, they will fine you heavily and escort you out of the region. They also make sure that foreigners stay only in hotels designated to accept foreigners. Otherwise, you may be in for a rude awakening in the early hours of the morning. The law also requires foreigners staying in a private residence to register with the local foreign affairs office, under penalty of fines and possible detention. However, the PSB can also be a good resource to turn to in case of crime or disputes. Their authority goes unquestioned throughout China, and they will generally have a friendlier face toward foreigners. In case of robberies or other crimes, the PSB should be notified immediately. Wherever possible, *Let's Go* lists the phone number and address of the local PSB, including the visa office or foreign affairs office. In an **emergency,** call ☎ 110.

DRUGS AND ALCOHOL

China's recent upsurge in drug trafficking and drug use has led the government to stern crackdowns upon offenders. Penalties concerning the possession, use, or trafficking of **illegal drugs** are particularly steep; drug dealers and smugglers are regularly sentenced to death. Yunnan and Guangxi, on the border with Myanmar, Laos, and Vietnam, are notorious gateways through which drugs pass into China. Guard your possessions carefully, especially on long-distance bus or train rides—don't be the unwitting scapegoat of a drug dealer. If you carry **prescription drugs** while you travel, it is vital to have a copy of the prescriptions themselves and a note from a doctor, which you should keep readily accessible whenever you cross national borders. If you carry your own syringes, also have a note from the doctor. **Avoid public drunkenness:** it can get you in trouble with the authorities, jeopardize your safety, and earn the disdain of locals. A high percentage of Chinese wines and liquors are estimated to be counterfeit—some say as high as 70%. Produced by peasants as a way to fast cash, these imitations range from the clumsy to the seemingly genuine. Usually the vendor can't even vouch for the liquor's authenticity, and large department stores often unknowingly sell imitations. Be aware that the poor distillation methods used to produce these illegally-brewed liquors sometimes lead to poisoning or death. Beer, on the other hand, is usually safe, being too cheap to profitably counterfeit.

SPECIFIC CONCERNS

NATURAL DISASTERS

China is in a seismically active region, and **earthquakes** occur mostly in the mountain provinces of Xinjiang, Qinghai, and Gansu in western China, as well as Yunnan, Tibet, and northeastern China. If a strong earthquake does occur, it will usually last only a few minutes. Open a door to provide an escape route, and protect yourself by sheltering beneath a sturdy doorway, table, or desk. In coastal or mountainous areas tidal waves and landslides may follow quakes. **Floods** have ravaged the banks of the Yellow River and the Yangzi River as long as people have lived by their banks. Flood season is in the months of May-August, the result of heavy summer rains. Dams and levees have reduced damage, but floods still regularly cause landslides, mudslides, and casualties. They may also temporarily suspend ferry service on the Yangzi and render sites inaccessible. **Typhoons** are severe tropical storms (equivalent to hurricanes in the Atlantic) with very high winds. Typhoons may occur in the coastal areas of Hainan, Guangdong, Fujian, and Zhejiang in the rainy season of May-October.

DEMONSTRATIONS AND POLITICAL GATHERINGS

The June 4, 1989 Tian'anmen incident certainly stands out as the most prominent example of the Chinese government's uncompromising and hostile attitude toward political demonstrations. Since then, the government has been vigilant about arresting dissidents and disbanding potential protests before they can escalate into another Tian'anmen. Beijing's strict policies have mostly succeeded. A large-scale Falun Gong protest in the same square in 2000 was quickly broken up by police. More recently, peaceful protesters marched in free-spirited Hong Kong as the CCP moved to deny the SAR the right to directly elect its own leaders.

The best policy for travelers is to stay clear of gatherings and demonstrations should they occur. Tensions still run high around the anniversary of Tian'anmen on June 4, especially in Beijing, and foreigners should be careful. It's wise not to air political opinions too loudly in public. The government is particularly suspicious of foreign travelers to the politically sensitive regions of Tibet and Xinjiang.

TERRORISM AND CRIME

With China swiftly changing from a planned economy to a market-driven one, the number of unemployed workers and struggling peasants is on the rise. The increase in crime has led the CCP to launch campaigns favoring swift justice and stiff punishments (including execution) against any "unstable factors" in society, including mafia-style gangs, currency counterfeiters, smugglers, and drug dealers.

China's violent crime rate is low by international standards, and it is rare for foreigners to be targets of such crimes. Travelers should be aware that property crimes most often occur in areas undergoing rapid economic development. Robberies of foreigners have occurred at night in the popular expatriate bar neighborhoods of Beijing and Shanghai. On the whole, though, China is a relatively safe country for foreigners, and local citizens will often watch out for the safety of travelers. If you are the victim of theft or assault, report immediately not only to the local PSB, but also to your embassy in China.

Terrorist activity in China is rare and usually not targeted at foreigners. It should not be a safety concern for travelers. Although political violence and terrorist bombings are largely the work of ethnic (mostly Uighur) separatist groups, the growing army of unemployed workers, underground pro-democracy organizations, and quasi-Buddhist sects are also involved.

EMERGENCY!   Police (PSB) ☎ 110. Fire ☎ 119. Ambulance ☎ 120.

PERSONAL SAFETY

EXPLORING AND TRAVELING

To avoid unwanted attention, try to blend in as much as possible. Respecting local customs (in many cases, dressing more conservatively than you would at home) may placate would-be hecklers. Familiarize yourself with your surroundings

TRAVEL ADVISORIES. The following government offices provide travel information and advisories by telephone, by fax, or via the web:

Australian Department of Foreign Affairs and Trade: ☎13 00 555135; faxback service 02 6261 1299; www.dfat.gov.au.

Canadian Department of Foreign Affairs and International Trade (DFAIT): In Canada and the US call ☎800-267-8376, elsewhere call ☎+1 613-944-4000; www.dfait-maeci.gc.ca. Call for their free booklet, *Bon Voyage...But.*

New Zealand Ministry of Foreign Affairs: ☎04 439 8000; fax 494 8506; www.mft.govt.nz/travel/index.html.

United Kingdom Foreign and Commonwealth Office: ☎020 7008 0232; fax 7008 0155; www.fco.gov.uk.

US Department of State: ☎202-647-5225, faxback service 202-647-3000; http://travel.state.gov. For *A Safe Trip Abroad,* call ☎202-512-1800.

before setting out, and carry yourself with confidence. Check maps in shops and restaurants rather than on the street. If you are traveling alone, be sure someone at home knows your itinerary, and never admit that you're by yourself. When walking at night, stick to busy, well-lit streets and avoid dark alleyways. If you ever feel uncomfortable, leave the area as quickly and directly as you can.

There is no sure-fire way to avoid all the threatening situations you might encounter while traveling, but a good **self-defense course** will give you concrete ways to react to unwanted advances. **Impact, Prepare, and Model Mugging** can refer you to local self-defense courses in the US (☎800-345-5425). Visit the website at www.impactsafety.org for a list of nearby chapters. Workshops (2-3hr.) start at US$50; full courses (20hr.) run US$350-500.

POSSESSIONS AND VALUABLES

Never leave your belongings unattended, as crime occurs in even the most demure-looking hostel or hotel. Bring your own **padlock** for hostel lockers, and don't ever store valuables in any locker. Be particularly careful on long-distance **buses** and **trains:** horror stories abound about determined thieves who wait for travelers to fall asleep. Carry your backpack in front of you where you can see it. When traveling with others, sleep in alternate shifts. When alone, use good judgment in selecting a train compartment: never stay in an empty one, and use a lock to secure your pack to the luggage rack. Try to sleep on top bunks with your luggage stored above you (if not in bed with you), and keep important documents and other valuables on your person.

There are a few steps you can take to minimize the financial risk associated with traveling. First, **bring as little with you as possible.** Second, buy a few combination padlocks to secure your belongings either in your pack or in a hostel or train station locker. Third, **carry as little cash as possible.** Keep your traveler's checks and ATM/credit cards in a **money belt**—not a "fanny pack"—along with your passport and ID cards. Fourth, **keep a small cash reserve separate from your primary stash.** This should be about US$50 (US$ are best) sewn into or stored in the depths of your pack, along with your traveler's check numbers and important photocopies.

In large cities **con artists** often work in groups and may involve children. Beware of certain classics: sob stories accompany requests for money, rolls of bills "found" on the street, liquid spilled (or saliva spit) onto your shoulder to distract you while they snatch your bag. **Never let your passport and your bags out of your sight.** Tourists are popular and easy targets for **pickpockets,** especially in city crowds, tourist destinations, buses, open-air markets, and stores, where they may be in cahoots with low-paid security guards. Robberies and crimes may be more likely along the borders with Pakistan, Vietnam, Laos, Burma, and Russia. In the rare cases when foreigners have been the target of crime, the culprits usually posed as well-dressed tourists, or used Chinese women to lure men with promises of sex. Be alert in telephone booths: if you must say your calling card number, do so very quietly; if you punch it in, make sure no one can look over your shoulder.

If you will be traveling with electronic devices, such as a laptop or a PDA, check to see if your homeowner's insurance covers loss, theft, or damage when you travel. If not, you might consider purchasing a separate insurance policy. **Safeware** (☎ US 800-800-1492; www.safeware.com) specializes in covering computers and charges $90 for 90-day comprehensive international travel coverage up to $4000.

PRE-DEPARTURE HEALTH

In your **passport,** write the names of people you wish to be contacted in case of a medical emergency and list any allergies or medical conditions. Matching a prescription to a foreign equivalent is not always easy, safe, or possible. If you take prescription drugs, consider carrying up-to-date prescriptions or a statement from your doctor stating the medication's trade name, manufacturer, chemical name, and dosage. While traveling, be sure to keep all medication with you in your carry-on luggage. For tips on a basic **first-aid kit** and other health essentials, see p. 23.

IMMUNIZATIONS AND PRECAUTIONS

Travelers over two years old should make sure that the following vaccines are up to date: MMR (for measles, mumps, and rubella), DTaP or Td (for diphtheria, tetanus, and pertussis), IPV (for polio), Hib (for *haemophilus* influenza B), and HepB (for Hepatitis B). Adults traveling to the developing world on trips longer than four weeks should consider the following additional immunizations: Hepatitis A vaccine and/or immune globulin (IG), an additional dose of polio vaccine, typhoid and cholera vaccines, particularly if traveling off the beaten path, as well as a meningitis vaccine, Japanese encephalitis vaccine, rabies vaccine, and yearly influenza vaccines. While yellow fever is endemic only to parts of South America and sub-Saharan Africa, China may deny entrance to travelers arriving from these zones without a certificate of vaccination. For recommendations on immunizations and prophylaxis, consult the CDC (p. 28) in the US or the equivalent in your home country, and check with a doctor for guidance.

INOCULATION REQUIREMENTS AND RECOMMENDATIONS. No vaccines are required to travel to China, except yellow fever if arriving from infected areas (parts of tropical South America and sub-Saharan Africa). Vaccines against measles, diptheria, tetanus, polio, typhoid, Hepatitis A, and Hepatitis B are all recommended. Visitors planning to stay longer than four weeks should get vaccines for typhoid. Visitors planning to stay longer than four weeks in the summer in a rural region should get vaccinations for Japanese encephalitis. Visitors who will be more than 24 hours away from major hospitals or will be in contact with animals should consider a rabies vaccine.

INSURANCE

Travel insurance covers four basic areas: medical/health problems, property loss, trip cancellation/interruption, and emergency evacuation. Though regular insurance policies may well extend to travel-related accidents, you may consider purchasing separate travel insurance if the cost of potential trip cancellation, interruption, or emergency medical evacuation is greater than you can afford. Prices for travel insurance purchased separately generally run about US$50 per week for full coverage, while trip cancellation/interruption insurance may be purchased separately at a rate of US$3-5 per day depending on length of stay.

Medical insurance (especially university policies) often covers costs incurred abroad: check with your provider. **US Medicare** does not cover foreign travel. **Canadian** provincial health insurance plans increasingly do not cover foreign travel. Check with the provincial Ministry of Health or Health Plan Headquarters for details. **Homeowner's insurance** (or your family's coverage) often covers theft during travel and loss of travel documents (passport, plane ticket, etc.) up to US$500.

ISIC and **ITIC** (p. 15) provide basic insurance benefits to US cardholders, including US$100 per day of in-hospital sickness for up to 60 days and US$5000 of accident-related medical reimbursement. See www.isicus.com for details. Cardholders have access to a toll-free 24hr. helpline for medical, legal, and financial emergencies overseas. **American Express** (US ☎ 800-528-4800) grants most cardholders travel accident coverage of US$100,000 on flights purchased with the card.

INSURANCE PROVIDERS

STA (p. 34) offers a range of plans that can supplement your basic coverage. Other private insurance providers in the US and Canada include: Access America (☎ 800-284-8300; www.accessamerica.com), Berkely Group (☎ 800-797-4514; www.berkely.com), Globalcare Travel Insurance (☎ 800-821-2488; www.globalcare-cocco.com), Travel Assistance International (☎ 800-821-2828; www.europ-assistance.com), and Travel Guard (☎ 800-826-4919; www.travelguard.com). Columbus Direct (☎ 020 7375 0011; www.columbusdirect.co.uk) operates in the UK, and AFTA (☎ 02 9264 3299; www.afta.com.au) operates in Australia.

USEFUL ORGANIZATIONS AND PUBLICATIONS

The US **Centers for Disease Control and Prevention** (**CDC;** ☎ 877-FYI-TRIP; fax 888-232-3299; www.cdc.gov/travel) maintains an international travelers' hotline and an informative website. The CDC's comprehensive booklet *Health Information for International Travel (The Yellow Book)*, an annual rundown of disease, immunization, and general health advice, is free online or US$29-40 via the Public Health Foundation (☎ 877-252-1200; http://bookstore.phf.org). Consult the appropriate government agency of your home country for consular information sheets on health, entry requirements, and other issues for various countries (see **Travel Advisories**, p. 26). For quick information on health and other travel warnings, call the **Overseas Citizens Services** (M-F 8am-8pm, ☎ 888-407-4747; after-hours 202-647-4000; from overseas 317-472-2328), or contact a passport agency, embassy, or consulate abroad. For information on medical evacuation services and travel insurance firms, see the US government's website at http://travel.state.gov/medical.html or the **British Foreign and Commonwealth Office** (www.fco.gov.uk). For general health info, contact the **American Red Cross** (☎ 800-564-1234; www.redcross.org).

STAYING HEALTHY

Common sense is the simplest prescription for good health while you travel. Drink lots of fluids to prevent dehydration and constipation, wear sturdy, broken-in shoes and clean socks, and use talcum powder to keep your feet dry. Never drink the tap water in China, although it's alright to brush your teeth with water from the tap, except in regions where the water is at risk from contamination.

ONCE IN CHINA

ENVIRONMENTAL HAZARDS

Air quality: A disproportionate number of the world's most polluted cities are in China. Most of the country burns coal for heat in the winter, and industrial emissions tend to be alarmingly high. This will aggravate existing respiratory problems such as allergies and asthma, and even healthy travelers will fall victim to chest colds, respiratory infections, and bronchitis. This is particularly the case in China's biggest cities, such as Beijing, Chongqing, Guangzhou, Shanghai, Shenyang, and Xi'an. If you suffer from respiratory difficulties, be certain to take inhalers and/or any prescription medication with you and consult with your doctor for advice before departure.

Heat exhaustion and dehydration: All areas of China, particularly the deserts of the northwest and the subtropical areas of the south and southwest, can be brutally hot in the summer. Heat exhaustion leads to nausea, excessive thirst, headaches, and dizziness. Avoid it by drinking plenty of fluids, eating salty foods (e.g. crackers), abstaining from dehydrating beverages (e.g. alcohol and caffeinated beverages), and always wearing sunscreen. Continuous heat stress can eventually lead to heatstroke, characterized by a rising temperature, severe headache, delirium, and cessation of sweating. Victims should be cooled off with wet towels and taken to a doctor.

Sunburn: If you're prone to sunburn, bring sunscreen with you, as it's hard to find when traveling in China. Always wear sunscreen (SPF 30 is good) when spending excessive amounts of time outdoors. If you are spending time near water, in the desert, or in the snow, you are at a higher risk of getting burned, even through clouds. If you get sunburned, drink more fluids than usual and apply an aloe-based lotion. Severe sunburns can lead to sun poisoning, a condition that affects the entire body, causing fever, chills, nausea, and vomiting. Sun poisoning should always be treated by a doctor.

Hypothermia and frostbite: A rapid drop in body temperature is the clearest sign of overexposure to cold. Victims may also shiver, feel exhausted, have poor coordination or slurred speech, hallucinate, or suffer amnesia. *Do not let hypothermia victims fall asleep.* To avoid hypothermia, keep dry, wear layers, and stay out of the wind. When the temperature is below freezing, watch out for frostbite. If skin turns white or blue, waxy, and cold, do not rub the area. Drink warm beverages, stay dry, and slowly warm the area with dry fabric or steady body contact until a doctor can be found. In China, be particularly careful on long-distance bus rides: faulty heaters and mechanical breakdowns can be deadly in cold weather or at high elevations at all times of the year.

High altitude: Travelers to high-altitude areas, particularly Tibet and parts of Sichuan, as well as areas on the border between Xinjiang and Pakistan, must allow their bodies a couple of days to adjust to lower oxygen levels before exerting themselves. Note that alcohol is more potent and UV rays are stronger at high elevations.

INSECT-BORNE DISEASES

Insects—mainly mosquitoes, fleas, ticks, and lice—transmit many diseases. Be careful in wet or forested areas, especially while hiking; wear long pants and long sleeves, tuck your pants into your socks, and use a mosquito net. Use insect repellents like DEET and soak or spray your gear with permethrin (licensed in the US only for use on clothing). **Mosquitoes**—responsible for malaria, dengue fever, yellow fever, and Japanese encephalitis, among others—can be particularly dangerous in wet, swampy, or wooded areas, like southern China, the coasts, and rivers.

Malaria: Transmitted by *Anopheles* mosquitoes that bite at night. The incubation period varies anywhere between 10 days and 4 weeks. Early symptoms include fever, chills, aches, and fatigue, followed by high fever and sweating, sometimes vomiting and diarrhea. See a doctor if any flu-like sicknesses occur after travel in a risk area. To reduce the risk of contracting malaria, use mosquito repellent, particularly in the evenings and when in forested areas. Make sure you see a doctor at least 4-6 weeks before a trip to a high-risk area to get up-to-date malaria prescriptions and recommendations. A doctor may prescribe oral prophylactics, like **mefloquine, doxycycline,** or **chloroquine.** Be aware that mefloquine can have very serious side effects, including paranoia, psychotic behavior, and nightmares. Risk is greatest in rural areas, so if hiking or staying overnight in certain areas, take weekly anti-malarials. The type of drug you should take depends upon the strain of malaria present in the region; chloroquine is generally recommended for travelers to most areas, while mefloquine is recommended for travelers to areas with chloroquine-resistant malaria (Hainan Island, Guangxi, and Yunnan).

 MALARIA RISK Malaria is a risk in most rural areas in China, with the notable exceptions of Qinghai, Tibet, and the northern provinces bordering Mongolia and Russia. For travelers visiting cities and tourist destinations, the risk is generally very small, and anti-malarial medication is usually not needed. In **Guangdong, Guangxi, Yunnan, Fujian,** and **Hainan,** malaria is a year-round risk. Most of the **Yangzi River** region (Anhui, Hubei, Hunan, Jiangsu, Jiangxi, Shanghai, and Zhejiang) and **Sichuan** are at risk from May to December. North of this area (Shandong), risk of infection is only from July to November. However, travelers going down the Yangzi River by boat are not at risk for malaria.

Dengue fever: An "urban viral infection" transmitted by *Aedes* mosquitoes, which bite during the day rather than at night. The incubation period is 3-14 days, usually 4-7 days. Early symptoms include a high fever, severe headaches, swollen lymph nodes, and muscle aches. Many also suffer from nausea, vomiting, and a pink rash. If you experience these symptoms, see a doctor immediately, drink plenty of liquids, and take fever-reducing medication such as acetaminophen (Tylenol). *Never take aspirin to treat dengue fever.* There is no vaccine for dengue fever, chiefly in the southern part of China.

Japanese encephalitis: Another mosquito-borne disease, most prevalent during the summer and the rainy season in agricultural areas near rice fields and livestock pens. Aside from delirium, most symptoms are flu-like: chills, headache, fever, vomiting, muscle fatigue. The disease has a high mortality rate, and it's vital to go to a hospital as soon as any symptoms appear. While the JE-VAX vaccine, usually given in 3 shots over a 30-day period, is effective for a year, it has been linked with serious side effects. According to the CDC, there is little chance of being infected if proper precautions are taken, such as using mosquito repellents containing DEET and sleeping under mosquito nets.

Other insect-borne diseases: Lymphatic filariasis is a roundworm infestation transmitted by mosquitoes. Infection causes enlargement of extremities. There is no vaccine. In scattered, localized areas of China, the **plague** and **relapsing fever,** transmitted through fleas and ticks, still occur. Treatment is available for both, and a vaccine can prevent the plague. The risk to travelers, however, is usually quite low.

FOOD- AND WATER-BORNE DISEASES

Prevention is the best cure: be sure that your food is properly cooked and the water you drink is clean. Peel fruits and vegetables and avoid tap water (including ice cubes and anything washed in tap water, like salad). One of the best (and cheapest) ways to sample China's culinary delights is at the nightmarkets and street stalls of every town, but travelers may want to watch out for food that may have been cooked in unhygienic conditions. Other culprits are raw shellfish, unpasteurized milk, and sauces containing raw eggs. **Never drink the tap water in China.** Buy bottled water, or purify your own water by bringing it to a rolling boil or treating it with **iodine tablets.** Note, however, that some parasites such as *giardia* have exteriors that resist iodine treatment, and boiling is more reliable. Some rural vendors will sell bottled tap water—check to make sure that the freshness seal is in place and the packaging looks clean and professional. When in doubt or when bottled water can't be found, drink tea, juice, or soda. Iced beverages are not part of the Chinese lifestyle, and should be avoided in general, as the ice cubes may be made from tap water. Always wash your hands before eating or bring a quick-drying purifying liquid hand cleaner.

Traveler's diarrhea: Results from drinking fecally contaminated water or eating uncooked and contaminated foods. Symptoms include nausea, bloating, and urgency. Try quick-energy, non-sugary foods with protein and carbohydrates to keep your strength up. Over-the-counter anti-diarrheals (e.g. Imodium) may counteract the problems. The most dangerous side effect is dehydration. Drink 8 oz. of water with ½ tsp. of sugar or honey and a pinch of salt, try uncaffeinated soft drinks, or eat salted crackers. If you develop a fever or your symptoms don't go away after 4-5 days, consult a doctor. Consult a doctor immediately for treatment of diarrhea in children.

Dysentery: Results from a serious intestinal infection caused by certain bacteria in contaminated food or water. The most common type is bacillary dysentery. Symptoms include bloody diarrhea (sometimes mixed with mucus), fever, and abdominal pain and tenderness. Bacillary dysentery generally only lasts a week, but it is highly contagious. Amoebic dysentery, which develops more slowly, is a more serious disease and may cause long-term damage if left untreated. A stool test can determine which kind you have; seek medical help immediately. Dysentery can be treated with the drugs norfloxacin or ciprofloxacin (commonly known as Cipro). If you are traveling in high-risk (especially rural) regions, consider obtaining a prescription before you leave home. Dehydration can be a problem; be sure to drink plenty of water or eat salted crackers.

Cholera: An intestinal disease caused by a bacteria in contaminated food. The risk is low in China, especially if food and water precautions are followed. Symptoms include severe diarrhea, dehydration, vomiting, and muscle cramps. See a doctor immediately: it may be deadly if untreated, even within a few hours. Antibiotics are available, but the most important treatment is rehydration. There is no vaccine available in the US.

Hepatitis A: A viral infection of the liver acquired primarily through contaminated water, including through shellfish from contaminated water. Symptoms include fatigue, fever, loss of appetite, nausea, dark urine, jaundice, vomiting, aches and pains, and light stools. Risk is high in China, especially in rural areas and the countryside, though it is also present in urban areas. Ask your doctor about the Hepatitis A vaccine (Havrix or Vaqta) or an injection of immune globulin (IG; formerly called gamma globulin).

Giardiasis: Transmitted through parasites (microbes, tapeworms, etc. in contaminated water and food) and acquired by drinking untreated water from streams or lakes. Symptoms include diarrhea, abdominal cramps, bloating, fatigue, weight loss, and nausea. If untreated it can lead to severe dehydration. Giardiasis occurs worldwide.

Schistosomiasis: A parasitic disease caused when the larvae of a certain freshwater snail species penetrate unbroken skin. Watch for itchy rashes, followed in 4-6 weeks by fever, fatigue, headaches, muscle and joint aches, painful urination, diarrhea, nausea, loss of appetite, and night sweats. Avoid swimming in fresh water in areas with poor sanitation. If exposed to untreated water, rub the area vigorously with a towel and apply rubbing alcohol. Risk is present in southern China and the central Yangzi River basin.

Typhoid fever: Caused by the salmonella bacteria; **common in villages and rural areas in south China.** While mostly transmitted through contaminated food and water, it may also be acquired by direct contact with another person. Early symptoms include a persistent, high fever, headaches, fatigue, loss of appetite, constipation, and sometimes a rash on the abdomen or chest. Antibiotics can treat typhoid, but a vaccination (70-90% effective) is recommended.

ESSENTIALS

Leptospirosis: A bacterial disease caused by exposure to fresh water or soil contaminated by the urine of infected animals. Able to enter the human body through cut skin, mucus membranes, and through ingestion, it is most common in tropical climates. Symptoms include a high fever, chills, nausea, and vomiting. If not treated it can lead to liver failure and meningitis. There is no vaccine; consult a doctor for treatment. Travelers who participate in water sports such as rafting or kayaking are at highest risk.

OTHER INFECTIOUS DISEASES

Rabies: Transmitted through the saliva of infected animals. Fatal if untreated. By the time symptoms (thirst and muscle spasms) appear, the disease is in its terminal stage. If you are bitten, wash the wound thoroughly, seek immediate medical care, and try to have the animal located. A rabies vaccine, which consists of 3 shots given over a 21-day period, is available and recommended for developing world travel, but is only semi-effective. Rabies is found all over the world, and is often transmitted through dogs.

Hepatitis B: A viral infection of the liver transmitted via blood or other bodily fluids. Symptoms, which may not surface until years after infection, include jaundice, loss of appetite, fever, and joint pain. It is transmitted through activities like unprotected sex, injections of illegal drugs, and unprotected health work. A 3-shot vaccination sequence is recommended for health-care workers, sexually-active travelers, and anyone planning to seek medical treatment abroad; it must begin 6 mo. before traveling.

Hepatitis C: Like Hepatitis B, but mode of transmission differs. IV drug users, those with occupational exposure to blood, hemodialysis patients, and recipients of blood transfusions are at highest risk, but it can also be spread through sexual contact or sharing items like razors and toothbrushes that may have traces of blood on them. No symptoms are usually exhibited, but if they are, they can include loss of appetite, abdominal pain, fatigue, nausea, and jaundice. If untreated, Hepatitis C can lead to liver failure.

Severe Acute Respiratory Syndrome (SARS): A viral respiratory illness transmitted through air droplets. Early symptoms include fever, chills, headache, and muscle ache. Steroids and antiviral agents such as oseltamivir and ribavirin have been used as therapy; in many cases, however, SARS is fatal. At the time of writing in September 2004, SARS is not a risk for visitors to China. Travelers should still take the common precautions for influenza and avoid wildlife markets in Guangdong and Hong Kong, where scientists hypothesize the virus originated.

Avian influenza: A variant of the common respiratory illness, caused by the Avian influenza A virus. Though carried by all birds, it can only kill domesticated ones. In outbreaks in Thailand and Vietnam, the virus has jumped from birds to affect humans, but in China and Hong Kong, the disease has been limited to chickens alone. So far there have been no cases of human to human transmission. As a precaution, travelers to southern China and Hong Kong should avoid poultry farms and bird markets.

AIDS and HIV: For detailed information on Acquired Immune Deficiency Syndrome (AIDS) in China, call the CDC's 24hr. hotline (☎800-342-2437), or contact the Joint United Nations Programme on HIV/AIDS (UNAIDS), 20, ave. Appia, CH-1211 Geneva 27, Switzerland (☎41 22 791 3666; fax 22 791 4187). The AIDS epidemic has hit China with such force that it will likely become one of the world's most critical areas of AIDS infection within the next decade. In Yunnan alone there are an estimated 50,000 AIDS victims, with Xinjiang a close second. Note that China screens incoming travelers for AIDS, primarily those planning extended visits for work or study, and denies entrance to those who test HIV-positive. Contact the Chinese consulate for information.

Sexually transmitted diseases (STDs): Gonorrhea, chlamydia, genital warts, syphilis, herpes, and other STDs are more common than HIV and can cause serious complications. Hepatitis B and C can also be transmitted sexually. Though condoms may protect you from some STDs, oral or even tactile contact can lead to transmission. If you think you may have contracted an STD, see a doctor immediately.

OTHER HEALTH CONCERNS

MEDICAL CARE ON THE ROAD

Pharmacies, indicated by green crosses, abound in larger cities. Few are open 24hr. a day. The selection of local and imported pharmaceuticals has increased in recent years, but you may still want to bring your own supplies. Drugs that require a prescription elsewhere, such as a wide variety of antibiotics, may be readily available over the counter. In an emergency, go to the nearest major hospital, which is almost certainly open all night with an in-house pharmacy. In rural areas, the going is a bit rougher, but major towns should have at least one pharmacy.

The quality of **hospitals** and other medical services varies greatly from urban centers to rural countryside. Some urban hospitals may have a special **foreigner ward** (wàibīn bìngfáng; 外宾病房), or a VIP ward (gāogàn bìngfáng; 高干病房), both of which accept foreigners and are generally of a higher quality. Hospitals in rural areas may be reluctant to treat foreigners in non-emergency situations. For non-emergency care, contact your embassy and ask for a suggested list of doctors.

There are a few foreign-operated hospitals and clinics in major cities geared toward international visitors. **Global Doctor** (24hr. ☎86 10 8456 9191; www.eglobaldoctor.com) runs clinics with the latest technology and telemedicine in Beijing, Chengdu, Shenyang, Changsha, Guangzhou, and Chongqing and also provides emergency evacuation. If you are concerned about obtaining medical assistance while traveling, you may wish to employ special support services. The *MedPass* from **GlobalCare, Inc.,** 6875 Shiloh Rd. East, Alpharetta, GA 30005, USA (☎800-860-1111; fax 678-341-1800; www.globalcare.net), provides 24hr. international medical assistance, support, and medical evacuation resources. The **International Association for Medical Assistance to Travelers** (**IAMAT;** US ☎716-754-4883, Canada 519-836-0102; www.cybermall.co.nz/NZ/IAMAT) has free membership, lists English-speaking doctors worldwide, and offers detailed info on immunization requirements and sanitation. If your regular **insurance** policy does not cover travel abroad, you may wish to purchase additional coverage (p. 27).

Those with medical conditions (such as diabetes, allergies to antibiotics, epilepsy, heart conditions) may want to obtain a **Medic Alert** membership (first year US$35, annually thereafter US$20), which includes a stainless steel ID tag, among other benefits, like a 24hr. collect-call number. Contact the Medic Alert Foundation, 2323 Colorado Ave, Turlock, CA 95382, USA (☎888-633-4298, outside US 209-668-3333; www.medicalert.org).

WOMEN'S HEALTH

Women traveling in unsanitary conditions are vulnerable to **urinary tract (including bladder and kidney) infections.** Over-the-counter medicines can sometimes alleviate symptoms, but if they persist, see a doctor. **Vaginal yeast infections** may flare up in hot and humid climates. Wearing loosely fitting trousers or a skirt and cotton underwear will help, as will remedies like Monostat or Gynelotrimin. Bring supplies from home if you are prone to infection, as they may be difficult to find on the road. **Pads** are available in most of China, though your favorite brand may not be stocked—bring extras of anything you can't live without. However, **tampons** are harder to find. **Reliable contraceptive devices** may also be difficult to find outside of large cities. Women on the pill should stock up to allow for possible loss or extended stays. Bring a prescription, since forms of the pill vary a good deal. Though condoms are available, consider bringing some, as availability and quality vary. **Abortion** in China is legal. Parental authorization is required for those under 18, and abortion may not be used to abort the fetus of an unwanted gender. Mifepristone, commonly known as RU-486, has been widely available in China since

1988. Women who need an abortion while abroad should contact the **International Planned Parenthood Federation**, European Regional Office, Regent's College Inner Circle, Regent's Park, London NW1 4NS, UK (☎44 20 7487 7900; fax 487 7950) for more information, or the **China Family Planning Association (CFPA)**, No. 35 Shaoyaoju, Chaoyang, Beijing 100029 (☎86 10 6441 3375; www.chinafpa.org.cn).

GETTING TO CHINA

BY PLANE

When it comes to airfare, a little effort can save you a bundle. If your plans are flexible enough to deal with the restrictions, courier fares are the cheapest. Tickets bought from consolidators and standby seating are also good deals, but last-minute specials, airfare wars, and charter flights often beat these fares. The key is to hunt around, to be flexible, and to ask persistently about discounts. Students, seniors, and those under 26 should never pay full price for a ticket.

AIRFARES

Airfares to China peak between late May and mid-September. Mid-week (M-Th morning) round-trip flights run US$40-50 cheaper than weekend flights, but they are generally more crowded and less likely to permit frequent-flier upgrades. Not fixing a return date ("open return") or arriving in and departing from different cities ("open-jaw") can be pricier than round-trip tickets and limits travel dates. Patching one-way flights together is the most expensive. Flights between China's capital or regional hubs—Beijing, Shanghai, and Hong Kong—tend to be cheaper.

If China is only one stop on a more extensive globe-hop, consider a round-the-world (RTW) ticket. Tickets usually include at least five stops and are valid for about a year. Prices range US$3400-5000. Try **Northwest Airlines/KLM** (US ☎800-447-4747; www.nwa.com) or **Star Alliance**, a consortium of 22 airlines, including United Airlines (US ☎800-241-6522; www.staralliance.com).

In the summer, **fares** for round-trip flights to Beijing, Shanghai, or Hong Kong from the US or Canadian east coast start at US$800-1600; from the US or Canadian west coast US$600-1400; from the UK UK$450-800; from Australia or New Zealand AUS$1000-1500. Fares are generally US$100-300 less in the low-season (late Sept.-early May). Tickets to Hong Kong are usually cheaper and easier to find than those to Beijing or Shanghai. Summer flights to China are cheapest when purchased in late February, March, and early April.

BUDGET AND STUDENT TRAVEL AGENCIES

Unlike many international destinations, the cheapest tickets to China are usually not offered by conventional student or budget travel agencies (i.e. Council Travel or STA), but by smaller **Chinatown** agencies that cater mainly to overseas Chinese. These agencies are often able to find prices as much as 20-30% lower than other budget travel agencies. We highly recommend scouring the phone book for travel agencies in your local Chinatown or picking up a copy of a local Chinese newspaper and flipping to the travel advertisements page to find an agency near you.

When this option is not feasible, budget travel agencies are your next best bet. Knowledgeable agents specializing in flights to China can make your life easy and help you save. Travelers with **ISIC** and **IYTC** (see p. 15) qualify for big discounts from student travel agencies. Most flights from budget agencies are on major airlines, but in high season some may sell seats on less reliable chartered aircraft.

CTS Travel, 30 Rathbone Pl., London W1T 1GQ, UK (☎0207 209 0630; www.ctstravel.co.uk). A British student travel agent with offices in 39 countries including the US: Empire State Building, 350 Fifth Ave., Suite 7813, New York, NY 10118 (☎877-287-6665; www.ctstravelusa.com).

STA Travel, 5900 Wilshire Blvd., Ste. 900, Los Angeles, CA 90036, USA (24hr. reservations and info ☎800-781-4040; www.sta-travel.com). A student and youth travel organization with over 150 offices worldwide, including US offices in Boston, Chicago, L.A., New York, San Francisco, Seattle, and Washington, D.C. Ticket booking, travel insurance, railpasses, and more. Walk-in offices are located throughout Australia (☎03 9349 4344), New Zealand (☎09 309 9723), and the UK (☎0870 1 600 599).

Travel CUTS (Canadian Universities Travel Services Limited), 187 College St., Toronto, ON M5T 1P7 (☎416-979-2406; www.travelcuts.com). Offices across Canada and the US, including Los Angeles, New York, Seattle, and San Francisco.

usit, 19-21 Aston Quay, Dublin 2 (☎01 602 1777; www.usitworld.com), Ireland's leading student/budget travel agency has 22 offices throughout Northern Ireland and the Republic of Ireland. Offers programs to work in North America.

COMMERCIAL AIRLINES

The commercial airlines' lowest regular offer is the **APEX** (Advance Purchase Excursion) fare, which provides confirmed reservations and allows "open-jaw" tickets. Generally, reservations must be made seven to 21 days in advance, with seven- to 14-day minimum-stay and up to 90-day maximum-stay restrictions. These fares carry hefty cancellation and change penalties (fees rise in summer). Book peak-season APEX fares early. Use **Microsoft Expedia** (msn.expedia.com) or **Travelocity** (www.travelocity.com) to get an idea of the lowest published fares, then use the resources outlined here to try and beat those fares. Low-season fares should be appreciably cheaper than the high-season ones listed here.

As more and more airlines fly to China, travelers have an increasingly large number of carriers to choose from. The airlines listed below often have cheaper fares than those offered by standard commercial carriers. Some flights may involve overnight stays or lengthy layovers in Tokyo or Seoul.

FLIGHT PLANNING ON THE INTERNET. The Internet may be the budget traveler's dream when it comes to finding and booking bargain fares. Many airline sites offer special last-minute deals on the web. Try **Air China** (www.airchina.com.cn); **China Eastern** (www.chinaeasternair.com); **Cathay Pacific** (www.cathaypacific.com); **Korean Air** (www.koreanair.com); **All Nippon Airways** (www.ana.co.jp); **Asiana Airlines** (www.asiana.co.kr).

STA (www.sta-travel.com) and **StudentUniverse** (www.studentuniverse.com) provide quotes on student tickets, while **Orbitz** (www.orbitz.com), **Expedia** (www.expedia.com), and **Travelocity** (www.travelocity.com) offer full travel services. **Asia Miles** (www.asiamiles.com) gives out mileage for doing business with their partners, including airlines, hotels, and restaurants, which travelers can then exchange for a variety of rewards. Booking flights to Hong Kong at **Zuji** (www.zuji.com) also earns Asia Miles. **Priceline** (www.priceline.com) lets you specify a price, and obligates you to buy any ticket that meets or beats it. **Hotwire** (www.hotwire.com) offers bargain fares, but won't reveal the airline or flight times until you buy. Other sites that compile deals for you include www.bestfares.com, www.flights.com, www.lowestfare.com, www.onetravel.com, and www.travelzoo.com.

To help sift through multiple offers, **SideStep** (www.sidestep.com; download required) and **Booking Buddy** (www.bookingbuddy.com) let you enter your trip information once and search multiple sites.

An indispensable resource on the Internet is the **Air Traveler's Handbook** (www.faqs.org/faqs/travel/air/handbook), a comprehensive listing of links to everything you need to know before you board a plane.

Air China: Australia ☎9232 7277; UK 7630 0919; US and Canada 800-986-1985; Beijing domestic 86 10 6601 3336, international 6601 6667; www.airchina.com.cn. Flies to both international and domestic destinations.

All Nippon Airways (ANA): Australia ☎1 800 00 1126; Ireland 850 200058; UK 870 837 8866; US and Canada 800-235-9262; Beijing 6590 9191; www.fly-ana.com.

Asiana Airlines: Australia ☎3 0076 7234; New Zealand 9 300 3630; UK 7514 0200; US and Canada 800-227-4262; http://flyasiana.com.

Air Canada: Australia ☎8248 5757; Ireland 1 679 3958; New Zealand 9 969 7470; UK 871 220 1111; US and Canada 888-247-2262; www.aircanada.ca.

Cathay Pacific: Australia ☎131 747; Canada 800-268-6868; New Zealand 800 800 454; UK 8834 8888; US 800-233-2742; www.cathaypacific.com.

China Eastern Airlines: Australia ☎9290 1148; US and Canada 800-200-5118; www.ce-air.com.

Korean Air: Australia ☎2 9262 6000; Ireland 1 799 7990; UK 800 0656 2001; US and Canada 800-438-5000; www.koreanair.com.

Japan Airlines (JAL): Australia ☎2 9272 1111; Ireland 1 408 3757; New Zealand 9 3799 906; UK 845 7747 700; US and Canada 800-525-3663; www.jal.co.jp/en. Flies to 14 destinations in China with stopovers in Japan.

TRAVELING FROM NORTH AMERICA

Basic round-trip fares to China range from roughly US$600-US$1600 to Beijing, US$500-US$1500 to Shanghai, and US$500-US$1600 to Hong Kong. Standard commercial airlines like American and United will probably offer the most convenient flights, but they may not be the cheapest, unless you grab a special promotion or airfare war ticket. One of the above airlines will probably offer better deals, if any of their limited departure points is convenient. **Northwest Airlines** (from the US and Canada ☎800-447-4747, from Beijing 86 10 6505 3505; www.nwa.com) also has cheaper fares. Most flights to China from North America go through New York, Chicago, Los Angeles, San Francisco, or Vancouver.

TRAVELING FROM THE UK AND IRELAND

Economy round-trip fares vary between £300-£800 to Beijing, Hong Kong, and Shanghai. British Airways generally provides convenient but expensive flights. You may find better deals with Air France, KLM, and airlines based in Asia. Austrian Airlines has affordable flights to Beijing and Shanghai via Vienna.

Air France: Ireland ☎1 605 0392, UK 845 359 1000; www.airfrance.com.

Austrian Airlines: ☎43 5 1789, Ireland 1 800 509 142, UK 870 1 24 26 25, Beijing 86 10 6462 2161; www.aua.com.

Royal Dutch Airlines (KLM): UK and Ireland ☎44 870 507 4074; www.klm.com.

Virgin Atlantic: ☎44 870 380 2007; www.virgin-atlantic.com.

TRAVELING FROM AUSTRALIA AND NEW ZEALAND

Fares for round-trip flights to Beijing run AUS$900-1400, to Shanghai AUS$900-1300, and to Hong Kong AUS$900-1200. **Qantas** flies to Shanghai from Sydney and Melbourne, and to Hong Kong from Sydney, Melbourne, Brisbane, Perth, and Cairn. **Japan Airlines (JAL)** tends to be cheaper, but requires a stopover in Japan. Flights from New Zealand cost about AUS$200 more than those from Australia.

Air New Zealand: New Zealand ☎800 737 000, from overseas 64 9 357 3000, from Australia 800 803 298; www.airnz.co.nz.

Qantas: Australia ☎13 13 13, Auckland 9 357 8900, Wellington 800 808 767; www.qantas.com.au.

AIR COURIER FLIGHTS

Those who travel light should consider courier flights. Couriers help transport cargo on international flights by using their checked luggage space for freight. Generally, couriers must travel with carry-ons only and must deal with complex flight restrictions. Most flights are round-trip only, with short fixed-length stays (usually at least one week) and a limit of one ticket per issue. Flights to Asia generally allow longer stays. Most of these flights also operate only out of major gateway cities, mostly in North America, including New York, Los Angeles, San Francisco, or Miami in the US, and Montreal, Toronto, or Vancouver in Canada. Round-trip courier fares from the US to Hong Kong (US$250-500) are the most common, though tickets to Beijing and Shanghai are sometimes available. Generally, you must be over 21 (in some cases 18). Traveling companions can pay full fare on the same flight, but those who fly courier usually travel alone. In summer, the most popular destinations often require a two-week advance reservation (you can usually book up to two months ahead). Super-discounted fares are common for "last-minute" flights (three to 14 days ahead).

Groups such as the **Air Courier Association** (☎ 800-461-8856; www.aircourier.org) provide members with lists of opportunities and courier brokers worldwide for an annual fee. Another organization to consult is the **International Association of Air Travel Couriers,** P.O. Box 847, Scottsbluff, Nebraska 69363-0847 (☎ 308-632-3273; www.courier.org). **Micom America** has branches in Los Angeles (☎ 310-670-1198) and New York (☎ 781-656-6242) with daily courier flights to Hong Kong and allows travelers to stay up to 30 days. **NOW Voyager,** 45 W. 21st St., Suite 5A , New York, NY 10010 (☎ 212-459-1616; www.nowvoyagertravel.com) arranges courier flights to Hong Kong. For more information, consult *Air Courier Bargains* by Kelly Monaghan (The Intrepid Traveler, US$15) or the *Courier Air Travel Handbook* by Mark Field (Perpetual Press, US$10).

STANDBY FLIGHTS

Traveling standby requires considerable flexibility in arrival and departure dates and cities. Companies dealing in standby flights sell vouchers rather than tickets, along with the promise to get you to your destination (or near your destination) within a certain window of time (typically 1-5 days). You call in before your specific window of time to hear your flight options and the probability that you will be able to board each flight. You can then decide which flights you want to try to make, show up at the appropriate airport at the appropriate time, present your voucher, and board if space is available. Vouchers can usually be bought for both one-way and round-trip travel. You may receive a monetary refund only if every available flight within your date range is full: if you opt not to take an available (but perhaps less convenient) flight, you can only get credit toward future travel. Carefully read agreements with any company offering standby flights as tricky fine print can leave you in the lurch. To check on a company's service record in the US, call the Better Business Bureau (☎ 703-276-0100). It is difficult to receive refunds, and vouchers will not be honored when an airline fails to receive payment in time.

TICKET CONSOLIDATORS

Ticket consolidators, or **"bucket shops,"** buy unsold tickets in bulk from commercial airlines and sell them at discounted rates. The best place to look is in the Sunday travel section of any major newspaper (such as *The New York Times*), where many bucket shops place tiny ads. Call quickly, as availability is typically extremely limited. Not all bucket shops are reliable, so insist on a receipt that gives full details of restrictions, refunds, and tickets, and pay by credit card (in spite of the 2-5% fee) so you can stop payment if you never receive your tickets. For more info, see www.travel-library.com/air-travel/consolidators.html.

TRAVELING FROM THE US AND CANADA

Travel Avenue (☎ 800-333-3335; www.travelavenue.com) searches for the best available published fares and then uses several consolidators to attempt to beat that fare. Other consolidators worth trying are **Rebel** (☎ 800-732-3588; www.rebeltours.com), **Cheap Tickets** (☎ 800-652-4327; www.cheaptickets.com), **Flights.com** (www.flights.com), and **TravelHUB** (www.travelhub.com). Keep in mind that these are just suggestions to get you started in your research; *Let's Go* does not endorse any of these agencies. As always, be cautious, and research companies before you hand over your credit card number.

TRAVELING FROM THE UK, AUSTRALIA, AND NEW ZEALAND

In London, the **Air Travel Advisory Bureau** (☎020 7306 3000; www.atab.co.uk) can provide names of reliable consolidators and discount flight specialists. From Australia and New Zealand, look for consolidator ads in the travel section of the *Sydney Morning Herald* and other papers.

CHARTER FLIGHTS

Charters are flights a tour operator contracts with an airline to fly extra loads of passengers in high season. These fly less frequently than major airlines, make refunds particularly difficult, and are almost always fully booked. Schedules and itineraries may change or be cancelled at the last moment (as late as 48hr. before the trip, and without a full refund), and check-in, boarding, and baggage claim are often much slower. However, they can also be cheaper. Discount clubs and fare brokers offer members savings on last-minute charter and tour deals. Study contracts closely: you don't want to end up with an unwanted overnight layover.

FROM RUSSIA, WITH LOVE

TRANS-SIBERIAN RAILROAD

The term Trans-Siberian Railroad is generally misused to refer to three different rail lines. The real Trans-Siberian line runs from Moscow to Vladivostok, connecting the gilded domes and tinted windshields of Moscow with the rest of her proud but crumbling empire. The two lines that are of interest to travelers in China are the Trans-Mongolian and the Trans-Manchurian. The **Trans-Mongolian** connects Beijing, Mongolia, and Moscow; the **Trans-Manchurian** runs north from Beijing, crosses the Chinese-Russian border via Manzhouli in Inner Mongolia, and goes straight to Moscow. The trip takes five or six days depending on the route (the Trans-Mongolian is the shorter of the two). Both trains roll through two continents, seven time zones, and thousands of miles of land.

LIFE ABOARD THE TRAINS. Food in dining cars (as well as that sold by locals) is priced according to local currency, so Russian rubles as well as Chinese *yuán* will be useful. Bringing US dollars is more convenient, as dollars are more easily exchanged at border crossings. Many travelers also bring their own food. Instant noodles are a good idea, as hot water is available. Try to avoid the first or last compartment in the car, which are next to the toilets; on trains without attendants, the stench can be unbearable. As always, remember to bring your own toilet paper.

VISAS

Because the Trans-Mongolian Railroad cuts through Ulaan Bataar, visas to both Russia and Mongolia are necessary to travel this route. The Trans-Manchurian Railroad only requires a Russian visa.

MONGOLIAN VISAS. Visitors can get a **transit visa** to Mongolia, which allows for a two-day stay, or a **tourist visa.** (Transit visa US$15, express US$30. Single-entry tourist visa valid for 3 months US$25/US$50; multiple-entry visa valid for 6 months US$65/US$130). A tourist visa requires visitors to have a **letter of invitation** from a travel agency in Mongolia. CITS gives travelers ticket vouchers to obtain the required visas. Visitors cannot obtain visas at the border, but must go to the **Mongolian embassy** in Beijing (p. 10), or apply for a visa through the travel agencies that also arranged for the train tickets. The transit visa requires that the applicant hold an onward ticket and a visa for their next destination, so you will have to get a Russian visa before you can get a Mongolian visa.

RUSSIAN VISAS. All Russian visas require an **invitation** stating the traveler's itinerary and dates of travel. Visas can be obtained with the help of the same travel agencies that book tickets, but it's cheaper to obtain visas from the Russian embassy in Beijing (p. 11). The **transit visa** is valid for only 10 days. Since the train ride takes about six, there is very little time to get off the train, especially since you will have to leave time to go from Moscow to your next destination. It is wise to arrange transportation out of Moscow in advance. To obtain a transit visa, you must already have a train ticket and a visa for your next destination. The **tourist visa** lasts 30 days but is a hassle to obtain. You must present tourist confirmations from hotels you will be staying in during your journey, which requires you to plan your itinerary in advance. Furthermore, you must stay in hotels that are registered with the Russian Ministry of Foreign Affairs, which tend to be expensive.

TRANS-MONGOLIAN RAILROAD

Tickets for the Trans-Mongolian can be obtained from **CITS** in Beijing, which allows you to reserve tickets in advance with a Y100 deposit. **Hualong International Travel Service** (p. 131) in the Beijing International Hotel also helps arrange tickets and Russian and Mongolian visas. In Hong Kong, the helpful **Moonsky Star Travel Agency** (p. 547) offers an assortment of packages and can help obtain visas.

FROM	DEPARTS	TO	ARRIVES	VIA	PRICE (Y)
Beijing	W 7:40am	Moscow	M 2:10pm (Moscow time)	Ulaan Batar (arrives Th 2:10pm)	2700-3200
Moscow	F 11:58pm (Moscow time)	Beijing	Th 3:49pm	Ulaan Batar (arrives W 8:31am)	2700-3200

TRANS-MANCHURIAN RAILROAD

Tickets for the Trans-Manchurian (route #19) are obtained in the same places and in the same manner as for the Trans-Mongolian (see above). Only the **CITS** head office in the Beijing International Hotel (p. 130) books tickets.

FROM	DEPARTS	TO	ARRIVES	VIA	PRICE (Y)
Beijing	Sa 11:10pm	Moscow	F 7:50pm (Moscow time)	Manzhouli (arrives M 4:54am)	2700-3200
Moscow	F 11:53pm (Moscow time)	Beijing	F 8:58am	Manzhouli (arrives W 10:58pm)	2700-3200

OTHER TRAINS INTO SIBERIA

Rail routes connect Harbin (p. 224) in Heilongjiang with Russia via Suifenhe (p. 239), a town on the China-Russia border. It's best to deal with visas in Beijing at the Russian embassy, but visas can also be obtained in Suifenhe, where the Railway Travel Agency can help travelers buy train tickets and obtain visas; note that US citizens cannot get visas in Suifenhe. Train #607 departs Harbin Main Station and branches off to Khabarovsk and Vladivostok. The return trains (#608) meet up, heading to Harbin together.

ROUTE	FROM	DEPARTS	TO	ARRIVES	PRICE (Y)
K607	Harbin	W, Sa 6:30pm	Khabarovsk	F, M 11:29am	about 1000
			Vladivostok	Th, Su 9:25pm	about 1000
K608	Khabarovsk	daily 7:48am	Harbin	3rd day 4:48am	same as above
	Vladivostok	daily 7:02pm			

A SLOW BOAT TO CHINA

FROM SOUTH KOREA. Many coastal cities have international ferry terminals with boats arriving from Inchon, particularly Dalian (p. 261) and Qingdao (p. 207). Citizens of Australia, Canada, South Africa, the US, most Western European countries, and New Zealand can stay in South Korea visa-free for 30 days.

FROM JAPAN. Ferries link Japan and several cities in China, including Tanggu (p. 170), Qingdao (p. 207), and Shanghai (p. 337). High-priced cruise lines offer trips from Osaka, Kobe, or Tokyo to Hong Kong or Beijing. Citizens of North America, Western Europe, and Oceanic countries can stay visa-free for 90 days.

BORDER CROSSINGS

In general, odd-numbered international trains depart from China, and even-numbered trains arrive in China. International train tickets are usually sold at **China International Travel Service (CITS)** or other travel agencies, not at train stations.

SOUTHEAST ASIA

LAOS. The border crossing between China and Laos is located at the town of **Mohan** in the Xishuangbanna region of Yunnan province. Mohan is accessible only by buses or minibuses (2hr.; buses Y10-15, minibuses Y60) from **Mengla** (p. 662). Leave early, as the border is open only 8am-5pm. Laotian visas are not issued at the border. They must be obtained in Beijing or at the Laotian consulate in Kunming (p. 644). For more information, see **Border Crossing into Laos: Mohan**, p. 662.

MYANMAR (BURMA). From **Ruili**, minibuses go to **Jiegao**, where the border between China and Myanmar has recently opened. You must obtain a visa from a consulate (try the Burmese Consulate in Kunming, p. 644), since border guards don't issue them. For more information, see **Border Crossing into Myanmar**, p. 668.

VIETNAM. Most travelers cross between Vietnam and China via one of two border posts: **Pingxiang** in Guangxi province or **Hekou** in Yunnan province (for more information, see **Border Crossing into Vietnam: Hekou**, p. 651). Trains and buses leave from Nanning to the crossing at Pingxiang (p. 600). Two buses per day go between Kunming and the crossing at Hekou. Direct trains no longer run between Beijing and Hanoi. Visas cannot be obtained at either crossing. The cheapest and safest plan is to take care of Vietnamese visas in Beijing or Hong Kong (p. 9). Chinese embassies in Hanoi and Bangkok process Chinese visas.

THE 'STANS

KAZAKHSTAN. Kazakh visas can be obtained at the embassy in Beijing, or at the **Kazakh Airlines Visa Office** in Ürümqi (see **Border Crossing into Kazakhstan**, p. 789). There are not only trains between Ürümqi and Altai, but also regular flight service and buses between the two cities. The trains below run only May-December.

ROUTE	FROM	DEPARTS	TO	ARRIVES	PRICE (Y)
K895	Ürümqi	Sa, M 10pm	Almaty	M, W 7:33am (Moscow time)	491
K896	Almaty	M, Sa 11:40pm (Moscow time)	Ürümqi	W, M 10:18am	96-192

PAKISTAN. Buses leave around noon from **Kashgar's** International Bus Station (p. 808) for Sost, Pakistan via Tashkurgan, Karakul Lake, and the Khunjerab Pass (16hr. plus overnight stay in Tashkurgan, summer daily, Y270). Visas are required and are not issued at the border. The Pakistani embassy in Beijing (p. 11) is the nearest source of Pakistani visas (p. 815).

KYRGYZSTAN. Buses also leave from Kashgar International Bus Station (p. 808) for Bishkek, Kyrgyzstan via the Torugut Pass (16hr., M, US$50). To take this bus, you'll have to obtain a transit permit (pīzhèng; 批证) beforehand. However, only travel agencies can issue these permits; they often require travelers to take a tour, but if you ask you may be able to purchase a permit separately (Y500 for groups less than 10). John's Information Cafe (p. 808) in Kashgar can also arrange permits and tours to Bishkek for US$280. Travelers to Kyrgyzstan must also obtain valid entry visas, which are available only in Beijing or Hong Kong (p. 11).

MONGOLIA

Travelers who want to visit Mongolia must have either a transit visa or a tourist visa (p. 39). Several **trains** go from China to Mongolia each week. In addition to the Trans-Mongolian train to Russia (p. 40), train #23 goes from Beijing to **Ulaan Bataar.** Tickets can be purchased in Beijing at CITS (p. 130) and Hualong Travel Service (p. 131). Trains #4602/4603 and #4601/4604/4605/4606 travel between Hohhot and Ulaan Bataar and cross the border at **Erinhot.** You can also take a **plane** to Ulaan Bataar from **Beijing** (2hr.; M, W-Th, Sa-Su; Y1767, round-trip Y2934).

ROUTE	FROM	DEPARTS	TO	ARRIVES	PRICE (Y)
#23	Beijing	Tu 7:40am	Ulaan Bataar	W 1:10pm (Ulaan Bataar time)	560
#4602/ 4603	Hohhot	M, F 10:30pm	Ulaan Bataar	W, Su 10:55am (Ulaan Bataar time)	500-551
#4601/ 4604/ 4605/ 4606	Ulaan Bataar	M, F 8:10pm (Ulaan Bataar time)	Hohhot	Tu, Sa 9:10pm	500-551

NEPAL

The **Friendship Highway** runs from Lhasa, in Tibet, to Kathmandu, crossing the border at **Zhangmu/Kodari.** Visitors travel in both directions, but in terms of visas and logistics, it's much easier to go from Tibet to Nepal than the other way around. Nepali visas are required and can be obtained at the border crossing for US$30, although it is far more convenient to get one at the Nepali consulate in Lhasa (p. 840). For more information, see **Border Crossing into Nepal,** p. 865.

NORTH KOREA

Views of North Korea from Changbaishan (p. 249) or from across the Yalu River in Dandong (p. 258) may be the closest you'll come to this isolated country. Generally, only organized tourist groups authorized by the North Korean government are permitted into the country. One such tourist group is the Beijing-based **Koryo Tours** (☎/fax 86 10 6416 7544; www.koryogroup.com), which has been in operation since 1993. Independent tourism is extremely limited, and visas are difficult to obtain, especially for US citizens (impossible for South Koreans). Travel to the DPRK is generally arranged through the North Korean embassy (p. 11).

GETTING AROUND CHINA
BY PLANE

China has enough geographical barriers and unbearably long bus and train rides for even the stingiest of travelers to consider domestic air travel. While the cost of flying is five to eight times the price of a hard sleeper, air travel saves precious time and energy. Air travel is also more convenient, thanks to the Chinese government, which has expanded flights, especially in the northwest. The new terminal at Beijing Capital Airport, Shanghai's Pudong Airport, and Hong Kong's Chep Lap Kok all have made air travel easier as well. Nearly all domestic flights are less than three hours in duration; *Let's Go* provides frequencies and approximate prices in **Practical Information** or **Transportation** sections for available destinations. Domestic airline schedules are revised in April and October.

DOMESTIC AIRLINES. The domestic airline industry is overseen by the state-run monopoly of the **Civil Aviation Administration of China** or **CAAC** (zhōngguó rénmín hángkōng gōngsī; 中国人民航空公司; usually shortened to "mínháng"). Once infamous for its suspect safety record, unsatisfactory service, and mismanagement, the CAAC has turned over a new leaf, spending millions on buying new aircraft and safety equipment, training air traffic controllers abroad, and improving its organization. Perhaps its boldest move yet has been decentralizing the industry by forming semi-independent regional airlines that will eventually assume complete autonomy. **Air China** is the CAAC's major airline and international carrier, flying to more than 300 destinations worldwide and within China (to contact Air China, see **Getting to China,** p. 35). Regional airlines in the CAAC fly mostly domestic route and international destinations in Asia.

- **China Eastern Airlines (MU),** domestic ☎86 21 6247 2255, Los Angeles 626-583-1500, San Francisco 415-982-5115, Shanghai international 86 21 6247 5953, Sydney 61 2 9290 1148, US and Canada 800-200-5118; www.ce-air.com. Centered in Shanghai, with daily flights to Los Angeles and domestic flights around the country.

- **China Northern Airlines (CJ),** Beijing ☎10 6601 7594, Hong Kong 852 2591 0626, Shanghai 21 6350 6088, Shenyang 86 24 2319 7188; www.cna.com.cn. Hubs in Shenyang, Changchun, and Harbin. Flights to Mongolia.

- **China Northwest Airlines (WH),** Beijing ☎10 6601 7755, Hong Kong 852 2827 7223, Nanjing 25 452 8188, Shanghai 21 6267 4233, Xi'an 29 8702 299; www.cnwa.com. Based in Xi'an and Lanzhou, it links the northwest to the rest of China.

- **China Southern Airlines (CZ),** Guangzhou ☎86 20 8668 2000, Hong Kong 852 2866 1331, Sydney 61 2 9231 1988, US and Canada 888-338-8988; www.cs-air.com. Based in Guangzhou, with flights to Japan, Southeast Asia, North America, and select destinations in Europe.

- **China Southwest Airlines (SZ),** Beijing ☎10 6601 7579, Chengdu 28 8666 8080, Hong Kong 852 2528 6898, Shanghai 21 6433 3355; www.cswa.com. Centered in Chengdu and Chongqing. Administers most flights to Tibet.

- **Major regional airlines include:** Great Wall (G8), Shanghai (FM), Shenzhen (4G), Sichuan (3U), Wuhan (WU), Xiamen (MF), Xinjiang (XO), Yunnan (3Q), Zhejiang (F6), and Zhongyuan (Z2). **Dragon Air (KA),** a non-CAAC domestic carrier, operates out of Hong Kong (Hong Kong ☎852 2868 6777; Beijing 86 10 6518 2533; Shanghai 21 6375 6375; www.dragonair.com).

ESSENTIALS

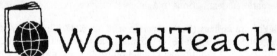

AIRCRAFT SAFETY. The airlines of developing world nations do not always meet safety standards. Flying in China is safer than it used to be, but crashes are still far more frequent than in more developed nations. When booking a domestic flight, be sure to inquire what type of aircraft is flying your route, as the CAAC fleet is a grab bag of some of the world's most advanced and most ancient planes. While flights in and out of more traveled regions utilize modern aircraft, flights in border regions (especially the southwest and northwest) often employ older, Russian-built aircraft, such as the accident-prone Tupolev 154s (Tu5) or Ilyusin 76 (ILW). The *Official Airline Guide* (www.oag.com) and many travel agencies can tell you the type and age of aircraft on a particular route. The **International Airline Passengers Association** (US ☎800-821-4272, UK 020 8681 6555) provides region-specific safety information. The **Federal Aviation Administration** (www.faa.gov) reviews the airline authorities for countries whose airlines enter the US. **US State Department** travel advisories (☎202-647-5225; travel.state.gov/travel_warnings.html) sometimes involve foreign carriers, especially when terrorist bombings may be a threat.

BUYING DOMESTIC AIR TICKETS. Standard rates are fixed between cities (i.e., Beijing to Shanghai costs the same as Shanghai to Beijing). The round-trip price is always double the one-way fare. Prices for foreigners and Chinese are the same. Children over the age of 12 must pay the adult fare, those between the ages of two and 12 pay half-price, and those under the age of two pay 10% of the adult fare.

While it is possible to purchase a limited selection of domestic airline tickets from travel agencies abroad, most travelers find it easier to buy them in China. Most airports have airline ticket offices that sell tickets for domestic flights on any carrier, and a CAAC ticket office usually operates in town as well. Although availability varies depending on the route, many travelers report no problems walking in and buying a ticket for the next departure. Note that it may be more difficult to obtain tickets during Chinese New Year and for some flights in the northwest, southwest, and to major tourist destinations. Be sure to reconfirm your reservation more than two days before departure; otherwise, your ticket may be cancelled. Most CAAC ticket offices take credit cards.

Domestic flights charge an **airport tax** of Y50, usually called an "airport construction fee," which you pay upon arriving at the airport. Children under 12 do not have to pay this fee.

CHANGES AND REFUNDS. Travelers wishing to modify the departure time, date, or class of a ticket may do so only once and must do so more than 24hr. before departure. If the new flight is also on the same carrier, then the change is straightforward. But if the new flight is aboard a different airline under the CAAC umbrella, then the passenger must buy a new ticket and cancel the old ticket at the airline office of the old ticket. Refunds requested less than 24hr. before departure are subjected to a 10% cancellation fee; if less than 2hr., the fee is 20%. No-shows are entitled to only 50% of the original ticket value.

BY TRAIN

With unbeatable prices, speed, convenience, and relative comfort, train travel is undeniably the transportation tool of choice in China for travelers and locals alike. Such popularity means that tickets can occasionally be hard to come by, and travelers are advised to buy tickets for their next destination as early as possible.

Paper **train schedules** (shíkèbiǎo; 时刻表) are available at most major stations for about Y1 or more. The **Chinese Ministry of Railways** (www.chinamor.cn.net) also offers comprehensive information on schedules and regulations. For those who read Chinese, www.tielu.org is a good resource for looking up train service, times, and durations between cities and stations. Most schedules, printed or online, are only in Chinese, but with some patience and reference to the characters for city names, anyone can decipher them. A good strategy is to figure out the characters for your destination ahead of time to avoid confusion in the crowded station.

IS THIS SEAT TAKEN? Chinese trains have 4 classes. Depending on the price, you can travel in any position, from squatting to sitting to supine.

Hard seat (yìng zuò; 硬座): Hard seat is the cheapest and most popular class. Generally, a hard seat ticket entitles the bearer only to a *space* on the train—the seat part is often optional, since many trains are overbooked. Moreover, crowded cars, clouds of cigarette smoke, and blaring loudspeakers also help to make the trip a less-than-soothing experience. Some of the more popular routes have new, more comfortable hard seat cars: perks include A/C, cleaner bathrooms, seats assignments, and, ironically, well-cushioned seats. These are usually on the express trains. Unless you reserved a seat in advance, you'll have to join the mad scramble for seats when boarding. Hold on to your hat.

Soft seat (ruǎn zuò; 软座): Soft seat cars exist only on certain routes, usually short trips between major cities and on express trains. The soft seat section is similar to the passenger sections of many Western trains. Seats are assigned, cars generally have A/C, and smoking is (allegedly) prohibited.

Hard sleeper (yìng wò; 硬卧): Hard sleeper cars consist of several doorless sleeping compartments off a main aisle. Each compartment has room for six people with three bunks on each side. Sheets, blankets, and pillows are provided. The choice of bunk is difficult. In summer, the claustrophobia-inducing top bunk (shàngpù; 上铺) can be too hot, too cold, or too loud, but does offer more privacy and a relatively safer place to store belongings. The middle bunk (zhōngpù; 中铺) is only slightly removed from the hubbub below. The bottom (xiàpù; 下铺) is convenient but inevitably becomes the communal bench during the day. Bunk assignments are printed on the ticket. It is possible to make requests at the ticket window (ticket prices drop with bunk elevation). Once on board, the attendant exchanges your paper ticket for a metal or plastic piece. Be sure to retrieve your ticket from the attendant before you disembark. As with the hard seat, hard sleeper cars are calmer and quieter on express trains.

Soft sleeper (ruǎn wò; 软卧): Soft sleeper passengers ride as close to the lap of luxury as is possible. Compartments are less cramped and more comfortable, with 4 well-padded bunks, a door, wall-to-wall carpeting, and curtains. For travelers faced with the unpleasant possibility of a night (or 2 or 3) in hard seat due to sold-out hard sleepers, soft sleeper present a comfy, albeit pricey, solution. Soft sleepers may cost nearly as much as airplane tickets.

TYPES OF TRAINS. The speed and type of Chinese trains can usually be deduced from the number on the train. Numbers prefixed by letters designate various express trains. The fastest and most luxurious of all the trains, **"T" trains** (tèkuài; 特快) are special express trains, usually with both soft and hard sleepers and seats. T trains can whisk you from Beijing to Shanghai in 12hr. flat; some international trains are also T trains. A **"K"** indicates a "regular" express train (kuàisù; 快

速), very similar to the T trains except slightly slower. **"Y"** (lǚyóu; 旅游) trains go to tourist destinations. The T, K, and Y trains all make the least number of stops, making for quick trips between major destinations. They all have air-conditioning, and their hard seat and hard sleeper cars are usually the cleanest and most orderly compared to hard seats and sleepers on other trains.

Trains lacking numbers descend in speed and increase in stops as the number increases (1-999, to give you an idea of all the trains criss-crossing China). Thus, trains numbered 1-299 are the fastest of the lot, receiving the designation "standard expresses" (pǔ kuài; 普快). As the numbers grow larger, the train becomes more and more of a regional train, stopping at every tiny town and local station.

TICKETS. Tickets can usually be purchased starting five days before departure—10 days in major stations such as Beijing. In some cities, same-day tickets are as early as they get. If you are having real trouble buying a ticket, most upscale hotels and travel agents can help for a fee (generally Y10-50). Train tickets do not differentiate by class, but instead by the type of seat, which ranges from the crowded, communal hard seat to the luxurious soft seat (see **Is This Seat Taken?,** p. 46).

Tickets all start at a fixed base price, to which extra costs are added as the train gets better. The T, K, and Y trains all have added fees for A/C and speed. However, the speed, convenience, and added comfort of an express train is usually worth the cost. Soft seats/and sleepers cost more, and the price of a hard sleeper decreases as the bunk (upper, middle, lower) rises in level. Children under 1.1m tall travel free, those between 1.1m and 1.4m pay half-price, while those taller than 1.4m pay the full fare. Tickets can be fully refunded up until departure.

You'll need to show your ticket to access the track area. Most train stations in China are chaotic (an understatement). Gates are generally closed about 3min. before departure. **Keep your ticket:** at your final destination, attendants scrutinize tickets before allowing you to exit the station.

TIP **A TICKET TO RIDE.** In summer, hard sleepers and soft seats are especially difficult to acquire for long-distance trains that originate in other cities, with all the best seats snapped up at the beginning. If you do not get the ticket type of your choice, you can buy a hard seat and sometimes **upgrade** (bǔ piào; 补票) once on board, depending on availability. Ask the conductor.

BY BUS

China's long-distance bus system has several advantages. It goes virtually everywhere. Tickets are almost always easier to purchase than train tickets, and they may even be cheaper than hard sleeper tickets. On the other hand, unpredictable road conditions, poorly maintained vehicles, and unreliable drivers can conspire to make bus trips long, uncomfortable, and even dangerous. It is not uncommon for roads, particularly in the northwest and southwest, to be washed out or otherwise impassable for weeks or months at a time.

Virtually every city or town has a **long-distance bus station** (chángtú qìchē zhàn; 长途汽车站) or designated location at which buses can drop off and pick up passengers. **Tickets** are sold at the station itself and need not be booked in advance. A number of routes are traversed by both rickety, old Chinese buses and newer, relatively posh, foreign buses (for which tickets are more expensive). It is generally a good idea to look at the bus in which you will be riding before you buy your ticket: a few travelers report having been charged the price for a trip on a higher-quality bus only to find themselves on a rattling, run-down vehicle. On overnight trips, more expensive **sleeper buses** with a semi-reclining bunk for each traveler now ply many routes. **Minibuses** run shorter routes, particularly between large, neighboring cities, and pick up passengers in front of train or bus stations or along major thoroughfares. Typically, you pay for your ticket once onboard the minibus, which leaves when full and stops when the driver feels like it.

Be sure to prepare yourself well for any long trip by bus. Trips often take longer than anticipated. For travel in cold or high-altitude areas, even in summer, bring plenty of warm clothing. Buses are all too frequently not equipped with working heaters, and mechanical breakdowns in remote areas can prove deadly for those not properly prepared (see **Environmental Hazards**, p. 29). It is also a good idea to bring enough food and water for the trip, since stops may be few and far between.

BY CAR

What are you, nuts? Most travelers to China wisely never get behind the wheel of an automobile. Foreign tourists are expressly forbidden to drive in and between most Chinese cities, more for their own safety than anything: drivers in China consider traffic laws to be no more than loose suggestions and routinely drive on both sides of the road, run traffic lights, speed, and are a general menace to society. When people do drive on the correct side of the road, however, they drive on the right in mainland China, while in Hong Kong and Macau they drive on the left. Cars can be rented in Hong Kong, Macau, Beijing, and Shanghai for local use, but the extensive train system, public transportation, and taxis will save you a great deal of time, money, and worry.

China's requirement that all drivers hold a Chinese driving license makes driving virtually impossible for foreign travelers anyway. China does not accept the **International Driving Permit (IDP)**. To apply for a Chinese driving license, foreigners must be over 18 and have a residence permit (p. 60) and a valid driving license from their home country. They must then pass a medical examination and a driving test. Chinese driving tests are often more difficult than those of other countries, and administrators do not hesitate to fail applicants. The entire process takes around two weeks and costs about Y680.

It may nonetheless be a good idea to get an IDP, in case you're in a situation (e.g. an accident or stranded in a small town) where the police do not know English; information on the IDP is printed in ten languages, including Chinese. Your IDP, valid for one year, must be issued in your own country before you depart. An application for an IDP usually requires one or two photos, a current local license, an additional form of identification, and a fee. To apply, contact the national or local branch of your home country's automobile association. Be careful when purchasing an IDP online or anywhere other than your home automobile association. Many vendors sell permits of questionable legitimacy for higher prices.

If, by some miracle, you do get a driving license in China and a car, then you are required by law to have auto insurance as well. Most credit cards cover standard insurance. If you rent, lease, or borrow a car, you will need a **green card**, or **International Insurance Certificate**, to certify that you have liability insurance and that it applies abroad. Green cards can be obtained at car rental agencies, car dealers (for those leasing cars), some travel agents, and some border crossings. Rental agencies may require you to purchase theft insurance in countries that they consider to have a high risk of auto theft. In China, drivers can contact the **People's Insurance Company (PICC)**, 69 Donghe Yan Jie, Xuanwu district, Beijing, 100052, for coverage options (☎86 10 6315 6688; www.picc.com.cn).

BY BOAT

Although they may be slow and inefficient, boats do give travelers the opportunity to explore regions of China not easily reached by land. A cruise down the **Yangzi River,** or the Changjiang, is often on the itineraries of many travelers, though the Three Gorges have been irrevocably changed by the colossal dam (now a sight in its own right). The boat trip begins in Chongqing (p. 727), winds down the Yangzi River through the Three Gorges, and stops at either Yichang (p. 465) or Wuhan (p. 459). The stretch from Yichang and Wuhan takes a day and is less scenic; most tourists choose to disembark at Yichang. A newer route lets travelers stay afloat all the way to Shanghai (p. 333), totaling a journey of over 2840km on the third longest river in the world. Along the way, the boat makes brief stops at several towns and tourist sights, allowing passengers to disembark and explore either independently or as part of a tour. Though most tourists choose to make the trip downstream, traveling east from Chongqing, for the best view of the Three Gorges, upstream journeys beginning in Wuhan and Yichang are also possible. It's also possible to take a fast boat, shortening the trip to one day. Several Chinese boat companies ply the river, with similar prices and accommodations. A few boats run by Westerners also make the journey in typical cruise-line comfort, but the prices skyrocket accordingly. For more information, see **The Three Gorges,** p. 734.

Ferry boats also traverse China's south coast, linking together Guangzhou, Hong Kong, Shantou, Xiamen, Fuzhou, Beihai, and the sunny beaches of Hainan Island.

KEEPING IN TOUCH

BY MAIL

SENDING MAIL HOME FROM CHINA

Airmail is the best way to send mail home from China. Write "airmail," "par avion," or 航空 (hángkōng) on the front. **Surface mail** is by far the cheapest and slowest way to send mail. It takes one to three months to cross the Pacific—good for heavy items you won't need for a while, such as souvenirs or other articles you've acquired along the way that are weighing down your pack.

Sending a post card airmail **out of China** to either Australia, Canada, Ireland, New Zealand, the UK, or the US costs Y4.50. Sending a letter airmail to the same nations costs Y6 for the first 20g and Y6 for each additional 10g.

Sending a postcard **within China** costs Y0.60. Sending letters within China costs Y0.80 for each 20g up to 100g, and Y2 per 100g thereafter until 2kg. Letters within the same city cost Y0.60 per 20g for the first 100g, and Y1.2 per 100g thereafter until 2kg. Registered mail is an additional Y8.

The most reliable way to ship documents and packages abroad from China is by **EMS** (Express Mail Service; tèkuài zhuāndì; 特快专递 ; ☎185), a service of China Post. Not all post offices offer EMS; *Let's Go* indicates if the service is available in the Practical Information section of each city. The rates listed below are for sending packages via surface mail and via EMS:

Australia and New Zealand: Allow 3-5 days for regular airmail home. Surface mail packages up to 1kg Y106, up to 2kg Y147. **EMS** letters up to 0.5kg Y160; packages up to 0.5kg Y140-210, 0.5-1kg Y210-250. Each additional 0.5kg over 1kg Y55.

Canada: Allow 4-7 days for regular airmail home. EMS does not serve Canada, but "medium speed" service charges Y180 for letters up to 0.5kg, packages Y240. Each additional 0.5kg Y75.

UK and Ireland: Allow 4-7 days for regular airmail home. Surface mail packages up to 1kg Y142, up to 2kg Y199. **EMS** letters up to 0.5kg Y220; packages up to 0.5kg Y160-280, 0.5-1kg Y280-315. Each additional 0.5kg over 1kg Y75.

US: Allow 4-7 days for regular airmail home. Packages up to 0.5kg Y102, up to 2kg Y145. **EMS** letters up to 0.5kg Y180; packages up to 0.5kg Y160-250, up to 1kg Y250-350. Each additional 500g after 1kg Y75.

SENDING MAIL TO CHINA

To ensure timely delivery, mark envelopes "airmail," "par avion," or " 航空 " (hángkōng). In addition to the standard postage system whose rates are listed below, **Federal Express** (Australia ☎ 13 26 10, Canada and US 800-463-3339, Ireland 1800 535 800, New Zealand 0800 733 339, UK 0800 123 800; www.fedex.com) handles express mail services from most countries to China. For example, they can get a letter from New York to Beijing in three days for US$36, and from London to Beijing in five days for UK£32.

Australia: Allow 4-6 days for regular airmail to China. Postcards and letters up to 20g cost AUS$1; packages up to 0.5kg AUS$6, up to 2kg AUS$34.50. EMS can get a letter to China in 3-4 days for AUS$30. www.auspost.com.au/pac.

Canada: Allow 4-7 days for regular airmail to China. Postcards and letters up to 30g cost CDN$1.40; packages up to 0.5kg CDN$12.20, up to 2kg CDN$37.35. Purolator International can get a letter to China in 3-6 days for CDN$48. www.canadapost.ca/personal/rates/default-e.asp.

Ireland: Allow 5-7 days for regular airmail to China. Postcards and letters up to 25g cost €0.65; packages up to 0.5kg €5, up to 2kg €16.

New Zealand: Allow 4-10 days for regular airmail to China. Postcards and letters up to 20g cost NZ$1.50; packages up to 0.5kg NZ$16, up to 2kg NZ$50. International Express can get a letter to China in 2-4 days for NZ$33. www.nzpost.co.nz/nzpost/inrates.

UK: Allow 5-7 days for regular airmail to China. Letters up to 20g cost UK£0.68; packages up to 0.5kg UK£5, up to 2kg UK£19. To get your mail signed for and shipped on the next available flight, purchase an International Signed For sticker for £3.30. www.royalmail.co.uk/calculator.

US: Allow 4-7 days for regular airmail to China. Letters up to 1 oz. cost US$0.80; packages up to 1 lb. US$9.25, up to 5 lb. US$15. Global Express Mail takes 2-3 days and costs US$19. http://ircalc.usps.gov.

RECEIVING MAIL IN CHINA

There are several ways to arrange pick-up of letters sent to you by friends and relatives while you are abroad. Mail can be sent via **Poste Restante** (General Delivery; cún jú hòu lǐng; 存局侯领) to almost any city or town in China with a post office, with varying reliability. When addressing letters to China, an attempt—however unskilled—to include Chinese characters will improve the letter's chances of arriving at the correct destination. *Let's Go* provides the characters for each province (shěng; 省) and city (shì; 市), and often many important streets as well. For the independent municipalities of Beijing, Tianjin, Shanghai, and Chongqing, no province name is needed. Address mail like the example below:

Sun Wukong

Poste Restante 存局侯领

Hubei Province, Wuhan 湖北省武汉市

China 中国 430014

The mail will go to a special desk in the central post office, unless you specify a post office by street address or postal code. It's best to use the largest post office, as mail will probably end up there regardless. It is usually safer and quicker, if more expensive, to send mail express or registered. Bring your passport (or other photo ID) for pick-up. There may also be a small fee (Y3). If the clerks insist that there is nothing for you, have them check under your first name as well. Sometimes it may help to write your name on a sheet of paper and hand it to the clerk. *Let's Go* lists post offices and postal codes in the **Practical Information** section for each city and most towns.

BY TELEPHONE

CALLING HOME FROM CHINA

A **calling card** is probably your cheapest bet. Calls are billed collect or to your account. You can frequently call collect without even possessing a company's calling card just by calling their access number and following the instructions. **To obtain a calling card** from your national telecommunications service before leaving home, contact the appropriate company listed below (using the numbers in the middle column). To **call home with a calling card,** contact the operator for your service provider in China by dialing the appropriate toll-free access number (listed below in the right-hand column). Before settling on a calling card plan, be sure to research your options in order to pick the one that best fits both your needs and your destination.

ESSENTIALS

COMPANY	TO OBTAIN A CARD, DIAL:	TO CALL ABROAD, DIAL:
AT&T (US)	800-364-9292	**108-888** from northern China and the Beijing region, **108 11** from southern and northern China, **800 96 1111** from Hong Kong, **0800 111** from Macau.
Canada Direct	800-561-8868	**108 186** from China, **800 96 1100** from Hong Kong, **0 800 100** from Macau.
MCI (US)	800-777-5000	**108 12** from China, **800 96 1121** from Hong Kong, **0800 131** from Macau.
Telstra Australia	13 22 00	**108 610** from Beijing, Shanghai, Guangzhou, and Shenzhen only; **800 96 0061** from Hong Kong; **0800 610** from Macau.

If you're staying in a hotel room of the grittier kind, the phone in the room may not allow international calls. In this case, you will have to first inform the front desk that you need to make an international call before they will "open" your phone line. Most **China Telecom** offices offer IDD service at expensive (but not exorbitant) rates. (See **Placing International Calls** below for instructions on how to place a direct international call.) Placing a **collect call** through an international operator is even more expensive, but may be necessary in an emergency. You can place collect calls through the service providers listed above even if you don't have one of their phone cards.

 PLACING INTERNATIONAL CALLS. To call China from home or to call home from China, dial:

1. The **international dialing prefix.** To call from **Australia,** dial 0011; **Canada** or the **US,** 011; **China,** 00; **Ireland, New Zealand,** or the **UK,** 00.
2. The **country code** of the country you want to call. To call **Australia,** dial 61; **Canada** or the **US,** 1; **China,** 86; **Ireland,** 353; **New Zealand,** 64; the **UK,** 44; **Hong Kong** and **Macau,** 852.
3. The **city/area code.** *Let's Go* lists the city/area codes for cities and towns in China opposite the city or town name, next to a ☎. If the first digit is a zero (e.g., 010 for Beijing), omit the zero when calling from abroad (e.g., dial 10 from Canada to reach Beijing).
4. The **local number.**

CALLING WITHIN CHINA

The simplest way to call within China is to use a **prepaid phone card** (diànhuà kǎ; 电话卡). Prepaid phone cards can be found at China Telecom locations throughout the country, at most newspaper stands, and on street corners everywhere. There are two types of phone cards, and they usually save time and money in the long run. **IP cards** carry a certain amount of phone time depending on the card's denomination. These can be used everywhere, although pay phones will levy a heavy surcharge that will eat up your minutes. Make sure that you buy a card that can be used throughout China, as there are IP cards that are limited to a single province or region; ask for the *"quán guó kǎ"* (全国卡). The characters will be printed on the back of the IP card; province IP cards will be labeled by the province name. The second kind of phone card, the **IC card,** can be used only at special IC phones. These resemble payphones and can be found on the streets of most cities. They are less convenient than IP cards and have less satisfactory rates. It's notoriously expensive to make international calls from China—a Y50 phone card will run out in no time. Watch out for phony phone cards, which are sometime sold in less official places. (China Telecom offices are the best bet for official cards).

In China there are **public telephones** at many newspaper kiosks and tiny corner shops. Look for small red-and-white sign with the characters " 公用电话 " (gōngyòng diànhuà). They are generally available for use for a fee and can be used to make both local and long-distance calls, with or without a phone card.

OPERATOR, PLEASE. China's telephone system is far from straightforward: even the number of digits in a telephone number varies between and within cities. Large cities and municipalities, like Beijing, have as many as 8 digits, while small border towns can have as few as 5. Macau has 6-, 7-, and 8-digit numbers. If you have trouble connecting to a number, try adding another digit to the beginning; "2," "6," and "8" are popular prefixes. If you still don't have any luck, China's **directory assistance** is a helpful resource: simply dial ☎114 from any phone. Or, consult an online directory, like www.chinabig.com.

ESSENTIALS

MOBILE PHONES

Mobile phones have become almost as ubiquitous in China as snack food stands. Coverage is surprisingly widespread, linking over 98% of inhabited areas—even faraway Xinjiang and Tibet—and nearly everyone, from the smartly-dressed businessman to the village farmer, totes a model.

China uses the international standard for mobile phones, **GSM,** a system that began in Europe and has spread to much of the world. To make and receive calls in China you will need a **GSM-compatible phone** and a **SIM (subscriber identity module) card,** a country-specific, thumbnail-sized chip that gives you a local phone number and plugs you into the local network. China's GSM network runs at 900MHz, which means that most European and Oceanic mobile GSM phones will work. The majority of GSM phones sold in the US operate on a different frequency (1900) than international phones (900/1800) and will not work abroad. Tri-band phones will operate through most of the world. Some GSM phones are **SIM-locked** and will only accept SIM cards from a single carrier. You'll need a **SIM-unlocked** phone to use a SIM card from a local carrier. For more info on GSM phones, check out www.telestial.com, www.vodafone.com, or www.planetomni.com.

Companies like **Cellular Abroad** (www.cellularabroad.com) rent mobile phones. It is not possible to rent a phone once in China, but phones are sold everywhere, and a basic phone can be purchased off the streets for as little as Y200-Y500. If you want a more reputable model, head to **China Mobile** (zhōngguó yídòng tōngxìn; 中国移动通信 ; hotline ☎1860; www.chinamobile.com) or **China Unicom** (zhōngguó liántōng; 中国联通 ; ☎1001; www.chinaunicom.com.cn). These two giants can fulfill your every mobile desire, with a mind-boggling array of phones, cards, gadgets, and other services. Once you have a phone, registering your phone number costs an additional Y100. The cheapest plans offer local calls at Y0.20 per minute and international calls at Y1.50 per minute.

Many SIM cards are **prepaid,** meaning that they come with calling time included so you don't need a monthly service plan. When you use up the prepaid time, you can buy additional cards or vouchers (available at China Mobile and Unicom), or you can recharge the SIM card. It is cheaper to buy SIM cards in China than from an outside provider. Using a phone card in conjunction with your mobile phone calls can help boost the lifespan of your SIM card. Text messaging **(SMS)** is also extremely popular in China.

WHICH SIM? While most SIM cards work throughout China, many cards can be recharged only in a specific region or province. The region of a SIM card is identified by the 3-digit area code of its number (from ☎130 to 139; for example ☎135 and 136 are Beijing, 137 Shanghai). For this reason, it's best not to buy SIM cards before you arrive in China, as you may unwittingly end up with a SIM card for Shanghai when you're trekking the Silk Road. Changing SIM cards is as easy as changing socks, but it will make things easier if you tell the store that you will be traveling and need a SIM card with as wide a range as possible. Also make sure you specify that you need a SIM card which can make and receive international calls. The most expensive SIM cards, *Shéntōng Xíng* (神通 行) work throughout China and are enabled for international calls.

TIME DIFFERENCES

China is nearly 5000km from east to west, but it has only one time zone. The entire nation runs on Beijing time, and as a result, the working day in western regions like Xinjiang starts long before sunrise. These areas sometimes keep different hours to compensate (p. 783). The country is officially eight hours ahead of **Greenwich Mean Time (GMT).** China doesn't follow **daylight saving time;** in summer the time difference will be an hour less for countries that do make the time change.

4AM	7AM	NOON	4PM	7PM	8PM	10PM	11PM
Vancouver Seattle San Francisco Los Angeles	Toronto Ottawa New York Boston	London (GMT)	Moscow	Hanoi Bangkok Jakarta Phnom Penh	China Hong Kong Manila Singapore	Sydney Canberra Melbourne	Auckland

BY EMAIL AND INTERNET

For the most convenient public Internet access venues, try China Telecom (zhōng-guó diánxìn; 中国电信) or Internet cafes (wǎngbā; 网吧). Other possible places include university campus computer rooms, higher end accommodations, and sometimes eateries and cafes oriented toward foreigners and backpackers. The Internet is ever popular in China, and *Let's Go* lists at least one establishment where travelers can surf the Net in almost every city's **Practical Information** section. The majority of Internet cafes charge Y2-10 per hour, and computer quality and connection speeds vary considerably. A fair selection of these are open 24hr.

Though in some places it's possible to forge a remote link with your home server, in most cases this is a much slower (and thus more expensive) option than taking advantage of free **web-based email accounts** (e.g. www.hotmail.com and www.yahoo.com). Travelers with **laptops** can call their home Internet service provider via a **modem.** Long-distance phone cards specifically intended for such calls can defray high phone charges; check with your long-distance phone provider to see if it offers this option. Be aware, though, that many calls go through switchboards or use antiquated phone systems, making dial-up access impossible. It is also possible to subscribe to a Chinese service provider, making long-distance dial-ups unnecessary. Some hotels in major cities also provide Internet access via the phoneline in individual hotel rooms; rates are charged according to the rates of the local Telephone Bureau.

Internet cafes may also allow laptops to connect directly to the Internet. Travelers with wireless-enabled computers may be able to take advantage of an increasing number of Internet "hotspots," where they can sign online for free or for a small fee. Websites like www.jiwire.com, www.wi-fihotspotlist.com, and www.locfinder.net can help you find them. In China, these wireless hotspots are limited to upscale hotels and business centers in Beijing, Shanghai, Guangdong, and Hong Kong. For info on insuring your laptop while traveling, see p. 26.

RULES AND REGULATIONS. In April 2001, the Chinese government enacted new Internet regulations to block surfers from sites relating to pornography, violence, gambling, and superstition. Surfers in China will also find that some sites of Western news sources and human rights organizations are blocked as well. It is illegal in China to use a computer to copy or publish material that harms government interests, spread viruses, or hack into databases. Recent rules have banned certain online computer games as well. Despite government warnings, however, most Internet dens are smoky and filled with teenagers immersed in online games.

ACCOMMODATIONS

Where else in the world can you get a dorm bed for US$3? Budget accommodations, when present, are often some of the best deals anywhere. Of course, quality may be somewhat lacking, and night-time visitors may include the eight-legged kind. In big cities and pricey tourist destinations, cheap lodgings are hard to find, and savvy travelers must bargain hard to lower the exorbitant rates. Since quality often varies more than price, choose carefully.

RESTRICTIONS. The Chinese government has strict restrictions governing where foreigners are allowed to stay. The only exception is in Beijing, where foreigners can supposedly stay in any hotel or hostel within the city. But in most cities, foreigners are barred from the cheapest lodgings. China has a five-star (wǔ xíngjí; 五星级) rating system for hotels. Most hotels authorized to accept foreigners (shèwài bīnguǎn; 涉外宾馆) are one star or higher. Those who speak Mandarin or are overseas Chinese sometimes talk the management into letting them stay in a place that officially does not accept foreign guests. In dire circumstances, hotel staff can sometimes be persuaded to call the local PSB to ask for permission to lodge you for one night, but this is by no means guaranteed. Some hotels accepting foreigners do not allow them to stay in dorm rooms. Most establishments also refuse to allow Chinese and foreigners to share a room, especially if of the opposite sex. Less frequently, unmarried foreign couples are forbidden to room together. A wedding band or marriage certificate, authentic or not, goes a long way in overcoming this regulation. Remember that an English sign outside does not always indicate a foreigner-friendly establishment.

If you plan on staying in a private residence while in China, you must register with the local branch of the PSB upon arrival (usually within the first day or two of your stay in the area). Violations of these rules may result in detainment or fines by the PSB (see **Local Laws and Police,** p. 24).

PRICES. The wave of renovations sweeping across China is converting many old budget standbys into high-end hotels. While backpackers in popular destinations like Yunnan, Guangxi, and Tibet continue to bed down in dorms for around US$2 per night, rooms rarely cost under US$20 a day in cities along the eastern coast. Fortunately, the low occupancy rate that plagues most Chinese hotels gives travelers bargaining power. At any type of establishment, **always ask for a discount:** you're likely to get at least 10-20% off, and lucky ones can enjoy 50% rates. Many low-end hotels use their price charts only as paperweights, giving discounts or padding room rates based on a guest's appearance. Although the two-tiered (foreigner and Chinese) pricing system is disappearing in most places (see p. 19), foreigners are still easy targets for price hikes. Telling the staff that you're a student may help.

ESSENTIALS

CHECKING IN. When checking in to your hotel, you will invariably be required to fill out a **registration form** (usually in English and Chinese, but sometimes only in Chinese) with vital statistics like your nationality (guójì; 国籍), passport number (hùzhào hàomǎ; 护照号码), and type of visa (qiānzhèng; 签证; see p. 15 for an explanation of visa types—most travelers have an "L"-type tourist visa). Should you be asked by hotel staff to leave your passport as a **deposit,** refuse and offer an expired one, some other form of identification, or cash instead. For any deposit you leave, remember to keep the receipt in order to get a refund upon check-out. Check-out is typically noon, while check-in is generally any time. Reservations for standard rooms may be accepted, but are usually necessary only around national holidays and in the high season (May-Sept. in most places).

HOTELS

UPSCALE HOTELS. These establishments generally offer on-site restaurants, business and travel services, IDD/DDD phones and TVs in every room, laundry, 24hr. hot water, A/C, private baths with Western-style toilets, massage parlor, salon, and just about every other amenity under the sun. The luxury doesn't come cheap, however: doubles typically go for US$40 (RMB320) and up.

MID-RANGE HOTELS. Perhaps the most common type of lodgings in China, mid-range hotels provide a decent night's rest at a friendlier rate than the luxury mega-hotels. A dime a dozen, these places usually come with a more limited selection of similar amenities (TV, A/C, phones, 24 hr. hot water) and a smaller price tag, usually US$15-40 (RMB120-320) for doubles. You may find, however, that in popular tourist destinations the price goes up and quality goes down. Many of these hotels are large, multi-storied buildings with worn linens and upholstery, aging Western-style bathrooms, and a faint musty odor. They often have several buildings, wings, or floors with different levels of quality, often called "economy" (jīngjì; 经济), "standard" (biāozhǔn; 标准; or pǔtōng; 普通), and "deluxe" (háohuà; 豪华). Receptionists will sometimes try to make you stay in the most expensive rooms, so always ask about cheaper options.

LOW-END HOTELS. Often near the train and/or long-distance bus stations, these establishments may not even have a star. Amenities may still include TV, sometimes phones, and perhaps Western-style toilets. These hotels, sometimes called hostels, often rent rooms by the bed, with most thrifty Chinese happy to bed down next to strangers at a fraction of the price of a room of their own. Some budget hotels let foreigners stay in these "dorm" rooms, especially when they're not full—the best of both worlds, since you pay for only the bed, but almost always get the room to yourself. In these dorm accommodations, bathrooms are usually communal, hot water available only during limited hours, and cleanliness questionable at times. But the price is right, usually US$3-8 per person per night.

 TYPES OF ACCOMMODATIONS. Mandarin has several words to distinguish between different types of establishments that are generally all translated as "hotel" in English. Strictly speaking, the five-star luxury hotels are called *jiǔdiàn* (酒店) or *fàndiàn* (饭店), and mid-range hotels are called *bīnguǎn* (宾馆). However, many establishments use the names interchangeably, making distinctions rather blurry. These 3 types of accommodations are usually the only places in town that accept foreigners. Low-end hotels are called *lǚguǎn* (旅馆), and hostels and guesthouses are called *lǚshè* (旅舍), *zhāodàisuǒ* (招待所), or *kèzhàn* (客栈); these establishments may not accept foreigners.

HOSTELS

Many hostels are laid out dorm-style, often with large single-sex rooms and bunk
beds, but many have a few private rooms as well. They sometimes have kitchens
and utensils for your use, bike rentals, storage areas, transportation, breakfast,
laundry facilities, on-site travel advice, and Internet access. There can be drawbacks: some hostels have a curfew, don't accept reservations, or less frequently,
require that you do chores. In China, there is usually a difference between a Western conception of a hostel (usually found in backpacker destinations like Yangshuo, Beijing, Hong Kong, and Shanghai) and simple dorm-style rooms. Dorm beds
in both average around US$2-6 (Y20-50), and a private room around US$5-20 (Y40-
160), with cheaper rooms outside of cities and tourist destinations.

 A HOSTELER'S BILL OF RIGHTS. There are certain standard features that we do not include in our hostel listings. Unless we state otherwise, you
can expect that every hostel has no lockout, no curfew, a kitchen, free hot showers, some system of secure luggage storage, and no key deposit.

HOSTELLING INTERNATIONAL

Joining the youth hostel association in your own country (listed below) automatically grants you membership privileges in **Hostelling International (HI),** a federation of
national hosteling associations. Non-HI members may be allowed to stay in most

hostels, but will pay more than members. HI hostels are scattered throughout China. Though the price may be slightly higher than those of dorm rooms, HI hostels provide a comforting familiarity. HI hostels also guarantee a certain standard of quality and cleanliness. HI's umbrella organization's web page (www.hihostels.com) lists the web addresses and phone numbers of all national associations.

Most student travel agencies (p. 34) sell HI cards, as do all of the national hosteling organizations listed below. All prices listed below are valid for **one-year memberships** unless otherwise noted.

An Óige (Irish Youth Hostel Association), 61 Mountjoy St., Dublin 7 (☎830 4555; fax 830 5808; www.irelandyha.org). €20, under 18 €10.

Australian Youth Hostels Association (AYHA), 422 Kent St., Sydney, NSW 200 (☎02 9261 1111; fax 9261 1969; www.yha.com.au). AUS$52, under 18 AUS$19.

Hostelling International-Canada (HI-C), 205 Catherine St. #400, Ottawa, ON K2P 1C3 (☎613-237-7884; fax 237-7868; www.hihostels.ca). CDN$35, under 18 free.

Hostelling International Northern Ireland (HINI), 22 Donegal Rd., Belfast BT12 5JN (☎02890 31 54 35; fax 43 96 99; www.hini.org.uk). UK£13, under 18 UK£6.

Hostelling International-USA, 8401 Colesville Rd., Ste. 600, Silver Spring, MD 20910 (☎301-495-1240; fax 495-6697; www.hiayh.org). US$28, under 18 free.

Scottish Youth Hostels Association (SYHA), 7 Glebe Cres., Stirling FK8 2JA (☎01786 89 14 00; fax 89 13 33; www.syha.org.uk). UK£6, under 17 £2.50.

Youth Hostels Association (England and Wales), Trevelyan House, Dimple Rd., Matlock, Derbyshire DE4 3YH, UK (☎0870 770 8868; fax 770 6127; www.yha.org.uk). UK£14, under 18 UK£6.

Youth Hostels Association of New Zealand (YHANZ), Level 1, Moorhouse City, 166 Moorhouse Ave., P.O. Box 436, Christchurch (☎0800 278 299 from NZ or 03 379 9970; fax 365 4476; www.yha.org.nz). NZ$40, under 18 free.

HOSTELLING INTERNATIONAL IN CHINA

The Chinese branch of HI is called the **Youth Hostel Association China (YHA China).** Locations are limited; HI can currently be found in Anhui, Beijing, Guangdong, Guangxi, Jiangsu, Macau, Sichuan, Shaanxi, Shanghai, Yunnan, and Zhejiang. For hostels in Hong Kong, contact the **Hong Kong Youth Association.**

Guangdong Youth Hostel Association of China, 185 Huanshi Xi Lu, Guangzhou 510010 (☎86 20 8666 6889, ext. 8719; gdyhac@public.guangzhou.gd.cn).

Hong Kong Youth Hostels Association, Room 225-227, Block 19, Shek Kip Mei Estate, Kowloon, Hong Kong (☎852 2788 3105, reservations 2788 1638; www.yha.org.hk).

Youth Hostel Association China (guójì qīngnián lǔshè; 国际青年旅舍), Moon Tower, Room 1803, 20 Mingyue Yi Lu, Guangzhou 510660 (☎20 8734 5080; www.yha.com). Search for hostels throughout China. Helpful information includes address, contact information, directions, descriptions, and photos of each hostel.

BOOKING HOSTELS ONLINE. One of the easiest ways to ensure you've got a bed for the night is by reserving online. Click to the **Hostelworld** booking engine through **www.letsgo.com,** and you'll have access to bargain accommodations from Argentina to Zimbabwe with no added commission.

OTHER TYPES OF ACCOMMODATIONS

YMCAS AND YWCAS

Young Men's Christian Association (YMCA) lodgings, though far from widespread in China, can be found in some of China's largest cities. Current locations are limited to Beijing, Chengdu, Guangzhou, Hangzhou, Nanjing, Tianjin, Wuhan, Xi'an, and Xiamen. YMCA accommodations are often more comfortable than many mid-range hotels, but the prices usually reflect this.

National Committee of YMCAs of China, 123 Xizang Nan Lu, Shanghai 200021 (☎86 21 6311 1765; fax 6320 3053; ymcachina@sohu.com).

World Alliance of YMCAs, 12 Clos Belmont, 1208 Geneva, Switzerland (☎41 22 849 5100; www.ymca.int). Search for YMCAs in China by address.

Y's Way International, 224 E. 47th St., New York, NY 10017, USA (☎212-308-2899; fax 308-3161). For a small fee (US$3 in North America, US$5 elsewhere), this "booking service" makes reservations for the YMCAs in Beijing, Chengdu, Guangzhou, Hangzhou, Nanjing, Shanghai, Tianjin, Wuhan, Xiamen, and Xi'an.

UNIVERSITY DORMS

Many **colleges and universities** have one or two residence halls open to travelers. Getting a room may take a couple of phone calls and require advanced planning, but rates tend to be low, and many offer free local calls and Internet access. A mix of students and foreign exchange students helps to create a friendly atmosphere for travelers staying the night. Beijing, Changsha, Hangzhou, Hefei, Nanjing, Suzhou, Tianjin, and Xi'an all have housing in dormitories. These lodgings are also often close to student areas—a good source for tips on things to do, cheap eats, and student bars and hang-outs—and can be great places to find English speakers. On the other hand, campuses are often far from the major sights of downtown areas. The quality of the accommodations varies widely, with some schools offering dorm beds for as little as US$7 a night and others with upscale, even swanky, rooms at rates equivalent to those of mid-range hotels.

MONASTERIES AND TEMPLES

Especially in remote areas, monasteries and temples often provide accommodations in peaceful simplicity for just a few *kuài* a night. These lodgings are particularly common on Buddhist mountains, but sometimes can be found in cities as well. Frequently lacking electricity and running water, these tend to be the most barebones of accommodations (essentially, a bed or a piece of the floor), but those who don't mind roughing it a little are often lured by the thought of trading in the noisy concrete high-rises of the cities for a little serene rusticity. Keep in mind, though, that on popular pilgrimage routes like Emeishan, every other traveler probably has the same idea, so spaces may be scarce.

HOME EXCHANGES AND HOSPITALITY CLUBS

Home exchange offers the traveler various types of homes (houses, apartments, condominiums, villas), plus the opportunity to live like a native and to cut down on accommodation costs. For more info, contact HomeExchange.com, P.O. Box 787, Hermosa Beach, CA 90254 USA (☎800-877-8723; www.homeexchange.com), or Intervac International Home Exchange (www.intervac.com). These listings are rare in China, usually offered only by expats in Beijing and Hong Kong.

ESSENTIALS

Hospitality clubs link their members with individuals or families abroad who are willing to host travelers for free or for a small fee to promote cultural exchange. In exchange, members usually must be willing to host travelers in their own homes. A small membership fee may also be required. **GlobalFreeloaders.com** (www.global-freeloaders.com) and **The Hospitality Club** (www.hospitalityclub.org) are good places to start. **Servas** (www.servas.org) is an established, more formal, peace-based organization and requires a fee and an interview to join. As always, use common sense when planning to stay with or host someone you do not know.

LONG-TERM ACCOMMODATIONS

Travelers planning to stay in China for extended periods of time may find it most cost-effective to rent an **apartment.** However, a string of regulations and bureaucracy make this difficult outside Beijing, Hong Kong, and Shanghai, where expats can rent only high-end apartments and condos designated especially for foreigners. Owned by Western companies, these classy apartments are astronomically more expensive than housing on the general market. Recently, Beijing and Shanghai loosened their restrictions, allowing foreigners to rent the cheaper apartments, which were formerly for locals only. Hong Kong has no restrictions, but does have pricey real estate. Some foreigners stay at Chinese homes as guests, although the practice is illegal if they do not register first at the PSB. All foreigners planning long-term residency in China must apply for a **residence permit** (hùkǒu; 户口) at the foreign affairs branch of the local PSB. The **Foreign Affairs Office** of Beijing Municipality publishes *The Handbook for Foreigners Living in Beijing*, a guide to entry and exit, registration for residency, housing, driving, employment, schooling, medical service, taxation, attractions, and entertainment. To find out more, call ☎86 10 6519 3228.

A basic one-bedroom (or studio) apartment ranges Y500-3000 per month. Landlords often request tenants to pay in three to six month chunks; some require a year's rent in advance. However, people report that price is negotiable. The following sites can help you get started on a search for an apartment.

Shanghai International Housing Management Center: ☎86 21 6224 0479; http://housingshanghai.home.sunbo.net. Limited to Shanghai. Y200-400 fee.

Sublet.com: www.sublet.com/city_rentals/China_Rentals.asp.

Wuwoo: www.wuwoo.com. In both English and Chinese. Membership (Y100) required.

CAMPING AND THE OUTDOORS

Camping in one of China's beautiful scenic areas and nature reserves might be an attractive option, but it is unfortunately a largely unfeasible one. Nowhere are there designated camping facilities. With limited exceptions, PSB frowns upon setting up your own site. *Let's Go* does not recommend camping in China. However, for a true rugged immersion in the wilderness, the best (and also legal) method may be to join an adventure tour (see **Organized Adventure Trips,** p. 64).

This does not mean, though, that there aren't opportunities for travelers to enjoy the great outdoors in China. Outdoor activities are gaining in popularity, many national parks have hiking trails, and trekking is the preferred method of travel in parts of southwest China. Rock climbing, a fledgling sport, is slowly taking hold in Beijing, but the strangely shaped karst formations in Guangxi remain the favorite of both local and foreign climbers. Skiing is possible in resorts in northeastern China, with the most well-known slopes in Heilongjiang province.

The **Great Outdoor Recreation Pages** (www.gorp.com) provides excellent general information for travelers planning on camping or spending time in the outdoors. Their guides to China have information on hiking and trekking in a range of rugged destinations, from the grasslands of Inner Mongolia to the tangled forests of Sichuan to the wildest sections of the Great Wall.

LEAVE NO TRACE. *Let's Go* encourages travelers to embrace the "Leave No Trace" ethic, minimizing their impact on natural environments and protecting them for future generations. Trekkers and wilderness enthusiasts should set up camp on durable surfaces, use cookstoves instead of campfires, bury human waste away from water supplies, bag trash and carry it out with them, and respect wildlife and natural objects. For more detailed information, contact the **Leave No Trace Center for Outdoor Ethics,** P.O. Box 997, Boulder, CO 80306, USA (☎800-332-4100 or 303-442-8222; www.lnt.org).

USEFUL PUBLICATIONS AND RESOURCES

Sierra Club Books, 85 Second St., 2nd fl., San Francisco, CA 94105, USA (☎415-977-5500; www.sierraclub.org). Publishes general resource books on hiking and camping and provides information about environmentalism and conservation in China.

The Mountaineers Books, 1001 SW Klickitat Way, Ste. 201, Seattle, WA 98134, USA (☎206-223-6303; www.mountaineersbooks.org). Boasts over 600 titles on hiking, biking, mountaineering, natural history, and conservation. Titles on China feature biking and mountaineering in China, including the Himalayas and Mt. Everest.

NATIONAL PARKS

Since 1979, the government has designated 177 national parks and scenic spots under the jurisdiction of the National Parks Agency of China. Sometimes, though, it may seem as if the designation of "national" is in name only. Management and administration continue to be locally determined and to vary widely in quality, from the environmentally friendly and unobtrusive, to the artificial and over-marketed. In places like **Jiuzhaigou** (p. 716) and **Huangshan** (p. 424), the government has done an excellent job of preserving the wilderness and minimizing the impact of human activity, despite the droves of tourists who descend upon the parks yearly. Other national parks exist in peaceful seclusion, due to their relative inaccessibility. Few visitors ever make it out to the Yarlungzangbo River Valley in Tibet, or hike up the trails to **Hailuogou Glacier** and the snow-frosted peak of **Gonggashan** in remote western Sichuan (p. 712). Sixteen of these national parks have been named United Nations Educational, Scientific, and Cultural Organization (UNESCO) World Heritage Sites, including the **Mogao Caves of Dunhuang** (p. 777), the **Temple of Heaven** in Beijing (p. 148), and the ancient villages of **Xidi** and **Hongcun** that have largely remained unchanged since the Ming Dynasty (p. 421).

A number of parks have also received the special designation of National Geographic Parks. **Weizhou** (p. 622), the youngest volcanic island in China, surrounded by a large coral reef, is the newest to join the list, which also include volcanoes in **Wudalianchi** (p. 234) and **Jingpo Lake** (p. 236). The **Stone Forest** in Yunnan province (p. 650), with its jagged labyrinth of stone pinnacles, and the **Three Gorges** (p. 734) on the Yangzi River are some of the better known National Geographic Parks.

Most parks charge admission, and prices vary, seemingly according to the popularity and fame of the park. Some parks are more tourist-friendly than others and have wide, paved roads welcoming busloads of visitors. Others require visitors to hire a guide and/or a 4WD vehicle. A few parks have strict regulations imposed in the interests of conservation and protection. Restrictions may limit the number of visitors per day, or prohibit the use of personal vehicles.

WILDERNESS SAFETY

THE GREAT OUTDOORS

Stay warm, stay dry, and stay hydrated. The vast majority of life-threatening wilderness situations can be avoided by following this simple advice. Prepare yourself for an emergency by always packing **raingear, a hat** and **mittens, a first-aid kit,** a **reflector,** a **whistle, high energy food,** and extra **water for any hike.** Dress in wool or warm layers of **synthetic materials** designed for the outdoors. **Never rely on cotton for warmth,** as it is useless when wet.

Check **weather forecasts** and pay attention to the skies when hiking, since weather patterns can change suddenly. Whenever possible, let someone know when and where you are hiking. Do not attempt a hike beyond your ability—you may be endangering your life.

WILDLIFE

China has over 4400 species of vertebrates, so it's no wonder that a few creatures can pose a threat to soft-skinned humans. China is home to pandas, snow leopards, tigers, takins, alligators, and more. Normally, though, these animals avoid humans. China also contains 57 species of **poisonous snakes,** including king cobras and sea snakes. In case of snake bite, the American Red Cross suggests that you wash the afflicted area with soap and water, keep it immobile and lower than the heart, and seek immediate medical attention.

Somewhat surprisingly, another potentially threatening animal is the **monkey.** In heavily touristed areas, monkeys grow accustomed to humans and are not afraid to come close enough to bite. Some travelers carry large walking sticks when in wilderness areas in order to discourage their approach. For minor bites, clean with soap and water and apply a dressing; for wounds with heavy bleeding, control the bleeding but do not clean the wound. Zoos and research facilities should be able to help you; in other areas seek immediate medical assistance.

Most other animal attacks in China occur in zoos, circuses, or reserves, usually when viewers taunt or hurt the animals in question. Be intelligent. **Teasing a tiger is never a good idea.** For more information, consult *How to Stay Alive in the Woods*, by Bradford Angier (Macmillan Press, US$12).

MOSQUITOES WILL SAVAGE YOU. All the big animals aside, **mosquitoes** may be travelers' main source of agony in China. While these tiny annoyances only feed upon northern China during the summer, they may be a year-round nuisance in the south. Mosquitoes can bite through thin fabric, so cover up as much as possible with thicker materials. **DEET** is useful, and mosquito netting is recommended for travelers going south of the Yangzi River. In China, department stores carry "mosquito fragrance" (wén xiāng; 蚊香), a plug-in that gives off an odorless smell that eliminates mosquitoes quite effectively.

CAMPING AND HIKING EQUIPMENT

WHAT TO BUY

Good camping equipment is both sturdy and light. North American suppliers tend to offer the most competitive prices. It's best to get these before you go, as selection will be more limited in China.

Sleeping Bags: Most sleeping bags are rated by season: "summer" means 30-40°C (86-104°F) at night; "four-season" or "winter" often means below -17°C (0°F). Bags are made of **down** (warm and light, but expensive, and miserable when wet) or of **synthetic** material (heavy, durable, and warm when wet). Prices range US$50-250 for a summer synthetic to US$200-300 for a good down winter bag. **Sleeping bag pads** include foam pads (US$10-30), air mattresses (US$15-50), and self-inflating mats (US$30-120). Bring a **stuff sack** to store your bag and keep it dry.

Backpacks: Internal-frame packs mold well to your back, keep a lower center of gravity, and flex adequately to allow you to hike difficult trails, while **external-frame packs** are more comfortable for long hikes over even terrain, as they carry weight higher and distribute it more evenly. Make sure your pack has a strong, padded hip-belt to transfer weight to your legs. There are models designed specifically for women. Any serious backpacking requires a pack of at least 4000 in. (16,000cc), plus 500 in. for sleeping bags in internal-frame packs. Sturdy backpacks cost anywhere from US$125 to $420— your pack is an area where it doesn't pay to economize. On your hunt for the perfect pack, fill up prospective models with something heavy, strap it on correctly, and walk around the store to get a sense of how the model distributes weight. Either buy a **rain cover** (US$10-20) or store all of your belongings in plastic bags inside your pack.

Boots: Be sure to wear hiking boots with good **ankle support.** They should fit snugly and comfortably over 1-2 pairs of **wool socks** and a pair of thin **liner socks.** Break in boots over several weeks before you go to spare yourself blisters.

Other Necessities: Synthetic layers, like those made of polypropylene or polyester, and a pile jacket will keep you warm even when wet. A **space blanket** (US$5-15) will help you to retain body heat and doubles as a groundcloth. Plastic **water bottles** are vital; look for shatter- and leak-resistant models. Carry **water-purification tablets** for when you can't boil water. Also bring a **first-aid kit, pocketknife, insect repellent,** and **waterproof matches** or a **lighter.**

WHERE TO BUY IT

The mail-order/online companies listed below offer lower prices than many retail stores. A visit to a local camping or outdoors store will give you a good sense of the look and weight of certain items. Although previously rare in China, a few adventure outfitters and sport equipment stores are cropping up in major cities.

Campmor, 28 Parkway, P.O. Box 700, Upper Saddle River, NJ 07458, USA (US ☎888-226-7667; www.campmor.com).

Discount Camping, 880 Main North Rd., Pooraka, South Australia 5095, Australia (☎08 8262 3399; fax 8260 6240; www.discountcamping.com.au).

Eastern Mountain Sports (EMS), 1 Vose Farm Rd., Peterborough, NH 03458, USA (☎888-463-6367; www.ems.com).

L.L. Bean, Freeport, ME 04033 (US and Canada ☎800-441-5713, UK 0800 891 297; www.llbean.com).

Mountain Designs, 51 Bishop St., Kelvin Grove, Queensland 4059, Australia (☎07 3856 2344; www.mountaindesigns.com).

Recreational Equipment, Inc. (REI), Sumner, WA 98352, USA (US and Canada ☎800-426-4840, elsewhere 253-891-2500; www.rei.com).

Sanfo Outdoors Sports, Bldg. 2, No. 3, Madian Nancun, Bei Sanhuan Zhong Lu, Beijing 100088 (☎86 10 6201 5550; www.sanfo.com.cn). Equipment for camping, hiking mountaineering, skiing, water sports, and other outdoors activities. A selection of both foreign and Chinese brands. Regional maps may be the best things here. Another loca-

tion near the World Trade Center at 1 Jianguomen Wai Dajie, Golden Bridge Plaza, 1st fl., Chaoyang District, Beijing (☎6507 9298). 3rd location at 1227-1229 Baizhang Dong Lu, Ningbo, Jiangsu Province 315040 (☎86 574 8792 3220).

YHA Adventure Shop, 19 High St., Staines, Middlesex, TW18 4QY, UK (☎1784 458625; www.yhaadventure.com).

ORGANIZED ADVENTURE TRIPS

Organized adventure tours offer another way of exploring the wild. Activities include hiking, trekking, horseback riding, biking, rafting, and mountain climbing. The most hard-core trips head into the deserts and peaks of Xinjiang, the forests and grasslands of Sichuan, and the minority villages of southwestern China. These organized trips also provide foreigners with an opportunity to journey into off-limits or difficult-to-access regions of China, such as the mountain ranges on the border with Pakistan and Tajikistan and the inner reaches of Tibet. Organizations that specialize in camping and outdoor equipment like REI and EMS (see above) also are good sources of info. The **Great Outdoor Recreation Pages** (www.gorp.com) and the **Sierra Club** (see p. 61) also lead guided adventure tours. In China, many travel agencies can help to arrange specific tours: see the travel agency listings in each city section for more detail.

Bike China (www.bikechina.com). Runs guided group bike tours (US$1200-5000) in China, with a range of difficulty levels and durations. Also designs custom tours, sells route maps, and features a selection of essays from bikers sharing stories and advice.

China Adventure Travel, 177 Renmin Xi Lu, Kunming, Yunnan 650031, China (☎86 871 531 2283; http://adventure.travel-to-china.net). Arranges trekking, biking, mountaineering, 4WD, rafting, and exploration trips in Xinjiang, Tibet, and the Southwest.

GAP Adventures, 355 Eglinton Ave. East, Toronto, ON M4P 1M5, Canada (☎800 465 5600; www.gap-china-adventures.com).

Golden Bridge International, 6/F Tak Woo House, 17-19 d'Aguilar St., Central, Hong Kong, China. (☎852 2801 5591; www.goldenbridge.net). Eco-tours, cycling, trekking, horsebacking, and camel riding across China.

iExplore, 600 W. Fulton St., Ste. 601, Chicago, IL 60661, USA (US and Canada ☎800-439-7567, from the rest of the world 1 312 492 9443; www.iexplore.com). Offers travel advice and lists regional tours and customer ratings on their website.

NAVO-Tour, 5F Ji Xiang Bldg., 49 Shang Nan Lu, Chengdu, 610041, China (☎86 28 8611 2277; www.navo-tour.com). Besides trekking and adventure tours, they also run mountaineering, photography, martial arts, and off-road tours.

Passion Asia, 23/84 (Block G) Soi Soonvijai, Rama IX Rd., Bangkapi, Huay Kwang, Bangkok 10320, Thailand (☎662 641 5619; www.passionasia.com).

Peregrine Adventures, 258 Lonsdale St., Melbourne, VIC 3000, Australia (☎61 3 9663 8611; www.peregrine.net.au). Trips starting from US$1100.

Sichuan China International Travel Service (CITS), Rm. 314, 65 Renmin Nan Lu, Chengdu, Sichuan Province, China (☎86 28 8665 2087 or 8665 2084; www.camptour.com). Specializes in trekking and camping tours in Tibet, Sichuan, and Xinjiang.

Specialty Travel Index, 305 San Anselmo Ave., Ste. 309, San Anselmo, CA 94960 (US ☎800-624-4030, elsewhere 415-455-1643; www.specialtytravel.com).

SPECIFIC CONCERNS

SUSTAINABLE TRAVEL

Unfortunately, tourism often comes at a cost to the land, despite efforts otherwise. **Ecotourism** focuses on the conservation of natural habitats and using them to build up the economy without exploitation or overdevelopment. Travelers can make a difference by doing advance research and by supporting organizations and establishments that strive to be environmentally friendly.

Consult the **Nature Conservancy** for a closer look at some of the issues that threaten China's wildernesses (US ☎703-841-8174, China 86 10 6603 4445 or 871 318 27 97; http://nature.org/wherewework/asiapacific/china/). Another good source of info on conservation and environmentalism is the **World Wide Fund for Nature in China,** Rm. 1609, Worker's Cultural Palace, Laodong Renmin Wenhua Gong Dongmen, Beijing 100006, China (☎86 10 6522 7100; www.wwfchina.org). To find out more about conservation in China, see **Alternatives to Tourism,** p. 105.

 ECOTOURISM RESOURCES. For more information on environmentally responsible tourism, contact one of the organizations below:

The Centre for Environmentally Responsible Tourism (www.c-e-r-t.org).

Earthwatch, 3 Clock Tower Place, Ste. 100, Box 75, Maynard, MA 01754, USA (☎800-776-0188 or 978-461-0081; www.earthwatch.org).

International Ecotourism Society, 733 15th St. NW, Washington, D.C. 20005, USA (☎202-347-9203; www.ecotourism.org).

ESSENTIALS

RESPONSIBLE TRAVEL

Travelers who care about the destinations and environments they explore should become aware of the social, cultural, and political implications of the choices they make when they travel. **Community-based tourism** aims to channel money from tourism into the local economy by emphasizing tours and cultural programs that are run by members of the community and benefit disadvantaged groups. Budget travelers invariably come closer to the local community in China than in the developed world. It's impossible to journey through China without stopping to sample food at a tiny snack stand, or to buy a map and some film from the old woman at the train station. Although visitors may complain about the commercialized nature of the experience, with vendors and hawkers everywhere, locals depend upon tourism for their income. Try to avoid packaged tours, which tend to whisk you through places. Choose local guides (if trustworthy and reliable), or tours owned and run locally, over national operators such as CITS. If people offer you lodgings in their homes, they may expect payment the next morning; it is polite to offer a small gift upon leaving in any case. In areas where tourists are uncommon, locals may view the visitors as a disruption. An excellent resource for general info on community-based travel is *The Good Alternative Travel Guide* (UK£10), a project of **Tourism Concern** (☎ 020 7133 3330; www.tourismconcern.org.uk).

TRAVELING ALONE

There are many benefits to traveling alone, including independence and greater interaction with locals. On the other hand, a solo traveler is more vulnerable to harassment and theft. Lone travelers need to be well-organized and look confident at all times. Try not to stand out as a tourist, and be especially careful in deserted or very crowded areas. Never admit that you are traveling alone. Use a cell phone to set up non-existent meetings with family and friends to curb unwanted attention. Maintain regular contact with someone at home who knows your itinerary. For more tips, pick up *Traveling Solo* by Eleanor Berman (Globe Pequot Press, US$17) or subscribe to **Connecting: Solo Travel Network,** 689 Park Road, Unit 6, Gibsons, BC V0N 1V7, Canada (☎ 604-886-9099; www.cstn.org; membership US$35).

WOMEN TRAVELERS

China is one of the safest parts of Asia for women travelers. Rape or assault of foreign women in China, although not unheard of, is rare. Women exploring on their own inevitably face some additional safety concerns, but it's easy to be adventurous without taking undue risks. Consider staying in hostels which offer single rooms with locks. Stick to centrally located accommodations and avoid solitary late-night treks or metro rides. Always carry extra money for a phone call, bus, or taxi. **Hitchhiking** is never safe for lone women, or even for two women traveling together. Look as if you know where you're going and approach older women or couples for directions if you're lost or uncomfortable.

Generally, the less you look like a tourist, the better. Dress conservatively, especially in less-touristed rural areas and in the Muslim areas of China's northwestern provinces. Some Chinese men assume that foreign women traveling alone are in fact seeking out sexual gratification—the chance to practice English and become "good friends" with a foreign woman can be too much too resist. In general, anyone who asks you to come visit in a hotel and any hotel that doesn't cast a second glance as you head upstairs without proper documentation should be viewed with a certain amount of skepticism. Unwanted late-night phone calls are best avoided by unplugging the phone. Also, never open your hotel door to strangers. Wearing a conspicuous **wedding band** sometimes helps to prevent unwanted overtures. Even the mention of a husband or group of male friends waiting back at the hotel can be enough to deter unwanted male attention. Some travelers report that pictures of a "husband" or "children" are extremely useful to help document marriage status.

Your best answer to verbal harassment is no answer at all. Feigning deafness, sitting motionless, and staring straight ahead at nothing in particular are often the most effective strategies. The extremely persistent can sometimes be dissuaded by a firm, loud, and very public "Go away!" or "*zŏukāi!*". Don't hesitate to seek out a police officer or a passerby if you are being harassed. Memorize the emergency numbers in places you visit, and consider carrying a whistle on your keychain. A self-defense course will both prepare you for a potential attack and raise your level of awareness of your surroundings (see **Self Defense**, p. 26). Also be aware of the health concerns that women face when traveling (see p. 33).

GLBT TRAVELERS

Attitudes toward gay, lesbian, bisexual, and transgendered (GLBT) travelers vary considerably in China, Hong Kong, and Macau. Both male and female Chinese may hold hands with members of the same sex as an expression of friendship, at times making it difficult to distinguish between heterosexual friends and homosexual couples. While heterosexual kissing and other romantic acts are becoming more acceptable in public, similar expressions of homosexuality are not. Nevertheless, many Chinese are tolerant of homosexual behavior as long as it does not interfere with one's responsibility to produce children and raise a family.

The official view of homosexuality is becoming more accepting: in 2001, homosexuality was removed from the Chinese Psychiatric Association's list of mental disorders. The government, however, continues to regard homosexuality as somewhat of a perversion brought to China by the decadent West, despite historical and literary evidence of its presence in ancient China. The legal status of homosexuality remains ambiguous; police persecution is not uncommon. Foreigners need not worry too much, but police raids of gay clubs and meeting places are becoming more frequent, especially in Beijing, Shanghai, Guangzhou, and Hong Kong.

To avoid hassles at airports and border crossings, transgendered travelers should make sure that all of their travel documents consistently report the same gender. Many countries (including the US, the UK, Canada, Ireland, Australia, and New Zealand) will amend the passports of post-operative transsexuals to reflect their true gender, although governments are generally less willing to amend documents for pre-operative transsexuals and other transgendered individuals.

Listed below are contact organizations, mail-order bookstores, and publishers that offer materials addressing specific concerns. **Utopia** (www.utopia-asia.com), "the Obi-wan Kenobi of the Asian gay cyber community," has extensive info about Chinese attitudes toward homosexuality, the Chinese gay, lesbian, and transgender community, and bars, clubs, and meeting-places around China. Their other site, **Utopia Tours** (www.utopia-tours.com), runs tours. **Out and About** (www.planetout.com) offers a newsletter addressing travel concerns and a comprehensive site addressing gay travel concerns. The online **365gay.com** (www.365gay.com/travel/travelchannel.htm), also has a travel section.

Gay's the Word, 66 Marchmont St., London WC1N 1AB, UK (☎44 20 7278 7654; www.gaystheword.co.uk). The largest gay and lesbian bookshop in the UK. Mail-order service available.

Giovanni's Room, 1145 Pine St., Philadelphia, PA 19107, USA (☎215-923-2960; www.queerbooks.com). An international lesbian/feminist and gay bookstore with mail-order service. Carries many of the publications listed below.

International Lesbian and Gay Association (ILGA), 81 rue Marché-au-Charbon, B-1000 Brussels, Belgium (☎32 2 502 2471; www.ilga.org). Provides political information, such as homosexuality laws of individual countries.

FURTHER READING: GBLT TRAVEL.

Spartacus 2003-2004: International Gay Guide. Bruno Gmunder Verlag (US$33).

Damron Men's Travel Guide, Damron Accommodations Guide, Damron City Guide, and *Damron Women's Traveler.* Damron Travel Guides (US$11-19). For info, call ☎800-462-6654 or visit www.damron.com.

Ferrari Guides' Gay Travel A to Z, Ferrari Guides' Men's Travel in Your Pocket, Ferrari Guides' Women's Travel in Your Pocket, and *Ferrari Guides' Inn Places.* Ferrari Publications (US$16-20).

The Gay Vacation Guide: The Best Trips and How to Plan Them, Mark Chesnut. Kensington Books (US$15).

TRAVELERS WITH DISABILITIES

China, including Hong Kong, is ill-equipped to deal with disabled travelers. Despite the efforts of Deng Pufang (son of Deng Xiaoping) and the China Disabled Persons Federation, improvements in disabled access are slow to be implemented. Attitudes toward the disabled have gradually improved, particularly in larger cities like Beijing, Shanghai, Nanjing, Guangzhou, and Hong Kong. The 2007 Special Olympics Games in Shanghai will hopefully raise public awareness, as did the earlier May 2000 Asian Special Olympics Game in Beijing.

Hospitals cannot be relied upon to replace broken braces or prostheses, and orthopedic materials are undependable. Public transportation and most budget hotels and guesthouses rely solely upon stairs, while more upscale hotels have elevators, and some airports can arrange wheelchairs and assistance. Lack of sidewalks and rundown roads in rural regions, and crowded streets in urban centers present more challenges. Before departure, check with your insurance provider to verify that they cover accidental injuries and medical expenses accrued in China.

Those with disabilities should inform airlines and hotels of their disabilities when making reservations: some time may be needed to make special arrangements. Call ahead to restaurants, museums, and other facilities to find out about the existence of ramps, the widths of doors, the dimensions of elevators, etc. **Guide dog owners** should inquire as to the quarantine policies of the country. At the very least, they will need to provide a certificate of immunization against rabies. The following organizations can provide additional resources and information.

Access Abroad, www.umabroad.umn.edu/access. A website devoted to making study abroad available to students with disabilities. Contact the Learning Abroad Office (☎612-626-9000) for more details. The site is maintained by Disability Services Research and Training, University of Minnesota, University Gateway, Ste. 180, 200 Oak St. SE, Minneapolis, MN 55455, USA (☎612-626-1333).

Accessible Journeys, 35 West Sellers Ave., Ridley Park, PA 19078, USA (☎800-846-4537; www.disabilitytravel.com). Designs tours for wheelchair users and slow walkers.

Directions Unlimited, 123 Green Ln., Bedford Hills, NY 10507, USA (☎800-533-5343). Books individual vacations for the physically disabled; not an info service.

Mobility International USA (MIUSA), P.O. Box 10767, Eugene, OR 97440, USA (☎541-343-1284; www.miusa.org). Books and other publications for travelers with disabilities.

Society for Accessible Travel & Hospitality (SATH), 347 Fifth Ave., #610, New York, NY 10016, USA (☎212-447-7284; www.sath.org). An advocacy group that publishes free online travel information and the travel magazine *OPEN WORLD* (annual subscription US$13, free for members). Annual membership US$45, students and seniors US$30.

MINORITY TRAVELERS

Every non-Asian traveler to China will find him- or herself in the minority. People will inevitably point and stare, crowds will gather, and you will be trailed by a constant murmur of *"lǎowài!"* (foreigner) wherever you go. People will want to practice their English with you or take your picture. Your best strategy is simply to take it all in stride and to go about your business politely but firmly. The Chinese reaction to you is usually more curiosity than malice.

Although the dual pricing system for foreigners is officially eliminated, merchants and vendors commonly overcharge tourists. Persistent bargaining is key, as it is often possible to slash an offered price by more than fifty percent.

For any foreign tourist, traveling in China means dealing with often incorrect assumptions about who you are based on your skin color; this problem is exacerbated if you are not white or not overseas Chinese. Non-white, non-Chinese tourists face a unique set of challenges and prejudices. Unfortunately, darker-skinned people may face more prejudice and curiosity. While incidents of racial violence or serious harassment are few and far between, discrimination on the basis of skin color does exist, be it from hotel owners, shopkeepers, travel agents, or government officials. Overseas Chinese may face a different set of challenges. People assume that anyone who looks Chinese can understand Mandarin like a native and are surprised and sometimes offended if the opposite is true.

DIETARY CONCERNS

Chinese cuisine believes in balance and often cooks meat and vegetables together, but **vegetarian** dishes abound. Buddhists constitute the largest group of Chinese vegetarians, and the nearest Buddhist monastery is often the best place for tasty vegetarian meals. Very few non-Buddhist Chinese are vegetarians, but meatless dishes, many of which use tofu (dòufǔ; 豆腐), are popular nonetheless. The abundance of tofu, tofu products, and soy milk make it easier for **vegans** (yángé sùshí zhě; 严格素食者) especially. Vegetarian restaurants can be found in many cities, and vegetarian dishes (sùcài; 素菜) are available at virtually every Chinese restaurant (see **Phrasebook**, p. 875). The restaurant chain **Gondelin** (功德林) excels particularly in creating delicious vegan dishes that mimics the taste of meat. Most Chinese homes cook with vegetable-based oils, but restaurants may prepare meatless dishes using animal-based cooking oils and other products; request that they use vegetable oil (zhí wù yóu; 植物油) instead. Strict vegetarians and **vegans** may want to consider preparing their own food while traveling. Vegans can enjoy soy milk (dòujiāng; 豆浆) at street vendors and grocery stores everywhere.

The travel section of the **Vegetarian Resource Group's** website (www.vrg.org), has a comprehensive list of organizations and websites that are geared toward helping vegetarians and vegans traveling abroad. For more information, visit your local bookstore or health food store and consult *The Vegetarian Traveler: Where to Stay if You're Vegetarian, Vegan, Environmentally Sensitive*, by Jed and Susan Civic (Larson Publications; US$16). Vegetarians will also find numerous resources on the web: try www.vegdining.com and www.happycow.net for starters. Vegetarian restaurants throughout China are listed at www.godsdirectcontact.com/vegetarian/veg.html and www.vegetarian-restaurants.net.

ESSENTIALS

Pork is the most popular meat in China and as a result **kosher** meals are practically nonexistent. A strong Muslim presence, however, makes **halal** (qīngzhēn; 清真) food a large part of the cuisine, especially in the north and west and in Xinjiang. Restaurants and stores certified *halal* are recognizable by their trademark green awnings and Arabic characters. They are also considered by some to offer more sanitary food than their non-*halal* counterparts.

Travelers who keep **kosher** should contact synagogues in larger cities for information on kosher restaurants. Your own synagogue or college Hillel should have access to lists of Jewish institutions across the nation. If you are strict in your observance, you may have to prepare your own food on the road. A good resource is the *Jewish Travel Guide*, by Michael Zaidner (Vallentine Mitchell; US$17). For a list of synagogues in China, see www.maven.co.il/synagogues/synagogues.asp.

OTHER RESOURCES

Let's Go tries to cover all aspects of budget travel, but we can't put *everything* in our guides. Listed below are books and websites that can serve as jumping-off points for your own research.

USEFUL PUBLICATIONS

China by Bike, by Roger Grigsby (Mountaineers Books; $15). Everything you'll need to bike your way through China. In addition to practical information and tips, there are also 9 suggested routes through China, Hong Kong, and Taiwan.

China by Rail, by Douglas Streatfeild-James (Trailblazer Publications; $20). A guide through 4 rail routes across the country and the cities and sights along the way.

Streets: Exploring Hong Kong Island, Jason Wordie (Hong Kong University Press; $28). Detailed walking tours of Hong Kong Island.

Trekking in Tibet, by Gary McCue (Mountaineers Books; $19). Highlights treks in Tibet of a variety of durations and difficulties. Provides valuable elevation information, pre-departure tips, and advice on safety and equipment.

Yunnan, by Patrick Booz (McGraw Hill; $20). A detailed guide through Yunnan's sights.

WORLD WIDE WEB

Almost every aspect of budget travel is accessible via the web. In 10 minutes at the keyboard, you can get advice on travel hotspots from other travelers or find out how much a train from Guangzhou to Shanghai costs. Unfortunately, the majority of the truly useful sites are in Chinese. If it exists, the English portal of the same site often offers much less information. There are websites for making hotel reservations and booking flights, but these sites usually only accept Chinese credit cards and require you to muddle through much Chinese.

Listed here are some regional and travel-related sites to start off your surfing; other relevant web sites are listed throughout the book. Because website turnover is high, use search engines to strike out on your own.

 WWW.LETSGO.COM Our freshly redesigned website features extensive content from our guides; community forums where travelers can connect with each other and ask questions or advice—as well as share stories and tips; and expanded resources to help you plan your trip. Visit us soon to browse by destination, find information about ordering our titles, and sign up for our e-newsletter!

THE ART OF TRAVEL

How to See the World: www.artoftravel.com. A compendium of great travel tips, from cheap flights to self defense to interacting with local culture.

Travel Library: www.travel-library.com. A fantastic set of links for general information and personal travelogues.

Backpacker's Ultimate Guide: www.bugeurope.com. Tips on packing, transportation, and where to go.

Travel Intelligence: www.travelintelligence.net. A large collection of travel writing by distinguished travel writers.

World Hum: www.worldhum.com. An independently produced collection of "travel dispatches from a shrinking planet."

BootsnAll.com: www.bootsnall.com. Numerous resources for independent travelers, from planning your trip to reporting on it when you get back.

INFORMATION ON CHINA

Atevo Travel: www.atevo.com/guides/destinations. Detailed introductions, travel tips, and suggested itineraries.

Beijing International: www.ebeijing.gov.cn. An indispensable resource for foreigners planning to travel or live in Beijing, with everything from recommendations of hotels and sights to information on how to find a doctor.

Beijing Portal: www.beijingportal.com.cn. More than just Beijing, this site has stories from all over China on news, culture, travel, and lifestyle. Also has up-to-date information on entertainment, events, and nightlife, as well as a classified section for those looking for employment, apartments, or language exchange partners.

China.org: www.china.org.cn. This general news-and-everything site has good coverage of travel, arts, and culture. Guides to each province and its sights.

China Today: www.chinatoday.com. A wealth of general information on China.

China Tour: www.chinatour.com. All the basic facts about traveling to China and more. The front page links to articles related to travel in China, collected from publications ranging from CNN to *The Guardian* to China's own Xinhua Agency.

China View: www.chinaview.cn. Straight from Xinhua News Agency, under direct government control. The news section may not be all that trustworthy, but the travel, entertainment, and metrolife sections are worth browsing through.

Discover Hong Kong: www.discoverhongkong.com. Several English language editions make this site a breeze.

Macau Government Tourist Office: www.macautourism.gov.mo. A comprehensive guide to the city in English, with detailed listings of local festivals and events.

China Through the Train Window

Few travelers recount their time in China without waxing poetic about the train rides. The tight quarters become the social space for a sampling of Chinese middle-class society. Laptops and Palm Pilots are rare sights; instead, the passengers are forced into close interaction. The train becomes a test tube where the commonalities and schisms of national politics and culture come to the forefront.

Riding the train from Beijing to Ürümqi (the capital of the Xinjiang Uighur Autonomous Region), I traveled across the length of China. In 48hr., we saw a near-total transformation. The crowded east-coast cities gave way to rice paddies and farmland on the first day. The second day, we arose to the view of a vast rocky desert. The following morning, we finally reached the oasis metropolis of Ürümqi.

I say "we" because China stubbornly holds onto travel as a collective experience. Contact between passengers was sparse during the first 12hr. of the train ride, with only brief communication to resolve issues of physical space. But the Chinese have a way of overhearing, staring, and interjecting into others' conversations that Americans might find rude. In time, however, these customs created moments of community with cross-generational discussions that one finds lacking in American life. It was not long before our living area had become a forum for debating all kinds of national issues, intertwined with loud games of Chinese poker.

Conversational topics included politics, the educational system, my Chinese name, the differences between local and "foreigner" culture, and the recent (but very limited) phenomenon of open homosexuality. During a discussion, the group would often split into two camps. There were the loud types, who loved to argue and to lead discussion, and then there were the quiet types, generally the elderly, who would participate with long, friendly smiles and affirmative nods.

It so happened that on this train ride, we were a week away from the International Olympic Committee's decision on the site of the 2008 Summer Games. A level of excitement filled China unlike anything I have ever seen in the United States. Amidst millions of T-shirts and daily news flashes, the train ride was the only time I heard skeptical opinions regarding the Beijing Olympics. I was reading a book when a medical student and recent addition to our group called on me by a joke name: "Mistah Leeee! What do you think of the Olympics?" I said I thought that people were perhaps making too big a deal of it, and asked him his opinion. He then began to describe *"luan shoufei."* According to him, *luan shoufei* or "unreasonable payments," is one of the largest problems in China. Whether the government is building a school, a road, or Olympic buildings thousands of miles away, the civilians are forced to contribute money. Former premier Zhu Rongji has publicly criticized the practice. However, he described it as a matter of *daode*, morals, rather than a political issue. Some of my conversational companions stressed the need for *falu*, or law, to end bureaucratic corruption. However, as the medical student said, "According to Confucian tradition, to make politicians operate by law would be to claim that they are immoral, and that would be disgraceful." Confucian philosophy maintains that the country should be governed by virtuous, paternalistic leaders. In turn, subjects should trust and obey officials. Thus, immorality can be self-perpetuating. The result has arguably been rampant corruption, which has pervaded much of Chinese history (yet we must not forget that this is also the history of the world's longest lasting civilization).

Our train pushed on into the evening. It was soon 10pm; lights out and music off. Conversation petered out, and everyone was soon asleep except for me and a businessman named Mr. Liu who was brushing his teeth. Unbuttoning my shirt, I remarked on how much I love Beijing night culture: "Everyone hangs out on the street and relaxes together. The men, out there with their shirts off, drinking bottles of beer to stifle the summer heat."

"Ah yes, but we can't do that right now," he said jokingly. "Nowadays, what would people think!" I took my shirt off anyway and lay down. We both laughed, and staring up at the ceiling, drifted off into sleep.

Josh Levin is a Harvard graduate and a veteran researcher-writer of Let's Go: China, 4th ed. *This article appeared previously in the* Harvard International Review *(February, 2001).*

LIFE AND TIMES

LAND

Children all over China learn from an early age that their country is shaped like a **rooster.** Or at least a rooster's torso. Add Southeast Asia as the legs, the Korean peninsula as the beak, and Japan as a helpless worm, and the picture is complete. But this is no mere barnyard fowl—China is the third-largest country in the world, dominating East Asia not only in size but also in the diversity of its landscape.

China is defined by its rivers and mountains more than any other geographic formation. The **Yangzi River,** or *Cháng Jiāng* (长江), the "Long River," flows 6500km from its lofty origins in the Tanggula Mountains of the Tibetan Plateau to the **East China Sea.** Along the way, the world's third-longest river carves its way through deep ravines in Yunnan and rugged peaks in southern Sichuan before winding through the **Three Gorges** and the fertile floodplains of the **Yangzi Basin.** Second to the Yangzi in length at 5464km, the **Yellow River** roars through northern China, though for more than 200 days of the year, the roar is more like a trickle, due to dams and overdevelopment. Its distinctive yellow loess gave the river its name, but its catastrophic floods earned it a more chilling title: China's Sorrow. Yet the Yellow River still holds a revered place in the hearts of its people, as the cradle of Chinese civilization and a symbol of the country itself.

The sheer peaks and snow-blanketed mountains of China present wonderful opportunities for the traveler but often mean poverty for its residents. A little more than 10% of the land can be cultivated; the rest is swallowed up by mountains, hills, deserts, and plateaus—but that doesn't stop one-fifth of the world's population from trying. The formidable **Himalayan, Pamir, Kunlun,** and **Tianshan** mountain ranges and the **Tibetan Plateau** guard China's western front. The deserts and depressions of **northwest China,** including the **Taklimakan** and the **Turpan,** create yet another barrier between China and Central Asia. **Subtropical rainforests** ramble over the southwest, giving rise to snowy peaks, which tilt up to shield the lush, mountain-ensconced **Sichuan Basin** at its southern edge. In the heart of **central China,** the land watered by the Yellow River is drier, defined by the yellow silt of the river. Meanwhile, the Yangzi flows through the warmer, wetter regions of southern China, *Jiāngnán* ("South of the River"), with its soft green hills, limestone peaks, and flooded rice paddies. Isolated at the far corner of the country, northeast China shares with its northern neighbor Russia deep poplar and pine forests, and deeper snows. Beyond China's historic northern border, the Great Wall, the **grasslands** of Inner Mongolia roll off to the horizon, fading into desert.

FLORA AND FAUNA

China's varied topography and climate make it home to many rare plants and animals. The district of **Xishuangbanna** in southern Yunnan province harbors most of China's tropical flora and fauna, including the **white-cheeked gibbon,** the **Asiatic elephant,** and the **flying frog,** as well as medicinal plants like the **Japanese snowbell** and the **sandal tree.** Farther north, the **giant panda** (p. 698) feasts on bamboo in the more temperate forests of Sichuan, Gansu, and Shaanxi provinces, sharing its distinctive habitat with the **golden snub-nosed monkey, takin, Asiatic black bear,** and **golden pheasant.** The Tibetan Plateau in far west China houses **snow leopards,**

Tibetan antelope, and **wild yaks.** Many of China's distinctive **crane** species live in the far north. The **Baiji dolphin,** unique to the Yangzi River, is the world's most endangered cetacean, with its population hovering at a precarious 50.

Nearly all of these animals are currently on the long list of endangered species, as too-rapid economic development and pollution threatens much of China's wealth. In recent years, the government has imposed steep penalties on **poachers** (one of the reasons behind the decimation of the pandas and tigers). The government has also created a network of **nature reserves.** These reserves are usually open to the public and many, like **Wolong** (p. 702), **Jiuzhaigou** (p. 716), **Zhangjiajie** (p. 456), **Wudalianchi** (p. 234), **Zhalong** (p. 234), and **Changbaishan** (p. 249), are prime spots to admire scenery and wildlife.

HISTORY

No matter where you travel in China, one thing will be immediately obvious: China is old. China's recorded history alone spans more than 5000 years, long enough to make Britain look like an impertinent upstart and the US like a toddler in a wading pool. What follows is a relatively short and sweet rundown of the Middle Kingdom's illustrious past. For more on the history of Tibet, see **Tibet: History,** p. 832.

ONCE UPON A TIME IN CHINA

In Chinese mythology, there's never been any doubt about which came first, the chicken or the egg. The primordial egg cracked open to reveal **Pan Gu,** the giant who started it all. From the chaos that spilled out as the "egg white," he separated earth from heaven. After he died, his breath became the winds and clouds, his voice the thunder, and his eyes the sun and moon. His blood flowed into rivers and streams; his bones were the metals of the earth. His body formed the holy mountains of the world, and the fleas on his body turned into humans.

The earliest civilizations (ca. 5000 BC) developed textiles, pottery, and more. One notable achievement is the working of **jade,** a particularly hard stone, into fine figurines, ornaments, and ritual objects. Legends tell of mythical kings and heroes who supposedly lived around this time and performed great deeds that immortalized them as forefathers of the Chinese. The most important of these, **Huangdi,** is said to have invented writing, silk, and ceramics.

The first two dynasties of China, the **Xia** (ca. 2200-1700 BC) and **Shang** (ca. 1700-1200 BC) only left behind legends and artifacts, which pointed to a complex and unified governing system. Large-scale tombs hinted at the power of its rulers, oracle bones at the importance of divination and the spiritual roles of kings, and bronze vessels at artistry and skill. The last of the three early dynasties, the **Zhou** (1027-771 BC) was the first to leave behind written records, including the earliest Chinese poetry and the story of its conquering of the Shang. The Zhou also evolved the concept of the ruler as the **Son of Heaven,** who retains power as long as he has heaven's mandate. The Eastern Zhou (770-256 BC), however, gradually dissolved into a prolonged conflict between states and vassals, better known as the **Warring States Period.** It was around this time that **Confucius, Laozi,** and other philosophers contemplated life, seeking a solution to the problems of the age.

CLASSICAL CHINA

EMPIRE RISING. From **Qin** (221-207 BC) comes China. The highly centralized and martial government of the **Qin** conquered the other warring states and transformed an isolated Shaanxi kingdom into a powerful empire with a common currency, a written language, and a standardized administrative system that lasted for 2000 years. The ruthless **Qin Shihuang**, "First Emperor," ruled with an iron hand, burning books (including those of Confucius) and enslaving thousands to build the **Great Wall**. He also suffered from paranoia and reputedly never slept in the same place for fear of assassins. Preoccupied with death, he searched for immortality but could only secure himself a massive tomb (constructed in secret, of course), complete with a personal army, the **Terracotta Warriors** (p. 276).

Qin Shihuang's tyrannical ways had not been popular, and his death sparked open rebellion. **Liu Bang** defeated his rivals and went on to be Emperor **Gaozu** of one of China's longest reigning dynasties, the **Han** (206 BC to AD 220). Thanks to the bartering power of precious silk, the Han extended its influence as far as the Pamirs and Ferghana. A string of tributary states stretched west along the **Silk Road**, kept in line by the lure of trade. The empire weakened briefly when Wang Mang usurped the throne, but the **Eastern Han** made its comeback 16 years later. Often compared to the glory days of the Roman Empire, the Han also gave its name to the Chinese people, 汉 , and the prized invention of paper.

WEI AND SUI PAVE THE WAY. More than 350 years of warfare and short-lived kingdoms followed the Han, beginning with the **Three Kingdoms** and ending with the **Northern and Southern Dynasties.** The empire fractured, and many Chinese fled south of the Yangzi. Northern China was gripped by a succession of non-Han tribes, who gradually assimilated into Chinese culture. The most influential of the foreign dynasties, the **Northern Wei** (AD 386-534) encouraged Buddhist scholarship and art, and sponsored many temples and grottoes that can still be seen today.

China was finally reunified by **Yang Jian**, a northern general of Chinese and Turkish ancestry. Under the **Sui Dynasty** (AD 581-618), the empire returned to the Confucian roots of the Zhou and Han. The dynasty set up civil service exams, created a lasting legal code, restored the Great Wall, and began the **Grand Canal.** But all good things must come to an end, and costly campaigns, conscription of millions, and repressive taxation led to rebellion just 40 years later.

GOLDEN TANG. When the dust settled in AD 617, **Li Yuan** (Emperor **Gaozu**) and his son **Li Shimin** (Emperor **Taizong**) emerged victorious and founded the **Tang Dynasty** (AD 618-907), launching China into its golden age. Early emperors were skilled tacticians, savvy diplomats, and fearless commanders. At the height of Tang power in the 7th century, Tang military protectorates stretched from western Iran to Vietnam, and diplomats forged alliances with Uighurs and Tibetans. For the first time, China became truly welcoming of foreign ideas and influences. As the country's capital and the world's largest city, **Chang'an** was a veritable cosmopolitan hub, humming with visitors and goods from Japan, Korea, India, Persia, and West Asia. Tang ships forayed into Southeast Asia, and camel caravans ferried Tang ideas down the Silk Road. Imperial courts flourished with an exchange of ideas and culture, attracting artists, musicians, and many of China's greatest poets. China's first (and only) female emperor, **Wu Zetian,** also came to power during this enlightened age, reigning for 51 years (ca. 654-705). A ruthless and skilled politician, she first ruled through the weak third emperor, her husband, and later deposed her two sons to proclaim her own dynasty, the **Zhou.**

The Tang court reached the height of its glory during the reign of **Xuanzong.** But love proved to be his downfall, as the emperor heeded the advice of his favorite concubine to shower favors upon **An Lushan,** who later rebelled and attacked Chang'an in 755. The resulting decade-long civil war left much of northern China in ruins. From then on, the Tang was never quite the same again. The empire withdrew from Central Asia, and the Tibetan sacking of Chang'an in 763 further weakened the dynasty. Though the Tang held on for another century or so, bandits, warlords, foreign enemies, and a corrupt bureaucracy plagued the country.

THE SONG. In 960, General **Zhao Kuangyin** (Emperor **Taizu**) reunified much of China and founded the **Northern Song Dynasty** (960-1126). The Song rulers concentrated on preserving Confucian culture and vastly expanded the meritocratic civil service examination system, creating an elite class of **scholar-officials.** Trade prospered, and ships carrying fine silks, ceramics, and books (first printed in the Tang) shuttled back and forth. Lyric poetry and landscape painting attained new depths, nourished by **Huizong.** Forced to become emperor when his brothers died, Huizong much preferred the arts over the throne. He was an accomplished artist and calligrapher, but his lack of political prowess led to the fall of the Northern Song.

Despite reforms and cultural richness at home, the Song was constantly threatened by northern "barbarians." Shortly after the founding of the Song, Mongolian **Khitan** nomads conquered Beijing and created the **Liao Dynasty** (916-1125). Unable to drive out the Liao, the Song collaborated with another tribe, the **Jurchen** of Manchuria, but the Jurchen not only conquered the Liao, they also turned upon the Song, overran their capital in 1126, and established the **Jin Dynasty** (1115-1234).

After Huizong's death, the remnants of his empire took refuge in southern China, establishing the **Southern Song** (1127-1279) in **Hangzhou** (p. 390). The Song never tried in earnest to regain the lost land: the court indulged themselves by the shores of the West Lake, while the literati withdrew into a inner world to explore nostalgia, loss, and identity through poetry and art. Soon, however, the Song would be jolted awake by a powerful nomadic nation to the far north: the Mongols.

THE MIGHTY KHANS. Before the 13th century, the Mongols were a nomadic people composed of dispersed, roving clans. In 1206, **Genghis Khan** unified the clans and subsequently stormed across Eurasia, sacking Baghdad, trampling Moscow, and pounding on the gates of Vienna. Genghis died in 1227, but his sons and grandsons finished the job, defeating the Song in 1279 with their ruthless tactics.

Kublai Khan's **Yuan Dynasty** court hosted guests including Italian explorer **Marco Polo** and also tackled major projects like Beijing's Beihai Park (p. 145), Zhongnanhai Compound, and an expanded Grand Canal system. To keep the populace under control, the Mongols employed harsh measures, treating Chinese as second-class citizens. The Chinese remained fiercely loyal to the fallen Song and the dream of a Han restoration. Loyalists fought to the end, restored the desecrated tombs of emperors, and formed underground pockets of resistance.

THE PEASANT EMPEROR. Unlike many emperors, **Zhu Yuanzhang** grew up in poverty and spent much of his youth wandering aimlessly. He joined the rebel group **Red Turbans** and eventually ousted the Mongols from Beijing, becoming Emperor **Taizu** of the **Ming Dynasty** (1368-1644). Though he reformed the tax system to take the burden off the poor and tried to cut costs, he could not run the government efficiently. His son **Yongle** (r. 1402-24) moved the capital to Beijing and oversaw ambitious public works projects. The empire also sought to expand into Central and South Asia, while **sea expeditions** ventured as far afield as Madagascar. But the Ming was plagued with internal problems. Despotic emperors purged scholar-officials for exercising their Confucian right to speak out and voice dissent. High inflation, constant fighting with Manchus and Mongols, and natural disasters created further problems, leading once more to public unrest.

LATE IMPERIAL CHINA: THE QING

GOING POSTAL. In 1644, a former postal official, **Li Zicheng,** led a rebel attack on Beijing and captured the capital city. In the final hours of the Ming, Emperor **Chongzhen** killed most of his family members before hanging himself on a tree in present-day **Jingshan Park** (p. 145). Loyalist general **Wu Sangui,** in a last-ditch

attempt to save the dynasty, invited Manchu armies into Beijing to quell Li's rel·
lion. The Manchus succeeded, but had no intentions of just quietly leaving. For the
fourth time in history, China fell under the folds of foreigners from the northern
steppes, this time under the dynasty name of **Qing** (清; "pure"). Understanding that
an empire could be won, but not ruled, on horseback, Qing emperors reigned in
the same guise as their Han predecessors, relying heavily on Chinese tradition and
Confucian administration while continuing to uphold the imperial examination
system, patronize the arts, and appoint Chinese to posts.

The Qing Dynasty produced two of the greatest and longest-reigning emperors
in Chinese history. **Kangxi** (r. 1668-1722), famous for his personal inspection tours
and ascetic habits, consolidated control over the empire and oversaw distant military campaigns in Russia, Mongolia, and Tibet. After the reign of Kangxi's able but
short-lived successor **Yongzheng** (r. 1723-1735), whose ascension and sudden death
were both mired in controversy and palace intrigue, **Qianlong** (r. 1736-1796) pre-
sided over a period of unprecedented wealth and territorial and population expansion. By the end of Qianlong's reign, however, all the familiar problems of
corruption and depleted imperial coffers were cropping up again and the new
problem of foreigners from the West was set to take center stage.

OPIUM FOR TEA. Although Westerners were eagerly knocking on the door, Qing
emperors remained wary of foreign interaction and short-sighted of the implications of a changing world. In the so-called **Canton system** (1760-1842), Qianlong limited foreign traders to the vicinity of Guangdong (Canton) province and channeled
all transactions through a select group of merchants. Britain initially accepted the
unfavorable trade restrictions in order to feed the English **tea** addiction, but the
tables soon turned when Britain assumed trade for an illegal Chinese addiction—
opium. By the 1820s, opium was alarmingly widespread and vast quantities of silver
were flowing out of China to pay for the narcotic, creating both a social and financial drain. In 1836, Emperor **Daoguang** started a vigorous campaign to stamp out
opium. Under Commissioner **Lin Zexu,** 50,000 pounds of opium were confiscated
and 16,000 Chinese dealers and users arrested. The purge was taken to the next
level in 1839 when Lin, after repeated unsuccessful entreaties to stop the opium
trade, blockaded foreigners into their factories, coercing the British to finally
relinquish their stash. His actions brought warships to the coast of Guangzhou.

The **Opium War** (1840-1842) was no contest. After several military conflicts and
failed negotiations, the Chinese consented to the stipulations imposed by Britain's
Treaty of Nanjing, the first in a long series of humiliating concessions and unequal
treaties with the Western world. Five ports were opened for trade, and the British
obtained, among other things, extraterritoriality, most-favored-nation status, and a
little island called Hong Kong. Tensions continued to flare leading to the **Second
Opium War** (1856-1858), which culminated in the **Treaty of Tianjin** and more concessions to Britain, France, Russia, and the US, including the legalization of opium.

WHEN IT RAINS, IT POURS. After 1850, floods, famine, and overpopulation combined with governmental neglect and corruption to create domestic unrest. Armed
uprisings broke out around the country, the most notorious of which was the **Taiping Rebellion,** led by militant evangelist **Hong Xiuquan.** After failing the civil exam
for the fourth time, Hong read some rudimentary Christian tracts, had some
visions, and naturally concluded that he was God's *other* son, called upon to save
China from the Manchurians. As a sign of the times, over 20,000 discontented Chinese responded to Hong's call to arms, creating a formidable army that eventually
numbered over one million. Hong captured the capital city of Nanjing in 1853,
establishing the **Heavenly Kingdom of Peace** (tàipíng tiān guó; 太平天国), which
lasted until 1864, when loyalist armies led by **Zeng Guofan** finally defeated the
rebels, giving the Qing government one last chance to get its act together.

RRAH. During the **Tongzhi period** (1862-1874), the Qing reformed on system, combatted corruption, and established a foreign affairs l with Western powers. China inched ahead in modernization, the **Self-Strengthening Movement** (1874-1894), which promoted Western for practical use, while retaining Chinese values. Reform was difficult nservative scholar class and a stagnant court; meanwhile, the world around continued to barrel ahead. In 1895 China was sent yet another humiliating wake-up call when it was defeated in the **Sino-Japanese War** and forced to cede Taiwan. Defeat inspired the short-lived **Hundred Days of Reform,** during which Emperor **Guangxu** finally broke free of the iron grip of his mother, the **Empress Dowager Ci Xi.**

Intellectuals and the ruling elite weren't alone in their desire for change. Throughout China, peasants formed **secret societies** (the roots of today's triads) that plotted against the Qing, foreigners, or both. The **Society of Righteous and Harmonious Fists,** dubbed the **"Boxers"** because of their shadow-boxing martial arts technique, gained support not only amongst commoners but also with members of the court. The Boxers attacked and looted Beijing in 1900 and killed foreign and Chinese Christians, prompting an allied force of international powers to descend upon the city and the Qing to declare war. The foreign powers, after proving that the Boxers were not, as they believed themselves to be, impervious to bullets, exacted hefty concessions from the Qing. At the turn of the century, China's inability to stand up to foreign powers indicated that the Qing's days were numbered.

THE REPUBLICAN ERA

BIRTH OF A NATION. In the final years of the Qing, the government made efforts to reform and modernize, including abolishing the imperial exams, banning foot binding, and moving towards constitutionalism, but it was too little too late for the dissident leaders who were busily debating the fate of China. On October 10, 1911, an armed uprising in Wuhan (p. 459) carried out by members of the **United League** brought down the half-dead Qing government once and for all, sparking a revolution that rippled throughout the country. In the midst of the turmoil, the foreign-educated, exiled revolutionary **Sun Yat-sen** (孙中山), the "father of modern China," returned and was inaugurated as president of the provisional government of the Republic of China. Sun had a comprehensive ideology for a revolutionary society based on his Three Principles of nationalism, democracy, and socialism, but knew that he lacked the military strength to keep the nation together.

In a series of compromises in 1912, the last Qing emperor, six-year-old **Henry Pu Yi,** abdicated, and Sun Yat-sen handed the presidency over to reformist general **Yuan Shikai,** believing that he would be able to head the government. Yuan, however, was a military man and a warlord. Faced with factionalism and a weak central government, he dissolved the legislature, purged the **Nationalist Party (GMD),** and declared himself emperor in 1916. A fresh round of rebellions commenced, as the nation sectioned off into regions and entered a **warlord era** (1916-1927).

THE SPIRIT OF MAY FOURTH. On May 4, 1919, 3000 students marched on Tian'anmen Square to protest the terms of the Treaty of Versailles, which transferred German concessions in Shandong to Japan rather than to China. Although the warlord government jailed more than 1000 students, widespread anger and frustration with imperialism and China's weak international standing ensured the spread of the **May Fourth Movement.** Intellectuals turned their attention to another vehicle for social change: **Communism.** In 1921, 11 delegates, including **Mao Zedong**

(毛泽东), attended the First Party Congress in Shanghai. Police raids forced the meeting to relocate to a boat, but could not prevent the establishment of the **Chinese Communist Party (CCP)** on July 1st of that year.

Meanwhile, Sun Yat-sen was busy trying to revitalize the nationalist cause. With the help of Soviet advisors, Sun streamlined the GMD and adopted Bolshevik methods of party organization and propaganda dissemination. Sun then established the **Huangpu Military Academy** in Guangzhou to assemble an army to wrest power from the warlords. His brother-in-law **Chiang Kai-shek** (蒋介石), fresh from training in Moscow, became the first commandant, and **Zhou Enlai** (周恩来), a capable young Communist, served as the political commissar. Sun did not live to see the fruits of his labor, however, dying of cancer in 1925.

THE LONG AND WINDING ROAD. In 1926, Generalissimo Chiang Kai-shek led a United Front of GMD-CCP forces on military campaigns against the warlords. In less than a year, the forces had subjugated all warlords south of the Yangzi River. But as Chiang's forces approached Shanghai, forces led by Zhou Enlai seized control of the city. In retaliation, the Generalissimo unleashed a bloody campaign that killed and jailed thousands of Communists and suspected Communist sympathizers. Chiang's regime in Nanjing took control, conquering Beijing in 1928.

The shock of Chiang's sudden purges left the Communist movement in disarray. With the CCP's morale hitting an all-time low in 1928, the tattered forces of Mao Zedong and Zhu De established a guerrilla base on **Jinggangshan** (p. 444) in Jiangxi province, where they bided their time fending off Nationalist guerrilla campaigns, but the under-equipped **Red Army** was eventually overwhelmed by the 700,000-member-strong GMD. Forced to retreat, in October 1935 the CCP embarked on the **Long March,** an epic journey across 8000km of China's most rugged terrain, which included 18 mountain ranges and 23 major rivers. By the time the ragged guerrillas limped into **Yan'an** (p. 281) one year later, fewer than 10,000 of the original 87,000 marchers had survived, and Mao had emerged as the clear leader of the CCP.

THE WORLD AT WAR. Japan didn't waste any time capitalizing on the chaos in China. Faced with Japanese aggression, Mao declared his willingness to unite with the GMD against the Japanese, but Chiang Kai-shek refused and insisted on fighting both at the same time. In what is known as the **Xi'an Incident,** GMD general **Zhang Xueliang** kidnapped Chiang and forced him to put aside the civil war and agree to a second United Front with the Communists.

WWII began in China on July 7, 1937, when Japanese troops clashed with Chinese guards on the **Marco Polo Bridge** outside Beijing (p. 165). Japan's all-out offensive took eastern China by storm. Chinese forces retreated into Sichuan while the Japanese raped and slaughtered thousands of surrendered soldiers and civilians in the capital city of Nanjing (p. 357), a massacre with scars so deep that its memory continues to mar Sino-Japanese relations today.

In the confusion, Communist guerrillas took control of rural areas, recruiting volunteers and carrying out small-scale raids against the Japanese and pro-Japanese militias. In 1941, Chiang Kai-shek, once again threatened by the Communists' burgeoning power, rescinded his promise of a United Front and attacked the Communist forces in southern China, re-igniting the civil war while the foreign war was still raging. Once Japan surrendered to the Allied forces, the two factions rushed to reclaim former Japanese territories. Despite efforts by the US to negotiate a settlement, full-scale civil war broke out in 1947. Eventually, the Nationalist cause, overwrought with inflation and corruption, gave way to Mao's prevailing **People's Liberation Army (PLA)**. Chiang Kai-shek and the Nationalists fled to **Taiwan** where they set up the provincial **Republic of China (ROC),** vowing to reclaim the mainland. On October 1, 1949, Chairman Mao stood over Tian'anmen Square and formally established the **People's Republic of China (PRC).**

THE COMMUNIST ERA

THE CAMELOT YEARS. Having won the civil war, the PRC faced the even more daunting task of transforming a war-torn and bankrupt country into a Communist state. In the early years of the PRC, Chairman Mao ruled with the help of his comrades-in-arms, including Zhou Enlai, **Liu Shaoqi** (刘少奇), and **Deng Xiaoping** (邓小平). From 1949 to 1957, the CCP made impressive gains, initiating a series of campaigns to solidify their hold on Chinese society. In the countryside, **land reform** and **collectivization** transferred private lands to public ownership and transformed the lives of the peasants. In urban areas, workers were organized into **work units**.

With the world split into two camps, Mao adopted a **"lean to one side"** policy, forging close ties with China's Marxist older brother, the Soviet Union. Such a policy alienated the PRC further from the established Western powers, who recognized the ROC as the legitimate government of China, but it brought in much-needed Soviet advisors and aid in the PRC's formative years.

LET THE FLOWERS WILT. In the early 1950s, the consolidation of economic power proceeded fairly smoothly. Reining in those pesky free-thinking intellectuals proved to be much more difficult. Sincerely or otherwise, in 1956 Mao launched the **Hundred Flowers Movement** to solicit the thoughts and suggestions of intellectuals concerning the party and their policies, famously declaring "Let a hundred flowers bloom, and a hundred schools contend." Cautious intellectuals initially stayed mum, but when the gates opened in 1957, criticism of party leadership, practices, and ideology came pouring out, to the great displeasure of Mao. His **Anti-Rightist Campaign** of 1957-58 moved swiftly to crush dissent. Hundreds of thousands of intellectuals and dissidents were rounded up and sent to labor camps for "thought reform" in the first of many campaigns that targeted intellectuals.

THE GREAT LEAP BACKWARD. By 1958, agricultural output was unable to keep up with population growth, and Mao was growing impatient with the slow pace of Soviet-style industrialization, which was proving to be unsuited for China. Instead of advocating technological improvements, as many advisors suggested, Mao turned to his favorite strategy—mass mobilization. As part of his infamous **Great Leap Forward** (1958-1960) plan, he ordered massive labor-intensive public works projects and organized enormous **People's Communes**, which housed as many as 1000 farmers and replaced smaller cooperatives. In the end, the Great Leap Forward, combined with a run of bad weather, led to one of the greatest catastrophes of the 20th century. An estimated 30 to 40 million people starved to death in the countryside from a largely manmade famine.

COMRADES NO MORE. Since the late 1950s, the alliance with the Soviet Union had been heading for the rocks. Russian leader Nikita Khrushchev was wary of Mao's uncomfortably fanatic domestic programs and increasingly cavalier international stance. Mao, in turn, was unhappy with playing second fiddle to the Soviets whose moderate position toward the United States and departure from orthodox Marxist-Leninist doctrine he deemed revisionist and inappropriately deferential to the Western capitalists. When the Soviets rescinded their original agreement to assist China with their nuclear program, the falling out was all but complete. By 1965, the **Sino-Soviet split** was an established fact, and relations between the two former comrades grew increasingly frosty.

THE STILL BEFORE THE STORM. In the aftermath of the disastrous Great Leap Forward, Mao was forced to take a step backward, handing over his position as head of state to second-in-command Liu Shaoqi, who, along with Deng Xiaoping, set about reviving China's dying economy and reversing previous policies. Mao turned to his wife **Jiang Qing** (江青), the notorious Madame Mao, and **Lin Biao** (林彪), the head of the PLA, to help him regain power. While Lin rallied his soldiers with copies of *The Quotations of Chairman Mao* **(The Little Red Book)**, Jiang spearheaded Mao's cultural reforms and tapped into a network of radical intellectuals from Shanghai. Having already purged landlords, capitalists, and intellectuals in his rise to power, Mao turned to his own party. At the instigation of propaganda saying that corrupt forces were trying to overthrow the beloved Chairman, radical students organized **Red Guard** groups to protect him and to struggle against party revisionists. Within a few short months, millions of youths had heeded Mao's call, launching the **Great Proletariat Cultural Revolution** (1966-69).

THE EAST IS RED. Mao's use of mass mobilization and personality cult to bolster his political power resulted in a complete upheaval of society. Under Mao's orders, the Red Guards purged Chinese culture of the **Four Olds:** old culture, old customs, old habits, and old ideas. Traditional books were burned, countless historical sites and temples ransacked, and cultural relics destroyed. But the greatest destruction was inflicted on people. "Reactionaries" were stripped of their pride and possessions and sent to hard labor camps. Academics were publicly humiliated, marched through streets with dunce caps and placards, beaten, interrogated, and tortured. Students struggled against teachers, children against parents. Hundreds of thousands of people perished, with many tortured to death or forced into suicide. At the height of the Cultural Revolution, all sense of social order was lost, as persecution and violence escalated to extreme levels in efforts to prove loyalty to Mao.

By 1968, the violence had veered out of even Mao's control and the Red Guards had fallen into fractious infighting. Chinese cities turned into war zones with militant factions fighting street battles with looted tanks and missiles. Mao brought the PLA in to restore order and repress the youth who had ransacked society at his beckoning. In mid-1968, some 15 million youths were transferred from the cities to impoverished farms in the vast countryside, where they were instructed to undergo re-education by the peasantry. Though the Cultural Revolution officially ended in 1969, many scholars date its end at Mao's death in 1976. Its psychological effects on Chinese society linger to this day.

A CHANGE IN THE WIND. Mao turned against his comrades who had dared to steer China from the proper socialist—that is, his—road. Liu Shaoqi was tried on trumped-up charges and eventually tortured to death; Deng Xiaoping was condemned to manual labor. Thousands of other cadres were sent to hard labor camps. With the CCP in tatters from repeated purges, the PLA moved to fill the power vacuum. By 1969, the PLA dominated the Party Congress, and Lin Biao was affirmed as Mao's chosen successor. After Lin staged a coup in 1971, however, subsequently dying in a suspiciously convenient plane crash while fleeing to the Soviet Union, Deng Xiaoping and Zhou Enlai reemerged in the forefront of politics.

After the turmoil of the Cultural Revolution, the country—partially due to the influence of Zhou Enlai—pursued a more moderate political and economic course that was markedly different from that of the past two decades. Zhou, the "diplomat," played an instrumental role in advancing **Sino-American relations.** Practical politics was overcoming ideological differences as a series of unofficial cultural and athletic contacts known as **ping pong diplomacy** paved the way for official interactions. After Secretary of State **Henry Kissinger**'s secret visit to China, **Richard Nixon** stunned the world by exchanging toasts with Chairman Mao in 1972. Though the road to rapprochement would be slow, the United States eventually formally recognized the PRC government in 1979.

THE POST-MAO ERA

THE PASSING OF AN ERA. 1976 saw the deaths of the PRC's two greatest leaders. Zhou Enlai passed away in early 1976 from cancer, creating a power vacuum. Mao at this point was indisposed by age and of questionable lucidity. Jiang Qing and her zealous cohorts, known as the **Gang of Four,** pounced on the moment, denouncing Zhou's policies and banning official mourning. Nevertheless, during the Qing Ming Festival in early April, millions of mourners gathered in Tian'anmen Square to remember the beloved premier and to vent anger at the radical leaders, a demonstration that the Gang of Four violently repressed. After the **April Fifth Incident,** Deng Xiaoping was again purged, charged as the mastermind behind the demonstrations. The Gang of Four did not, however, hold onto power very long. On September 9, 1976, the Great Helmsman passed away at the ripe old age of 83, and a month later the Gang of Four was arrested.

NEW CAT IN CHARGE. Prior to his death, Mao handpicked the nondescript **Hua Guofeng** (华国锋) as his successor, but Hua's conservative plans for China, uncharitably labeled the **Two Whatevers** ("whatever Mao said and whatever Mao did") would not fly with a population eager for change. Political posters sprang up on public bulletin boards in Beijing demanding economic and political change, in what came to be known as the **Democracy Wall Movement.** Deng Xiaoping, on the final upswing of his roller-coaster political career, rode a surge of popular support and quickly used his old connections to oust Hua and take control of the country.

With the pragmatic Deng in control, reform and not revolution was the path of progress. He pursued Zhou Enlai's policy of **Four Modernizations,** focusing on improvements in industry, agriculture, science, and defense. The speed and scope of liberalization and Deng's brand of "socialism with Chinese characteristics" quickly became a topic of national and international debate. While conservative hardliners urged the maintenance of state control, Democracy Wall activist **Wei Jingsheng** advocated the fifth modernization—democracy—without which the previous four modernizations would be useless. Deng responded with a familiar hard hand, outlawing the Democracy Wall Movement, jailing key activists, and starting a campaign against "spiritual pollution" from the West. It soon became clear that China's liberalization would be limited to the economic sphere.

The government did, however, relax cultural restrictions. Western fashions replaced Mao suits and the domestic travel industry revived. Foreign products invaded the mainland and celebrities like Michael Jackson and Michael Jordan became familiar names and faces to most Chinese citizens. Deng himself visited the United States and donned a cowboy hat.

KNOCKIN' ON HEAVEN'S GATE. In the late 1980s, the Chinese economy slumped as soaring inflation eroded consumer savings and undermined public confidence. Moreover, the economic boom had created unemployment and great disparities in wealth unheard of in the egalitarian Maoist era. As the public simmered, party chief and former Deng protege **Hu Yaobang** (胡耀邦) was fired for being too liberal and permissive. Not particularly popular in office, Hu was eulogized after his death on April 15, 1989 as a progressive leader suppressed by the old guard.

Thousands of college students marched to **Tian'anmen Square** (p. 142) in memory of Hu, again using mourning as a forum of political protest. Student leaders called on the party to root out corruption and implement democratic reforms, including the institution of freedom of the press, freedom of speech, and open elections. What started as a student movement quickly gained support from a broad sector of society, including workers and intellectuals. With an internally torn government scrambling for an appropriate response and moderate leaders like secretary-general **Zhao Ziyang** expressing sympathy for the students' cause, the tide for change seemed positive. The protestors, with the help of Beijing residents, repeatedly stared down troops sent in to remove them from the square.

The number of protestors in Beijing ballooned to millions by mid-May, with hundreds of thousands occupying the square, upstaging the summit meeting between Deng and Soviet leader Mikhail Gorbachev. Journalists in town to cover the summit found themselves in the midst of a revolution. Their presence bolstered the **Tian'anmen Movement** into an international media spectacle, placing greater pressure on the government. Students led by Wang Dan, Wu'er Kaixi, Chai Ling, and others staged hunger strikes in the square and pushed for dialogue, but internal factions both within the government and among the student leaders impeded progress, as attempts at negotiation continuously failed. Meanwhile, the political tide was changing as conservatives consolidated power and ousted Zhao Ziyang.

On the night of June 3rd, Beijing called in outside PLA units to disperse the demonstrators, violently cracking down on the students' six-week occupation. Television audiences around the world watched in horror as tanks plowed through the streets on the morning of June 4th, and the iconic image of a lone man in front of a tank would be imprinted in public memory. It is unclear how many people died from the massacre, though many scholars cite a number around 3,000. Much of the bloodshed actually occurred on the rioting streets of Beijing, and most of the victims were residents rather than student protestors. The violence extended well beyond Beijing and June 4th, with similar crackdowns occurring throughout the country and the government staging highly public witch hunts and executions in the aftermath. To this day the Chinese government has failed to adequately address the events of Tian'anmen.

END OF THE CENTURY. At the start of the 1990s, China began to focus more and more attention on the "rogue province," Taiwan. **Lee Teng-hui,** the president of Taiwan, embarked on a series of democratic reforms, instituting free elections and freedom of the press, moves that the PRC saw as an unacceptable move toward independence. Tensions escalated in 1996 with Taiwan's first direct presidential election, and the PRC blasted missiles a mere 25km from the coast of Taiwan, causing the US to send aircraft carriers to the straits. Though the **Taiwan Missile Crisis** was never a great threat, it showed China's dedication to the One China policy.

The economy continued to expand at a dizzying pace, maintaining double-digit GDP growth for much of the 90s. China scored more victories with the successful returns of Hong Kong in 1997 and Macau in 1999 to Chinese hands as **Special Administrative Regions.** After Deng Xiaoping's death in 1997, his successor **Jiang Zemin** proceeded with the same trend of controlled market reforms. Though slowed down, China emerged from the Asian financial crisis relatively unscathed and its economy continued to forge ahead with reckless abandon.

TODAY

China has emerged onto the international stage in a major way. From its admission into the World Trade Organization in December of 2001 to the launching of its first astronaut into space in October 2003, today's China is undoubtedly a world power. The humiliating defeats of the previous century are things of the past, but the challenges of the present are as daunting as ever, as China comes to terms with its evolving global role, political system, and economic development.

Relations with the rest of world continue to be a diplomatic see-saw. Sino-US relations started out rocky in the new millennium with the US's accidental bombing of the Chinese embassy in Yugoslavia in late 1999 and the EP-3 spy plane incident in 2001. In the aftermath of 9/11, China has displayed a greater willingness to participate proactively in the international community and has been playing a key role mediating between North Korea and other powers. Nevertheless, China's spotty human rights record, continued border disputes with neighbors, belligerent stance on Taiwan, aggressive exporting, and rising nationalism draw wary eyes.

China has more than its share of domestic issues to deal with, from overpopulation and pollution to AIDS crises and separatist movements. **Xinjiang** (p. 86), in northwestern China, is just one of the chronic problem areas. With a long history of Uighur **separatism**, the region is often inflamed with ethnic tensions that at times lead to riots. The government's battle against terrorist bombings and increasingly militant separatist groups in Xinjiang has drawn criticism for its harsh blanket repression of political dissent. In Xinjiang and many other parts of China, the **AIDS** infection rate is quickly approaching crisis levels, a problem that the government has been slow to acknowledge, let alone address, although recent efforts indicate that the PRC may be finally moving in the right direction.

In 2003, China garnered a lot of unwanted attention with the outbreak of **SARS** (Severe Acute Respiratory Syndrome), which broke out most prominently in Hong Kong and spread quickly throughout the world. China's initial cover-up of the incidence drew global criticism, prompting newly elected president **Hu Jintao** to oust high-level bureaucrats and establish more transparency. In addition, widespread **demonstrations** in Hong Kong in 2003 and 2004 expressed dissatisfaction with Beijing-backed Chief Executive **Tung Chee Hwa** and the government's continued reluctance to set up democratic elections. The protests have put the much-lauded **"one country, two systems"** policy into question, undermining the PRC's credibility as it courts an increasingly independent **Taiwan,** which continues to be the singularly most volatile issue surrounding China.

In the midst of all the chaotic political, economic, and social forces acting upon China, the country continues to chug forward with modernization and industrialization, while the economic gap between urban and rural areas, and eastern and western China, widens by the day. Beijing is whole-heartedly and happily preparing to host the **2008 Summer Olympic Games,** a source of great national pride. Taking aggressive steps to ease its pollution and transportation problems, the city, like the country, is determined to show its best face to the world.

PEOPLE

China has approximately 1.3 billion people in an area only slightly larger than the US. If you squash three-quarters of China's population into less than half of its land mass, you have a rough idea of the population density in the east. Yet the crowds are still thickening. In order to stimulate economic growth, the government is moving away from its Communist roots into a market-driven economy, displacing workers when their skills are no longer needed. Almost 100-150 million peasants float in and out of China's major cities looking for work, hoping for a higher standard of living. At this rate, over 60% of the country will become urbanized within the next 30 years. That's double the current rate of about 30%. City dwellers blame migrants for all sorts of urban social problems, including rising crime rates and disease outbreaks (not to mention longer bathroom lines and overcrowded karaoke bars). Along with the grime and grit of city life, urbanites are also adopting the modern materialism and independence that come with Western capitalism. Rural China, however, is in a standstill.

POPULATION GROWTH

Every year China grows by about 7.3 million people, approximately half the population of Shanghai. When he founded the People's Republic in 1949, Mao Zedong was all for Stalin's "the more, the merrier" approach to baby-making. Mothers who had five or more children were honored as "revolutionary mothers" and awarded government subsidies. Mao loved mass mobilization, even if it extended to the bedroom, and the population ballooned from 550 million in 1950 to an out-of-control 900 million near the end of the 70s.

In 1978, China instituted its **one-child policy,** implementing new regulations and propaganda campaigns that urged parents to use family planning. Posters of smiling mothers and cherubic babies proclaimed, "Mama only had me; having one is good." Beyond the billboards, economic incentives enforced the decree. Compliant families received stipends, along with medical and educational benefits, while the threat of demotion, job loss, forced sterilization, or heavy social compensation fees forced women to abort after the first child.

A dark side effect of the one-child policy is the practice of abandoning baby girls. Especially in rural areas, where boys can contribute to the family farm and carry on the family name, the traditional preference for sons lives on. Every year, more than a million girls are aborted, and hundreds of thousands of female infants abandoned. Consequently, the gender imbalance is significantly more severe than the worldwide averages—a whopping 1.17 boys born to every girl (compared with the global average of 1.06). As millions of men slowly realize that they will not find wives, a black market trafficking in females has emerged. An estimated 250,000 women and girls were trafficked in China last year.

Recently, the one-child rule has been relaxed, especially in rural areas. Ethnic minorities and couples that are both only children can have two, while parents without special status beg bureaucrats for the same luxury. Estimates show that the population will increase to 1.4 billion by 2010, then peak at 1.6 billion by 2050. Even with a decreasing growth rate, population control remains a top priority: controlling the inflating population is a first step to tackling environmental and social issues.

ETHNIC COMPOSITION

Most of what is considered to be Chinese culture comes from the Han, who trace their ancestry back to the Han Dynasty (see **Empire Rising,** p. 74). During the Republican Era, Sun Yat-sen envisioned a nationalist state ruled by China's five main ethnic groups: the Han, Manchu, Tibetan, Mongolian, and Uighur peoples. That failed. When Mao took over, he followed Stalin's model and decided to offer minority groups significant autonomy. As long as each minority accepted the Communist government, it would be allowed semi-self-rule. Those who rebelled faced the PLA, which routinely squelched ethnic rebellions. Not surprisingly, there have been relatively few dissenters. Han Chinese migration into minority areas has further marginalized minorities in their homelands and contributed to ethnic tension.

China's population is 92% Han Chinese; the 55 officially recognized ethnic groups making up the remaining 8% number approximately 160 million people. National minorities receive some special government benefits, including exemption from the one-child policy, tax breaks, and subsidies. In general, Han Chinese relations tend to be better with groups that have assimilated (Manchu, Zhuang, Korean) and worse with those that have not (Tibetan, Uighur).

MINORITY NATIONALITIES

NORTHEASTERN MINORITIES

The **Manchus** (numbering 10 million) were once the kings of the Northeast (p. 76). Due to the popular and political strength of the Han majority and the political machinations of the Qing emperors, the Manchus adopted much of Chinese culture. Even though there are many Manchus in Liaoning province and Beijing today, their language is mostly limited to towns in Heilongjiang province, and as a people they are almost indistinguishable from the Han.

A large number of ethnic **Koreans** live in eastern Jilin, Liaoning, and Heilongjiang provinces along the Yalu River (see **The Northeast,** p. 223). Many are descendants of those who fled when the Japanese annexed the Korean peninsula in 1895. The Koreans have lived peacefully and prosperously, mostly as agricultural workers, and share strong cultural ties with the Chinese. Since the 90s North Koreans have fled to Chinese-Korean communities to escape the famines that are ravaging their homeland; since 2000, those who arrive risk deportation.

NORTHERN MINORITIES

Although caravans from Central Asia have been trickling into China since the Tang Dynasty, the 13th-century Mongol invasions sparked a mass influx of Muslims to China, where they mingled with the local Chinese to form the distinct **Hui** minority. The Hui uses Han script but practices Islam. Currently, the Hui ethnic group is found throughout China but are most heavily concentrated in Ningxia province, Beijing, and Shanghai. During Mao's guerrilla war in Yan'an, many Hui locals joined the Communist cause, eventually rising to power with the establishment of the Ningxia Hui Autonomous Region in 1956. Although the Hui and Han usually coexist peacefully, religious differences still cause strife.

Like their 12th-century leader Genghis Khan, the **Mongols** are often viewed as hardy, horse-loving yurt dwellers who follow their grazing herds across the steppes of Central Asia. In their heyday, the Mongols ruled much of Asia. Today, Mongols in China live mostly in the northern regions, stretching from Xinjiang to Heilongjiang. Although many Mongols have become sedentary farmers or city dwellers, many clans still live in yurts and villages and maintain age-old traditions.

NORTHWESTERN MINORITIES

The Uighur, Kazakh, Tatar, Tajik, Uzbek, and Kyrgyz peoples share something other than their hard-to-pronounce monikers. They all live in Xinjiang, a land dominated by **Islam** (p. 90). The **Uighur,** seven million strong, are by far the most numerous. They use Arabic script and are known to burst into spontaneous song and dance. Many depend on irrigation agriculture, building elaborate underground channels and planting their crops in the desert.

Since 1949, the percentage of Han Chinese in the Northwest has risen from 3.7% to over 50% of the total. This demographic shift has led to a good deal of conflict, as the Uighurs struggle to preserve their culture in the face of massive immigration. In the 1950s, the PLA executed thousands of separatists, GMD sympathizers, and nomads. Ethnic tensions during the Great Leap Forward (p. 80) led to the exodus of 20,000 Uighurs to the Soviet Union. When the Soviet power collapsed in the 90s, Uighurs saw their cultural relatives, Kazakhstan, Uzbekistan, and Kyrgyzstan, declare independence, and separatists in Xinjiang were tempted to do the same. In 1990, the PLA crushed uprisings in several cities, and rebel organizations went underground. After terrorist bombings in Beijing and Ürümqi in 1997 by Uighur separatists, the government cracked down with Operation Strike Hard, in which police infiltrated mosques, apprehended suspected insurgents, and performed public executions, effectively breaking the underground alliances. Since 9/11, the Chinese government has, with some success, been pushing the UN to classify Uighur separatist movements as Al-Qaeda related terrorist movements.

SOUTHWESTERN MINORITIES

Over three dozen minority groups inhabit the mountains of southwest China. For centuries, many of these people lived in familial clans, planting rice and raising livestock. Most of these minority groups originally lived in the lower Yangzi valley, but Han expansion forced them into their present mountain homes.

The relationship between these minorities and their Han neighbors varies widely. The **Zhuang,** China's largest ethnic minority with over 17 million people, live mainly in Guangxi province. They speak Mandarin, study Chinese, and are virtually indistinguishable from the Chinese in physical appearances. The **Yi,** more resistant to Han influence, have worked hard to uphold their traditions. Before the 1950s, the Yi lived under a caste system of hereditary nobles, serfs, and slaves, but their practice of enslaving captives has since been outlawed. The **Li** on Hainan Island are famed for their medicinal and practical knowledge of herbs.

Larger, more widespread minorities have villages dispersed throughout the southwest, including the **Miao** and the **Dong** (see **Kaili Minority Villages,** p. 634). During festivals, Miao women don heavy silver headdresses weighing up to several pounds, while musicians play the *lúshēng*, a bamboo pipe organ. The smaller, but equally festive, **Dong** minority are easily distinguishable by their drum towers, built without nails and almost entirely for the purpose of a "carousing central," where courtship, dancing, music, and more somber town meetings take place.

The **Dai** in Xishuangbanna (p. 652) share a language and cultural kinship with the peoples of Thailand, Laos, and Myanmar, practicing both Buddhism and animism. Six- or seven-year-old Dai boys train as monks for five years, after which most choose to return to the secular lifestyle. The matriarchal **Naxi** in Yunnan wove a fascinating architecture from Tibetan and Han elements, the best of which flourished in Lijiang old city (p. 674).

LANGUAGE

The official language of the People's Republic is **Mandarin Chinese.** The official pronunciation is called *pǔtōng huà* (普通话; "common language"), which is based on the Beijing enunciation. However, a vast number of dialects exist—cities only 80km apart may speak two different dialects. Some are fairly similar, while others, like **Shanghainese,** are virtually unintelligible to non-locals.

Mandarin is spoken in most parts of China, as a kind of universal second language to the local dialect, but often sounds nothing like standard *pǔtōng huà* because of regional accents. In Hong Kong, **Cantonese,** which is about as close to Mandarin as French is to Italian, is dominant (see p. 542). Most minority groups have their own spoken language, and twenty-three have their own writing systems. In the west, especially in rural areas, local languages like Uighur, Tibetan, and Kazakh are widely spoken and often more welcome than Mandarin.

Even a basic knowledge of Mandarin makes a visit to China much easier and more rewarding. Although English is the hands-down favorite among language students in China, few people speak English fluently outside of major cities. If you need the assistance of an English speaker, your best bet is to ask a young student or urban professional. *Let's Go* provides the pronunciation and characters for most establishments and place names, as well as other handy words. If no one understands you, you can always point at the Chinese characters in the book. See also the phrasebook (p. 867) in the **Appendix** for help.

TONES

Each Chinese word is assigned a certain **tone** that determines its pronunciation. Mandarin only has five tones, but Cantonese has a tongue-twisting seven or more (depending on whom you ask). Different dialects play it fast and loose with tones, but most people should understand standard *pǔtōng huà*. For more information on **pronunciation,** see the pronunciation guide in the **Appendix** (p. 867).

TONE	PINYIN	PRONUNCIATION
First (high)	ā	A doctor tells you to say "AHHH."
Second (rising)	á	A confused "Huh?"
Third (falling-rising)	ǎ	Inviting further explanation: "Go on..."
Fourth (falling)	à	"[Insert the expletive of your choice]!"
Fifth (neutral)	a	A thoughtful "hm." (used rarely)

GRAMMAR

Compared to its pronunciation, Chinese grammar is remarkably simple. You don't have to conjugate verbs or decline nouns. Usually, word order is **subject, time, verb, object.** This is not to say that Chinese is a flat, simple language. Though efficient, the language is far from inelegant. Even short phrases embody images and moods, and proverbs or idioms are expressed with **four-character phrases** that convey a wealth of meaning—sometimes entire stories—in only four words.

WRITING

Perhaps the greatest uniting factor of China today (apart from a predilection for sentimental pop songs) is its written language. Regardless of the spoken dialect, all Chinese is expressed with one common written language. Unfortunately, its universality is the only convenient thing about it. The non-alphabetic **Chinese writing system** includes 40,000 to 80,000 characters, torturing earnest language students who spend years acquiring fluency (though one only needs 3000-4000 characters to muddle successfully through a Chinese newspaper).

The earliest characters, pictographs and ideographs, appeared 4000 years ago carved into oracle bones. Over time, they evolved to take on radicals and compounds, making many of their pictograph derivations completely unidentifiable. Of course, for some words, anyone can see the relationship between character and meaning. Take, for instance: 串 (kebab), 山 (mountain), 口 (mouth), and 磷 (phosphorus). Or: 木 (one tree, wood), 林 (wood, grove), 森 (forest), and 树 (tree).

The ancient Chinese sometimes used the same character to represent different words with similar pronunciations. Not surprisingly, this led to confusion and some serious strife between long-distance penpals. To resolve the homonym horror, extra characters called **radicals** were added to each word. Today about 90% of today's Chinese characters have two parts: the radical, which helps clarify the meaning, and the original character, which aids in indicating the pronunciation. For example, many words that have to do with water (水), contain the water radical (氵), three drops of water: river (河), ocean (海), wave (浪), and flow (流). Because spoken Chinese has changed so drastically over the centuries, characters that today share a phonetic radical are not always pronounced the same way.

Until 1949, the Chinese writing system used **traditional** characters (fántǐzì; 繁体字). In order to simplify the written language and increase literacy rates, the CCP reduced the number of strokes for many commonly used characters, introducing the system of **simplified** characters (jiǎntǐzì; 简体字). This system does not originate with a bunch of bespectacled Party members sitting around, cutting strokes willy-nilly—simplified characters actually date back to the **Qin Dynasty,** when they were used in handwriting, and to a later cursive form of calligraphy (see **Calligraphy,** p. 97). The government also established the **pinyin** (拼音) romanization system as a more accurate way to romanize Chinese sounds, replacing the confusing-as-all-hell **Wade-Giles** system (from which we get "Peking" for Beijing).

RELIGION AND PHILOSOPHY

Until the Communists arrived, China was dominated by three major faiths: Confucianism, Daoism, and Buddhism. These faiths coexisted quite peacefully, and most people subscribed to some combination of the three.

CONFUCIANISM. Be it as a philosophy, a religion, or a political theory, Confucianism has had a profound impact on Chinese society. Confucius's humanistic understanding of the importance of roles, relationships, and rituals in maintaining a moral social order was applied to daily interactions, studied as a scholarly pursuit, and adopted as a philosophy for governance. Ironically, though the basis of Confucian thought was a secular organization of society, it evolved in the popular realm into something of a religion, inspiring the creation of temples and shrines and reaching a much vaster audience than purely philosophical systems.

Born in 551 BC in the city of **Qufu** (p. 203), **Confucius** (kǒng fūzǐ; 孔夫子) spent years in various government posts fruitlessly searching for a ruler who would respect his ideas, but he did not find a receptive audience during his lifetime. Confucius eventually settled down and devoted himself to teaching. After his death in 479 BC, his pupils compiled the **Analects,** a loose collection of his oral teachings. Master Kong himself did not leave behind any writings.

Confucius believed in nothing short of the perfection of society. In his social hierarchy, everyone has a role to fulfill: sons should obey fathers, wives should obey husbands, and subjects should obey rulers. In turn he who rules must set an example of benevolence, virtue, and morality. Individuals are bound to each other in sacred rituals and mutual obligations. According to Confucius, as long as everyone plays their roles properly, society would be peaceful and enlightened. In the centuries after Confucius's death, other thinkers, most notably **Mencius,** contributed to his doctrine, which came to be widely adapted as a guide for everyday family decisions and for the behavior of rulers and bureaucrats.

Confucianism took a hit in the late 19th century. Chinese intellectuals and Communist leaders rejected its conservatism and political nepotism in favor of Western ideologies, blaming Confucian ideals for the oppressive customs and backward ideas that were stifling society and preventing China from modernizing. Confucianism has been in limbo since then, too often cited for every possible positive and negative aspect of Chinese society. In recent years, scholars have again recanted, suggesting that the recent economic success of East Asian countries like South Korea and Singapore is due in part to their Confucian heritage.

DAOISM. Unlike Confucianism's emphasis on social relations, Daoism focuses on the individual, his relation to nature, and metaphysical reality. It dates back to around 300 BC, when the **Dao De Jing** *(Tao Te Ching)* is thought to have been written. The *Dao De Jing* is a complex, poetic text, with many possible interpretations. To vastly simplify, its main assertions concern the inadequacy of language and the power of the *Dao*, an invisible, all-encompassing force that is the source of all things. Daoists value the individual over society, nature over man, silence over words, and the useless over the useful. They believed that humans disturbed the natural order, that the best governments did as little as possible, and that everything is relative. The quintessential Daoist philosophers are **Laozi** and **Zhuangzi.**

As with Confucianism, scholars draw a line between philosophical and religious Daoism. The distinction, however, is a bit blurry. Philosophical Daoism is based on intellectual exploration and occasional forays into mystical and alchemical practices. Religious Daoism takes elements from age-old Chinese folk beliefs and the supernatural. Local gods and spirits, fortune-telling, magic, alchemy, and the pursuit of immortality are all part of popular Daoism. Other aspects of Chinese culture have also made their way into the religious practice of Daoism, including ancestor worship. The language and practices of Daoism mixed easily with those of Buddhism, creating a set of beliefs that many could embrace.

Daoism may never have enjoyed the state patronage that Confucianism did, but its influence on Chinese culture was immense. Early alchemists, working to find the elixirs of immortality, helped advance Chinese science. Daoist ideas of man's relation to nature influenced many generations of landscape artists, and Daoist ideals colored many a personal and philosophical expression of classical poets.

Buddhist temples vastly outnumber Daoist ones, but today visitors can still see active Daoist temples in many parts of China, where Daoist monks (*dàoshì*) still abide by all the old traditions, neither cutting their hair nor eating meat. There are major Daoist temples on each of the **Five Sacred Daoist Mountains.**

BUDDHISM. Unlike Confucianism and Daoism, Buddhism originated outside China. **Siddhartha Gautama,** the man who became **Buddha** (Enlightened One), was born a prince around 560 BC in Lumbini (present-day Nepal). In his youth, Gautama was awakened after witnessing various images of suffering during his forays into the outside world. At the age of 29, he left his family and posh life behind for good to wander the forests of India as an ascetic. He eventually found a moderate path of meditation (the **Middle Way**), achieved **nirvana** (enlightenment) under the Bodhi tree, and spent the rest of his life preaching.

The Buddha advocated total detachment from the present world. Because material possessions, physical desires, and individual existence are fleeting illusions that bring pain, the only way to escape the perpetual cycle of human suffering is to renounce all worldly desires. Through the right understanding, thought, speech, action, livelihood, effort, mindfulness, and concentration (the **Eightfold Path**), individuals could attain nirvana. Buddhism preserves Hindu doctrines of *karma* and reincarnation, according to which actions in the present life determine one's position in the next. Buddhist sects differ in practice and doctrine. Chinese Buddhism, a part of the **Mahayana** ("Great Vehicle") school, stresses compassion and the quest for nirvana as a society. Worship of Buddhist figures such as **Amitabha,** Buddha of Infinite Light, and **Guanyin,** Goddess of Mercy, is widespread.

Buddhism was introduced to China in the later half of the Han Dynasty (p. 75) and caught on quickly, intermingling with Daoism. By the Sui Dynasty, Buddhism had become the state religion. Toward the end of the Tang Dynasty, however, Emperor Wuzong undertook a large-scale **persecution** of Buddhism, out of fear of the fiscal and political power of the Buddhist clergy. Chinese Buddhism never quite recovered from this blow. Although it continued to flourish as a religion, its power was tightly controlled, and the state frequently liquidated Buddhist assets.

In modern times, the Cultural Revolution took a heavy toll on Buddhism, as Red Guards destroyed temples and the government disbanded monasteries. Buddhism has since rebounded and monasteries are again active centers. Very few Chinese identify themselves as strict Buddhists, but many visit temples or pilgrimage sites.

OTHER RELIGIONS. Depending on whom you ask, nearly 20-100 million Chinese practice **Islam.** Among the 55 ethnic minorities in China, 10 practice Islam as the prevailing religion. See also **Minority Nationalities** (p. 86).

Christians make up 4% of the total population, concentrated mostly in the southeast. Missionaries first arrived in the 16th century, and despite the Catholic penchant for missionaries, today the majority of Chinese Christians are Protestant. Recently, Christianity began to revive after a long hiatus that began when the CCP took power. Foreign missionaries and a lax government policy against underground Christian meetings contribute to two million new converts each year.

COMMUNISM AND RELIGION. Communist China is officially atheist. Faith in the state and the working people is supposed to eliminate the need for any deities. The Cultural Revolution marked the height of state-sponsored religious persecution. Red Guards destroyed temples and churches, and monks and nuns of all faiths were forced to renounce their vows. Confucianism was attacked as a remnant of feudal oppression, and Daoism and Buddhism were branded as reactionary superstitions. Christianity was condemned as a vestige of Western exploitation.

In the years following Mao's death, the intense anti-religiosity of the Cultural Revolution began to fade away. Buddhism and Daoism are now officially (and proudly) considered national relics. The government now actively promotes the restoration of temples and holy mountains. In 2001, President Jiang, a temple-goer himself, met with top officials to discuss the integration of religious activity into socialist society. The groundbreaking meeting prompted authorities to relax the monitoring of churches and monasteries that are deemed unthreatening. However, the Catholic Church, which asserts the supremacy of the Pope over all temporal authorities, Tibetan Buddhism, which claims the Dalai Lama as its spiritual and political leader, and independence-seeking Muslim groups in Xinjiang have clashed frequently with the government in recent years.

GOVERNMENT

The political structure of China has remained largely unchanged since 1949. China is a Communist, one-party republic controlled primarily by the **Chinese Communist Party** or **CCP.** A few government-approved "opposition" parties exist, mainly to showcase how tolerant the government is than to present actual opposition. The Chinese government and CCP are *officially* separate institutions, but leaders of the former are always leaders of the latter. Since 2003, China's top party and government leadership has been transitioning to a younger generation of politicians who are more willing to speak the language of reform, though still slow in making actual changes. The government's main legislative body is the **National People's Congress** (governed by the **Politburo,** the CCP's executive committee, and the **Secretariat**), and the chief executive body is the **State Council.** Local governments follow a similar pattern, with power formally in the hands of government bodies and effectively in the hands of local Communist Party leaders.

	NAME/DOB	TITLES	PERSONAL AD
H E A D	Hu Jintao 胡锦涛 Dec. 1942	President CCP General Secretary Chairman of Central Military Committee	"Compassionate reformer," enjoys ballroom dancing, has a photographic memory, best-looking man in Chinese politics; degree in hydraulic engineering.
H O N C H O S	Zeng Qinghong 曾庆红 July 1939	Vice President	Jiang Zemin protege, son of veteran revolutionaries, strategist, knows how to play hardball; degree in engineering.
	Wen Jiabao 温家宝 Sept. 1942	Premier Prime Minister	Political survivor, economic guru, meticulous, less than charismatic, has a funky smile; degree in geomechanics.
	Jiang Zemin 江泽民 Aug. 17, 1926	Former President	Just won't go away, fluent in 4 languages, plays bamboo flute; degree in electrical engineering.

ECONOMY

As the saying goes, if you're not a Communist before you're 30 you don't have a heart, but if you're not a capitalist after you're 30 you don't have a brain. The CCP have taken this to heart. For nearly 30 years after the founding of the PRC, the nation had a highly centralized planned economy based on the Soviet model. Under Mao's rule, the country aimed to modernize industries through a series of **Five-Year Plans,** which, although successful at first, eventually led to famine, low levels of production, and a sluggish economy. As the People's Republic neared its 30th birthday, Deng Xiaoping rose to power and immediately began to implement new free-market economic reforms. In 1979, the government named the southeastern coastal cities of Shenzhen, Zhuhai, Xiamen, and Shantou **Special Economic Zones (SEZs).** The national government allowed the local SEZ governments to foster economic growth and develop governmental infrastructures without first getting the approval of the central government. The phenomenal success of the first four SEZs has prompted the government to establish others all along the south coast and down the Yangzi River.

China managed to keep the *yuán* on the straight during the **financial crisis** that sent most of Asia into a tailspin in late 1997. China obtained **Permanent Normal Trade Relations** with the US in 2000 and membership in the **World Trade Organization (WTO)** in 2001. The economy grows at an increasing rate (about 9% in 2003), although signs of overheating prompt policy makers to slow down the economy. Since 1978, output has quadrupled, and China's economy has become the second-largest in the world. Still, these promising indications only mask underlying troubles. With a hybrid system, China often suffers the worst of both socialism (corruption and a bloated bureaucracy) and capitalism (income disparities and unemployment). Open trade comes at a price, as inefficient **state-owned enterprises** risk collapse from international competition. The government precariously keeps these industrial dinosaurs afloat through massive subsidies, while sustaining adequate job growth for the rising population of unemployed. Economic development also leads to soil erosion and the loss of arable land—trouble for the agricultural sector, which comprises half of the country's labor force. Half of the population, mostly rural farmers, live on US$2 per day; 19% live under US$1. Regardless, the government presses forward, anxious to make its way in the global economy.

HUMAN RIGHTS

China's human rights violations have been cause for considerable international concern. The government maintains that stability and social order are more important than individual freedom. People have been detained, arrested, and jailed for peacefully expressing dissident political, religious, and social views.

Since the crackdown on the **Tian'anmen Square Democracy Movement** in 1989 (p. 82), the world has kept a close eye on China's individual rights profile. In September of 1998, the UN High Commissioner for Human Rights visited China for the first time and, one month later, the Chinese government signed—but did not ratify—the **United Nations Covenant on Civil and Political Rights.** The signing of the covenant coincided with Beijing's first international human rights conference.

Beginning in November and December of 1998, the authorities conducted rounds of arrests, detaining dissidents who were registered with opposition political parties. Repression continues for unauthorized religious organizations, including the quasi-religious sect **Falun Gong.** The government also tightened control over the Internet and print publications, blocking as many as 50,000 Internet sites and mandating reporters to write news as "80% positive and 20% negative."

Despite restrictions on the press, a high-profile, recurrent issue for the Chinese government has been the human rights abuses in Tibet. Dissidents, led by the Dalai Lama and backed by many Western groups like Free Tibet (including Hollywood stars like Richard Gere) have proved remarkably successful at rallying support abroad. At home, however, they have been threatened, arrested, detained, sentenced to hard labor, imprisoned, and even tortured (see **Tibet: History,** p. 832). The plight of the Uighurs of Xinjiang is less well known overseas, in no small part because they lack a prominent figure to champion their cause.

Nevertheless, China is in the midst of **judicial reform,** sponsoring judicial independence and better-trained legal professionals. The courts still hold close ties with the central government, however, and defendants still lack due process. Additionally, Chinese lawyers often cannot adequately represent their clients, due to government pressure. In 2003, two lawyers were sentenced to several years in prison for actively defending their controversial clients. Moreover, those accused are often detained for months and years in prison without a trial. China's stance on human rights has affected its foreign relations. When protestors opposed China's bid for the 2008 Olympics, they pointed to the country's human rights violations.

CULTURE

CUSTOMS AND ETIQUETTE

BATHROOMS. Culture shock can't be measured in volts, but the jolt sent through most Westerners the first time they see and smell a Chinese toilet is roughly equivalent to sticking a fork in a socket. Most Chinese toilets are squat toilets: basically, a hole in the ground. Some toilets are recessed porcelain basins, with running water; some are noxious, stagnant pits. Many stall partitions are at knee-height, few have doors, and none have toilet paper. As the final insult, some toilets charge admission (Y0.2-0.5). Public toilets are marked with signs, usually in Chinese (公用厕所 , gōngyòng cèsuǒ; or 公厕), but sometimes as "WC" as well. Sometimes, the facilities are separated by gender: male (nán; 男) and female (nǚ; 女). In preparation for the 2008 Olympics, Beijing is "beautifying" its bathrooms and building "three-starred toilets." In the meantime, *Let's Go* advises travelers to seek relief at posh department stores, shining hotels, and Western fast-food restaurants.

SPITTING. Polluted cities and poor sanitation mean that respiratory flus are common for anyone living through a Chinese winter, and the Chinese tend to be fairly up front about how they take care of their phlegm. No one is shy about hawking back and letting it fly on streets, sidewalks, trains, buses, and even restaurant floors. Increasingly more cities are enacting anti-spitting regulations and hanging "No Spitting" signs, but all of this has had little actual effect. It's best to get used to the characteristic hawking sound and get out of the way.

STARING. Staring is not quite the social faux pas in China that it is in the West, to put it mildly. Be prepared for intense, prolonged scrutiny, especially if you're obviously a foreigner and in a rural area that sees few Westerners. There is little that you can do to ward off the spectators. Take solace in the fact that you have achieved a special place in the pantheon of Chinese tourist sights. Unobtrusive clothing is recommended; body piercing and brightly dyed hair will make you stand out more. Yelling (in any language) or showing obvious annoyance will just make people stare more. If you speak Chinese, talking to onlookers is often the best way to deal with unwanted attention. Remember that staring usually represents friendly curiosity, nothing more. See also **Minority Travelers** (p. 69).

LIFE AND TIMES

BEGGARS. At some point you're likely to be approached by beggars, whether in Beijing or in poverty-stricken rural regions. With rising unemployment, more and more people throughout the country are going hungry. In crowded areas like train and bus stations, the elderly, the disabled, young children, and mothers with babies frequently beg for money. The children are quite tenacious, often grabbing hold of the legs and arms of passersby and hanging on. If you do give money, you run the risk of being thronged by more hopeful beggars. Keep a handful of spare change in your pockets to avoid drawing attention to cash. Buying food for beggars is also a good alternative.

TAIWAN. China and Taiwan have—how should we say—strained relations. In order to avoid an embarrassing or even hostile situation, take care how you refer to Taiwan. When on the mainland, avoid mentioning Taiwan at all if possible. Never explicitly refer to it as a separate country, as it will likely offend the Chinese. However, when in Taiwan, avoid calling it "The Republic of China" or "Nationalist China," which will offend the Taiwanese, who consider themselves citizens of a separate country. You might be the safest simply saying "Taiwan."

FOOD AND DRINK

According to a Chinese proverb, to the common man, food is as sacred as the heavens. China has one of the most distinctive and varied cuisines in the world. Food has commanded the interest and respect of intellectual and political leaders throughout China's extensive history. Traditionally, when a new emperor ascended the throne, one of his first duties was to appoint a personal chef. Even among commoners, "Have you eaten yet?" was used as the equivalent of "How are you?" And in perhaps the most vivid proof of China's illustrious culinary past, the great Song poet Su Dongpo wrote the lyrical poem "In Praise of Pork."

Chinese cuisine stresses the importance of a balance between *fàn* (rice) and *cài* (vegetables and meat dishes). Rice is the staple crop in most of southern China, but in the north wheat is the principal crop, and *cài* is often accompanied by steamed buns called *mántóu* or buns stuffed with meat and veggies, *bāozi*. A meal in China is a communal affair, with the whole family gathered around the table sharing three or four dishes of *cài* (well divided between meat and vegetables) and bowls of rice or a *mántóu* for everyone. And of course, everyone adeptly maneuvers their food with chopsticks.

Pork may be the favorite meat, but crabs, fish, shrimp, and more fish are prized delicacies everywhere in China. In Beijing, elaborate banquets historically kept emperors and CCP officials well fed with **Beijing duck** and a host of cuisines from all over China and the world. **Shandong** is especially famous for its hearty dumplings. In the northeast, cuisine is influenced by nearby Korea, but noodles are still the big favorite.

Chefs in Hong Kong and Guangdong province like to slice up whatever's handy: snake, pigeon, frog, turtle—you name it, they eat it. Don't be intimidated, however—Cantonese cuisine is among the best in China. The former British colony is also famous for the safer **dim sum,** a selection of appetizer-sized dishes of meats, pastries, and dumplings eaten with tea.

Swinging west, Sichuan and Hunan locals test their wills against food laden with spices and chilis, and the most searing **hotpot,** found all over China but especially "hot" in Sichuan and Chongqing. A pot is kept bubbling over an electric or gas stove, while raw meats and veggies are dropped into the soup until cooked, then scooped out and eaten. In the northwest, Muslim influences dominate, and bread replaces rice as a staple. Street stalls vend noodles, soups, **lamb kebabs,** roasted lamb, lamb dumplings, lamb everything. The **yak** is Tibet's answer to the ubiquitous lamb in the northwest, and from **yak butter tea** to roasted yak and *momo*, Tibetan dumplings filled with—you guessed it—yak.

China's favorite beverage comes in hundreds of flavors and varieties, with two main types: **green tea** (lǜchá; 绿茶) and **black tea** (hóngchá; 红茶). Prices range from Y1 per bag to hundreds of dollars per ounce for the most prized varieties. Hot water, on the other hand, is free and available everywhere. Some notable teas include **Longjing** of Hangzhou, **oolong,** and **Iron Goddess** (tiěguān yīn). **Soy milk** is a breakfast favorite. Grain-based **báijiǔ** (白酒), a traditional spirit with an extremely high alcohol content, is popular among adults, especially the elderly. China also produces beer, the most famous of which is exported **Tsingtao,** made in Qingdao (p. 207). Most towns have their own local brews, including Yibin's **Wuliangye.**

THE ARTS

LITERATURE

ANCIENT AND PREMODERN

The keystone of classical Chinese literature, **lyric poetry** is also the oldest. Confucius himself supposedly edited the first anthology of poetry, a collection of 10th-to 7th-century-BC lyrics called the **Classic of Poetry** (*Shijing*, also translated as *Book of Songs*). It set the foundation for all later poetry and remains a vital part of a traditional education. Poetry eventually lost its original ritualistic role, and writers created individualistic, expressive works, a sort of diary for the literati. Lyrical poetry reached its height in the Tang and Song Dynasties. Poets rarely wrote about themselves directly, but meditated on images of nature to reflect on everything from personal emotions to events and politics. Many poets from this era are still revered: **Li Bai** wrote bold, individualistic poems; **Du Fu** dealt with social, historical, and personal issues; **Wang Wei** created deeply imagistic poems on landscapes; and **Bai Juyi** retold legends. A new genre of lyrical poetry, the **ci,** was created in the Song Dynasty. Usually about love and desire, these lyrics were set to music and sung by courtesans. **Su Dongpo** (Su Shi) was the greatest of the Song poets.

Personal essays expressing individual philosophies complete the classical Chinese literary canon. The **Analects** of Confucius and the **Dao De Jing** of Laozi, along with the writings of **Zhuanzi** and **Mencius,** are classics in this category.

Long regarded as lowly art forms due to their popularity with the lower classes, **drama** and **fiction** gained respect in the Yuan and Ming Dynasties. Plays became popular with the Mongol rulers. The rise in vernacular works, as opposed to classical Chinese, opened up the book market to a wider audience. In the late Ming, the intellectual elite recorded traditional stories and eventually composed original fiction, many of which advocated individual passion over Confucian ideals.

The great **novels** of the Ming and Qing Dynasties are written in a combination of vernacular and classical language. Of these, the **"Four Great Works"** have become required reading for educated Chinese. *Romance of the Three Kingdoms* is an epic tale of the wars following the end of the Han Dynasty, comparable to the *Iliad* in size and scale; *Water Margin* tells the story of a band of virtuous rebels that resisted the Mongol incursion during the Song; and *Journey to the West* recounts the legend of the monk Xuan Zang's journey to India to obtain Buddhist scriptures, aided by the famous Monkey King. Perhaps the best-known of these four novels is Cao Xueqin's tragic love story of two youths in a declining noble family, called the *Dream of the Red Chamber* or *The Story of the Stone*.

MODERN

In the early 20th century, intellectuals campaigned for the use of vernacular writing, rather than archaic, classical writing, to make literature and learning more accessible. Embroiled with May Fourth ideals and the grand goal of saving China, young writers addressed contemporary social and political problems, popularizing revolutionary thought and criticism to awaken and educate the people. China's first and most famous modern writer, **Lu Xun,** produced short stories *(The Story of Ah Q)* that satirized Old China's oppressive customs, social ills, and defeatist psyche, engaging the conflicts of tradition and modernization. Such themes were also explored in the works of **Lao She** *(Rickshaw Boy)* and **Ba Jin's** renowned trilogy *(Family, Spring,* and *Autumn)*. Other prominent writers include **Mao Dun** *(Midnight)*, **Guo Moruo** *(Goddesses)*, and **Eileen Chang** *(Love in a Fallen City)*, a popular writer who painted stories of love and decadence in a time of upheaval.

During the Mao era, writing was strictly controlled and only works that advanced the Communist cause were published. After the Cultural Revolution, the government allowed the emergence of a diverse range of literature, albeit one that continues to be limited by the reality of censors and state-owned publishing houses. As a natural fallout of years of anguish, literary loosening prompted an abundance of writing obsessing over root-searching and suffering. Writers like **Feng Jicai, Su Tong** *(Raise the Red Lantern)*, and **Mo Yan** *(Red Sorghum)* explored a vibrant, amorphous feudal past in satire-laden novels. The controversial **Zhang Xianliang** pressed buttons with his labor camp memoir *Grass Soup* and the sexually explicit *Half of Man Is Woman*. Popular punk novelist **Wang Shuo** *(Playing for Thrills)* gave voice to a generation of disillusioned youth, with cynical, irreverent novels that celebrated vice and mocked society.

In recent years, established writers have been contending with a general trend of declining readership, while new players have touched upon a more successful formula. For today's subversive young writers, it's no longer about correct politics, but rather no politics, as the rise of **linglei** (alternative) culture pushes the boundaries of what's acceptable. **Wei Hui** *(Shanghai Baby)*, **Han Han** *(The Third Way)*, and **Chun Shu** *(Beijing Doll)* write candidly about sexuality, corruption, alienation, materialism, and other worldly concerns of fast-track urbanites. Many young writers skip the grind altogether by publishing directly onto the Internet. Standing the test of time and politics, the martial arts novels of **Gu Long** and the legendary **Jin Yong** are loved by all generations; it helps that their works have been adapted into popular television dramas in China, Hong Kong, and Taiwan.

PERFORMING ARTS

MUSIC

Legend has it that music was created in 2697 BC, when Emperor Huangdi sent an advisor to find bamboo pipes that could sound the call of the phoenix and harmonize the universe. Records confirm that music has been around for at least this long: relics from the Shang Dynasty (1600-1050 BC) include instruments for ritual music, the **Record of Rites** (2nd century BC) mentions court ceremonies with music, and the **Classic of Poetry** (see **Literature,** p. 95) was originally set to music.

Traditional Chinese music uses a 12-tone system. Major **traditional instruments** include the zither, the *pipa* (lute), and *erhu* (two-stringed violin). Most Chinese music is indigenous, but traces of Muslim music, popular during the Tang Dynasty, can be found. Traditional instruments are often integrated into contemporary music. Its influences can be heard in the music of veteran rock band **Tang Dynasty** and pop instrumental group **12 Girls Band.**

In the early years of the PRC, communal choruses adapted folk songs and rewrote lyrics to reflect the lives of the "common people." **The East is Red** (dōng fāng hóng; 东方红) is perhaps the most famous of these tunes, due in no small part to the ubiquitous kitschy Chairman Mao lighters that play the song when lit. Even now, revolutionary music still holds a special place in nostalgic hearts. At the polar opposite, the influx of Western influences in the 1980s fostered the development of a famously gritty **underground rock** scene in Beijing, starting with China's first rocker **Cui Jian**, whose politically charged melodies, notably *Nothing to My Name* (yī wú suǒ yǒu; 一无所有), were anthems for the Tian'anmen generation.

Among China's youth, more modern sounds from Hong Kong, Taiwan, and beyond have taken hold. Proving that music can indeed cross all boundaries, Taiwanese music has traditionally been well received. At the height of her fame, when her ballads could be heard from every street stall, it was said that China was ruled by two Dengs: Deng Xiaoping by day and **Deng Lijun** (Teresa Teng) by night. Today the sounds of R&B sensation **Jay Chou** and the Taiwanese boy bands of the moment have a wide audience in the mainland. Hong Kong has popularized its own indigenous form of music dubbed **Canto-pop,** which has a faithful following in China and the Chinatowns of the world. The **Four Heavenly Kings** of Canto-pop—Jacky Cheung, Andy Lau, Leon Lai, and Aaron Kwok—reigned supreme for much of the 1990s. In recent years, the music scene has opened into a free-for-all of established artists and young pre-fab idols, with the rise of stars like Nicholas Tse, Eason Chan, Joey Yung, and the inexplicably popular **Twins,** whose pretty mugs hawk every possible product in Hong Kong. In comparison, China's domestic music scene is rather limited and less far-reaching, due to its rampant pirating industry. It does, nonetheless, have its share of superstars, including pop divas Han Hong and Na Ying, crooner Sun Nam, and brooding singer-songwriter Pu Shu.

THEATER

Chinese theater is well-known for its **opera,** a combination of vocal and instrumental music. Operas of different regions and dialects boast varying singing styles and instruments, but common features include bare stages, set role types, dancing, acrobatics, elaborate costumes, and heavy face paint. Chinese opera began with the **zaju** (杂剧 ; variety plays) of the Northern Song and the **nanxi** (南戏 ; southern opera) of the Southern Song, which were written in the vernacular and set to music. **Kunqu** (昆曲), a form of *nánxì* originally performed for the lower classes, gradually gained a following among literati; some are still read as classics today. **Jingju** (京剧 ; Beijing opera) rose to prominence at the end of the 18th century. Like *kūnqǔ*, it primarily uses flutes instead of percussion, but its plot is quicker and its acrobatics more elaborate. Although less poetic than *kūnqǔ*, *jīngjù* is the most famous form of opera today (p. 155). Other popular forms include the more folk- music-based **yueju** (粤剧 ; Cantonese opera) and **huangmei** (黄梅).

Introduced to Western drama in the early 1900s, the Chinese added folk songs and dances to spoken drama and created a uniquely Chinese genre called **huaju** (画剧), which was easily accessible to the masses and a handy tool for nationalist propagandists. During the 1950s, operas of inspirational socialist stories were also common forms of propaganda. In the 1960s, the revolutionary **model operas** commissioned by Madame Mao were the only ones allowed during the Cultural Revolution. After 1980, however, traditional opera edged back into the public sphere and is still popular among the older generation.

VISUAL ARTS

CALLIGRAPHY

The ancient Chinese considered calligraphy to be the highest and most refined of the arts, a true scholar's pursuit. Traditionally, a calligraphy artist uses the "Four Treasures of the Study"—brush, ink, inkstone, and paper. Meaning was not only conveyed through words, but more importantly through the style of the brush strokes: their boldness, spontaneity, grace, elegance, naturalness, and beauty. The most "cursive" of the calligraphy styles, *cǎoshū*, is loose and almost wild in its strokes and is said to be writing that "listens to one's mood." Beautiful calligraphy was the hallmark of a fine education and temperament, and students then and now practiced their characters for hours on end. Emperors wrote scrolls of calligraphy and appointed officials based on their calligraphic skills, while literati held "calligraphy gatherings." Even Jiang Zemin has jumped on the bandwagon and rushed about China leaving his brush strokes at various mountains and sights.

PAINTING

Closely related to calligraphy, classical Chinese painting uses the same brushes, ink, and paper (or sometimes silk), and is also judged by the expressiveness and style of the brush strokes. The classical painter was less concerned with depicting outer realities than the subject's inner life. With a few simple splashes of ink, the artist could evoke entire mountain ranges. The scholarly official loved to paint bamboo, pine, and orchids, all symbols of the scholar. Perhaps the most important genre, **landscape painting** captures not only natural beauty, but also the inner mood of the artist. Light washes of black ink with tinges of blue and green became vast expanses of water, mountain, and clouds—the quintessential Chinese landscape.

In the early 1920s, many Chinese artists visited Europe, and movements like Impressionism helped to fuse modern Western and traditional Chinese styles. The influential **Xu Beihong** used a traditional Chinese brush to mimic the realistic effect of pencil and chalk. After the Communist takeover, socialist realism became the rule of the day. Sentimentalized and idealized revolutionaries, workers, and farmers striking heroic poses found their way onto everything—from canvases to propaganda to stamps. In the tumultuous decades that followed, art production ground to a halt. Art could be construed as remnants of the "decadent imperialistic past" and incriminated artists were oppressed during the Cultural Revolution. Later, Chinese painting primarily adopted non-political subject matter to safely weather government scrutiny. Artistic freedom increased in the years leading up to the 21st century, and many artists adopted Western styles and subject matters, including abstraction and the nude. However, censorship hasn't died down completely. Today, the art community is reviving again, and galleries in Beijing and Shanghai display the latest works. Some artists return to classical painting or explore minority art, but many freely experiment with a fusion of Western and Chinese art, looking at age-old subject matters through avant-garde styles and changing modern China through traditional mediums of brush and ink.

SCULPTURE

In ancient China, sculpture never attained the form of high art and was seen as an artisan's trade. Sculptors did not work for purely aesthetic reasons, but to adorn architecture, temples, and tombs, though that's not to say their creations lacked aesthetic value. One of the largest-scale sculptural works, the Terracotta Warriors in the tomb of Qin Shihuang consists of more than 7000 life-size statues of warriors and horses. Since the introduction and spread of Buddhism at the end of the Han, China has gone on a Buddha sculpturing frenzy, resulting in more Buddhas than you could shake a stick at—sitting, sleeping, standing, reclining, many-armed, Buddhas 70m-tall and 4cm-tall, Buddhas of stone, bronze, jade, gold, and every material imaginable.

Pottery dates back to the Shang, when lacquer glazes and jade carvings decorated coffins and weapons. By the Tang, whiteware and tricolored glazes were highly prized. Ming ceramics were coveted in places as far away as Europe, and the degree to which *Zhōngguó* became equated with its product can be seen in the English name "china." Still in business today, **Jingdezhen** (p. 436) made the distinctive blue-and-white Ming vases, and Yixing ceramics come from **Suzhou** (p. 366).

ARCHITECTURE

Five thousand years of development and countless stylistic and religious influences have resulted in an extraordinary architectural variety, from ancient earth-covered houses and magnificent underground tombs, to towering pagodas and ornate imperial residences, to modern skyscrapers and cookie-cutter housing projects. Common traditional Chinese architectural elements include arching roofs with **flying eaves,** timber structures, and the use of columns for support rather than walls. Most important buildings face south. Compounds, be it imperial, religious, or residential, tend to center around **courtyards,** with thick outer walls. This can be seen most prominently in **hutong** (alley) residences like those in Beijing, where courtyard homes are linked by adjoining walls. Cities were also protected by walls, and their remnants can still be found around Xi'an, Nanjing, and Pingyao, with the most prominent being the massive **Great Wall.**

Imperial **palaces** are elaborate labyrinths of courtyards, terraces, halls, and courts connected by pathways, gardens, and gateways. **Mausoleums,** usually built against hills or mountains over plains, recreate the grandeur of palaces underground. Buddhist architecture includes multi-storied, pavilioned **pagodas, grottoes,** cliffside caves with elaborate engravings, and **temples** ranging from neighborhood altars to grand **monasteries** in Tibet and on sacred mountains. Daoist temples adapt to natural topography. **Gardens** usually feature an elegant combination of landscaping, natural scenery, and pathways and pavilions set over ponds. Structures and styles change from region to region in accordance with local cultures, geography, and climate; **mosques, yurts,** and **minority wooden houses** are only the beginning.

In the 20th century, Chinese architecture adapted European designs to modern needs. After 1949, Soviet-style practicality beat out aesthetics (hello gray buildings) while massive political structures like the Great Hall of the People (p. 143) and Mao Zedong's Mausoleum (p. 143) were functional but grand, in the Greek tradition. Recently, China has joined the race for the skies with high-rises sprouting up left and right in a stylistically disjointed manner, ranging from award-winning designs in magnet cities like Shanghai and Hong Kong, to awkward amalgams of modernity and tradition (drab blocks capped with flying eaves).

FENG SHUI. The traditional practice of feng shui (风水 ; "wind and water"), referring to geomancy or divination according to geographic features, has persisted into the modern era. To maximize auspiciousness, *feng shui* masters determine placement of elements by balancing the metaphysical energies of a physical space with its functions and inhabitants. Popularly used for interior design, *feng shui* can also be applied on a large scale for building sites and floorplans. It is taken rather seriously in places like Hong Kong, where any major building project (even Disneyland) necessitates a *feng shui* consultation.

FILM

Cinema, or "electric shadows" (diànyǐng; 电影), was introduced to China in 1896. By the 1920s, a vibrant domestic film industry had developed in Shanghai, producing China's golden age of film. After the CCP took over, much of the Shanghai contingent transplanted in full to Hong Kong. Those who stayed behind were only allowed to produce party-appropriate socialist propaganda films of heroic peasants and class struggle. During the Cultural Revolution, the film industry all but disappeared, as only 10 films were played in the entire 10-year period.

After the Cultural Revolution, the illustrious **"Fifth Generation"** of filmmakers emerged with China's two most prominent directors. **Chen Kaige,** whose *Yellow Earth* was the first Chinese film to break through at international festivals, produced speculative, political pieces while **Zhang Yimou** provocatively interpreted China's vibrant, torturous past *(Raise the Red Lantern)*. Both directors followed an arc of receiving accolades abroad while being banned at home, and eventually shifted towards more epic or mainstream films within the government's censors. In the 1990s, the **"Sixth Generation"** splashed onto the scene. Like their predecessors, Sixth Generation directors were acclaimed internationally but banned domestically, but that's where the similarities end. Directors like **Zhang Yuan** *(Beijing Bastards)*, **Jia Zhangke** *(Platform)*, and **Wang Xiaoshua** *(The Days)* painted bleak, disaffected, allegorical urban tales of the darker side of Chinese society, touching on controversial topics like homosexuality and suicide. Many of these novice films were very raw and filmed on low budgets, but their higher profile has opened up more opportunities and funding for these directors.

Thanks to Bruce Lee, the Shaw Brothers, and the successful crossover of Jackie Chan, Jet Li, John Woo, and others, martial art flicks have long enjoyed a well-established international reputation. Hong Kong cinema, however, has a personality that extends beyond just action movies. The bizarre satire of **Fruit Chan** *(Made in Hong Kong)*, the hard-boiled thrillers of **Johnny To** *(The Mission)*, the pop confections of **Joe Ma** *(Love Undercover)*, the high-jinks, word-play comedies of **Stephen Chow** *(Shaolin Soccer)*, the crowd-pleasing spectacles of **Tsui Hark** *(Zu Warriors)*, and the lyrical dramas of **Stanley Kwan** *(Center Stage)* all occupy a unique niche in Hong Kong's spectrum of film. Meanwhile, eccentric auteur **Wong Kar-wai**'s hypnotically beautiful and thoroughly incomprehensible essays of yearning, transience, and isolation simply create a world all their own.

SPORTS AND RECREATION

GAMES

Popular among children, **tiaoqi** (checkers) is a competitive game involving marbles on a star-shaped board. Those who'd rather not get involved in the sheer brutality of children's games can opt for the more sedate **xiangqi** (Chinese chess). Similar to international chess, *xiàngqí* uses wooden pieces and is by far the most popular board game. Also ubiquitous is **weiqi** (or Go), the ancient "game of encirclement." Players use white and black pebbles on a grid board, with each side trying to secure "territory" by surrounding and conquering opponent stones. *Wéiqí's* emphasis on strategy makes it ideal training for military students. **Mahjong** is a four-person game using ceramic, ivory, or plastic tiles. Players pick up and replace tiles to form certain patterns (similar to gin rummy). A gentle form of gambling, *mahjong* is especially popular among women. Amble to a local park to see games of all types in action.

SPORTS

Despite the worldwide popularity of Chinese kung fu, the most popular spectator sports in China are **basketball** and **soccer** (football). The NBA is a hot topic of conversation, especially since the Houston Rockets drafted **Yao Ming,** a 7'5" center, as their first pick in 2002. As a testament to his popularity, the basketball superstar carried the Olympic torch on its last stretch to Beijing before the 2004 Athens Games, and also led the Chinese delegation at the opening ceremony. Local basketball games are also popular, with many major cities sporting their own teams. Ping pong and badminton are the most widespread urban sports in China, although bowling, billiards, and tennis are gaining popularity.

As for soccer, the Chinese women's teams have continuously succeeded at the international level, where their male counterparts have not (a cause of deep frustration among fans). The women's team has won numerous Asian championships and consistently advances to the Olympics.

In the Olympic Games, China performs especially well in diving, gymnastics, women's volleyball, weight-lifting, and ping pong. The successful 2008 Olympic bid (p. 83) sparked an even greater interest in athletics. On January 13, 2004, Premier Wen Jiabao signed the country's first anti-doping decree.

Wushu is a traditional form of self-defense as well as an art form incorporated into many dances and operas. The Buddhist Shaolin Monastery (p. 289) and the Daoist Wudangshan temples (p. 471) are the most famous centers for *wushu*. The style of Shaolin is generally more energetic and acrobatic, while Wudang claims an internal style, using weapons such as the legendary Wudang sword. *Tai chi*, a slower version of *wushu*, is popular among the elderly, who practice in parks every morning. Fans claim that *tai chi* results in various health benefits to the cardiovascular, immune, and skeletal systems. Have you *tai chi*'ed today?

KARAOKE

As inevitable as staring and suffocating crowds, karaoke (kǎlā OK; 卡拉 OK) is simply something visitors to China cannot avoid. Invented by the Japanese, karaoke first became a hit in China in the 1980s. Soon, restaurants, bars, hotels, and even some private homes flashed karaoke rooms. Today, karaoke bars (**"KTV"**) can be found on nearly every street corner in cities and even in remote frontier towns. They are often filled with large, drunken crowds, where singers of all ages croon unsteadily to anything from pop songs to old revolutionary tunes. A night in one room can range in cost from a mere Y20 to thousands of dollars.

HOLIDAYS AND FESTIVALS

In addition to these festivals and holidays, many minority groups have their own celebrations and festivals, such as the Miao's **Sisters' Meal Festival** in Guizhou, the Dai's **Water Splashing Festival,** and the **Naadam Festival** in Inner Mongolia (see p. 321).

DATE	FESTIVAL	DETAILS
Feb. 9, 2005 Jan. 29, 2006	Lunar New Year (*Chūn Jié*) 2005 Year of the Rooster, 2006 Year of the Dog	On the 1st day of the 1st month of the Lunar year. The most important and liveliest holiday. Families gather, enjoy special treats, exchange gifts, light fireworks, and celebrate being together.
Feb. 23, 2005 Feb. 12, 2006	Lantern Festival (*Yuánxiāo Jié*)	On the 15th day of the 1st month. People light colorful paper lanterns in the streets, perform lion dances, and eat sweet stuffed sticky rice balls.
Apr. 4-5	Qingming (Tomb-Sweeping) Festival	A traditional holiday when the Chinese visit and beautify their ancestors' graves.
May 4	International Youth Day	A state holiday honoring the student demonstrators of the May 4 Movement (p. 78).
June 1	International Children's Day	A state holiday when children get the day off from school, and special activities offer toys and fun.
June 11, 2005 May 31, 2006	Dragon Boat Festival (*Duānwǔ Jié*)	The 5th day of the 5th month of the lunar year. Memorializes poet and patriot Qu Yuan (p. 605). People race dragon boats and eat *zòngzi*, sticky rice wrapped in reed and bamboo leaves.
July 1	Anniversary of the CCP's Founding	A patriotic state holiday.
Aug. 1	Anniversary of the PLA's Founding	A state holiday honoring the armed forces.
Oct. 1	National Day	A state holiday commemorating the CCP's victory of October 1, 1949, and prime traveling time.
Sept. 18, 2005 Oct. 6, 2006	Autumn Moon (Mid-Autumn) Festival; *Zhōngqiū Jié*	Celebrated the night of the 15th day of the 8th lunar month, when the moon is at its fullest and brightest. Activities include moon-gazing (especially at lakes) and eating mooncakes.

LIFE AND TIMES

ADDITIONAL RESOURCES

GENERAL HISTORY

A Concise History of China, by J.A.G. Roberts (Harvard Univ. Press, US$12). Condenses 4 millennia of China into 300 pages. Includes ten maps.

China: A New History, by John King Fairbank and Merle Goldman (Harvard Univ. Press, US$13). A comprehensive account of China, its people, and their cultural history.

China: Empire and Civilization, by Edward Shaugnessy (Oxford Univ. Press, US$36). Covers the most interesting facets of Imperial China and its legacy in the 20th century.

The Cambridge Illustrated History of China, by Patricia Buckley Ebrey and Kwan-Ching Liu (Cambridge Univ. Press, US$24). Explores recurring themes in Chinese history.

FICTION AND NON-FICTION

A Dream of Red Mansions, by Cao Xueqin, Gao E, Yang Xianyi (translator) (Foreign Language Press, US$24). A celebrated 18th-century Chinese classic novel about a tragic love story and a degenerating empire.

Bad Elements, by Ian Buruma (Random House, US$15). A collection of the author's encounters with notable Chinese dissidents, exiled rebels, and democrats dispersed around the world, including Wei Jingsheng and Tian'anmen leaders.

Becoming Madame Mao, by Anchee Min (Mariner Books, US$10). A historical fiction of Madame Mao, known as the White-Boned Demon during her reign of terror in China.

China Dawn: The Story of a Technology and Business Revolution, by David Sheff (Harper Business, US$17). An investigation into the high-tech revolution in China today as it faces heavy government censorship and regulation.

Diary of a Madman and Other Stories, by Lu Xun, William Lyell (translator) (Univ. of Hawaii Press, US$20). Lu Xun's 1st collection of short stories, including *Story of Ah Q*.

Peony, by Pearl S. Buck (Moyer Bell, US$5). This quiet, beautiful novel chronicles the life of Peony, a bondmaid sold to a wealthy Chinese-Jewish family.

Wild Swans: Three Daughters of China, by Jung Chang (Anchor World Views, US$8). A history of 3 generations of women who braved China's 20th-century political scene.

TRAVEL WRITING

A Truthful Impression of the Country: British and American Travel Writing in China, 1880-1949, by Nicholas R. Clifford (Univ. of Michigan Press, US$40). An accurate representation of the unfamiliar and exotic, by a college professor.

Inscribed Landscapes: Travel Writing From Imperial China, by Richard E. Strassberg (Univ. of California Press, US$15). An anthology of impressions of Chinese landscape from native citizens, covering several centuries.

The Myth of Shangri-La: Tibet, Travel Writing and the Western Creation of a Sacred Landscape, by Peter Bishop (Univ. of California Press, US$40). Examines travel writings on Tibet to delineate the relationship between culture, landscape, and the sacred.

Red Dust, by Ma Jian (Anchor, US$14). A stark, gritty portrait of a China that travelers never see, told by a dissident artist who left his Beijing home to drift for 3 years.

River Town: Two Years on the Yangtze, by Peter Hessler (Perennial, US$14). A volunteer tells of his life teaching English in a small town on the Yangzi River.

PHOTOGRAPHY

A World Away, by Larry Snider (Pegasus Publishing, US$45). Photographs taken over 10 years in Tibet, China, Bhutan, and Ladakh.

Children in China, by Michael Karhausen (Orbis, US$19). 90 black and white photographs of China's children and their worlds.

Marc Riboud in China: Forty Years of Photography, by Marc Riboud (Harry N. Abrams, US$25). Contrasting old and new China with images that mark the country's evolution.

Spectacular China, by Nigel Cameron (Hugh Lauter Levin Associates, US$40). China's natural beauty, culture, and architecture, all in one book.

FILMS

Farewell My Concubine (1993, dir. Chen Kaige). Bleak but powerful epic of the complex relationship between 2 Beijing opera stars over a jarring historical backdrop.

Gate of Heavenly Peace (1995, dir. Carma Hinton). Compelling, comprehensive documentary of the events and figures surrounding the Tian'anmen protests.

Happy Together (1997, dir. Wong Kar-wai). The late Leslie Cheung and the great Tony Leung falling together and apart in a beautiful tango of love in Argentina.

Infernal Affairs (2002, dir. Andrew Lau, Alan Mak). Stylishly tense cat-and-mouse thriller with the police and triads racing against time to find dual moles in their ranks.

In the Heat of the Sun (1994, dir. Jiang Wen). Based on a Wang Shuo novel, irreverent youth come of age in the hazy, dazy days of the Cultural Revolution.

Once Upon a Time in China (1991, dir. Tsui Hark). The banging of drums, the swelling of music, and Jet Li doing his thing in an uplifting, patriotic period flick.

Quitting (2001, dir. Zhang Yang). Actor Jia Hongshen and family star as themselves, reliving Jia's journey from drug-induced paranoia to recovery. Meta.

Suzhou River (2000, dir. Lou Ye). A melancholy love triangle, mesmerizingly rendered with vibrantly contrasting colors and a shaky subjective camera.

To Live (1994, dir. Zhang Yimou). One family's trials and tribulations through 3 turbulent decades of Communist rule.

LIFE AND TIMES

ALTERNATIVES TO TOURISM

A PHILOSOPHY FOR TRAVELERS

Let's Go believes that the connection between travelers and their destinations is an important one. Over the years, we've watched the growth of the 'ignorant tourist' stereotype with dismay, knowing that many travelers care passionately about the communities and environments they explore—but also knowing that even conscientious tourists can inadvertently damage natural wonders and harm cultural environments. With this "Alternatives to Tourism" chapter, *Let's Go* hopes to promote a better understanding of China and to enhance your experience there.

In the developing world, there are several different options for those who seek alternatives to tourism. Opportunities for **volunteerism** abound, both with local and international organizations. Those wishing to **study abroad** can enroll directly in a local university or in an independent research project. *Let's Go* discourages **working** in the developing world due to high unemployment rates and weak economies.

Though China has been pegged by many as the up-and-coming nation in Asia, behind all the rising skyscrapers and hype of China's new century, the crushing truth of poverty remains. The country has one of the largest wealth gaps in the world, with more than 270 million people struggling in destitution. Even as China's run-away economy continues its reckless dash forward, unemployment is on the rise. As a result, a discontented population of jobless and migrant workers roams the streets, a heart-rending testimony to the pains of growth and development. China's headlong rush toward modernization has had other consequences as well. By most estimates, 15 of the world's 20 most polluted cities are in China. Dust clings to the air, and erosion and waste choke rivers into relentless muddy slogs. Not only the giant panda and the Baiji dolphin, but also hundreds of other animal species are on the verge of extinction.

All of this leaves ample opportunities for the volunteer. Either on a short-term basis or as the main component of your trip, you can live and work with Tibetan herders in the highlands of Qinghai, build a school for a rural village in Shaanxi, provide health care for villagers, or educate the community on issues such as AIDS. Teaching English is the most common volunteer activity for Westerners, though it can be done as a salaried position as well. Later in this section, we recommend organizations that can help you find the opportunities that best suit your interests, whether you're looking to pitch in for a day or a year.

Studying at a college or in a language program is another option. With the immersion in a Chinese-speaking environment, students find that their language abilities improve rapidly. Electives such as Chinese painting, calligraphy, martial arts, and cooking deepen the cultural experience in a way unattainable to travelers simply passing through. The few months, semester, or year spent in one city provide a priceless opportunity to form lasting friendships with locals, host-families, and fellow students. Waking up every morning to grab a steamed bun before heading off to class, jostling with the crowd to get on the city bus, and ending the day over a glass of Tsingtao with friends at the local bar—all this lets students experience life as the Chinese live it.

104

VOLUNTEERING

China, while rich in culture and history, has significant concerns about the environment, poverty, and the side-effects of rapid development, particularly in the rural regions. Many volunteer programs are run by Western organizations specializing in sending volunteers to developing nations. These organizations generally try to minimize the distance between the volunteer and the local community, but also try to provide a comparatively comfortable standard of living and an extensive support network. Conditions range from an apartment in a city like Beijing or Xi'an to a yurt on the grasslands or traditional village-style housing. All the usual difficulties of a developing country may be expected, from transportation hassles to adjustments to lodgings, food, and other difficulties. Yet volunteers gain the opportunities to live and work extensively with a community for a period of time, providing aid and sharing skills, while learning from the people they seek to help.

People who volunteer in China often do so on a short-term basis, usually with organizations that run programs lasting from two or three weeks to several months. The best way to find opportunities that match up with your interests and schedule may be to check with the organizations listed below. Chinese volunteer organizations are relatively new, and many of them are happy to accept foreigners. Be sure to plan out the logistics before you go: contact the organization directly to work out visas and transportation. Make sure that they know you're coming and that there is in fact a position for you; also inquire about housing and meals.

For a more structured experience, it may be best to go through a volunteer placement agency, which will take care of logistics and frequently provide a group environment and support system. Many of these programs charge you a fee to participate. This amount can range from a simple application fee to surprisingly hefty costs (although they frequently cover most, if not all, expenses in the country).

CONSERVATION

While the environment has largely been overlooked in China's push for progress in the last 50 years or so, conservation has recently come into focus as a crucial issue. A multitude of organizations in China has sprung up in response to the new spotlight on environmental issues. From educating the public, to publishing newsletters, to studying Tibetan antelope on the distant highlands of Qinghai province, a variety of opportunities awaits the eager traveler.

ENVIRONMENTAL CONSERVATION

Earthwatch Institute, 3 Clock Tower Place, Ste. 100, Box 75, Maynard, MA 01754, USA (North America ☎800-776-0188 or 978-461-0081; www.earthwatch.org). Sends out research and conservation expeditions to assist scientists and researchers in their work. Current programs in China involve studying desertification and water resources in the Gobi Desert in Inner Mongolia and preserving ancestral temples in Zhejiang province.

Friends of Nature, Gonghe Business Bldg., Ste. 301, 10 Qihelou Bei Xiang, Beijing 100006, China (☎86 10 6526 1382 or 6526 1384; fax 6523 3134; www.fon.org). One of the largest conservation organizations in China, Friends of Nature always welcomes volunteers to help with their many projects. In addition, they also have domestic and international ties to many other conservation and environmental groups. Volunteers teach children in rural villages throughout China about environmental issues and sustainable development, train teachers to do the same, encourage students to come up with their own solutions and projects, plant trees, raise funds for the Tibetan antelope and other projects, publish a newsletter, and work in the office.

Global Village of Beijing, 86 Beiyuan Lu, Jiaming Garden, Chaoyang District, Beijing 100101, China (☎86 10 8485 9669; www.gvbchina.org). Based in Beijing, the Global Village aims to educate citizens about a responsible lifestyle and encourage them to think about the environmental impact of their decisions. Volunteers help organize and run meetings and forums to raise awareness, run programs to educate students, work on the newsletter *Voices of Grassroot,* and help translate and write essays for publication. Many volunteers also work at the training center, centered in an NGO-run wilderness conservation area in Yanqing county. Tasks at the center include participating in conservation methods, educating citizens, and leading outdoors activities and tours to help visitors better understand biodiversity and sustainable development.

Greener Beijing, Rm. 402, Unit 1, Bldg. 1, Section 6, Tiantongyuan, Beijing 102209, China (☎86 10 8482 0743; www.grchina.net). Part of a greater organization called "Greener China." Involved with many projects, including planting trees and cleaning up Beijing, researching grasslands in Inner Mongolia, studying sustainable use of energy and resources, saving the Tibetan antelope, and educating the public on environmental issues. Volunteers can help in a variety of capacities and locations.

Green Stone, 183 Huju Bei Lu, Nanjing, Jiangsu province 210011, China (☎86 25 5877 0224; www.green-stone.org). Green Stone works to bring together several environmental groups working in Jiangsu, Zhejiang, and the mouth of the Yangzi River. They are based in regional universities, in particular Nanjing University. One of their main focuses is the Baiji dolphin, also known as the Yangzi dolphin, of which fewer than 50 are estimated to be living today. Green Stone seeks volunteers to help with education, communication, and coordination. English skills welcomed.

Snowland Great Rivers Environmental Protection Association, Tibetan Medicine University of Yushu Prefecture, Jiegu, Yushu Prefecture, Qinghai province 815400, China (☎86 138 9716 1833 or 976 882 9066; www.snowland-great-rivers.org). The Snowlands Association focuses on the Three Rivers in the Yushu Tibetan Autonomous Prefec-

ESSAY CONTEST WINNER!

beyondtourism.com

Last year's winner, Eleanor Glass, spent a summer volunteering with children on an island off the Yucatan Peninsula. Read the rest of her story and find your own once-in-a-lifetime experience at **www.beyondtourism.com!**

"... I was discovering elements of life in Mexico that I had never even dreamt of. I regularly had meals at my students' houses, as their fisherman fathers would instruct them to invite the nice gringa to lunch after a lucky day's catch. Downtown, tourists wandered the streets and spent too much on cheap necklaces, while I played with a friend's baby niece, or took my new kitten to the local vet for her shots, or picked up tortillas at the tortilleria, or vegetables in the mercado. ... I was lucky that I found a great place to volunteer and a community to adopt me. ... Just being there, listening to stories, hearing the young men talk of cousins who had crossed the border, I know I went beyond tourism." - Eleanor Glass, 2004

LET'S GO

ture, a wilderness of grasslands, forest, highlands, glacier-capped peaks, and mountain lakes, and the source of the mighty Yangzi, Yellow, and Lancang Rivers. Volunteers here work to protect the biodiversity and ecological richness of the region. They collaborate with Tibetan villages to model sustainable economic development without damaging the environment. Many college students live and work with herdsmen to experience first-hand the issues they face. Wildlife conservation is another project of the association to protect the hundreds of species in the Three Rivers. Those with scientific backgrounds or interest in the highlands of China are also welcome to conduct research. Volunteers will be matched to tasks according to ability, background, and interest. Ask to speak with Zhaxi Duojie for more information on volunteering.

World Wide Fund for Nature: China, Rm. 901, The Gateway, 10 Yabao Lu, Chaoyang District, Beijing 100020, China (☎86 10 8563 6538; www.wwfchina.org). The WWF's projects include restoring the ecological balance in threatened regions, reducing green-house emissions and encouraging the use of alternative energy sources, controlling the illegal trade of endangered species, and educating the population on the importance of conservation. The WWF has a wide network of volunteers, based in 10 cities in China and abroad. They help coordinate and manage activities and raise awareness of environmental issues in China. Volunteers in the field must be fluent in Chinese.

WILDLIFE CONSERVATION

Beijing Human and Animal Environmental Education Center (☎86 10 6178 6778; www.animalschina.org). The BHAEC focuses on the humane treatment of animals and hosts a variety of programs in the community. Volunteers help educate the public, instruct children on proper pet care, and help with pet therapy and fund-raising events. The center is located in the Changping district of Beijing, between Litang Lu and the Badaling Expressway, west of the Aviation Museum.

China Wildlife Conservation Association (CWCA), 18 Hepingli Dong Jie, Beijing 100714, China (☎86 10 8423 9016; www.cwca.org.cn). The largest organization dedicated to the protection and conservation of wildlife and endangered species, the CWCA has 622 offices around the country. Volunteers can work at their headquarters in Beijing in the office, or do field work regionally in wildlife and natural preserves and wildlife centers throughout China. When calling about volunteering, ask to speak to Zhong Yi.

Greenriver, 3 Biyun Lu, 4 Danyuan No. 17, Chengdu, Sichuan province 610041, China (☎86 28 8505 6595; www.green-river.org). Every summer, the Suonandajie Natural Reserve in Qinghai province asks college students to help the Tibetan antelope that have just given birth to cross the Qinghai-Tibetan highway safely in their summer migrations. There are 3 different sessions, each lasting 2-3 weeks, June-Sept. Applications can be downloaded from the Green River website. Inquire about year-round volunteer positions. Contact the organization directly if interested; the application is in Chinese.

Hong Kong Dolphin Conservation Society, P.O. Box 156, Tung Chung, Hong Kong (☎2366 2652; www.hkdcs.org). Established in December 2003, the HKDCS is a non-profit organization dedicated to the conservation of white dolphins (they're actually pink), porpoises, and whales in Hong Kong. Foreign students, preferably with a background in biology or environmental science, are welcome to participate in the research internship program, which includes sea-, land-, and even air-based field surveys and observations of the marine mammals. Minimum 1-month commitment. Volunteer positions that require a shorter commitment in technical, administrative, and educational capacities are also available. Membership fee HK$200.

Lamma Animal Welfare Center, G/F Flat A, 25B Main St., Yung Shue Wan, Lamma Island, Hong Kong (☎852 2982 0800; www.lammaanimals.org). Based on Hong Kong's Lamma Island, the animal center concerns itself mainly with the fate of homeless dogs and cats in the city. Ideal for animal lovers, the center offers a range of volunteer activities, including walking and training dogs, counseling potential adopters, working with pet therapy, educating the community, providing care for abandoned animals, and carrying out day-to-day administrative and animal-related tasks in the center.

Wolong Giant Panda Reserve (☎837 624 6615). The Wolong Giant Panda Reserve and Research Center focuses on caring for these cuddly creatures, as well as studying them, their breeding, and bamboo ecology. Potential volunteers should contact the reserve directly. The Sichuan branch of **China International Travel Service (CITS),** Rm. 314, 65 Renmin Nan Lu, Er Duan, Chengdu, China (☎86 28 8665 2087; www.4panda.com/panda/volunteer.htm), can also arrange volunteering positions for a fee of US$20 per application. The reserve charges $50 per day. Lodgings $25 per day, with food $35.

RURAL DEVELOPMENT

Over 800 million people live in rural areas, where the standard of living is starkly different from the bustling centers of Beijing, Shanghai, or the wealthy SEZs in Guangdong. Even a few hours out from one of these cities, villages struggle for survival without adequate health care, schools, a sustainable economy, or infrastructure. Though China requires at least nine years of schooling, lack of space and teachers, as well as the demands of agriculture, often prevent village children from attending school for the full time. Many volunteer organizations focus on these rural villages on the brink of existence, building schools, training teachers, and taking the time to read, educate, and play with local children.

CARE-Venture International, Tampines Central Post Office, P.O. Box 87, Singapore 915203 (☎871 652 0050; www.careventure.org). Volunteers work in a variety of projects, all based in Yunnan province. Run summer camps for children of minority villages, help build showers, toilets, and other infrastructure for rural villages, and work in a center to help homeless children in Kunming. Volunteers are responsible for their own transportation, lodgings, and food costs.

Global Volunteers, 375 East Little Canada Rd., St. Paul, MN 55117, USA (☎800–487-1074 or 651-407-6100; www.globalvolunteers.org). Join Project Peace and help build a school and library for the children of Anshang Village, in rural Shaanxi. Other tasks include teaching English in Anshang and elsewhere in Shaanxi. Free time to explore Xi'an and beyond. 2-week program fee $2220, students $2120; 3-week $2295/$2195. 2-week teaching in Xi'an and Bo'ai $2295/$1995; 3-week $2595/$2295.

Rokpa UK Overseas Project, Eskdalemuir, Langholm, Dumfriesshire DG13 0QL, Scotland, UK (☎44 13 8737 3232, ext. 3; Canada 604-733-1055; Ireland 353 1 473 1223; US 703-642-2248; www.rokpauk.org). Rokpa runs over 100 projects in Tibet and regions populated by Tibetans, including Sichuan, Qinghai, Gansu, and northern Yunnan. Projects focus on education, the environment, employment, and health care.

Voluntary Service Overseas, 317 Putney Bridge Rd., London SW15 2PN, UK (☎44 20 8780 7241; www.vso.org.uk). VSO works in the poorest regions of western, southern, and central China. Teaching English to students in rural areas, educating communities on HIV/AIDS and environmental conservation, working for sustainable rural livelihood, and promoting environmentally sustainable tourism. Applicants must be at least 20 years old and be qualified.

Volunteers for Peace, 1034 Tiffany Rd., Belmont, Vermont 05730, USA (☎802-259-2759; www.vfp.org). VFP sends out small teams of volunteers to "work camps" internationally, where they live with the local people and participate in community service projects. The current camp for China is in Xinjing Village, on Hainan Island. Volunteers teach the children English, and help with construction, health care, farm work, and environmental issues. Program fee of US$200 and additional fee of $185.

Yunnan Institute for Development, 49-51 Ni'er Lu, Yuxi 653100, Yunnan province, China (☎86 877 205 9695; www.volunteerchina.org or www.drh-movement.org). Formed with the Humana People to People Movement (www.humana.org), the Yunnan Institute of Development aims to help improve the lives of children in rural areas through a unique structure. After 6 months of training in the school in Yunnan, volunteers are sent into the field for another 6 months, either in China or in Africa. At the end, volunteers have 2 months back in Yunnan, where they reflect on their work and produce material in print, in writing, or through exhibits.

MEDICAL OUTREACH

In much of rural China, residents are often kilometers away from the nearest hospital. Village clinics and hospitals in smaller towns and cities lack the latest medical technology, and supplies and doctors are often limited, especially in the undeveloped regions of western China. The volunteer organizations below send humanitarian missions to China to provide care and training for people who lack regular access to medical care. Volunteers almost always must be qualified professionals, but occasionally there are positions in non-technical capacities.

Medical Expeditions International, 1235 N. Decatur Rd., Atlanta, GA 30306, USA (☎404-815-7044; http://medexinternational.org). Sends medical professionals of all fields to provide health care to the nomadic Tibetan peoples and children in a local orphanage in Qinghai province. Also trains local health care professionals. The trip lasts about 2 weeks, including traveling in Beijing, Qinghai, Lhasa, and Shanghai, and costs US$2535, which covers all expenses except the airfare to China.

Médicins du Monde, 29th fl., One Canada Sq., London E14 5AA, UK (☎44 20 7516 9103; www.medecinsdumonde.co.uk). Volunteers, usually medical professionals such as doctors, nurses, midwives, and technicians, work in the field to provide care to the the people of rural China and improve the local health care infrastructure. Volunteers without medical experience also accepted to work as administrators and coordinators. Check their website for current openings. Duration 4 months and up. All transportation, accommodations, food, and insurance costs paid for, in addition to a monthly allowance and compensation.

World Association for Children and Parents (WACAP), P.O. Box 88948, Seattle, WA 98138, USA (☎206-575-4550; www.wacap.org). WACAP runs the Peony Project to help children with disabilities. They seek volunteer occupational therapists, physical therapists, and special education teachers to improve medical care and education for these children. They also train parents and teachers. Based in Henan province. Minimum requirements include a bachelor's degree and experience with children with developmental disabilities. Minimum stay 3 months, though 1 year or longer is preferred. Lodgings, travel expenses, and stipend provided.

URBAN ISSUES

These organizations tackle a variety of problems in the city, ranging from working with children, to educating the public about AIDS and environmentalism, to youth outreach, to planting trees in the city and around.

Cross-Cultural Solutions, 2 Clinton Pl., New Rochelle, NY 10801 USA; Tower Point 44, North Rd., Brighton, BN1 1YR, UK (US ☎800-380-4777, UK and all other countries 44 845 458 2781; www.crossculturalsolutions.org). 2-10 week programs in Xi'an place volunteers with a local organization. Possible tasks include taking care of children in orphanages and daycares, teaching English to teenagers, and observing and assisting with local medical institutions. The program also provides for activities, outings, and free time for independent exploration. 1st 2 weeks US$2175, each additional week US$248. Fee covers lodgings, meals, transportation, language assistance, travel insurance, emergency evacuation insurance, and local phone calls.

Hong Kong Youth Hostels Association (HKYHA), Rm. 225-227, Block 19, Shek Kip Mei Estate, Sham Shui Po, Kowloon, Hong Kong (☎852 2788 1638; www.yha.org.hk). Seeks volunteers to help the association in promotions and operations, as well as organizing recreational activities and tours for hostel members. An application can be downloaded at the website. Contact Bobby Leung at the above phone number.

Peking Volunteers, 288 Jinjiachun, Fengtai District, Beijing 100036, China (☎86 130 5192 0619; fax 86 10 6818 7462). This non-governmental Beijing organization focuses on educating the community about AIDS/HIV, encouraging forestation and greenification, and helping the underprivileged gain job skills and education opportunities, especially in the field of foreign language instruction.

TEACHING ENGLISH

There are many opportunities to teach English in China in different settings, ranging from kindergarten to university level, from Beijing and Shanghai to far-flung villages in western China. Many are on a volunteer basis. For salaried positions, the compensation may seem minimal by Western standards, but the stipend is usually more than adequate when considered against China's cost of living. Housing with a host family, in a dorm, or in an apartment is almost always provided.

China tends to have relatively lenient qualification requirements for English teachers. Full-fledged teachers are often expected to be native English speakers with a bachelor's degree, though in many cases a high school degree is the minimum requirement. A few summer programs offer college undergraduates the chance to teach or tutor. Experience and Chinese language fluency are usually unnecessary. Most schools in China do not require teachers to have a **Teaching English as a Foreign Language (TEFL)** certificate, though some placement agencies may prefer applicants to be certified. Not having one certainly doesn't exclude you from finding a teaching job, but a TEFL may mean higher salaries. Native English speakers working in private schools are most often hired for English-immersion classrooms where no Chinese is spoken. Those volunteering or teaching in poorer public schools are more likely to be working in both English and Chinese.

To find a teaching job in China, it's possible to apply directly to a Chinese school or university. Occasionally job openings are posted on the web. The most reliable method may be to go through a Western organization, placement agency, or university fellowship program, which will help you with visas, logistics, and paperwork. You can also try your luck once you get there, though this is risky and you'll have to obtain a work visa. Most people enter with a tourist visa and have it converted to a work visa once employment has been arranged.

A multitude of organizations help volunteers find teaching positions, so choose carefully to find one that matches your interests.

VOLUNTEER POSITIONS

BUNAC, 16 Bowling Green Ln., London, EC1R 0QH, UK (☎44 20 7251 3472; www.bunac.org). Citizens of the UK can apply to the Teach in China volunteer organization. If applicants do not hold the TEFL, TESOL, RSA/Cambridge, or Trinity College London certificate, they must first take a 4-week teacher training course. Programs approximately 10 months, Sept.-June. Cost UK£1700, including the training course, visa fees, accommodations, insurance, and travel costs.

Involvement Volunteers, P.O. Box 218, Port Melbourne, Victoria 3207, Australia (☎61 3 9646 9392; www.volunteering.org.au). Places volunteers in a variety of English-teaching positions throughout China. Requirements, durations, and fees depend on each institution. Check their online database of positions. Registration fee AUS$250.

i-to-i, Woodside House, 261 Low Ln., Leeds, LS18 5NY, UK (UK ☎44 870 333 2332, US 800-985-4864; www.i-to-i.com). Teaching English projects currently in primary schools, high schools, and colleges in Guangzhou, Beijing, and Yanqing, with a special focus on children from unemployed and low-income families. Other teaching programs in Guangzhou involve working at a center for children with learning disabilities and a university summer camp run for children ages 7-12. Programs last 8-12 weeks and cost US$1500-2100 with a US$295 deposit.

Global Volunteer Network, P.O. Box 2231, Wellington, New Zealand (☎64 4 569 9080, Australia 800 005 342, UK 800 096 7864, US 800-963-1198; www.volunteer.org.nz). Places teachers in Shandong schools in the Yantai area (Sept.-Jan. or Mar.-June). Summer school sessions (July-Aug.) are only in primary and secondary schools. Housing, meals, orientation, and weekend sightseeing included. Application fee NZ$297; program fee NZ$450-1000, depending on length of stay.

Project Trust, Hebridean Centre, Isle of Coll, Argyll PA78 6TE, UK (☎44 1879 230 444; www.projecttrust.org.uk). This gap year program only accepts UK and EU citizens ages 17½-19½. Opportunities to teach English at middle schools and colleges in Guangdong, Gansu, and Shandong. Participants must be able to begin the 1-year program in Aug., Sept., or Jan. of their gap year. Accommodations provided by the host school.

Teaching and Projects Abroad, Aldsworth Parade, Goring, Sussex BN12 4TX UK (☎44 1903 708 300; www.teaching-abroad.co.uk). Limited to Shanghai, the program arranges English-teaching positions in secondary schools, vocational schools, and colleges. Other opportunities include the chance to work with a variety of businesses in fast-growing Shanghai, hospitals, publications, and even a wildlife zoo. Basic price covers 3 months of accommodations with a local host, food, insurance, and emergency support. Teaching program US$3000, other programs US$3000-4000.

WorldTeach, Inc., Center for International Development, Harvard University, 79 John F. Kennedy St., Cambridge, MA 02138, USA (☎800-4-TEACH-0 or 617-495-5527; www.worldteach.org). Volunteers primarily teach classes in conversational English to students of all ages in China. Fee includes airfare, health insurance, training, room, and board. Fees US$4000-6000.

PAID POSITIONS

Asia/US Public Service and Educational Exchange Programs, P.O. Box 20266, Stanford, CA 94309, USA (☎650-723-3228; www.viaprograms.org). Places college graduates in teaching positions in technical universities and colleges. Provides round-trip airfare, accommodations, monthly stipend, travel allowance, and Chinese language training. Applications due Feb.-Mar. US$975-1975 depending on length of stay, undergraduate summer program $975.

China Education Exchange, ASM Overseas Corporation, 2434 W. Main St., Ste. 102, Alhambra, CA 91801, USA (☎626-458-8009; www.chinaeducationexchange.org). Works in partnership with China State Council to place college graduates. Also maintains a limited database of schools that directly post positions. Monthly salary of Y2500-4500 plus housing. 3-day Beijing orientation US$300; optional network support fee $500 per year. Application fee $85, non-native English speakers $300.

Colorado China Council, 4556 Apple Way, Boulder, CO 80301, USA (☎303-443-1108; www.asiacouncil.org). Places US college graduates and professionals in universities (Sept.-June or Feb./Mar.-June) to teach English, American/British literature, history, culture, and special fields like business, economics, or law. 2-week intensive training in

Shanghai, medical insurance, housing, and a monthly stipend of Y2200-8000. Fee US$2950, $4450 for professionals, reduced fees for married couples. Reduced spring semester fee of $1150 does not include training.

Council of International Educational Exchange (CIEE), 7 Custom House St., 3rd fl., Portland, ME 01401, USA (☎207-553-7600 or 800-40-STUDY; www.ciee.org). Places college graduates in schools ranging from kindergarten to university for 5 or 10 months. Provides for housing, insurance, 7-day training and orientation in Shanghai, and monthly salary of at least US$2600. Application fee $50; 5-month program fee $1400, 10-month $1800.

Footprints Recruiting, 55 Vancouver St., Ste. 314, Vancouver, B.C. V68 1A1, Canada (☎888-677-3166 or 694-677-6556; www.footprintsrecruiting.com). Places teachers in schools in various Asian countries, including China, free of charge. Must submit a lesson plan with application.

Global Crossroad, 8772 Quarters Lake Rd., Ste. 9, Baton Rouge, LA 70809, USA (North America ☎800-413-2008, UK 800 310 1821; www.globalcrossroad.com). Program places teachers in schools in Hebei. Includes monthly salary of Y2000-5000, depending on qualifications and length of stay, Chinese lessons, housing, and meals. Can arrange to live with host family. Minimum 1-month commitment. Also offers volunteer teaching positions in 2-week summer and winter camps for 5- to 12-year-olds in Inner Mongolia; yurt housing and meals provided. Program fee US$600; camp fee $670.

International Exchange Programs, P.O. Box 1786, Shortland St., Auckland, New Zealand (☎64 9 3666 255; www.iepnz.co.nz). Based in New Zealand, the IEP arranges teaching positions in China. Commitment from 4 months to 2 years. Requires applicants to take their TESOL certification course (NZ$1595). Positions available in both China and Hong Kong. Airfare and accommodations taken care of by the schools; monthly salary ranges $500-2500.

International Schools Services (ISS), 15 Roszel Rd., Box 5910, Princeton, NJ 08543-5910, USA (☎609-452-0990; www.iss.edu). Places experienced teachers into more than 200 overseas schools including ones in Beijing, Hong Kong, Guangzhou, Shanghai, and Tianjin. Monthly salary, round-trip airfare, and housing included. 2-year commitment expected. Candidates should be willing to be placed in at least 2 continents. Application fee US$150.

Sinoculture, P.O. Box 2231, Wellington, New Zealand (☎64 4 569 9080; www.sinoculture.com). Candidates with teaching experience are placed in secondary schools and universities, mainly for conversational English classes. May be asked to teach linguistics, literature, and Western culture at university level. TEFL preferred, at least 6-month commitment expected. Monthly salary of Y2200-4000 per month; housing and travel allowance provided. Application fee NZ$300.

US-China Education and Culture Exchange Center, 600 University Ave., Rennel Hall #234, Bridgeport, CT 06601, USA (☎203-576-6709; www.uschinaedu.org). Places college graduates for ½-year or 1-year programs. No experience needed, but must participate in teaching camp. Round-trip airfare, in-country transportation, and salary of at least Y3000 per month. Also offers TEFL summer camp program, which has no salary but includes meals. Fee US$250; summer camp fee 5-6 weeks $640, 7 weeks $490; reduced fee for certified teachers; college professors and staff free.

STUDYING

Study abroad programs range from basic language and culture courses to college-level classes, often for credit. In order to choose a program that best fits your needs, research as much as you can before making your decision—determine costs and duration, as well as what kinds of students participate in the program and what sort of accommodations are provided. Often, international students have their own dormitory within a Chinese university and live in singles or doubles, but sometimes students live with a host family or in apartments off campus.

In programs that have large groups of students who speak the same language, there is a trade-off. You may feel more comfortable in the community, but you will not have the same opportunity to immerse yourself in a Mandarin-speaking environment or befriend other international students. For accommodations, dorm life provides a better opportunity to mingle with fellow students, but there is less of a chance to experience the local scene. If you live with a family, there is a potential to build lifelong friendships and experience day-to-day life in more depth, but conditions can vary greatly from family to family.

VISA INFORMATION

Students studying abroad in China must have a passport and a student visa. Type **"F" visas** are for students staying less than 6 months; **"X" visas** are for stays of 6-12 months. In addition to the requirements for the standard visa, student visa applicants must also fill out a J-W202 form issued by the Chinese Ministry of Education, as well as have their doctor fill out a physical examination record form (Q-2) to prove that they are in good health. Applicants must also submit both the original and a photocopy of the letter of acceptance from the school or university. For more information on Chinese consulates, procedures, and visa fees specific to your country, refer to **Essentials** (p. 9).

UNIVERSITIES

Most university-level study-abroad programs are conducted in Mandarin Chinese, although many programs offer classes in English and beginner- and lower-level language courses. Those relatively fluent in Mandarin may find it cheaper to enroll directly in a university abroad, although getting college credit may be more difficult. You can search www.studyabroad.com for various semester-abroad programs that meet your criteria, including your desired location and focus of study. The following is a list of organizations that can help place students in university programs abroad or that have their own branch in China.

AMERICAN PROGRAMS

Central College Abroad, Office of International Education, 812 University, Pella, IA 50219, USA (☎800-831-3629 or 641-628-5284; www.central.edu/abroad). At Zhejiang University in Hangzhou, students take intensive Chinese courses, cultural electives, and other university courses. 1 semester US$10,250. Application fee US$25.

Council on International Educational Exchange (CIEE), 7 Custom House St., 3rd fl., Portland, ME 01401, USA (☎207-553-7600 or 800-40-STUDY; www.ciee.org). Spend a semester or a year at Beijing University, Nanjing University, or the East China Normal University in Shanghai. Besides language classes, the universities offer culture and history courses, trips, electives, peer language tutors, and homestays, depending on the program. Applicants must be college students with at least 1 completed semester. 1 semester US$8250-9600; 1 year approximately US$15,800. Summer programs in Beijing and Shanghai US$4500.

Princeton in Beijing, 211 Jones Hall, Princeton University, Princeton, NJ 08544-1008, USA (☎609-258-4269; www.princeton.edu/~pib). In this intensive 8-week program, students pledge to only use Mandarin Chinese to communicate. Based in Beijing Normal University, but all course materials, teaching, and evaluation methods are from Princeton. US$4400 includes tuition, textbooks, room, extra-curricular activities, trips and cultural activities, and twice weekly "Chinese table" meals with teachers.

School for International Training (SIT), Kipling Rd., P.O. Box 676, Brattleboro, VT 05302, USA (☎800-257-7751 or 802-257-7751; www.sit.edu). The **Languages and Cultures** program is a semester of intensive language courses in Kunming, Yunnan province, supplemented by cultural courses, seminars, study-trips to Dali and Lijiang, and other activities. 1 semester about US$13,000, including room and board. During the summer **Public Health and Traditional Program,** also in Kunming, students work with a local hospital to study Chinese traditional medicine and public health issues. Program fee US$5874, including room and board. Also runs the **Experiment in International Living** (☎800-345-2929 or the SIT phone number; www.usexperiment.org) for high school students. The 4-week summer program (US$5200) includes cross-cultural homestays, community service, ecological adventure, and language training. Contact Chris Frantz (☎802-258-3446), former China group leader, for more information.

University Studies Abroad Consortium, Virginia Street Gym, #5, USAC/323, Reno, NV 89557, USA (☎775-784-6569; http://usac.unr.edu). Term-time program at Southwest University for Nationalities in Chengdu offers a language-intensive track, comprised of language courses and cultural electives, and a China track, with courses in history, government, literature, anthropology, and business. The same 2 tracks also offered by 4-week summer programs. Fall or spring semester US$4260, 1 year $6860; June or July summer session $1680, both sessions $2980. Fee does not include room and board.

CHINESE PROGRAMS

Foreign students constitute one of the largest parts of China's expatriate population. Summer-, semester-, and year-long programs, especially for Chinese language and culture study, are increasing in number all the time. Most students study abroad in Beijing, but universities in almost every province accept international students. Some universities also require applicants to submit a **Chinese Proficiency Test (HSK)** along with their application, letters of recommendation, and copies of transcripts and degrees. At the university, students can study Chinese or pursue a degree. Usually, candidates for a full degree must pass the HSK or first take a year of language courses before enrolling. Tuition and room and board costs will typically be inexpensive by Western standards. Students will generally stay in a dormitory or guesthouse designated for international students; rooms typically are a single or a double with private bath and cost about US$5-12 per day. The **China Scholarship Council,** 160 Fuxingmen Nei Dajie, Beijing 100031, China (☎86 10 6641 3249; www.csc.edu.cn), a division of the Ministry of Education, offers scholarships and financial aid for foreign students studying in China.

The Chinese academic year begins in early September for the fall semester and in early February to early March for the spring semester. Most colleges ask you to apply at least 5-6 months before the start of the term. The following universities represent only a small selection of universities in China; visit the China Scholarship Council's website for a full list of schools with international programs.

Beijing University (Peking University), International Students Division, Office of International Relations, Shaoyuan Bldg. 3, Beijing University, Beijing 100871 (☎10 6275 1233 or 6275 1230; http://en.pku.edu.cn). The foremost college of China, Beijing University offers the full range of degrees, language programs, and short-term options. Their English website is extensive and helpful. Students wishing to start school in Sept. must submit their application by Feb. of the same year. Applicants must be at least a high-school graduate and pass the entrance exams, administered in Apr. (contact the Student Enrollment Office, ☎10 6275 9027). Applications can be downloaded online. Annual tuition US$3700 for a science degree and $3200 for a humanities degree.

Chengdu University of Traditional Chinese Medicine, 37 Shi'erqiao Lu, Chengdu, Sichuan province 610075 (☎28 8771 7385 or 8776 8611; www.cdutcm.edu.cn/english/all.htm). The international education College division accepts candidates for bachelor's, masters, and doctoral degrees in a wide range of fields in Chinese traditional medicine. Short-term programs available for students already familiar with medicine. Annual tuition for an undergraduate degree Y21,000.

Fudan University, Foreign Students Office, 220 Handan Lu, Shanghai 200433 (☎21 6511 7628 or 6564 2258; www.fso.fudan.edu.cn). Undergraduate and graduate degrees and language programs for international students. B.A. in Chinese Language is available for foreign students. Annual tuition Y23,000-42,000. Non-degree and research scholar programs also available. Summer language programs supplemented by classes on culture and trips: Y3300 for 4 weeks, Y700 for each additional week. Courses on a single subject can also be arranged.

Jingdezhen Ceramics Institute, Art and Design School, and **Department of Sculpture,** Jingdezhen, Jiangxi 333001 (☎798 848 1476 or 139 7983 0451; www.jci.jx.cn). Ask for Shao Changzong. Jingdezhen has been famous for its china since the Ming and Qing dynasties. The institute is happy to welcome foreign students to study ceramics, art, or sculpture with them, both on a temporary basis and for a degree.

Shanghai University of Foreign Trade, 620 Gubei Lu, Shanghai (☎21 6274 8210; www.shift.edu.cn). Tuition for language courses at all levels Y7830 per semester. 1- to 2-week oral expression classes also available.

Shenyang University, International Culture and Education Exchange Center, 21 Wanghua Nan Jie, Dadong district, Shenyang, Liaoning province 110044 (☎24 6226 8729; www.syu.edu.cn). Short-term language courses 1-3 months US$300-600; long-term 5 months ($750) and 10 months ($1000). Annual tuition for a science degree $2000, humanities degree $1800. Download an application online, or call, email, or write.

Wuhan University, College of Foreign Students Education, Wuhan, Hubei province 430072 (☎27 8786 3154; www.whu.edu.cn/en/index.html). Students at Wuhan University's College of Foreign Students Education division can pursue bachelor's degrees in Chinese language and other fields. Masters and doctoral degrees and short-term Chinese language programs also available. Also qualified to administer the HSK test. Fall applications due June 15; spring applications due Dec. 15 of the previous year.

Zhejiang University, 38 Zheda Lu, Hangzhou, Zhejiang province 310027 (☎571 8795 1718 or 8795 1717; www.zju.edu.cn/english). Degree-granting Chinese language and culture programs focus on either Economics and Trade or Tourism. Non-language program offers bachelor's, masters, and doctoral degrees. Multi-level Chinese courses are required for foreign degree-seeking students. Language program also available. Annual tuition US$1800-5800.

LANGUAGE SCHOOLS

Language schools can be independently run international or local organizations or divisions of foreign universities. They sometimes offer college credit. They are a good alternative to university study if you desire a deeper focus on the language or a slightly less rigorous courseload. These programs are also good for younger high-school students who might not feel comfortable with older students in a university program. Full-fledged universities listed above also offer similar language immersion opportunities. Some good programs include:

Beijing Language and Culture University, Admission Office for Foreign Students, 15 Xueyuan Lu, Haidian District, Beijing 100083, China (long-term students ☎86 10 8230 3086, short-term students 8230 3951; www.blcu.edu.cn/english). Offers many options, from a 4-week language program (US$420), to a 3-year certificate program in Chinese calligraphy or Chinese painting ($3000 per year), to a full-fledged undergraduate degree ($2800 per year), to a doctorate in linguistics ($3400 per year).

Beijing University of Aeronautics and Astronautics (BUAA) Study Abroad Program, 241 Cliff St., Cliffside Park, NJ 07010, USA (☎201-313-7132; www.us-china.org). 5-week program offers 3 levels of language classes, electives, field trips, and excursions to Inner Mongolia, Shanghai, Zhengzhou, and Xi'an. All meals, accommodations, airfare from New York, and other transportation costs included. US$3250.

Hong Kong Language Learning Center, Rm. 1602-3, Emperor Group Center, 288 Hennessy Rd., Wan Chai, Hong Kong (☎852 2572 6488; www.hkllc.com). Language school in Hong Kong specializing in Mandarin and Cantonese. Branch at Beijing Language and Culture University. 4-week to full-semester programs. Fee ranges HK$2300-7600. Can also arrange homestay with a Mandarin or Cantonese family for 2-8 weeks (HK$1500 per week, including breakfast and dinner).

Study Abroad International, 3646 W. Brown St., Ste. A, Phoenix, AZ 85051, USA (☎602-942-6734; www.studyabroadinternational.com). Runs a Chinese Mandarin language school in Xiamen, Fujian province. Tuition (Y680-880 per week) gives you the opportunity to live and learn in your teacher's home. Materials, insurance, and weekly excursions to surrounding sights included in the cost. Application fee US$75.

Yuxi Teacher's College, Yuxi, Yunnan province 653100, China (☎86 877 205 9585; www.yuxitc.org). Located in the heart of Yunnan, only 1hr. away from Kunming. Chinese courses and electives cater to all levels and interests. Fall semester Sept.-Jan., spring early Mar.-July. Tuition US$725 per semester. Dorms $40 per month; apartments $105-140 per month. Download an application from the website.

MARTIAL ARTS

Dozens of martial arts films have romanticized China as the land of *gongfu* (known as "kung fu") and *wushu* in the Western imagination. While not everyone you see on the streets can pull out Jackie Chan-style moves, the tradition of *wushu* has a long history in China, beginning with the monks of Shaolin Monastery, who defended a Tang Dynasty emperor from bandits. Besides Shaolin *wushu*, martial arts schools also teach a variety of other styles, from techniques involving swords, spears, or just bare fists, to the more peaceful *qigong*, a deep breathing exercise that channels energy throughout the body, and *taiji quan (tai chi)*, a series of controlled movements often practiced by the elderly in parks. Both beginning students and those with previous knowledge are welcomed. To be fully adept, years of study are needed, but students can train for as little as a few weeks. Below is a selection of martial arts schools in China.

Academy of Wudang Daoism Martial Arts (wǔdàngshān dàojiào wǔ xuéyuàn; 武当山道教武学院 ; ☎86 719 568 9243 or 567 8243; www.wdgf.com). Located on Wudangshan (p. 471), a Daoist mountain famed for its martial arts, the academy currently has around 10 masters and 100 students. Compared to the more spectacular martial arts style taught at Shaolin Monastery, Wudang offers more traditional training, with an emphasis on internal power. Lessons in Wudang boxing, *qigong*, and sword- and fist-fighting. Classes taught throughout the year. Short term options range from 3 days to 1 month (US$120-500); more long term classes 2 months and up (US$500-900 per month; the longer you stay, the lower the monthly fee).

Beijing Zongxun Yiquan Institute, Bldg. 26 6-903, 21 Beixiao Jie, Dongzhimen Nei Dajie, Dongcheng, Beijing 100007, China (☎86 10 6404 0895; www.yiquan.com). *Yiquan* is a style that emphasizes form and strength. Options include an individual training program (elementary US$280, intermediate $840, advanced $490); a full-time professional program (6 months $800); part-time intensive course; and an after-hours course of 3hr. meetings, 3 times per week. ($75 per month).

Shaolin Monastery (☎130 1462 5369), on Songshan, near Zhengzhou, Henan province. Foreigners are welcome to come to Shaolin Monastery (p. 289) to learn the great art of *wushu*. Those who are serious should consider attending for 1-3 years, though less time is also fine. 1 year Y8000, including lessons, food, and lodgings.

Siping City Shaolin Martial Arts Academy, Yehe Ancient Castle, Siping City, Jilin province 136523, China (☎86 434 549 0348; www.shaolins.com). Teaches a wide range of techniques in the traditional Shaolin-style. Monks next to the academy also teach optional classes on Chinese language, Buddhist and Daoist theory, and acupuncture. Accepts students 16 or older to the academy; students under 16 may attend if accompanied by a parent, guardian, or relative. Min. stay 2 months. Application fee US$50, 1-time administration fee $350. Monthly tuition $350, room and board $270. Fee (excluding application cost) for long-term students $4550 for the 1st year, $3990 for the 2nd, $3500 for the 3rd, $3300 for the 4th, and $3000 for the 5th.

WorldLink Education, 1904 3rd Ave., Ste. 735, Seattle, WA 98101, USA (☎800-621-3085; www.worldlinkedu.com). Intensive martial arts immersion programs in Beijing teach a variety of martial arts styles, including broadsword, fist fighting, staff, and spear. Short-term programs run 1-12 weeks; long-term 1 semester or 1 academic year. Program fees for those who live in a double on campus range from US$560 (1 week) to $7210 (1 year); additional costs depend on type of accommodation (student residence, host family, apartment, or hotel). Fee includes visa, accommodations, tuition, after-class tutorials, electives in calligraphy, painting, and *taiji quan* (*tai chi*), language partners with Chinese students, tours, social events and dinners, emergency travel and medical insurance, membership with the SOS Clinic in Beijing, and a trip to Shaolin Monastery for those who study for 8 weeks or more. WorldLink also offers a Chinese language program, which can be combined with the martial arts program.

Wuwei Monastery (wúwéi sì; 无为寺 ; ☎136 0872 4904), Dali, Yunnan province. From Dali (p. 668), take any bus heading north on Dianzang Lu and tell them you're going to Wuwei Monastery. From the base of the hill where the bus stops, a 40min. walk up the road leads to the temple, marked by a stone sign with red Chinese characters on the right of the road. Arranging a minibus from town costs Y10-20. Tucked away in the mountains, Wuwei Monastery is one of Dali's least-known but most unique temples. The monks at the temple teach *gongfu* and their own style of *taiji quan* to those willing to forgo the luxuries of material culture so readily available in Dali. More and more foreigners arrive for lessons every year (at peak times there may be 10 foreigners among the 30 students). No electricity and cold showers ensure that only serious students study here—don't expect to be coddled. Typical days begin with a 5am run to a nearby stream. 5hr. of lessons per day, room, and board are all included for Y300 per week.

Yuedong Shaolin Wushu School, Dongjiao Chang, Meizhou, Guangdong province, China (☎223 3530, ext. 988; www.ydshaolin.com.cn). Though not officially affilated with Shaolin Monastery, this school also teaches the Shaolin style of martial arts. As an alternative to traditional schooling, students ages 7-23 can enroll full-time; *wushu* classes are supplemented by normal coursework (elementary-school-aged students Y1800 per semester, high-school-aged students Y2800). The full program lasts 3 years and teaches the 72 variations of Shaolin *wushu,* among other styles (ages 15 and above; Y2000 per semester). A special program for those who wish to be security guards or simply learn self-defense runs for 1 year (ages 17-25, Y3600). A summer program may be the most affordable for travelers (45 days, ages 7 and older, Y380). Room and board per month Y300, extra Y60 for A/C.

Ziboce Kungfu Box, P.O. Box 87067, Tok Wa Wan Post Office, Hong Kong (☎852 9755 6313; www.geocities.com/zibocecom). Peter (Zi Boce) teaches *taiji quan, qigong, yiquan,* and other martial arts styles to individuals, groups, and corporate organizations. Weekly classes HK$100 per class and $300 per month.

FOR FURTHER READING ON ALTERNATIVES TO TOURISM

Alternatives to the Peace Corps: A Directory of Third World and U.S. Volunteer Opportunities, by Joan Powell. Food First Books, 2000 (US$10).

How to Live Your Dream of Volunteering Overseas, by Collins, DeZerega, and Heckscher. Penguin Books, 2002 (US$17).

International Directory of Voluntary Work, by Whetter and Pybus. Peterson's Guides and Vacation Work, 2000 (US$16).

Invest Yourself: The Catalogue of Volunteer Opportunities, published by the Commission on Voluntary Service and Action (☎718-638-8487).

ALTERNATIVES
TO TOURISM

BEIJING AND THE NORTH COAST

The north coast is in a perpetual race to prove itself as the ideal model for a forward-thinking China in control of the reigns of stability and progress. In fact, with Beijing sitting smack dab in the center, the region could hardly be anything else. After all, China revolves around Beijing, an independent municipality, the nation's capital, and the *crème de la crème*. Not surprisingly, Beijing has drawn its neighboring provinces along with it into Olympic fever, and the whole region seems to be swept up by Olympic preparations. The Games are only fueling what has long been coming—a massive reconstruction of regional infrastructure and renewed ecological awareness.

Of course, despite all that hard work, the region hasn't forgotten how to have fun. After Beijing's bigwigs finish writing the rules, they saunter over to Hebei province for a little relaxation. Indeed, Hebei has had a long tradition as the vacation spot of choice for the busy folk at the nation's center. Emperors lounged in the shade of their personal playground, the Summer Villa in Chengde (p. 184), and government officials continue to cavort and sunbathe in Beidaihe (p. 189). Today, pleasure-seekers from all over the world flock to the legacies of China's long history. The Forbidden City, Summer Palace, Great Wall, and the Temple of Heaven stand as enduring reminders of China's dynastic splendor, while rising skyscrapers point to the nation's future. The north coast isn't just the political center, but also the cultural capital of China, and it has no intention of giving up that title. Or giving up the right to boast about it.

BEIJING

HIGHLIGHTS OF BEIJING

FLY A KITE in **Tian'anmen Square** (p. 142), take a boat onto the lake of **Summer Palace** (p. 152), surround yourself in lotus flowers in **Yuanmingyuan** (p. 153) and climb up the white marble steps and admire the resplendent **Temple of Heaven** (p. 148).

KICK BACK WITH A BEER on the beaches of **Qingdao** (p. 207).

SCRAMBLE UP THE WILD WALL at **Huanghuacheng** (p. 168), the unrestored section of the Great Wall.

BEIJING 北京 ☎ 010

Beijing isn't China's oldest city, nor is it the richest, or even the biggest. Beijing knows itself to be something infinitely more important—the heart, hope, and future of this vast nation. A tiny touch of melodrama aside, everything here happens on a grand scale, with boulevards more sprawling, monuments more magnificent, and energy more intoxicating. The city has taken center stage for more than

700 years, and today it's more than accustomed to the limelight. But Beijing has been the focus of the nation's struggles as well as its greatness. The same streets that witnessed the patriotic protests of May Fourth also saw the turmoil and chaos of "Bloody August" at the height of the Cultural Revolution. From displays of Communist extravaganzas to the lone man silently defying the line of tanks in 1989, Beijing has come a long way.

Today the city is fiercely proud of its illustrious past. Perhaps because Beijing is confident enough to carry off any and all contradictions with a flair and a swagger, the bright red walls and white marble obelisks of imperial palaces and pagodas fit in perfectly with the constantly evolving cityscape of steel and cement. A recent storm of construction has raised up dozens of new buildings and torn down tiny alleys and old neighborhoods, but the core of Beijing refuses to change. Like their city, the people of Beijing are always on the move, slowing down only in the evenings to play chess on street corners and stroll in the city's parks, where children play badminton and old men exercise in the former haunts of emperors. Taxis lurch down Chang'an Jie past eager crowds by day and a swathe of glittering plazas and neon by night. With the Olympics approaching in 2008, Beijing is more conscious than ever of the eyes of the world and as ready as ever to dazzle.

◪ INTERCITY TRANSPORTATION

BY PLANE

Beijing's **Capital Airport** (shǒudū jīchǎng; 首都机场 ; toll free direct dial ☎ 962580) is about 1hr. from the city. A taxi to the city costs at least Y80-100 (tolls Y15). Taxis from the airport are notorious for overcharging and getting "lost"; insist that the ride be metered. Or, take the **CAAC shuttle bus** (1-1½hr., Y16), which runs to and from various points in Beijing. The most reliable places to be picked up are in front of the **Aviation Building**, 15 Xi Chang'an Jie (every 30min. 5am-8pm), or at the west entrance of the **Beijing International Hotel,** near the main train station (every 30min. 6:30am-6:30pm). Travelers flying internationally must pay a departure tax of Y90, domestic flights Y50. For more information on international flights to Beijing, see **Getting to China: By Plane,** p. 34.

TO	PER DAY	PRICE	TO	PER DAY	PRICE
Changsha	2	Y1213	Lanzhou	2-3	Y1345
Chengdu	11	Y1433	Lhasa	1	Y2430
Chongqing	5	Y1563	Nanjing	5-6	Y1017
Dalian	3-5	Y720	Qingdao	7	Y1134
Fuzhou	2	Y834	Shanghai	19	Y1134
Guangzhou	8	Y1700	Shenyang	6-7	Y800
Guilin	1	Y1786	Ürümqi	2	Y2413
Harbin	5	Y963	Wuhan	2	Y1075
Hong Kong	5-6	Y1600-2000	Xiamen	2-3	Y1720
Kunming	3	Y1813	Xi'an	6	Y1050

Domestic Airlines: CAAC headquarters (domestic ☎ 6256 7811, international 6601 6667, 6656 9118, 6656 9166, or toll-free 800 810 1111), Aviation Bldg., 15 Xi Chang'an Jie, 1st fl. Take the bus or subway to Xidan and walk 5min. east; look for the airline symbol (a large red star framed by a pair of blue wings and bordered on the bot-

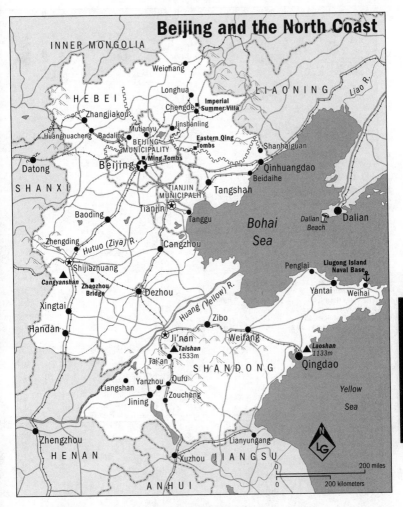

Beijing and the North Coast

INNER MONGOLIA

Weichang

Longhua

H E B E I

Chengde · Imperial Summer Villa

L I A O N I N G

Liao R.

Zhangjiakou

Mutianyu · Jinshanling

Huanghuacheng Badaling · BEIJING MUNICIPALITY · Eastern Qing Tombs

Shanhaiguan

Beijing · Ming Tombs

Qinhuangdao

Beidaihe

Datong

S H A N X I

TIANJIN MUNICIPALITY

Tangshan

Bohai Sea

Dalian L Beach

Dalian

Baoding

Tianjin

Tanggu

Zhengding Hutuo (Ziya) R.

Cangzhou

Shijiazhuang

Penglai

Liugong Island Naval Base ⚓

Cangyanshan

Zhaozhou Bridge

Dezhou

Yantai

Weihai

Xingtai

Huang (Yellow) R.

Zibo

Handan

Ji'nan · Weifang

Taishan 1533m

Laoshan 1133m

Tai'an

S H A N D O N G

Qingdao

Yanzhou · Qufu

Liangshan

Zoucheng

Yellow

Jining

Sea

Zhengzhou

Lianyungang

H E N A N

Xuzhou J I A N G S U

200 miles

A N H U I

0   200 kilometers

N

tom by 4 smaller stars) on the building. Most tickets can be purchased at any counter in the foyer or the right wing. Open daily 8am-9pm. Counters for other domestic airlines are in the left wing. During summer and winter holidays, 40% discounts are possible on domestic flights for exchange students with ID. **Dragon Air,** Henderson Center, 18 Jianguomen Nei Dajie, Tower 1, Ste. 1710-1712 (☎6518 2533).

Asian Airlines: Air Macau, SCITECH Tower Place, 22 Jianguomen Wai Dajie, Ste. 807 (☎6515 8988 or 6515 9398). **All Nippon Airways,** Fortune Bldg., 5 Dong Sanhuan Bei Lu, 2nd fl. (☎6590 9191). **Asiana Airlines,** Lufthansa Center, Kempinski Hotel, 50 Liangmaqiao Lu, Ste. W102 (☎6468 4000). **Japan Airlines,** Changfugong Office Bldg., Hotel New Otari, 26 Jianguomen Wai Dajie, 1st fl. (☎6513 0888, international 800 810 5553). **Malaysian Airlines,** China World Trade Center, 1 Jianguomen Wai Dajie, Tower 2, Ste. 1005 (☎6505 2681 or 6505 2683). **MIAT Mongolian Airlines,** China

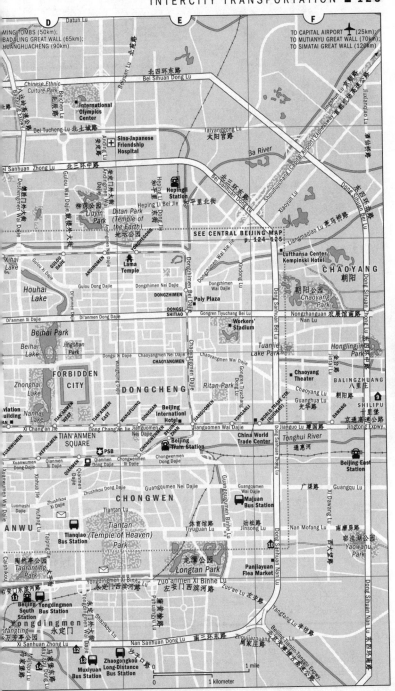

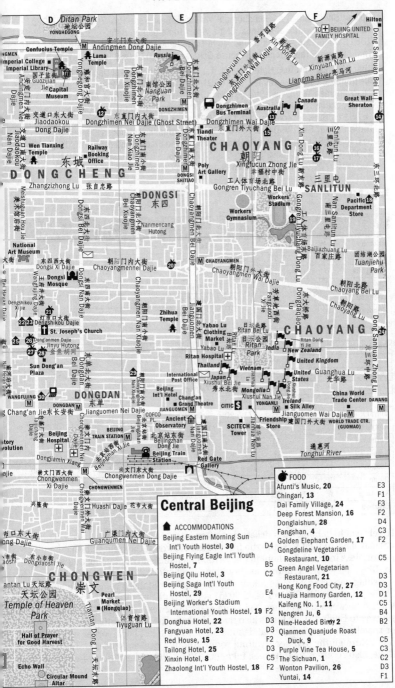

BEIJING

Central Beijing

🏠 **ACCOMMODATIONS**

Beijing Eastern Morning Sun Int'l Youth Hostel, **30**	D4
Beijing Flying Eagle Int'l Youth Hostel, **7**	B5
Beijing Qilu Hotel, **3**	C2
Beijing Saga Int'l Youth Hostel, **29**	E4
Beijing Worker's Stadium International Youth Hostel, **19**	F2
Donghua Hotel, **22**	D3
Fangyuan Hotel, **23**	D3
Red House, **15**	F2
Tailong Hotel, **25**	D3
Xinxin Hotel, **8**	C5
Zhaolong Int'l Youth Hostel, **18**	F2

🍎 **FOOD**

Afunti's Music, **20**	E3
Chingari, **13**	F1
Dai Family Village, **24**	F3
Deep Forest Mansion, **16**	F2
Donglaishun, **28**	D4
Fangshan, **4**	C3
Golden Elephant Garden, **17**	F2
Gongdeline Vegetarian Restaurant, **10**	C5
Green Angel Vegetarian Restaurant, **21**	D3
Hong Kong Food City, **27**	D3
Huajia Harmony Garden, **12**	D1
Kaifeng No. 1, **11**	C5
Nengren Ju, **6**	B4
Nine-Headed Bird, **2**	B2
Qianmen Quanjude Roast Duck, **9**	C5
Purple Vine Tea House, **5**	C3
The Sichuan, **1**	C2
Wonton Pavilion, **26**	D3
Yuntai, **14**	F1

Golden Bridge Bldg., A1 Jianguomen Wai Dajie, East Gate, Rm. 705 (☎6507 9297). **Pakistan International Airlines,** China World Trade Center, Bldg. 1, Ste. 617 (☎6505 1681). **Singapore Airlines,** China World Trade Center, Tower 2, 8th fl. (☎6505 2233). **Thai Airways International,** Lufthansa Center, Ste. S102B (☎6460 8899).

Other Airlines: Aeroflot, Hotel Jinglun, 1st fl., 3 Jianguomen Wai Dajie (☎6500 2412). **Air Canada,** Lufthansa Center, Ste. C201 (☎6468 2001). **Air France,** Fenglian Plaza, Chaoyangmen Wai Dajie, Ste. 515 (☎4008 808 808). **Austrian Airlines,** Lufthansa Center, Ste. S103 (☎6462 2164). **British Airways,** SCITECH Tower Place, Ste. 210 (☎8511 6699, reservations 8511 5599). **KLM Royal Dutch Airlines,** China World Trade Center, Ste. W501 (☎6505 3505). **Lufthansa,** Lufthansa Center, Ste. S101 (☎6465 4488). **Northwest Airlines,** China World Trade Center, Ste. W501 (☎6505 3505). **Qantas,** Lufthansa Center, Ste. S120 (☎6467 3337). **Swissair,** SCITECH, Ste. 608 (☎6512 3555). **United Airlines,** Lufthansa Center, 1st fl. (☎6463 1111).

BY TRAIN

TO	站	PER DAY	HR.	PRICE (Y)
Baotou	B, W	3	14	113, 209
Changchun	B	2	10	130, 239
Changsha	W	1	14	191, 345
Chengde	B	2	5	20-41
Chengdu	W	2	28	231, 418
Chongqing	W	2	30	238, 430
Dalian	B	2	10	140, 257
Dandong	B	2	15	143, 263
Datong	W	3	8-9	46, 94
Fuzhou	B	1	35	253, 458
Guangzhou	W	2	24	253, 458
Guilin	W	1	28	238, 430
Guiyang	W	1	31	271, 490
Hangzhou	B	2	12	200, 363
Harbin	B	2	11	158, 290
Hefei	B	2	8	143, 263
Hohhot	W	1	12	92, 170
Ji'nan	B	1	6	73, 137
Kunming	W	1	40	320, 578
Lanzhou	W	1	21	215, 390

TO	站	PER DAY	HR.	PRICE (Y)
Luoyang	W	1	12	106, 197
Manzhouli	B	1	31	197, 380
Nanchang	W	3	16	175, 319
Nanjing	B	3	10	150, 274
Qingdao	B	2	10	116, 215
Shanghai	B	8	10	88-179, 327, 499
Shenyang	B	2	10	191
Shenzhen	W	2	30	257, 467
Shijiazhuang	W	3	4	50
Suzhou	B	2	14	170, 309
Taiyuan	B, W	3	8	79, 179
Tianjin	B	13	1½	11-35
Ürümqi	W	1	60	363, 652
Wuhan	W	6	13	154, 281
Xiamen	W	1	34	253, 458
Xi'an	W	4	29	150, 274
Xining	W	1	33	238, 430
Yantai	B	1	14	126, 231
Yinchuan	W	1	21	143, 262
Zhengzhou	W	3	7-11	94, 175

Hotels can help book train **tickets,** but often charge a Y30-50 commission. Travelers may have to fight to get to the front of the crowds at the train station counters, but ruthless individuals shouldn't have too much difficulty obtaining a ticket. **CITS** (p. 130) handles reservations and booking for all international train travel.

Beijing has several train stations. The **Beijing Train Station** (běijīng huǒchē zhàn; 北京火车站; ☎6512 8931 or 6232 0025) is just southeast of the city center, sandwiched between Jianguomen Nei Dajie and Chongwenmen Dong Dajie. Take the subway to Beijing Zhan; buses also make the trip. The **booking office** for foreigners or travelers with international destinations is in the left back corner on the first floor, through the soft seat waiting room. Another **booking office,** 88 Dongsi Bei Dajie, also reserves boat tickets; take bus #13 to Chuanban Hutong. (☎6403 0473 or 6405 3642. Open daily 8am-5pm.) International trains include the Trans-Mongolian (p. 39) to **Moscow** (6 days, W and Sa, Y2054-3283) and trains to **Ulaan Bataar, Mongolia** (30hr., Tu and F, Y1440-3031).

Beijing West Train Station (běijīng xī zhàn; 北京西站 ; ☎6321 6253) is on Lianhuachi Dong Lu near Lianhuachi Park (莲花池公园), at the southern end of Yangfangdian Lu, accessible by buses #5, 48, 52, 320, and 845. Take the subway to the Military Museum (jūn bó; 军博) and walk down Yangfangdian Lu; take a Y5-10 pedicab to the station; or take a minibus from Beijing Train Station. Destinations include **Kowloon, Hong Kong** (28hr., every other day 12:47pm, Y253-705) and **Hanoi, Vietnam** (3 days, M and F 8pm) via **Nanning**. The **foreigners' ticket office** is on the second floor, immediately to the left of the escalators.

Beijing South Station (běijīng nán zhàn; 北京南站 ; ☎6303 0031), off Yong'anmen Dong Binhe Lu, is accessible by buses #20 and 102. Trains to **Shidu** leave from here via Laiyuan (5½hr., 5:40pm) and Taiyuan (15hr., 6:37am). The station serves a few other destinations, including Shijiazhuang (3hr.; midnight, 1:55am, 1:27pm), and Tianjin (1½hr., 5:53am). **Beijing North Station** (běijīng běi zhàn; 北京北站 ; ☎9510 5105) is on the northwest corner of Erhuan Lu; take the subway to Xizhimen.

The table on p. 126 provides the departure station, number of direct trains per day, duration of travel (in hours), and the price (in *yuán*) for major Chinese cities serviced by trains from Beijing Train Station **(B)** and West Station **(W)**. Prices listed are for hard seat and hard sleeper; short routes may only have hard seats available. Travel times vary. Faster trains and guaranteed seating are more expensive.

BY BUS

Only two of Beijing's bus stations are major long-distance hubs, though local bus stations, such as Tianqiao, also send buses to Hubei province. The **Xizhimen Long-Distance Bus Station** (xīzhìmén chángtú qìchē zhàn; 西直门长途汽车站 ; ☎6217 6075) is a long way from the Xizhimen subway stop; either walk straight and take the first left, or take bus #16 one stop. Buses go to Chengde (4hr., every 20-30min. 6am-6pm); Dalian (15-17hr., daily); Shenyang (9hr., 3 per day). The **Zhaogongkou Long-Distance Bus Station** (zhàogōngkǒu chángtú qìchē zhàn; 赵公口长途汽车站 ; ☎6722 9491) is off Nan Sanhuan Lu, in Fengtai district. Take the subway to Qianmen and hop on bus #17. Buses go to Qingdao (16hr.; 5, 7pm; Y159) and Tianjin (1½hr., every 15min., Y31).

✦ ORIENTATION

Beijing is huge. Sprawling. Immense. Really, really big. But for all its size, Beijing is surprisingly symmetrical, with **five ring roads** radiating out from the city's geographic center of Tian'anmen Square and the Forbidden City. Knowing these ring roads is integral to navigating Beijing—almost everything is oriented around them. The first ring road, around the Forbidden City, does not exist for all practical purposes. The second ring road, **Erhuan** (二环), is more often called by its various component names, which change many times according to its gates as you follow the loop. The third ring road goes by **Sanhuan** (三环), the fourth by **Sihuan** (四环).

Most other roads are named in relation to landmarks and former city gates; *běi* (north), *nán* (south), *xī* (west), *dōng* (east), *nèi* (inner), *wài* (outer), *qián* (front), and *hòu* (back) are added to names to indicate their relative locations. In general, address numbers increase as you go west and south; even numbers are on east and north sides, odd on west and south.

The most important thoroughfare is **Chang'an Jie** (长安街), which bisects the city horizontally, running east-west between the Forbidden City and Tian'anmen Square. It changes names continually: moving from east to west, it becomes Jianguo Lu (建国路), Jianguomen Wai Dajie, Jianguomen Nei Dajie, Dong Chang'an Jie, Xi Chang'an Jie, Fuxingmen Nei Dajie, Fuxingmen Wai Dajie, and finally Fuxing Lu (复兴路). Driving down its wide length is an eye-opening experience, especially at night, when skyscrapers and towers funded by big money from Hong Kong all light up in glittery splendor.

Even though the gates themselves no longer exist, Beijing's neighborhoods and addresses are still determined in relation to their nearest city gate, or *mén* (门). Some of the most important gates on the second ring road are: **Qianmen** (前门), directly south of Tian'anmen, anchored by its busy traffic circle; **Xuanwumen** (宣武门); **Fuxingmen** (复兴门), on the west, at the intersection with Fuxing Lu/Fuxingmen Wai Dajie; **Xizhimen** (西直门), where the second ring road turns to form the north edge; **Dongzhimen** (东直门), directly opposite Xizhimen, where the second ring road turns to form the east edge; **Chaoyangmen** (朝阳门), the western border of Sanlitun; and **Jianguomen** (建国门), at the intersection with Jianguo Lu/Jianguomen Wai Dajie.

The metropolitan crux centers around the **Forbidden City** and **Tian'anmen Square**, on either side of Chang'an Dajie. From the south side of the square, at the traffic circle, **Qianmen Dajie** (前门大街) runs south through the crowded business district and markets of **Dazhalan** (大栅栏) to Tiantan Park before connecting travelers to budget hotels in the southern district of **Fengtai** (丰台). Directly east of the Forbidden City, busy **Wangfujing** (王府井) and **Dongdan** (东单) are full of the latest fashions and prime shopping; their counterpart, **Xidan** (西单), lies west of the Forbidden City and Beihai Park. North of these humming districts, neighborhoods of gray-bricked *hútòng* and courtyards make up the best-preserved example of "Old Beijing," near **Houhai** (后海), bounded in by Erhuan.

North of the Forbidden City and parallel to Chang'an Dajie, Chaoyangmen Dajie and **Gongren Tiyuchang Bei Lu** (工人体育场北路 ; say **"Gongti Bei Lu"** to sound like a local), help define the embassy and expat districts of Chaoyang and **Sanlitun** (三里屯), east between the second and third ring roads. Beijing and Qinghua Universities, the **Summer Palace,** and the **Old Summer Palace** form a cluster in the far northwest, just beyond the fourth ring road in the northern district of **Haidian** (海淀).

⊫ LOCAL TRANSPORTATION

BY BUS

The Beijing bus system (☎ 6396 0088, toll-free 96166; www.bjbus.com) can be mystifying, but using the crowded buses, especially in combination with the subway, is a cheap and convenient way to get around. Most buses run from 5am to 10 or 11pm. Fare is generally Y1 regardless of destination; buses with A/C cost Y2. Bus stop signs list the name of the stop in characters and pinyin on the front; the back of the sign lists out the complete route in characters, with the name of each stop running vertically down. Knowing the characters for your destination is helpful for finding the right bus when reading the signs. If all else fails, ask the ticket taker to tell you when you arrive at your stop. The scramble for seats at each stop can prevent disembarking, so hover by the door before you reach your stop.

There is a method to the madness of Beijing's more than 400 **bus routes.** As a general rule, buses #1-124 navigate the city center while #300-500s ply Beijing's periphery, including the Summer Palace; #600s and 700s traverse even more far-flung destinations, connecting the city center with such sights as the Fragrant Hill Park. Bus #200s are late-night buses; #800s are air-conditioned. The #900s (☎ 6336 0283) head to the most distant outskirts and daytrip destinations, leaving from Dongzhimen, Deshengmen, and Tianqiao (fare Y5-10). The table below lists some main bus routes and the areas they serve.

BUS #	ROUTE DESCRIPTION	BUS #	ROUTE DESCRIPTION
1, 4, 52, 802	Chang'an Jie (Xidan-Tian'anmen-Dongdan-Beijing Main-Jianguomen)	5	South-North: Qianmen-Beihai-Gulou-Di'anmen-Deshengmen
14	Jiaomen Nan Zhan-Yangqiao-Taiping Jie-Hepingmen-Houhai	20	Beijing Main-Tian'anmen-Qianmen-Tiantan-Beijing South Station
21	Beijing West-Fuchengmen-Xizhimen	24	Beijing Main-Dongdan-Chaoyang-Dongzhimen
44, 800	Loop line subway (follows 2nd ring)	66	Beijing West-Yangqiao-Qianmen
101, 109	Chaoyang/Sanlitun-Forbidden City-Beihai-Fuchengmen	103	Beijing Main-Wangfujing-Forbidden City-Beihai-Zoo
120	Yongdingmen-Tiantan-Qianmen-Beijing Main-Jianguomen-Chaoyang	300	Sanhuan Lu-Liangmaqiao-Sanlitun
331	Xinjiekou-Yuanmingyuan-Summer Palace-Fragrant HIlls	808	Beijing Main-Qianmen-Xidan-Zoo-Beijing University-Summer Palace

Beijing also has a number of **tourist bus lines** (☎8729 9990) serving major tourist destinations. These are numbered 1-18 and are distinguished from the regular buses with the prefix " 游 " (yóu; "travel"). A number of buses depart when full in the early morning and return to Beijing around 4-5pm; you must return with the bus on which you arrived. Tourist buses #1-4 run daily to **Badaling Great Wall** and the **Ming Tombs** (round-trip Y50); #1 is the most convenient, departing 6-10am from the northeast corner of Qianmen; 2 leaves 6-10am from Beijing Train Station, Tian'anmen, and Dongzhimen; 4 leaves 6-10am from the Beijing Zoo and the Summer Palace. Tourist buses #6-18 depart from Qianmen and the Xuanwumen church 6:30-8am April 5-October 15 on weekends and holidays; 6 runs to **Mutianyu Great Wall** (round-trip Y50); 7 runs to **Tanzhe** and **Jietai Temples** (Y60); 10 runs to **Shidu**; and 12 runs to **Simatai Great Wall** (Y60).

BY SUBWAY

Despite a relatively limited reach, Beijing's subway is a clean and reliable way to escape the traffic and construction. Trains run frequently 5am-11pm and cost Y3 regardless of destination. The system currently has three intersecting lines. **Line #1** (red) runs directly under Fuxingmen Dajie/Chang'an Dajie/Jianguomen Dajie, all the way from Pingguoyuan to Sihui East; **Loop Line** (#2 or blue) cruises beneath the old city wall, circumnavigating the center of Beijing and stopping at all the main gates; and **Line #13** makes an extensive loop north to Beijing's newly developed northern suburban districts, going up from **Xizhimen** to Huilongguan and Lishuiqiao in Changping and back down to **Dongzhimen.** To transfer between lines, follow the English signs and rushing crowds at the **Fuxingmen** or **Jianguomen** stops (to change from #1 to 2 and vice versa), and at the **Xizhimen** or **Dongzhimen** stops (to transfer from line #2 to 13). Signs are in both characters and pinyin, and stops are announced in Chinese and English. Construction work is ongoing on new subway lines, set to open before the 2008 Beijing Olympics.

BY TAXI

Base fare is Y10 (11pm-5am Y11) and each additional km is Y1.2-2. Cheaper taxis are smaller and do not have A/C; pricier ones are slightly nicer, larger, and have A/C. Always insist that drivers use the meter. Almost no cabbies speak English, and few read pinyin. Most taxi drivers are familiar with Beijing's districts (i.e., Chaoyang or Haidian), but may not know specific locations (this or that restaurant). Almost all drivers carry cell phones, so bring the telephone number of your destination and have them call to get good directions. Mention nearby landmarks or the actual address, and you're good to go. If you're going a considerable distance

BEIJING

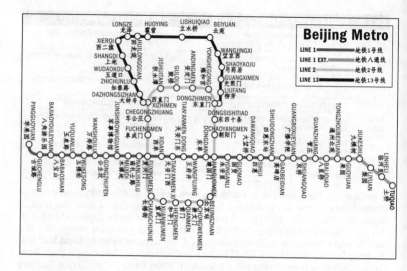

across the city, ask your cabbie to take the ring roads, which are the quickest and fastest ways to get around. You may want to keep your receipt, in case you forget your belongings in the taxi. Call **Beijing Taxi** (☎6837 3399) or **Beijing Tourism Taxi** (☎6832 2561) for pickup. For **taxi complaints,** call ☎6835 1150.

BY BIKE

As millions of locals know, a bike is a handy way to get around Beijing. Be warned, however, that there are no road rules here—motorists, cyclists, and pedestrians cross, weave, dash, cut, and crash at their own risk. Bike lanes are nominally on the side of the street closest to the curb, but few follow this rule. Be especially careful crossing the streets—weaving bikes are far less noticeable than oncoming cars. Many hotels and hostels that rent bikes often lend out only the dregs; ensure that the bicycle is rideable before paying. Also be aware that bike theft is common in Beijing. Hotels have been known to lend out a bicycle and a lock, only to send someone with another set of keys to trail the hapless biker and make off with the bike, so use a different lock if you have one. A rusty, grizzled bike seemingly on the verge of disintegration attracts wandering hands much less than a shiny new model. Bike parking generally costs Y0.2.

⁊ PRACTICAL INFORMATION

TOURIST AND FINANCIAL SERVICES

Tourist Offices: The vast majority of accommodations in Beijing have on-site travel agencies or arrange tours to popular sights. They can also book air and train tickets. There is a **tourist information service** in Beijing (☎6513 0828), but no tourism bureau. The **Beijing Tourism Administration,** Tourism Bldg., 28 Jianguomen Wai Dajie (☎6515 8252), handles tourist complaints and large groups.

CITS: Beijing International Hotel, 9 Jianguomen Nei Dajie, west lobby. Airline office (☎6512 1368 or 6512 0507). International train office (☎6512 0507; fax 6512 0503). Commission Y50. Both open M-F 8:30am-noon and 1-5pm, Sa 9am-noon and 1:30-4pm. A **branch** in the World Trade

Tower #2, 1 Jianguomen Wai Dajie, Rm. 301 (☎6505 3775 or 6505 3776; fax 6505 3105) books airline tickets. Open M-F 9am-noon and 1-5:30pm, Sa 9am-noon. A 3rd **branch** (☎6606 2336 or 6601 1122), next to the Parkson at Fuxingmen. Open M-F 9am-noon and 1-5:30pm.

CYTS, 17F, Avic Tower, 2 Dong Sanhuan Nan Lu, at Guomao Qiao, Chaoyang (☎6567 9900; fax 6568 0990). Headquarters.

Hualong International Travel Service (huálóng guójì lǚxíng shè; 华龙国际旅行社), Beijing International Hotel, 9 Jianguomen Nei Dajie, 1st fl. (☎6522 9444, 6512 1486, or 6512 1487; beijinghualong@163.com), at what looks like a reception desk. Open daily 7:30am-10pm.

Jinghua Hotel (jīnghuá fàndiàn; 京华饭店), Xiluoyuan Nanli, Yongdingmen Wai (☎6722 2211, ext. 3359; fax 6721 6383), off Nan Sanhuan Lu. Books domestic train (Y50 commission) and plane tickets. Open daily 8am-midnight.

Beijing Hotel Travel Service (běijīng fàndiàn lǚyóu bù; 北京饭店旅游部), Beijing Hotel, 33 Dong Chang'an Jie (☎6523 2370; fax 6523 2372). Open daily 8am-10pm.

Embassies: Sanlitun and Jianguomen Wai, near the Silk Market, are the main embassy compounds. See **Essentials: Consular Services in China** (p. 10) for complete listings.

Banks: Bank of China, 410 Fuchengmen Nei Dajie, 2nd fl., Counter #1 or 2 (☎6601 6688). Open M-F 9am-noon and 1-5pm. Other branches: **Capital Airport; Asia-Pacific Bldg.,** 8 Yabao Lu, Chaoyang; **Lufthansa Center,** 50 Liangmaqiao Lu, 1st fl.; **China World Trade Tower,** 1 Jianguomen Wai Dajie, Ste. L204; **1 Dong Chang'an Jie** at Wangfujing (☎8518 1155); **Chang'an Building,** 7 Jianguomen Nei Dajie; **19 Dong'anmen Dajie** near Wangfujing; **CITIC Industrial Bank** (zhōngxìn shíyè yínháng; 中信实业银行), CITIC Bldg., 19 Jianguomen Wai Dajie, Chaoyang; the **Friendship Store** (yǒuyí shāngdiàn; 友谊商店), 17 Jianguomen Wai Dajie. All exchange currency and traveler's checks. Most branches open M-F 9am-5pm.

ATM: There are over 250 ATMs in Beijing, with more sprouting up. Nearly all accept **AmEx, Cirrus, MC, Plus,** and **V.** Locations include: **Bank of China,** 8 Yabao Lu, Chaoyang; 138 Wangfujing Dajie, in the Sun Dong An Plaza; 1 Dong Chang'an Jie, at Wangfujing; **Palace Hotel,** 8 Jinyu Hutong, Dongdan Bei Dajie; **Landmark Towers,** 8 Dong Sanhuan Bei Lu, Chaoyang; **Central Garden Hotel,** 18 Gaoliangqiao Lu, Haidian; **Capital Airport; SCITECH Shopping Center,** 22 Jianguomen Wai Dajie; **China World Hotel,** 1 Jianguomen Wai Dajie, basement entrance.

American Express: China World Trade Center, 1 Jianguomen Wai Dajie, Ste. 2101 (☎6505 2888), deals with lost American Express credit cards. For lost checks, first call the office in Sydney, Australia (toll free ☎ 1080 0610 0277).

LOCAL SERVICES

Bookstores: The following bookstores have a wide selection of English-Chinese dictionaries and other foreign literature. **Wangfujing Xinhua Bookstore,** 218 Wangfujing Dajie (☎6525 2592), left of the escalators. Beijing's largest and most impressive bookstore, with a fantastic selection of English-language classics, Chinese literature, and popular novels from *Harry Potter* to *The Hitchhiker's Guide to the Galaxy.* On the 1st fl., on the right, stacks of Beijing guidebooks await the weary and disoriented. English-speaking staff. Open daily 9am-9:30pm. **Friendship Store** (yǒuyí shāngdiàn; 友谊商店), 17 Jianguomen Wai Dajie, 1st fl., has a great bookstore and sells magazines.

Library: National Library (guójiā túshū guǎn; 国家图书馆), 39 Baishiqiao Lu (☎8854 4114), Haidian, near the zoo, next to Purple Bamboo Park. Take bus #332 or other buses to Purple Bamboo. Large foreign-language section. Open daily 9am-5pm.

Weather Conditions: ☎ 121 in Chinese and English. Y0.3 per min.

EMERGENCY AND COMMUNICATIONS

PSB: 9 Qianmen Dong Dajie (☎6524 2063, foreigners' section 8401 5292, visa extensions 6532 3861).

Medical Services: All have English-speaking staff members. **Beijing International SOS Clinic** (formerly **Asia Emergency Assistance International**), BITIC Leasing Center, 1 Bei Lu, Xingfu Sancun, Bldg. C, Sanlitun (24hr. ☎6462 9100, clinic 6462 9112). The state-of-the-art **Sino-Japanese Friendship Hospital** (zhōngrì yǒuhǎo yīyuàn; 中日友好 医院 ; ☎6422 1122, foreigners ext. 5121), on Heping Jie Bei Kou, Chaoyang, just north of Sanhuan Lu, is renowned for treating foreign dignitaries. Accessible by bus #119 from Andingmen or 62 from Yonghegong. **Beijing United Family Hospital** (běijīng hémù fù'ér yīyuàn; 北京和睦妇儿医院), 2 Jiangtai Lu, Chaoyang (24hr. ☎6433 3960), 5min. east of the Holiday Inn Lido, specializes in family medicine.

Internet Access: Qianyi Internet Cafe (qiányì wǎngluò kāfeīwū; 前艺网络咖啡屋 ; ☎6705 1722), in the Station Shopping Mall (lǎochēzhàn shāngchéng; 老车站商城), 3rd fl., opposite the southeast corner of Tian'anmen Square. The climb up is worth it: artistic layout, lots of breathing space, and computers equipped with printers and CD drives. Y10 per 30min. Open daily 9am-midnight. **Science City Plaza Internet Cafe** (kēchéng dàshà wǎngbā; 科城厦网吧), 19-2 Haidian Lu, 2nd fl. above the convenience store. Y2 per hr. Open 8am-midnight. **Century Internet Garden** (shìjì jiāshuò wǎngbā; 世纪嘉硕网苑), 218-3 Wangfujing Dajie (☎8512 0907), right behind the Wangfujing Xinhua Bookstore. Sleek, shiny, and snazzy, but only Y3 per hr. Y10 deposit. Open daily 8am-midnight. **Zhaolong International Youth Hostel** (see **Accommodations,** p. 134) has a pair of networked computers, but it'll cost you. Y5 per 30min., Y5 min. Open to public, but there's often a line. Open daily 7am-midnight.

Post and Telecommunications: International Post Office (guójì yóujú; 国际邮局 ; ☎6512 8120), on the west side of Jianguomen Bei Dajie. EMS, IDD service, and Poste Restante. Open daily 8am-6:30pm. **Post and Telecommunications Office of the New Century** (☎6519 6630), on Jianguomen Nei Dajie, west of the Henderson Center, at Beijing Zhankou bus stop. EMS, IDD service, and Poste Restante. Open daily 8am-7pm. A **China Post** at 8-18 Dongdan Santiao, next to the Beijing Eastern Morning Sun Hostel. Open daily 8am-7pm.

Western Union: International Post Office, in the Postal Savings Money Order Hall; China Post, 7 Qianmen Dong Dajie. Post and Telecommunications Office of the New Century (see above).

Private Couriers: DHL Worldwide Express, China World Trade Center, Ste. 217, Sinotrans Express Center (☎6505 2173, ext. 8103, or 6466 2211). Supposedly open daily 8am-9pm, but certain shipping services stop before 5pm. **UPS,** Sinotrans International Express Co., Ltd. (liánhé bāoguǒ yùnshū; 联合包裹运输), Shouqi Bldg., 3 Zaoying Lu, 3rd fl., Maizidian, Chaoyang (☎6530 2233 or 6530 1234). Open M-F 8:30am-5:30pm, Sa 8:30am-noon. Another location at the Scitech Tower, 22 Jianguomen Wai Dajie, 1st fl. (☎6512 2288). **Federal Express** (liánbāng kuàidì; 联邦快递), Gaolan Plaza, 32 Liangmaqiao, 3rd fl., Chaoyang (☎6468 5566).

⚑ ACCOMMODATIONS

In Beijing, "budget" usually means "bad location"—most cheap accommodations cluster around the city's southern periphery. University hotels are often far from the city center, may have annoying curfews, and need to be reserved well ahead of time. Many hotels that used to have relatively cheaper prices have been renovated, and managers have gladly increased prices to accommodate the ever-growing waves of foreign tourists.

The exceptions to the price binge are the **international youth hostels,** many of which have just opened recently. Teeming with backpackers, these outposts provide dirt-cheap dorms, bike rental, ticket and tour booking, Internet access, and plenty of fellow foreigners. In general, conditions are clean and comfortable, making these hostels the best deals in the capital city. **Beijing Saga International Youth Hostel, the Gongti International Youth Hostel,** and **Zhaolong International Youth Hostel** are shining examples of the growing merger of budget and convenience.

During the summer, cheap rooms are snatched up quickly, and hotels generally don't accept reservations. Your best bet is to suck it up, take a more expensive room for one night, and ask them to hold a cheaper room for you when one becomes available (and it inevitably will) in the morning. Those willing to splurge can find four- and five-star hotels everywhere. Most hotels have on-site restaurants and currency exchange, but only hotels with more stars to their name accept foreign credit cards (V and MC, but usually not AmEx).

ACCOMMODATIONS BY PRICE

CC City Center **CW** Chongwen **CY** Chaoyang **FT** Fengtai **HD** Haidian **XC** Xicheng **XW** Xuanwu

UNDER Y80 (❶)		**Y181-Y250 (❸)**	
Beijing Medical School Doctorate Hotel (137)	HD	Fangyuan Hotel (134)	CC
Eastern Morning Sun Hostel (133)	CC	Lihua Hotel (136)	FT
Flying Eagle Hostel (HI) (135)	XW	Sea Star Hotel (136)	FT
🏠 Jinghua Youth Hostel (135)	FT	Tailong Hotel (134)	CC
Qiaoyuan Hotel (136)	FT		
🏠 Saga Hostel (HI) (133)	CC	**Y251-Y350 (❹)**	
🏠 Workers' Stadium Hostel (134)	CY	Beijing Qilu Hotel (134)	CC
Xinxin Hotel (135)	XW	Donghua Hotel (134)	CC
Zhaolong Hostel (HI) (134)	CY	Evergreen Hotel (137)	XC
		Leyou Hotel (135)	CW
Y81-Y180 (❷)		Red House (135)	CY
Beijing Institute of Education (136)	XC	Zhongguancun Hotel (137)	HD
🏠 Beijing Univ. Shaoyuan Hotel (137)	HD		
Furong Hotel (135)	CY		

CITY CENTER

North of Chang'an Jie, clustered around the Forbidden City, and all conveniently inside the second ring road (Erhuan), these hotels are within easy reach of many sights, bus and subway stops, restaurants, and shopping—everything a traveler could want. They have the prices to match: only a few are affordable.

🏠 **Beijing Saga International Youth Hostel (HI)** (běijīng shíjiā guójì qīngnián lǚshè; 国际 实佳青年旅舍), 9 Shijia Hutong, Dongcheng (☎6527 2773; fax 6524 9098), behind the Beijing International Hotel. Walk down Chaoyangmen Nan Xiaojie from the Beijing International Hotel and turn left onto Shijia; English sign directs you. Accessible by bus (#1, 4, 20, 808) or subway to Beijing Zhan; airport shuttles drop off and pick up at the hotel. Extremely neat rooms, wooden bunk beds, and A/C for unbeatable prices. Table football, energetic lounge, and chatty backpackers keep the place buzzing. Friendly, English-speaking staff. Bike rental (Y10 for 4hr., Y20 per day; deposit Y300), Internet (Y4 for 30min., Y10 per hr.), and laundry facilities (Y10). Tours start at Y180. Be sure to book 10 days ahead in the summer, 7 days in winter. 8-bed dorms Y60, members Y50; 4- and 5-bed Y80/Y70; doubles Y200/Y180; triples Y230/Y210. ❶

Beijing Eastern Morning Sun International Youth Hostel (HI) (běijīng dōngfāng chén-guāng qīngnián lǚshè; 北京东方晨光青年旅舍), Dongdan Santiao 8-16, East Bldg., Dongfang Plaza (☎6528 4347; fax 6528 4350). In the midst of all the action at Wang-fujing Dajie, 10min. walk from Forbidden City and Tian'anmen Square. Cramped conditions, but price and location make up for it. Hard to make reservations, so it's best to appear in person to check for availability. A/C. 24hr. hot water. 24hr. reception. Checkout 2pm. Singles Y80; doubles Y120-140; triples Y150; quints Y300. ❶

Tailong Hotel (tàilóng bīnguǎn; 泰龙宾馆), 51 Dong'anmen Dajie (☎6525 7908), right behind the Donghuamen nightmarket. Excellent location and recently renovated rooms, complete with spruced up furnishings and unsoiled carpets. Clean baths with standing showers have great water pressure. Informative and accommodating hotel staff fret over all your wants. Doubles Y220; triples Y360. Discounts can drop prices down to Y160 and Y280, respectively. ❸

Beijing Qilu Hotel (qílǔ fàndiàn; 齐鲁饭店), 103 Di'anmen Xi Dajie (☎6618 0966; www.qiluhotel.com), near Houhai Lake, at the north gate of Beihai Park. Accessible by buses #13 to Beihai Beimen, and 107, 111, or 118 to Dongguanfang; look for the huge billboard. Imitation antique furniture in grainy colors, incense-scented hallways, white sheets, and free fruit bowls. Great location within walking distance of Beihai Park and all the Andingmen sights. Breakfast included. 24hr. hot water. Reservations recommended. Standard doubles Y270; triples Y298-318. Ask for discounts. ❹

Fangyuan Hotel (fāngyuán bīnguǎn; 芳园宾馆), 36 Dengshikou Xi Jie (☎6525 6331; fangyuan_hotel@sohu.net). Walk north on Wangfujing Dajie past the Starbucks; it's on the 1st street on the left. Frenzy of foreign tourists crowding the lobby and hallways. Claustrophobic rooms need brighter lights. Breakfast included. Laundry and Internet access (Y10 per hr., 9:30am-10pm). Bike rental Y20 per day; deposit Y100. Travel services on 1st fl. Reserve in advance in the summer. Deposit Y5. Doubles Y238-298. Discounts up to 20% off. ❸

Donghua Hotel (dōnghuá fàndiàn; 东华饭店), 32 Dengshikou Xi Jie (☎6525 7531 or 6525 7532), near Fangyuan Hotel. Unbeatable location. Renovations in 2003 replaced the squeaky old furnishings with classical Chinese creations of cherry wood and floral carvings. Rooms are small but clean. Breakfast included. Internet, TV, A/C, 24hr. hot water, standing showers. Check-out 2pm. Reservations highly recommended, especially for fought-over singles. Singles Y260; doubles Y388. Discounts up to 20% off. ❹

CHAOYANG (SANLITUN)

Scattered throughout the fun-loving expat district of Chaoyang, east of the city center and the second ring road, these hotels are the perfect place to stay if you're planning a late night out in Sanlitun. Their location near many foreigner-oriented plazas and services doesn't hurt either.

Beijing Workers' Stadium International Youth Hostel (HI) (běijīng gōngtǐ guójì qīngnián lǚshè; 北京工体国际青年旅舍), 9 Tai (台 ; Platform), Workers' Stadium, East Gate, Chaoyang (☎6552 4800; gongti@hotmail.com). Take buses #110, 113, 115, 118, 120, 403, 813, or 834 to Tiyuchang (stadium). Uniquely curved hallways due to location inside stadium. Co-ed or single-sex dorms with summer-camp bunk beds. Spacious and airy rooms. Perpetually swept floors and grime-free Western-style common bath. 24hr. hot water, A/C, and Internet on the 1st fl. Free laundry, kitchen, luggage storage, and safe deposit box. Getting in and out of the hostel may be confusing and troublesome whenever football games are in play. They're reluctant to accept reservations; best way to secure a room is to appear in person. Deposit room rate plus Y100. 4-bed dorms Y60, members Y50; 2-bed dorms Y80/Y70; singles Y100-120. ❶

Zhaolong International Youth Hostel (HI) (zhàolóng qīngnián lǚshè; 兆龙青年旅舍), 2 Gongren Tiyuguan Bei Lu (☎6597 2299; fax 6597 2288), at Dong Sanhuan Lu, just behind the Zhaolong Hotel. Take bus #113 or 115 from the Dongsi Shitiao subway stop to Nongzhanguan; 701 and 801 also stop there, or try 403 or 703 to Tuanjie Hu. A cozier, less crowded, multi-level version of the Beijing Youth Hostel. Mostly friendly backpackers, but also some long-term residents. Bunk beds, chilly A/C, tiled floors, kitchen, TV room, 2 slow computers (Internet Y5 per 30min.), coveted Western-style toilet on the 2nd fl., and common showers with fantastic water pressure. Breakfast toast Y10. Curfew 1am, but there's a back door. Deposit without reservations Y2000—make reservations! 6-bed dorms Y60, HI members Y50; 4-bed Y70/Y60; 2-bed Y80/Y70. ❶

Furong Hotel (fúróng bīnguǎn; 芙蓉宾馆; ☎6557 2921; www.furonghotel.com), off Chaoyang Lu, on Shilipu, next to Huatang Shopping Center (华堂商场). Take bus #9 to Xiaozhuang and then #112, 115, or 117 to Balizhuang. Ridiculously far from everything, though nearby Sihui East subway stop makes the distance tolerable. Soft beds, but management should do something about the exceedingly dull, sleep-inducing pastel decor. 24hr. hot water. Breakfast included. Deposit depends on duration of stay. Singles and doubles Y180; doubles with computer and Internet access Y298. ❷

Red House (ruìxiù bīnguǎn; 瑞秀宾馆), 10 Chunxiu Lu (☎6416 7810 or 6416 7500; www.redhouse.com.cn), off Gongti Bei Lu, a 10-15min. walk west of Sanlitun. Look for the building with the glaringly obvious red facade. High ceilings and neat architecture. Rooms are less impressive, but are recently renovated and surprisingly comfortable (A/C, TV, phone, you name it). Singles Y300; doubles Y350-500; 4-person suites Y800. Ask for discounts in the winter. ❹

XUANWU AND CHONGWEN

Hotels in Xuanwu and Chongwen are far enough from the center to have budget-friendly prices, but aren't far enough to be inconvenient. The vital artery of Qianmen Dajie feeds into the area, and the subway loop line runs along the northern edge of these two districts, sandwiched between the second and third ring roads.

Beijing Flying Eagle International Youth Hostel (HI) (běijīng fēiyīng guójì qīngnián lǚshè; 北京飞鹰国际青年旅舍 ; ☎6315 1165 or 6317 1116; iyhfy@yahoo.com.cn), in Xuanwu, on Changchun Jie, behind Bldg. 10 on Xi Dajie/Erhuan (西大街十号楼后街). Changchun Jie subway stop on the loop line (#2) is 100m to the west; buses #25, 48, 337, 703, and 848 stop nearby. Clean, well-kept co-ed dorms. Singles and doubles have private bath. A/C, kitchen, laundry, Internet (Y10 per hr.), and 24hr. hot water. Travel services galore. Make reservations about 5 days in advance. 10-bed dorms Y30; 5-bed Y60, members Y50; singles Y320; triples Y360. ❶

Xinxin Hotel (xīnxīn bīnguǎn; 新新宾馆; ☎6303 1381), 24 Xi Heyan (西河沿), west of Qianmen Dajie, 5min. walk from Qianmen subway station. Walls keep out the persistent clamor of traffic (but not of guests). More decent than you'd expect from the disreputable-looking exterior. Dim hallways and slightly dirty floors, but clean sheets. 2- to 5-bed dorms Y80; singles Y180; doubles Y260-368; triples Y398. ❶

Leyou Hotel (lèyóu fàndiàn; 乐游饭店), 13 Dong Sanhuan Nan Lu (☎6771 2266 or 6771 2547; fax 6771 1636), at the southeast corner of the third ring road, in the Panjiayuan area east of Longtan Park. Take bus #28, 35, 52, or 368 to Jinsong Dong Kou. Panjiayuan Flea Market only a 10min. walk away. Rooms lack breathing space and toilets don't really flush well. Clean sheets and a safe environment are a plus. 24hr. hot water. Breakfast included. Deposit depends on room. Doubles Y288-430; triples Y398. ❹

FENGTAI

These hotels fall around both sides of the third ring road in the south of the city.

🎖 **Jinghua Youth Hostel** (jīnghuá fàndiàn; 京华饭店), Xiluoyuan Nanli, Yongdingmen Wai Dajie, Fengtai (☎6722 2211; fax 6721 1455), off Nan Sanhuan Zhong Lu, east of the smelly canal and McDonald's, to the southeast of Yangqiao (洋桥). Take bus #66 from Qianmen or 14 from Hepingmen to Yangqiao. With co-ed dorms, a pool, and an unending flow of travelers, the Jinghua is a cauldron of carousal and arousal. Cheaper dorms downstairs are basic; newer ones feel more like home, with spacious compartments

FLYING HIGH

Leng Shixiang (冷世祥) *is a traditional kite-maker who has practiced his art for over 40 years. His work has been showcased in museums, on TV, and in art shows throughout the world.*

On his interest: I've been making kites since childhood. I first delved into paper-cutting just for fun. Then I was introduced to kite-making. My family wasn't very supportive. In the 60s, kite-making wasn't seen as a profession, just an amusing hobby. But this is real for me—I make kites because it's a love, not an occupation.

On the history of kite-making: Kite-making dates back over 2300 years. There's an ancient story about an old man who spent three years making a wooden bird that could fly. You see, even then, the Chinese already had the wish to fly into the sky. Reality did not satisfy them, so they wrote prayers for long life and good fortune on kites and sent them into the heavens. Only later did kites become useful for the military and then recreation.

On how to make kites: Sometimes it takes me months or years to think up the design or concept for a kite, even though it'll only take a few days to actually create. But really, anyone can make kites. The basics are simple. Kite-making is just like any other art form—you achieve the highest level of art in your creations when inspiration arises from the self.

and cleaner pillows. Better bring your own bedsheets and towel though. 24hr. Waley's Bar serves french toast, french fries, and other Western fare (Y10-25). Tourist services galore. Internet Y10 per hr. 20-bed dorm Y25; 11-bed Y30; 6-bed Y35-40; standard doubles Y240-300; triples Y230; suites with A/C Y480. ❶

Qiaoyuan Hotel (qiáoyuán fàndiàn; 侨园饭店), 135 You'anmen Wai Dong Binhe Lu, Fengtai (☎6301 2244, ext. 3161 or 6303 8861; fax 6303 0119). Walk 500m west down the main street from the South Train Station (bus #20 from Tian'anmen East or Beijing Zhan, or #102). Chock full of foreigners looking for cheap, clean rooms. Common baths for dorms (remember your flip-flops). Quality doubles with all the essentials (TV, A/C, bath, 24hr. hot water) that make the hotel feel like a 3-star resort. Internet access (Y10 per hr.), discount airline tickets, bike rental (Y10 per day), and cheap tours. Deposit Y200. 4-bed dorms Y31-50; doubles Y132-260; triples Y192-360. ❶

Lihua Hotel (lìhuá fàndiàn; 丽华饭店), 71 Majiapu Dong Lu, Fengtai (☎6756 1144; fax 6756 1367), off Nan Sanhuan Lu, near Yangqiao. Accessible via bus #14, 66, 343, 957, or 724 from Lihua and bus #300, 324, or 368 from Yangqiao. Still has the spotlessness and odor of fresh paint that come hand in hand with recent renovations. Interior decorator had a good sense of style. Higher-priced doubles have bath and standard amenities. Lower-priced doubles Y200. ❸

Sea Star Hotel (hǎixīng dàjiǔdiàn; 海兴大酒店), 166 Haihutun, Yongdingmen Wai Dajie, Fengtai (☎6721 8855, ext. 3358; fax 6722 7915), in Muxiyuan. Accessible via bus #40, 54, 324, or 366. Plush carpeting, TV, A/C, phone, and all the amenities, with the price tag to match. Doubles Y220 and up; suites Y480. ❸

XICHENG

Enjoying the best of both worlds, the hotels near the zoo, west of the second ring road, are within easy reach of the city center, but also offer convenient access to buses departing to more distant sights, including the Summer Palace, Fragrant Hills, and the Great Wall.

Beijing Institute of Education (běijīng jiàoyù xuéyuàn; 北京教育学院), 2 Wenxing Jie (☎6835 2701). Take a bus to the zoo, then walk through the bus station across the street from the zoo's main gate. Cross the street behind the station, and continue down Wenxing Dong Jie (文兴东街), the alley left of the shopping complex. Follow the street as it curves to the right. Walk about 50m, and the entrance is on the left. Go to either the East or West Bldg. (you may need to tell them about your "friend" who is a student here). Great prices for clean, spacious doubles with A/C. Usually home to picky CET foreign-exchange students. Frequently scrubbed common showers and Western-style toilets. Laundry Y10 per load. Call ahead, but you may be told that there are no rooms when there actually are. Your best bet is to actually go and beg. Doubles Y100. ❷

Evergreen Hotel (wànniánqīng bīnguǎn; 万年青宾馆), 25 Xi Sanhuan Bei Lu (☎6842 5154). Take bus #300 or 323 to Wanshousi; or take bus #360 from the zoo to Beiwai Lu, walk east to Sanhuan Lu, and head north for 10min. Tell them that someone recommended the hotel to you and you may get a room more quickly. Rooms have a dormitory feel, with clean sheets and (for once) unsoiled carpets. Rooms face a courtyard with the loudest cicadas known to man. The only convenient sight is the Wanshou Temple that houses the Beijing Art Gallery. Singles and doubles Y260; triples Y280. ❹

HAIDIAN

Plan on at least 1hr. to reach anything in the heart of Beijing if you stay around Haidian, along the northern stretch of the fourth ring road. However, if you have friends in Beijing University or other colleges, or just want to be close to the Summer Palace and the Old Summer Palace, Haidian is the perfect choice.

▨ **Beijing University Shaoyuan Hotel** (běijīng dàxué sháoyuán bīnguǎn; 北京大学勺园宾馆), Bldg. 7 (☎6275 2218 or 6275 2200). Take bus #106, 320, 332, 355, 732, 832, or 808 to Beida Ximen (West Entrance of Beijing University), and enter the gate on Yiheyuan Lu. Continue along the path and over the bridge; turn right and walk straight for about 7min. Look for a plaque that reads Bldg. 7; hotel is directly across from the tennis courts. Although small and bare of all decoration, dorm singles with a great deal of privacy are perfect for long-term residents. Actual singles and doubles are overly spacious with TV, A/C, bath, and the works. Safe, well-maintained grounds, lakeside surroundings, and relatively peaceful atmosphere more than make up for distance to the city center. Pleasant chatter of students buzzes from basketball, tennis, and volleyball courts right outside. Close to the Summer Palace. Make reservations early, especially in the summer. Singles in single-sex dorm suites (only for those around college age or younger) with common room and bath Y90; other singles Y200; doubles Y110–320. ❷

Beijing Medical School Doctorate Hotel (běiyī bóshì yuàn bīnguǎn; 北医博士苑宾馆), 38 Beijing Xueyuan Lu (☎6202 7771). Take bus #331 or 375 from Xizhimen to Beiyi Sanyuan. On school grounds; go to one of the gates and ask for directions. Host to visiting professors and students, the hotel has a safe, scholarly atmosphere. Walls are paper-thin and rooms are on the small side, but they're cleaned daily. You may want to mention you know a student of the school who recommended the place. TV, A/C, 24hr. hot water. Tacit curfew at 11:30pm when the receptionists go to sleep. Deposit room rate plus Y100. Singles Y100; doubles Y120. ❶

Zhongguancun Hotel (zhōngguāncūn jiǔdiàn; 中关村酒店), 19 Haidian Lu (☎6256 5577, ext. 2001 or 2002), about 2 blocks east of the smaller Beijing University south gate. Take bus #320, 332, or 808 to Zhongguancun; turn left and walk down any street or alley on your right to Haidian Lu; the hotel is on your left. Typical rooms with TV, A/C, standing shower, and the occasional insect. Wooden floors and vibrant surroundings. Deposit depends on duration of stay and room. Doubles Y268-298. ❹

◨ FOOD

The streets of Beijing sell dirt-cheap, delicious food options. Almost every little road-side restaurant serves standard *jiāchángcài* (everyday family food; 家常菜). Few of these places have English menus, but they offer a wide selection of tasty, filling meals for about Y10-20 per person. Avoid being charged ridiculously inflated prices by asking to see the menu with listed prices first.

Beijing is full of can't-miss culinary experiences. The two **nightmarkets** off Wangfujing Dajie are filled with delicacies and all the bubble tea you can drink. Red-and-white carts line **Dong'anmen**, off the north end of Wangfujing Dajie, tempting passersby with sugared fried bananas and more exotic fare. (Open daily around dusk to 10:30 or 11pm.) Near the south end of Dong'anmen is the **Wangfujing Snack Street** (wángfǔjǐng xiǎochī jiē; 王府井小吃街), where excited vendors grill lamb, chicken, and every kind of meat imaginable, stab a stick through it, and cover it with mouth-watering spices. Grab a seat and devour sizzling plates of rice and noodles (Y8), while singers perform on the outdoor balcony. To satisfy **late-night** cravings, take the subway to Dongzhimen. Popular 24hr. restaurants, decorated by glowing red lanterns, line **Dongzhimen Dajie**, known among locals as **Ghost Street** (guǐjiē; 鬼街). Help yourself to a mug of beer (Y5 for a large pint), heaps of crayfish (Y10 and up), and platefuls of sumptuous food (practice your haggling skills).

Western-style bakeries, like their fast-food counterparts, are spreading like wildfire. **Délifrance** bakes authentic croissants and other pastries, while some Sanlitun bakeries sell convincing French loaves. **Mrs. Shanen's Bagels** (shuānglóng wùzī gōngsī; 双龙物资公司), A3 Zhaojiu Lu, Jiuxianqiao, Chaoyang, turns out bagels by the dozen. (Delivery ☎ 6435 9561. Open M-Sa 8am-6pm, Su 8am-4pm.) For an overpriced and overcommercialized Western experience, try the **Hard Rock Cafe**, at Landmark Towers, 8 Dong Sanhuan Bei Lu. (☎ 6590 6688, ext. 2571. Open Su-Th 11:30am-2am, F-Sa 11:30am-3am.) **TGI Friday's** (xīngqīwǔ cāntīng; 星期五餐厅), Huafeng Mansions, 19 Dong Sanhuan Bei Lu, Chaoyang, also dishes up generic Western fare for those hungry for home. (☎ 6597 5314. Open daily 11am-midnight.)

For fans of self-catering, supermarkets and shopping centers are scattered throughout the city. Some convenient locations include the food court in the basement of the **Sun Dong'an Plaza**, at Wangfujing; **Park N Shop**, COFCO Plaza, 8 Jianguomen Nei Dajie, in the basement of Tower B, diagonally opposite the Beijing International Hotel (open daily 8am-10pm); and the **Hualian Shopping Center**, across from the Vantone New World Plaza.

FOOD BY TYPE

BEIJING DUCK	
Huahua (142)	Xicheng ❷
🏮 Qianmen Quanjude (141)	Qianmen ❹
CANTONESE	
Golden Palace (142)	Xicheng ❹
Hong Kong Food City (140)	Wangfujing ❸
CHINESE	
Deep Forest Mansion (142)	Chaoyang ❸
🏮 Fangshan (139)	city center ❺
Haiwan Dian (142)	Xicheng ❸
🏮 Huajia Garden (140)	city center ❸
DAI	
🏮 Dai Family Village (141)	Chaoyang ❸
DUMPLINGS	
Kaifeng No. 1 (141)	Qianmen ❷
Wonton Pavilion (140)	Wangfujing ❷

HOTPOT	
Donglaishun (140)	Wangfujing ❸
Nengren Ju (141)	Qianmen ❷
HUBEI	
Nine-Headed Bird (140)	city center ❷
INDIAN	
Chingari (142)	Chaoyang ❸
Golden Elephant Garden (141)	Chaoyang ❹
MUSLIM	
🏮 Afunti's Music (139)	city center ❹
SICHUANESE	
The Sichuan (140)	city center ❹
🏮 Yuntai (141)	Chaoyang ❸
VEGETARIAN	
Gongdelin (141)	Qianmen ❷
Green Angel (140)	Wangfujing ❸

BEIJING

BEIJING SPECIALTIES

BEIJING DUCK. A delicacy fit for a king at a price budget travelers can stomach, Beijing duck (běijīng kǎoyā; 北京烤鸭) is as dear to Beijing hearts as the Forbidden City. Roasted until a crispy golden brown, the duck is sliced into delectably thin pieces and served with paper-thin crepes (often lotus-leaf cakes or just plain pancakes), seasonings, slivers of cucumber or scallion, and a dish of sweet brown sauce. Wrap several slices of duck in a pancake, along with a few pieces of cucumber or scallions and several daubs of sauce, and savor what Beijing does best.

JIANBING. If there is one dish close to the heart (or stomach) of every Beijing local, it's the orgasmic *jiānbǐng* (煎饼; sometimes called *jiānbǐng guǒzi* or 煎饼 果子), a grilled pancake wrapped around fried, crispy dough—the mother of all snack foods. Look for the ubiquitous white carts with black round frying skillets and feast on these delicious concoctions, made with globs of batter, an egg, tasty brown sauce, a pinch of scallions, and—if you're lucky—sesame seeds. At Y2-3 per *jiānbǐng*, it doesn't get any better than this.

BEIJING HOTPOT. With vats of bubbling soup, vials of sauces, and heaps of raw meat, hotpot (huǒguō; 火锅) is like fondue on steroids. Vegetarians need not despair—veggie broths and non-meat ingredients (see **Appendix**, p. 875) are available. Eating hotpot is a simple, personalized affair—you can go as spicy and as well-done as you like. The soup (savory clear or spicy red) is kept boiling, while you drop in raw meat and veggies. Wait impatiently for the rare stuff to cook and then use chopsticks (or even smarter, a sieve-like ladle) to scoop out the goods.

MUSLIM. Beijing is blessed with many Uighur neighborhoods, though sadly, high-rises have replaced the largest one, which was near the zoo. Typical Muslim fare includes noodles (*miàn*; 面), flatbread *(nang)*, sumptuous kebabs (ròu chuàn; 肉串), and Uighur tea. Find Muslim restaurants on the street by looking for " 清真 " (qīngzhēn) or Arabic writing.

FOOD BY NEIGHBORHOOD

CITY CENTER

▨ **Afunti's Music from the Hometown** (āfántí jiāxiāng yīnyuè cāntīng; 阿凡提家乡音乐 餐厅), Chaoyangmen Nei Dajie ("Chao Nei"), 2A Houguaibang Hutong, Dongcheng (☎6525 1071, 6527 2288, or 6525 1545; www.afunti.com), in an alley just south of the (Chaonei) Xiaojie stop; take bus #101, 109, 110, or 112. This Uighur funhouse serves up delectable Xinjiang fare, like melt-in-your-mouth "fried mutton with toothpick" (kebabs; Y32 and up). A wild song-and-dance troupe performs daily 7:30-8pm, accompanied by women in Uighur dress and enthusiastic *lǎowài* trying to dance on tabletops. Entrees Y30-90. 40% off lunch options. Open daily 10am-10:30pm. ❹

▨ **Fangshan** (fǎngshàn fànzhuāng; 仿膳饭庄 ; ☎6401 1879 or 6401 1889), inside Beihai Park, halfway along the corridor that runs around Qiong Island. The elegant dining area, with gold silks and Qing-Dynasty decor, was originally reserved for emperors, as was the exquisite food. Fangshan opened to the public in 1925, and now you too can enjoy Empress Dowager Ci Xi's favorite 108-course banquet—if you can afford the outrageous price. Try the next best thing, *wōwōtóu*, dry little corncakes eaten by Ci Xi after she fled Beijing and had nothing to eat for 3 days; she liked it so much it became a permanent on the imperial menu. Royal recipes included, Fangshan has 800 dishes to satiate even the most refined tastes. 14- to 16-course set banquets Y150-400 per person. Slightly more feasible lunch menu starting at Y100 per person. Open daily 11am-1:30pm and 5-7:30pm. ❺

BEIJING

🗺 **Huajia Harmony Garden** (huājiā yíyuán; 花家怡园), 235 Dongzhimen Nei Dajie, Dongcheng (☎6403 0677 or 6405 1908), on Ghost Street. Take the subway to Dongzhimen. Ever-busy, with an open courtyard, caged birds, floral wreaths, and greenery all around. Bright-red crayfish stream out of a gigantic cauldron (medium-sized platter Y20). Deep-fried chrysanthemum-shaped fish (júhuā yú; 菊花鱼) smothered in sweet-and-sour fruit sauce Y80. Most dishes Y20-60. Picture menu. Open daily 24hr. ❸

Nine-Headed Bird (jiǔtóuniǎo jiǔjiā; 九头鸟酒家), 141 Di'anmen Xi Dajie (☎6651 9001), northwest of Beihai, in front of the Beihai Hotel. Take bus #13, 42, 107, 111, or 823 to Changqiao. This monstrous creature was once a derogatory term for Hubei province residents, who have come to embrace their name just as Beijing has embraced their food. Nearly every table has a plate of *dòupí* (豆皮 ; sticky rice, meat, scallions, and maybe some veggies, all wrapped within thin layers of crispy bean-flour crepes; Y5), as well as some variation of lotus root (ǒu; 藕 ; Y18 and up), both popular Hubei specialties. English menu. Open daily 11am-10pm. ❷

The Sichuan (sìchuān fàndiàn; 四川饭店), 14 Liuyin Jie (柳荫街), Xicheng (☎6615 6924 or 6615 7061; fax 6615 6925), a short walk north from Prince Gong's Former Residence, behind Beihai Park; follow the blue-and-white signs from Di'anmen Dajie. The facial tissue market owes itself to The Sichuan. Zhou Enlai himself oversaw the restaurant's establishment in 1959. A political bigwig favorite, but also host to oversized tour groups. Friendly service. Entrees Y20-90. Open daily 9am-2pm and 5-9pm. ❹

WANGFUJING

Green Angel Vegetarian Restaurant (lǜsè tiānshí cāntīng; 绿色天食餐厅), 57 Dengshikou Dajie, 2nd fl., Dongcheng (☎6524 2476 or 6524 2349), east of Wangfujing Dajie. This lovely little restaurant's specialty is "the imitation of real meat, not only in appearance, but also in taste," achieved with ingredients like soy bean protein, taro, mushrooms, and tofu. A very convincing endeavor, with dishes and vegetable-carvings of phoenixes that are too beautiful to eat. The "prawn" is interesting in the very least. Picture menu has helpful explanations of specific dishes and of the magic of tea. Most dishes Y30-70. Extremely popular, so make reservations in advance or prepare for waitresses to pull out the folding tables. Open daily 10am-10pm. ❸

Donglaishun (dōngláishùn fànzhuāng; 东来顺饭庄), Sun Dong'an Plaza, 138 Wangfujing Dajie, 5th fl. (☎6528 0932), to the right of the escalators. A change of location and scenery would make the experience more worth talking about, but this busy restaurant with over 100 years of history, once the only place to go for hotpot, still deserves its first-rate reputation. Spirited waiters with digital gear to order your dishes make for most efficient service. Hotpot broth Y15; most meat Y16-30; vegetables Y4. Prepared dishes Y15 and up. Open daily 11am-2pm and 5-9pm. Many other locations throughout Beijing, including in Chaoyang, Fengtai, and the city center. ❸

Hong Kong Food City (xiānggǎng měishí chéng; 香港美食城), 18 Dong'anmen Dajie (☎6525 7349 or 653 6668, ext. 3102 or 3103), east of Wangfujing Dajie. This huge, posh restaurant holds its own against the nightmarket across the street. Lots of Hong Kong businessmen and Cantonese chatter. A dining experience worth the cost if you try the specialties, such as bamboo cooked rice and shark fin soup. Small dim-sum appetizers (Y6-20) available 11am-5pm and 9pm-1am. Try the chilled sweet red tofu (Y6), a chef's specialty. Bring your own drink to avoid the exorbitantly priced fresh fruit blends (Y16+). Most dishes Y25-100. 10% service charge. Open daily 11am-1am. ❸

Wonton Pavilion (húntun hóu; 馄饨侯), 11 Dong'anmen Dajie (☎6525 1892 or 6525 4953), at Wangfujing Dajie. Come mealtimes, the relatively quiet atmosphere transforms into a feeding free-for-all. Watch the chef create delectable wontons in a stuffing frenzy. Sesame cakes (Y3) and pickles are welcome sides. 20 different filling options (Y8-14 per dish), but the most popular is still the pork. Soups Y3-6. Open daily 7am-1am. ❷

QIANMEN AND QIANMEN DAJIE

▨ Qianmen Quanjude Roast Duck (qiánmén quánjùdé kǎoyā diàn; 前门全聚德烤鸭店), 32 Qianmen Dajie (☎6511 2418 or 6701 1379). Take a bus or subway to Qianmen; walk south. Founded in 1864, the Qianmen location is the oldest of 25 branches and cooks 2000 quackers per day to fill the bellies of demanding patrons. Former guests include Fidel Castro and Yanni. If you're going to splurge on a duck, do it with style—head through the archway to the fancier section. A duck can feed 3 people (Y168; with sauce, scallions, and pancakes Y184; carving extra). More complete meals including soups and entrees start at Y300 per person. Make reservations, as the place is packed. The fast-food area in front serves the same delicious duck (Y68 per person), but with less panache (read: paper plates). Meals Y75-100. "Fancier" part open daily 11am-1:30pm and 4:45-8pm; "less fancy" part 10am-9pm. ❹

Gongdelin Vegetarian Restaurant (gōngdélín sùcài fànzhuāng; 功德林素菜饭庄), 158 Qianmen Nan Dajie (☎6702 0867 or 6511 2542). Take a bus (20, 59, 110) to Zhushikou or take the subway to Qianmen and walk about 15min. down Qianmen Nan Dajie. Established in 1922, the Gongdelin is a pro at culinary deceit, recreating popular meat and seafood dishes with tofu, potatoes, and fresh greens. Unlike most restaurants, even the cooking oil is vegetable. Meals Y20-34. Open daily 10:30am-10pm. ❷

Kaifeng No. 1 (kāifēng dìyīlóu; 开封第一楼), 83 Qianmen Dajie (☎6303 0268). Renowned for its traditional *bāozi* (stuffed buns; Y10-20 per dozen) and tasty fillings. Dip the duck-filled buns into the bowl of spices—it's delicious. Don't forget the spoon or else you'll spill all the savory juices the moment you bite into the *bāozi*. Not as memorable as the real No. 1 in Kaifeng. Environment is a little too cozy, as you're seated inches away from your neighbor. Open daily 8:30am-10:30pm. ❷

Nengren Ju (néngrén jū; 能仁居), 135 Qianmen Xi Dajie (☎6605 7485). From Xuanwumen, walk about 10min. east on Qianmen Xi Dajie. This humble branch of the popular chain store is located in a quieter part of city, making for a peaceful meal. Beijing-style hotpot sauce Y5; animal parts Y18-40; veggies Y5. Open daily 11am-10pm. ❷

CHAOYANG

▨ Dai Family Village (dǎijiā cūn; 傣家村), Guandongdian Nan Jie, Chaoyang (☎6585 8709), near Sanhuan Lu, about a block north of the Kerry Center Hotel. Also at 80 Tiantan Dong Lu (☎6714 0145 or 6711 1616). All in the style of the Dai minority tribe of Yunnan, meals of mushroom, turtle, snake, and other treats are complemented by booze served in fat bamboo trunks and dance performances in the aisles to the sound of lutes. Most dishes Y30-70. More expensive, more bizarre entrees also available: crispy scorpions Y80, sauna bullfrogs Y48, eels stuck in bamboo pipes Y38, and smoked young pigeons Y18. Delectable pineapple porridge with 8 essences Y25. Yum... Performances at 11:30am, 6:30, 7:30pm. Open daily 10:30am-2:30pm and 4:30-9:30pm. Reservations highly recommended. ❸

▨ Yuntai (yúntái cāntīng; 云台餐厅), Great Wall Sheraton Hotel, 10 Dong Sanhuan Bei Lu (☎6590 5566, ext. 2295). The 3-pepper dishes here are hot enough to melt glass. Those with guts and tastebuds to spare should sample the ultra-spicy, tear-inducing *fūqī fèipiàn* (夫妻肺片 ; Y38), chilled slices of beef and other cow parts. The posh 21st fl. location, hanging lanterns, floating candles, stellar food, superb service, and English-speaking waiters dressed in black and gold make the prices (Y45-88) palatable. 15% service charge. Open daily 11:30am-2pm and 6-10:30pm. ❸

Golden Elephant Garden (jīnxiàng yuàn dōngfāng cāntīng; 金象苑东方餐厅 ; ☎6417 1650 or 6417 1651; fax 6416 9363). Turn west off Sanlitun Lu onto Sanlitun Hou Jie; look for the sign. Master chefs from Thailand and India cook tempting South Asian cuisine like mandarin fish and shish kebabs. Trendy ambience, with red lanterns, star lights, and bamboo and wicker furnishings. Thai shark fin (Y288) feeds 4. Entrees Y28-98. Weekday lunch buffet Y48. Open daily 11:30am-10:30pm. ❹

Deep Forest Mansion (shèng lín fǔ jiǔlóu; 盛林府酒楼; ☎6415 9274 or 6415 9233), south of Bldg. No. 18, Bei Sanlitun, near the Golden Elephant. Take a right before you reach the Golden Elephant; look for the sign. Out of the way, but atmosphere and authentic Taiwanese cooking make up for the search. Nifty bamboo furnishings and a profusion of flora and fauna. Home-style hot-and-sour soup Y25. Sizzling black pepper beef Y28. Slightly bizarre combo of ribs and pineapple Y28. Roasted eels Y55. ❸

Chingari (xīngélǐ cāntīng; 鑫格里餐厅), 27 Dongzhimen Wai Dajie, 4th fl., Chaoyang (☎8448 3690; www.chingari-restaurant.com), west of the Australian Embassy. Specializes in Thai, Bangladeshi, Pakistani, and Indian cuisine. Overwhelming variety of curry dishes like lamb *vindaloo* for Y50-75, veggie options like *pilaf* (Y35), and Indian bread (Y10-15). Pleasantly dim lighting. Open daily 11:30am-2:30pm and 5:30-10:30pm. ❸

XICHENG

Golden Palace, New Century Hotel, 6 Shoudu Tiyuguan Nan Lu, 3rd fl. (☎6849 2001, ext. 1155; or 6849 2001, ext. 1159). Take bus #105 or 111 to Baishi Qiao and look for the white high-rise just south of Xizhimen Wai Dajie. Behind its glitzy facade, Golden Palace offers melt-in-your-mouth dim sum lunches Sa-Su (Y8-17 per dish). Eat to your heart's content, but skip the drinks (can of Coke Y20). Teeming with crowds, so make reservations early. Entrees and entrails Y30-80. 15% service charge. Open daily 11:30am-2:30pm and 5:30-10pm. ❹

Haiwan Dian (hǎiwǎn diàn; 海碗店), 11 Zengguang Lu, East End, Haidian (☎8837 4993), near the zoo (walk south on Sanlihe Lu). Bus #102, 103, or 114 to Ganjiakou Shangchang stops nearby. Look for a bright red awning and lanterns. Dozens of young male waiters shout greetings as you enter (or break into spontaneous yelping just for the hell of it) and serve big bowls of Beijing *zhájiàng miàn* (炸酱面), a noodle dish topped with veggies and savory brown sauce. The place is packed, the menu English, and the service exciting. Entrees Y6-25. Noodles Y8-10. Open daily 11am-11pm. ❷

Huahua Restaurant (huāhuā jiǔdiàn; 花花酒店; ☎8837 2129 or 136 4130 1912), on Wenxing Jie, a 5min. walk west of the Beijing Institute of Education and 10m from the western end of Wenxing Jie. Good family environment and family-style food. Beijing duck serves 3 (Y38 with pancakes and other accessories). Open daily 10am-11pm. ❷

👁 SIGHTS

CITY CENTER

TIAN'ANMEN SQUARE 天安门广场

Between Chang'an Dajie and Qianmen Dajie. Take the subway to Qianmen (blue line) or to Tian'anmen East (red line). Buses #1, 4, 10, and 20 stop along Chang'an Jie to the north, while #5, 9, 17, 22, 47, 53, 54, 59, and 307 reach Qianmen to the south. Bus #116 runs along the side of the square.

Tian'anmen Square (tiān'ānmén guǎngchǎng), the largest and possibly the most famous public meeting space in the world, has created enough historical and political cannon fodder to last for generations. As the political epicenter of popular protest in modern China, the square witnessed the May Fourth anti-imperialist demonstrations (p. 78), anti-Japanese protests, Mao Zedong's proclamation of the People's Republic of China, Red Guard rallies of the Cultural Revolution, politically charged outpourings of grief for Zhou Enlai, and, of course, the 1989 pro-democracy protests (p. 82). For most Chinese, Tian'anmen Square is an ideological mecca, a place to pay tribute to the heroes and victims of China's tumultuous history. Despite its complicated past, the square seems rooted in an eternally celebratory atmosphere, a prime site for kite-flying and picture-taking. On special occasions, when crowds fill this vast expanse of cement, as they did after the announcement of Beijing's victorious Olympic bid, nationalistic fervor and contagious enthusiasm will rouse even the most skeptical.

TIAN'ANMEN GATE (tiān'ānmén; 天安门). On the gate, a huge banner proclaims "Long Live the People's Republic of China, Long Live the Unity of the World's Peoples." It was on the rostrum of this gate, literally the "Gate of Heavenly Peace," that Chairman Mao declared the founding of the PRC in 1949, and his portrait (touched up yearly) still gazes serenely over the square. Most admire the imposing structure of red walls and golden tiles from a distance. The climb to the top of the gate is not very interesting—there's only an off-limits collection of dining tables. It does allow you to gaze over the square, just as Mao does every day. Two stone lions guard each of the five bridges of **Jinshui River,** a manmade moat encircling the Forbidden Palace. *(At the northern end of Tian'anmen Square. Open daily 8:30am-5:30pm. Y15, students Y5; mandatory bag deposit Y2.)*

ZHENGYANGMEN GATE (zhèngyángmén; 正阳门). Of the nine imperial gates *(mén)* that once guarded Beijing, only Zhengyangmen's character for *mén* (门) lacked the little hook at the lower corner. The emperor often passed through this gate, and it was believed that the hook may snag him, as emperors are the descendants of the dragon, an aquatic creature. In 1964, when the Beijing walls were torn down to make room for the subway and second ring road, only Zhengyangmen, better known as **Qianmen,** was left standing. A small exhibit has photos of Old Beijing. *(At the south end of Tian'anmen Square. Open daily 8:30am-4pm. Y10, students Y5.)*

GREAT HALL OF THE PEOPLE (rénmín dàhuìtáng; 人民大会堂). Home to the National People's Congress, this hall features a selection of province-themed reception rooms amid chandeliers and marble pillars. Room after room of chairs and rolled-up carpet quickly loses its appeal, but the Grand Auditorium is worth a look for its seating capacity of 10,000. *(On the western edge of the square. Open daily 8am-4pm, except when the Congress is in session. Y30, students Y15.)*

CHINESE HISTORY AND REVOLUTION MUSEUMS (zhōngguó gémìng lìshǐ bówùguǎn; 中国革命历史博物馆). This large museum with six halls housing exhibits from around the world is rather sparse, with the notable exception of the wonderfully curated Selected Treaures of the National Chinese Museum. In the Selected Treaures Hall on the second floor, neat and beautiful displays showcase Chinese artifacts dating from the Neolithic period. Next door, the Wax Museum, quite obviously sponsored by the Party and State Council, has wax figures of the "far-sighted statesmen and strategists" who shaped China. Though there's not much to see right now, signs promise significant additions as the 2008 Olympics approach. *(On the east side of the square. Open daily 8:30am-4:30pm; last admission 3:30pm. Y20; F noon-4:30pm free.)*

CHAIRMAN MAO MAUSOLEUM (máozhǔxí jìniàn táng; 毛主席纪念堂). Chairman Mao has lain flag-draped and preserved in splendor in his final resting place since 1976. Tourists from all over flock to the mausoleum for a quick peek. The cult-like adoration that Mao enjoyed during his lifetime has obviously been little diminished by his current waxy state. Strict white-gloved authorities shepherd epic lines of visitors through the dimly lit, red-carpeted tomb. Inappropriate attire (no slippers!) is forbidden, and signs and speakers enjoin viewers to take off their hats and remain silent so as not to disturb the Great Embalmed One. Don't expect to see much—you're rushed in and out of the building within 5min., thanks to the no-nonsense PLA. *(In the middle of Tian'anmen Square, before the Monument to the People's*

Heroes; use the north door. Prepare for long lines, unless you time it right; try going at opening time. No bags or cameras allowed; mandatory bag check across the street Y5-10. Open daily summer 7-11:30am, later depending on size of crowd; winter Tu and Th 8-11:30am. Free.)

FORBIDDEN CITY 故宫

From Tian'anmen Square, go under Tian'anmen Gate to the ticket booths for the Palace Museum. For the North Gate, take bus #101, 103, or 109. ☎6525 0614. All halls have English captions; English tour guides (Y200) and highly recommended audio tours in 10 languages (Y40, deposit Y100) give more in-depth knowledge. Open daily summer 8:30am-4pm; winter 8:30am-3:30pm; last admission 1hr. before closing. Palace Y60, students Y20, children under 1.2m free. Additional halls around the palace extra Y5-10.

During the palace's 500-year history, only 24 emperors and their most intimate attendants were privy to every part of its 800 buildings and 9000 chambers. Because common folk could not enter its gates, the palace was named the Forbidden City (zǐjìn chéng; 紫禁城). Now known as the **Former Palace** (gù gōng; 故宫), the complex opened to the public in 1949, and is the largest and most impressive example of traditional architecture in China. The signs in the Forbidden City usually give at least three dates—those of construction, destruction, and reconstruction. The palaces have seen so many face-lifts that it is hard to tell what is original anymore, but no amount of fresh paint can diminish the epic weight they carry.

Construction of the Forbidden City began in 1406, the fourth year of Ming Emperor Yongle's reign. During the Qing Dynasty, the palace saw significant expansion. The first few halls of the Outer Court are the largest and most magnificent. Within these ceremonial halls, the Son of Heaven conducted his stately affairs, seated atop his imperial throne at the **Hall of Supreme Harmony.** Auspicious signs of royalty are all around, from lions at the gates (for loyalty), to crane and tortoise incense burners (for good luck and longevity), to winding dragons (symbolizing the emperor himself). The Inner Court, where the royal couple, eunuchs, and concubines lived, was naturally a place of passion and intrigue. Peek through windows at the silk-flowered beds of the wedding chamber in the **Empress' Palace of Earthly Tranquility.** In the **Imperial Garden** out back, visitors linger in the once quiet beautiful and shady grounds.

When the Nationalist Party fled China, they stole most of the palace treasures, now displayed at the National Palace Museum in Taipei, Taiwan. What remains, however, still inspires awe. The **Hall of Paintings** to the west, just before Qianqing-gong, is a dimly lit cavern of famous scriptures and paintings. Unabashedly ostentatious European timepieces fill the must-see **Hall of Clocks,** behind the Hall of Preserving Harmony; some are so cluttered with gold leaf and dancing mechanical animals that it's impossible to tell the time. (Open daily 8:30am-4pm. Y10.) Head north to the **Hall of Jewelry** and its splendid imperial relics. Visitors must shuffle about in neon orange overshoes (Y2) to preserve the brick floors. Within the courtyard, a large **theater** hosted extravagant productions of Beijing opera to entertain emperors and concubines. Before leaving, visitors pass a small well, where a beloved concubine of Emperor Guangxu was drowned by orders of Empress Dowager Ci Xi. (Open daily 8:30am-4pm. Y5.)

Outside the Forbidden City, two parks offer an unexpected respite from the hordes of camera-clicking tourists. Emperors made sacrifices to the gods of land and grain at the Altar of Five-Colored Soil in **Zhongshan Park** (zhōngshān gōngyuán; 中山公园) to the southwest. The flower garden (Y5) is only worthwhile in the summer. (Open daily 6am-10pm; last admission 9pm. Y3, students Y1.5, children under 1.2m free.) To the southeast are the **Working People's Cultural Palace** (láodòng rénmín wénhuà gōng; 劳动人民文化宫) and **Imperial Ancestral Temple.** For those who haven't seen enough, the temple showcases a small museum of imperial relics. The inner court is like a tiny Forbidden City, surprisingly resplendent with marble terraces and stairways, but admission is an unjustifiable Y15. (Open daily 6am-9pm; temple 9am-4pm. Park Y2, students Y1, children under 1.2m free.)

OTHER SIGHTS IN THE CITY CENTER

BEIHAI PARK (běihǎi gōngyuán; 北海公园). Constructed about 1000 years ago during the Jin Dynasty, this park is one of the world's earliest imperial gardens, though it was never heavily regarded until its massive expansion and construction under Qianlong (1735-1796). Most of the park is taken up by the lake, dotted with boats and lotus flowers in the summer. A bridge, ferries, and rental boats link the shores to **Qionghua Island,** made from the mud collected as the lake was dug out by hand. The centerpiece of Beihai, the **White Dagoba** (bái tǎ; 白塔), a Tibetan-style pagoda, rises up from the island in the middle of the lake. Other sights include the **Nine-Dragon Screen** (along the Eastern Shore), a 5m-long depiction of nine dragons batting pearls in the turquoise water, and the **Jade Buddha** (in Round City), carved out of a single piece of white jade. The eastern and western shores hold gardens, religious buildings, and a small temple where Empress Dowager Ci Xi raised silkworms. From the eastern shore, you can also get a beautiful view of the whole lake, with the pristine White Dagoba rising out of the greenery and reflected in the waters. *(Northwest of the Forbidden City. Buses #5, 101, 103, 109, 111, 124, 202, 812, and 814 stop outside its main gate in the south. Buses #13, 42, 107, 111, 118, and 810 stop at the less crowded North Gate entrance. Open daily summer 6am-10pm; winter 6:30am-8pm. Most sights inside Beihai close by 5pm. Rental boats Y30 per hr., Y200 insurance. Park Y10, Chinese students Y5. White Dagoba Y5. Round City Y5.)*

JINGSHAN PARK (jǐngshān gōngyuán; 景山公园). Built from the debris of old palaces and dirt from the Forbidden City's moat, Jingshan Park was an imperial garden during the Ming and Qing Dynasties. Climb up the hill to Jingshan's highest pavilion, perhaps the best place from which to appreciate the grand and beautifully symmetric scale of the Forbidden City. The picture-perfect views of the emperor's domain seem to go on forever, a capsule of history set against the backdrop of modern Beijing. Here, the Emperor Chongzhen, wracked with despair after insurgents captured the Forbidden City, hanged himself from a locust tree, ending the Ming Dynasty. As a "punishment" for killing the Son of Heaven, the tree was placed in chains. The original tree is long gone, but a liberated replacement now stands unimpressively in its place at the foot of the mountain. *(Jingshan Qianjie, directly opposite the north rear gate of the Forbidden City. Accessible by buses #101, 103, 109, 111, 202, 211, 802, 810, and 812. ☎6404 4071. Open daily 6am-10pm. Y2.)*

AROUND THE SECOND RING ROAD

The second ring road roughly traces Beijing's old city wall. Subway stops are marked by the old locations of the city gates. Although the gates are no longer standing, *Běijīngrén* still use the gate names as landmarks. Most sights around the second ring road are easily accessible by subway. Beginning with Deshengmen north of city center, the following gates are arranged clockwise.

DESHENGMEN 德胜门

PRINCE GONG'S MANSION (gōngwáng fǔ huāyuán; 恭王府花园). One of the few royal Qing residences remaining in Old Beijing, this jewel would be an idyllic paradise, were it not jam-packed with summer tour groups. The tourism bureau has taken over, and though the surrounding *hútòng* (胡同) remain unscathed (save for the bumper-to-bumper tour buses), you'll find yourself squeezing for

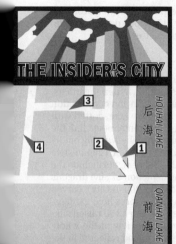

后海 HOUHAI LAKE

前海 QIANHAI LAKE

INTO OLD BEIJING

Beneath Beijing's rapidly changing skyline, traditional *hútòng* (alleys) and *sìhéyuàn* (residential courtyards) still linger. Once home to both commoners and nobles, the alleys are best preserved in Houhai, near the Drum and Bell Towers. From the bridge separating Houhai and Qianhai Lakes, head to the alley parallel to the lakeside path by Houhai for an afternoon exploring these living museums of Old Beijing.

1 The **doorway** to a private courtyard reveals the owner's prestige. This one has two knobs above the door, but if there were four, the *sìhéyuàn* behind would have belonged to a wealthy man or a general of rank. Flanking both sides of the entry gate are two **drum stones,** once used to prop the door open. If the drum stones are curved and lion-shaped, then the resident was of high military standing.

2 The sharp, square stone pillars by this **entrance gate** indicate that the resident was a civil

space in the nine small courtyards of Prince Gong's hideaway. The residence is reputedly the model for the setting of the 18th-century literary classic *Dream of the Red Chamber*. Bamboo-shaded paths open onto gardens of fuchsia flowers, surrounded by a haze of white moths and dragonflies. You can study the intricate floral detail on the Xiyang Gate, or avoid (some of) the mob at the Mid-Lake Pavilion (湖心亭), set right in the center of a lake tinged a troubling murky green. *(14 Liuyin Jie, north of Beihai Park. Hard to get to except by taxi or pedicab. Take bus #13 or 103 from Fuchengmen, or 107 or 111 from Xizhimen to the closest bus stop at Beihai Bei Men, "Beihai Park North Gate"; cross Ping'an Dajie, and start asking the locals for directions. Open daily 8:30am-4:30pm. Guided tours with tea and performance Y60. Y20, students Y10.)*

DRUM TOWER (gǔ lóu; 鼓楼). This vast structure has seen a few face-lifts since 1272, including a major one in August 2001. Nevertheless, you can still climb the steep, dimly lit 600-year-old stairs for a peek at the surrounding city. Skip the splurge at the downstairs "art museum" (i.e., comprehensive tourist shop)—the ancient drums upstairs are more worthwhile. Young men dressed in proper regalia give a riveting 10min. drum concert. Take lots of photos—the high ceiling, colorful attire, and gargantuan drums make for a great composition. Nearby is the **Bell Tower** (zhōng lóu; 钟楼) and its 63-ton bell. These two towers once kept the time in Beijing and signaled the daily closing of the city gates. *(At the northern tip of Gulou Dajie. Take bus #5, 58, 60, or 107; or take the subway to Gulou Dajie, then walk south on Jiugulou Dajie. Drum performances daily every 30min. 2-5pm. Open daily summer 9am-6pm; winter 9am-4:30pm; last admission 30min. before closing time. Y20.)*

SONG QINGLING MUSEUM (sòng qìnglíng gùjū; 宋庆龄故居). Pu Yi, China's last emperor, was born in this park-mansion, but after the end of imperial rule, it became the official residence of Song Qingling, the politically active wife of Sun Yat-sen. Named Honorary President of the PRC at her death, Song was a proponent of democracy and civil rights. After her death in 1981, her home was turned into a museum. English translations describe photos, artifacts, and meticulously preserved rooms and gardens. Blessed with considerably fewer tourists than Prince Gong's Mansion, the Song Qingling grounds retain a much more peaceable, somber mood. *(46 Houhai Beiyan. On the north edge of Houhai Lake, heralded by an ornate gateway. Take bus #5, 210, or 819 to Guozishi; or take the subway to Jishuitan and walk south on Gulou Xi Dajie. ☎6404 4205. Open Tu-Su 9am-5pm; last admission 4pm. Y20, students Y8.)*

XU BEIHONG MUSEUM (xú bēihóng jìniàn guǎn; 徐悲鸿纪念馆). Hailed as the father of modern Chinese painting and realist art, Xu Beihong enjoyed a long and distinguished career of "making ancient things serve the present" and "making foreign things serve China." Among the most celebrated of his works are his large, traditional Chinese-style scrolls of wild, prancing horses, reproductions of which now overflow many a market stall and decorate many a home. More tantalizingly, this large, tastefully arranged museum also showcases Xu's lesser-known works, revealing an evolving style that successfully takes from European and Chinese traditions. (*53 Xinjiekou Bei Dajie. South of the Jishuitan subway stop; or take bus #22 from Qianmen. ☎6225 2187. Open daily 9-11:30am and 1-5pm; last admission 4pm. Y5, students Y2.*)

BEIJING HUTONG TOUR. As Hong Kong tycoons turn vast swaths of Beijing's old neighborhoods into office buildings and hotels, tourism may be the last savior of the city's urban cultural heritage. For those not confident enough to navigate the narrow maze of *hútòng* (alleyways) alone, this 2½-3hr. rickshaw tour traverses one of Beijing's best-preserved graybricked neighborhoods, with stops at Prince Gong's Residence, the Drum and Bell Towers, and sometimes private residences for an additional fee of Y10. (*☎6615 9097. Tours depart at 9am and 2pm from 26 Di'anmen Xi Dajie, at Qianhai Xi Jie, 200m west of Beihai Park's North Gate; take buses #13, 107, 111, or 118 to Beihai Bei Men. English tours available. Reservations sometimes not necessary—just walk up to an empty rickshaw. Y180 per person, admission to sights included.*)

ANDINGMEN 安定门

LAMA TEMPLE (yōnghé gōng; 雍和宫). Wafting clouds of incense do little to obscure the brilliance of the blue, green, and gold detail of the red pagodas. The intricacy of the decoration both inside and out of this colorful Tibetan monastery, also called **Yonghe Lamasery,** is breathtaking. Constructed in 1694 and converted into a lamasery in 1744, Yonghe blends Han, Mongol, Manchu, and Tibetan architectural elements. The temple boasts three "matchless treasures:" an 18m-high sandalwood **Buddha statue,** with a plaque from the Guinness Book of World Records certifying that the Buddha was carved from one tree; the **Mountain of 500 Arhats,** made of precious stones and less-precious metals; and the **"niche of Buddha"** carved out of wood. One exhibition hall displays portraits of Dalai Lamas; the other, more interesting one chronicles (in English) the life of Emperor Qianlong, who promoted the spread of Tibetan Buddhism. Even the unavoidable crowds, all fortified with arm-

officer in the imperial government. The vermillion paint and hefty door rings of copper are classic features of courtyards. The elevated **stone step** in the doorway wards off evil spirits, which are believed to be short, and therefore unable to jump over high steps.

3 If you've practiced your charming smile, you may be able to persuade the owners of this **private courtyard** to let you in. The gate is at the southeast corner; when you enter, you'll first see a screen-wall that shields the interior to protect against evil spirits and to create more privacy. The main house is at the north, facing south, and side buildings line the other three sides. Traditional courtyards and alleys all have gray tiles and stones.

4 This beautifully restored **private sìhéyuàn** is open to the public for Y10. The screen-wall is decorated with an intricate floral carving. There is not much of a courtyard inside, but the traditional gray eaves are carved into scholar slippers. This courtyard also serves as a **bed and breakfast.** (*Contact Jimmy Jing. 12 Dajinsi Hutong, Gulou Jie. ☎6618 5660; fax 6657 0371. Y200 per night.*)

loads of 0.5m-long incense sticks, instill the temple with a vibrancy that enhances rather than diminishes the sense of active spirituality. *(28 Yonghegong Dajie. Take bus #13, 116, or 807 to Yonghegong or Guozijian, or walk south from the Yonghegong subway stop. Buses #56, 816, and 819 also stop nearby. Enter at the tail end of the temple. Open daily 9am-4:30pm. Y25, students and seniors Y12.)*

CONFUCIUS TEMPLE (kǒng miào; 孔庙) **AND IMPERIAL COLLEGE** (guózǐ jiān;国子监). Less grand and much calmer than its counterpart in Qufu (p. 203), this quiet refuge is mostly overlooked by tourists. Inside, 198 stone stelae list the names of over 50,000 successful candidates for the *jìnshì* degree, the highest level of academic achievement in the imperial civil service examination system. Like most academic records, these heavy tablets are stored in an old, dim warehouse in the back. The complex also houses the small **Capital Museum** (shǒudū bówùguǎn; 首都博物馆), which traces the history of Beijing, beginning 400,000 years ago with *Sinanthropus Pekinensis* (Peking Man; see p. 166) and ending with "liberation" in 1949. Continuing that proud history, there is now a 2008 Olympics Beijing exhibit with the requisite torch, jogging outfit, and commemorative plaques on display. *(13 Guozijian Jie. Diagonally opposite the main gate of the Lama Temple. Enter through a decorated archway and walk straight for 3min. ☎8401 1977 or 6401 2118; www.confucius-bj.org.cn. Open daily 8:30am-5pm; last admission 4:30pm. Y10, seniors Y6, students Y3.)*

JIANGUOMEN 建国门

BEIJING ANCIENT OBSERVATORY (běijīng gǔ guānxiàngtái; 北京古观象台). Within Beijing's busy financial district lies one of the world's oldest observatories. Built in 1442 and still in terrific condition, this sanctuary displays amazingly sophisticated navigational and astrological instruments—works of art in their own right—with dragon-encrusted pillars and turtle-shaped pedestals. Skip the ground-level exhibition, which has a few uninspiring displays narrating the history of astronomy, and climb to the rooftop to see eight ancient astrological instruments, bearing exotic names like "Azimuth Theobolite," "Equatorial Armilla," and "Celestial Globe." *(West of the Friendship Store, southwest of the intersection of Erhuan Lu and Jianguomen Nei Dajie. Ride the subway to Jianguomen and take the southwest exit; it's around the corner. Open Su, Tu-Sa 9-11:30am and 1-5pm. Y10, children Y5.)*

RITAN PARK (rìtán gōngyuán; 日坛公园). Sheltered from the bustle of Jianguomen, Ritan Park is one of Beijing's most pleasant parks. Built in 1530, its winding paths and bamboo fences lead to craggy rock formations and sleepy waterways near the south gate. Emperors of the Ming and Qing Dynasties once made sacrificial offerings at Ritan ("Temple of the Sun"). Now, the park is a sanctuary for the elderly and for the occasional expat sporting tank top and jogging shorts. The lack of tour groups guarantees a rare serenity. *(South and main gates at the end of Jianhua Lu, in the heart of the embassy district behind the Friendship Store. West gate at the end of Yabao Lu, opposite the Russian shopping district. Buses #1 and 4 stop nearby on Jianguomen Wai Dajie. Open daily 6am-9pm. Y1, students Y0.5; monthly ticket Y3.)*

CHONGWENMEN 崇文门

▧ TIANTAN (TEMPLE OF HEAVEN) 天坛

South of the city center, between Erhuan Lu and Sanhuan Lu. Bordered by Tiantan Lu (north gate), Tiantan Dong Lu (east gate, at Tiyuguan Lu), Yongdingmen Dong Jie (south gate), and Qianmen Dajie/Yongdingmen Nei Dajie (west gate, at Nanwei Lu). Buses #2, 6, 15, 17, 20, 34, 35, 36, 105, 106, 110, 120, 803, and 814 all stop at least 1 of the 4 gates. Park open daily 6am-8pm; sights open 8am-6pm. Park high season Y15, low season Y10; students Y8/Y5. Ticket including all 3 sights Y35/Y30.

Emperors of the Ming and Qing Dynasties built a total of four imperial shrines (tán; 坛) in Beijing, one each for *tiān* (heaven), *dì* (earth), *rì* (sun), and *yuè* (moon). The largest and grandest of the four, **Tiantan** (tiāntán gōngyuán; 天坛公园) remains a lasting symbol of Beijing, immortalized in Chinese memory as a resplendent remembrance of dynastic splendor.

The imperial architects designed the Temple of Heaven to be the altar for the annual imperial ceremony to appease the heavens, secure good harvests, atone for sins, and receive divine direction. The 273-hectare complex is rounded at its northern edge and square along its southern edge, reflecting the traditional Chinese belief that the earth is square and the heavens are round. Imperial processions passed "from earth to heaven" along a long, elevated boulevard paved with smooth slabs of stone, linking the Circular Mound Altar in the south to the Temple of Heaven in the north. Constructed in 1420 and opened to the public in 1949, Tiantan draws crowds of tai chi practitioners, bird-cage bearers, and traditional Chinese musicians at dawn. During the day, crowds congregate at the three major sights, but the vast forested grounds promise plenty of breathing room—and the cleanest air in Beijing. Striking out on many of the dirt paths scattered throughout the park leads to quiet woods, unfrequented save for the rare elderly local. Once within Tiantan's red walls and strolling down its pathways shaded by tall pines and cypresses, you'll completely forget about the city beyond the walls.

HALL OF PRAYER FOR GOOD HARVEST (qí nián diàn; 祈年殿). With its gleaming blue-, yellow-, and green-glazed tiles, the three-layered eaves crowning the Hall of Prayer can be glimpsed from most places in the park, as long as there's a clearing in the trees. The three colors represent the heavens, earth, and mortal realm, appropriate for this temple, where the emperor prayed for blessings from heaven. The Hall of Prayer is Tiantan, a hallmark of Ming engineering and an image of China recognized the world over. Constructed entirely without the use of nails, cement, or beams, the hall has kept its proud pose for more than 500 years, held up only by an elaborate network of interlocking pillars. Inside, four gigantic "dragon" pillars represent the seasons, and two dozen smaller ones symbolize the 12 months of the year. At the very center of the hall, set in the floor, is the propitious stone, a slab of marble with the natural likeness of a dragon and phoenix. A wooden carving high up on the ceiling reflects the same image. Three tiers of exquisitely carved white marble rings raise up the hall even higher, adding elevation to its grandeur. The clamoring tourists, the gimmicky vendors, the loudspeaker-touting tour guides—nothing can reduce its majesty. *(From the east or west gate, walk toward the center of the park; it's impossible to miss.)*

ECHO WALL (huíyīn bì; 回音壁). Thanks to its perfect curvature, a mere murmur at one side of this circular wall will supposedly travel with perfect clarity all the way around. But with visitors hooting and howling everywhere, it's impossible to put that theory to the test. The **Triple Echo Stones** (sānyīn shí; 三音石), immediately in front of the hall, are similarly hindered by all the din. Stand on the first stone and clap, and the echo comes back once; on the second stone, the sound returns twice; and on the third, three times. Though you might be hard-pressed to hear an echo, what you will hear is a continuous, "I think I heard something..." murmur throughout the courtyard. Clamor aside, this courtyard was designed to enclose the **Imperial Vault of Heaven** (huáng qióng yǔ; 皇穹宇), which housed tablets for sacrificial rites. A smaller version of the Hall of Prayer, this vault is likewise topped by a blue-tiled, mushroom-capped roof, upon which a blue-green gilded dragon plays with a pearl. *(Walk south on the stone boulevard from the Hall of Prayers for Good Harvest.)*

BEIJING

CIRCULAR MOUND ALTAR (yuán qiū; 圆丘). This sight will tickle a numerologist's fancy: its structure, surrounding stairs, and railings are all based on the lucky imperial number nine. The three tiers of the altar represent the heavens, earth, and mortal realm. Join the other stamping, yelling, and occasionally mooing visitors eager to test out the timeless qualities of physics from the central stone on the top tier; the sound will reverberate off the stones. *(Farther south along the main park axis.)*

DOUBLE PAVILION (shuāngtíng; 双亭). An architectural oddity that you'll probably never see elsewhere, this structure consists of two round pavilions fused together in the middle. Built by Emperor Qianlong in 1741 as a gift for his mother's 60th birthday, the twin pavilions symbolize two longevity peaches. The theme of pairs continues through the double-eaved roofs, topped by brilliant peacock-blue tiles. The gilded rounded tips represent "harmony, auspiciousness, and longevity." Follow the pavilioned walkways to gardens and peaceful woods, or admire the stately pines and rambling rocks directly across. *(Northeast of the west gate; walk down the main path, past the 2nd pair of gates, and turn left at the sign a few min. down.)*

OTHER TIANTAN SIGHTS. Popular myth claims that the **Seven Star Stones** (qīxīng yán; 七星岩) fell from heaven as meteors, but visitors may be disappointed to learn that history is slightly more grounded. The Ming emperor Jiajing placed these mastodonic rocks in Tiantan during his reign. Inscribed with designs of mountains, they symbolize the peaks of the sacred Taishan. *(Southwest from the Hall of Prayer.)* Three days before sacrificial rites, emperors would sequester themselves in the **Fasting Palace** (zhāigōng; 斋宫), away from the wily reaches of meat, drink, and women. As one might expect of a place of asceticism, the buildings are not terribly exciting, save for some original furniture from Qianlong's reign. *(After entering the west gate, turn right from the main path shortly after passing the 2nd pair of gates.)*

OTHER SIGHTS IN CHONGMENWEN

NATURAL HISTORY MUSEUM (zìrán bówùguǎn; 自然博物馆). Though the largest museum of its kind in China, this place hardly takes itself seriously—it even quotes Maxim Gorky ("Man, oh what an arrogant creation!"). The main halls focus on plant, animal, and human evolution. There is a graphic excess of pickled worms and deformed fetuses swimming in formaldehyde, but you can easily avoid them and spend your time with enormous dinosaur fossils. On ground level, there's a rather sad aquarium, with tanks more suitable for restaurants than for exotic, endangered fish. English translations are patchy if you can't decipher Latin genus names. *(126 Tianqiao Nan Dajie. An ivy-covered building 7min. north of Tiantan Park's West Gate. Take bus #2, 6, 20, 54, 120, or others to Tianqiao or Tiantan. ☎6702 4431. Open daily 8:30am-5pm; last admission 4pm. Y15, students and seniors Y10.)*

XUANWUMEN 宣武门

GRAND VIEW GARDEN (dàguān yuán; 大观园). Planned and built according to descriptions in Cao Xueqin's *Dream of the Red Chamber*, the Grand View Garden meticulously replicates the mansion and garden of the tragic novel. It also served as the set for the popular TV series based on the story. The landscape is surreally pristine, with sights bearing romantic names like "Spilling Jade Pavilion," "Seeping Fragrance Bridge," and "Grave of Flowers." The most charming sight on the grounds may be the "Paddy Sweet Cottage," a secluded thatched hut, encircled by a wooden fence and a thick tangle of bamboo shoots. Even if some of the rock formations and buildings seem artificial due to the lack of wear and tear, lakeside paths make for a gorgeous walk in this imagined world. Familiarizing yourself with the story beforehand is a good idea, given the lack of English translations. *(12*

Nancaiyuan Jie, west of Taoranting along Yongdingmen Dong Binhe Lu. Buses #53 and 59 make the trip from Qianmen; 122 from Beijing Station and Jianguomen; 351 from Fengtai; 395 from Fuxingmen; 800 from Jianguomen, Deshengmen, and Xizhimen. ☎6354 2299, 6354 4993 or 6354 4994. Open daily 8:30am-5:30pm; last admission 4:30pm. Y15, students Y8.)

NIUJIE MOSQUE (niújiē lǐbài sì; 牛街礼拜寺). Built in AD 996 by Arab scholar Nasuratan, the mosque combines Arab and traditional Chinese palace architecture. The intricately decorated main hall opens onto panel after panel of gold Arabic script on a red background. The breathtaking hall spills into a courtyard of green plants and pink flowers. The mosque is fully operational, and visitors must respect all rules regarding personal appearance. Don't despair—the mosque lends out garish checkered pants to the one or two inappropriately dressed visitors, to the amusement of its friendly inhabitants. *(On Niu Jie, south of Guang'anmen Nei Dajie. Look for the wall with painted dancers in traditional Arab garb; the mosque is right across the street. Bus #10 from Xidan, Dongdan, and Tian'anmen stop in front; 6, 40, 50, 53, and 109 stop nearby at Guang'anmen or Niu Jie. No skirts or shorts. Open daily 8am-4pm. Y10, students Y5.)*

WHITE CLOUD TEMPLE (báiyún guān; 白云观). White Cloud, Beijing's most active Daoist temple complex, is a sleeper of a tourist attraction. Monks with distinctive topknots inhabit the grounds, but otherwise, only the occasional foreigner makes an appearance. The **Shrine Hall for the Jade Emperor** houses two light-up, revolving cones, strangely reminiscent of large Christmas trees, with rows upon rows of miniature Buddhas, individually labeled to honor patrons of the temple. Beyond that, White Cloud's biggest attraction is the "wind-containing" bridge, nothing more than a white, stone arch with a large coin hanging from its crest. Visitors can hurl tokens (Y10 for 50) at the coin, which has a bell in its center; hitting the bell brings good luck, granted to you by a tiny voice that booms metallically out from under the bridge. *(6 Baiyun Lu, Xibianmen Wai. Take bus #19, 40, 49, or 848 to Tianning Si and head north; or take 48 or 308 to Baiyun Lu. Open daily May-Sept. 8:30am-5pm; Oct.-Apr. 8:30am-4pm. Last admission 30min. before closing. Y10.)*

TAORANTING PARK (táorántíng gōngyuán; 陶然亭公园). Taoranting is one of the city's most serene parks (but only when the kids are at school). Behind the amusement parks and waterslides, lovers snuggle and the elderly stroll along lakeside paths. Look for the Yuan-Dynasty **Temple of Mercy,** used as a base by May 4th revolutionaries. *(19 Taiping Jie, between Taoranting Lu and Yongdingmen Dong Binhe Lu. Buses #20, 54, 59, 102, and 106 stop in front; 1 and 40 stop nearby. Open daily summer 6am-10pm; winter 6am-8:30 or 9pm. Pool Y15. Y2, students Y1.)*

FUXINGMEN 复兴门

NATIONAL MILITARY MUSEUM (jūnshì bówùguǎn; 军事博物馆). Tanks, planes, and war galore! With an overwhelming number of camera flashes and enough artillery to start a revolution, this museum is a military junkie's dream come true. They've got missiles, tanks, mine-layers, and fighter planes on the ground floor, and every type of handheld weapon known to mankind on the second. Just to remind people that peace is better than war (it's easy to get a bit carried away downstairs), the top floor has a quiet display of friendship gifts presented to China from various countries. But few make it up this far, preferring to drool over the grenade and torpedo displays. Beware of overactive little boys sitting in missile launchers. *(9 Fuxing Lu. ☎6686 6135. Take subway line #1 to Junshi Bowuguan "Jūn Bó"; accessible by bus #1, 4, or 728 from Tian'anmen; it's the huge building with the unmistakable PLA star perched atop. Open daily 8:30am-5:30pm; last admission 4:30pm. Y20, students Y10.)*

BEIJING

FUCHENGMEN 阜成门

GUANGJI TEMPLE (guǎngjì sì; 广济寺). When Beijing was but a vacant stretch of land during the 12th century, villagers built this temple, known as the Liu Village Temple, but it was soon abandoned until the 15th century, when the Ming government sponsored its reconstruction. The small temple now features images of Buddha, stone turtles, and pillar fragments that confirm the ruined temple's original location. The Chinese Buddhist Association has used this quiet, humble refuge as its headquarters since 1953. Be sure to note the unique roof ridge of Daxiong Hall: the combination of water, lotus flowers, and Sanskrit represents the everlasting world. Bright red columns enclose a library (closed to the public) of 100,000 volumes of rare scripture, including a complete set of the Ming Dynasty "Grand Collection of Scriptures." *(25 Fuchengmen Nei Dajie, at Xisi Dajie. Bus #13, 101, or 103 to Xisi; or walk east from the Fuchengmen subway stop. ☎ 6617 1074. Open daily 6am-4:30pm. Free.)*

WHITE PAGODA TEMPLE (báitǎ sì; 白塔寺). The ancient Indian-inspired temple has a huge chalky body, designed to look like an upside-down alms bowl, with an intricate, gold-gilded Buddhist *stupa* resting on top. The temple houses a small collection of Qing Buddhist relics, with one particular room overflowing with more Tibetan-style Buddha statues than imaginable. Going around the pagoda clockwise, from west to east, is said to bring happiness and dispel disease. *(171 Fuchengmen Nei Dajie. Take bus #13, 38, 101, 103, 812, 814, or 850 to Baitasi, or walk 8min. east from the Fuchengmen subway stop, or walk west from Guangji Temple. Open daily 8:30am-5pm; last admission 4:30pm. Y10, Chinese students and seniors Y5.)*

LU XUN MUSEUM (lǔxùn bówùguǎn; 鲁讯博物馆). This museum, which houses the acclaimed revolutionary writer's self-designed Beijing residence, has over 30,000 Lu Xun relics, including pens, photographs, original manuscripts, and his personal library. *(19 Gongmenkou Ertiao. ☎ 6615 6548 or 6616 4169. Take the 1st left at the KFC as you walk east on Fuchengmen Nei Bei Dajie from the Fuchengmen subway stop; it's at the end of the road. Open Su, Tu-Sa 9am-3:30pm; last admission 3:30pm. Y5, students Y3.)*

XIZHIMEN 西直门

BEIJING ZOO (běijīng dòngwùyuán; 北京动物园). Willow-shaded paths, placid lakes, and chirping birds make the zoo a pleasant spot for a stroll. Adorable pandas are the major tourist attraction and live in more comfortable surroundings than other animals. *(Northwest of city center, on Xizhimen Wai Dajie. Buses stop directly outside: #7 from Hepingmen; 15 from Fuximen; 27 from Deshengmen; 102 and 105 from Xuanwumen; 103 from Wangfujing or Beijing Train Station; 107 from Dongzhimen; and 111 from Chongwenmen. Subway to Xizhimen; switch to buses #7, 27, 105, 808, or 904. Open daily mid-Mar. to mid-Nov. 7:30am-5:30 or 6pm; mid-Nov. to mid-Mar. 7:30am-5pm. Pandas Y5. Admissions Apr.-Oct. Y15, students and seniors Y8; Nov.-Mar. Y10/Y5. Children under 1.2m free.)*

PURPLE BAMBOO PARK (zǐzhúyuàn gōngyuán; 紫竹院公园). Beijing's lovers come here to grow drowsy in one another's arms. The park is an emerald maze of waterways and footbridges, with sprawling lawns, pavilions, and lots of bamboo. *(Just west of the zoo, on Zizhuyuan Lu, continuation of Xizhimen Wai Dajie. Walk from zoo; or take bus #114, 300, 323, 374, or 817 to Zizhuyuan; or bus #320, 332, 347, or 360 to Baishiqiao to the west gate. ☎ 6842 5851. Open daily 6am-8:30pm; last admission 7pm. Y2, students Y1.)*

BEYOND THE THIRD RING ROAD
SUMMER PALACE 颐和园

Minibus #375 (from Xizhimen) is the quickest, stopping at the road to the east gate. **Bus** #332 and 732 from the zoo, and 726 and 826 from Qianmen terminate at the east gate. 817 (Fuchengmen) stops at the east gate and ends at the north gate, also served by 801

(Old Summer Palace), 904 (Xizhimen, zoo, Fragrant Hills), and 808 (Qianmen). 331 links the Palace with the Old Summer Palace heading to the city and to Fragrant Hills heading away. From Qianmen, the Palace is 2hr. away by bike. Open daily Apr.-Oct. 6:30am-6pm; Nov.-Mar. 7am-5pm. All halls close 1hr. earlier. Park Apr.-Oct. Y30, students Y15, through ticket Y50 (includes Garden of Virtue and Harmony Y5, Tower of the Incense of Buddha Y10, and Suzhou Jie/Hall of Serenity Y10); Nov.-Mar. Y20/Y10/Y40. English maps Y5.

First constructed by Qianlong in 1750, the magnificent **Summer Palace** (yìhé yuán) contains over 3000 halls, pavilions, towers, courtyards, and most eye-catching of all, a sweeping lake. The park only gained true splendor under Dowager Empress Ci Xi, who embezzled money intended for the imperial navy to build her pleasure palace. The navy lost to the Japanese, but today tourists and locals can take advantage of Ci Xi's dishonesty and revel in her elaborate summertime playground.

Entering from the main (east) gate, travelers first encounter a series of rooms and courtyards, many of which contain relics left over from Ci Xi's day, including old carriages. The side rooms display "everyday" artifacts and many rooms are furnished as they would have been 150 years ago. Backtrack a bit and turn left past the Hall of Benevolence for a stroll along the stunning 728m **Long Corridor** (cháng láng; 长廊), a pavilion-archway meandering along **Kunming Lake** (kūnmíng hú; 昆明湖). Admire the intricate 14,000 pastoral pictures painted on the ceiling as you head toward the **Tower of the Incense of Buddha** (fóxiāng gé; 佛香阁), atop Longevity Hill. Perfect for emperors seeking spiritual guidance without leaving their vacation resort, this octagonal structure also provides a gorgeous, all-encompassing view of the lake. Nearby is the **Buddhist Tenants' Hall** and the **Pavilion of Fragrant Rocks,** where you can duck in and out of the oddly shaped stone passageways.

Along the back lake is a must-see, albeit very artificial, re-creation of the southern Chinese city of Suzhou (p. 366) where empresses would go "shopping" for fine silk. Within **Suzhou Jie** (苏州街), cool green water laps the sidewalks, stylized gondolas idle beside dumpling restaurants, and stone walkways wind between water on one side and shops, snack stands, and street artists on the other. With all the picture-taking, backpack-sporting, sunglass-wearing daytrippers, this remade town is more like a modern carnival.

To steer clear of the most concentrated crowds, walk south along the lakeshore in the direction opposite **Longevity Hill,** *away* from all the temples—use the Tower of the Incense of Buddha as a landmark. Weepy willows, quaint little stone bridges arched over rivulets, and a few lovey-dovey couples share these backwaters. Or, follow the signs to the less-traveled, northern park area. Here, the **Hall of Serenity** displays a collection of imperial furniture. Waterside pavilions and tranquil lily ponds make up the **Garden of Harmonious Pleasures,** a "garden within a garden," whose best attribute is its relative peacefulness.

Other sights include Empress Dowager Ci Xi's infamous **Marble Boat,** a stationary edifice built courtesy of embezzled funds, the **Seventeen-Arch Bridge** topped with 544 stone lions, the **Pavilion for Listening to Orioles,** and the **Porcelain Pagoda.** *(Paddleboat stations open daily 8am-around 6pm; Y30-40 per hr., deposit Y200-400. Small, imperial-style ferries make one-way trips to different areas along the lake 9am-6pm; Y6.)*

OTHER SIGHTS BEYOND THE THIRD RING ROAD

OLD SUMMER PALACE (yuánmíng yuán; 园明园). Unlike its splendid younger counterpart, the desolate Old Summer Palace remains in ruins from its plunder and pillage by French and British troops during the Second Opium War. Only the winding stone labyrinth, an imitation of a European-style maze, was left unscathed. During the Mid-Autumn Moon Festival, emperors held celebrations here: maids clutching lanterns would run through the maze, and prizes would be heaped on whomever reached the center of the maze first.

BEIJING

Unlikely Families

A famous Chinese saying holds that "When the moon is full, mankind is one." The spirit of this proverb pervades the celebration of the Mid-Autumn Festival, also called the Moon Festival, which marks the middle of autumn, when the moon is at its largest. Embellished with the mystery of ancient legends, the Mid-Autumn Festival—at its core a harvest celebration marking the equinox—is a poetic evening during which friends and family gather together outside to eat mooncakes, enjoy the cooling air, and gaze at the full moon, a symbol of harmony and reunion.

On the evening of the Mid-Autumn Festival a few years ago, I found myself madly bicycling in and out of Beijing's rush-hour traffic along tree-lined streets on my way to the Summer Palace. I had spent the last month and a half in Beijing, studying Mandarin at the Beijing Language and Culture University in Haidian District. Learning the language was proving to be a challenge. Four hours of class each day didn't feel like enough time—though sitting in a spartan, windowless classroom from 8am until noon certainly felt like an eternity. My limited linguistic ability meant that what I could see and do in the afternoons after class only scratched at the surface of what Beijing had to offer. In the faces of those I passed on the street, I saw hundreds of thousands of stories waiting to be shared, and for the first time in my life, I was literally at a loss for words—all I seemed able to muster was "Hello, my name is Emma. I am from the United States. Are you from Beijing?"

"Hang in there," friends who had been in Beijing longer told me. "One day, everything suddenly clicks." So I let myself get dragged to dinners, nodding dumbly, laughing politely, struggling to catch key words or phrases. I eavesdropped on conversations on the bus. I kept the TV on all the time when I was in my apartment in the hope that I would absorb the sound of the language. I started spending a great deal of time with a Chinese friend who would, in broken English, patiently explain measure words or auxiliary verbs over and over again to me as we sipped eight-treasures tea at a downtown teahouse.

And so it was that I found myself en route to the Summer Palace that evening in the middle of October. When my friends and I arrived, giddy from the near-death experience of bicycling in Beijing, the sun was setting in a brilliant flash of color over Kunming Lake. We bought several bottles of beer and a box of mooncakes filled with lotus seed paste and sprawled out on the grass nearby. The Palace grounds were filled with people: families strolling sedately arm in arm, high school kids in their uniforms jumping around to the latest hits blaring from a boom box, and tourists toting cameras and posing by each pagoda.

As the sky began to darken and the moon became visible, my Korean friend turned to me and said in Chinese, "Look at all those Chinese families! And look at us—we're like one big, crazy family!" I laughed and responded, "And what an unlikely family we are."

It wasn't until a few minutes later that I realized I had just had my first real exchange in Mandarin. I recreated it in my mind: a comment had been made in Mandarin, and I had understood it, reacted to it, and responded in Mandarin.

I looked around at my friends lounging on the grass, stuffing their faces with mooncakes and drinking cheap Chinese beer, and realized that what I had just said so casually had actually been true: thousands of miles from home, stranded in a foreign language, and surrounded every day by things we didn't understand, we had become a family of sorts. Among the 15 of us, we spoke seven languages natively. Our homes spanned the globe—from Britain to Indonesia, Italy to Ghana. And yet here we were, sitting together on the grounds of a centuries-old Chinese palace, laughing at the world, and staring at the full moon.

Over the next several months, my Mandarin proficiency improved exponentially. At the same time, I discovered that knowing the local language can sometimes be as much of a liability as it is an asset. I learned that not all of the stories behind the faces of those I met on the street were ones I wanted to hear. Throughout the trials and tribulations of life in Beijing, however, I kept fresh the memory of sitting under the full moon with a group of sudden friends and discovering a common language.

Emma Nothmann has traveled China from Beijing to Yunnan, on her own and as a researcher-writer for Let's Go: China, *4th ed. She is a Harvard graduate with a degree in East Asian Studies, the publishing director of the* Let's Go 2005 *series, and editor of* Let's Go: Southeast Asia, *8th ed.*

Today, only broken stone fragments and the gardens' pretty names (like Eternal Spring Garden) offer a glimpse of the palace's former grandeur. There is a wild, untamed quality about these ruins, half-overgrown with grass, that grant them a sad, haunting grace. During late July and August, stroll to the **Lotus-Viewing Area,** where the lake surface vanishes beneath blossoming lotus flowers and wide green leaves, all in wild disarray. *(Northeast of the Summer Palace. Many buses stop outside: #716 from the zoo; 722 from Xizhimen; 810 from the Forbidden City or Chaoyangmen; 826 and 726 from Qianmen or Summer Palace; 331, 801, and 973 from the Summer Palace; 331 and 318 from Fragrant Hills. Minibus costs Y5 from the Summer Palace, taxi Y10. Open daily 7am-7pm. Grounds Y10, students Y5; European palaces and labyrinth Y15/Y5.)*

GREAT BELL TEMPLE (dàzhōng sì; 大钟寺). This endearing temple believes that "every bell is a nutshell of a part of history and culture." The "bell forest," a veritable museum, contains several hundred bells, from primitive pottery bells of the Warring States Period (475-221 BC) to utilitarian Mao-era bells. Few tourists stop by the temple, but it's worth the trip just to see the **Great Bell,** the fifth-largest bell in the world and one of the oldest. Over 230,000 characters from Buddhist scriptures and prayers adorn the interior of the bell; duck your head inside for a look. Suspended in mid-air, the Great Bell rings every Spring Festival, and its peals can supposedly be heard throughout much of Beijing proper. For Y2, visitors can climb a set of stairs to toss a coin in the hole of the bell for good luck. *(31A Bei Sanhuan Xi Lu. Buses #300, 367, and 601 from the zoo stop outside. Buses #8, 201, 836, and 967 also stop nearby. Open daily 8:30am-4:30pm. Y10, students Y5.)*

🎭 ENTERTAINMENT

ACROBATICS

Chinese acrobatics is a dizzying pinnacle of artistic achievement: plates whirl on poles and grinning contortionists fold in half while trapeze artists, tumblers, and dozens of girls perch precariously on unicycles and other frail contraptions.

Chaoyang Theater (cháoyáng jùchǎng; 朝阳剧场), 36 Dong Sanhuan Bei Lu, Hujialou, Chaoyang (☎6507 2421). Tickets Y100-300. Performances nightly 7:15-8:30pm.

Tiandi Theater (tiāndì jùchǎng; 天地剧场), 10 Dongzhimen Wai Dajie (☎6502 3984 or 6502 2649), 3min. north of the Poly Plaza. Features the **Children's Team of the China Acrobatics Troupe.** Tickets Y100-300. Performances nightly 7:15-8:30pm.

Wansheng Theater (wànshèng jùchǎng; 万胜剧场), 95 Tianqiao Shichang, Xuanwu (☎6303 7449 or 6702 2324). From the west gate of Tiantan Park, turn right onto Qianmen Dajie and walk north. Features the **Beijing Acrobatics Troupe.** Tickets Y100-300. Performances nightly 7:15-8:45pm.

BEIJING OPERA

There are as many types of Chinese opera as there are Chinese dialects, but Beijing opera (jīngjù; 京剧) is by far the most well-known. Performers in elaborate costumes and colorful facial makeup (configurations for different personalities and characters) act, sing, and dance out dramatic accounts of Chinese history and classical tales to a flurry of music and acrobatics. An orchestra of wind, string, and percussion instruments accompanies the performances. As a concession to the modern era, the traditional all-night affair has been toned down to 2hr. versions, with translations flashing on electronic screens.

Huguang Guild Hall (húguǎng huìguǎn; 湖广会馆), 3 Hufangqiao, Xuanwu (☎6351 8284 or 6352 9134), at the southwest corner at Luomashi Dajie. Take bus #6, 14, 15, 25, 34, 53, or 102 to Hufangqiao. From Liulichang, walk about 20min. south down Nan Xinhua Jie. Segments of famous operas presented in a beautiful traditional theater once visited by Mao Zedong. Within the authentically Chinese stone and red wood complex, you'll also find a small museum and a courtyard with wandering ducks and roosters. If you don't want to read subtitles, English and Japanese translation headphones are available for rent. Tickets, including snacks, tea, and fruit platter, Y150-580; Chinese students Y120. Ticket office open 9am-4pm. Performances nightly 7:30-8:30pm.

Liyuan Theatre (líyuán jùchǎng; 梨园剧场), Qianmen Hotel, 175 Yong'an Lu (☎6301 6688, ext. 8860), at the northeast corner at Hufang Lu. Take the bus to Hufangqiao or Hufang Lu. Opera segments accompanied by senseless English subtitles performed in a clean-cut, Western-style theater. Tickets Y40-180. Pictures with actors Y10. Ticket office open 9am-8pm. Performances nightly 7:30-8:45pm.

Chang'an Grand Theatre (cháng'ān dà xìyuàn; 长安大戏院), Chang'an Bldg., 7 Jianguomen Nei Dajie, Dongcheng (☎6510 1309 or 6510 1308). Buses #1, 4, 20. 2½hr. performances with scenes from various operas in a Western-style theater. Little acrobatic work apart from swordplay. Possibly the only theater also offering full-length operas aside from segment performances. Closed for renovations at time of writing in Aug. 2004. Tickets Y20-380. Ticket office open 9am-8:30pm. Performances daily 7pm.

Zhengyici Theatre (zhèngyìcí xìlóu; 正乙祠戏楼), 220 Xi Heyan (☎8315 1649). Take the subway to Hepingmen; head south and turn left down the narrow road at the Quanjude Roast Duck Restaurant. Follow the string of flags and red lanterns. China's 1st opera house is closed for renovation until 2005. Performances nightly 7:30-9pm.

GALLERIES AND ART MUSEUMS

National Art Museum of China (zhōngguó měishù guǎn; 中国美术馆), 1 Wusi Dajie (☎6401 7076; fax 8403 4953). Take buses #101, 103, 109, 111, 112, 803, or 810 to Meishu Guan. This spacious museum is one of China's best. 21 halls display well-curated exhibits of remarkable scroll paintings, folk paper cut-outs, foreign spotlights, and contemporary art. Open daily 9am-5pm; last admission 4pm. Y20, students Y10.

Red Gate Gallery (hóngmén huàláng; 红门画廊 ; ☎6525 1005; www.redgategallery.com), Dongbianmen Watchtower. Ask for Dongnan Cheng Jiaolou (东南城角楼). From the Jianguomen subway stop, walk about 15min. south on Jianguomen Nan Dajie, well past the Gloria Plaza Hotel; look for the towering stone building with a red temple to the right. One of the first private galleries in Beijing to challenge the boundaries of acceptable art. A small but wonderful collection of recent works by local artists on 1st and 4th fl., exorbitantly expensive rocks on 2nd fl. Exhibits change monthly. Open Su, Tu-Sa 9am-5pm. Y10, students Y5.

Courtyard Gallery (sìhéyuàn huàláng; 四合苑画廊), 95 Donghuamen Dajie, basement (☎6526 8882; www.courtyard-gallery.com), next to the moat east of the Forbidden City, behind a wall of bamboo. Short walk from the Forbidden City or Jingshan Park. This funky, 1-room gallery displays mixed-media modern art installations. Congregation spot for young, energetic artists. Overhanging eaves shelter a posh Western restaurant. Exhibits change about twice per month. Open M-Sa 11am-7pm, Su noon-7pm. Free.

Poly Art Museum (☎6500 8117; fax 6501 0263), on Dongzhimen Nan Dajie, 2nd fl. of the posh Poly Plaza. Take the subway loop line to Dongsi Shitiao. Extensive collection of Sui and Tang sculptures, well-preserved *bodhisattvas*, flying *apsaras*, and ancient scrolls make up for the expensive admission. Open Tu, Th, Sa 9:30am-4:30pm. Y50.

◪ TEA HOUSES

Typical Beijing tea houses not only serve tea and traditional snacks like sunflower and watermelon seeds, but also feature Beijing opera, acrobatic performances, magic tricks, traditional music, and more. Tea ceremonies (chá dào; 茶道) take place at several venues.

Lao She Tea House (laǒshě cháguǎn; 老舍茶馆), Dawancha Bldg., 3 Qianmen Xi Dajie, 2nd fl. (☎6303 6506 or 6303 4748 ; www.laosheteahouse.com), about 5min. west of Qianmen; take the bus or subway to Qianmen. The 2nd fl. is a grassy, contemplative retreat of private tea rooms starting at Y60. Tea Y30 and up. The lacquered wood and covered lanterns on the 3rd. fl. evoke an air of days long past. Performances include opera segments, instrumental music, acrobatic swordplay, magic tricks, and comedy routines. Restaurant across from performance room serves dishes ranging Y10-160; open daily 9am-9pm. Jīngjù karaoke W and F 2-4pm; Y10 includes cup of tea. Tickets Y40-130. Free snacks. Shows daily 7:50-9:20pm.

Sanwei Bookstore (sānwèi shūwū; 三味书屋), 60 Fuxingmen Nei Dajie (☎6601 3204), at an alley corner off the main street, across from the Minzu Hotel (民族饭店). Take the subway or bus to Xidan and head west. Candles, bird cages, and expensive tea await on the 2nd fl. of this ancient, dusty bookstore. Chinese folk music with translated explanations of the history of each traditional instrument on Sa; Western music on F. Eight-treasures tea Y25. Cover Y30. Open daily 9:30am-10:30pm, F 9:30am-11:30pm.

Purple Vine Tea House (zǐ téng lú; 紫藤庐), 2 Nanchang Jie (☎6606 6614), on the corner of Xihuamen, between the Forbidden City and Beihai. Heading west from the Forbidden City on Chang'an Jie, turn right on Nanchang Jie, or take bus #5 to Xihuamen. Cozy little wooden rooms serve cups of tranquility starting at Y40 per person. 40min. tea ceremonies conducted in both English and Chinese Y188. Open daily noon-2am.

▥ SHOPPING

Wangfujing Dajie, an upscale street with lots of stores and lots of action, runs north-south east of Tian'anmen Square. The street sells real designer labels and boasts the huge **Oriental Sun Dong An Plaza.** West of Tian'anmen off Chang'an Jie, **Xidan** is home to cheap European and American fashions. The vast **Friendship Store** (yǒuyì shāngdiàn; 友谊商店), 17 Jianguomen Wai Dajie, is a self-contained commercial cosmos with exorbitant prices (read: tourist trap for unsuspecting foreigners) but an incongruous dollar-store feel. (Open daily 9am-9pm.)

For upscale products, try **Watson's** (wòtèsēn; 沃特森), at the Holiday Inn Lido; the **Lufthansa Center** (yànshā shāngchéng; 燕沙商城), 50 Liangmaqiao Lu, also known as the **Kempinski Hotel** (kǎibīnsījī fàndiàn; 凯宾斯基饭店); the **China World Trade Center,** 1 Jianguomen Wai Dajie; or the **Pacific Department Store** (tàipíngyáng bǎihuò yíngkēdiàn; 太平洋百货盈科店), A2 Gongti Bei Lu (☎6539 3888), about 2min. west of the Zhaolong Hotel. The glitzy **Hualian Shopping Center** (huálián shāngshà; 华联商厦), across from Vartone New World Plaza at Fuchengmen Wai Dajie, also has designer goods, as well as a sprawling basement supermarket.

■**PANJIAYUAN FLEA MARKET** (pānjiāyuán jiùhuò shìchǎng; 潘家园旧货市场). Wake up at the crack of dawn to peek at one of Beijing's best shopping spots. Antiques and not-so-antiques stretch for what seems like miles beneath a vast overhead canopy. Nowhere else will you find such a huge selection of high-quality, dirt-cheap goods (large art scrolls Y30-35, giant scrolls go up to Y100). Unique wares like traditional Chinese shadow puppets go for Y50 and up, or hopefully lower if you're a bargainer extraordinaire. *(At Panjiayuan, in the southeast part of the city, near Dong Sanhuan Nan Lu. Accessible by buses #34, 51, 63, 64, 368, 730, 800, 810. Open M-F 8:30am-6pm, Sa-Su 4:30am-4:30pm; busiest from 5am to around 1pm.)*

SILK ALLEY (xiùshuǐ shìchǎng; 秀水市场). Oceans of silk spill into the street in the form of shirts, lingerie, teddy-bear pajamas, and traditional Chinese dresses. The market also peddles brand-name (sometimes authentic) merchandise that might fall apart before you even get home. Shifty characters lead customers down alleys to reveal duffle bags full of pirated CDs and movies (Y7-10). Accustomed to rich tourists, vendors scrutinize their potential prey with a practiced eye, on the prowl for easily swindled shoppers. The clientele is almost completely foreign, resulting in much higher prices than what a local would ever dream of paying. Nevertheless, it's a whole lot cheaper than anything you could find at home. Don't buy anything for more than Y100; most goods are imitation products, no matter how convincingly made they are. *(On Xiushui Dong Jie, a tiny street stretching from the north side of Jianguomen Wai Dajie, between the Friendship Store and the Jianguo Hotel next to the US Embassy. Take bus #1,4, 120, or 802 to Yong'an Li. Just look for the crowds.)*

LIULICHANG (liúlìchǎng; 琉璃厂). The antique market of Liulichang combines the brilliant reds, blues, and golds of sleek traditional restoration with the timeless art of the con. Stores overflow with vases, scrolls, calligraphy, and carpets, both genuine antiques and convincing imitations. Liulichang is a well-known tourist trap and prices are exorbitantly high—compare prices and bargain up a storm. *(Off Nan Xinhua Jie, perpendicular to Erhuan, southwest of Qianmen. Bus #14, 15, or 66. Or take the subway to Hepingmen and walk south on Nan Xinhua Dajie. Most stores open daily 9am-5pm.)*

PEARL MARKET (hóngqiáo shìchǎng; 红桥市场). Rows of pearls in every color, style, and quality imaginable fill the third floor of this indoor market. Real pearls should have a grainy surface that you can test by scraping; it should retain its shiny quality. It is quite possible to snatch a deal here after bargaining down the high starting costs. The lower levels of the market sell "Prada" handbags and other brand-name imitations for a fraction of the prices at the Silk Market. The basement has a seafood market, no doubt to make use of all those oysters. *(A few min. northeast of Tiantan's east gate. Take bus #39 from the train station; 60 or 106 from Dongzhimen; or 812 from the zoo to Hongqiao. Open daily 8:30am-7pm.)*

YABAO LU CLOTHING MARKET (yábǎolù shìchǎng; 雅宝路市场). This bizarre bazaar is a veritable Little Russia; store signs are written in Cyrillic, and Russian salutations fill the air. Russian immigrants have been running import businesses on Yabao Lu since the early 90s. Now, many store owners and clerks are Chinese, but stores still parade tons of cheap clothing, handbags, and neck-to-ankle-length furs (think imitation minks). *(Off Jianguomen Bei Dajie, opposite the west entrance to Ritan Park. Accessible by bus #44 from Qianmen or subway to Jianguomen.)*

DAZHALAN (dàzhàlán; 大栅栏) **AND QIANMEN DAJIE** (qiánmén dàjjiē; 前门大街). Stalls crowd these two action-packed streets, selling virtually every article of clothing and clothing-related product known to mankind, including "leather" jackets, luggage, purses, shoes, custom-made clothing, toys, and more. Two larger shops in the Dazhalan Pedestrian Zone are **Zhangyiyuan Tea House** (zhāngyīyuán cházhuāng; 张一元茶庄), where you can sip teas (Y10-30) or indulge in a tea ceremony (Y50-150) at lower prices than most other places, and **Tongren Medicinal Hall** (tóngrén táng; 同仁堂), the place to buy antlers, cicada shells, and other traditional herbal remedies. *(Just south of Tian'anmen. Bus #20, 54, 59, 110, or 120 to Dazhalan, or subway to the Qianmen stop. ☎6303 4001.)*

🎵 NIGHTLIFE

Welcome to China, Beijing Journal offers an insider's look at fun stuff to do, from bungee-jumping to bar-hopping. *City Weekend* and *Metro* also list great night spots and restaurants. You can pick up these free magazines in shopping districts, universities, and large hotels. The best source is still word of mouth—the hostel grapevine hums with talk of the newest and trendiest hotspots in town.

The decadent embassy district of **Sanlitun** (sānlǐtún; 三里屯) in northeast Beijing should be called "*lǎowài* central"—every bar and street is bursting at the seams with foreigners and yuppie businessmen. There are two main bar streets in Sanlitun: **Sanlitun Lu,** frequented mainly by local night owls, and **Nan Sanlitun Lu,** packed with expat bars and expats. The south gate of **Chaoyang Park** is a veritable mini-Las Vegas, but the new favorite place is a few minutes away by foot, near the **west gate** of Chaoyang Park. There, in the shadows of sky-scraping apartment towers (appropriately nicknamed the "international compound" due to the overwhelming number of foreign residents), restaurants and bars wrestle for space and the spotlight. Just don't expect to find the "real China" here.

For a much more intimate, relaxed feel, go to the streets that line the north and south sides of Houhai Lake, near the Bell and Drum Towers behind Beihai Park. Unpretentious yet elegant, the bars and teahouses in this relatively secluded neighborhood are becoming known as the place to go for a quieter night out, filled more with good company than trendy dance moves. Bars have an organic feel—less government planning and more small-time entrepreneurship. Plenty of rooftop terrace bars open onto the night air, hosting a clientele of more locals than expats. Try **Vanilla Sky** (xiāngcǎo tiānkōng; 香草天空), 43 Yandai Xie Jie, Houhai (☎6402 6440). From Di'anmen Wai Dajie, go west on Yandai Xie Jie (烟袋斜街) to find cheap beer and slightly more less cheap mixes.

BARS

🎵 **The Big Easy** (kuàilè zhàn; 快乐站), 8 Chaoyang Gongyuan Lu (☎6508 6776 or 6415 8420; fax 6591 1844), at the south gate of Chaoyang Park. A piece of New Orleans dropped in China. Large portions of delicious and authentic Cajun and Creole food (Y38-138), green neon lights, the sexy ambience of music and candlelight, an outdoor terrace, classy clientele, and superb service. One of the best bars around. The Big Easy band plays feel-good Motown, R&B, and blues F-Sa 10pm. Happy hour daily 5-8pm. Open daily 5pm-2am. Accepts credit cards.

The World of Suzie Wong (☎6593 6049), at the west gate of Chaoyang Park. In the same building as The Phoenix; look for the sign. Arguably the most popular haunt to be seen and heard for expats and affluent locals alike. Strong techno beats inside, more ventilation outside on the rooftop terrace. Arrive before 9pm for an intimate tête-à-tête; after 10pm, forget about personal space. Drinks Y20-60. Blue kamikaze Y52. Sex on the beach Y25. Open daily 7pm-2am.

Alfa, 6 Xingfu Yicun (☎6413 0086), across Gongti Bei Lu, north of the Workers' Stadium. Go down Chunxiu Lu, turn right onto Xingfucun Zhong Lu; Alfa is on the right. Quickly becoming a favorite hangout for barhoppers. Faux zebra-, leopard-, and tiger-prints draped under lights and over whitewashed walls. Backrooms for more intimate gatherings. Giant plush sofas outside for those who want a breather. Drinks from margaritas to high-proof liquors (Y20-80). A somewhat odd array of shrimp specialties, including coconut shrimp in sweet-and-sour soup (Y35), vanilla shrimp rolls (Y20), and shrimp toast (Y25). Open daily 5pm-2am.

The Flair Chivas Bar (☎6500 5888), at the north gate of the Workers' Stadium (Gongren Tiyuchang), across from Outback Steakhouse and right next to the Mix. Flair Chivas plays host to both expats and aspiring yuppies in their 20s and 30s. Daily cocktail-making show, friendly service, DJs, and a dance floor where you can actually get your groove on. Drinks cost a pretty penny (Y30-100). Appetizers Y35-60. Open daily 8pm-4am.

The Loft (cáng kù; 藏酷), 4 Gongren Tiyuguan Bei Lu (☎6501 7501 or 6506 5637; www.theloft.com.cn). Follow the signs next to Pacific Century Place around to the bar. Easily one of the coolest hangouts around, this sexier-than-thou bar features bamboo chairs, leafy plants, black leather and marble decor, and a glass-encased patio with unobstructed views of the night sky. Often host to large, organized functions. Drinks Y10-120. Cocktails and Loft specials Y41-49. Entrees Y42-120. Open daily 11am-2am.

Hidden Tree, 12 Dongdaqiao Xi Jie (monkeychina@compuserve.com), down the street from Durty Nellie's, on Nan Sanlitun Lu. More secluded and less raucous, but still afflicted by Chinese renditions of Western pop. Vast collection of imported drinks from Belgium (Y20-40). Awesome pizza. Especially crowded on weekends. Open daily Su-Th 10:30pm-2am (or when the last guest leaves), F-Sa 10:30pm-4am.

Cloud Dream Bar (yún mèng jiǔbā; 云梦酒吧), 16 Dong Sanhuan Lu, Chaoyang (☎6586 5532 or 6592 3398), next to the Beiguojie Qiao, 5-10min. south of the Great Wall Sheraton. Drinks (especially the tequila!) are cheap (Y10 and up) and plentiful, drawing local and exchange students on a daily basis. Manager knows her stuff—ask her to recommend some favorite brews. Nightly revelers encouraged to go onstage to perform; otherwise, stereos blast Western hits. Packed F-Sa nights. Open daily 5pm-3am.

Durty Nellie's (dūbólín xī cāntīng; 都伯临西餐厅), 12 Nan Sanlitun Lu (☎6502 2808), on Dongdaqiao Xi Jie off Gongren Tiyuguan Bei Lu. Everything here has the flavor of an old Irish pub, even if drinks are a bit weak. In the winter, people come in to warm up (and end up staying); in the summer, they come to get liquored up (before hitting the dance clubs). Drinks Y20-30. Open Su-Th 5:30pm-1:30am, F-Sa noon-2:30am.

CLUBS

Latinos (☎6507 9898; www.latinosclubchina.com), south gate of Chaoyang Park, Nonzhanguan Nan Lu (农展馆南路) at Jiuba Jie, a few meters from The Big Easy. A live 8-piece band from Venezuela plays sultry, sexy melodies while adept dancers sashay on the dance floor. Y50 cover (unless you're a regular) includes a free drink. Dance lessons 6-9pm, Y60. Open M-Th 9pm-2am, F-Su 9pm-3 or 4am.

Vics (wēikèsī; 威克斯; ☎6593 6215), at the north gate of Workers' Stadium, next to the Outback Steakhouse. Entrance is at ground level, but all the action is subterranean. Scantily clad women, bouncers dressed in black, ultra-professional bartenders, and a good mix of locals and expats. Couples get (a little too) slinky on the dance floor to R&B and the thumping beats of hiphop. Cover Y30. Shooters Y10, cocktails Y15 before midnight. Ladies free on Th. Busiest on F. Open daily 8pm-6am.

The Den (dūnhuáng xī cāntīng; 敦煌西餐厅), 4A Gongti Dong Lu, Chaoyang (☎6592 6290; www.theDen.com.cn), next to the City Hotel in Sanlitun. Go before midnight and you'll be sorely disappointed. On weekends, arrive fashionably late (past 1am) to a packed dance floor upstairs. Gravitate downstairs to a smoky chamber decorated with Eurocup jerseys for drinks, sustenance (Y20-50), and breathing space. Cover Y30, free for hardy, heavy-drinking regulars. Open Su-Th 10:30am-3am, F-Sa 10:30am-7am.

Lakeside Rock & Roll (☎6592 9856 or 6503 4301; www.rockroll-bj.com), on Gongti Bei Lu, next to the Loft. Dance floor filled to capacity. Slow songs and live dance performances interspersed between pounding techno beats. You've probably seen better shows, so saunter over to 1 of 3 separate bars offering other diversions (drinks Y20-50; fruit salads Y30 and up). Mainly Asian crowd, but the expat community is getting a whiff of the place. Cover Y20. Open daily 8pm-5:30am.

Mix (☎6530 2889), at the north gate of Worker's Stadium. Hip-hopping, table-scratching DJs. Eardrum-popping volumes and vibrations bouncing off the walls. Strobe lights flash to disco. A good mix of foreigners and locals sporting 'fros. Cover Y50. Open Su-Th 9pm-4am, F-Sa 8pm-6am.

Nightman (láitè màn; 莱特曼), 2 Xibahe Nanli, Chaoyang (☎6466 2562). Features dizzying lights, strobes, smoke, TV screens, multiple levels, and unremittingly erotic dancers. Full of Chinese students hopping to English pop and techno. Drinks Y20-30. No cover for foreigners, otherwise Y20-30. Open Th-Su 8:30pm-5am, but full only F-Sa.

◢ DAYTRIPS FROM BEIJING

FRAGRANT HILLS AND ENVIRONS

FRAGRANT HILL PARK

Several buses go to Fragrant Hills Park and the adjoining Azure Clouds Temple. Bus #318 (30min., Y1-2) departs from Pingguoyuan; from the subway stop walk down Pingguoyuan Nan Lu and take a right at the 1st intersection. Other buses stop here: #331 (Xinjiekou and the Summer Palace on Yiheyan Lu), 360 (Beijing Zoo), 733 (Balizhuang), and 904 (Xizhimen and the zoo). The bus terminus is at the foot of the hills, where a handful of

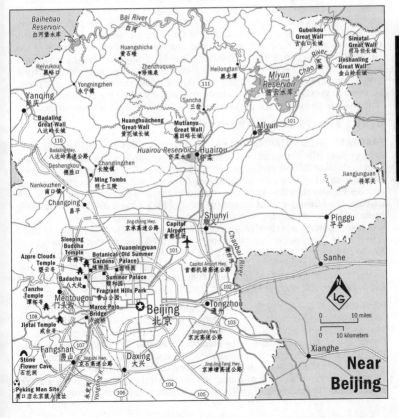

BEIJING

cabs await to take you to the park's north entrance (Y3-5 or a 15min. walk). Open daily summer 6am-7pm; winter 6am-6pm. Cable car runs daily 9am-4pm (one-way Y30, children under 1.2m Y10). Admissions Y10, students Y5.

Cloudy mists reminiscent of the haze of incense swathe **Fragrant Hills Park** (xiāngshān gōngyuán; 香山公园). An impressive peak resembling an incense burner, ripe cherry tree blossoms, a dash of history, a smattering of architecture, and a lot of retired folks make up the rest of the scenery. Built in 1745 under Emperor Qianlong and ravaged by foreign forces in 1860 and 1900, the park underwent some cosmetic surgery after 1949 and is now one of Beijing's most idyllic spots.

It's best to enter through the north entrance, visit the Azure Clouds Temple just within the park, and then ascend to the top of the mountain. Originally built in 1331 as a convent during the Yuan Dynasty, the **Azure Clouds Temple** (bìyún sì; 碧云寺) contains several halls, including the Hall of Lokapalas, with 18 *arhats* surrounded by rolling clouds and seas, and a memorial hall to Sun Yat-sen, whose remains were temporarily housed here. The red walls and tiled roofs of the other buildings give way to the cool white marble and Indian-style *stupas* of the Vajra **(Diamond Throne Pagoda)** in the back. Come late in the day, and you might find yourself the only one wandering the grounds. Most tourists skip over Azure Clouds in favor of the mountain, and an ambience of mysticism pervades the entire temple. *(Open daily 8am-6pm; last admission 5pm. Y10.)*

If the hike up to the summit, via a long and winding path with little to see save trees, doesn't tickle your fancy, a **cable car** can whisk you up, up, and away in 18 exertion- and perspiration-free minutes. Walk back down, and the park's greenery opens up to reveal an architectural gem or two—namely the faux-Tibetan **Temple of Brilliance** and a glazed-tile pagoda—that managed to escape the razings of the last century. The park's natural harmony is sullied only slightly by the vendors hawking the plastic-encased red maple leaves that lend the Fragrant Hills their fiery autumnal glow. Fall and spring, with their glorious colors, are the most popular times to visit the park, but the shady greens and well-kept gardens of summertime will still please the eye and reward the visitor with a pinch more privacy.

OTHER SIGHTS IN FRAGRANT HILLS

FRAGRANT HILLS BOTANICAL GARDENS (xiāngshān zhíwù yuán; 香山植物园). A huge scientific and ornamental complex, these gardens are home to, at last count, a total of 620,000 plants, including 30 varieties of bamboo and 2000 Chinese herbaceous peony trees. From monstrous ferns to hanging orchids, thousands of species grow within the space-age, climate-controlled conservatory. Within the gardens, the **Sleeping Buddha Temple** (wòfó sì; 卧佛寺) has a 250,000kg, 5.3m-long bronze statue of a reclining Sakyamuni, contentedly passing the years beside several pairs of enormous cloth shoes—only 7000 people had to be enslaved to build it in 1321. *(A 15min. walk or short cab ride from the foot of Fragrant Hills Park. From the city center, the Zhiwuyuan "Botanical Gardens" stop is 1 stop before the Fragrant Hills terminus. Buses #331 and 904 stop at Wofosi "Sleeping Buddha Temple," 1 stop before Fragrant Hills. Open daily summer 6am-9pm, last admission 7pm; winter 6am-8pm, last admission 5pm. Tropical conservatory and gardens Y50, students Y40; gardens Y5/Y2.5; Sleeping Buddha Temple Y5.)*

BADACHU (bādà chù; 八大处). A short ride from Fragrant Hills, Badachu, the "eight great sites," is really only an arbitrary assortment of sights that the tourism bureau decided to advertise. From the main gate, the easternmost path leads to the cable-car station climbing to the **Precious Stone Cave.** The western path weaves through a series of temples and nunneries. Perhaps the best idea for a full exploration is to take the cable car up and hike down the western route (3-5hr.). Those short on time can run up the west trail and check out the recently refurbished **Lingguang Temple** (língguāng sì; 灵光寺) and the 13-story pagoda that houses a relic of the Buddha: his tooth. *(From Beijing Zoo, take bus #347; or take subway line #1 to Ping-guoyuan and switch to bus #972. From Fragrant Hills or the Botanical Gardens, take bus #318 to Pingguoyuan Dong Kou and switch to 389. A taxi from the Botanical Gardens costs about Y20. Cable car Y30, round-trip Y60. Open daily 5am-8pm. Y10, students Y5.)*

MING TOMBS

About 50km northwest of Beijing proper, not far from Badaling Great Wall. Take bus #5 or 44 from Qianmen to Deshengmen (or subway to Jishuitan); from the Watch Tower, walk a few min. west, under the pedestrian overpass, to the bus terminal. Take bus or minibus #345 or the faster 345 (支) to Changping (昌平) or Changping Dongcheng (50-80min.). Tour buses 1-4 visit both the tombs and Badaling (p. 167). The 3 tombs that are open to the public (Changling, Dingling, and Zhaoling) are far apart and hard to get to by any means save taxi (Y20 from bus stop to Changling, Y10 between tombs; cheapest to hire a cab to take you around to all 3 sites). High season Apr.-Oct., low season Nov.-Mar. Tombs open daily 8am-5pm. Changling Y45, students Y22; Dingling (including museum) Y60/Y30; Zhaoling Y30. Sacred Way open daily 7am-8pm, Y15-20. Children under 1.2m free.

At the foot of the Tianshou Mountains lie the famed Ming Tombs (míng shísān líng; 明十三陵). Shortly after moving the capital to Beijing, in 1409 Zhu Di (Emperor Yongle) commissioned his tomb to be built on the outskirts of the new capital. This who's who of entombed corpses includes 13 emperors, 23 empresses, eight concubines, and one prince. Thirty-six white stone ministers, soldiers, and mythical beasts pave the famed **Sacred Way** (shéndào; 神道), also called the **Divine Road to the Changling Tomb.** It once stretched 4km north, crossing the **Seven-Arch Bridge** before reaching its final destination, but has since been shortened to a 20min. willow-shaded stroll past a veritable circus of animals. **Changling** is the first and largest tomb here, built for the emperor who started it all. **Zhaoling**, the resting place of the 12th Ming emperor, is just a miniature Changling. Most tours head instead to **Dingling,** (about 3km from Changling) the only tomb where you can actually descend into the Underground Palace and discover what's beneath all that dirt.

The Ming Tombs should be a reflection of Ming achievements in artistry and engineering, but most of the artifacts, including the corpses, were smeared with duck blood and burned by the Red Army. The **Upper Palaces** are no more extraordinary than any other temple. The one actual tomb you can see (Dingling) has large, damp tunnels leading to chambers decorated with replicated coffins and scattered money from visitors tossing somewhat belated offerings to the emperors. The descriptions offer a brief history, but it's much better to listen in on tour guides.

EASTERN QING TOMBS

150km east of Beijing. Near Zunhua and Hebei province, but best reached from Beijing. On weekends and holidays, a tourist bus (3hr., 8:30am, round-trip Y60) departs when full from Xuanwumen Church; arrive at least 30min. earlier to guarantee a spot. Bus departs for Beijing around 3:30pm, arriving 7pm. A round-trip Y10 pedicab ride should cover several tombs, including the Ci An and Ci Xi Tombs. ☎6501 4925; www.qingdongling.com. Open daily 8am-5:30pm. 10-tomb admission Y90, students Y35-45, children under 1.3m free. If you're not a local, try going to the back door for Y71 tickets.

The Eastern Qing Tombs (qīng dōng líng; 清东陵) are China's largest and most complete set of imperial tombs. Supposedly, the first Qing emperor, Shunzhi, chose the site for its abundant *feng shui* properties: bordered by mountains in the south and north, and by hills and cliffs to the east and west, with two rivers meeting at the center. Although the Qing Tombs are more of a hassle to reach than their Ming counterparts (you're basically stuck there until your bus returns), they also offer more to see, even if only a few underground tombs are actually opened. The tombs are home to two princesses, three princes, five emperors, 15 empresses, 136 concubines, and an impressive entourage of dust bunnies.

Superstars among the interred include the **Empress Dowager Ci Xi,** the dragon lady who ruled China through two puppet emperors (p. 78). She really spoiled herself rotten upon her own death: gold-glazed paintings and statuesque dragon-carved pillars decorate the three halls of her mausoleum. A deathly, goosebump-inducing chill pervades her underground tomb, appropriately lit with spooky green fluorescent lights. **Emperor Qianlong,** China's longest reigning emperor (p. 77), also rests here. Besides many architectural projects and poetic inspirations, he also left behind the most impressive tomb of the Qing emperors. His three magnificently carved chambers boast Tibetan and Sanskrit engravings, beautiful and elegant in the dimness.

The sprawling 15-tomb estate has been turned into an impromptu, somewhat run-down, collection of bejeweled knicks, knacks, clocks, and corpses. At least the coffins and bodies here are the real thing. "Imperial performances" showcase a gaggle of ruffians donning faded costumes and pretending to be royalty. These spectacles take place at **Xiaoling Tomb,** the tomb farthest to the north. (Performances Su, Tu-Sa 10am and 2pm.)

SHIDU

Southwest of Beijing. Trains (2½hr., 2 per day) go to Shidu from Beijing South Train Station: "dirty" train (one-way Y9) leaves at 6:36am and returns at 5:40pm; A/C train (one-way Y12) leaves at 7:30am and returns at 4:50pm. Bus #917 (3hr.; 10 per day depart from Tianqiao 6am-5pm, from Shidu 5:30am-5:30pm; Y9) runs from Tianqiao Bus Station, off Qianmen Dajie; take bus #59 from Qianmen to Beiwei Lu (北纬路), or take 2, 15, 17, 20, 34, 35, 106, 110, or 120 to Tianqiao or Tiantan. Tourist bus #10 (2hr., round-trip Y60) departs 6:30-8am from Xuanwumen Church on weekends and holidays; it may take a while to attract enough passengers for the driver to leave. Private minivans (Y15-25 for the entire day, depending on group size and bargaining abilities) and horse buggies wait at the Shidu Train Station to take you wherever you want.

You've hiked the Great Wall, gazed at Taishan's sea of clouds, and conquered Wudangshan's peak. So you think, what's another mountain range? Think again. A masterpiece of natural landscaping, **Shidu** (十渡) is painted with rippling mountains and layered trees and stones, all rising above a twisting river that must be crossed 10 times (hence its name, "10th Crossing") to reach the next city.

At the train station, throngs of private minivans and horse-drawn carriages greet new arrivals. If you want to see more sights, choose a reputable-looking minivan and driver for a faster trip to **Solitary Hill Village** (gūshān zhài; 孤山寨). Following the winding path through mountain valleys and bubbling creek beds, you'll happen upon herds of snow-white **goats,** nibbling on grass, resting by the flowing water, or blocking traffic by occupying all lanes of the road. The walk leads to the **Thread of Sky,** a fissure in the rocks just wide enough for one person to pass through to peek at the thin sliver of sky high above. (Open daily 7am-7pm. Y25.)

A short cab ride away is **Immortal Peak Gorge** (xiān fēng gǔ; 仙峰谷) and the wonderful chance to scramble through a dry river bed to a small pool tucked away in a niche in the mountain. (Open daily 7am-7pm. Y22.) At **Xihu Gong,** a hike along a sinuous riverside trail leads to the Dragon Pool Waterfall, a rather unimpressive cascade of little spurts. Continue trudging on the path to a larger-than-life sculpture of the multi-armed Goddess of Mercy, a makeshift shrine for the mountain spirits, and views of lofty peaks encircling this sanctuary. Prepare for the all-too-friendly locals selling armloads of incense and charms. (Open daily 7am-7pm. Y32.)

Finally, head back to **Badu** or **Jiudu** (8th and 9th crossings) to find more pure tourist traps. A **cable car** (Y25, round-trip Y40) from Jiudu blesses you with a heart-wrenching view of the surroundings (even if the peaks aren't that high), as well as the chance to see a moss-covered rock that bears an uncanny resemblence to Buddha. At Jiudu, zip down a **glider** (Y35), sail along a **bamboo raft** (Y15-35), or leave all sense of sanity behind and try **bungee jumping** (Y150-180). If you're lucky, your driver will know the regulars and can bargain down the prices.

TANZHE AND JIETAI

Tour bus #7 (6:30-8am, Y60) leaves Apr.-Oct. weekends and holidays from the northeast corner of Qianmen and the Xuanwumen church, stopping at the 2 temples and the beautiful Stone Flower limestone cave. Otherwise, take the subway to Pingguoyuan (the last stop), turn right from the station exit, walk down the street for about 5min., and hop on bus #931, which stops at both temples (about 1hr., leaves every 10min. about 6am-6pm, Y2-2.5). Bus not always on schedule; you may wait quite a while. Unregistered cabs scout the bus stop for stranded travelers (Y10 to Tanzhe or Jietai); metered cab from the subway station costs about Y35 one-way, although drivers will try to charge much more.

TANZHE TEMPLE (tánzhè sì; 潭柘寺). This 1700-year-old Jin-Dynasty temple lies at the end of a scenic drive up mountains and through valleys. Here presides the ancient Emperor's Gingko Tree, named by Qianlong himself, with numerous trunks growing from the same root. The Empress's Gingko Tree stands to its left. The temple takes its name from **Dragon Pool** (lóng tán; 龙潭), a 20min. hike behind the complex, and the mulberry trees (zhè shù; 柘树) on the surrounding hills. The central section houses the largest and most ornate of the buildings. The eastern section contains the **Floating Cup Pavilion.** The etching on the pavilion floor supposedly resembles a dragon from the south and a tiger from the north. It is quite possible that the Qing-Dynasty poets who saw these images were delusional. *(Open daily summer 8am-6pm; winter 8:30am-4:30pm. Y35, students Y17, children under 1.2m free.)*

JIETAI TEMPLE (jiètái sì; 戒台寺). Also known as **Temple of the Ordination Altar,** Jietai didn't acquire its famed white marble altar until several hundred years after its building in AD 622. This three-storied altar, with over 100 niches featuring the carved God of Ordination, was once used to celebrate novices' graduation into full monkhood. The artistically twisted pine trees have individual names such as the **Chinese Scholar Tree,** the protector of Buddhism, the Phoenix-Tailed Pine, and the Sleeping Dragon Pine, all of which are over 1000 years old. Though the others may not resemble their poetic titles, **Embracing Pagoda Pine** is true to its name, wrapping its branches around a small pagoda. *(11km southeast of Tanzhe, on Ma'an Hill. From the #931 bus stop in front of the large sign, it's a 10min. walk up. Open daily summer 8am-5:30pm; winter 8:30am-4:30pm. Y35, students Y20, children under 1.2m free. You may be able to get in for free by entering through the hotel entrance on the left.)*

MARCO POLO BRIDGE AND ENVIRONS

88 Lugouqiao Chengnei Xi Jie. 15km southwest of Beijing. Accessible by taxi from Tanzhe and Jietai Temples (Y30-40). From the city, take bus #1, 4, 6, 38, or 702 to Liuliqiao and switch to bus #309, 339, or 964 to Lugou Xin Qiao.

MARCO POLO BRIDGE (lúgōu qiáo; 卢沟桥). This bridge is famous for its many stone lions, each unique. Legend has it that you can't count how many lions there are because they frolic about at night, but the official tally is 501. Built in 1192, the bridge, the oldest in Beijing, is also known for its role in stories that Marco Polo brought to Europe and for Qianlong's original calligraphy. But it is best remembered for the Marco Polo Bridge Incident of July 7, 1937, when Japan attacked Beijing, catapulting China into the fray of WWII (p. 79). *(Walk straight from the bus stop and take the 1st right; follow the river until you reach the bridge. ☎8389 4614 or 8389 2521. Open daily summer 7am-7pm; winter 8am-5pm. Y10, students Y5.)*

BEIJING

MUSEUM OF THE ANTI-JAPANESE WAR (zhōngguó rénmín kàngrì zhànzhēng jìniànguǎn; 中国人民抗日战争纪念馆). In the old Ming-Dynasty garrison town of Wanping, this museum looms ominously over the narrow, surrounding streets. Exhibits do not shirk from showing disturbingly bloody images of war victims. A screening of the Japanese invasion shows Japanese armies swarming over some of Beijing's renowned tourist sights. The musem is closed for renovation and will reopen in 2005. (*101 Lugouqiao Cheng Nei Jie, 10min. east of the Marco Polo bridge.* ☎8389 4614 or 8389 2521. Mandatory bag check. Open daily summer 8am-5pm; winter 8:30am-4:30pm; last admission 1hr. before. Y15, students Y8.)

PEKING MAN SITE AT ZHOUKOUDIAN

50km southwest of Beijing, on the boundary between Taihang Range and the North China Plain. Take bus #917 (1½-2hr., Y4.5) from the Tianqiao bus station to Fangshan; then grab a taxi (Y10). Open daily 8am-6pm; last admission 5pm. Site admission Y15, students (through high school) Y8; with museum Y20/Y10.

Half a million years ago, *homo erectus pekinensis* liked it here so much he left his bones and artifacts, discovered in 1921. The Peking Man Site at Zhoukoudian (zhōukǒudiàn běijīng yuánrén yízhǐ; 周口店北京猿人遗址) is an exciting site in theory, but the original findings that set archaeological hearts aflutter have since been "lost" at sea. All that remains are excavated, fenced-off caves and a dismal museum housing some bone chips and stone tools. Only **Cave #1**, huge and separated from the outside world, is of any interest. Outside the site, plastic dinosaur exhibits and two mummies give off an overwhelming stench of decayed flesh.

GREAT WALL 长城

From Shanhaiguan (p. 187) on the Bohai Sea to its last pass at Jiayuguan (p. 772) in Gansu province, the Great Wall winds across China's northern periphery. Once thought to stretch over 6700km—a distance longer than the width of the United States—this imposing dragon just got a little longer, with the discovery of new sections buried beneath the desert sands in Xinjiang province. Its length now totals over 7200km, coiling over green mountains, craggy peaks, and desert steppes.

Kingdoms of the Warring States period (5th century BC) built the earliest sections of the wall, but it was Qin Shihuang, the first emperor of the Qin Dynasty, who linked them together to create the Great Wall in 221 BC. For thousands of years, the wall protected China from barbarian attacks and aided communication between central China and the most far-flung outposts of the country. Although the skeleton of the Great Wall is more than 2000 years old, much of the wall you see today dates to the Ming Dynasty, when the threat of Mongol invasion spurred emperors to fortify and extend it.

At the Mutianyu portion of the Great Wall, a plaque reads, "Once intended to ward off enemy attacks, today it brings together peoples of the world." To facilitate this exchange and capitalize on its huge money-making potential, the government has opened three sections in Beijing to tourists: **Badaling, Mutianyu,** and **Simatai. Huanghuacheng,** typically referred to as the "Wild Wall," is the most remote section, so far untouched by tourism. Each section has its own personality and its own majesty, but no matter where you stand, you can gaze at this stone monument weaving atop mountainous peaks for as far as the eye can see. Although it can no longer be described as the only manmade structure visible from space—China's first astronaut Yang Liwei debunked the myth—the Great Wall is undeniably one of the greatest achievements of civilization. Its epic legacy and colossal scale is an unparalleled testament to the strength and perseverance of an entire people, making the debate over its fate all the more poignant.

The Great Wall straddles a delicate balance of tourism, preservation, and restoration. Over the years, natural forces, unregulated development, careless destruction by locals, and floods of tourists have inflicted great damage to the wall, causing the government to section off the wildest, unrestored sections, including parts of Simatai. Meanwhile, the debate between protection versus restoration continues without much resolution. Many people object to the government's brand of rebuilding for tourist consumption, considering a modern makeover to be a mockery of the wall's original grandeur. However, if left alone, the wall will inevitably crumble away, as much of it already has. With an estimated two-thirds of its length already destroyed, the Great Wall is simultaneously one of China's most endangered and most revered artifacts.

BADALING GREAT WALL 八达岭长城

*Take **bus** #5 or 44 from Qianmen or 800 to Deshengmen; hop on bus #919 in front of the Watchtower to Badaling (1½hr., approx. every 10min. 6am-6pm). Official **tourist buses** #1-4 (round-trip Y50) leave daily for Badaling Great Wall and the Ming Tombs from bus #1 station at Qianmen (6-10am), northeast corner of Qianmen (6:30-9am), Xuanwumen Church (6:30-9:30am), Beijing Train Station in the 103 bus station (6-10am), Xizhimen (6-10am), and the zoo (6-10am). It's best to arrive early; also possible to arrange a pickup if you call ahead (☎ 6845 7170). See **Local Transportation: Bus**, p. 128. Hotel services and tour guides are the most expensive way of getting there. ☎ 6912 1988. Cable cars (daily 8am-4pm; Y40, round-trip Y60). Museum open daily 9am-4pm. Badaling open daily summer 7:30am-5pm; winter 8am-5pm. Admission including museum and film Y45, students and seniors Y25.*

Badaling is the part of the wall to visit if you want to take pictures that look like "official" photos and documentary stills. Getting that elusive shot without souvenir shops and other tourists, however, is a whole other feat. You'll get to rub elbows (literally) with tourists from all around the world, all of whom flock to the most accessible section of the wall. The government has taken great pains to restore Badaling to its "original" condition. Every tower and turret stands just as it did when the Mongols overran the country 700 years ago, give or take a few massive shops and gaudy pastel flags. Guard rails and cable cars make Badaling the safe—almost easy—way to see the Great Wall. A **museum** displays a brief history of the Wall alongside a barebones collection of artifacts. It culminates in photos of dozens of world leaders huffing and puffing up the wall and the 360° **Great Wall Circle Vision Theatre,** which shows a 15min. film on the history of and legends surrounding the wall. (Open 9am-5:45pm.) Despite scant English subtitles and the feeble artificial battle reenactments, the stomach-wrenching bird's-eye view of the sweeping mountains and valleys leaves visitors satisfied.

MUTIANYU GREAT WALL 慕田峪长城

70km northeast of Beijing. Tourist bus #6 from the Xuanwumen church (2hr., Apr.-Oct. weekends and holidays 6:30-8am, round-trip Y50) is probably the best way to get to Mutianyu. On weekdays, take the subway to Dongzhimen (use the northeast exit) and turn left; from the long-distance bus station about 7min. down on your left, take bus #916 (with A/C, Y8) to Huairou. Minibuses (Y20-30) take passengers to Mutianyu. Cable cars (daily 8am-4pm; one-way Y35, students Y17.5; round-trip Y50/Y25). Mutianyu open daily summer 6am-6pm; winter 8am-4pm. Y35, students Y17.5; insurance additional Y1.

Constructed during the Northern Qi Dynasty over 1400 years ago, the Mutianyu section of the monumental edifice has been richly preserved, with a little help from its friends in the government tourism bureau. Opened to take the pressure off Badaling, Mutianyu is less overrun with tourists and peddlers, but plenty of both still exist. Look no further for an "I climbed the Great Wall" t-shirt (Y5-20). Higher up in the mountains than Badaling, Mutianyu has a much more dramatic view of steep mountain slopes, the valley below, and the Great Wall itself, curling into the distance. This section of the wall also features unusual double-serrated ramparts. A cable car near the No. 1 parking lot runs to one of the towers. Walking the wall past the eight or nine towers to the next cable-car station (which returns to the same parking lot) takes about 1½-2hr. Those with a little dough and a hankering for festivities can rent out the platform at the cable-car station up top—for a cocktail party, a movie-screening, anything. All in all, Mutianyu is less accessible and more expensive than Badaling, but worth it. Even the trip there on a twisting bus route into the mountains is gorgeous and photo-worthy.

SIMATAI GREAT WALL 司马台长城

Tourist bus #12 (Y60) departs from Xuanwumen Church Apr.-Oct. on weekends 7-8am and leaves Simatai at 4pm. Jinghua Youth Hostel (p. 135) runs tours daily (6-person minimum; depart 8am, return 2:30pm; Y60 excluding admission; yu-ding@jing-hua-hotel.com); if inclement weather, only 50% refund. Chartering a miàndī taxi costs around Y360. Cable car one-way Y30, round-trip Y50. Climbing train Y15/Y20. Open daily 8am-5pm. Y30, students Y15.

Reputedly the most dangerous part of the Great Wall, Simatai is also hands-down the most majestic in terms of scenery. Unfortunately, the government sectioned off the most treacherous stretch, claiming wobbly rocks. Trying to bribe the guards to let you pass won't work, so you might as well take as many pictures as you can of the unrestored, crumbling stones before the tourism bureau transforms all of Simatai into a scalable passageway.

Despite the restoration beginning on this section of the wall, Simatai still presents a glimpse of what the old wall once looked like. There are few guardrails or handholds along the wall. If you walk far enough, parts of the wall sport 70° inclines and 500m drops, bringing many hikers down on all fours. Simatai's high elevation grants an absolutely glorious view of the surrounding mountains. Stairways lead to cloud-enshrouded turrets, and unrestored sections curl away 19km into the distance, hugging the narrow, precipitous cliffs.

A stretch of rolling hills stands between you and the wall. Save your time and energy to conquer Simatai itself and use the cable car, especially since most buses only give you 3 or 4hr. to explore. The remaining hike from the cable car station is short but painful for the knees with all the 1-ft.-high steps. If you're willing to shell out a bit more, a "climbing train" can finish the job.

Although Simatai is still rough and undeveloped, hawkers and restaurants are quickly starting to capitalize on the tourists. As one of the last wild sections of the Great Wall, Simatai deserves a visit before it entirely loses its rugged beauty.

HUANGHUACHENG GREAT WALL 黄花长城

About 90km north of Beijing, 22km from Mutianyu. Take the subway to Dongzhimen (northeast exit) and turn left. From the long-distance bus station about 7min. down on your left, take bus #961 (7:40, 9:40am, 3:30, 5pm; return 5:20, 6:50am, 1, 2:30pm; Y7-8) to Huanghuacheng. Alternatively, bus #916 (with A/C, Y8) frequently leaves Dongzhimen for Huairou (about 2hr.), where you can catch bus #961 (1hr., approx. every hr. 5:30am-5:40pm, Y2.5) to Huanghuacheng. From Huairou, a taxi is much faster and costs Y20-30. No tourist infrastructure or hours of operation—only locally run checkpoints (Y2).

Built by General Cai Kai, Huanghuacheng took so long to construct that the unfortunate general was deemed inefficient and beheaded. As testament to his tenacity, his headless body stood vigilant without toppling for three days and three nights before the locals had him interred. When the Mongols attacked, Cai Kai's efforts paid off—Huanghuacheng was the only fortress that successfully warded off the enemy. Abashed, the government reburied Cai Kai with honor near the wall.

Even today, Huanghuacheng is the part of the Great Wall that you conquer to become, as the Chinese say, a true man (or woman). This is un-restoration at its very best. Overgrown patches of brush lay a moss-green carpet on the wall's surface, while many of the steps have dissolved into treacherous bits of crumbly pebbles that slip and slide beneath your feet. Be careful, put on your hiking boots, and don't walk the wall alone. No sissy cable cars or guardrails here. Some areas are so steep that the descent leaves climbers clinging to the crumbling wall for dear life. The danger makes it exciting, the beauty makes it breathtaking, and the damage of time makes it real. This is the Great Wall experience of choice for hardy backpackers who scorn rampant commercialism, as there are few vendors and no tour groups. While most locals are more interested in their sheep than you, some have set up shop and charge Y2 for maintenance of ladders and for walking on their private land. Rumors say that the tourism bureau plans to move in within a few years' time.

The most adventurous of hikers choose to spend the night on the wall, but don't do it alone. Alternatively, there's the **Jintang Mountain Lodge ❹** (jīntāng shān zhuāng; 金汤山庄), across from the reservoir. Unfortunately, a face-lift has transformed dorms to relatively luxurious standards with a corresponding price hike, but after a long trek, it might be worthwhile for your tired feet. (☎6165 1134 or 6165 1188-809; fax 6165 1442. Doubles Y298; triples Y328.) A couple family-run bed-and-breakfast lodgings line the road to the reservoir. Dormitory-like housing comes without much privacy, but at great prices (around Y20 per bed). Just show up at the door and ask for accommodations for the night.

TIANJIN 天津   ☎022

A center of trade during the Ming Dynasty, Tianjin is China's fourth largest city, a major manufacturing center, and the largest port in northern China. From 1860 to 1945, nine foreign powers held concession territories in Tianjin, and remnants of their architectural legacy have left a distinctive European mark upon the city. Downtown, megastores and trendy shops jostle each other for space, while 30-floor residential complexes rise in the outskirts. Even though Tianjin has lost much of its small-town mentality, the city's remaining narrow streets and alleys are still infused with the culture and history of old China. For every high-priced restaurant, 10 cheap fried dough vendors dish up the old breakfast favorite; for every fancy yellow minivan, hundreds of bicycles weave through the streets. Despite its unusual affluence, Tianjin has managed to retain a charm all its own.

BEIJING

◤ TRANSPORTATION

Flights: Zhangguizhuang Airport (zhāngguìzhuāng fēijīchǎng; 张贵庄飞机场; ☎2490 1114 or 2490 2924). Book tickets at **Tianjin CITS Ticketing Centre,** 22 Youyi Lu (☎2835 8866; fax 2835 4653), directly in front of the Friendship Store. Open M-F 9am-5pm, Sa-Su 9am-4pm. To: **Chengdu** (Su-Th and Sa, Y1390); **Guangzhou** (2 per day, Y1101); **Kunming** (6 per week, Y1700); **Qingdao** (daily, Y660); **Shanghai** (3 per day, Y1030); **Xi'an** (daily, Y960).

Trains: The 24hr. bus #24 serves both the Tianjin and West Stations, shuttling passengers between Heping Lu and the 2 stations (Baihuo Dalou stop). 5-day advance purchase for tickets. Tickets are cheaper and easier to obtain at the Tianjin (Main) Station.

Tianjin (Main) Railway Station (tiānjīn zhàn; 天津站; ☎6053 6053), on Haihe Dong Lu, just across Jiefang Qiao. To: **Beijing** (1½hr., every hr., Y11-50); **Nanjing** (19hr., daily, Y215); **Shanghai** (16-18hr., 3 per day, Y301); **Tangshan** (3hr., daily, Y20).

West Railway Station (xī zhàn; 西站 ; ☎2618 9803), on Xizhan Qian Jie. To: **Beijing** (1½hr., 15 per day, Y20-30); **Guangzhou** (19hr., daily, Y301); **Harbin** (18hr., daily, Y122); **Nanjing** (14-19hr., 10 per day, Y100-300); **Shanghai** (12-17hr.; 1-3 per day; Y200, express Y400).

North Railway Station (tiānjīn běi zhàn; 天津北站 ; ☎2618 1162), off Zhongshan Bei Lu. To: **Beijing** (1½hr., every hr., Y25-35); **Tangshan** (2hr., 4 per day, Y10-15); **Tianjin Railway Station** (few minutes, every hr., Y2.5-9).

Buses: There are 2 main bus stations in Tianjin and 1 that only services Beijing.

Balitai Bus Station (bālǐtái chángtú qìchē zhàn;八里台长途汽车站 ; ☎2334 4749), near Shuishang Park, runs buses to **Ji'nan** (7hr., 2 per day).

West Station (tiānjīn chángtú xī zhàn;天津长途西站), 2 Xiqing Dao (☎2732 0688), down the road from the West Train Station, runs buses to **Shijiazhuang** (4hr., daily, Y86-100) and **Zhengzhou** (9hr., daily, Y149).

Beijing Zhao Gong Kou Bus Station (北京赵公口站 ; ☎138 2000 4683), on Rongye Dajie in front of Food St. To: **Beijing** (1½hr., every hr. 7am-6:30pm, Y30).

Tianjin Harbor Passenger Terminal (☎2570 6728). Take the train from the Tianjin Railway Station to the Tanggu Passenger Terminal (tánggū xīngǎng kèyùn mǎtóu;塘沽新港 客运码头); take bus #102 from there. Open Tu, Th, Sa 8:30am-4:30pm; M, W, F 8:30am-6:30pm. Ferries only go to **Kobe, Japan** (48hr., 1 per week, Y1540-2000).

Local Buses: Tianjin's labyrinth-like bus system is intimidating and sometimes unreliable, but can be worth deciphering. Fare Y1, with A/C Y2. Hours of operation and bus routes are listed on bus stop signs. Most buses run 5am-11pm; buses numbered 1-100 tend to run later than others. The following buses stop near the end of Heping Lu at Baihuo Dalou (百货大楼) before trundling on to other major locations:

#8: Main Train Station, Balitai (right beside Nankai University on Weijin Lu), Shuishang Park.

#24 (24hr.): Tianjin Railway Station, West Railway Station.

#904: Hubei Lu, Yingkou Dao.

Subway: At the time of printing, the subway was under reconstruction. It is due to open some time in 2005.

Taxis: Minivan taxis are cheapest. Red minivans Y5 for the first 3km, each additional km Y1.50; yellow minivans Y5 for the 1st 5km, each additional km Y1.30.

✳ 🛈 ORIENTATION AND PRACTICAL INFORMATION

Tianjin is big enough to be interesting but a horrendous nightmare to navigate, unless you master the major roads. Streets labeled *Lu* run east-west; those labeled *Dao* go north-south. The city center is formed by a jumble of commercial streets and old-style alleys branching off **Heping Lu** (和平路) and **Binjiang Dao** (滨江道), Tianjin's main shopping arteries and pedestrian thoroughfares. Dubbed **"Chinatown"** by Europeans, the old city northwest of downtown is boxed in by **Bei** (北), **Nan** (南), **Dong** (东), and **Xi Malu** (西马路). Three universities converge on **Qilitai** and **Balitai,** in the southwest corner of the city.

The **Hai River** cuts through the city diagonally. Some of Tianjin's large temples are sprinkled along its northwest corner. The famed architectural legacy of the European concessions is visible throughout the city, but the largest collection of international styles is concentrated together along **Jiefang Bei Lu,** perpendicular to Machang Dao (literally, Race Horse Road) and the Hai road. The **Tianjin Railway Station** is north of the Hai, just across Jiefang Qiao (Liberation Bridge). Phone numbers are provided where possible, but the best way to get in touch with any establishment or agency is to dial the operator (☎114) and ask to be transferred.

Travel Agency: CITS, 22 Youyi Lu (☎2835 8499 or 2835 8309), opposite the Friendship Store. Prepares travel plans but has little information on Tianjin itself. Shares the office with **Tianjin Overseas Tourist Corporation** (tiānjīnshì hǎiwài lǚyóu zǒnggōngsī; 天津市海外旅游总公司). Both are open M-F 9am-6pm.

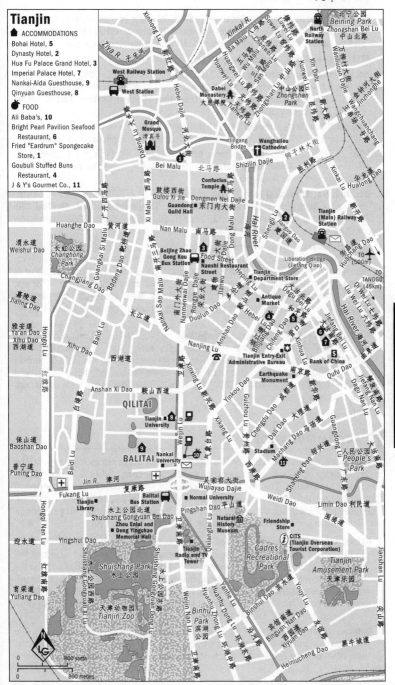

Tianjin

ACCOMMODATIONS

Bohai Hotel, **5**
Dynasty Hotel, **2**
Hua Fu Palace Grand Hotel, **3**
Imperial Palace Hotel, **7**
Nankai-Aida Guesthouse, **9**
Qinyuan Guesthouse, **8**

FOOD

Ali Baba's, **10**
Bright Pearl Pavilion Seafood
 Restaurant, **6**
Fried "Eardrum" Spongecake
 Store, **1**
Goubuli Stuffed Buns
 Restaurant, **4**
J & Y's Gourmet Co., **11**

Bank of China: 80-82 Jiefang Bei Lu (☎2710 2208), near intersection of Jiefang Bei Lu and Dagu Bei Lu. Exchanges traveler's checks and currency. Credit card advances may also be issued. Open M-F 9am-noon and 1:30-5pm. Many other locations.

ATM: Bank of China, 80-82 Jiefang Bei Lu. Cirrus/MC/Plus/V.

Bookstore: Xinhua Bookstore (☎2712 9784), on the corner of Binjiang Dao and Xingan Lu. The 5 floors cover everything from picture books to economic theory. Decent selection of classic English literature, with a "Learn How To Speak Chinese" section for foreigners. Open daily 9:30am-8pm.

Shopping: Tianjin Department Store (tiānjīn bǎihuò dàlóu; 天津百货大楼), 172 Heping Lu (☎2730 0723, ext. 3106). Open daily summer 9am-9pm; winter 9am-8pm.

PSB: 26 Tangshan Dao. The **Foreigners Office** (wàiguǎn chù; 外管处), located at the **Tianjin Exit-Entry Administrative Bureau,** 19 Shou'an Jie, grants visa extensions. Open M-Th 9am-5pm, F-Sa 9am-4pm.

Hospital: No. 1 Hospital (dìyīzhōngxīn yīyuàn; 第一中心医院 ; ☎2336 6914), on Fukang Lu. Right next to the main entrance is the **Tianjin International Medical Center,** 24 Fukang Lu (8am-10pm ☎2362 6360, 10pm-8am 2362 6365). Supposedly has English-speaking staff. Open 24hr.

Internet Access: Friends Internet Bar (péngyǒu wǎngbā; 朋友网吧), 133 Weijin Lu, down the road from Tianjin University. Address is misleading, look for sign and entrance into small alley. On the 2nd fl. of red brick building, this hole in the wall has 50 or so computer stations. Y2 per hr. Open 11am-midnight. **Ali Baba's** (see **Food,** p. 173) also has a computer with Internet available for patrons. Many hotels also offer Internet access from standard rooms and charge the regular telephone usage fee, but do not supply wires/cables.

Post Office: China Post Dongzhan Post Office (☎2401 3075). Gigantic building right next to the Tianjin Railway Station. EMS. English-speaking staff. Open daily 24hr. The **China Post** across from the Nankai University main entrance also has EMS. Open daily 8:30am-6:30pm. **DHL,** 35 Liujing Lu (zhōngguó wàiyùn dùnhào guójì hángkōng kuàijiàn gōngsī; 中国外运顿号国际航空快件公司; ☎2430 3388), is a private courier service. Open daily 8am-5:30pm.

Postal Code: 300000.

🏠 ACCOMMODATIONS

Tianjin is a great place to visit for the day, but can be quite pricey if you spend the night. The city does not cater to occasional backpackers, and budget options for foreigners are limited. To stay in the city center, your best bet is to head for one of Tianjin's consistently high-quality hotels, which usually require a Y100+ deposit. The more affordable but far-off dormitories at Nankai and Tianjin University combine friendliness with private baths, 24hr. hot water, TVs, and A/C.

Nankai-Aida Guesthouse (nánkāi àidà huìguǎn; 南开爱大会馆; ☎2350 1832 or 2350 5339). Follow Dazhong Lu from the main university entrance and take a second left onto Yiyuan Lu. Check-in at the off-white brick building on the left. That building and the red brick complex on the right are the dormitory residences. The lively college campus atmosphere and friendly local and foreign-exchange students make visitors feel right at home. Bathroom facilities are old but kept clean and functional. Fantastic water pressure. 3-bed dorms Y70; doubles Y200; suites Y400. ❶

Qinyuan Guesthouse (qìnyuán lìshǔ; 沁园隶属; ☎2740 7711 or 2740 7508). The white-gray building on the Tianjin University campus, right next to the School of Architecture, down Beiyang Dao (北洋道). Rest on silky golden bed covers and enjoy the picturesque surroundings of small, waterlily-covered lakes. Ask about mini-fridges. Reception 6am-midnight. Inform the receptionist if you're planning a late night out. Reservations recommended. Doubles Y196. ❸

Hua Fu Palace Grand Hotel (huá fù gōng dà fàndiàn; 华富宫大饭店 ; ☎2735 0066 or 2734 7594; www.hfghotel.com.cn.), on Nanshi Hotel St., close to Rongye Dajie and Food St. Hard to miss with the pagoda-shaped exterior. Impeccable service and amenities, including free safety deposit boxes, Western-style bathrooms, and lint-free, dust-free sheets. Internet access charged according to the Telephone Bureau. Noon checkout. 5% service charge and deposit of at least Y100 for foreigners. Singles Y160; doubles Y180; triples Y240. AmEx/MC/V. ❷

Bohai Hotel (bóhǎi dàlóu fàndiàn; 渤海大楼饭店), 277 Heping Lu (☎2711 2422), conveniently located at the intersection of Heping Lu and Chifeng Dao, next to many shops and just a walk away from Binjiang Dao. Bedsheets are slightly worn but unsoiled. Reservations recommended. Singles Y150-200; doubles Y190-270. ❸

Dynasty Hotel (wángcháo dàjiǔdiàn; 王朝大酒店), 42 Jianguo Dao (☎2403 1617), a 5min. walk from the main train station and local bus stations. Rooms are on the small, cramped side, and the facilities are aged, but the hotel is a convenient base from which to explore the city. Internet available in the lounge. Y400 deposit. Standard singles Y138-150; doubles Y180; triples Y218. ❷

Imperial Palace Hotel (huánggōng fàndiàn; 皇宫饭店), 177 Jiefang Bei Lu (☎2319 0888), near the intersection with Taian Dao. Those willing to splurge can indulge themselves in the posh district of Jiefang Bei Lu. The Imperial is no exception from its upscale neighbors, with its renovated, spotlessly clean suites and deluxe rooms. But the most impressive feature is its trendy location. Internet access. Singles Y360; standard Y420; deluxe Y530. ❺

🗗 FOOD

Tianjin is a great place for epicureans, and snacking is perhaps the best way to discover all that the city has to offer. Vendors throughout the city sell crunchy **deep-fried dough twists** (guìfāxiáng máhuā; 桂发祥麻花) with or without sesame seeds, and **fried "eardrum" spongecake** (ěrduǒyǎn zhágāo; 耳朵眼炸糕), filled with sweet red bean paste. But Tianjin is still most renowned for its **Goubuli Baozi** (gǒubùlǐ bāozi; 狗不理包子), buns stuffed with savory meats and veggies. Goubuli can now be found everywhere in the city, but all the locals still point to **Nanshi Restaurants Street** or **Food Street** (shípǐn jiē; 食品街), a snacker's Shangri-La for cheap, delicious fare. On weekends crowds fill the street complex, a pagoda-shaped mall of food stores off Rongye Dajie and Qingge Dajie. Though not as crowded as in years past, dozens of stores still sell a variety of pastries, fruits, herbs, and candies. Aquarium tanks alive with fish, crabs, frogs, and snails ensure the freshest meal at any of the numerous seafood restaurants. Be sure to pick up baked goods from the Austrian-founded **Kiesseling's Bakery** for a taste of century-old gastronomic history.

Goubuli Stuffed Buns Restaurant (gǒubùlǐ bāozidiàn; 狗不理包子店), 77 Shandong Lu (☎2730 2540), pagoda-style building between Binjiang Dao and Changchun Dao. Famous for its mouth-watering *bāozi*, Goubuli is stuffed with devoted patrons. Grab beef- or pork-filled buns to-go at the counter right inside the entrance (meals Y12-18). The upstairs has pricier entrees like calamari and salty duck (Y20-40). Freshly-made pork-filled *bāozi* Y6 per dozen; red-dotted specialty *bāozi* with pork, eel, vegetable, and catfish fillings Y10-20 per dozen. Downstairs and counter open daily 7am-10pm; upstairs 11am-2pm and 5-8:30pm. Downstairs ❶, upstairs ❸.

Fried "Eardrum" Spongecake Store (ěrduǒyǎn zhágāodiàn; 耳朵眼炸糕店), near the intersection of Beimenwai Dajie and Bei Malu. Some of the tastiest, cheapest eardrum cakes—a regional favorite—can be bought here. 25 appetizing varieties for your culinary pleasure. Creative fillings you won't find on the streets include beef (Y1.50), lettuce (Y1.20), and duck (Y12). Open daily 8am-midnight. ❶

Ali Baba's (ālǐ bābā; 阿里巴巴 ; ☎2351 3976), right outside the Nankai University campus. Turn right off of Weijin Lu onto Tong An Dao, at the Tianyu video store, then another right and walk down the alley. Ali Baba is on the right. A messy college atmosphere, walls plastered with Western movie posters, and an earnest attempt at American food draw crowds of foreign exchange students. Many stay late to down beers (Tsingtao Y8) and watch Chinese music videos. Main courses Y12-20, pizza and pasta Y7-22, noodles Y8-25. A computer in the corner with Internet access, free for patrons, provides good distraction. Open daily 11am-2am. ❷

J & Y's Gourmet Co., 125 Machang Dao (☎2325 6000). After a stroll through the lantern-lined streets of European concessions, enjoy a sumptuous meal of Shanghai cuisine surrounded by English architecture. Dinners look and taste much more expensive than they actually are, and the English menu makes ordering a breeze. Try the yellow croaker (Y22) or the lotus seeds (Y8). For the daring, there's pork blood (Y16) and tiny mud snails cooked in beer (Y28). Open daily 11am-9:30pm. ❷

Bright Pearl Pavilion Seafood Restaurant (míng zhū gé hǎixiān jiǔlóu; 明珠阁海鲜酒 楼), 58 Chifeng Lu (☎2711 1888). This seafood restaurant takes advantage of Tianjin's seaport status, serving pricey but delectable fresh seafood dishes, such as crab (Y25), sea cucumber (Y10), fish (Y16-50), and snails (Y20). Other options are available at startling Y100+ prices. Horseshoe crabs for display only. Reservations recommended. Open daily 10am-8pm. ❸

◎ SIGHTS

Colorful streets near the city center and museums make up Tianjin's tourist sights, though most museums are best reached by taxi. The city itself has been called a living museum of international architecture, and the energetic walker can explore either bank of the **Hai River** to see the 19th-century British, French, German, Russian, and Italian buildings, reminders of the old days of foreign concession in the late 19th and early 20th centuries.

DABEI MONASTERY (dàbēi chányuàn; 大悲禅院). A colorful array of red charms and miniature figurines line the way to the entrance of this Buddhist monastery. Inside, the well-preserved prayer rooms are still lively sites of worship. Amidst solemn chanting, people gather in the incense-wreathed air, bearing offerings of fruits and cakes. Arrive early to avoid the craze of the afternoon rush, or come around 2pm on Wednesdays to catch a glimpse of prayer rituals. *(40 Tianwei Lu. To the north of Jingang Bridge, Tianwei Lu is the first left off Zhongshan Lu. ☎2626 1768 or 2626 1769. Open daily 9am-4pm. Y4.)*

SHUISHANG PARK (shuǐshàng gōngyuán; 水上公园). The park is one of the few remaining places in Tianjin where the sounds of water and chirping birds can overpower the clamor of city life. Entrance fees have gone up in recent years, but residents gladly pay to relax beneath makeshift pavilions and stroll down shady cobblestone walkways. A meandering boat ride goes for Y20-40 per hour, though the aged Tianjin Zoo in the south end of the park may not be worth your time. On nights of national holidays, water fountain shows light up with hundreds of strobe lights. *(Bordered by Shuishang Gongyuan Dong Lu, south of Nankai University, across Weijin Nan Lu from the TV tower. ☎2335 8454. Open daily 5am-9pm; winter 5:30am-6:30pm. Y25.)*

ZHOU ENLAI AND DENG YINGCHAO MEMORIAL HALL (zhōu ēnlái dèng yǐngchāo jìniàn guǎn; 周恩来邓颖超纪念馆). Students, elderly tour groups, and die-hard history aficionados can enjoy the old photographs, revolutionary scripts, wax figures, and documentary films that fill this ultra-modern museum dedicated to the life and achievements of China's two most revered revolutionary heroes, Zhou Enlai and his wife Deng Yingchao. While the latter worked for women's liberation in China, former Premier Zhou is especially respected for his lifelong work in the Chinese Communist Party and for being the sole voice of reason and moderation during the turmoil of the Cultural Revolution. The downstairs hall showcases their life and achievements, while the upstairs Qing Huai Hall displays personal trinkets and eerily life-like wax figures. Zhou's personal jet sits outside. (Near the end of Shuishang Gongyuan Lu. Southeast of Nankai University, just across from Shuishang Park. ☎ 2359 2257 or 2359 1256. Open Su, Tu-Sa 8:30am-5pm; last ticket sold at 4pm. Y10, students Y5. Admission to jet Y10. Wheelchair accessible.)

SHENYANG DAO ANTIQUE MARKET (shěnyángdào gǔwù shìchǎng; 沈阳道古物市 场). A complex neighborhood of winding alleyways, beginning at Shenyang Dao, where bustling vendors display their wares on roadside mats. Ceramics and antiques galore (some real, some laughable) provide an opportunity to practice your bargaining skills. On Thursday and Friday mornings this place truly gets going when the traveling merchants put up shop. (Shenyang Dao, south of Heping Lu. An alley directly opposite the Shijie Shangsha leads to the market. Open daily 9am-4pm.)

GULOU STREET MARKET (gǔlóu jiē; 鼓楼街). The faux antique pagodas that house several dozen small shops and vendors are like the goods for sale—more imitation than genuine. Though they may be barred from airports, well-made, sturdy-looking Chinese swords fetch Y40-200, porcelain figurines Y50, and jade bracelets a mere Y10. (At the intersection of Chengxiang Zhong Lu (城厢中路) and Bian Gulou Jie, (鼓楼街) Open daily 9am-8pm.)

OTHER SIGHTS. Tianjin's **Confucius Temple** (wénmiào; 文庙) sits on the northern side of Dongmen Nei Dajie, under the shadow of the huge Carrefour megastore. No longer as peaceful as in days past, the temple grounds now house busy vendors, as well as umbrella-shaped trees, chirping birds, and an arched stone bridge leading to some beautifully ornate (but rather dusty) pagodas dedicated to the life of Confucius. (☎ 2727 2812. Open Su, Tu-Sa 9:30am-4pm. Y4.)

The **Tianjin Radio and TV Tower** (tiānjīn guǎngbō diànshì tǎ; 天津广播电视塔) on Weijin Nan Lu is an impressive sight from afar, especially when lit up at night (until 10pm). The fee for an elevator ride to the open skyspace is as steep as the ascent. The view of Tianjin's flat, building-filled landscape in the haze may fail to dazzle, but it does give a startling idea of how rapidly the city is changing. (☎ 2335 5775, 2334 3557, or 2335 5314; fax 2334 9673. Elevator on 2nd fl. Open daily 8:30am-10pm. Tower Y50, children under 1.3m Y25.)

📷 NIGHTLIFE

Not too many years ago, Tianjin was a quiet little town; today, however, reckless carousers abound in the ever-changing nightlife scene. Foreigners congregate near the universities in the southwest corner of the city at hangouts such as **Ali Baba's** (see p. 174), where the music is loud and the beer plentiful. Talking to the students here is a good way to find out where the latest hot spots are. Youth, yuppies, and the young at heart strain their vocal cords at KTV centers along Jiefang Bei Lu (cover Y50-100). Try the **Banana KTV Disco** (bānànà díbā; 巴那那迪吧 ; ☎ 2332 5788), 78 Jinshe Lu. An exploration of Tianjin's fountains and nightmarkets that stretch along the north side of the river reveals even cheaper delights. Over 20 bars cater to revelers on Youyi Lu. Some merit special notice, including the intimate and relaxed **Western Heaven** and **Man!la,** where the clientele have dance fever and express their superstar tendencies with lively karaoke.

Sky Dragon Disco (tiānlóng díbā; 天龙迪吧), 103 Qiongzhou Dao (☎8381 6666). Best bet is to take a taxi there and back. Join the lively Tianjin locals as they yell and cheer for crowd favorites performing parodies of Chinese opera and Western and Chinese pop music. On some nights, the stage gives way to dance and disco, accompanied by the top hits on MTV-Asia. Corona Y25, Budweiser Y20. Cover Y10. Open daily 8pm-3am.

Western Heaven (xībù dàtáng jĭubā; 西部大堂酒吧), Bar Street, Youyi Lu (☎2837 1533). Local performers croon Western tunes in Chinese and heavily-accented English. In the corner, people play chess and relax. Scented candles, oak decor, and friendly service create a cozy and welcoming atmosphere. Serves food and beer (Y15-30). No cover charge. Open daily 8pm-2:30am.

▶ DAYTRIP FROM TIANJIN: TANGGU 塘沽

Buses leave for Tanggu from many locations, including the Tianjin Railway Station and the South Bus Station (1½hr., bus #612 leaves when full, Y4). Trains from Tianjin Railway Station (Y5.5) cover the distance in 30min. and leave frequently. Tanggu is surprisingly vast and quite difficult to get around. Taxis are the best bet, but beware of swindlers.

Tanggu lacks the comfort and luxury of nearby Tianjin. Many of its buildings are under construction but never seem to reach completion. The biggest draw of Tanggu is not even within the proper city limits. Over 16km from the city center, the **Seaside Amusement Park** (hǎibīn yùchǎng; 海滨浴场) is home to waterslides and the largest manmade beach in China. Visitors can breathe in the pungent aroma of seawater and look out over the brown waters of the Bohai Gulf as happy music blares from speakers. On bad days, smog can obscure even the closest buildings. (On Haifang Lu, across the Haihe Bridge. ☎2531 9020 or 2531 9558. A 20min. taxi ride costs about Y50. Open daily June-Oct. 24hr. Y10, swimming Y30, crab- and shrimp-catching Y15.) **Dagu Fort** (dàgū pàotái; 大沽炮台) boasts little more than a rusty old war plane and several decaying cannons. Though not much to the casual viewer, the lonely fort still stands as a remembrance of China's defeat in the Second Opium War and the ransacking of Beijing by Western forces. Climb up the solitary preserved post for an unobstructed view of the desolate landscape. (☎139 0214 2038. Open daily 8am-5:30pm. Y10, students Y5.)

Travelers consigned to Tanggu's shores overnight have an ever-increasing range of options. Across from the oceanic passenger terminal is the **International Seamen's Club ❷** (tiānjīn xīngǎng guójì hǎiyuán jùlèbù; 天津新港国际海员俱乐部). Rooms are slightly cramped but offer TV and bath. (☎6577 0333. Singles Y160; doubles Y218-240; suites Y360. Several newer hotels on Shanghai Dao welcome foreigners. Though affordable, **Santai Dajiudian ❷** (sāntái dàjiŭdiàn; 三泰大酒店) does not stand out from other hotels in terms of cleanliness, but it does have 24hr. security and a central location. (TV, bath, 24hr. water pressure. Economy rooms Y150; singles Y168; standard doubles Y226.)

HEBEI 河北

With the powerful municipalities of Beijing and Tianjin geographically (but not administratively) within its borders, Hebei is the understudy, never the star. While this province may not be hip or fashionable, it stands firmly on its own with a rugged appeal that has hardly endured the years. But perhaps it's precisely this distance from the limelight that has made the province such a sanctuary for the emperors of yore and the baton-wielders of today. After all, for centuries, Hebei has been the vacation spot of choice for the ruling elite. During the 18th century, Qing emperors, laid low by heat and boredom, jaunted off to the expansive land-scaped beauty of the Imperial Summer Villa (literally "Flee-the-Heat Villa"). These days, the beach and surf of Beidaihe and Shanhaiguan lure city-weary CCP hot-shots and throngs of heat-stricken vacationers. In the end, Hebei's less than glam-orous reputation may be its saving grace.

SHIJIAZHUANG 石家庄 ☎ 0311

The economic and political capital of Hebei usually doesn't make the travel itiner-ary—and for good reason. Besides being the burial place of revolutionary martyrs and home to the country's largest People's Liberation Army academy, there's not much else to see, little to eat, and even less to do. But Shijiazhuang is not com-pletely without its appeal, even if it doesn't have the flashy, neon glitz of nearby Beijing or Tianjin. Without the tumult that often plagues those teeming metropoli-tan centers, Shijiazhuang has been able to concentrate on completely rebuilding its infrastructure—and becoming a nice place to *live*. Neat, orderly streets, trees that have been around for longer than five years, an abundance of no-smoking signs, and trucks that hose down the streets and sidewalks at 9am all make life comfortable and easy in the province's aspiring capital. Major railway lines all con-verge at Shijiazhuang, providing travelers an ideal base from which to see the sur-rounding sights and neighboring cities.

▐ TRANSPORTATION

Flights: Shijiazhuang Airport (shíjiāzhuāng jīchǎng; 石家庄机场), 40km northeast of city center, 35km from its edge. **China Eastern Airlines** (zhōngguó dōngfāng hángkōng gōngsī; 中国东方航空公司), Aviation Bldg., 128 Zhongshan Dong Lu (☎ 698 1824 or 698 1124; fax 864 1533). Ask about shuttle buses to the airport. Open 9am-5:30pm. To: **Chongqing** (W, Sa; Y990); **Guangzhou** (Tu, W, F, Sa; Y1560); **Shanghai** (7:40am, Y990); **Shenzhen** (Th, Y1510).

Trains: Shijiazhuang Railway Station (shíjiāzhuāng huǒchē zhàn; 石家庄火车站 ; ☎ 702 2227) is accessible by almost every bus in the city. Tickets available 10 days in advance; recommended purchase at least 24hr. before departure. Luggage storage Y3-5 per day. To: **Anyang** (2-4hr., a couple per day, Y19-56); **Beijing** (2½hr., 4 express trains, Y44); **Datong** (12hr., 2 per day, Y79-144); **Guangzhou** (10hr., 10am, Y226); **Shanghai** (17-19hr., 2pm, Y308); **Tianjin** (7hr., 1 per day, Y31-68); **Xi'an** (10hr., 2 per day, Y250).

Buses: Long-Distance Bus Station (chángtú qìchē zhàn; 长途汽车站 ; ☎ 702 2570), south of the train station. Turn left in front of the train station and head as far south as you can on the pedestrian street immediately in front of the train station. The bus sta-tion is at the very end of the street, past the jungle of minibuses. Ticket counter open daily 5am-5:30pm. To: **Beijing** (4hr., every hr. 7am-5pm, Y45); **Qinhuangdao** (8-12hr., 3 per day, Y105); **Tianjin** (6hr., several per day, Y42). **Yunhe Bridge Bus Station** (yùn-héqiáo zhàn; 运河桥站 ; ☎ 683 4318), 1.7km north of the train station, down Shengli Dajie, past Heping Lu. Buses make local stops in the city outskirts before heading to smaller towns in the province. Open daily 5am-7pm. To: **Beitai** (7:30am, Y17); **Gaoy-ang** (many per day, Y25); **Tangshan** (2 per day, Y60).

Public Transportation: Local **buses** ply the streets of downtown Shijiazhuang; most of them start from, stop at, or run past the train station. Routes are mapped out on bus stop signs and convenient to navigate. Buses run until 7pm. Two major bus depots are on Zhanqian Lu, just south (in front of and to the left) of the train station. Buses #1, 5, and 6 run east-west along Zhongshan Lu; #4 runs east-west along Heping Lu; #7 runs north-south along Ping'an Lu; #13 runs north-south along Zhonghua Dajie.

BEIJING

Taxis: Base fare Y5. Y10-15 should suffice for most places around the center of town. Round-trip Y1.4 per km; one-way Y2.1 per km.

■ ✦ 🔢 ORIENTATION AND PRACTICAL INFORMATION

Many of the streets are arranged in a grid-like pattern, which makes for easy navigation and transportation. Most activity is centered around the plaza outside the train station; along **Zhongshan Xi Lu** (中山西路) and **Zhongshan Dong Lu,** which run west and east from the station; and on **Shengli Bei Jie** (胜利北街) and **Shengli Nan Jie,** which run north and south from the station. Zhanqian Jie (站前街) goes past the train station and nearly all of the town's affordable hotels and 24hr. Western-style fast-food restaurants. Yucai Jie (育才街) branches off Zhongshan Dong Lu, just past the Provincial Museum.

Travel Agencies: CITS (☎581 6629) and **CTS** main offices are in the Tourism Bldg., 175 Yucai Jie, 4th and 6th fl., opposite the Hebei Grand Hotel. Both open M-F 8am-noon and 2-6pm. **CTS branch,** 140 Yucai Jie, 2nd fl. (☎621 6663). English-speaking staff. Open daily 8am-noon and 2-6pm. **Bailin Hotel guest services** (☎702 1937; fax 702 1884) helps book tickets and plan travel itineraries. Open daily 9am-5pm. See **Accommodations,** p. 179.

Bank of China: 83 Zhongshan Xi Lu, Dongfang Plaza, 1st fl. (☎861 1299), a short walk northwest of the train station, around the corner from the Dongfang Shopping Plaza main entrance. Exchanges currency and traveler's checks. Credit card advances. Open M-F 8:30am-noon and 2:30-5:30pm.

Shopping: Dongfang City Plaza Shopping Center (dōngfāng chéngshìguǎngchǎng gòuwù zhōngxīn; 东方城市广场购物中心), 83 Zhongshan Xi Lu (☎861 1061), about a block west of the train station. Open daily M-F 9am-7:30pm, Sa-Su 9am-9pm. Head east to reach the **Beiguo Commercial Building** (běiguó shāngchéng; 北国商城), 188 Zhongshan Dong Lu (☎697 4448), at the intersection of Zhongshan Dong Lu and Jianshe Bei Dao. Open daily 9am-10pm.

Internet Access: In general, Internet bars have short lifespans but always seem to cluster on the same street. Several exist along and around Yucai Jie. **Red Earth Coffee & Internet Bar,** 171 Yucai Jie (☎657 1686), close to the CITS main office. Receive a free hr. of net access for each Y5 you spend on milk, dark or spiced coffee, and drinks (Y10-20). Open 24hr. **Shenshenlan Internet Bar,** 265 Yuhua Dong Lu, caters more to the college crowd. Go east from the intersection between Yucai Jie and Yuhua Dong Lu. Y2 per hr., Y10 deposit for Internet card. Open daily 9am-2am.

PSB: 216 Zhongshan Dong Lu.

Post Office: China Post, 1 Gongli Jie (☎702 5736), on the corner of Gongli Jie and Zhongshan Xi Lu, just across the bridge from the train station. Main entrance on Gongli Jie; at later hours, use the entrance around the corner on Zhongshan Lu. EMS, IDD service, and Poste Restante. Open 24hr.

Postal Code: 050000.

ACCOMMODATIONS AND FOOD

If you're in Shijiazhuang, you're probably a reluctant itinerant. Dormitory-style hotels and those that charge by the hour refuse foreign guests, and the hotels that do welcome foreigners know that you're stuck here. As a result, budget options are limited, and the quality may not merit the price tag. Many hotels are near the train station and are fiercely competitive; it won't hurt to check out several options before making a choice.

Shijiazhuang is not known for any gastronomic delights, and what it does have is mediocre at best. The biggest food fads in town are fill-me-up-quick box lunches and stuff-me-to-the-brim buffets. **Kiosks** lining Zhanqian Jie cook up strips of chicken teriyaki for Y1 per stick, while small **shops** ladle out big helpings of beef noodles for Y5. Get a taste of **farm produce** on Donghua Lu, off Zhongshan Dong Lu. Vendors offer a variety of fresh fruits and vegetables for Y1-3 per kg, but be sure to check for insects and wash all purchases carefully. For sit-down meals in more orderly environments with actual menus, a strip of **restaurants** serves up aquatic delicacies along Yucai Jie, south of the Hebei Teachers' University.

Bailin Hotel (báilín dàshà; 柏林大厦), 24 Zhanqian Jie (☎702 1398; fax 702 1887), opposite the train station. Within spitting distance of the next train out of town and unofficial winner of the best and the biggest baths in town award. More costly rooms have newer bedcovers and offer more refuge from the din of downtown traffic. Laundry, Internet, and an automatic shoe polisher available. Breakfast included. Check-out noon. Deposit Y120 and up. Doubles Y126-260; triples Y280-420. ❷

Silver Spring Hotel (yínquán jiǔjiā; 银泉酒家), 12 Zhanqian Jie (☎702 6981), across the street from the long-distance bus station. Convenient location, with well-kept rooms that have A/C, bath, phone, Internet, and TV. Water pressure at specific hours of the day; do not try to take showers after 2am. Reservations recommended. Economy singles Y88; doubles Y128-200; triples Y198. ❷

Hebei Hotel (héběi fàndiàn; 河北饭店), 10 Zhanqian Jie (☎702 5991), across from the area between the train station and the bus station, next to the Hualian Commercial Building. Room amenities and cleanliness do not vary much with price, although baths are noticeably better in more expensive options. Rooms may smell of cigar and cigarette smoke, but the busy front desk will let you change rooms. Check-out 2pm. Deposit starting at Y100. Standard economy Y130; doubles 180-360. ❷

Hebei Huiwen Hotel (héběi huìwén jiǔdiàn; 河北汇文酒店), 6 Zhanqian Jie (☎787 9988; fax 786 5500), right next to the Hebei Hotel. Out of all the hotels in the train station's immediate area, the only one whose quality—and cost—will knock your socks off. For those who want to live in the lap of luxury and don't mind triple-digit numbers, all rooms are well-lit, with opulent, silk wheat-design bedcovers. Teak furniture polished to a gleam, and rooms kept meticulously dust- and grime-free. Economy rooms start at Y260 and skyrocket from there. ❹

BEIJING

⊙ SIGHTS

Within the city, few sights hold visitors' interests for long. If you just want to kill some time, wander through the bustling markets south of **Xinhua Dong Lu** (新华东路) and along **Shengli Bei Jie** (胜利北街). More exciting sights lie outside the city proper, but getting there can be an expensive and difficult endeavor, often requiring chartered taxis that cost Y50-100.

HEBEI PROVINCIAL MUSEUM (héběi shěng bówùguǎn; 河北省博物馆). This massive columned building is an impossible-to-miss local landmark. Skip the free commercial exhibition downstairs unless you collect pamphlets. The main gallery space upstairs features exhibits on modern and ancient Hebei, with just enough relics to make the visit worthwhile for the amateur archaeologist. Spotlighted artifacts include a suit of jade armor, a terracotta army, oracle bones, and gilt bronze statues of the Goddess of Mercy. *(Zhongshan Dong Lu, 3 blocks east of the Beiguo Commercial Building. Take bus #1, 5, 25, or 29 from the train station. ☎ 603 9534. Open Tu-F 8:30-11:30am and 2:30-6pm, Sa-Su 9am-5pm. Y10. Last admission 40min. before closing.)*

MARTYRS MEMORIAL (lièshì língyuán; 烈士陵园). In this perfectly geometric, expansive park, superhuman statues and busts are set off by rampant overgrown greenery. Several stately buildings display all sorts of weaponry, including glass-encased machine guns and rusted shells. The photo collections and relics depict in astounding detail every aspect of the lives of those who dedicated themselves to the revolution. Now frequented by mandatory student tour groups and the elderly, the memorial is mainly dedicated to exhibits on the guerrilla physician Dr. Bethune, who fought on the side of the Communist Party against the Japanese during WWII. *(343 Zhongshan Xi Lu. Take bus #1, 25, or 29 from the train station; #25 stops right in front of the memorial. ☎ 702 2904. Open daily 8:30-11:30am and 2-5:30pm. Y5.)*

GREAT BUDDHA TEMPLE (dàfó sì; 大佛寺). First built in 586 AD, **Longxing Monastery** (lóngxīng sì; 隆兴寺) is more popularly known as the Great Buddha Temple. Back in the Song Dynasty (960-1279 AD), when the town of Zhengding (正定) flourished as a religious hub, the temple teemed with monks and worshippers alike. Today, the monks have long gone, but tourists still flock here to see the remnants of well-preserved, priceless Buddhist sculptures. The multi-armed, bronze statue of Guanyin, the Goddess of Mercy, dominates the Main Hall at a towering 21.3m. Built in seven stages, the Goddess of Mercy boasts "one thousand hands and eyes." During the Song Dynasty, it was known as the highest statue in China, and locals still proudly name it one of the "four wonders of Hebei Province." According to popular belief, a climb into the upper rafters to shake one of the Buddha's many burnished hands, touch the nose, or risk injury in any way, demonstrates one's piety. *(15km northeast of Shijiazhuang. Take bus #201 from the south side of the train station to the last stop. From there, jump aboard (or get shoved into) bus #1 to Dafo Si. ☎ 878 6560; www.longxingsi.com. Open daily 8am-5:30pm. Y30, children under 1.4m Y15.)*

▶ DAYTRIP: CANGYANSHAN MOUNTAIN 苍岩山

About 70km southwest of Shijiazhuang. Circuitous bus route through small towns and markets takes 2-3hr. Take bus #9 or 114 to Xiwang Bus Station (xīwángzhàn; 西王站 ; ☎ 366 1780). Ticket counter open daily 6am-5:30pm. 5 buses leave for Cangyanshan daily (2-3hr.; 7, 8, 9:50am, 1, 5pm; Y13). Make sure to ask about return trips in advance: times vary depending on which bus you take.

This complex of pagodas and monasteries, sheltered against a dramatic landscape of mountain peaks and marvelously twisted 500-year-old cypresses, has been precariously stitched upon the steep cliff precipices and narrow ridges. The hike up the mountain passes 16 designated scenic spots and should take about 1½-2hr. An 8min. cable car ride can also take you directly to the summit, but the power may be out occasionally. It is best to go in the early morning or afternoon for safety and to avoid the heat and crowds. (Open daily 24hr. Cable car round-trip Y40.) The sheer vertical cliffs and dizzingly steep ascent on certain paths may be more memorable than some of the crumbling, manmade structures. Gatekeepers at temples along the way and at the top of the summit charge further admission fees (Y5). Luckily, the free hike provides enough to see, as these generic sights aren't worth the extra time or money. The one exception that you *do* want to visit, the **Hanging Palace** straddles a narrow cleft between two cliffs. Those more foolhardy can follow signs to the **Tomb of the Princess,** gracing the summit of Cangyanshan. Supposedly, the Princess Nanyang, daughter of Emperor Yang (AD 581-618) of the Sui Dynasty, knelt in prayer to Buddha here. Beware: the rusty, rickety guard rail that outlines the spiraling ascent may not be enough to prevent a precipitous drop.

Booths offer popsicles and bottled water along the climb, and a shack sells cookies and bread (Y1-3) at the base of the mountain, but there is little else available in terms of sustenance. Should you find yourself stranded for the night, the rooms at the **Cangyanshan Hotel ❷** (cāngyánshān bīnguǎn; 苍岩山宾馆) gaze out at the cable cars and the pagodas adorning the tips of the mountains—arguably the best view from a hotel in the entire province. (☎ 232 4114. Reception 6am-11pm; let the receptionist know if you intend to come back later. Doubles and triples Y180.)

CHENGDE 承德　　　　　　☎ 0314

Three hundred years ago, Chengde was but a small, remote village, quietly nestled 200km northeast of Beijing. In the early 18th century, however, the region's untamed grasslands caught the imperial eye. The Qing emperors Kangxi and Qianlong began to develop Chengde as an elaborate summer villa for hunting and relaxing, replete with lavish gardens, pagodas, and shaded lakes. Pleasure alone was not the motivation: the shrewd emperors constructed the elaborate temples and palaces at the empire's northeastern border as a symbol of political unity.

Unfortunately, in the 19th century the mountain resort fell into disgrace as the site of imperial deaths and humiliating treaties. But not even years of corruption and neglect can harm the beauty of Chengde. The mountainous terrain and vistas that once captured the hearts of emperors are as breathtaking as ever. Today, as in the past, Chengde's promise of a cool refuge draws city-dwellers away from Beijing's summer heat and traffic to follow in the footsteps of emperors past.

TRANSPORTATION

Trains: Chengde Train Station (chéngdé huǒchē zhàn; 承德火车站 ; ☎ 208 4499), east of the river. 24hr. luggage storage (xíngbāo fáng; 行包房) Y2 per day. Ticket office open daily 5-7:45am and 8:10am-11pm; advance tickets 8:40-11am and 2-4pm. To: **Beijing** (4-7hr., 5 per day, Y17-41); **Shenyang** (12hr., daily, Y45); **Shijiazhuang** (12hr., daily, Y38); **Tianjin** (9hr., daily, Y30).

Buses: Chengde Long-Distance Bus Station (chéngdé chángtú qìchē zhàn; 承德长途汽车站). Located outside of the city, accessible by bus #16. Luggage storage 5:30am-10pm (Y10 per day, depending on size). Open daily 24hr. To: **Beijing** (3½hr., every 20min. 6am-6pm, Y45); **Qinhuangdao** (6hr., 4 per day, Y65); **Tianjin** (6hr., 3 per day, Y66). Private **minibuses** also depart frequently for **Beijing** (3hr., Y45) from the front of the building.

Local Transportation: Public buses (#1-15) run 6am-7pm. Bus #5 goes from the train station to the Imperial Summer Villa; #6 from Nanyingzi Dajie to the Northern Temples via the Villa; #7 between the train station and Nanyingzi Dajie; #10 from Nanyingzi

Dajie to the Eastern Temples. More frequent are the **private buses** (numbered in the 100s), which run later, but travel only to central locations. Unnumbered **minibuses** run along the main streets between the train station and the city center.

Taxis: Base fare officially Y5; each additional km Y1.4. To most sights in the city Y10; agree on the price in advance.

Bike Rental: (☎202 6827). Look for a stand on the right side of Tiaoli Jie near the intersection with Xinhua Lu, 100m in, across from a local school. Knock on the door at night. Y5 per day. Open daily 24hr. Another stand at the southwest corner of the train station square, left of the post office, has a limited selection. Y5 per day, deposit Y100-200. Open daily approx. 6am-6:30pm.

✴❼ ORIENTATION AND PRACTICAL INFORMATION

Chengde rests in a valley bisected by the Wulie River. Its principal roads, Nanyingzi Dajie (南营子大街), Xi Dajie (西大街), Dong Dajie (东大街), and Lizhengmen Dajie (丽正门大街) all intersect in a cross at the city center, about a 5min. walk west of the gates of the Imperial Summer Villa. The Eight Outer Temples sprawl throughout the surrounding mountains further east.

Travel Agency: CITS, 11 Zhonghua Lu, 2nd fl. (☎202 6827), in the right wing of the courtyard of a gray building, 2min. up the street from the Summer Villa's Dehuimen Gate. Organizes foreign language tours (Y200 and up per day). Staff members speak impeccable English. Open daily 8:30am-noon and 2-5pm.

Bank of China: 3 Dong Dajie. Exchanges traveler's checks. Credit card advances. Branches throughout the city.

Hospital: Chengde Central Hospital (chéngdéshì zhōngxīn yīyuàn; 承德市中心医院), on Xi Dajie, 1½ blocks west of Nanyingzi Dajie. English-speaking staff. Open 24hr.

Internet Access: The 2 most centrally located Internet cafes are on Nanyingzi Dajie, left of the cinema. Follow the signs leading to the **Mingxing Hotel** (míngxíng bīnguǎn; 明行宾馆). Enter on Nanxinglong Food St., between Lizhengmen Dajie and Dong Dajie. Y2 per hr. Open daily 10am-2am. **Huafeng Computer** (huáfēng diànnǎo; 华峰电脑 ; ☎139 0314 2165), at the intersection of Xinhua Lu and Nanyingzi Dajie, fixes computers in addition to providing Internet access. Y2 per hr. Open daily 8am-3pm.

Post Office: About half a block north of the southern tip of Nanyingzi Dajie. EMS. Open daily 8am-6pm.

Postal Code: 067000.

⌂ ACCOMMODATIONS

If traveling from Beijing to Chengde, chances are that hotel touts will accost you before you've even departed. They'll guarantee a free ride from the train station and often help get discounts at the better hotels.

Jiaoshi Hotel (jiàoshī bīnguǎn; 教师宾馆), 16 Tiaoli Jie (☎215 3268), a 7min. walk south of Xinhua Lu. These pleasant rooms are hard to beat in terms of price, atmosphere, and location. Doubles are a decent size, and quads are extremely spacious with 2 attaching rooms that share a common bath. Clean bathrooms, A/C, and TV. Hot water 8:30-10:30pm (longer in the summer). 4-bed dorms Y30, with bath Y80; doubles Y120, but may be pricier in the summer. All prices negotiable. ❶

Jingcheng Hotel (jīngchéng fàndiàn; 京承饭店 ; ☎208 2027), on the southeast side of the train station square. Its proximity to the train station is an immediate plus, but a taxi to the city center costs Y5-10. Rooms are clean, bright, and neat. Large bathrooms, but no separated showers. Restaurant on the 2nd fl. A/C, TV, and 24hr. hot water. 4-bed and 3-bed dorms Y50; 2-bed Y65; singles Y100. Low-season discounts available. ❶

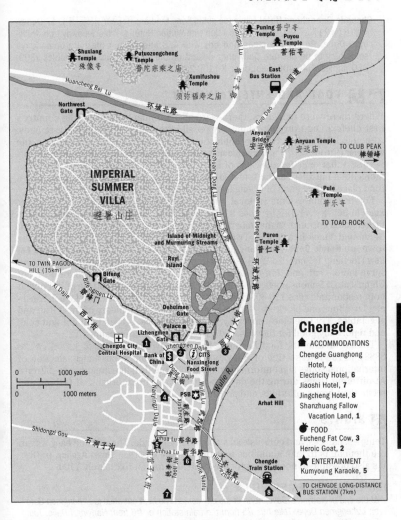

Chengde

🏠 ACCOMMODATIONS

Chengde Guanghong
Hotel, 4
Electricity Hotel, 6
Jiaoshi Hotel, 7
Jingcheng Hotel, 8
Shanzhuang Fallow
Vacation Land, 1

🍎 FOOD
Fucheng Fat Cow, 3
Heroic Goat, 2

★ ENTERTAINMENT
Kumyoung Karaoke, 5

TO CHENGDE LONG-DISTANCE
BUS STATION (7km)

Shanzhuang Fallow Vacation Land (shānzhuāng xiūxián dùjiǎcūn; 山庄休闲度假村;
☎ 203 7858 or 203 5770; cdhldjc@163.com), in Liangshi Beishan Building #6, next to
the statue of emperor Kangxi, hidden among the growing apartment blocks. Elevated
along the mountainside, this former residential apartment has now been converted into
a guesthouse. A quieter, more homey stay ideal for longer visits. Hard to find, but worth
the search. Doubles Y400-508. Bargaining may be necessary. ❹

Electricity Hotel (diànlì bīnguǎn; 电力宾馆; ☎ 217 3735), at the busy intersection of
Xinhua Lu and Wulie Lu, about 10min. from Nanyingzi Dajie, near the train station.
Rooms are neat, clean, and well-lit, but the bathrooms may be dirty and dim. Shower
not separate. TV, A/C, and 24hr. hot water. 5-bed dorms with bath Y50; 3-bed dorms
Y80; 2-bed dorms Y30, with bath Y50, depending on season. ❶

Chengde Guanghong Hotel (chéngdé guānghóng fàndiàn; 承德光宏饭店), 17 Dongxing Lu (☎217 3735), at the intersection with Wutiao Hutong, 2 blocks away from Nanyingzi Dajie. Rooms are clean and tidy with A/C and TV, but the bathrooms leave something to be desired. Daily price posted on the counter. July-Aug. doubles Y300-360; triples Y340-400. Sept.-June 2 Y100-200/Y130-240. ❸

📷 🎵 FOOD AND ENTERTAINMENT

Where there were emperors, there were also attendant armies of the country's best chefs doing everything humanly possible to tickle the imperial taste buds. Although little of that culinary sophistication survives into the present day, the **wild deer** (lùròu; 鹿肉) and **mushroom-braised baby chicken** (xiǎojī dùn mógū; 小鸡炖蘑菇) that once fed the Sons of Heaven are still local specialties. **Almonds,** an indigenous nut that can be found all along the city's mountainsides, also hold a fond place in the hearts of Chengde's chefs.

For true connoisseurs of local cuisine, **Nanxinglong Food Street** (nánxīnglóng xiǎochī jiē; 南兴隆小吃街) has it all. The bustling, bubbling, street opposite the Lizhengmen entrance to the Imperial Villa dishes up hotpot (Y8-18) and every kind of almond snack imaginable. Two restaurants that are currently the craze of the town are **Heroic Goat** (bātè yáng jié zǐ; 巴特羊羯子 ; ☎202 9259) and **Fucheng Fat Cow** (fúchéng féi niú; 福成肥牛). Both are along Nanxinglong Food Street and serve lamb, veal, and *dōngpō ròu* (东坡肉), a pork dish named after one of China's most famous poets, Su Dongpo, who wrote a poem in praise of it. Food at both restaurants runs Y20-30. In the evening, **open-air stalls** on Yihua Lu and Xinsheng Lu, about one block west of the bus station, serve up plenty of fresh fruit and vegetables. Try Chengde's specialty, **Lulu Almond Juice,** served both hot and cold, and reportedly good for the skin. (Y0.5 from street vendors, canned Y2.)

To ease off after the food, **Kumyoung Karaoke** (jīnyǒng gēchéng; 金永歌城 ; ☎206 3888), at the intersection of Nanyingzi Dajie and Xinhua Lu, has a selection of international songs and uniformed youth who shout drill-like greetings to patrons. At different times during the day, they march out in an organized fashion and recite their hours, offerings, and policies.

🔆 SIGHTS

Temples, palaces, and curious rocks abound in Chengde. The fast and easy way to see them all is to take a minibus tour through the city (see **Travel Agency,** p. 182). It's also possible to book a taxi for the entire day for approximately Y100.

IMPERIAL SUMMER VILLA

At the end of Nanyingzi Dajie, north of the city center. The best entrance is Lizhengmen Gate on Lizhengmen Dajie. Take bus #5 from the train station or #6 from Nanyingzi Dajie. Tour buses (40min., 8am-5pm, Y40) leave from the area between the courtyards and the lake. Open daily summer 7am-5:30pm; winter 8am-4:30pm. Y90, children under 1.2m free.

The 18th century Imperial Summer Villa (bìshǔ shānzhuāng; 避暑山庄) is twice the size of Beijing's Summer Palace and has seen nearly as many Qing intrigues. Though the once resplendent retreat has slipped slowly into a state of neglect, it's still the must-see main attraction of Chengde. With its 300th anniversary celebration in 2002, the massive estate has undergone major renovations.

The Villa is divided into four separate regions: the main palace, the mountains, the lakes, and the plains. Each represents a different aspect of China. Of the 120 groups of ancient buildings, only 40-50 are open to the public. The main palace, including the elegant **Hall of Frugality and Sincerity,** has been converted into a museum of weaponry and furniture. In the side halls, the walls are lined with shelves that hold an encyclopedic collection of books and illustrations. The sickly Emperor Xianfeng signed the 1860 Treaty of Beijing and took his last breath in the lavish **Hall of Refreshing Mists and Ripples,** behind the courtyard. His demise allowed the Dowager Empress Ci Xi to co-reign with her young son, thus wresting political control from the male-dominated court.

The pride and joy of the villa are its lakes, mountains, and Mongolian plains, which take up the majority of the estate. Emperors tested their hunting prowess on mountain grounds (where deer abound) and rolling grasslands. It would be unwise to explore the land alone, though, unless you want to wander lost in the hills. A winding paved road offers a 3hr. walk to breathtaking views of the city and the neighboring temples of Putuozongcheng and Xumifushou. A cart ride (1hr., Y40) with a short musical performance of ancient Chinese instruments is also available for a worthwhile run around the mountains.

While the summer villa may get its name from the mountains, the lakes are perhaps the most strikingly beautiful part. Eight distinct, manmade lakes flow into one another to form a patchwork of islands, the prettiest of which are **Ruyi Island** and the **Island of Midnight and Murmuring Streams.** You can walk to all of the islands, but renting a boat (Y50 per hr., deposit Y100-200) is more fun.

EIGHT OUTER TEMPLES

There were once 12 great temples built around Chengde, but four have fallen gracefully into disrepair. Of the Eight Outer Temples (wài bā miào; 外八庙) that remain, only four are open to visitors. Built according to various ethnic styles, these temples were commissioned by Emperors Kangxi and Qianlong more for political than religious reasons. Constructed out of Tibetan, Mongolian, and Han Chinese elements, the temples brought the country together in architectural form. In their lavish prime, they were a visual reminder to visiting Tibetan and Mongol emissaries and religious leaders of the magnificence of the Qing empire.

The older and smaller **Eastern Temples** (Anyuan, Pule, and Puren), on the east bank of the river, are a perfect place to escape the boisterous tourist crowds. The big money-makers are the **Northern Temples** (Putuozongcheng, Xumifushou, Puning, Puyou, and Shuxiang). The smaller Puren Temple (pǔrén sì; 普仁寺) and Shuxiang Temple (shūxiàng sì; 殊像寺) are not open to the public. While it may be tempting to strike out independently to cover all the temples, it is easy to overdose; most organized tours only take in two or three. If pressed for time, the mustsees are Puning and Putuozongcheng Temple.

TEMPLE KNOW-HOW. Before entering a temple, take off your hat and put away your camera. While it's fine to take shots of the exterior, once inside pictures are generally not allowed. As you enter the temple, there will be three doors. Never go through the middle door—it is reserved for high monks. Enter through the left door, and exit from the right. Do not step on the elevated wooden planks that line the doorways; these are considered to be part of the deities' bodies. Temple attendants may ask that you pay respects to the presiding deity, which usually consists of burning incense and kowtowing. Do not point at the statues, as that is considered disrespectful.

PUNING TEMPLE (pǔníng sì; 普宁寺). Of the Northern Temples, this is the only one where the religious chanting isn't pre-recorded. Called the "Temple of Universal Peace," this active temple commemorates Qianlong's defeat of the Mongolian rebels in 1755. The star of the temple is the 42-armed, 110-ton Guanyin (Goddess of Mercy) residing in the hall of Mahayana. At 22m tall, it is the largest wooden

Buddhist statue in the world. Accompanying it are two smaller Buddha statues of Guanyin's attendants, Boy of Good Wealth and Dragon Girl. *(At the end of Puningsi Lu, east of the villa. Take bus #15 to the end or get off at Dafosi 大佛寺.* ☎ *202 4548. Open daily 7:30am-6pm; last admission 5:30pm. Y50.)*

PUYOU TEMPLE (púyòu sì; 菩佑寺). This small, quiet compound, originally the center for the study of Buddhist scripture, is closed for renovations as of summer 2004. In 1937, Japanese occupation forces moved 500 statues here from Arhat Temple. Unfortunately, many were destroyed in a lightning fire in 1964: 178 remain today. See such disciples as Liu Haichan, who teased toads, "The Crazy Monk," who swept up treacherous officials with his trusty broom, and "Crazy Ji," who "acted like a lunatic and gave no damn to rules." *(A 2min. walk east from Puning Temple, to the right of the gate. Open daily 8am-6pm; last admission 5:30pm. Y50.)*

XUMIFUSHOU TEMPLE (xūmífùshòu zhī miào; 须弥福寿之庙). The outstanding features of Xumifushou Temple are the eight dragons made of sparkling gold, each weighing over 1000kg, that perch on its roof. This "Temple of Happiness and Longevity" was built in 1780 for the Sixth Panchen Lama when he came to celebrate the emperor's 70th birthday. It was to be a quiet place of study for the Lama who unfortunately enjoyed neither happiness nor longevity as he died, en route, in Beijing. *(On Shizigou Lu, the 1st of the Northern Temples, north of the Imperial Villa and a 10min. walk west from Puning Temple. Open daily 8:30am-5:30pm; last admission 5pm. Y50.)*

PUTUOZONGCHENG TEMPLE (pǔtuózōngchéng zhī miào; 普陀宗乘之庙). The oldest of the Chengde temples, Putuozongcheng is generally considered a happy alternative for those who can't make it to Tibet. Also known as the Temple of Potaraka Doctrine, it is a one-third scale model of the Dalai Lama's Potala Palace in Lhasa (p. 843). Built in honor of the emperor Qianlong's 60th birthday, the temple also served as an offering to those of lama faith and housed visiting Tibetan dignitaries. There are six vertical buddhas along the first level of the temple. Inside, there is a special shrine and seat for the planned coming of the Eighth Dalai Lama, who was never able to make the visit. *(A few hundred meters west of Xumifushou. Open daily 8:30am-5:30pm; last admission 5pm. Y50.)*

EASTERN TEMPLES. Pule Temple (pǔlè sì; 普乐寺) is a quiet spot with a circular pavilion in the back that resembles Beijing's Temple of Heaven (sp. 148). The building was constructed by visiting Mongols, and the architecture is a mixture of Mongolian, Tibetan, Chinese, and Islamic styles. From within, observe the tale of Princess Ming who became the Buddha Mother of Wisdom in one day. Admire the Central Asian architecture of **Anyuan Temple** (ānyuán miào; 安远庙) from afar, as this replica of a Xinjiang Temple is currently closed for renovations. *(Bus #10 drops you off at a big square, where English signs show the way to Pule, Anyuan, and Club Peak. Pule Temple open daily 8am-6pm; last admission 5:30pm. Y30.)*

OTHER SIGHTS

CLUB PEAK (bàngchuí fēng; 棒锤峰). Resembling a large sore thumb sticking out of the eastern horizon, Club Peak is Chengde's most beloved rock formation, which, according to legend, was created by a dragon. It can be seen from most scenic points in town. **Toad Rock** (hámá shí; 蛤蟆石) lies 2km south. From the right angle and with the right imagination, it does indeed mildly resemble a toad. The climb up is especially enjoyable in the early morning, when the paths lack mounds of tourists. Early birds can watch the sun rise over the countryside. *(At the end of Hedong Lu, between Anyuan and Pule Temples. Take bus #10 to its terminus. Open daily 6:30am-6pm. Y35. Cable car up Y35, down Y20.)*

TWIN PAGODA HILL (shuāngtǎ shān; 双塔山). More secluded than the widely visible and widely visited Club Peak, Twin Pagoda Hill seems like a better deal to most travelers. It has not just one but two exciting protuberances. You can either take the stone staircase or the cable cars to reach the top of the hills. There are 365 steps, one for each day of the year. The path is shaded by trees, including Chengde's favorite, almond. A small squat rock resembles a tortoise bowing before the two pagodas. Another formation looks like a pair of kissing lovers. *(About 15km west of Chengde. Accessible by bus #5. Open daily 24hr. Museum and cable cars 6am-7pm. Park Y35, cable car up Y35, down Y20, round-trip Y50.)*

SHANHAIGUAN 山海关 ☎ 0335

Famed as the place where the Great Wall meets the sea, Shanhaiguan challenges the visitor with all sorts of sights and tastes. The newly paved outer roads and modern buildings juxtapose the narrow inner streets and poor city housing. For all its renovations and modernization, Shanhaiguan maintains an air of calmness. Maybe it's the looming old city walls or the dusty inner city, but Shanhaiguan seems to have half a foot caught in the past, walking to a unique time and rhythm.

✈ ⚡ TRANSPORTATION AND PRACTICAL INFORMATION

The center of Shanhaiguan is the small village within the city walls, plus the few blocks to the south and east where the train station and the **First Pass Under Heaven** are found. The center of town is divided into a grid pattern, anchored by **Bei Dajie** (北大街), **Nan Dajie** (南大街), **Dong Dajie** (东大街), and **Xi Dajie** (西大街). The entire village is easily navigable on foot. Around it blooms the new Shanhaiguan, an impressively uniform and unexciting flower of post-modern Chinese architecture. The whole town is encircled by mountains, the sea, and sights, many of which are beyond the reach of public transportation.

Trains: Shanhaiguan Train Station (shānhǎiguān huǒchē zhàn; 山海关火车站; ☎504 4102), at the end of Nanguan Dajie. Luggage storage Y3 per hr. To: **Beijing** (3-7hr., 21 per day, Y50-65); **Changchun** (7-9hr., 3 per day, Y49-99); **Harbin** (10-12hr., 6 per day, Y62-120); **Shenyang** (4-7hr., 7 per day, Y31-63); **Tianjin** (4-5hr., 3 per day, Y24-47).

Local Transportation: The bus station at the junction of Guangcheng Dong Lu and Guangcheng Nan Lu serves **city buses** (Y1), which can also be caught on any major street outside the city walls. Bus #25 runs from Qinhuangdao to Old Dragon Head. The seasonal #24 goes to Yansai Lake; #23 to the Mengjiangnu Temple.

Taxis: The only way to get to Longevity Mountain and Jiaoshan Great Wall. Base fare Y5, each additional km Y1.4.

Travel Agency: CITS (☎505 2952), above the restaurant next to the ticket booth for the First Pass Under Heaven. English-language tours. Open daily 8:30am-5:30pm.

Bank of China: 60 Diyiguan Lu (☎505 2195). Exchanges traveler's checks. Credit card advances. Open M-F 8:30-11:45am and 3-5:30pm. In winter, times subject to change.

PSB: 23 Guangcheng Nan Lu. (☎507 3727).

Hospital: People's Hospital (rénmín yīyuàn; 人民医院), 46 Nan Dajie (☎505 1023).

Internet: A small **cafe** (wǎng bā; 网吧) at 24 Nan Dajie, halfway up the street through the South Gate. Y2 per hr. Several other establishments along the street are open as late as 2am.

Post Office: 31 Nan Dajie. EMS and Poste Restante. Open daily 8am-6pm.

Postal Code: 066200.

ACCOMMODATIONS AND FOOD

Shanhaiguan puts Beidaihe to shame when it comes to inexpensive places to stay. The elegant **Ronghua Hotel** ❷ (rónghuá jiǔdiàn; 荣华酒店), 1 Nanguan Dajie, has nice, clean rooms with 24hr. hot water, A/C, and attached baths. (☎507 7698. Singles Y168; doubles Y188-288; triples Y368.) Don't be fooled by the not-so-elegant entrance of the **Shanhaiguan Hotel** ❹ (shānhǎiguān dàjiǔdiàn; 山海关大酒店), 107 Guangcheng Nan Lu, outside and east of the South Gate. The rooms are very clean and brightly lit, and the central location is hard to beat. (☎506 4488, ext. 0 or 506 4988. Doubles Y300-430, extra bed Y100; triples with living room Y520.) The **First Pass Hotel** ❸ (dìyīguān bīnguǎn; 第一关宾馆), 1 Dong Dajie, is conveniently located right within the gates of the First Pass (thus sparing the need to pay for admission), and boasts impeccably clean rooms with large bathrooms. (☎513 2188 or 513 2199; firstpasshotel2188@tom.com. Singles and doubles Y200; triples Y200-300; quads Y420. All prices are negotiable.)

Shanhaiguan burns with love for **Middle Eastern cuisine.** Many restaurants have Arabic signs or call themselves Islamic taverns. Unlike most places in China, bread is a street vendor staple (Y2) and is served with most meals. The local specialty, *mènxiōngkǒu* (braised meat; 焖胸口), can be found at any of the family restaurants within the old city walls or on Nanguan Dajie. *Bōluó bǐng* (饽椤饼), a local favorite, can be found along Guangcheng Nan Lu at Wangyang Lou. *Bōluó bǐng* is a pastry wrapped in the leaves of the Bōluó tree, which grows on the Shanhaiguan mountainside. There are two types of filling, vegetable and meat. (Y8 for a box of 10.)

SIGHTS

Out of the many sights in Shanhaiguan, the most popular is probably the **Old Dragon Head** that fronts the Great Wall of China. Beijingers also flock to the coast for its **beaches.** Don't expect luxurious white sand and crystal clear water. There's a reason why Shanhaiguan is much cheaper than its neighbor, Beidaihe. From the city center to the coast, a taxi ride costs Y10.

FIRST PASS UNDER HEAVEN (tiānxià dìyī guān; 天下第一关). Along Diyiguan Lu, you will find three sites for the price of one, the main attraction being First Pass Under Heaven. This gate was China's outermost gate to the world—at least until the Manchu armies stormed in, soon followed by souvenir vendors. The main sight is an imposing tower of the Great Wall that now looms tall and lonesome amid the crowds. (*At the end of Diyiguan Lu on the eastern edge of town. Open daily 6am-7pm. Y50, includes admission to the Great Wall Museum and the Ice Sculpture Museum.*)

GREAT WALL MUSEUM (chángchéng bówùguǎn; 长城博物馆). One of the most interesting place to visit in Shanhaiguan, the museum features a well-curated and well-displayed history of the Great Wall. If you can read Chinese, there's enough information here to answer any Great Wall trivia questions that backpackers can sling. Even for the Chinese-illiterate, the excellent pictures should be enough to make you itch to adjust your travel itinerary. (*On Diyiguan Lu, 3min. south of the First Pass Under Heaven, following the Old City Wall. Open daily 7:45am-6:30pm. Included in the admission price to the First Pass Under Heaven.*)

ICE SCULPTURE MUSEUM (bīng xuě dàshìjiè; 冰雪大世界). Living under the wings of Harbin, Hebei residents have a fascination with ice sculptures. This small, somewhat random, ice sculpture museum is located at the front of Diyiguan Lu. These well-lit, impressive sculptures include dragons, temples, the Great Wall, and fictional characters like the Monkey King Wukong (悟空). (*Open daily 8am-6pm. Admission included in First Pass Under Heaven. Warm coats Y2.*)

JIAOSHAN GREAT WALL (jiǎoshān chángchéng; 角山长城). Stately and breath-taking, Jiaoshan surges up along the precipitous peaks of a mountain ridge that faces the Bohai Sea, earning itself the name "Horn Mountain" for its resemblance to the ridges on the back of a writhing dragon. Legend has it that this section of the Great Wall spontaneously dissolved to reveal the bones of human workers that had been used to fill in its base. Even with the extensive restorations since then, determined hikers must scramble hard past the laborers mending the mountain path to make it up to **Qixian Monastery,** built during the Ming Dynasty for scholars to study in seclusion. When it rains atop the mountain, you can see "Buddha light" (fó guāng; 佛光), a rare atmospheric trick of the sunlight and mists. Monastery aside, just the gorgeous view of Yansai Lake is well worth your sweat. *(3km north of Shanhaiguan. Accessible by taxi for Y10. Open daily from dawn until 2hr. before dusk. Cable car 8am-4pm. Y35, includes a cable car ride.)*

GREAT WALL CULTURAL CENTER (chángchéng wénhùa yóudōngyuán; 长城文化游东园). The exhibitions include a giant *papier maché* Great Wall and 5 rooms with life-sized illustrations of stories about the architectural marvel. One of the more famous stories tells of the Qing Dynasty Mengjiangnu (mèngjiāngnǚ: 孟姜女), a woman who cried for three days and three nights until a part of the Great Wall collapsed to reveal the bones of her beloved husband. Ever since, people have said that "water changes, sky changes, but Mengjiangnu's heart will never change." A temple in her name can be found 6km east of Shanhaiguan. The tour includes free admission to the Buddha Light Temple, a dimly lit, catacomb-like structure of Buddhist gods in rooms decorated with intricate and beautiful murals. *(Mengjiangnu's temple is accessible by bus #23 in July and August. Buddha Light Temple is at the head of the 500m strip leading to the Old Dragon Head. Open daily 7am-6pm. Y25.)*

OLD DRAGON HEAD (lǎo lóng tóu; 老龙头). You don't go to Shanhaiguan without seeing its claim to fame. This easternmost edge of the Great Wall juts out 124m into the Bohai Sea and is a perfect juxtaposition of manmade miracle and gorgeous natural scenery. Where a large stone dragon head once overlooked the sea, today there remains but a small fortress and temple. To get a better view of the entire structure, you can head over to the neighboring beaches. For Y30 you can take a high-speed boat tour around the shores, snapping perfect pictures. *(3km from Shanhaiguan. Minibuses leave from South Gate for Y2. Bus #25 takes forever to get to the same place. Park open daily 4am-7:30pm; the wall opens at 7:30am. Y50.)*

LONGEVITY MOUNTAIN (chángshòu shān; 长寿山). Longevity Mountain, part of the Yanshan Mountains, is mostly made of granite that was uplifted during the Himalayan movement. Grotesque rock formations (look for the turtle and the giant bull's head), caves, and precipitous mountains make it a truly unique hike. For those not interested in hiking, cars can drive through designated roads. On your way up to the mountain entrance, take note of **Nine Cave Mountain** (jiǔménkǒu shān; 九门口山) to your right. The road between Longevity and Nine Cave Mountain forms the border between Hebei and Liaoning Province. *(9km northeast of Shanhaiguan. Accessible by taxi Y30. ☎ 507 5110. Ticket office open daily 7am-sunset. Park open 24hr.)*

BEIDAIHE 北戴河 ☎ 0335

Until Europeans living in Tianijn "discovered" Beidaihe in the 19th century, it was just a little fishing village. The foreigners' proclivity for sun and surf, however, quickly turned Beidaihe into China's equivalent of the Riviera. Westerners have since fled, and the coastal city has become a watering hole for Communist cadres and *yuán*-laden Chinese vacationers. If the promise of Party bigwigs shedding their comrade garb is too much to resist, join the scantily clad mainlanders and head to this sparkling oceanic oasis. Be sure to pack lots of money with your swimsuit—seaside fun has its price.

■▮ **TRANSPORTATION AND PRACTICAL INFORMATION.** Beidaihe's two main streets, **Xi Haitan Lu** and **Dongjing Lu,** run along the seashore, from which branch a bunch of numbered alleys, named **Bao "number" Lu** (Baoyi Lu, Bao'er Lu, etc.; 保"X"路). One of the fastest ways to get to **Beijing** is to take a **minibus,** which leaves daily from the square near the post office on Haining Lu (every 30min.; summer Y80, winter Y60). Otherwise, **trains** run from the remote, though modern-looking, **Beidaihe Train Station** to: Beijing (2-6hr., 13 per day, Y50-60); Changchun (10hr., 2 per day, Y81 and up); Dalian (10hr., daily, Y81); Harbin (13hr., 2 per day, Y160 and up); and Tianjin (4hr., 4 per day, Y18 and up).

While **trains** to Qinhuangdao depart almost constantly, during the day a more practical option is to take one of the frequent **local buses** (6:30am-5pm, Y1). Useful routes include #5, 15, and 22 (every 5min. from the Beidaihe Train Station via West Beach to the Beidaihe Haibin Bus Station, a few blocks from Dongjing Lu up Haining Lu); and #34 from Beidaihe to Qinhuangdao (1hr., Y2; to get to Shanhaiguan, hop on #25 when you reach the downtown area). Some routes are seasonal but all are open during the summer. A **taxi** from the train station to most hotels costs Y10 (base fare Y5, each additional km Y1.2). Expensive **bike rentals** are necessary only if you intend to venture to quieter beaches in the east, where taxis and buses are not allowed. Check out the array of tandems, tridems, and specials at the entrance to East Beach at Qiqiao Nan Lu, opposite the Bank of China. (Up to Y10 per hr.)

Bank of China, 17 Dongjing Lu, between Anwu Lu and Liuchi Lu, exchanges traveler's checks and issues credit card advances. (☎404 0397. Open daily 8am-noon and 2-6pm.) The local **PSB,** on Lianfeng Lu, can be reached at ☎404 4841. The **Qinhuangdao No. 8 Hospital** is across from the PSB. **China Telecom,** 76 Dongjing Lu, has IDD service and Internet access for Y0.3 per min. (☎404 1029. Open 24hr.; Internet access may be out at certain times, so it's best to try 6am-10pm.) **China Mobile,** on Kangle Lu, also offers both phone and Internet services. (Open 8am-9pm. Y3 per hr.) The **post office,** on Hai'er Lu, about half a block north of Dongjing Lu, has EMS and Poste Restante, and it also books tickets. (☎404 2781 or 403 3999. Open daily 8am-6pm.) **Postal Code:** 066100.

▮ **ACCOMMODATIONS.** Those not willing to shell out Y600-700 per night have few options. In fact, if you're coming here during the busy season from July to August, no amount of money will buy you even a bed in Beidahe. Be sure to plan ahead and book early. During the low season, however, prices conveniently fall and the beaches are wonderfully uncrowded.

A drastically less expensive and worthwhile option is the **Jinshan Internationals Youth Hostel ❶,** conveniently located within 3min. of the beach, but slightly hidden in the spread of the more expensive **Jinshan Binguan** (金山宾馆). Both stand at the intersection of Dong San Lu (东三路) and Zhong Haitan Lu (中海滩路). Well-kept and extremely well-lit bare-bones dorms have access to clean public bathrooms and 24hr. hot water. (☎404 1338 6100. Open from May to early Oct. July-Aug. 6-bed dorms Y60, May-June and Sept. to early Oct. Y30.) The **Guesthouse for Diplomatic Missions ❹** (wàijiāo rényuán bīnguǎn; 外交人员宾馆), 1 Baosan Lu, off Dongjing Lu, uses a different definition of "budget," offering decadent oceanfront bungalows with access to a pool and tennis courts. The house is gated and guarded, remnants of its past purpose of housing and entertaining foreign diplomats. (☎404 4287. Open Apr.-Oct. Doubles and triples from Y280, depending on the season.) The plush **Yuehua Hotel ❹** (yuèhuá bīnguǎn; 悦华宾馆), 90 Dongjing Lu, is in a big white building at the intersection with Baosan Lu. (☎404 0470. Singles Y600; doubles Y380, newer rooms Y500; triples Y520. Credit cards accepted.)

◘ **FOOD.** The quality of the **seafood** in Beidaihe is nothing short of spectacular; pick out the creature of your choice from the red and green tubs on the sidewalk. The **Ju'an Restaurant** ❷ (jū ān cāntīng; 居安餐厅), a favorite among travelers, is at the intersection of Dongjing Lu and Haining Lu, in front of the pavilion. For Y20, the delicious local fish, *jìngyú* (镜鱼) and *qìpào yú* (气泡鱼), can't be missed. (☎ 403 8299. Open 9am-11pm.) From Haining Lu all the way down Baoer Lu toward Tiger Rock is a row of clean, lively, and airy seafood restaurants. **Kiesslings** ❷ (qǐshílín cāntīng; 起士林餐厅), a branch of the famous Tianjin chain, is near the Guesthouse for Diplomatic Missions, where Baosan Lu and Dongjing Lu meet. Feast on borscht, caviar, and the sinfully good pastries that the Austrians brought to Tianjin during the concession days. (☎ 404 1043. Dishes Y5-35. Open July-Aug. daily 9am-11pm.) **Kangle Market Place,** on Kangle Lu, is the place where the locals go for fresh fruits and cheap but tasty foods. While nothing is particularly unique to the area, the food is very affordable (under Y10). Small stores also offer better prices on foods than beachside stands.

◙◪ **SIGHTS AND BEACHES.** You don't come to Beidaihe for much more than the beach, but if you start to yearn for something other than blue skies and green seas, **Lianfengshan Park** (liánfēngshān gōngyuán; 联峰山公园), also locally known as **Xi Shan** (西山), is a pleasant refuge, offering elevated views of the city and sea. Here, locals take walks and engage in early morning exercises before the massive arrival of tourists. Get there before 7am and you can try to kindly talk your way into getting in for free to enjoy a refreshing morning stroll. (Bus #5 will bring you to the gate. Get off when the bus takes a turn at the top of a hill. Open daily 7am-6pm. Admission Y22, students Y12.)

The new **Olympic Park** in the Beidahe city center will feature statues, fountains, and gardens. It is an addendum to the main soccer stadium in Qinhuangdao, about a 20min. taxi ride away.

Of the three stretches of beach in Beidaihe, the closest and busiest is **Middle Beach.** The **West** and **East Beaches** offer more tranquility, perhaps owing to the abundance of men in uniform who cordon off choice sections for party leaders.

SHANDONG 山东

With good company, good dumplings, and most importantly, good beer, Shandong has surprisingly plenty to be cheerful about. The province has traditionally been one of China's poorer regions, due in no small part to the caprices of the Yellow River, which regularly spills across its banks and into the sea. Yet scrappy little Shandong has held on and refuses to fall into neighboring Beijing's shadow. Over the millennia, it has made quite a name for itself, with everything from early Shang Dynasty relics to the Great Sage Confucius. Perhaps more dear to travelers' hearts, however, is the internationally renowned brewery that churns out bottle after bottle of Tsingtao. Throw in the beaches and turf breaking off the long coastlines, and you've got the perfect makings for a sandy party or two.

JI'NAN 济南   ☎ 0531

For most travelers, Ji'nan, the capital of Shandong province, is just a convenient stopping point en route to Qingdao or Taishan and Qufu, not a place that you would want to stick around for long. Congestion at all hours of the day and the hammering of constant construction at every corner testify to the city's growing pains. Although nothing much within dusty downtown Ji'nan captivates the traveler's interest, the city's edges harbor unexpected beauties. Removed from the ceaseless hustle of the train station, rampant steel and cement finally give in to the unruffled mystic wonder of the Thousand Buddha Mountain and the quiet grace of the forested hills surrounding the Four Gate Pagoda.

▐ TRANSPORTATION

Flights: Yaoqiang International Airport (yáoqiáng guójì jīchǎng; 遥墙国际机场 ; ☎688 1767), about 25km away from the city proper. Tickets can be booked by calling the **Shandong Airlines Co. Ltd.,** 588 Jingqi Lu (☎603 3747 or 603 3737; www.shandongair.com), at the corner of Jingqi Lu and Weiba Lu. **Shuttle buses** run from the **Silver Plaza Shopping Center** (yínzuò shāngchéng; 银座商城), at the intersection of Luoyuan Dajie and Qianfoshan Lu. To: **Beijing** (2 per day, Y640); **Chengdu** (2 per day, Y1360); **Chongqing** (8am, Y1100); **Dalian** (daily, Y910); **Guangzhou** (2 per day, Y1590); **Haikou** (daily, Y2030); **Harbin** (1-2 per day, Y1130); **Nanjing** (daily, Y800); **Shanghai** (3 per day, Y760); **Shenyang** (daily, Y860).

Trains: Ji'nan Train Station (jǐnán huǒchē zhàn; 济南火车站 ; ☎242 4572 or 242 8862), on Jingyi Lu, in the city center. Ticket counters open daily 7:30am-7:40pm. Information office open daily 6:30am-10pm. To: **Beijing** (3½-4hr., several per day, Y90); **Harbin** (17hr., several per day, Y170); **Nanjing** (11-12hr., 2 per day, Y70); **Qingdao** (4hr., 2 per day, Y50); **Shanghai** (15-17hr., 2 per day, Y120); **Shenyang** (14hr., 2 per day, Y170); **Tianjin** (3½hr., several per day, Y60).

Buses: The station opposite the train station (☎691 0789) is the most centrally located and convenient. Very helpful staff at information desk. To: **Beijing** (5½-6hr., several in the morning, Y96); **Qingdao** (4½-5hr., several per day, Y52-95); **Shanghai** (20hr., 8:30am, Y169; express train 12hr., daily, Y216); **Tai'an** (1½hr., every 30min., Y8-13); **Yantai** (5-6hr., every hr., Y66-80); **Weihai** (6-8hr., many per day, Y78-138).

Local Transportation: Many **buses,** including #3, 9, 11, 18, and 34, run to and from the train and bus stations. Buses #2, 48, and 51 run along Jingshi Lu to the Thousand Buddha Mountain; #11 goes from the train station to Daming Lake Park. Bus fare Y0.5-4. Buses do not always follow signs and will make additional stops.

Taxis: Base fare Y6, each additional km Y1.2. Expect to "tip" the driver an additional Y1.

❀ ? ORIENTATION AND PRACTICAL INFORMATION

Ji'nan's **train station** is in the western part of town, on **Jingyi Lu** (经一路), a major east-west street. **Daming Lake** (大明湖), encircled by Daming Lake Park, is the major landmark in the eastern half of the city. **Daming Hu Bei Lu** (大明湖北路) to the north and **Daming Hu Lu** to the south outline the lake and park. **Quancheng Square** (quánchéng guǎngchǎng; 泉城广场), the main business and shopping center, is to the south of the lake. The major north-south thoroughfare of **Lishan Lu** (历山路) is to the east. **Qianfoshan Lu** (千佛山路) runs through the southern half of the city toward Thousand Buddha Mountain, intersecting with **Jingshi Lu** (经十路), which runs from east to west past the Shandong Provincial Museum.

In the southwestern part of the city, the east-west streets are designated as **Jing (number) Lu:** from north to south, the traveler encounters Jingyi Lu, Jinger Lu, Jingsan Lu, and so on. The north-south streets are designated **Wei (number) Lu,** and the numbers increase from east to west. A number of smaller, often unlabeled streets in between are prefixed with a **Xiao** (小).

Travel Agency: CITS, 88 Jingshi Lu (☎296 5858 or 296 2750; fax 296 5651), at the intersection of Jinshi Lu and Lishan Lu. Open M-F 8am-6pm. **Ji'nan Tourism Bureau,** 117 Jingqi Weisi Lu, 5th fl. (☎793 0899), at the intersection with Weisi Lu.

Bank of China: 22 Luoyuan Dajie (☎699 5026). Exchanges currency and traveler's checks. Credit card advances. Open M-F 8am-noon and 1:30-6pm.

PSB: 145 Jingsan Lu (call ☎114 and ask to be transferred), east of Weiwu Lu.

Hospital: Shengli Hospital (shènglì yīyuàn; 省立医院), 324 Jingwu Lu (☎793 8911), opposite the intersection with Weiqi Lu. 24hr. emergency care. Pharmacy available.

Internet Access: Several Internet bars litter the complex of buildings right in front of the train station. **Sanheren Internet Cafe** (sānhérén wǎngbā; 三和人网吧; ☎830 1821 or 830 1822) is right across from the train station, on the 2nd fl. above the convenience store. Y2 per hr. Open 8am-11:30pm.

Post Office: China Post, 162 Jing'er Lu (☎626 1074), at Wei'er Lu. EMS and Poste Restante. Open daily summer 8am-7:30pm; winter 8am-7pm. China Post (☎691 4151) also available on the 1st fl. of the **Ji'nan Post Hotel** (see **Accommodations**, p. 193). EMS. Open daily 8:30am-6pm.

Postal Code: 250001.

ACCOMMODATIONS

In general, affordable accommodations in Ji'nan are pretty much identical. All come with A/C, phone, TV, and a slightly stained carpet. Baths, however, are less common. Hotels near the train station are generally the cheapest in town, catering to those who just need a wink of sleep and a quick bite to eat. More creature comforts can be found further out.

Ji'nan Post Hotel (jīnán yóuzhèng bīnguǎn; 济南邮政宾馆 ; ☎605 7777; fax 605 5678), to the left of the train station and directly in front of the bus station. Walls may be slightly discolored, but bedsheets are fresh and the furniture may even seem luxurious. Check-out noon. Hourly stay up to 4hr. Y80; economy rooms Y120-180. ❷

Shandong Longqiantan Hotel (shāndōng lóngqiāntán jiǔdiàn; 山东龙千潭酒店), 11-15 Jingyi Weisan Lu (☎605 7777; fax 605 5678), on Weisan Lu, 10min. southeast of the train and bus stations. Major buses, including #51 to Thousand Buddha Mountain, all stop outside. Rooms that go for the same rate vary greatly in quality (especially the baths), so request room change if unsatisfied. Friendly, helpful staff makes up for the occasional cockroach. Internet access. Restaurant on 1st and 2nd fl. Deposit depends on room and duration of stay. Standard economy Y180; doubles 280. ❸

Shandong Hotel (shāndōng bīnguǎn; 山东宾馆), 92 Jingyi Lu Weisan Lu (☎605 7881 or 605 7881; fax 605 7881), about a block south of the train station. All rooms have water cooler and bathroom fixtures that need a healthy dose of cleaning agent. Renovated rooms fetch a slightly higher price. 24hr. reception. Breakfast included. Deposit Y150. 1hr. rest Y30; singles Y130; doubles Y150-180; triples Y210-240. ❷

Ji'nan Hotel (jīnán fàndiàn; 济南饭店), 240 Jingsan Lu (☎793 8981; fax 793 2906), between Weiliu Lu and Weiqi Lu. Reception in Bldg. 4, the farthest from the entrance. A little hard to find behind all the foliage, but far enough from the street for a little peace and quiet. Sparse electricity usage. Clean rooms and bathtubs. Courtyard. Breakfast included. Deposit depends on room and duration of stay. Singles Y120; doubles Y160-220; triples Y240. ❷

FOOD

Luscious produce fills Ji'nan's alleys, as **fruit** and **vegetable vendors** dish up lots of fresh imported produce. A succession of restaurants, all nearly identical to each other and specializing in **fresh-water seafood**, crowds Jingqi Lu, and a strip of **bars** and eateries is on Qianfoshan Lu, right down the street from the Thou-

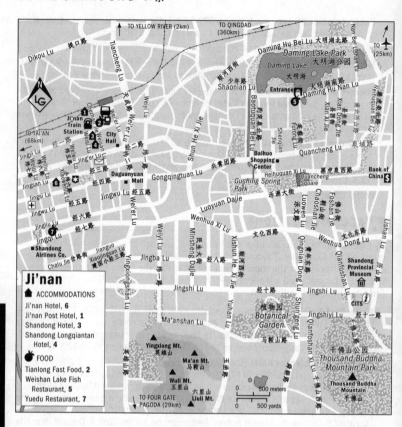

Ji'nan

▲ ACCOMMODATIONS
Ji'nan Hotel, 6
Ji'nan Post Hotel, 1
Shandong Hotel, 3
Shandong Longqiantan
Hotel, 4

● FOOD
Tianlong Fast Food, 2
Weishan Lake Fish
Restaurant, 5
Yuedu Restaurant, 7

sand Buddha Mountain entrance. Locals gather for on-the-spot snacks and noo-dle dishes in the Weiwu Lu alley opposite the hospital. **Stalls** around the **Silver Plaza Shopping Center,** 6 Luoyuan Dajie, at the intersection of Luoyuan Dajie and Qianfoshan Lu, offer a wide selection of clean, palate-pleasing foods for ultra-cheap prices (Y1-10).

Weishan Lake Fish Restaurant (wēishān hú yú guǎn; 微山湖鱼馆; ☎793 4825), on Daming Hu Lu, right in front of the south gate of Daming Lake. Classier than most, with a kind, attentive staff and chefs ready to personalize your meal. Plenty of delights for the fish connoisseur, fresh from the tank. Try the carp soup (Y28) or braised fish with lotus leaves (Y30), or swallow your fear and indulge in some hot snake head (Y30). ❷

Yuedu Restaurant (yuèdū jiǔlóu; 粤都酒楼), 588 Jingqi Lu (☎790 6908 or 708 8567). Seafood galore, as aquariums chock-full of the local catch await the frying pan. Patrons choose their dishes (Y8-20) from a window display and wait as they're freshly prepared. Larger meals go for Y15-30. Open daily 10am-10pm. ❷

Tianlong Fast Food (tiānlóng kuàicān; 天龙快餐; ☎602 3742), opposite the train sta-tion, to the left. Bright neon lights beckon hungry arrivals and departees alike to this tin tray, cafeteria-style eatery where your chosen, styrofoam-wrapped dishes are cooked in front of you at a supersonic pace. Dishes Y1-11. Open daily 5:30am-10pm. ❶

⊙ SIGHTS

THOUSAND BUDDHA MOUNTAIN (qiānfó shān; 千佛山). At a mere 285m, this mountain hardly intimidates; a climb up its hills is more a leisurely stroll than a real hike. But its dark, chilly caverns hide a veritable cache of ageless gems—thousands of Buddhas, ranging in shape and size from the miniscule to the hefty, chiseled into the stone in the Sui Dynasty (AD 581-618). Carry a flashlight with you when crossing through a smoky passage into an incense-filled cave that houses a massive gold- and bronze-plated Buddha. Surrounded by the quiet emptiness of the dark caverns, you may feel like a trespasser in a timeless sanctuary.

Outside, ancient gingkos and cypresses shade the temples and stairways. A hike to the summit takes about one hour; a 7min. cable car ride to the temples halfway up (Y15, round-trip Y25) passes over two giant statues of Buddhist deities, heads poking through the foliage. *(18 Jingshiyi Lu, on the southern edge of town. Accessible via buses #2 and 48, which run along Jingshi Lu and Lishan Lu, and 51, which runs along Jingshi Lu. ☎266 2321. Ticket office open daily 6am-7pm. Park Y15, cave additional Y15.)*

FOUR GATE PAGODA (sìmén tǎ; 四门塔). Officially, the pagoda is only 29km south of town, but the mode of transportation—a bus that stops for each and every weary traveler on the road—will make you feel like it's much farther away. Nevertheless, the trip is well worth the time. The pagoda is a small square stone hut built in AD 611, impressive for its unassuming dignity and gracious sense of history. Like an ancient scroll painting come to life, pagodas and staircases embroider the surrounding green hills, all in gentle harmony with nature. *(A 1½hr. ride on bus for Y3. ☎284 3051 or 284 1444. Chinese tour guides available. Open daily summer 6:30am-7:30pm; winter 6:30am-7pm. Y20, student Y10.)*

SHANDONG PROVINCIAL MUSEUM (shāndōng shěng bówùguǎn; 山东省博物馆). This imposing concrete block houses one of China's more intriguing provincial museums. View a Ming Dynasty ship, huge dinosaur fossils, Buddhist carvings, and truckloads of thousand-year-old pottery, some of which include stone tablets from the Han Dynasty (206-220 BC). The animal exhibit upstairs can be skipped (unless you want to see two-headed frogs and other bizarre misfits of creation). The exhibits are on rotation, so not all displays are open. *(14 Jingshiyi Lu. 5min. walk from Thousand Buddha Mountain; accessible via buses #2, 31, and 48. Open daily 9-11:30am and 2-4:20pm, last ticket sold at 4pm. Y10, students Y5.)*

ily Chronicle

IN RECENT NEWS

THUMB WARS

China's ever-growing population of mobile phone users sent more than 220 billion text messages in 2003, accounting for over half of the world's text messages. With such a wave of chatter, the government recently stepped in with regulations allowing mobile phone companies to monitor text messages. Although the abbreviated nature of the text message makes it seem like a poor tool for stirring up trouble, it has already found surprising ways to undermine government authority.

Text messages were instrumental in breaking the cover-up of the SARS epidemic in 2001 and 2002. With the state instituting a media blackout, many people in China actually learned about the outbreak through text messages. In February 2003, a state-run news agency published a report stating that text messaging may be a threat to state security. Others criticize the growing trend as an obsession that alienates people from personal relationships, distracts them in school, and even leads to poor health—doctors report of patients with injured tendons in their thumbs due to excessive button-pushing. By 2007, China is expected to have more than 400 million mobile phone users. And whatever the regulations, this ubiquitous technology is being put to use in unexpected new ways: writer Qian Fuchang's novel *Outside the Fortress Besieged* was released exclusively as text messages.

DAMING LAKE (dàmíng hú; 大明湖). During the Tang Dynasty (AD 617-907), Daming Lake was the worthy topic of poetic literature, as the master poet Du Fu rhapsodized about its tranquil waters. But recent construction, including the amusement park in the northeast corner, detract from the lake's once-pristine beauty. Local residents still seek calm and comfort in the paths that meander throughout the surrounding park and the breezy willow trees that hint at the lake's former grandeur. *(271 Daminghu Nan Lu. Take bus #11 or 41. ☎ 608 8906. Paddle boats Y40 per hr. Open daily 6am-6:30pm. Y15.)*

TAI'AN 泰安   ☎ 0538

Tucked humbly at the base of the illustrious Taishan Mountain, compact little Tai'an could easily be mistaken for nothing more than a gateway to—if not some puny wart on the foot of—its giant companion. But every emperor who conquered Taishan's summit stopped first at Tai'an's glorious and much revered Dai Temple. Climbing Taishan has long been a Chinese rite of passage, which has instilled in the temple and the city a proper sense of its own worth. Fully aware that it has been earmarked a special spot in history (and in the guidebooks), Tai'an is jump-starting its own economic progress, using Taishan as the spark. Hotels, souvenir shops, and tour groups crowd, smother, and run amuck. When a cloudy haze obscures the mountain from view, as is often the case, Tai'an's own trendy, plexi-glas-covered buildings instead glitter and gleam for the benefit of visitors.

▚ TRANSPORTATION

Trains: Taishan Station (tàishān zhàn; 泰山站; ☎ 219 6222) is in the western half of the city, just south of Dongyue Dajie. To: **Beijing** (6-6½hr., many per day, Y85-Y170); **Changchun** (10hr., several per day, Y100); **Ji'nan** (1hr., every 30min., Y7-14); **Qingdao** (5hr., 2 per day, Y80).

Buses: Tai'an Long-Distance Bus Station (tài'ān chángtú qìchē zhàn; 泰安长途汽车站), on Dongyue Dajie, about 3 blocks east of the train station (☎ 210 8600). To: **Beijing** (6-7hr., daily, Y115); **Ji'nan** (1½hr., every 30min., Y20); **Qingdao** (7hr., 2 per day, Y68); **Qufu** (1½hr., every 20min., Y8-14); **Tianjin** (5hr., daily, Y100); **Weihai** (8hr., 3 per day, Y83).

Public Transportation: Several **buses** ply downtown Tai'an, but their routes are rather limited and bus sightings are infrequent, so consider yourself lucky if you can avoid a taxi ride. Fare Y1. Bus #3 runs along Hongmen Lu from the station area to the east and west entrances of Taishan; #4 bumps along Dongyue Dajie.

Taxis: Y5 for the 1st 3km, each addition km Y1.5.

▰▱ ORIENTATION AND PRACTICAL INFORMATION

With barely 500,000 residents and a compact center, Tai'an is quite manageable. The mountain, positioned directly north of town, is a useful landmark when not hidden by haze. Activity is concentrated along **Hongmen Lu** (红门路), which runs directly south of the mountain before ending at the entrance to the Dai Temple and **Dongyue Dajie** (东岳大街), the major east-west street. The train station is just south of Dongyue Dajie, but everything else of interest to visitors is in the north-eastern portion, just south of the base of Taishan.

Travel Agency: CITS, 22 Hongmen Lu, 2nd fl. (☎ 822 3259 or 822 3259; fax 833 2240), a 2min. walk from the Taishan Guesthouse. Open M-F 9am-5pm. **Tai'an Tourism Information Center** (☎ 827 2114), right in front of the train station, provides information and helps acquire tickets. Look for the English sign.

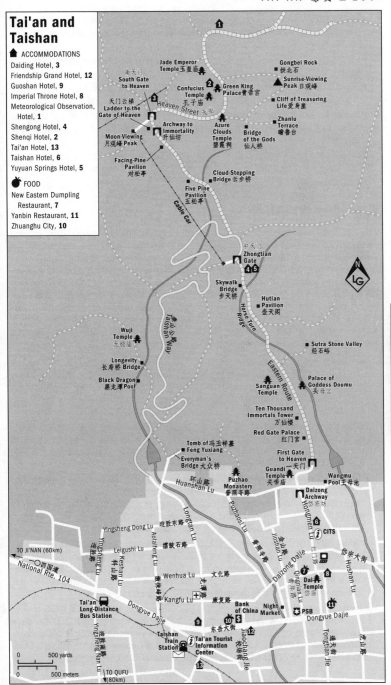

Tai'an and Taishan

🏠 **ACCOMMODATIONS**

Daiding Hotel, **3**
Friendship Grand Hotel, **12**
Guoshan Hotel, **9**
Imperial Throne Hotel, **8**
Meteorological Observation, Hotel, **1**
Shengong Hotel, **4**
Shenqi Hotel, **2**
Tai'an Hotel, **13**
Taishan Hotel, **6**
Yuyuan Springs Hotel, **5**

🍎 **FOOD**

New Eastern Dumpling Restaurant, **7**
Yanbin Restaurant, **11**
Zhuanghu City, **10**

BEIJING

Jade Emperor Temple 玉皇庙
南天门
South Gate to Heaven
Confucius Temple 孔子庙
天门云梯
Ladder to the Gate of Heaven
Heaven Street 天街
Archway to Immortality 升仙坊
Moon-Viewing 月观峰 Peak
Facing-Pine Pavilion 对松亭
Five Pine Pavilion 五松亭
Cable Car

Gongbei Rock 拱北石
Sunrise-Viewing Peak 日观峰
Green King Palace 青帝宫
Cliff of Treasuring Life 爱身崖
Azure Clouds Temple 碧霞祠
Zhanlu Terrace 瞻鲁台
Bridge of the Gods 仙人桥
Cloud-Stepping Bridge 云步桥

中天门
Zhongtian Gate
Skywalk Bridge 步天桥
Hutian Pavilion 壶天阁
Horse Turn Ridge
Taishan Way 泰山公路
Eastern Route
Sutra Stone Valley 经石峪

Wuji Temple 无极庙
Longevity 长寿桥 Bridge
Black Dragon 黑龙潭 Pool
Palace of Goddess Doumu 斗母宫
Sanguan Temple
Ten Thousand Immortals Tower 万仙楼
Red Gate Palace 红门宫

Tomb of 冯玉祥墓 Feng Yuxiang
Everyman's Bridge 大众桥
Puzhao Monastery 普照寺路
First Gate to Heaven 一天门
Guandi Temple 关帝庙
Wangmu Pool 王母池
Daizong Archway 岱宗坊
环山路 Huanshan Lu

TO JI'NAN (60km)
National Rte. 104
泰山大街 Taishan Dajie
Yingsheng Dong Lu 迎胜东路
迎胜北路
Leigushi Lu 擂鼓石路
Aolaifeng Lu 擂鼓石路
Keshan Lu 科山路
Yingsheng Lu 迎胜路
Wenhua Lu 文化路
Kangfu Lu 康复路
Dongyue Dajie 东岳大街
Tai'an Long-Distance Bus Station
Yingsheng Nan Lu 迎胜南路
Longtan Lu 龙潭路
Puzhaosi Lu 普照寺路
Jinshan Lu 金山路
Dongyue Dajie 东岳大街

Bank of China
Night Market
Taishan Train Station
Tai'an Tourist Information Center
TO QUFU (80km)

CITS
Hongmen Lu 红门路
Dai Temple 岱庙
PSB
Dongyue Dajie 东岳大街
Hushan Lu 虎山路
岱宗大街 Daizong Dajie
Qingnian Lu 青年路
Dongyue Dajie 东岳大街
Tongtian Jie 通天街
Hushan Lu 虎山路
Jinglian Jie

0   500 yards
0   500 meters

Bank of China: 48 Dongyue Dajie (☎829 6701), on the corner of Dongyue Dajie and Zhaotong Jie. Exchanges currency and traveler's checks. Credit card advances. Open M-F 8:30am-5pm, Sa-Su 8:30am-noon and 2-5pm.

PSB: 71 Qingnian Lu (☎827 5264). The main gate is around the corner on 2 Dongyue Dajie.

Hospital: Central Hospital (zhōngxīn yīyuàn; 中心医院), 29 Longtan Lu (☎822 4161), near the intersection with Daizhong Dajie. English-speaking doctors. Pharmacy.

Internet Access: Big World Internet Bar (dà shìjiè wǎngbā; 大世界网吧), 8 Hongmen Lu (☎821 8598), on the 2nd fl. in a small alley, right across from Xin Restaurant. Open daily 8am-midnight.

Post Office: China Post (☎853 8709), to the left of the train station's main entrance. EMS and Poste Restante. Open daily summer 8am-7pm; winter 8am-6pm.

Postal Code: 271000.

▚ ACCOMMODATIONS

The traffic of pilgrims and tourists through Tai'an keeps accommodation pricing competitive. Dongyue Dajie in particular is crawling with hotels. Hotels at the base are considerably cheaper and more comfortable than those at the summit, though most spend the night up there anyway, so as not to miss the famous sunrise. Most hotels at the base will store your belongings while you climb (Y1 per piece of luggage), but some do not offer overnight storage, so be sure to check. If traveling with a small group (less than five or so), some Chinese-only hotels may accept foreigners who attempt Mandarin, although success is entirely dependent upon luck and personal charm. Deposits vary but are often based on the difference between room price and the next hundred yuan.

Guoshan Hotel (guóshān dàjiǔdiàn; 国山大酒店), 1 Longtan Lu (☎219 0777 or 219 0077). Not an unpleasant place to stay, considering the price. Toilet flushing needs more oomph (pour your own water!), but lighting works and sheets are changed daily or upon request. 24hr. reception. Reservations recommended. Wheedle for lower prices. Standard economy singles Y80-120; doubles Y100; triples Y150. ❶

Tai'an Hotel (tài'ān bīnguǎn; 泰安宾馆 ; ☎833 3183), to right of the train station's main entrance. Cheapest option out there that accepts foreigners. Best to stay with friends and share the nuisance of leaky toilets. Flip-flops recommended. Singles Y80; doubles Y80-200; small triples Y50. ❶

Friendship Grand Hotel (yǒuyì dàjiǔdiàn; 友谊大酒店), 49 Dongyue Dajie (☎822 2288; fax 822 4100), 2 blocks from the train station. Caters mostly to businessmen. The impressive lobby features a "Beer City" lounge and bar. Rooms aren't quite up to par, with somewhat dirty baths and a serious lack of electrical outlets. TV, A/C, 24hr. hot water. Doubles Y280-360; economy Y180 available, but ask for them early. ❸

Taishan Hotel (tàishān bīnguǎn; 泰山宾馆), 26 Hongmen Lu (☎822 4678), within spitting distance of Taishan. The only real 3-star in town, a typical plush tourist hotel with typical high tourist prices for every luxury on hand, and an indulgent staff. Best feature: the cleanest bathrooms in all of Tai'an; mold-free tiles, plush towels, and cathartic hot showers. Breakfast included. Singles Y300-380; doubles 300-420. ❹

Imperial Throne Hotel (yùzuò bīnguǎn; 御座宾馆), 3 Dabei Lu (☎826 9999 or 822 3180), right next to the Dai Temple. The complex is comprised of a cluster of two-story buildings, hidden from public view. Safe and secure environment. Lobby is misleadingly elegant. Somewhat tacky room decor consists of pastel, polka-dotted bedsheets. 24hr. hot water, laundry. Check-out noon. Standard economy Y280; triples Y380. ❹

BEIJING

🔲 FOOD

Summer heralds a splendid harvest, which Tai'an is more than happy to share with the weary climber. Along the trail up the mountain, many stalls proudly display piles of reddish-green peaches, ready-to-burst tomatoes, and crunchy cucumbers. Fruits and veggies cascade down makeshift fountains, tempting sweat-soaked hikers. Hearty Shandong cuisine, usually dumplings galore, is supplemented by a few specialties unique to Tai'an, most notably **red-scaled fish** (hóng lǐ yú; 红鲤鱼), a species said to be found only in the waters around Taishan. At night, small alleys branching off of **Dongyue Dajie** dispense simple pleasures such as scallion pancakes (Y1-3), braised chicken wings (Y5), and beef noodle soup (Y5 per bowl).

Zhuanghu City (zhuānghù chéng; 庄户城), 54 Dongyue Dajie (☎833 3373). Polynesian-style decor with eye-catching red-flowered walls and straw-roofed dining halls. Pick an appetizer from the window and dinner from the aquariums while it's still swimming, be it fish, shellfish, or sea slug. Private dining rooms upstairs. Dinners average Y20-30. Open daily 9am-10pm. ❷

Yanbin Restaurant (yàn bīn dàjiǔdiàn; 宴宾大酒店), 9 Yanxun Jie (☎823 1515 or 828 1513). A lot of open space, so you'll be able to breathe and relax among the other patrons. Friendly, welcoming staff dressed in candystriped uniforms. Lots of fishy options (Y15-30), such as sea cucumber, red-scaled carp, and heaps of shrimp. Fruit dishes are too pretty to eat (Y5-10). ❷

New Eastern Dumpling Restaurant (xīn dōng jiǎozǐ wáng; 新东饺子王), 1 Hongmen Lu (☎828 1788 or 689 2238). Right at the base of Taishan, this is the perfect haunt to rest and recuperate after climbing. Sizzling dumplings of chicken, pork, beef, or vegetable fillings go for Y15-20 per dozen. Tsingtao beer (Y5 per bottle) graces the surface of each table. Meals Y6-30. Try the spicy chicken, courtesy of the local farmers. ❶

🧭 SIGHTS

There *is* more to Tai'an than the mountain. Follow the example of the first emperor of China and head to the **Dai Temple** (dàimiào; 岱庙) before you tackle the mighty ascent. Here, over 2200 years ago, Emperor Qin Shihuang held sacrifices before he set out to climb Taishan. Not wanting to feel inferior, emperors came here regularly to pay homage to the gods of Taishan after Qin Shihuang's historic visit. As guardians of the eastern edge of the empire, the Taishan deities were thought to exercise a crucial influence over the fate of a ruler and his dynasty.

The main hall of the Dai Temple, known as the **Hall of Celestial Gifts,** was built in the Song Dynasty. Murals featuring 657 distinct figures of deities and ancient warriors festoon its walls. What makes them memorable is that these murals have not been "restored" by garish attempts at repainting. Those on the eastern side depict the god of Taishan (often associated with the sun) setting out on a journey, while those on the western side show him returning home. Cover your shoes in ridiculous-looking plastic bags (Y1) before going inside; resourceful penny-pinchers can bring hotel shower caps instead. The **Dongyue Throneroom** dominates the main hall and was once the emperors' resting place between sacrifices. There's also the **Han Cypress Courtyard** (hànbǎi yuàn; 韩柏院), home of five ancient cypresses planted by a Han Dynasty emperor. Some of the well-preserved calligraphic stelae, carried on the back of stone turtles dotting the courtyard, are rumored to be from the emperor's own hands. Even the massive tour groups do not disturb the Dai Temple's ancient ambiance and regal dignity. (The North Gate is at the bottom end of Hongmen Lu; the South Gate is on Dongyue Dajie. ☎626 5055 or 626 5053. Open daily 7:30am-6:30pm; last ticket sold 6:10pm. Y20.)

CLIMBING TAISHAN MOUNTAIN 泰山

This is it. The fabled Taishan, the easternmost and holiest of China's five sacred Daoist mountains, the revered peak that brought emperors to their knees. Confucius climbed it. The founder of the Qin Dynasty climbed it. Seventy-two emperors and their retinues lined up to climb it. Even Mao lumbered up in his day. Now it's your turn. Countless Chinese travel for miles to offer prayers to the various deities associated with the mountain and to watch the first rays of morning light, as the sunrise from the summit is an indispensable part of the Taishan experience. Scaling the mountain has never been considered "off the beaten path," but trust us, this is one bandwagon you do want to jump on.

Stone stairs, built into the side of the mountain hundreds of years ago, line the trails to the summit. Wide railings provide ample sitting space for rests. A succession of temples and shrines mark visitors' upward progress. Souvenir shops, food vendors, and photographers stake out every trailside spot from base to summit. Prices rise with the altitude.

While Taishan remains an active place of worship, the temples and shrines that line the paths are frequented by all people of all sorts—from businessmen to tourists to teenagers in platform shoes. Both tradition and the spell-binding beauty at the summit urge visitors up the mountain's steep steps. Those lucky enough to come during July or August will enjoy waterfalls and streams. Above the clouds, an ocean of haunting mist floats through the forest and slowly evaporates as it drifts toward the mountaintop. It's as if you've stepped into heaven.

🛈 PRACTICAL INFORMATION. The climb can take anywhere from three to eight hours. The 6600 stairs are not to be trifled with. Only those accustomed to severe leg beatings should consider going up and coming down in one day. Food and drink are exorbitantly priced but readily available along the trail or at the summit. Private guides—usually young locals—will give a roundabout tour and help you with your bags (Y10-20). Unfortunately, park administrators are now tightening admissions and actually checking tickets at a stop before Zhongtian Gate, so new friends will have to be left behind.

Naturally, the temperature at the summit is quite a bit cooler than at the base. Bring warm, waterproof clothing. If climbing in autumn, bring at least three layers as temperatures may dip below freezing. Some hotels offer complimentary big, cozy PLA coats, which can also be rented at the summit for Y2-5. The exhausted can hop on a **cable car** to the summit from Zhongtian Gate, the halfway mark. (Open daily summer 6:30am-7pm; winter 7:30am-5pm. One-way Y45, children Y20.) You can also take a **bus** (Y18) from the west entrance up to Zhongtian Gate.

The ticket gates are open 24hr., and some frugal pilgrims often make the climb at night to arrive in time for the sunrise. Those daring a night climb should carry a flashlight, as lampposts are scarce and usually not working. Year-round admission from the East Entrance is Y80, students Y50, payable at **Ten Thousand Immortals Tower.** Admission from the West Entrance is Y90. (☎621 5013.)

EASTERN ROUTE

This is the more traveled of the two routes to the summit, dotted with an endless collection of sights to engross any and all explorers. To get to the trailhead, follow Hongmen Lu north from the Dai Temple to the **Daizong Archway** (dàizōng fáng; 岱宗坊), the first Taishan landmark, built during the Ming Dynasty. Calligraphic carvings extolling the traditional virtues of generosity and beneficence decorate the arch. Hongmen Lu ends at the **First Gate to Heaven** (yì tiān mén; 一天门), which marks the beginning of the ascent.

The next major landmark is the **Red Gate Palace** (hóng mén gōng; 红门宫), named for the two, door-like scarlet stones on the southern face of the nearby peak. Skip the Y5 admissions fee: there are plenty of other temples, littered with money and offerings to their affiliated deities, that surround the gate and line the path. Before passing through, stop and gather your strength and count your blessings before the real strain begins.

Next is the **Ten Thousand Immortals Tower** (wànxiān lóu; 万仙楼), built in 1620 and dedicated to Wangmu, the popular "mother goddess" or Queen of Heaven. Entrance fees are paid here. One kilometer farther up is the **Palace of Goddess Doumu** (dǒumǔ gōng; 斗母宫), a dusty temple that houses a statue of the child-faced goddess, sitting atop a lotus leaf. More likely than not, you'll also see a parade of 70-year-old women, whipping out incense sticks and red threads. More minor sights (the Sutra Stone Valley, Feng'an Stele, and Cypress Cave) line the path up to the midpoint of the hike.

WESTERN ROUTE

Temples, calligraphy, and fellow climbers are much more scarce along the western route, but it's less strenuous and more meandering than the eastern path. The western route begins at the northern tip of Longtan Lu, runs through **Tianwai Village** (tiānwài cūn; 天外村), then follows a winding path up to **Zhongtian Gate.** The western and eastern routes converge between Zhongtian Gate and the summit.

After entering through Tianwai Village, the first major sight is the **Black Dragon Pool** (hēilóng tán; 黑龙潭), home to Tai'an's famed red-scaled carp. Farther along the trail, the **Longevity Bridge** (chángshòu qiáo; 长寿桥) stretches between craggy cliffs. The brook flowing beneath it feeds a tall waterfall. The bridge is known by some as "the boundary between life and death." The last major sight before Zhongtian Gate is **Wuji Temple** (wújí miào; 无极庙). Built in 1925 by the warlord Zhang Zongchang in memory of his late wife (who he hoped would become a Daoist immortal), the temple is a testament to the endurance of Taishan's mystique.

ABOVE ZHONGTIAN GATE

Zhongtian Gate (zhōngtiān mén; 中天门) marks the midpoint of the ascent, perched 850m above sea level. Here, the eastern route intersects with the western route, and a village of trinket shops awaits visitors. Take another breather here before continuing the ascent, because the stone steps suddenly become 10 degrees steeper and any edible products undergo their own price hike. The truly spent can hop on a cable car to the summit or collapse at one of the few hotels at the midpoint. Accommodations are uniform in quality, or in their lack thereof, with dirty baths and dirty sheets; opt for the cheapest. Bring a plentiful supply of mosquito repellent—you'll soon wish you had more. Try the **Shengong Hotel** ❸ (shéngōng bīnguǎn; 神宫宾馆), identical to its fellow hotels, but more deserted. (☎ 139 5488 3722. Doubles Y200; triples Y240). The **Yuyuan Springs Hotel** ❶ (玉源泉宾馆) is a cheaper alternative. (☎ 822 6740. Dorms Y60; doubles Y100; triples Y120.) Not many people stay in the midpoint hotels. If you can make it, it's better to stay at the summit, where hotels are safer and only marginally more expensive.

The first major sight along the second half of the climb is the **Cloud-Stepping Bridge** (yúnbù qiáo; 云步桥), about 1km past Zhongtian Gate. The bridge offers striking views of a waterfall and glistening streams full of water in July and August. When mist settles in the early morning, wispy vapor clouds float along the rocky crevices, wafting above and under the bridge. Crossing it is supposed to be like "stepping among the clouds" (though these clouds look an awful lot like vertigo-stricken tourists snapping photos like there's no tomorrow). A sprinkling of temples and smaller shrines like **Facing-Pine Pavilion** gather along the final stretch.

Before the final ascent, Nantianmen Gate proudly smirks down from its precarious perch high up on the mountain ridge. Even the most sluggish trekker will experience a much needed spurt of vigor when he catches sight of that glorious beacon in the distance. The very last landmark before the summit, and the bane of tired climbers, the **Ladder to the Gate of Heaven** (tiānmén yúntī; 天门云梯) comprises of 18 bends and 1600 very steep steps that must be conquered before the weary pilgrim can reach "heaven." From afar, the Ladder is an almost-vertical 400m ascent, so hold on to that rail, lest you slip and fall. Don't give up. If that little grandmother with her walking stick beside you can make it, surely you can too.

SUMMIT

The **South Gate to Heaven,** or **Nantianmen Gate** (nántiān mén; 南天门), built during the Yuan Dynasty, marks the very end of the Ladder. From there, walk along wide **Heaven Street** (tiān jiē; 天街), lined with shops, restaurants, and stalls.

Continue onto the *raison d'etre* of modern Taishan, the **Azure Clouds Temple** (bìxiá cí; 碧霞祠). The **Goddess of the Azure Clouds** (bìxiá yuánjūn; 碧霞元君), lovingly known as **Grandmother Taishan** (tàishān nǎinǎi; 泰山奶奶), is Taishan's premier cult figure, a Daoist deity with a fanatical following among the elderly peasant women who make the difficult climb. Myths claim she was the daughter of the Taishan god, while others list her as one of seven special women sacrificed by the mythical Emperor Huangdi to the Taishan gods. Over 40 Daoist devouts, identifiable by their distinctive topknots, live and study here. (Y5; fortune telling Y5.)

Other highlights on the summit include the **Green King Palace** (qīngdì gōng; 青帝官). Emperors and commoners alike have gathered here to ask for the blessings of this god, who, according to legend, controls mankind. Another one of the many scenic spots is **Aishen Cliff,** or the Cliff of Treasuring Life. Filial duty in days of yore were extreme, to say the least. In order to ensure their parents' happiness, children would pray to the gods, and then fling themselves off this cliff. The final destination is the **Jade Emperor Temple** (yùhuáng miào; 玉皇庙), the true summit of Taishan, where emperors past would have held the sacrifices to heaven.

In the pre-dawn stillness, crowds of tourists appear seemingly out of nowhere, tumbling out of bed and stumbling over to the **Sunrise Viewing Peak** (rìguān fēng; 日观峰). Those who are more foolhardy perch themselves on Aishen Cliff. Make sure to pick a spot and get there at least half an hour earlier than projected sunrise time. Some diehard enthusiasts will stake out their positions the night before by camping out. Unfortunately, clear days are a rarity in this part of Shandong (concentrated mostly in spring and autumn), and only the very lucky will view an unobscured sunrise from Taishan. Still, seeing that great orb surging out of the east, even shrouded in haze, harks back to all the ancients who embarked upon the path before you. It was, after all, the legendary Taishan sunrise that inspired Mao to proclaim, "The east is red."

Hotels tend to get crowded by the late afternoon, so secure rooms early. Dorm rooms are cheap, but anything close to comfortable demands an outrageous price. As always, check out the rooms before agreeing to stay at any place. The crowded **Daiding Hotel** ❶ (dàidǐng bīnguǎn; 岱顶宾馆), at the end of the alley up the stairway from Nantianmen Gate, features beds decorated with cartoon sheets. The rooms are small but comfortable, with decent public baths. (☎823 6519. 24hr. hot water. Laundry. Dorm beds Y10; doubles with bath Y120, renovated doubles Y160-180.) The most expensive of the contenders, and the safest for lone travelers, the **Shenqi Hotel** ❷ (shénqì bīnguǎn; 神憩宾馆), next to the Green King Palace, about 15min. past the South Gate, is everything you'd expect from a three-star hotel. Close to the peak, you're paying for the fabulous view. (☎822 3866 or 833 7025; fax 820 7619. A/C, TV, 24hr. hot water. Quads without bath Y160; doubles with bath Y580. Call early and ask about reserving one of the few singles for Y200.) For privacy on Sunrise Viewing Peak, head for the lofty, slightly intimidating **Meteorological Observation Hotel** ❶ (rìguānfēng qìxiàngtái bīnguǎn; 日观峰气象台宾馆). Enjoy the panorama from this hotel perched at the peak; rooms that face east are pricier. (☎822 6995 or 822 2818. 8-bed dorms Y20; 4-bed dorms Y40-80; doubles Y240-300; triples with Chinese-style toilets Y380-460.)

QUFU 曲阜   ☎ 0537

In the *Analects*, Qufu's famed former resident Confucius said, "Is it not a joy to have friends come from afar?" The rhetorical question seems to have proven quite prophetic for this once-tranquil little town, its city center now swollen with tour groups eager to pay homage to Master Kong. Their overwhelming presence and loud chatter can be a bit distracting to the otherwise scholarly atmosphere. Nevertheless, present-day Qufu is a miracle of preservation, part of its enduring allure. The town is a rare skyscraper-free zone full of traditional streets and wooden buildings, where the main mode of transportation is still of the two-wheeled variety. The Great Sage, born during the Zhou Dynasty (1066-256 BC), stressed that descendants are the key to immortality, and his words did not go unheeded. In a town where one in every five residents shares Confucius' surname, Kong, the reflections of his life lived 2500 years ago still proudly manifest in the hardworking ethics of Qufu's inhabitants.

▐▐❓ TRANSPORTATION AND PRACTICAL INFORMATION

Qufu is compact and easily navigable; pedicabs or your own two feet should get you anywhere. The Confucius Temple and Confucius Mansions are right in the center of town, bordered to the east and west by **Gulou Jie** (鼓楼街) and **Banbi Jie** (半壁街), respectively. Gulou Jie becomes **Lindao Lu** (林道路) in the north, where the Confucius Forest sits. Farther south on Gulou Jie is the bus station, near the intersection with **Jingxuan Lu** (静轩路). **Shendao Lu** (神道路) runs between it and the south end of the Confucius Temple.

Trains: The nearest train station is a 20min. cab drive away in **Yanzhou** (兖州). Travelers are probably better off making connections in Ji'nan (p. 191).

Buses: Qufu Long-Distance Bus Station (qūfù chángtú qìchēzhàn; 曲阜长途汽车站), 1 Jingxuan Lu (☎441 1241). To: **Beijing** (6hr., 3 per day, Y90-120); **Ji'nan** (2½hr., every 30min. Y21); **Qingdao** (5½hr., several per day, Y90-110); **Shanghai** (15hr., daily, Y140-160); **Tai'an** (1-1½hr., every 30min. 6am-6pm, Y14); **Xi'an** (11hr., daily, Y110); **Zhengzhou** (7hr., 2 per day, Y100); **Zoucheng** (40min., every 20min. 6:30am-6pm, Y5).

Local Transportation: Pedicabs run to anywhere in town for Y2-5; bargain and set the price beforehand. Tours of all of Qufu's sights average Y30-40. Red minivan **taxis** start at Y5, but many are unwilling to use the meter and charge Y10-15 to go anywhere. Local buses are non-existent; any bus that you do see is a tour bus from out of town.

Travel Agency: CITS, 1 Jingxuan Lu (☎441 2491), off Dacheng Lu. Easiest access is straight through the lobby of Luyou Hotel. Open daily 8am-5pm. **CTS,** 23 Gulou Jie (☎441 2647 or 498 1519), in the Qufu Hotel, helps buy tickets and plan itineraries. Open daily 8am-5pm.

Bank of China: 96 Dongmen Dajie (☎441 5862), east of Gulou Jie. Exchanges currency and traveler's checks. Credit card advances. Open daily 8am-6pm.

PSB: 1 Wuyuan Tan Lu (☎441 1403).

Hospital: People's Hospital (rénmín yīyuàn; 人民医院; ☎441 2440), on Tianguandi Dajie.

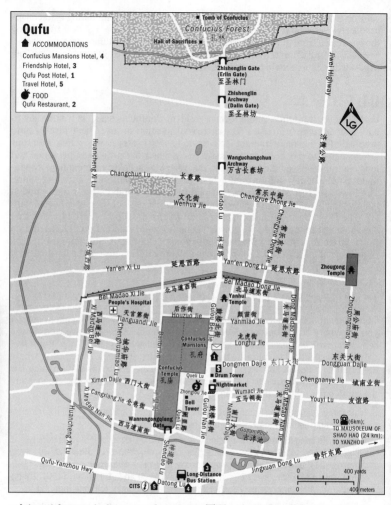

Qufu

🏠 ACCOMMODATIONS

Confucius Mansions Hotel, **4**
Friendship Hotel, **3**
Qufu Post Hotel, **1**
Travel Hotel, **5**

🍴 FOOD
Qufu Restaurant, **2**

Internet Access: An **Internet cafe** (wǎngbā; 网吧) is near the intersection of Queli Lu and Gulou Nan Jie, on the 2nd fl. of a small bldg. Y10 deposit. Y2 per hr.

Post Office: China Post, 8 Gulou Bei Jie (☎ 441 2214), near the Qufu Post Hotel. EMS. Open daily summer 8:30am-6pm; winter 8:30am-5pm.

Postal Code: 273100.

🏠🍴 ACCOMMODATIONS AND FOOD

Qufu has a decent range of accommodation options, most of which are conveniently close to sights. Since most travelers make a whirlwind daytrip to Qufu from Tai'an, hotels may lower prices by at least Y20 if you ask for a cheaper room. All listed hotels have A/C and TV.

Across the street from the Confucius Temple and Mansions is a bustling **night-market**. Dozens of carts offer fresh *jiǎozi* (dumplings) and barbecued pork sticks over hot coal furnaces. Stuff yourself for under Y10. For a sit-down meal right next to the Confucius Temple, try the **Qufu Restaurant ❷** (qūfù dàjiǔdiàn; 曲阜大酒店), 23 Gulou Jie. With a light and airy environment, you won't feel besieged by all the tour groups crowding the other tables. Stay healthy and hale with plenty of vegetable dishes, such as a plate of spinach and asparagus roots (Y6). Meaty options go for Y12-25. (☎441 2647 or 498 1519. Open daily 10am-8pm.)

Qufu Post Hotel (qūfùshì yóuzhèng bīnguǎn; 曲阜市邮政宾馆), 8 Gulou Bei Jie (☎448 3888), just opposite the Confucius Mansions (the real ones, not the hotel listed below). The spacious rooms feel much, much more expensive than they actually are. Amenities and services include 24hr. hot water, spotless bathrooms, and an amiable staff whose utmost priority is your comfort. The convenient location doesn't hurt either. Doubles Y180-280; triples Y160. For longer stays, ask for discounts. ❷

Friendship Hotel (yǒuyì bīnguǎn; 友谊宾馆), 129 Gulou Nan Jie (☎442 8998), a 3min. walk from the bus station. Sparsely furnished rooms and a slight mothball odor that doesn't come from your luggage case. Right on a major road, but the walls do a decent job of blocking out the racket. Standing showers and garish red carpeting. Singles Y50-180; doubles Y160-180; triples Y140-180. ❶

Confucius Mansions Hotel (kǒngfǔ fàndiàn; 孔府饭店), 9 Datong Lu (☎441 2686 or 441 1783; fax 442 1473), opposite the bus station; enter through a stone gateway on Jingxuan Lu, right before its intersection with Gulou Dajie/Datong Lu. Hardly as resplendent as the real Confucian Mansions, but newly renovated rooms that still smell of paint and plaster are better kept than the run-down exterior suggests. All have bath and 24hr. hot water. Singles Y100; nicer singles and doubles Y120. ❷

Travel Hotel (lǚyóu bīnguǎn; 旅游宾馆), 108 Jingxuan Lu (☎486 9719 or 286 9400; fax 486 9719), opposite and right of the bus station. Comfortable, if slightly deserted; lobby is ritzy, but rooms are a step down in quality. More expensive rooms are much nicer (read: more electrical outlets and better smell) than cheaper options. Phones in rooms. Hot water 8am-midnight. Curfew midnight. Doubles Y280-320; triples Y300. In the low season (any time that's not July-Aug.) ask for discounts. ❹

◉ SIGHTS

Confucius is the hot topic in town, and that seems unlikely to change any time soon. With nothing else to tout, Qufu flaunts its Confucian legacy with relish. The recent surge in scholarly interest of the Great Sage is reflected in hiked-up admission prices for sights and in the tenacity of persistent tour guides. Watch out for unending streams of tourists coming in motorcades of tour buses, wearing t-shirts, hats, and any other gear that proclaims, in Chinese, "I paid homage to Confucius." Do your best to fend off tour guides ready to pounce on the bewildered traveler. Politeness does not work; stern rejections might, but running away may be best. Despite all this, the old haunts of the Great Sage pass on memories of tradition and the origins of profound wisdom.

CONFUCIUS FOREST (kǒnglín; 孔林). North of town, the forest contains the tomb of Confucius and the graves of a mere 100,000 of his ancestors and descendants. Not surprisingly, it's the largest, oldest, and best-preserved single-family cemetery in China. After running the gauntlet of vendors, cross over an arched stone bridge to the resting place of Confucius himself. Surprisingly unpretentious and set far back in the cemetery, away from the flurry of haggling peddlers, the 2500-year-old grave of the famous philosopher-scholar is simply built and carved

BEIJING

with ancient characters painted in yellow. Peaceful and perfectly conducive to meditative thoughts, the forest is a memorial worthy of Master Kong. Even the occasional tour group, easily picked out by their uniform sun-hats, does not disturb the solemn serenity of these hallowed grounds. Along the many paths, other graves and stone inscriptions peek out through the untamed overgrowth. *(Hiring pedicabs and taxis to the forest is nice for your feet. Alternatively, walk north along Gulou Jie, which turns into Linda Lu and runs directly to the forest. Persistent Chinese-speaking guides Y10. Minibus tour Y10. Open daily 7:30am-6:30pm. Y22.)*

CONFUCIUS TEMPLE (kǒng miào; 孔庙). It didn't take long for Confucius, largely neglected during his lifetime, to start getting his due; this temple was first built in 478 BC, when the soil had barely settled over the sage's grave. For someone who advocated modesty, the temple built in Master Kong's honor is quite extravagant. Arranged along a perfect north-south axis, the temple is a stately introduction to Confucianism. Miniature figurines of creatures in the Chinese zodiac decorate the intricate flying eaves.

Ten monolithic columns, each adorned with well-preserved, gorgeously carved dragons, border the imposing **Dacheng Hall** (dàchéng diàn; 大成殿). It's not the actual shrine inside, but the architectural design, sheer size, and cavernous interior that gives the hall its eye-catching monumentality. Confucius is said to have lectured his disciples in the **Apricot Altar Pavilion** (xìngtán gé; 杏坛阁), proclaiming those maxims that would eventually be compiled in the *Analects*. Centered in a courtyard, the pavilion shelters several calligraphic steles that only those well-versed in Chinese wordplay will appreciate. *(In the center of Qufu, off Gulou Jie, an unmistakable sea of red roofs. Guides Y10. Open M-Th 8am-5pm; last admission at 4:30pm. Y52.)*

CONFUCIUS MANSIONS (kǒngfǔ; 孔府). Confucius may not have been appreciated in his lifetime, but the imperial favors and aristocratic authority bestowed upon his descendants more than make up for past wrongs. Thanks to their illustrious ancestor, those of the direct male line lived a rather cushy life in the Confucius Mansions, said to have been the second-most luxurious residence in all of ancient China, after that of the imperial family. The mansions themselves are a wealth of individual halls and gardens, all set out in a maze-like design. Peering through smoky windows into the now-blocked-off rooms and hallways reveals the enduring grandeur of these quarters. Features of the mansions include the **Front Chamber**, where patriarchs lived with their wives; the **Upper Front Chamber**, where celebrations were held; the **Third Hall**, where important family affairs were handled; and the **Great Hall**, where official decrees were received. Many members of the Kong family milked their glorious genetic heritage to the fullest, at times ruling western Shandong as their own private fiefdom. The last of Kong's direct descendants did not leave the mansions until 1949, when they fled to Taiwan in fear of Communist persecution. *(Off Gulou Jie in the town center. Open daily 8am-5pm; last admission at 4:30pm. Y22.)*

MAUSOLEUM OF SHAO HAO (shǎohào líng; 少昊陵). A deserted retreat, the Mausoleum of Shao Hao lies to the northeast, a short ride away over wheat-covered roads and onion fields. Shao Hao, the son of the mythical king Huangdi, ruled for 84 years and died at the ripe old age of 100. His little-known mausoleum isn't all that memorable; a short jaunt should suffice. The groundskeepers seem to have retired, and birds have made the memorial their permanent nesting grounds. The only noteworthy mention is the bizarre pyramid marking the tomb. According to tradition, well-wishers clamber up the 9m pyramid and pay homage to a statue of Shao Hao at the top. *(Pedicab Y6-10. Taxi-ride Y10. Open daily 8am-5pm. Y20.)*

⚑ DAYTRIP FROM QUFU: ZOUCHENG

*Buses leave from the long-distance bus station (40min., every 20min. 6:30am-6pm, Y5).
☎ 522 1377. Temple open daily 8am-5:40pm; mansions open daily 8am-5pm. Ticket sellers leave at 4pm sharp. Admission includes temple and mansion, Y20.*

Zoucheng (zōuchéng; 邹城), formerly Zouxian, is a tiny, struggling town less than
one hour from Qufu. Its claim to fame is that it was the hometown of the philosopher Mencius, one of Confucianism's greatest proponents. The whole place is
something of a poor man's Qufu, less grand and far calmer, hardly worth visiting
unless you wish to avoid businessmen wearing requisite tour caps.

The **Mencius Temple** (mèng miào; 孟庙), on Yashengfu Jie, is just a pedicab ride
from the bus station (Y3). No longer on any tourist map, the temple has fallen into
disarray, with crumbling stone paths, fallen trees, and weeds invading any
exposed space. Several steles remain, such as one from the Qing Dynasty
inscribed by Emperor Kangxi in AD 1687. The temple would be peaceful were it
not for a particular raucous species of bird that dominates the remaining, statuesque trees. Walk fast or carry an umbrella unless you want to be victimized by the
same white goop covering the pathways and temple tops. Around the corner, the
Mencius Mansions (mèng fǔ; 孟府) are impeccably manicured reminders of the
glory once bestowed upon the descendants of the "other" semi-divine philosopher.

QINGDAO 青岛   ☎ 0532

Before the Qing imperial court began garrisoning troops in the area in 1891,
Qingdao was just an unpretentious, undiscovered fishing village. In 1897, along
came a German concession, which gave this modest beauty a full-scale makeover
and—more importantly—some full-bodied beer. By the time the Japanese invaded
in 1937, Qingdao had blossomed into the stunning temptress that it is today, with a
healthy resort-driven economy, an eclectic mix of Western shingles and Chinese
eaves, and a breezy attitude.

Qingdao is a celebrity in the West, thanks to its famous export, Tsingtao beer.
Many people enjoy the beer, and even more enjoy Qingdao, whose charms are as
richly satisfying as a good brew. Red-roofed Bavarian buildings, hills of foliage and
flora, and kilometers of rock-strewn beaches add to the appeal of this beautiful
coastal city. Chinese tourists flock here on holidays, while foreign travelers pour
in at increasing rates. Seductive, enchanting Qingdao won't hesitate to take advantage of those inebriated by its charms.

BEIJING

▐ TRANSPORTATION

Flights: Liuting International Airport (liútíng guójì jīchǎng; 流亭国际机场 ; ☎ 597
6176), on Kaiyang Lu, 32km northeast of the city. Shuttle buses (every 30min., Y10)
take passengers from the airport to 30 Xianggang Lu, where buses #25 and 316 run to
the train station. For more info, contact the **CAAC ticket office,** 29 Zhongshan Lu
(☎ 289 5577 or 287 4275, international office 577 4249; www.airqingdao.com), or
the **Shandong Airlines** office at the train station (☎ 288 9160 or 286 5870). Taxis from
the airport to the city center cost at least Y90. Open daily 8am-6pm. To: **Beijing** (2-3
per day, Y710); **Chengdu** (several times per day, Y1510); **Chongqing** (several times
per week, Y1300); **Dalian** (2 per day, Y540); **Guangzhou** (1 per day, Y1780); **Shanghai** (1-2 per day, Y740). International flights vary extensively with season. To: **Seoul,
South Korea** (2hr., 2 per day, Y1300); **Singapore** (6hr., a couple per week, Y5100);
Tokyo, Japan (2-3 per week).

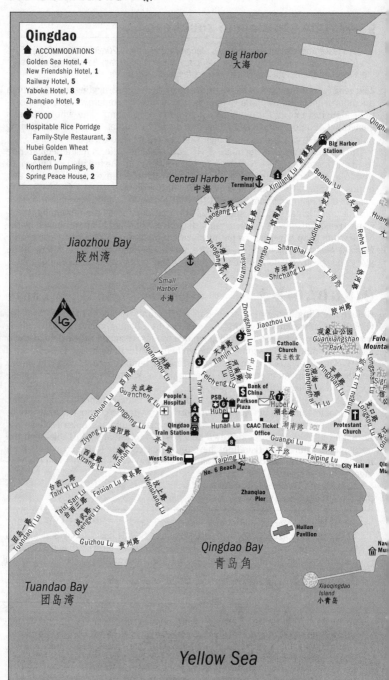

Qingdao

🏠 ACCOMMODATIONS
Golden Sea Hotel, 4
New Friendship Hotel, 1
Railway Hotel, 5
Yaboke Hotel, 8
Zhanqiao Hotel, 9

🍎 FOOD
Hospitable Rice Porridge
  Family-Style Restaurant, 3
Hubei Golden Wheat
  Garden, 7
Northern Dumplings, 6
Spring Peace House, 2

Big Harbor
大海

Big Harbor
Station

Central Harbor
中海

Ferry
Terminal

Jiaozhou Bay
胶州湾

Small
Harbor
小海

Xiaogang Er Lu 小港二路
Xiaogang Yi Lu 小港一路

Xinjiang Lu 新疆路
Baotou Lu 包头路
Wuding Lu 武定路
Rehe Lu 热河路

Guantao Lu 冠县路
Zhifu Lu 芝罘路
Guantao Lu
Shanghai Lu 上海路
市场路 Shichang Lu

Guanxianlu
Zhongshan Lu 中山路

胶州路
Jiaozhou Lu

观象山公园
Guanxiangshan
Park

Fulo
Mounta

Guangzhou Lu 广州路

天津路 Tianjin Lu
河南路 Henan Lu
Feicheng Lu
Tai'an Lu 泰安路

Catholic
Church
天主教堂

湖南一路
Pingyuan Lu
Guangzhou Lu

Longshan Lu
Sigr
信江路

Bank of
China

PSB
Parkson
Plaza

People's
Hospital
🏥

Qingdao
Train Station
🚉

Hubei Lu
湖北路

R 🍎 7
Hubei Lu
湖北路

Protestant
Church

Yi Lu

关成路 Guancheng Lu
Sichuan Lu 四川路
Dongping Lu 东平路
Ziyang Lu 滋阳路
Yunnan Lu 云南路
Xizang Lu 西藏路

Hunan Lu
CAAC Ticket
Office
Guangxi Lu
广西路

Taiping Lu 太平路

West Station 🚌

台西一路 Taixi Yi Lu
台西三路 Taixi San Lu
Feixian Lu 费县路
威宁路
Chengwu Lu 成武路

Guizhou Lu 贵州路

Wenshang Lu

No. 6 Beach

Zhanqiao
Pier

Huilan
Pavilion

Taiping Lu
广西路
City Hall ■

Navi
Mu

Tuandao Bay
团岛湾

Tuandao Lu 团岛路

Qingdao Bay
青岛角

Xiaoqingdao
Island
小青岛

Yellow Sea

BEIJING

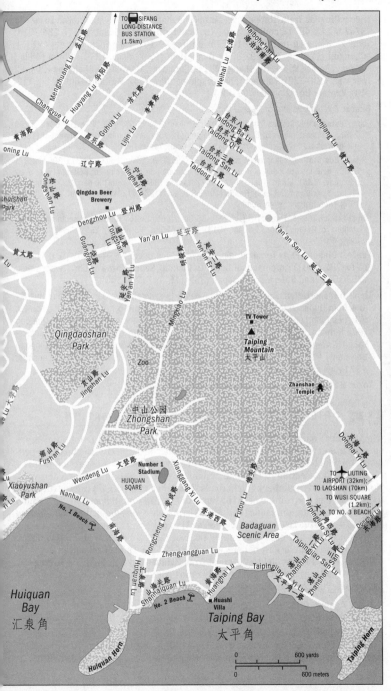

TO SIFANG
LONG-DISTANCE
BUS STATION
(1.5km)

Mengzhuang Lu 孟庄路

Huayang Lu 华阳路

Changyue Lu

青海路

oning Lu

Chengwu Lu 城武路

Guhua Lu 古化路

Lijin Lu

法化路

李村路

昌乐路

辽宁路

Weihai Lu 威海路

Haibohehan Lu 海泊河南路

Zhenjiang Lu 镇江路

台东八路 Taidong Ba Lu
台东七路 Taidong Qi Lu
Taidong San Lu
Taidong Yi Lu
台东三路
台东一路

Songshan Lu

崂山路

shuishan
Park

黄大路

Lu

Qingdao Beer
Brewery

Dengzhou Lu 登州路

Guangbo Lu

徐州路

Tongshan
Lu

通山路

Yan'an Lu 延安路

Yan'an Er Lu 延安二路

延安路

Yan'an Yi Lu

Yan'an San Lu 延安三路

Mingxiao Lu

Qingdaoshan
Park

Zoo

Jingshan Lu

青山路

Lu 大学路

TV Tower

▲
Taiping
Mountain
太平山

Zhanshan
Temple

Yan'an San Lu 延安三路

Fushan Lu
福山路

中山公园
Zhongshan
Park

Wendeng Lu 文登路

Number 1
Stadium

HUIQUAN
SQARE

Xiangang Xi Lu

香港西路

Futou Lu 浮头路

韩水路

Donghai Yi Lu 东海一路

Xiaoyushan
Park

Nanhai Lu

南海路

Yi Lu

No. 1 Beach

Badaguan
Scenic Area

TO LIUTING
AIRPORT (32km);
TO LAOSHAN (70km)
TO WUSI SQUARE
(1.2km);
TO NO. 3 BEACH

Rongcheng Lu

Zhengyangguan Lu

乐成路

Huiquan
Bay
汇泉角

Huiquan
Lu

Shanhaiguan Lu

山海关路

汇泉角

No. 2 Beach

黄海路

Huanghai Lu

Huashi
Villa

Taipingjiao
Zhanshan Lu

Taipingjiao Si Lu

Taiping
Bay
太平角

Taipingjiao Yi Lu
太平角一路

Taipingjiao San Lu

Zhanshan
Lu

Zhansan

Huiquan Horn

0   600 yards
0   600 meters

Taiping Horn

BEIJING

Trains: Qingdao Train Station (qīngdǎo huǒchē zhàn; 青岛火车站), 4 Tai'an Lu (☎286 5741 or 286 4571), north of Taiping Lu. **Ticket offices** at 9 Guantao Lu (☎284 3014) and 2 Fuqing Lu (☎587 1814). To: **Beijing** (9-10hr., a couple per day, Y215); **Chengdu** (12hr., daily, Y292-303); **Guangzhou** (15hr., daily, Y330); **Ji'nan** (4-6hr., several per day, Y55-106); **Shanghai** (15-18hr., daily, Y290-300); **Shenyang** (20hr., 2 per day, Y100-232); **Taishan** (5hr., couple per day, Y34); **Weihai** (4-6hr., daily, Y12-46); **Yantai** (4hr., 2 per day, Y22-35).

Buses: 3 main bus stations serve Qingdao.

Long-Distance Bus Station (chángtú lǚyóu qìchē zhàn; 长途旅游汽车站; ☎267 6842 or 289 2498), at the terminus of bus #8. To: **Beijing** (12-15hr., every other day); **Shanghai** (18hr., daily); **Weihai** (4-6hr., every 30min. 6am-noon, 6pm); **Yantai** (3½hr., every 30min., 6am-6pm).

Sifang Bus Station (sìfāng qìchē zhàn; 四方汽车站), 2 Wenzhou Lu (☎371 8061 or 371 8060), is at the other end of route #8, in the northern part of the city. To: **Beijing** (16hr., every other day, Y146); **Ji'nan** (4hr., every hr., Y97); **Nanjing** (8-9hr., several per day, Y153); **Shanghai** (18hr., 3 per day, Y198-218); **Tianjin** (10hr., 8:30am, Y126-152); **Weihai** (5-6hr., every 30min., Y68); **Yantai** (3½hr., every 30min., Y50).

West Station (qìchē xī zhàn; 汽车西站), 36 Guantao Lu (☎267 6842), just south of the train station. To: **Beijing** (12hr., 7:50pm, Y218); **Ji'nan** (4-5hr., 4-5 per day, Y95); **Shanghai** (19hr., daily, Y201).

Ferries: Qingdao Ferry Terminal (qīngdǎogǎng kèyùn zhàn; 青岛港客运站), 6 Xinjiang Lu (☎282 5001). International boats to **Inchon, South Korea** (15hr., 3 per week, Y750-1090) and **Shimonoseki, Japan** (36hr.; M, Th; Y1200-1400).

Local Transportation: Bus fare Y1, with A/C Y2. In general, runs 6am-8 or 9pm. Bus #1 runs from Hubei Lu to Sifang District via Yan'an Lu; #2 and 5 run down Zhongshan Lu; #8 goes from Lundu Dock to the Sifang Bus Station via the train station and Qingdao Ferry Terminal; #26 runs from the train station to eastern Qingdao along the coastal Yang Lu, Wendeng Lu, and Xianggang Lu; #31 connects Zhongshan Park and Qingdao University; #317 runs along the coast to the Stoneman Scenic Area, close to Laoshan; #321 runs along Taiping Lu, all the way to Wusi Sq.

Taxis: Base fare Y7, each additional km Y1.2.

✦ 🛈 ORIENTATION AND PRACTICAL INFORMATION

Qingdao isn't easy to navigate; its seven urban districts and five counties are spread far and wide along the coast. The western side of the city, the tip of the peninsula on which Qingdao sits, is a jumble of hilly streets that loop around in tortuous paths. This section of Qingdao contains the train station, the ferry terminal, No. 6 Beach, and a number of main roads. **Zhongshan Lu** (中山路) runs north-south to **Zhanqiao Pier** and is intersected by **Hubei Lu** (湖北路) and **Hunan** (湖南路), which lead to the train station. **Taiping Lu** (太平路) runs east-west along the coast. **Jiangsu Lu** (江苏路), **Daxue Lu** (大学路), and **Yan'an Yi Lu** (延安一路) run north-south along the coast, eventually crossing Taiping Lu. No. 1 and 2 Beaches and the Qingdao World Trade Center lie east of here. **Nanhai Lu** (南海路) and **Shanhaiguan Lu** (山海关路) are roughly parallel to the coast from **Huiquan Bay** (汇泉角) to **Taiping Bay** (太平角). **Xianggang Lu** (香港路) also runs parallel to the coast, starting from Zhongshan Park and heading west.

Travel Agency: CITS, 73 Xianggang Xi Lu (☎389 3005), in the eastern part of town, at the intersection of Xianggang Lu and Donghai Lu. Open daily 8am-5pm. Ticket offices also available at the **IATA office** (☎288 9160; fax 286 5870) at the train station.

Bank of China: 68 Zhongshan Lu (☎286 1106). Exchanges currency and traveler's checks. Credit card advances. Open daily M-F 8:30am-5pm, Sa-Sun 9:30am-4pm.

Bookstore: Foreign Language Bookstore (wàiwén shūdiàn; 外文书店), 165 Zhongshan Lu (☎282 8230). Open daily 9am-5:30pm.

PSB: 29 Hubei Lu, between Tai'an Lu and Zhongshan Lu. **Foreign affairs office,** 272 Ningxia Lu (☎579 2555), in the eastern part of town. Take bus #301 from the train station to Xiaoyao Lu. Open M-F 8:30-11:30am and 1:30-5pm.

Pharmacy: No. 1 Pharmacy (huá dìyī dà yàodiàn; 华第一大药店), 14 Hubei Lu, has Chinese and Western medicines. 24hr. window. Open daily 8:30am-9pm.

Hospital: Qingdao Southern District People's Hospital (qīngdǎoshì shìnán qū rénmín yīyuàn; 青岛市市南区人民医院), 29 Guangzhou Lu (☎261 9783), west of the train station. English-speaking doctors. Open 24hr.

Internet Access: Flying Skies Internet Cafe (fēixiáng tiānkōng wǎngbā; 飞翔天空网 吧), 22 Henan Lu (☎286 0791), right next to Northern Dumplings. Y1.5 per hr. Open daily 8am-midnight.

Post Office: China Post, 51 Zhongshan Lu, slightly diagonal from Parkson Plaza. EMS and Poste Restante. Open daily 8am-6pm.

Postal Code: 266001.

ACCOMMODATIONS

Cheaper establishments crowd the train station and ferry terminal areas. More upscale resort hotels line the south coast and the No. 1 and No. 2 beaches. Reservations are recommended for all hotels. Most hotels offer discounts up to 50%, except during the busiest months of July and August. All listed hotels have 24hr. hot water and A/C, unless otherwise noted.

Zhanqiao Hotel (zhànqiáo bīnguǎn; 栈桥宾馆), 31 Taiping Lu (☎288 8666 or 287 0502; fax 287 0936). A 5min. walk to the end of Zhanqiao Pier and a bus stop away from everything else. The 1st guesthouse to receive foreigners in Qingdao, Zhanqiao maintains a consistently high standard of excellence. Constructed in the German Bavarian style, it has elegance and superb service to match. TV, clean sheets, full bath, laundry, and currency exchange. Call early to get the Y200 non-seaside double; seaside doubles Y298; triples Y398. Discounts rare but it never hurts to ask. ❸

Golden Sea Hotel (jīnhǎi dàjiǔdiàn; 金海大酒店), 14 Tai'an Lu (☎297 6110, 808 1168, or 297 8609), has a very nice and helpful staff. Ever busy; arrive early and call ahead to guarantee yourself a room. Ask to see rooms before registering; avoid rooms facing the railroad but snap up the newly renovated ones. TV. Doubles begin at Y280 but discounts of up to 50% are possible; triples Y360. ❹

Yaboke Hotel, 1 Mengyin Lu (☎286 5388 or 287 1288), directly across from the train station square, next to Agricultural Bank of China. Among the better-kept options near the train station. Quieter, calmer environment. Standing showers. Singles Y380, low-season (Sept.-June) can be marked down to Y120; doubles Y480/Y200. ❺

Railway Hotel (qíngdǎo tiědào dàshà; 青岛铁道大厦), 8 Tai'an Lu (☎606 7888 or 606 7999; fax 286 0497), just north of the train station exit. Bright recently renovated rooms, complete with paint-like smell, clean bathroom tiles, spruced-up furniture, and TV. A glass elevator offers great views. Doubles with bath Y280, can be brought down to Y160; quads Y480. 30% discount during low season. ❸

New Friendship Hotel (yǒuyí bīnguǎn; 友谊宾馆), 12 Xinjiang Lu (☎284 4888 or 282 4686), next door to the Friendship Store. Right on the coast, near the piers, in a very Korean neighborhood. Tacky decor, poor lighting, somewhat far from all the essential sights, and a vertigo-inducing elevator—perfect for the adventurous budget traveler. No A/C. Economy rooms Y50 per hr.; doubles Y248-288; triples Y338. Discounts up to 50% always available. ❸

🔲 🔟 FOOD AND ENTERTAINMENT

A Chinese saying proclaims, "Live by the mountain, eat off the mountain; live by the water, drink the water." Visitors should take this to heart—even if the hot temperatures make liquid diets tempting—and indulge in Qingdao's fruitful mountain-grown produce and famed Laoshan springs. To quench your thirst, sample the carts of peaches, apples, and **lychee.** Seafood restaurants scatter all over Qingdao, especially along **No. 1 Beach, Tai'an Lu,** and **Hubei Lu,** near the train station.

Fresh fish from the sea results in **sushi** eateries in the neighborhood east of Zhongshan Lu and to the south of the Catholic Church (especially Boshan Lu). Hearty Shandong cooking, including **roasted corn** (Y0.8-1) and **dumplings** (Y5-10 per dozen), can be sampled anywhere. Locals tend to load these treats with more soy sauce and garlic than you'd expect. International tastes, including Muslim, Japanese, and the ever-exotic Kentucky, also abound.

Besides hotel dining options, the city center is surprisingly bereft of notable mid-range, sit-down restaurants. Travelers may find themselves stuck between overpriced delicacies (Y50+ per plate) or a nourishing kebab meal (Y1 per stick).

Night-owls may enjoy the numerous **movie theaters** that line Zhongshan Lu. Hong Kong imports and dubbed US flicks cost less than Y25. Other nightlife options feed off the cool ocean breezes. When the sun sets, resourceful entrepreneurs drag out television sets, microphones, and stacks of VCDs, setting up shop along the coastal walkway stretching alongside Taiping Lu. Locals come out in droves to **impromptu karaoke** centers in order to listen to idol-wannabes croon pop melodies and revolutionary classics (Y1 per song).

Spring Peace House (chūnhé lóu; 春和楼), 146 Zhongshan Lu, at the intersection of Tianjin and Zhongshan Lu, a 5-10min. walk north from the waterfront. The fast-food section (Y5-12) on the 1st fl. combines lightning speed with the cleanliness and tastiness of a real restaurant. The restaurant on the 2nd fl. offers great local specialties (Y10-50). Savor duck with skin roasted to a perfect state of crispness, dipped in the accompanying pungent spices (Y25). Dumplings Y6 for 6. Open daily 6am-10pm. ❷

Hubei Golden Wheat Garden (húběilù jīnmàiyuán; 湖北路金麦园), 18 Anhui Lu (☎289 3070), on the corner of Hubei Lu and Anhui Lu. Feast on some classic Shandong cuisine, prepared with alacrity and flourish in a cafeteria-style interior. Beef noodles (Y5 per bowl) and gargantuan vegetable dumplings (Y1 for 4). Freshly steamed *bāozi* (Y5 each) from the take-out window. Open daily 6am-9pm. ❶

Hospitable Rice Porridge Family-Style Restaurant (kèlái zhōudào jiāchángcài guǎn; 客来粥到家常菜馆), 85 Beijing Lu (☎283 2628), a 10min. walk from the train station. A familial, sit-down find, popular with locals. Friendly staff. Limited display of dishes to choose from, but portions are large for the hungry and weary. Open 8am-10pm. ❶

Northern Dumplings (běifāng shuǐjiǎo; 北方水饺), 24 Hubei Lu (☎286 3494), a block west of Zhongshan Lu. True northern dumplings with a variety of fillings (pork Y6-8 for 20; beef or more tasty options Y10-15 for 20). Stir-fried dishes upstairs (entrees Y15-30). Soy milk for breakfast Y1. Open daily 6am-9pm. ❶

🔘 SIGHTS

Qingdao locals accurately describe their colorful peninsula with eight little words: "red roofs, green trees, aqua water, blue sky." Take in the scenery at **No. 2 Beach** and **Signal Hill Park,** and join in the commercial action of **Zhongshan Lu** and the intimate **German-style neighborhood** east of Zhongshan Lu and north of the Catholic Church. Every year, beer-guzzling fanatics stumble to the **Qingdao Beer Festival** (held in late summer) to do what beer fans do best: drink.

⧉ QINGDAO BEER BREWERY (qīngdǎo píjiǔ chǎng; 青岛啤酒厂). Qingdao's most famous export has been fermenting since 1903, when German expats established the country's best-known brewery. Mineral water from nearby Laoshan is said to be the secret ingredient behind the beer's great taste and purported medicinal properties. Just inside the main entrance, a fountain designed in the shape of a Tsingtao beer bottle, with accompanying shot glasses, makes a great photo-op. The brewery museum, modern in design and function, displays several exhibits on the history of the company and on beer-brewing. All signs have English translations. Artifacts, such as old wort thermometers and measuring instruments, are lovingly preserved, and the requisite wax figures, poised to brew, add a comical touch to the elegant showcases. Sweet, redolent aromas of fermenting barley waft from the "mystic yeast garden," priming your tastebuds—and your wallet—for the beer bar and Tsingtao shop at the end of the tour. Drink Tsingtao—live forever. *(56 Dengzhou Lu. Take bus #1 or 25 from the train station to Shiwuzhong on Yan'an Lu.* ☎ *383 3437. Open daily 9am-4:30pm. Call ahead. 30min. tour of the bottling workshop and up to 4 glasses beer-tasting Y30, children Y15. Tour guide additional Y20.)*

WUSI SQUARE (wǔsì guángchǎng; 五四广场). A twisted structure, covered by red panels, is the most eye-catching landmark of Wusi (literally "May 4th") Square. Illuminated at night, it's a true example of the Chinese penchant for all things red. The square features several fountains, including one you can walk through. Jazz instrumental music, emanating from cleverly disguised loudspeakers, infuses the skies with romantic ambience. Closer to No. 3 beach, 12 marble pillars (representing China's 12 dynasties) welcome visitors. Take a leisurely stroll from the beach and enjoy Qingdao's skyline or walk along the jetty and feel the crashing waves tickle your feet. *(East of #2 and #3 beaches; take bus #321 directly to Wusi Sq.)*

SIGNAL HILL PARK (xìnhàoshān gōngyuán; 信号山公园). This park derives its name from a former beacon that once sat atop the steep hill. The park offers precious little in terms of excitement. All-encompassing views of the city reward those who make the 20min. hike to the top on one of several meandering pathways. Ascend the **Rotary Sightseeing Building,** an onion-dome-like structure that rotates for a 360° panorama. Be careful not to disturb the elderly meditating in small hillside plots. *(*☎ *279 4141. 18 Longshan Lu, just east of Jiangsu Lu. Open daily 7am-7pm. Y12, including Rotary Sightseeing Building.)*

NAVY MUSEUM (hǎijūn bówùguǎn; 海军博物馆). On the foot of Xiaoqing Island, this is the first and only museum in China dedicated to the country's naval fleet. The indoor exhibition hall, with little else but uniforms and commemorative plaques, can be skipped. Battleship lovers will appreciate the demobilized warships, guided missiles, cannons, and tanks crowding the open-air display area. Anshan 101, the first destroyer, floats proudly in the water. Stretching 112.5m, the 2600-ton craft is surprisingly distinctive. A series of other vessels, including a submarine and a frigate, Nanchong 502, are only a short walk away. *(8 Laiyang Lu.* ☎ *287 4786 or 286 6784. Open M-Sa 9am-4pm. Summer Y30, winter Y20; individual sights Y10.)*

CATHOLIC CHURCH (tiānzhǔ jiàotáng; 天主教堂). Officially called **St. Michael's Cathedral,** this neo-Gothic and Roman cathedral was built in 1934 by German architects. Heavily damaged during the Cultural Revolution, the church was renovated and reopened in 1981. Today it is an active but essentially empty place of worship, with few priests and nuns in residence. *(At Zhejiang Lu and Feicheng Lu, east of Zhongshan Lu.* ☎ *591 1400. Open M-Sa 8am-5pm, Su noon-5pm. Service Su 7-9:30am. Y6.)*

BEIJING

🌊 BEACHES

NO. 2 BEACH (dì'èr hǎishuǐ yùchǎng; 第二海水浴场). Finding a beach in Qingdao is only marginally harder than finding a disgruntled bureaucrat in Beijing. Of them all, No. 2 runs circles around the competition. Leafy green hills hem the beach on three sides, and clean sands and sapphire water take care of the fourth. Only algae, seaweed, and the occasional sharp rock litter the shores. Little except the crash and hiss of waves disturbs the quiet. Free of the distractions that plague beach No. 1, you can just unwind, bathe, loll in the sun, or rummage for hermits and shells with bucket in hand. *(Open 24hr. Y2; free after 5pm. Locker and shower Y10.)*

At the eastern end of the beach is **Huashi Villa** (huāshí lóu; 花石楼), or "Granite Castle." This old-world stone villa was built in 1930 for a Russian aristocrat and later owned by a succession of Chinese cadres. Apart from its lookout tower, the villa is only mildly interesting; one exhibit displays some of Chiang Kai-shek's belongings. Sadly, the surroundings gardens have been spoiled by flowery pink "I Love You" wreaths and cartoon-like swing-sets. *(18 Huanghai Lu, at Shanhaiguan Lu. Open daily 7:30am-6pm. Y5.)*

Over 200 European-style villas of the concession era line the broad avenues winding through the thick greenery of **Badaguan Scenic Area** (bādàguān fēngjǐngqū; 八大关风景区), set into the surrounding hills. *(South of Zhongshan Park, in the eastern part of town. Accessible by buses #6, 26, 214, 219, and 304.)*

NO. 1 BEACH (dìyī hǎishuǐ yùchǎng; 第一海水浴场). Qingdao's longest beach is flooded with tourists, hotels, restaurants, and shark-proof nets. Because the beach's slope is rather flat, swimmers can wade out far into the bay, away from the masses of the less daring. Beware tight-fitting Speedos. This kind of high-drama swimming and sunbathing can be avoided at the more deserted No. 2 Beach. *(In the eastern part of town, just south of Nanhai Lu. Accessible by buses #6, 15, 26, 312, and others. Open July-Sept. Free; swimming Y3.)*

THE REAL DEAL. In Qingdao, any walkable stretch of coastline is much too often invaded by kiosks all selling the same trinket, strings upon strings of "real cultured pearls." When a potential victim (that's you) halts in front of one of the stalls, vendors will immediately latch on and throw out a high price—often for bogus goods. Authentic nuggets do exist among the fray, but swindlers are much too common. A few things to keep in mind:

Under bright light, real pearls should gleam an off-white, somewhat hazy luster. Only fake pearls shine a brilliant white.

No two pearls are identical in shape or color. Rarely are they perfectly circular.

Real, cultured pearls are significantly heavier than the counterfeit samples.

Rub the pearls in a strand together. There should be friction and no slipping.

Qingdao pearls are grown in saltwater instead of freshwater. As a result, they are supposed to age differently. Instead of yellowing with age, these jewels should gleam brighter with wear.

NO. 6 BEACH (dìliù hǎishuǐ yùchǎng; 第六海水浴场). Far too close to the downtown area, the No. 6 Beach is number one in terms of population density, litter, and noise level. It is, however, the gateway to **Huilan Pavilion** (huílán gé; 回澜阁) and **Zhanqiao Pier** (zhàn qiáo; 栈桥). Don't waste your money on the unimpressive aquarium (Y4). The pier, built in 1891, is one of the most well-known symbols of Qingdao, and the octagonal pavilion at the far end echoes with the pounding rhythms of the ocean and the sound of chattering tourists. *(At the southern end of the city center, south of the train station. The pier is on Taiping Lu at Zhongshan Lu. Open 24hr. Ticketing time ends earlier in the winter. 8:30am-6pm Y2, after 7:30pm free.)*

■ DAYTRIP FROM QINGDAO: LAOSHAN 崂山

*40km east of Qingdao. Laoshan is most conveniently seen with a **tour bus** (Y25 for guide and transportation, admission extra); megaphone-toting ticket sellers abound near the train station. All tours are in Chinese and may include annoying stops at pearl shops, but you can ditch the group after arrival. There are 3 **park entrances: Liuqinghe** (流清河), near Weizhu Nunnery, Liuqing River, and Jufeng Peak; **Yakou** (垭口), near Taiping Palace, Shangqing Palace, Mingxia Caves, and Longtan Waterfall; and **Yangkou** (仰口), near a beach, Mitian Cave, and several small temples. Tour buses usually go only to Yakou. To explore on your own, **bus #304** runs from the train station (Y6.5) to Yakou, and #312 runs from the train station (Y6.5) or Zhongshan Park (Y6) to Yangkou. The last bus to Qingdao departs Yangkou at 4:40pm and Yakou at 5pm. **Cable car** to Taiping Palace (one-way Y30, round-trip Y50). **Minibuses** (30min., every 30min. 7am-4pm, Y3) link Yakou and Yangkou. Y50; individual sights Y10-15.*

The fabled Daoist fairyland of Laoshan Mountain (láo shān; 崂山) makes a magical daytrip from Qingdao. Rising 1133m above sea level, the source of Laoshan Mineral Spring Water is dotted with waterfalls and limestone cliffs hanging over the Yellow Sea. In its prime, Laoshan was home to 9 palaces, 8 temples, and 72 convents, many of which are still intact and active. Sights along the scenic paths are staggeringly numerous, and the arduous hikes are an incomparable experience. All sights are spread out on Laoshan, so unless you're with a tour group, prepare to make allowances for the cost and inconvenience of transportation. To explore the expanse of mountains and waterfalls fully, plan on staying a week.

Accommodations are impossible to find on the mountain itself. All lodgings belong to the peasants who call Laoshan home, and unless you can convince one to house you for the night, good luck. (Note that it's illegal to stay in a resident's house without the permission of the PSB.) Sit-down dining options are also rare, unless you happen to be driving down and out of the park. Your best chance is to grab some price-inflated snacks and other edible treats from the vendors at the **Yakou** and **Yangkou** bus stops. Those with foresight and tolerance for heavy packs can buy sustenance in Qingdao and tote the weight along. At the **Yakou** bus stop, you may want to try **Laoshan tea** (láoshān chá; 崂山茶), which comes in several varieties and is brewed from herbs grown on the hillside by local farmers. The tea supposedly has a wealth of medicinal benefits and a light, slightly bitter flavor, with a sweet, refreshing aftertaste.

YAKOU (yàkǒu; 垭口). From the Yakou bus stop, you can walk to the Eight-Water River (bāshuǐ hé; 八水河) checkpoint, where a steep climb leads to **Dragon Pool Waterfall** (lóngtán; 龙潭), the site of many a rainbow skimming the water. The entire climb takes less than an hour and is well worth the sore muscles. During the months of July and August, the roaring waters rush through the mist to create a breathtaking (and slightly moist) sight. Continue up the path for an additional 30min. to reach the **Shangqing Palace** (shàngqīng gōng; 上清宫), the oldest monastery in the area. The incline becomes steeper as you trudge for another hour to the **Bright Clouds Caves** (míngxía dòng; 明霞洞).

Laoshan is also home to the **Taiqing Palace** (tàiqīng gōng; 太清宫), a famous monastery with an active Daoist community that abides by all the ancient rules—no meat, marriage, and haircuts. First built during the Northern Song Dynasty, the palace now consists of 140 rooms and halls. A recent fire closed the palace to visitors, but reconstruction is set to finish at the end of 2004. Walk to the cable-car station from the Yakou bus stop for a quick ride up (one-way Y30, round-trip Y50).

YANGKOU (yángkǒu; 仰口). Take the tour bus, taxi, or bus #312 (Yangkou stop, then walk to Huayan Si stop), and head to the north side of Laoshan, where **Huayan Temple** (huáyán sì; 华严寺) beckons, fronted by a gate adorned with Buddhas bearing enigmatic smiles. It's an effortless 20min. hike to the temple, but the best scenery is at the bottom at the gate. The sharp, ragged mountains surround you like petals of a gigantic lotus flower. At the Yangkou bus stop, a 2hr. hike takes you through a series of deep-set caves, including **Mitian Caves** and **White Dragon Caves.**

JUFENG PEAK (jùfēng; 巨峰). A hike up to **Jufeng Peak,** the highest point of Laoshan, is a tortuous but thrilling affair, though few visitors are daring enough to risk the time and effort. The entire trek takes 3-5hrs., and should only be made when the weather is fair and the rocks not slippery. Your best bet is to find a driver who is willing to stop at **Dahedong** (dàhédōng; 大河东), climb to Houlaoqing (hòulǎoqīng; 后老清), and proceed from there.

YANTAI 烟台 ☎ 0535

Yantai should not be dismissed as a simple stopover on the way to the marvelous Penglai castle, Dalian, or Tianjin. Once nothing more than a jumble of grime-coated Communist concrete architecture, Yantai has undergone a modern makeover, a marked divergence from its gray past. An affluent residential district and vibrant nightlife along its beaches paint the city with a splatter of neon-glow, while a few outdoor markets and a neighborhood of well-preserved Western-style buildings give the city a surprising dose of charm.

⊏ TRANSPORTATION

Flights: Yantai Airport (yāntái jīchǎng; 烟台机场 ; ☎624 1330), 17km south of Yantai. A taxi from the city costs Y40. Shuttles (Y10) leave 2hr. before flights from the **CAAC ticket office**, 6 Dahaiyang Lu (☎624 5596), just south of the train station. Open daily 8am-6pm. To: **Beijing** (5-6 per day, Y590-800); **Changchun** (F, Y720); **Guangzhou** (Tu-Th, Y1650); **Hong Kong** (W, Sa; Y1870); **Ji'nan** (Tu-Su, Y230); **Shanghai** (2 per day, Y550); **Shenyang** (daily, Y620).

Trains: Yantai Train Station (yāntái huǒchē zhàn; 烟台火车站), 135 Bei Malu (☎624 3917 or 666 6111). To: **Beijing** (15hr.; 10am, 10pm; Y103-117); **Ji'nan** (8hr., several per day, Y38-66); **Qingdao** (4hr., 4-5 per day, Y22-36); **Shanghai** (20hr.; 5am, 8pm; Y88-190); **Xi'an** (15hr., 2 per day, Y96).

Buses: Yantai Bus Station (yāntái qìchē zhàn; 烟台汽车站), 86 Xi Dajie (☎624 2716 664 1441 or 666 6994), at Qingnian Lu, 2 blocks west and 1 block south of the train station. To: **Beijing** (13-16hr., 7 or 10:45am, Y105-150); **Ji'nan** (5½hr., 6am-noon, Y101); **Penglai** (1½hr., every 15-30min. 6am-6pm, Y10-14); **Qingdao** (4-5hr., every hr., Y42); **Shanghai** (15-16hr., 7:15am, Y193); **Tai'an** (6-10hr.; 6:45, 8:30am; Y74-102); **Tianjin** (15-16hr.; 7, 10:45am; Y103-113); **Weihai** (1hr., every 15min., Y17). The **Train Station Bus Station** (huǒchē zhàn qìchē zhàn; 火车站汽车站) is not a formal station but a collection of buses in front of the train station. Times and prices vary by bus. To: **Beijing** (15-17hr., several per day, Y150); **Ji'nan** (6½hr., every 40min., Y65); **Weihai** (1hr., every 15min. 5:30am-6pm, Y16-20).

Ferries: Yantai Passenger Ferry Terminal (yāntái kèyùn zhàn; 烟台客运站), 155 Bei Malu (☎674 1774), east of the train station. Ticket office is on Dahaiyang Lu, 50m south of Bei Malu. To **Dalian** (express 3hr., 4 per day 8:30am-2pm, Y192; regular 8hr., 6 per day 8am-9:30pm, Y72-560) and **Tianjin** (16hr., July-Aug. 4pm, Y76-214).

BEIJING

Local Transportation: Minibuses (Y5), **public buses** (Y1), and **double-decker buses** (Y1-4) go almost anywhere. Buses #2, 48, and 52 ply Nan Dajie; #10 and 17 from train station to the beaches to Yantai University; #21 and 22 to the Development Zone.

Taxis: Base fare Y5, each additional km Y1.3-1.5.

ORIENTATION AND PRACTICAL INFORMATION

Yantai spreads along the southern shore of the Yellow Sea. **Bei Dajie** (北大街) turns into **Bei Malu** (北马路) 5min. east of the train station and runs east-west, parallel to **Nan Dajie** (南大街). **Dahaiyang Lu** (大海洋路), **Xinanhe Lu** (西南河路), **Shengli Lu** (胜利路), and **Jiefang Lu** (解放路) all run north-south.

Travel Agency: CITS, 180-181B Jiefang Lu, 2nd fl. (☎623 4144), at Si Malu, south of the Bank of China. Organizes English tours of Penglai. Some staff members speak English, Japanese, or Korean. Open M-F 8:30am-5:50pm. **Yantai City Tourism Information Office,** 32 Hai Wan Jie (☎663 3222 or 663 3522; www.chinatravel168.com), right in front of the admissions into Yantai Hill Park.

Tourist Information: ☎624 7534.

Bank of China: 166 Jiefang Lu (☎623 8888), next to the International Hotel, south of Nan Dajie. Exchanges currency and traveler's checks. Credit card advances. Open M-F 8:30am-5pm.

PSB: 78 Shifu Jie, at Chaoyang Jie. **Foreign affairs office** (☎621 7744) is on the 5th fl. Open M-Sa 8:30am-5pm.

Pharmacy: Sailors' Pharmacy (hǎiyuán yàodiàn; 海员药店), 68 Bei Malu, in the same building complex as the Haiyuan Hotel. Open daily 8am-8pm.

Hospital: Yantaishan Hospital (yāntáishān yīyuàn; 烟台山医院), 1 Jiefang Lu (☎660 2108), at Binhai Bei Lu. Some English-speaking staff members. Open 24hr.

Internet Access: Starlight Internet Cafe (xīngguāng wǎngbā; 星光网吧; ☎662 3845), in an alley off Bei Dajie, on Xinglong Jie. Y1.5 per hr. **Hongxing Internet Cafe** (hóngxīng wǎngbā; 宏兴网吧), 8 Lifeng Jie, 2nd fl. Y2 per hr. Both open 8am-midnight.

Post Office: China Post, 172 Nan Dajie, at Dahaiyang Lu. EMS, IDD service, and Poste Restante. English signs. Open daily 8am-6pm.

Postal Code: 264000 or 264001.

ACCOMMODATIONS

Several hotels crowd the train and bus station exits. In general, the closer to the coast, the more expensive the rooms. All listed rooms have A/C and TV.

Joyful Fortune Hotel (yífú bīnguǎn; 怡福宾馆), 172 Bei Malu (☎621 6495). Slightly removed from the stations, but buses stop right outside. Furnishings in newly renovated rooms exude a luxury that's worth far more than the price you're paying. Prepare to be pampered: the complementary plate of plums and pears each morning is just the beginning. 24hr. hot water. Reservations recommended. Singles and doubles Y128-218. ❷

Scenic Hotel (fēngguāng bīnguǎn; 风光宾馆), 2 Haiwan Jie (☎620 7340; fax 622 6521). Old, rusty-looking building with rooms only slightly better. Bring your own slippers for stained carpets, bathrooms with somewhat mucky floors. Location close to the beach makes up for it though. Hot water 8am-11:30pm. Reservations recommended. Deposit Y80. Doubles Y200; triples Y280. Discounts possible Jan.-June and Oct.-Dec. ❸

Sailor Hotel (hǎiyuán bīnguǎn; 海员宾馆), 68 Bei Malu (☎ 624 3425), across from the train and ferry stations. The old hotel is labeled as the "International Seamen's Club," but the sailors look more like Korean businessmen. Well-kept rooms. Singles and doubles have 24hr. hot water. Singles Y100; doubles Y160-200; triples Y260. ❷

🔾 FOOD

Thoroughfares like **Bei Malu** and **Nan Dajie** and Yantai's oceanfront street, **Hai'an Lu,** are strewn with eateries that serve local seafood. Bars, including a spin-off of Beijing's **Keep In Touch,** line Chaoyang Jie north of Bei Malu. **Shengli Lu** offers great sit-down lunch and dinner options.

The popular **Haojiaxiang Restaurant** ❷ (háojiāxiāng fàndiàn; 豪佳香饭店), 51 Shifu Jie, in front of Taipingyang Hotel, specializes in dim sum. Arrive early or you may have to fight for seating. Have a plate of three fat dumplings (Y5), or check out the veggies (Y1-6). Bar opposite the entrance serves a great fresh fruit mix, starting at Y6—try the watermelon. (☎ 662 7588. Most dishes Y5-6. Open 24hr.) Eat the chicken at **Jincheng Restaurant** ❷ (jǐnchéng dàjiǔdiàn; 锦城大酒店), 174 Xi Nanhe Lu, and you'll wonder why people ever go to KFC. Just watch out for the slightly unnerving chicken head that comes with the plate. (☎ 661 7333. Most entrees Y14-30. Vegetable dishes Y3-10. Open 24hr.)

🔾🔾 BEACHES AND SIGHTS

Beaches, not sights, are Yantai's appeal. **Yantai Museum** (yāntáishì bówùguǎn; 烟台市博物馆), 257 Nan Dajie, at Shengli Jie, was built in 1884 by merchants from Fujian. The architecture and decoration warrant a closer look than the few displays. Colorful carvings of dragons, phoenixes, flowers, and figurines inspired by the *Romance of the Three Kingdoms*, *Eight Immortals*, and other Chinese folk stories adorn the buildings and the stone pillars. The main hall in the complex features a 19th-century temple built for the "Heavenly Queen" Mazu, goddess of the sea. (Take bus #1, 2, 3, 5, 12, 45, 48, or 52 to Hualian Dept. Store and walk down Nan Dajie. ☎ 622 2877. Open daily 9am-noon and 1:30-4:30pm. Y10, students Y5.)

North of Bei Malu, the intimate streets lined with Western-style architecture lead to **Yantai Hill Park** (yāntáishān gōngyuán; 烟台山公园). Park ticket includes admission into several buildings with rather small and boring exhibitions on Chinese nautical history. Spend your time roaming one of the two major trails to the summit. The climb is short and easy, and the grounds are meticulously maintained. The remains of a fort and a 1905 lighthouse are among the attractions. (Open daily summer 6:30am-7:30pm; winter 7am-5:30pm. Fort Y2. Lighthouse Y3 to climb, elevator-ride up the 6 stories Y5. Park Y20.)

No. 2 Beach (dì'èr hǎishuǐ yùchǎng; 第二海水浴场) pales in comparison to **No. 1 Beach** (dìyī hǎishuǐ yùchǎng; 第一海水浴场), with its attractive, clean path winding along the waterfront. The man-in-the-moon statue, in the next cove, is a popular spot for marriages and parties. The No. 2 is a bit down the road. This unfortunate runner-up is simply wanting: fewer people, scrawnier waves, more rocks, but lots of fishing boats docked offshore. The **Yellow Sea Beach** (huánghǎi hǎishuǐ yùchǎng; 黄海海水浴场) is even farther down the coast, and more secluded than the rest. After sunset, when the weather is fair, the coast comes alive as locals collect en masse along the waterfront, especially around No. 1 Beach. Dancing and karaoke are popular pastimes, as sprays of fountain water and lights illuminate the skies. All three beaches are accessible by bus #17 and free.

◪ DAYTRIP FROM YANTAI: PENGLAI

Buses to Penglai leave 6am-6pm from the Yantai Bus Station and the station on Bei Malu (1½hr.; every 15min. Y10, every 30min. Y14). Buses return from the Penglai Long-Distance Bus Station, 166 Zhonglou Bei Lu (☎564 2018), at Beiguan Lu (1½hr., every 30min. 6am-6pm, Y8). The admissions office is a 10min. walk or Y5 taxi ride away; just follow the tourists. ☎564 8106 or 564 3012; fax 566 6911. Pavilion open daily summer 7am-6pm; winter 8am-5pm. Cable car one-way Y10, round-trip Y18. Y70.

Those who know Chinese mythology will recognize the name Penglai (pénglái; 蓬莱). According to legends, Qin and Han Dynasty emperors, including Qin Shihuang and Han Wudi, came here to find the secrets of immortality and to appease the gods of the sea. Scholars also made the pilgrimage to Penglai, seeking not immortality but inspiration in the ocean and cliffs, and left legacies of poetry and calligraphy that now adorn many of the stones.

Visitors today may not find the fountain of youth or hoary immortals of many a folktale, but at least there's the **Penglai Pavilion** (pénglái gé; 蓬莱阁), perched atop oceanside cliffs in regal majesty. The garden- and temple-lined path to the pavilion coils over bridges and hills, rewarding patient trekkers with a beautiful, unobstructed ocean view. The two-story pavilion is closed to public viewing downstairs, but the upstairs exhibit, complete with requisite wax figures, is open. From the ledge, you can get a great view of temple tops and the ocean beyond. The grounds also host a fort, museums, and a maritime history exhibition.

A hike or cable car ride takes you up to **Haishi Pavilion,** from which you can take a path on the cliffs to the fantastically unexciting **demarcation line** between the Bohai and Yellow Seas. A pair of stone dragons, their teeth clenching a wire that supports a pearl-like sphere in the center, marks the boundary between the seas. Walk past the statues and take the steep path down to the thunderous waves below. At the base, you can scramble up rocks jutting out into the ocean or stroll in mid-air, upon a wood-plank path suspended from the cliff face.

Penglai is also famous for the **Penglai Mirage,** said to occur every few decades. When mist drapes over the cliffs and the sunlight hits at just the right angle, refraction of the light creates an illusion in the distance. Some see just a hazy mist, but others claim to glimpse entire cities through the clouds, complete with busy villagers, intricate temples, and mule-drawn carts.

WEIHAI 威海   ☎0631

Originally a fortified port from which the Chinese fleet fought off Japanese pirate raids, Weihai is now home to some of China's most beautiful beaches. The city became a dramatic battleground in 1895, when a smaller Japanese flotilla destroyed the Qing Dynasty's entire North Sea Fleet, the most advanced armada in Asia. Now eclipsed by the larger ports of Qingdao and Yantai, Weihai tenaciously holds onto its small niche as a hub for ferry connections to South Korea, which explains the sizable Korean population (especially businessmen). Shandong University, claiming a fair share of acreage in the city, promises throngs of students and a scholarly atmosphere. Not yet inundated by tourism, Weihai remains a residential haven for those who crave a slower, more leisurely way of life.

▣ TRANSPORTATION

Flights: Weihai Airport (wēihǎi jīchǎng; 威海机场), 80km away in neighboring Wendeng County, is accessible by taxi (1hr., Y70-80). **CAAC ticket office,** 24-1 Qingdao Bei Lu (☎531 7915), just south of the Bank of China. Open daily 8am-8pm. To: **Beijing** (7:50am, Y890); **Changchun** (2 per week, Y700); **Shanghai** (daily, Y760).

BEIJING

Trains: Weihai Train Station (wēihǎi huǒchē zhàn; 威海火车站), off Qingdao Zhong Lu in the south of the city. Take bus #1 or 12 from downtown. To **Beijing** (15hr., 9:30pm, Y126-246) and **Ji'nan** (13hr., 3-4 per day, Y110).

Buses: Weihai Long-Distance Bus Station (wēihǎi chángtú qìchē zhàn; 威海长途汽车站 ; ☎522 2867), at the intersection of Jiefang Lu and Dongcheng Lu, at the terminus of buses #3, 4, 6, 7, and 9. A kiosk next to the bus station's ticket counter also sells train and boat tickets. To: **Beijing** (15hr., 2-3 per day, Y155); **Ji'nan** (8hr., every 30min. 8am-6pm, Y90); **Qingdao** (3½hr., every 15-30min. 6am-6pm, Y50); **Yantai** (1½hr., every 15min. 6am-6pm, Y10-18).

Ferries: Weihai Passenger Ferry Terminal (wēihǎi kèyùn zhàn; 威海客运站), 53 Haibin Bei Lu (☎523 3220). To **Dalian** (7-8hr.; 9am, 8:30, 9pm; Y92-790) and **Inchon, South Korea** (16hr., 2-4 per day, Y750-1650).

Local Transportation: Buses usually run about 6am-7pm, major lines 6am-9pm. Fare Y1, exact change only. Bus #1 runs from the ferry terminal to the south of the city, along Qingdao Lu; #2 runs along Huangshan Lu; #4 hugs the coast along Haidongshan Lu; #7 runs from the International Beach, past the ferry, to the long-distance bus station; #12 runs to the train station.

Taxis: Base fare Y5, each additional km Y1.2-1.5.

■✷ 🤖 ORIENTATION AND PRACTICAL INFORMATION

The city sits on a rugged outcropping that juts into the Yellow Sea, forming a natural harbor with **Weihai Gulf** to the east. **Haibin Lu** (海滨路) runs along the gulf shore and intersects **Kunming Lu** (昆明路) in front of the ferry terminal. **Qingdao Lu** (青岛路), **Xinwei Lu** (新威路), and **Tongyi Lu** (统一路) are roughly parallel to Haibin Lu. **Wenhua Lu** (文化路) runs east-west from the **City Government Square** (shìfǔ guǎngchǎng; 市府广场) to the International Beach.

Travel Agencies: CITS, 96 Guzhai Dong Lu (☎581 8616), across from the broadcasting station. Open M-F 9am-5:30pm. **CTS,** 46 Haibin Beilu (☎520 3477 or 522 3856). Open 8am-6pm. **Weihai Ticket Center** (☎523 1874 or 523 1577), on Xinwei Lu, 100m north of Weihaiwei Mansion. Arranges tickets for tours, trains, buses, and flights. Open daily 8am-7pm.

Bank of China: 38 Xinwei Lu, next to the Weihai Communications Corporation. Exchanges currency and traveler's checks. Credit card advances. Open daily 8:30am-5:30pm.

PSB: 111 Chongqing Jie (foreigner affairs section ☎527 2253).

Hospital: Central Hospital (zhōng yīyuàn; 中医院), 29 Qingdao Bei Lu (☎532 1811), south of the Bank of China and north of the train station.

Internet Access: Internet Cafe (wǎngbā; 网吧), down the nondescript alley that leads to the Weihai Hotel, on the 3rd fl. of the building next to the hotel. Y20 deposit for Internet card. Y2 per hr. Open 24hr. Find university students, and you've got Internet cafes: A few hundred meters from Shandong University, **Jovial Internet Cafe** (kāixīn wǎngbā; 开心网吧) is at the intersection of Huoju Lu and Shenyang Lu.

Post and Telecommunications: China Post, 178-12 Tongyi Lu (☎580 7213). Open daily 9am-5pm. **China Telecom,** 40 Xinwei Lu. IDD/DDD service. Open daily summer 7:30am-6:30pm; winter 7:30am-5:30pm.

Postal Code: 264200.

ACCOMMODATIONS AND FOOD

Most of Weihai's accommodations are quite expensive, but a few bargains exist. Unfortunately, one of the cheapest options in town for foreigners, **Shandong University Foreign Students Dormitory** (shāndōng dàxué liúxuéshēng sùshè; 山东大学留学生宿舍), is currently undergoing renovation. The construction is set to be finished in the middle of 2005, but its completion will also mean a corresponding hike in prices. The dormitory is off Wenhua Xi Lu, just east of the International Beach; take bus #7 to the Shandong stop and walk through campus. For now, the **Shandong University Academics Building ❸** (shāndōng dàxué yuànshì lóu; 山东大学院士楼) can serve as a substitute. A house-turned-hotel, the Academics Building is right down the street from the remains of the Foreign Students Dormitory. Rooms are small but have standard amenities. (☎568 8328. TV, A/C. Doubles Y240, but discounts possible except July-Aug.)

Near the International Beach, on Shenyang Lu, a few hotels that look like holes-in-the-wall are surprisingly good deals, given their proximity to the waves. Try the **Cloud Dragon Hotel ❷** (yúnlóng bīnguǎn; 云龙宾馆), 1-4 Shenyang Lu. (☎569 6346, ext. 8888. 24hr. hot water, TV, A/C. Only 28 rooms, so call and grab early. Doubles Y160-200; triples Y200. Discounts up to 40% possible anytime except July-Sept.) **Xixiangjun Hotel ❶** (xǐxiàngjūn bīnguǎn; 喜相君宾馆), 31 Shenyang Lu, has recently renovated rooms that disappear quickly during summer. (☎130 3457 4559. Doubles Y70-160; triples Y40-100.) **Weihai Hotel ❸** (wēihǎi dàfàndiàn; 威海大饭店), 9 Dongping Jie, in an alley east of Tongyi Lu, is right next to a too-popular karaoke bar, a beer bar, and an Internet cafe. Rooms aren't entirely soundproof, so be prepared to fall asleep to the music of Teresa Teng or not-so-pleasurable imitations. (☎523 3888 or 366 5999. Singles Y198; doubles Y228-248; triples Y298.)

Restaurants are dispersed throughout the downtown area, especially on side streets off **Xinwei Lu.** Small seafood eateries congregate near the International Beach. Among the numerous Korean food options is **Han Xiangfu Restaurant ❷** (hán xiāng fú fàndiàn; 韩香福饭店), 44 Guangming Lu, east of Xinwei Lu. Amid the intimate atmosphere, diners can choose to sit down or go Korean and kneel on the floor. Meals range from Y6 to Y30, with small complementary dishes of radishes, pickled lettuce, and anchovies. (☎523 8667 or 599 0978. More extravagant meals with unpronounceable names Y60-80. Open daily 8am-10:30pm.) Locals frequent the **Sumptuous Garden Restaurant ❶** (fēngshēngyuán càiguǎn; 丰盛园菜馆), 61-1 Tongyi Lu, which serves up a variety of small dishes (xiǎocài, 小菜). Despite the cafeteria-style interior, the cooking is well-done and doesn't taste or feel like fast food. (☎520 1988 or 521 4449. Dishes Y3-5. Open daily 5:30am-9pm.)

SIGHTS AND BEACHES

Weihai itself has few notable sights, but a walk through its coastal streets provides a respite from the rushed pace of urban life. In the city center, south of the grandiose city government building, **People's Square** is a popular gathering spot, especially at night when ballroom dancers take to the streets.

The ■ **International Beach** (guójì hǎishuǐ yùchǎng; 国际海水浴场), on Beihai Lu, is perfect for strolling, swimming, or sunbathing. With fine smooth sands and crystal-clear waters, this beach alone makes a trip to Weihai worthwhile. Test your reflexes by catching crabs submerged in the sand. The nearby university guarantees that you'll only share the waters with students and locals—thankfully the tour buses have not yet found this secluded, natural cove. (Accessible by buses #7 and 12. Open 24hr. Inflatable boats Y10-20 per hr., water bikes Y25 per hr. Public changing room with shower and lockers Y5.)

▶ DAYTRIP FROM WEIHAI: LIUGONG ISLAND

Summer tourist ferries (20min., every 10min. 7am-5pm, round-trip Y40) shuttle visitors to the island from Weihai Tourist Dock (wēihǎi lǚyóu mǎtóu; 威海旅游码头; ☎ 523 1985), 100m south of the main ferry terminal. On foggy days, all boats remain docked; call ahead to check conditions. There are no accommodations on the island, so don't miss the last boat back to Weihai at 6pm.

Weihai's biggest attraction, the former fortress-island of Liugong (liúgōng dǎo; 刘公岛) lies 5km off the coast and played an important role in history not too long ago. Weakened by corruption and embezzlement in the Qing courts, the Chinese navy suffered humiliating defeats in the Opium Wars (p. 77). China was further embarrassed when its navy, one of the strongest in Asia, surrendered to the Japanese in 1895 here in Weihai Gulf. The war ended with the infamous Maguan Treaty, in which China ceded control of Dalian, Lushun, and Taiwan to Japan.

Not surprisingly, the island is best known for the **Museum of the 1894-95 Sino-Japanese War** (jiǎwǔ zhànzhēng bówùguǎn; 甲午战争博物馆), housed in the old offices of the North Sea Fleet. Photos of warships, a couple of battleship models, and relics salvaged from ships sunk in Weihai Gulf make up the few exhibits on display. Among the preserved artifacts is a bleak reminder of undiminished pride, despite the corrupt Qing government—the stateroom in which Ding Ruchang, commander of the naval fleet, committed suicide rather than surrender. (West of the ferry exit. Some English translations. Open daily 8:30am-5:30pm. Y30.)

Unless you share the museum designers' penchant for wax figures, travelers should bypass the **Sino-Japanese Sea War Hall** (jiǎwǔ hǎizhàn guǎn; 甲午海战馆). Visitors walk through modern exhibits that dedicated lots of wax and painted scenery to depict snapshots of history. Wait for the free tour if you don't want to walk around in the dark. (East of the ferry exit. Open daily 9am-5pm. Y30.) As an alternative to waxy statues, head up to the six 20-ton Krupp cannons atop the forested hills and hiking trails of **Liugong Island Park** (liúgōngdǎo gōngyuán; 刘公岛公园) on the rugged north coast. (Open 24hr. Y10. Cannons Y8-10.)

If the museums are too depressing, seek some solace in the form of delicious seafood. You'd be remiss to skip the several stalls of makeshift **restaurants** just past the museum, proudly displaying dozens of plastic buckets containing veritable aquariums of seafood. Treats include crab (Y5), bass (Y10), and much more rare and expensive delicacies like hammerhead shark and sea urchins.

THE NORTHEAST

China's northeast, known as Manchuria to Westerners and *Dōngběi* to the Chinese, is a region oft overlooked. Lacking in mainstream tourist attractions, its humble sights and industrial cities give way to rugged, unexplored landscapes, with a historical and cultural diversity that has been quietly brewing for thousands of years. Isolated for the most part from centerstage China, people don't come to this far corner to see flocks of foreign tourists, but to experience *Dōngběi*'s own "foreigner" status. Sandwiched by Russia, North Korea, and Mongolia, this border land and its people have embraced neighboring cultures to create multi-faceted communities completely outside traditional conceptions of China.

Lying at the geographic edges of a far-reaching empire, the northeast has always had a unique flair, different and even alien from the rest of China. Since the 3rd century BC, Han Chinese have been trying to control these hinterlands, but the region's plucky, stubborn, and just plain volatile denizens refused to give in. Over the centuries, Khitans, Manchus, Mongols, Jurchen, and a host of other peoples fought (and usually beat) the Chinese. In the 17th century, the Manchus burst through the Great Wall to found the Qing Dynasty, uniting Manchuria with the rest of China for the first time (see **Going Postal**, p. 76). Foreign invasions, civil wars, and modern ills like unemployment made the 20th century a particularly tumultuous time in the northeast. Nevertheless, its hardy, laid-back inhabitants continue to carve out life and fight the harsh winters upon the vast relentless land. Volcanic mountains, endless grasslands, forests of pines and birches, and jagged coastlines hint only at the beginning of what the northeast has to offer.

HIGHLIGHTS OF THE NORTHEAST

PEEK INTO THE COLONIAL PAST of **Harbin** (p. 224), as you stroll past the 19th-century European-style buildings, the last remnants of Russian influence.

CATCH A GLIMPSE OF KIM IL SUNG, or at least his picture, while traversing along the border of North Korea in **Dandong** (p. 258).

CAMP ON A VOLCANO at the shores of a giant crater lake in wild and unexplored **Changbaishan Mountain** (p. 249).

HEILONGJIANG 黑龙江

Despite China's northernmost province's extreme climates and occasional industrial ugliness, Heilongjiang has seen Russians, Koreans, Manchus, and sub-Arctic minorities within its ice-rimmed borders, turning this unlikely region into something of a cultural crossroads. Harbin's grand onion-domed cathedrals, Jingpo Lake's luminous waters, and Wudalianchi's volcanic terrain can't quite block out the aesthetic drab of mammoth-sized factories and gloomy commercial districts, earning the province a rather cold, grimy reputation. But for those willing to venture into the deep north and look past the concrete, Heilongjiang has a graceful side. Be it in sweltering heat or in snowbound winter, the majestic peaks and sprawling plains are testaments to its isolated beauty.

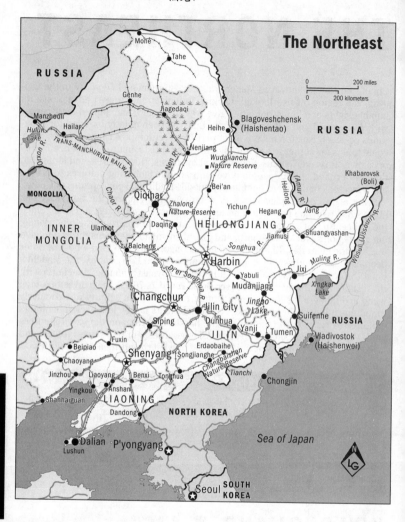

The Northeast

HARBIN 哈尔滨 ☎ 0451

Once the "town of fishing nets," Harbin is now often dubbed the "Moscow of the Orient" for its heroic Russian architecture, or "Little Paris" for its acute fashion sense. Were it not for the 1890s construction of the Far Eastern Railway, Harbin might still be the sleepy village that it was before the turn of the 20th century. Instead, Harbin is now the second-largest city in the northeast and capital of Heilongjiang province, with a population 4.5 million. Much of the city was built in the early 20th century by European expats, and the downtown area exhibits an eclectic mix of neo-classical Russian domes, traditional Chinese architecture, and industrial concrete eyesores amid the broad and lively avenues.

Most people visit Harbin in the winter to see its world-famous ice sculptures. The six-month-long season easily reaches lows of -30° C (-22° F), though hot and heavy Russian dishes, accompanied by a healthy shot of vodka, warm up all chilly fingers and toes. Harsh winters give way to pleasant summers, filling Harbin's Sun Island and Songhua River with tourists in search of a cool respite from the heat.

⬛ TRANSPORTATION

Flights: Harbin's **Taiping International Airport** (tàipíng guójì jīchǎng; 太平国际机场 ; ☎8289 4219), 45km southwest of the city center. Airport shuttles (Y20) leave from the CAAC ticket office about 2hr. before departures; taxis cost Y120-150. Plane tickets can be booked at the **CAAC Harbin Ticket Office** (mínháng shěngjú hā'ěrbīn shòupiàochù; 民航省局哈尔滨售票处), 99 Zhongshan Lu (24hr. domestic ☎8265 1188, international 8266 1924 or 8289 6874). Take bus #2 to Tian E Hotel. Open daily 6am-9pm. To: **Beijing** (at least 10 per day, Y960); **Dalian** (3-4 per day, Y840); **Guangzhou** (2 per day, Y2540); **Hong Kong** (daily, Y1750); **Nanjing** (2-3 per day, Y1650); **Qingdao** (2 per day, Y950); **Shanghai** (3-4 per day, Y1560); **Shenyang** (2-3 per day, Y510); **Tianjin** (5 per week, Y990); **Xi'an** (2 per day, Y1680); **Yantai** (2-3 per day, Y950). International flights to **Seoul, South Korea** (daily, Y1820).

Trains: Virtually every train passing through Harbin stops at both stations; the **East Train Station,** however, is not of much use to travelers. **Harbin Central Station** (hā'ěrbīn zhàn; 哈尔滨站 ; ☎8643 4152 or 8643 1642), at the intersection of Songhuajiang Jie and Hongjun Jie, near Museum Sq. Travelers should buy tickets in advance; dealing with the station's busy ticket and information booths is not very pleasant. Printed schedules (Y5) are particularly hard to find. Some station employees provide information and allow you to buy tickets without standing in line for a Y30-50 commission; **Harbin Railway International Tourist Agency** (see **Travel Agencies,** p. 226) is another option. To: **Beijing** (13-24hr., at least 8 per day, Y88); **Changchun** (4½hr., 10 per day, Y22); **Dalian** (13hr., 2 per day, Y32); **Dandong** (13hr., 9:40pm, Y55-140); **Heihe** (11hr., 2 per day, Y56) via **Bei'an** (6-8hr., Y14); **Mudanjiang** (4½-7hr., 6 per day, Y30); **Qiqihar** (3hr., 10 per day, Y22); **Shanghai** (29hr., 10:30pm, Y276); **Shenyang** (8hr., 12 per day, Y38). To go to **Russia,** you must travel to **Suifenhe** (6hr., Y76).

Buses: The **Nangang Highway Public Bus Station** (nángǎng gōnglù kèyùn zhàn; 南岗公路客运站), just opposite the train station, halfway between Hongjun Jie and Haiguan Jie. The station is divided into 2 sub-stations, whose mutual enmity is reflected by the fact that the corridor leading from one to the other is marked "toilet." The station to the right serves state-run buses that go longer distances. Open daily 8am-5pm. To: **Changchun** (4hr., every 30min., Y76); **Dalian** (14hr., 3:40pm, Y178); **Mudanjiang** (5hr., every hr., Y81); **Qiqihar** (5hr., every hr., Y61); **Tonghua** (2hr., 6:30am, Y100). The smaller station (☎363 4528) to the left has deluxe buses with A/C. Open daily 5am-6:30pm. To: **Jiamusi** (4½hr., every hr., Y90) via **Two Dragon Mountain** (1½hr.); **Mudanjiang** (4hr., every hr., Y58) via **Yabuli** (3hr.); **Qiqihar** (3-4hr., 9 per day, Y60); **Shenyang** (7hr., every 1½hr. 8am-4pm, Y140); **Tonghua** (1½hr., every hr., Y24); **Wudalianchi** (5hr.; 7:30am, 1:30pm), Y69).

Local Transportation: On routes numbered 28 or lower, fare is Y1-2, with A/C (indicated by a snowflake next to the route number) Y2. All **buses** run through train station. Bus #2 travels along Hongjun Lu and Zhongshan Dajie from the train station past the CAAC ticket office; #6 goes from the train station to the temple area; #8 runs between Daoli and Nangang districts; #10 connects the zoo with Museum Sq. and the temple area. **Minibuses** are numbered 50-99 and in the 300s. Fare Y1-2. Minibus #64 runs between Museum Sq. and Daoli district; #338 and 343 go from the hub on Tielu Jie near the train station to the Germ Warfare Base via the zoo. **Trolley buses** (Y1-2) are numbered in the 100s. Trolley #101 runs between Dongli and Daoli districts via Museum Sq.; #104 runs from Daowai district to the temple area; #109 goes from Daowai district to the Children's Park via the train station. All buses run approx. 5am-8pm.

Ferry: Boats cross the Songhua River from the Flood Control Monument and travel to Sun Island from the riverbank along Stalin Park in Daowai district. Cheaper passenger boats (Y2) depart from the docks beneath the funicular railway; taxi-boats (Y10) run from farther down the river. Boats run 6am-1hr. after dusk.

Cable car: Run daily 8:30am-5:30pm from the station in Stalin Park to Sun Island. Round-trip Y70, children 1.1-1.4m free.

Taxis: Base fare Y7-8, each additional km Y1.6-1.9. Taxis between districts Y9-20.

✈ 🛈 ORIENTATION AND PRACTICAL INFORMATION

The railway is the city's economic and geographic center, but crossing the tracks to get from one district to another can be cumbersome. The **main train station** and **Museum Square** (bówùguǎn guǎngchǎng; 博物馆广场) comprise the center of the commercial **Nangang District** (南岗区), bisected by **Xi Dazhi Jie** (西大直街) and **Dong Dazhi Jie** (东大直街). The latter leads toward the distant **Taiping District** (太平 区) in the east via the **temple area**. The city's architectural treasure trove, **Daoli District** (道里区), is on the west side of the railroad, bisected by **Zhongyang Dajie** (中央 大街). Just east of Daoli district is its counterpart, **Daowai District** (道外区), full of street markets and Russian architecture. Both Dao districts rest on the bank of the **Songhua River** (sōnghuā jiāng; 松花江), which marks the northern border of the city; beyond it lie the attractive **Sun Island** and **Siberian Tiger Parks**. In the confusing cobweb of Harbin's alleys, rivers, channels, and railways, it can be difficult to find other districts. Hop on a bus to get to the southern **Dongli District** (动力区), home to the zoo and botanical garden, and to **Pingfang District** (平房区), farther south and home to the Germ Warfare Base. Harbin is in a constant state of road construction and renaming, but this shouldn't affect navigation too much.

Travel Agencies: CITS (domestic ☎5366 7388, international 5366 1919), Yuanda Business Bldg., 101 Jianshi Jie, 10th fl., 10min. from train station. Arranges tours to ski resorts and ice sculpture festivals. Also has tour packages for Russia (does not process US passports). English-, Japanese-, Korean-, and French- speaking staff. Has branches in most major hotels. Open daily 8:30am-5:30pm. **Harbin Railway International Tourist Agency** (hā'ěrbīn tiědào guójì lǚxíngshè; 哈尔滨铁道国际旅行社), 8 Tielu Jie, 7th fl. (☎5364 3264 or 8469 6543), behind the Hushi Bldg., in the Kunlun Hotel; look for the swarm of minibuses. Sells domestic as well as international tickets. To **Khabarovsk** (Y1750) and **Vladivostok, Russia** (Y1400). Open M-F 8am-5pm. **Heilongjiang Overseas Tourist Corp.,** Hushi Bldg., 182 Haiguan Jie, 11th fl. (☎5366 1159; fax 5366 1190), next to the train station. In winter, they can arrange 1-day trips to Yabuli, Two Dragon Mountain, and other ski-resorts (Y180 includes transportation and ski-pass), along with independent ski-trips for groups of 10 or more (Y300 and up). Organizes flights to Russia starting at Y900 and trains starting at Y600. Open M-F 8:30am-5pm.

Bank of China: 19 Hongjun Jie (☎ 5363 3518), near Museum Sq. in a clearly marked, tall building. Exchanges currency (1st fl.) and traveler's checks (M-F, 3rd fl.). Credit card advances. Open M-F 8:30am-noon and 1-5pm, Sa-Su 8:30am-4pm. Convenient branch at 29 Xishi Daojie (☎2463 7043), between Zhongyang Dajie and Shangzhi Dajie. Open M-F 8:30am-5pm, Sa-Su 9am-4pm. Many other branches on Zhongyang Dajie.

PSB: 9 Hongxing Jie (☎8466 1144), near the intersection of Zhongyang Dajie and Jingwei Jie. Foreign affairs, 26 Duan Jie (☎8464 3497), is hidden behind the building. Processes visa extensions. Open daily 8:30-11:30am and 1:30-5pm.

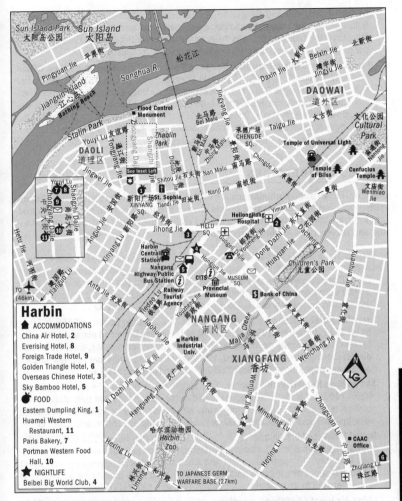

Harbin

⌂ ACCOMMODATIONS
China Air Hotel, 2
Everising Hotel, 8
Foreign Trade Hotel, 9
Golden Triangle Hotel, 6
Overseas Chinese Hotel, 3
Sky Bamboo Hotel, 5

⬤ FOOD
Eastern Dumpling King, 1
Huamei Western
   Restaurant, 11
Paris Bakery, 7
Portman Western Food
   Hall, 10

★ NIGHTLIFE
Beibei Big World Club, 4

NORTHEAST

Bookstore: Xinhua Bookstore, at the intersection of Hongzhuan Jie and Zhongyang Dajie. Open daily 9am-7:30pm.

Market: A couple of markets are along Zhongyang Dajie. **Third Grocery Store** (zhōngyāng shāngchéng; 中央商城), 118 Zhongyang Dajie. Open daily 9am-9pm.

Pharmacy: Zhongyang Dajie is dotted with 24hr. pharmacies. **Baofeng Medical Co.** (☎8465 0129) has a multi-story pharmacy on Zhongyang Dajie at Xi Shisi Daojie.

Hospital: Heilongjiang Medical University Hospital (hēilóngjiāng yīkēdàxué fùshǔ yīyuàn; 黑龙江医科大学附属医院 ; ☎5364 3829), at the intersection of Youzheng Jie and Longjiang Jie.

Internet Access: Many small Internet cafes branch off Zhongyang Dajie. **First Degree Dimension Internet Cafe** (yīdù kōngjiān wǎngbā; 一度空间网吧), 27 Hongzhuan Jie, has over 60 computers. Y2 per hr. In **Nangang,** 2 cafes at 49 Xuefu Lu (open daily

8:30am-10pm) and 399 Guogeli Dajie (open daily 8:30am-8pm), near McDonald's. Building facing the train station houses a fast, clean, and amazingly quiet 24hr. Internet cafe; enter the courtyard between the entrances to Beibei Hotel and the bus station. Y3 per hr. Small, noisy hole-in-the-wall cafes are ubiquitous; usually Y2 per hr.

Post and Telecommunications: Nangang Post and Telecommunications Office (nángǎng yóudiànjú; 南岗邮电局), 104 Dongda Zhi Jie (☎5363 3137), just east of Museum Sq. at Guogeli Dajie. Film processing and currency exchange. Open daily summer 8am-7pm; winter 8am-6:30pm. A large post office, 12 Tiedao Lu, near the train station. Open daily 8am-10pm. Open daily until 8pm. In Daoli district, on Xi Shisi Daojie. Open daily summer 8am-6:30pm; winter 8am-6pm. All have EMS and Poste Restante.

Postal Code: 150001 for Poste Restante, 150000 for the city.

ACCOMMODATIONS

Most of Harbin's accommodations are expensive, but a few bargains can be found. The most conveniently located hotels cluster around the main train station and Zhongyang Dajie. During the Ice Lantern Festival, the prices may more than double and reservations are highly recommended.

Foreign Trade Hotel (wàimào dàjiǔdiàn; 外贸大酒店), 9 Xi San Daojie (☎8464 8568). A 2min. walk from the Ice Lantern Festival and extremely near historical Zhongyang Dajie. Comfortable rooms may be dimly lit, but are a good size with large windows and slightly dusty, dark mahogany furniture. Travel agency, store, and dining room on the 1st fl. 24hr. hot water and A/C. Doubles Y120; prices negotiable. ❷

Everising Hotel (xīnhéng jī bīnguǎn; 新恒基宾馆), 38 Xitou Daojie (☎8488 1000 or 8488 1111; fax 8488 1199), 1 block east of Zhongyang Dajie and across from the Ice Lantern Festival. 5 reasons for excitement: the 1913 Russian building, the central Daoli district location, breakfast included, free local calls, and individual A/C remotes for each (very green) room. Doubles Y160-268, depending on season. ❸

Sky Bamboo Hotel (tiān zhú bīnguǎn; 天竹宾馆), 6 Songhuajiang Jie (☎5363 7261 or 5363 7262; fax 5364 3720), opposite and to the right of the main train station. Bellboy out front ushers you into comfy rooms with a wide range of amenities. Best value near the train station. Doubles Y100, with A/C Y168; triples Y180; quads Y200. ❷

Beibei Hotel (běiběi dàjiǔdiàn; 北北大酒店), 2 Chunshen Jie (☎8257 0960 or 8257 0963), right across from the main train station. You can't get much closer to transportation than this. The rooms are bright and functional, but accompanied by busy street noise that staff claim is barely audible. Well-advertised Y100 rooms (see red banner at entrance) tend to be booked solid. Doubles Y78, with bath Y100, with A/C Y130. ❷

China Air Hotel (zhōngháng zhāodàisuǒ; 中航招待所), 122 Youzheng Jie (☎8257 6288), 200m from Guogeli Dajie, across from the hospital. Don't get confused: Youzheng Lu extends on both sides of Guogeli Dajie. Economical, especially for this area, and comfortable rooms. As an alternative to the elevator and normal staircase, have fun climbing the winding staircase to the right. All rooms have A/C. Hot water 7pm-11am. Doubles Y150; triples Y150; quads Y200. ❷

Overseas Chinese Hotel (huáqiáo fàndiàn; 华侨饭店), 72 Hongjun Jie (☎8257 1888). From the train station, walk 5min. up Hongjun Jie (3 blocks); it's on the right, opposite the glass towers of the North Sinoway Hotel. The range of prices doesn't quite capture the extremely wide range in rooms. Y108 doubles are spartan and look like they are crumbling, with dank, dim bathrooms. Y128 rooms across the hall are a significant upgrade. Y168 rooms in a separate tower and probably not worth the price. Y128 and Y168 doubles have A/C and 24hr. hot water. ❷

Golden Triangle Hotel (jīnsānjiǎo bīnguǎn; 金三角宾馆), 15 Zhujiang Lu (☎8232 7101), a few blocks from the Swan Hotel; take a bus along Zhongshan Lu to Tian E Hotel. Distinguished by the glass pyramid on its side, this hotel is vaguely reminiscent of the Louvre. Rooms are surprisingly unpolished but cheap. 3-bed dorms Y40; singles Y60; doubles Y100, with A/C 160. Prices negotiable. ❶

FOOD AND ENTERTAINMENT

Local specialties in Harbin tend toward the rich and hearty. **Mongolian hotpot** (shuàn yángròu; 涮羊肉) is a do-it-yourself mutton dish (usually Y50 for an ample dinner for two). Local *jiǎozi* (dumplings) are first-rate and available everywhere. The price range of a restaurant is easily determined with a system unique to Harbin: the more **lanterns** in front of an establishment, the more expensive the meal. Most restaurants have red lanterns; blue lanterns indicate Muslim restaurants, which serve a range of mutton dishes; white lanterns with Korean flags indicate a Korean restaurant, notable for healthy *bibimbap* (bànfàn; 拌饭). The best places to satisfy your appetite for Western or fast food are **Zhongyang Dajie** and the corner of **Guogeli Dajie** and **Dong Dazhi Jie,** near Museum Sq. The latter area, especially on small streets behind the main post office, houses a peculiar Little Russia, in which borscht (dubbed "red soup;" Y3-10) and *golubtsi* (cabbage rolls; Y3-5) are standard dinner items. **Zhaolin Park,** at the end of Zhaoyang Jie, hosts the Ice Lantern Festival in the winter, but also peddles extremely cheap outdoor food for Y1-5 during the summer. Pick and choose from fried scorpion and starfish to Xinjiang bread and bubble tea. (Open 9am-9pm. Park admission Y2).

For some dancing and rollerskating fun, follow the techno music and glow-in-the-dark murals to the **Beibei Big World Club** (běiběi hànbīng dīshìgāo; 北北旱冰迪 士高), in an underground passageway on the corner of Hongjun Jie at Tielu Jie, across from the train station. (Open daily 9am-midnight. Cover Y20 includes skate rental.) If you'd prefer to not shell out the expensive cover, grab your own pair of skates and head out to **City Government Square** (shì zhèngfǔ guǎngchǎng; 市政府广 场), where people gather in celebration of good weather. For movie buffs, the square by Xijiu Daojie has outdoor screenings at night (starting at 8-9pm).

Eastern Dumpling King (dōngfāng jiǎozi wáng; 东方饺子王), 39 Zhongyang Dajie (☎8465 3920 or 8465 3921). Food fit for a king. Even at off-peak hours, this branch of the well-known chain draws a persistent crowd. The cabbage and pork dumplings (báicài zhūròu shuǐjiǎo; 白菜猪肉水饺) are a sure bet. A number of other locations throughout town. Entrees Y4-60. Tea Y10. Open daily 10am-10pm. ❷

Portman Western Food Hall (bōtèmàn xī cāntīng; 波特曼西餐厅), 63 Xiqi Daojie (☎8468 6888), overlooking an open-air seating area off Zhongyang Dajie. This snazzy little joint has an English menu of salads, pasta, burgers, pizza, and baby-back ribs amid a few Russian specialties, including a whole roast pig, apple and all (Y300). Live music noon-midnight. Entrees Y10-70. Open daily 11am-2am. ❷

Paris Bakery (bālí miànbāo fáng; 巴黎面包坊), 4 Xi Dazhi Jie (☎5362 6838) and 174 Zhongyang Dajie (☎8464 9109). Escape the bustling streets of China in this small, cornerstone "Parisian" cafe with jazz music, photos of Paris, coffee (Y5-20), and a small sampling of pastries and ice cream (Y5-7). Open daily 9am-9pm. ❶

Huamei Western Restaurant (huáméi xīcāntīng; 华梅西餐厅), 112 Zhongyang Dajie (☎8467 5574 or 8467 5573), directly across from the Modern Hotel. Huamei offers Russian specialties and other fine continental dishes like french fries. Try the *golubtsi* (Y15) and borscht (Y3). Entrees Y15-30. Open daily 11am-8pm. ❷

◎ SIGHTS

WINTER SIGHTS. The **Ice Lantern Festival** (bīng dēng jié; 冰灯节) takes place each winter, and a remarkable number of tropic-dwellers make it all the way to Harbin for this exceptional ice show in **Zhaolin Park** (zhàolín gōngyuán; 兆林公园), near the end of Zhongyang Dajie in Daoli district. Officially, the festival runs January 5 to February 25, but the ice sculptures that glow from within (with the help of colored lights) can be viewed from the end of December until early March. *(Admission to the park during the festival Y50; in summer Y2. Tickets to special exhibits up to Y200; buying through a travel agency may be easier and cheaper, especially for groups.)*

The Ice Lantern Festival is not without competition. A short ferry ride away, the run-down **Sun Island Park** (tàiyáng dǎo gōngyuán; 太阳岛公园) houses the **Snow Sculpture Festival,** which occurs year-round, but tends to only attract confused winter tourists or overheated summer visitors looking for a place to cool off. *(Park Y10, snow sculptures Y50.)* Many come to Harbin to ski at the nearby resorts. The most prominent skiing areas are **Two Dragon Mountain** (èrlóng shān; 二龙山), on the road to Jiamusi (includes summer skiing facilities), **Jade Fountain Ski Resort** (yùquán huáxuě chǎng; 玉泉滑雪场), and **Yabuli Ski Resort** (yàbùlì huáxuě chǎng; 亚布力滑雪场), on the road to Mudanjiang (p. 236). Each area is fairly difficult to reach using public transport, especially during the low season. The best option may be to go through CITS, which offers skiers a convenient Y200 per day deal.

For the vertically challenged, pony rides and sleighing are slippery but fun diversions when the Songhua River freezes over. There may be no carols, but you can hum along to the ballroom music as locals dance on the frozen riverbanks.

ZHONGYANG DAJIE (zhōngyāng dàjiē; 中央大街). The oldest street in Harbin, the pedestrian Zhongyang Dajie is unique for its cobblestones and historic Russian buildings. The street was originally paved with stones so that it could support the weight of heavy merchandise and railway materials as they were transported from the dock to the train. Zhongyang Dajie is now a haven from taxis and city pollution. Locals stroll the street, loll in cafes, or enjoy street performances. As you wander the area, don't forget to look down at the 1350m of cobblestones. Each stone cost US$1, a price equivalent to the annual salary of an average Chinese citizen at the time of its construction.

The street ends at **Stalin Park** (sīdàlín gōngyuán; 斯大林工园) extending along the riverbank. The **Flood Control Monument** (fánghóng shènglì jìniàn tǎ; 防洪胜利纪念塔), a curious combination of classic Greek and social realist styles, stands here in commemoration of the victory of man over nature during the Songhua River deluge of 1957. Two additional water-level marks on the monument mark the 1932 flood (ignored due to the Japanese invasion) and the 1998 record-high level.

CHURCH OF SAINT SOPHIA (shèng suǒfēiyà jiàotáng; 圣索菲亚教堂). This massive Russian church sticks out like a sore but beautiful thumb in an otherwise commercial area. It's almost hard to believe that when the church was first built in 1907, the nearest building was on today's Zhongyang Dajie, and the plains to the north sprawled uninhabited all the way to Europe. Now in the thick of the metropolis, the decaying church is home to a fascinating photographic exhibition on Russian influences in Harbin, with a limited gallery of artwork and antiques circling the back of the church. Come at night to see the structure illuminated by evening lights. *(On Toulong Jie. Open daily 8:30am-9:30pm, Y25, students and after 7pm Y15.)*

JAPANESE GERM WARFARE BASE, 731ST DIVISION (qīnhuá rìjūn qīsānyī bùduì zuìzhèng chénlièguǎn; 侵华日军 731 部队罪证列馆). This solemn museum is located on the grounds of a former secret biological warfare research station built by the Japanese army in 1933 to conduct tests on Chinese subjects. Under the rather ironic name of the "Kuantong Army of Epidemic Prevention and Water Supply Unit," the site tested human reactions to tuberculosis, bubonic plague, heat endurance, and amputation. Because the troops blew up the camp before fleeing in 1945, the exhibits are primarily limited to illustrations and videotaped personal accounts of the horrors these grounds have witnessed. The exhibits also include some controversial documents implying that the US government traded the freedom of the perpetrators for their research results. *(20km south of the city center. 1hr. bus ride on #337 or 343 from Tiedao Lu near the train station to the terminus. English and Chinese captions. Open daily summer 9am-6:30pm; winter 9am-6pm. Last admission 1hr. earlier. Y20, students Y10.)*

TEMPLE AREA. These temples are a welcome alternative to the Slavic atmosphere of Harbin. Near the Cultural Park, the doors of the **Temple of Universal Light** (pǔzhào sì; 普照寺) may be closed (try the little dirt road passage to the left). Those who make it in will see beautiful traditional constructions and a large ceremony if you're lucky. *(☎8252 2635. Open daily 7am-3pm. Free.)* Nearby, in the **Pagoda Courtyard** (tǎ yuàn; 塔院), listen to the chanting *(ah-mi-tuo-fo)* of diligent monks. *(Open daily 8am-4pm. Y10.)* The **Temple of Bliss** (jílè sì; 极乐寺) attracts more visitors despite its rather mundane look. *(Open daily 8am-4pm. Y10, booths within may charge an additional Y2.)* Past the noisy intersection and a 10min. walk down Wenmiao Jie (文庙街), the **Confucius Temple** (wén miào; 文庙) is visited by few, but praised by all. It is home to the only jade bridges in Harbin. *(Open daily 8am-4pm. Y15.)*

RENT-A-TAXI. When getting a taxi, agree on a price beforehand to avoid being taken on a longer ride than you bargained for. Ask around for average prices. You can also *bāo chē* (包车), or book a taxi for the entire day (Y100)—useful when seeing many sights around the city. Some taxi drivers can also serve as travel guides. Always jot down the license number and name. To be extra cautious, write up a mini contract with the driver.

◪ DAYTRIP FROM HARBIN: YABULI 亚布力

Buses depart from Harbin to Mudanjiang (4hr., every hr., Y58) via Yabuli (3hr.). A taxi ride (60km, Y30-35) brings visitors to the skiing grounds. Arriving in Yabuli via public transportation is difficult during low season. To return, take a taxi to Yabuli town and then catch a bus. After 4:30pm, transportation is difficult to find; take a taxi (15km, Y25) to the Harbin-Mudanjiang Hwy. and hunt for passing buses (last bus approx. 8:30pm.) Admission Y10. Skiing pass 2hr. Y100, half day Y150; ask around for better package deals from employees. Ski rental from hotel Y100-200. Chairlift and luge ride Y50.

If you want to ski in China, you want Yabuli. In the summer, Yabuli is just another sleepy town, but in the winter it comes alive, attracting skiers from all over China. The infrastructure is somewhat less developed than it could be, given that Yabuli hosted the 1996 Asian Winter Games, but it's about as good as skiing gets in China. Buses drop off confused skiers in the small town of Yabuli situated on flat plains, but the skiing area, where posh hotels line both sides of the road, is up the village road. Ski-lifts ascend four levels, although the highest is restricted to experts. A **luge** facility is up the little road to the right. Speeding down **the longest tobogganing lane in the world** can quench anyone's thirst for adventure.

Yabuli is desolate in the summer, with only the most expensive hotels open for business conferences. Rooms are but slightly cheaper than winter ones, which are not only sky-high in cost but often booked solid. Those who opt to spend the night can try the **Yalin Hostel ❸** (yàlín zhāosuǒ; 亚林招所), one of the affordable places

NORTHEAST

in town. (☎ 139 4512 4373. Dorms Y200 and under. Open Oct.-Mar.) A more neighbor- and wallet-friendly option is to bed down on one of the 50- to 60-person *kàng* (炕), communal heated platform beds, located near the base of the mountain.

QIQIHAR 齐齐哈尔 ☎ 0452

Like many cities in Heilongjiang, Qiqihar was a Russian outpost in the early years of the Trans-Siberian Railroad. Unfortunately, it boasts none of the graceful Russian architecture of Harbin. Qiqihar's designers seemed to prefer unpaved roads and masses of concrete. Cool name aside, if you do go to Qiqihar, it's probably for the city's proximity to the Zhalong Nature Reserve.

▐ TRANSPORTATION

Flights: Qiqihar Airport (qíqíhā'ěr fēijīchǎng; 齐齐哈尔飞机场 ; ☎ 234 6338), 15km from downtown Qiqihar. Taxis (Y20) to the airport take 20min. **CAAC ticket office** (☎ 618 6618 or 246 8444), inside the White Crane Hotel. Open daily 8am-5:30pm. To **Beijing** (Tu, Th, Sa 7:20am; Y1110) and **Shanghai** (Tu and F 4:30pm, Y1850).

Trains: Qiqihar Train Station (qíqíhā'ěr huǒchē zhàn; 齐齐哈尔火车站 ; ☎ 212 3111 or 292 9115), on the corner of Zhanqian Dajie and Longhua Lu. Luggage storage (up to Y8 per day) in the inconspicuous basement waiting room. Ingenious English signs will entertain you while you wait. To: **Beijing** (21hr., 4 per day, Y81-182); **Changchun** (7hr., 3 per day, Y34-66); **Dalian** (19hr., 5 per day, Y70-73); **Harbin** (3-6hr., 17 per day, Y22-50); **Manzhouli** (11hr., daily, Y61).

Buses: Qiqihar Long-Distance North Bus Station (qíqíhā'ěr chángtú kèyùn běi zhàn; 齐齐哈尔长途客运北站), about 10min. from the train station on Longhua Lu (☎ 213 3166). Open daily 5:30am-4:30pm. To: **Heihe** (5:30pm, Y79) and **Wudalianchi** (6hr., 8:30am, Y40). Buses to **Harbin** (Y62) and **Shenyang** depart from the train station (☎ 212 6012). Both the **East Bus Station** and **West Bus Station,** off Longnan Jie, near the North Bus Station, serve local towns and are not really of use to tourists.

Local Transportation: Most **buses** run 6am-7pm; buses service major streets until 10pm. Fare Y1. On Longhua Lu and Longsha Lu, all buses except #8 and 12 go from the train station to Longsha Park; hop on either bus to get from one side of town to the other. Bus #100 runs from West Bus Station to **Zhalong** (fare Y6); the last bus leaves Zhalong at around 1pm.

Taxis: Base fare Y6, sporadically negotiable to Y5; each additional km Y1.5. Destinations within city limits up to Y10. One-way to Zhalong costs Y20-25 for locals and Y25 and up for tourists. Be sure to bargain your way down.

✳ ▐ ORIENTATION AND PRACTICAL INFORMATION

Every visitor in Qiqihar goes to northern **Longsha Lu** (龙沙路) for food and southern **Longhua Lu** (龙华路) for shelter. Both streets run near the train station and are the backbone of Qiqihar's tourism industry; they lead right to **Longsha Park** (lóngshā gōngyuán; 龙沙公园) and to the city center, concentrated around **Bukui Dajie** (卜奎大街). The area between Bukui Dajie and the park is filled with perpetually busy little streets, stuffed with street vendors and travel agencies.

Travel Agencies: Xinsheng Lu and the surrounding area between Longsha Park and Bukui Dajie is dense with travel agencies, all of which organize English and Russian tours to the Zhalong Nature Reserve. **Qiqihar Great Light Travel Company** (qíqíhā'ěr guāngdà lǚyóu gōngsī; 齐齐哈尔光大旅游公司), Jinggu Hotel, 35 Gongyuan Lu, Rm.

201, across from the Xinsheng Lu entrance to Longsha Park. The **Dongfang Travel Company**, on Bukui Dajie, is located across from the PSB and takes passport photos for the visa dept. Open daily 8-11:30am and 1:30-4pm.

Bank of China: 3 Bukui Dajie (☎240 9933), in a towering building near Longhua Lu. Exchanges currency and traveler's checks (M-F). Credit card advances. Open M-F 8am-6pm, Sa-Su 8:30am-4:30pm.

PSB: ☎242 5981. On the corner of Bukui Dajie at Longsha Lu. The **Foreign Affairs Office** (wàishì; 外事; ☎248 6227), on the 2nd fl. Open daily 8-11am and 1:30-4pm.

Hospital: No. 1 Hospital (dìyī yīyuàn; 第一医院; ☎242 5981), on Gongyuanhou Hutong, north of Longsha Park. Staff speak English, Japanese, and Russian.

Pharmacy: New Medicine (xīn tè yào; 新特药), 1 Longbei Jie (☎240 9304), off Longhua Lu and next to the Military District Hotel. Open daily 8am-9pm. Many other pharmacies are also along Longhua Lu.

Internet Access: The pink building in the left corner of the train station houses a 24hr. **Internet cafe** (wǎngbā; 网吧). Y2 per hr. The giant **Sports Center** (wénshì zhànqián tǐyùguǎn; 文市站前体育馆), about 5min. down Zhanqian Lu from the train station has Y1.5 per hr. Internet, in addition to pool and ping pong. Open daily 8am-midnight.

Post and Telecommunications: China Post and **China Telecom**, 1 Junshao Jie, just down Longhua Dajie from the train station. Open daily 8am-5pm.

Postal Code: 161000.

ACCOMMODATIONS

The most expensive hotels are near the train station and along Bukui Dajie, while Longhua Lu has the best budget accommodations.

White Crane Hotel (bái hè bīnguǎn; 白鹤宾馆), 25 Zhanqian Dajie (☎292 1111; fax 212 7639), across the street and south of the train station. Few hotels offer such nice public bathrooms. The rooms are incredibly spacious and well maintained by courteous staff. The sauna, bar, revolving restaurant, CAAC ticket office, and other conveniences are sure to satisfy the needs of any traveler. Doubles Y100, with bath Y220. ❷

Military District Hostel (jūn fēnqū zhāodàisuǒ; 军分区招待所), 2 Longbei Jie (☎610 2800, 610 2810, or 610 2820), off Longhua Lu. Great central location accompanied by lots of lights to make sure that it is noticeable at night. Appropriately spartan and neat rooms. 24hr. hot water. Make sure to book ahead. Doubles with bath and A/C Y78; quads Y120, with bath Y150. ❶

Old Workers' Guesthouse (qítiě lǎogànbù zhāodàisuǒ; 齐铁老干部招待所; ☎292 2957), across from the train station and near the White Crane Hotel. Perfect for a night's rest. Small, somewhat dilapidated rooms with hard beds and TV. Showers across the street for Y2. Public telephones and a small food shop conveniently located on the 1st fl. 5-bed dorms Y8-10; 2-bed Y30. Prices may be negotiable. ❶

Military Rule Hostel (jūnzhèng zhāodàisuǒ; 军政招待所), 11 Longhua Lu (☎212 2821 or 212 8100), near the train station. Clean dorm-like rooms and sterile atmosphere. 24hr. hot water. 4-bed dorms Y18; 3-bed Y20; doubles Y80, with bath Y160. ❶

FOOD

Qiqihar's main food street is **Longsha Lu.** For great Cantonese food 24hr. a day, check out **Bifeng Tang** ❷ (bì fēng táng; 避风塘), 1 Longnan Jie, across from the Military District Hotel and the New Medicine Pharmacy. The clean-cut bamboo decor creates a comfortable atmosphere that becomes nothing short of hectic during meal times. Great prices, large servings, and music performances during dinner

NORTHEAST

pack guests into this popular restaurant. Be sure to book ahead. (☎247 0608. Meals Y10-30.) For a more hands-on experience, fry your own dishes at **Hongchang Barbecue ❷** (hóng chāng shāokǎo; 宏昌烧烤), on the second floor of Eastern Market Mini District (dōng shìchǎng xiǎo qū ; 东市场小区). Order plates of raw meats and vegetables and test your culinary skills over the charcoal grill unique to each table. (☎256 4444. Plates Y8-30. Half-plates are half the price.) Many Chinese and Korean restaurants, decked with flags, are on Longsha Lu and in the area between the park and Bukui Dajie, around Xinsheng Lu. At night, the latter area also houses outdoor crustacean extravaganzas.

◉ SIGHTS

Locals like to while away their idle hours in the tree-lined lanes of **Longsha Park** (lóngshā gōngyuán; 龙沙公园), a pleasant retreat from the bustle of the train station and the noise of city streets. A small amusement park is also located in the park. (Open daily 24hr. Free.) Markets fill the streets east and northeast of the park. After dinner, locals (those not at the nightmarket) gather in large crowds along Longhua Dajie to dance everything from ballroom to the Electric Slide.

ZHALONG NATURE RESERVE

26km southeast of Qiqihar. Buses to Zhalong leave the West Bus Station 7am-midnight; buses from Zhalong to Qiqihar depart from the area before the hotel 8am-1pm. In both cases, show up early to get a seat. Fare Y6 one-way. Taxis one-way Y30. Y20.

Established in 1979, the Zhalong Nature Reserve (zhālóng zìrán bǎohùqū; 扎龙自然保护区) is home to over 200 different bird species with several varieties of rare **cranes,** including the endangered red-crowned and white-naped cranes. During the spring and summer, tens of thousands of birds stop here en route to southern migration areas. Due to industrial growth, the wetlands are quickly disappearing, but during the summer, the cranes seem as abundant as ever. A short walk into the waist-high grass will quickly lead you to families of cranes that are only slightly wary of humans. For those who miss the wild cranes, there are plenty of caged ones. Short crane performances occur daily at 2pm.

The park's two narrow paths encourage more avian than human visitors. A better place to absorb the size and beauty of the reserve's wetlands, the observation deck (Y1) offers free binoculars. Motor boats are also available for rent (Y10 per person for a short ride), but engine noise tends to scare the birds away. Morning or, better yet, sunrise is the best time for birdwatching.

In the **hotel ❷** on the reserve grounds, you may be the only visitor, but you'll have peace, fresh air, and a beautiful hardwood-floored room, not to mention the upper hand when it comes to bargaining down hotel prices. The hotel also has a restaurant and souvenir shop. (☎138 3622 7566. Doubles Y100, with A/C and sporadic hot water Y125-180.)

WUDALIANCHI 五大连池 ☎0456

Wudalianchi—"the five great linked lakes"—was formed 500 years ago after the eruption of a nearby volcano stopped up the Bai River. While no eruptions are due in the near future, this active volcanic site is China's youngest, giving tourists an eyeful of barren landscapes. Spacious plains separate the numerous volcanoes poking abruptly out of flat, fertile farmland. The small, rustic town sharing the nearby lake's name is down-to-earth, with low mountains, a slow lifestyle, and humble, friendly residents happy to offer rides on their tractors or donkeys. Don't expect red flags and tourist brochures. Sleepy Wudalianchi sees few visitors beyond those seeking its famous spring water, believed to have medicinal benefits.

☎🚌 TRANSPORTATION AND PRACTICAL INFORMATION. If you don't notice when you've arrived in Wudalianchi, don't be surprised—a drab traffic circle encompasses the tourist village in its entirety. Long-distance **buses** depart from the traffic circle or from the adjacent parking lot. Getting to Wudalianchi is easy; getting back is a little harder. Buses leave from Wudalianchi to Bei'an (1½hr., every hr. 5:30am-3:30pm, Y11), where you can catch another bus to Harbin (5hr.; 6:30am, 2pm; Y70). A **train** from Bei'an to Harbin (6-7hr.; 7:27am, 1pm; Y25-29) is also an option, especially if you want to get to Harbin by noon. There is one small **Internet cafe** near the central intersection on Zhanqian Dajie. (Y2 per hr.) There is a **first aid center** and a **post office** in the village. (Open daily 8am-5pm.) **Postal Code:** 164185.

☎🍴 ACCOMMODATIONS AND FOOD. Two family-run hostels at the main intersection accept foreigners. The **Rice Paddy Hotel ❶** (shuǐ hétián jiǔdiàn; 水禾田 酒店) sits at the corner of the intersection. A busy restaurant downstairs claims to give hotel customers discount meals, while small dorm-like rooms upstairs make for a nice, hard-bedded stay. Public baths have no showers; the nearby shower costs Y5. (☎722 2837. 4-bed dorms Y20; doubles Y50.) **Mineral Guesthouse ❶** (dìkuàng zhāodàisuǒ; 地矿招待所), up an outdoors staircase, offers less privacy but more air flow. The public baths (also lacking shower) aren't as nice as the Rice Paddy's, but the staff are friendlier. A row of cheap eats below makes for convenient meals and friendly company—hang out with the vendor from Xinjiang who joyfully roasts meats every evening. (☎722 2310. Beds Y8-10.) For comfort-seekers, expensive hotels abound along the main street; doubles with bath (but not hot water) cost about Y150. **Silver Lake Vacation Village ❷** (yín chí dùjià cūn; 银池度假 村), farther down the road from Rice Paddy, has particularly attentive staff members. Book early during the summer. (☎722 2913 or 722 1635. Posh, clean rooms, hardwood floors, private baths. Doubles Y160.) Be warned: the bus from Harbin likes to drop passengers off in the parking lot of overpriced inns.

Cheap eateries are everywhere. The **restaurant** at the Rice Paddy Hotel is a sure bet. The specialty is **preserved tofu** (jiàng dòufǔ; 酱豆腐), along with the town's famous—and rather mysterious—**mineral water.** Locals will demonstrate to you why the water may not be mixed with tea: a chemical reaction forms an allegedly poisonous black precipitate, even though the water is said to have health benefits.

◙ SIGHTS. Aside from the many healing springs, the most frequented places in Wudalianchi are Old Black Mountain and Medicinal Springs Mountain. From the heavily touristed peak of **Old Black Mountain** (lǎo hēi shān; 老黑山 ; Y60), you can see the famed five lakes and a vast horizon of volcanic mountains. While you're here, be sure to make the 120m descent to **Fairy Cave,** a glistening ice cave formed entirely from molten lava, rumored to be inhabited by fairies. The short climb up **Medicinal Springs Mountain** (yào quán shān; 药泉山 ; Y10) brings visitors to a temple (Y10) occupying the mouth of the volcano. A small path leads around the rim of the mountain to a bird's-eye view of the cities and plains below. Admission to the mountain is free before 7am, when the ticket office has not yet opened.

Other sights include **Geqiu Mountain** (gé qiú shān; 格球山 ; free), which may be worthwhile if there is water in the **Tianchi** (天池), one of the country's largest volcanic lakes, and the **Underground Ice River** (dìxià bīng hé; 地下冰河 ; Y30). The Undergound Ice River, a large, natural ice cave, showcases the usual Northeastern fascination with fluorescently lit ice sculptures. Though not too thrilling, the sight is a cool summer retreat from the slopes and plains. Your admission ticket actually covers two caves, so don't let your driver fool you into only going to one!

Locals and tourists alike drink the famed **mineral water.** To avoid tourist stands and admission fees, ask a local to take you through the backroads. The path roughly heads down Zhanqian Dajie from the central traffic light. Take the first left

NORTHEAST

onto a narrow road filled with street vendors and small shops. Follow this road to the end until you reach the dirt road, with fields visible in the distance. Turn left and follow the dirt road in the midst of a forest for about 5min. until you reach the stone bridge. Cross the stone bridge and walk ahead for less than 100m to the crowded rock springs flowing with mineral water for the taking.

> If you join a tour, don't let your guide, who gets commission from restaurant owners, take you for an exorbitantly priced meal or charge extra admission at sights. Don't pay for the tour until you're satisfied with the service. It is generally easier to book a taxi for the day, which should cover most major destinations including Old Black Mountain, Medicinal Springs Mountain, Underground Ice River, and a few add-ons. The bare minimum taxi fare for a day is around Y50, but expect to pay more. Some may accept the Y50 fare provided that they sell you the admission tickets (which they previously purchased for a lower price). The price they offer should be the same as if you were going solo.

MUDANJIANG 牡丹江 ☎ 0453

Five hours southeast of Harbin, dust-laden Mudanjiang is not exactly a tourist town. Dirt road villages and farmland aside, this is actually one of the larger cities in Heilongjiang, complete with a modern city center. Those few travelers who do stumble into Mudanjiang are usually en route to Jingpo Lake or Russia. Happily, the city's transportation is convenient, and there are a few reasonably priced hotels from which to choose. The lively street markets add a refreshing dash of watermelon flavor to an otherwise bland city.

■ **TRANSPORTATION.** This transportation hub offers plenty of options to get away. **Mudanjiang Airport** (mǔdānjiāng jīchǎng; 牡丹江机场) is 10km south of the city. CAAC airport buses (Y10) leave 1½hr. prior to departure from the **CAAC Ticket Office**, on the corner of Dong Ertiao Lu and Aimin Jie. (☎ 693 9627. Open daily 8am-5pm.) Airplanes fly to: Beijing (1-2 per day, Y1190); Shanghai (3 per week, Y1460); Shenyang (2 per week, Y450). The **train station** (mǔdānjiāng huǒchē zhàn; 牡丹江火车站 ; ☎ 882 4852 or 882 4732) is at the intersection of Guanghua Lu and Taiping Lu. Trains go to: Beijing (22hr., 11:42am, Y79-550); Dalian (21hr., 9:34am, Y65-217); Harbin (4½-7hr., 11 per day, Y21-50); Ji'nan (28hr., 10:14am, Y90-600) via Tianjin (23hr.); Shenyang (12¼hr., 4 per day, Y39 and up); Tumen (6hr., 9:26am, Y22). The **bus station** is in the parking lot outside the train station. (Open 5am-6pm.) Frequent **minibuses** to Jingpo Lake (2-4hr.; Y20, round-trip Y40) leave from the left parking lot. All other buses depart from the right parking lot to: Harbin (5hr., every 30min., Y59); Suifenhe (2hr., every 20min., Y26); Tumen (8hr., 2pm, Y37); Yabuli (2hr.; usually 2:20pm, but time varies; Y17); Yanji (7hr., noon, Y41). **Sleeper buses** travel to Shenyang (13hr., 1pm, Y103). **Public buses** (Y1) run approximately 5am-7pm and span all major streets. **Taxi** base fare is Y5, each additional kilometer Y1.6. Destinations within the city shouldn't cost more than Y10. **Motorcycle-taxis** (Y2) are more convenient for short distances.

■ **ORIENTATION AND PRACTICAL INFORMATION.** The train tracks cut Mudanjiang into two, with most city spotlights to the south. The **train station** is in the center, at the intersection of east-west **Guanghua Lu** (光华路) and north-south **Taiping Lu** (太平路). The heart of the commercial district is the pedestrian street **Dong Yitiao Lu** (东一条路), one block away from and parallel to Taiping Lu. **CITS**, 34 Jingfu Lu, between Dong Yitiao Lu and Dong Ertiao Lu, arranges group tours to Jingpo Lake or Changbaishan in Jilin province. (☎ 695 0061; fax 695 0064. Open daily 8am-5pm.) The **Bank of China**, 9 Taiping Lu, 200m from the train station, exchanges currency and traveler's checks. (☎667 8005. Open daily 8am-6pm.) The **PSB**, 96 Guanghua Lu, has a visa department at the corner. (☎628 2402. Open M-F 8am-11:30pm and 1:30-6pm.) Other services include: **24hr. pharmacy** at 108 Dong Yitiao Lu (☎692 0094); **No. 2 People's Hospital** (dì èr rénmín yīyuàn; 第二人民医院 ; ☎692 3422 or 692 2035), at the intersection of Taiping Lu and Ping'an Jie; and 24hr. **Internet** cafe (wǎngbā; 网吧), on Ping'an Jie, past the hospital. The **post office**, 33 Taiping Lu, offers EMS. (Open daily summer 8am-5:30pm; winter 8am-5pm.) **Postal Code:** 157000.

▮▮ ACCOMMODATIONS AND FOOD. Most cheap, foreigner-friendly hotels are within a 10min. walk of the train station. Don't mistake the **PSB Hostel ❶** (gōngānjú zhāodàisuǒ; 公安局招待所), 100m from train station on Guanghua Lu, with painted yellow caution tape along the windows, for the actual PSB, another 100m down the road. Hardwood floors and marble-like hallways give a sterile feel to the very clean rooms. (☎628 2011. Doubles Y40, with bath Y80.) **Big Hotel Garden ❷** (dàguǎn yuán; 大馆园), 98 Guanghua Lu, just behind the PSB, has comfort, elegance, and A/C, but somewhat dim rooms. The doubles are very standard but the suites are amazingly large with not only two rooms, but also two bathrooms. Staff are very willing to bargain. (☎693 5068. Doubles Y100; quads Y204.) The **Imperial City Hotel ❶** (jīn chéng bīnguǎn; 金城宾馆), 139 Guanghua Lu, offers spacious, hardwood-floored rooms at dirt cheap prices, but the bathrooms have rusty showers. The building looks like it's crumbling, much like its already fallen neighbor. Night train whistles rattle walls and wake sleepers. Staff are more than friendly and extremely excited about new visitors. (☎691 6845 or 692 3236, ext. 8071. 8-bed dorms Y10; 6-bed Y12; 5-bed Y15; 4-bed Y20; 3-bed Y25; 2-bed Y30; singles Y40; doubles Y60 and up; triples Y75 and up.)

Many small restaurants line the side streets off Taiping Lu and Guanghua Lu; most department stores along Taiping Lu and Dong Yitiao Lu also have food halls. Nearby **nightmarkets** offer fruit-, meat-, and seafood-on-a-stick (Y1) in the summer. The second floor of **House Property Flats** (fángchǎn gōngyù guǎn; 房产公寓馆), 75 Qixing Jie, right near Dong Yitiao Lu, has cheap meals in a more upscale sit-down environment. Large windows allow you to look down onto the busy pedestrian Dong Yitiao Lu. Dishes run Y3-15; a plate of 12 dumplings costs but Y3. Locals also like to boast about their extraordinarily juicy **watermelons**, with shells so crisp that they can easily be cracked open by hand. In mid- to late July, hundreds of stands line the highways outside of Mudanjiang, selling watermelon (Y2.5-5 per *jīn*).

JINGPO LAKE 镜泊湖   ☎0453

Jingpo, or "Mirror," Lake, south of Mudanjiang, was formed by volcanic explosions near the Mudan River over 5000 years ago. Despite throngs of summer tourists, Jingpo Lake Reserve can be surprisingly peaceful due to its sprawling size. Dotted with hotels and retirement homes, the lake's 90km circumference is navigable only by electric cars. Aside from swimming and treks to the waterfall, there's not much to do in the reserve, but tours can be arranged to visit the nearby sights.

▮▮ TRANSPORTATION AND PRACTICAL INFORMATION. The most convenient way to reach Jingpo Lake is to take one of the frequent **minibuses** (round-trip Y40) that depart from the square in front of the **Mudanjiang Train Station.** Otherwise, you'll need to travel by train through the town of Dongjing, either from Mudanjiang (2hr., 2 per day, Y4) or Dunhua (3hr., daily, Y6). A **bus** also makes the trip from Dunhua to Dongjing (3hr., many per day, Y19). Frequent minibuses go from Dongjing train station to the front gate of Jingpo Lake (45min., Y7).

The grand stone entranceway to Jingpo Lake marks the termination point of all outside vehicles. Upon paying the Y60 **admission,** you'll immediately be charged another Y8 for each electric car ride within the reserve. The main tourist access point, with parking lots, a beach, and a dock, is **Jingpo Village,** 5min. past the round-about, marked by signs reading "**Villa.**" A **waterfall** is north of the village, 1.2km up a road from the traffic circle; sporadic electric cars (Y5-10) connecting the village and waterfall leave only when full. The village has a **first aid center** and a **post office.** (Open daily 8:30am-5:30pm. It may be locked but ask around the nearby restaurants if you need them to open it.) **Postal Code:** 157438.

ⓘ⃞ ACCOMMODATIONS AND FOOD. Many hotels do not open until mid-May, so if you visit in low season, call in advance. Prices are significantly lower in May and June than they are later in the summer. The best places to budget crash are the two **Harbin Industrial University Dorms ❶** (hāgōng dà dìyī tǐyǎngsuǒ; 哈工大第一体养所; and hāgōng dà dì'èr zhāodàisuǒ; 哈工大第二招待所), 2min. up the road from the docks. Trade stories with students in English and Chinese. No matter how many guests they have, they'll always find you a bed in the small but functional rooms, complete with squat toilets and crusty TVs. (☎627 0015 and 627 0039, respectively. Y30 per bed.) The same owners offer a slightly more upscale (and less sociable) alternative around the corner at the **Mountain Villa Hotel ❷** (shān-zhuāng bīnguǎn; 山庄宾馆), facing the dock and lake. The clean rooms with polished floors are a good size. (☎627 0012. Open May-Sept. Doubles May-June Y100-120, July-Aug. Y150-180 after bargaining.) You can also try the retirement homes scattered throughout (Y40-100).

For food, the best options are at hotel restaurants. Note that fish is often over-priced and poorly prepared. For a pleasant splurge, head over to the **International Hotel ❸** (guójì jùlèbù; 国际聚乐部). This four-star hotel is only slightly more expensive than the (before bargaining) prices of cheaper restaurants, but it employs some of the best chefs in the province. Fish is still pricey at Y100, but meats are around Y20. Fresh, handmade meat pancakes (ròu bǐng; 肉饼) are only Y3. The gorgeous dining area has giant two-story windows and a balcony over-looking the sights along the lake (a boat tour to see the sights costs Y60).

◉ SIGHTS. Although most tourist facilities and beaches are in Jingpo Village on the northeastern shore of the lake, attractions are scattered all over the lake-shores. To see the **Solitary Mountains** (gūshān; 孤山), **White Precipice** (bái shí luòzi; 白石落子), and the favorite **Mao Zedong Mountains** (two mountains that, from the right angle, supposedly look like the resting body of the beloved Chairman), take a 1½hr. boat ride on the A route (Y80) or a 3hr. ride on the B route (Y60). Tours run 7:30am-5pm but are easiest to organize in the morning, when busloads of tourists arrive from Mudanjiang. The B route tends to depart more frequently.

Infrequent minibuses run from the village to the **Diaoshuilou Waterfall** (diào shuǐ lóu pùbù; 掉水楼瀑布), formed from a volcanic eruption about 10,000 years ago. In mid-summer, water from the river cascades over the lava rock into the 60m-deep crater left by the eruption. Free water-diving performances are given daily at 10am and 2pm sharp. Those who don't take the minibus to Jingpo Lake directly from Mudanjiang might see some attractions on the way to the village. A 4km motorcycle ride (Y5-10) from Dongjing visits the ruins of **Shangjing,** the 7th- to 10th-century capital of the Bohai Kingdom (Y10). Aside from overgrown grass and the stone foundation of the city, little remains of this small kingdom. A complete reconstruction of the city is due in the near future. In the meantime, take a not-so-worthwhile peek at the small museum of antique replicas. The only real Bohai relics sit in a rundown temple about 10km away. There, children jump and swing from the thousand-year-old giant stone Buddha and light tower.

Thirty kilometers farther along the road, about 15km from the village, is Heilongjiang's own **Underground Forest** (dìxià sēnlín; 地下森林), a wild garden located in a volcanic dip. The road to the forest branches right off the road from Dongjing to Jingpo and continues for about another 60km; it's clearly marked—in Chinese. Don't forget to drop by the underground cave temple, also on this road. There's no admission charge and you can see an icy shrine to Buddha along with the 18 luóhàn. Make sure the staff know you're down there, as it is impossible to navigate the icy cave if they accidently turn off the lights. Transportation is difficult to arrange if you're not willing to pay the Y75 taxi fare from Dongjing or join an overpriced CITS tour from Mudanjiang. Groups coming from Jingpo Lake can arrange a tour to see the outside sights. Otherwise, a private taxi will cost around Y300 to see the Bohai Ruins and the Undergound Forest. Going with a taxi that has connections with the reserve employees will save you the Y60 readmission price. If you're approaching Jingpo Lake from the south, stop at Dunhua and hop in a taxi (Y10) to Asia's second-largest Buddhist temple, **Six-Peak Mountain Zhengjue Temple** (liù dǐng shān zhèngjué sì; 六顶山正觉寺 ; Y10).

SUIFENHE 绥芬河   ☎ 0453

Nothing is on level ground in hilly Suifenhe. Fifty years ago, when Mao and Stalin defined the Sino-Soviet borders, they unwittingly designated the task of cushioning the impact of cross-border travel to Suifenhe, a little commercial city caught between cultures. The many Russian-themed, Chinese-run, but foreigners-only establishments create an odd double standard in which visitors take precedence over locals. If you're heading to Russia, or just curious about its culture, spend some time on the beautiful, winding roads of Suifenhe.

TRANSPORTATION. The **train station** (huǒchē zhàn; 火车站) on Zhanqian Lu, down Wenhua Jie from Central Sq., has domestic trains to Harbin (11hr., 1pm, Y101) and Mudanjiang (every 20min., Y30), and international trains to Khabarovsk and Vladivostok (8:50am, 12:10pm; Y1400; show up at least 1½hr. before departure for ticket and passport control). Ticket booths (☎392 3050) are open 6am-5pm. International tickets may be easier to buy at the **Railway Travel Agency** (tiědào lüxíngshè; 铁道旅行社 ; ☎392 1029) across the street. The **bus station** (kèyùn zhàn; 客运站 ; ☎392 4933), at the intersection of Tongtian Lu and Xinxing Jie, 10min. from Central Sq., has buses to Yanji (10hr., 4:40am, Y55) and Harbin (6hr., 9:10am, Y120). **Minibuses** go to Mudanjiang (2hr., at least every 20min. 6am-6pm, Y26); sleeper buses to Harbin (17hr., 8:30pm, Y70) depart from the square in front of the train station. Local **buses** (6am-7pm; Y1) all stop at the train station. **Taxi** base fare is Y5, each additional kilometer Y1.6; many are unmetered. Trips within town should be about Y5.

ORIENTATION AND PRACTICAL INFORMATION. Central Square (zhōngxīn guǎngchǎng; 中心广场) is at the intersection of Tongtian Lu (通天路) and Wenhua Jie (文化街), which runs to the train station. In the north, separated from the city center by the Harbin-Vladivostok Highway, the **Temple of Light** (guāngmíng sì; 光明寺) is a conspicuous landmark that can help travelers get their bearings.

The **Railway Travel Agency** (see above) offers package trips to **Russia** (Y1500). The **Bank of China,** 134 Wenhua Jie, in Central Sq., has 24hr. self-service banking. (Open daily 8am-5:30pm.) The **PSB,** 22 Guanghua Lu, is 200m from Wenhua Jie. Xinhua Lu, the street leading from Central Sq. to the bus station, has a large **supermarket** with a **pharmacy.** (Open daily 9am-9pm.) Farther down Xinhua Lu, many **Internet** cafes are easily found. (Y3 per hr.) The New China Internet Cafe（xīn dàlù wǎngbā; 新大陆网吧）, 64 Xinhua Lu, right next to **CITS**, is open daily 8am-4pm. The main **post office,** 25 Yinxing Jie, is a block away from Wenhua Jie and Central Sq. (☎392 2103. Open M-F 7:30am-5:30pm.) A smaller post office is more conveniently located in Central Sq. next to Bank of China. **Postal Code**: 157300.

█▐█ ACCOMMODATIONS AND FOOD. Most hotels in Suifenhe are fairly similar and target businesspeople, with rates around Y150-200. A good place to check out is **Suifenhe Business Hotel ❷** (suífēnhé shì huálóng shāngwù jiǔdiàn; 绥芬河市华龙商务酒店）, 35 Xinglong Lu, right next to Central Sq. Despite somewhat worn carpeting, spacious rooms have balconies overlooking the lively square. (☎392 1119 or 395 8884. Doubles Y180.) Cheaper rooms in home-like settings (Y40) are on any of the smaller roads along the hillside between the PSB and the bus station.

Russian food is an integral part of the Suifenhe bicultural experience, but sadly enough, the majority of the local Russian establishments fall short of expectations. **MAKCNM** (makcim) on Shancheng Lu（山城路）is hands-down the tourist favorite. Despite the American folk music and Chinese staff, its Russian cuisine is the best in town and all Russian visitors make a stop here at some point. While enjoying the elegant setting, be sure to try the red-beet borscht (борщ; Y5) with Armenian goat cheese (армянский сыр). For a more raucous culinary experience, go to **Restoran Wanda** (Ванда), a block from Central Sq., down Tongtian Jie. The dark, underground club is easy to find (head for the noise) and filled with apoplectic Caucasians. (Open daily 10pm-dawn.)

JILIN 吉林

Much like its northern neighbor Heilongjiang, Jilin province is an innocuous blend of industrial banality and scenic wonder. Formerly known as Kirin, the area was once the home of the steppe- and forest-dwelling Hurka tribe. The Manchus conquered the region in the late 16th century, and Han Chinese began settling here in the 18th century. These days, the sooty cities of Jilin and Changchun reveal lifestyles less tainted by Western influence and more embracing of its ethnic Korean population. Though visitors may be less than enthralled with Jilin City, the stunningly beautiful mountain scenery of Changbaishan continues to justifiably draw scores of travelers to its majestic peaks.

CHANGCHUN 长春 ☎0431

Changchun literally means "eternal spring," and although springtime indeed arrives here in a burst of green, this designation ignores the reality of the long frigid winters preceding the spring. Fortunately, the ubiquitous beauty and spa centers are sure to provide glamour, comfort, and "eternal spring" to the city's residents throughout the year. During the Japanese occupation from 1931 to 1945, Changchun was the capital of Manchukuo. The somewhat neglected palace from which the puppet emperor Pu Yi ruled remains the city's biggest claim to tourist fame. Changchun may lack dazzling must-see sights, but its unexpected mixture of greenery and urbanity are great for travelers seeking a Chinese city undisturbed by Western influences.

█ TRANSPORTATION

Flights: Changchun Airport (chángchūn jīchǎng; 长春机场）, 28 Luyuan Chuyingbin Lu (☎799 5606), west of the city. Bus #364 connects the airport with People's Sq. Taxi Y20-25. **CAAC,** 23-1 Changbai Lu, 2nd fl. (☎298 8888), between the train station and the Post Hotel. Open daily 8am-4:30pm. To: **Beijing** (6-9 per day, Y880); **Chengdu** (3 per week, Y1780); **Dalian** (1-3 per day, Y520); **Fuzhou** (3 per week, Y1600); **Guang-zhou** (1-3 per day, Y2100); **Nanjing** (1-2 per day, Y1320); **Qingdao** (1-2 per day, Y730); **Shanghai** (2-4 per day, Y1280); **Yantai** (2 per week, Y730).

Trains: Changchun Train Station (chángchūn huǒchēzhàn; 长春火车站; ☎612 2222), at the north end of Renmin Dajie. 24hr. luggage storage (Y5). To: **Beijing** (11-14hr., 8 per day, Y83-165); **Dalian** (11hr., 5 per day, Y61-121); **Dandong** (8-10hr., 2 per day, Y71); **Harbin** (3-4hr., 11 per day, Y25-75); **Jilin** (2-4hr., 6 per day, Y9-53); **Shanghai** (29hr., 2 per day, Y158-312); **Shenyang** (4hr., 3-4 per day, Y29-75); **Tonghua** (9hr., daily, Y21-48); **Tumen** (10-11hr., 3 per day, Y32-43).

Buses: Changchun Highways Passenger Transport Center (chángchūn gōnglù kèyùn zhōngxīn zhàn; 长春公路客运中心站), 6 Renmin Dajie (☎279 2544), a block from the train station, on the left. To: **Beijing** (3pm, Y180); **Dalian** (8hr., 5 per day, Y157); **Erdaobaihe** (3hr., 6am, Y52); **Harbin** (4hr., every 30min. 5:30am-5pm, Y60); **Jilin** (2hr., every 10min. 5:10am-6pm, Y14); **Shenyang** (4hr., 5 per day, Y35); **Yanji** (10hr., 7:30am, Y85).

Local Transportation: The frequent local **buses** ply every street of the city 6am-10pm; some lines only go until 6 or 8pm. Buses numbered below 100 tend to stay on the larger roads, while the 200s and 300s cover obscure neighborhoods and dirt roads. Bus #6 spans Renmin Dajie; #25 and 62 go from the train station to South Lake Park via Tongzhi Jie. Fare Y1.

Taxis: Base fare Y5, each additional km Y1.3. Most destinations Y7-16.

✦🛈 ORIENTATION AND PRACTICAL INFORMATION

Changchun is a sprawling city blessed with wide streets and plenty of open space. The main street **Renmin Dajie** (人民大街) bisects the city from the train station and through **People's Square** (rénmín guǎngchǎng; 人民广场). Most major streets are arranged on a grid around Renmin Dajie, with a few thoroughfares extending radially from People's Square. All in all, the center is easy to navigate. The highly visible shapes of the skyscrapers serve as helpful landmarks.

Travel Agency: JPTG (Jilin Provincial Tourism Group) (jílín shěng lǚyóu jítuán; 吉林省旅游集团), Yinmao Bldg., 14 Xinmin Dajie, 1st fl. (☎690 9039). Open M-F 8:30-11:30am and 1:30-5pm.

Bank of China: Yinmao Bldg., 14 Xinmin Lu, 1st fl. Exchanges currency and traveler's checks. Credit card advances. Open M-F 8:30-11:30am and 1-5:30pm.

Bookstore: Foreign Language Bookstore (wài wén shūdiàn; 外文书店), 44 Tongzhi Jie (☎897 0241), at Huimin Lu. Open daily summer 8:30am-8:30pm; winter 9am-5pm. **Learner's Bookstore,** 126 Renmin Dajie (☎566 2793), near Ziyou Sq., has a large collection of bilingual books. Open daily 10am-6pm.

PSB: (☎898 2107). A large station occupies the area in the southwest corner of People's Sq. An impressive exhibition in the square illustrates the PSB's success in tracing and handling public enemies. **Visa extensions** processed at the branch on Guangming Lu. Open M-F 8:30am-5pm.

Hospital: Jilin Province People's Hospital (jílín shěng rénmín yīyuàn; 吉林省人民医院 ; ☎559 5114), on Hongqi Jie. **24hr. pharmacy.**

Internet Access: Worker's Cultural Palace Internet Cafe (láodòng rénmín wénhuà gōng wǎngbā; 劳动人民文化宫网吧), 74 Renmin Dajie, 3rd fl. (☎891 3369). Over 40 computers. Y2 per hr. Open daily 8am-10pm. **Earth Village Internet and Coffee Bar** (dìqiú cūn wǎngluò kāfēi tīng; 地球村网络咖啡厅), 47 Tongzhi Jie (☎565 3704), at Huimin Lu, across from the Foreign Language Bookstore. Y5 per hr. Open 24hr. **Sunshine Zone** (yángguāng dìdài; 阳光地带), 12 Qinghe Jie. Open until late.

NORTHEAST

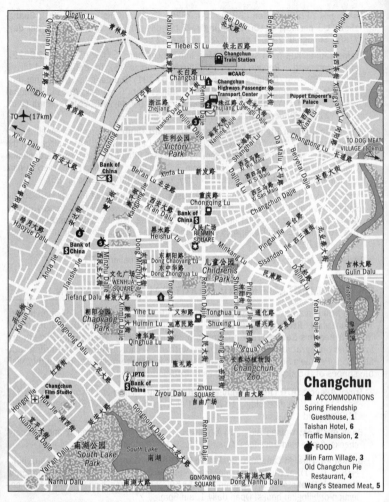

Changchun

🏠 **ACCOMMODATIONS**
Spring Friendship
  Guesthouse, **1**
Taishan Hotel, **6**
Traffic Mansion, **2**
🍴 **FOOD**
Jilin Farm Village, **3**
Old Changchun Pie
  Restaurant, **4**
Wang's Steamed Meat, **5**

Post Office: 18 Renmin Dajie (☎271 4269), south of the train station. EMS and Poste Restante daily summer 8am-5pm; winter 8am-4:30pm. IDD service daily 8am-9pm.
Postal Code: 130000.

ACCOMMODATIONS

Business travelers are the city's most frequent visitors. Changchun's budget options are distinguishable only by whether or not the rooms have attached baths. Most are near the train station or on Tongzhi Jie and have 24hr. hot water and A/C.

Spring Friendship Guesthouse (chūnyì bīnguǎn; 春谊宾馆), 80 Renmin Dajie (☎209 6888; fax 896 0171), across the square from the train station. Rooms are nice and neat, and bathrooms have a shower instead of the typical oversized bathtub. Try getting a room in the older building as they seem to offer slightly better service. Good buffet breakfast included. Doubles Y218-280. ❸

Taishan Hotel (tàishān dàjiǔdiàn; 泰山大酒店), 35 Tongzhi Jie (☎563 4991; fax 563 6025), at Jiefang Dalu. Friendly staff, clean rooms, large bathrooms, and superb location. Suites are extremely spacious with plush leather couches. Cheaper rooms are available but they may not allow foreigners to stay there. Doubles Y160; suites Y230. ❷

Traffic Mansion of Changchun (chángchūn jiāotōng dàshà; 长春交通大厦), 238 Renmin Dajie (☎611 5888; fax 277 4990). Attached to the ever busy long-distance bus station and down the street from the train station. While the 1st fl. may be a bit busy, the upper levels are extremely calm. Rooms and bathrooms are decent but in slight disrepair. Breakfast included. Doubles Y110-130. ❷

🍴 FOOD

Small, home-style eateries filling Changchun's streets serve standard fare and close very late at night, if at all. In the evenings, the entrance to **Victory Park** is the best place to find a stick of seafood, sweets, or sausage. The nearby Xinfa Lu boasts a kingdom of **dumpling houses. Wang's Steamed Meat** ❷ (wáng shì zhēng ròu; 王氏蒸肉), 17 Xi Minzhu Dajie, has great food and a friendly waitstaff. Their claim to fame is the tasty stewed pork. (☎854 6888. Dishes around Y20. Open daily 10am-10pm.) The **Old Changchun Pie Restaurant** ❶ (lǎo chángchūn bǐng diàn; 老长春饼店), on the corner of Dongjing Lu, serves fried 2-*liǎng* portions of dumplings for Y8-16. (☎277 8896. Open daily 10am-midnight or later.) At the **Jilin Farm Village** ❷ (jílín nóngjiā fànzhuāng; 吉林农家饭店), 23 Beijing Dajie, a meal for two won't exceed Y50. (☎273 4137. Open daily 10:30am-11pm.) But Changchun's real culinary treat is the dusty and remote **Dog Meat Village** (gǒuròu tún; 狗肉屯), a collection of restaurants accessible from Renmin Sq. by bus #259; get off when bus enters a dirt road. After the bus stops running at 8pm, a taxi ride costs a fixed Y15. A savory meal including a soup with a distinctly canine look and smell should cost about Y30. Mmm...puppies. **Datong River Dog Meat Restaurant** (dàtóng jiāng gǒuròu guǎn; 大同江狗肉馆; ☎464 5804), possibly the least hole-in-the-wall of the lot, is said to be the best, but dozens of neighboring establishments are also fido-licious.

👁 SIGHTS

Changchun's main attractions are its streets and people, best savored in Changchun's parks. Full of busy metropolitan denizens seeking a place to relax, **Vic-**

ON THE MENU

DOGGONE IT

Visitors to China may cringe at the thought of consuming man's best friend, but dog meat is simply a part of the local palate. Though it is not even close in popularity to beef, pork, and other "generic" meats, dog meat is also not out of the ordinary. Dogs are raised for consumption in much the same way that cows and pigs are. Han Chinese in the Northeast are actually less charmed by Fido's succulent flavors than Chinese people elsewhere. The heavy presence of ethnic Koreans and the central role of dog meat in some regional Korean cuisines, however, translates into "Dog Meat Villages," dog hotpot, and dog everything.

Dog meat emerged as a staple in the northeast because it was difficult to raise cattle, and cows were invaluable in the fields, not in the pot. With its "warming" qualities (locals warn against consuming dog meat when running a fever), dog hotpot or broth is the rage when temperatures drop below freezing, as they often do in the northeast's grueling winters. In addition, dog meat is lean and believed to benefit the circulatory and digestive systems. In terms of quality, yellow-furred dogs are considered the most tasty, followed by black-, and then white-furred dogs. This delicacy comes at a price, though. Restaurant owners report that a full dog goes for Y300 or more. Chefs often impress tourists by showcasing the uneaten tail, paws, and head. Yum...

tory Park (shènglì gōngyuán; 胜利公园) offers a taste of China's city life, culinary and otherwise. (Open daily sunrise to late night. Y3, after dusk free.) The remote **Moonlight Pond Recreation Area** is a more pastoral alternative. (Take bus #102 from San Malu near People's Sq.)

> **BULK BUYS.** If you're running low on batteries, paper, mannequins, or other miscellaneous items, join the masses at Changchun's famous market, **Heishui Lu** (黑水路), to buy at wholesale prices. At least 3 buildings are devoted entirely to clothing, and the streets are lined with vendors shouting out extremely low prices. Open daily 4am-2pm.

PUPPET EMPEROR'S PALACE (wěi huánggōng; 伪皇宫). After the Japanese invaded Manchuria in 1931, they installed Henry Pu Yi, the last Qing ruler, as puppet emperor of the new state of Manchukuo. Bernardo Bertolucci's film *The Last Emperor* was filmed here. Do not, however, mistake the palace for another Chinese-miniseries-set-turned-tourist-attraction. The palace consists of the inner court (the prison-like private residence of the emperor and his family) and the outer court, where public affairs and ceremonies were handled. The ironically named **Mansion of Serving the Populace,** where Pu Yi signed treaties that cemented Japanese control over northern China, and **Pavilion of Joint Virtue,** where the "last concubine" Li Yuqin lived, have both been restored. Due to wartime destruction and subsequent reconstruction, it desperately lacks any genuine artifacts, but walking through the sterile halls that staged the glamorously tragic stories of Pu Yi and his wife and concubine is a haunting experience. The palace is very accessible and has English captions. *(In the northeastern part of the city, close to the train station. Bus #268 stops at nearby Guangsha Lu; from here, go down a long dirt road. The palace is nearly impossible to find; consider taking a taxi for Y5. Open daily summer 8:30am-5pm; winter 8:40am-4:30pm. Last admission 40min. before closing. Y50, student Y30.)*

CHANGCHUN FILM STUDIO (chángchūn diànyǐng zhìpiān chǎng; 长春电影制片厂). Locals take much pride from the crumbling remains of the cradle of the Chinese film industry, but the glamor seems to be long gone. Nevertheless, you can experience the old but ingenious methods of film-making and even film your own movie. The tour and captions are in Chinese only. *(28 Huxi Lu, west of South Lake Park. Take bus #13 from People's Sq. or catch #120 on the nearby streets. ☎594 8427. Open daily 8am-4:30pm. Live movie show in Chinese Y10. Y35, students Y20.)*

JILIN CITY 吉林市 ☎0432

Jilin's name means "lucky forest," an ironic misnomer for this industrial monster that seems to despise the color green. Even Jilin's trees are most impressive during the winter, when their branches are frosted with dignified "ice rims," the product of frozen evaporation from nearby hydroelectric plants. Still, the surrounding mountains liven up the horizon, and a few sights provide more intimate respite from the expansive avenues of the city.

▐ TRANSPORTATION

Flights: Gudianzi Airport (gūdiànzǐ jīchǎng; 孤甸子机场 ; ☎306 7450), on the city's western outskirts, a Y30 taxi ride from the city center. Free shuttle buses leave 2hr. before departure from the **CAAC ticket office,** Dongmei Hotel, 199 Tianjin Jie, 2nd fl. (☎254 3638). Open M-Sa 8am-4:30pm, Su 9am-2pm. To: **Beijing** (daily, Y870); **Guangzhou** (2 per week, Y2090); **Shanghai** (2 per week, Y1320).

Trains: Jilin Train Station (jílín zhàn; 吉林站 ; ☎292 1222), at the end of Zhongkang Lu. To: **Beijing** (15-19hr., 2 per day, Y75-262); **Changchun** (2-4hr., 8 per day, Y10-30); **Dalian** (14½hr., 2 per day, Y56-174); **Harbin** (5½-7hr., 2 per day, Y20-170); **Shenyang** (6-9hr., 8 per day, Y31-115); **Tianjin** (18hr., 2:38pm, Y80-280); **Tumen** (8-12hr., 7 per day, Y30-115) via **Yanji.**

Buses: Main Passenger Bus Station (kèyùn zǒngzhàn; 客运总站 ; ☎255 5401), on Zhongkang Lu near Tianjin Jie, 5min. from the train station. To: **Dalian** (8½hr., 8:30am, Y135); **Harbin** (5-6hr., 7 per day, Y31); **Shenyang** (4½hr., 8 per day, Y95). **Linjiang Long-Distance Bus Station** (línjiāng chángtú qìchē zhàn; 临江长途汽车站 ; ☎484 0121), on Xi'an Lu, between Jiefang Dalu and Songjiang Lu. Buses go to **Changchun** (1½hr., 7 per day, Y30). In addition, **sleeper buses** (☎139 0444 6898) leave for **Dalian** from the square next to the train station (12hr., 6pm, Y100).

Local Transportation: Most **buses** run from early morning until 8pm, and many terminate at the Jilin Train Station. Fare Y1-2. Buses #7 and 107 go to Beishan Park; #8 and 101 run between the train station and the Linjiang Bus Station; #13 runs along Tianjin Jie between the train station and the riverfront; #49 goes from Songjiang Lu to the terminus at Dragon Pond Mountain Park; #103 runs from the train station down Jilin Dajie.

Taxis: Base fare Y5, each additional km Y1.3-1.5. Train station to Songjiang Lu Y5-10.

■✳🛈 ORIENTATION AND PRACTICAL INFORMATION

Jilin's major streets run along the **Songhua River** (松花江), and most of the city streets fan out from the river. **Songjiang Lu** (松江路) winds along the northwestern bank of the river bend. The main artery, **Jilin Dajie** (吉林大街), runs north-south, while **Jiefang Lu** (解放路) connects the city's western and eastern neighborhoods.

Travel Agency: CITS, 2 Gangwan Lu (☎245 3773 or 2435673; www.jlcits.com), inside the Dongguan Hotel. Organizes 3-day trips to Changbaishan's Southern Pass by train via Yanji (Y500 per person). Open M-F 8:30am-5pm. Many travel agencies cluster around and in **Wenmiao Alley,** dubbed "Travel Market" by locals.

Bank of China: 1 Shenchun Jie (☎467 0277), across the Linjiangmen Bridge, near the Linjiang Long-Distance Bus Station. Exchanges traveler's checks. Credit card advances. Open M-F 8:30am-5:30pm, Sa-Su 9am-5pm.

PSB: At the intersection of Beijing Lu and Nanjing Lu. **Foreign affairs department** (☎240 9323). Open M-F 8:30am-4pm.

Hospital: Jilin's largest hospital is at 4 Nanjing Jie (☎216 7114; fax 244 0643). **24hr. pharmacy.**

Internet Access: China Telecom Internet Bar (☎249 2757), at the intersection of Chongqing Jie and Jiefang Dalu. Take bus #3. Y2 per hr. Open daily 8:30am-9:30pm. **Aide Internet Cafe** (àidé wǎngbā; 爱德网吧 ; ☎248 9388), at the intersection of Shanghai Lu and Chongqing Jie. Y1.5 per hr.

Post Office: China Post, 2 Songjiang Lu (☎248 9619). EMS. Phone cards sold on 2nd fl. Open daily 8am-6pm.

Postal Code: 132001.

▟ ACCOMMODATIONS

Jilin suffers from the northeast's chronic lack of budget accommodations. Even hotels near the train station are pricey.

Tourism Hotel (lǚyóu bīnguǎn; 旅游宾馆), 88 Chaoyang Jie (☎248 2087), overlooking Cultural Sq. One of the most central locations in Jilin, within walking distance of Henan Jie, Jilin Dajie, and Jiefang Lu. Great standard rooms for an equally great price are quiet and clean. Mini water dispensers in every room. Friendly staff. Doubles Y128. ❷

Angel Hotel (tiānshǐ bīnguǎn; 天使宾馆), 2 Nanjing Jie (☎248 1848; fax 248 0323), just north of the Catholic Church. The location makes it a prime spot for easy access to the scenic Songhua River. Neat rooms offer comfortable beds and an elegant atmosphere. Tea house in the lobby. Doubles Y228; triples Y248. ❸

Jilin Changlin Hotel (jílín chánglín bīnguǎn; 吉林常林宾馆), 113 Tianjin Jie (☎255 7780), near the train station. Not only do you get a clean room, but you also get to make a spectacle of yourself in the very public showers that offer no separation between the line of showerheads. Leave your modesty at the door. Doubles Y160, easily negotiable to Y100; quads Y220, negotiable to Y160. ❷

🍴 FOOD

At night, **Jiefang Dalu** bathes in neon light and prepares for food and fun. The pedestrian street **Henan Jie** (河南街) fulfills your needs with everything from bakeries to dumpling houses to Sichuanese restaurants. Chongqing Jie (重庆街) is closed to automobile traffic, and local **hotpot** restaurants abound north of Shanghai Lu. **Tea houses** cluster around Tianjin Jie, and fresh fruit vendors line Qingnian Lu, which links Tianjin Jie and Jilin Dajie in the temple area.

🍴 **Green Garden Restaurant** (lǜshēng yuán dàjiǔdiàn; 绿生园大酒店 ; ☎481 7711 or 481 7722), 2km from Wende Sq. Take bus #9 to Wende Sq., and walk down the dirt path for 15min., or grab a taxi (Y5). A refreshing change from Jilin, this large farm restaurant is definitely worth the trip to the countryside. Catch your own fish in the pond, watch the sun set over the mountains, and eat your fresh, deliciously prepared meal inside a spacious, elegant greenhouse. Be sure to check out the peacocks out front, the giant dragon carved from a tree, and the cheesy mini waterfall. Most dishes Y8-50. Open daily 8:30am-11pm or when the last customer leaves. ❷

Village Farm Restaurant (zhuāngjià yuàn fàndiàn; 庄稼院饭店), 143 Jilin Dajie (☎467 1536 or 467 8315). Tikki huts, animal skins, and a dirt courtyard welcome you to this rowdy restaurant. Chefs cook up a storm in steaming pots right before your eyes. Bobbing giant fish heads for your viewing pleasure. Entrees Y20-60. ❸

👁 SIGHTS

Jilin City dazzles most in the winter, sub-zero temperatures notwithstanding. Thanks to the manipulations of hydroelectric power plants, the Songhua River does not freeze, allowing water droplets to condense and drift up in a fine mist, clinging to tree branches. When the foggy vapor freezes, a shimmering coat of ice glazes the trees, transforming Jilin into a winter wonderland. Locals call this spectacle *wùsōng* (雾凇), or "ice flowers." The **Zhuque Mountain Forest Park** (zhūquè shān sēnlín gōngyuán; 朱雀山森林公园) is a treat for skiers. In the summer, there are plenty of opportunities to get out of town for a pleasant day-hike.

SONGHUA LAKE (sōnghuā hú; 松花湖 ; ☎468 1316). Prized for its not-so-natural beauty, this manmade lake is a popular place to take a stroll, catch some fish, or enjoy the scenery. Crystal-clear waters reflect the surrounding forest like a mirror. Nearby ski grounds come to life during the winter season. *(24km south of the city center, a 1½hr. ride away. Take bus #33. Taxi Y50. Y5.)*

CONFUCIUS TEMPLE (wénmiào; 文庙). The Confucius Temple offers respite from concrete urbanity. Though crumbly-looking on the outside, it is actually quite peaceful and beautiful on the inside. The large and rarely visited temple houses a small museum and statues of the 12 disciples of Confucius. In mid-June to July, little white papers, tied by local students praying for academic success, flutter along the surrounding pear trees. *(Near the intersection of Jiangwan Lu and Tianjin Jie, tucked away in Wenmiao Xiang. Open daily 8:30am-4:30pm. Y15, students Y5.)*

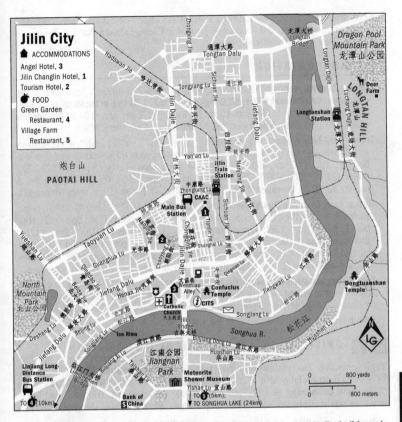

Jilin City

🏠 ACCOMMODATIONS

Angel Hotel, **3**
Jilin Changlin Hotel, **1**
Tourism Hotel, **2**

🍴 FOOD

Green Garden
   Restaurant, **4**
Village Farm
   Restaurant, **5**

CITY PARKS. The temples and sights of the **Dragon Pool Mountain Park** (lóng tán shān gōngyuán; 龙潭山公园 ; ☎8923 0082) date back to the reign of Emperor Kangxi in the Qing Dynasty. Locals outnumber tourists in this serene park. Head to the peak, where legend has it a dragon once lived. While you probably won't see a dragon, you will find a Daoist Temple and an open cage full of monkeys that frolic on the mountain during summer. *(Take bus #49 from Songjiang Lu to the terminus or #112 from the train station. Y2.)* The few hills of **North Mountain Park** (běishān gōngyuán; 北山公园) are sprinkled with Buddhist temples and pavilions and offer panoramic views of both the city and the surrounding mountains. The dilapidated **Children's Park** sullies the spiritual atmosphere somewhat with the usual park amusements, including small zoos, paddleboats, and even bungee jumping by the fake waterfall. *(Take bus #7 from the train station. Open daily 6am-5:30pm. Paddleboats Y20-30 per hr. Zoos Y3-5. Park Y5, children Y3. Children's Park Y15/Y10. Temples and pavilions Y1-2.)*

YANJI 延吉 ☎ 0433

As the largest city in Jilin province's ethnic Korean minority region, Yanji may seem more Korean than Chinese, with bilingual residents and Korean signs. Though Chinese is still the *lingua franca*, the customs and language of the *cháoxiǎn rén* (朝鲜人) have a substantial presence in Yanji, creating an interesting cultural crossroads. Beyond this, Yanji offers little more than cheap, comfortable accommodations and an access point for Changbaishan Nature Reserve's Southern Pass (p. 249), 300km away.

⌐ TRANSPORTATION

Flights: Yanji Airport (yánjí fēijīchǎng; 延吉飞机场; ☎223 4433), 10min. west of the city center. **CAAC ticket office,** 62 Gongyuan Lu (☎271 5118), in the lobby of the Civil Aviation Mansion. Open M-F 8am-10pm. To: **Beijing** (1-2 per day, Y1040); **Changchun** (daily, Y430); **Dalian** (5 per week, Y880); **Shenyang** (5 per week, Y590).

Trains: Yanji Train Station (yánjí huǒchēzhàn; 延吉火车站; ☎221 2600), at the southern end of Zhanqian Jie, south of the rivers. Ticket booths open daily 4:50am-11:30pm. To: **Beijing** (25hr., 11:25am, Y80-588) via **Tianjin; Changchun** (9-10hr., 2 per day, Y29-220); **Dalian** (21hr., 6:05pm, Y76-275); **Harbin** (12hr., 7:40pm, Y36-170); **Jilin City** (7-10hr., 5 per day, Y22-114); **Shenyang** (14hr., 3 per day, Y45-254); **Tumen** (1½hr., many per day, Y3).

Buses: Long-Distance Bus Station (kèyùn zǒng zhàn; 客运总站; ☎290 9345), in the square in front of the train station. Sleeper buses to: **Changchun** (7hr., 5pm, Y85); **Harbin** (12-13hr., 4pm, Y96); **Mudanjiang** (6hr., Y48); **Shenyang** (14-15hr., 2pm, Y120). Buses to **Changbaishan** (5hr.; depart 5:30am, return 4pm; round-trip Y101) are labeled **Tianchi** (天池) and leave from another **bus station** 2 blocks away. **Minibuses** to **Dunhua, Tumen** (1¼hr., 10 per day, Y8-10) and other cities also depart from here.

Local Transportation: Buses run 6am-7pm. Fare Y1. Buses #2, 3, 4, and 5 go between the train station and the long-distance bus station; #3 travels along Guangming Jie; #35 runs along Zhanqian Jie between the train station and the CAAC and CITS offices.

Taxi: Base fare Y5. Most taxis do not use meters.

✱ ? ORIENTATION AND PRACTICAL INFORMATION

Yanji sprawls on both sides of the **Yanji** (延吉河) and **Buerhatong Rivers** (布尔哈通河). The commercial center of the city is at the intersection of **Renmin Dajie** (人民大街) and **Guangming Jie** (光明街), northeast of the rivers. The train and long-distance bus stations are across the **Yanji Bridge** (延吉桥) from the city center.

Travel Agency: CITS, 4 Yanxi Jie, 6th fl. (☎271 5018; fax 271 7906), almost directly across from CAAC. Organizes guided tours to the Southern Pass of Changbaishan. Individual travelers may join 1-day tours (5am-9pm, Y270); 2-day tours to the waterfall and Underground Forest are available for groups of 10 or more (Y470). Open daily 8am-6pm. **Taxi drivers** offer expensive but more flexible packages for Y700-1600; they will stop at sights that are further away and not on tour group itineraries.

Bank of China: On Renmin Dajie, 2 blocks east of Guangming Jie, next to the PSB. Exchanges traveler's checks. Credit card advances. Open daily summer 8-11:30am and 1:30-5pm; winter 8-11:30am and 1-4:30pm.

PSB: On Renmin Dajie, 1 block east of Juzi Jie. The **visa department** (☎252 1372) is in the small, yellow building to the right, on the 3rd fl. Open 8am-5pm.

Pharmacy: Teyao Pharmacy (tèyào dàyàofáng; 特药大药房), 40 Guangming Jie (☎252 2488), on the corner of Renmin Dajie. Open daily 7:30am-6pm.

Internet Access: Internet Cafe, on Tuanjie Lu, a block north of Renmin Lu, just east of Juzi Jie. Over 100 fast computers. Y2 per hr. Open 24hr. **Yanji Post** has limited Internet access on the 2nd fl. Y3 per hr. Open daily 8am-4:30pm. **Zhengli Internet Cafe** (zhèng lì wǎngbā; 正力网吧), on the 2nd fl. of Zhengli Bldg., 1 block from the post office, has a surprisingly modern and user-friendly environment despite the shabby, narrow stone steps to the entrance. Y1.5 per hr. Open 24hr.

Post and Telecommunications: Yanji Post, on Renmin Dajie, on the corner of Juzi Jie (☎252 6989). EMS and Poste Restante. **Western Union** on 1st fl., phone cards and Internet on 2nd fl. Open daily summer 8am-5:30pm; winter 8am-6pm.

Postal Code: 133000.

 ## ACCOMMODATIONS AND FOOD

The center of Yanji, especially along Xinxing Jie (新兴街), has mid-range hotels with exceptionally comfortable rooms. Several cheap hostels cluster near the train station square, many without hot water or showers, but some as cheap as Y10.

Korean restaurants are ubiquitous in Yanji. Eateries specializing in **dog** dishes (gǒu ròu; 狗肉) line Jiefang Lu, east of Juzi Jie. **Pama's ❷** (pāimǎsī; 拍玛斯), on the corner of Xinxing Jie and Hailan Lu, three blocks south of Renmin Dajie, serves tasty American and European cuisine. A favorite of locals, this bar also occasionally hosts live music. (☎251 2419. Entrees Y15-36. Open daily 8:30am-2am.) For a popular local hangout constantly tuned into Korean pop, **Shanhe Hall ❷** (shànhé huìguǎn; 善和会馆 ; ☎255 7588 or 252 8304), 5min. from Renmin Square, seems to remain open even when others are closed. It offers free appetizers, large quantities of good, inexpensive Korean food (Y8-20), and wooden screens for privacy.

> **TIP**
> **SHOES OFF!** Note that in some Korean establishments, you may need to take off your shoes. Watch out for a foyer at the entrance of rooms and avoid stepping on mats and elevated platforms with shoes on.

Kaoshimao Hotel, 122 Xinxing Jie (☎291 7828), 2 blocks north of Renmin Dajie. The classy marble lobby is a good indication of what's to come. Incredibly spacious rooms are freshly painted and very bright. Caters to English speakers. Bargaining is more difficult here. Doubles Y180-290. ❷

Golden City Towers (jīnchéng dàshà; 金城大厦), 114 Tuanjie Lu (☎251 9337 or 290 1866), just east of Juzi Jie. Huge, shining bathrooms dwarf the clean and comfortable rooms. Sumptuous breakfast included. Hot water 6-8am, 11am-2pm, and 6-11pm. Doubles Y180, can be bargained down to Y140 depending on room availability. ❷

Liujin Hotel (liújīn fàndiàn; 流金饭店), 124 Xinxing Jie (☎291 2228; fax 256 1563), next to Kaoshimao. The neat rooms are a study in making the most out of a little: stairs and mirrored walls make tiny rooms look like giant 2-story chambers. Elevator and hallways could use some improvement. Breakfast included. Singles and doubles Y150. ❷

SIGHTS

From the bridge at Renmin Dajie, bus #43 runs south to **Cat Mountain Park** (māo'ér shān gōngyuán; 猫儿山公园), a fairly pleasant retreat with the usual paddleboats (Y10-20) and a not-so-usual ski jump. Chinese-Korean cultural events enliven the area during festivals and holidays. Even if you don't have the luck of visiting during a holiday, the woods and wildlife still make it a worthwhile experience. Families may prefer to lodge here in a little house with electricity and hot water (Y100).

CHANGBAISHAN 长白山

No one could have said it better than Deng Xiaoping: "Not climbing atop Changbaishan will be a regret harbored for life." Located in the southeast of corner Jilin and spilling over the North Korean border, Changbaishan features dramatic cliffs, waterfalls, grasslands, and the crater lake of Tianchi, its most famous remnant of past volcanic activity. With snow year-round, the ice-cold waters of Tianchi cascade into a roaring,

NORTHEAST

silvery waterfall and give rise to three major rivers in the Northeast. Aside from its highly touristed lake, spa-like hot springs, and family-friendly accessibility, Changbaishan is also a beautiful nature reserve. The forests are deep and piney and animals roam freely, while hardcore campers and hikers explore the untrodden paradise.

AT A GLANCE	
AREA: 1965 km²	**CLIMATE:** Temperate and sub-polar
GATEWAYS: Songjianghe, Erdaobaihe, Yanji (p. 247)	**FEES:** Entrance to the nature reserve Y60
FEATURES: Tianchi Lake (p. 252), Changbaishan Gorge (p. 253), Changbai Waterfall (p. 251)	**HIGHLIGHTS:** Camping on the shores of Tianchi Lake (p. 251); gazing across the North Korean border (p. 253)

⌐ TRANSPORTATION

The easiest way to travel to Changbaishan's **Southern Pass** is to go directly from **Yanji** (p. 247); buses leave from Yanji's long-distance bus station (5hr., 5:30am, Y55). If you don't come from Yanji, you'll have to travel through **Erdaobaihe**, a small, mysterious city 30km south of the entrance to the nature reserve. From Erdaobaihe, **trains** go to Changchun (17hr., 11:40pm), Dandong (19hr., 4:40am), and Tonghua (8hr., 4 per day), all via Songjianghe (2hr., Y5-8), the access point to the Western Pass. The ticket office (☎571 980) keeps sporadic hours. **Buses** from Erdaobaihe travel to Dunhua (4hr., multiple departures 6am-noon, Y22), Songjianghe (3hr., 2pm, Y6), and Yanji (5hr., 7:10am, Y45). Between 4 and 6pm, buses en route to Yanji and Jilin pass through the town; although they're not listed on the bus schedule, they'll still pick up passengers.

Songjianghe, three hours from the nature reserve, is the main access point for the **Western Pass.** The train station is at the end of the main street. **Trains** go to Erdaobaihe (2hr., 2 per day, Y3), Changchun (15hr., 1:48am), Dandong (17hr., 6:55am), and Tonghua (8hr., 4 per day). **Buses** depart from the Songjianghe station on the main street to Erdaobaihe (3hr., 8am, Y6), Changchun (6:35am), and Jilin (6am). As of June 2004, the only way to get from Songjianghe to the Western Pass is to join a tour offered by one of Songjianghe's hotels or take a private taxi that may charge exorbitant rates.

✳ ? ORIENTATION AND PRACTICAL INFORMATION

Changbaishan is actually a gigantic volcano, surrounded by immense plains and a dozen other peaks. From China, two roads lead to the edge of the crater: one runs from **Songjiang River** (松江河) to the **Western Pass** (xī pō; 西坡); the other runs from **Erdaobaihe** (二道白河), commonly called the **Northern Pass** (běi pō, 北坡; or èrdào běipō, 二道北坡), to the **Southern Pass** (nán pō; 南坡). These two access towns are separated by 350km of road, but geographically are only 7km (a strenuous 10hr. hike) apart. Hikers must take care not to trespass into land beyond the white border stones; there are better things to do in Changbaishan than be interrogated by North Korean border guards.

Tours: For tours beginning at the Southern Pass, contact the **Tianchi Hotel** (tiānchí bīnguǎn; 天池宾馆; ☎0439 631 3077) or the **Railway Hostel** (tiědào zhāodàisuǒ; 铁道招待所; ☎0439 631 3742) in Songjianghe. Each arranges 1-day tours for groups of 20 or more (depart approx. 5am, return 2-5pm; Y120 per person, including admission). Individual travelers may be able to join a previously established group. For tours of the Western Pass, contact the **CITS** offices in Jilin (p. 245) or Yanji (p. 248).

Bank of China: In Erdaobaihe, on the main street, near the bus station; in Songjianghe, on the main street.

Emergency: ☎ 0433 575 0120.

Post Office: In Erdaobaihe, near the bus station (☎571 9011). Another branch, near the Southern Pass gate to the nature reserve, is open daily 8am-5pm. In Songjianghe, near the bank. Open daily summer 8am-5:30pm; winter 8am-5pm.

Postal Code: Erdaobaihe 133613, Songjianghe 134504.

ACCOMMODATIONS

SOUTHERN PASS

If you enter Changbaishan via the Southern Pass, stay in the nature reserve itself to cut transportation and admission costs. Accommodations are pricey (Y400 and up) during the summer months but there are rooms available for as low as Y80 if you book ahead. Due to the number of affluent Japanese and Korean tourists who visit the area, fairly expensive establishments (Y400-800) crowd the Southern Pass. In general, the farther up the road to Tianchi you go, the more expensive the accommodations. To circumvent the lofty prices, some hardy travelers pitch **tents** along Tianchi, making sure to stay near the shore, since large rocks frequently slide down the mountainsides. A local guide maintains two semi-permanent tents (one for his dog) along the shores May to October and sells food and water.

A more comfortable and arguably more exotic option are the Korean heated floors of **Jilin Hot Springs ❶** (jílín chángbáishān yuèhuá wēnquán; 吉林长白山岳桦温泉 ; ☎13 8044 8956, 574 6068, or 574 6069), 500m below the waterfall ticket booth in the second parking lot, a 10min. walk from the last (third) parking lot. Small, windowless rooms with floors heated by hot springs water are an incredible steal at Y80 per person. You also get free access to the hot spring spas, which cost nonresidents Y40. This place is booked solid in July and August. The **Flying Fox Mountain Villa ❶** (fēihú shānzhuāng; 飞狐山庄) has dorm rooms in a neat wooden structure, inconveniently located outside the ticket gate, though closer to the outside attractions. (☎0422 571 8740. 30-bed dorms Y50; standard rooms Y220.)

WESTERN PASS

If you enter via the Western Pass, **camping** is the only option within the park. Otherwise, you'll have to spend the night in Songjianghe, in which case a few expensive and comfortable hotels (doubles Y260) can be found by the town's rotary. Try the **Baiyuan Hotel ❷** (báiyuán bīnguǎn; 白原宾馆), on the main street near the train station, past the bank and post office. (☎0439 632 4055. Doubles with bath Y150.) The best values can be found at the **Fenglou Travel Hotel ❶** (fēnglóu lǚ fàndiàn; 丰楼旅饭店), which also houses a disco. (☎0439 631 3087. Singles and doubles with TV and bath Y20 per person; triples Y30.) There is also a **bathhouse** (Y10) in the center of town and a **"bath palace"** at the Railway Hostel (Y3).

TREKKING IN CHANGBAISHAN

The bus depot in the parking lot 25km past the ticket gates is the hub for hitting all Southern Pass trails and destinations.

FOR NOVICES AND DAYTRIPPERS

A 4.3km road begins at the parking lot, to the right of the Main Peak road, and continues along the stream to **Changbai Waterfall** (chángbái pùbù; 长白瀑布), the largest and most famous of Changbaishan's many waterfalls. A jeep ride to the waterfall costs Y50 or less per car, but the fairly deserted road (beware of the occasional speeding car) isn't steep and makes for a pleasant walk. Fifteen minutes from the parking lot, the road also passes on the left the **hiking path** to the Main Peak (zhǔ fēng; 主峰). The road to **Small Tianchi** and the top of **White Cloud Mountain** is clearly marked and on the right. The last parking lot is located here and usually fills with tourists during the summer months. Take a last glance at the joyfully hectic environment of food, hotels, and spas before you make your trek up the quieter mountainside. The road ends at a ticket booth (Y15) past the steamy **hot springs.** Off to the left, you can find more spectacular geysers before continuing on to the waterfall. Eggs boiled in hot spring waters can be bought for Y3. The walk from the ticket booth to the waterfall takes 10-15min.

From the waterfall, continue along the same steep path to the heavenly shores and sapphire waters of Changbaishan's most popular attraction, **Tianchi** (天池), an enormous crater lake located 2189m above sea level, cradled by golden peaks. The path to Tianchi (Y40) is covered and railed, making the climb fairly safe, if tiring. The 1hr. hike leads to the top of the waterfall and opens up to reveal green plains with towering volcanic mountains on both sides. Batches of dirty snow left over from the winter decorate the way to the lake shores, where guides maintain a permanent tent and photographers sell their pictures. A stony trail leading to **Dragon Gate Peak** and **White Cloud Peak** branches off to the right. Just before Tianchi, a footbridge marks the beginning of a path to the left that leads to the Main Peak.

You can also get to the **Underground Forest** (dìxià sēnlín; 地下森林) from the main access road (Y15, after 5pm free). Take care when walking on the narrow main road, as cars move fast and the road has many blindspots. A 1.5km woodboarded path, branching to the right 5km before the first parking lot, winds through the forest of conifers and pines growing over the craters, gradually descending 100m until it reaches the river. The trek from the waterfall to the forest takes a good 2hr. At the river, the path abruptly diverges into two. The right side leads you further into the forest, while the left meanders to the **Dongtian Waterfall.** This path is not strenuous, and it takes approximately 20-30min. to reach the falls. Concealed under soil and roots, the tumbling water carves out a 50m gorge.

If you want to appreciate Changbaishan's beautiful views without having to sweat or toil, you're not alone. Jeeps take passengers straight to the top of **Tianwen Peak** (tiānwén fēng; 天文峰; 2670m), also known as the Main Peak. (30min., Apr.-Sept. approx. 4:30am-4pm, Y80.)

FOR EXPERIENCED HIKERS

For those up for a greater challenge, two paths head for the **Main Peak,** one running to the left of the Changbai Waterfall, the other to the right. Though more difficult and dangerous, these trails are also a lot more rewarding, as you are actually surrounded by untamed nature and varied terrain, rather than tourists. It is illegal to travel these paths without a guide due to safety and nature preservation. Ask the officers at the first parking lot for more information on guides. Travelers are strongly advised to have a companion when hiking here, as there will be points when you may need assistance to scale rocks. Paths are not clearly marked, making it easy to get lost. Wild animals, including tigers, bears, and boars, have been sighted in the forests; even mosquitoes are more vicious in these parts of the woods. It is best to start early in the morning, prepared for sporadic weather conditions.

The trail climbing up the left side of Changbai Waterfall can be accessed through any of the somewhat overgrown footpaths along the left of the main road. The trail ascends through the forest and then follows the paved road to Main Peak for about an hour. At **Black Wind Pass** (hēi fēng kǒu; 黑风口), a pavilion with a panoramic view of the waterfall, the path swerves left and continues straight across to the peak. The route is about 6km long and takes 3hr. to ascend and 2½hr. to descend.

The path to **Tianchi** branches to the left (about 5min. before reaching the lake) to reveal a footbridge, this hike's starting point. The first section, up a steep mountain gorge, is gritty and dangerous; after it reaches a grassy slope, the walk becomes a monotonous, albeit scenic, stair-climb. The ascent takes 2½hr., the descent 1½hr. After reaching the Main Peak, you can continue on to **Huagai Peak** (huágài fēng; 华盖峰 ; 2640m). The beautiful route spans a quarter of Tianchi's 13km circumference and passes some of Changbaishan's most interesting geological quirks. The well-defined path soon disappears, but the easy-to-follow trail continues along the main crest. Near the summit, the lack of trees makes it easy to spot a temple-like structure on top of White Cloud Peak, marking the border between China and North Korea. Take care not to cross it, although white border stones and guards will help those who stray. The hike takes 4-6hr. each way.

The second and more difficult trail is a small path right of the main road from the parking lot to Changbai Waterfall. This path will bring you to **Small Tianchi** (xiǎo tiānchí; 小天池). From here, a path leads to the majestic **Dragon Gate Peak** (lóngmén fēng; 龙门峰 ; 2595m) and **White Cloud Peak** (báiyún fēng; 白云峰 ; 2691m). Follow the trees labeled with white pieces of cloth; once you pass the tree line, the path is clearer. On a hollow alp, the path splits into two: the branch to the left leads to Dragon Gate Peak and another path to Tianchi (1hr.); the trail to the right continues along the main crest to White Cloud Peak and beyond to the Western Pass. The area around White Cloud Peak is particularly difficult, and some rock-climbing experience may be necessary. The hike between Small Tianchi and the junction takes 3hr. to ascend, 1½hr. to descend; Small Tianchi and White Cloud Peak 6hr./3hr.; Small Tianchi and Western Pass 10hr./8hr.

A path connects the road between Tianchi and Changbai Waterfall with the junction of the paths leading to Dragon Gate and White Cloud Peaks. It begins at the stone embankment and climbs all the way up to the pass, turning slightly to the left. This dangerous path bisects a fragile rubble slope and should only be used to evacuate from the higher sections of Dragon Gate Peak. It takes 1hr. to ascend, 30min. to descend.

THE WESTERN PASS

The rugged attractions of the Western Pass are scattered along the access road from Songjianghe. There is a junction 10km before the end of the road, from which a dirt road branches to the left to the 100m deep, precipitous **Changbaishan Gorge** (chángbáishān dàxiágǔ; 长白山大峡谷). The path overlooking the gorge passes a unique tree, actually the merging trunks of three different species. After 30min., the path leads to a bridge over a chasm. A nearby junction attracts jump-happy daredevils. Pass the end of the road, paved stairs reach the spectacular scenery of the pass, from which a path descends to Tianchi (1hr.). A difficult trail to **White Cloud Peak** and **Southern Pass** starts on the left (facing Tianchi), just below the pass. Mountains to the right are easier to hike, but the North Korean border cuts them in half, and wandering hikers are stopped by vigilant PSB offices.

OUTSIDE CHANGBAISHAN

There are a few places right outside of the reserve (6km south) that are still considered Changbaishan sights, though you have to repay the admission fee to return to the reserve. At **Tiger Park** (hǔ línyuán; 虎林园), customers are caged while the tigers roam free. If the picture-perfect surroundings make you crave gory nature, you can buy live animals—chickens (Y35) or small cows (Y500 and up)—to feed the tigers. Holding a baby tiger costs Y10, but be careful because, like all babies, they are extremely irritable. (Admission Y35.) If you can't make it to the Western Pass, the **Fushilin Gorges** (fú shílín; 浮石林) are the next best thing. Volcanic activity carved these natural cliffs, chasms, slopes, and rock formations. The unguided paths can be slippery and may extend to the very edges of the gorges, so take care when trying to angle for the best views. (Admission Y30.)

LIAONING 辽宁

With a long coastline, a booming economy, and a mild climate, Liaoning is the golden child of the northeast. The beautifully varied and untamed landscape of plains, mountains, and waters has historically inspired much admiration—and greed—in its neighbors, from the Qing emperors who chose Liaoning as the site of their first capital, to the Japanese who wrested it from the Qing. While it suffered heavily during the Japanese occupation in the 1930s and 40s, the province now seems blissfully unfettered by recollections of darker eras. Today, despite growing unemployment and lagging development in the countryside, Liaoning's crown jewels—the warm-water seaports of Dalian and Lushun—still shine.

SHENYANG 沈阳   ☎024

Amid the endless wheat fields of Liaoning province, Shenyang is a promising metropolis. History singled out the city as the home of the Manchu court (1625-1644) at the beginning of the Qing Dynasty. In 1931, Shenyang, along with the rest of Manchuria, landed itself in the history books once again, when the Japanese launched their invasion of China from the region. With a population of 6.8 million, Shenyang is the largest and arguably the most important city in the northeast. Modernization is more than just a buzz word here: main streets are gutted and repaved and high-rises are constructed and demolished at a frenzied pace. Luckily, the populace appears to be taking it all in stride. Proudly embracing its imperial past, the enterprising city knows that its biggest draw is not high-rises but history.

▎ TRANSPORTATION

Flights: Taoxian International Airport (táoxiān jīchǎng; 桃仙机场; ☎8938 2520), on the southern fringe of the city, off the main highway to Dalian. **CAAC shuttle buses** (Y10) depart from the corner of Taiyuan Jie and Zhonghua Lu. Taxi Y60. **IATA ticket office** (guójì hángxié hángkōng shòupiào chù; 国际航协航空售票处), 229 Zhongshan Lu (☎2284 2925). Other ticket offices abound. To: **Beijing** (5 per day, Y640); **Dalian** (1-2 per day, Y170); **Guangzhou** (1-2 per day, Y2000); **Harbin** (1-4 per day, Y470); **Hong Kong** (6 per week, Y2130); **Qingdao** (5 per week, Y620); **Shanghai** (1-3 per day, Y1190); **Xi'an** (9:25am, Y1350). International flights to: **Khabarovsk, Russia** (2 per week); **Osaka** (4 per week) and other major destinations in **Japan** (1-2 per week); **Seoul, South Korea** (2 per week).

Trains: Shenyang has 2 main train stations. Most trains pass through both stations.

Shenyang Main Train Station (shěnyáng huǒchē zhàn; 沈阳火车站 ; ☎6206 4222 or 2351 4122), at the end of Zhonghua Lu, on the corner of Shengli Dajie, Heping district. To: **Baihe** (9hr., 4:30am, Y39-80) via **Songjianghe** (7hr.); **Beijing** (10-12hr., 8 per day, Y51-300); **Changchun** (5hr., 7 per day, Y20-75); **Dalian** (4-6hr., 8 per day, Y28-124); **Dandong** (5hr., 9 per day, Y18-54); **Harbin** (8hr., 12 per day, Y32-159); **Tumen** (16hr., 2 per day, Y47-254).

Shenyang North Station (shěnyáng běizhàn; 沈阳北站 ; ☎2252 2085 or 6204 3522), on Beizhan Lu, Shenhe district. To: **Dalian** (15 per day); **Dandong** (4½hr., 4 per day); **Guangzhou** (48hr., 8pm, Y286-900); **Jilin** (6-9hr., 6 per day, Y31-115); **Shanghai** (34hr., 4 per day, Y204-800); **Tianjin** (10-14hr., 4 per day, Y49-290).

Buses: 2 main bus stations, along with a slew of private vehicles, service Shenyang.

Shenyang South Long-Distance Passenger Transport Station (shěnyáng nánzhàn chángtú qìchē kèyùn zhàn; 沈阳南站长途汽车客运站 ; tickets ☎2251 1223, information 2251 7871), on 120 Huigong Jie, near the train station. To: **Beijing** (13hr., 6 per day, Y190); **Dalian** (4½hr., 13 per day, Y72); **Harbin** (12hr., 6 per day, Y130); **Tianjin** (13hr., 1pm, Y62-114).

Express Bus Station (kuàisù kèyùn zhàn; 快速客运站 ; ☎2251 1222) on Huigong Jie. From Shenyang North Station, walk down Youhao Jie to a roundabout; it's on the left. To: **Beijing**

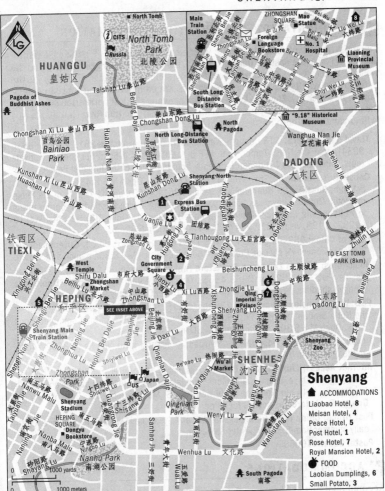

Shenyang

♦ **ACCOMMODATIONS**
Liaobao Hotel, **8**
Meisan Hotel, **4**
Peace Hotel, **5**
Post Hotel, **1**
Rose Hotel, **7**
Royal Mansion Hotel, **2**
● **FOOD**
Laobian Dumplings, **6**
Small Potato, **3**

(12hr., 2 per day, Y190); **Changchun** (4hr., 8 per day, Y75); **Dalian** (4½hr., 7 per day, Y99); **Dandong** (4hr., 6 per day, Y65); **Harbin** (7hr., 2 per day, Y130); **Jilin** (4½hr., 8 per day, Y96).

Private buses depart from the square in front of the North Train Station. Frequent buses to: **Beijing** (Y185); **Dalian** (Y98); **Harbin** (Y80). Buses in the parking lot next-door run to: **Changchun** (3 per day, Y70); **Qingdao** (3:30pm, Y198); **Tianjin** (4, 6pm; Y221). Destinations in Liaoning province are easily reached on **private cars** that depart when full. Many ply the area between the Main Train Station and the Long-Distance Station. Rides to **Dandong** (3hr.) cost Y80 after bargaining.

Local Transportation: Buses and most **minibuses** cost Y1-2; larger A/C buses and minibuses numbered 500-plus Y2. Buses run on major streets until 10:30pm. The **first ring bus** (yī huán; 一环) loops from the Main Train Station to North Station via Xi Shuncheng Jie; #202 runs between the Main Train Station and North Tomb Park via City Government Sq.; #225 loops from the Main Train Station to South Lake Park and up Qingnian Dajie to City Government Sq.

Taxis: Base fare Y7, with A/C Y8; each additional km Y1.6-2.

✦🛈 ORIENTATION AND PRACTICAL INFORMATION

The most important districts are the west-central **Heping** (和平), the east-central **Shenhe** (沈河), the eastern **Dadong** (大东), the northern **Huanggu** (皇姑), and the western **Tiexi** (铁西). **City Government Square** (shìfǔ guǎngchǎng; 市府广场) is the hub of the city. Heping and Shenhe districts are commercial and tourist centers. **Taiyuan Jie** (太原街), **Zhongjie Lu** (中街路), Shenyang's oldest pedestrian street, and the areas nearby will likely interest visitors the most. The **Hun River** (hún hé; 浑河) is Shenyang's southern border.

Travel Agency: CITS, 113 Huanghe Nan Dajie, Huanggu district (☎8612 2445 or 8680 9834), near the North Tomb. Open M-F 8-11:30am and 1-5pm. For cheaper, private tours, minibuses (Y140) depart frequently from the gates of the Imperial Palace.

Consulates: Japan, 50 Shisi Wei Lu (☎2322 7490). Open M-F 8:45am-noon and 1-5:15pm. **Russia,** 109 Huanghe Nan Dajie (☎8611 4963), on the 10th fl. of the Phoenix Hotel. Organize day visas here if you are planning to visit Russia from border towns in Heilongjiang Province. Open M-Tu and Th-F 9am-4:30pm. **US,** 52 Shisi Wei Lu (☎2322 1198, visas 2322 2147). Open M-F 8:30am-5:30pm.

Bank of China: 253 Shifu Dalu (☎2285 7563 or 2285 7595), on City Government Sq. Exchanges traveler's checks. Credit card advances. Open M-F 8:30am-noon and 1-5pm.

Bookstores: Foreign Language Bookstore (wài wén shūdiàn; 外文书店), 43 Taiyuan Bei Jie (☎2340 9324 or 2383 4565). Open daily 9am-6pm. **Dongyu Bookstore** (dōngyǔ shūdiàn; 东宇书店), 2 Heping Nan Dajie. Open daily 9am-8pm.

PSB: Visa extension department, 73 Zhongshan Lu, 4th fl., post 6 (☎2253 4850), near the North Station, opposite Post Hotel. Enter through the lobby of the Communications Bank. Open M-F 8:30-11:30am and 1-4:30pm.

Hospital: Great No. 1 Hospital (yī dà yīyuàn; 一大医院), Nanjing Jie (☎8699 2401), at Zhongshan Sq.

Internet Access: Linxi Internet Cafe (línxī wǎngbā; 林夕网吧), 367 Zhongshan Lu, near Qingnian Dajie. Open 10am-midnight or later. Another **Internet cafe** is on Taiyuan Jie, 2nd fl., between Nan San Malu and Nan Si Malu. Open 24hr. Both Y2 per hr. **Dongyu Bookstore** has access for Y3 per hr.

Post Office: China Post, 54 Zhongshan Lu, at Taiyuan Jie. EMS and IDD service. Open daily summer 8am-5:30pm; winter 8am-5pm.

Postal Code: 110000.

⌂ ACCOMMODATIONS

Accommodations in Shenyang tend to be upscale, but there are some relatively cheap places in good locations. Construction is the hobby of choice and hotels are often fully booked, so call ahead.

SHENHE DISTRICT

Post Hotel (yóuzhèng dàshà; 邮政大厦), 78 Beizhan Lu (☎2259 3333), just west of the North Train Station. The humble Post Hotel is functional and affordable, if a bit spartan, with bare walls, worn carpeting, and fans. Prime location and prominent self-promotion (red banner advertising its Y60 dorms) make it a popular spot, so book ahead. Relatively clean public baths. Travel agency and convenience store on 1st fl. 2-bed dorms Y60; doubles Y100-120 and up. ❶

Rose Hotel (méiguì dàfàndiàn; 玫瑰大饭店), 201 Zhongjie Lu (☎2489 8188; fax 189 8060). 10min. from the train station, across from Laobian Dumplings. On the pricey side, but amenities and attentive service make it worthwhile. Fairly large rooms with big windows and great city views. Bathrooms are somewhat cramped. 24hr. hot water, mini water dispensers, free Internet from room. Breakfast included. Doubles Y300-368. ❹

Meisan Hotel (méisǎn bīnguǎn; 梅糁宾馆), 48 Xiaoxi Lu (☎227 35548; fax 2273 5548). Within walking distance of City Government Sq. and the Imperial Palace. Hardwood floors add a touch of class. Doubles Y140; triples Y200; quads Y240. ❷

Royal Mansion Hotel (wángfǔ bīnguǎn; 王府宾馆), 5 Youhao Jie (☎2273 5867), south of the North Train Station. A reliable option with standard services, relatively clean rooms, and decent public baths. Possibly the best prices in town. 2-bed dorms Y30; 3-bed dorms Y45; doubles Y100; triples Y150. ❶

HEPING DISTRICT

Peace Hotel (hépíng bīnguǎn; 和平宾馆), 104 Shengli Bei Jie (☎2349 8888; www.hpbg.com.cn), just north of the Main Train Station. On the musty and yellowing side, but a decent place for a night's sleep. Doubles with 2 rooms don't get much bigger than this. Small baths. Carpeted floors creak. Doubles with bath Y190-260. ❸

Liaobao Hotel (liáobào dàjiǔdiàn; 辽报大酒店), 15 Bei Sanjing Jie (☎2271 4779 or 2284 4824), next door to the Liaoning newspaper building on Zhongshan Lu, a bit removed from the noise of Taiyuan Jie. Dimly lit rooms are rather small and bathrooms are leaky, but staff is very friendly. Hot water until midnight. Doubles Y120. ❷

🔾 FOOD

Western restaurants and bars cluster in the Heping district and near Dongbei University. **Zhongshan Market** (zhōngshān shìchǎng; 中山市场), on Beiliu Lu off Zhongshan Lu, is a good place for fresh fruit. The neighboring streets branching off Taiyuan Jie are packed with stalls selling *bāozi* (Y0.5). The **Civic Convenience Shop** (xìnméng biànlì diàn; 信盟便利店) has 24hr. branches scattered throughout the city, including one on Xiaoxi Lu across from the Meisan Hotel.

🦑 **Li Liangui Smoked Meat-Stuffed-Pancake Restaurant** (lǐliánguì xūnròu dàbǐng jiǔdiàn; 李连贵熏肉大饼酒店), 4 Zhenyang Jie, 2nd fl. (☎2383 5111). Almost as old as Laobian Dumplings, Li Liangui's specialty is *xūnròu bǐng*, a fried doughy pancake with smoked meat rolled in, a deliciously greasy dish unique to Shenyang. It also has a variety of other dishes in large portions at extremely affordable prices. Y3-10 per dish. ❶

🦑 **Laobian Dumplings** (lǎo biān jiǎozǐ guǎn; 老边饺子馆), at the intersection of Zhongjie Lu and Chaoyang Jie. Another branch in Heping district, across from the Peace Hotel. With a history of close to 200 years, Shenyang's most famous and beloved restaurant has itself become a historical site. Originating in 1829 during the rule of Qing emperor Daoguang, Laobian through the years has grown to offer a seemingly endless variety of mouthwatering, incomparable dumplings. 1 *liǎng* (50g or 1.8 oz.) Y30; 2 *liǎng* Y50. ❸

Nationalities of China Village (huáxià mínzú cūn dàjiǔlóu; 华夏民族村大酒楼), 11 Bei Wu Malu, Heping district (☎2340 9334 or 2383 2173), a short walk north along Nanjing Bei Jie from Zhongshan Sq. A great place to get local food, hang out with resident folk, and play with children's blow-up toys. Entrees Y10-40. ❷

Small Potato (xiǎo tǔdòu; 小土豆), 37 Xiaoxi Lu (☎2291 5040). This restaurant's potato dishes are so popular with locals that it's often hard to find empty tables. Entrees Y10-25. Open daily 10:30am-10:30pm. ❷

👁 SIGHTS

QING IMPERIAL PALACE (gù gōng, 故宫 ; officially tàiqīng gōng, 太清宫). In the early 1600s, this splendid complex was the home of Nurhaci and Hong Taiji, the Manchu founders of the Qing Dynasty. The palace looks like a small version of Beijing's Forbidden City, with 300 rooms constructed largely using Han Chinese architectural principles and Manchu and Mongol elements blended seamlessly into the grounds. Swallows swoop here and there in this surprisingly peaceful space. Guides in Qing attire give tours. *(On the pedestrian Zhongjie Lu, Shenhe district.* ☎ *2484 3001. Open daily 8:30am-7pm, last ticket 6:15pm. Y50.)*

NORTH TOMB PARK (běi líng gōngyuán; 北陵公园). With acres of old pines and elegantly sculpted manmade lakes, this park is the biggest and best in Shenyang. If you have a couple of hours, join the locals for some kite flying or a relaxed game of badminton. During the summer, take your pick of cutesy animal paddleboats. Within the park lies the vaunted tomb of Hong Taiji (also known as Abahai), second emperor of the Qing. The tomb itself hasn't been opened yet, making for a somewhat anticlimactic experience, but the characteristic architecture of the Qing Dynasty is interesting in its own right. English subtitles provide a thorough history. *(Encircled by Taishan Lu and Huanghe Nan Dajie, at the end of Beiling Dajie, in Huanggu district. Take bus #220 from the North Train Station or bus #227 from Xi Shuncheng Jie, just west of the Imperial Palace. Open daily summer 6am-6pm; winter 8am-5pm. Boats foot paddle Y40, hand paddle Y30. Park Y6, tomb Y30.)*

EAST TOMB PARK (dōng líng gōngyuán; 东陵公园). The founder of the Qing Dynasty, the "Dragon Tiger General" Nurhaci (1559-1626), is buried in these woods with his empress. Perhaps because of the tomb's remote location or because he was genuinely less popular, Nurhaci sees fewer visitors than does his late partner Hong Taiji. Remarkably similar in appearance to the North Tomb, but less intricate, East Tomb is worth a visit only for those who prefer the road less traveled. *(45min. east of the city center by bus. Take bus #218 from Xi Shuncheng Jie just east of the Imperial Palace. Open daily 6am-6:30pm. Y30.)*

"9.18" HISTORICAL MUSEUM (jiǔyībā lìshǐ bówùguǎn; 九一八历史博物馆). Named after the "9.18 Incident," the seizure of Shenyang by the Japanese on September 18, 1931, the museum explores the occupation of Manchuria. Though predictably biased, the haunting war images, supplemented by English captions, present a compelling and touching recounting of Japanese oppression. *(46 Wanghua Nan Jie. Accessible by bus #212 from Xi Shuncheng Jie, west of the Imperial Palace. Tickets sold 8:30am-4pm. Y20, students Y10.)*

DANDONG 丹东 ☎ 415

A small, unassuming city, Dandong would make its way onto few tourist itineraries if not for its prime location on the Sino-Korean border. Japanese, South Korean, and Chinese tourists crowd onto its shore, into boats, and along the Yalu River Bridge to catch a glimpse of the forbidden Communist kingdom beyond. The transformation of the world's most isolated nation into a tourist spectacle is a phenomenon every bit as bizarre as the view of North Korea itself.

▣ TRANSPORTATION

Flights: Dandong Airport (dāndōng jīchǎng; 丹东机场 ; ☎ 617 6569), 13km from Dandong. A taxi from the city costs Y25-30. **Shuttle buses** (Y5) leave 1½hr. before departure from the **CAAC ticket office,** 50 Jingshan Dajie (☎ 212 3427), at San Wei Lu. Open daily 8am-5:30pm. To **Beijing** (Sa, Y570) and **Shanghai** (Tu, Th, Sa; Y990).

Trains: Dandong Train Station (dāndōng huǒchē zhàn; 丹东火车站 ; ☎ 202 1222), at the intersection of Shi Wei Lu and Qi Jing Jie. Ticket booths open daily 6am-6pm. To: **Beijing** (14-22hr., 2 per day, Y73-400); **Changchun** (11hr., 7am, Y41-71); **Dalian** (11hr., daily, Y53-170); **Qingdao** (24½hr., daily, Y100-330); **Shenyang** (4hr., 7 per day, Y29-54).

Buses: Dandong Long-Distance Passenger Bus Station (dāndōng chángtú kèyùn zhàn; 丹东长途客运站), 98 Shiwei Lu (☎ 213 4571), a short walk to the left from the train station. To: **Beijing** (18hr., 10am, Y165); **Dalian** (6hr.; frequent minibuses 5:30am-

2:30pm, a deluxe coach 4pm; Y54-64); **Harbin** (at least 20hr., 10am, Y154). **Huayuan Passenger Station** (huàyuán kèyùn zhàn; 化园客运站), on Huayuan Jie in north Dandong. Take local bus #11, 12, or 21. To **Shenyang** (6hr., frequent, Y54-98).

Local Transportation: Local buses usually run 5am-7pm. Fare Y1.

Taxi: Base fare Y5, each additional km Y1.8. **Pedicabs** within the city generally cost Y2.

✴ 🛈 ORIENTATION AND PRACTICAL INFORMATION

East of the railroad, central Dandong is a grid of roads. Numbered **"Wei Lu"** roads run north-south, and numbered **"Jing Jie"** roads run east-west. Buildings are rarely marked with their street number. Much of the city's drama takes place along the **riverbank,** past Yi Jing Jie, where cruise ships and restaurants line the shore. The pedestrian **Xin'an Lu** (新安路), ten minutes from the train station, is Dandong's take on a Western thoroughfare.

Travel Agency: CITS, 1 Zhanqian Dalu, 3rd fl. of CITS Hotel (☎213 7473 or 212 7721; fax 212 6377), Zhanqian Sq., south of the train station. English-speaking staff. Offers tour packages to North Korea, including visas; allow a few days for processing (see **North Korea,** p. 42). Open M-F 8-11:30am and 1:30-5pm.

Bank of China: 60 Jingshan Dajie, at Er Wei Lu. Exchanges traveler's checks. Credit card advances. Open M-F summer 8-11:30am and 1:30-5pm; 8-11:30am and 1-4:30pm.

PSB: Along Shi Wei Lu (☎213 0110), a block from the Yalu River. Open M-F 8am-noon and 1:30-5:30pm.

Hospital: No. 1 Hospital (dìyī yīyuàn; 第一医院 ; ☎281 4132), on Qi Jing Jie, past the pedestrian Xin'an Lu. **Pharmacy** inside.

Internet Access: Coffee Internet Cafe (kāfēi wǎngbā; 咖啡网吧), on Qi Jing Jie, at Qi Wei Lu. Cake and tea on the left, fast connections on the right. Open daily 10am-midnight or later. There is another cafe with a slower connection on Wu Jing Jie, at Liu Wei Lu, on the 2nd fl. Open 24hr. Both charge Y2 per hr. **China Mobile,** at the intersection of Wu Jing Jie and Liu Wei Lu, has 2 free, albeit slow and unreliable, Internet stations.

Post Office: China Post, on Qi Jing Jie, at Qi Wei Lu. EMS. Open M-F 8am-5:30pm. Phone booths next door in front of **China Telecom.**

Postal Code: 118000.

🏠 ACCOMMODATIONS

Most of Dandong's hotels are standard and stodgy. The best locations are near the train station and the Yalu River, but the city is small enough that it doesn't matter much. The most upscale hotels are on the riverbank, west of the railroad tracks, near the Yalu River Bridge.

Dandong Railway Hotel (dān tiě dàshà; 丹铁大厦), 3 Shiyi Wei Lu (☎230 7777), in the tower attached to the train station. Enjoy a perfect view of trains passing below. Also across from the bus station and a mere 10min. walk from Yalu River. With clean but cramped rooms and small bathrooms, this hotel favors convenience over class. Horn-happy taxis can make for a noisy stay. Dorms Y25-40; doubles Y150 and up. ❶

CITS Hotel (jīnshuāngxīng shāngwù bīnguǎn; 金双星商务宾馆), 1 Zhanqian Sq., 2nd fl. (☎230 7888). Somewhat upscale rooms are a good value for the price. CITS travel agency dominates the 5th fl. 24hr. hot water. Doubles Y260-880. ❹

Dandong Hotel (dāndōng fàndiàn; 丹东饭店), 31 Qi Jing Jie (☎212 3529), 1 block east of the post office. Great prices and location, but dark hallways lead to creaky dorms. Doubles are more roomy; some have private toilets. Not-so-clean public bathrooms. Almost 24hr. hot water. Dorms Y25-40; singles Y80; doubles Y120. ❶

THE BIG SPLURGE

THE OTHER SIDE

If peering over the riverbank doesn't satisfy your curiosity, here's your chance to see more of the hermit kingdom. From Dandong, you can cross the infamous China-North Korea Bridge and experience the rare view from the other side of the Yalu River. But everything comes at a price, and this one starts at around Y8000.

The standard tour package touches down at Pyongyang, the capital city and the country's cultural, economic, and political center. You'll get more than your fill of North Korea's two rulers: statues and memorials devoted to the Great Leader Kim Il Sung and the Dear Leader Kim Jong Il abound. From Pyongyang, choose a route that fits your tastes. To the south lie Nampo, Kaesong, and the DMZ. Hardier travelers can try scaling Mt. Myohyang or Mt. Kumgang, which feaures North Korea's highest peak, Piro (1639m). For a quick fix, there are also cheaper one-day tours for Sinoju, right at the border of North Korea and China.

Tours in North Korea are extremely structured. Visitors are accompanied at all times, may not speak to locals, and are only allowed in designated areas. Violation of protocol could have serious consequences.

*Citizens of Israel, South Korea, and the US cannot enter North Korea. Contact the **Dandong CITS** (☎213 7473; www.ddcits.com) for more information. Ask for Zhang Runfu.*

Zhonglian Hotel (zhōnglián dàjiǔdiàn; 中联大酒店), No. 1, 2A Business and Tourism Section (☎317 0666). Hands down the nicest hotel in Dandong with prices to match. Depending on how much you love the China-North Korea Bridge, it may or may not be worth it. These clean and decently sized rooms are right along the river with large windows for checking out Dandong's main attraction, the elusive country on the other side of the Yalu. Singles Y398; doubles Y498, extra bed Y150. ❺

🍴 FOOD

Dandong's wealth of dining options, though a testament to the power of international trade, does not ensure culinary mastery. Small **Korean** restaurants line Shi Wei Lu between the train station square and the river, serving cold noodles (lěng miàn; 冷面 ; Y3-5) and *bibimbap* (bànfàn; 拌饭 ; Y5-8). For sleepwalkers and night-eaters, **Qi Jing Lu,** which runs from the train station, has food stalls open until 3am. Several fancy restaurants line **Liu Wei Lu.**

Andong Pavilion Restaurant (āndōng gé; 安东阁), along the riverbank, a 5min. walk past the railroad and the Yalu River Bridge. The large pavilion is easy to spot from afar. This elegant establishment has an original no-menu style of ordering: the waiter walks you through a display of living creatures from which you pick and choose. The best non-bridge view of North Korea. Most entrees Y20-50. Open daily 11am-9:30pm. ❷

Deheng Fat Cow City (déhēng féiniú chéng; 德亨肥牛城), E40 Business and Tourism Section (shāngmào lǚyóu qū; 商贸旅游区). On the little street parallel to the riverbank, between Andong Pavilion and the big square. Run by a Hui family, this restaurant serves Muslim dishes and hotpot. Dishes Y10-60. Open daily 10am-10pm. ❷

Italy Pizza (yìdàlì bǐsābǐng; 意大利比萨饼), on Qi Jing Jie, at San Wei Lu. An Italian master chef awarded Italy Pizza the "New Kind Of Pizza Invention Award," now proudly framed and displayed. Popular among locals, the over-priced Western food might just hit the right spot for travelers as well. Entrees Y12-30. Open daily 8am-midnight. ❷

🔆 SIGHTS

Dandong's most interesting sights are near the Yalu River and the Democratic People's Republic of Korea. Nature-lovers can explore the hills surrounding Dandong, but even these are best known for their bird's-eye views of The Other Bank.

YALU RIVER CRUISES. All along the Yalu River, cruises take passengers within 10m of North Korea, one of the most isolated places on earth. Photos are allowed, but don't expect picturesque scenery: old boats, children at play, a few soldiers on patrol, and one discreetly hidden picture of Kim Il Sung constitute the entire visible slice of North Korean life. *(Boats run 6am-6:30pm, occasionally later. 20min. cruise on a big boat Y8. 10min. speed boat rides get closer to the North Korean shore for Y18. If you're coming along Shi Wei Lu, don't wander right into the uninteresting park, which charges extra admission; there are docks on other side of the rail tracks.)*

YALU RIVER BRIDGE (yālù jiāng qiáo; 鸭绿江桥). The unconventional bridge still bears evidence of 1950s "US aggression" against North Korea: look for shrapnel and some damage. Visitors can wear a Chinese Volunteer Anti-Imperialist Force uniform and pose with a gun in front of the North Korean border (Y5). *(West of Yalu River Park, extending halfway over the Yalu River. Open daily 6:30am-7pm. Y15.)*

▶ DAYTRIPS FROM DANDONG

▩ PHOENIX MOUNTAIN

50km northwest of Dandong, near the city of Fengcheng (凤城). Buses (1½hr., approx. every 10 min. 4am-4pm., Y8) go from Dandong Long-Distance Bus Station to Fengcheng; ask to be dropped off at Fenghuangshan Gate (凤凰山门), a few km before Fengcheng city. Buses (Y5) shuttle visitors between the gate and the ticket office. Open May to early Oct. Y30.

Reputed to be China's most challenging *via ferrata* (a rock-climbing route made more accessible with the addition of steel railings), Phoenix Mountain (fènghuáng shān; 凤凰山) offers mountaineering excitement that rivals some of the world's most famous routes. Don't expect sky-high altitudes, even though scenic vistas abound; the real treat is the solid rock. The path's metal protectors cut through nearly vertical, polished, vertiginous rock faces and slice through dark, cramped caves, challenging agoraphobes and claustrophobes alike.

Good hiking shoes are an absolute must. There are at least four main routes, each taking 1½-6½hr. to complete. The shortest and flattest route involves dark tunnels that require flashlights or candles that can be bought outside for Y5. A cable car rescues fledgling hikers halfway. (Y25. One-way ascent Y15. Round-trip Y40.) Guides charge Y100 to walk less confident visitors around the loop. When you return to comfortingly horizontal surfaces, check out the Qing and Ming Dynasty Daoist temples scattered between the ticket gate and the last parking lot.

TIGER MOUNTAIN GREAT WALL

15km northeast of Dandong, past the town of Jiuliancheng (九连城). Minibuses (20min., 4am-4pm, Y4) depart irregularly from the corner of Shi Wei Lu and Jingshan Dajie, near the bus station. Or, instead of waiting for the erratic minibus, take local bus #15 (Y1). Chinese speakers can take bus #13 (Y1) to the other side of the river; from there, take a boat (Y10) to the wall. Do not stray into the North Korean grasslands on the right. Round-trip taxis cost Y80. Open daily 7:30am-5:30pm. Y30, museum Y10.

Built by the Ming Dynasty in 1469, Tiger Mountain Great Wall (hǔshān chángchéng; 虎山长城) constitutes the northernmost edge of the piecemeal Great Wall, with a half dozen towers snaking along the North Korean border. Swallows swoop as you make your way up to the mountain peak. Along the rocky mountainside, the wall disappears into a steep narrow staircase with steel railings. At the top, the wall reappears, offering beautiful views of China in the front and North Korea in the back, before descending into the mountain peak.

DALIAN 大连 ☎ 0411

In many parts of China, economic prosperity comes at the price of clean air and charm. Not so in Dalian, whose natural blessings are its biggest economic asset. Dalian made its money through the vast shipping traffic that passes through its harbor, the third largest in China. But if you plan on getting a taste of traditional Chinese lifestyle, don't look here. The city owes its strikingly European architecture to its days under the Japanese empire, which designed Dalian to imitate Western cities. After Dalian returned to Chinese rule, the government continued the faux European legacy and banned traditional Chinese architecture. Today, the city is vivid, rich, and cosmopolitan, filled with Japanese, Korean, and Russian tourists who flock here to enjoy the beaches, nightlife, and of course, the shopping.

▐ TRANSPORTATION

Flights: Dalian Zhoushuizi International Airport (dàlián zhōushuǐzǐ guójì jīchǎng; 大连周水子国际机场 ; ☎8361 2888) is about 2km northwest of the city. Domestic departure tax Y50. **CAAC ticket office,** Civil Aviation Hotel, 143 Zhongshan Lu (☎363 7480), in Xiwang Square. Open daily 8am-6:30pm. To: **Beijing** (10 or more per day, Y720); **Changchun** (2 per day, Y530); **Chengdu** (1-3 per day, Y1600); **Guangzhou** (3 per day, Y1790); **Harbin** (2-5 per day, Y770); **Hong Kong** (2-3 per day, Y2870); **Qingdao** (3-5 per day, Y430); **Shanghai** (5-6 per day, Y980); **Shenyang** (1-2 per day, Y170); **Xi'an** (1-2 per day, Y1050). International flights to **Seoul, South Korea** (daily, Y1950) and **Tokyo, Japan** (2-4 per day, Y2200).

Trains: Dalian Train Station (dàlián huǒchē zhàn; 大连火车站 ; ☎1682 3456), at the head of Victory Square. To: **Beijing** (18½hr., 2 per day, Y62-373); **Changchun** (11hr., daily, Y51-121); **Dandong** (11hr., 7:31pm, Y53-99); **Harbin** (14hr., 3 per day, Y62-352); **Jilin** (14½hr., 6pm, Y57-200); **Shenyang** (4-6hr., 8 per day, Y28-124).

Buses: Dalian Long-Distance Bus Station (dàlián chángtú qìchē zhàn; 大连长途汽车站), 20 Anshan Lu (☎8362 8681), at Xinkai Lu, west of the train station. To: **Dandong** (6hr., frequent departures, Y46-58). Buses to other cities leave from the train station area, including the front parking lot and in front of the Bohai Pearl and Post Hotels. To: **Beijing** (14hr., several per day, Y150-210); **Changchun** (8hr., Y156); **Harbin** (13hr., Y180); **Shenyang** (4½hr., frequent departures, Y98); **Tianjin** (13½hr., Y150).

Ferries: Dalian Passenger Ferry Port (dàlián kèyùn gǎng; 大连客运港 ; ☎263 6061), on Gangwai Jie, at the north end of Renmin Lu. To: **Qinhuangdao** (5pm, Y120-390); **Shanghai** (36hr., 3-4 per week, Y122-662); **Tianjin** (13-15hr., 5:30pm, Y160-690); **Weihai** (7hr., frequent departures, Y80-800); **Yantai** (express 3hr., Y48-590; regular 6-7hr., Y190; both depart frequently). International ferries travel to **Inchon, South Korea** (18hr.; Tu, F 11am; Y897-1543).

Local Transportation: Buses run until midnight. Fare Y1-2. Bus #2 runs along Jiefang Lu; #13 runs between the train station and the ferry port; #19 runs from Shandong Lu to Zhongshan Square; #23 runs along Zhongshan Lu between Zhongshan Square and Xinghai Park; #701 shuttles from Zhongshan Sq. to the airport.

Taxis: Base fare Y8, at night Y10.4; each additional km Y1.2, at night Y1.56. From the city center to the beach Y15-30. From the train station, **motorcycle-taxis** take arriving passengers to the central hotels for Y5.

▐ ORIENTATION AND PRACTICAL INFORMATION

Dalian's public squares, complete with greenery and flocks of pigeons, date back to the time of Japanese rule. **Victory Square** (shènglì guǎngchǎng; 胜利广场) is opposite the train station and close to a number of hotels. To the east is **Friendship Square** (yǒuhǎo guǎngchǎng; 友好广场), home to hotels, cinemas, and bars. From here, **Zhongshan Lu** (中山路) runs farther east to the city's main square, **Zhongshan Square** (中山广场). A number of major thoroughfares radiate from here: **Yan'an Lu** (延安路) runs south from the square; **Renmin Lu** (人民路) runs northeast to the

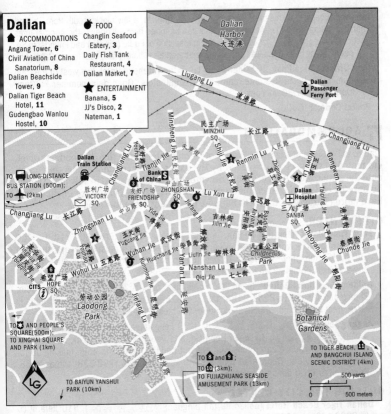

Dalian

▲ ACCOMMODATIONS
Angang Tower, 6
Civil Aviation of China
  Sanatorium, 8
Dalian Beachside
  Tower, 9
Dalian Tiger Beach
  Hotel, 11
Gudengbao Wanlou
  Hostel, 10

🍴 FOOD
Changlin Seafood
  Eatery, 3
Daily Fish Tank
  Restaurant, 4
Dalian Market, 7

★ ENTERTAINMENT
Banana, 5
JJ's Disco, 2
Nateman, 1

ferry port; and **Minsheng Jie** (民生街) and **Shanghai Lu** (上海路) intersect the pedestrian **Tianjin Jie** (天津街). West of the main train station is the stately **People's Square** (rénmín guǎngchǎng; 人民广场). Dalian's beaches and scenic drives are in the south along **Jiefang Lu** (解放路). To avoid the busy ground traffic between 9am and 9pm, take the lively underground pedestrian tunnels, centers of activity in their own right, filled with cheap shopping and food.

Travel Agency: CITS, 1 Changtong Jie (☎8368 7843), off Hope Sq., opposite the Civil Aviation Hotel on Zhongshan Lu. For foreigners, the most official way to go to Lushun begins here. Open M-F 8am-5pm.

Bank of China: 9 Zhongshan Square (☎280 5711), in a green-domed building. China's largest Bank of China exchanges traveler's checks (window #27) and issues credit card advances (window #2). M-F 8:30am-6pm, Sa-Su 9am-6pm.

PSB: (☎280 5711). At the intersection of Zhongshan Lu and Beijing Jie. Open daily 8:30am-5:30pm.

Hospital: No. 1 Hospital of Dalian Medical University (dàlián yīxuéyuàn dìyī fùshǔ yīyuàn; 大连医学院第一附属医院), 222 Zhongshan Lu (☎8363 59631), just west of People's Square.

Pharmacy: Dalian Medicine Market (dàlián yàofáng; 大连药房), 207 Tianjin Jie (☎8263 0203). Open daily 8:30am-9pm.

Internet Access: Dalian's main Internet hub is on **Qiqi Jie,** a few blocks south from Zhongshan Sq., along Yan'an Lu. At least 10 cafes can be found here, all open 24hr. Another Internet cafe (wǎngbā; 网吧) is located at the intersection of Pu Jie (普街) and Friendship Sq. Y3 per hr. Many hole-in-the-wall places are scattered elsewhere throughout town. Y2-4 per hr.

Post Office: China Post, 261 Changjiang Lu, in the Youzheng Hotel, just west of the train station. EMS, Poste Restante, cafe, and a small store. Open daily summer 7:30am-7:30pm; winter 7:30am-7pm.

Postal Code: 116000.

ACCOMMODATIONS

Dalian is bursting at the seams with hotels that cater to the rich, but budget travelers may find themselves displaced by the expensive accommodations that dominate the scene. Most budget places downtown are fully booked in July and August; be sure to call ahead. Accommodations outside of city center are cheaper and have more character. Be sure to bargain, especially in the low season.

CITY CENTER

Feng Yuan Hotel (fēngyuán jiǔdiàn; 丰源酒店), on Qingni Lu (☎280 7718; fax 280 2902), one block from Zhongshan Lu. Despite the dim and musty hallways, the loud and lively atmosphere is enough to brighten up any stay. Rooms have a great view of city activities, complete with city noise. Doubles Y358. ❺

Golden Plaza Hotel Dalian (dàlián tiānfú dàjiǔdiàn; 大连天富大酒店), 189 Tianjin Jie, Zhongshan District (☎8281 3188; fax 264 8288). Large, clean rooms with equally large, neat bathrooms. Breakfast included. Doubles Y298-328. ❹

Angang Tower (āngāng dàshà; 鞍钢大厦), 33 Fengguang Jie (☎8365 1888; fax 362 4479), at Zhongshan Lu, between Hope Sq. and People's Sq. Central location without the city noise. Fairly clean rooms with elegant bedding, A/C, and bath, making up for the aging corridors. Renovated rooms are pricier. Doubles Y298-328; triples Y368. Prices fall to Y100 during the winter season. ❹

OUTSIDE THE CITY CENTER

Dalian Tiger Beach Hotel (dàlián hǔ tǎn bīnguǎn; 大连虎滩宾馆), 810 Jiefang Lu (☎8268 1734 or 8268 1001, ext. 208), right across from the bus station. Take the #2 bus to Laohutan. Extremely bright, beachy rooms with soft colors and oceanside views. 24hr. hot water. Breakfast included. Doubles Y120-180. ❷

Dalian Civil Aviation of China Sanatorium (zhōngguó mínháng dàlián liáoyǎngyuàn; 中国民航大连疗养院), 48 Xi Binhai Lu (☎240 1412 or 240 6100), within the retirement complex. While this may be a sanatorium for recuperating aircrew and ground service personnel, 1 bldg. is devoted entirely to paying guests. Large rooms in a peaceful environment with an absolutely breathtaking ocean view (possibly the best money can buy). 24hr. hot water, TV, and microwave. Y120. ❷

Dalian Beachside Tower (dàlián bīnhǎi dàshà; 大连滨海大厦), 2 Xi Binhai Lu. (☎240 1945; fax 240 0873). Spacious rooms with expansive windows and scenic views. This pricey hotel also has Chinese- and Western-style restaurants and arranges tours for guests. Fully booked from June-Aug.; call ahead. Doubles Y388, ocean view Y428. ❺

Gudengbao Wanlou Hostel (gǔdēngbǎo wánlóu zhāodàisuǒ; 古登堡沩楼招待所), 58 Linmao Jie (☎249 6223), perched like a little castle on a hill, near Changchun Lu in a residential neighborhood south of the city. Take bus #706 from Zhongshan Sq. and get off when the bus turns uphill to a small road. The extremely gaudy rooms festooned with plastic grapevines will satisfy everyone's appetite for kitsch. Dimly lit, dirty public bathrooms with no showers. Call Ms. Li (☎8213 7051) for budget rooms located elsewhere in the city. 3-bed dorms Y25-35. ❶

◢ FOOD

Dalian is a port city, and it shows in the food. **Seafood** restaurants pepper ▨ **Xiangqian Jie**, between Kunming Jie and Friendship Square, and the streets close to the shore. **Captain Nemo's ❸**, 1 Jiefang Jie, on the ground floor of the Grand Hotel, just south of Zhongshan Sq., serves up a Y38 Western breakfast buffet (7:30-10am). Tasty, reasonably priced restaurants line Wuwu Lu. The underground mall at Victory Square has an extensive **food court**; enter from Tianjin Jie.

Dalian Market (dàlián shāngchǎng; 大连商场), at the intersection of Jiefang Lu and Wuhan Lu. Brace yourself for a bustling experience. This large department store's 1st fl. market is filled with all the food you can stomach, served in plastic bags. From sweets and meats to live seafood and yummy drinks, you can sample Dalian at a price that won't break your purse. Arrive late and everything may be going at half-price, but food may have been lying around for a while. Y0.5-20. Open daily 11:30am-9pm. ❶

Changlin Seafood Eatery (chánglín hǎixiān dàpáidǎng; 长林海鲜大排挡), 13 Youhao Lu (☎8263 2071), a 10min. walk from the train station. To experience good seafood at reasonable prices, this small *dà pái dǎng* serves up giant portions. Seafood sold by the *jīn* (0.5kg) Y16-60. Vegetable and meat dishes around Y5. Open daily 11am-9pm. ❷

Daily Fish Tank Restaurant (tiāntiān yú gāng jiǔdiàn; 天天鱼缸酒店), 41 Yan'an Lu (☎8280 1111), 3 blocks from Zhongshan Sq. Not cheap, but this is justifiably Dalian's best seafood restaurant. In fact, it's so popular that it expanded to at least 6 other stores scattered throughout city center. 1 *jīn* of fish Y40-500 and up; the frog (Y45 per *jīn*) is a treat, too. Open daily 10am-11pm. ❹

Yixin Roast Meat Restaurant (yīxīn kǎoròu diàn; 一心烤肉店), 56 Yan'an Lu (☎265 5878), at Nanshan Lu, south of Zhongshan Sq. Also at 216 Youhao Lu (☎263 8202) and 246 Tangshan Jie (☎362 9203). Roast meat aficionados mob the place during peak hours, so prepare to wait. Waiters place metal stoves full of burning coal under a rack in the center of the table, allowing customers to cook their own pre-seasoned meats (Y15-18). Great food and great fun. Open daily 11am-10:30pm. ❷

◉ SIGHTS

Dalian is not about musty museums or ossified temples. Tourists come here for the sea air, great shopping, glamorous atmosphere, and beaches. After all, markets, malls, and skylines don't require admission fees. **Victory Square**, on Zhongshan Lu, is a large elevated plaza with an underground shopping center, soccer field, and outdoor cafe. To the right of the Holiday Inn is **Tianjin Jie**, a jam-packed pedestrian street. A left turn on Shanghai Lu points you toward **Zhongshan Square**, lined with grandiose Western-style buildings. For a bird's-eye view of Dalian, take the **cable car** (Y25-40) over the hills of **Baiyun Yanshui Park** (báiyún yánshuǐ gōngyuán; 白云妍水公园). To reach the park, take bus #407 from Changchun Lu or Go'erji Lu at People's Square to the end of the route.

FUJIAZHUANG SEASIDE AMUSEMENT PARK (fùjiāzhuāng hǎishuǐ yúlè chǎng; 傅家庄海水娱乐场). Barking loudspeakers, screaming children, crowded tents, and the sharp, pebbled ground temper the beach fun just a bit. To avoid the crowds, walk past a string of trinket vendors and seafood restaurants to a path that leads to a clifftop. It's a good spot for those desperate for some ocean exposure. *(Take bus #401 from Victory Sq. or a taxi for Y15-20. Entry 8am-6pm Y5, 6-10pm Y3; passes for 1 month Y10; 1 summer Y15; 1 year Y22.)*

SOUTHWESTERN DALIAN. Once a garbage dump, **Xinghai Square** (xīnghǎi guǎngchǎng; 星海广场) is now reputedly the largest oceanfront square in Asia. A kilometer away, the cheesy, rickety rides of **Xinghai Park** (xīnghǎi gōngyuán; 星海公园) are supplemented by a few record-holding attractions, including the world's tallest **bungee jumping tower.** Walk through Asia's longest water-tank tunnel at **Sun Asia Ocean World.** From July to August, you can swim with the fishies for an extra Y150. If weather permits, test your piloting skills and take two flights around the square in a motorized **parachuting cart.** *(Both Xinghai Square and Xinghai Park are accessible via buses #22 from Victory Square and bus #23 from Zhongshan Square. Xinghai Park Y4. Bungee tower open 8am-5:30pm, Y180. Sun Asia Ocean World open M-F 8am-5pm, Sa-Su 8am-5:30pm; Y130. Roller-coaster Y80. Parachuting cart Y200.)*

SOUTHEASTERN DALIAN. While it's not much more than a bay and a small **amusement park,** no trip to Dalian seems complete without a visit to the ballyhooed **Tiger Beach** (lǎohǔtān; 老虎滩). Most tourists will make their way to this pit stop, which can be covered within an hour. There is also a small bird sanctuary. *(Accessible by bus #2. ☎ 8239 9298. Open daily 6am-9pm. Amusement park Y15, rides Y5-10, bird sanctuary Y30.)* To get away from the beach holiday atmosphere, head to **Bangchui Island Scenic District** (bàngchuí dǎo jǐngqū; 棒棰岛景区), with its picturesque routes and less-touristed beaches. *(Ferry to Banchui Island Y30. Take a taxi from Laohutan to the dock for Y20. Open daily 24hr.)*

🎵 ENTERTAINMENT

Dalian's harbor brings both foreign business people and sailors to town, and most nightlife is frequented by one or the other. **JJ's Disco** (jiéjié dísīkē; 杰杰迪斯科), on Wuwu Lu, is a popular spot for students and foreigners. (Cover Y15 for men, free for women.) Other popular clubs include **Nateman** (nàtèmàn; 纳特曼) on Renmin Lu and **Banana** (bānǎnǎ; 巴娜娜) at Hope Square. A handful of intimate cafes and bars line **Yan'an Lu,** just south of the PSB, across the street from the **Night Cat** music club. A few blocks away, across from the Grand Hotel, patrons listen to live performances or sing in private karaoke rooms at the extravagantly decorated **Xanadu.** Dalian's champion **soccer team** plays every other Saturday from September to June. The stadium is in Olympic Square, one bus stop along Zhongshan Lu past People's Square. For more low-key spectator sports, check out the daily **soccer** matches in **Victory Square,** or head to the ever-packed **Zhongshan Square** at night to play **hacky-sack** and **badminton** with the student population. In the summer, the square screens outdoor films and soccer matches at 9pm every day.

CENTRAL CHINA

Watered by the life-giving Yellow River, Central China has been a hive of cultural and political activity for millennia, producing countless works of art, temples, and remnants of empires and civilizations still visible today. As the "cradle of Chinese civilization," the Yellow River Valley nourished the earliest villages with its gift of fertile loess soil, irrigating the otherwise parched land. The villages grew up into kingdoms, and all early dynasties planted roots here. From the city of Chang'an (modern day Xi'an), the Qin were the first to rule a united China, and a millennium later the Tang reigned over China's Golden Age. But in times of flood, "The Ungovernable" destroyed everything and everyone in its path. As if withstanding devastating floods was not enough, Central China has also spent centuries warding off repeated northern invasions, serving as a buffer for the rest of China.

Not surprisingly, Central China has been one of the country's most impoverished regions. Things started to pick up in the 1950s, with the industrialization of coal- and iron-rich cities. Economic development has made some of the world's finest archaeological discoveries accessible, and many visitors flock to flourishing Xi'an to see the Terracotta Warriors buried with Emperor Qin Shihuang. But in a landscape sprawling from the alpine valleys of Wutaishan, where serene temples and mountain scenery stretch as far as the eye can see, to the timeless grasslands of Inner Mongolia, dotted by flocks of sheep and yurts, ancient tombs are only the beginning of Central China's attractions.

HIGHLIGHTS OF CENTRAL CHINA

CLIMB THE ANCIENT RAMPARTS of beautiful, stone-walled **Pingyao** (p. 308), the site of Zhang Yimou's *Raise the Red Lantern*.

MEASURE YOUR HEIGHT against the 17m-tall Buddhas of **Longmen Grottoes** (p. 295) and **Yungang Grottoes** (p. 315), chock-full of statues of all shapes and sizes.

RIDE INTO A SEA OF GRASS and watch the sun set over the vast grasslands near **Hohhot** (p. 322) or **Manzhouli** (p. 329).

SHAANXI 陕西

Though constantly threatened with bad weather, floods, and attacks from the north, emperors of the Zhou, Qin, Han, Sui, and Tang Dynasties were all happy to maintain their capitals in Shaanxi, the geographical center of the Middle Kingdom. The soft silt of the Yellow River valley in north Shaanxi allowed farmers to settle, giving rise to one of the earliest civilizations. During the Tang Dynasty, the ancient capital city of Chang'an (now Xi'an), at the start of the Silk Road, thrived as a cosmopolitan hub. By the end of the 9th century, however, Shaanxi's glory days came to a swift end when the city was sacked. The next millennium left the region in a state of dreadful impoverishment, plagued by drought, rebellion, and famine. It wasn't until the Communists ended their Long March in Yan'an in 1937 that Shaanxi regained some of its former political significance. Today, Shaanxi is poised for a comeback. The dry, dusty northern region of the province is still quite poor, but in the southern region, an influx of foreign and domestic investment has breathed new life into the entire province.

XI'AN 西安   ☎029

When tourists think of Xi'an, they immediately picture the Terracotta Warriors, but this ancient city harbors dozens of sights, small and large, from the looming city wall to neighborhood temples. Chang'an, as Xi'an was known in its heyday, was the capital city during a long procession of dynasties, culminating in the golden age of the Tang Dynasty, when it had bragging rights as one of the world's wealthiest, largest, and most sophisticated cities. After the city was sacked by Tibetans in AD 783 and the Tang dissolved in chaos, Xi'an lost its prominence, although it continued to broker trade with Central Asia.

A latecomer on the industrialization bandwagon, the Shaanxi's capital now leads the region in construction and development, turning itself into a modern metropolis, while taking care to preserve its dynastic heritage. Xi'an also contains a vibrant Muslim quarter, adding an element of architectural and cultural diversity to the city. Xi'an has something for everyone, and you'll realize that a few days is hardly enough to explore its wealth of historic ruins, temples, and back alleys.

▐ TRANSPORTATION

Flights: Xi'an Xianyang Airport (xī'ān xiányáng guójì jīchǎng; 西安咸阳国际机场; ☎8879 8450), about 50km northwest of Xi'an. Taxi from airport to city center Y100-120; many hotels also arrange transportation. Shuttle bus (1hr., every hr. 8am-6pm, Y20) leaves from the **CAAC ticket office**, 231 Laodong Lu (☎8870 2299). Open daily 8am-9pm). Discounts are common and often increase when tickets are bought the day before or the day of travel. To: **Beijing** (8-9 per day, Y840-1050); **Chengdu** (3-5 per day, Y500); **Chongqing** (5 per day, Y350-700); **Dunhuang** (3 per day, Y1510); **Fuzhou** (1-2 per day, Y1450); **Guangzhou** (4 per day, Y1490); **Harbin** (M, W, Su; Y1680); **Hohhot** (1-2 per day, Y830); **Hong Kong** (2 per day, Y1910); **Jiayuguan** (daily, Y1210); **Kunming** (3 per day, Y1050); **Lanzhou** (4-6 per day, Y600); **Nanjing** (2 per day, Y1080); **Shanghai** (4-6 per day, Y1600); **Ürümqi** (3-4 per day, Y1660); **Wuhan** (1-2 per day, Y690); **Xining** (1-2 per day, Y650).

Trains: Most commute to Xi'an by train, and tickets are often difficult to acquire, particularly May-July. Hotels and hostels sometimes buy up tickets and jack up prices. If only hard seats are available at the time of purchase, upgrading is often possible on board. **Xi'an Train Station** (xī'ān huǒchē zhàn; 西安火车站; ☎8213 0402) is at the north end of Jiefang Lu. Taxi to city center Y8-12. Lost and Found is on the 1st fl., on the west side of station. Information with English-speaking staff directly inside the main hall. To buy tickets more than 2 days in advance, go to Dongli Dasha (东立大厦), the building directly to the west of the train station. Storage Y5 per bag. Open 24hr. To: **Beijing** (12hr., 4 per day, Y150-417); **Chengdu** (17hr., 3 per day, Y55-316); **Chongqing** (15hr., daily, Y53-184); **Guangzhou** (24hr., daily, Y238-658); **Lanzhou** (9hr., 3 per day, Y71-264); **Luoyang** (6hr., many per day, Y28-162); **Nanjing West** (15hr., 2 per day, Y170-429); **Shanghai** (17hr., daily, Y182-511); **Taiyuan** (12hr., 4 per day, Y45-156); **Tianshui** (4hr., 4 per day, Y39-128); **Ürümqi** (38hr., daily, Y135-467); **Yinchuan** (14hr., 2 per day, Y55-294); **Zhengzhou** (8hr., many per day, Y36-205).

Buses: Jiefang Men Bus Station (jiěfàngmén qìchē zhàn; 解放门汽车站; ☎8742 7420), opposite the Xi'an Train Station. Open daily 4:30am-8:30pm. Storage Y2 per bag. To: **Huashan** (2-3hr., every hr. 6am-4pm, Y20); **Lanzhou** (8-10hr., 4 per day 7am-1pm, Y110); **Luoyang** (4hr., every hr. 6am-5pm, Y60); **Taiyuan** (8hr., 10 per day 7am-9:40pm, Y128); **Tianshui** (5hr., every hr. 7:30am-3:30pm, Y60); **Yan'an** (8hr., every hr. 6am-3:30pm, Y59-78); **Yinchuan** (20hr., 8 per day, Y110); **Zhengzhou** (10hr., every hr. 7:30am-5pm, Y120). **Minibuses** to surrounding towns leave from the parking lot east of the train station.

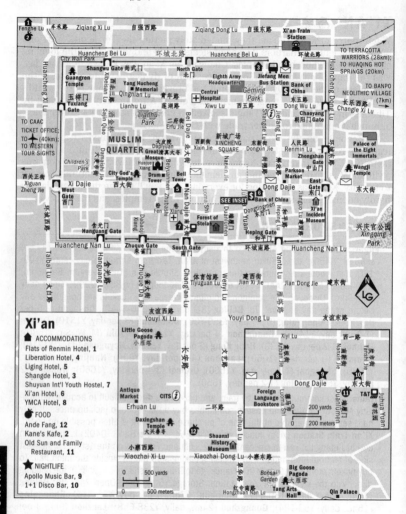

Xi'an

ACCOMMODATIONS
Flats of Renmin Hotel, **1**
Liberation Hotel, **4**
Liging Hotel, **5**
Shangde Hotel, **3**
Shuyuan Int'l Youth Hostel, **7**
Xi'an Hotel, **6**
YMCA Hotel, **8**

FOOD
Ande Fang, **12**
Kane's Kafe, **2**
Old Sun and Family
Restaurant, **11**

NIGHTLIFE
Apollo Music Bar, **9**
1+1 Disco Bar, **10**

Local Transportation: Local **buses** usually cost Y1, with A/C Y2; many routes have no fare collectors and can't make change. **Minibus** prices vary with distance (Y0.5-5). Several key routes, including #5 (train station to Yike Daxue) and 18 (Xiaozhai to Zhangjiabao), run 6am-11pm, but most run 7am-8pm. Some have shorter winter hours. Buses #5 and 41 serve Jiefang Lu and Heping Lu, while #43, 201, and 205 run the Xi and Dong Dajie corridor. **Tourist minibus** #610 runs from Jiefang Men Bus Station and stops at the Bell Tower, Drum Tower, Little Goose Pagoda, Big Goose Pagoda, and the Shaanxi History Museum. Runs daily 7am-8pm.

Taxis: Base fare Y5, each additional km Y1.2-1.7. 10pm-6am Y0.3 per km surcharge.

Bike Rental: Flats of Renmin Hotel (see **Accommodations,** p. 272) rents bikes (Y5).

ORIENTATION AND PRACTICAL INFORMATION

Although the modern metropolis has long since outgrown the confines of its ancient walls, Xi'an remains remarkably compact for a city with an urban population close to four million. Streets inside the walls are arranged in a grid pattern that ends abruptly in the narrow alleys of the **Muslim Quarter** in the west and the pebble-paved streets in the southeast. The **Bell Tower** (zhōng lóu; 钟楼) marks the city center; from this point, **Bei Dajie** (北大街), **Nan Dajie** (南大街), **Dong Dajie** (东大街), and **Xi Dajie** (西大街) extend like a cross to the city gates. **Jiefang Lu** (解放路), east of Bei Dajie, runs south from the main train and bus stations to **Heping Gate** (和平门), becoming **Heping Lu** (和平路) south of Dong Dajie. Dong Dajie, Nan Dajie, the area around the Bell Tower, and the surrounding quarters are lined with hotels and shops, but many of the major attractions are outside the city walls.

Travel Agencies: CITS, 48 Chang'an Bei Lu (☎8524 1864). Arranges tours and books tickets (commission Y50). English-speaking staff member. Open daily 8am-10pm. Other branches at the Sheraton and Bell Tower (Rm. 227) Hotels and the airport. **China Golden Bridge Travel Service** (xī'ān jīnqiáo guójì lǚxíng shè; 西安金桥国际旅行社), Bell Tower Hotel, Rm. 219 (☎8725 8863 or 8725 7975), has similar but more expensive services and arranges discounts at many hotels. Commission Y60. Open daily 8am-8pm. The **Flats of Renmin Hotel** and **Kane's Kafe** (see **Food,** p. 273) arrange tours to the Terracotta Warriors and help obtain train tickets in Xi'an's competitive market.

Bank of China: 306 Dong Dajie (☎8726 1726). Exchanges currency and traveler's checks. Open M-F 8am-8pm, Sa-Su 9am-4pm. Another branch, 157 Jiefang Jie (☎8745 5374), exchanges currency and traveler's checks.

ATM: At the Bank of China below the Kaiyuan Shopping Center in the southeast corner of the Bell Tower intersection. Also at the Jiefang Jie and Dong Dajie locations. MC/V.

Bookstore: Shaanxi Foreign Language Bookstore (shǎnxīshěng wàiwén shūdiàn; 陕西省外文书店), 349 Dong Dajie (☎8814 2678). 3rd fl. has decent selection of English classics, mysteries, Shakespeare, newspapers, and dictionaries. Open daily 9am-6pm.

Market: Parkson (bǎishèng gòuwù zhōngxīn; 百盛购物中心), 237 Dong Dajie, east of Jiefang Lu, kitty-corner to the Hyatt Regency. 4th fl. has a supermarket with a large selection of Western brands. Open daily summer 9:30am-10pm; winter 9:30am-9pm.

PSB: 138 Xi Dajie (☎8723 4500, ext. 51810). Visa extensions and English-speaking staff. Open M-F 8am-noon and 2-6pm.

TIP **FOLLOW THE PAPER TRAIL!** Stamping, ticketing, scribbling, checking, tagging—China's infamous, pervasive bureaucracy can leave the hapless traveler thoroughly bewildered, clutching fistfuls of translucent paper wondering which way to turn. Stuffing them into a back pocket, or indeed, into the nearest trashcan, is not the best move. Although the endless receipts may seem excessive and unnecessary to you, they are actually quite priceless. In many hotels, a receipt is needed to reclaim a deposit and will be requested upon check-out. Retrieving luggage from the lower compartments on buses depends on whether or not you can produce that highly prized sticker. At train stations, a ticket is just as necessary to exit as it is to enter. Generally speaking, misplacing the paperwork will earn you little more than a quick-fire question round in the local dialect, but to save yourself the hassle, make the extra effort to carefully store all receipts, tickets, and stamps so that you can proceed quickly along your way.

CENTRAL CHINA

Hospital: Xi'an No. 1 Hospital (xī'ān shì dìyī yīyuàn; 西安市第一医院), 30 Fen Xiang (☎8763 0799), 1 block west of Nan Dajie. **Central Hospital** (xī'ān shì zhōngxīn yīyuàn; 西安市中心医院), 161 Xiwu Lu (☎8726 8341), on the corner of Bei Dajie, is more modern but has few English speakers.

Internet Access: Like most of China, Internet cafes are reaching epidemic proportions in Xi'an. On Dong Dajie, the large and air-conditioned **T&T Internet Bar**, on the 2nd fl., down an alleyway next to Dallas Bar, is the cheapest at Y1.5 per hr. **Potman Club** (bōtèmàn huìsuǒ; 波特曼会所), 9 Nan Dajie, across from Shuyuan Hostel. Y2 per hr.

Post Office: China Post, at the Bell Tower. For EMS and Poste Restante, inquire at the foreign mail counter on the right. Open daily 8:30am-8pm.

Postal Code: 710003.

ACCOMMODATIONS

Hotels that accept foreigners cater primarily to business travelers and tour groups. Backpackers and budget travelers can choose between two hostels and several relatively inexpensive options clustered near the train station. More upscale establishments line Dong Dajie and Xi Dajie in the city center.

Flats of Renmin Hotel (HI) (rénmín dàshà gōngyù; 人民大厦公寓), 11 Fenghe Lu (☎8624 0349), about 5min. from Xinghuo Lu. Bus #9 makes the 30min. trip from the parking lot on the right side of the train station; exit at Xinghuo Lu (9th stop). Or take bus #501 from Nan Dajie. Somewhat curt English-speaking staff and relatively inconvenient location, but spacious rooms in this backpacker enclave have A/C and large windows. Ask for clean sheets. Internet access Y9 per hr. Rents bikes (Y5). Arranges tours (see **Sights,** p. 273). 8-bed dorms without bath Y35; 4- and 6-bed dorms Y40, with bath Y45; doubles with bath Y120. ❶

Xi'an Shuyuan International Youth Hostel (HI) (xī'ān shūyuàn guójì qīngnián lǚshè; 西安书院国际青年旅舍 ; ☎8728 7720), 20m directly west of the South Gate (Nan Men), along the inner wall. Just a 10min. walk south of the Bell Tower, this hostel occupies some prime real estate. Located in a charming courtyard house, but rooms are small, bare, and often windowless. Those with windows look over a small courtyard. Public baths are cramped. Travel desk arranges tours; small business center has printing and faxing. Dorms Y50, HI members Y40; doubles Y140-160. ❶

Shangde Hotel (shàngdé bīnguǎn; 尚德宾馆), 228 Shangde Lu (☎8210 8101), directly west of the Jiefang Men Bus Station and a block south of the city wall. Dorm rooms are impressively clean for the price. 3-bed dorms without showers Y25-40; singles Y158; doubles Y158-178; triples Y188. ❶

Liging Hotel (lìjīng jiǔdiàn; 丽晶酒店), 20 Xi Dajie (☎8728 8731, ext. 100), at the southwest corner of the Bell Tower Sq., between Zhubashi and Nan Dajie. Clean and tidy rooms with A/C, TV, IDD, and bath. More expensive rooms have great views of the Bell Tower, Drum Tower, and Square. Courteous staff, tropical tea house, and milk steam rooms. Singles Y180-240; doubles Y180-240. ❷

Liberation Hotel (jiěfàng fàndiàn; 解放饭店), 181 Jiefang Lu (☎8769 8881; www.jiefanghotel.com), left of the train station's main exit, across the parking lot. Standard rooms with A/C, TV, and bath. Rooms in the back building (hòulóu; 后楼) are less worn. More expensive doubles are brighter, with newer appliances and more luxurious furnishings. Large, pleasant atrium with bar. Doubles Y120-380; triples Y380. ❷

YMCA Hotel (qīngniánhuì bīnguǎn; 青年会宾馆), 565 Dong Dajie (☎8767 3000), a 5min. walk east along Dong Dajie from the Bell Tower; a red sign points guests down a covered alley. Central location and good deals on very small, windowless rooms with TV, A/C, and phone. Some rooms have private baths. 24hr. hot water. Singles Y118-128; doubles Y298-318. Staff is very willing to bargain. ❷

Xi'an Hotel (xī'ān fànzhuāng; 西安饭庄), 298 Dong Dajie (☎8768 0769), between Juhua Lu and Nanxin Lu. Bus #201 from the train station stops on Dong Dajie, not far from the entrance. Large standard rooms with nice baths make this centrally located hotel appealing, if somewhat pricey. Singles Y176; doubles Y265; triples Y303. ❷

▌ FOOD

The quality, variety, and price of Xi'an's cuisine will impress the budget-conscious food connoisseur. West Xi'an boasts excellent **Muslim food.** Damaishi Jie (大麦市 街), Zhubashi Market (竹笆市), and the other streets near the Great Mosque are lined with small food stalls designated as *qīngzhēn* (清真; Muslim). An especially popular Xi'an specialty, **yángròu pàomó** (羊肉泡馍) is a savory mutton soup, eaten with pieces of lightly toasted flour buns (usually Y4-7). Other Xi'an specialties include **rice cakes with sweet filling** (mǐgāo; 米糕; Y1-2), **steamed mutton with bread crumbs** (fěnzhēngròu; 粉蒸肉 ; Y2-3), a sweet, refreshing **sour plum juice** (suān-méitāng; 酸梅汤), and **dark noodles** (hēi lāomiàn; 黑捞面 ; Y2-3). Many alleys off the main roads house food peddlers. The largest, Tanshi Jie, across from the bank on Dong Dajie, teems with vendors selling everything from dried spices to live fish.

Xi'an is full of quick, food-court-style establishments. Check out Dong Dajie, near the Bell Tower and May First Hotel, for over a dozen stations with hot noodles, *bāozi* (steamed meat buns), kebabs of all kinds, and street food particular to Xi'an. **Ande Fang** (āndé fáng; 安德坊), 215 Chang'an Lu, is a large food-court restaurant specializing in Muslim local specialties. Next to the Xi'an Hotel, **Shaanxi Food Village** ❷ provides all you can eat for Y18.

▨ **Jiasan Steamed Buns Restaurant** (jiǎsān bāozi guǎn; 贾三包子馆 ; ☎8725 7507), on Beiyuanmen, Muslim Quarter. Customers come for the dumplings (Y5 for 10) and the uniquely flavored *zhōu*, or rice porridge (粥 ; Y2). The staff stays on their toes serving up dishes, *suānméitāng*, and a lot of energy to families and friends out for a good time. Open daily 7:30am-2 or 3am. ❶

▨ **Kane's Kafe,** 11 Fenghe Lu, conveniently across from the lobby of the Flats of Renmin Hotel. Friendly owner Kane dishes up Chinese and Western specialties, as well as free travel advice in English. English music and movies upon request. The extensive English menu includes Kane's special pita bread with pork, beef, or chicken filling (Y10), beer (Y4-6 per bottle), and a delicious banana yogurt shake (Y10). Good company for free. Kane works with the Flats Hotel to arrange tours. Open daily 7:30am-2am. ❷

Old Sun and Family Restaurant (lǎosūnjiā fànzhuāng; 老孙家饭庄), 364 Dong Dajie (☎8721 0936). Owner Ma Mingyan was schooled in Marxism, Leninism, Maoism, and yes, even Deng Xiaoping-ism. The famous establishment has 5 "feature foods," including Muslim *jiǎozi* (Y0.7), salt-cured beef and mutton (Y13), beef and mutton buns, and *yángròu pàomó*. Banquet rooms serve delicacies like peacock (Y98) and fawn (Y58). Brochures explain their employee indoctrination methods. Open daily 7am-10pm. ❷

◉ SIGHTS

Tourist agencies and hotels arrange one-day tours of Xi'an's famous landmarks that finish in time to catch the next train out of town. The more popular **Eastern Tour** (p. 276) generally includes the Terracotta Warriors, Banpo Village, Tomb of Qin Shihuang, and sometimes Huaqing Hot Springs. The **Western Tour** (p. 277) includes the Xianyang City Museum, several (though usually not all) of the imperial tombs, and Famen Temple.

CENTRAL CHINA

THE LOCAL STORY

IRON LADY

n China's 2000 years of dynastic history, 243 emperors reigned over China, but one name stands apart—Wu Zetian, the one and only female emperor. She was born to a merchant family in Wenshui in Shanxi province. Her father, a follower of Tang Dynasty founder Li Yuan, had a hand in the overthrow of the Sui, earning him a position in the new Tang court. He brought his daughter to Chang'an, the city that would become her stage.

At the age of 14, Wu Zetian became a concubine to Emperor Taizong. After his death, rather than accepting her widow status, she became the concubine of Taizong's son, newly crowned Emperor Gaozong. She ruled from behind the curtain for many years through her sickly husband and various sons before declaring herself emperor of a new dynasty.

Wu Zetian reigned over a period of peace and prosperity, but the controversy surrounding her throne overshadowed her accomplishments. Her climb up the imperial ladder was a bloody ascent. To become empress, she had to have two other wives beheaded. To maintain power, she sentenced her most promising son to death. Wu's decadent lifestyle—including male concubines—also suited her fondness for power. After her death, a blank tablet was placed before her tomb, supposedly at her behest, so that later generations could be the judges of her reign.

XI'AN CITY SIGHTS

GREAT MOSQUE (qīngzhēn dà sì; 清真大寺). One of 20 mosques in Xi'an, the Great Mosque is the best known. Though none of it speaks of Islamic architecture, the mosque is gorgeous nonetheless. Established in AD 742, the Great Mosque has four courtyards, each with historically fascinating religious records, among them the "Moon Tablet," a stele that bears Arabic inscriptions about the Muslim calendar. Other treasures include a handwritten copy of the Qur'an and Chinese tablets inscribed by famous Chinese calligraphers, considered to be some of the best works of art in the country. Arabic inscriptions from the Qur'an are carved into the ceiling of the hall of worship, but non-Muslims are not allowed inside. The parts of the mosque accessible to the general public are popular among foreign visitors. *(Just minutes from the Bell Tower. Buses #201, 205, and 610 from the train station stop at the Bell Tower. From Xi Dajie, take the 1st right onto Beiyuanmen and continue north 1 block until just past the covered tunnel; red signs point the rest of the way. The entrance is down an alley called Huajue Xiang, on the left. Open daily 8am-8pm. Y12, including an English guidebook.)*

SHAANXI HISTORY MUSEUM (shǎnxī lìshǐ bówùguǎn; 陕西历史博物馆). Large Tang-style stone buildings with white tile eaves look out onto the wide courtyards of this relatively new museum. The huge space stores over 3.7 million historical relics, well preserved by elaborate environmental control systems. The central hall features a permanent exhibit on Shaanxi's history and culture, while other exhibits display Bronze Age artifacts, ancient pottery, and sculptures. The exhibits all have English captions. *(91 Xiaozhai Dong Lu. Take bus #610 from the train station. ☎8525 4727. Open daily 8am-6:30pm. Y25, students Y12.)*

BELL TOWER (zhōng lóu; 钟楼). First erected in 1384, this 36m pavilion was moved to its present central location at the intersection of Bei, Nan, Dong, and Xi Dajie in 1582 and then repaired and rebuilt in 1740. The second floor houses an exhibit of ancient musical instruments, and the third floor displays calligraphy scroll paintings. From the top, visitors get a bird's-eye view of the former capital. Elaborate musical performances drown out the traffic below. *(Take bus #201, 205, or 610 from the train station to Zhonglou; enter through the pedestrian tunnel. Music performances every 30min. 9-11:30am and 2:30-5:30pm. Open daily 8am-9pm. Y15.)*

BIG GOOSE PAGODA (dàyàn tǎ; 大雁塔). This expansive park is comprised of temples, beautiful landscaping, and, of course, the Big Goose. Built in AD 652, the pagoda houses over 600 sets of Buddhist scriptures brought to China from India by Xuan Zang, the most famous monk of the Tang Dynasty. Over the last 1200 years, the 64m tall pyramidal structure of blue brick has been restored many times. On the first story, two stelae offer a Tang-era treatise on Xuan Zang's translations. The pagoda was also known in the Tang for its walls, on which imperial exam degree recipients inscribed autobiographical poems. *(Bus #610 from the train station stops outside the main entrance. ☎8521 5014. Open daily 8am-6:30pm. Y25.)*

LITTLE GOOSE PAGODA (xiǎoyàn tǎ; 小雁塔). Contrary to what its name would indicate, Little Goose Pagoda is actually bigger than Big Goose Pagoda. Completed in AD 709, the structure originally shot up 15 tiers, but an earthquake reduced its height to 13 perspiration-inducing flights. Earthquakes have been a theme in the pagoda's history: it has survived over 70 of them. A particularly violent quake in 1487 reputedly left a foot-wide fissure that ran from the top to the bottom of the temple. The crack is rumored to have been mended by an equally violent quake in 1521. *(Bus #610 stops on Youyi Xi Lu, at Xiao Yan Ta stop; from the train station, walk east about 1 block. Open daily 8:30am-6pm. Park Y18; park and pagoda Y28, students Y14.)*

CITY WALL (chéngqiáng; 城墙). Constructed in 1370, long after Xi'an had fallen from imperial capital to mere Ming outpost, the 14km long city wall bristles with 5984 battlements, 98 defense towers, and a moat. While Beijing and other cities tore down city walls to build highways and subways, Xi'an chose to restore the

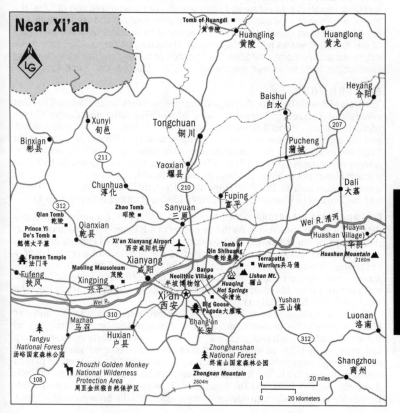

walls and turn them into tourist attractions, complete with Chinese and English explanatory signs. The city wall can be climbed from any of the four gates. South Gate is most approachable on foot, though the North Gate is the most visually impressive. *(From the train station, bus #9 goes to the North Gate, #3 goes to the South Gate, and #5 and 41 go to Heping Gate. ☎8727 1081. Open daily 8am-7pm. Y10, students Y5.)*

PALACE OF THE EIGHT IMMORTALS (bā xiān ān; 八仙庵). This active Daoist temple features two huge stelae with gorgeous, intricate etchings on their upper sections. Under Yuxian Bridge hangs the "lucky and peaceful bell." According to legend, if you hit the bell with a coin, you have a predestined relationship with Daoism and will always be lucky and peaceful. Unfortunately, the bell is only around 4 in. tall and 3 in. wide. *(East of Zhongshan Gate. Take bus #22 from the train station to the intersection with Dongxin Jie; walk east 2½ blocks. Open daily 6am-5:30pm.)*

DRUM TOWER (gǔ lóu; 鼓楼). Since 1380, drum beats from this tower have signaled the arrival of dusk. The tower's carved beams and painted columns have held up well, with a little help from the restorations bureau. Climb to the top to look out over the city. Colorful exhibits display beautifully restored drums, furniture, and vases from the Ming and the Qing. *(On Beiyuamen, across a broad square from the Bell Tower. 8 drum performances per day. Open daily 8am-9pm. Y12.)*

XI'AN FOREST OF STELAE (xī'ān bēi lín; 西安碑林). Amid the traditional Ming and Qing Dynasty architecture and antique shops of the southern part of Xi'an, the Forest of Stelae is a veritable theme park for philosophers and etched stone lovers. The collection of over 1000 inscribed stone slabs includes tablets from copies of the *Analects*, works by Mencius, and the Dictionary of Terms. *(15 Sanxue Jie. Go east on the last street before the South Gate; turn right at the dead end and follow the curving street another 3min.; the museum is on the right. ☎8721 4459. Open daily 8am-6:45pm. Y30.)*

EASTERN TOUR

The **Flats of Renmin Hotel** (p. 272) organizes transportation for an Eastern Tour that consists of Terracotta Warriors, Tomb of Qin Shihuang, and Banpo Village (departs 8:30am, returns 3:30pm; Y35). Individual admission fees are not included, and the group must have at least four people. **Kane** (p. 273) can also arrange an English-speaking guide and transportation to the same sights for Y100 per person. Almost every travel agency in Xi'an offers the same tour with "more" included for a much higher price. Many visitors opt for the flexibility and economy of public transportation instead. Bus #306 stops at the Huaqing Hot Springs, the Qin Tomb, and the Terracotta Warriors (approx. every 15min., shuttling between sites Y1).

TERRACOTTA WARRIORS (bīngmǎyǒng; 兵马俑). In 1974, a group of peasants digging for water stumbled upon the discovery of a lifetime—the Terracotta Warriors. Emperor **Qin Shihuang** (p. 74), founder of the first unified dynasty in 221 BC, strove to construct an underground empire that would reflect the glory and dignity of his empire long after his death. He immortalized his soldiers by directing artisans to carve out a terracotta army for his tomb in their images. Little did he know that centuries later, his efforts would restore the glory and dignity (or at least the tourist draw) of his capital city.

The army consists of over 7000 slightly larger-than-life clay warriors and war horses waiting in battle formation, posed according to Qin Dynasty directives on the art of warfare. Each face is unique, and the clay men's hands grasp still-sharp and still-poisoned Qin-era weapons, which excited archaeologists quickly whisked away. Though impressive, the collection is not as sprawling as brochure photos would make you think. The first vault, measuring 210m by 60m, houses 6000 soldiers; the second 1000; and the third only 68, accompanied by a war chariot. Despite the sea of soldiers on display, some suggest that the excavated army is just one part of an even more magnificent system still buried in Qin Shihuang's tomb. *(45min. drive away. Bus #306 from the train station stops outside. Minibuses make the trip for Y5, sometimes dropping people off at the small amusement park about a 15min. walk from the entrance. A movie explains the history of the warriors, and displays in each vault have English and Chinese explanations. Photography is not allowed in the largest vault. ☎ 8391 1954. Open daily summer 8:30am-5:30pm, last admission 5pm; winter 8:30am-5pm. Y90.)*

TOMB OF QIN SHIHUANG (qínshǐhuáng líng; 秦始皇陵). The Terracotta Warriors form only one section of the tomb of Emperor Qin Shihuang. The famous emperor ascended the throne of the Qin kingdom at age 13 and immediately began the construction of his tomb at Mt. Lishan. Seven hundred thousand conscripts built the tomb, which contained model palaces and offices, vessels, jewels, and a number of unlucky prisoners, builders, and palace maids who were buried alive with Qin Shihuang. All that visitors can see today is a large mound approximately 1.5km from the vaults of the terracotta warriors. The steps to the top lead to a spectacular view of the surrounding mountains. The actual tomb remains unexcavated, and the (booby-trapped) treasures of this 200km^2 underground palace remain hidden. Historian Sima Qian wrote that mercury was circulated mechanically to represent the rivers of China, the ceiling was inlaid with pearls to symbolize the heavens, and figures of gold, silver, and carved jade recreated the earth. *(Bus #306 stops a short distance away; walk in the direction of the souvenir stands. If coming from the Terracotta Warriors, continue in the same direction taken by the bus back to Xi'an. Walking from the Warriors is not recommended; a minibus is only Y0.5-1. A 10min. English audio and visual guide of the underground tomb available. Open daily 7:15am-6:30pm. Y25.)*

HUAQING HOT SPRINGS (huáqīng chí; 华清池). Dating back more than 2000 years, the Huaqing Hot Springs have been enjoyed by a succession of emperors and other important figures. Qin Shihuang dubbed the area the "Hot Spring of Lishan Mountain." In AD 747 Emperor Xuanzong of the Tang expanded it into Huaqing Palace and made it famous by allowing his concubine, Yang Guifei, one of the four legendary beauties in Chinese history, to bathe there. In 1936, Chiang Kaishek came here to set up his field headquarters against the CCP but was captured in a coup known as the Xi'an Incident (p. 79). To get a panoramic view of the area and beautiful Mt. Lishan, take the cable car up the mountain. *(Bus #306 stops outside the cable car entrance. A minibus back to the train station costs Y3-4 and takes 35min. Cable car open 8am-6pm; round-trip Y40. Open daily 7am-7pm. Y30; hot springs Y20-40 extra.)*

BANPO NEOLITHIC VILLAGE (bànpō bówùguǎn; 半坡博物馆). Part dry archaeological exhibit and part kitschy theme park, Banpo is on most tour itineraries. The village is the remains of a 6000-year-old matriarchal clan community in the Yellow River valley, discovered in 1953. The **Great Hall,** the excavated dwelling area of the Banpo people, is closed for renovation until 2005. Four houses have been reconstructed at the site, and the graves of individuals, groups, and children have been unearthed. Near the back, enter the "authentic" reproduction of the matriarchal village. Banpo also houses a slightly voyeuristic photograph exhibition of "primitive man." *(Bus #105 from the train station stops at Banpo. Take a right onto Banpo Lu at the first intersection; the museum is about 5min. ahead on the left. Open daily 8am-6pm. Y20.)*

WESTERN TOUR

The Xianyang Museum is the only Western Tour sight reasonably accessible by public transportation. Minibuses (with Chinese-speaking guides) leave from the parking lot to the east of the train station around 8 or 9am and return around 7pm. For everything else, you'll have to join a tour. Tours follow a tight schedule and won't allow passengers much flexibility. Average cost is Y45 for transportation. As

CENTRAL CHINA

always, if asked to pay a flat fee in advance, be sure to clarify which sights and admission fees this covers—many tourists report being overcharged or under-tombed. Also be prepared to visit some sights not included in the following list.

■ **FAMEN TEMPLE** (fǎmén sì; 法门寺). Unlike some of the other sights on the Western Tour, this temple and museum houses not only dead bodies, but also an amazing collection of relics. In fact, the collection is so extensive that tour guides claim the 1700-year-old Eastern Han Dynasty temple holds more historical value than all of Hong Kong. The extraordinary complex encompasses 24 courtyards, made all the more impressive by its long history. The final resting place for four of Buddha's finger bones (*sarira*), this temple was one of the four ancient sacred Buddhist sanctuaries. In 1981, the *sarira* crypt was restored, yielding more than 1000 sacrificial objects preserved for over 1000 years. They are now kept in an on-site museum. The downstairs vault, in white stone and with elaborate gold decora-tion, is absolutely gorgeous. *(In Fufeng County, a bumpy 115km northwest of Xi'an. Open daily 8am-6pm. Temple Y28; museum Y32. Inquire about student tickets.)*

XIANYANG MUSEUM (xiányáng bówùguǎn; 咸阳博物馆). The museum pays trib-ute to the long and impressive history of Xianyang. The city witnessed the found-ing of the Qin in 221 BC, housed 11 ensuing dynasties, and gave rise to cutting-edge cultural and economic achievements. Originally a Confucian temple, the museum was reconstructed in 1371 during the Ming Dynasty and today features over 5000 objects, primarily relics from the Qin and Han dynasties, rare colored pottery, and 3000 miniature terracotta soldiers. *(Bus #3 goes from the train station to the terminal. From here bus #59 takes you to Xianyang. At the clock tower on the left, turn right; when you reach Xining Jie, turn right again. ☎ 096 321 3015. Open daily 8am-6pm. Y20.)*

QIAN TOMB (qián líng; 乾陵). The largest of the surrounding tombs, the Qian Tomb is the burial ground of the third Tang emperor and his more famous wife, Empress Wu Zetian, the first and only female emperor in Chinese history. A pleas-ant 15-20min. walk leads from one end of the tomb to the other on a long walkway lined with sculptures of lions and other figures. Other nearby sites include the 17 smaller tombs of princes, princesses, and ministers. Most notable is the tomb of Princess Yongtai, reportedly beaten to death on the order of her grandmother Wu Zetian, who caught her gossiping about the empress's indulgent lifestyle. The tomb is adorned with still vivid frescoes. *(Open daily 7:30am-7pm. Y31, students Y16.)*

PRINCE YI DE'S TOMB (shǎnxī gānlíng yìdé tàizǐmù bówùguǎn; 陕西干陵懿德太子墓博物馆). In AD 701, 19-year-old Li Zhongren, eldest son of Emperor Zhong-zong, demanded to know why certain nobles were favored in the courts. Empress Wu Zetian had him flogged to death for his insubordination. When Zhongzong assumed the throne four years later, he honored his son with the title Yi De "The Virtuous" and reburied him alongside an eligible (if deceased) young lady. Exca-vated in 1971, the tomb was spectacularly refurbished in 1996. Besides the gor-geous Tang-style buildings, restaurants, exhibition halls, and the burial vault itself, corridors, tunnels, and chambers display the pride of the tomb: $450m^2$ of frescoes. *(Open daily 8am-6:30pm. Y21.)*

MAOLING MAUSOLEUM (màolíng bówùguǎn; 茂陵博物馆). Referred to as the crown jewel of Western Han Dynasty mausoleums, the Maoling houses the tombs of Emperor Wudi (157-87 BC) and his relatives and assistants. Perched dramati-cally on a 47m high hill overlooking the museum's gardens and large, ornamental fountain, Emperor Wudi's tomb once contained many ancient stone sculptures that are now lost or absent. The well-preserved artifacts, including a bronze rhi-noceros-shaped vessel used for drinking wine, are now on display. *(40km northwest of Xi'an. Open daily 7:30am-6:30pm. Y25.)*

NIGHTLIFE

Most bars, discos, and clubs are concentrated along Dong Dajie and Nan Dajie. The **Bell Tower Square** is especially lively on warm summer nights when it fills with children, couples in love, and elderly locals out for a stroll. Enjoy Western films at the newly-constructed **International Cinema,** at Zhongda International Place on Nan Dajie. **Apollo Music Bar,** 348 Dong Dajie, hosts live music beginning at 10pm, while relaxed, well-dressed patrons sit in intimate conversation. (☎8721 3661. Beer Y15-20. Wine Y110-158. Open daily 8pm-2am.) For some good old-fashioned grooving, head to **1+1 Disco Bar** (yī jiā yī dīsīkē jiǔbā; 1+1迪斯科酒吧), 285 Dong Dajie, on the left before Tanshi Jie as you come from the Bell Tower area. Around 10pm, the young crowd, complete with pole dancers, begin grinding to house, trance, and disco. (☎8197 6242. Imported beers Y25-28. Open daily 8pm-2am.)

HUASHAN MOUNTAIN 华山 ☎0913

Proclaimed one of the five sacred Daoist mountains by Emperor Wudi over 2000 years ago, Huashan, also known as *Xīyuè*, or "Western Mountain," guards the eastern gateway to Shaanxi. With near-vertical cliffs and plunging ravines, the impenetrable mountain repelled countless invaders over the centuries. The exhilarating and terrifying climb to the 2158m summit makes clear why would-be attackers always gave up and went home. Romanticized in public imagination as the legendary setting of martial arts epics, Huashan may not actually be the stomping ground of mythical heroes, but its knife-sharp precipices are still formidable foes for would-be adventurers daring its trails. In the valley of the towering peak, the village of Huashan is but the beginning of the mountain's breathtaking surprises.

TRANSPORTATION AND PRACTICAL INFORMATION

Huashan village lies at the base of the mountain, approximately 120km east of Xi'an, not far from the main Xi'an-Zhengzhou rail line. **Yuquan Lu** (玉泉路) is perpendicular to **Xitong Gonglu** (西铜公路), the highway along which buses from Xi'an approach the village. Yuquan Lu continues up the hill to Yuquan Temple and the entrance to the mountain behind it. A number of hotels, restaurants, and souvenir stands line this mainly pedestrian road. The cableway terminus is about 15min. by minibus southeast of Huashan village. Huashan's administrative center is north of the rail line and mountain.

Trains: Huashan Train Station (huáshān huǒchē zhàn; 华山火车站), 15km away in Mengyuan, linked with Huashan village by frequent minibuses (Y3-5). A taxi may be necessary during the evening or for return trips (Y15). To: **Luoyang** (4-5hr., 10 per day, Y31); **Taiyuan** (9hr., 4 per day, Y56); **Xi'an** (2-3hr., 12 per day, Y16). Despite its convenient location in Huashan Village, **Huashan West Train Station** (huáshān xī huǒchē zhàn; 华山西火车站) is only for cargo.

Buses: Minibuses to **Xi'an** (2-3hr., Y20) leave when full from Yuquan Lu at Xitong Gonglu. **Huashan Bus Station** (huáshān qìchē zhàn; 华山汽车站) is on Xitong Gonglu, west of Yuquan Lu. Due to the infrequency of departures, most travelers find it more convenient to take the minibus or the train.

Local Transportation: Minibuses stop at the train station. **Taxis** are easily accessible and do not use meters; Yuquan Lu to the train station costs Y15-20.

Hospital: Huashan Xiahe Hospital (huáshān xiàhé yīyuàn; 华山夏和医院 ; ☎435 2815), a 5min. walk toward Xi'an from Yuquan Lu at Xitong Gonglu, on the left side.

Internet: Joyful Computers (kāixīn diànnǎo; 开心电脑). Walk up Yuquan Lu from Xitong Gonglu and take the 1st left; it's 2min. on your right. Y2 per hr.

Post Office: On Yuquan Lu, across from Huayuan Hotel. Open daily 8am-6pm.

Postal Code: 714200.

■ ◐ ACCOMMODATIONS AND FOOD

Huashan's cheap hotels line Yuquan Lu near the trailhead. Rates under Y50 per person are possible, but quality varies considerably. Many hotels charge much higher rates for foreigners. Discounts or the lower rate may be possible when business is sluggish. Even in high season, proprietors are willing to bargain. Those who want to stay on the mountain have only one option, the **North Peak Hotel ❶** (běifēng fàndiàn; 北峰饭店), a 5min. walk up North Peak from the cable-car station. Overrun with people, it's not exactly a peaceful mountain retreat, but its clean, rustic rooms grant magnificent views. Common baths lack showers and are less than fragrant. (☎ 138 9254 2429. During the day, beds Y10 per hr. 14- and 30-bed dorms Y35; 8-bed Y50; doubles Y300-480; quads Y400.) All the hotels listed below are in Huashan village.

Restaurants abound along Yuquan Lu in Huashan village, but proprietors are quite aware of exploitable tourists. Nearly every hostel and hotel has a small restaurant, and the food varies little place to place. On the other side of Xitong Gonglu, roadside stands dish up noodles and soups (Y3 per bowl). Refreshment vendors are also plentiful along the trail, but the offerings at the summit are much more limited (read: instant noodles).

Huayin City Golden Bureau Hostel (huáyīnshì huángjīnjú zhāodàisuǒ; 华阴市黄金局招待所 ; ☎436 3087), a 2min. walk up Yuquan Lu from Xitong Gonglu, on the right. This small, endearing family-run hostel provides rooms with larger than usual bathroom. More expensive rooms have A/C and TV. Doubles Y40-80. ❶

Huayang Hotel (huáyáng dàjiǔdiàn; 华洋大酒店 ; ☎436 5802) on Yuquan Lu, a 5min. walk on the right. Simple but clean rooms with equally clean baths make this small hotel stand above the rest. Singles and doubles Y100-120; triples Y150. ❷

Huayue Hotel (huáyuè bīnguǎn; 华岳宾馆 ; ☎436 9099). When facing the mountain, it's on the righthand corner of the Yuquan Lu-Xitong Gong Lu intersection. Spotless rooms with A/C, TV, carpet, and bathtub. Hotel store sells cigarettes, sneakers, and more. Singles and doubles Y120-218; triples Y150. ❷

Xiyue Hotel (xīyuè fàndiàn; 西岳饭店 ; ☎436 8298; fax 436 4559), on the right side of Yuquan Lu, about 2min. below the Yuquan Temple entrance. Reception is down the driveway and to the right. Rooms have all the standard amenities, including bathtub. Singles and doubles Y198; quads Y320. ❸

◪ CLIMBING HUASHAN

Minibuses between the cable car base and Huashan village Y10. Buses leave and return to the bottom of Yuquan Lu. ☎436 2683. Cable car to North Peak runs daily 7am-7pm (Y60, round-trip Y110). Ticket gate open daily 24hr. Park Y70, students Y60.

Breathtaking peaks, dense vegetation, and an inspiring summit vista leave no doubt as to why many consider Huashan sacred. Though the trail is well-defined with pebble-paved paths and stone stairs, the climb is challenging, arduous, and seemingly endless. The path begins as a steep ascent, and certain stretches near the top are steep enough to transform the handrail from a simple metal chain into a lifeline. Wearing dark clothing and a pair of gloves from the village is advisable; it's hard to keep clean when you're hanging on a rusty guardrail for dear life.

Yuquan Temple (yùquán yuàn; 玉泉院), at the trailhead, is an obligatory first stop. From there, a 3-5hr. climb (just over 6km) leads to **North Peak** (běi fēng; 北峰), taking up the lion's share of the hike. This climb is not recommended for children. The ascent is eased by numerous overpriced refreshment stands selling cucumbers, and hard-boiled eggs for a protein kick. It's a good idea to bring your own water, but they also sell beverages such as beer and Red Bull.

When not shrouded by fog or mist, the sheer, white granite cliffs are quite imposing. The **Thousand-Foot Cliff** (qiānchǐ chuáng; 千尺幢) is steep and narrow and just keeps on going. But the wind that whips off these cliffs can be chilly, even in the summer. Bringing an extra layer of clothing is a good idea, especially at night.

From the North Peak (also accessible by cable car), you can turn around or continue along the **Green Dragon Ridge** trail, which connects the North Peak to the West, South, and East Peaks. These trail hikes are shorter and more suitable for children or less experienced hikers. The signs, though in English, can be misleading; ask a fellow climber rather than rely on inaccurate markers. Most visitors continue to the **East Peak** (dōng fēng; 东峰), at least 1½hr. from the North Peak and accessible by the trail above the number "6" sign. The **West Peak** (xī fēng; 西峰) is about 1½-2hr. away; the **South Peak** (nán fēng;南峰) is about 45min. beyond. Take care on the descent, especially at night. While the hike up is an athletic challenge, the climb down is one of balance, patience, and poise. Remember that the cable car is always an option.

If you want to see the **sunrise** from East Peak but don't want to pay for accommodations, join the crowds of thrifty tourists on a night climb. A group of at least 50 climbers sets off between 11pm and midnight, finishing up on East Peak as the sun comes up. Flashlights for purchase or rental (Y3) are available on Yuquan Lu in Huashan village. Be extremely careful if hiking in the dark, or dawn won't be the only thing breaking. Climbing Huashan by day is a strenuous endeavor; by night, it can be very dangerous, especially for lone hikers. While many hikers, porters, and enterprising refreshment sellers frequent the trails during the day, next to nobody will linger on the trails at night apart from the intrepid sunrise group.

TURNIN' UP THE HEAT. Take the sun into consideration when planning your climb and deciding how many extra layers of clothing to bring. The trail from Yuquan Temple to North Peak is in the shade during the early morning, but the summer sun hits it full on in the late morning and afternoon. The trail from the bottom of the cable car station to North Peak is in the sun all morning and most of the afternoon. The sun beats down on Green Dragon Ridge trail nearly all day.

YAN'AN 延安 ☎0911

The final stop of the Long March in 1937, Yan'an is now the terminus for countless sojourners making the same pilgrimage as Chairman Mao. For nine years, Yan'an's stark landscape of wind-swept sandstone cliffs was the backdrop for the "birthplace of the revolution" and the headquarters of the fledgling Chinese Communist Party. Today, this modern city in the middle of nowhere symbolizes the less complicated, more heroic and idealistic phase of the revolution (p. 79). Even though "Yan'an Spirit" has since diminished, massive construction projects prove that the city has not been completely forgotten. With over 20 tourist sites, there is more than enough Communist idealism and Mao paraphernalia to go around.

CENTRAL CHINA

📠 ❷ TRANSPORTATION AND PRACTICAL INFORMATION

Yan'an's main commercial areas and streets run parallel to the Yan and Nanchuan rivers, with the city center lying west of the confluence. **Zhongxin Jie** (中心街), which becomes **Beiguan Jie** (北关街) farther north, is the main street. It intersects with **Daqiao Jie** (大桥街), which becomes **Dongguan Jie** (东关街) on the east side of the river, next to the bus station. While the bus station, several parks, and a few sites are located near the city center, the train station and many attractions are several kilometers away.

Flights: Yan'an Airport (yán'ān jīchǎng; 延安机场), about 5km northeast of the city. Limited flights. Buses to the airport depart from the **CAAC ticket office** (☎211 1111), a 10min. walk from the bus station, on the left down Dongguan Jie, away from the city center. Taxi Y10. Open daily 7:30am-7pm. To **Beijing** (1½hr., 4 per week, Y850).

Trains: Yan'an Train Station (yán'ān huǒchē zhàn; 延安火车站 ; ☎249 6976), at the far southern end of town on Qilipu Dajie. Buses #1, 3, and 12 stop right outside, as do numerous minibuses. The ticket office is to the right of the waiting room when facing the station. Tickets sell out fast, so buy early. Same day sales only. Open daily 4:30-6:30am and 10:30am-10:30pm. To **Xi'an** (8-9hr., 2 per day, Y70-84).

Buses: Yan'an Bus Station (yán'ān qìchē zhàn; 延安汽车站; ☎211 2534), on the right of Dongguan Jie as you head away from the city center. Buses #4, 6, and 8 serve the station. To: **Beijing** (22hr., 11am, Y160); **Lanzhou** (20hr., 5:30am, sleeper Y150); **Xi'an** (9hr, every 30min. 9:15am-5pm, Y56-69).

Local Transportation: 11 bus routes run 6am-8pm. Fare Y1. Frequent **minibuses** between the train station and other key areas follow the same routes as public buses. Fare Y1-3. Service until at least 10pm.

Taxis: Base fare Y5, each additional km Y1.

Travel Agency: CITS, in the Yan'an Tourism Bldg. on Zhongxin Jie. **Yan'an Red Capital Travel Service** (yán'ān hóngdū lǚxíng shè; 延安红都旅行社), Beifeng Tower, 4th fl. (☎223 3020), on Zhongxin Jie. Books plane and train tickets.

Bank of China: On the right side of Beiguan Jie (☎211 2423), a few minutes past the Yan'an Hotel. Exchanges currency and traveler's checks. English-speaking staff member at window #11. Open M-F 8am-6pm.

Hospital: Yan'an Region People's Hospital (yán'ān dìqū rénmín yīyuàn; 延安地区人民医院 ; ☎211 3522), on Zhongxin Jie, just down from the Yan'an Hotel.

PSB: On the left side of Beiguan Jie, across from the Bank of China.

Post and Telecommunications: On Zhongxin Jie, away from Daqiao Jie toward the Yan'an Hotel; it's on the left. EMS. Open daily 8am-midnight. **China Telecom** (☎211 2829) is next door. Open 8am-7pm.

Postal Code: 716000.

🏠 🍴 ACCOMMODATIONS AND FOOD

Yan'an has many nice hotels catering to the growing number of Chinese tourists. Most are located to the west of the confluence of the two rivers.

Good eating in Yan'an is easy to come by. Two **nightmarkets,** on either side of Yan'an Bridge (yán'ān dàqiáo; 延安大桥), serve a number of northern Shaanxi specialties. Dark noodles (hēi lāomiàn; 黑捞面) are about Y2-3 per bowl. Several Mongolian **hotpot** restaurants, mostly along Daqiao Jie and Zhongxin Jie, supplement the local cuisine. Across from Traffic Hotel and 3min. toward town, helpful waiters at **Old Chengdu Hotpot City** (lǎo chéngdū huǒguō chéng; 老成都火锅城 ; ☎211 7001 8008), 71 Dongguan Jie, guide novices through the steps of Sichuan hotpot.

Traffic Hotel (jiāotōng fàndiàn; 交通饭店 ; ☎212 5270). From the bus station, turn right; the hotel is a 1min. walk down the right side of Dongguan Jie. The staff is friendly. TV. Dorms Y10-50, with bath Y90. ❶

Yasheng Hotel (yàshèng dàjiǔdiàn; 亚圣大酒店 ; ☎213 2778; fax 213 2779). From the train station, take bus #3 to the intersection between Erdao Jie and Zhongxin Jie; it's straight ahead on Erdao Jie. With a business center, karaoke room, and revolving restaurant, the Yasheng Hotel offers large rooms with A/C and TV. Rooms above the 7th fl. have a great view. Singles and doubles Y238-398. ❸

Yan'an Hotel (yán'ān bīnguǎn; 延安宾馆 ; ☎211 3122), on Beiguan Jie. Bus #3 from the train station stops in front; a taxi costs Y7-8. The first 4-star hotel in northern Shaanxi—and it shows. Spacious rooms with A/C, sparkling baths, and TV. Extensive facilities include sauna, karaoke, swimming pool, ping-pong room, and 16 restaurants. Singles Y348; doubles Y380. ❹

🔎 SIGHTS

A slew of well-maintained exhibits brings visitors up close and personal with not only the Chairman, but also former premier Zhou Enlai and other key members of the Communist Party. Most attractions are outside the city center, but the city's compactness makes it possible to get your Mao fix in one day.

📷 YANGJIALING REVOLUTION HEADQUARTERS (yángjiālǐng gémìng jiùzhǐ; 杨家岭革命旧址). Seeking refuge after the Long March, the Central Committee set up camp in this series of buildings and cave dwellings carved into the dry hillsides outside Yan'an. The meeting hall, offices, and propaganda and policy research divisions are the first stop for many Chinese tour groups retracing Mao's legendary steps. To truly get into the revolutionary spirit, pay Y10 to don a Mao suit and have your picture taken at the podium where the Chairman spoke. *(Take bus #1 or 3 from the train station to the last stop, then walk back toward the city for 10min. Taking a left at the 1st vendor-lined alley leads to the large stone gates of the entrance. Open daily 7am-7:30pm. Y16.)*

YAN'AN REVOLUTION MUSEUM (yán'ān gémìng jìniànguǎn; 延安革命纪念馆).
After taking the obligatory picture of the massive stone carving of Mao, visitors slowly meander through the museum and its impressive collection of maps, relics, and old photographs, all unfortunately without English captions. Mao's horse (stuffed, of course) holds a place of honor here; legend says that when its death was near, the horse turned toward Zhongnanhai, the residential complex of top CCP officials in Beijing, and gave three cries as a final farewell to its rider. *(The big orange building at the northern end of Wangjiaping Bridge. Take bus #1 or 3 from the train station and walk across the bridge. ☎211 2610. Open daily summer 8am-6pm; winter 8am-5pm. Y12.)*

BAO PAGODA (bǎo tǎ; 宝塔). Built in AD 766-778, the 44m high pagoda is such a fixture in the Yan'an skyline that its silhouette often appeared on Mao buttons in the 1960s. The climb up the claustrophobic staircase is tiring (think large steps and many of them), but has its rewards: on clear days visitors can glimpse the city, cradled between several mountains, and the distant desert beyond. *(On the east side of Nanchuan River. Take bus #1 to Xiao Dong Men. The walk up to the pagoda takes 15-20min.; taxis also make the trip. Open daily 6am-10pm. Park entrance Y20, pagoda climb Y5.)*

YULIN 榆林　　　　☎0912

Well-preserved architecture graces Yulin, a remote, friendly town on the outskirts of the Mu Us desert in northern China. A former Ming Dynasty garrison and Great Wall patrol post, Yulin's present attractions are limited, although the ride through the countryside to the town passes pleasant landscapes. The town's loca-

CENTRAL CHINA

tion provides travelers with a peaceful stopover en route to Xi'an, Yinchuan, or Baotou and the chance to gaze upon the Great Wall in its glorious, unpreserved state, but not much else.

▉ ▉ TRANSPORTATION AND PRACTICAL INFORMATION. Yulin spans both sides of the **Yuxi River** (榆溪河), but most sites of interest are on the easily navigable east side. **Yuyang Zhong Lu** (榆阳中路) runs east-west past the **bus station** and is the southern end of **Nan Dajie** (南大街), the commercial thoroughfare of **Xinjian Lu** (新建路), and **Changcheng Lu** (长城路; "Great Wall Road"). These streets run north until they terminate at **Renmin Lu** (人民路). Three towers line **Bei Dajie** (北大街), which turns into Nan Dajie, culminating in the imposing **Southern Gate** (nán mén; 南门) at the intersection of Nan Dajie and Yuyang Zhong Lu.

The small and deserted **Yulin Airport** (☎388 4777 or 3888 4666) is a Y10 cab ride east of the city, with flights serving Xi'an (daily, Y500-600). The **bus station** is on Yuyang Zhong Lu, just west of Xinjian Lu. Buses congregate frequently at the rotary at the east end. Since few people work at the station, just find your bus and pay the driver. Buses go to: Baotou (5hr.; 5:30, 8:30, 10:10am; Y38-53); Daliuta (1½hr., every 20min., Y27); Xi'an (12hr.; 7:30am, 6:30pm; Y112-121); Yan'an (4½hr., every 20min. 6:40am-11pm); Yinchuan (7-8hr.; 5:30, 8, 9:20am, 3pm; Y81). Within Yulin, **bus** #2 follows Xinjian Lu to Renmin Lu and circles back along Changcheng Lu; #4 patrols Nan Dajie. The base fare for a **taxi** is Y4-5, for a **moped** Y2.

The **Bank of China,** on Renmin Lu, just west of Changcheng Lu, is the only bank in town that exchanges currency and traveler's checks. (☎325 8365. Open daily 8-11:30am and 2-6pm.) The **PSB** (☎326 1442) is on Nan Dajie, just north of the middle tower. **Changtong Internet Cafe** is south of the post office, on the second alley to the right, across from Agricultural Bank. (Y3 per hr. Open daily 8am-2am.) The **post office** is on Xinjian Nan Lu, south of Renmin Square Park, and has EMS. (☎323 5196. Open daily summer 8am-8pm; winter 8am-7pm). **Postal Code:** 719000.

▉ ▉ ACCOMMODATIONS AND FOOD. Yulin, rarely visited by tourists, has few accommodations. **Guangji Tower ❷** (guǎngjì dàshà; 广济大厦), on the northwest corner of Renmin Lu and Changcheng Lu, has rooms with large windows, clean baths, TV, and A/C. (☎389 5158. Singles Y110-198; doubles Y110-168; triples Y150.) **Yuxi Hotel ❷** (yúxī dàjiǔdiàn; 榆溪大酒店), on Renmin Lu, has worn but clean rooms with well-maintained baths. Turn right out of the bus station and right onto Changcheng Lu, make a left onto Renmin Lu, and continue for half a block. (☎336 3700 or 336 3800. Singles Y100-140; doubles Y120-150; triples Y120.)

Pricey food joints line Xinjian Lu, but inexpensive, authentic local fare can be found east of the bus station on Yuyang Zhong Lu at Nan Dajie, or along Nan Dajie itself (large bowls of dumplings Y1).

▉ SIGHTS. Meandering down the pebble-paved alleys of **East Yulin** is a bit like traveling through time. Low brick walls encircle what were once the courtyards of Ming-Dynasty homes. Leaving South Gate behind, walk from south to north along Nan Dajie, and you will encounter three towers, each more ornate and grander than the last. Climb to the top of the last tower, **Bell Tower** (zhōnglóu; 钟楼), to view the surrounding desert and the **Great Wall.** Follow the winding path of the first paved alley south of the middle gate, either by foot or taxi (Y4). For the more agile, shimmy up the southeast corner of the last rotary on Yuyang Zhong Lu. Subtle hints of Islamic influence in the tower's architecture underscore the town's proximity to the northwest provinces. The Great Wall to the east of Nan Dajie also provides views of the city and surroundings. Fully integrated into the needs of the population, this section of the Great Wall serves as a ready-made fourth wall or roof for small houses and an easy mount for telephone poles. This is the real Great Wall for free, without the restoration and reconstruction of the more touristed portions of the wall. Finding a place to scramble up can be difficult, but worth it to see old Yulin unfold beneath you.

It's easy to forget that a harsh desert lies beyond the city walls, especially when strolling through the ancient streets of Yulin. Just outside the city, 7.5km from downtown Yulin, sits the three-tiered fortress of the **North Tower** (zhèngběi tái; 正北台). This former stronghold still projects an imposing appearance, testimony to Yulin's past strategic importance. The hike to the top is worth it for the best view of the green fields fading to desert sands. (Taxi Y20. Open 7:30am-8pm. Tower Y10.) Down the road is another tourist-free, and generally people-free, site, the **Red Stone Gorges** (hóngshí xiá; 红石峡), where you can duck through caves and visualize the lives of desert-dwellers.

HENAN 河南

Over 90 million people call Henan home, making it the second most populous province in China. The three ancient national capitals (Luoyang, Kaifeng, and Anyang) that once distinguished the province have left behind enough artifacts to satisfy even the most rapacious history buff. The unearthing of even more treasures, such as bone flutes dating back to 7000 BC and ruins of the Xia Dynasty (2200-1800 BC), has only prompted the government (and thus, its tourism industry) to adopt a more active, financially-driven interest in the preservation of such historical legacies. A number of foreign investors have added their money to the economic boom; as a result, the province seems to be perpetually under construction. Its main cities, Zhengzhou and Luoyang, have been highly image-conscious in their development: tree-lined boulevards stretch as far as the eye can see, and wide promenades of polished concrete encourage visitors to look beyond the traffic chaos. But tradition here remains alive and well. The first Buddhist temple in China, the White Horse Temple, keeps up its role as an important place of worship, and the world-renowned Shaolin monks continue to perfect their kung fu fighting skills, just as they have done for over 1500 years.

ZHENGZHOU 郑州 ☎ 0371

Droves of Chinese and foreign travelers pass through Zhengzhou en route to Shaolin Monastery, Luoyang, or Kaifeng, but few stick around this transportation hub for more than a night or two. The Erqi Pagoda shopping district, encircled by its wrap-around pedestrian overpass (which glows blue neon after dark), is Henan's retail haven, with every imaginable store within walking distance. The city itself hasn't much that is unique to offer the tourist, with the notable exception of the Henan Provincial Museum.

▭ TRANSPORTATION

Flights: Zhengzhou Airport (zhèngzhōu jīchǎng; 郑州机场), 5km east of the city center. The CAAC bus (45min., every hr. 6am-6pm, Y15) goes to the airport from the Aviation Hotel (mínháng dàjiǔdiàn; 民航大酒店), 3 Jinshui Lu (☎599 1111). To: **Beijing** (5 per day, Y480); **Guangzhou** (5 per day, Y810); **Hong Kong** (M-W, F, Su 9am; Y1800); **Kunming** (4 per day, Y1010); **Shanghai** (5 per day, Y560). Buy tickets from the friendly staff at the **IATA ticket office** (☎594 1222), on the corner of the intersection of Renmin Lu and Jinshui Lu. Open 24hr.

CENTRAL CHINA

Trains: Zhengzhou Train Station (zhèngzhōu huǒchē zhàn; 郑州火车站 ; ☎835 1111, ticket info 698 8988), in the big square at the end of Datong Lu and Xinlong Jie, southwest of the main commercial center. Tickets (especially sleepers) for trains not originating in Zhengzhou are difficult to obtain. To: **Beijing** (7hr.; many per day, 4 originating; Y95-175); **Guangzhou** (16hr.; 7 per day, 1 originating; Y353); **Luoyang** (2½hr.; 5 per day, 3 originating; Y20); **Nanjing** (8hr., daily, Y103-163); **Shanghai** (10hr.; 7 per day, 2 originating; Y240); **Taiyuan** (10hr., 3 per day, Y85); **Wuhan** (5½hr.; 4 per day, 1 originating; Y65); **Xi'an** (6hr.; 10 per day, 1 originating; Y82-120).

Buses: Zhengzhou Bus Station (zhèngzhōu qìchē zhàn; 郑州汽车站 ; ☎698 3995), on Xinlong Jie, across the square from the train station. To: **Anyang** (4hr., every 20min., Y36-45); **Beijing** (8hr., every 1½hr., Y150); **Ji'nan** (8hr., 5 per day 7:30am-2:30pm, Y125); **Shanghai** (20hr., 5:20pm, Y236); **Taiyuan** (8hr., 3 per day, Y140); **Xi'an** (6hr., 9 per day, Y120).

Local Transportation: Datong Lu, opposite and to the right of the train station entrance, is a hub for local **buses.** Nearly every bus stops here before heading back to the Erqi Pagoda (via Fushou Jie) and then onto their individual routes. Fare Y1. Bus #2 leaves from Datong Lu, navigating a circular route that extends as far east as Dongming Lu and north to Nongye Lu; #32 also leaves from Datong Lu and, once past the Erqi Pagoda, travels north to the end of Jingqi Lu before turning east down Nongye Lu; #4 and 201 head west from the train station to the Zhengzhou University area. **Minibuses,** including #16 to the Yellow River, ply many routes 6am-8 or 9pm. Fare Y4 and under.

Taxis: Base fare Y7, each additional km Y1.

▚ 🛈 ORIENTATION AND PRACTICAL INFORMATION

Zhengzhou, about 30km south of the Yellow River, is a crowded regional rail hub. Most activity concentrates around the train station square, a choked-up mesh of buses, taxis, vans, and bicycles. Northeast, **Erqi Pagoda,** a notable landmark with streets that radiate from it in five directions, is a 15min. walk from the train station. This area and, to a lesser extent, the neighborhood around the intersection of Jinshui Lu and Zijingshan Lu are home to department stores, boutiques, restaurants, and hotels. **Erqi Lu** (二七路) and **Renmin Lu** (人民路) are main thoroughfares that begin at the pagoda.

Travel Agency: CITS, Haitong Bldg., 50 Jinqi Lu, 7th fl. (☎534 6711 or 534 6722), at Wei Wu Lu. Arranges tours to Shaolin Temple (Y98, not including admission). Train ticket commission Y30-50. Free airline booking. Open M-F 8am-6pm.

Bank of China: At the intersection of Chengdong Lu and Jinshui Lu. Exchanges currency and traveler's checks. Credit card advances. Open daily 9am-5pm.

ATM: At **Guangdong Development Bank** (guǎngdōng fāzhǎn yínháng; 广东发展银行), 8 Jinshui Lu, to the right as you exit the Bank of China.

Market: Zhengzhou Department Store (zhèngzhōu bǎihuò dàlóu; 郑州百货大楼), 49 Erqi Lu, north of Erqi Pagoda. Open daily 9am-8pm.

PSB: 110 Erqi Lu (☎622 2023), near People's Park. Open M-F 8:30am-noon and 3-6:30pm.

Hospital: Erqi People's Hospital (èrqī rénmín yīyuàn; 二七人民医院; ☎696 5663), on your left as you walk down pedestrian Dehua Jie from Erqi Pagoda.

Internet Access: Internet access is available on the second fl. of the train station. Facing the station, head to the ticket purchasing section on the far left. The staircase is immediately to the left as you enter. Fast connections at Y3 per hour. Open 24hr.

Post Office: Zhengzhou Post Office, on the south side of the train station square. EMS, Western Union, Poste Restante. Open daily 8am-7pm.

Postal Code: 450000.

Zhengzhou

🏠 ACCOMMODATIONS
Dehua Buxing Jie Hotel, 3
Golden Sunshine Hotel, 5
Jinyu Hotel, 4
Zhongyuan Mansions, 6

🍴 FOOD
Haoxianglai Restaurant, 1
Home-Cooked Meal, 2

🏠 ACCOMMODATIONS

Though there is no shortage of hotels in the train station square, most carry a high price tag. Such an abundance of top-end establishments, however, makes for fierce competition, putting the traveler in a strong bargaining position. Price haggling is also a must for those seeking budget accommodations. Hotel hawkers, with their insider's knowledge of which hotels quietly harbor cheaper options, can help you find a more affordable alternative.

Dehua Buxing Jie Hotel (dé huà bùxíng jiē lǚguǎn; 德化步行街旅馆), 79 Dehua Jie (☎696 5880 or 618 5300). With your back to Erqi Pagoda, walk down pedestrian Dehua Jie. It's on the right just after a light-green colored optician store. Despite a dark and somewhat dingy exterior, these rooms are reasonably comfy and clean, located in a shopping district just a 2min. walk from the city center. Rooms have A/C, TV, and shared bathrooms and showers. Doubles Y30. ❶

Jinyu Hotel (jìnyù bīnguǎn; 晋豫宾馆), 6 Fushou Jie (☎705 0201). Look for a small white entrance, flanked by 2 large vases. Simply furnished rooms with cozy beds. Basic but clean bathrooms with bathtubs. Although rooms at the back face another building and get no sunlight, they are a good deal quieter than those at the front. Doubles Y60 and up. ❶

Zhongyuan Mansions (zhōngyuán dàshà; 中原大厦 ; ☎676 8481), directly opposite the main entrance to the train station. A cavernous high-rise in which you won't want to spend more than a night. Noise from the train station in front and the central bus system in back makes sure that you wake up in time. Basic but spacious rooms. Deposit Y10. Singles Y80, with bath Y138; doubles Y100, with bath Y168; quads Y50. ❷

Golden Sunshine Hotel (jīn yángguāng dàjiǔdiàn; 金阳光大酒店), 86 Er Malu (☎696 9999; fax 699 9534), 3min. left of the entrance to the train station. All rooms have TV and A/C. Large standard rooms with mini-bars and comfortable queen-sized beds. Health club and other amenities. Breakfast included with standard rooms. Suites generally increase in quality and price with distance from the ground fl. Singles Y120 and up; doubles Y228-504. ❸

☕ FOOD

Aside from its famous **No. 3 hybrid watermelon,** Zhengzhou isn't particularly well known for any local food. Fortunately, there are a number of small nightmarket stalls around the alleys near the Erqi Pagoda. For your slurping delight, be sure to sample a bowl of *shāguō miàn* (砂锅面) or *huìmiàn* (烩面), wavy noodles flavored with seaweed and cooked in a clay pot (Y3). Stalls sell both in a small alley off Renmin Lu, near the base of the pedestrian overpass; most close up around 9pm. Late-night munchies can be found at another market that calmly sets up at 10pm along Dehua Jie, near the McDonald's. Many restaurants and street stands serving Muslim or Sichuanese cuisine line Ziyou Lu and Minzhu Lu off Jiefang Lu.

Home-Cooked Meal (jiā cháng cài; 家常菜 ; ☎622 8290), at the intersection of Erqi Lu and Renmin Lu, facing Erqi Pagoda. The swinging, suspended garden chairs alone, adorned with flowers and peacock feathers, make this restaurant worth a visit. A vast, globe-spanning range of dishes, from beef noodles (Y8) to pizza (Y45), as well as a colorful selection of fruit juices and ice cream. Open daily 9am-8pm. ❷

Haoxianglai Restaurant (háoxiǎnglái; 毫享来), 21 Minggong Lu (☎622 6038), a 10-min. walk south of the entrance to People's Park. Take bus #2 from the station to Minggong Lu and walk north for a few minutes. The restaurant's on the left. This clean, cheery place serves everything from curried chicken to dim sum, but the most worthwhile are the set meals (Y25), bubbling plates of egg, pasta, and meat. Open 24hr. ❷

⊙ SIGHTS

Mostly a jumping-off point for tours of Songshan Monastery, Zhengzhou itself has little of interest, beyond the ultra-modern ▨ **Henan Provincial Museum** (hénán shěng bówùguǎn; 河南省博物馆). The most interesting and best-preserved relics discovered in Henan province have found their way to this gigantic pyramidal museum, whose impressive collection fills four floors of exhibition space. Oracle bone inscriptions, a full-body jade suit, fantastic replicas of classical architecture, and even the occasional vegetable (ivory cabbage and radishes from the Qing Dynasty) grace the halls. Fascinating English captions enhance the experience. Tuesday through Sunday, at 10am and 4pm, you can enjoy a 30min. musical performance that uses ancient instruments. *(8 Nongye Lu, at the north end of Jinqi Lu. Bus #32 stops one block to the east. ☎3511 237. Open daily summer 8:30am-6:30pm. Last admission 30min. before closing. Audio tours in English Y30, deposit Y400 or passport. Y20, students Y10.)*

▣ DAYTRIP FROM ZHENGZHOU: SONGSHAN AND SHAOLIN

Songshan Mountain (1492m), stretching 500km across central Henan, has been a center for Daoist worship ever since the Zhou Dynasty (1066-256 BC), when it was designated as one of the five sacred Daoist mountains of China. But today, the biggest draw is Buddhist—travelers from around the world flock to Shaolin Monastery. No longer quite so secluded, the mountain also sees thousands of young boys eager to master the techniques of Shaolin kung fu. Travelers don't have to face a weary climb to the top of Songshan, making the mountain an easy daytrip from either Luoyang or Zhengzhou.

SHAOLIN MONASTERY 少林寺

Minibuses make the trip from Zhengzhou, departing from the long-distance bus station (daily 8am, returning 4pm; Y21 each way, return tickets available at Shaolin). Most hotels arrange their own tours. The standard price for round-trip tickets is Y40, low season Y30. Although tickets are purchased directly from the bus station ticket office, the majority of buses operate as tour groups, often turning a 2-2½hr. trip into a 5hr. ride with many extra stops along the way (the Han Tombs, Zhongyue Temple, a souvenir store, a kung fu performance, the gas station, or a restaurant). A faster option would be to take a minibus, leaving from the bus station next to the entrance of the train station (1½-2hr., many each morning based on demand, Y40). Stops generally include a tourist shop and the White Horse Temple. Question drivers closely ahead of time to find out what kind of trip you're in for, though you may not get a forthright answer. It may be a good idea to ask your driver to write down the planned arrival time. Upon arrival, you can stay with the tour bus (Y80 including admission) or visit the sights yourself (Y40, student price Y40 for 2 students, children under 1.3m free). The latter option is certainly feasible: all the attractions, save only the Bodhidharma Cave, lie along the main road and are within 15min. walking distance from each other. Motorcabs can also take you around for Y3-5, but they tend to overcharge. Make sure to confirm the place and time to meet up with your original bus or you might have trouble finding a way back and have to pay extra. Most buses meet in the parking lot directly outside the Pagoda Forest (塔林).

The cult of kung fu (gōngfū; 功夫) is going strong in Shaolin Monastery. Although brightly colored uniforms have replaced monastic robes, the thousands of young trainees who fill the neighborhood still practice the kicks and jabs that made this tradition famous. Vigorous exercise certainly pays off—where else can you find dozens of 8-year-olds who could kick your butt? Almost every technique imaginable has been used to instill discipline in Shaolin martial arts (wǔshù; 武术) students. Training methods include ramming logs into a volunteer's stomach, meditating while suspended from a tree, using stones to crack walnuts over each others' heads, and other strength-testing and character-building exercises.

SHAOLIN MONASTERY (shàolín sì; 少林寺). Opened in AD 495, the monastery is known as the birthplace of Chan Buddhism (popularized in the West under its Japanese name, Zen), after a visit by Bodhidharma in AD 527, when it began to adapt local martial arts to Buddhist teachings. These monks were far from secluded, showcasing their fighting prowess by helping Tang Emperor Taizong vanquish bandit rebels. The halls and shrines within the temple are in excellent condition, as most were rebuilt after 1928. In **Daxiong Hall** (大雄殿), the main hall of worship, three large golden Buddhas sit cross-legged under a beautifully ornate ceiling. **Wenshu Hall,** a smaller building near Daxiong Hall, contains a stone supposedly emblazoned with the image of Bodhisattva Wenshu. **Li Xue Pavilion** (Standing-in-the-Snow Pavilion; 立雪亭) marks the place where the master monk Huike stood deep in the snow and cut off his own left arm in order to understand the essence of Chan Buddhism. Within **Pilu Pavilion,** colored frescoes of the story of the 500 *arhats* adorn the walls. Forty-eight footprints cover the brick floor, where monks have gathered and worshipped in the same spot for centuries. **Chuipu Hall,** an easy-to-miss courtyard to the left of the entrance to the temple, was built in 1984 and has 216 lively plaster figurines depicting Shaolin martial arts and famous temple legends. *(15min. walk on main road from the entrance, on the right. Open daily 8am-6:30pm.)*

SHIFANG MONASTERY (shífāng chányuàn; 十方禅院). This small monastery features a collection of 500 dusty, faded Buddha statues with lively expressions and varied poses. As a neat fortune-telling exercise, visitors can pick the *arhat* that they find particularly appealing, count down the same number as their age (plus one year), and then read the explanatory note (in Chinese) on the Buddha statue. *(Across the street from Shaolin Temple. Open daily 8am-6:30pm.)*

OTHER SHAOLIN SIGHTS. The **Pagoda Forest** (tǎ lín; 塔林), at the end of the parking lot, a 15min. walk from the Shaolin Temple, forms a maze of many small pagodas and provides a nice view of the surrounding mountain range. Immediately to your right as you pass the main entrance ticket checkpoint, **Wushu Hall** (wǔshù guǎn; 武术馆) hosts martial arts demonstrations. (30min. Show times daily 10, 11:30am, 1:30, 3, 4pm. Y20.) Hardly anyone makes the two-hour trek up to **Science Fiction Hall** (kēhuàn guǎn; 科幻馆) and **Bodhidharma Cave** (dámó dòng; 达摩洞), which is better seen with binoculars (Y1). Watching the martial arts classes and checking out the beautiful fields just inside the main entrance are far more worthwhile. *(All included in admission fee to Shaolin.)*

OTHER SONGSHAN SIGHTS

ZHONGYUE TEMPLE (zhōngyuè miào; 中岳庙). At the foot of Songshan Mountain, Zhongyue Temple is the oldest Daoist place of worship in China. Its name comes from Songshan's famed position as the center peak of the five sacred Daoist mountains. Inside the compound, a bit off to the side, stand four figures known as the "Iron Men of the Song." Supposedly, rubbing the figures and then touching a sore spot on your own body will magically eliminate the pain. *(Open daily summer 7am-7pm; winter 7am-6pm. Y15.)*

YONGTAI TEMPLE (yǒngtài sì; 永泰寺). A short taxi or minibus ride away, Yongtai Temple, a beautifully preserved building dating from 521 AD, offers a glimpse into a Buddhist nunnery. Remove your shoes before entering the Princess Building, where you will find an impressive jade stone statue of Yongtai, an emperor's daughter who entered the nunnery. *(Open daily summer 7am-7pm; winter 8am-8pm. Y16.)*

LUOYANG 洛阳　　　　　　　　　　　　　☎ 0379

A fast-paced and energetic city, Luoyang hides many more peaceful, shaded parks and leafy boulevards behind its noisy streets. Escaping from the hustle and bustle, people exercise in the morning, play cards in the afternoon heat, and waltz through the cool summer nights. Visitors can find serenity at the nearby Longmen Grottoes and the White Horse Temple, surrounded by ancient Buddhist sculptures and carvings. In mid-April, tourists and city folk alike gather for the annual Peony Festival, when the Royal City Park showcases over 500 varieties of Empress Wu Zetian's favorite flower.

▐ TRANSPORTATION

Flights: Luoyang Airport (luòyáng jīchǎng; 洛阳机场 ; ☎ 393 5301, ext. 510), over 10km north of the city. **CAAC ticket office,** 196 Chundu Lu (☎ 231 0121 or 231 4666), west of the train station, at the intersection with Shachang Bei Lu. Open daily 8am-5:30pm. To **Beijing** (Y890) and **Shanghai** (Y890).

Trains: Luoyang Train Station (luòyáng huǒchē zhàn; 洛阳火车站 ; ☎ 256 1222), at the top of Jinguyuan Lu. To: **Beijing** (11hr., 7pm, Y191); **Guangzhou** (24hr., 5pm, Y331); **Shanghai** (17hr., 10pm, Y246); **Wuhan** (8hr., 10pm, Y154); **Xi'an** (5-6hr., several per day, Y55-87).

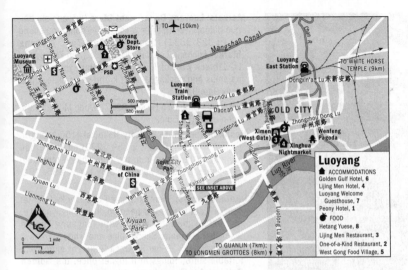

Buses: Luoyang Bus Station (luòyáng chángtú qìchē zhàn; 洛阳长途汽车站; ☎323 2945), on the corner of Jinguyuan Lu and Daonan Lu, diagonally opposite the train station. To: **Anyang** (4hr., every hr. 7:30am-4pm, Y60); **Guangzhou** (27hr., 12:30pm, Y320); **Ji'nan** (9hr., 8am, Y110); **Kaifeng** (3½hr., every 30min., Y35); **Taiyuan** (8hr., 3 per day, Y90); **Xi'an** (4hr., several per day, Y61); **Zhengzhou** (1½hr., every 30min. 7am-7pm, Y30).

Local Transportation: Most **buses** stop running around 8-9pm. **Minibuses** run along Zhongzhou Zhong Lu late into the night. Fare for both Y1. Buses #5, 48, 56 and 81 run from the train station, down Jinguyuan Lu, before turning left to head east along Zhongzhou Zhong Lu; #83 goes north from the main train station to the Ancient Tombs Museum and the airport; #102 and 103 run along Zhongzhou Xi Lu and up Jinguyuan Lu to the train station.

Taxis: Base fare Y6. Motorcycle taxis cost at least Y3.

✳ 2 ORIENTATION AND PRACTICAL INFORMATION

Luoyang sits on the northern bank of the Luo River, and covers an area of nearly 500km². Most of the city's hotels, shops, and restaurants are near **Zhongzhou Lu** (中州路), which runs east-west across the city. **Jinguyuan Lu** (金谷园路) runs south from the train station before reaching **Wangcheng Square** (王城广场). The main railway and bus stations are on the northern edge of the city. The airport is to the northwest. By far the best way to navigate the city is by bus. Luoyang's local bus service is a model of efficiency: quick, clean, cheap, and very easy to use.

Tourist Services: Luoyang Tourist Information (☎431 3824).

Travel Agency: CITS (☎432 3212 or 431 3701), in the Tourist Mansion on Jiudu Xi Lu. Free airline reservations; Y30 commission for train tickets. Open daily summer 8am-6pm; winter 8am-5:30pm.

Bank of China: 439 Zhongzhou Zhong Lu (☎432 3212), in the Int'l Finance Bldg. Exchanges currency and traveler's checks. Credit card advances. Open summer M-F 8am-6pm; winter M-F 8am-5:30pm.

NO AID FOR AIDS?

More than a decade ago, millions of poor Chinese farmers in Henan sold pints of blood to collecting stations, both government-sponsored and underground. Contaminated samples, unsanitary collecting practices, and unregulated blood transfusions ultimately resulted in the widespread AIDS epidemic that now haunts much of Henan and the surrounding provinces. Most estimates put the number of infected at half a million or higher.

In the village of Shuang Miao (pop. 3000), more than 1200 farmers sold their blood regularly. Now, more than 600 have AIDS, and, without treatment, villagers die every week. Zhu Jingzhong, an HIV-positive farmer, likens the tragedy to an atomic bomb gone off. People are dying at the same time, with some committing suicide upon diagnosis. The situation is the same elsewhere, with more than half the population affected in many villages.

The United Nations estimates that more than one million people in China are HIV-positive, and by 2010, more than 20 million will be infected. Yet, until recently, the government has refused to acknowledge the AIDS epidemic. By 1994, government officials in Henan were already aware of the problem, but they suppressed the information and even reported improvements in blood safety. In the years of cover-up, many villagers died without treatment.

Markets: Luoyang Department Store (luòyáng shì bǎihuò dàlóu; 洛阳市百货大楼), 287 Zhongzhou Zhong Lu (☎323 3531). Open daily 9am-7pm. **Xicheng Market** (xīchéng liàngfàn; 西城量贩), on Zhongzhou Lu 1 block west of Jinguyuan Lu. Here you can find pajamas and packaged meat in the same aisle. Open daily 9am-9pm.

PSB: 1 Kaixuan Xi Lu (☎394 8257). Open M-F 8:30am-noon and 2:30-5pm.

Hospital: The **150th Military Hospital** (150 zhōngxīn yīyuàn; 150 中心医院 ; ☎389 2222) on Zhongzhou Lu, across the street from the bank, has a reputable Foreigner's Building. Accessible by buses #55, 101, and 103.

Internet Access: There is a small and smoky Internet cafe on your left as you head south on Jinguyuan Lu, just before the intersection with Tanggong Lu and Wangcheng Square. Simple blue and white sign says 网吧 (wǎngbā). Y3 per hr. Open 24hr. For more comfortable surroundings at a higher price, the **Golden Gulf Hotel** on Zhongzhou Lu (see **Accommodations**, p. 293) provides Internet services at Y10 per hr.

Post Office: East of Wangcheng Sq. at the intersection of Jinguyuan Lu and Zhongzhou Zhong Lu (☎393 8683). EMS and Poste Restante. Open daily 8am-5:30pm for packages, 8am-6:30pm for all other services.

Postal Code: 471000.

ACCOMMODATIONS

Accommodations open to foreigners generally fall into one of two categories: cheap, noisy hotels near the main train station, or relatively posh establishments along Zhongzhou Lu in the city center. Brochure-wielding hotel hawkers await new arrivals at the train station. Though convenient for those passing through, the area immediately south of the train station is by far the grimiest part of town. Veer left upon exiting the station and hop aboard one of the local buses to make your way to more appealing alternatives.

Lijing Men Hotel (lìjīngmén bīnguǎn; 丽京门宾馆 ; ☎350 3381). As you approach the Old City's main West Gate (xīmén; 西门) from the city center, follow the pathway sloping down to the right. With small but cozy bedrooms built into the base of Luoyang's restored Old City walls, this hotel brings novelty to a night's sleep. Fully furnished, carpeted, pleasantly decorated, and with private baths, Lijing offers unbeatable value for your money. Singles Y100; doubles Y160; triples Y160. ❷

Peony Hotel (mŭdān bīnguăn; 牡丹宾馆), 4 Jiefang Bei Lu (☎256 0188 or 137 0388 5812). With your back to the train station exit, walk straight and veer slightly to the right to reach Jiefang Lu. It's about half a block down Jiefang Lu, on the right. Forget the pretty name—cheap, cheerless rooms await off dark corridors. Shared bathrooms aren't the cleanest but they have showers. Friendly, helpful staff. Deposit Y20. Dorm rooms (available for groups only) Y20; singles Y60; doubles Y80. ❶

Luoyang Welcome Guesthouse (luòyáng yíng bīnguăn; 洛阳迎宾馆), 6 Renmin Xi Lu (☎330 8788; fax 391 9295), about 3min. south of Zhongzhou Lu. Take bus #2 or 16 from the train station to Xi Gong Youyuan; the hotel entrance is on the right side of the street, marked by 2 imposing lion statues at the door. Very comfortable rooms all come with standard amenities. Singles Y230; doubles Y460. ❸

Golden Gulf Hotel (jīn shuĭwān dàjiŭdiàn; 金水湾大酒店), 319 Zhongzhou Zhong Lu (☎339 5588; fax 339 5678), in the high-rise near Renmin Xi Lu. Accessible by bus #103 from train station. This 3-star beauty offers huge carpeted rooms with comfy pillows. A/C, Internet access, and currency exchange. Friendly staff. Doubles Y400-Y572, but 30% discounts usually available except during the Peony Festival (mid-Apr.). ❺

◪ FOOD

Luoyang is famous for its 24-course **Water Banquet,** but those who have neither the time nor the appetite have plenty of other options. Crowded street stalls and outside tables are set up at night in the city's compact alleys. There are markets off **Renmin Dong Lu,** just south of Zhongzhou Zhong Lu, **Wangcheng Lu** opposite Wangcheng Park from Zhongzhou Lu to Kaixuan Xi Lu, and at the **Xinghua Nightmarket** (xìng-huá yèshì; 兴华夜市) in the Old City. Don't look too closely at the fascinating food displays—they're probably still alive.

Popular snacks include lamb kebabs, *jiānbāo* (fried pastry stuffed with herbs, garlic, and other fillings; 煎包; Y0.5-2), and *jiàngmiàntiáo* (starched noodles; 浆面条 ; Y1), made from mung bean milk, noodles, vegetables, and various other seasonings. Another popular local dish, *tàngmiànjiăo* (steamed dumplings in the shape of crescent moons; 烫面饺 ; Y0.5-1), was first prepared in Henan province, and is known for its thin wrappings and jade-like color.

▨ **Lijing Men** (lìjīngmén; 丽京门 ; ☎350 3382). Take bus #5 or 56 to Ximen or the Old City and go right a block. It's hard to miss the enormous gates. Both of the 2 dining options at the Old City walls host an Ancient Royal Show to entertain diners. On the 3rd and 4th floors,

As news of the rising AIDS problem leaked out, the government gradually changed its stance. Most recently, at the July 2004 AIDS Conference in Thailand, Premier Wen Jiabao stated the problem in the most straightforward terms yet, and admitted that China was already in the midst of an AIDS epidemic.

Some steps have already been taken. According to the state news agency, most of the AIDS cases in Henan are being treated. The blood stations have all been closed down. Programs have been implemented that will provide housing, free education, and treatment for the orphans of AIDS victims. In March 2004, the US Center for Disease Control and China's own CDC began working together to create HIV prevention, treatment, and support programs. Officials were sent to live in the 38 crisis villages and overlook AIDS-prevention programs, which provide free anti-retroviral medicine to victims.

But even with Wen Jiabao's appeal to the extensive bureaucracy to make AIDS a top concern, real benefits have yet to be seen. With boxes full of medicine and no doctors to administer them, many villagers do not know what to do. Due to the severe side efffects, many stop taking the drugs, overwhelmed by the need to support their family while they still can. In villages across Henan, the death rates remain as high as ever. Meanwhile, in faraway Yunnan and Xinjiang, the infection rates for AIDS are also rising.

animated, cheery locals enjoy sizzling hotpot favorites (Y10-20) in an open-air setting with sweeping views. Exuberant and colorful performances kick off at 8pm and last 30min. For those who prefer an indoor location, downstairs on the opposite side of the Gate, the Water Banquet and Fujian-style dishes (Y50-100) are cooked up in a beautifully decorated restaurant. 2hr. shows held daily at noon and 7pm. Both restaurants open 11am-9pm. Open-air restaurant ❷, indoor restaurant ❹.

▨ **One-of-a-Kind Restaurant** (zhēnbùtóng fàndiàn; 真不同饭店), 359 Zhongzhou Dong Lu (☎399 5080), near the nightmarket. Take bus #5 to just past the Old City and go left about 1 block. Don't miss the 4-course mini Water Banquet (Y20; serves 2). Open daily 9:30am-9pm or until the last guest leaves. ❷

West Gong Food Village (xīgōng fànzhuāng; 西工饭庄), off Renmin Dong Lu. Local specialties served lightning fast. Patrons slurp down bowls of hot, creamy *jiàngmiàntiáo* (Y0.8) and munch on *tàngmiànjiǎo* (10 for Y2.5). Open 24hr. ❶

Hetang Yuese (hé táng yuè sè; 荷塘月色), 28 Kaixuan Xi Lu (☎391 3988). Walk south along Jiefang Lu past Zhongzhou Lu. Turn right onto the next main road, Kaixuan Xi Lu, and continue for half a block. Delicious food served up by friendly staff. The pork in eggplant (Y16) tastes a great deal better than it sounds and looks. The eight-treasures tea (bābǎochá; 八宝茶) is a real treat: refills come squirting out of a teapot with a foot-long spout, balanced by a waiter with impeccable aim. Entrees Y8-Y30. ❷

◎ SIGHTS

Luoyang, with its ancient Buddhist temples, recently-excavated tombs, and impressive stone grottoes, attracts a great many Chinese tourists.

GUANLIN (guānlín; 关林). This temple commemorates Guan Yu, a legendary warrior who lived from AD 160-219. In the *Romance of the Three Kingdoms*, Guan Yu was defeated, captured, and executed by the ruler of the Kingdom of Wu. He was buried with full honors beneath a great mound surrounded by a stone wall. The "lin" in the name of this site refers not to cypress trees, as many assume, but instead to the burial place of a sage or saint. Only the tombs of Confucius (see **Qufu**, p. 203) and Guan Yu have received this designation. Stone lions, each unique in their design, line the pathway to the Great Hall. Guan Yu certainly reigns supreme here: nearly every hall contains a statue of his ruddy-faced, green-robed figure or murals of his heroic adventures. *(Bus #81 stops here on the way to the Longmen Grottoes. Get off where the bus makes a U-turn. Open daily 8am-6pm. Y25, children Y12.50.)*

WHITE HORSE TEMPLE (báimǎ sì; 白马寺). The oldest of all Chinese Buddhist temples, the White Horse, built in AD 68, marks the site of the first Buddhist monastery in China. Two Indian monks who came to Luoyang to spread the Mahayana gospel carried their scriptures on a white horse—and the name stuck. Vendors sell glazed horse figurines of every color and style as two slightly droopy stone horse statues welcome you at the entrance. Many of the halls and statues are authentic works dating back hundreds of years to the Yuan or Ming Dynasties. In spite of their age, they are remarkably well preserved. In the Pilu Pavilion, 42 chapters translated from the *sutra* are inscribed on the stone walls. *(12km east of Luoyang, a 45min.-1hr. bus ride. Take bus #56 which runs from the train station before turning east along Zhongzhou Lu; bus #58 from Xiguan also works. Open daily summer 8am-6:30pm. Y35.)*

TIANZI JIA LIU MUSEUM (tiānzǐ jià liù bówùguǎn; 天子驾六博物馆). A somewhat harrowing burial ground built following the death of a young prince during the Eastern Zhou Dynasty, this site, excavated in 2002 (roughly 2700 years later), contains the remarkably well-preserved remains of several dogs, horses, and chariots, laid out in formation. Guided tours available in English (Y50) and Chinese (Y20). *(Located in Wangcheng Square. Open daily 8am-10pm. Y20.)*

OTHER SIGHTS. The **Luoyang Museum** (luòyáng bówùguǎn; 洛阳博物馆), 298 Zhongzhou Lu, charts the city's history as the seat of past empires and showcases artifacts from the various dynasties. (☎393 7107. Y15.) Continue east along Zhongzhou Lu to the **Royal City Park,** where visitors can stroll in leafy green gardens and find peace away from the bustling streets. Snooze in the shady hammocks or take a paddleboat along the river. The Peony Festival is held here every April. (Open daily 5:30am-9pm. Y3.) Most other tourist attractions are a short bus ride outside the city center, making independent daytrips relatively simple.

▶ DAYTRIP FROM LUOYANG: LONGMEN GROTTOES 龙门石窟

South of Luoyang. Take bus #81 from Zhongzhou Zhong Lu to the last stop, Longmen Qiao (30-40min., Y1). The Grottoes are a 15min. walk away through a "trade street." Visit in the morning when the crowds and the heat haven't picked up yet. Open daily summer 6am-6:30pm; winter 7:30am-7:30pm. Y80; children, students, and seniors Y40.

The site of the Longmen Grottoes (lóngmén shíkū; 龙门石窟) was originally just a typical lake surrounded by hills. According to legend, one day a young shepherd heard a mysterious voice call from the hills, "*Kāi bù kāi* (shall I open)?" Perplexed, he sought out his mother, who told him to respond in the affirmative should the voice ask again. When the boy heard the voice once more, he shouted "Open!" and the earth trembled. The hills split open and the lake flowed out into the East Sea. In its place, small streams gurgled from cracks in the cliffs, which now contained caves, miraculously filled with thousands of stone statues.

History tells a slightly different story. It took over 400 years of back-breaking construction to complete the grottoes. Begun in AD 493 by Emperor Xiaowen of the Northern Wei Dynasty, the grottoes once housed over 100,000 Buddhist statues. Now, many of the 2100 niche shrines, 3600 tablets and inscriptions, and innumerable sculptured figures are missing, limbless, or in poor condition. Nevertheless, the detailed carvings and niches, ranging from tiny indentations to sizable caverns, leave visitors in awe. Most of the largest caves and sculptures are found on the Western Hills, although a few temples and the possibility of a good panoramic view draw some visitors to the other side of the Yi River.

CAVES. The **Ten Thousand Buddhas Cave** (wànfó dòng; 万佛洞) actually contains over 10,000 figurines carved into the walls, many only 4cm tall. The cave took six years to complete and was supervised by two female officials from the imperial court. Nearby, the **Lotus Flowers Cave** (liánhuā dòng; 莲花洞) houses the smallest statues (2cm) of the Longmen Grottoes and has a distinctive lotus flower carved high above its dome. Empress Wu Zetian financed **Fengxian Temple** (fèngxiān sì; 奉先寺) with a generous donation. Her entire annual cosmetics budget resulted in Longmen's largest shrine, containing the 17m-high Buddha Losana, whom some say was modeled after the empress herself.

The walls of the **Medical Prescription Cave** (yàofáng dòng; 药房洞) are covered with hundreds of ancient treatments and prescriptions. The smiling statue of Sakyamuni presides over **Guyang Cave** (gǔyáng dòng; 古阳洞), the oldest and best-preserved of the Longmen Grottoes. Numerous sculptures depict the process by which Siddhartha Gautama, the founder of Buddhism, attained enlightenment.

KAIFENG 开封 ☎ 0378

About a thousand years ago, Kaifeng was *the* place to have your dynastic capital. Ever since King Zhengzhuanggong built a barn here, seven dynasties, from 364 BC to AD 1233, followed his lead and set up their capitals in the city. In Kaifeng's heyday, the Northern Song (AD 960-1127) settled here for 168 years on the pleasant, breezy banks of the Yangjia and Panjia Lakes. Under the reign of the nine Song emperors, Kaifeng became the largest city in the world and the most important commercial center in all of Asia. The famous scroll painting, *Up the River on Qingming Festival*, depicts the bustling life of this age in minute detail.

Today, Kaifeng's population of 600,000 pales in comparison to the 1.5 million people who lived there at the height of its splendor. But with its thousands of miniature kiosks, traditional wood-eaved buildings lining the narrow backstreets, and light-hearted bustle, the scene at Gulou Square captures the lively spirit animating the scroll painting. Kaifeng has not allowed its proud thousand-year-old history to remain trapped within the ruins of the bygone dynasties and glories. Modern Kaifeng is still very much a living history that does more than just emulate its past.

▐ TRANSPORTATION

Trains: Kaifeng Train Station (kāifēng huǒchē zhàn; 开封火车站 ; ☎ 257 2222), on Zhongshan Lu, about 1km south of the old city walls. Take bus #1, 3, 4, or 9. To: **Beijing** (11hr., several per day, Y130-160); **Ji'nan** (6-8hr., several per day, Y47-80); **Luoyang** (3hr., several per day, Y15-30); **Taiyuan** (13hr.; 7am, 4pm; Y130-170); **Zhengzhou** (1½hr., several per day, Y5.5-13).

Buses:

Kaifeng Bus Station (kāifēng qìchē zhàn; 开封汽车站 ; ☎ 565 3755), at the southern tip of Jiefang Lu, less than 2min. walk from the train station. The terminus for bus #3 is right outside. To: **Anyang** (3hr., several per day, Y40-45); **Beijing** (9hr., a couple per day, Y160); **Luoyang** (3hr., every hr., Y3.5-5); **Zhengzhou** (1½hr., every 15min. 6am-7pm, Y12-13).

Kaifeng West Bus Station (kāifēng kèyùn xī zhàn; 开封客运西站), 8 Yingbin Lu, south of Baogong Lake. Buses #1, 4, and 9 stop outside at Xi Zhan. To: **Anyang** (4hr.; 8:40am, 2:40pm; Y24); **Luoyang** (3hr., every hr. 7am-6pm, Y35); **Zhengzhou East Station** (1hr., every 15min. 6am-7pm, Y10-11); **Zhengzhou West Station** (2hr.,7:36am, Y10).

Local Transportation: Gulou Square on Gulou Jie is a major **bus** hub. Bus #1 from the train station runs up Zhongshan Lu and past the west bus station and Song Dynasty St. before terminating 2min. from the Iron Pagoda. #3 runs parallel to #1 along Jiefang Lu, terminating at the Iron Pagoda bus station; #4 runs from Gulou Jie to the train station.

Taxis: Base fare Y5, each additional km Y1.3.

Bike Rental: Small shops line the north side of Baogong Lake. Look for elderly women wearing white hats and pocketing cash. Deposit Y100. Y10 per hr.

▐ ORIENTATION AND PRACTICAL INFORMATION

The heart of Kaifeng lies within the old city walls, about 3km long on each side. Streets are sometimes unlabeled, one street may have five different names, and many streets are undergoing reconstruction. Major roads include **Zhongshan Lu** (中山路), which runs north-south from Dragon Pavilion Park, through the center of town, and past the city wall to the long-distance train and bus stations. **Shengfu Jie** (省府街) turns into **Sihou Jie** (寺后街), **Gulou Jie** (鼓楼街), and finally **Mujiaqiao Jie** (穆家桥街) as it heads east. The town center is **Gulou Square** (gǔlóu guǎngchǎng; 鼓楼广场), where **Shudian Jie** (书店街) intersects with Sihou Jie, Gulou Jie, and **Madao Jie** (马道街). **Jiefang Lu** (解放路) bisects the town down the middle.

Kaifeng

▲ ACCOMMODATIONS
Dajintai Hotel, 6
Dazhong Hotel, 5
Kaifeng Hotel, 7
Yingbin Hotel, 1

🍎 FOOD
No. 1 Dumpling
　Restaurant, 2
Tianli Cake Shop, 3
You Yi Xin Restaurant, 4

Travel Agency: CITS, 98 Yingbin Lu (☎398 0084 or 388 6660), to the left of the Dongjing Hotel, near the West Bus Station. Open M-F 8:30am-noon and 2-6pm. **Kaifeng Hotel Travel Service** (kāifēng bīnguǎn lǚxíngshè; 开封宾馆旅行社), 66 Ziyou Lu (☎595 1255), left of the hotel entrance. Open daily 8am-6:30pm. Commissions on train tickets Y20-40; airline booking free. Both have English-speaking staff members.

Bank of China: 31 Zhongshan Bei Lu, on the west side of the street. Open daily 8am-6pm. Exchanges currency and traveler's checks. Another branch can be found at 64 Gulou Jie (☎288 4529). Open daily summer 8am-6:30pm; spring and autumn 8am-6pm; winter 8am-5pm.

Hospitals: No. 1 Hospital (dīyī yīyuàn; 第一医院; ☎567 1288). At corner of Shudian Jie and Xufu Jie. Open 24hr.

PSB: 86 Zhongshan Lu. Open 24hr.

Post Office: China Post, 33 Ziyou Lu, east of Zhongshan Lu. EMS and Poste Restante. Open daily 8am-6pm.
Postal Code: 475000.

ACCOMMODATIONS

Several hotels along Gulou Jie, Sihou Jie, Ziyou Lu, and Zhongshan Lu are close enough to the nightmarket that visitors can hop out of their hotel rooms to satisfy their midnight cravings. Prices for accommodations are higher in the city center than around the train station, but quality and convenience more than make up for it. Several more expensive establishments are near Baogong Lake.

Dajintai Hotel (dàjīntái bīnguǎn; 大金台宾馆), 23 Gulou Jie (☎595 6677), east of the intersection with Madao Jie and Shudian Jie. Buses #4 and 7 from the train station stop at Gulou Jie. Walk east; the entrance is on the right, marked by a red archway. Hard to avoid the clamor of local traffic, but an easy landmark and arguably the best in terms of location. Standard doubles have twin-sized beds, complete with functioning TV and the occasional small bug. Breakfast included. Doubles Y60, with bath Y130-160. ❶

Kaifeng Hotel (kāifēng bīnguǎn; 开封宾馆), 66 Ziyou Lu (☎595 5589; fax 595 3086), east of Madao Jie. The entire, enclosed complex of this 3-star beauty deserves more than its official rating. The buildings are designed in the traditional style of pagodas and tiered roofs. But don't be misled—the interior is purely modern, with ethernet and modem, TV, teak and maple furniture, and lots of light fixtures. Reception is under the main gate to the left. Doubles Y180-248; triples Y210-240. ❸

Dazhong Hotel (dàzhòng bīnguǎn; 大众宾馆), 8 Gulou Jie (☎596 2796 or 598 1262), a couple of buildings over from the Dajintai Hotel. The rooms are small but cozy enough, and the beds still have some bounce. The water thankfully runs 24hr., and the prices are unbeatable. Doubles Y50, with A/C and bath Y90. ❶

Yingbin Hotel (yíngbīn fàndiàn; 迎宾饭店), 96 Yingbin Lu (☎393 1943), 2min. diagonally opposite the West Bus Station. Buses #1, 4, and 9 from the train station stop nearby at West Bus Station. Removed from the city center, this hotel is more like a dorm. Institutional atmosphere with long hallways and rooms that look like converted classrooms. Run-down school charm, minus chalkboard and desks. A/C and TV. Dorms Y22; doubles Y80, with bath up to Y200; triples Y100-180. ❶

FOOD

For adventure, excitement, and food, zigzag your way past indecisive pedestrians, swerving bicycles, and lurching minivans to Kaifeng's **nightmarket,** centered around the brightly lit, smoky Gulou Square. Join fellow night-revelers as you browse through precariously packed stalls and outdoor tables, soaking in the frenzied atmosphere while eagerly awaiting your spicy lamb skewers (Y1 each). Roll up your sleeves and loosen your belt as you gorge through *shāguō* (砂锅), transparent noodles (chǎo liángfěn; 炒凉粉), meat-stuffed bread, and dumplings galore, and all for less than Y5 each. If you've practiced your adorable smile, brushed up your bargaining skills, or learned a few useful phrases of Chinese, you can haggle down the already unbeatable prices or up the portion size. For dessert, eight-treasures rice (bā bǎo fàn; 八宝饭) is an easy-to-find delicacy, but most prefer to munch on rice ice cream with flavored ice and red beans (Y3).

No. 1 Dumpling Restaurant (dìyīlóu bāozi guǎn; 第一楼包子馆), 8 Sihou Jie (☎565 0780), just east of Zhongshan Lu. This local, hundred-year-old landmark serves up pork and soup-filled dumplings (xiǎolóng bāo; 小笼包) for Y10 per steamer. You'll want to use the soup spoon to catch every drop of that savory, succulent filling. Plenty of vegetable options available (Y5-15). Ever-full tables and ever-scurrying staff keep this classy place churning. Upper floors have private rooms and more expensive entrees, as well as an expansive beer stock. Open daily 7am-10:30pm. Downstairs ❷, upstairs ❸.

You Yi Xin Restaurant (yòuyīxīn fàndiàn; 又一新饭店), 22 Gulou Jie (☎255 5186). Perfect place to bring some comrades and sit around the lazy susans, graze on appetizers (xiǎocài; 小菜 ; Y5-10), and feast on the main courses of rabbit meat, transparent noodles, and freshwater fish (Y20-40). Healthy servings of beer and liquor. Try the green tea with wild bamboo leaves (Y10-30). Open daily 7-9am, 11am-2:30pm, and 6-9pm. ❷

Tianli Cake Shop (tiānlì miànbāo xībǐngwū; 天力面包西饼屋), 43 Gulou Lu, just west of Shudian Jie. Let your nose guide the way to this small bakery under a red awning. Fluffy sponge cake, sugary enough to satisfy those with a sweet tooth, sprinkled with coconut flakes (Y2). A large selection of breads and pastries (mostly under Y3). Open daily 7:30am-9pm. ❶

EAT, DRINK, AND BE MERRY. If you're fortunate enough to be the guest of some overly generous host(ess), and the locale of choice is a fine restaurant like **Kaifeng No. 1 Dumpling** or **You Yi Xin**, there are a few rules of etiquette to keep in mind:

Always have a drink in hand, whether it be Tsingtao, bamboo-leaf tea, or peach-flavored milk. The host is bound to toast you and your presence at the table. Each toast is accompanied by a chug of beer or a good, healthy sip of milk.

The host(ess), or rather, anyone seated next to you, will recommend certain dishes. You are expected to immediately try them, and even if the taste does not agree well with your buds, compliment the host's selection. Do not be disgruntled if your neighbor also takes his or her chopsticks, and plops an extra helping of sea cucumber or fresh fish onto your plate.

Never finish the meal with an empty plate. To wipe your plate clean suggests that you're still hungry and that the host has not provided you with enough satisfying food. Leave some morsel to show that you are oh-so-full and content.

⊙ SIGHTS

A good pair of sandals and a bottle of sunscreen is all you need to sightsee in Kaifeng. Many of the city's attractions are either within a 30min. walk of the city center or easily reached by local buses. Be prepared to get lost, so take along a trusty dictionary and get ready to charm the locals.

IRON PAGODA (tiě tǎ; 铁塔). Hundreds of glazed brick tiles, burnt umber and dark olive in color, aged so that they have the look and feel of tarnished iron, give this pagoda its name. Each tile is meticulously carved with images of the Buddha, ancient musicians, and celestial scenes. Built in AD 1049, this exquisitely beautiful 13-story, 55.88m tall pagoda has survived a millennia of war, earthquakes, and floods. The structure overlooks the surrounding park and portions of the Kaifeng city wall. Skip the Y10 climb, as the top view (through tiny barred openings) is not all that stirring. The rest of the park consists of several lily-covered ponds, bonsai gardens, a palace hall that has a curious growth of shrubbery on its roof, and a lake in which you can wade with freshwater fish. But don't expect moments of revelation: large tour groups of businessmen have caught on, and the sound of camera shutters compete with the trills of native birds. (*175 Jiefang Lu, at Tieta Xi Jie. Buses #1, 3, 6, and 20 terminate a block away. ☎282 6629. Open daily 7am-7pm. Y20, students Y15; climbing pagoda additional Y10.*)

GRAND XIANGGUO MONASTERY (dàxiàngguó sì; 大相国寺). One of China's most famous Buddhist temples, this monastery was originally built in AD 555, but was later flooded and damaged by war before being rebuilt in 1661. At its proudest moments in the Northern Song Dynasty, it had 64 halls and over 1000 monks in residence. Today, the monastery still attracts more worshippers than tourists. The oddly-shaped **Hall of Arhat** houses 500 *arhats* with expressions ranging from serene to devilish. In the main hall stands the monastery's most prized possession, an awe-inspiring Goddess of Mercy statue with 1048 hands and 1048 eyes that took 58 years to complete. Nearby, **Cangjing Hall** (藏经楼) houses a white Burma jade statue of Sakyamuni and calligraphic steles written by Sun Xingyan, a famous calligrapher during the Qing Dynasty. Once run by the state, the monastery has since returned to the care of the monks, who lovingly preserve every piece of art in the complex. The no-photography rule is strictly enforced within the halls. *(35 Ziyou Lu, west of Madao Jie. Open daily summer 8am-6pm; winter 9am-5:30pm. Y25.)*

DRAGON PAVILION PARK (lóng tíng gōngyuán; 龙亭公园). Built on the ruins of the imperial palaces of the Song, Jin, and Ming Dynasties, the park overlooks two scenic lakes. The Imperial Road, a 500m stone pathway, leads to the main hall. Inside, the exhibit of a life-sized, wax-figure scene of the "Founding Ceremony of Northern Song," is worth only a quick glance. You're better off spending your time on the pavilion's terrace, where you can see almost all of Kaifeng, including parts of the ancient wall. Touring the grounds during off-peak times (early morning) is the best opportunity to have unobstructed views of the surrounding lakes and greenery. When the crowds start arriving around noon, serenity (and sight) gives way. And who can forget the kitschy duck and dragon boats (20-30min., Y20) that circle the lake? **Song Dynasty Street** (sòng dū jiē; 宋都街), just south of the main entrance, is lined with restaurants and souvenir shops, some of which are exorbitantly priced and only for the budget-unconscious. *(At the north end of Zhongshan Lu. Take bus #1, 15, or 20 from the train station, or walk from the Gulou Square area. ☎ 566 0142. Open daily summer 7am-7pm; winter 7:30am-5:30pm. Y35, students Y15.)*

PO PAGODA (pó tǎ; 繁塔). It may be difficult to find, but this structure, the oldest in Kaifeng, is well worth the trouble if you're in the vicinity. One of the last unmarketed historical sights in the city, the pagoda hasn't yet fallen prey to the camera-crazy tourists. When it was first built in AD 974, the pagoda stood nine stories tall; by the Ming Dynasty, only three stories remained. Now, the pagoda has six stories built with 7000 bricks that feature 108 different designs of Buddhas in meditation, many of which had their faces smashed during the Cultural Revolution. If you risk a climb, be sure to ask the guard to turn on the lights. The ascent is brief but steep, and the inside of the pagoda is more cavernous than most would expect. *(☎ 292 1167. Hidden in a neighborhood in southeast Kaifeng; once you're in the vicinity, get a local to show you the way. From Yu Terrace, walk down Tielu Beiyan Jie and turn left onto Pota Xi Jie; follow the Chinese characters painted in red on the lefthand alleys. Open daily 8am-7pm. Y5.)*

MEMORIAL TEMPLE TO LORD BAO (bāo gōng cí; 包公祠). The temple documents the life and legend of Lord Bao (AD 999-1062), a magistrate renowned for his noble character and unyielding principles. The main hall features a bronze statue of Lord Bao, and more impressively, $68m^2$ of intricately made glazed pottery frescoes that depict Lord Bao as he crushes corruption, punishes criminals, and feeds the hungry. Though the wax figures in nearby halls are more realistic than most, you would probably get more of a kick observing the ancient instruments of torture—including fearsome tiger- and dragon-shaped blades meant to behead criminals daring enough to risk Lord Bao's unwavering sense of justice. The rock gardens and lakeside views from the pavilion are not much more scenic than what travelers can enjoy by **Baogong Lake** for free. *(On the corner of Xiangyang Lu and Xibo Bei Jie. Buses #8, 10, and 20 stop nearby en route to Gulou Jie or the station. ☎ 393 1595. Open daily summer 7am-7pm; winter 7am-5pm. Y20.)*

QINGMING RIVERSIDE LANDSCAPE GARDEN PARK (qīngmíng shànghé yuán; 清明上河园). At 9am every day, performers clad in Northern Song costume parade outside the main gate of this newly built historic theme park, welcoming the flock of exuberant tourists and locals alike. Based off a single scroll painted by Zhang Zeduan, *Up the River on Qingming Festival*, the park recreates the painting in minute and kitschy detail. Architectural design includes a rainbow-shaped bridge, dozens of pavilions built five inches above the water, and Shangshanmen Gate (上善门), whose monstrous crimson doors prove most intimidating. Nowhere else will you be able to learn first-hand the immense (and perspiring) tasks of churning wheat and weaving silk strands, or buy hand-made crafts in the Northern Song style created by traditional methods. *(5 Longting Xi Lu, north of Baogong Dong Hu. ☎ 566 4874; http://qingmings.com. Open daily summer 9am-6pm; winter 9am-5pm. Y35.)*

TERRACE OF YU THE GREAT (yǔwángtái gōngyuán; 禹王台公园). First named the "Playing Terrace" in honor of the blind musician Shi Kang, the terrace was renamed in 1522 to commemorate the sage king who tamed the Great Flood. The terrace itself is rather deserted, populated only by lackluster wax figures of the musician playing the zither. Hundreds of years ago, poets like Kang You Wei (康有为) found inspiration in the cypresses, but that golden font of genius has since dimmed down. Tree-lovers can still appreciate the arboretum-like role that the park has now adopted. *(Near Tielu Beiyan Jie. ☎ 267 8761. Open daily summer 7am-7pm; winter 7am-6pm. Y10.)*

MEMORIAL TO LIU SHAOQI (liú shàoqí chénlièguǎn; 刘少奇陈列馆). This small memorial is dedicated to Liu Shaoqi, Chairman Mao's heir apparent until he was purged at the start of the Cultural Revolution (p. 81). Visitors may leave aghast and nauseated after seeing the contrast between early photos of a robust Liu Shaoqi and those of the ailing man at an interrogation session during the Cultural Revolution. The left room in the inner building is where he actually died in 1969. The chamberpot is propped up on the floor, the deathbed, complete with sheets, still stands, and plastic flowers cover the pillow. In the main hall, Liu Shaoqi's final days are detailed down to his last dose of medication, body temperature readings, and the price of his cremation. *(10-12 Jiefang Lu. Walk from Gulou Jie or take bus #3. ☎ 338 8022. Open daily 9am-6:00pm. Y10, students Y5.)*

ANYANG 安阳 ☎ 0372

Modern Anyang sits on the site of Yin, one of China's seven ancient capital cities, a fact confirmed by the oracle bones unearthed by local peasants over 100 years ago. Subsequent excavations revealed tombs and ruins, as well as bronzes, chariots, pottery, jade, and thousands of oracle bones, the first hard evidence to support the existence of the legendary Shang Dynasty (p. 74). Although Anyang is of great interest to scholars and archaeologists, this small city has few things to see and may hold visitors' attention for a day or two at most.

▐▟ TRANSPORTATION AND PRACTICAL INFORMATION

Anyang is mostly to the south of the **Huan River** (huán hé; 洹河), near the border of Henan and Hebei provinces. **Jiefang Dadao** (解放大道), a major east-west thoroughfare, extends from the train station to People's Park and runs parallel to **Ren-**

min Dadao (人民大道). **Hongqi Lu** (红旗路), perpendicular to Jiefang Dadao and Renmin Dadao, becomes **Bei Dajie** (北大街) and then **Zhongshan Jie** (中山街). The Yin Ruins are in the northern part of the city.

Trains: Anyang Train Station (ānyáng huǒchē zhàn; 安阳火车站 ; ☎593 7216 or 327 1252), at the western end of Jiefang Lu. To: **Beijing** (5-6½hr., several per day, Y73); **Kaifeng** (3hr., several per day, Y25-40); **Taiyuan** (8hr., 2 per day, Y90); **Shijiazhuang** (2-3hr., several per day, Y40-50); **Zhengzhou** (2-3hr., many per day, Y15-30).

Buses: Anyang Bus Station (ānyáng chángtú qìchē zhàn; 安阳长途汽车站 ; ☎591 3951), on Heping Lu. From the train station, go south to the end of Yinbin Lu. To: **Beijing** (6hr., 6 per day 9:30am-11:50pm, Y108); **Luoyang** (3hr., several per day 7am-4:30pm, Y53-59); **Shijiazhuang** (3hr., every 40min. 8am-4:30pm, Y45); **Taiyuan** (6½hr., 7:20am-6:20pm, Y70-90); **Zhengzhou** (3hr., every 20min. 6am-7pm, Y33).

Local Transportation: Fare Y1. Bus #2 runs from the train station along Jiefang Lu, up Hongqi Lu, past Renmin Lu; #3 and 27 run down Jiefang Lu to People's Park; #11 goes from the train station up Zhangde Lu, and down Renmin Lu and Dongfeng Lu past People's Park; #26 runs down Dongfeng Lu.

Taxis: Base fare Y4-5 for the 1st 2km, each additional km Y1.30.

Travel Agency: CITS, Anyang Hotel, Bldg. 4 (☎592 5650). Open M-F 8am-noon and 2-6pm. Train ticket commission varies with purchase.

Bank of China: (☎592 4286), on Jiefang Dadao, just east of Hongqi Lu. Exchanges currency and traveler's checks. Open daily summer 8am-6pm; winter 8am-5pm.

PSB: 35 Hongqi Lu. Open 24hr.

Hospital: Anyang People's Hospital (ānyángshì rénmín yīyuàn; 安阳市人民医院 ; ☎592 3331), on Jiefang Lu, about 1 block east of Hongqi Lu near the Anyang Hotel.

Post Office: China Post, 1 Yinbin Lu (☎595 1100), just south of the train station. EMS and Poste Restante. Open daily 8am-7pm. Another branch on Dengta Lu, about half a block west of Hongqi Lu. Open daily 8am-9pm.

Postal Code: 455000.

🏠🍴 ACCOMMODATIONS AND FOOD

Several lodgings cluster around the train and long-distance bus stations. Unfortunately, many of the cheaper dormitory-style options do not accept foreigners. A few classier places are off Jiefang Dadao. Accommodations are nearly identical in terms of their consistently high quality and differ only slightly in prices.

The nightmarkets near the Drum Tower and in front of the Workers' Cultural Palace offer a wide variety of noodles and fried dishes (Y3-5), as well as lamb skewers (Y1), stuffed pitas (Y1.5), and other snacks. A scattering of vendors appear in the evening near the train station along Jiefang Dadao, serving cafeteria-style food. For a sit-down meal, try the **Three Tastes Restaurant** ❷ (wèisānxiān; 味三鲜), on Hongqi Lu (☎511 0866), near the intersection with Jiefang Dadao. Appetizer-size portions of spicy seaweed, sliced beef and pork, and snails go for Y4-16. (Open daily 10am-3pm and 5-10pm.)

Anyang Hotel, Building #3 (ānyáng bīnguǎn; 安阳宾馆), 1 Youyi Lu (☎592 2219; fax 592 2244), just north of Jiefang Dadao, a 15min. walk from the train station. Bus #3 or 16 from the train station stops nearby at Hongqi Square. Frequented by businessmen, the full-fledged baths have great water pressure and the spacious rooms offer beds larger than the standard single size. A/C, TV, Internet, and laundry service. Breakfast included. Reservations definitely recommended. Doubles Y188-280. ❸

Great Wall Hotel (cháng chéng bīnguǎn; 长城宾馆), 5 Xinxing Jie (☎591 0669; fax 593 1663), between Jiefang Dadao and Heping Lu. A 3-star, often-overlooked hotel that's a 5min. walk from the train and long-distance bus stations. Friendly and welcoming staff more than make up for the sometimes dysfunctional Internet service. Cheaper doubles lack great vantage points, but are otherwise identical to their more expensive counterparts. Breakfast included. Check-out 2pm. Reservations recommended. Doubles Y180-280, half off for 4hr. rest. Ask for discounts and cheaper economy rooms. ❸

Flying Eagle Hotel (fēiyīng dàjiǔdiàn; 飞鹰大酒店), 119 Renmin Dadao (☎593 5888; fax 592 3037), west of Hongqi Lu. Take bus #2 from the train station to Er Baihuo; go north up Hongqi Lu and take a right at the 1st intersection. The pricier the room, the cleaner the windows. A work in progress, the hotel has already-renovated rooms with new televisions, Internet access, and the whitest bedsheets you'll ever see on the road. Breakfast included. Economy singles and doubles Y118-148; small triples Y208. ❷

👁 🎵 SIGHTS AND ENTERTAINMENT

By day, the sights are limited. By night, not too surprisingly, full-fledged entertainment options are also rather scarce. The **Workers' Cultural Palace** (gōngrén wénhuà gōng; 工人文化宫), 5min. east of the train station at Zhangde Lu and Jiefang Dadao, has a movie theater and, when the weather is warm, a huge number of *mahjong* tables out in front.

TIANNING PAGODA (tiānníng sì tǎ; 天宁寺塔). Also known as Wenfeng Pagoda (wénfēng tǎ; 文峰塔), the 39m pagoda built in AD 925 is impossible to miss as a landmark due to its unique shape. Be sure to duck your head and tuck your tummy—some parts of the steep climb are less than 5.25 ft. high and 2.5 ft. wide. As you climb the pagoda, the radius of the structure grows wider, making the Tianning Pagoda look strangely like a mushroom from afar. At the top, an observation platform provides bird's eye views of the remains of Anyang's Old City. *(The pagoda can be reached on foot from the train station. From Jiefang Dadao, walk 4 blocks south on Bei Dajie; turn right onto Dasi Qian Jie and continue for a couple of blocks. ☎592 3227. Open daily summer 9am-6:30pm; winter 9am-5:30pm. Y10.)*

MUSEUM OF YIN RUINS (yīnxū bówùyuàn; 殷墟博物苑). Sitting in a dusty and barren part of town, this museum is slightly difficult to reach but is worth the effort. History buffs will be delighted by the cornucopia of artifacts, and the average onlooker may be fascinated as well by unearthed horse chariots, complete with bones of horse and rider. Study the ruins of the majestic Shang Dynasty, and perplex yourself by trying to understand scapulimancy, the study of oracle bones. Some disturbing pictures of human sacrifices, skulls dislocated from the rest of their bodies, complete the museum trip. *(On Yinxu Lu north of Anyang Lu. From the People's Park, take bus #18, which stops 1km away from the museum entrance. ☎393 2171. Open daily summer 8am-6pm; winter 8am-5:30pm. Y21, students Y10.)*

SHANXI 山西

Shanxi boasts a unique type of ugliness that leaves many visitors slightly smoggy. Fortunately, its rough roads, barren mountainsides, and unremarkable coal mining cities hide a few delightful pieces of history, both ancient and recent. Residents of this mountainous province have spent a lot of time resisting invasion. Bounded in the north by the Great Wall, Shanxi played a key role in protecting China from northern nomadic tribes during the Qin and Han Dynasties. During the Japanese occupation in the 1930s, Communist soldiers bided their time among the caves and crevices of Shanxi's barren mountainsides before launching guerrilla offensives. Now that all the excitement's died down, Shanxi is back to its old peaceful—and dull—self. But underneath the layer of dust and soot coating much of the province, some spectacular sights exist, hidden well off the beaten path, from the quaint town of Pingyao to the verdant valleys of Wutaishan to the Yungang Grottoes and Hanging Monastery of Datong.

TAIYUAN 太原 ☎ 0351

Founded in the ancient dynasty of Zhou in 479 BC, Taiyuan witnessed the military beginnings of Tang founder Li Yuan's conquest of China some 1000 years later. But don't expect too many historical sights: the struggle against the Nationalists reduced many of the city's relics to rubble. Instead, foundries and furnaces, thriving on the city's rich iron and coal deposits, belch out a smoky backdrop for this fast-paced, highly polluted industrial and commercial center.

Although gritty and in-your-face by day, Taiyuan sparkles by night. Visitors flock to Yingze Dajie for brightly lit hotels and restaurants and to May First Square for romantic encounters and quick snapshots in front of the fountains. The city's refreshing "easy come, easy go" spirit sees lively card games springing up on any bit of sidewalk large enough to support a group of four. The capital of Shanxi province, Taiyuan maintains a casual charm, a high-energy attitude, and an impressive overabundance of karaoke bars.

▐ TRANSPORTATION

Flights: Taiyuan Airport (tàiyuán jīchǎng; 太原机场 ; ☎ 701 2355) is far from the city center. Taxi to the airport Y50. Shuttle buses (30min., 5:30am, Y10) leave from the **China Eastern Airlines Ticket Office** (zhōngguó dōngfāng mínháng shòupiào chù; 中国东方民航售票处), 158 Yingze Dajie (☎ 404 2903), 10min. west of May First Sq., on the south side of the street. Open daily 8am-8pm. To: **Beijing** (1-2 per day, Y540-590); **Guangzhou** (2 per day, Y1000-1430); **Shanghai** (daily, Y840-1200). Walk next door to **Shanxi Airlines** for flights to **Xi'an.**

Trains: Taiyuan Train Station (tàiyuán huǒchē zhàn; 太原火车站 ; ☎ 418 2913), on the corner of Yingze Dajie and Jianshe Lu. Ticket office and information booth to the right of main entrance. To: **Beijing** (8-10hr., 5 per day 7:30am-9pm, Y73-131); **Datong** (7-9hr., 5 per day, Y26-104); **Guangzhou** (32hr., daily, Y236); **Shanghai** (22hr., daily, Y170); **Xi'an** (11-12hr., 2 per day, Y47-163).

Buses: Taiyuan Bus Station (tàiyuán qìchē zhàn; 太原汽车站 ; ☎ 404 2346), on the south side of Yingze Dajie between the train station and Bingzhou Lu. Tickets can be purchased directly from bus drivers behind the bus station, or on the 2nd fl. of the station. Buses often stop on the way to each destination, making most surrounding cities easily accessible. To: **Beijing** (6hr.; 6:30am, every 15min. 7am-7pm; Y120); **Datong** (5hr., every 30min. 7am-6:30pm, Y71); **Shijiazhuang** (4hr., every 30min. 6:30am-6:30pm, Y48-53); **Wutaishan** (4-5hr., 7 per day 6:30am-1:30pm, Y44-51); **Yan'an** (9hr.; 6:30, 8:45am; Y83); **Yulin** (8hr., 5 per day 9:15am-2:30pm, Y74); **Zhengzhou** (8-9 hr., 4 per day, Y139-141). **Minibuses** wait in the train station parking lot. To: **Datong** (Y50); **Pingyao** (Y30); **Shijiazhuang** (Y53); **Wutaishan** (Y43).

Local Transportation: Most **buses** run approx. 5:30am to 7 or 8pm. Bus #1 shuttles incessantly along Yingze Dajie past May First Sq.; #3 and #102 go up Wuyi Lu; #103 runs until 10pm from just south of the square to Shanxi University. **Minibuses** (Y1-2) also troll the city streets.

Taxis: Base fare Y7, each additional km Y1.2. From train station Y1 tariff.

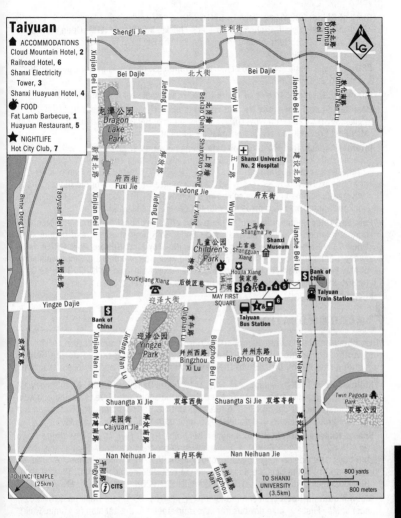

Taiyuan

▲ ACCOMMODATIONS
Cloud Mountain Hotel, **2**
Railroad Hotel, **6**
Shanxi Electricity
 Tower, **3**
Shanxi Huayuan Hotel, **4**
🍎 FOOD
Fat Lamb Barbecue, **1**
Huayuan Restaurant, **5**
★ NIGHTLIFE
Hot City Club, **7**

Shengli Jie 胜利街
Bei Dajie 北大街 Bei Dajie
Xinjian Bei Lu
Jiefang Lu
Beixiao Qiang 北小墙
Shangxiao Qiang 上肖墙
Wuyi Lu
Jianshe Bei Lu
Dunhua Bei Lu
Dunhua Nan Lu

龙潭公园
Dragon
Lake
Park

✚ Shanxi University
No. 2 Hospital
五一路

Taoyuan Bei Lu
Xinjian Bei Lu
Jiefang Lu
府西街 Fuxi Jie
Fudong Jie
府东街
Wuyi Lu
Lu Xiang
吕巷

Binhe Dong Lu

桃园北路

上马街
Shangma Jie

儿童公园
Children's
Park

上官巷
Shangguan
Xiang
Shanxi
Museum 🏛

Houtiejiang Xiang
后铁匠巷
侯家巷
Houjia Xiang

Bank of
China

Yingze Dajie
迎泽大街
五一
广场
MAY FIRST
SQUARE

$ R ★ 🍎 ⊠
Taiyuan
Train Station

$
Bank of
China

Taiyuan
Bus Station

Qingnian Lu
Bingzhou Bei Lu
赛牛路
并州西路
Bingzhou
Xi Lu
并州东路
Bingzhou Dong Lu
Jianshe Nan Lu

迎泽公园
Yingze
Park

Xinjian Nan Lu
Jiefang Nan Lu

汾河东路

Shuangta Xi Jie 双塔西街
Shuangta Si Jie 双塔寺街

Twin Pagoda
Park
双塔公园

菜园街
Caiyuan Jie

新建南路
解放南路

Nan Neihuan Jie 南内环街
Nan Neihuan Jie

早南路
Pingyang Lu
ℹ CITS

TO JINCI TEMPLE
(25km)

Bingzhou
Nan Lu

TO SHANXI
UNIVERSITY
(3.5km)

0 ___ 800 yards
0 ___ 800 meters

CENTRAL CHINA

✳ ORIENTATION AND PRACTICAL INFORMATION

Yingze Dajie (迎泽大街) runs west from the train station through Taiyuan's main commercial district. Transportation and accommodation options are on the eastern edge of the city, at the intersection of Yingze Dajie and **Jianshe Lu** (建设路). Ten minutes to the west, **May First Square** (wǔyī guǎngchǎng; 五一广场) marks the busy intersection with **Wuyi Lu** (五一路), which runs north, and **Bingzhou Bei Lu** (并洲北路), which runs south. Most tourist attractions are near May First Square.

   Travel Agency: CITS, 38 Pingyang Lu (☎724 4126). English-speaking staff member, but not much information. Commission Y20. Another branch, next to the main Bank of China. Both open M-F 8:30am-noon and 2:30-6pm.

Bank of China: 288 Yingze Dajie (☎826 6268), 5min. walk west of Yingze Park. Friendly English-speaking staff. Exchanges traveler's checks. MC/Plus/V **ATM**. Open daily 8am-noon and 2:30-5:30pm. Another branch on Jianshe Bei Lu, 3min. north of the train station, exchanges currency.

PSB: 9 Houjia Xiang (☎202 3011), 1 block northeast of May First Sq. Open M-F 8am-noon and 2:30-5:30pm.

Pharmacy: On the north side of Yingze Dajie, 1min. walk east from May First Sq.

Hospital: Shanxi University No. 2 Hospital (shānxī dàxué dì'èr yīyuàn; 山西大学第二医院; ☎307 4231), on Wuyi Lu, 1½ blocks south of Bei Dajie. Take bus #3 north from May First Sq. until you see the hospital on the right.

Internet Access: Red Fox Internet Cafe (hóng hú wǎngbā; 红狐网吧; ☎406 6929), conveniently located inside the Hot City Club bldg., upstairs on the left. Y2 per hr. Open 24hr. **Oasis Internet Cafe** (lùzhōu wǎngbā; 绿洲网吧; ☎812 4765), on Wucheng Lu near Shanxi University. Take bus #103 from Yingze Dajie and Bingzhou Lu to Shanxi University's Nanmen (南门; also known as Xinmen, 新门); cross the street and double back for 5min. Large and pleasant, with flat panel screens. Y2-3 per hr.

Post and Telecommunications: The **main post office** is opposite the train station on the northern corner of Jianshe Lu and Yingze Dajie. EMS, English signs, and helpful staff. Open daily 8am-8pm. The less foreigner-friendly **May First Square Post Office** (wǔyī guǎngchǎng yóujú; 五一广场邮局), is on the west side of Wuyi Lu, a 3min. walk north of May First Sq. Poste Restante and EMS. Open daily 8am-7pm. **CNC,** 213 Yingze Dajie (☎806 9999), at northeast corner of Jiefang Lu. IDD service. Open 24hr.

Postal Code: 030001.

ACCOMMODATIONS

Most cheaper places that accept foreigners are near the train station. Although comparable accommodations can be found along Wucheng Lu, bordering Shanxi University, the 30min. bus ride to the city center makes this option less attractive.

Railroad Hotel (tiělù bīnguǎn; 铁路宾馆), 18 Yingze Dajie (☎404 0624), a 5min. walk west from the train station down Yingze Dajie on the south side. True to its name, a well-maintained budget option close to the train station. Hallways are dirty, with clean but cramped rooms. Singles and doubles Y75, with bath Y130; triples Y160. ❶

Shanxi Huayuan Hotel (shānxī huáyuàn bīnguǎn; 山西华苑宾馆), 9 Yingze Dajie (☎404 6201; fax 404 6980), a ½ block west of the train station. Although noise from the busy street below might disturb some guests, the large windows, spacious rooms, and sparkling bathrooms are a step above the rest. Rooms include A/C, TV, and bath. Breakfast included. Singles Y218-248; doubles Y238-288; triples Y238. ❸

Cloud Mountain Hotel (yún shān fàndiàn; 云山饭店), 99 Yingze Dajie (☎496 4862), east of May First Sq. Take any bus from the train station to the 1st stop (a 10min. walk). Clean rooms are small and bathrooms are very basic. All rooms include TV, A/C, and bath. Breakfast included. Singles Y138; doubles Y190; triples Y210. ❷

Shanxi Electricity Tower (shānxī diànlì dàshà; 山西电力大厦), 39 Yingze Dajie (☎404 1784; fax 404 0777), a 5-10min. walk west of the train station. Though not exactly electrifying, the rooms are clean and well furnished, with rather worn baths. Doubles Y180, with windows Y220; triples Y380. ❷

FOOD AND ENTERTAINMENT

From slices of watermelon and cantaloupe as big as your forearm to styrofoam bowls of noodles, dining in Taiyuan is casual and made to eat on the go. The city is best known for its **knife-cut noodles** (dāoxiāo miàn; 刀削面), available for just a few *kuài* per bowl. If you're lucky, you'll get to see the knife-wielding chef in action. When dusk falls, the aroma of grilled meat and sizzling vegetables fills the city as **street markets** cook up a variety of noodles and fried dishes. On summer nights, stands crowd **Jiefang Lu** and **May First Square.** Farther south along **Wucheng Lu,** near the Shanxi University campus, fruit, steamed corn, and kebab vendors fight for space with noodle stalls. (Take bus #103 from May First Square.) A block west of May First Square, anything from designer shoes to kittens can be bought on **Luxiang Nan Lu;** its nearby alleys teem with meat and vegetables on grilled sticks, hotpot, noodles, sweet rice, and even the odd pool table.

One place worthy of a special visit is **Huayuan Restaurant ❷** (huáyuàn dàjiǔlóu; 华苑大酒楼), 11 Yingze Dajie, next to the Shanxi Huayuan Hotel. Appearances can be deceiving; this prosaic restaurant has an extensive English menu, listing cheap standard dishes as well as more exotic fare. Order anything from knife-cut noodles (Y3-5) to pig's brains (Y68), or try the northwest specialty **banyou noodles** (bànyóu miàn; 拌莜面), a garlic- and vinegar-laden appetizer with noodles made from a unique kind of wheat grown in northwestern China (Y10). (Open daily 11am-10:30pm.) Taiyuan also hides a number of delicious kebab joints. **Fat Lamb Barbecue** (féi yáng shāokǎo; 肥羊烧烤), on Wuyu Lu, on the first left corner north of May First Sq., has great atmosphere and great food, grilling up beef tendons, lamb, and soybean kebabs, among other options.

It's hard to avoid the **karaoke** bars that line all the major streets (and many minor ones); beyond that, nightlife options are rather limited. Shanxi University students frequent the bars on **Wucheng Lu,** but if the popularity of bars serving up Internet access instead of alcohol is any indication, Taiyuan students seem to prefer a Saturday night chatting online to an evening crooning at a karaoke bar. For those who'd rather meet people face to face, the **Hot City Club** (dà mēng chéng; 大蒙城), directly west of Huayuan Hotel, is festooned with neon green lights, a mere preview of the overstimulating colors and lighting effects inside. A friendly and peppy staff strives to put customers at ease, as they groove to 70s and 80s music and European house. (Drinks Y20-60. No cover. Open 8:30pm, dancing starts at 11pm.)

◉ SIGHTS

Though not generally known as a tourist destination, Taiyuan has a surprising number of attractions, both in the city and in nearby towns. At **Children's Park** (értóng gōngyuán; 儿童公园), rambunctious children, *mahjong*-playing senior citizens, and young couples alike share the shade and pleasant environment. Though the lake is more mud than water, families are not deterred from enjoying the bumper cars (Y5). The entrance is off alleyways from Wuyi Lu and Luxiang Nan Li. *(Open daily 4am-11pm. Free.)* The gardens of **Shanxi Museum** offer a respite from city crowds and pollution. From May First Square, walk along Wuyi Lu and take a right on the first cross-street after the post office. Continue about 5min. until the dead end. *(Open daily summer 9am-noon and 2:30-6:30pm; winter 9am-5pm. Y2.)*

YINGZE PARK (yíngzé gōngyuán; 迎泽公园). With large, fake rock formations and scenery blocking out the surrounding streets, this gateless park is a green refuge for singing toddlers in daycare groups, cuddling couples, impromptu Beijing opera performers, and locals seeking hot dogs on a stick. *(On the southern side of Yingze Dajie, between Jiefang Lu and Qingnian Lu. Buses #1 and 6 from the train station stop at Da Nan Men 大南门 . Golf cart and boat rentals Y10-40 per hr. Free.)*

TWIN PAGODA PARK (shuāngtǎ gōngyuán; 双塔公园). The striking twin pagodas, also called **Yongzuo Monastery** (yǒngzuò sì; 永祚寺), were constructed during the Ming Dynasty and have recently been renovated. The noisy approach through commercial and industrial streets makes the garden courtyard all the more peaceful and beautiful. *(On a small street running east from Chuangta Bei Lu. Bus #19 from the train station stops at Xingyue Ge Xiecheng, the 1st stop after the railroad tracks. Turn right on the 1st street, then left before the dead end. The entrance is another 10-15min. down the road, to the right. A taxi from the train station costs about Y10. Open daily 9am-4pm. Y20.)*

JINCI TEMPLE (jìncí sì; 晋祠寺). This rambling complex, first constructed in AD 1023-1031, is filled with a diverse jumble of buildings from various dynasties and, come the summer months, plenty of tourists as well. Wandering through the maze of gardens may be more rewarding than trying to follow the twists and turns on the map. As always, visitors must run the gauntlet of souvenir stands and postcard hawkers outside the main entrance. *(☎602 0038. 25km outside the city. From Yingze Dajie in front of the train station, minibus #804 takes 1hr. and costs Y2. Jinci Park open daily 7am-sunset. Y5. Jinci Temple open daily summer 8am-6pm; winter 8:30am-5:30pm. Y16.)*

⚑ DAYTRIP FROM TAIYUAN: PINGYAO 平遥

*Easily accessible from Taiyuan. The first **train** leaves at 5am (2½hr, 10 per day, Y6-8). **Buses** to Pingyao usually lurk near the train station in the mornings or park behind the bus station. **Minibuses** (2hr., approx. Y15) leave frequently from the Pingyao Train Station for Taiyuan when full. Open daily 8am-6:30pm. Bicycle rental Y5 per hr. at various shops in the city. Bicycle rides Y25 at the top of the wall. Comprehensive admission ticket covers over 20 attractions within the city. Tickets can be bought at Beimen, Ximen, the Government Office museum, and the City God Temple. Y120, students Y60.*

Since its construction in the 9th century BC, the 6km brick wall surrounding the ancient city of Pingyao has warded off numerous threats, from invasion to modernization. The amazingly well-preserved city is full of outstanding examples of Ming and Qing architecture, and it's easy to envision Pingyao flourishing during these dynasties as China's premier banking center. This beautiful, bustling city retains many of its archaic features (as seen in Zhang Yimou's film *Raise the Red Lantern*), but manages to escape a static museum atmosphere.

The layout and scale of Pingyao make it easy to travel on foot. The four main roads are named after the directions in which they stretch: **Dong Dajie** (东大街), **Nan Dajie** (南大街), actually several hundred meters east of the intersection with Bei Dajie, **Xi Dajie** (西大街), and **Bei Dajie** (北大街) cover the old city and all main tourist attractions. Visitors first encounter the 6km **city wall** surrounding these streets. To get to the city wall from the train station, continue straight down **Shuncheng Lu** (顺城路), perpendicular to the train station, to the first intersection with **Xiguan Dajie** (西关大街); make a left, and a 10min.walk brings you to the West Gate of the city wall. Visitors can only ascend the wall from the north and west gates. From the North Gate, the center of the city is down Bei Dajie and left onto Xi Dajie. Farther north, Xi Dajie becomes Mingqing Jie. Museums, restaurants, and hotels can be found on Nan Dajie, two blocks further from the city center.

The city wall was built with rammed earth beginning in 827 BC, but the Song army set it on fire in AD 960. After the first attack, the residents of Pingyao learned their lesson and rebuilt again using bricks in 1370. It's no wonder that this sturdier version is still standing today, with its many watchtowers and imposing cannons bristling from the impenetrable ramparts. According to legend, the 3000 embrasures built into the wall represent the disciples of Confucius. His most venerated sages are embodied by the 72 small watchtowers. A walk around the top from the west gate (turn right at the top of the stairs) to the small exhibition at the north gate takes about 30-45min. and affords many peeks into the courtyards of the city's traditional tile-roofed houses and narrow alleyways.

The **Chinese Financial House Museum** (rìshēng chāng piàohào; 日升昌票号), housed in a now-defunct bank next to 40 Xi Dajie, exhibits relics dating back to its 1823 establishment. *(Open daily summer 8am-7pm; winter 8:30am-5pm. Y10.)* Continue down Xi Dajie to find the ornate traditional-style buildings along touristy **Mingqing Jie** (明清街). These buildings house various museums, antique stores, and other enterprises. After paying Y5 to scale the **Town Tower** (shì lóu; 市楼), visitors can see the city almost as it was a thousand years ago: a sea of dark gray roofs dotted with Pingyao's trademark red lanterns.

WUTAISHAN MOUNTAIN 五台山 ☎ 0350

A slightly harrowing ride along high alpine roads eventually deposits tourists and pilgrims alike in Taihuai, the small village nestled peacefully in the valley of Wutaishan's five mountain peaks. Thanks to its near inaccessibility, Wutaishan, one of China's four sacred Buddhist mountains, kept its many temples and monasteries safe from destruction during the Cultural Revolution.

Bright wildflowers and grazing livestock line the path to Taihuai, where the sound of jangling bells and melodic Buddhist chants fill the streets. Monks in colorful garb and pilgrims from across China, Tibet, and Mongolia mingle with camera-toting tourists hoping to bask in the area's monastic glow. Despite the unholy number of visitors at times, most find that Taihuai's location and reasonably priced rooms make it an ideal place from which to appreciate Wutaishan's breathtaking scenery. Mists cloak the peaks until mid-morning, keeping visitors guessing at the mountain's true size and adding mystery to its already hallowed air.

🖼️ TRANSPORTATION AND PRACTICAL INFORMATION

All vehicles entering Taihuai must stop at the gate to the Wutaishan Scenic Area to pay the **admission fee** (Y90 per person, students Y45). Think of it less as the heavy hand of the tourist industry and more as a way to get in touch with your spiritual side (by relinquishing all worldly possessions).

Taihuai is a narrow, oval-shaped town organized around the main road **Taihuai Lu** (台怀路), which turns into **Yingfang Jie** (营坊街) at the northern end, and runs north-south parallel to **Qingshui River** (qīngshuǐ hé;清水河). Most tourist attractions and services are spread along the western side of Taihuai Lu, with the notable exception of Dailuo Peak, accessible by **Dailuo Peak Bridge,** which crosses the river on the eastern side. The **Big White Pagoda** on the western side of the main road is a useful landmark when navigating Taihuai.

Trains: Wutaishan Train Station (wǔtáishān huǒchē zhàn; 五台山火车站). 1hr. from Taihuai (bus Y20, taxi Y60). To: **Bejing** (6-7hr., 2 per day, Y97); **Datong** (5hr.); **Taiyuan** (4-5hr.)

Buses: The best way to get to Wutaishan, via Taiyuan or Datong. The **long-distance bus station** (chángtú qìchē zhàn; 长途汽车站), at the southern end of Taihuai Lu, a 20min. walk from town center, runs buses to **Taiyuan** (5hr., nearly every hr., Y50). Buses from the main road, 2min. south and opposite of Dailuo Peak Bridge, go to **Datong** (4hr.; 5 per day 6:30am-1pm, 10pm; Y50). The station is in a small courtyard with a blue banner. **Minibuses** to Taiyuan (4hr., approx. every 30min. until 4pm, Y43) leave when full from the station at the southern tip of town, 30min. walk from the Dailuo Peak Bridge.

Travel Agency: CITS, 18 Mingqing Jie (☎654 3138). Arranges special (read: overpriced) full- and half-day English tours. Open daily 8am-6pm. Another branch, 18 Yingfang Jie (☎654 5218), offers the same services.

Bank of China: 10min. walk from the center of town west of the main road. Exchanges foreign currency only. Open daily 8am-noon and 2:30-6pm.

Internet Access: Flying Space Internet Cafe (fēi yǔ wǎngbā; 飞宇网吧), on the street branching east across from Shizi Jie. Operated by a young monk. Y3 per hr.

Post and Telecommunications: On Yanling Jie, parallel to and 1 block west of the main road, 5min. south of the Dailuo Peak Bridge. Open daily summer 8am-8pm; winter 8am-6pm. A **"telephone cafe"** (huà bā; 话吧) on Shizi Jie (十字街), the 1st right off Taihuai Lu heading south from the bridge, has IDD service.

Postal Code: 035515.

ACCOMMODATIONS AND FOOD

Small hostels in the north end of town compete with larger "luxury" hotels in the south. Most budget travelers spend their nights in the former, giving in to the seductively low prices offered by relentless hostel owners. When rooms aren't full, prices may be flexible, especially at smaller places. Many small vegetarian and standard Chinese restaurants scatter throughout town, most pushing expensive specialty dishes featuring the local leafy vegetable. Prices are slightly higher than in nearby towns, as nearly all food must be trucked into this mountain hideaway.

Precious Silver Hotel (bǎoyín bīnguǎn; 宝银宾馆 ; ☎654 5648), supposedly on Yingfang Jie, but actually 3min. down Shizi Jie, across from and slightly south of the bridge. The 1st building (yībù; 一部) contains clean and spacious doubles and triples with TV and bath; 3rd fl. rooms get a great view of the town. Avoid the musty 2nd building (èrbù; 二部) around the corner. Singles Y40; doubles Y50; triples Y60. ❶

Traffic Hotel (jiāotōng bīnguǎn; 交通宾馆 ; ☎654 5840), 1min. north of the bridge to the Dailuo Peak cable car parking lot, on the west side of the main road. Rooms are clean, tidy, and well ventilated, all with TV and bath. 2-bed dorms Y40. ❶

Xianhe Hotel (xiānhé bīnguǎn; 先和宾馆), 25 Taiping Jie (☎654 5531). Heading north from the post office, take a left and then a quick right at the dead end; Xianhe is two-thirds of the way up on your left. Doubles are clean, though getting on in years, with TV and new bathrooms. Doubles Y100. ❷

Leap Forward Hostel (yuèjìn zhāodàisuǒ; 跃进招待所), 32 Yingfang Jie (☎654 5586), just before the Precious Silver Hotel. The inconspicuous entrance is on the right side of the street. Worn rooms, but owners are receptive to bargaining. 2-bed dorms Y20. ❶

Jinwei Hotel (jīnwēi bīnguǎn; 金威宾馆 ; ☎654 2791), on Mingxing Jie, a 15min. walk south from the center of town and across the bridge. The 1st in a long line of "luxury" hotels on Mingxing Jie. Doubles sport new carpeting, immaculate baths, and TV. Friendly staff. Doubles Y240. ❸

SIGHTS

TAIHUAI VILLAGE (táihuái zhèn; 台怀镇). For such a little town, Taihuai Village contains an impressive number of temples. Wandering aimlessly among them guarantees a mix of large temples popular with tour groups and smaller, more personal ones. The grandeur of the encircling mountains is mirrored in the beauty and craftsmanship of temple architecture, down to the details of the smallest paintings under the eaves. Admission to most temples is Y6 or less; some are free.

The most visually striking sight is the **Tayuan Temple** (tǎyuàn sì; 塔院寺), which houses the **Big White Pagoda** (dà bái tǎ; 大白塔), a Tibetan-style pagoda topped with a bronze cap, currently under renovation. *(Open daily 7am-6:30pm. Y4.)* Northeast of the pagoda, the graceful and expansive **Xiantong Temple** (xiǎntōng sì; 显通

寺) is noteworthy for the simplicity of its "beamless hall," constructed entirely out of brick. The shiny **Copper Palace** (tóng diàn; 铜殿) is on the hill at the north end of the compound. *(Open daily 6:30am-7pm. Y6.)* Those who climb the 108 steps leading to the **Bodhisattva Hill** (púsà dǐng; 菩萨顶) will be rewarded with a panoramic view of the surrounding temples and countryside. *(Open daily 5:45am-7:30pm. Y5.)*

From the **Dailuo Peak** (dàiluó dǐng; 黛螺顶), east of the main road in the northern part of the village, catch a glimpse of the fog-shrouded mountains or a dramatic landscape on sunny days. The robust route to the top clambers over the south face's 1080 steps, carefully planned to be a multiple of the lucky Buddhist number 108. *(Cable cars Y25 up, Y23 down. Horses Y25 up, Y15 down; Y60 for a 1hr. tour of the surrounding area. Open daily summer 6:30am-7:30pm. Temple grounds at the top Y4.)*

OUTLYING SIGHTS. Several temples are on the bus route from Wutaishan to Taiyuan. Ask the bus driver for suggestions on which temples are the most accessible and time-worthy and request stops (Y10-20). Or take a half-day **taxi tour** departing from the stand on the main road, north of the Bank of China. Prices vary wildly; expect to pay Y40-165, depending on how many peaks are included. **CITS** also arranges half-day (Y150 per person) and full-day tours (Y270).

The breathtaking ⬛ **Nantai Temple** (nántái sì; 南台寺), 2485m high on the South Peak, looks out onto the rugged alpine valleys. Equally impressive but more of a challenge to reach, **Thousand Buddha Cave** (qiān fó dòng; 千佛洞), also known as **Fomu Cave** (fómǔ dòng; 佛母洞), takes about 1½hr. to climb. A round-trip taxi to the two sights should cost about Y80 per person. To get to the more remote and seldom-visited **Nanchan Monastery** (nánchán sì; 南禅寺), take a Taiyuan-bound bus and get off at **Dongyue** (东岳). From here, eager taxi drivers provide bumpy 20min. rides to Nanchan (approx. Y25-30). Alternatively, take a full taxi (4 people) directly to Nanchan for Y80 per person. The temple's main draw is its roof, which was constructed during the Tang Dynasty entirely without nails.

DATONG 大同 ☎ 0352

Although Datong had a luminous past as the capital of the Northern Wei Dynasty (AD 383-534), its current reputation is distinctively dingy, appropriately mirroring its name: "all the same." Not that long ago, the city was the stage for legendary imperial exploits. A popular folk tale and catchy opera song tell of Ming Emperor Zhengde, the "wandering dragon" who came to Datong on an imperial inspection tour and fell in love with Li Fengjie, the "phoenix," the daughter of a hotel owner. Sadly, the city's charm does not extend beyond this legend. Today's Datong leads the country in coal production, for which it earns a thick layer of smog. Outside the bustling commercial areas, the streets are a dusty maze of half-completed construction projects punctuated by mule-carts and lurching minibuses. Visitors venture to industrial Datong not to see the city itself, but for the magnificent Yungang Grottoes, Hanging Monastery, and Huayan Monastery.

▶ TRANSPORTATION

Flights: The nearest airport is in **Taiyuan** (p. 316).

Trains: Datong Train Station (dàtóng huǒchē zhàn; 大同火车站 ; ☎ 712 2922), at Xinjian Bei Lu at Zhanqian Jie, in the northern part of the city. Tickets, especially those to Beijing, can be hard to come by if the train doesn't originate in Datong; some travelers have better luck at CITS or hotels. The ticket office is next to the clock tower; both same-day and advance tickets are sold. Open daily 24hr. in theory, but the staff might not always be there. Luggage storage near ticket office Y5 per piece per day. To: **Beijing**

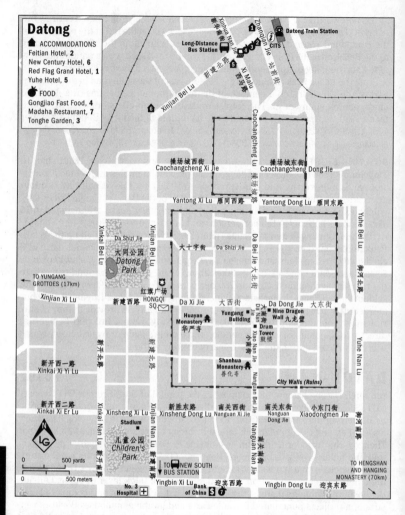

Datong

▲ ACCOMMODATIONS
Feitian Hotel, **2**
New Century Hotel, **6**
Red Flag Grand Hotel, **1**
Yuhe Hotel, **5**

🍎 FOOD
Gongjiao Fast Food, **4**
Madaha Restaurant, **7**
Tonghe Garden, **3**

TO YUNGANG
GROTTOES (17km)

TO HENGSHAN
AND HANGING
MONASTERY (70km)

(6½-8hr., 7 per day, Y27-74); **Hohhot** (5hr., 6 per day, Y19-37); **Nanjing** (30hr., daily, Y159-308); **Taiyuan** (5-8hr., 3 per day, Y30); **Xi'an** (18hr., daily, Y164). The **Trans-Mongolian** rail (p. 40) also has a stop in Datong.

Buses: There are 2 bus stations in Datong at opposite ends of town.

Datong Long-Distance Bus Station (dàtóng chángtú qìchē zhàn; 大同长途汽车站; ☎281 8411), at Xinhua Jie and Xinjian Bei Lu, a 10min. walk from the train station. Open daily 6am-6:30pm. Most people buy their tickets on the bus, and most buses leave in the mornings. To **Hohhot** (4-5hr., 2-3 per day, Y36-41) and **Taiyuan** (3hr., 2 per day, Y71). Minibuses to **Wutaishan** (4hr., few per day 6:10am-2pm) run less frequently in winter.

New South Bus Station (xīn nán zhàn; 新南站; ☎502 5222), on Xinjian Nan Lu in the far southern part of town. Accessible by bus #30 from the train station. Open 6:30am-7pm. To **Beijing** (4½hr., 4 per day, Y91) and **Taiyuan** (3hr., every 40min. 7am-6:30pm, Y51-71).

Local Transportation: Most **buses** run approximately 6am-7:30pm. Some (including #15) run 5:30am-8:40pm. Base fare Y1. Buses that leave the city (including #3) cost Y1.5. Bus #15 runs from the train station along Xinjian Lu to Yingbin Lu and several hotels; #2, 4, 8, 14, 15, 16, and 201 all originate at the train station; #30 runs between the train station and the New South Bus Station.

Taxis: Base fare Y5, each additional km Y1.2. From train station to Yingbin Lu Y10-12.

■ ⚡ ORIENTATION AND PRACTICAL INFORMATION

From the town center, the main commercial streets **Da Xi Jie** (大西街), **Da Dong Jie** (大东街), **Da Bei Jie** (大北街), and **Da Nan Jie** (大南街) extend to the west, east, north, and south, respectively. The **Drum Tower** (gǔ lóu; 鼓楼) lies south of the traffic circle. **Xinjian Lu** (新建路) runs from the train station to the southern reaches of the city and the terminus of several bus routes.

Travel Agency: CITS (☎712 4882 or 510 1326; fax 510 1326), in the train station between the 2 waiting rooms. Staffed by friendly, knowledgeable, and English-speaking staff, this is the 1st stop for most foreign travelers. Guided minibus tours of Yungang Grottoes, Hanging Monastery, and other sights (Y100 and up per person for groups of 2 or more, not including admission). Sleeper ticket commission Y30. Bargain for discounts. Open daily summer 6am-8:30pm; winter 6:30am-6:30pm.

Bank of China: 62 Yingbin Xi Lu (☎504 4114), across the street from the Datong Hotel. Bus #15 stops in front. Exchanges currency and traveler's checks. Open M-F 8am-1:30pm and 2-5:30pm.

Market: Yungang Building, at the southwest corner of Da Xi Jie and Da Nan Jie. Large selection of toiletries and food on the 1st fl. Open daily 6:40am-8:30pm.

PSB: On the east side of Xinjian Bei Lu (☎205 0778, ext. 4231), just north of Da Xi Jie. Visa extensions. Open M-F 8am-noon and 3-6:30pm.

Pharmacy: Tongren Pharmacy (tóngrén táng; 同仁堂), 118 Da Xi Jie, has a few Western brands. Open daily summer 7:30am-10:30pm; winter 7:30am-9:30pm.

Hospital: No. 3 Hospital (dàtóngshì dìsān yīyuàn; 大同市第三医院 ; ☎502 1001), on the corner of Xinjian Nan Lu at Yingbin Lu. Accessible by bus #15.

Internet Access: Wangyuan Internet Cafe (wǎngyuán wǎngbā; 网缘网吧 ; ☎280 5063), on Xinjian Bei Lu, about half a block from the train station on the left. Y5 per hr. Open daily 8am-midnight.

Post and Telecommunications: ☎203 3937. On the southeast side of the intersection of Xinjian Lu and Da Xi Jie. EMS and Poste Restante. Open daily 8am-6:30pm.

Postal Code: 037006.

▶ ACCOMMODATIONS

Most of the hotels are near the train station or on Yingbin Lu. Those near the train station conveniently span the cheaper than cheap to three-star hotels.

Feitian Hotel (fēitiān bīnguǎn; 飞天宾馆), 1 Chezhan Qian Jie (☎281 4348), immediately to the left of the train station square. Cheap, clean rooms popular among backpackers. Delicious hotpot next door. Scrubbed communal baths and showers. 4-bed dorms Y35; doubles Y140, with A/C Y160. ❶

New Century Hotel (xīn shìjì bīnguǎn; 新世纪宾馆 ; ☎243 3000), on the north corner where Xinjian Bei Lu turns. From the train station, take bus #2, 15, or 16; or walk straight down Xinjian Bei Lu for 20min. With a distinctly "homey" feel, this once grand hotel is now rather worn. The rooms are still clean, however, and the staff are friendly. Baths are somewhat small and dark. 3-bed dorms with communal showers Y30. ❶

Red Flag Grand Hotel (hóngqí dàjiǔdiàn; 红旗大酒店 ; ☎536 6111 or 536 6666). From the train station, head straight ahead and to the right. More expensive than its railside neighbors, but makes up for it with additional perks such as a bar and a coffee shop. Rooms are spotless and comfortable, with newly renovated baths. Doubles with bath and A/C Y288. Discounts available in the low season. ❹

Yuhe Hotel (yǔhé lǚguǎn; 雨禾旅馆 ; ☎281 4124), on Xinjian Bei Lu, across the street and just east of the long-distance bus station. Spartan but clean rooms with tiled floors, but beds are extra hard; small communal baths. No elevator. 24hr. hot water and fans. 2-bed dorms Y23 (if there are no other foreigners to share the room, you must buy both beds); doubles with bath Y60. ❶

🍴 FOOD

Datong folks are rough with their noodles. **Hand-pulled noodles** (lāmiàn; 拉面), **knife-cut noodles** (dāoxiāo miàn; 刀削面), and the more peaceful **oat flour noodles** (yóu miàn; 莜面) are popular. They're usually served cold with vegetables in a tasty sauce in the summer and hot with meat in the winter. Vendors are everywhere, dishing home-cooked noodles to hungry customers waiting at adjacent picnic tables. Food stalls cluster around the intersection of **Baibowa Dong Jie** (near the train tracks) and **Xinjian Xi Lu** to the west of Hongqi Sq. Great breakfast joints and casual outdoor dining are available near the train station on **Xinhua Nan Jie,** north of Xinjian Bei Lu. Those yearning for more choices should head to the restaurant district at **Da Xi Jie** and **Da Dong Lu,** near the main square and Drum Tower.

Tonghe Garden (tóng hé yuán; 同和园 ; ☎280 8111), next to Feitian Hotel. All the amenities and atmosphere of an expensive restaurant, but at more reasonable prices. The left side of the restaurant is for hotpot, complete with lively families and free cold appetizers and vegetables; right side is more expensive and has an English menu. Vegetables Y3 and up. Meat Y8 and up. Open daily 11:30am-2:30pm and 6-9:30pm. ❶

Gongjiao Fast Food (gōngjiāo kuàicān; 公交快餐), between Feitian Hotel and Wangyuan Internet Cafe. A great place for a cheap meal near the train station. If you need your staples, try the tasty stewed beef with potatoes (tǔdòu dùn niúròu; 土豆炖牛肉 ; Y12). Friendly staff speak no English, but will gladly work with you to find an appropriate dish. 15-dumpling plate Y3.5. Open daily 6am-10:30pm. ❶

Madaha Restaurant (mǎdàhā fàndiàn; 马大哈饭店), on Yingbin Lu, across from the Datong Hotel. Busiest in the mornings, when it cooks up piping hot bowls of knife-cut noodles (with hard-boiled egg) for Y2. Dumplings and other noodles available. Open daily from 7:30am. ❶

👁 SIGHTS

Though Datong is not a typical Great Wall destination, it provides the opportunity to see the Great Wall completely unpreserved. Join the CITS Ancient Great Wall tour (Y100), or hire a taxi at the train station (approximately Y50). The view of the low mound snaking through a dry landscape of villages, fields, and remnants of watchtowers offers a priceless understanding of the Wall's former importance and current challenges.

▧ HUAYAN MONASTERY (huáyán sì; 华严寺). Built in the Liao and Jin Dynasties, only a few of the original buildings remain. During later dynasties, the complex was divided into upper and lower portions. The ancient, towering Buddhist sutras in the main **Bhagavan Stack Hall** of the Lower Monastery are reason enough to visit this quiet gem, though the Upper Monastery is where the "treasure" resides in the immense Daxiong Treasure Hall. Many large statues fill the hall, and detailed colorful frescoes cover every inch of the walls. *(South of Da Xi Jie and west of Da Nan Jie. To get to both the Upper and Lower Monasteries, walk east on Da Xi Jie, take a right on the 1st through street; the monasteries are on the right. Open daily summer 8am-6pm; winter 9am-5pm. Upper and Lower Monasteries both Y20, students Y10.)*

NINE DRAGON WALL (jiǔlóng bì; 九龙壁). In imperial China, dragon walls served as screens to conceal palace and temple interiors from outsiders. Constructed in 1392, Datong's Nine Dragon Wall hid the palace of Prince Zhugui, the 13th son of the founder of the Ming Dynasty. Fire destroyed the accompanying temple, but the sturdy wall still stands, with sections of it scattered throughout Datong. Unfortunately, the section open to tourists is smaller than the one dedicated to souvenir shops. Remember to peek at the pond below the wall—as the water moves, the dragons come alive. Most tour buses skip the wall's majesty, but the colorful teal-blue sight definitely has its charm. *(About 1 block east of Da Nan Jie and Da Dong Jie, on the south side of the street. Bus #17 stops at Jiulong Bi, and bus #4 from the station stops nearby at Sipailou. Open daily 8am-6pm. Y10, students Y5.)*

SHANHUA MONASTERY (shànhuà sì; 善化寺; ☎205 2898). Built in 713 during the Tang Dynasty, this monastery was ravaged by war in 1122 and rebuilt a few years later. Thanks to the monk who diligently oversaw its reconstruction, the immense, incense-filled **Hall of Mahaviva** remains. The highlight of the complex, this hall is a slightly less well-preserved version of Huayan's Upper Monastery, housing a magnificent collection of Buddha statues. Apart from a small section of Datong's Nine Dragon Wall, there is little more to see. *(From the Drum Tower, take a right on the 1st street down south of Hualin Dept. Store and the 1st left down the alley for about 5min. Blue signs point the way. Accessible by bus #17. Open daily 8:30am-6pm. Y20, students Y10.)*

◪ DAYTRIPS FROM DATONG

YUNGANG GROTTOES 云冈石窟

About 17km west of Datong. Buses (Y4) leave from the train station directly to Yungang Grottoes throughout the day until early afternoon. Chinese and English descriptions. ☎302 6229, ext. 8831. Open daily summer 8:30am-6:30pm; winter 8:30am-5:30pm. Y60, students Y30.

Among the finest examples of Buddhist art, the spectacular Yungang Grottoes (yúngāng shíkū; 云冈石窟) take cave-carving to a new, mind-blowing level with 20 caves and 51,000 Buddhist statues. Dating back more than 1500 years, these grottoes were carved out of the mountains west of Datong during the Northern Wei Dynasty. The rulers wished to atone for their earlier persecution of Buddhism and ordered this massive project, which took 40,000 sculptors 50 years to complete. The sculptural styles here are primarily borrowed from Indian Buddhist art, which itself was created from a synthesis of various foreign styles, including Persian, Byzantine, and Greek. With its international bent, Yungang is quite unlike the later Longmen Grottoes (p. 295), which feature uniquely Chinese designs.

After running the gauntlet of souvenir shops, visitors enter a small gallery that describes the restoration of the caves and then come face-to-face with the pride of the Grottoes—**cave #5**'s imposing 17m tall Buddha. The figure is allegedly large enough for 120 people to stand on its knees, but testing this with 119 of your friends might not be appreciated by grotto staff. The soft sandstone made carving easier, but also rendered painting a difficult task. The holes in many of the statues and cave walls were made from wooden poles between which grass was woven. Mud, and then paint, was laid on top of the grass. Thus the remaining paint seen today is not from the Northern Wei period, but rather the Qing Dynasty, just over a 100 years ago. Fortunately, no number of camera-toting tourists can detract from the awe that these magnificent caves inspire.

HENGSHAN AND THE HANGING MONASTERY 悬空寺

*70km from Datong. Unscheduled **minibuses** (Y25-30) leave each morning from the train and old bus station areas in Datong, according to demand. For independent travelers, this unreliable option is the cheapest. A more secure method is to take a CITS tour, which often includes the monastery and may actually be cheaper. ☎0352 832 7795. Open daily summer 7am-7:30pm; winter 8am-5:30pm. Y60, students Y30.*

One of the five sacred Daoist mountains, Shanxi's Hengshan Mountain (héngshān; 恒山) is often referred to as **Beiyue** (běiyuè; 北岳) to distinguish it from *Nányuè*, the Hengshan of Hunan (p. 447). Rising 2017m into the air, Hengshan is known for its treacherous cliffs and calligraphy by Tang poet Li Bai. The most dramatic of the Eighteen Scenes of Hengshan, the Hanging Monastery (xuánkōng sì; 悬空寺) precariously suspends from an overhanging precipice. Some of the 40 halls in this temple are held up by only a single supporting pillar. Signs indicate the proper path as visitors wind their way up, down, and around to reach over 80 Buddha statues and other treasures. In the monastery, if there are a large number of tourists, this relaxed viewing can turn into a forced march. Looking down through the cracks in the flooring provides an exhilarating rush (or sheer terror). Hengshan Reservoir is up the stairs about 5 or 10min. beyond.

INNER MONGOLIA 内蒙古

The words "Inner Mongolia" evoke images of burly men with long wild hair billowing in the winds, riding their trusty steeds on brazen exploits, like Genghis Khan, Kublai Khan, and their fearsome roving armies, which carved out a grand empire in a path of carnage (p. 76). But the mighty Khans were buried centuries ago, and things haven't been quite the same since. The unified Mongol Empire collapsed in the 14th century, and by the 1900s, China and Russia were busily splitting up the nation. Inner Mongolia itself (not to be confused with the country Mongolia, to the north) became the PRC's first autonomous region in 1947.

Despite its size (China's third-largest regional- and province-level territory), Inner Mongolia is sparsely populated, and even more sparsely populated by ethnic Mongolians, who only make up about 10-20% of the region's residents. While some inhabitants maintain their traditional nomadic lifestyles upon the steppes, visitors are much more likely to encounter Han Chinese on horseback. Still, a decidedly non-Chinese feel pervades the region, especially in the uninterrupted grasslands surrounding Hohhot. People remain quite proud of the region's Mongolian heritage, keen to display pictures of Genghis Khan and the flying horse symbol. Although organized grasslands tours may seem somewhat contrived and far from authentic (concrete-floored yurts don't fool us) most travelers who venture north beyond the urban cityscape find something with which to fall in love—be it the endless stretches of blue sky, the knee-high grass and wildflowers waving in the wind, the potent kick of local liquor, or those dashing Mongolian tour guides.

HOHHOT 呼和浩特 ☎0471

The name Hohhot derives from the Mongolian word for "blue city," and indeed, the skies above this bright, clean city are beautifully azure. But for many visitors to Inner Mongolia's capital, the sky is even bluer and the grass even greener on the other side, on the grasslands about 100km away. Hordes of grass-loving steppe-seekers use Hohhot as a convenient point from which to explore the surrounding plains. Residents of this former frontier trading post welcome travelers open-heartedly, making the stay all the more pleasant. The summer months are green and balmy, perfect for cultivating the coniferous trees along the boulevards, and the town holds well-preserved architecture dating back to the early Ming Dynasty, when Han Chinese first moved into the city. Hohhot's current population, hovering around one million, is predominantly Han, but shop signs with Mongolian script scrolling alongside Chinese characters suggest that, while the Mongol presence is outnumbered, it is by no means overshadowed.

TRANSPORTATION

Flights: Hohhot Airport (hūhéhàotè jīchǎng; 呼和浩特机场), about 15km east of the city center. The **CAAC ticket office,** 35 Xilinguole Bei Lu (☎696 4103), just south of Xinhua Sq., next to the Air China office, has airport buses (Y5) leaving 1½-2hr. before scheduled departures beginning at 5:30am. Taxis from the airport to the train station cost about Y25. English-speaking staff members. Open daily 8am-8pm. To: **Beijing** (at least 6 per day, Y500); **Chengdu** (4 per week, Y1350); **Guangzhou** (M, Th, Sa; Y1880); **Shanghai** (at least 1 per day, Y1350); **Xi'an** (daily, Y830).

Trains: Hohhot Train Station (hūhéhàotè huǒchē zhàn; 呼和浩特火车站 ; ☎224 3222), at the north end of the square, at Chezhan Jie and Xilinguole Bei Lu, in the north part of the city. Train tickets to Beijing sell out quickly. Luggage storage Y4 per piece per day. To: **Baotou** (2½hr., 10 per day, Y12-25); **Beijing** (10hr., 5 per day, Y45-75); **Datong** (5hr., 10 per day, Y22-44).

Buses: Hohhot Bus Station (hūhéhàotè qìchē zhàn; 呼和浩特汽车站 ; ☎696 5969), on the west side of the train station, has 2 entrances, one facing the square and one off Chezhan Xi Jie. Open daily 6am-6pm. To: **Baotou** (2-3hr., every 20min. 8am-8pm, Y17-26); **Beijing** (12hr., 4 per day, Y80-100); **Datong** (6hr., 9 per day, Y40).

Local Transportation: Most **buses** run about 7am-7pm; winter hours slightly shorter. Bus fare Y1 (exact change only); **minibus** fare to most destinations Y1.5. Bus #1 runs from the west side of the train station and travels down Xilinguole Lu, Zhongshan Xi Lu, and Gongyuan Xi Lu before terminating at Shiyangqiao Lu at Nan Chafang Jie; #3 and 4 run from Zhongshan Lu to Xinhua Dajie, but do not directly serve the train station area.

Taxis: Base fare Y6, each additional km Y1.

Bike Rental: Cheap bike rental is available on the east side of Xilinguole Lu, about 5min. from the train station (Y3 per day, deposit Y100).

ORIENTATION AND PRACTICAL INFORMATION

Hohhot is fairly easy to get around. The train and bus stations are in the north at the intersection of **Xilinguole Lu** (锡林郭勒路) and **Chezhan Jie** (车站街). **Hulunbei'er Lu** (呼伦贝尔路) runs east of the train station and parallel to Xilinguole Lu. **Xinhua Dajie** (新华大街), which turns into **Xincheng Jie** (新城街), runs east-west through the main shopping districts. **Zhongshan Lu** (中山路), a commercial street lined with useful services, runs southwest from Xincheng Xi Jie, near the Inner Mongolian Museum. To the west, **Tongdao Jie** (通道街), which becomes **Da Bei Jie** (大北街) and **Da Nan Jie** (大南街), runs north-south through the older section of the city.

Travel Agencies: There are many travel agencies here, some specializing in grasslands tours. For packaged 1-night trips to Xilamuren (Y230-450, depending on number of people), as well as multi-night options that include the Singing Sands Gorge, you can try: **TYTS** (tiěyùn lǚxíng shè; 铁运旅行社 ; ☎691 8716), west of the train station, past Xinyi Hotel, under the building on the left side of the parking lot to the right; **365 Travel Center,** west side of Xilinguole Lu, directly south of Nanma Lu; **train station travel**

agency (☎139 4719 7024), west of the hall for ticket sales. None have English-speaking staff. For longer and more flexible stays in the grasslands, the easiest option is to organize a tour through a large hotel, such as **Inner Mongolia Outline Travel Service** (☎635 0737) in Holiday Inn or the agency (☎687 8761) in **Xincheng Hotel** (新城宾馆), which has accommodating English-speaking staff and offers very competitive rates.

Bank of China: 44 Xinhua Dajie (☎696 6738), east of Xilinguole Lu, opposite the Zhaojun Hotel. Exchanges currency and traveler's checks M-F. MC/V **ATM.** Open 8am-6pm.

Bookstore: Foreign-Language Bookstore (wàiwén shūdiàn; 外文书店), 52 Xincheng Xi Jie, just west of the bank. Good selection of dictionaries.

PSB: 39 Zhongshan Lu (☎669 0586), on the south side of the street. The office of the **Division of Aliens Exit-Entry Administration** is to the left, just inside the gate. Visa extensions at counters #1 and 2. Open M-F 8:30am-noon and 2:30-5:30pm.

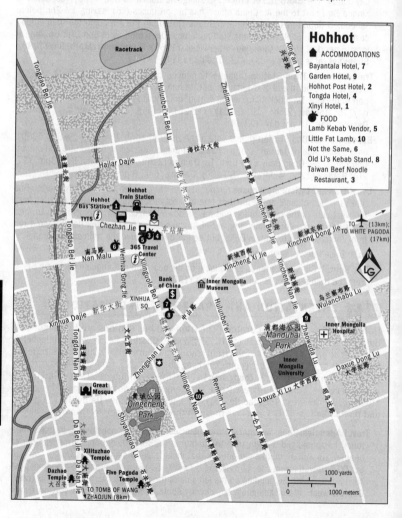

Hohhot

🏠 ACCOMMODATIONS
Bayantala Hotel, **7**
Garden Hotel, **9**
Hohhot Post Hotel, **2**
Tongda Hotel, **4**
Xinyi Hotel, **1**

🍴 FOOD
Lamb Kebab Vendor, **5**
Little Fat Lamb, **10**
Not the Same, **6**
Old Li's Kebab Stand, **8**
Taiwan Beef Noodle Restaurant, **3**

CENTRAL CHINA

Hospital: Inner Mongolia Hospital, 20 Zhaowuda Lu, a 10min. walk south of the intersection with Wulanchabu Lu. Bus #4 stops in front.

Internet Access: Internet Cafe (wǎngbā; 网吧), across from the train station on the southeastern corner of Chezhan Jie. Walk 2min. east past Xilinguole Bei Lu; entrance is on the right down a small alleyway. Open 8am-midnight. Y2 per hr.

Post and Telecommunications: Immediately east of the train station. EMS, Poste Restante, and IDD service. Open daily 8:30am-6:30pm.

Postal Code: 010050.

ACCOMMODATIONS

Without a doubt, the cheapest accommodations open to foreigners are near the train station. More expensive hotels with better rooms can be found near Xinhua Sq. During the summer months, hotels often fill to capacity, and reservations are recommended, especially at more upscale establishments.

Xinyi Hotel (☎ 225 0642), directly west of the train station and north of the bus station. The best dorm rooms in town, though the large common baths with showers make the hotel a bit humid. Central courtyard has ping-pong tables. Convenient location. 24hr. hot water, fan, and TV. 4-bed dorms Y25; 3-bed Y30; 2-bed Y35; doubles Y150. ❶

Hohhot Post Hotel (húshì yóuzhèng fàndiàn; 呼市邮政饭店 ; ☎696 6872), to the left exiting the train station, marked by a green China Post logo. Cheap, convenient, and well-kept. More expensive rooms are spacious and carpeted, with bath and TV. Dorms are clean, as are common baths. Rooms in back of hotel hear less train station noise. Overall helpful staff. 24hr. hot water. 3-bed dorms Y30; doubles Y40, with bath Y80. ❶

Bayantala Hotel (bāyàntǎlā fàndiàn; 巴彦塔拉饭店), 13 Xilinguole Bei Lu (☎696 3344), across from Xinhua Sq. Take bus #1 from train station. Clean and roomy dorms; immaculately kept, even luxurious, doubles. Reserve early, especially in summer. 2-bed dorms Y86; doubles and triples Y240-380. Low-season discounts available. ❷

Tongda Hotel (tōngdá fàndiàn; 通达饭店), 28 Chezhan Dong Jie (☎696 8731), across the street, a half block to the left when you exit the train station. Just out of reach of the obnoxiously early train station loudspeaker. Worn rooms come with dark and somewhat dingy attached baths. 5th fl. is slightly nicer. No elevator or A/C. Hot water 7-8:30am and 9-11pm. Free luggage storage. Doubles and triples Y70-100. ❶

Garden Hotel (huāyuán bīnguǎn; 花园宾馆), 83 Zhaowuda Lu (☎496 5478), at Wulanchabu Lu. From the train station, take bus #4 to the Inner Mongolia Hospital and backtrack a half block; a taxi costs about Y8. Friendly staff, but rooms are small and run-down. Passable common bath. 24hr. hot water. Breakfast included. 2-bed dorms Y88 per room; doubles Y168; triples Y280. ❶

FOOD

A trip to Inner Mongolia without **Mongolian hotpot with sliced mutton** (shuàn yángròu; 涮羊肉) would be a grievous culinary faux pas. Although most people find the idea of boiling broth appetizing only in cold winter, giant hotpot palaces, hoping for more year-round business, turn on their A/C full-blast in the summer to create a frigid feel. If the weather is warm and you're sick of sheep, there are several good areas for outdoor dining. Stands selling *bāozi* (Y2.5-3 per steamer) set up by the **Bayantala Hotel,** south of Xilinguole Lu at Xinhua Dajie. Various hotpot and dumpling restaurants line **Xilinguole Lu,** south of the train station, as well as the first pedestrian road to the west off Xilinguole Lu. The unofficial hotpot district is on **Nanma Lu,** the first street on the right after crossing Chezhan Dong Jie. For *jiǎozi* and kebabs, follow your nose to **Wulanqiate Dong Jie** and **Guoziban Xiang,** south of Bayantala Hotel, where restaurants and impromptu stands dish out both.

Old Li's Kebab Stand (lǎo lǐ kǎoròu yǎkè; 老李烤肉雅客), directly south of the Bayantala Hotel. You can't miss the bright orange-and-yellow tablecloths at this family-style joint. Mr. Li mans the portable grill while his wife, daughter, and son-in-law take care of everything else. Very tasty standards like lamb and chicken wing kebabs are accompanied by snails and silkworms (Y5). Most goodies are displayed in front, so pointing is not a problem. Open daily 7pm-3am. ❶

Not the Same (dà bù tóng; 大不同 ; ☎626 3898), on the northwest corner of Nanma Lu and Wenhua Gong Jie. As its name implies, this 3-story restaurant is quite special. A local hot spot, it serves hotpot with a little flare and a lot of confidence. When the A/C breaks down, men strip off their shirts to continue downing lamb and assorted veggies. Vegetables Y3-6. Meat Y6-10. Open daily until 10:30pm. ❷

Little Fat Lamb (xiǎo féi yáng; 小肥羊 ; ☎668 7799), on Xilinguole Nan Lu, on the east side north of Daxue Xi Jie. This slightly more upscale version of hotpot has moved on to electric plates and reliable A/C, but without losing any of the flavor. 2 branches in Hohhot. Vegetables Y3-8. Meat Y8-15. Open daily until 9:30pm. ❷

Taiwan Beef Noodle Restaurant (táiwān niúròu miàn guǎn; 台弯牛肉面馆), across from the train station, on the east side of Xilinguole Bei Lu. Quick, flavorful bowls of dumplings in soup (tāng jiǎo; 汤铰 ; Y5) or beef noodle soup (Y6) can satisfy any hungry traveler. Standard cold appetizers (Y3-5) sit at the ready. Open daily 7am-10pm. ❶

Lamb Kebab Vendor, on the east side of Xilinguole Bei Lu, a 2min. walk south of the train station. Enormous mouth-watering hunks of meat (Y1) that put the skinny kebabs of other vendors to shame. Kick back with beer and friends at the picnic table. ❶

👁 SIGHTS

Most visitors come to Hohhot with the intention of trekking out to the famed grasslands outside the city. Many sights within the city are interesting enough to be justifiably included on grassland tours, but because they are easily accessible by public bus or bike, independent visits are possible as well.

▩XILITUZHAO TEMPLE (xílìtúzhào sì; 席力图召寺). Situated off a maze of winding alleyways lined with squat adobe houses, this temple features the largest *stupa* in Inner Mongolia. Brightly colored dragon carpets and the overwhelming smell of incense fill the large and imposing main hall, and banners hang from the ceiling. More secluded than the neighboring Dazhao Temple, Xilituzhao also squares off many courtyards worth exploring and is the home of the Living Buddha responsible for Buddhist affairs in Hohhot. *(On a small street just east of Da Nan Jie. From Dazhao, turn left onto Dazhao Qianjie and cross the road, then continue directly across to the lane on the other side. Open daily 7am-7pm. Y10, students Y5.)*

DAZHAO TEMPLE (dàzhào sì; 大召寺). Dating back to the Ming Dynasty, this large complex houses a complete set (108 volumes) of Buddhist scriptures and a rare silver statue of Sakyamuni. The colorfully decorated main hall of this active temple sometimes plays host to large prayer gatherings. The sprawling courtyards often play host to camera-clicking tourists. *(On Dazhao Qianjie off Da Nan Jie, the main south street. Bus #6 from Tongda Bei Jie and Chezhan Xi Jie, west of the train station, stops nearby; from the bus stop, walk straight ahead for 3min., and then turn right onto Dazhao Qianjie. Peek down the alley from Da Nan Jie. ☎597 3154. Open daily 7am-7pm. Y15, students Y7.)*

WHITE PAGODA (bái tǎ; 白塔). Originally known as the Ten Thousand Avatamska Sutras Temple, this isolated, carefully restored pagoda towers more than 50m over the nearby fields. Although the lime on the outside gives the structure a brilliant sheen, the inside of the pagoda is almost pitch-black, making for a treacherous climb. Visitors may want to bring matches to the top to burn incense and pray for a safe descent. The climb is worth it, however, for the commanding vista of the rolling countryside and the flower and vegetable gardens below. The smell of summer flowers and the sight of gourds dangling in the arbors are nearly as good reasons to visit this out-of-the-way pagoda. *(About 15km east of Hohhot beyond the airport. Minibus #12 to Hexi from the eastern end of Dongfeng Lu goes past the site. Some buses are unnumbered, so just catch any bus to Hexi. Bus #2 from the train station stops at the terminus for bus #12. Not many buses troll the country, so you may want to catch a taxi back to the train station for Y20.* ☎901 1027. *Open daily 8am-6pm. Y5, climbing the pagoda extra Y5.)*

GREAT MOSQUE (qīngzhēn dàsì; 清真大寺). A must-see sight, if not for the gorgeous mosque itself, then for the lively atmosphere inside and outside its walls. Friendly, boisterous Muslim vendors cluster outside the mosque, providing visitors with sweet rice and dried apricots to munch on as they stroll through the courtyards. Non-Muslims are not allowed inside the various worship halls. The mosque is under renovation until 2005. *(Just east of Tongdao Jie at Zhongshan Xi Lu. Bus #13 from the southeast corner of Xinhua Sq. terminates just beyond. Free.)*

FIVE PAGODA TEMPLE (wǔtǎ sì; 五塔寺). These five pagodas are all that remain after the destruction of the Ci Deng Temple, the original anchor of the site. Despite their orphaned status, the five little buildings are beautifully maintained and worth a visit. The pagodas display Mongolian, Chinese, and Sanskrit script against beautifully carved pictures in styles originating from India. The astronomical chart with Mongolian inscriptions on the back wall is the only one of its kind in China. *(48 Wutasi Houjie, west of Gongyuan Xi Lu. Bus #1 from the train station stops at Wujing Yiyuan; from the stop, continue walking south for a few blocks until the pagodas become visible down an alley on the right.* ☎597 2640. *Open daily 8am-6:30pm. Y15.)*

INNER MONGOLIA MUSEUM (nèi ménggǔ bówùguǎn; 内蒙古博物馆). Spanning Inner Mongolia's history from prehistoric times to the Communist Revolution, an incredible number of artifacts and pictures is crammed into this two-story museum. Exhibits cover everything from dinosaurs to yurts.

NAADAM

Naadam (那达幕) is the largest annual Mongolian event, celebrated locally all over Mongolia and Inner Mongolia in July and August. Dating back to the days of Genghis Khan, Naadam is some three days of singing, dancing, and feasting. The biggest party is the National Naadam Festival in Ulaan Bataar, but for those who can't make it that far north, there's always the grasslands of Inner Mongolia. Naadam traditionally occurs when the grass is longest, making for rather spontaneous festivals. Check with a travel agency for dates.

The word *naadam* means "games," and Beijing could take some pointers from this festival for the Olympics. It opens with a colorful parade of horses, costumes, and flags before shifting to competitions in the "three manly sports" of wrestling, archery, and horseracing. Competitions are open to females, except for wrestling. Supposedly, a woman in male guise once won in wrestling, infuriating the men so much that they required all participants henceforth to wear the open chested *zodog* vest, ensuring that no woman could participate. Wrestlers are awarded titles from the respectable "falcon" to the almighty "lion." The victorious archer is named *mergen* (marksman), and the racer *tumny ekh*, or "leader of ten thousand." The final day is devoted to closing ceremonies and merrymaking, with plenty of milk tea and vodka.

The first floor features colorful clothing, tools, and other items of the minority nationalities living in Inner Mongolia, in particular ethnic Mongolians. *(2 Xinhua Dajie. Take bus #20 or minibus #33 from the train station. The main entrance is on Hulunbei'er Lu between Xinhua Dajie and Zhongshan Dong Lu. ☎ 696 3766. English and Chinese explanations. Tickets sold at a small window to the right of entrance. Open M and W-Su 9am-5pm. Y10, students Y5.)*

TOMB OF WANG ZHAOJUN (zhāojūn mù; 昭君墓). The 98m hill offers decent views of the countryside, red-roofed villages, and well-landscaped courtyards, in addition to being the final resting place of the imperial concubine who brought peace to the Han Dynasty. In 33 BC, the fearsome Hun chieftain extended an olive branch by proposing a marriage alliance with the Han. Wang Zhaojun, languishing at the bottom of the concubine hierarchy, volunteered. Noting her unflattering portrait, the Han emperor agreed, but little did he know she had been too proud to bribe the imperial painter. When Wang Zhaojun entered the palace to be handed over to the chieftan, the emperor gasped for he had never seen such beauty, but it was too late. The emperor could only watch glumly as the chieftan swung Zhaojun onto his horse and rode off into the sunset. As the "queen" of the Huns, Wang Zhaojun used her influence to encourage peace between her homeland and her adopted home. The Huns did not try to attack again for 50 years. *(About 10km south of the city. At the terminus of minibus #44. Bus #1 from the train station terminates at Shiyang-qiao Xi Lu at Nan Chafang Jie. ☎ 515 0061. English captions. Open daily summer 8am-6pm; winter 8am-5pm. Park Y35, students Y10.)*

HOHHOT GRASSLANDS 草原

The grasslands near Hohhot simultaneously feel remote and touristy. You can spend a few days wallowing in the simple beauty of the seemingly endless wild-flower prairie, but you'll have to share the experience with loads of other tourists. Grazing flocks of sheep roam the green expanses, but the only horses here are ones that cost Y50 per hour to ride. The dancing, singing, and wrestling, like the concrete-floored, electric-wired yurt lodgings, present varying degrees of authenticity. Despite the summer camp-meets-Club Med atmosphere, the yurt camps themselves are only small dots upon the enormous lands. A 5min. walk in any direction to watch the sunset lands you in the midst of a stark, lonely landscape, with grass stretching to the horizons. Visiting the grasslands is a must from Hohhot and a worthwhile long-weekend excursion from Beijing.

GRASSLANDS AREAS. Of the three main grassland sites around Hohhot, **Xilamuren** (希拉穆仁; 80km from the city) is the most visited, **Huitengxile** (辉腾锡勒; 120km) is the most beautiful, and the quiet, unassuming **Gegentala** (格根塔拉; 160km) just is. The best months to visit are August and September, when the grass is highest and greenest. In winter, temperatures dip below -20°C; even in summer, the weather can get chilly, so bring warm clothes. At times, even the less-touristed Huitengxile and Gegentala can resemble a long string of yurt-motels. For more remote grasslands, head to the Hulun Buir Grasslands near Manzhouli (p. 329).

GRASSLAND TOURS. Just about everyone who visits the grasslands signs on with an official tour (p. 317). Numerous tour operators—some extremely unscrupulous—solicit business throughout Hohhot. While it's certainly no trouble to book a tour, be cautious and clarify many times what is included. Keep in mind also that some tourists have paid for tours to Huitengxile (easily identified by the large white windmills nearby) only to be taken to the less remote Xilamuren instead. Tour prices depend on where you want to go, how long you want to stay, the number of people accompanying you, and the tour agency itself. Arranging a tour is cheaper with more people, since transportation is often the most expensive part (vehicle Y500 and up for 2 nights). When traveling alone or in a small group, save money by finding a guide (Y50 per day) who is already leading a larger tour. (2-day tour to Xilamuren Y200-300 per person, to Huitengxile Y250-350.)

Most tours last one, two, or three nights and include transportation, yurt accommodations, food, admission to a wrestling match or horse race, and often temple admission. While they provide the opportunity to go horseback riding across the steppes, they do not include the fee (Y50 per hr.). Food often features the traditional mutton dish *shǒu bǎ ròu* (手把肉 ; Y20), eaten with a large knife and your hands. Don't fret about etiquette—all is forgotten by the time the evening meal culminates in the *hādá* (哈达), in which local spirits are poured into goblets and passed around to the strains of Mongolian melodies. After dipping your fingers and pointing first to the sky, then to the ground, and finally touching your forehead, it's time to imbibe. Try not to gag—this stuff is potent.

VISITING INDEPENDENTLY. Good bargaining skills can result in a significantly more enriching guided tour only marginally more expensive than an independent grasslands visit. However, for those tight on time or budget (or just plain tourgroup wary), the Xilamuren grasslands are easily reached by public transportation. Buses (2hr., from 8am, Y15) leave from the Hohhot bus station in the morning for **Zhaohe**, the access point for Xilamuren. You can enjoy horseback riding (Y20-30 per hr. with bargaining), sample traditional Mongolian foods, visit the local Mongolian Buddhist temple (Y5), and still get home in time (buses leave regularly until dusk). It is also possible to arrange cheap lodgings; negotiate a reasonable per-day rate (Y50 per bed) and you can avoid tour groups altogether. Such ease has its price though: Xilamuren's grasses are closer cousins to your front lawn than the knee-high beauties of other grasslands, and wildflowers are hard to spot.

BAOTOU 包头   ☎ 0472

In the spirit of Chinese modernization, Baotou is inconveniently divided into two parts, old and new. West Baotou is the new, lazily spreading itself across boulevards and spacious parks and busily constructing imposing hotels and offices. East Baotou, however, was there first, and its small, winding streets, crowded with wares of every kind, will certainly make sure you don't forget it. Non-business travelers have little reason to venture to Baotou, and those who do usually use the city as a base for trips to Singing Sands Gorge and Wudangzhao Monastery. Counterintuitively, this coal-reliant city is extremely clean, and travelers leave remembering its pleasantly neat streets and nearby natural scenery.

▄ TRANSPORTATION

Flights: Baotou Airport (bāotóu jīchǎng; 包头机场 ; ☎ 460 0160), is about 2km south of the Baotou East Train Station. **CAAC ticket office,** 26 Gangtie Dajie, Kunqu (☎ 513 5492), in the Aviation Bldg. east of the Bank of China in the Xingyuan Hotel. Open daily 8:30am-6:30pm. To **Beijing** (3-4 per day, Y590) and **Shanghai** (2 per day, Y1350).

Trains: Baotou East Station (bāotóu dōng zhàn; 包头东站 ; ☎ 222 4012), in Donghe. Tickets sold under the large clock. **Baotou Train Station** (bāotóu zhàn; 包头站 ; ☎ 160 5678), West Baotou, 1.5km south of Kunqu. Trains run to and from both stations; check times for your preferred station. Beijing trains sell out quickly in the summer. To: **Beijing** (12hr., 3 per day, Y54-106); **Hohhot** (3hr., 9 per day, Y12-25); **Lanzhou** (14hr., daily, Y63); **Xi'an** (24hr., daily, Y89); **Yinchuan** (8hr., daily, Y45).

Buses: The most convenient bus station is in Donghe, just north of the east train station. Most people buy tickets once on board. To: **Dongsheng** (3hr., every 20min. 6:40am-8pm, Y14-22); **Hohhot** (3hr., every 20-30min. 6:20am-7:20pm, Y17-26); **Yulin**.

Local Transportation: Buses are slow and crowded; most run from 6-7am to 7-8pm. Bus #1 runs 9am-9pm; #5 runs 6:30am-10:30pm. Base fare Y1; East Baotou to West Baotou buses Y2, minibuses Y2.5. Be sure to hold onto the ticket until you get off the bus. Bus #1 runs from Baotou Train Station up A'erding Dajie to Gangtie Dajie; #5 and 10 leave every 5min. and make the 50min. trip from the far eastern parking lot in Baotou East Station to Gangtie Dajie in Kunqu, West Baotou.

Taxis: Base fare Y5-8, each additional km Y1.2. Very accessible. Taxis between East and West Baotou cost Y35-45.

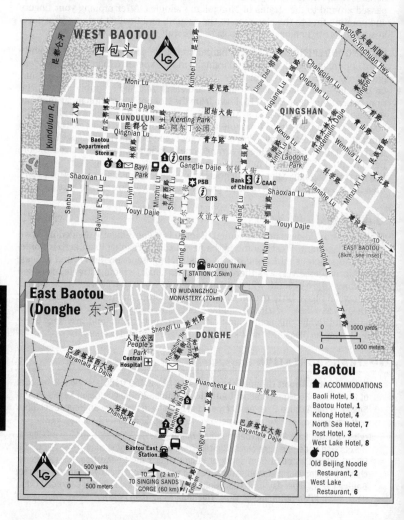

ORIENTATION AND PRACTICAL INFORMATION

East Baotou, or **Donghe** (东河), is small and compact. The east train station, long-distance bus station, and airport are all in the southern part of the city. **Nanmen Wai Dajie** (南门外大街) runs north from the train station, intersects **Huancheng Lu** (环城路), and forms the commercial center of the district. Though most transportation options are in East Baotou, more essential services are located in West Baotou. West Baotou consists of two districts, **Qingshan** (青山) and **Kundulun** (昆都仑), called **Kunqu** (昆区) for short. **Gangtie Dajie** (钢铁大街) runs east-west through Qingshan and Kunqu. **A'erding Dajie** (阿尔丁大街) intersects Gangtie Dajie near the city government building and continues south to the train station.

Travel Agencies: CITS, 14 Shaoxian Lu (☎516 1415; fax 511 6824). English-speaking staff. Open M-Sa 8am-6:30pm. A more convenient branch is in the **Baotou Hotel** compound, 64 Gangtie Dajie, Kunqu (☎516 3606). No local tours, but they can provide information for other parts of Inner Mongolia. Open daily 8am-6:30pm.

Bank of China: 28 Gangtie Dajie, Kunqu (☎512 8888), in Xingyuan Hotel. Exchanges traveler's checks. Another **branch** next to the Baobai Supermarket exchanges currency. MC/V **ATM**s at both Bank of China branches. Both open daily 7:30am-5:30pm.

Market: The **Baotou Department Store,** known as **Baobai** (bāobǎi; 包百), 61 Gangtie Dajie, Kunqu, west of Linyin Lu. Open daily summer 9am-8pm; winter 9am-7:30pm. In Donghe, a **supermarket** is next to the West Lake Hotel. Open daily 8:30am-8:30pm.

PSB: On Shaoxian Lu (☎518 0772), in the Jiaojing Zhihui Ctr., kitty-corner from CITS. Visa extensions. Open M-Th 8am-noon and 2:30-6:30pm, F 8am-noon.

Hospital: No. 2 Municipal Hospital (shì dì'èr yīyuàn; 市第二医院 ; ☎417 1084), also called **Central Hospital** (zhōngxīn yīyuàn; 中心医院), off Huancheng Lu facing People's Park, Donghe.

Internet Access: Internet cafe, on the southwestern corner of Gangtie Jie at Minzhu Lu. In Donghe, a **cafe** is on the corner of Zhanbei Lu at Nanmen Wai Dajie. Both Y2 per hr.

Post and Telecommunications: In Donghe, on the corner of Huancheng Lu at Tongshun Jie. EMS. Open daily 7:30am-7pm. **China Telecom** is in the same building. Open daily summer 8am-6:30pm; winter 8am-6pm. In Kunqu, on the southwest corner of Gangtie Dajie at Linyin Lu. EMS and Poste Restante. Open daily 8am-7pm. **China Telecom,** on the other side of the Post Hotel. Open daily 8am-6pm.

Postal Code: Donghe 014040, Kunqu 014010.

ACCOMMODATIONS

Donghe has cheap and convenient accommodations, while Kunqu's hotels in quieter surroundings have higher price tags and cater to less thrifty businesspeople.

DONGHE

West Lake Hotel (xīhú fàndiàn; 西湖饭店), 10 Nanmen Wai Dajie (☎418 7101), on the east side of the street, a 5min. walk from the train station. Scrubbed baths with good water pressure complement well-maintained and spacious rooms. Common showers and baths on the 6th fl. have locks for increased privacy. 3-bed dorms Y93 per room; doubles Y128-188. Bargaining can be fruitful. ❷

Baoli Hotel (bǎolì dàshà; 保利大厦), 8 Nanmen Wai Dajie (☎220 2666), a 10min. walk from the train station, on the east side. The best budget option in Donghe. Large, clean rooms have tile floors, and spacious bathrooms feature standing showers. No elevator. Doubles Y60; triples Y60, with A/C and sitting room Y180. ❶

North Sea Hotel (běiyáng fàndiàn; 北洋饭店; ☎412 4246), opposite West Lake Hotel on the west side of Nanmen Wai Dajie. Relatively clean worn rooms and cramped bathrooms with bathtubs. A good deal for dorms, though standard rooms are overpriced. 2- to 4-bed dorms Y20; doubles Y78, with A/C Y138. ❶

KUNQU

Baotou Hotel (bāotóu bīnguǎn; 包头宾馆), 64 Gangtie Dajie (☎216 6818), near Shifu Xi Lu. Buses #1 from Baotou Station and 5 from Donghe stop nearby. Baotou Hotel is comprised of 2 buildings, each with its own front desk. The big building facing the street has large, pristine rooms with immaculate bath. Singles Y310; doubles Y310-Y365. ❹ The older building to the left when entering the gate has no bathtubs, but rooms are quite spotless. Book ahead. Singles Y140; doubles Y160; triples Y220. ❷

Kelong Hotel (kēlóng dàjiǔdiàn; 科隆大酒店; ☎515 2211 or 510 3385), across the street from the Baotou Hotel, on the corner of Gangtie Jie at Minzhu Lu. Spic-and-span carpeted dorms and rooms may be a bit small. Exceptionally clean common toilets, but no showers. Finicky hot water. Front rooms face a loud street; back rooms face a factory. Dorms Y45 per room; standard rooms Y148. ❶

Post Hotel (yóudiàn dàshà; 邮电大厦), 64 Gangtie Dajie (☎216 6818 or 216 6828), at Linyin Lu opposite Bayi Park, sandwiched between the post office and China Telecom. Bus #1 stops at the park. Courteous staff, A/C, bathtubs, and yummy extras in the room. Breakfast included. Reservations recommended. Doubles economy Y160, standard Y196 and up; triples Y266-320. Discounts on pricier rooms. ❷

☐ FOOD

The diverse cuisine of Baotou caters to all dining styles and tastes. In the summer, vendors crowd the intersection of Huancheng Lu and Nanmen Wai Dajie in Donghe. On **Zhanbei Lu** west of the train station, street stands sell watermelons, hot pastries, and every roastable part of a pig (hoofs Y3). Next to the West Lake Hotel, the **West Lake Restaurant ❶** packs in customers who yearn for extensive soups (Y5-10) and impressive cold appetizer buffets boasting over 20 varieties of pickled, hot, and sweet dishes. (Vegetarian plate Y4. Meat dishes Y10.)

In Kunqu, both **Minzu Lu** (just south of Gangtie Dajie) and the small lane west of the Sawa Hotel on Gangtie Dajie are lined with restaurants offering noodles, fried dishes, and more. During the day, small stands set up on the side streets near the Bayi Park and Baotou Department Store, selling everything from noodles to shaved ice to Mongolian souvenirs. ▨ **Old Beijing Noodle Restaurant ❶** (lǎo běijīng zhájiàng miàn guǎn; 老北京炸酱面馆), 66 Gangtie Dajie, next to the post office in Kunqu, specializes in noodles topped with tasty brown sauce (Y3-8 per bowl), but also has a decent selection of regional cuisine and the occasional singing waiter.

▨ DAYTRIPS FROM BAOTOU

▨ SINGING SANDS GORGE 响沙湾

*Independent travel from both Baotou and Dongsheng is easy. From the Donghe Bus Station, **buses** to Dongsheng depart every 20min. Disembark at the turn-off, recognizable by its white gate with "Singing Sands" written on it in red characters. Fare should be Y8. From there, it is an additional 8km over a dirt road. **Taxis** and **minibuses** will usually stop and pick up travelers for about Y10, but you can also walk under the railroad bridge. A more reliable strategy is to disembark at Daqi (达旗), the 1st bus station between Baotou and Dongsheng (approx. 1hr., Y5-6). From there, hire a taxi (approx. 30min.; Y30, round-trip Y50). To return, it's fairly easy to flag down a Baotou- or Dongsheng-bound bus from the side of the main road. Activities office ☎0477 396 3355. Y25, students Y15.*

Legend has it that a mean-spirited monk once found himself caught in the middle of a sandstorm with only his trumpet by his side. In an attempt to escape Heaven's sandy wrath, he blew hard on his trumpet in hopes that villagers would hear his call for help, but no one came, and the monk perished in the desert. Despite this lamentable tale, the dunes of Singing Sands Gorge (xiǎngshā wān; 响沙湾) offer nothing but pleasure to visitors today, with a number of low-key adventure activities for fun-seekers of all stripes. Those who wish to create a wailing, singing sound themselves can slide down the sandy slides via bum or sled.

The more adventurous can climb up the rope ladder from the lower parking lot and slide down the gorge (sled Y10 per trip), or lose themselves in the sea of dunes on the far side, perhaps perching atop a secluded peak for a picnic lunch. Those who don't want to trudge through sand can take the chairlift from the upper parking lot (Y50 including 1 slide down). On the far side of the gorge, a kitschy playground atmosphere of camel rides (Y35 for 30min.), sand-skiing (Y10), hang-gliding (Y80 per trip), and horseback riding (Y20 for a little run around the track) awaits. In the summer, colorful knee-high booties are worth the Y5 fee, as the sand gets unbearably hot.

WUDANGZHAO MONASTERY 五当召

*70km northeast of Baotou. 2 **minibuses** leave from the parking area between the East Baotou train and long-distance bus stations (2½hr.; 10, 11am; Y10). They depart 50min. after their arrival. A few other buses and a taxi or 2 depart the lamasery for Shigui or Baotou, but it is best to ask when before losing yourself in the dark rooms or surrounding hills. More reliably, **bus #7** travels from the Donghe bus station parking lot to Shiguai (every 30min. 7:45am-5:40pm, Y4), a small town 1½-2hr. north of Baotou. From there, hire a **taxi** for the remainder of the trip (round-trip Y40-50). Open daily 8am-6pm. Y30.*

The bumpy riverbed road to Wudangzhao (wǔdāngzhào; 五当召) builds up many a traveler's expectations, and luckily this Tibetan Buddhist monastery doesn't disappoint. Though not an extremely large compound, there are eight visitable temples and schools laid out over the side of a hill. Built in 1749, Wudangzhou Temple is the largest in Inner Mongolia and one of the most famous in China. The six halls house a friendly school of monks. The white Tibetan-style buildings extend up the hillside and contain some exquisitely detailed Buddhist statues and well-maintained, colorful frescoes. Beautiful surrounding scenery complements the architectural and stylistic details. Pine trees and grazing sheep speckle the softly shaped hills in every direction. Several trails leading up various hills begin near the parking lot, offering nature lovers the chance to walk and picnic, not to mention soak in the serenity of this holy retreat.

DONGSHENG 东胜 ☎ 0477

Dongsheng lies in the middle of the Ordos Plateau, and like its northern neighbor Baotou, it has an economy based on coal production. Despite their best efforts, the city's clean streets, new buildings, and friendly inhabitants have little to offer sight-seeing tourists. The few who choose to journey out here usually just spend the night before heading to the Mausoleum of Genghis Khan.

▄▗ TRANSPORTATION AND PRACTICAL INFORMATION

Dongsheng is small, with an urban area of just 8.6km². **Hangjin Lu** (杭锦路) traverses the city north-south and intersects **Yijinhuoluo Dong Jie** (伊金霍洛东街), a street full of shopping options. Navigation is easy: the bus station is at the north end of Hangjin Lu, and the intersection with Yijinhuoluo Dong Jie is one block south. Most of the city's cheap lodgings, shops, and services are within a couple of blocks of the intersection of Hangjin Lu and Yijinhuoluo Dong Jie.

Buses: Dongsheng Bus Station (dōngshèng qìchē zhàn; 东胜汽车站 ; ☎834 1333), on the west side of Hangjin Lu, 1 block south of Etuoke Jie and 1 block north of Yijinhuoluo Dong Jie. Most travelers buy tickets once on board. Open daily 5:30am-6pm. To: **Baotou** (2hr., every 15min. 7am-7pm, Y22); **Beijing** (16hr., 2 per day, Y140); **Hohhot** (3-4hr., approx. every hr. 7am-5:20pm, Y48).

Local Transportation: Given Dongsheng's small size, walking is often the best way to get around. **Minibuses** #1, 2, and 3 all stop just south of the train station; #1 and 3 serve the eastern and western parts of the city, respectively; #2 runs down Hangjin Lu to the Tianjiao Hotel at the southern tip of the city. Fare Y0.2-1.

Taxis: Base fare technically Y5, but many cars are not metered.

PSB: ☎832 3470. On the northeastern corner of Etuoke Jie at Hangjin Lu, north of the bus station. Open M-F 8:30am-noon and 2:30-5:30pm.

Bank of China: On the south side of Yijinhuoluo Jie (☎836 3100), just before the hospital. Exchanges traveler's checks. Open daily 8:30am-noon and 2:30-5:30pm.

Hospital: E'erduosi Central Hospital (è'ěrduōsī shì zhōngxīn yīyuàn; 鄂尔多斯市中心 医院 ; ☎836 7180), on the north side of Yijinhuoluo Xi Jie between Wendu'er Lu and Hangjin Lu. This self-proclaimed "baby friendly" hospital is a 10min. walk west from the Yijinhuoluo Dong Jie and Hangjin Lu intersection.

Internet Access: Internet Cafe (wǎngbā; 网吧), at the southeast corner of Hangjin Lu and Yijinhuoluo Dong Jie. Y2 per hr. Open daily 8am-midnight.

Post and Telecommunications: East of Hangjin Lu (☎832 9957), on the northwest corner of Yijinhuoluo Dong Jie at Zhunge'er Bei Lu. EMS. **China Telecom,** in the same building, has IDD. Both open daily 8am-6pm.

Postal Code: 017000.

ACCOMMODATIONS AND FOOD

Most of Dongsheng's reasonably priced accommodations are on **Yijinhuoluo Jie**, within a block of Hangjin Lu. The overpriced **Tianjiao Hotel** at the southern end of the city caters primarily to businessmen and wealthy tourists. Restaurants line Yijinhuoluo Dong Jie and its side alleyways closer to the post office. The bus station area offers corn and quick bites.

Wuzhou Hotel (wǔzhōu dàjiǔdiàn; 五洲大酒店 ; ☎832 1532), on the south side of Yijinhuoluo Dong Jie, 3min. east of Hangjin Lu. A large sign above the hotel proclaims "Grand Continental Hotel." Clean and well-lit doubles. Cheaper rooms are small with attached baths that redefine the word cramped. Larger doubles are new and impressively clean. Doubles Y150 and up. ❷

Traffic Hotel (jiāotōng bīnguǎn; 交通宾馆 ; ☎832 1414), 2min. south of the bus station's main entrance; take a right when exiting. A relatively clean budget option. Rooms have either carpet or linoleum. Spartan baths. Common showers consist of a large room with a lock. 2-bed dorms Y50-60; doubles Y88-96. ❶

Dongsheng Hotel (dōngshèng dàjiǔdiàn; 东胜大酒店 ; ☎399 6688). On the northwest corner of Yijinhuoluo Dong Jie at Hangjin Lu. Dongsheng's nicest hotel without the big-city luxury price tag. Spacious, spotless rooms. Bathrooms have either a bathtub or a deluxe full-body shower (multiple nozzles at different heights). Business center. Doubles Y198-238. Bargaining is a must. ❸

DAYTRIP FROM DONGSHENG

MAUSOLEUM OF GENGHIS KHAN 成吉思汗陵

*50km from Dongsheng. From the Dongsheng Long-Distance Bus Station, take a **minibus** (2hr., approx. every 30min. from 7am, Y8) that drops off at the Mausoleum on the main road. Flag down a Dongsheng–bound bus to return to Dongsheng. Open 24hr. English-speaking guides Y30. Admission Y35, students Y20.*

After the passing of Genghis Khan in 1227, his underlings went to great lengths to ensure the secrecy of his tomb's location. Grisly tales say that all 2,000 people who attended his funeral were killed by 800 soldiers, who were then in turn also executed. To this day, the location of Genghis Khan's burial site is unknown. Of course, that didn't deter the Chinese government from setting up a mausoleum (chéngjísī hàn líng; 成吉思汗陵 ; or chéng líng, " 成陵 ") in his honor in 1955, celebrating the establishment of the Inner Mongolia Autonomous Region.

The mausoleum's main claim to authenticity are relics left behind by the mighty Khan. These relics had been guarded by a group of dedicated followers who continued to hold memorial services for their deceased patron right up until WWII, when the prized objects were seized by the Japanese government to contribute to the legitimacy of their Mongolian puppet state. Eventually, the Chinese government took the relics back and created this tourist attraction—ahem, shrine.

A gigantic bronze statue of the Great Conqueror himself watches over the entrance of the tomb, followed by a marble statue in the main hall, with a map of his extensive empire serving as the backdrop. Behind the grand entrance is a mourning room with an altar and the Khan's supposed remains. One side hall contains the remains of the Great Man's daughter-in-law, mother of the almost-as-great Kublai Khan, who completed his grandfather's conquest of China. The other side hall contains his bow and arrow and a silver saddle. The walls of both halls are decorated with vivid murals detailing Genghis Khan's military exploits, Mongolian culture, and the various kingdoms of Central Asia and the Middle East with whom he had "established contact."

To the left of the mausoleum, visitors can pay their respects at the **Sacrificial Altar to Suled** (sūlèdé jìtán; 苏勒德祭坛). "Suled" is the banner of the ancient Mongolian army. The **Gandeli Obo** (gāndélì áobāo; 甘德利敖包), a large stone pile used for prayer, affords a nice view of the surrounding valley. Those with more time on their hands might prefer to make the 30min. trek to the **Reviewing Stand** (diǎnjiàng tái; 点将台), on the edge of the grasslands.

The **Genghis Guesthouse ❶** (chéngjísī bīnguǎn; 成吉思宾馆 ; ☎896 1009) has accommodations for those who just can't get enough of the Khan. Reception is next to the parking lot, to the right of the entrance. Standard doubles have tile floors, TV, and attached bath (Y100-200); yurts are more rustic (Y80 for 5 people).

MANZHOULI 满洲里　　　☎0470

Manzhouli, in the far northeast of Inner Mongolia, bordering Russian Siberia to the north and Mongolian deserts to the west, is a temptation for travelers heeding the call of untamed nature. The remote city is neatly laid out and attractive in its own right, but lacks the wild beauty and open skies of the surrounding Hulun Buir grasslands. For the many Russians who fill the streets of Manzhouli, piling loads of Chinese goods into their vans, Manzhouli's main appeal lies not in its boundless steppes, but rather in its bustling commerce and rowdy, drunken nights.

CENTRAL CHINA

TRANSPORTATION

Flights: The **Manzhouli Airport** is due to open by 2005, but currently the closest airport is **Hailar Airport** (hǎilā'ěr fēijīchǎng; 海拉尔飞机场; ☎827 0004). Y3 shuttle buses leave 1½hr. before departures from the **CAAC ticket offices**, 35 Er Daojie, 2nd fl., in the International Hotel, Manzhouli (☎622 1436), and 31 Qiaodan Jie, Hailar (☎833 1010). To **Beijing** (16 per day, Y1150) and **Hohhot** (5 per day, Y1310).

Trains: **Manzhouli Train Station** (mǎnzhōulǐ huǒchē zhàn; 满洲里火车站), on Yi Nan Daojie, south of the train tracks (☎228 2852, 225 2592, or 225 2661). To: **Beijing** (33hr.; 12:33pm; hard seat Y227, soft sleeper Y800); **Hailar** (3-4½hr., 6 per day, Y12-29); **Harbin** (17hr., 2 per day, Y120); **Qiqihar** (11hr., 9am, Y61). Note that only hard seats and soft sleepers are available for trains originating in Manzhouli. There is also a weekly train to **Moscow** (M 7am; purchase ticket through a travel agency).

Buses: **Manzhouli Long-Distance Bus Station** (mǎnzhōulǐ chángtú qìchē zhàn; 满洲里长途汽车站), at the west end of Yi Daojie. Frequent departures to **Hailar** (3hr., Y26). Useful if you're heading to Hulun Lake, **minibuses** to **Zha Qu** (扎区; 30min., Y3) depart regularly from the square at Si Daojie at Xinhua Lu, in front of Xinhua Bookstore.

Taxis: To any destination on the same side of the railroad tracks Y5; crossing the tracks or going to the train station is an extra Y5.

ORIENTATION AND PRACTICAL INFORMATION

Train tracks to the south and **North Lake Park** (běihú gōngyuán; 北湖公园) to the north define the city center. **Xinhua Lu** (新华路), **Haiguan Lu** (海关路), and **Shizheng Lu** (市政路) run north-south, and a series of numbered (yī, èr, etc.) **Daojie** (道街) stretches east-west; **Yi Daojie** (一道街) is the closest to the train tracks. Everything on the lively northern side of the rail tracks is within walking distance.

Travel Agency: CITS, 35 Er Daojie (☎624 8244 or 624 8276; fax 622 4540), is officially limited to organizing overpriced tours (Y450 and up) for groups of 20 or more. Independent travelers are better off directly contacting Shi Zhouyu (史轴寓), on the 3rd fl. Open M-F 8am-noon and 2:30-5:30pm.

Bank of China: On the corner of San Daojie and Xinhua Lu. Exchanges currency and traveler's checks. Credit card advances M-F 8am-5pm. Open daily summer 8am-noon and 2:30-5:30pm; winter 8am-noon and 2-5pm.

PSB: 39 San Daojie, 2nd fl. (☎626 1050 or 626 1030, visa dept. ext. 7913). **Visa extensions.** Open daily 8am-noon and 2:30-6pm.

Hospital: No. 1 Hospital (dìyī yīyuàn; 第一医院), 14 San Daojie (☎622 2121).

Internet Access: Internet cafe (wǎngbā; 网吧), on Si Daojie between Xinhua Lu and Haiguan Lu. Fast connections. Y3 per hr. Open daily morning-midnight. A few other establishments line the central streets, particularly on Xinhua Lu.

Post and Telecommunications: China Post (☎622 9177), on Haiguan Lu at Si Daojie. EMS, Poste Restante, and IDD service. All packages must go through the **customs office,** which is a taxi ride away. Open summer M-F 8am-6pm, Sa-Su 9am-4pm; winter M-F 8am-5pm, Sa-Su 9am-4pm.

Postal Code: 021400.

ACCOMMODATIONS

Travelers can easily find hotels north of the railroad tracks, particularly on San Daojie. Due to the chilly climate, A/C is rare. Rooms with A/C begin at Y300 in the posh **International Hotel ❹**, 35 Er Daojie (☎622 2225; fax 622 2976). Russian is spoken in all hotels.

Electricity Hotel (diànlì bīnguǎn; 电力宾馆), 1 San Daojie (☎624 8718, 624 8768, or 624 8778), at Shulin Lu. Comfortable, chic rooms, with high ceilings, good lighting, and clean bathrooms. Energetic atmosphere. Includes free access to the popular Banana Club next door. 2-bed dorms with no bath Y30; doubles Y150. ❶

Shipment Training Center Hostel (huànzhuāngsuǒ péixùn zhōngxīn zhāodàisuǒ; 换装所培训中心招待所; ☎225 3729 or 225 2729), on Daokou Lu, north of the railroad tracks (you can see the trains from the door). Large but spartan rooms. Restaurant below. Book ahead in the summer. 4-bed dorms Y16; 3-bed with bath Y61. ❶

Golden Wok Hotel (jīn dìng dàshà; 金锭大厦; ☎624 8532), on the 15th fl., across the street from Electricity Hotel. Large standard doubles with neat bathrooms, though the rooms are not as well lit as Electricity's. Friendly elevator attendee whom you'll appreciate when you travel up and down the 15 floors. Doubles Y150. ❷

Huamei Hotel (huáměi dàshà; 华美大厦), 96 San Daojie (☎622 5225, 622 5224, or 622 5096). Small rooms are sectioned off into corners so that 2 separate rooms can share a bath. Somewhat dark and stale but very functional, with a central location. Massage and beauty salon on lower levels. Doubles Y88. ❷

🌑🎵 FOOD AND ENTERTAINMENT

Despite the city's proximity to Mongolia, Mongolian food is hard to come by. Manzhouli's best cuisine is **Russian,** but that's not saying much—most Russians seem to stick with french fries or steaks. The **International Hotel** cooks a range of options, from southern Chinese on the second floor to cheaper northeastern food on the first floor. If you're willing to pay Y70 for a meal and 2hr. of entertainment, be sure to check out the famous medley of Russian and Chinese performances every night 6-8pm. The eateries on Er Daojie, San Daojie, and Xinhua Lu are also excellent. Seize the opportunity to have an exotic (in China, at least) apple dessert, a roll of fried dough with apple filling (Y2), at the **PECTOPAH PyCb,** 38 San Daojie (☎622 2008). In all establishments, be sure to ask for a Russian menu, or your choices will be limited to Russian-style Chinese cuisine. If you crave more genuine Chinese food, head to the hole-in-the-wall restaurants in the city center.

🌐 SIGHTS

A quick walk through Manzhouli soon proves that the only activities in town are shopping for souvenirs of very questionable Russian origin and admiring the occasional Russian-style buildings. Nearby sights prove to be more entertaining. For many, the call of the wild and the proximity of the **Hulun Buir Grasslands** (hūlún bèi'ěr dàcǎoyuán; 呼伦贝尔大草原) are overpowering. Punctuated by lakes, ridges, and rolling hills, the steppe is home to the Ewenki and Oroqen people in the northeast and a few Han minorities in the south. Mongolian yurt villages further enrich this ethnic and cultural kaleidoscope. Individuals may tell you about staying in "authentic" housing, but it's better to use official companies (see **Travel Agencies,** p. 330). In the winter, most minority-inhabited areas are inaccessible.

▨**HULUN LAKE** (hūlún hú; 呼伦湖). About 90-100km from Manzhouli, the Hulun Lake is a mere 50km from the Mongolian border. For those seeking wild beauty, tourist-free open spaces, and pink quartz-like rocks for souvenirs, the lake is very much worth the long journey. Known locally as **Dalai Lake** (dálài hú; 达赉湖), Hulun is the fifth-largest lake in China. Rare birds inhabit the protected wetlands and grasslands encircling this salt-water lake. During the summer, sunbathers, swimmers, and avid birdwatchers line the shores. A few short months later, ice fishermen battle the bitter cold. Overpriced seafood restaurants cluster near the parking lot of the **hotel** ❺. (☎653 1997; doubles Y360 and up.) It is also possible to arrange a stay in small, one-room log cabins (Y100), located near the end of the row of restaurants lining the crowded beach. According to legend, Genghis Khan once tied his horse to the Horse-Tethering Stake, a rock standing over 20m high on the western bank of the lake. With waves crashing against the abrupt cliffs, the opposite bank offers a different perspective of the seemingly endless Hulun Lake. *(45km southeast of Manzhouli. Take a Y3 minibus to Zha Qu and then a taxi to the lake; taxi should cost Y30 one-way, Y50 round-trip after bargaining. Or take a taxi directly from Manzhouli for Y150–300. From the booth, walk 5min. to reach the beach. Y10, extra Y10 to enter with taxi.)*

SINO-RUSSIAN TRADE AREA (zhōng é hùshì màoyì qū; 中饿互市贸易区). The trade area and Mother Russia, or at least the 50km stretch of shared land between China and Russia, are only a 12km taxi ride away. There's not much to see aside from train tracks, a few monuments, and lots of dirt, but the watchtower does afford beautiful views of the endless grasslands below. *(Y20, students free.)*

▶ DAYTRIP: JIN ZHANG HAN VILLAGE 金帐汗

Take the train or the 3½hr. bus from Manzhouli Long-Distance Bus Station to Hailar. From Hailar, 30min. taxi to Jin Zhang Han Village (round-trip Y110). Open June-Sept. Y10.

Despite the obvious tourist trappings—massive, stylized wooden constructions presumptuously imitating traditional yurts and faux-Mongolian clothing for rent—Jin Zhang Han Village (jīn zhàng hàn; 金帐汗) is redeemed by its beautiful location in the **Hulun Buir grasslands.** Views encompass the vast grasslands, meandering streams, and jagged mountains beyond. Temperatures fall below -40°C in the winter, freezing the steppe in snow and ice. Regardless of the season, it's always a good time to sip Mongolian **milk tea** (nǎi chá; 奶茶 ; Y5), bricks of red tea brewed with salt and mare's milk and fat, while enjoying slabs of mutton (yáng ròu; 羊肉). You can spend the night in a yurt for Y100. Although bathrooms and hot water are lacking, the midnight sky and morning sunrise make up for everything.

You can also stay overnight in **Hailar,** a decidedly more Mongolian city than Manzhouli. Mongolians from far and wide congregate in Hailar mid-July through August for the **Naadam Festival** (see p. 321), a traditional raucous Mongolian festival.

SHANGHAI AND THE YANGZI DELTA

At the tail of the mighty Yangzi River, Shanghai Municipality and Jiangsu and Zhejiang provinces make up China's most densely populated and prosperous region. But to most Chinese, the defining characteristic of the area is something very different: many would inform you that the residents here are China's most shameless penny-pinchers. Perhaps the Yangzi Delta's tight-fisted mentality stems from its centuries-old contact with money, tourists, traders, and luxury goods. Shiploads of silk, ceramics, grains, and imperial riches have traversed the Grand Canal and the extensive network of waterways for centuries. Villages popped up here as early as 5000 years ago, and cities like Suzhou, Wuxi, and Shaoxing have been lively commercial and cultural centers since the 7th and 8th centuries. Hangzhou soared above them all when the Southern Song Dynasty (1127-1279) set up shop by the West Lake and attracted a court of literati. But it would be Shanghai—city of 1930s glam, Westernized mannerisms, and nonstop commercial energy—that would usher the Yangzi region into modernity.

Through all this flow and flux, the people of the Yangzi Delta have managed to hold onto something distinctly theirs. Revolution and urbanization have altered the landscape where China's greatest poets, writers, and artists once thrived, but trade continues to line the pockets of the region's wealthiest residents with money. Still prospering and still energetic, the people here can comfortably and proudly ignore whatever the rest of the nation may say.

HIGHLIGHTS OF THE YANGZI RIVER DELTA

SCOPE THE CROWDS by day on the **Bund** (p. 348), Shanghai's glittering waterfront promenade, and dance the night away on **Maoming Lu** (p. 354).

LOSE YOURSELF in the mazes of **Suzhou's** (p. 366) gardens, full of rocky spires, zig-zagging bridges, rambling waters, and a riot of greenery.

STEP INTO A PAINTING by the willowy shores of Hangzhou's **West Lake** (**P. 395**).

SHANGHAI 上海 ☎021

Shanghai is no stranger to change, with a host of powers sweeping in and out. Once christened the "Paris of the East" by 19th-century European colonists, the city claimed Old World glamor and a well-deserved reputation as China's most free-spirited metropolis. The tumult of world war, civil war, and new CCP rulers pressed the city into a short-lived slumber, but when Deng Xiaoping loosened China's shackles in the 1980s, Shanghai was one of the first to awaken, exploding into a free-market wonder. Skyscrapers leap up faster than Nanjing Lu's designer boutiques can change their window displays, and its young, cell-phone-toting

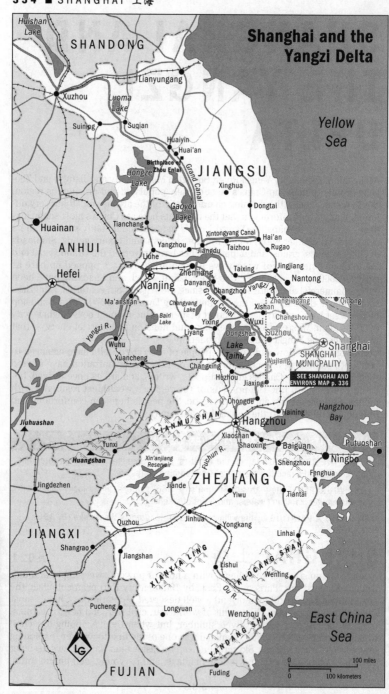

Shanghai and the Yangzi Delta

inhabitants epitomize the youthful energy of a city only just getting started. Take a peek at the city planners' blueprints in the exhibition hall, hear Shanghainese boast of the APEC in 2001 or the upcoming World Expo, and you will feel not only Shanghai's potent presence, but its even more tremendous potential.

The ambition of the city seeps into the lives of its ordinary folks. No one in China is a bigger fan of Shanghai than the Shanghainese themselves—a Shanghainese dialect is the ticket to the club, and outsiders are here to be impressed (or feel lost in the barrage of syllables). To the Shanghainese, change is a point of pride, and nostalgia only a glamorous indulgence. Even today, homesick expats can find something reminiscent of home on its boulevards adorned with intricate European facades and open-air cafes steaming pricey cups of espresso. Elsewhere, incense clouds the temples of this one-time fishing village, and eager hawkers shout out bargain prices over the clamor of crammed-to-bursting markets.

✈ INTERCITY TRANSPORTATION

BY AIR

In October 1999, Shanghai opened its second major airport, **Pudong International Airport,** on the east side of the Huangpu River in the Pudong district. Although both Pudong and **Hongqiao International Airport** currently serve foreign airlines, it is expected that all foreign airlines will eventually operate out of Pudong only. Both airports feature roughly the same design: arrivals are on the lower level and departures on the upper level, with separate check-in areas for international and domestic travelers. Airline counters are generally on the upper level, while hotel, bus, and tourist information can be found on the lower level. For more information on international flights to China, see **Getting to China: By Plane,** p. 34.

For **flight** information, call **Air China** (☎5239 7227), **Air France** (☎6360 6688), **Canadian Airlines** (☎6375 8899), **China Eastern Airlines** (☎6247 2255), **DRAGONAIR** (☎6375 6375), **Japan Airlines** (☎6288 3000), **Lufthansa** (☎5830 4400), **Northwest Airlines** (☎6884 6884), **Shanghai Airlines** (☎6255 0550), **United Airlines** (☎6279 8009), or **Virgin Atlantic** (☎5353 4600).

TO	AIRPORT	PER DAY	PRICE	TO	AIRPORT	PER DAY	PRICE
Beijing	Hongqiao	30	Y1130	Kunming	Hongqiao	6-7	Y1900
Changsha	Pudong	4	Y890	Lanzhou	Hongqiao	2-3	Y1750
Chengdu	Hongqiao	13	Y1610	Lhasa	Hongqiao	1	Y2760
Chongqing	Hongqiao	12	Y1490	Qingdao	Hongqiao	30	Y740
Dalian	Pudong	5-8	Y1060	Sanya	Pudong	5-6	Y1890
Fuzhou	Hongqiao	8-11	Y780	Shenyang	Pudong	8-9	Y1300
Guangzhou	Pudong	43	Y1280	Shenzhen	Pudong	40	Y1400
Guilin	Hongqiao	5-8	Y1300	Tianjin	Hongqiao	6-8	Y1030
Harbin	Pudong	6-7	Y1760	Wuhan	Hongqiao	8-9	Y810
Hefei	Hongqiao	2	Y490	Xiamen	Hongqiao	9-12	Y890
Hong Kong	Pudong	26	Y2660	Xi'an	Hongqiao	9-10	Y1260

HONGQIAO AIRPORT. Hongqiao International Airport (shànghǎi hóngqiáo guójì jīchǎng; 上海虹桥国际机场 ; ☎6268 3659), is about 10km west of Shanghai. The airport handles domestic and international flights to Asia and Southeast Asia. **Luggage storage** (Y5-20 per day) is located beside the No. 1 door of the arrival hall in Terminal A and the No. 3 door of the departure hall in Terminal B. The **tourist center** in the international arrivals lounge offers free maps, brochures, and helpful

advice in Chinese and English. (☎6268 8899, ext. 56750. Open daily 10am-9:30pm.)

A **taxi** ride to central Shanghai (45-90min., depending on traffic) costs Y50-70, but if you go far enough east, you have to pay an extra Y15 toll to take the Yan'an Elevated Rd. **Buses** line up outside the domestic arrivals area. The **airline shuttle** (mínbān zhuānxiàn; 民班专线) goes to the Shanghai Exhibition Hall in central Shanghai. Bus #925 goes to People's Sq., while #941 goes to the train station (1hr., every 20-30min., Y14-36). Bus #1 runs from Hongqiao to Pudong Airport.

PUDONG AIRPORT. Pudong International Airport (pǔdōng guójì jīchǎng; 上海国际机场 ; ☎3848 4500), 30km from downtown Shanghai, is bright and clean. All maps, signs, and announcements are in both Chinese and English. An automated machine to pay the departure tax (Y90) is on the upper level. For a fee, luggage deposit (open 24hr.) will hold your bags for up to 30 days, after which they will be moved to a storage depot.

A **taxi** to the Bund in central Shanghai (45-90min.) averages Y150, not including the Yan'an Elevated Road toll. **Shuttle buses** leave to Central Shanghai and Hongqiao Airport from outside the lower level (every 20-30min.). Bus #1 goes to Hongqiao (Y30); #2 goes to Exhibition Hall in central Shanghai (Y19); #5 goes to Yan'an Zhong Lu and the train station via People's Sq (Y18). Big signs show bus number and the next departure time. Tickets are sold on board.

BY TRAIN

The main train station is **Shanghai Train Station** (shànghǎi huǒchē zhàn; 上海火车站), 330 Moling Lu (☎6354 3193, schedules 6317 9090, toll-free booking 800 820 7890), north of Suzhou Creek, near Tianmu Xi Lu at Hengfeng Lu. Buses #64, 104, 109, and 113 terminate in the station's square near the main Metro entrance. The ticket office is just east of the main square on the southern side of the station. If traveling to Suzhou, Hangzhou, or Wuxi, avoid long lines by buying same-day tickets from the little booth to the right of the security checkpoint (look for the green-and-white Chinese sign). No-nonsense ticket sellers prefer exact change. (English-speaking window at #10. Open daily 6:15am-11:30pm.) Most hotels book tickets with a commission, including the Longmen Hotel just west of the station (commission Y5-10). Some trains depart from the **Shanghai West Train Station** (shànghǎi xī huǒchē zhàn; 上海西火车站), 1 Taopu Lu (☎6214 8479), at the intersection of Jiaotong Lu and Caoyang Lu. Bus #106 connects the two train stations.

The following table provides the departure station, number of trains per day, duration of travel (in hours), and the price (in *yuán*) for all major Chinese cities serviced by trains from Shanghai. Shanghai Main Train Station is indicated by "S," and Shanghai West Train Station by "W." Prices listed range from the cheapest hard seat to the most expensive sleeper. For more information on train types and train travel, see **Trains**, p. 45. Look for "check room" or "left luggage" signs to **store luggage**. Price ranges from Y4-15 depending on size and duration. Lockers are only available inside the security checkpoint for Y15 for the first 12hr., Y30 for the next 12hr., and Y10 more for every 12hr. thereafter.

TO	站	PER DAY	HR.	PRICE
Beijing	S, W	3	15	Y263-281
Changsha	S	1	12-22	Y283-499
Chengdu	S	2	35-40	Y276-499
Chongqing	S	1	38½	Y271-490
Fuzhou	S	1	17½	Y234-249
Guangzhou	S	2	24½	Y208-379
Guilin	S	2	25	Y194-353
Hangzhou	S	16	2-4	Y33-57
Hefei	S	3	9	Y87-162
Hong Kong	S	1	24	Y559-583

TO	站	PER DAY	HR.	PRICE
Huangshan	S	1	11	Y94-175
Kunming	S	2	41-42	Y288-519
Nanjing	S, W	39	3-6	Y41-68
Qingdao	S	1	18	Y170-309
Suzhou	S	35	1	Y13-19
Tianjin	S, W	7	18½	Y165-301
Ürümqi	S	1	46½	Y389-699
Wuhan	S	1	20	Y154-281
Xiamen	S	1	18	Y170-309
Xi'an	S	2	16½	Y182-333

BY BUS

Buses head to destinations along the east coast and beyond. However, this may not be the best way to travel, due to the region's overly congested roads, not to mention the lack of clear signs, maps, and schedules in English (and even in Chinese). There are two main long-distance bus stations, as well as several smaller ones spread throughout the city. Booths at the airport and main train station also handle departures for some destinations within the area.

North District Bus Station (běiqū kèyùn zhàn; 北区客运站), 80 Gonghexin Lu (☎6324 6464), at Zhijiang Lu, handles buses to Anhui, Fujian, Hubei, Hunan, Jiangsu, Shandong, and Zhejiang provinces.

South District Bus Station (nánqū kèyùn zhàn; 南区客运站; ☎6484 7561), Longhua Xi Lu at Zhongshan Nan Er Lu, near the Shanghai Stadium Metro, serves the same destinations as the North District Station.

Shanghai Public Transportation Long-Distance Bus Station (shànghǎi chángtú qìchē zhàn; 上海长途汽车站), 1015 Zhongshan Bei Lu (☎5653 8064), at Hutai Lu, serves Anhui, Jiangsu, and Zhejiang provinces.

Zhijiang Lu Bus Station (zhījiāng lù qìchē zhàn; 芷江路汽车站), 865 Zhijiang Lu (☎5662 6224), has buses to Anhui, Jiangsu, and Zhejiang provinces.

BY BOAT

The **Shiliupu Passenger Terminal** (shíliùpù kèyùn zhàn; 十六铺客运站), 111 Zhongshan Dong Er Lu, is south of the Bund. (☎5657 5500. Open daily 7am-5:30pm.) Bus #64 from the main train station terminates just south of the terminal. Boats depart to Chongqing (4 days, Y200-900), Nanjing (18½hr., Y35-200), Wuhan (60hr., Y60-300), and other ports of call along the Yangzi, but they may be canceled when the water level is high. Slow boats to Putuoshan depart daily at 6pm (13hr., Y92-420).

Boats to Dalian and Guangzhou dock at the **Gongping Lu Passenger Terminal** (gōngpínglù kèyùn zhàn; 公平路客运站), 50 Gongping Lu (☎6326 1261), just south of Daming Dong Lu. Bus #37 from Nanjing Lu stops nearby. The **International Passenger Terminal** (guójì kèyùn zhàn; 国际客运站), 100 Yangshuipu Lu, is not far beyond the point where Suzhou Creek empties into the Huangpu River. The **Passage Booking Office of the Port of Shanghai** (shànghǎi gǎng chuánpiào chù; 上海港船票处), 1 Jinling Dong Lu, just across the street from the main CITS office, sells tickets to boats sailing to Osaka and Yokohama, Japan. (☎6595 7788 or 5657 5500. Open daily 7-11:30am and 12:30-5pm.) All tickets are sold at the Jinling Lu office; domestic service is on the first floor, while international is on the second floor.

Central Shanghai

🏠 ACCOMMODATIONS

Captain Hostel, 16	E3
Education Hotel, 4	B4
International Center for Cultural	
Exchange, 21	F1
Love Inn, 5	C1
Pujiang Hotel, 22	F2
Shengxianju Hotel, 8	D1
Star of the Sea Conch	
Hotel, 17	E4
Wugong Hotel, 15	E3
YMCA Hotel, 12	D4
Zhongbai Hotel, 9	D3
Zhongya Hotel, 6	C1

Shanghai Train Station

Foreign Language Bookstore

TRAIN STATION

静安 JING'AN

Tianmu Xi Lu

HANZHONG LU 汉中路

Jade Buddha Temple 安远路

Anyuan Lu

Haifang Lu

昌化路 Changhua Lu

江宁路 Jiangning Lu

Children's Hospital

Changping Lu 昌平路

陕西北路 Shaanxi Bei Lu

康定路 Kangding Lu

Xikang Lu 西康路

Xinzha Lu

新闸路

泰兴路 Taixing Lu

Xinxia Lu

Central District Hospital

Beijing Xi Lu

Majestic Theatre

北京西路

石门一路 SHIMEN YI LU

南京西路 Nanjing Zhong Lu

CITS 上海商场 Shanghai Centre

南京西路

Wujiang Lu (Food Street)

石门二路 Shimen Er Lu

成都北路 Chengdu Bei Lu

AMEX Shanghai Exhibition Centre

Weihai Lu

威海路

Jing'an Temple 静安寺

TO ✈ HONGQIAO AIRPORT (10km)

万航渡路 Wanhangdu Lu

Nanjing Xi Lu

JING'AN TEMPLE 静安寺

Yan'an Xi Lu

Yan'an Zhong Lu

延安中路

CTS

巨鹿路

新乐路 Xinle Lu

Huahan Lu

Huanshan Hospital

Julu Lu

Shanghai No. 3 Hospital 长乐路

Xiangyang Park 襄阳公园

Julu Lu

Changshu Lu 常熟路

Changle Lu

FORMER FRENCH CONCESSION

Changle Lu

陕西南路 SHAANXI NAN LU

瑞金一路 Ruijin Yi Lu

Nanchang Lu 南昌路

复兴公园 Fuxing Park

复兴西路 Fuxing Xi Lu

Huaihai Zhong Lu

淮海中路

Conservatory of Music

陕西南路 CHANGSHU

茂名南路 Maoming Nan Lu

Sun Yat-sen's Former Residence

US Consulate

Shanghai Library

TO SONG QINGLING'S FORMER RESIDENCE (600m)

Hengshan 衡山路

复兴中路 Fuxing Zhong Lu

Zhou Enlai's Former Residence

HENGSHAN

Yueyang Hospital 岳阳医院

Flower Market

瑞金二路 Ruijin Er Lu

思南路 Sinan Lu

Ruijin Hospital

重庆南路 Chongqing Nan Lu

He

Yongjia Lu

Wulumuqi Nan Lu 乌鲁木齐南路

Yueyang Lu 岳阳路

太原路 Taiyuan Lu

襄阳南路 Xiangyang Nan Lu

陕西南路 Shaanxi Nan Lu

建国东路 Jianguo

Jianguo Dong Lu

Xujia

Zhaojiabang Lu 肇嘉浜路

Liyuan Lu

丽园路

肇家浜路

重庆南路

大浦路 Dapu Lu

鲁班路 Luban Lu

Liyu

Shanghai Medical University

Pediatric Hospital

枫林路 Fenglin Lu

小木桥路 Xiaomuqiao Lu

Damaqiao Lu 大马桥路

Xietu Lu

Ruijin Nan Lu 瑞金南路

Dapu Lu 大浦路

斜土路

N

0   400 yards

0   400 meters

SHANGHAI

SHANGHAI

FOOD

Badlands, **2**	B4
FAD, **14**	E3
Fengyu Shengjian, **13**	D5
Gino Cafe, **3**	B4
Gongdelin Vegetarian Restaurant, **10**	D3
Little Fat Lamb Hotpot, **1**	B2
Nanxiang Steamed Buns, **20**	E4
Old City Mid-Lake Pavilion Tea House, **19**	E4
Sichuan Water-Cooked-Fish Restaurant, **7**	C4
Songyue Lou Vegetarian Restaurant, **18**	E4
Yunnan Garden, **11**	D3

⚡ ORIENTATION

Shanghai occupies the southern portion of the Yangzi Delta, bordered by the East China Sea to the east, Jiangsu province to the northwest, and Zhejiang province to the southwest. Although Shanghai Municipality is vast—almost 6000km^2—most of Shanghai's sights and residents are found in the much smaller district known as Shanghai proper or **Central Shanghai**. In Central Shanghai, the **Bund** (wàitān; 外滩), a 1.5km waterfront promenade, runs parallel to **Zhongshan Dong Lu** (中山东路) and intersects **Nanjing Lu** (南京路) in front of the Peace Hotel. A veritable circus of shops, fast-food restaurants, offices, and pedestrians, Nanjing Lu runs west for 6km before arriving at **Shanghai Centre** (shànghǎi shāngchǎng; 上海商场), the home of upscale shops, expats, and the Portman Ritz-Carlton.

The former French Concession, anchored by **Huaihai Zhong Lu** (淮海中路) and lined with several Metro stops, runs west from the Bund and has trendy shops and clubs. Zhongshan Lu circles much of Central Shanghai, changing name as it slips across the river into the Special Economic Zone of **Pudong** (浦东). The **Old Chinese City**, circled by **Renmin Lu** (人民路) and **Zhonghua Lu** (中华路), is home to the Yuyuan Garden and Bazaar. A confusing array of narrow, winding streets makes traveling on foot the best way to get around this area.

Western Shanghai contains few places of tourist interest and is reputed to be somewhat unsafe. But if the stadium complex and nearby industrial areas inspire curiosity, Metro line #1 has several stops in the area. North of Suzhou Creek and beyond Hongkou Park, the surroundings become more industrial, much like the area around the main train station. Fudan University at **Wujiaochang** (五角场), has cheap food and drinks. Chinese maps (Y3-8) are widely available, and bilingual maps (Y6-15) can be bought from foreign-language bookstores and street vendors.

⊟ LOCAL TRANSPORTATION

BY BUS. When tackling the behemoth of Shanghai's bus system, only a small percentage of bus lines is relevant to the traveler; the rest comb residential neighborhoods. Although it's impossible to find a bilingual bus map, most city buses have English announcements at every stop. The newer buses even scroll the English names of stops electronically above the driver. Bus stop signs show operating times, names of stops along the route, and the direction the bus is going. Buses start disappearing around 10pm, after which taxis are the best alternative. The chart below details some of the most important buses.

BUS #	ROUTE DESCRIPTION	BUS #	ROUTE DESCRIPTION
18	Lu Xun Park-People's Sq. (by Fuzhou Lu)	20, 37	Nanjing Lu-People's Sq.
42, 126, 926	Bund down Huaihai Lu-Library-Stadium	64	Shiliupu Terminal-Bund-Main Train Station
113	Main Train Station-Huaihai Lu	917	Nanjing Lu-People's Sq.-Shanghai Centre
923	Main Train Station-Jingan Temple-Nanpu Bridge	930	Main Train Station-Yuyuan Area

Fares are usually flat; most buses cost Y1, with A/C Y2 (indicated by a snowflake beside the route number). Fares on double-decker buses heading to more distant corners of the city (such as #910 to Wujiaochang) depend on the destination (Y1-5). There will be a circulating fare collector who can provide change, but paying with anything higher than a Y10 bill might not trigger a warm reaction. Some buses have collection boxes in front of the bus driver that require exact change.

Faster and more comfortable **minibuses** also ply many of the same routes as the buses. To catch one, wait at the regular bus stop and shout out your destination as unmarked minibuses slowly cruise past (often with a tout hanging out an open door). Prices vary, but Y2-5 is reasonable.

BY METRO. The Shanghai Metro is one of the world's few subways with velvet cordons. Clean, speedy trains serve the hub of the city on three lines. Another three new lines extending to the outskirts of the city are in the works. All stations have manned ticket booths and ticket vending machines, which only take small bills. Announcements and signs are in both Chinese and English.

Line #1 runs south from the main train station, underneath People's Sq. and along Huaihai Zhong Lu, before ending in Xinzhuang. (Open 5am-11pm.) When completed, **Line #2** will run from Hongqiao to Pudong airports. As of August 2004, it only runs from Zhangjiang High Tech Park, in the south of Pudong district, to Zhongshan Xi Lu, west of the French Concession. (Open 7am-8pm.) The Longyang Lu stop connects with airport bus #3 to Pudong Airport. Half circling central Shanghai, the **Pearl Line,** or elevated line, is entirely done up in chrome and serves the main train station, stadium, and the west train station. Fares on all three lines range Y2-5; route maps at ticket vending machines show fares to specific stops. While it's possible to transfer from Line #1 to #2 with the same fare card, a new ticket is required for the Pearl Line. Monthly pass for the Pearl Line is Y50. To jet off in style, shell out Y50 and the **Maglev** will whip you from the Longyang Lu station to Pudong Airport in seven blurry minutes. (Every 30min., round-trip Y80.)

BY TAXI. Taxis are a convenient and generally hassle-free alternative to public transportation. Base fare is Y10, each additional kilometer Y2 (after 10km Y3); from 11pm to 5am, base fare is Y13. Taxis rule the streets after public transportation shuts down. Major cab companies operating 24hr. include the sherbet-green **Dazhong Taxi** (dàzhòng chūzū qìchē; 大众出租汽车; ☎96822), and the yellow **Shanghai Qiangsheng Taxi** (shànghǎi qiángshēng chūzū qìchē; 上海强生出租汽车; ☎6258 0000). The **complaint hotline** for taxis (save your receipt) is ☎6323 2150.

⁊ PRACTICAL INFORMATION

TOURIST AND FINANCIAL SERVICES

Tourist Hotline: The **Hotline for Tourist Consultancy** (☎6439 3615) gives advice and information in Chinese and English. Open daily 8:30am-8:30pm, English after 9am.

Tours: CITS and CTS offer various guided tours, including visits to family apartments and local schools as well as main tourist attractions. For those who want more transportation flexibility, **Shanghai Tour Bus Lines** (☎6426 5555), based at Shanghai Stadium, has 10 lines to sights within the city proper as well as the outer counties. Bus #1 to Songjiang district; #3 to the Pearl Tower and Pudong sights; #4 to the Shanghai Zoo and Zhujiajiao; #6A to the Jiading district; #7 to Shanghai Library, Shanghai Museum, and all the sights in the former French Concession; #9 to Wuxi and Lingshan; and #10 to the tourist attractions in the city center.

Travel Agencies: CITS, Guangming Bldg., 2 Jinling Dong Lu (☎6323 8770 or 6323 8749), near the Bund's southern end, a block south of Yan'an Lu. Open daily 9am-5:30pm, train ticket purchase until 4:30pm. Another **branch,** 1277 Beijing Xi Lu (☎6289 8899). Open daily 9am-noon and 1-5:30pm. **CTS,** 129 Yan'an Zhong Lu (☎6248 3330). Open daily 8:30-11:30am and 1:30-5pm.

Consulates: See **Essentials: Consular Services in China,** p. 10.

SHANGHAI

TALL TALES

"Going under the knife" just doesn't cut it any more as a phrase describing plastic surgery: women all over China are having their legs broken for beauty. The increasingly popular procedure, known as "growth surgery," is designed to make patients 3 to 10cm taller. During the procedure, the patient's tibia (shin bone) is broken so that 27cm-long steel pins may be inserted and attached to a metal frame by screws. Over the next 4-6 months, the screws are tightened little by little to lengthen the bone. The procedure costs upwards of Y20,000 and carries significant risk. The *Shenzhen Daily News* reported in June 2004 that a 20-year-old woman in Zhuhai became unable to walk as the result of a growth surgery aiming to add 10cm to her 1.48m height.

Over the past 10 years, there have been more than 200,000 malpractice lawsuits filed because of faulty cosmetic operations. Despite the risk and the pain of recovery, the procedure is gaining popularity. Vanity is not the only reason: Chinese society values height in some surprisingly institutionalized ways. Many schools require their female applicants to be taller than 5'1", driving tests often call for people 5'3" or taller, and job advertisements may list height as a criterion. Cosmetic surgery is a way to improve one's lot in life: when there are 1.3 billion people in your country, it helps to stand out.

Bank of China: 23 Zhongshan Yi Lu (☎6529 9556), on the Bund. Exchanges currency and traveler's checks. Open daily 9am-4:30pm.

ATM: Just about every ATM is connected to Cirrus and V/Plus networks. **Citibank** has 2 ATMs (Cirrus/DC/Plus/V) in Shanghai: 1 conveniently close to the Bund, 19 Zhongshan Yi Lu, and 1 across the river in Pudong, in the Marine Tower, 1 Pudong Dadao. Most banks, shopping centers, and hotels have ATMs. Bank of China will give cash advances on credit cards; be sure to bring your passport.

American Express: 1333 Nanjing Xi Lu (☎6426 7317). Card replacements and mail holding. Open daily 9am-5:30pm.

LOCAL SERVICES

Bookstores: Shanghai Foreign-Language Bookstore (shànghǎi wàiwén shūdiàn; 上海外文书店), 390 Fuzhou Lu (☎6322 3200, ext. 231), a block east of Fujian Lu. A paltry selection of travel books, maps, and paperbacks. Expat magazines may include 10% discount coupons. Open Su-Th 9:30am-6pm and F-Sa 9:30am-7pm. **Shanghai Book City** (shànghǎi shūchéng; 上海书城), 465 Fuzhou Lu (☎6352 2222), has several branches around town. This megastore has mostly Chinese books, but also an impressive section of imports (mostly in English) for Y12-20. Open daily 9am-9pm.

Library: Shanghai Library (shànghǎi túshūguǎn; 上海图书馆), 1550 Huaihai Zhong Lu (☎6445 5555). Over 13 million volumes. Internet available. Passport and proof of long-term residency required for foreign students to enter. Temporary card grants access but not check-out, Y10 per month; library card Y50 per year, deposit Y1000. Most rooms open daily 8:30am-8:30pm; apply for new cards 8:30am-4:30pm.

Ticket Agencies: Shanghai Centre Theatre Ticket Office (shànghǎi shāngchéng jùcháng shòupiào chù; 上海商城剧场售票处), 1376 Nanjing Xi Lu (☎6279 8606), just right of the main entrance. Sells tickets for performances at Shanghai Centre, the Music Hall, and other venues. Open daily 9am-7:30pm. The **Shanghai Grand Theatre** has several reservation offices around town selling tickets for cultural events. Main office on the lower level of the theater, 300 Renmin Dadao (☎6372 8701), on the edge of People's Sq., next to the exit of the underpass. Open daily 9am-7:30pm. Soccer fans can try for tickets to matches at the **Shanghai Sport Stadium** (☎6438 5200), but games are usually sold out far in advance. Open daily 8:30am-5pm.

Markets: Lianhua Supermarket (liánhuá chāoshì; 联华超市), with a branch at Fuzhou Lu at Zhejiang Lu, has a decent but slightly pricey selection of Western food. Open daily 8am-9pm. A better choice, **Jiadeli** (jiā dé lì;家得利) has locations on Wulumuqi Lu and at 245 Zhapu Lu. Open daily 8:30am-10:30pm. **Kedi** (kědi; 可的), a 24hr. convenience store, has many **branches,** including Henan Zhong Lu at Ningbo Lu.

Weather Conditions: ☎121.

EMERGENCY AND COMMUNICATIONS

Pharmacies: Shanghai No. 1 Dispensary Co. (shànghǎi shì dìyī yīyào shāngdiàn; 上海市第一医药商店), 616 Nanjing Dong Lu (☎6322 4567), a few blocks east of Xizang Lu, near Zhejiang Lu at Nanjing Dong Lu. Several floors of Western and Chinese medicines and 24hr. emergency service. Open daily 9am-10pm. **Watson's,** the Hong Kong pharmacy chain, sells Western over-the-counter medicine. Locations include on the 1st fl. of Shanghai Centre and in the Pudong Airport. Open daily 9am-10pm.

Hospitals: Huashan Hospital (huáshān yīyuàn; 华山医院), 430 Huashan Lu (☎6248 9999, ext. 1921). The **Worldwide Medical Center,** 1068 Changle Lu (☎6248 3986), caters especially to foreigners. **No. 9 People's Hospital** (dìjiǔ rénmín yīyuàn; 第九人民医院), 639 Zhizaoju Lu (☎6313 8341). **WorldLink Medical Centers,** Shanghai Centre, 1376 Nanjing Xi Lu, Ste. 203 (☎6279 7688), specializes in non-emergency expat medical care. English speaking doctors offer 24hr. care for members; for non-members M-F 9am-7pm, Sa 9am-4pm, Su 9am-3pm. Nurses available after hours. **New Pioneer International Medical Centre,** 252 Xikang Lu (☎6407 3898), provides 24hr. medical and dental services.

Telephones: China Telecom, 547 Tianmu Xi Lu (☎6321 1001), just west of the Peace Hotel, a half-block from the Bund. Open daily 8:30am-8pm. Most hotels now have IDD/DDD phones; many offer free local calls.

Internet Access: Internet cafes are everywhere. Look into any shop with a huge sign marked "网吧" in the front, and bring a photo ID. Average rates Y3-5 per hr. **China Telecom** sells Internet cards (Y50 per 20hr., occasional offers of Y20 per 15hr.) for computers in their Nanjing Dong Lu office and other branches. Open daily 7am-10:30pm. **Hola.net.coffee,** 333 Tangren Lu (☎6247 5559). Y4 per hr. Open daily 9am-2pm.

Post Office: The **main post office,** 1 Sichuan Bei Lu, between Tiantong Lu and Bei Suzhou Lu, just north of Suzhou Creek. Open daily 7:30am-10pm. **Western Union.** International service, including EMS (☎6393 6666); open daily 9am-5pm. Poste Restante at counter #17 from the Tiantong Lu entrance; open daily 8-11:30am and 1-5pm. A branch, 276 Suzhou Bei Lu (☎6393 6666). Open daily 7am-7pm.

Private Courier: DHL Worldwide Express has several locations around town, including one at Shanghai Centre, 1376 Nanjing Xi Lu, B02 (☎6536 2900). Open M-Sa 8:30am-6pm. Pick-up service available; call ahead.

Postal Code: 200085.

▐ ACCOMMODATIONS

Many of the city's accommodations cater to business travelers or tour groups, and rates tend to be high, especially along Nanjing Lu and in other central locations. A number of small places around the train station offer cheap rooms but almost always refuse foreigners. A new breed of lodgings called "holiday hotels" (jiàrì bīnguǎn; 假日宾馆) is springing up all over the city and caters to wealthy Chinese families. Their central location, quality rooms, and affordable prices make them worthwhile alternatives to the hard-to-find dorms. Most hotels have laundry service and will book train and plane tickets.

CITY CENTER (THE BUND AND NANJING LU)

Pujiang Hotel (pǔjiāng fàndiàn; 浦江饭店), 15 Huangpu Lu (☎6324 6388; www.pujianghotel.com), across Suzhou Creek from the Bund. Take bus #64 from the main train station stops on Beijing Dong Lu at Jiangxi Zhong Lu. Continue along Beijing Dong Lu until you reach the Bund, then take a left and cross Waibaidu Bridge. Pujiang is on the 1st street on the right. High ceilings, hardwood floors, and etched glass windows whisper its past as one of the first and most luxurious Western hotels in China. Originally built in 1854, it housed China's first lightbulb and telephone. As one might expect, rooms are clean and well kept. A/C, lockers in some rooms (key deposit Y100). Luggage storage Y2 per bag per day. 8- to 12-bed dorms (many with baths) Y70; 5-bed Y100; doubles with bath Y420. Try to score room #507 to experience Shanghai's 1930s elegance. Albert Einstein's room Y880. AmEx/DC/MC/V. ❶

Captain Hostel (HI) (chuánzhǎng qīngnián jiǔdiàn; 船长青年酒店), 37 Fuzhou Lu (☎6323 5053; www.captainhostel.com.cn). Take bus #64 from the train station to Beijing Dong Lu at Jiangxi Zhong Lu. Walk toward the Bund; take a right on Zhongshan Lu and another right on Fuzhou Lu. True to the nautical spirit, rooms look like cabins and staff sport sailor suits. Dorms are fully sea-going with mini-port holes and "Sailor Bunks" in light wood. Shared bath (bring your own toilet paper), self-service laundry, 24hr. hot water (great water pressure!). Take in the sunshine on the rooftop bar. Bike rental Y10 per 4hr., deposit Y200. Internet Y5 per 15min. Luggage storage Y1 per day per piece. Locker deposit Y100. 5- or 10-bed dorms Y60, HI members Y55; doubles Y400 plus 10% service charge. AmEx/DC/MC/V. ❶

YMCA Hotel (qīngnián huì bīnguǎn; 青年会宾馆), 123 Xizang Nan Lu (☎6326 1040; www.ymcahotel.com), between Jinling Lu and Yan'an Lu, overlooking People's Sq. Dorms feature dense mattresses, spotless bathrooms, and central A/C. Vigilant staff and well-lit corridors. Currency exchange and ticket booking. Internet Y1 per min. 4-bed dorms Y125; singles Y455; doubles Y530. 10% service charge. AmEx/DC/MC/V. ❷

Wugong Hotel (wúgōng dàjiǔdiàn; 吴宫大酒店), 431 Fuzhou Lu (☎6326 0303), at Fujian Zhong Lu, about halfway between the Bund and People's Sq. Great location in the hubbub of city proper. Spacious rooms with appealingly sophisticated decor. TV, 24hr. hot water, standing showers, and A/C. Ticket booking service. Breakfast included. Doubles Y280-500; extra bed Y66. AmEx/DC/MC/V. ❹

Education Hotel (jiàoyù bīnguǎn; 教育宾馆), 3 Fengyang Lu (☎6466 3147; fax 6466 3149), near Huaihai Zhong Lu. This friendly hotel offers 47 quiet and clean rooms with hard beds. Other perks include A/C, fridge, dry cleaning service, free local calls, and breakfast included. Deposit Y100. Economy rooms without bath Y200; standard doubles Y380 (bargain to Y280); extra bed Y100. ❸

Star of the Sea Conch Hotel (hǎiluó zhī xīng jiàrì jiǔdiàn; 海螺之星假日酒店), 491 Jinling Dong Lu (☎6328 7070; conchstar@citiz.net). From People's Sq., walk toward the Bund (east) on Yan'an Lu; turn right and walk a block on Yongshou Lu; the hotel is on Jinling Lu at Yongshou Lu. Proximity to the Bund may make up for dim, smoke-scented rooms. Bath, A/C, TV, and IDD phones. Doubles Y248-278. 20% discount. ❸

Zhongbai Hotel (zhōngbǎi dàjiǔdiàn; 终百大酒店), 462 Xizang Zhong Lu (☎6360 9898; fax 6351 0146). Near People's Sq., at Xizang Lu and Nanjing Dong Lu. Lobby on the 3rd fl. Central location, but bony mattress, spotted carpet, and windowless rooms. A/C, TV, IDD/DDD phones, and bath. Singles Y200-250; doubles Y258, with windows Y280; triples Y340. ❸

OUTSIDE OF CITY CENTER

International Center for Cultural Exchange SISU/Shangwai Hotel (shàngwài bīnguǎn; 上外宾馆), 555 Chifeng Lu (☎6531 8882; fax 6544 8106), 1 block east of the Chifeng Lu station on the Pearl Line. Take bus #15 from the train station. Nearby public transportation redeems the considerable distance from the city center. Heavy drapes, good beds, and bath in every room. English-speaking staff. A/C, bath, free self-service laundry, and IDD/DDD phones with free local calls. Bowling alley. 24hr. convenience store. Make reservations 2-3 days in advance. Doubles Y172-286; extra bed Y50. Student discount 20%. AmEx/DC/MC/V. ❷

Love Inn (héjiāhuān jiàrì bīnguǎn; 合家欢假日宾馆), 1555 Zhongxing Lu (☎5672 2998; happyb@online.sh.cn), less than 5min. from the north entrance of the main train station. A modern oasis among northern Shanghai's stacked shacks and industrial haze. Dusty corridors and peeling wallpapers lead to clean and spacious rooms. Bath, TV, and IDD/DDD phones. Chinese-style breakfast included. Remote-controlled A/C. Singles Y129; doubles Y189; triples Y159; extra bed Y40. Y50-90 discounts. ❷

Zhongya Hotel (zhōngyà fàndiàn; 中亚饭店), 330 Meiyuan Lu (☎6317 2317), near the main train station, down a tunnel at Tianmu Xi Lu. Tidy, roomy doubles but small baths. A/C, Internet, cable TV, and IDD, as well as access to a ticket-booking agent, sauna, salon, night club, and billiards room. Singles Y260-480; doubles Y260-500. 10% service charge. Ask for 35% discount. MC/V. ❹

Shengxianju Hotel (shèngxián jū bīnguǎn; 圣贤居宾馆), 1032 Zhongxing Lu (☎5662 9157). Take bus #928 or 929 from the train station to the next stop. Continue down the street; it's little more than a block away on the right. Neat rooms show slight signs of age. Toiletry collection features bath salts, razors, and shaving cream. Doubles Y388-438. Perennial 20% discount, but be bold and try for more. ❺

FOOD

Good food starts in Shanghai's rooftop steakhouses and ends in its steamy, packed alleys. Grilled meats from Xinjiang, rice noodles from Guilin, popsicles from Inner Mongolia, and Shanghai's own small **pan-fried buns** (shēng jiān; 生煎) all meet up in the numerous food courts (xiǎo chī diàn; 小吃店). Customers can point to what they like through the kitchen windows displaying noodles, **soup-filled meat buns** (xiǎo lóng bāo; 小笼包; Y4-5 per dozen), wonton soup (húntún tāng; 馄饨汤; check for clean bowls), and **spareribs with rice cakes** (páigǔ niángāo; 排骨年糕).

The side streets around People's Sq. host street stalls and sit-down eateries. From Yan'an Dong Lu to Jinling Dong Lu, **Yunnan Lu Food Street** (yúnnán lù měishí jiē; 云南路美食街) sees restaurant hoppers until midnight. Chinese fast food can be found on **Sha Market Food Street** (shāshì shíjiē; 沙市食街), running south from Jiujiang Lu. **Zhapu Lu Food Street,** north of Suzhou Creek and east of Sichuan Bei Lu, sells dumplings, buns (Y1 for 5), and **fried pancakes** (jiān bǐng; 煎饼; Y1.5-2). On Wujiang Lu, right outside the Metro stop at Shimen Yi Lu (石门一路), vendors pat rounds of dough to make sesame-studded **Xinjiang-style flatbread** (Y0.3-0.7).

Dim sum makes its presence felt throughout Shanghai with the many branches of ▨ **Bi Feng Tang** ❷ (bì fēng táng; 避风塘), 1 Hongqiao Lu, fifth floor of the Ganghui Plaza outside the Xujiahui Metro stop. All dim sum items are Y6 per plate during the weekday lunch special (11:30am-4pm). Succulent prawns inside translucent rice flour skins (xiā jiǎo; 虾饺), taro balls cocooned in sweet dough, and golden fried pigeon (Y38) are delicious options. (Branches at 1717 Nanjing Xi Lu, 2nd fl., and 98 Huaihai Zhong Lu. ☎6447 8677. Open daily 11am-10pm. Credit cards accepted.) For award-winning delicacies in national culinary competitions, head to the **Yuyuan Gardens and Bazaar.** Open markets sell **sticky rice balls** stuffed with sweet sesame paste (tāng yuán; 汤圆 ; Y3-5 for 10), while century-old restaurants offer duck tongues (yā shé; 鸭舌 ; Y10-20), among other fancy dishes.

NANJING LU AND ENVIRONS

Pedestrians on Nanjing Lu, the ritzy promenade near People's Sq., cool down from the heat with iced mung bean drinks and cantaloupe-on-a-stick. Restaurants serve local fare on **Huanghe Lu,** between Nanjing Lu and Beijing Lu, north of People's Park. The residential area around **Wulumuqi Zhong Lu** sees markets and vendors.

Gongdelin Vegetarian Restaurant (gōngdélín sù shí chù; 功德林素食处), 445 Nanjing Xi Lu (☎6327 0218). Turn your karma around by feasting on Gongdelin's famed vegetarian dishes. A little shrine is home to a smirking Buddha, while incense wafts throughout. With a few clever tricks, tofu, mushrooms, and bamboo transform into meats and seafood. Most entrees ("saute-shaped hair vegetable ball" and delicious "crab") Y15-45. Cold dishes Y7-14. Fermented sticky rice Y14. Jujube and pumpkin Y12. Open daily 6:30-9:45am, 11am-4pm, and 5-9:30pm (stir-fried dishes until 9pm). ❷

Yunnan Garden (yúnnán měishí yuán; 云南美食园), 268 Xizang Zhong Lu (☎6340 3076), in the Raffles City Plaza next to People's Sq. The Across-the-Bridge Noodle (guò qiáo mǐxiàn; 过桥米线 ; Y15) served here is a close rival to that in Yunnan (p. 646). Savory broth made each morning with free-range chicken, snake, bamboo, dozens of herbs, and a secret recipe. Stir the rice noodles into the piping hot soup, top it with 12 saucers of ingredients (from quail eggs to bean sprouts), and slurp away. Other Yunnan-style dishes Y10-35. Open daily 10am-9pm. ❷

FAD (xiān guǒ fāng; 鲜果坊), 500 Nanjing Dong Lu (☎6322 3921), right across from the Hotel Sofitel, on the 2nd fl. Delectable fresh and fruity concoctions, from mango pudding (Y20) to large dishes of seasonal fruits to smoothies with tapioca pearls (Y38). Dumplings and sandwiches (Y18 and up). Great service and an intimate escape from the din below. Open daily 10am-midnight. ❷

OLD CHINESE CITY AREA

Kiosks inside **Yuyuan Commercial City** scoop out large bowls of wonton soup (Y8), soup-filled stuffed buns (crabmeat Y15 per dozen, vegetable Y1 per bun), and other small delights (xiǎochī; 小吃) that are large enough to be meals. Those willing to shell out a bit more can enjoy century-old recipes and A/C.

🏶 **Nanxiang Steamed Buns** (nánxiáng mántóu diàn; 南翔馒头店), 85 Yuyuan Lu (☎6355 4206 or 6326 5265), across from the Mid-Lake Pavilion Tea House. Renowned for its tiny xiǎo lóng bāo (Y8 for 16, with crabmeat Y15), Nanxiang has a perpetual line outside its take-out window. Popular restaurant upstairs serves set meals consisting of a potpourri of tiny buns and soups. Reserve a day ahead. Open daily 8am-10pm. ❷

Songyue Lou Vegetarian Restaurant (chūnfēng sōngyuè lóu; 春风松月楼), 23 Bailin Lu (☎6355 3630), a small block down the street from Mid-Lake Tea Shop. Since 1920, vegetarians and gourmet lovers alike have alighted here for its "vegetable assorted noodles" (sù miàn; 素面; Y8), with a delicious sauce of fungi and tubers. Side take-out window sells vegetable and mushroom-filled buns (Y1) and shaved ice with sweet red beans (Y2). Entrees Y5-20. Open daily 8am-9:30pm. ❶

Old City Mid-Lake Pavilion Tea House (shànghǎi lǎochéng húxīntíng chálóu; 上海老城湖心亭茶楼), 257 Yuyuan Lu (☎6373 6950). In a pagoda over the pond, the most famous tea shop in town plays to both world leaders (Bill Clinton and Queen Elizabeth) and to tourists. Popular brews like green and jasmine come by the pot on the lower level (Y15-25). More exotic concoctions, some requiring special brewing methods and teaware, are upstairs (Y40 and up per cup). Shows (F-Su until 9:30pm) featuring traditional music or tea ceremonies are usually scheduled by large tour groups, but with a cup of tea and an extra seat, you can watch as well. Open daily 8am-10pm. ❷

Chang'an Dumplings (cháng'ān jiǎozi guǎn; 长安饺子馆), 279 Nong, Ninghai Dong Lu (☎6374 4034). 108 kinds of dumplings from the bizarre (taro or amphibian) to the traditional fillings. Personalized dumpling for a fee. Huge set meals on the 1st fl. for 2-10 people (Y20 and up), with more stylish (and expensive) dining on the 2nd fl. 1st fl. open daily 6am-2am; 2nd fl. 11am-2pm and 5-9pm. ❷

FORMER FRENCH CONCESSION

Street vendors aren't as numerous here as elsewhere. The **No. 2 Food Market,** on Huaihai Zhong Lu at Shaanxi Lu, sells dried plums, squid, beef—you name it—as well as Chinese pastries, prepared poultry, vegetables, and pig ears. (Open daily 8am-9pm.) Numerous **hotpot** spots park along Huaihai Zhong Lu.

Fengyu Shengjian (fēng yù shēng jiān; 丰裕生煎), 485 Jianguo Dong Lu, (☎6386 9891) near its intersection at Huangpi Nan Lu. The small, pan-fried buns (shēngjiān; 生煎 ; Y1.8 for 4), with fluffy flour skin and tasty meat and broth filling top everything else on the menu. Noodles, soups, and rice with sauces (Y3-8). More gourmet options like crab and tofu stew (Y16; 白蟹豆腐煲). Branches all over. Open daily 7am-10pm. ❶

Sichuan Water-Cooked-Fish Restaurant (bāshān shǔguó shuǐzhǔyú jiǔlóu; 巴山蜀国水煮鱼酒楼), 41 Sinan Lu (☎5306 5777), on the corner of Fuxing Lu. Delicious and fiery dishes of authentic Sichuanese cuisine. Despite the bland-sounding name, the water-cooked fish (Y29) is braised to tender perfection in a tongue-tingling soup of hot chili peppers. For the choicest part of the creature, try the classic fish head simmered in an earthenware pot (Y38). Open daily 10am-9pm. ❸

Little Fat Lamb Hotpot (xiǎo féi yáng huǒguō; 小肥羊火锅), 777 Jiangning Lu (☎5289 1717), down the street from and south of Jade Buddha Temple. The delicious broth and fresh ingredients explain this hotpot sensation's success throughout China. A whole page of ingredients in small print promises adventurous picks. Thin slices of lamb (Y8) and egg dumplings are staple favorites. Shrimp squirming on a stick (Y16) is rather macabre. Broth Y30-40. Branches on 169 Nandan Lu and 33 Caobao Lu, both in Xujiahui. Open daily 10am-9:30pm. ❸

Gino Cafe (jìnuò yìdàlì xiūxián cāntīng; 季诺意大利休闲餐厅), 918 Huaihai Zhong Lu (☎6415 5245), in the Parkson Shopping Center at Shaanxi Nan Lu. This wanna-be *ristorante* betrays itself with yuppie Chinese clientele and pizzas (Y30-40) sporting bizarre toppings of shrimp or green beans. Still, the casual atmosphere, tasty Italian food (salads and minestrone both Y15 and up), and caffeinated drinks make this place a relaxing stop. **Branches** right across from the Shanghai Times Sq. on Huaihai Zhong Lu, and at 66 Nanjing Lu, 2nd fl. Open daily 9am-11pm. Credit cards accepted. ❷

Badlands (bǎilán; 百岚), 897 Julu Lu (☎6467 0773), near Changshu Lu, about 10min. north of Huaihai Zhong Lu. Though quite good, Tex-Mex food is only a secondary concern here. Look out back at the "Belgian Beer Garden" or check out the "Nutty Irish Man" (Y50) to discover Badland's true passion. Set meals Y65. Tacos Y10 on Tu. 2 tequila shots Y30 on F. Open daily 6pm-midnight. Make reservations for other hours. ❹

NEAR THE TRAIN STATION

Chinese fast-food places across the square (on the south side) sell big bowls of fried rice (Y6), small buns (Y1 for 4), and noodle soup (Y5 and up). Try **Naf** ❶ (watch for the big red-and-white sign) or **Xinya** ❶ (xīnyà; 新亚), right across the street with the red-and-yellow Chinese sign. (Both open 24hr.) A **Nanxiang Steamed Buns** ❶, 1509 Zhongxing Lu, next to Love Inn, serves the same steamed buns as the one in Yuyuan Garden, but at a mere Y3.5 for eight, with crab meat Y7.

◎ SIGHTS

Shanghai's main sights are architectural, from the sculpted and spired traces of the international past to towers of glass and steel. Religious sites, museums, and lively neighborhoods are thrown in for good measure. At present, Shanghai is "greenifying," and most park fees have been abolished. Within various quarters of the city, walking is often preferable to using the overcrowded public buses.

THE BUND AND PUDONG NEW AREA

THE BUND 外滩

Postcards like to showcase the stately waterfront embankment, lit with neon and graced by European architecture. Stretching 1.5km along Zhongshan Dong Lu, all the way from Waibaidu Bridge to Jinling Lu, the Bund (wàitān; 外滩) traces the Huangpu River past some of Shanghai's oldest reminders of foreign influence. European banks and trade houses along the Bund date back to the 1840s, when the Treaty of Nanjing opened the city to international commerce.

In early mornings, fan dancers and waltzers glide across the promenade along the Huangpu River. At night, young couples share the benches, and roving families and tourists add laugh and chatter to festive summer evenings. Barges floating down the Yangzi contribute baritone horns. At one end of the Bund, just north of Waibaidu Bridge, the towering **Shanghai Mansions** (shànghǎi dàshà; 上海大厦) served as the military headquarters for both Japan and the US, and now shelters tourists before they foray into the wilds of Shanghai. The modern, triangular **Monument to the People's Heroes** (shànghǎi shì rénmín yīngxióng jìniàn tǎ; 上海市人民英雄纪念塔) stands on the corner of Suzhou Creek and Huangpu River. The 1993 inscription on the tower pays tribute to martyrs to the Socialist cause.

At the base of the tower lies the entrance to the **Bund History Museum** (wàitān lìshǐ jìniàn guǎn; 外滩历史纪念馆), where old photographs of the Bund chronicle the opening of Shanghai as a treaty port, the introduction of gas lighting, and the upheaval of the 1920s and 30s, before moving on to recent events. (Open daily 9am-4:15pm, last admission 4pm. Free.) Just beyond the museum, **Huangpu Park** (huángpǔ gōngyuán; 黄浦公园) was initially opened as the British Public Gardens after the Opium War. A source of Chinese indignation and a symbol of imperialist snobbery, the infamous sign at its gate declared, "Chinese people and dogs are not allowed." In 1928, the park was truly opened to the general public, and it has since become a popular place for all the usual park activities. (On the corner of Zhongshan Dong Lu and Beijing Dong Lu. ☎5308 2636. Open daily 5am-11pm. Free.)

The platform of the **Bund Observatory** (wàitān tiānwéntái; 外滩天文台) yields a panoramic view of the glittering length of the Bund. The building houses the **Bund History Exhibition** (wàitānshǐchénliè shì; 外滩史陈列室), a collection of documents and photographs from Shanghai's earlier days. Purchase a drink at the Museum Club 1865 bar (see **Nightlife**, p. 353) in exchange for the view. (1A Zhongshan Dong Er Lu. Open daily 8:30am-6am.)

The Pudong Development Bank, 12 Zhongshan Dong Yi Lu, dazzles with a **ceiling mural** saved from destruction during the Cultural Revolution. Another 51 buildings representing various architectural styles include the former **English Consulate**, 33 Zhongshan Dong Lu, the **City Government Building,** and the **Customs House,** 13 Zhongshan Dong Lu, all of which date from the 1910s and 20s. These now house Chinese government offices and are not open to tourists.

Frequent **boat tours** depart from 222 Zhongshan Dong Er Lu, a Bund-side dock, providing a watery escape from the Shanghai traffic. The longer rides go all the way to the mouth of the Yangzi. (Buy tickets along the Bund. Shorter trips 1hr., 6 per day 9:15am-8pm, Y25-30. Longer tours 2-3hr., mainly in the afternoon, Y45-100.) The newest thing on the Bund is an underground cable car beneath the river, offering views of nothing but kitschy neon light displays. (One-way Y35.)

PUDONG NEW AREA 浦东新区

ORIENTAL PEARL TV TOWER (dōngfāng míngzhū diànshì tái; 东方明珠电视台). Restaurants, KTV parlors, and several observation decks top the 468m tower, the tallest in Asia. However, if the sky is overcast, it's better seen from the other side of the river—the admission fee is almost as high as the tower. *(On the Pudong side of the Huangpu River. Take the metro to the Lujiazui stop, or bus #985 from the Stadium or Xujiahui. Buy tickets along the northern end of the Bund. Open daily 8:30am-10pm. Y50-100; price rises with the height of the view.)*

OLD CHINESE CITY

In the Southern City district, seven main gates mark the boundaries of the Old Chinese City, whose narrow streets and labyrinthine alleyways are best explored on foot. Old Shanghai'ers gathered here in days past to burn incense for the gods, but crowds now come to revel in shopping and food. The **Yuyuan Bazaar** (yùyuán shāngshà; 豫园商厦) has both upscale stores and lone street vendors—chances are that they're both selling the same overpriced souvenirs or not-so-gold jewelry. Of particular note are the stores selling only fans and chopsticks. At night, the Bazaar buzzes with lights and sounds, and stores and stalls stay open until 10pm.

YUYUAN GARDEN (yùyuán; 豫园). The garden is an oasis of greenery and relative calm amid the carnival atmosphere of the adjoining Bazaar. Built in the 16th century by wealthy Ming Dynasty officials, Yuyuan suffered during the Opium War and the Taiping Rebellion, but was eventually restored to its traditional style. Contemplate the Tower of Happiness or the Hall of Observing Quietness, surrounded by jagged rocks, water lily pools, and picture-perfect walkways. Walk quickly, lest mastodonic Japanese tour groups overwhelm you. *(218 Anren Lu, in the northeast part of the district, bounded by Fuyou Lu. Open daily 8:30am-5pm, last admission 4:30pm. Y30.)*

NANJING LU AND ENVIRONS

NANJING LU (nánjīng lù; 南京路). Shanghai's answer to Hong Kong's Golden Mile (p. 562) stretches across six upscale kilometers, from the Bund to Jingan Temple just beyond the Shanghai Centre. Every day, thousands parade past the glamorous setting of the historic **Peace Hotel** (hépíng fàndiàn; 和平饭店). On Saturday afternoons, the street closes to all vehicles, and the energetic crowds spill over the sidewalks and into the streets.

Back in 1850, this neighborhood formed the heart of the English Concession, but it was horseracing, not shopping, that caught people's fancy. These days, **Shanghai No. 1 Department Store** (shànghǎi dìyī bǎihuò shāngdiàn; 上海第一百货商店), 870 Nanjing Dong Lu, anchors the corner of Xizang Lu. (☎ 6322 3344. Open daily 9:30am-10pm.) Numerous other upscale shopping meccas crowd nearby. Just a few blocks south on Xizang Lu, **People's Square** (rénmín guǎngchǎng; 人民广场), the former site of the Shanghai Racecourse, invites tourists, locals, and groups of kite-toting children to enjoy its greenery and fountains.

North of People's Sq. and People's Park, Nanjing Lu winds west to the **Shanghai Centre** (shànghǎi shāngchéng; 上海商城). **Jingan Temple** (jìngān sì; 静安寺), the "Temple of Peace and Quiet," marks the official end of this raucous road and the beginning of industrial Shanghai. As of 2004, remodeling efforts have dunked the temple in fresh paint and filled it with construction shacks, making the Y10 admission absurd. *(1686 Nanjing Xi Lu, at Wanhangdu Lu. Open daily 7:30am-4:45pm.)*

SHANGHAI MUSEUM (shànghǎi bówùguǎn; 上海博物馆). This modern building houses a sizeable collection of ancient Chinese bronzes, the most notable of which are the intricately etched, two-millennia-old wine vessels as big as a small bathtub. The second floor displays exquisite ceramics from the Qing Dynasty. The Eight Immortals Vase features a donkey whose hairs are fine enough to count. Home decor enthusiasts should check out the bas reliefs on furniture from the Qing Dynasty, ceramic pillows, and a berserk "evil spirit exorciser" from the Han Dynasty pottery collection. (201 Renmin Dadao, in People's Sq. ☎6372 3500. Audio tours in 8 languages Y40; deposit Y400, US$50, or passport. Open 9am-5pm. Y20, students with IDs Y5. Those with fake IDs are chastised and risk fines.)

SHANGHAI ART MUSEUM (shànghǎi měishù guǎn; 上海美术馆). The museum's newly renovated home has a small collection of Western oils, contemporary Chinese art, and works by Shanghainese artists. Visitors can attend art lectures. The building itself is a work of art. (325 Nanjing Xi Lu, just west of People's Sq. ☎6327 2829; www.sh-artmuseum.org.cn. Open daily 9am-5pm, last admission 4pm. Y20, students Y5.)

SHANGHAI URBAN PLANNING EXHIBITION HALL (shànghǎi chéngshì guīhuà zhǎnshìguǎn; 上海城市规划展示馆). The real gem, on the third floor, is the sprawling model of Shanghai, detailed enough to find your hotel room. Models of things to come (in 10 or 20 years) are in the side wings. Photographs document the city's past on the second floor, and the top floor has a special exhibit on the history of the Jewish people in Shanghai. (100 Renmin Dadao, across Xizang Lu from People's Sq. ☎6372 2077. Open M-F 9am-5pm, Sa-Su 9am-6pm. Y25, students Y5.)

FORMER FRENCH CONCESSION

The glitzy boutiques on Huaihai Zhong Lu may lure masses of salivating shoppers each day, but much of the area's historical significance and atmosphere is best absorbed on side streets a few blocks away from the glitter. The blissful canopy of plane trees hint at the French past, and sky-high Dior ads show that the French still hold quite a bit of sway here. Once the haunt of gangsters and revolutionaries, the neighborhood now puts out a more proper image, particularly in the foreign diplomatic area west of Changshu Lu.

FORMER RESIDENCE OF ZHOU ENLAI (zhōu gōngguǎn; 周公馆). China's well-loved former premier lived here from 1946 to 1947, when he led meetings with communist revolutionaries, printed pamphlets, and held press conferences for foreign journalists. A GMD espionage unit, based in a hospital overlooking the openly communist building, wrote reports on his activities every other day. The spartan quarters and Zhou's briefcase of 20 years speak to the practical mindset of the early CCP. (73 Si Nan Lu, south of Fuxing Lu. ☎6473 0420. Free tours in Chinese only. Open Su and W-Sa 9-11:30am and 2:15-5pm; last admission 4:30pm. Y2, students with ID Y1.)

FORMER RESIDENCE OF DR. SUN YAT-SEN (sūn zhōngshān gù jū; 孙中山故居). GMD founder and leader of the republican revolution against the Qing, Sun Yat-sen (p. 78) moved into this house in 1920 and lived here for five years. After his death, his wife Song Qingling reconstructed the layout of the rooms from memory, and most of the furnishings are originals. The two floors of the eerily well-preserved house hold many old portraits, a study with brushes and ink wells, and guest rooms once frequented by visiting dignitaries. (7 Xiangshan Lu, off Si Nan Lu between Nanchang Lu and Fuxing Lu. ☎6437 2954. Open daily 9am-4:30pm. Y8, students Y6.)

FORMER RESIDENCE OF SONG QINGLING (sòng qìnglíng gù jū; 宋庆龄故居). Sun's widow spent much of her time here after 1948. The items on display include a limo presented to her by Stalin, a painting by the most celebrated artist of modern China, Xu Beihong, her student visa to the US, and letters of love and revolution to Sun. Also showcased are correspondences to Stalin, Mao Zedong, and other figures. *(1843 Huaihai Lu, between Yuqing Lu and Wanping Lu. Take bus #920 from Xizang Lu to Wukang. ☎ 6437 6268. Open daily 9-11am and 1-4:30pm. Y8, students Y6.)*

FIRST NATIONAL CONGRESS OF THE CHINESE COMMUNIST PARTY (zhōng gòng yīdà huìzhǐ jìniànguǎn; 中共一大会址纪念馆). On July 23, 1921, 11 representatives, including Mao Zedong and Chen Duxiu, initiated secret proceedings to found the CCP here—secret, that is, until they were discovered by French police who forced the delegates to flee to a boat on South Lake in Zhejiang province. The building opened as a museum in 1952. *(76 Xingye Lu, at Huangpi Nan Lu. ☎ 5383 2171. Open daily 9am-4pm, closed M mornings. Y3.)*

WESTERN SHANGHAI

There are fewer obvious tourist attractions in this area of Shanghai than elsewhere in the city, and the distances between sights are comparatively greater. **Xujiahui Cathedral** (xújiāhuì tiānzhǔtáng; 徐家汇天主堂), 158 Puxi Lu, was built in 1906; take the Metro to Xujiahui and use exit #3. Daily mass begins at 6:15am, with several services open to all worshippers. (Open to visitors Sa-Su 1-5pm.) The imposing **Shanghai Stadium** (shànghǎi tǐyùguǎn; 上海体育馆 ; ☎ 6438 5200), at Tiyuguan Metro (one stop beyond Xujiahui), is part of a complex that includes a swimming pool, playing fields, and other training facilities.

LONGHUA MARTYRS' MAUSOLEUM (lónghuá lièshì língyuán; 龙华烈士陵园). The verdant gardens here are a soothing counterpoint to the tombstones and the industrial grime of the surrounding area. An eternal flame in honor of those who died supporting the Communist cause burns in front of a giant sculpture emerging from the hillside. The **Longhua Martyrs' Museum** (lónghuá lièshì jìniànguǎn; 龙华烈士纪念馆) features exhibit after heroic exhibit about the lives and achievements of those who fought against imperialists and Nationalists back in the 1940s. *(2887 Longhua Lu. Mausoleum open daily 6:30am-5pm, last admission 4:30pm; Y1. Museum open daily 9am-4pm, last admission 3:30pm; Y5.)*

The Longhua complex continues on grounds close to the main building. The halls of the illustrious **Longhua Temple** (lónghuá sì; 龙华寺) are filled with the heady scent of incense and the occasional clanging of the large bell near the entrance—ring it yourself and eliminate all worries, or wait until New Year's day when it rings 108 times. *(Vegetarian restaurant open daily 11am-2pm and 5-8pm. Temple open daily 7am-4:30pm. Admission Y10. Bell-ringing Y10.)* Across the street stands **Longhua Pagoda** (lónghuá tǎ; 龙华塔), a seven-story octagonal tower.

AROUND SUZHOU CREEK

HONGKOU PARK (hóngkǒu gōngyuán; 虹口公园). Also known as **Lu Xun Park** (lǔxùn gōngyuán; 鲁迅公园), this park sees locals dozing on its shady grounds or floating in its boats. Bridges and covered pathways wind past a tea house. The **Tomb of Lu Xun** (lǔxùn mù; 鲁迅墓), complete with museum exhibits, is open to visitors. *(Museum ☎ 6540 2288. Open daily 9am-5pm, last admission 4pm. Y5.)* Though the first-floor signs are entirely in Chinese, English captions on the second floor enlighten travelers on the life of the influential satirist and left-wing political activist (see **Modern Literature,** p. 95) who passed away here on October 19, 1936. *(2288 Sichuan Bei Lu, bordered by Dalian Lu on the north and Jiangbei Dong Lu on the west. Take bus #18 from People's Sq. Open daily 6am-9pm. Y2.)*

OHEL MOISHE SYNAGOGUE (móxī huìtáng; 摩西会堂). Much of the neighborhood north of Suzhou Creek is part of Shanghai's international settlement. Ohel Moishe Synagogue was a center in the "Designated Area for Stateless Refugees" during the 1930s and 40s. The museum features a few small exhibits. *(62 Changyang Lu, 3rd fl. ☎6512 1934. Open daily 9am-4pm. Y50.)*

JADE BUDDHA TEMPLE (yùfó sì; 玉佛寺). This temple is renowned for a 2m-tall Buddha carved from a single piece of white jade, brought to China by a Burmese monk in 1822. The statue would not be around, however, were it not for the quick wit of an abbot. During the Cultural Revolution, the abbot of the Jade Buddha Temple closed its gates and plastered them with pictures of Chairman Mao. Because tearing down pictures of Mao was an offense punishable by death, the Red Guards could not enter and the temple was saved. Today, this big Buddha is surrounded by 688 little golden Buddhas all mounted along the ceiling. *(170 Anyuan Lu, west of Jiangning Lu. Take bus #506 one stop from the train station and follow the trail of incense sellers. Vegetarian restaurant serves noodles for Y5-8 and wontons for Y6; open daily 11am-2pm and 5-8pm. Temple ☎6266 3668. Open daily 8am-4:30pm. Y10, students Y5; additional Y5 to see the Jade Buddha.)*

🎭 ENTERTAINMENT

That's Shanghai is the preferred entertainment magazine for young expats. The monthly publication discovers hip bars and restaurants within a week of their arrival, and lists cultural events, movies, and more importantly, where to get down. Most movies in Shanghai are dubbed, but check *That's Shanghai* or *City Weekend* for current listings on English movies (magazines Y35). In June, the **Shanghai International Film Festival (SIFF)** brings in many foreign films (Y25-35). Tickets for the following listings (except sometimes the Yifu Theater) can be purchased at the Shanghai Centre box office (p. 342). Acrobatic show tickets sell out fast because of tour groups; purchase yours in advance.

Shanghai Acrobatic Theatre (shànghǎi shāngchéng jùyuàn; 上海商城剧院), 1376 Nanjing Xi Lu (☎6279 8948), in the Shanghai Centre Theatre. The current venue is relatively small, and even the cheapest seats enjoy decent views. The theater caters to tour groups, showcasing teeterboard, various comic acts, and a monkey thrown in for good measure. Performances are almost every night at 7:30pm. Box office open daily 9am-7:30pm, if no show 9am-5pm. Tickets Y100-200.

Shanghai Concert Hall (shànghǎi yīnyuè tīng; 上海音乐厅), 523 Yan'an Dong Lu (☎6386 9153), near Xizang Lu. Primarily hosts classical music performances by local groups, but sometimes sees visiting orchestras and ensembles. Tickets average Y280-500 but can go higher.

Yifu Theatre (yìfū wǔtái; 逸夫舞台), 701 Fuzhou Lu (☎6351 4668), near People's Sq. For those craving the sweet sounds of Chinese opera, Yifu shows Beijing opera and Shanghai's own "Hu" opera on Su afternoons. Purchase tickets at box office outside.

Majestic Theatre (měiqí dàxìyuàn; 美琪大戏院), 66 Jiangning Lu (☎6217 4409). Shanghai's oldest theater shows a variety of programs, including ballet, tango, and revolutionary operas.

Shanghai Grand Theatre (shànghǎi dàjùyuàn; 上海大剧院), 300 Renmin Dadao (☎6386 8686; www.shgtheatre.com), on the edge of People's Sq. A sight in itself, this theater shows everything from Irish dancing to Russian ballet. Tickets sold at the 1st fl. box office (☎6372 8701; open daily 9am-7:30pm) and other locations around town.

FESTIVALS

FESTIVAL	TIME	LOCATION	ACTIVITIES
New Year's Festival	Dec. 31–Jan. 1	Longhua Temple	New Year celebrations flourish under fireworks.
Temple Gathering	early Apr.	Longhua Temple	Street fairs feature guessing riddles and lots of food.
Shanghai International Tea Festival	last Saturday in Apr.	Zhabei Park (admission to park covers fee for festival)	Park-goers savor exotic and traditional blends of tea
International Food Festival	last weekend of June	Yandang Lu (Y100 to enter)	Sample foods from all over China and the world.
Shanghai Beer Festival	Last Friday in June	a designated city park	The 2nd national drink of China gets primary attention.
Autumn Moon (Mid-Autumn) Festival	Sept. 18, 2005 Oct. 6, 2006	major streets	Nibble Shanghai's famous mooncakes under the full moon while guessing the riddles printed on lanterns.
Shanghai Seafood Festival	late Sept. to early Oct. (week-long)	Xujiahui District	Foodfest sells crustaceans, mollusks, and the gilled.
Shanghai Tourism Festival	1st week of Nov.	Nanjing Lu	A celebration of you—the mighty tourist! Glossy brochures and parades down Nanjing Lu.

▚ NIGHTLIFE

The former French Concession hosts the heart of Shanghai's nightlife, on the streets leading south off the long stretch of Huaihai Lu, from Huangpi Lu to Hengshan Lu. *Shanghai Talk, That's Shanghai, City Weekend,* and the Shanghai edition of *Metrozine* are English-language monthlies with extensive listings of establishments and feature articles. Free copies are available at many hotels, hangouts, and travel agencies. Although new spots pop up all over, Shanghai's nightlife is struggling. Tightening regulations and more lucrative ventures such as restaurants have prompted owners to shut the doors of many clubs. Police frequently raid clubs and bars on Maoming Lu, citing a 50-decibel sound limit, and Julu Lu has as many women of ill-repute as club-goers. Even worse, persistent rumors hint that the entirety of Maoming Lu is slated for bulldozing and redevelopment, with strict regulations on its future occupants. But never fear: plucky Shanghai'ers are already seeking out new joints (and building their own) while revisiting old haunts. Movie stars and expats pack the classic **Xintiandi** (新天地), near the site of the first CCP congress, while classy bars crop up on **Hengshan Lu,** and the side streets off **Si Nan Lu** offer enduring gems like **Park 97** and **Shanghai Sally's.**

THE BUND

Noah's, on the top fl. of Captain's Hostel. Cheap beer (pitcher for 2 Y65), lounging backpackers, and an unobstructed rooftop view of the neon-painted Bund at night. Its Green Monster (Y35), a slightly sweet concoction of Malibu and rum, is very patron-friendly.

Museum Club 1865, 1A Zhongshan Lu (☎ 3313 0871). Sip martinis atop the terrace of the observatory north of the Bund. Think of the Y10 cover as the price for an unobstructed view of the Pearl TV tower and the glowing architecture rising up on all sides. Sodas Y20. Beer and cocktails Y30 and up. Open daily 9am-midnight.

FORMER FRENCH CONCESSION

SI NAN LU

Park 97, 2 Gaolan Lu, Fuxing Park (☎ 5383 2208; www.lankwaifong.com), on the corner of Si Nan Lu. Entry on Si Nan Lu. Run by the Lan Kwai Fong group of Hong Kong fame, this chic Art Deco hangout features 2 restaurants and a tiny dance floor that somehow manages to pack in hundreds of screaming expats.

Shanghai Sally's, 4 Xiangshan Lu (☎ 5382 0738), a few blocks south of Huaihai Zhong Lu, at Si Nan Lu. Don't be fooled by this lady's reserved exterior. Sure, the top floor may offer patrons the chance to sip a beer (Y20-35) in a pub-like setting, but live music blares from the basement with DJs on weekends. Because the dancing is downstairs, sometimes you can be let in after 2am, even after it looks dark and closed upstairs (to fool the police). Cocktails (downstairs only) Y45-50. Half-priced drinks for ladies on weekends. Open daily 5:30pm-2am.

Fairy Forest (xiān zōng lín; 仙踪林), 37 Yandang Lu, south of Huaihai Lu. This chic and relaxed watering hole of lime green chairs and wooden tables woos an equally chic and relaxed crowd. Sip from large glasses of bubble tea (Y10-15) and hypnotize that cute girl/guy across the room with the slow and sensuous rocking motion of the swing. If that's a bit much, chat and people-watch on chrome chairs outside. Open daily 12:30pm-1am.

MAOMING LU

1931 Pub, 112 Maoming Nan Lu (☎ 6472 5264). A time capsule of 1930s Shanghai, with delicate cups and yellowing posters of faded movie stars. Sophisticated patrons in their late 20s and early 30s indulge in "nostalgia" with Y10-60 teas and Y45-50 cocktails. Open daily 11am-2am.

Blues & Jazz Club, 159 Maoming Nan Lu, near Fuxing Zhong Lu. Long known among expats as a house of quiet down-time, quality live music emanates almost nightly from this atmospheric club. The artsy and casual coexist in harmony. Open daily 6pm-1am.

dkd, 172 Maoming Nan Lu (☎ 6415 2688). Cool decorations, a laid-back Buddha statue, and pillowed alcoves set the mood for lounging. Features 2 fl. of music (the top floor is more chill). Come on weekends.

HENGSHAN LU

Cotton Club, 1428 Huaihai Zhong Lu (☎ 6437 7110), at Fuxing Lu. A favorite of local jazz lovers. The lights are dim, the tables intimate, and the music sublime. Unfortunately, the sight of the mainly expat, middle-aged male crowd flirting outrageously with the younger local women tends to break the spell. Regulars swear by Cotton Gin, a heady potion of cherry brandy and gin. Cocktails Y45. Beer Y40. Shots Y35. Min. tab Y25. Live music Su-Th 9pm-midnight, F-Sa 9:30pm-1:30am. Cover Y10. Open daily 7pm-3am.

O'Malley's Pub, 42 Taojiang Lu (☎ 6474 4533), between Hengshan Lu and Wulumuqi Lu. This would be the quintessential neighborhood bar—if it were in England. The mostly expat crowd seems to be having a good time, enjoying summertime patio seating and homestyle dishes like cottage pie (Y120) and fish and chips. Guinness flows freely—or, as freely as Guinness can flow (half-pint Y40, pint Y65). Open daily 11am-2am.

⚡ DAYTRIPS FROM SHANGHAI

These days, dust, fresh paint, and admission booths take the place of streams flowing around rice paddies and ancient houses nestled by droopy willows. If daytrippers from the city poked around the designated tourist sights with some patience, they'd still find the arched stone bridges and winding alleys of traditional Chinese paintings. The counties and districts surrounding Shanghai are linked to the city proper by bus and minibus service; many leave from People's Sq. Even the farthest townships are generally no more than 75km from the city center.

SONGJIANG COUNTY 松江县

*In southwestern Shanghai Municipality. The Huhang Gaosu Gonglu, an expwy. linking Shanghai with Hangzhou, passes Songjiang city. Direct **buses** to Songjiang leave from Songshan Lu, across from Wusheng Lu and People's Sq., or from Shanghai Stadium (1hr., every 20min. 6am-8pm, Y5). Take a **tour bus** from Shanghai Stadium to Sheshan or a **minibus** (30min., Y3.5) from the Songjiang county seat to Qingpu; get off at the large sign that says **Sheshan Tourist District.***

Mt. Sheshan, about halfway from Songjiang to Qingpu, draws nature lovers, with its blooming vegetation and Christian pilgrims with its cathedral at festival times. Sheshan's Mediterranean-style cathedral, the **Sheshan Holy Mother Cathedral** (shéshān tiānzhǔ jiàotáng; 佘山天主教堂), was built in 1871 by French missionaries. The slope leading up to the cathedral bears images of the 14 Stations of the Cross, and a "path of suffering" winds to a shrine. (Open daily until 3:30pm. Y2.) The greenery of Sheshan National Forest is soul-soothing, though not as unique as its pricey admission suggests. A cable car to the cathedral and forest provides views of greenery and heartstopping experiences during brisk winds. (Open daily 7:30am-4pm. ☎5765 3423. Cable car round-trip to cathedral Y15, to forest Y10, both Y20. Forest Y28, children Y22.) **Sheshan Observatory,** next to the cathedral, records earthquakes and other natural phenomena. (Open daily 8am-4pm. Y6.)

The Square Pagoda and Screen Wall stand inside **Square Pagoda Park** (fāngtǎ gōngyuán; 方塔公园), 235 Zhongshan Zhong Lu, in the county seat. The town buses go in circles, and bus #2 (Y1) will eventually arrive at the park no matter where one boards. The nine-story pagoda has a history spanning over 900 years. The low ceilings and narrow wooden stairs of the pagoda make the climb a head-bumping experience if attempted by those towering over six feet. The large screen wall to the north was built in 1370 during the Ming Dynasty. A huge, beastly animal called Tao is carved into the center of the wall. The greedy animal swallowed all the treasures in the world but still craved the sun. He made a desperate leap over the sea for the sun, but, as it shone too high for his reach, he fell and drowned, or so the legend goes. (Open daily 7am-9pm. Park Y12. Pagoda Y5.)

The **Pond of the Drunken Bai Juyi** (zuìbái chí; 醉白池), 64 Renmin Nan Lu, in the county seat, is named for Bai Juyi, the famous Tang Dynasty poet who loved drinking almost as much as he loved writing. Walk east from the bus station until Renmin Bei Lu; turn right and walk south for 15min., past the Drunken Bai Restaurant. The pond was originally the private residence of the Ming artist Dong Qichang, who enjoyed Bai's poetry so much that he designed a garden in his honor. Empty and a little overgrown, the paths and lotus ponds make a pleasant escape from the usual madness. (☎5772 2415. Open daily 6:30am-4:30pm. Y12.)

The **Songjiang Mosque** (sōngjiāng qīngzhēn sì; 松江清真寺), the oldest in the Shanghai area, was built in the mid-1300s. Surrounded by houses, the mosque is difficult to find. From Zhongshan Zhong Lu, turn south onto Renmin Lu, and look for a small golden dome topped by a moon and a star immediately to the right. The mosque is to the left of the dome. (☎5781 1957. Open daily 2-5pm. Visitors pay a Y5 admissions fee, though worshippers wander in for free.)

NANHUI COUNTY 南汇县

*Southeast of city center. A special tour **ferry** departs from Shiliupu Passenger Terminal to Luchao Port, and a tour **bus** from the stadium (2hr., every 15min. 6:30am-9pm, Y5). During the Peach Blossom Festival, buses (7, 7:30am) leave from People's Sq. to Nanhui.*

Known locally as the "Land of Peach Blossoms," Nanhui boasts over 333 hectares of orchards all decked out in bold pastels at harvest time. From late-March to mid-April, the **Peach Blossom Festival,** followed by the **Peach Festival,** draws tourists from near and far to smell and savor ripening peaches. At the Peachland Folk Custom Village and the Fairy Land of Peaches in Shenxi, professional actors play out scenes of daily life from past and present on outdoor stages. **Luchao Port** (lúcháo gǎng; 芦潮港), on the northern coast of Hangzhou Bay, features a natural harbor and several miles of beach.

JIADING DISTRICT 嘉定区

In northwestern Shanghai Municipality, linked to city center by the Shanghai-Jiading Freeway. **Buses** *(M-F 6am-6pm, Sa-Su 6am-10pm) go to Jiading from Weihai Lu at Huangpi Lu, Yan'an Lu at Weihai Lu, and Hengfeng Lu near the Shanghai Train Station. Buses (daily 5am-8pm, Y6) to* **Nanxiang** *leave from the Shanghai North Station on Zhongshan Bei Lu.* **Tour buses** *depart from the stadium (1hr., every 20min.).*

Jiading's **Nanxiang Town** (nánxiáng; 南翔) teems with pagodas and temples that should please both history buffs and casual tourists. The **Confucius Temple** (kǒng-miào; 孔庙), 183 Nan Dajie, was first built in 1219 and today houses the **Jiading Museum** (jiādìng bówùguǎn; 嘉定博物馆). Those with a penchant for poetic names will enjoy a stroll through here. Even memorial archways bear such names as "Cultivating the Talents" and "Encouraging the Virtuous." The 72 carved lions outside the temple represent the 72 disciples of Confucius. (☎5953 0379. Open daily 8-11am and 1:30-4:30pm. Y10.)

Just east of the temple, the **Dragon Meeting Pond** (huì lóng tán; 汇龙潭) bears the shape of "five dragons snatching at a pearl." Five small streams (the dragons) run into a pond, from which Yingkui Hill (the pearl) rises. Visitors can listen to a cicada chorus under the shade in the **Garden of Autumn Clouds** (qiūxiá pǔ; 秋霞圃 ; 3144 Dong Da Lu. ☎5953 1949. Open daily 8am-5pm. Y12.) The **Garden of Ancient Splendor** (gǔ yī yuán; 古猗园), in the eastern part of town, has the only pavilion in China with an intentionally missing corner. The patriots who built the pavilion during the Japanese invasion of the 1930s left the northeast corner incomplete to symbolize the enemy occupation of China's northeast. The Zigzag Bridge leading up to the Pavilion with a Missing Corner crosses a pond abloom with lotus flowers in the summer. (2 Minghu Dong Lu. ☎5912 4916. Open daily 7am-6pm.)

QINGPU COUNTY 青浦县

In western Shanghai Municipality, bordered by Songjiang County to the south and Jiading to the north. Huqingping Lu (State Hwy. 318), a continuation of Yan'an Lu, is the main thoroughfare. **Buses** *(approx. 5am-8pm, Y8) go from Shanghai West Station on Wuzhong Lu and from People's Sq. to the Qingpu county seat or to Zhujiajiao.* **Minibuses** *(Y6) travel to the surrounding area from the Qingpu county seat.*

Once removed from the hordes of fried crepe vendors and motorcycle taxis patrolling Qingpu's bus stop, the county offers a few pleasant retreats. **Grand View Garden** (dà guān yuán; 大观园), on Dianshan Lake, 65km west of Shanghai, reproduces the gardens from the classic novel *Dream of the Red Chamber* (p. 95). Visitors can discuss the significance of buildings that are "Fraught with Favor, Basking in Kindness" or just take in the scenery. (Open daily 8am-4:30pm.)

In the ancient town of **Zhujiajiao** (zhūjiājiǎo; 朱家角 ; Y10), willows shade the narrow stone paths, cicadas chirp all summer long, and a peek through mossy, wooden doors reveals Qing-era courtyards. Arrive in the early morning ahead of the tour groups, when you can watch fishermen catch, gill, and de-scale fish using traditional methods. Sticky rice wrapped in reed leaves (zòngzi; 粽子), filled with meat, red bean paste, egg yolk, or chestnuts, is the town's specialty; grab the best from **Ge Saijin's Shop**, 308 Bei Dajie. (Meat Y2, meat and egg yolk Y2.5. Try the braised pork feet, *zhūtí*.) The **Setting Free Bridge** (fàng shēng qiáo; 放生桥), in the ancient town of Zhujiajiao (zhūjiājiǎo; 朱家角), is the largest stone bridge in the municipality and draws numerous visitors. Buddhists believe that setting living things free builds good karma. Somewhat ironically, local fishermen peddle tiny fish caught (and re-caught) expressly for this purpose

JIANGSU 江苏

With rich soils and mild temperatures, Jiangsu enjoys abundant harvests and fresh breezes from the Yellow Sea, earning itself an extremely vivid and exciting moniker—the "Land of Fish and Rice." Rest assured that Jiangsu has much more to offer. With industrious silkworms busily spinning the nation's prized fabric and mazes of industrial canals, the province's foremost city, Suzhou, lays claim to Jiangsu's enduring images. Meanwhile, smaller villages like Tongli have preserved their classic tiny bridges arching over equally tiny waterways. Jiangsu itself sits upon a silt bed of the long, snaking Yangzi River, its gateway to maritime trade. Living at the whims of the flood-prone Yangzi, those who managed to step out of the knee-deep waters of the rice fields often headed down the scholarly path at the dynastic capital of Nanjing. Today, the studious bent continues with the prominent Nanjing University, but industrialization has given the sleepy lands a jolt. Smoking factories dot the meandering rice paddies, and the Grand Canal is choked more with hulking metal barges than wooden fishing junks. Nevertheless, Jiangsu isn't exactly an economic boomtown, and all the construction and industry takes a backseat to the cultural and historic relics. Travelers come for a slice of southern China's ancient charm—intricate gardens and pagodas, misty lakes, and of course, trickling streams and waterways.

NANJING 南京　　　　　　　　☎025

Legend has it that an ancient Chinese poet once described Nanjing (formerly Jinling, or "golden hills") with this verse: "Oh, what a beautiful place, Jinling! Deservedly the home for many a king." And many a king did make Nanjing his home. Literally "Southern Capital," the city served as the seat of the Ming Dynasty for 50 years, when it became the first (and only) city south of the Yangzi River to preside over a united China. In the early half of the 20th century, the city ruled a fragmented Republic of China (1928-49), led by Sun Yat-sen and Chiang Kai-shek.

Now the capital of Jiangsu province, Nanjing has shaken off, but not forgotten, its turbulent past. Somber memorials and historical ruins recall darker days, even as modern Nanjing moves forward to greet the future. Though it lacks the grandeur of Beijing and the scenic delight of Hangzhou, Nanjing exemplifies the evolution of a growing city (thin coat of dust included). Luxurious hotels and decadent restaurants sprout up throughout the city, catering to pampered tourists and the business elite, but Nanjing remains a city for the people who live in it. The lakes, parks, museums, and six million trees lining the boulevards are more local haunts than touristed national treasures. Life flourishes in the small alleys off Xinjiekou, where people scrub laundry on traditional wooden washboards and families set up dinner tables in front of shops. Nanjing is promisingly, unabashedly regular—a regular city for regular folk.

▐ TRANSPORTATION

Flights: Nanjing International Airport (nánjīng lùkǒu guójì jīchǎng; 南京禄口国际机场; ☎5248 0488). The only regular international flights serve Southeast Asia. Starting at 6am, buses (Y25) leave from Xinhan Mansion, 180 Hanzhong Lu. Taxi to the city center costs Y150. Shuttle buses (1hr., every 30min. 6:30am-6pm, Y25) to the airport

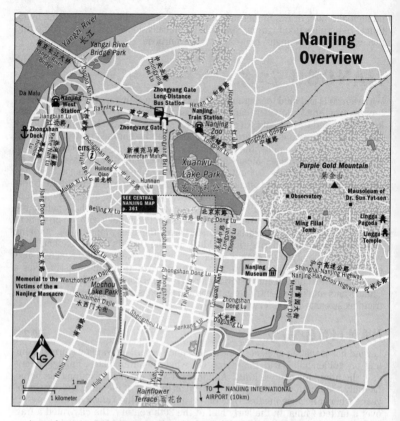

Nanjing Overview

leave from the **CAAC ticket office,** 52 Ruijin Lu (☎8449 9378, international 8449 9410). A 2nd ticket office, 1 Beijing Xi Lu (☎331 1747), is 200m west of Gulou Sq. Open daily 24hr. To: **Beijing** (6-7 per day, Y1010); **Guangzhou** (5-6 per day, Y1180); **Hong Kong** (2 per day, Y1600); **Kunming** (2-3 per day, Y1750); **Qingdao** (daily, Y620); **Tianjin** (Tu, Th-F, Su; Y800); **Wuhan** (2-3 per day, Y580).

Trains: Nanjing Train Station (nánjīng huǒchē zhàn; 南京火车站), 264 Longpan Lu (☎8582 2222), at the terminus of buses #1, 17, 32, and 33. Buy tickets within 17 days of departure, and as early as possible in late June to Aug., to avoid the rush of holidaying students. The **Gulou Ticket Office,** 223 Zhongshan Bei Lu (☎8330 1692), does not charge commission and also sells tickets for **Nanjing West Station.** Open daily 8am-5pm. To: **Beijing** (9½-17hr.; 7 per day, Y270-400); **Chengdu** (31-36hr.; 4 per day; Y380-650, A/C Y405); **Shanghai** (3-5hr., 40 per day, Y47-72); **Xi'an** (13-20hr.; 6:41, 7:28pm; Y280-420).

Buses: There are 2 main bus stations in Nanjing.

Zhongyang Gate Long-Distance Bus Station (zhōngyāngmén chángtú qìchē zhàn; 中央门长途汽车站), 1 Jianning Lu (☎8550 4973), a 10min. walk west of Nanjing Train Station. Accessible via buses #1, 17, 32, and 33. Ticket window open daily 24hr. To: **Changsha** (13hr., 1pm, Y246); **Guangzhou** (20hr., 8pm, Y337); **Hefei** (2-3hr., every 10min. 6:15am-7:50pm, Y38-54); **Jiuhua-shan** (4hr.; 7:20, 9:30am, 2pm; Y57); **Nanchang** (9hr.; 9am, 12:30, 9, 10pm; Y198-263); **Shanghai** (3½hr., every 30min. 6:30am-7:30pm, Y88).

Hanfu Jie Long-Distance Bus Station (hànfǔ jiē chángtú qìchē zhàn; 汉府街长途汽车站), 25 Daxing Gong (☎8454 0786), east of Xinjiekou off Zhongshan Dong Lu. Also known as **Hanzhongmen** (hàn zhōng mén; 汉中门). Take bus #5, 9, 25, or 29 to Daxing Gong. To: **Hangzhou** (5-6hr.; 1:30, 9:30am, 12:30pm; Y98); **Shanghai** (3½hr., every hr. 7:40am-5:50pm, Y75-88); **Suzhou** (2½hr., every hr. 7am-5:40pm, Y55-64); **Wuxi** (2hr., every hr. 6:30am-5:50pm, Y44-52).

Local Transportation: The **public bus** system extends as far as Zijinshan (Purple Gold Mountain) and the Yangzi River Bridge. Several buses (like #9, 11, and 13) run 5am-11pm, but most operate 6:30am-8 or 9pm. Fare Y1, with A/C (denoted by a "*" in front of the bus number) Y2; price is marked on the outside of the bus, near the door, or on the fare box. 4 **tour buses** shuttle between the main train station, bus stations, and all the sights. Buses #1, 9, and 34 run along Zhongshan Lu; #1, 7 and tour bus 2 run along Fuzimiao and connect to other attractions. **Minibuses** (Y1-4) follow popular bus routes. A **subway** is scheduled to be completed in 2006; it will run north-south through the city center, with 13 stops, including Xinjiekou, Gulou, and the train station.

Taxis: Base fare Y7, each additional km Y2.4-2.6. Xinjiekou to the main train and bus stations Y20-25, to the airport Y120.

Bike Rental: Rental shops are few; explore the Nanjing University area for options. A **stand,** in a small alley 1 block south of Beijing Dong Lu, has a few bikes; come either early in the day or at night. Y2 per hr. Open daily 6:30am-9pm. **Nanjing Fuzimiao International Youth Hostel** (p. 360) rents bikes. Y5 per hr., Y20 per day.

✴️ 🛈 ORIENTATION AND PRACTICAL INFORMATION

Nanjing's 10 districts and five counties cover more than 6500km² on the south side of the **Yangzi River,** about 200km from Shanghai. The city is bounded by the river to the west and **Zijinshan Mountain** to the east. Thriving commercial districts cluster in the 10km stretch between Zhongyang Gate in the north and Zhonghua Gate in the south. In the heart of the city, there are two large traffic circles at **Gulou** (鼓楼) and **Xinjiekou** (新街口). The Gulou traffic circle is the intersection of **Beijing Dong Lu** (北京东路), **Beijing Xi Lu** (北京西路), **Zhongshan Bei Lu** (中山北路), and **Zhongyang Bei Lu** (中央北路). Zhongyang Bei Lu and Zhongshan Bei Lu run south to become **Zhongshan Lu** (中山路), which intersects **Hanzhong Lu** (汉中路) and Zhongshan Dong Lu at the Xinjiekou traffic circle. Another major street, **Longpan Zhong Lu** (龙蟠中路), runs north, parallel to Zhongshan Lu, until it turns west at Beijing Dong Lu; after it intersects Zhongyang Lu, it turns into **Jianning Lu** (建宁路), running along the city's northern edge, past the Nanjing Train Station and the Zhongyang Gate Bus Station, near the West Train Station, before finally hitting the Yangzi River near the docks.

TOURIST AND FINANCIAL SERVICES

Tourist Office: Nanjing Municipal Tourism Bureau (nánjīngshì lǚyóuchù shìchǎng kāifāchù; 南京市旅游处市场开发处), 4 Nan Donggua Shi alley, 4th fl. on Shanghai Lu (☎8360 8901; fax 5771 1959). Take bus #31 to near the Foreign Students' Dorm. Open M-F 8:30am-noon and 2:30-5:30pm. Sheraton and Jinling hotels sell English maps of Nanjing (Y4-5).

Travel Agencies: CITS, 12 Baiziting, 3rd fl. (☎8336 6224), near Xinmo Lu, north of the Hongqiao Hotel. Take bus #15, 26, or 30 and get off at the Nanjing Hotel Stop. English-speaking staff. Average train ticket commission Y30; no commission for plane tickets. Open M-F 9am-5pm, Sa-Su 9am-4pm. **CTS,** 12 Baiziting, 3rd fl. (☎8336 6227, tickets 8441 5347). Average commission Y30. Open M-F 9am-noon and 2-5pm.

Bank of China: 29 Hongwu Lu (☎8441 7999). From Xinjiekou, walk 1 block east on Zhongshan Dong Lu and turn right on Hongwu Lu; it's on the left, 1 block down. Open M-F 8:30am-5:30pm.

ATMs: Cirrus/Plus ATMs can be found at the Bank of China on Hongwu Lu and many other branches scattered along Zhongshan Nan Lu.

LOCAL SERVICES

Bookstore: Xinhua Foreign-Language Bookstore, 126 Zhongshan Lu (☎8664 8852). English classics and best-sellers. Open daily 8:20am-7pm.

Department Store: Xinjiekou Department Store (xīnjiēkǒu bǎihuò shāngdiàn; 新街口 百货商店), 3 Zhongshan Nan Lu. The grande dame of Nanjing department stores, with just about every product imaginable. Open M-Th 9:15am-10pm, F-Su 9am-10:30pm.

Markets: SGCS (sūguǒ chāoshì; 苏果超市), 26 Hongwu Lu, 1 block east of Xinjiekou traffic circle, off Zhongshan Dong Lu, opposite the Bank of China building. Open daily 7am-10pm. A good selection of snacks and ready-to-go meals. Another **branch** at Xinjiekou Traffic Circle. Open 24hr. Many other locations around town.

EMERGENCY AND COMMUNICATIONS

PSB: 1 Honggongzi Lu (☎8442 0114), south of Xinjiekou. Open 24hr. The **Foreigners' Bureau** (chūrùjìng guǎnlǐ chù; 出人境管理处 ; ☎8442 0004) has English-speaking staff. Open M-F 8:30am-5:30pm.

Pharmacies: Sarow Pharmacy (☎8330 6810), on Haining Lu, a block south of Beijing Xi Lu. Open daily 24hr. **Baixin Pharmacy,** 34 Gongyuan Xi Jie (☎5226 3612) at Fuzimiao. Open daily 8am-9pm. Other locations throughout the city (look for bright green-and-white signs), with everything from Tylenol to herbal elixirs.

Hospital: Gulou Hospital (gǔlóu yīyuàn; 鼓楼医院), 291 Zhongshan Lu (☎8330 4616). From the Gulou traffic circle, the hospital is a short distance down Zhongshan Lu on the right. Affiliated with Nanjing University Medical School. English-speaking staff.

Internet Access: Nanjing's large student population means numerous Internet options, all Y2-6 per hr. An **Internet cafe,** 53 Gongyuan Xi Jie, in an alley 200m from the main gate to the Confucius Temple, has fast connections. Y2 per hr. Open daily 8am-midnight. **Internet Impression** (yīngpàishēng wǎngluò;英派升网络), 152 Shanghai Lu, between Beijing Xi Lu and Hankou Xi Lu. Y4 per hr.; multiple-use cards offer great savings. **Nanjing Normal University Hotel** and the **Fuzimiao Hostel** both have Internet (see below).

Post and Telecommunications: Nanjing Post Office (☎8379 7012), in the high-rise building south of Gulou traffic circle, at Beijing Dong Lu at Zhongshan Lu. EMS. Address Poste Restante to the Gulou Post Office (鼓楼邮局). Open daily 8:30am-6:30pm. **China Telecom** (toll free ☎1000), 2 Zhongyang Bei Lu, just off the Gulou traffic circle. IDD and telegram service at the first counter to your right. Open daily 8am-6pm. Side office with separate entrance provides the same services 24hr.

Postal Code: 210005, Poste Restante 210008.

⌐ ACCOMMODATIONS

Apart from Nanjing's two university dormitories, most establishments that accept foreign guests are pricey three-star hotels. If posted room rates seem too good to be true, they very well may be; chances are the place does not accept foreigners.

Nanjing Fuzimiao International Youth Hostel (HI) (nánjīng fūzǐmiào guójì qīngnián lǚguǎn), 39 Dashiba Jie (☎8662 4133 or 5226 4434; www.yhananjing.com). From the train station, take bus #1 to the last stop, Fuzimiao. Walk in the same direction for 100m and turn right at Pingjiang Fu; cross the bridge, and the hostel is on the left. Friendly and young staff host lively pool games and stargazings on the 2nd fl. Clean rooms, hard beds, and roomy single-stall baths await on the 3rd fl. Dorms are co-ed

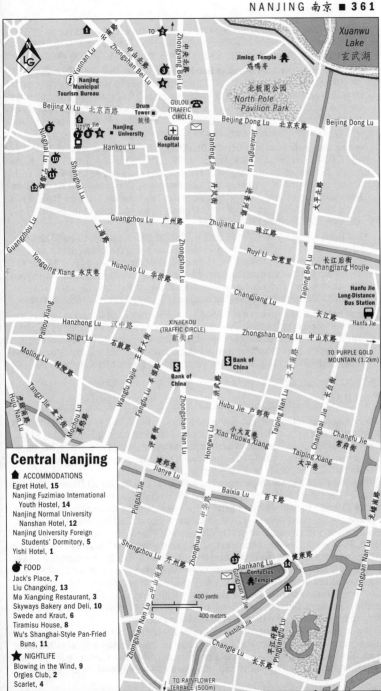

Central Nanjing

⌂ ACCOMMODATIONS
Egret Hotel, **15**
Nanjing Fuzimiao International
  Youth Hostel, **14**
Nanjing Normal University
  Nanshan Hotel, **12**
Nanjing University Foreign
  Students' Dormitory, **5**
Yishi Hotel, **1**

🍎 FOOD
Jack's Place, **7**
Liu Changxing, **13**
Ma Xiangxing Restaurant, **3**
Skyways Bakery and Deli, **10**
Swede and Kraut, **6**
Tiramisu House, **8**
Wu's Shanghai-Style Pan-Fried
  Buns, **11**

★ NIGHTLIFE
Blowing in the Wind, **9**
Orgies Club, **2**
Scarlet, **4**

Map labels:
Xuanwu Lake 玄武湖
Jiming Temple 鸡鸣寺
北极阁公园 North Pole Pavilion Park
Beijing Dong Lu 北京东路
Beijing Xi Lu 北京西路
Yunan Lu
Zhongshan Bei Lu
中山北路
中央北路 Zhongyang Bei Lu
中央路
Nanjing Municipal Tourism Bureau
Drum Tower 鼓楼
GULOU (TRAFFIC CIRCLE)
Jipyin Jie
Nanjing University
Ninghai Lu
Shanghai Lu
Hankou Lu
Gulou Hospital
Danfeng Jie 丹凤街
Jinxianghe Lu
太平北路
Guangzhou Lu 广州路
Zhujiang Lu 珠江路
Zhongshan Lu
Huaqiao Lu 华侨路
Yongqing Xiang 永庆巷
Ruyi Li 如意里
长江后街 Changjiang Houjie
Changjiang Lu 长江路
Taiping Bei Lu
Hanzhong Lu 汉中路
XINJIEKOU (TRAFFIC CIRCLE) 新街口
Shigu Lu
Zhongshan Dong Lu 中山东路
Hanfu Jie Long-Distance Bus Station
Hanfu Jie
TO PURPLE GOLD MOUNTAIN (1.2km)
Moling Lu 秣陵路
Wangfu Dajie 王府大街
Fengfu Lu 丰富路
Bank of China
Bank of China
Hubu Jie 户部街
Taiping Nan Lu
Changbai Jie
Changfu Jie 常府街
Tangzi Jie 堂子街
Mochou Lu 莫愁路
Zhongshan Nan Lu
Hongwu Lu
小火瓦巷 Xiao Huowa Xiang
Taiping Xiang 太平巷
Huju Nan Lu
Pingshi Jie
Jianye Lu 建邺路
Baixia Lu 百下路
Shengzhou Lu 升州路
Zhonghua Lu 中华路
Jiankang Lu 健康路
Confucius Temple 夫子庙
Gongyuan Xijie
Longpan Nan Lu
Dashiba Jie 大石坝街
平江府路 Pinglangfu Lu
Changle Lu 长乐路
TO RAINFLOWER TERRACE (500m)
Zhongshan Nan Lu 中山南路
400 yards
400 meters

when crowded. Closet-sized lockers, 24hr. hot water, and A/C. Bikes Y5 per hr., Y20 per day. Laundry Y5 per hr. Internet Y2-5 per hr. Reception 7am-midnight. 4- to 16-person dorms M-F Y40, HI members Y30; Sa-Su Y45/Y35. Doubles Y120/Y100. ❶

Nanjing Normal University Nanshan Hotel (nánjīng shīfàn dàxué nánshān zhuānjiā lóu; 南京师范大学南山专家楼), 122 Ninghai Lu (☎8371 6440), a block south of Hankou Xi Lu. Enter the main gate of the campus; turn left at a large flagpole and follow the blue sign to the right and up a hill. Compact singles with bright bath. A/C, phone (free local calls), and TV. Internet Y0.53 per min. Laundry service Y5. Rooms go fast (especially singles); reserve early. Singles Y100; doubles Y170. ❷

Nanjing University Foreign Students' Dormitory (nánjīng dàxué xī yuàn; 南京大学西苑), 20 Jinyin Jie (☎359 3589; fax 359 4699). Coming from Gulou, it's 1 block to the right of the intersection of Shanghai Lu at Beijing Xi Lu. Take bus #813 to Yunnan Lu. In a lively quarter, close to eateries and bars catering to foreign and Chinese students. Mattresses aren't plush, and plumbing pipes may be visible, but baths are cheerful and rooms clean. A/C, TV, phone. Self-service laundry Y2 per kg. Deposit Y10. Singles Y140, with bath Y280; doubles Y160, Y280. ❷

Yishi Hotel (jiāngsū yìshì yuán; 江苏议事园), 81 Zhongshan Bei Lu (☎8332 6826; yshotel@public1.ptt.js.cn), behind a yellow wall bordering Zhongshan Bei Lu and Yunnan Lu, off Sanxilu Sq. From Gulou, 1 stop on northbound buses #16 or 34. Or #13 (from train and bus stations) to Dafang Xiang. Smaller, traditional Chinese-style hotel has attentive staff and a convenient location. Breakfast included. Currency exchange. Singles Y200; doubles Y240. Student discounts possible. Credit cards accepted. ❸

Egret Hotel, 68 Dashiba Lu (☎8687 9588; fax 8662 1895), off Gongyuan Jie in Fuzimiao. Overlooking the Qinghuai River, the Egret has the same great location as its pricier neighbors. The south building is chock-full of amenities, while cheaper rooms in the north building show wear and tear. Breakfast included. Post-discount rates: singles Y300; doubles Y280-340. 30% student discount, but always bargain for more. ❹

📷 FOOD

According to a Chinese saying, Sichuanese food is like a hot woman, Beijing food a refined young lady, and South Yangzi food a humble farm girl. Yet Nanjing's elaborate menu of age-old delicacies and mouth-watering snacks is anything but plain. Small restaurants and family-run stalls reach their culinary peak at night, and an evening stroll can quickly become a scrumptious foodfest.

The stretch of **Ninghai Lu** between Hankou Xi Lu and Beijing Xi Lu near Nanjing Normal University is normally crammed with vendors serving everything from *bāozi* (Y0.6-1) to salted duck's head (Y9). Vendors offer delectable Macau-style caramelized custard tarts and fresh seasonal fruits at Y2-3 per *jīn*. After sunset, the street doubles as a nightmarket with vegetables and fruits just carted from the farm. Take bus #13 or 45 to Yunnan Lu, walk down Shanghai Lu away from Beijing Xi Lu, and turn right on the first large street, Hankou Xi Lu. The nightmarket in **Xinjiekou,** on a lane right behind the Xinjiekou Department Store off Zhongshan Nan Lu, specializes in smelly tofu (Y1-2) and grilled or fried poultry and meats (Y2). The area around **Fuzimiao Temple** also teems with vendors selling traditional Nanjing and southern Chinese favorites at night. Take bus #1 from Xinjiekou's east bus stop to the end and cross the street to the large gate.

Soy-sauce goose and roasted chicken (Y9-12) hang in rotisseries in residential neighborhoods such as Hankou Lu. The ultimate Nanjing specialty is **salted water duck** (yán shuǐ yā; 盐水鸭), available both freshly made and vacuum-packed. Subtly salted, but incredibly juicy, half of a duck can be enjoyed for a mere Y9-10.

Other specialties are also duck-related, such as roasted duck (guìhuā yā; 桂花鸭) and duck blood rice noodle soup (yāxuě fěnsī tāng; 鸭血粉丝汤 ; Y3-4), served with bits of duck innards, scallions, and fried tofu skin.

Liu Changxing (liú chángxīng fànguǎn; 刘长兴饭店), 127 Jiankang Lu, across from the main gate to the Confucius Temple pedestrian area. Just Y3 will get you 4 "thin-skinned steamed mini-buns." Equally tempting are the dumplings with curried beef filling. Noodle soups Y4-8.5. Open daily 9:30am-midnight, takeout window 6am-8:30pm. ❶

Wu's Shanghai-Style Pan-Fried Buns (wújiā shēngjiān bāo; 吴家生煎包), 143 Ninghai Lu. The sizzle of ludicrously good bite-sized meat buns attracts long lines. Many locals come daily for Nanjing's best squirt-prone snack (Y2 for 4). Noodle soups Y2.5-12. ❶

Jack's Place (jiékè dìfāng; 杰克地方), 160-4 Shanghai Lu (☎8332 3616), at Jinyin Jie, opposite the Nanjing Univ. Foreign Students' Dormitory. Open daily 9am-3am. **Jack's Place II** is on Hunan Lu. **Jack's Place III,** 35 Wangfu Dajie, at Fengfu Lu, is more expensive than its siblings. All are cheery, with brightly colored awnings and the chatter of students. Jack's french toast (Y6) gets rave reviews. Extensive Chinese and Western dishes include club sandwiches (small Y29, large Y52) and banana splits (Y18). Lunchtime delivery within 3km. Versions II and III open 9am-11pm. ❶

Swede and Kraut (yún zhōng cān; 云中餐), 14 Ninghai Lu (☎8663 4843), about halfway between Beijing Dong Lu and Hankou Lu. Expensive pasta (Y40 and up) and subs (around Y20 and up) earn high marks at this student-friendly restaurant owned by a German and a Swede (hence its name). Th pizza nights feature individual pizzas or a meat entree and drinks for Y45. Open Su, Tu-F 5:30-10pm, Sa 11am-2pm and 5:30-10pm. Credit cards accepted. **Skyways Bakery & Deli,** 3-6 Hankou Xi Lu (☎8663 4834), is a new Swede and Kraut venture baking authentic German bread (Y5), apple cake (Y30), and whiskey truffle (Y32 per 100g). Open daily 9am-9:30pm. ❸

Tiramisu House (wēiquè tílāmīsū cāntīng; 威雀提拉米苏餐厅), 19 Jinyin Jie (☎8323 1353), between Blowing in the Wind and the Nanjing Univ. Foreign Students' Dormitory. Dim lighting, crimson walls, and wine racks welcome backpackers and students, who nibble on tiramisu (Y20). Chocolate fondue with fruit and cookies Y48. Cheese fondue Y88. Sashimi Y20. French-style baked snails Y58. Spinach and meat lasagna Y38. Modest selection of beer and wine Y20-65. Open daily 10am-1am. ❸

Ma Xiangxing Restaurant (qīngzhēn mǎxiángxìng càiguǎn; 清真马祥兴菜馆), 42 Hubei Lu (☎8320 3865), near Gulou Sq.; look for the green-and-yellow Chinese sign. Established in 1840, this halal restaurant's longevity is well deserved; its famed pickled vegetables and fish stew tops any banquet. A simpler meal of meat sauce and cold noodles costs Y2.5. 2nd fl. open daily 10am-2pm and 5-8pm. Lower level serves buns (Y0.5-0.8) and dumplings (Y1.2); open daily 6:15am-8:15pm. ❷

◉ SIGHTS

Most of Nanjing's main attractions are scattered around the outskirts of the city. Places of reflection and remembrance, they recall Nanjing's imperial, revolutionary, and war-torn past, but also hint at its thriving future. In July and early August, there are daily musical performances (7-10pm) at the **Open-Air Music Concert Hall** and at **Baima Park** (báimǎ gōngyuán; 白马公园 ; open 8-10pm. Free.)

PURPLE GOLD MOUNTAIN 紫金山

East of Nanjing. Take bus #9 from Xinjiekou to its last stop, Zhongshanling, or take tour bus #1 from the train station. Bike ride 30-40min. from Xinjiekou, down Zhongshan Dong Lu, to where the road forks just in front of the Zhongshan Gate. Bear left and take Mingling Lu (明陵路); bike storage available. Tour buses #2 and 3 (Y2) shuttle between sights 9am-5:30pm. A Zhongshan Fengjing sightseeing bus (Y10) also links the sights. Open daily summer sunrise-sunset; winter 7am-5:30pm. Mountain free; all 3 sights Y80.

While neither purple nor gold, the densely wooded, untarnished Purple Gold Mountain (zǐjīn shān), east of the city, hosts Nanjing's most renowned sights.

MAUSOLEUM OF DR. SUN YAT-SEN (zhōngshān líng; 中山陵). This grandiose mausoleum has become something of a pilgrimage site for thousands of Chinese every day. A plaque at the bottom of the memorial commemorates Sun Yat-sen's devotion to the revolutionary cause (see **The Republican Era,** p. 78). A small picture exhibit in the garden behind the mausoleum documents the building of the memorial. Inside the mausoleum is a life-sized marble statue of Sun lying in his coffin. After the arduous climb to the top—complete with a breathtaking view of Nanjing and its surrounding hills—most visitors will be convinced that the scale of this structure does indeed do justice to Sun's memory. *(☎8444 6111. The Tourist Info Center offers simple English help, but no tours. Open daily 6:30am-6:30pm. Y40.)*

LINGGU PARK (línggǔ gōngyuán; 灵谷公园). Built in 514 and moved to its present site by the first Ming emperor, **Linggu Temple** (línggǔ sì; 灵谷寺) makes up for its small size with intricacy and numerous Buddhist relics. The **Beamless Hall** (wú liáng diàn; 无梁殿), the only remnant of the original structure, is constructed entirely of stone and brick, its arched ceiling supported only by paste and ingenuity. The hall contains a wax figure exhibit on the history of Chinese revolutions from the reign of the Qing emperor Kangxi to liberation in 1949. Carved on the walls are the names of 33,224 soldiers who died between 1926 and 1933. From **Linggu Pagoda** (línggǔ tǎ; 灵谷塔), visitors can see the whole park. *(A 30min. walk or a 10min. ride east of Sun Yat-sen's Mausoleum. Park open daily 6:30am-6:30pm. Y15.)*

MING FILIAL TOMB (míng xiào líng; 明孝陵). This is the tomb of the first Ming emperor Zhu Yuanzhang, Empress Ma, and 46 sacrificed concubines. Twelve pairs of stone animals (horses, camels, and elephants) guard the **Sacred Avenue** (mínglíng shéndào; 明陵神道) to the tomb entrance. A nearby stone tablet features an inscription by Qing emperor Kangxi. West of the tomb, a **cable car** goes to the top of the mountain. *(Four stops from the mausoleum on the sightseeing bus. Cable car Y45, at the last bus stop Y45. Near the 天文台 observatory. Open daily 6:30am-6:45pm. Y50.)*

OTHER SIGHTS

GULOU SQUARE (gǔlóu guǎngchǎng; 鼓楼广场). The heart of Nanjing before all the action moved to Xinjiekou, Gulou Square remains the more aesthetically pleasing of the two traffic circles. The **Drum Tower,** built in 1302, sits on a traffic island, west of the traffic circle. Visitors can climb to the second level to see the drums, which once signaled changes in the night watch. Stop by **Gulou Tea House** for some tranquility. *(☎8336 6838. Buffet daily 10am-2am.)* Opposite the Drum Tower on the other side of the traffic circle, **Gulou Park** (gǔlóu gōngyuán; 鼓楼公园) sees happy families on balmy summer evenings. *(On Zhongshan Lu, 2km north of Xinjiekou. Accessible via buses #1, 16, 26, and 34. Open daily 6am-10pm. Free.)*

CONFUCIUS TEMPLE (fūzǐ miào; 夫子庙). This riverside temple, temporarily closed at the time of writing, was built in AD 103 and houses a statue of Confucius and eight of his disciples. In the past, hopeful scholars flocked here to take the civil service exam in the small rooms behind the main tower. No longer frequented by anxious students, the streets now market everything from parakeets to cheap clothing. Come in the lively hours of early evening, when lantern-lovers, diners, and shoppers stroll the brightly lit river banks. *(From Xinjiekou, take bus #1 east to the last stop, opposite the main temple gate. Area around temple open daily dawn-10pm. Rent a boat to view the architecture from the Qinghua River; motor boats Y20 per 30min, 4-person paddleboats Y15 per 30min. A 15min. narrated boat tour costs Y20 per person.)*

RAINFLOWER TERRACE (yǔhuā tái; 雨花台). Famous to students of Communist history, Rainflower Terrace is a memorial to revolutionaries killed by Chiang Kai-shek in 1927. Shaded paths and rainflower pebble stands dot the elegant gardens, and a stoic monument to the Revolutionary Martyrs completes the scene. Many groups of 30-somethings come here for their initiation into the Communist Party. Head to the surrounding mountain and the Yuhua Pavilion for great views. Over 15 birds strut in the peacock zoo. *(Just beyond Zhonghua Gate at the terminus of bus #16 from Gulou and Xinjiekou. Zhonghua Lu becomes Yuhua Lu as it leads to the entrance of the Rainflower Terrace. Open daily 6am-9pm. Y15, students Y7. Memorial open 8am-6pm.)*

MEMORIAL TO THE VICTIMS OF THE NANJING MASSACRE (qīnhuá nánjīng dàtúshā yùnàn tóngbao jìniànguǎn; 侵华南京大屠杀遇难同胞纪念馆). Located in one of the former execution sites, this memorial is a somber and austere reminder of the hundreds of thousands of Nanjing residents terrorized and killed by Japanese troops in December 1937. The memorial contains outdoor exhibits, a historical museum, and a building housing the remains of some victims. English audio tapes and documentary available. *(418 Shuiximen Dajie. Take bus #37 or 41 from Xinjiekou, 3 stops past Mochou Lake. ☎8661 0931. Open daily 8:30am-4:30pm. Free.)*

ZHONGHUA GATE (zhōnghuá mén; 中华门). One of the best-preserved pieces of the old Nanjing city wall, Zhonghua Gate consists of four large archways, each with a wooden door and a 1000kg iron gate that shuts automatically when the door shatters, effectively trapping retreating enemy soldiers within the city. The cement mixture for the wall is especially strong—a healthy combination of lime, tung oil, and sticky rice juice gives the mixture an extra kick. Built during the Yuan and Ming Dynasties, the gate has been restored to its original condition. The observation platform at the top provides the closest thing there is to a bird's-eye view of Nanjing. *(Take bus #16 south along Zhonghua Lu to Zhonghua Men Nei, the 2nd-to-last stop. Open daily 8am-6pm. Y15, children under 1.3m free.)*

Far from any of Nanjing's other tourist attractions, the **Yangzi River Bridge** (nánjīng chángjiāng dàqiáo; 南京长江大桥) stretches 4km over the Yangzi River. An elevator at the base of the bridge takes you to the top, where zooming cars and an expansive view of Nanjing awaits. *(Off Daqiao Nan Lu. Take bus #12, 15, or 67 from Nanjing West Train Station. Open daily 8am-6pm. Y5.)*

■ NIGHTLIFE

Nanjing's many students frequent a constantly evolving nightclub and bar scene. New watering holes open every few months, replacing those that lost their mojo. The area near the Nanjing University Foreign Students' Dormitory offers casual drinks and fun: croon to karaoke favorites, jump and jive to East-West hip-hop, or simply guzzle beer in a laid-back bar. Many Nanjing universities lock their gates at 11pm, so clubs popular among students fill up by 9:30pm and empty at the stroke of 11. Then the foreigners rush in, along with foreign DJs. If the time-conscious nightclub scene doesn't float your boat, try the movie theaters in the Fuzimiao area or the ever-popular bowling lanes. (Chinese and Cantonese films Y15 and up.)

Blowing in the Wind (dá'àn jiǔbā; 答案酒吧), 13 Jinyin Jie (☎8323 2486), down the street from the Nanjing Univ. Foreign Students' Dormitory. A roomy atmosphere, pictures of past shenanigans, and reasonable drink prices (Y10 and up) make this a lively hangout for students, foreigners, and jazz lovers. The owner and his bass guitar player often join in impromptu jam sessions. Monthly performances feature local bands. Live music nightly 9:30pm. Open daily 5pm-2am.

Orgies Club, 202 Zhongshan Bei Lu (☎8341 5529), next to Rainbow Bridge Hotel. Mostly Chinese students ensure a non-stop run-down of Chinese and Cantonese songs. Larger dance floor than Scarlet. A separate karaoke area and small snack area. Reservations needed for live jazz on weekends. Open daily 9pm-2am.

Scarlet (luànshì jiārén yīnyuè xīcāntīng jiǔbā; 乱世佳人音乐西餐厅酒吧), 34-1 Hubei Lu (☎8320 6090), off the northwest corner of Gulou, behind Gulou Dept. Store. With unusual staying power, Scarlet has been the disco of choice for at least 6 years among locals and foreigners. International DJ spins hip-hop after 1am. Drinks Y30 and up. Foreigners get in free. Open M-F 6:30pm-2am, Sa-Su 6:30pm-4am.

SUZHOU 苏州 ☎0512

One of China's oldest cities, Suzhou dates back to 514 BC, when King Helu of Wu settled here, dug numerous canals, and began the private gardens that earned Suzhou the title "Venice of the East." But the city really flourished about 1500 years later, when the Grand Canal funneled pioneering traders to Suzhou for its storied silk production. By the 12th century, the slinky fabrics were among Suzhou's top exports, and wealthy merchants and officials were able to elaborate upon old gardens and build new ones—making more than 280 in total. Lured by the gardens, scholars and artists trickled in to add cultural fame to Suzhou's already considerable list of assets. Although the city has lost some of its elegance with modernization, its carefully landscaped gardens still delight visitors with mazes of greenery, pavilions, streams, and rocks. Just don't expect solitude—tour groups hit the paths by late morning—although relative seclusion does exist among its more anonymous, but no less beautiful gardens. Construction is in full swing downtown, but far from the city center, rustic canals recapture the charm of Suzhou's old nickname. The shady streets and winding lanes are ideal for aimless wandering, from gardens and canals to tea houses and nighttime trinket stands.

▶ TRANSPORTATION

Trains: Suzhou Train Station (sūzhōu huǒchē zhàn; 苏州火车站 ; ☎160 1234), on the north side of town, just west of Renmin Lu after the moat. To: **Beijing** (12-21hr., 2 per day, Y83-300); **Hangzhou** (4½-5hr., 12 per day, Y44); **Nanjing** (3½-4hr., Y17-30) via **Wuxi** (30min., Y10-15); **Shanghai** (30-60min., Y7-15).

Buses: Suzhou has 1 bus station in the north of town and 2 in the south.

Pingmen Long-Distance Bus Station (píngmén zhàn; 平门站 ; ☎160 1088), on the east side of the traffic circle at the head of Renmin Lu. Take bus #29 from Guanqian Jie, in the city center. Open daily 5:15am-7:30pm. To: **Hangzhou** (many per day, Y33-52); **Nanjing** (2½hr., many per day, Y53-64); **Shanghai** (1½hr., many per day, Y26-30); **Wuxi** (1hr., every 30min. 6:10am-6:10pm, Y20); **Yangzhou** (5 per day, Y51).

South Gate Long-Distance Bus Station (nán mén qìchē zhàn; 南门汽车站 ; ☎160 1088), on the east side of Renmin Lu, just before the southern part of the moat. Ticket office is the 1st building on the right as you walk down Renmin Lu. Open daily 5am-7:30pm. To: **Hangzhou** (every 30min. 6:20am-7pm, Y55); **Shanghai** (13 per day, Y30); **Yangzhou** (7 per day, Y62).

Wuzhong Bus Terminal (wúzhōng qìchē zhàn; 吴中汽车站), farther south on Renmin Lu. A 5min. walk past the moat, near the terminus of buses #43 and 103, or take 102. Frequent minibuses leave unpredictably for **Dongshan, Xishan,** and other **Lake Taihu** destinations.

Ferries: Suzhou Shipping Terminal (sūzhōu lúnchuán gōngsī; 苏州轮船公司), 8 Renmin Lu (☎6520 6681), just south of the South Gate Bus Station, on the outer moat near the Renmin Lu bridge. Open daily 7am-5pm. A boat leaves daily for **Hangzhou** (14hr., 5:30pm, Y70-150). Passengers must board 30min. prior to departure. The nighttime trip may not offer much in terms of river views, but it does feature entertainment on board (read: alcohol and karaoke) for Y10.

Public Transportation: City **buses** run to the most popular sights. Most lines run 6am-8pm and have a flat fare of Y1. Exact change. Bus #1 goes down Renmin Lu from the train station to Wuzhong district; #4 begins in the southeast, just outside the moat, and zigzags northwest, passing the Master of Nets Garden and the Twin Pagodas before terminating on Xi Zhongshi Lu; #9 goes east-west on Ganjiang Lu through the center of town. **Tour bus** #2, " 游 2" (Y1, with A/C Y2), covers just about every major sight between Tiger Hill and Panmen Gate.

Taxis: Base fare Y10, each additional km Y2.1. Taxi from one of the Shiquan Jie hotels to the train station about Y20-22. Bike **rickshaws** (base fare Y2, each additional km Y2), affectionately labeled "tourist pedicabs," can be found almost everywhere.

Bike Rental: Major streets have separate bike lanes. Many bike **rental places** near the train station offer bikes of all sizes and conditions for Y2 per 3hr. or Y5 per day. Look for groups of bikes lined up on Renmin Lu opposite the North Temple Park. **Yang Yang Bike**

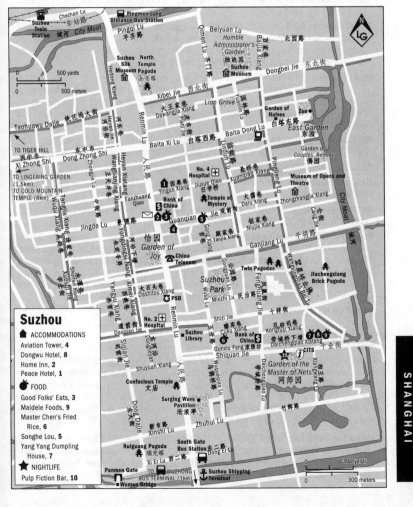

Suzhou

🏠 ACCOMMODATIONS
Aviation Tower, **4**
Dongwu Hotel, **8**
Home Inn, **2**
Peace Hotel, **1**

🍴 FOOD
Good Folks' Eats, **3**
Maidele Foods, **9**
Master Chen's Fried
Rice, **6**
Songhe Lou, **5**
Yang Yang Dumpling
House, **7**

⭐ NIGHTLIFE
Pulp Fiction Bar, **10**

S H A N G H A I

Rental, run by a PLA veteran, has reliable bikes and friendly service. On Renmin Lu, a 5min. walk past the northern moat; or from the train station, the 1st stop on bus #102 or 103. Open daily 6am-7pm. Y2 for 4hr., Y3 for 6hr., Y5 per day. **Stands** on Shiquan Jie charge Y10-15 per day. All bike rentals require a deposit of Y200-300.

⚡🛈 ORIENTATION AND PRACTICAL INFORMATION

Suzhou's layout follows the original grid of its canals and is neatly confined within a rectangular outer moat. Two streets form the commercial heart of the city: **Renmin Lu** (人民路), the major thoroughfare cutting north-south through the city; and **Guanqian Jie** (观前街), a pedestrian shopping and eating zone. Most of Suzhou's hotels are in the southeastern part of town, near or along **Shiquan Jie** (十全街), a tree-lined street running east-west.

Tourist Hotline: CITS Tourist Complaints ☎6522 3377. Information ☎6520 3131. Both have English-speaking staff.

Travel Agency: CITS (☎753 0782), on the east side of the train station. Open daily 8am-5pm. Another **branch,** 18 Dajin Xiang (☎6515 9177), in the Lexiang Hotel on Guanqian Jie, has English-speaking staff. Travel agencies offer little help, however; it's easier to purchase a map from a gift shop at any of the major sights.

Bank of China: 1450 Renmin Lu (☎6720 1326), north of Guanqian Jie. Exchanges foreign currency and traveler's checks. Open daily 8:15am-5:15pm. Another **branch,** at Shiquan Jie at Fenghuang Jie, offers the same services. Open daily 8:30am-5:10pm. 24hr. **ATMs** (Cirrus/Plus) at both branches. Most of Suzhou's larger hotels also exchange currency.

Bookstores: Foreign-Language Bookstore (wàiwén shūdiàn; 外文书店), 44 Renmin Lu (☎/fax 6519 7355), north of Zhuhui Lu. Dictionaries. Open daily 9am-7:30pm.

PSB: 7 Dashitou Xiang, at Renmin Lu, north of Daoqian Jie.

Hospital: Suzhou No. 2 Hospital (sūzhōu dì'èr yīyuàn; 苏州第二医院 ; ☎6515 7565), half a block west of Renmin Lu on Daoqian Jie.

Internet Access: Three-Footed Bird Internet Cafe, 76 Baita Xi Lu, near Lindun Lu, has speedy access for Y2 per hr. Open daily 8am-midnight.

Post and Telecommunications: China Post, 1401 Renmin Lu, at Jingde Lu. Lovely branch with EMS, Poste Restante, newsstand, and an English chart of postage rates. Open daily 8am-8pm. **Suzhou Renmin Lu Telecommunications Business Department,** on the east side of Renmin Lu, north of Daoqian Jie. IDD service Y8 per min. to most countries in Asia, Y15 per min. everywhere else. Open 24hr. **China Telecom** also has several offices on Renmin Lu, south of Daoqian Jie, with IDD/DDD service.

Postal Code: 215005.

🏠 ACCOMMODATIONS

Suzhou's gardens are the playgrounds of choice for daytripping bureaucrats and businessmen, as well as local and international visitors. The prosperous tourism scene is reflected in the dearth of budget options. Interspersed among ritzy resorts, a few mid-range spots along the east end of Siquan Jie are more likely to offer discounts. The stretch of Renmin Lu between Baita Lu and Shiquan Jie offers clean lodgings along the city's artery. All listed hotels offer A/C, TV, and bath.

Home Inn (rújiā lǚguǎn; 如家旅馆), 246 Guanqian Jie (☎6523 8770, toll free 800 820 3333), at Renmin Lu. Trusty chain offers bright and spacious rooms, complete with soft duvet covers and sliding glass shower doors. Friendly staff. Phone. Reserve ahead. Singles Y158; doubles Y198. 8% discount with free membership. ❷

Dongwu Hotel (dōngwú fàndiàn; 东吴饭店), 24 Wuya Chang (☎6519 4437; fax 6519 4590), at the eastern end of Shiquan Jie, near the bridge. Renovations have raised this student residence to the quality of a starred hotel, but prices are still relatively cheap. Room deposit equal to price of stay; key deposit Y50. With half the dorms set aside for long-term foreign students, travelers should reserve well in advance. Reception open 24hr. Singles and doubles Y80-100, with bath Y180-280; triples Y360. ❶

Aviation Tower (hángtiān dàshà; 航天大厦), 1 Jiusheng Xiang (☎6511 6200; fax 6511 4806). In the heart of Suzhou's pedestrian shopping zone; enter on the little pedestrian street off Renmin Lu, south of Guanqian Jie. Dark bedrooms but bright, clean baths. Phone. Singles Y250-300; doubles Y260. Low-season discounts available. ❹

Peace Hotel (hépíng fàndiàn; 和平饭店), 50 Yinguo Xiang (☎6729 6356; fax 6729 4167), a block south of Baita Lu at Renmin Lu. Sunlit, relatively clean rooms of moderate size show wear and tear, but convenient location buoys up its price. Phone and water boiler. Doubles Y298; triples Y350. Discounts are rare, but try for 10% off. ❹

▐ FOOD

Suzhou's culinary history dates back to the exquisite delicacies enjoyed by Tang emperors while cruising down the Grand Canal on their dragon boats. As might be expected from its vaunted origin, Suzhou is known for creative, flavorful, subtle cuisine pleasing to both the eye and the stomach. The city's most renowned street for eats is **Taijian Nong** (太监弄), off Guanqian Jie, next to Renmin Shangchang, lined with hundred-year-old restaurants flaunting the best of Suzhou specialties. Where Taijian Nong ends, **Bifeng Fang** (碧凤坊) begins, sporting delicious dumplings, noodles, and buns down its length. A walk down Guanqian Jie's **Buxing Jie** (pedestrian section) isn't complete without a stop at the age-old **Huangtian Yuan** (huángtiān yuán; 黄天源) for the quintessential **Suzhou sticky rice cakes** (sūzhōu gāo tuán; 苏州糕团). Made from rice flour, these gently molded cakes come in more flavors and varieties than you can imagine. Farmers on the street carry baskets full of *yángméi* (杨梅), fuzzy red fruit similar to lychee. Ingesting the pit supposedly cleans your stomach of any hairballs you may have swallowed.

Good Folks' Eats (hǎo rén mínjiān xiǎochī; 好人民间小吃 ; ☎6727 3236), at Guanqian Jie at Renmin Lu. This popular eatery combines Sichuanese spice with slightly sweet Suzhou flavors to create spareribs in a spicy bamboo sauce (Y15). Don't be startled by fried milk (Y3), a dessert with crisp pastry skin and a rich, creamy filling (think fried ice cream). Noodles Y5-18. Appetizers Y2-18. Open daily 9am-11pm. ❶

Songhe Lou (sōng hè lóu càifàn; 松鹤楼菜饭), 141 Guanqian Jie (☎6727 7006), 1 block east of Renmin Lu. Like so many things in China, this restaurant got its start with Emperor Qianlong. Extensive (and expensive) menu includes the Suzhou-style soy-sauce duck (Y18). Its most famous dish, *sōngshǔ guìyú* (松鼠桂鱼 ; Y160), fish fried 'til golden and drenched in sweet-and-sour sauce, is made with a 100-year-old recipe. Best of all, unlike most Chinese fish, *sōngshǔ guìyú* is served without bones. Pine-nut-studded red rice cakes (Y12) showcase what Suzhou does best: rich, sweet desserts. Stir-fries Y13-38. Desserts Y10-35. Open daily 11am-1:30pm and 5-8:30pm. ❸

Maidele Foods (màidélè shípǐn; 麦德乐食品), 86 Shiquan Jie (☎6519 8468), next to the Dongwu Hotel. Serves warm mooncakes with flaky skin and juicy meat filling (Y1) to those in the know. Modest selection of breads and cakes (Y1-2.8), some filled with shredded pork or raisins. Bubble tea Y2. Iced soy milk Y1.5. Open daily 7am-9pm. ❶

Master Chen's Fried Rice (chén shīfù chǎofàn; 陈师傅炒饭 ; ☎6515 5871; www.chinabelly.com), on the corner of Renmin Lu and an alley, a block south of Daoqianjie Bridge, across from the Suzhou Library; look for yellow lanterns outside. Wicker chairs and fake wood arbors aim for a quaint charm. The fluffy egg-fried rice is a universal favorite. Fried rice platters Y4-6, served with pickled vegetables and soup. ❶

FROM THE ROAD

A TRIP TO THE HAIRDRESSER

China's suffocating heat had been wearing me down. As I trudged on, I had the misfortune of seeing my reflection in a shop window. Perspiring furiously, forehead withered like a dried prune, unkempt hair straggling in all directions—one thing had become clear: life on the road was taking its toll. There was only one thing left to do, I acknowledged grimly. needed a haircut.

Now, I've always believed that a chopping need only take 5min. With this in mind, I ventured into a salon and made hopeful scissors gestures toward my head. A flurry of dialect ensued and I was ushered into a leather seat, a gown fastened neatly around my neck—so far so good.

A lady with a towering hairdo approached. Smiling, she seized a wash bottle and set to work. Though I hadn't intended on getting my hair shampooed, there was little to be gained by objecting: already a generous lather was foaming. Hair-washing in China, it soon transpired, is no mere lather, rinse, repeat—a thorough massage is critical. Digging her nails into my scalp, my attendant delivered. Though at times I felt sure she must be drawing blood, the whole experience was remarkably soothing. As my worries started to ebb away, I closed my eyes... Suddenly she began an elaborate head slapping technique, which sounded very much

Yang Yang Dumpling House (yángyáng jiǎoziguǎn; 洋洋饺子馆), 144 Shiquan Jie (☎6519 2728), across from the Suzhou Hotel. A haven of cheap gourmet cooking. The owners imported the secrets of *jiǎozi* from northern China, serving up tender and delicious dumplings (Y5 per dozen). Also southern staples like sweet-and-sour pork (Y18). Try the homemade hot pepper sauce. Open daily 6am-2am. ❶

🧭 SIGHTS

In Suzhou, ponds become seas, and rocks mountains, harmoniously set amid classical Chinese architecture and groves of bamboo. A garden is not just a pleasant enclosed space of greenery—the grounds often contain subtle allusions to art and literature and represent entire inner worlds. Each turn of the path brings visitors to a wholly different scene, making the gardens seem much larger than they actually are, and thus recreating the world in miniature. To understand these "silent poems" and "three-dimensional paintings" requires an appreciation of classical Chinese ideas of art, beauty, and man's relation to nature and society. They exist not only to please the eye, but also to stimulate the mind and provide a refuge from the chaotic world without. Of course, knowledge of Chinese language and culture isn't necessary to enjoy the serenity of the gardens.

Suzhou's 70 or so gardens each holds its own reasons for a visit, and their accessible locations around the city proper make sightseeing easy. The most worthwhile ones are probably **Lion Grove** and the **Humble Administrator's Garden** in north Suzhou, **Garden of the Master of Nets** in south Suzhou, and **Tiger Hill** and **Lingering Garden,** both beyond the moat. Arrive early in the morning or late in the day to beat the crowds. If possible, tag along with a tour group or pick up brochures to enjoy the anecdotes and history of each garden. Prices and hours fluctuate between the "winter" (mid-Nov. to Feb.) and "summer" (Mar. to mid-Nov.) seasons. Some daytrippers short on time prefer a pedicab tour (Y60-80) that leaves each morning from Suzhou's major hotels, including the Nanlin Hotel. A more flexible option is to rent a bike and navigate the slew of gardens and pagodas at a more leisurely pace. For a breather, stop in one of the teahouses of Suzhou's past.

NORTH SUZHOU

LION GROVE (shīzi lín; 狮子林). A showcase of Yuan Dynasty architecture, this "kingdom of rockery" was built by the monk Tianru in memory of his teacher, who lived in Lion Crag in Zhejiang province.

The expansive labyrinth of craggy rocks from Lake Taihu supposedly trapped Emperor Qianlong with his concubines for 2hr. before he managed to find the way out; apparently, he wasn't in a hurry to leave. Lion Grove does not see as much traffic as its fame and ancient rocks merit, mostly because tour groups prefer the more picturesque ponds and pavilions. Some of the rambling, rippled rock formations look like lions; others simply look like rocks (albeit very exciting ones). Many of the garden's buildings display paintings and etchings by famous artists. *(About 250m south of the Suzhou Museum. Open daily 7:30am-5:30pm; last admission 5pm. Y20, children under 1.2m free.)*

HUMBLE ADMINISTRATOR'S GARDEN (zhuózhèng yuán; 拙政园). This name was given in irony: the "Humble" Administrator's Garden is actually the largest in Suzhou and the crown attraction of Suzhou. After being cast out of his job, Wang Xianchen, a corrupt Ming Dynasty official, sought solace in governing nature and built this garden. "Building houses, planting trees, watering gardens, and growing vegetables," he wrote, "are a way for a humble man to manage administrative affairs." Water covers three-fifths of the garden. Wandering the paths and bridges twisting and turning to the maze of waters is a great way to stumble into the more isolated corners. Robust willows and lilacs hide some of the architecture. The overflowing lily ponds host an annual lily show (June-Aug.) with some 70 exotic varieties from around the world. *(On Dongbei Jie, 1km east of the North Temple. Free tours in Chinese every 30min. Open daily 7:30am-5:30pm; last admission 5pm. Y50.)*

NORTH TEMPLE PAGODA (běi sì tǎ; 北寺塔). Supposedly Suzhou's first pagoda (the original main temple was built in AD 238-251), this 76m structure is the tallest pagoda south of the Yangzi. Unfortunately, the top floor has been sealed off due to safety concerns. Regardless, a climb up the pagoda allows a bird's-eye view of Suzhou, overlooking a belt of green rice paddies stretching to the distant horizon. A small garden next to the pagoda hosts occasional amateur opera performances in its tea house. *(On the corner of Renmin Lu and Xibei Jie, take tour bus #1, 101, 103—just about anything going to the train station—and get off at Beisita. Open daily summer 7:45am-5:30pm; winter 7:45am-5pm. Last admission 30min. before closing. Y25.)*

SUZHOU SILK MUSEUM (sūzhōu sīchóu bówùguǎn; 苏州丝绸博物馆). Suzhou first gained prosperity as the silk-producing center of China, a status the city enjoys to this day. This museum claims to be the only silk-centric museum in the world, and its well-presented exhibits (with English captions) spin the tale

like eggs were being cracked on my skull. This continued with vigor while she struck up a lively conversation, which I barely followed, given the dialect, the whirring hairdryers, and the head wallops. My chair was spun around at last, and she pointed to the sink. Ah, rinsing, I guessed, and ambled over, leaving a trail of suds.

But it's never that simple. The rinse turned into another massage, including the earlobes. We continued our dialogue, though it was becoming clear that neither party understood the other. Lest I felt that I wasn't getting my money's worth (Y15), I was passed to a third chair, where a lady dealt swift blows to my back and shoulders. I had at this stage long forgotten the haircut itself.

It was at least 45min. in before there was any sign of scissors. A young man appeared and danced about my head with clippers as if he were trimming an ice sculpture. The background music changed to the mellow "Country Roads, Take Me Home," which seemed particularly appropriate.

Thirty minutes later, the hair-artiste stepped back with a flourish. I thanked him kindly and muttered my appreciation to all involved in staging this event. Running my fingers through my hair, I noticed hardly anything had been taken off. I rejoiced, as this signaled a return trip in the not-too-distant future. The pampering, though at times disturbing, had put a spring in my step—truly a therapy for the weary traveler.

—Gary Cooney

of Suzhou's silk trade, which dates back to the Neolithic Age. The weaving room offers a try at the looms, while the "Sericulture House" teems with plump silkworms hard at work. A display room tempts visitors with the brilliant colors and sleek textures of the finished product, but many prefer buying more stylish items in the silk boutiques along Renmin Lu north of Guanqian Jie. *(2001 Renmin Lu, across the street from the North Temple Pagoda and about a half-block north. Open daily 9am-4:45pm; last admission 4:15pm. Y7, students Y3.5.)*

OTHER SIGHTS. The now privatized **Garden of Couple's Retreat** (ǒu yuán; 偶园) is more than just a lover's lair. Built by a provincial governor who wanted a place to sit with his wife, the garden today remains a secluded hideaway, with gondola rides, local story-telling, and folk music. *(East of Lion Grove. Open daily summer 7:30am-5:30pm; winter 8am-5pm. Last admission 30min. before closing. Gondolas Y10 per person. Y15.)* In the unique **Garden of Halves** (bàn yuán; 半园), half of everything is missing, from the pavilion to the bridge. The owner designed the garden according to the ancient Chinese saying, "It is better to be satisfied and not seek perfection." This perhaps explains why the garden is dusty and overgrown. *(60 Baita Dong Lu. Open 24hr. Just walk in.)* Old pine trees and not much else fill the **East Garden** (dōng yuán; 东园), at the end of Baita Dong Lu, near the Outer Moat. Boats are available, a sure treat if you want to examine the pond in closer detail. *(Open daily summer 7:30am-5:30pm; winter 8am-5pm. Boats Y10 per hr. Y10, children under 1.2m free.)*

CENTRAL SUZHOU

GARDEN OF JOY (qià yuán; 恰园). Once the private residence of Qing bureaucrat Gu Wenbin, this garden was built using stylistic elements from other gardens in the area. There are caves from Lion Grove, a stone boat like the one in the Humble Administrator's Garden, and so on. The plum groves make a fragrant stop if you're in the area to send mail or change money. *(1265 Renmin Lu. Open daily 7:30am-11pm; last admission 5pm. Y45, includes a drink at the tea house and opera performances.)*

TWIN PAGODAS (shuāngtǎ yuàn; 双塔院). Part of the Arhat Temple complex, the Twin Pagodas are all that's left of a temple built by three brothers in AD 1410. The site was ransacked in the early 20th century, but the pagodas were restored in 1954. The current garden is designed around the ruins of the former "Great Hall." Two large tea houses are left of the sculpted stelae. *(Half a block east of Fenghuang Jie, just south of Ganjiang Dong Lu. Open daily 7:30am-5:30pm. Y8, children under 1.2m Y4.)*

SOUTH SUZHOU

GARDEN OF THE MASTER OF NETS (wǎng shī yuán; 网师园). During the 12th century, Shi Zhengzhi (better known as the "Fishing Hermit") owned the **Hall of Ten Thousand Volumes.** About 600 years later, a retired bureaucrat claimed the area and built the garden in its current form as his "Fisherman's Retreat." The Garden of the Master of Nets certainly knows how to cast a net—the 1.5-acre plot squeezes in pavilions, a lily pond, a stone mountain, chambers for musical performances, Suzhou's tiniest stone bridge, and a resonating boulder, and all without alarming claustrophobes. Visit during the day and again at night, when Chinese folk music wafts through the garden (see **Entertainment and Nightlife,** p. 374). *(On Shiquan Jie, near Fengshuang Jie. Enter through the alley between 491 and 482 Shiquan Lu; follow the English signs. ☎6520 3514. Musical performances Y80. Free guided tours in Chinese. Open daily summer 7:30am-5:30pm; winter 7:30am-5pm. Summer Y30, winter Y20; children under 1.2m free.)*

PAN GATE SCENIC AREA (pán mén jǐng qū; 盘门景区). Thanks to renovations, this ancient water-land defense system lights up the southern part of the city at night and greets visitors with fresh paint and red lanterns during the day. Climb to the fifth floor of **Ruiguang Pagoda** (ruìguāng tǎ; 瑞光塔) for Y6. At the far corner, the **Tower of City Gates** displays the portcullises, cannons, stone walls, and "murder holes" used to fend off attackers. The semi-circular and oft photographed **Wumen Bridge** (wǔmén qiáo; 午门桥) is on the southern edge of the park. *(At far southwest corner of the old city. Enter from outside the moat to the south or from east of the Sheraton Hotel on Zhuhui Lu. Open daily 8am-5pm; last admission 4:30pm. Y25, children under 1.2m free.)*

SURGING WAVE PAVILION (cāng làng tíng; 沧浪亭). This is Suzhou's oldest garden, built over 1000 years ago. The pavilion is bigger and more natural and woodsy than others, but not as tidily kept. Suffice it to say the facade is more impressive than what's inside. Notable features include the **Temple of 500 Sages**, which showcases prominent figures in Suzhou's history, and the **Green and Delicate Hall**, surrounded by several varieties of thick bamboo. *(East of Pan Gate, off the east side of Renmin Lu, south of Shiquan Jie. Open daily summer 7:30am-5:30pm; winter 8am-5pm. Last admission 30min. before closing. Y15, children under 1.2m free.)*

BEYOND THE OUTER MOAT

TIGER HILL (hǔqiū gōngyuán; 虎丘公园). Strange legends surround this hill and Suzhou's founder, Helu of Wu, who was buried here with his sword in 550 BC. Three days after his burial, people saw a white tiger crouching by his tomb, and the hill became known as Tiger Hill. Since then, the temple has experienced destruction seven times, and provided the backdrop for an unbelievable number of strange and sordid tales. The park's claim to fame is its 28m-tall pagoda, which tilts precariously from atop the hill. The huge cleft of the **Sword-Testing Rock** is said to come from King Helu's swords, and Sword Pond was supposedly created when subsequent kings all searched for Helu's tomb with no success. Helu's son must have done his job well: he killed the 1000 workers who built his father's tomb to hide the grave from future gold-diggers. When it rains, the morbid **Thousand-Man Rock** bleeds red streaks—the blood of the 1000 murdered, or so the stories say.

For a less grisly experience, climb up to the **Giant Buddha Temple** atop the hill. The truly devout are supposed to kneel and bow on each of the 53 steps leading up to the Buddha. The less devout can hire people to carry them from the entrance to the top in a red palanquin (Y20) or opt for a horse-drawn carriage that goes to the bottom of the hill (Y5). *(Buses #2 and 5 from the train station stop outside. By bike, take Xi Zhongshi Lu west from the city, turn right after the moat, then turn left on Shantang Jie, which follows a path to Tiger Hill. From the Lingering Garden, head west, and then take Huqiu Lu, the 1st major right off Liuyuan Lu. After about 3 blocks, bear left, and then cruise to Tiger Hill on the tree-lined road. English audio guides Y400 deposit. Open daily summer 7:30am-6pm; winter 7:30am-5:30pm. Last admission 30min. before closing. Summer Y60; winter Y40.)*

LINGERING GARDEN (liú yuán; 留园). Refurbishment has restored much of the original beauty of this 400-year-old garden. The original owner's homes, dating back to the Qing Dynasty, are richly decorated with scrolls, plaques, delicately latticed and carved windows, and dark cherrywood furniture. A bridge with nine bends zigzags over the water, past rocky mountains, groves, and an extensive bonsai collection—miniature gardens within an already tiny garden. *(1km west of the city's outer moat. 15min. by bike from city center. Follow Xi Zhongshi Lu west until it turns into Fengqiao Lu; turn right on Guangli Lu, and then left onto Liuyuan Jie. Open daily summer 7:30am-5:30pm, winter 7:30am-5pm; last admission 30min. before closing. Summer Y40; winter Y30.)*

COLD MOUNTAIN TEMPLE (hánshān sì; 寒山寺). Tang poet Zhang Ji immortalized this temple in verse: "The moon sets, crows call, a frosty sky/Sleepless the fishing lights drift in the river by Maple Bridge/Beyond Gusu, from Cold Mountain Temple, the cold chime of midnight floats to the wanderer's boat." Thirteen hundred years later, Gusu (the ancient name of Suzhou) and this temple have lost their

SHANGHAI

ethereal air. The Maple Bridge is only a reconstruction, and the tolling bell a replica (the original is in Japan, and the replacement is also "Made in Japan"). First built in the 6th century, Cold Mountain Temple is named after a Tang Buddhist monk poet known as Hanshan (Cold Mountain), but whatever hermetic asceticism is implied by the name has since been trampled by busloads of tour groups. Red lanterns and curry-yellow paint give the grounds a ghastly carnivalesque air. **Maple Bridge Garden**, across from the arched bridge in front of the temple, has the surreal feel of a movie set, with brand-new traditional houses. At least the maple tree is real. An "artisan street" inside the garden has clay teapots and silk scarves on sale for prices higher than in the city proper. *(About 8km from Suzhou. Baita Xi Lu becomes Fengqiao Lu west of the Outer Moat. Temple is next to the canal. Open daily 8am-4:50pm. Ringing temple bell Y5. Temple Y20, children under 1.2m free. Maple Bridge open daily 7:30am-5pm. Y25, children under 1.2m free.)*

🎭🎵 ENTERTAINMENT AND NIGHTLIFE

Suzhou's summer evenings are its finest hours. By far the best entertainment is the nightly **cultural performance** inside the **Garden of the Master of Nets** (p. 372). Busloads of tourists move through this multi-part assembly line from opera to flute to lute, with Suzhou's architectural masterpieces shimmering in the evening light. Just tag along with whichever group you fancy. (May-Oct. nightly 7:30-10pm. Y80.)

Norm, the Australian owner of the **Pulp Fiction Bar**, 169 Shiquan Jie, plies his mostly male, mostly international patrons with beer (Y25 and up) and music. The first floor of this intimate establishment plays oldies and classic rock, while the second floor features darts, pool, and a TV lounge area. Keep an eye on the pool table: tradition here dictates that those with seven balls left on the table must drop their pants and bunny-hop around the table. (☎520 8067. Happy hour 7pm-midnight.) Night spots on **Shiquan Jie** charge high prices, and few are full enough to be lively. Some places get busy in an entirely different way: be wary of "bars" displaying a photo of a couple in a snazzy bedroom. It may be flattering to be chatted up by attractive women, but buy them drinks and watch prices skyrocket.

🔖 DAYTRIPS FROM SUZHOU

DONGSHAN 东山 AND XISHAN 西山

*About 40km southwest of Suzhou. Getting there is simple, but finding reasonably priced transportation once there can be a hassle. Catch a **minibus** (Y5) from the train station, where bus #20 (Y4) also leaves for the area. From the Wuzhong station, **buses** (Y10-15) depart when full during daylight hours to both Dongshan and Xishan; they should have Chinese labels on them (" 东山 " and " 西山 "). Bringing a bike on board is Y5 extra. A warning: the roads on Dongshan are often steep, rocky, and not particularly well suited to low-quality bikes. With a bike, you'll have to travel exclusively by land; the **motorboats** that cross the lake are usually too small to carry bicycles. To return to Suzhou, minibuses leave from the parking lot by the tower on **Xishan** to the main street in **Xishan Zhen** (Xishan's largest town). Buses to Suzhou depart from where minibuses drop passengers off in Xishan Zhen, or in front of the Xishan Hotel at the ferry dock. Dongshan Y35. Xishan Y68.*

The **Dongshan** (东山) peninsula stretches out into **Lake Taihu**, and the island of **Xishan** (西山 ; or xī dòngtíngshān; 西洞庭山) sits not far off the coast. Far from the fume-belching industries of the city, these areas are home to fishermen, fruit farmers, fragrant countryside, and not much else—a peaceful escape for those who overdosed on gardens. Once in Dongshan, buses stop near an intersection in the town proper, from which a 15min. walk leads to **Purple Gold Nunnery** (zǐjīn ān; 紫金俺). Hidden amid pines, bamboo, and wildflowers, the 1400-year-old nunnery displays 16 masterpiece arhats of colored clay. (Open daily 8am-5pm; last admission 4:30pm. Y12.) A right at the intersection brings visitors to a small dock renting **motorboats** to Xishan (30min., Y80) and the Dongshan Hotel, just behind the dock.

From either direction, it's about 10km from the ferry dock to **Xishan** by land, going around the hilly bulwark of Moli. Once on Xishan, make towards the large hill with a tower on top. The **Linwu Caves** provide relief from the summer heat, but the steps are slick and treacherous. From here, a short hike uphill arrives at the **Jiatu Tower.** Points beyond the souvenir and tea shops see idyllic vistas of the green countryside and plum trees. (Open daily 8am-4:30pm; last admission 4pm. Y25.)

Taxis from Dongshan to Xishan cost Y20-30. If the two scheduled ferries (daily, Y120) aren't running, it may be possible to hire a motorboat on the spot. The asking price will always be higher than the minimal price drivers are willing to accept; a reasonable fare is one-way Y80, round-trip Y150. Be sure to indicate your desired destinations on the map, so that you don't end up at other spots. Bus #91 (Y4) runs to Xishan from the train station.

TONGLI 同里

*About 25km southeast of Suzhou. Take a **bus** from Wuzhong Lu and ask for Tongli (1½hr., frequent departures, Y7); get off across the street from the stone gate entrance that leads to the pedestrian village. The **Tourist Service Center** (☎800 828 2990), near the entrance to Tuisi Garden, can book a Y50 tour including guide and admissions. Open daily 9am-noon and 1-6pm. **Gondolas** (Y60 per 8 people) offer 30min. tours of Tongli. **Motor boats** (6 people; one-way Y180 per boat, round-trip Y250) jet to Zhouzhuang, Tongli's more celebrated (and touristed) neighbor. To return to Suzhou, buses and minibuses (Y20) depart from the stone gate. Y50, from Suzhou bus stations Y45.*

If you've ever seen Chinese postcards of little bridges arching over water, most likely they're photos of Tongli (同里) and its watery, more crowded neighbor Zhouzhuang (周庄). These two villages, along with Suzhou, are the unofficial "Venice of the East." Tongli is a lovely retreat, with a scenic tourist area compact enough for an hour or two of wandering. The village is most famous for three bridges, **Taiping Bridge** (tàipíng qiáo; 太平桥), **Jili Bridge** (jílì qiáo; 吉利桥), and **Changqing Bridge** (chángqìng qiáo; 长庆桥), representing peace, luck, and lasting celebration, respectively. Crossing them all in a row (guò sān qiáo; 过三桥) is good luck; elderly Tongli locals partake in this tradition on their 66th birthdays. Another worthy sight, the famous **Retreating into Meditation Garden** (tuì sī yuán; 退思园), was built as a spot for uninterrupted contemplation. Tiered rows of pavilions surround the quiet pond. The outer edges of Tongli are not as well kept, but they're unfrequented by tour groups. Throughout the village, you can snack on delicious flat flaky cakes and pastries, both salty and sweet. Roasted pigs are just as good.

WUXI 无锡 ☎0510

Many consider Wuxi to be an industrial wart on the beautifully scenic shores of Lake Taihu, one of China's largest freshwater lakes. The city has never been a center of culture or innovation, and its early glory was forged from deposits of tin. By the time the Han Dynasty rolled around, the mines had already been stripped, earning the city the name of Wuxi, or "without tin." Since then, Wuxi has functioned mainly as a trade and transportation center en route to Lake Taihu, just a few kilometers away. Still, the city manages to hold on to a lazy resort town feel, helped by the wide, tree-lined avenues and surrounding greenery. Wuxi has even caught the attention of China's film industry, which spruces up the lakeshores as backdrops for the latest flicks on ancient emperors and dashing kung fu heroes. The movie sets in constant flux have become attractions as popular as the lake itself. Wuxi is beginning to flourish economically, with the busiest intersection resembling a mini-Shanghai in the works, with sleek high-rises and sleeker girls and guys. Further out, the pace dramatically slows, with old men chirping to their caged birds and streetside venders scrubbing vegetables.

▣ TRANSPORTATION

Flights: Wuxi Airport (wúxī jīchǎng; 无锡机场 ; ☎532 2067), about 25km outside the city. Accessible only by taxi (approx. Y60). A very limited number of destinations. Book tickets at CTS for **Beijing** (11:10am, Y810), or contact **Air China** (☎5501 1160).

Trains: Wuxi Train Station (wúxī huǒchē zhàn; 无锡火车站 ; ☎230 1217), at Tonghui Dong Lu and Wuhu Lu. Open daily 6:30am-11:30pm. **Luggage storage** (Y2-4 per day) to the left of the exit; open 6am-midnight. Many trains per day to: **Nanjing** (2-3hr., Y14-44); **Shanghai** (1-2hr., Y20-30); **Suzhou** (30min., Y10); **Zhenjiang** (2hr., Y20).

Buses: Wuxi Main Bus Station (wúxī qìchē zhàn; 无锡汽车站 ; ☎230 0751), just west of the train station. Buy tickets at the ticket office on the east side of the station (open daily 4am-9pm) or the kiosk in the square in front of the train station. To: **Nanjing** (2hr., every 12min. 5:50am-7:30pm, Y44-52); **Shanghai** (1½-2hr., every 18min. 6:30am-6:30pm, Y31-43); **Suzhou** (1hr., every 15min. 6:35am-6:25pm, Y19); **Zhenjiang** (1½hr., every 40-60min. 7:25am-6:05pm, Y28-38). Buses from the **West Bus Station** (qìchē xī zhàn; 汽车西站 ; ☎580 2297), on Hubin Lu across the Liangxi Bridge, only serve destinations in Yixing county and Anhui province.

Ferries: ☎370 7796. Boats run to **Hangzhou** (13hr., several per day, Y60-300) from the dock southwest of Liangxi Bridge.

Local Transportation: Buses in Wuxi are easy to use. Many lines terminate just west of the train station and most run 6am-6pm. A/C buses display " 空调 " (kōngtiáo) in front. Fare Y1, with A/C Y2; exact change only. Bus #1 runs across Baojie Bridge to Turtle Head Island; #4 cuts through town to Liangxi Bridge, near the South Bus Station; #11 connects the train station and the city; #20 links the North and South Bus Stations; #88 goes to the giant Buddha in Lingshan; K83 shuttles around Lake Taihu sights. **Motor pedicabs** are everywhere; agree on a price in advance.

Taxis: Y8 for the 1st 2km, each additional km Y1.6-2. From the train or either bus stations to the city center Y10-15. Larger taxis Y10 base fare; prices indicated on window.

Bike Rental: A few shops are around the train station, but none have English signs.

✺ ▤ ORIENTATION AND PRACTICAL INFORMATION

The **Grand Canal** meanders along the west side of Wuxi and several smaller canals run through the city. Across the canal, farther west, is the **Xihui Park** area, visible from much of the city. **Jiefang Lu** (解放路) circles the downtown area. The north-south **Zhongshan Lu** (中山路) and the east-west **Renmin Lu** (人民路) intersect at the commercial (and culinary) center of the city. All the tourist sights are to the west of the city center. Trains (and most buses) arrive in the northern end of town, across the **Gongyun Bridge** (gōngyùn qiáo; 工运桥) and just a few blocks from Jiefang Bei Lu. The **Liangxi Bridge** (liángxī qiáo; 梁溪桥) connects the area near the South Bus Station to the city proper.

Travel Agencies: IATA, 88 Chezhan Lu, 1st and 4th fl. (☎270 5369), across the train station, next to the CTS Hotel. Look for the large "Wuxi Tourist Guide Center" sign. Booking services and an **automated information kiosk** with all sorts of info (and tourist propaganda) in English on the 1st fl. Open daily 7:30am-8:30pm. Main **CITS** office, 18 Zhongshan Lu (☎270 5369), at the terminus of bus #12. Open daily 8:30am-5pm. You can also find English maps at major hotels like the Sheraton on Xianqian Jie and Zhongshan Lu. Act important and the concierge might be fooled into giving you one for free.

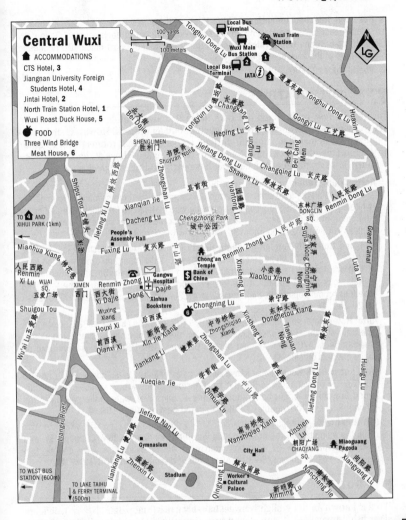

Central Wuxi

⬤ ACCOMMODATIONS
CTS Hotel, 3
Jiangnan University Foreign
   Students Hotel, 4
Jintai Hotel, 2
North Train Station Hotel, 1
Wuxi Roast Duck House, 5

🍴 FOOD
Three Wind Bridge
   Meat House, 6

Tourist Complaint: ☎ 16081 (24hr.).

Bank of China: 258 Zhongshan Lu (☎ 270 5888), just south of Renmin Lu. Exchanges currency and traveler's checks. **24hr. ATM,** left of the building. Open daily 8am-5pm.

Bookstore: Xinhua Bookstore, 185 Renmin Zhong Lu (☎ 270 1212). English pulp fiction on the 1st fl. Open daily 9am-9pm.

Hospital: Gangwu Hospital, 181 Renmin Lu (☎ 270 8118), across from the Xinhua Bookstore. 24hr. emergency. Open daily 8am-5pm.

Internet Access: There is a small **Internet cafe,** 148 Huihe Lu, in the direction of Xihui Park from Jiangnan University Foreign Students Hotel. This friendly joint is run by students and features old machines with speedy access. Y1.5 per hr. Open 8am-midnight.

Post and Telecommunications: China Post, 226 Renmin Lu (☎272 9227), about 2 blocks east of Jiefang Lu. English list of services offered at each counter. Open daily 7:30am-6:30pm. **China Telecom,** down the street from the post office. IDD phones to the right of the entrance. Open daily 8:30am-5pm.

Postal Code: 214001.

🏠 ACCOMMODATIONS

In the past few years, Wuxi has built several soaring hotels in the heart of the downtown area, making it hard to find good budget options. However, since supply exceeds demand, it's not too difficult to bargain great rooms down to a fair price. Staff members in Wuxi hotels often speak English (those at the Sheraton are superb), a welcome relief in a city that has nearly no English speakers.

North Train Station Hotel (běi zhàn bīnguǎn; 北站宾馆), 15 Chezhan Lu (☎232 3888), west of the train station. Spartan dorms and musty doubles manage to maintain white linens and wiped furnishings. Dorms may be off-limits to foreigners, depending on the mood of the front desk, but reserve ahead for the cheaper singles. Dorms Y20-40; singles Y50, with A/C and bath Y80; doubles with A/C and bath Y120. ❶

Jiangnan University Foreign Students Hotel (jiāngnán dàxué liúxuéshēng lóu; 江南大学留学生楼), 170 Huihe Lu (☎586 1034), across the moat and down the road from Xihui Park. Take bus #2 from the train station to Qingshan Wan (5th stop); the hotel is a half-block up the street, on the left. Far from the city, but closer to the lake. The cheaper rooms come with their costs. No A/C in 1st-fl. dorms. Singles Y80; doubles Y120-200. ❶

Jintai Hotel (jīntài dàjiǔdiàn; 金泰大酒店), 17 Chezhan Lu (☎232 8338), across from the train station. Crazy pastel-colored tiles on the exterior disguise simple rooms and spartan beds. A/C, bath, TV, and phone. Doubles Y130-150. Bargains advertised on huge banners outside. ❷

Wuxi Roast Duck House (wúxī kǎoyā diàn; 无锡烤鸭店), 222 Zhongshan Lu (☎270 8222), 1½ blocks south of Renmin Lu. Spacious rooms with stainless carpets, dark wood furnishings, bright bath, sturdy mattress, hair dryer, water boiler, A/C, TV, and phone. Singles Y208; doubles Y228-288, in the west building Y168. ❷

CTS Hotel (zhōnglǚ dàjiǔdiàn; 中旅大酒店), 88 Chezhan Lu (☎868 9888), across from the train station. The ritziest pad in Wuxi has airy rooms with A/C, phone, TV, and in-bed breakfasts (Y8-15). Huge bathroom mirror and sparkling tiles. A few doubles feature balconies. Doubles Y288-338. 40% student discount. AmEx/DC/MC/V. ❹

🍴 FOOD

Wuxi is known for juicy, slightly sweet **baby back ribs** (xiǎopáigǔ; 小排骨), delicate **silver fish** (yínyú; 银鱼), and chewy **frogs** (literally "field chicken;" tiánjī; 田鸡). Hotel restaurants specialize in Jiangsu-style seafood dishes, cooking just about anything with gills, flippers, or shells. The area around the intersection of Zhongshan Lu and Renmin Lu is filled with fast food. Duck into a side street, however, and you're likely to find larger sit-down restaurants. In the summer, smaller streets hawk fresh peaches and produce. Student-friendly cafes abound on Huaihe Lu around Jiangnan University (jiāngnán dàxué; 江南大学), near Xihui Park.

Three Wind Bridge Meat House (sānfēngqiáo ròuzhuāng; 三风桥肉庄), 240 Zhongshan Lu. This carnivore heaven has it all: poultry, pork, beef, and its nationally famous baby back ribs (Y25). No place to sit; choose your meats—from frozen to ready-to-gnaw—to savor elsewhere. Prepared meat starts at Y14 per 300g. Deli open daily 8am-6:30pm; pre-packaged section open daily 8am-8pm. ❷

Wuxi Roast Duck House (wúxī kǎoyā diàn; 无锡烤鸭店), 222 Zhongshan Lu (☎270 8222). Duck feet and geese dangle in display window. Downstairs dishes up meaty specialties (Y10-39). Locals go for Beijing duck (Y18 per 0.5kg) or Taihu smoked fish (Y25 per 0.5kg). Vacuum-sealed ribs are Y16. Upstairs serves the same deal, but with fancier displays and at twice the price (Y25-90). Open daily 8:30am-7:30pm. ❷

Jiangnan University Foreign Students Hotel (jiāngnán dàxué liúxuéshēng lóu; 江南大学留学生楼), 170 Huihe Lu. Front desk takes customized orders the day before for table-sized breakfasts for a mere Y5. A la carte entrees for lunch and dinner (Y3-6) in the dining room on the 2nd fl. Open daily 7-8am, 11am-noon, and 5-7pm. ❶

🔍 SIGHTS

Wuxi has almost no sights of its own, mainly because Lake Taihu compensates with an overwhelming amount of tourist pizzazz.

XIHUI PARK (xīhuì gōngyuán; 锡惠公园). The large hill of **Xishan** (锡山) sits here, accessorized with a distinctive pink pagoda. Its many forgettable attractions include tea houses, fountains, a zoo, an azalea garden, and a sad amusement park with a dying carousel (what the management calls "turning luxury hobbyhorses"). However, Xihui sells unforgettable souvenirs—small clay figurines (usually of plump senior citizens or children cuddling fish, symbols of wealth and good fortune). One of the more famous sights in Xihui is a **spring** that inspired the blind composer A Bing (阿丙) to write *Two Springs Reflecting the Moon* (èr quán yìng yuè; 二泉映月). A plaque proclaims this odorous little pool as the "world's second best spring," second only to the one in Zhenjiang.

Once a shelter from Japanese air raids, the **Dragon Light Cave** echoes with digital whistles and roars of a hundred scattered robotic creatures, all lurking in dark rooms off an intimidatingly long corridor. Other than kitschy blinking lights, the cave holds little interest. No wonder it's free. Blandness aside, one attraction does stand out: a ski-lift-style **cable car** that connects the hill with **Huishan,** the other large hill visible from Wuxi. On clear days, the ride offers soaring views of the city and lake; beware of vertigo, as the trip is remarkably high and long. *(Park open daily 5:30am-5:30pm. Cable car 8:30am-5pm, weather permitting. Admission with clay figurine museum/shop Y30, with zoo Y35, with cable-car ride or 7 rides in a small amusement park plus zoo Y45. Separate admissions for zoo Y10, azalea garden Y5, clay museum Y6, cable car Y28.)*

▶ DAYTRIP FROM WUXI: LAKE TAIHU 太湖

*Take **bus** #1 or K83 from the North Bus Station (about 45min.) and get off either at Turtle Head Island or near the Li Garden. Bus #2 stops at Plum Garden. Otherwise, travel by **bike** and beware of long stretches on a busy road. Follow either Liangxi Lu (toward Plum Garden) or Hubin Lu to the south, which bends right and runs along the lake to Baojie Bridge. **Accommodations** abound, although most tourists return to Wuxi for the night.*

Covering more than 2250km², Taihu (tàihú; 太湖) is the third-largest freshwater lake in China. The lake is famous for the "purple sand" (zǐshā; 紫砂) found at its bottom that actually comes in several different colors. It flavors the unique local blend of green tea and is also used to make some of the finest pottery around. Not surprisingly, the cool air of Lake Taihu attracts droves of summer tourists. Dozens of lush islands peer through gauzy (albeit polluted) haze, blossoming grapes, peaches, and plums paint the coasts in bright colors, and fish leap about in the shallow waters. If you need one more excuse, locals love to down fresh seafood with cold bottles of tàihú shuǐ (太湖水), a tasty regional beer. Spring, when flowers bloom, and autumn, with its mellow harvests, are the best times to visit Lake

SHANGHAI

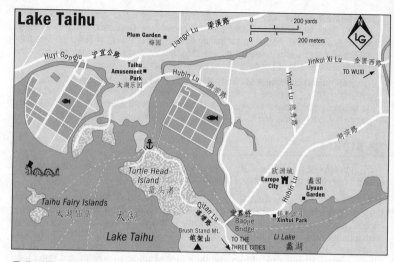

Taihu. The summer months can be unforgivingly hot, despite the lake breeze. At any time, though, the folks who inhabit these misty coasts will throw out the welcome mat—just take the time to sample their seed-stuffed wares.

PLUM GARDEN (méi yuán; 梅园). Across the street is the middle gate for the Plum Garden, established in 1912 by two industrialists who planted 5000 plum trees to mark their retirement. Since then, more features have been added, including the "In Suddenly Enlightened Hole," a large, dank cave; a garage-like perfumery and greenhouse toward the back; the Nianqu Tower, the highest point in the garden; and Kaiyuan Temple, a Buddhist complex with statues of snarling deities (Y3). Early spring sees plum trees in full bloom, while in mid-autumn, fragrant osmanthus trees rule the hillsides. The garden has the occasional tourist, but it mostly provides solitude and serenity for locals—be careful not to disrupt the couples. (*Accessible by bus #2, 88, 91, or 206. Open daily 6am-6pm. Y30.*)

THREE CITIES. These recently built TV production sets have now been transformed into tourist sights. **Tang City,** the oldest of the three, was the set of a late 80s TV series about a Tang Dynasty emperor. Daily grandiose re-enactments of movie scenes and an "imperial procession" feature song and dance. Dress up in period gear to get into the mood. (☎ 555 0117. *Open daily 8am-6:15pm. Y32.*) **Three Kingdoms City** was the set for the popular series *The Romance of the Three Kingdoms.* Actors stage famous battle scenes, ship burnings, and jousts. (☎ 555 0117. *Open daily 8am-6:15pm. Y35.*) Last, and possibly least, is **Water Margin City,** set of the TV series of the same name. It's bigger and more naturalistic, but not better. (*Bus K83 goes to all 3 cities. Y35, with Three Kingdoms Y60, all 3 cities Y80.*)

TURTLE HEAD ISLAND (yuántóu zhǔ; 鼋头渚). Perhaps the most renowned part of Lake Taihu is Turtle Head Island, a peninsula shaped like a turtle head extending into the northwest part of the lake about 8km from Wuxi. This old reptilian noggin contains hidden natural gems for the daring explorer; to all others, it represents the unstoppable sprawl of pavilions and hokey attractions, such as the free Monkey King performances by circus folk in the afternoon. The island can also be reached via Baojie Bridge, which connects the head to land near the Li Yuan Garden. Near Turtle Head Island's east entrance is **Space City** (tàikōng chéng; 太空城),

a surreal, ramshackle amusement center that seems to be on the verge of permanent retirement. Much farther east is the **East Aquarium,** with seven exhibition halls showcasing all sorts of sea-bound beasties. Especially cool is the "sci-popularization video room." *(Open daily 7am-5:30pm. Y15.)*

Admission to Turtle Head Island includes ferry access to the **Taihu Fairy Islands** (tàihú xiān dǎo; 太湖仙岛), also called **Three Mountain Islands** (sānshān dǎo; 三山 岛). While Turtle Head Island holds some natural treats (such as the "Sino-Japan Flowery Cherry Woods") to balance out the manmade pavilions, the Fairy Islands are dominated by tourist-oriented statues, caves, and pagodas. Still, the trip out is a minor adventure with great views of the lake (especially on misty days), and there's no need to stay on the beaten path. *(Ferries run daily every 20-40min. 8:30am-6pm. Bike parking Y1, motorcycle parking Y3. Y70, children 1.1-1.4m Y35.)*

ZHENJIANG 镇江　　　　　　　　　　　☎ 0511

Some cities have distinctive landmarks or landscapes, but Zhenjiang has a distinctive smell. Step a block or two away from Zhenjiang's railway station, and you'll find yourself in a pickle—or, at least, the stuff of which pickles are made. The sharp, pungent scent of vinegar drifts through the town, swirling about the jars sold at nearly every street corner and slinking through the doors of every local restaurant. It originates at the famed Heng Shun Sauce and Vinegar Factory, the home of a 1400-year-old recipe for China's most prized fragrant vinegar. In 1908, the recipe won the gold prize at the World Expo in Panama—a feat it repeated in Paris in 1985. These bottles of vinegar have since made their way around the world, and are as easy to find in any Chinatown as in China. Today, Zhenjiang lives in relative obscurity, attracting the occasional tourist who seeks nothing more than a few bottles of top vintage for the trip home.

⌐ TRANSPORTATION

Trains: Zhenjiang Train Station (zhènjiāng huǒchē zhàn; 镇江火车站), west of the city center. Buy tickets on the far right side of the station; hours vary, but windows #8 and 9 should be open all night. Zhenjiang is another convenient city on the Nanjing-Shanghai line and has frequent trains to: **Hangzhou** (5½-8hr., 10 per day, Y57-103); **Hefei** (5-5½hr., 2 per day, Y48); **Nanjing** (40min., Y13-19); **Shanghai** (2½-4½hr., Y38-57); **Suzhou** (1½-3½hr., Y24-37); **Wuxi** (2-3hr., Y9-24).

Buses: Long-distance buses leave from 1 of 2 stations across from each other on Jiefang Nan Lu, about 3 blocks south of Dashi Kou. The **bus station** (☎ 523 2762) east of the train station runs buses to: **Hangzhou** (4 per day 6:45am-2:45pm, Y68); **Nanjing** (every 10min. 6:05am-6:45pm, Y22); **Shanghai** (8 per day 7:30am-5pm, Y56-75); **Wuxi** (12 per day 7am-5:30pm, Y38). Privately-run **minibuses** have no posted schedule; just hop on one pulling out from a station on Zhongshan Lu, a few blocks from the train station. To: **Hangzhou** (4½hr., 6 per day, Y68); **Nanjing** (1hr., Y22); **Shanghai** (3½hr., 8 per day, Y64-75); **Wuxi** (1½hr., 14 per day, Y28-38). Buses to **Yangzhou** (40-60min., Y13) are everywhere; catch one at the ferry terminal or at either bus station. You also can hop on a minibus to Yangzhou as it waits to cross the Yangzi.

Local Transportation: Buses are useful for getting to major sights and transport hubs in town. Most of the 23 lines run 6am-6pm, but some, like bus #2, run until 11pm. Buses with a "W" in front of their numbers lack fare collectors and require exact change. Fare usually Y1. Bus #2 goes up Daxi Lu in the old neighborhood, past the museum, and ends at Jinshan Temple; #4 goes to Beigushan and out to Jiaoshan; #10 goes to the ferry dock; #13 shuttles between the train station and the main bus station. **Ferries** (Y8) cross the Yangzi regularly from the **dock** (dùkǒu; 渡口) in the northwest corner of town. A **taxi** from the center of town costs Y20-25.

SHANGHAI

Bike Rental: Bikes are everywhere, but the city is small enough that they're unnecessary. There are no decent bike rental shops. Those desperate for a bike can buy a cheapie (Y70-90) and resell it before leaving.

ORIENTATION AND PRACTICAL INFORMATION

Zhenjiang stretches along the south bank of the **Yangzi River**. The **Grand Canal** runs north through town, cutting through the city center before making its way to the river. The busiest part of town is in the southeast, centered around **Dashi Kou** (大市口), where the east-west **Zhongshan Lu** (中山路) and north-south **Jiefang Lu** (解放路) intersect. Almost all buses pass through Dashi Kou, the perfect reference point and home to most useful tourist services. Trains and minibuses arrive in western Zhenjiang, near Zhongshan Lu, Heng Shun factory, hotels, and restaurants. Most buses arrive at the bus station on Jiefang Nan Lu, a few blocks south of Dashi Kou.

A maze of tiny shops and large-scale construction projects make up the oldest part of the city in the west, near the river. Here, the streets become narrower and more closely packed. **Jinshan Temple,** farther west, marks the end of the main city.

Travel Agencies: CITS, 92 Zhongshan Xi Lu (☎522 6063 or 524 7315). The staff is friendly. Open daily 8am-noon and 2-6pm. **Zhenjiang China Culture Tourist Agency** (zhènjiāng zhōngguó wénhuà lǚxíngshè; 镇江中国文化旅行社), 25 Jiankang Lu, Bldg. 3 (☎523 1806). Open daily 8am-noon and 2-6pm.

Bank of China: 235 Zhongshan Dong Lu (☎502 6789), half a block east of Dashi Kou, on the north side of the street. Open daily 8-11am and 3-5:30pm.

PSB: Off a small lane next to the McDonald's near Dashi Kou.

Pharmacy: Zhongshan Pharmacy (zhōngshān yàodiàn; 中山药店), 61 Zhongshan Xi Lu. Carries Western medicine. 24hr. emergency. Open daily 7am-8pm.

Hospital: Jingkou Hospital (jīngkǒu qū yīyuàn; 京口区医院), 230 Zhongshan Dong Lu (☎502 4009), next to the Bank of China. 24hr. emergency. Open daily 8am-6pm.

Internet Access: Fantasy Life Internet Cafe (xūnǐ rénshēng wǎngbā; 虚拟人生网吧), 63 Zhongshan Xi Lu (☎524 0365), 200m east of the train station. Speedy access for Y2 per hr. Open daily 8am-midnight. **Hengdeli Internet Cafe** (hēngdélì wǎngbā; 亨得利网吧), 1 Runzhoushan Lu (☎523 7156), at the bottom of the hill leading up to Pearl Buck's former residence. Y2 per hr. Open daily 8am-midnight.

Post Office: 423 Zhongshan Dong Lu. English signs and EMS. Open daily 8am-7pm. Another **branch,** 65 Zhongshan Xi Lu (☎523 5420), 100m east of the train station. Open daily 8am-6pm.

Postal Code: 212000.

ACCOMMODATIONS

Hotels cluster around Dashi Kou and the train station. Most post rates around Y400-500, but in the low season (and Zhenjiang doesn't really have a high season), hotels willingly grant discounts of up to 50%. Rooms tend to be cheaper if reservations are made ahead of time; hotels are less willing to bargain later in the day.

Jingkou Hotel (jīngkǒu fàndiàn; 京口饭店), 407 Zhongshan Dong Lu (☎522 4866), about 100m from the gate on the east bank of the Grand Canal. Cheaper rooms have A/C, bath, and TV. Newer rooms are bright and happy. Breakfast included. Doubles Y280. If the front desk asks the posted price, bargain for up to 40% discount. ❷

Great Wall Hotel (chángchéng dàjiǔdiàn; 长城大酒店), 59 Jiefang Nan Lu (☎501 8999), 2-3 blocks south of Dashi Kou, past the Yanchun Restaurant. This hotel's old age explains dim showers and yellowing tubs, but also the ornate lamp shades and high ceilings. Staff clean and polish daily. Exchanges currency at a slightly inferior rate to those of banks. Doubles Y140-210; triples Y200-300. Discounts start at 30%. ❷

Zhenjiang Hotel (zhènjiāng bīnguǎn; 镇江宾馆), 92 Zhongshan Xi Lu (☎523 3888; zjhotel@public.zj.js.cn), 500m east of the train station. 4-star rooms in Bldg. 1 have free high-speed Internet ports, bright and spacious rooms, and an indoor swimming pool. 3-star rooms in Bldg. 2 offer equally spacious but older rooms with phone lines for modems. Doubles Bldg. 2 Y230, Bldg. 1 Y328. Discounts start at 20%. ❹

🍴 FOOD

Zhenjiang is a veritable bonanza of food stalls and street markets. A walk down Zhongshan Lu reveals the pickled delights of the **Heng Shun Sauce and Vinegar Factory** (héngshùn jiàng cù chǎng; 恒顺酱醋厂). Since 1840, the factory has been pickling everything from turnips to cucumbers to "sacred pagoda vegetables." A **Heng Shun Hotel Takeout Window** (héngshùn bīnguǎn wàixiāo bù; 恒顺宾馆外销部) to the right of the factory entrance sells hot snacks like buns filled with pickled vegetables and meats. (Buns Y0.6. Open daily 6-9am, 10:30am-1pm, and 4-7:30pm.) Zhenjiang is also famous for its **freshwater delicacies,** including long-tailed fishes (huíyú; 回鱼), rare Yangzi herring (shíyú; 鲥鱼), and another trout-like creature that locals call knife fish (dāoyú; 刀鱼). If seafood doesn't appeal, then Dashi Kou can soothe the fast-food addict's soul. Many Chinese fast-food joints serve *tāngbāo* (汤包), buns stuffed with filling and soup. Poke a hole in the dumpling, suck out the filling—be careful, it's hot—then eat the skin dipped in vinegar.

Spring Banquet (yàn chūn jiǔlóu; 宴春酒楼), 17 Renmin Jie (☎501 0478 or 501 0477), 2 blocks east of the museum. Arguably Zhenjiang's most famous restaurant, this place has been around since 1938. Its beloved specialty is the crabmeat and pork *xièfěn tāngbāo* (蟹粉汤包 ; Y5-20). Open daily 6:15-10am, 11am-2pm, and 5-9pm. A newer **branch,** 212 Zhufang Lu (☎563 5779), west of the train station, 2 blocks south of Dashi Kou, has the same hours. ❷

Xinhua Cuisine Garden (xīnhuá měishí yuán; 新华美食园), Zhongshan Lu at Jiefang Lu. This neighborhood snack joint serves Zhenjiang favorites like duck blood soup (Y3) and meat-filled wontons (Y2) to a packed lunch-time crowd. The popular fried sticky rice (Y1) is a slab of red-bean-paste-filled sticky rice, fried french-toast style. ❶

👁 SIGHTS

Zhenjiang's sights could easily be ingested in the course of a long day. If you have time to kill, dawdle in the **Daxi Lu** neighborhood near the museum and explore the labyrinthine alleys and street markets shaded by 100-year-old trees. For less conventional amusements, try your luck on the sidewalks. Fortune tellers give face readings (kàn xiàng; 看相) for Y2.

PEARL S. BUCK HOUSE (sài zhēnzhū jiùjū; 赛珍珠旧居). Pearl S. Buck (1892-1973), the Nobel-prize-winning American author who astounded the world with her portrayals of traditional Chinese families, spent a total of 18 years in Zhenjiang. The house where she grew up has been replaced by a factory, but the home in which she spent her later years still stands. In 1991, with the encouragement of Zhenjiang's American sister-city, Tempe, Arizona, the house was turned into a small museum. The museum contains original furniture from Buck's residence, captioned photos and paintings, a small collection of books, and two rooms of relics from the author's houses in America and Japan, including an assortment of Santa Clauses and "I Love Tempe" mugs. *(6 Runzhoushan Lu, near the train station. From the station, head down Zhongshan Xi Lu toward Dashi Kou. Take the 1st left onto Daxi Lu, a narrow street packed with snack stands. At the 2nd left, head up the road going up the hill; the house is at the top. Open daily 8:30-11:30am and 2:30-5pm. Free.)*

JINSHAN TEMPLE (jīnshān sì; 金山寺). This temple and park complex in the northwest part of town has as much water as land. The park area contains ponds, the "Number One Spring in China," a slew of souvenir stands, and, most impressively, a 1500-year-old Buddhist temple with a towering pagoda and an active community of monks. Buddhists from Hong Kong and Singapore come all the way to Jinshan because they believe praying to the Buddha here is more effective than praying elsewhere. The main temple is lavishly stuffed with icons and Buddhas of all sorts. The 18 arhats surrounding the three main Buddhas are worth a peek, especially the one picking ear wax with a stick.

Peer out from the top of the eight-sided, seven-storied, 36m-tall **Cishou Pagoda** (císhòu tǎ; 慈寿塔) for a view of Zhenjiang's other hilltop sights, fish ponds, farmland, and the mighty Yangzi to the north. A temple was first built on this site 1400 years ago. The current pagoda was constructed in 1900 to mark the Empress Dowager's birthday. An inquiry office offers help in English. *(At the terminus for bus #2. ☎551 2992. Open daily 6am-6pm. Park Y42, children under 1.4m Y20. Cishou Pagoda Y4.)*

JIAOSHAN (jiāoshān; 焦山). In the far eastern portion of the town hulks a jungly island with pavilions, historical remnants, and a large tower. The mainland side of this park has a few diversions of its own, including a waterfall, but the island is the main attraction. Free ferries shuttle visitors across the river. Motorboats put visitors close enough to the river to spit in it and see it spit back. The most scenic route is via the **cable car,** which lifts you far above the river to gaze below at the Yangzi's vast flood potential. *(Ferries every 20min. May-Oct. 7:30am-6pm, Nov.-Apr. 7:30am-5:30pm. Motorboats across the river if you have 3 people Y4, to Beigushan Y10. Cable car runs daily 8:30am-4:30pm. One-way Y15, round-trip Y20.)*

The **Wanfo Pagoda** ("10,000 Buddhas Pagoda;" wànfó tǎ; 万佛塔) glistens after recent restorations, which seem to be as much a cause for pride as the existence of the pagoda itself. You can even sponsor a Buddha (prices vary depending on your Buddha's size and tier), but hurry before the 10,000 run out. *(Y15, but the views from the base are just as lovely.)* Near the river side tower is a small **calligraphy museum** (Y2), and not far away are some old **gun batteries** from Zhenjiang's days as an active stronghold. You can also wander the island's winding paths, enjoy the fragrance of ancient trees rich with centuries of river dew, and relish those final moments of sweet life before you get back on that big, scary cable car. *(Take bus #4, or head northeast on city streets until you hit Zhenjiao Lu, which winds toward the front entrance. Open daily 7:15am-6pm; last admission 4:45pm. Y20.)*

BEIGUSHAN MOUNTAIN (běigù shān; 北固山). *The Romance of the Three Kingdoms* tells the story of Liu Bei, King of Shu, who was offered the hand of Sun Shangxiang, the sister of his enemy Sun Quan, King of Wu. As Liu Bei floated down the Yangzi for his wedding, Sun Quan and his treacherous advisors plotted to kill the bridegroom and annex his lands. They planted the ambushers inside the **Ganlu Temple** atop Beigushan. But the assassination plot failed, and the royal hitch peacefully cemented. The rock in the courtyard with a gash in the middle is where the two kings reportedly sealed their allegiance. Without the story, Beigushan would be just an overgrown garden, with silly statues and an ancient temple. Ganlu Temple, however, houses the lightning-blitzed **Iron Pagoda** and **Qinghui Pavilion,** both overlooking the river. *(Open daily 7am-6pm; last admission 5:30pm. Y10.)*

YANGZHOU 扬洲 ☎ 0514

Scholars, artists, and salt merchants have flocked to Yangzhou for centuries. The avenues exude a subdued and even peaceful air, and not just because of the ordinance against honking. Residents are easy-going and more than willing to chat. After all, vocal braggarts have a history here: one of Yangzhou's cultural legacies is *píng huà* (评话), a lively form of storytelling. The city also basks in its reputation for beautiful women. Many emperors supposedly came here as much for the selection of concubines as for the scenery. Imperial heart-flutterers aren't Yangzhou's only gifts to the rulers of China—former president Jiang Zemin also hails from this port on the Grand Canal. He may not quite have the looks, but he's definitely still the toast of the town. After all the talking is done, Yangzhou's serene atmosphere inspires contemplation—a good thing, as there's precious little else to do. Walk long enough, and you'll come across quiet, simple distractions: a scattering of gardens, a small monastery, and tiny bridges arched over flowing streams.

🖪 🛪 TRANSPORTATION AND PRACTICAL INFORMATION

Yangzhou is a relatively small city next to the **Grand Canal.** The grid-like streets make navigation easy, even though many streets change names along their length. Most hotels and services are on **Wenhe Lu** (汶河路) and **Wenchang Lu** (文昌路), intersecting at the **Wenchang Pavilion** (wénchāng gé; 文昌阁) in the center of town. Most buses arrive at the station in the south of town, just past the Grand Canal. Buses into the city proper travel along a major street that changes names from **Dujiang Nan Lu** (渡江南路) and **Dujiang Lu** (渡江路) in the south to **Guoqing Lu** (国庆路) and **Shi Kefa Lu** (史可法路) in the north. In the northwestern part of town is **Shouxi Lake Park,** the town's most popular attraction. **Yanfu Lu** (盐阜路) runs east from the park, along a smaller canal where imperial boats used to dock; now a market thrives upon its shores.

Buses: Yangzhou Bus Station (yángzhōu qìchē zhàn; 扬洲汽车站 ; ☎ 796 3658), at Hanjiang Lu at Jiangyang Xi Lu, 2km southwest of town. Take bus #1 or 2 (northeast Yangzhou) or 5, 15, or 20 (Wenhe Lu or the northwest near Shouxi Lake). There are 3 types of long-distance buses: *kuàikè* " 快客 " (fastest, A/C, priciest); *zhōngbā* " 中巴 " (mid-sized, more stops and less comfy, about 20% cheaper); and *dàbā* "大巴" (bigger, slower, another 20% cheaper). Ticket office open daily 5:30am-6pm. To: **Hangzhou** (5hr., every hr. 6:20am-6:20pm, Y90-98); **Hefei** (3½hr., 6 per day 7am-3:40pm, Y58); **Huai'an** (almost every hr., Y38-40); **Nanjing** (*zhōngbā* 70min., 6am-6:30pm, Y21; *dàbā* 1½hr., 6:30am-6:30pm, Y27); **Shanghai** (4-6hr., 5:45am-5:10pm, Y40-69); **Wuxi** (2hr., 18 per day 6:20am-5:30pm, Y26-53). The **West Bus Station** (qìchē xī zhàn; 汽车西站), accessible via bus #8 (Guoqing Lu) or 22 (Wenhe Lu), sends buses to **Zhenjiang** (40-60min., every 20min. 6:20am-7pm, Y13) and nearby towns. Long-distance buses from the main station also stop here sometimes.

Local Transportation: Some of the more popular sights are best reached by **bus.** Most buses run 7am-7pm, but some are few and far between. Fare Y1-2. Buses **#4 and 12** run along Wenchang Lu; **#5** goes from the bus station to Shouxi Lake; **#15** runs from the far north of town, past Shouxi Lake and along Wenhe Lu to the main bus station; **#22** follows a similar route in the south and continues to Daming Temple. **Tourist buses** shuttle to the Imperial Dock, Shouxi Lake Park, Daming Temple, and other attractions (6 per day 8:30am-4pm, Y5).

Taxis: Base fare Y5-7, each additional km Y1.6-2.4. Taxis are hard to find on the city outskirts, but **pedicabs** are everywhere (Y3 to start). Bargain up a storm.

Travel Agency: CTS, 8 Fengle Shang Jie (☎ 736 3909). Helpful English and French speakers. Tickets, tours, and visas. Open daily 8:30am-noon and 3-6pm.

SHANGHAI

Tourist Complaint Line: ☎ 732 5601.

Bank of China: 28 Wenhe Bei Lu. The exchange counter will make even the most paranoid traveler feel safe, but be prepared for extensive examinations of your signature and documents. Open daily 8:30am-5pm. **24hr. ATM** (Cirrus/MC/Plus/V).

Bookstores: Yangzhou Old Books Store, 10 Yanfu Xi Lu (☎ 734 3916). Piles of dictionaries, stacks of English novels, and translated Chinese classics. Open daily 9am-6pm. **Xinhua Bookstore,** 112 Wenhe Nan Lu (☎ 734 4427), has maps, dictionaries, and well-thumbed English classics. Open daily 8:30am-9pm.

PSB: ☎ 734 2097. On Huai'hai Lu between Siwangting Lu and Yanfu Xi Lu.

Hospital: Municipal No. 3 People's Hospital (shì dìsān rénmín yīyuàn; 市第三人民医院), 61 Wenhe Lu (☎ 732 2776), across from the Blue Sky Hotel.

Internet Access: A few Internet places north of Friendship Hall (next to Xiyuan Hotel). **Connecting Friends Internet Cafe** (liányǒu wǎngbā; 联友网吧), 82 Desheng Qiao (☎ 731 3629), right before the Yanchun Restaurant. Y1.5 per hr. Open 8am-midnight.

Post Office: China Post, 162 Wenchang Zhong Lu. EMS and Poste Restante. Open daily 8am-6pm.

Postal Code: 225002.

⌂ ACCOMMODATIONS

Yangzhou has plentiful high-end hotels, but there are few budget options. Hotels in the center and north of town are convenient to sights. May is Yangzhou's high season; discounts are more liberal later in the summer.

Cuiyuan Hotel (cuìyuán fàndiàn; 萃园饭店), 209 Wenchang Zhong Lu (☎ 780 1999; fax 734 8315). Known as Yangzhou Municipal Government's No.1 Guesthouse in its non-privatized days, this recently renovated hotel features spacious rooms, thick mattresses, and clean fixtures. A popular snack stand outside sells delicious, freshly made sugary buns, sausage rolls, and stuffed buns (Y0.6; open daily 7-8:30am and 4:30-6pm). Singles Y248; doubles Y238-480; triples Y218. ❸

Xiyuan Hotel (xīyuán dàjiǔdiàn; 西园大酒店), 1 Fengle Shang Jie (☎ 780 7888; yzx-iyuan@public.yz.js.cn), north of Yanfu Xi Lu and a block east of Wenhe Bei Lu, behind CITS. The exterior may resemble a riot-proof monstrosity, but it's quite luxurious on the inside, with large rooms, huge white-linen beds, and bright baths. Recent renovations in the main building brought pink carpeting and wallpaper. Free detergent. Older buildings: doubles Y240-280; triples Y260. AmEx/DC/MC/V. ❸

Yiyuan Hotel (yíyuán fàndiàn; 怡园饭店), 1 Siwangting Lu (☎ 780 1588; fax 731 6888), at Wenhe Bei Lu. High ceilings, duct-taped wallpaper, and eerie blue bathroom light decorate these sizeable but old rooms. A/C, TV, phone, and water boiler. Singles Y150; doubles Y240-350; spartan triples Y150-190. ❷

Blue Sky Hotel (lántiān dàshà; 蓝天大厦), 42 Wenhe Bei Lu (☎ 736 0000). Bright hallways lead to airy sherbet-green rooms and clean baths. Pricier doubles even have a comfortable recliner with footrest. A/C, phone, and TV. Reservations recommended. Doubles Y360-598; triples Y460. 30% discounts possible. ❺

◨ FOOD

In the pantheon of Chinese cuisine, Yangzhou food enjoys a special place thanks to its delicate flavors and clear broths. The desserts and cakes are divine, often layered with egg custard, red bean paste, and flaky pastry. Street carts trundle around in the southeastern part of town with the best of Yangzhou tastes. The bazaar-like area near the Imperial Dock features several sit-down places, as well

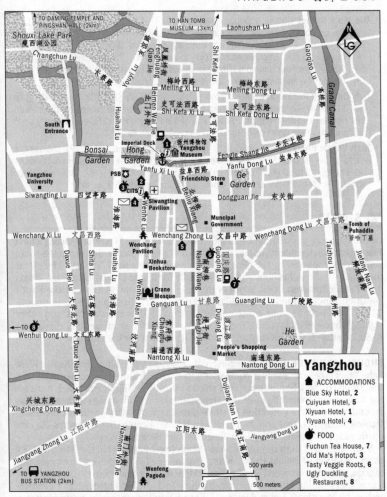

as a busy market with puppies and goldfish. In the evenings, small stalls and carts line Wenhe Lu, between Wenchang Lu and Yanfu Lu. A festering fast-food rash of McDonald's and KFCs has also afflicted this street. **Yangzhou fried rice** (yángzhōu chǎofàn; 扬州炒饭), famous overseas, makes the menus of most reasonably priced restaurants on **Food Street** (měishí jiē; 美食街), a section of Siwangting Lu.

🥢 **Fuchun Tea House** (fùchūn cháshè; 富春茶舍), 35 Desheng Qiao (☎ 723 3326), down an alley branching east off Guoqing Lu, between Guangling Lu and Wenchang Lu. Founded in 1885, Fuchun is *the* Yangzhou restaurant. The 10- to 15-piece sampler (Y12-28) features classic Yangzhou delicacies like soup-filled crabmeat buns and thousand-layer cake. Try the 3 award-winning specialties: meatballs with bits of crab (xièfěn shīzitóu; 蟹粉狮子头 ; Y8), fish-head soup (Y45), and shredded tofu medley (dà zhǔ gānsī; 大煮干丝 ; Y10-20). Or aspire to Emperor Qianlong's favorite, buns stuffed with 3 ingredients (sāndīng bāozi; 三丁包子). Open daily 6:15am-2pm and 3:45-8pm. ❷

S H A N G H A I

Old Ma's Hotpot (lǎomā huǒguō; 老妈火锅), 48 Siwanting Lu (☎732 7777), at Huai'hai Lu. Look for the sign with red peppers. Tourists and locals alike descend upon Old Ma for its silky tofu soup (Y5) and bubbling cauldrons of hotpot (Y18-48). Ingredients range from farm-fresh vegetables (Y1) to squid (Y20). Plump dumplings (Y3) noodles (Y3-8), taro flour dim sum filled with sweet red bean paste (Y1), and snails (Y5). Just like Mom's. Another location, 139 Wenchang Zhong Lu (☎793 6777). ❶

Ugly Duckling Restaurant (chǒu xiǎoyā jiǔlóu; 丑小鸭酒楼) 108 Wenhui Dong Lu (☎731 8528). Tantalizing interpretations of Yangzhou cuisine served on tables with fresh flowers and linen napkins. Squid with pickled vegetables Y26. Iced snow lily soup in a pumpkin Y18. Open daily 9am-2pm and 4:30-9pm. ❷

Tasty Veggie Roots (càigēnxiāng; 菜根香), 115 Guoqing Lu (☎734 2079). The humble name belies its sumptuous menu. Meatballs with crab (Y10) accompany centerpieces like whole pig's head (Y120). Great for lavish banquets or casual meals. Stir-fried dishes Y8-60. "Family-style" dishes Y6-20. Open daily 9am-2pm and 5-9pm. ❷

👁 SIGHTS

One of the more unusual sightseeing tours, dragon boats of **Emperor Qianlong's Boat Tour** (qiánlóng shuǐshàng yóulǎn;乾隆水上游览) ferry passengers down the route supposedly followed by the Qing Dynasty ruler during his 1757 visit. They float past many of the sights constructed especially for him in Shouxi Lake Park. Boats board at the Imperial Dock, south of the Xiyuan Hotel, and at Shouxi Lake Park's south entrance. (Open daily 6:30am-5:30pm. 1½hr.; 4 people Y800, 10 people Y1100. Fee includes tour guide and admission to Shouxi Lake Park and other sights.) Clustered all around Shouxi Lake Park, Yangzhou's attractions are easy to see in one day. If visitors stay an extra day, it's usually for the dim sum.

SHOUXI LAKE PARK (shòu xīhú gōngyuán; 瘦西湖公园). Literally "Slender West Lake," this lake is an explicit comparison to the much more famous West Lake in Hangzhou (p. 395). Shouxi's rippling waters mirror the willow and peach trees on the shores, and footpaths meander along the lake. A walk passes a canal, a playground, a zoo, and a collection of white pagodas and breezy pavilions, including Dahong Bridge, Lotus Pond, and Southern Breeze. Keep to the walkways. As one poetic plaque cautions, "Fragile is the grass, merciless your steps."

A salt merchant built the vase-shaped **White Tower Pagoda** (bái tǎ; 白塔) in 1784 as an imitation of Beihai Park's White Pagoda (p. 145) in Beijing. Just past the pagoda, cross the crowded **Five Pavilion Bridge** (wǔ tíng qiáo; 五亭桥), a local aristocrat's welcoming gift to Emperor Qianlong in 1757. This bridge has 15 roofed arches, or "cavities." A sign declares, "When it's full moon, every cavity carries a moon, so the goldenness on the water sways and the moons contend for splendor, which is impossible to put into words." So we won't even try. Beyond the bend at **Xichu Pavilion,** the path enters a less crowded strip of the park, with pavilions spanning all the way to the north entrance. Daming Temple is right outside the gate. (On Liuhu Lu, off Siwangting Lu; another entrance on Pingshantang Lu, near the Daming Temple. Accessible by buses #1, 4, 6, 16, and 18. ☎734 2901. Open daily 6am-6:30pm. Paddle boats Y12 per hr. Bicycle boats Y18 per hr., deposit Y100. Motor boats Y25 per hr. Admission Y45, children 1.2-1.4m Y20, under 1.2m free.)

DAMING TEMPLE (dàmíng sì; 大明寺). The well-kept "Great Brightness Temple" was named after the enlightened Ming Dynasty during which it was built (AD 457-465). Among the highlights are **Pingshan Hall** (píngshān táng; 平山堂), built in 1048, the nine-story **Qiling Pagoda,** and **Jian Zhan Memorial Hall** (Y5), built in 1973 in honor of the monk Jian Zhan, who was invited to Japan to share secrets of Chinese Buddhism. Unfortunately, high tides and rough storms at sea constantly frustrated his efforts. Finally, on his sixth attempt, at age 66, he reached Japan, where he and his followers impressed all sorts of knowledge into their Japanese colleagues. A sign at the front reads, "Monks, emperors, sages, poets, men of letters...all pious pilgrims who said their prayers [at Daming Temple], without exception, have had their prayers answered." *(Across from Shouxi Lake Park's north entrance. Take bus #21 or 22. Open daily 7am-5pm. Y30, children under 1.4m Y20.)* The area northeast of the temple has a few ponds, the **Tang City Wall** (tángchéng yízhǐ; 唐城遗址), and the **Han Tomb Museum** (hànmù bówùguǎn; 汉墓博物官), built over an archaeological site off Xiangbie Lu. **Qingling Pagoda,** originating from the Sui Dynasty and rebuilt in 1993, grants gorgeous views of surrounding rice paddies, Shanxi Lake, and old men fishing. *(Open daily 7:30am-5pm. Climbing the pagoda Y8.)*

OTHER SIGHTS. Qianlong's boat is said to have docked at the **Imperial Dock,** on the canal at the north end of Guoqing Lu, during his visit 245 years ago. Thatch-roofed buildings line Yanfu Lu all the way to the **Yangzhou Museum.** On summer evenings, a plaza in the front is converted into a rink for roller-skating. *(Bring your own skates. Free.)* About 500m farther east, **Ge Garden** (gè yuán; 个园), 10 Yanfu Lu, is another leftover from the days when salt merchants were the fat cats of Yangzhou. Built in 1818 by Huang Yintai, a bamboo lover, the garden is bursting at the seams with 40 species of bamboo, growing thickly among stones, gullies, and ponds. *(Take buses #1 and 8. Open daily 7:30am-6pm. Y30, children under 1.4m Y10, under 1.2m free.)*

On the south side of Yangzhou, the **Crane Mosque** (xiānhè qīngzhēnsì; 仙鹤请真寺), a rarity in this part of China, has a stark courtyard highlighted by a prayer room with a large wooden wall covered in gilded Arabic inscriptions. *(Enter the building off an alley, about 10m east of Guoqing Lu and 1 block north of Ganquan Lu. Gate is sometimes locked for 30-60min. in the afternoon. Open M-Th and Sa-Su sunrise-sunset.)* Farther northeast on Wenchang Lu, just across the Grand Canal, stands the **Tomb of Puhaddin** (pǔhādīng mùyuán; 普哈丁墓园), the resting place of a 16th-century descendent of Muhammad who served as a missionary in China. Look for the small, golden onion-domes; the tomb is through several gates, beyond the garden and pond and atop the hill. Beware the ravenous mosquitoes. *(Accessible via bus #12.)*

The lovely Fu Zhuang island teems with chirping birds and willows. If you visit in late June, nary a soul will interrupt your solitary stroll. The northern end sports several secluded pavilions. *(Y10, includes bonsai garden across Hongqiao Bridge.)*

ZHEJIANG 浙江

Most Chinese will agree that people in Zhejiang have it easy. With balmy weather, coastal wealth, an enviable cultural heritage, and natural scenery, Zhejiang deserves its reputation in every way. The ancients must have felt the same: classical poets composed odes upon the shores of Hangzhou's West Lake, and artists captured its beauty in pale washes of ink, while emperors of the Southern Song (1127-1279) made the lake their home. Today, the province leaps into the new capitalist market with the same eager aplomb it dedicated to cultivating the atmosphere that so entranced the literati of long ago. Once blessed by fertile rice fields and ocean trade, the province now prospers with big-name corporations and a runaway tourism industry. Along the way, Zhejiang doesn't forget what gave it its fame and carefully preserves its lakes, pagodas, and temples. From the Buddhist isle of Putuoshan to the literary haven of Shaoshan, Zhejiang takes travelers through storybook settings teeming with natural and cultural charm.

SHANGHAI

HANGZHOU 杭州 ☎0571

A famous Chinese saying declares, "Above there is heaven, below there are Suzhou and Hangzhou." Indeed, there is something transcendent about Hangzhou's willow-lined West Lake, ancient pagodas, and gently curving hills. The city, or, more specifically, its lake, has captivated artists and literati for centuries, inspiring outpourings of calligraphy, paintings, and poetry.

From its days as the capital of the Southern Song Dynasty (AD 1127-1279), Hangzhou has been one of China's most important cultural and political centers. These days, as the capital of Zhejiang province, Hangzhou juggles commercial and industrial developments without disrupting West Lake's silhouette of hills and bridges too much. The energy of the city center complements the serenity of the lake, and in the tradition of dynasties past, locals stroll the banks of the West Lake

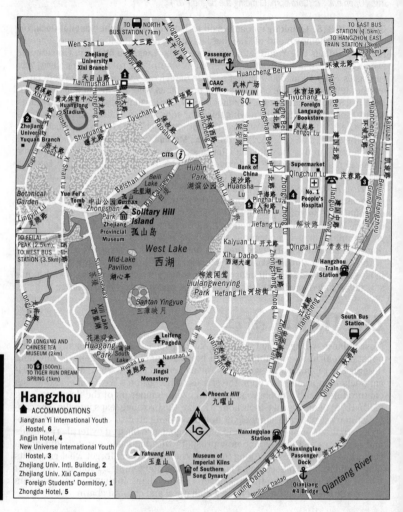

Hangzhou

🔺 ACCOMMODATIONS
Jiangnan Yi International Youth
Hostel, 6
Jingjin Hotel, 4
New Universe International Youth
Hostel, 3
Zhejiang Univ. Intl. Building, 2
Zhejiang Univ. Xixi Campus
Foreign Students' Dormitory, 1
Zhongda Hotel, 5

with ease and contentment. Walk by the lake in spring and gaze at its rain-misted far shores, or catch the autumn moon rippling the waters, and you'll understand why so many poets chose to call Hangzhou home.

▣ TRANSPORTATION

Flights: Hangzhou Airport (hángzhōu jīchǎng; 杭州机场 ; ☎8666 1236), northeast of central Hangzhou. Taxi to the city center (about Y100) takes 30min. Shuttle buses (every 30min. 6am-8pm, Y15) run between the airport and the **CAAC ticket office,** 390 Tiyuchang Lu (domestic info ☎8515 4259, international 8515 2575), off Wulin Sq. in the downtown area. Open daily 8am-8pm. To: **Beijing** (every hr. 7am-late, Y1150); **Fuzhou** (2-3 per day, Y740); **Guangzhou** (every hr. 8am-7pm, Y1050); **Hong Kong** (4-5 per day 8:30am-3:20pm, Y1460).

Trains: Hangzhou Train Station (hángzhōu huǒchē zhàn; 杭州火车站 ; ☎8782 9418), an ark-shaped building on Huancheng Dong Lu just south of Xihu Dadao. At the terminus of buses #2, 7, 11, and 39. Ticket office open 24hr. To: **Beijing** (23hr.; 6:03, 10:10pm; Y363); Fuzhou (14hr.; 7:02, 9:03pm; Y209); **Guangzhou** (21hr., 2 per day, Y353); **Hefei** (8hr.; 2:36, 5:10, 8pm; Y106-197); **Nanchang** (10hr.; 3:58, 7:40, 11:03pm; Y170); **Nanjing** (5-7½hr.; 5 per day 10:10am-3am; Y64-120) via **Suzhou** (3hr., Y44); **Shanghai** (2-3hr., many per day 6:15am-7:35pm, Y33); **Xiamen** (27hr., 1:55pm, Y274). **Hangzhou East Train Station** (hángzhōu huǒchē dōngzhàn; 杭州火车东站 ; ☎5672 7342, ticketing 5672 7462), at the end of Tiancheng Lu, at the terminus of buses #5, 28, and 518. Open 24hr. To **Beijing** (23hr., 3:59pm) and **Guangzhou** (21hr., 6:10am). Also serves nearby cities.

Buses: 4 bus stations provide different services.

East Long-Distance Bus Station (chángtú qìchē dōng zhàn; 长途汽车东站), 71 Genshan Lu (☎8694 8251 or 8694 8252), accessible by buses #19, 31, and 56. Currently fields the most traffic because of its size and proximity to the new expressway. Tickets sold 5-11:30am and 11:40am-8pm. To: **Ningbo** (2hr., every 8-10min. 6:30am-7:40pm, Y49); **Shanghai** (2hr., every 10-20min. 6:50am-7:35pm, Y54); **Shaoxing** (1hr., every 10min. 5:30am-7:45pm, Y19); **Suzhou** (4hr., every 20-30min. 6:50am-7pm, Y29-54).

North Long-Distance Bus Station (chángtú qìchē běi zhàn; 长途汽车北站), 758 Moganshan Lu (☎8809 7761), far from city center. Accessible via buses #155, 503, and 555. Open daily 5:30am-7:35pm. To: **Hefei** (6½hr., 10 per day 7:20am-5:40pm, Y98-138); **Nanjing** (5hr., every 30min. 7am-6:50pm, Y67-100).

West Long-Distance Bus Station (chángtú qìchē xī zhàn; 长途汽车西站), 357 Tianmushan Lu (☎8522 1304), at Yugu Lu. Accessible via buses #30, 49, and 502. Open daily 5:30am-6:50pm. To: **Huangshan City** (15 per day 6:30am-6pm, Y30-66); **Huangshan Scenic Area** (4-7hr., every 50min. 6:20am-2:40pm, Y54-73); **Jingdezhen** (9:30am, 3:20pm; Y115-117); **Wuhan** (4:50pm, Y200).

South Long-Distance Bus Station (chángtú qìchē nán zhàn; 长途汽车南站), 407 Qiutao Lu (☎8604 6666 or 8606 4785), accessible by buses #14, 20, and 39. Ticket window open 6am-7:30pm. To: **Fuzhou** (9½hr., 3pm, Y243) and smaller cities within Zhejiang, including **Dongyang** (2½hr., every hr. 6:50am-7:30pm, Y45).

Boats: Passenger Wharf (kèyùn mǎtóu; 客运码头), 138 Huancheng Bei Lu (☎8515 3185), north of Wulin Sq., near the intersection of Huangshan Bei Lu and Zhongshan Bei Lu. Accessible via buses #22, 502, and 517. All boats have A/C. Open daily 7am-5:30pm. To: **Suzhou** (13½hr., 5:30pm, Y70-130).

Local Transportation: Most **buses** run 6:30am-8 or 9pm; hours for each route are marked on signs at designated stops. Base fare Y1, with A/C (denoted by a "K" in front of the route number) Y2. **Tour bus** #2 runs from the train station, loops around the lake, and stops at several scenic spots; #27 shuttles between the northern edge of the lake and the Longjing tea village. Tour buses #1, 2, and 3 serve West Lake and the surrounding forest area. Fare Y2-3. **Minibuses** (Y2) follow popular bus routes.

Taxis: Base fare Y10, 1st 4km free, each additional km Y2. From Yan'an Lu to the airport Y65-100; to the train and bus stations Y10-30. **Pedicabs** make short trips (under 1km) for Y5-10.

■✹ 🛈 ORIENTATION AND PRACTICAL INFORMATION

Hangzhou has built its reputation and tourist industry around **West Lake** (xīhú; 西 湖), the approximate geographic center of the city. The major downtown area lies to the east. **Hubin Lu** (湖滨路) begins at the northeastern tip of the lake and hugs its banks as it continues south and becomes **Nanshan Lu** (南山路). East of and roughly parallel to Hubin Lu is the commercial **Yan'an Lu** (延安路), which intersects with the east-west running **Qingchun Lu** (庆春路), **Pinghai Lu** (平海路), and **Jiefang Lu** (解 放路). The area bounded by these four streets contains many of Hangzhou's more upscale hotels and stores.

Travel Agency: CITS, 1 Shihan Lu (☎8515 2888; citszj@mail.hz.zj.cn), on a small lane off the corner of Beishan Lu and Baoshu Lu. Average commission Y30-40. "English Department" (☎8505 9026) offers tours, interpreters, and tickets. Main office and English Dept. open daily 8:30am-5pm, ticketing open 8am-8pm.

Bank of China: 320 Yan'an Lu (☎8707 7996), a half-block north of Qingchun Lu. Exchanges traveler's checks. Credit card advances. **ATM** inside. Open daily 9am-5pm. Few other branches exchange traveler's checks.

Bookstore: Zhejiang Province Foreign Language Bookstore (zhèjiāng shěng wàiwén shūdiàn; 浙江省外文书店), 466 Fengqi Lu (☎8516 5987), at Yan'an Lu. Fair selection of bilingual tourist maps (Y5) and good pickings in English classics and translated Chinese literature section. Open daily 8:45am-9pm.

Markets: Family Friend Supermarket (jiāyǒu chāoshì; 家友超市), 86 Qingchun Lu (☎8725 1169), across from the No. 1 People's Hospital. Open daily 9am-9:30pm.

PSB: 35 Huaguang Xiang (☎8728 0114, visa extensions 8728 0539). Open daily 8:30am-noon and 2:30-5pm.

Hospitals: Hangzhou Central Hospital (hángzhōushì zhōng yīyuàn; 杭州市中医院), 453 Tiyuchang Lu (☎8582 7888). Open daily 8-11:30am and 2:30-5:30pm. **Hangzhou No. 1 People's Hospital** (hángzhōushì dìyī rénmín yīyuàn; 杭州市第一人民医 院), 261 Wangsa Lu (☎8706 5701). Open daily 8am-noon and 2-5:30pm. English speakers at both hospitals.

Internet Access: Many of the newer university guesthouses and foreign student dorms offer on-site access; some are free to guests while others require the purchase of an Internet card. Both the HI hostels offer Internet access (see **Accommodations,** p. 392). **Internet Cafe,** across from the Zhejiang University Xixi Campus. Y2 per hr. Open 24hr.

Post and Telecommunications: Hangzhou International Post Office, 147 Qingchun Lu (☎8722 8213), slightly west of the Family Friend Supermarket. Take bus #31 from the city center. EMS and Poste Restante. Open daily 8:30am-6pm. **China Telecom,** 87 Qingchun Lu (☎8517 4318, hotline 10000). IDD service. Open daily 8:30am-5pm. Another location in Wulin Sq. is open 24hr.

Postal Code: 310003.

🏠 ACCOMMODATIONS

Two HI hostels opened in 2002, creating more budget places to stay in addition to the university dormitories. Travelers looking to skip the journey to the city center (10-15min. by bus) may be pleasantly surprised to find affordable and comfortable options surrounding the lake. Big spenders have their pick of luxury hotels, including the **Shangri-La Hotel** (xiānggélǐlā fàndiàn; 香格里拉饭店), 78 Beishan Lu (☎8707 7951), where US President Richard Nixon met with Zhou Enlai on his historic 1972 visit to China. At Y880 plus 15% service charge per night, it's quite a steal.

■ **New Universe International Youth Hostel (HI)** (xīnyǔ guójì qīngnián lǚguǎn; 新宇国际 青年旅馆), 21 Qingchun Lu (☎8724 4888). Take bus #31 from the city center to Zhejiang Yiyuan. The sparkling lobby of this 15-story hostel reflects the cleanliness of its rooms. If large dorms, twin beds, and big storage lockers aren't enough, the friendly staff and complimentary toilet paper win additional points. In fact, you won't even know that you're in a hostel. Free broadband Internet plugs in all rooms; Internet cable rental Y10 per day. Vegan restaurant on the 15th fl. 8-bed dorms Y40, HI members Y35; 4-bed dorms Y50/Y40; doubles Y360/Y180. AmEx/DC/MC/V. ❶

■ **Jiangnan Yi International Youth Hostel (HI)** (jiāngnán yì guójì qīngnián lǚshè; 江南驿 国际青年旅舍), 32 Xiajiangnanyi Lu (☎8715 3273; www.jiangnanyi.com). Take tour bus #1 or 2 to the zoo. Then backtrack 50m and take a left on Manjuelong Lu (满觉陇 路). Walk 50m more and go up the 1st slope to the right. Wooden bunks, hardwood floors, funky lights, and bright green sheets give the cheerful dorms extra personality. Distinctive wash basins, traditional wooden furniture, and spacious beds justify the price for doubles. Start your day with sprigs of real bamboo in the shared baths. Rooms on top floor have skylights. Hot water heats up in 10min. Self-service laundry Y5 per load. **Internet** Y3 per hr. Bike rental Y5 per hr. or Y20 per day; deposit Y200. Free luggage storage. 2- to 6-bed dorms Y40-50, HI members Y35-40; doubles Y200/Y180. AmEx/DC/MC/V. ❶

Zhongda Hotel (zhōngdá fàndiàn; 中达饭店), 1 Changsheng Lu (☎8707 8366), a block south of the intersection between Qingchun Lu and Huansha Lu, within 2 blocks of West Lake. This family-oriented hotel offers clean, roomy doubles with A/C, bath, and TV. Doubles Y180. Ask for at least a 50% discount off the posted price. ❷

Zhejiang University Xixi Campus Foreign Students' Dormitory (zhèjiāng dàxué xīxī xiàoqū liúxuéshēng lóu; 浙江大学西溪校区留学生楼) 48 Tianmushan Lu, Bldg. 3 (☎8827 3784), at Hangda Lu. Bus #K11 from the train station or K21 from city center to Zhejiang Xixi. From main gate, bear right along the main path, past the basketball courts on the left. Rowdy international students and a no-nonsense staff inhabit these spotless, spacious, and newly renovated rooms. Often full June-Aug. No reservations; call before arrival. 2-bed dorms Y40; doubles with A/C and bath Y150. ❶

Jingjin Hotel (jīngjìn dàshà; 京晋大厦), 228 Zhonghe Zhong Lu (☎8701 9663), just north of Pinghai Lu, a 10min. walk from West Lake. This comfortable hotel has big, bright rooms. A/C, bath, TV, and filtered water dispensers. Doubles Y200-280. ❸

Zhejiang University International Building (zhèjiāng zhúkězhēn guójì dàlóu; 浙江竺可 桢国际大楼), 38 Zheda Lu (☎8795 1122), at Yuquan Campus. From the train station, take bus #K21 to the last stop. A 10min. walk through campus, at the end of the 1st road right of the main gate. Despite floors swept daily and crisp linen, the slightly cramped rooms occasionally sport a petrified mosquito on the wall. Rooms with A/C, bath, good water pressure, and TV. Singles Y98; doubles Y180. ❷

🔲 FOOD

With an impressive list of specialty dishes and enough history attached to rival West Lake itself, a routine meal in Hangzhou can easily turn into an extravaganza. Most restaurants will serve Hangzhou's fabled delicacies, and pared-down versions are available in any street stall (Y1-4).

The side streets off **Zhonghe Lu** (east of and parallel to Yan'an Lu), especially near the Jiefang Lu intersection, are lined with good, cheap restaurants. **Hubin Lu** establishments are characterized by tourist kitsch and hefty prices, but **Renhe Lu,**

ON THE MENU

HEAVEN ELEVEN

The West Lake's 11 famous dishes are visually stunning and mouth-wateringly delicious. **Louwailou** (see right), Qianlong's favorite, is the place to go for a taste of heaven.

Start with **West Lake Pure Greens Soup** (西湖纯菜汤), a refreshing soup made from a local lake plant. Or try the vinegary **Aunt Song's Fish Stew** (宋嫂鱼羹). Aunt Song also made Hangzhou's most famous dish, **West Lake Fish** (西湖醋鱼), in a sweet-and-sour sauce. **Sweet Ham** (蜜汁火方) features rock candy. Tender, roasted **Dongpo Pork** (东坡肉) is said to have been created by poet Su Dongpo, writer of "In Praise of Pork."

Pine Nut Fish (松子桂鱼) and **Shrimp with Eel** (虾爆鳝面) both star lake residents. After Longjing tea was spilled onto the emperor's shrimp, the accidental but fragrant **Shrimp with Dragon Well Tea** (龙井虾仁) was born. Strangely named **Fried Bells** (干炸响铃) is nothing more than tofu skins fried in the shape of bells. The plainly titled **Hangzhou Rolled Chicken** (杭州卷鸡) is actually more interesting, a golden crispy concoction of bamboo and beancurd skin.

A beggar stole a chicken, and lacking cookware, he ingeniously wrapped up his fowl in lotus leaves, paper, and clay and baked it in the fire. **Beggar's Chicken** (叫化童鸡) was thus born, proving that West Lake cuisine isn't an imperials-only affair.

running east off Hubin Lu, is one of the most exciting culinary streets around, with many small, perpetually packed restaurants that sell a dazzling variety of favorites, from Beijing duck to small snacks (xiǎochī; 小吃) such as stinky or crispy tofu. Along the heavily commercial and touristed stretch of Yan'an Lu, vendors sell cheap buns filled with pork, vegetables, and red bean paste (Y1-2). The restaurants along Qingchun Lu, between Hubin Lu and Zhonghe Lu, are ideal for larger groups that want to sample some of Hangzhou's finest cuisine. **Wahaha Gourmet Palace ❸** (wāhāhā měishí huánggōng; 哇哈哈美食皇宫), 169 Qingchun Lu, part of the mega-beverage company, dishes up inhabitants of the deep in a gargantuan building. Braised yellow eel starts at Y20. (☎8721 9898. Open daily 11am-3am.)

On hot, sticky Hangzhou nights, join locals at the **nightmarket** on Wushan Jie (吴山街), a tiny alley off Pinghai Lu, in the quest for frivolous trinkets and antiques. Lots of restaurants and street stalls also surround the area, selling countless juicy meat-stuffed buns (xiǎolóngbāo; 小笼包 ; Y5-6) and skewered meats, tofu, seafood, and mushrooms (Y1-3). **Teahouses** line the streets north and northeast of the lake, particularly on Beishan Lu and Hubin Lu. At the **Lakeside Pavilion ❶** (wànghú lóu; 望湖楼), 12 Baochu Lu, near CITS, you can enjoy inexpensive tea (about Y10) and nibble on sunflower and watermelon seeds, all while gazing at the West Lake. (☎8515 5843. Also serves meals. Open daily 8:30am-11pm.)

🍴 **Louwailou Restaurant** (lóuwàilóu càiguǎn; 楼外楼菜 馆), 30 Gushan Lu (☎8796 9023), near the southern end of Solitary Hill Island. Opened in 1848, this restaurant is said to be the oldest in China and, some would argue, the best. Emperors and poets have all dined here, praising Louwailou to the skies, but the food, while slightly ahead of the pack in taste and presentation, does not quite live up to its considerable reputation. It is, after all, the restaurant that created Hangzhou's famous 11 dishes: Dongpo pork; Beggar's Chicken (Y89); West Lake Pure Greens Soup (Y20); Longjin Baby Shrimp (Y98). Open daily 10:30am-2:30pm and 4:15-8:30pm. Customers can stay as late as needed to finish meals. ❹

Zhiweiguan (zhīwèiguān; 知味观), 83 Renhe Lu. The take-out window of this famed Hangzhou staple sells almond-paste cookies (Y2) and sticky rice-covered meatballs (Y1.5) in addition to the roasted hind and front quarters of all kinds of poultry (Y12-55). Small meat-filled wontons (Y4), the restaurant's claim to fame, are served inside. Purchase food tickets in the front. ❶

Nine Hundred Bowls of Noodles Restaurant (jiǔbǎiwǎn miànguǎn; 九百碗面馆), 115-1 Pinghai Lu (☎8703 9677), at Hubin Lu. Young couples and friends pack this casual eatery on weekends. Just the scent of the wide variety of noodle soups slowly simmering on charcoal stoves is appetizing enough. Also serves rice plates (Y10-20), chewy pan-fried noodles (Y10-18), and flavorful snacks like made-from-scratch lamb dumplings (Y5 for 6). Open daily 9am-10:30pm. ❷

Heaven on Earth Restaurant (tiāntáng rénjiān; 天堂人间), 36 Hubin Lu (☎8706 2288). Rich and authentic Italian fare for those hankering for Western food. The oxtail and black olives with homemade *pappardelle* (Y48) beats most of what one would find outside of Italy. Entrees Y42-158. Salads Y22-158. Open daily 11am-12:30am. ❸

🅒 SIGHTS

Hangzhou's sights mostly come down to one: West Lake. A good chunk of the day and a casual stroll would lead from stone bridges to ponds of red carp to swaths of lotus flowers (late-July to Aug.). Large tour groups tend to mill about docks and entrance to ticketed parks, but the expansive lake and less vaunted parks allow for plenty of secluded wandering.

▓ WEST LAKE 西湖

Bordered by Beishan Lu to the north, Hubin Lu to the east, and Nanshan Lu to the south. Bus #K7 runs along Beishan Lu and the northern end of Hubin Lu; get off at any stop along that stretch. Numerous buses run along Hubin and Yan'an Lu, including #38 and 151. Sights are connected by public transportation. Walk 1 block west from Yan'an Lu to reach the eastern shore. The lake and its shores are free, but some individual sights require an admission fee.

West Lake (xī hú; 西湖): heaven on earth, Hangzhou's *raison d'être*. For centuries, men have compared the lake to women and women to the lake. Of course, some have succeeded more eloquently than others. Poets wrote that West Lake's weeping willows are as softly arched as the eyebrows of Xi Shi, one of China's four legendary beauties, and its rippling waves as sparkling as her eyes.

Stroll along any portion of the West Lake shore or along **Bai Causeway** (bái dī; 白 堤) to the north and **Su Causeway** (sū dī; 苏堤) to the west for views of the lake. Bai Causeway connects Solitary Hill to the north shore; Su Causeway, shaded by willow trees, leads from the western end of the north shore to the south shore, linking the Tomb of Yue Fei to Huagang Park.

ISLANDS. As you set out across the waters by boat, arguably the best way to see the lake, keep an eye out for the three Lover's Bridges, the backdrop to some of China's most well-known love stories. The small, forested grounds of the **Mid-Lake Pavilion** (hú xīn tíng; 湖心亭), not far from Solitary Hill Island, make for peaceful strolls, although views are better from the shore. *(Open daily 8am-5pm. Free.)*

To the south lie the stone paths and zigzagging bridges of **Santan Yingyue** (sāntán yìngyuè; 三潭映月) and the **Small Immortal Isle,** an island within a lake with a lake within that island. Every turn on the island yields a carved tablet with imperial handwritings or delicate, breezy pavilions. The island's namesake, three stone towers, jut from the water. During the **Mid-Autumn Moon Festival,** the 15th day of the eighth month of the lunar calendar (Sept. 18, 2005 and Oct. 6, 2006), a candle lights in each tower; the reflection of the candlelight thrown upon the lake by the four round windows in each tower creates 12 "moons." The candles themselves form three additional moons, making a total of 15. *(Island Y15.)*

Several water vehicles can reach these islands and cross the lake. Passenger **ferries** leave from the eastern shore, midway along the Su Causeway, and from a dock between the Su and Bai Causeways on the northern shore, opposite the Tomb of

Yue Fei. Tickets are sold at the dock. *(Every 30-40min. 7:50am-4:50pm. Round-trip to the Mid-Lake Pavilion and Santan Yingyue including admissions Y35. Boats leave all the time from the 2 islands.)* **Night cruises** are also available, weather permitting. *(Tickets sold F-Su 6:30-9:30pm. Y20-25.)* **Private boats** can also be arranged. *(Y60-80 per hr.)*

HUAGANG PARK (huāgǎng guānyú; 花港观鱼). A private garden in the early Song Dynasty, the park now draws visitors with its peony gardens and hyperactive fish. The attention-loving inhabitants of **Red Carp Pond** (hóng yú chí; 红鱼池) give the park its name, *guānyú* (观鱼 ; "to view fish"), leaping out of the water constantly, especially if encouraged with food. *(At the southwestern tip of West Lake. Enter off Nanshan Lu or the southern end of Su Causeway. Take bus #315 from Hubin Lu to Su Di. ☎8796 3033. Open 24hr. Free.)*

SOLITARY HILL ISLAND (gū shān dǎo; 孤山岛). This "island" extending from the northern shores of the West Lake has some of the best vistas of willow trees, lotus ponds, and jagged pagoda roofs spangling the hills encircling the lake. **"Autumn Moon on a Calm Lake"** (píng hú qiū yuè; 平湖秋月), on the southeast corner, is touted as the area's best location for twilight lake-gazing (Hangzhou's sport of choice). Stop by the **Zhejiang Provincial Museum** (zhèjiāng shěng bówùguǎn; 浙江省博物馆) to see its letters and relics documenting the revolutions of modern China, including the first Chinese women's magazine; copies of "New Youth," with articles penned by Lu Xun; and a Texaco sign in Chinese. *(☎8797 0617. Audio guide Y10, deposit Y100. Open M noon-4pm, Tu-Su 9am-4pm. Free.)* Gushan Park (gūshān gōngyuán; 孤山公园), in the center of the island, also known as Sun Yat-sen Park, first entertained the upper-crust in 1752 as a private imperial resort. Within the park, the pavilions, half-hidden by greenery and overgrown paths of Solitary Hill, shelter locals from the clamor of tourists. *(Open daily sunrise-sunset. Free. Bike rental outside the park entrance Y10 per hr. Bargain for a 60% discount.)*

FEILAI PEAK 飞来峰

At the end of Linyin Lu, 15-20min. northwest of West Lake. Tour Bus #2 circles the lake, stopping at Lingyin Temple. ☎8796 4426. Open daily 5:30am-6pm. Y25, children 1-1.3m Y12.5, under 1m free. Lingyin Temple Y20.

To many, **Lingyin Temple** (língyǐn sì; 灵隐寺), the "Monastery of the Soul's Retreat," is the real draw of Feilai Peak. At the entrance of the temple, twin stone pagodas dating from AD 326 and two 1000-year-old sutra pillars stand guard, while peddlers sell tea leaves, trinkets, and incense sticks. China's largest wooden (19.6m) sleeping Buddha snoozes in the main **Mahavira Hall,** watched over by thousands of Buddhas carved into the wall.

To the left of the entrance to Feilai Peak (fēilái fēng; 飞来峰), the **Park of Selected Grotto Carvings** (zhōnghuá shíkū jícuìyuán; 中华石窟集翠园) displays free-standing Buddhist sculptures and images culled from far-away caves and temples. Farther up the road on the left, signs point the way to **Feilai Peak Grottoes** (fēiláifēng shíkū; 飞来峰石窟). According to legend, the peak was dubbed "Flown from Afar" in AD 326, when the Indian monk Hui Li marveled that the jagged summit must have "flown" from his native land because of its distinctive shape, common to peaks in India. More than 470 Buddhist carvings, dating mainly from the 10th to 14th centuries, festoon the hill. Visitors can test their luck in the almost pitch-black **Deep Dragon Cave** (lóng hóng dòng; 龙泓洞), where supposedly only a select few can see a tiny shaft of light through a pinhole opening on top (the "thread of heaven"). The **Cave of Milky Icicles** contains carvings of the characters for peace, fortune, and love; many a hopeful tourist rubs them for good luck.

SHANGHAI

OTHER SIGHTS

TOMB OF YUE FEI (yuèfēi mù; 岳飞墓). This tomb bears the famous phrase "loyalty to one's country to the end," characters that were supposedly tattooed onto Yue Fei's back by his mother when he joined the army. Yue Fei (1103-1142) proved to be a brilliant general, but his services were lent to a corrupt and inept Song court. The jealous prime minister Qin Hui framed Yue Fei for defying military orders and executed the legendary general. It took another 20 years, several disastrous defeats at the hands of the Jin, and strong public sentiment to convince a later emperor to finally give Yue Fei a ceremonial reburial. **Yue Temple** (yuèwáng miào; 岳王庙), first constructed in 1221, memorializes Yue and his son. Murals recount his childhood bravery and the kindness to peasants that endeared him to the common folk. An impressive amount of drool and phlegm cover the iron statues of Qin Hui and his cohorts, kneeling in disgrace before Yue Fei's tomb, despite a "spitting is forbidden" sign. Be careful while crossing the steep Bridge of Good and Evil. Qin Hui tripped here on his way to his victim's funeral, and tripping on the bridge has since been an indication of a guilty conscience. *(On Beishan Lu, near the northwest corner of West Lake. Take bus #7 to Yue Miao.* ☎ *8797 2651. Open daily 7am-6pm. Y25, children 1-1.3m Y12.5, under 1m free.)*

TIGER RUN DREAM SPRING (hǔ pǎo mèng quán; 虎跑梦泉). Tea connoisseurs once ranked these spring waters the third-best in China—but that was more than 1000 years ago. These days one look at the murky pools at the top of the hill will deter any thought of drinking the water. Vendors sell cups of filtered versions (Y0.5) at the "source," covered with pumps. Near the spring sits the **Jigong Temple,** named after a legendary half-crazy monk, the **Hall of the Arhats,** and a simple **Hupao Temple.** *(10min. south of West Lake, accessible by bus #504 and K4 from Yan'an Lu to Hupao. Open daily 6am-6:30pm. Y15, children under 1.3m Y7.5. Guides Y20.)*

▶ DAYTRIP FROM HANGZHOU: LONGJING 龙井

Take bus #27 from Pinghai Lu downtown or from along the northern shore of West Lake to Longjing Cha Shi, the next-to-last stop.

Worlds away from the pandemonium of the city, the Longjing (lóngjǐng; 龙井) tea plantations, hidden in the hills west of the lake, cultivate one of China's most revered teas. The roads from Hangzhou to Longjing village wind through terraced tea fields, passing the occasional tea planter moving between green boughs. An hour-long stroll or half a day spent sipping tea and admiring the bird's-eye view of the city should convert anyone into a tea enthusiast. The refreshing and fragrant "Dragon Well" tea gets its name from the limestone Longjing Spring, just past the central courtyard of **Longjing Tea Room** (lóngjǐng chá shǐ; 龙井茶室), a few meters from the bus stop. Myth has it that a dragon with special powers inhabits the well, which explains why it never dries up, even during a drought. The water here is

CHOOSE YOUR DRAGON WELL. Selecting superior Longjing is tricky—even the locals don't always come home with the real thing. When purchasing from a villager, always perform a taste test first. Drink the sample slowly so you have time to see if the tea turns a red tinge. If it does, the tea is stale and has absorbed too much moisture. Make sure your selection is measured out from the same stock that you sampled from and that it's sealed in front of you. A good rule of thumb is to avoid sellers with flashier homes, who may employ polished sales tactics to cajole higher prices from naive buyers. A reasonable price for quality Longjing is Y250-350 per *jīn,* though the sky is the limit.

SHANGHAI

cold and clean (if unfit for drinking); it's customary to splash water from the well on your face and hands for good luck. A short walk along the hills passes the houses of tea farmers, which double as business venues to sell their tea harvests.

Two stops before Longjing village, at Shuangfeng, the elegant **Chinese Tea Museum** (zhōngguó cháyè bówùguǎn; 中国茶叶博物馆) traces the history of tea from the Tang Dynasty to the present. (☎ 8796 4221. Free.) The road down the hill, Longjing Lu, leads to **Shuangfeng Village** (shuāngfēng cūn; 双峰村), home of the famed Hangzhou pearl and silk factories.

SHAOXING 绍兴   ☎ 0575

Lu Xun wrote stories about his native Shaoxing, a hometown of slow pace, remote from the epicenters of change, but affected by their ripples nonetheless. Perhaps in deference to modern China's greatest writer, the town has stayed much the same nearly a century later. While its frenetic, skyscraper-encrusted neighbors host one world-class exhibition after another, Shaoxing is content to read about them in the news and occasionally voice a few comments, in the tradition of its intellectual past. This is, after all, the birthplace of many of China's greatest minds, including Wang Xizhi, a master of calligraphy, and Cai Yuan, founder of Beijing University. Travelers come not for sensory shock, but to savor the bridges where great poems were once composed and the wine shops that inspired mighty pens.

▐ TRANSPORTATION

Trains: Shaoxing Train Station (shāoxīng huǒchē zhàn; 绍兴火车站 ; ☎ 802 2584), on Chezhan Lu, at the terminus of buses #1, 2, 3, 4, 11, and 14. Facing the main building, the ticket office is slightly to the right. Open daily 6am-10:30pm. To: **Guangzhou** (24hr., 1:40pm, Y200); **Hangzhou** (50min., frequently 9am-9:20pm, Y13-19); **Ningbo** (1½hr., 12 per day 2:10am-10:20pm, Y17-28); **Shanghai** (3-5hr.; 10:30am, 2, 4:40, 6:30pm; Y22-63).

Buses: Shaoxing Passenger Transit Center (shāoxīngshì gōnglù kèyùn zhōngxīn; 绍兴市公路客运中心 ; ☎ 801 8852, ext. 8004), 15min. northeast of the city center, at the northernmost end of Zhongxing Bei Lu. Accessible via bus #107. One of China's most luxurious bus stations, with impeccable service. To: **Fuzhou** (18hr., noon, Y179); **Hangzhou** (70min., every 10-20min. 6:30am-7:35pm, Y19); **Ningbo** (1½hr., every 40min. 6:40am-6pm, Y38); **Shanghai** (3hr., 17 per day 6:15am-7:25pm, Y66-70).

Local Transportation: Public **buses** run roughly 6am-8pm (Y1). Bus #2 runs along Jiefang Lu to the Yu Mausoleum and #3 travels down Shengli Lu to the Orchid Pavilion. **Huanxian Bus** (huánxiàn bāshì; 环线巴士), a private minibus line, services Jiefang Lu (Y1). Jiefang Lu is not very long, so for those unfazed by the summer heat, walking often takes the same amount of time as, if not less than, the bus.

Taxis: Base fare Y5, each additional km Y2. Most destinations under Y5-6. **Pedicabs** from Renmin Lu to the station area Y6-7, shorter distances Y3. Negotiate in advance.

▐ ORIENTATION AND PRACTICAL INFORMATION

Jiefang Lu (解放路) is the city's main thoroughfare, lined with numerous shops and hotels. It runs north-south through the city, intersecting **Shengli Lu** (胜利路), **Dong Jie** (东街), **Renmin Lu** (人民路), **Lu Xun Lu** (鲁迅路), and **Yan'an Lu** (延安路). **Huancheng Lu** (环城路) circles the city proper. Some of Shaoxing's major sights lie outside city limits but are easily accessed by public transportation. The train station, slightly north of the city, is connected to Jiefang Bei Lu by **Chezhan Lu** (车站路); the transit center, or the long-distance bus station, is 10min. northeast of the city, accessible via **Zhongxing Bei Lu** (中兴北路).

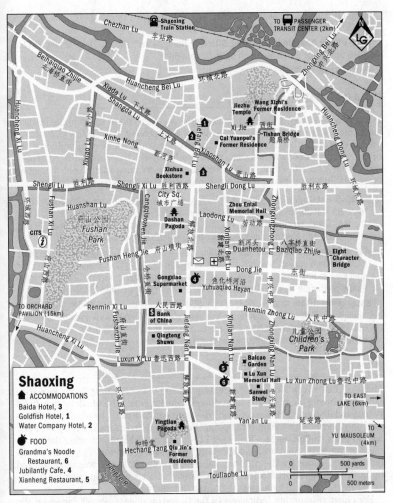

Shaoxing

🏠 ACCOMMODATIONS

Baida Hotel, **3**
Goldfish Hotel, **1**
Water Company Hotel, **2**

🍎 FOOD

Grandma's Noodle
  Restaurant, **6**
Jubilantly Cafe, **4**
Xianheng Restaurant, **5**

Travel Agency: CITS, 341 Fushan Xi Lu (☎515 5669), 2½ blocks south of Shengli Xi Lu. Accessible via west-bound bus #7 from the train station. No commission for plane tickets; average train ticket commission Y40. Open daily 8am-5:30pm.

Bank of China: 201 Renmin Zhong Lu (☎522 2888), 1 block west of Jiefang Lu. Exchanges traveler's checks. Credit card advances. **ATM.** Open daily 8am-8pm. Another **branch,** 41 Lu Xun Zhong Lu (☎513 5404), offers the same services. Open daily 7:40am-5:10pm.

Bookstore: Xinhua Bookstore, on Jiefang Bei Lu, 1 block north of Shengli Xi Lu, opposite the Baida Hotel. One of the only places in Shaoxing that sells bilingual maps. English-Chinese dictionaries available. Open daily 8am-8:30pm.

Market: Gongxiao Supermarket (gòngxiāo chāoshì; 供销超市), 219 Jiefang Bei Lu (☎511 7434). Open daily 8:15am-9pm.

Hospital: Municipal People's Hospital (shì rénmín yīyuàn; 市人民医院), 61 Dong Jie (☎522 8888), about 20m from the post office.

Post Office: Shaoxing Main Post Office, 1 Dong Jie (☎513 5000), at Jiefang Bei Lu. EMS and Poste Restante. Open daily 7:30am-6pm.

Postal Code: 312000.

ACCOMMODATIONS

Budget digs are easy to find, especially in the northern end of town. In the last few years, concerns over safety have led to tighter enforcement of the policy that foreigners can only stay in hotels with three stars or better. With luck, one can still score one of the cheaper run-down rooms in a three-star hotel, which are often in need of mosquito nets. A bit more cash (Y100-150) will secure creature comforts at the upper-crust establishments closer to the city center. All listed hotels have A/C and TV.

Goldfish Hotel (jīnyú bīnguǎn; 金鱼宾馆), 128 Jiefang Bei Lu (☎2626 2688). From the train station, take bus #1 to Qiche Zhan; walk 75m south on Jiefang Bei Lu; it's on the left. Clean rooms and large doubles with big windows are worth the price. Phone, water filter, and electric mosquito repellent. Singles Y170; doubles Y150-190. ❷

Water Company Hotel (shuǐlián bīnguǎn; 水联宾馆), 127 Jiefang Lu (☎522 7998). From the train station, take bus #7 to Diwu Yiyuan (第五医院). Crisp, white linen and spacious rooms make this hotel a steal. Run by the water company: 24hr. hot water guaranteed. Free filtered water and phone. Singles Y100; doubles Y120-140. ❷

Baida Hotel (bǎidà fàndiàn; 百大饭店), 258 Jiefang Bei Lu (☎511 1818), just north of Shengli Lu. Convenient location on the main street, a 15min. walk from the train station. Bright and clean rooms with baths. Breakfast included. Singles Y150; doubles Y198 and up. 40% discounts off the displayed price frequently available. ❷

FOOD

Much of Shaoxing's local cuisine centers around wine. **Shaoxing Yellow Rice Wine** (shāoxīng huáng jiǔ; 绍兴黄酒), produced from a special kind of sticky rice, has a potent and distinctive flavor. Drinking the brew can be a fairly heady experience—probably because it's meant for cooking. For a less intoxicating taste, try the aptly named **Drunken Chicken** (zuì jī; 醉鸡 ; Y15-30), prepared by marinating the breast meat in the wine. Another local specialty, **lima beans** (chándòu; 蚕豆) are admittedly more famous for their literary value—the culinary staple was immortalized by Lu Xun in his short stories. Many Chinese who grew up studying his works swear by the spiritual experience of eating this simple dish.

For cheap restaurants, look along **Lu Xun Lu** and on side streets off Yan'an Lu, the next major street south of Lu Xun Lu, intersecting Jiefang Lu. The intersection of Jiefang Lu and Renmin Lu has a smattering of **bakeries** (individual pastries Y2-4, small breads and cakes Y5 and up). At night, look for unusual food on **Xiada Lu**, off Jiefang Bei Lu, where stalls (dàpáidǎng; 大排档) sell an endless array of fresh seafood (Y12-14 per *jīn*), pig's stomach (Y8 per *jīn*), and various other goodies.

Grandma's Noodle Restaurant (āpó miànguǎn; 阿婆面馆), 100 Lu Xun Zhong Lu (☎513 0826), near Lu Xun Memorial Hall. Xianheng's equal in authentic Shaoxing cuisine, though without the latter's crowds. Grandma's Noodle Soup (Y15; 阿婆面), with toppings of pan-fried fish, pig's stomach, and fresh mushrooms and veggies, is the popular house specialty. Fish steamed over chicken (Y15; 白扣鸡) is another delicious and healthy option. Noodle dishes Y6-10. Noodle soups Y4-17. Stir-fried dishes Y6-20. Open daily 7am-2am. ❶

Xianheng Restaurant (xiánhēng jiǔdiàn; 咸亨酒店), 179 Lu Xun Zhong Lu (☎511 6666, ext. 8877), across from Grandma's Noodle Restaurant. This award-winning 100-year-old establishment is a recurring character in the stories of Lu Xun. It's said that every Shaoxing native eats here at least once in his life. The 1890s-style teahouse architecture and the statue of the anonymous restaurant manager, to whom Lu Xun was once apprenticed, make great photo ops. Shaoxing wine Y2-18 per *jīn*. Drunken chicken Y15. Lima beans Y6. Open daily 7:30am-8pm. ❷

Jubilantly Cafe (jùnlěi měishí; 俊磊美食), 558 Jiefang Bei Lu (☎513 9718), close to Dong Jie. Overshadowed by the KFC next door, but boasting a more extensive selection of fast food. The popular fresh wonton soup is only Y3. Noodle dishes Y3-12. Dumplings Y4 for 10. A la carte dishes Y3-7. Open daily 7am-9pm. ❶

🎦 SIGHTS

Shaoxing is peppered with the former residences of scholars and the scenes that inspired their works. A stroll around the city center can be a thrilling experience for lovers of Chinese art and literature.

EAST LAKE (dōng hú; 东湖). More a river than a lake, East Lake, with its single-stone causeways and pavilions over the water, is a pleasant retreat from Shaoxing. One of the most enjoyable ways to see the lake is to take a ride on a *wūpéng chuán* (乌蓬船). Unique to Shaoxing, these famed boats rely only on the foot-power of the boatman to push and steer one oar. The boats can go to areas of the lake that would otherwise be impossible to reach. The **Immortal Peach Cave** (xiāntáo dòng; 仙桃洞), **Trumpet Cave** (lǎbā dòng; 喇叭洞), and **Taogong Cave** (táogōng dòng; 陶公洞) all feature cliffs with near-vertical rock faces, legacy of millennia of rock quarrying since the Han Dynasty 2000 years ago. *(Bus #1 to Dong Hu Fengjing Qu, which runs until 6:15pm; or a 45min. boat ride from the Yu Mausoleum, Y80. ☎864 9560. Wūpéng chuán Y50 per boat; each boat seats 3. Open daily 7:30am-5:30pm. Y25, children 1.1-1.4m Y12, under 1.1m free.)*

ORCHID PAVILION (lán tíng; 兰亭). Built during the Han Dynasty, the pavilion sits at the foot of Lanzhu Hill and was named in honor of the orchids planted here by an emperor. The pavilion is sacred to devotees of Chinese calligraphy, but even those less reverent about their brush and scroll may find enlightenment in the refreshing grounds, with tufts of bamboo and grass growing in the cracks between glistening slabs of stone. In AD 353, renowned calligrapher Wang Xizhi and 41 of his closest friends played a drinking game along the nearby creek. Those unable to compose a sufficiently brief and witty poem on command were required to down three shots of wine. Wang's account of the 37 poems that the amusing game produced, the **Preface to the Orchid Pavilion** (lántíng xù; 兰亭序), has come to be revered as the quintessential example of superb calligraphic style and lucid prose. Visitors can find numerous copies of Wang's Preface, including one by Emperor Kangxi, scattered around the various pavilions and within the **Ancestral Shrine to Wang Xizhi** (wáng yòujūn cí; 王右军祠). Wang, also called Wang Youjun, doted on geese as pets and even devoted a small pavilion in their honor. *(On Shaoda Gonglu, 14km southwest of Shaoxing. Bus #3 from the train station takes 35-40min. and stops at Lanting. ☎460 9035 or 401 1035. Bamboo raft rental Y15 per 30min.; 4 per raft max. Open daily 8am-5:30pm. Y25, children 1.1-1.4m Y12, under 1.1m free.)*

LU XUN MEMORIAL HALL (lǔ xùn jìniàn guǎn; 鲁迅纪念馆). Shaoxing was the birthplace and childhood home of Lu Xun (1881-1936), generally considered to be the best satirical fiction writer and essayist of modern China. His criticism of feudal customs and outdated traditions is particularly studied. The memorial hall documents Lu Xun's life and works, from his use of literature to "wake up the Chinese

SHANGHAI

people" to the original handwritten copy of his autobiography. Note that the meticulously detailed museum has no English translations. Across from the museum, **Lu Xun's Ancestral Home** (lǔxùn zǔjū; 鲁迅祖居), the site of his wealthy family's home, features a courtyard and an interior of traditional Shaoxing architecture. The writer spent his childhood in **Lu Xun's Former Residence** (lǔ xùn gù jū; 鲁迅故居), west of the memorial hall. **Baicao Garden** (bǎicǎo yuán; 百草园), a small vegetable garden described as Lu Xun's "paradise," is also on the grounds. **Sanwei Study** ("three-flavor study"; sānwèi shūwū; 三味书屋), the school that Lu Xun attended as a child, lies diagonally across the street from the other sights. Visitors can still ogle the character for "early" (早) that Lu Xun carved into his desk when his teacher reprimanded him for being late. The saying "From Baicao Garden to Sanwei Study" (cóng bǎicǎoyuán dào sānwèishūwū; 从百草园到三味书屋) is still used today to describe the process of becoming educated. If Lu Xun were alive today, he might frown upon the overt commercialization here. Those unfamiliar with the famous author may not find the recreations interesting. *(393 Lu Xun Zhong Lu. Take bus #5, 9, or 12 to the intersection of Jiefang Lu and Lu Xun Zhong Lu; the hall is a 5min. walk to the east. ☎ 513 2080. Open daily 8am-5pm; last admission 4:15pm. Chinese-only guides Y60. All 4 buildings Y60, children 1.1-1.4m Y40, under 1.1m free.)*

OTHER SIGHTS. The **Zhou Enlai Memorial Hall** (zhōu ēnlái jìniànguǎn; 周恩来纪念馆) commemorates the first premier of the CCP, respected for his moderate position during the tumultuous years of the Cultural Revolution. The Hall itself is a large square. His ancestral home across the street details his life story and houses some of his letters, furniture, and clothing. *(369 Laodong Lu, near Zhongxing Zhong Lu. ☎ 513 3368. Open daily early June-Sept. 8am-5:30pm; Oct.-early June 8am-5pm. Both buildings and Tang poet He Zhitang's museum Y18, children 1.1-1.4m Y9, under 1.1m free.)* Southeast of here is the unique **Eight Character Bridge** (bā zì qiáo; 八字桥), named for its arched shape, which resembles the Chinese character for the number eight (八).

To the north of the city center, west of Zhongxing Lu, lies Jiezhu Temple, the site of **Wang Xizhi's Former Residence** (wáng xīzhī gùzhái; 王羲之故宅). This tiny museum holds preserved examples of the venerated calligrapher's works, including copies of the famous poems in his *Preface to the Orchid Pavilion. (72 Xi Jie. Open daily 8am-5pm. Y5.)* Slightly farther south on Caishan Jie is the **Tishan Bridge** (tíshàn qiáo; 题扇桥). While crossing the bridge one day, Wang Xizhi saw an aged fan vendor sobbing over not being able to sell even one fan. Sympathetic, Wang grabbed a brush from a nearby stand, scrawled five characters on each fan, then told the perplexed vendor that she could now sell the fans for a hundred times their original prices. This she did, and from that day on, she waited every day on the bridge with hundreds of fans for Wang to autograph, leading to the name, "Avoiding Old Woman Alley" (避婆弄). To the east of Jiefang Bei Lu, near Xiaoshan Jie, is **Cai Yuanpei's Former Residence** (càiyuánpéi gùjū; 蔡元培故居). The first president of Beijing University is an important figure in Chinese academic history. The museum documents his life story, complete with English translations. The house also showcases traditional Shaoxing architecture. *(13 Bifei Nong. Open daily 8am-5:30pm. Y8.)*

NINGBO 宁波 ☎ 0574

Once a port on the Silk Road of the Sea, Ningbo sent ships laden with precious cargoes of silks and porcelains to India, Persia, and beyond during the Tang Dynasty. By the mid-19th century, however, Ningbo's importance as a trading harbor began to decline, while Shanghai flourished, thanks to its more direct link to the sea. But sleek, modern Ningbo doesn't need to dwell on its past. Full of luxurious hotels and ever-growing skyscrapers, the city races ahead of the pack in the competition

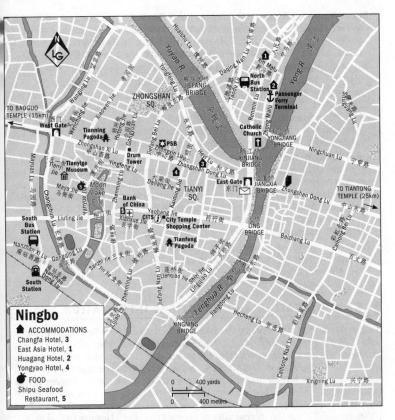

Ningbo

ACCOMMODATIONS
Changfa Hotel, **3**
East Asia Hotel, **1**
Huagang Hotel, **2**
Yongyao Hotel, **4**

FOOD
Shipu Seafood
    Restaurant, **5**

to be the brightest star on the east coast. Slick, fast, and perpetually under construction, Ningbo flaunts its urban dash, but holds little appeal for those not interested in a cosmopolitan life. Many visitors glide through the port city en route to Putuoshan, a Buddhist island in the East China Sea.

TRANSPORTATION

Flights: Ningbo Lishe Airport (níngbō lìshè jīchǎng; 宁波栎社机场 ; ☎8783 6750, 8742 7888; www.ningbo-airport.com), a 30min. taxi ride (Y50) from the city. Buses (30-45min., every hr., Y10) shuttle between airport and the **CAAC ticket office,** 91 Xingning Lu (☎8742 7700). Open daily 8am-6pm. To: **Beijing** (2hr.; 8, 11am, 4:50, 8:30pm; Y1180); **Fuzhou** (1hr.; Tu-W, F, Su 1:55pm; Y690); **Hong Kong** (3 per day 8:45am-2:35pm, Y1530); **Shanghai** (30min.; 7:50, 8, 11:50am, 7:30, 9pm; Y380).

Trains: South Station (nán zhàn; 南站 ; ☎8731 2084, tickets 160 6161), in the southwestern corner of the city, in a plaza at the terminus of Nanzhan Xi Lu, Mayuan Lu, and Gongqing Lu. Accessible by bus #1 from the ferry terminal and 518 from Jiefang Lu. Ticket window open daily 7:20-11am and 12:30-6pm. To: **Hangzhou** (2hr., many per day 7:35am-9pm, Y14-44); **Nanjing** (8-10hr., 4 per day 8am-5:30pm, Y80-169); **Shanghai** (5-7hr., many per day 8:13am-5:30pm, Y27-91).

Buses: Ningbo has 3 bus stations, but the **South Bus Station** (qìchē nán zhàn;汽车南站 ; ☎8713 0585), across the street from the train station's main entrance, handles almost all long-distance traffic. Open daily 5:20am-8pm. To **Hangzhou** (2hr., every 10-15min. 5:50am-7:50pm, Y42-48) and **Shanghai** (4hr., many per day 6am-8pm, Y98).

Boats: Ningbo Harbor Passenger Ferry Terminal (níngbōgǎng kèyùn mǎtóu; 宁波港客运码头), 142 Zhong Malu (☎8735 6332), in the northeastern part of the city. Also known as the **Boat Dock** (lúnchuán mǎtóu; 轮船码头). Accessible by bus #1 from the train station. Ticket windows open daily summer 5:45am-4:30pm; winter 6:15am-4:30pm. To **Putuoshan** (2hr., many per day 5:50am-3:40pm, Y58). Many agents here offer hotel rooms on Putuoshan, but fierce competition among hotel salespeople at the Putuoshan ferry terminal often pushes down rates even more.

Local Transportation: Bus fare Y1, with A/C Y2. Bus #1 connects the bus and train stations with the ferry terminal in the north; #517 travels along Zhongshan Lu, linking the eastern and western parts of the city; #820 runs down Liuting Jie, passing the train station, Moon Lake, Chenghuang Temple, and the intersection with Jiefang Bei Lu. For outlying areas, bus #332 from Renmin Lu, just south of the ferry terminal, serves Baoguo Temple and 601 runs to Ningbo University. Private **minibuses** offer direct services between the station area and the ferry terminal (sunrise-sunset, Y1-2).

Taxis: Base fare Y8, each additional km Y1.5. From bus and train stations to ferry terminal approximately Y8; from city center to airport Y50. **Pedicabs** go to most places for Y5-8, but many drivers charge more for the long uphill climb to the ferry area.

■✳❼ ORIENTATION AND PRACTICAL INFORMATION

Ningbo city is split into three by the Y-shaped formation of the **Yuyao** (yúyáo jiāng; 余姚江), **Yong** (yǒng jiāng; 甬江), and **Fenghua** (fènghuà jiāng; 奉化江) rivers. Travelers will most likely encounter only two of these three sections: the western, where the railway station, bus stations, and several sights are; and the northern, the location of the ferry terminal. These two areas are connected by **Xinjiang Bridge** (xīnjiāng qiáo; 新江桥). The western section of the main east-west street, **Zhongshan Xi Lu** (中山西路), is bookended by two significant junctions: the **East Gate** (dōng mén; 东门), at the intersection of Zhongshan Lu and **Lingqiao Lu** (灵桥路), and the **West Gate** (xī mén; 西门), at the intersection of Zhongshan Lu and **Changchun Lu** (长春路). The other major east-west thoroughfare is **Liuting Jie** (柳汀街), home to numerous shops and eateries; Liuting Jie becomes **Yaohang Jie** (药行街) east of its intersection with **Jiefang Nan Lu** (解放南路).

Travel Agency: Ningbo CITS, 48-130 Nong, Liuting Jie (☎8719 3018), past the main gate of Chenghuang Temple and immediately to the right. Train ticket commission Y20; no commission for plane tickets. Helpful international dept. provides interpreters and tour guides. Open M-F 8:30am-5pm.

Bank of China: 15 Liuting Jie (☎8719 6666), between Moon Lake and Fenghua River, 2 blocks east of the No. 1 Municipal Hospital. Accessible from ferry terminal by southbound bus #20. Exchanges currency and traveler's checks. Credit card advances. MC/V **ATMs.** Open daily 8:30-11:30am and 2-6pm.

Bookstore: Xinhua Bookstore, 99 Zhongshan Dong Lu (☎8724 6719). A 4-fl. megastore with a wide variety of English fiction and bilingual English-Chinese maps. Open Su-Th 8:30am-9pm, F-Sa 8:30am-9:30pm.

PSB: 658 Zhongxing Lu (☎8706 2000), in the municipal government's building complex (shì zhèngfǔ; 市政府), at the northeastern corner of Zhongshan Lu at Jiefang Bei Lu. **Visa extensions** ☎8706 2505. Open daily 8:30-11am and 2:30-6pm.

Hospital: No. 1 Municipal Hospital (shì dìyī yīyuàn; 市第一医院), 90 Xianxue Jie (☎8708 5588), off Liuting Jie between Moon Lake and Jiefang Nan Lu. English-speaking staff members. Open 24hr.

Post and Telecommunications: 258 Zhongshan Zhong Lu (☎8736 5701), at the southeast corner of Lingqiao Lu at Zhongshan Zhong Lu. EMS and Poste Restante. IDD and calling card service on 2nd fl. Open daily 8am-8pm.

Postal Code: 315000.

ACCOMMODATIONS

Although most hotels in Ningbo are mid-range establishments, there are a few budget options outside the city center. Hotels in the northern part of town, near the ferry terminal, are reasonably priced and very convenient. Call in advance to double-check addresses, because the pace of construction in Ningbo means short lives for buildings outside of the main commercial districts.

Huagang Hotel (huágǎng bīnguǎn; 华港宾馆), 146 Zhong Malu (☎8767 7977), left of the ferry terminal ticket office. Short walk to local bus stops, banks, and post office. Clean rooms and windows with an enchanting view of construction sites. A/C, TV, and phone. Doubles Y120. Aim for 30% discount. ❷

East Asia Hotel (dōng yà fàndiàn; 东亚饭店), 183 Xin Malu (☎8735 6224). Take bus #1 from the station area to Lunchuan Matou (ferry terminal). From the terminal, turn right on Zhong Malu, take a left at the 1st intersection, and walk 2 long blocks; or take a pedicab for Y5. Showcases sparkling, airy rooms at a new location. Buffet breakfast included. Singles and doubles Y150. Discounts of Y20-50 possible. ❷

Yongyao Hotel (yǒngyào jiǔdiàn; 永耀酒店), 341 Kaiming Jie (☎8710 1888; fax 8710 1121), near Zhongshan Dong Lu in the city center. Spacious rooms with light-colored furnishings, thick mattresses, shiny bathrooms, lucky bamboo, and big windows looking out to Ningbo's skyline. Attentive staff. TV, phone, A/C, mini-fridge. Doubles Y248. ❸

Changfa Hotel (chángfā jiǔdiàn; 长发酒店), 151 Zhongshan Dong Lu (☎8725 1828), adjacent to the Ningbo Grand Hotel, in the city center. Take bus #518 going east on Zhongshan Dong Lu to Jiefang Lu; it's 2 blocks east on the left. The cheapest rooms are windowless, but a few extra *yuán* secures a spacious pad, windows, and a big, spotless bath. Doubles Y228-268. AmEx/DC/MC/V. ❸

FOOD

Ningbo has a wide variety of local **seafood**, both fresh and dried. Small restaurants with creatures from the deep, including snails, eels, and squid, line Renmin Lu and Zhong Malu, south of the ferry terminal. Farther south, by the Moon Lake area, local favorite ▧ **Shipu Seafood Restaurant** ❷ (shípǔ hǎiwèi fàndiàn; 石浦海味饭店), 60 Yanyue Jie, serves the famous yellow fish (huángyú; 黄鱼 ; starting at Y60 per *jīn*) and turtles (hǎiguī; 海龟 ; Y58 per *jīn*) in classic Chinese-banquet style, complete with a legion of waitstaff. Diners sentence to the chopping block whatever aquarium-bound creature strikes their fancy. Shipu also serves ▧ **níngbō tāngyuán** (宁波汤圆; Y8), sticky rice flour balls stuffed with sweet sesame paste. Come early (☎8732 8777. Meat and vegetable dishes Y12-40. Gelatinous marinated pig's nose Y22. Open daily 10am-10pm.)

For land-dwelling options, try the **City Temple Shopping City** ❶ (chénghuáng miào shāngchéng; 城隍庙商城), at the southwest corner of Yaohang Lu at Kaiming Jie. A dining area is at the southern end of this jampacked block, serving everything from Sichuanese kebabs dipped in spicy broths to pumpkin-filled rice balls. Large restaurants across the alley dish up Ningbo's favorite foods, including **smoked fish** and the ubiquitous sweet rice balls. After dark, the scents of skewered barbecued meat and **smelly tofu** waft around the street stalls. In the summer, vendors also sell desserts like **shaved ice** with sweet toppings (bào bīng; 刨冰 ; Y2-4).

👁 SIGHTS

For those with extra time in Ningbo, the temples in the surrounding countryside may be worth a visit. In the Jiangbei district, 15km northwest of Ningbo, the 970-year-old **Baoguo Temple** (bǎoguó sì; 保国寺) is an all-wood structure holding up a 50-ton ceiling. Bus #332 (Y3) runs from Xinjiang Bridge. Partly obscured by century-old forests, the **Tiantong Temple** (tiāntóng sì; 天童寺) is simply built with dark wood. Monks live and work in its serene buildings, some of which date to 300 AD. Bus #362 (Y4) leaves every 15min. 6:15am-5:35pm from Ningbo East Bus Station to Tiantong Temple, some 25km east of the city. (Temple Y3.)

TIANYIGE MUSEUM (tiānyìgé bówùguǎn; 天一阁博物馆). Set amid a maze of streams, gardens, and meticulously arranged rock formations, the museum is centered around the famed **Tianyige Library** (tiānyìgé bǎoshū lóu; 天一阁宝书楼), the oldest private library in China. Built between 1561 and 1566, the library originally held the collection of defense minister Fan Qing. Most of the current 300,000 titles were retrieved after the Cultural Revolution, and only a few manuscripts from the Ming and Qing Dynasties are open for public viewing. There are numerous other pavilions and exhibits to explore, including a **Painting and Calligraphy Hall** (tiānyìgé shūhuà guǎn; 天一阁书画馆), with period art and scrolls for sale; the **Former Residence of Fan Qing** (fànshì gùjū; 范氏故居), with books and printing woodblocks; and the small **Ningbo History Museum** (níngbō shǐ bówùguǎn; 宁波史博物馆). The real highlight, however, is the **Mahjong Museum**, built in honor of the game's inventor, a Ningbo native. The museum details the evolution of *mahjong*, with beautiful game sets from China and Japan on display. The courtyard features giant *mahjong* tiles, reminiscent of Alice in Wonderland. (*10 Tianyi Jie. Take bus #560 from Chenghuang Miao, "city temple," to the Tianyige stop.* ☎ *729 3526. Open daily May-Sept. 8am-5:30pm; Oct.-Apr. 8am-5pm. Y20, children under 1.4m or students with ID Y10.*)

OTHER SIGHTS. Near the Tianyige Museum, the oblong **Moon Lake** (yuè hú; 月湖) offers a willow-shaded respite from decidedly urban Ningbo. The open-air pavilions and winding corridors on the bank draw crowds, who gather around chess players and makeshift barber chairs. In mid-summer, retirees hold impromptu Chinese opera performances. A popular after-dinner sport of Ningbo families is crossing the lake on paddleboats. (*Boats Y15-20 per 30min., deposit Y20. Boat office open daily 7:30am-5:30pm and 6-10:30pm, last boat 10pm. Park open daily dawn-dusk. Free.*) The area north of **Xinjiang Bridge** is the site of the former Portuguese and British concessions. With its red bricks and tapered spires, the 17th-century **Catholic Church** (tiānzhǔ jiàotáng; 天主教堂) stands proudly out of place among rows of residential houses and small storefronts. (*22 Zhong Malu. From the ferry terminal, head south on Zhong Malu for about 5min.; the church is in a gated area on the left.* ☎ *8735 5903. Free.*)

PUTUOSHAN 普陀山 ☎ 0580

Saturated with the fragrance of incense and sounds of Buddhist chants, the air on the tiny island of Putuoshan is worlds away from the chaotic fumes of the mainland cities. Here, ochre-tinted rocks stand unwavering against the waves of the East China Sea. A mecca for both devout Buddhist pilgrims and tourists, the island has an abundance of temples, shrines, and monasteries. With rolling hills, rugged cliffside beaches, and ocean stretching into the distant haze, Putuoshan promises

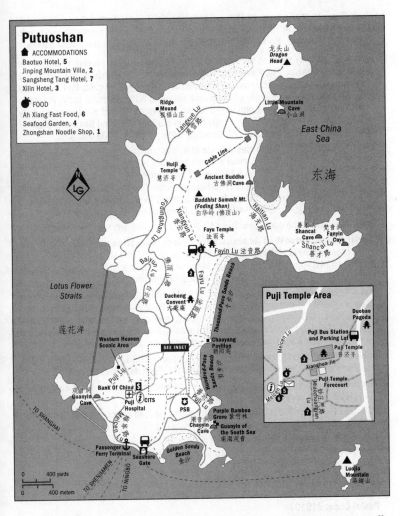

Putuoshan

ACCOMMODATIONS
Baotuo Hotel, **5**
Jinping Mountain Villa, **2**
Sangsheng Tang Hotel, **7**
Xilin Hotel, **3**

FOOD
Ah Xiang Fast Food, **6**
Seafood Garden, **4**
Zhongshan Noodle Shop, **1**

Dragon Head
龙头山

Ridge Mound
祖福山庄

Little Mountain Cave
小山洞

East China Sea

东海

Huiji Temple
慧济寺

Cable Line

Ancient Buddha Cave
古佛洞

Buddhist Summit Mt. (Foding Shan)
白华岭 (佛顶山)

Fayu Temple
法雨寺

Fayin Lu 法音路

Shancai Cave
善财洞

Fanyin Cave
梵音洞

Shancai Lu 善才岭

Langxue Lu 澜雪路

Foudingshan Lu

Xiangyun Lu 祥云岭

Haitian Lu 海天路

Baiyun Lu 白云路

Thousand-Pace Sands Beach 千步沙

Dacheng Convent
大乘庵

Lotus Flower Straits

莲花洋

Western Heaven Scenic Area

SEE INSET

Chaoyang Pavilion
朝阳阁

Hundred-Pace Sands Beach 百步沙

Puji Lu

Bank Of China

Puji Hospital

Guanyin Cave
观音洞

CITS

PSB

Chaoyin Cave
潮音洞

Purple Bamboo Grove 紫竹林

Guanyin of the South Sea
南海观音

Passenger Ferry Terminal

Seashore Gate

Golden Sands Beach
金沙

Meicen Lu 梅岑路

TO SHANGHAI

TO SHENJIAMEN

TO NINGBO

Luojia Mountain
洛迦山

0   400 yards
0   400 meters

Puji Temple Area

Duobao Pagoda

Puji Bus Station and Parking Lot

Puji Temple
普济寺

Meicen Lu

Xianghua Jie

Miaozhuangyan Lu 妙庄严路

Puji Temple Forecourt

timeless spots for quiet reflection. Enterprising carts selling sutra beads, scrolls, and exorbitantly priced bottles of water add a touch of commercialism, but most travelers are too wonderstruck to notice.

TRANSPORTATION AND PRACTICAL INFORMATION

Off the coast of northern Zhejiang in the East China Sea, Putuoshan is compact enough to be traversed on foot in 3-4hr. Most major roads run north-south. The **ferry terminal** is at the southern tip of the island. The most direct route to Puji Temple and the island's eateries is via **Meicen Lu** (梅岑路), running west and then north from the terminal. **Puji Lu** (普济路) runs east and then north along the eastern coast. From the Puji Temple area, several roads run north: **Fayu Lu** (法雨路) leads to Fayu Temple at the base of Putuoshan's principal peak, **Fodingshan** (佛顶山); and **Foding Shan Lu** (佛顶山路) scales the western side of the mountain and ends near the Huiji Temple. Footpaths run through the hills and link the major routes.

Ferry: The only way to reach the island is by ferry from Shanghai, Ningbo, or one of the larger islands nearby. The **Passenger Ferry Terminal** (lúnchuán mǎtóu; 轮船码头), 1 Puji Lu (☎ 609 1121), also known as *kèyùn mǎtóu* (客运码头). Tickets for Ningbo may only be purchased on the day of travel and sell out quickly, so come early. Tickets to other destinations may be purchased 1 day in advance. Ticket window open daily 6:20am-5pm. To **Ningbo** (2-2½hr., every hr. 7am-5:30pm, Y58) and **Shanghai** (Express 4hr.; 12:30, 1:15, 2pm; Y192-222. Overnight 12hr., 4:40pm, Y108-230.).

Local Transportation: Minibuses operate from dawn to about 4:30pm, but service to destinations other than the 3 main temples and dock is erratic. From ferry terminal to Puji Temple parking lot (Y3); Puji Temple to Fayu Temple (Y4); Puji Temple to the base of Fodingshan, near Huiji Temple (Y6). Upscale hotels like the Putuoshan Grand Hotel also rent vans for guests. Walking from the terminal to Puji Temple takes 40-50min.; Puji Temple to Fayu Temple 30-40min.; Fayu Temple to Huiji Temple 40-50min.

Taxis: Taxis wait at the dock. Base fare Y40. Negotiate a price with the driver beforehand.

Tourist Office: Putuoshan Administrative Offices, Reception and Welcome Office (pǔtuóshān guǎnlǐ jú jiēdàisuǒ; 普陀山管理局接待所), 115 Meicen Lu (☎ 609 1224 or 609 1414), opposite and a bit south of the post office, in a large courtyard overlooking a pond. A good place to gather free maps and brochures.

Travel Agency: CITS, 117 Meicen Lu (☎ 609 1414), opposite the Bank of China, immediately right of the entrance to the courtyard. Friendly staff arrange tours of Putuoshan (1-day tours Y187 and up) and book ferry tickets to Ningbo and Shanghai (commission Y10-15). English-speakers available. Open daily 8-11am and 1:30-5:30pm. Most hotels also book plane, bus, and boat tickets with 1-day notice (commission Y10-20).

Bank of China: 106 Meicen Lu (☎ 609 1591), opposite CITS. Exchanges currency and traveler's checks. Credit card advances. **24hr. ATM.** Open daily 8-11am and 2-5:30pm.

Markets: Several small **supermarkets** cluster on Xianghua Jie (the street east of Puji Temple) and the alleys running south from it.

PSB: 231 Puji Lu (☎ 609 3186), on the right side of the road as you head south from the Puji Temple parking lot. 24hr. service.

Hospital: Puji Hospital (pǔjì yīyuàn; 普济医院), 95 Meicen Lu (☎ 609 2388), just past the Bank of China. Friendly staff, but no English-speakers. Open daily 7:30-11:30am and 2-5pm. Emergency open 24hr.

Post and Telecommunications: 126 Meicen Lu (☎ 609 1190), on the corner with Meicen Lu. EMS and Poste Restante. Open daily 8am-5pm. **China Telecom** is next door.

Postal Code: 316107.

◤ ACCOMMODATIONS

Like everything else on the island, hotels tend to be expensive, and the quality of the costly mid-range hotels pales in comparison to their mainland counterparts. The best chance to lock in a good price is at the dock, where representatives from hotels undercut each other's prices in a shouting match. Make sure to ask about amenities. The best options are the hotels clustered on small alleys near the main temples, especially Puji and Fayu Temples. Some locals make pocket money by opening up their homes to Chinese tourists, posting "accommodation available inside" (nèi yǒu zhùsù; 内有住宿) signs throughout the island. Foreigners, however, will have little success at these and most other cheap establishments.

If all else fails, resort to these two top-end hotels: the **Xilei Little Villa** (xīlěi xiǎo zhuāng; 息耒小庄 ; ☎609 1505), on the corner of Puti Lu and Meicen Lu, and the **Putuoshan Grand Hotel** (pǔtuóshān dàjiǔdiàn; 普陀山大酒店 ; ☎609 2828), on Meicen Lu next to Puji Hospital. These luxury options start at a whopping Y1080 per night, but often slash rates by 50% on weekdays. Hotels are often filled to capacity on weekends and prices jump Y100 on average. Reservations are recommended in the summer. The establishments below all have A/C, bath, and TV.

Jinping Mountain Villa (jīnpíng shān zhuāng; 锦屏山庄), 107 Fayu Lu (☎609 1500; fax 609 1698), a few min. south of Fayu Temple. Large windows in spacious rooms look out to green hills, small villages, and clotheslines. Doubles Y130-200. 50% discounts possible on low-season weekdays. ❷

Sansheng Tang Hotel (sānshèngtáng fàndiàn; 三圣堂饭店), 121 Miaozhuangyan Lu (☎609 1277; fax 609 1140). From Meicen Lu, turn right onto the post office road; the hotel is 10min. ahead on the left. A vast monastery-turned-hotel, with equally vast rooms and bright baths. Doubles Y260-280. 40% low-season discounts. ❹

Xilin Hotel (xīlín fàndiàn; 锡麟饭店), 9 Xianghua Jie (☎609 1303; fax 609 1199), next to the western end of Puji Temple. Newly renovated, with idyllic courtyards and sparkling rooms. Singles Y308; doubles Y428-488; triples Y488. Low-season 20-40% off. ❹

Baotuo Hotel (bǎotuó fàndiàn; 宝陀饭店), 118 Meicen Lu (☎609 2090), across from CITS. Central location, thick mattresses, and stainless bathrooms make this hotel a pleasant deal. Doubles Y300; Oct.-Apr. Y240-250. ❹

🍴 FOOD

Not surprisingly, Putuoshan is famous for its seafood. Specialties include **Zhoushan yellow fish** (zhōushān huáng yú; 舟山黄鱼), steamed or sautéed with a side dish of tofu and fish-head soup (Y80 per kg), and **Zhoushan snails** (zhōushān wōniú; 舟山蜗牛 ; Y20), stir-fried in a special vinegar sauce. Virtually identical seafood restaurants display basins of fish, crawlies, and mollusks along Meicen Lu and Puji Lu. A large **market** on Meicen Lu, opposite the row of banks, has fresh seafood. Besides seafood, there are scant budget options. On Xianghua Jie, **fruit vendors** share space with shops selling everything from dried seahorse to Guanyin statuettes.

Seafood Garden (hǎixiān yuán; 海鲜园 ; ☎609 1505), where Puji Lu meets Meicen Lu. Regal banquet-style restaurant reputed for its taste, freshness, and variety. Zhoushan yellow fish Y120 per jīn. Drunken crab Y68. Vegetarian dishes Y12-24. ❷

Zhongshan Noodle Shop (zhōngshān miànshí diàn; 中山面食店), opposite and 100m to the right of Fayu Temple's main exit. Piping hot fried and seafood noodles (Y6-20) are the cheapest on the island, or so they claim. Vegetarian treasures noodle soup topped with mock chicken, mushrooms, and leafy greens Y10. ❶

Ah Xiang Fast Food (āxiáng kuàicān; 阿祥快餐 ; ☎609 1557), opposite the Putuoshan Grand Hotel. Generous tofu, vegetables, pork, and seafood dishes for Y5-10 per platter. Open daily 9am-10pm. ❶

📷 SIGHTS

Admission to Putuoshan is Y110, children under 1.4m and students Y55; pay upon arrival at the ferry terminal. A simple stroll around the island takes you past bamboo groves, gilded Buddhist statues, and misty horizons in the distance. With their intense spirituality and majestic architecture, the three major temples (Puji, Fayu, and Huiji) are the major attractions for lay and devout alike.

PUJI TEMPLE (pǔjì sì; 普济寺). Puji Temple is the oldest and most popular of the three principal temples on Putuoshan. Legend holds that when Emperor Zhuang visited this temple dressed as a peasant, a monk wouldn't let him in through the main (middle) door and instead showed him the side entrance. Furious, the emperor ordered that no one else be allowed to use the main entrance. Later, three bridges were constructed over the nearby **Haiyin Pond**—the middle one for the emperor, the arched one for nobles, and the plain one for commoners. Haiyin Pond (also known as Freeing-the-Soul Pond) itself is a large lotus flower reservoir and gathering place for tour groups, *tai chi* practitioners, and souvenir vendors.

Built in 1080, Puji Temple is not only the geographical heart of the island, but its spiritual center as well. It houses the Divine Guanyin (shèng guānyīn; 圣观音), the only representation of Guanyin made by Putuoshan natives. A grand Buddha flanked by the **Eighteen Arhats** sits in the main hall. Other halls house other buddhas and bodhisattvas, including Wenshu, the golden bodhisattva of learning, better known as the bodhisattva of university entrance examinations for many of the students who visit. Puji gets rather crowded during the summer; the temples higher up on the mountain are more isolated. *(From the terminal exit, follow Meicen Lu north as it becomes Xianghua Jie; temple is half a block down on the left. Or take bus from terminal. Open daily summer 5:30am-6:30pm; winter 6am-5pm. Y5, children under 1.4m free.)*

FAYU TEMPLE (fǎyǔ sì; 法雨寺). At the foot of **Fodingshan** (Buddhist Summit Mountain), Fayu Temple enjoys a breezy feel in its terraced halls and buildings, quite unlike the dense and compact Puji Temple. Built in 1580, Fayu greets visitors with the unique **Nine-Dragon Screen** (jiǔ lóng bì; 九龙壁), carved from 60 stones pieced together like an interlocking jigsaw. Visitors will only see eight dragons, however—as "descendants of the dragon," the people represent the ninth dragon. A miniature golden pagoda stands between the wall and the first of the temple's several halls, where visitors can toss coins through five tiers of windows for good luck. In one hall sits the imposing **Thousand-Hand Guanyin** (qiān shǒu guānyīn; 千手观音) statue. The main **Nine-Dragon Hall of Treasures** (jiǔ lóng bǎo diàn; 九龙宝殿), was moved from Nanjing to Putuoshan during the Qing Dynasty. *(1 Fayin Lu. Take minibus from Puji Temple parking lot, or walk 30min. north. Also accessible from Huiji Temple by descending Fodingshan along a trail of 1080 steps. ☎ 669 0141. Open daily 5:30am-6pm. Y5.)*

HUIJI TEMPLE (huìjì sì; 慧济寺). Approachable only by cable car or an arduous climb to the very top of Fodingshan, Huiji attracts only the most devout pilgrims. Consequently, it's also the least crowded. The temple's terraces and walkways swing past breathtaking ocean vistas to the west and the mountainside and valley to the south and east. Lotus leaves and ancient calligraphy pave the long path leading to the temple; this represents Guanyin's presence and is believed to purify visitors of worldly sins. The temple has two main halls off an inner courtyard. The murmur of praying monks emanates from side halls. Out the west courtyard door, monks planted little patches of vegetables. *(208 Xiangyun Lu. Take a minibus to Fayu Temple and climb for 30-45min. up the 1080 steps. Cable car operates 6:30am-7pm. Cable car up Y25, down Y15; round-trip Y35, children Y18. ☎ 609 0136. Open daily sunrise-sunset. Y5.)*

PURPLE BAMBOO GROVE (zǐzhú lín; 紫竹林). Ironically, the purple bamboo is the least exciting of this grove's many attractions. Inside a small temple, flanked by a frieze of colorful miniature murals, sits a statue of Guanyin carved entirely from a solid block of jade. Near the murals, intrepid visitors can peer into **Chaoyin Cave** (cháoyīn dòng; 朝音洞), a spine-tingling drop that many devoted followers have thrown themselves into in a dubious bid for enlightenment. The small pavilion on the rocks looks out over **Luojia Mountain** (luòjiā shān; 洛迦山), shaped like a sleeping Buddha. The rock depression on the beach represents the footprint left by Guanyin when she stepped over to Putuoshan to admire its view. The **Courtyard**

of the **Cannot-Bear-To-Leave Guanyin** (bùkěnqù guānyīn yuàn; 不肯去观音院), a tiny shrine to the left of Chaoyin Cave, acquired its name when a Japanese monk tried to take a Guanyin statue from Wutaishan to Japan. When his raft sailed past Putuoshan, a sudden storm threw him on the beach beneath Chaoyin Cave. The monk interpreted the shipwreck as the deity's choice to remain in her homeland. Sheltering the statue in a local villager's home, the monk began Putuoshan's temple building tradition. *(Minibuses stop here on the way from the Puji Temple parking lot to the ferry for Y2. Or walk south on Puji Lu for 10min.; when the road forks, turn left onto Zizhu Lu. Few min. walk down the road, a footpath leads to the entrance. ☎ 669 8221. Open daily 5am-5:30pm. Y5.)*

GUANYIN OF THE SOUTH SEA (nánhǎi guānyīn; 南海观音). This 33m-tall statue, set amid white limestone and marble, is visible from much of the island. Guanyin's statue raises her fingers in benediction over the ocean. Around the base of the statue, halls show art and artifacts. The lower-level walls are covered with intricate wall-to-ceiling murals made with bronze, dark wood, and even colored jade. The murals illustrate scenes from the story of Putuoshan's origin and familiar pictures of present-day Putuoshan. The second level has hundreds of glass-encased icons of Guanyin. *(Take Puji Lu south from the Puji Temple parking lot and follow the left fork that becomes Zizhu Lu. Bear right as Zizhu Lu becomes a footpath leading uphill for another 5-10min.; the entrance is on top of the hill. Open daily 5:30am-6:30pm. Y6.)*

OTHER SIGHTS. Putuoshan hosts more caves, temples, and pavilions than the average tourist has the leisure (or the energy) to explore. Both the small **Hundred-Pace Sands Beach** (bǎi bù shā; 百步沙), opposite and a bit north of the Puji Temple parking lot, and the more spacious **Thousand-Pace Sands Beach** (qiān bù shā; 千步沙), with its entrance along a gardened path opposite Fayu Temple, have pristine waters and velvety sands perfect for escaping the religiosity of the rest of the island. During the summer, you can **camp** in rented tents on Hundred-Pace Sands. Sunrise- and sunset-watching and tea sampling are popular hobbies for locals and tourists. *(☎ 609 1414. Deck chairs, umbrellas, and other beach equipment rental Y15-30 per hr., deposit Y100. Hundred-Pace Sands open for swimming 8am-6pm, strolling 24hr. Swimming Y15, children under 1.4m Y8; beach Y5/Y3. Thousand-Pace Sands open dawn-dusk; free.)*

YANGZI BASIN

The third-longest river in the world, the Yangzi River flows 6380km from the Geladandong Glaciers of Tibet to the East China Sea, rushing through the Three Gorges in Chongqing and Hubei, before giving way to sleepy hamlets and rapidly developing industrial cities. Its many moods determine the fates of the countless people who dwell along its banks. Summer floods bring torrents of muddy rapids, threatening to overwhelm dikes and deluge even the most massive cities. Even in flood-free years, the rushing waters bring unbearably humid summers and damp, chilly winters to the riverside provinces of Anhui, Jiangxi, Hunan, and Hubei. Nevertheless, the Yangzi is much gentler than its northern brother, the Yellow River. The land along its banks is among China's most populous and fertile, showcasing some of China's most dramatic scenery. Away from the mighty river, flood plains stretch out toward haunting mountains wreathed in seas of mist. For centuries, these ethereal peaks have entranced poets and painters, and today they attract scores of visitors in search of the splendor of times past.

HIGHLIGHTS OF THE YANGZI RIVER BASIN

CHANT IT LIKE A MONK on the sacred mountains of Buddhist **Jiuhuashan** (p. 429) and Daoist **Wudangshan** (p. 471), where incense wafts and all is calm.

ROUGH IT LIKE AN OUTLAW in the ghostly forests and crags of **Zhangjiajie** (p. 456).

LIVE IT LIKE THE CHAIRMAN from Mao's boyhood days in **Shaoshan** (p. 452) to his college days in **Changsha** (p. 447) to his fighting days in **Jinggangshan** (p. 444).

LOVE IT LIKE AN IMMORTAL above a sea of clouds on **Huangshan Mountain** (p. 424)—you'll never want to come down again after a sunrise upon its peaks.

ANHUI 安徽

Travel south through Anhui and marvel as the country transforms before your eyes. The unfolding beauty of the province will soothe the frazzled nerves of any weary tourist in search of China's rural charm. Leaving behind dusty, lethargic northern towns, the journey winds through pastoral countryside, expanses of flooded rice paddies tiered across the landscape, herds of water buffalo languishing in mud baths against dark, shadowy distant hills. Gradually, the land becomes more forested and mountainous, sculpted with a soaring loveliness reflected in the many lakes and rivers. The scenery is simply idyllic. Little wonder, then, that for centuries it inspired Chinese poets, philosophers, and artists.

Anhui's beauty is no secret. Chinese and overseas tourists alike flock to famed Huangshan Mountain to catch a glimpse of the mesmerizing Beihai sunrise. Nearby Jiuhuashan, one of China's four sacred Buddhist mountains, is also a popular destination. A small village with winding streets and crisp mountain air, it manages to embrace tourism without losing its peaceful, secluded grace.

HEFEI 合肥 ☎ 0551

The main streets of Hefei might serve well as a metaphor for the country as a whole. The moneyed stroll the boulevards with designer clothing, highlighted hair, and a cellphone tucked in every pocket. They sidestep the dozens of homeless people sprawled across the pavement, too exhausted to lift their begging bowls. The very old rummage through trash cans, and the very young clutch at your knee with imploring eyes hoping for *jǐ kuài qián*. The contrast between the upwardly mobile and the down-and-out is rarely so evident—a stark reminder that behind the glitz and glamor of a strong economy, abject, pervasive poverty still exists.

With well over one million inhabitants, Hefei still manages to run at a less frantic pace than most cities its size. After dark the city takes on something of a technicolor glow, as almost every park and bridge turn on their blinking, colored lights. As Anhui's capital, it's sure to serve many as a major transportation hub to Jiangsu or Huangshan, but from its bustling retail streets to its hushed Buddhist temples, it offers much to remedy those bus shelter blues.

⌐ TRANSPORTATION

Flights: Luogang Airport (luògǎng jīchǎng; 骆岗机场 ; ☎288 6626), 7km south of town. Bus #11 (Y1) runs from the train station to near the airport; a faster minibus runs between the two for Y5; taxis cost Y10-12. **Anhui Foreign Trade International Travel Service** (wàimào guólǔ; 外贸国旅), 304 Jinzhai Lu (☎283 698), sells tickets. Open daily 8:30am-7pm. To: **Beijing** (3 per day, Y900); **Chengdu** (M, F; Y1100); **Guangzhou** (2 per day, Y950); **Huangshan** (1-2 per day, Y300-400); **Kunming** (daily, Y1520); **Shanghai** (3 per day, Y440); **Xiamen** (2 per week, Y790); **Xi'an** (2 per day, Y920).

Trains: Buses #1 and 119 run along Changjiang Lu to and from the station, and #101 links it to the southwest part of the city. The ticket office is to the left of the station; windows #6 and 7 are open all night. To: **Beijing** (11-12hr., 4 per day, Y263); **Guangzhou** (15-16hr., 2 per day, Y314); **Nanjing** (4-5hr., 2 per day, Y49); **Shanghai** (8hr., 3 per day, Y87); **Tianjin** (10hr., 2 per day, Y200); **Zhenjiang** (4½-5hr., 2 per day, Y50).

Buses: About 4 long-distance bus stations are south of the Shengli Lu and Mingguang Lu intersection, near the old train station. The **ticket office,** 168 Mingguang Lu (☎469 3763), is 5min. west of Shengli Lu. To: **Huangshan** (5hr.; 7:10, 8:20am; Y55); **Nanjing** (2½hr., every 20min. 6am-7:50pm, Y52); **Shanghai** (7½hr., 12 per day 6:30am-5:40pm, Y140); **Wuhan** (6½hr., 6 per day 7am-8pm, Y140); **Wuxi** (4½hr., 8 per day 7:10am-3:20pm, Y90); **Yangzhou** (3½hr., 6 per day 7:30am-3:30pm, Y58); **Zhenjiang** (4½hr.; 8am, 12:50pm; Y56).

Local Transportation: Fare Y1. Buses #1 and 101 both run from the train station to the bus stations before heading toward the city center along Changjiang Lu and Jinzhai Lu.

Taxis: Some taxis, particularly around the train station, are not metered. Base fare Y5-6, each additional km Y1.2; with A/C Y7/Y1.4. From the city center to the train station or airport Y10-12.

🔁 🔓 ORIENTATION AND PRACTICAL INFORMATION

Hefei is in the northern part of Anhui province, about 80km north of the Yangzi River. The smaller **Nanfei River** runs along Hefei's northern edge and, along with a handful of parks and ponds, encircles the main part of the city. The industrial suburbs recede quickly into farmland. Hefei is largely explorable by foot. Three ring roads wind their way around Hefei, one of which, **Huancheng Lu** (环城路), follows the parks and waterways near the city center. **Changjiang Lu** (长江路) runs east-west through the main commercial district. **Shouchun Lu** (寿春路), **Huaihe Lu** (淮河路), and **Meishan Lu/Wuhu Lu** (梅山路 / 芜湖路)are roughly parallel to Changjiang Lu. **Jinzhai Lu** (金寨路), **Meiling Dadao** (美菱大道), and **Suzhou Lu** (宿洲路) run north-south through the city. Both the train station and the main long-distance bus station are on **Shengli Lu** (胜利路), in the northeast part of the city.

The Yangzi Basin

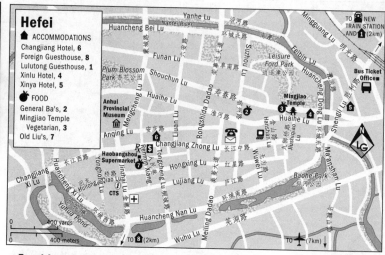

Hefei

🏠 ACCOMMODATIONS
Changjiang Hotel, 6
Foreign Guesthouse, 8
Lulutong Guesthouse, 1
Xinlu Hotel, 4
Xinya Hotel, 5

🍎 FOOD
General Ba's, 2
Mingjiao Temple
  Vegetarian, 3
Old Liu's, 7

Travel Agency: CTS, Jiuzhou Bldg., 381 Jinzhai Lu, 1st fl. (☎265 1952; fax 265 4308), near Lujiang Lu. Staff members speak English, French, German, Spanish, and Japanese. Mrs. Jane Liu in the airline booking office readily offers advice and speaks wonderful English. Open 8am-6pm.

Bank of China: 313 Changjiang Lu (☎292 6116 or 292 6117), at Renmin Xiang. Exchanges currency and traveler's checks. Credit card advances. Open M-F 8:15am-5pm; summer hours until 5:30pm.

Hospital: Hefei Red Cross Hospital (héféishì hóngshízihuì yīyuàn; 合肥市红十字会医院; ☎363 4794, 24hr. 365 1919), near Anhui University. From the train station, take bus #119 to Jiuhu stop and walk up a small alley. Another **hospital,** 346 Jinzhai Lu (☎262 5623; fax 262 8303), on the left as you walk south past Lujiang Lu. Open 8am-noon and 2-6pm.

Pharmacy: Changjiang Pharmacy (ānhuī chángjiāng dàyàofáng; 安徽长江大药房), 315 Changjiang Lu (☎264 8063), at Renmin Xiang. The 1st fl. offers a wide selection of pharmaceuticals. Upstairs you'll find medicinal herbs, wheelchairs, and surgical instruments. 1st fl. open 24hr., upstairs 8am-8:30pm.

Telephones: China Telecom, 99 Suzhou Lu (☎265 502). IDD service. Open 8am-6pm.

Internet Access: There is no shortage of Internet cafes along Huaihe Lu, though you may have to disappear down a back alley to get to one. **Pacific** (tàipíng yáng; 太平洋 ; ☎265 3931) is a popular venue, with comfy chairs and well over 100 terminals. As you head east on Huaihe Lu, turn left between Pizza Hut and Baleno before you reach Suzhou Lu. It's in the basement, a few doors down to the right. Y2 per hr. with a Y10 deposit. Printing Y2 per page. Open 24hr.

Post Office: Hefei Post Office, on the corner of Suzhou Lu and Changjiang Lu, near Sipai Lou bus stop. EMS and Poste Restante. Open daily 8am-8pm.

Postal Code: 230001.

ACCOMMODATIONS

Hotels in Hefei are primarily located along **Changjiang Lu,** near Yuhua Pond in the southwest, and near the train and bus stations.

Foreign Guesthouse of the University of Science and Technology of China (zhōng-guó kējì dàxué zhuānjiā lóu; 中国科技大学专家楼), 96 Jinzhai Lu (☎360 2881). Take bus #1 or 101 from the train station to the university stop. The university is 5min. up the road, on your left. Go through the main university gate, turn left at the dead end, turn right at the end of the road, and take the 2nd path to the left. It's past a large lily pond, near the north campus gate. The more expensive rooms are new, and some even have balconies. Quiet and very clean with desks. A/C, bath, TV. Rooms can be tough to get, so consider booking in advance. Singles Y150; doubles Y240; triples Y290. ❷

Xinya Hotel (xīnyà dàjiǔdiàn; 新亚大酒店), 18 Shengli Lu (☎220 3388; fax 220 3000). Fluffy bedspreads, pristine bath, and well-furnished rooms high up enough to escape the incessant street din. A/C, TV. Singles Y198; doubles Y168-198. ❸

Changjiang Hotel (chángjiāng fàndiàn; 长江饭店), 262 Changjiang Lu (☎265 6441; fax 262 2295), near Tongcheng Lu. Buses #1, 3, 29, and 46 stop outside. Relatively clean rooms and a central location. Cheaper 3rd fl. rooms. Somewhat dull, however, with white walls and brown bedcovers. Singles and doubles Y180-320; triples Y260-440. ❸

Xinlu Hotel (xīnlù fàndiàn; 欣路饭店), 9 Shouchun Lu (☎264 9349), on the corner of Huancheng Dong Lu. Large, run down rooms, but conveniently located. Traffic noise will wake you bright and early. No hot water. A/C, attached bath, TV. Singles and doubles Y90; triples Y100. ❷

Lulutong Guesthouse (lùlùtōng zhāodàisuǒ; 路路通招待所). Handy if you're overnighting at Hefei with no time to see the city, this very small hotel is part of the train station complex. Upon exiting the station, turn left immediately and look for the large sign above the door, near the China Mobile store. Small, makeshift rooms, but clean and cheerful. Singles Y30; doubles Y60; triples Y70. ❶

▶ FOOD

Hefei's liveliest eating areas are hidden off the main roads. At the western edge of the city center, one block south of Changjiang Lu, small stands line the street from Jinzhai Lu almost to Gongwan Lu. A bit east of Jinzhai Lu, **Renmin Xiang** stretches south from Changjiang Lu, where small, friendly restaurants spill out onto the streets, inviting passersby in with their bright, upbeat atmospheres. Other cheerful eateries can be found along the side streets heading south from Wuhu Lu, near the entrance to Baohe Park. Restaurants and stalls on **Suzhou Lu** between Huaihe Lu and Shouchun Lu focus on tasty lunchtime munchies. **Street markets** are scattered throughout the city, with several right off Changjiang Lu. In all of these places, Y10 will buy a hearty meal for one. Hefei's regional specialty, **freshwater crab** from Lake Chao, is heaven at a reasonable price. Look for the frisky critters at sidewalk restaurants throughout the city.

The 24hr. **Haobangshou Supermarket** (hǎobāngshǒu chāoshì; 好帮手超市 ; ☎265 7342), two doors down from the Changjiang Pharmacy on Renmin Xiang, has a good selection of food and drinks, especially noodles and alcohol. On the right side when coming from Changjiang Lu, the small door to the market is next to a set of stairs leading to a restaurant on the second floor.

Old Liu's (dàlǎoliú xiǎochībù; 大老刘小吃部 ; ☎261 1461), next to 15 Renmin Xiang, proves the power of specialization. The friendly owners of this local favorite serve only noodle soups. The result is a bowl of basic beef noodles (Y3.5) that may well be the best you'll ever have. Soups Y2.50-14. Open daily 6am-10pm. ❶

General Ba's (bā jiāngjūn; 巴将军 ; ☎261 3777), on Suzhou Lu at Huaihe Lu. A more classy hotpot restaurant, with bubbling broths of spicy sauces. The chili packs a powerful punch; small damp towels for brow-mopping provided. Free dessert if you smile pathetically enough. A vast range of flavors and a vast range of prices. Y8-Y180. Open daily 9:30am-4:30am. ❶-❺.

Mingjiao Temple Vegetarian Restaurant (míngjiàosì sù cāntīng; 明教寺素餐厅), 44 Huaihe Lu (☎139 6669 5045), inside the Mingjiao Temple entrance on the corner of Jiushiqiao Lu. Serves imitation meat dishes (Y5-25), soups (Y10), cabbage soaked in vinegar (Y5). Open daily 7am-8:30pm. ❶

🔘 SIGHTS

What Hefei lacks in tourist panache, it makes up for with its lush and lovely parks. In fact, the ring of parks surrounding the city center earned Hefei the honor of a "National Garden City" designation in 1992. If you're here during the hot season, you'll quickly come to appreciate these cool, shaded retreats.

BAOHE PARK (bāohé gōngyuán; 包河公园). With well-kept, leafy gardens and twittering birds, this lakeside park is a local favorite. The park contains the **Tomb of Lord Bao** (bāozhěng mù; 包拯墓), a Song Dynasty judge posthumously honored for honest and upright service. The fact that he became the protagonist of a wildly popular Taiwanese TV show hasn't affected Hefei denizens' pride in him. A climb up the **Clear Wind Pavilion** (qīng fēng gé; 清风阁), an impressive and imposing pagoda opposite the entrance to the tomb, brings visitors to a bird's eye view of the city. *(Entrances to park at Ma'anshan Lu, south of Changjiang Lu; on Huancheng Lu and Wuhu Lu, off Meiling Dadao. Open daily 24hr. Free. Tomb of Lord Bao and Qing Feng Ancient Building open 8am-6pm. Y15 each.)*

ANHUI PROVINCIAL MUSEUM (ānhuīshěng bówùguǎn; 安徽省博物馆). The museum may inspire little interest with its dilapidated exterior and lackluster displays, but it still merits a quick look. Near the entrance, the skull of a locally found ape-man is on view. Further on, you'll find inscriptions from Han Dynasty tombs, as well as a study showcasing the "Four Scholastic Treasures" (ink, paper, brush, and stone). A walk through the museum takes around 30min., but be sure to allot time to rummage through its eclectic gift shop. *(268 Anqing Lu, at the northern end of Jinzhai Lu. ☎282 3465. English captions. Open daily 8:30-11am and 2:30-5pm. Y10.)*

MINGJIAO TEMPLE (míngjiào sì; 明教寺). With very few visitors, this small temple escapes the flag-following tour groups. The genuine atmosphere of tranquil prayer remains undisturbed. The halls date from the 16th century and were recently restored after being damaged during the Cultural Revolution. *(Huaihe Lu, at Jiushiqiao Lu. Open daily 7am-6pm. Y10.)*

OTHER SIGHTS. On the northeast side of town, **Leisure Ford Park** (xiāoyáojīn gōngyuán;逍遥津公园) was the site of a famous battle between the nations of Wu and Wei during the Three Kingdoms period (AD 220-80). A statue commemorates the Kingdom of Wei's General Zhang Liao, whose 10,000-man fighting force defeated an army 10 times its size. With a children's playground and some amusements, the park has left behind its martial past and now nicely combines a carnival atmosphere with more secluded lakeside trails. *(16 Shouchun Lu. Open daily 5am-6pm. Y5.)* **Plum Blossom Park** (xìnghuā gōngyuán; 杏花公园) is bordered on the east by Mengcheng Lu, with an entrance between Shouchun Lu and Huaihe Lu. Other parks include **Yuhua Pond** (yǔhuā táng; 雨花塘), a popular spot for evening walks on the southwest side of the city.

TUNXI 屯溪 ☎ 0559

Tunxi, also called Huangshan City, is the main transportation hub for the mighty Huangshan. Most travelers just pass through on their way to Huangshan, although some buses drive directly to the base town of Tangkou. Though the city itself is grimy and unkempt, it serves as an excellent springboard for exploring the surrounding areas. Nearby Yixian county shelters extraordinarily well-preserved architecture from the Ming and Qing dynasties and may prove a peaceful respite from the constant Huangshan hoopla.

▐ TRANSPORTATION

Flights: Huangshan City Airport (huángshānshì fēijīchǎng; 黄山市飞机场), about 5km west of the city center. Tickets available at the **CAAC ticket office,** 23 Huangshan Bei Lu (☎254 1222). Open daily 8am-5pm. To: **Beijing** (1 per day, Y760); **Guangzhou** (1-3 per day, Y580); **Shanghai** (2-3 per day, Y290).

Trains: Huangshan City Train Station (huángshānshì huǒchē zhàn; 黄山市火车站), at the north end of Qianyuan Bei Lu, near the traffic circle on Guojing Lu. **Ticket office** (☎211 6222) in the small adjoining office on the left side as you face the station. Open 24hr. To: **Beijing** (20hr., 10:17am, Y333); **Fuzhou** (14hr.; 5:37am, 5:37pm; Y197); **Kunming** (50hr., 1 per day, Y450); **Nanjing** (7-11hr., 7 per day 4:30am-12:30am, Y108); **Shanghai** (10hr., 10:38pm, Y175); **Xiamen** (24hr., 6:21am, Y360).

Buses: Huangshan City Long-Distance Bus Station (huángshānshì chángtú qìchē zhàn; 黄山市长途汽车站), at the eastern end of Hehua Dong Lu. Ticket office (☎2535 3952) is in the building to the left as you face the station. Open daily 5am-6pm. To: **Hangzhou** (5hr., 6 per day 5:40am-3pm, Y55); **Hefei** (6hr., 6 per day 6am-3:20pm, Y77); **Shanghai** (8hr., 4 per day 5:50am-2pm, Y90).

Local Transportation: Bus #12 passes just south of the intersection in front of the train station, before heading down Qianyuan Lu, turning right onto Huangshan Lu, which connects to the main commercial center. Fare Y1. **Minibuses** travel throughout the city during daylight hours. Most stop at both the train and bus stations and go along Huangshan Lu. With all the ticket sellers hanging out of buses and calling to pedestrians, chances are you'll find one that's going your way. Fare Y1.

Taxis: Taxis, pedicabs, and minibuses run throughout the region. Be careful—drivers have no qualms about ripping you off. Tunxi to Tangkou should cost about Y50-100. A pedicab from the train station to the west of the city should not be more than Y5. Always negotiate the fare in advance.

▐ ORIENTATION AND PRACTICAL INFORMATION

The train station and **Huancheng Lu** (环城路) mark the far north of town. **Qianyuan Lu** (前园路) runs south to the **Xinan River** (xīn'ān hé; 新安河). Several major east-west streets intersect Qianyuan Lu, including **Hehua Lu** (荷花路), which runs to the long-distance bus station in the east, and **Huangshan Lu** (黄山路), which connects **Xinan Lu** (新安路) and the commercial heart of the city in the west.

Travel Agency: CITS, 6 Xizhen Jie, 3rd. fl. (☎254 2110), across from the Huaxi Hotel in the southwest part of town, just across the bridge from Ancient Street; entrance through the restaurant under the long vertical CITS sign. The exceptionally helpful Johnson Yeh speaks fluent English and is a mine of information on Anhui's tourist attractions. His comprehensive website (www.huangshantour.com) is an excellent resource for the traveler, with English maps, transport schedules, links to accommodations, and weather reports. Staff also speaks French, German, Korean, and Japanese. Open M-F 8am-5pm.

Tourist Complaint Line: ☎251 7464.

Bank of China: 9 Xinan Bei Lu (☎251 4859), at Huangshan Lu. The only bank in town that exchanges currency and traveler's checks. Open daily 8am-8pm.

ATM: At the Bank of China on Xinan Bei Lu.

PSB: (☎231 8768). At the south end point of Qianyuan Lu. **Travel permits** to Yixian County (Y50) available. Bring your passport. Very short processing time. Open daily 8-11:30am and 2:30-5:30pm.

Internet Access: Zhengda Internet Bar (zhèng dà wǎngbā; 正大网吧), on a side street just where Ancient St. meets the junction of Huangshan Lu and Xinan Bei Lu. Y1.5 per hr. Open daily 8am-midnight.

Post Office: Huangshan City Post Office, 39 Qianyuan Nan Lu (☎231 5554), directly opposite the PSB. EMS and Poste Restante. Open daily 8am-8pm.

Postal Code: 245000.

ACCOMMODATIONS

Tunxi is well aware of its role as a tourist gateway, so the bar is set high on hotel prices, though not always on quality. Still, don't let that perturb you—a little haggling can go a long way, and with a bit of luck, prices can plummet by as much as half the original. The high season lasts from March 16 to November 15. All rooms listed here have A/C, TV, and private bath.

Huangshan International Youth Hostel (HI) (huángshān guójì qīngnián lǚguǎn; 黄山国际青年旅馆 ; ☎211 4522), on Huancheng Bei Lu, which runs behind the bus station, 1 block south of the train station. Walk east along Huancheng Lu for about 3min. with your back to Huangshan Jingwei Hotel. It's on the right. Opened in 2004, this is set to be a favorite among backpackers. Smooth, glossy wooden flooring, a comfortable lounge area, sturdy bunkbeds, and no shortage of amenities. Canteen, bar, Internet access, 24hr. hot water. High season 6-bed dorms Y35; singles and doubles Y120. Low-season Y30/Y100. HI members Y5 less for 6-bed dorms, Y10 less for singles and doubles. ❶

New Pine Breeze Hotel (xīn sōng fēng bīnguǎn; 新松风宾馆), 21 Qianyuan Bei Lu (☎211 3588). Further away from the train station than Huangshan Jingwei Hotel and on the opposite side. Rooms are small but clean with new wooden furniture. A quiet night's sleep at a very reasonable price. Singles Y70; doubles Y100; triples Y90. ❶

Huangshan Sanctitude Athens Hotel, 6 Qianyuan Bei Lu (☎235 8755 or 235 8766). Situated 500m south of the train station, to the left, next to "The New Swan Rummery." This hotel offers large and comfortable doubles. Smiling staff are happy to give discounts. Doubles Y180. ❷

Huangshan Jingwei Hotel (huángshān jīngwěi jiǔdiàn; 黄山经纬酒店), 18 Qianyuan Bei Lu (☎234 5188; fax 234 5098). It's the huge, glass cylindrical building 1 block south of the train station. Costs big bucks, but ultra-convenient. Large rooms have curved walls and sweeping views. Doubles Y360-480; triples Y980. ❺

Huaxi Hotel (huāxī fàndiàn; 花溪饭店), 1 Xizhen Jie (☎232 8000; fax 251 4990), in the southwest part of the city, across the bridge at the western end of Ancient Street. A 300-room monster, complete with restaurants, supermarkets, and stores. Plain rooms are comfortable but not worth the price. Staff in floral shirts are exceedingly friendly. High-season doubles in the old building Y480, in the new Y580. Low-season Y384/Y464. AmEx/MC/V. ❺

FOOD

Small **food stands** cluster near the train and bus stations, especially along Hehua Dong Lu, where giant bowls of *jiǎozi* sell for as little as Y2. The street west of the bus station has oodles of **noodle** and **dumpling vendors.** Qianyuan Bei Lu has bigger (and more expensive) eateries. The primary nighttime activity is **karaoke**, but the tone-deaf may prefer the hopping **morning market** near the bus station. Frogs are Y3; get 'em while they're hot. **House of Good Food** ❶ (měi shí rén jīa; 美食人家; ☎251 2222) is at the main, lion-guarded arch leading into Ancient St. A favorite among local families, this restaurant allows you to select food from a counter of exhibited, cellophaned samples, convenient for those who fear a menu of Chinese characters. Staff cook up a wide range of vegetable, meat, dumpling, and noodle dishes right before your eyes. Dishes range from Y0.5 to Y10.

🌀 SIGHTS

Tunxi's **Ancient Street** (túnxī lǎo jiē; 屯溪老街) begins near the bridge in the far western part of town and winds south toward the Xinan River. Many of the buildings lining the street date all the way back to the Song Dynasty (some of the tourist maps sold here can't be much younger). Tour leaders herd their groups through this narrow lane before taking them to the mountain, so expect to see plenty of kitschy, overpriced merchandise. Some shops specialize in traditional local products, including medicine, tea, scrolls, and carved bamboo heads. Most unusual are the bottles of wine (Y30-150) with large, dead snakes inside, a delicacy that puts every tequila worm to shame. All in all, this famed street is a let-down unless you intend on some serious shopping, although the place is a lot livelier at night.

　　▨ Cheng's Three Mansions (chéngshì sānzhái; 程氏三宅), just off Huangshan Dong Lu near Ancient St., may be a more rewarding sight. A well-preserved example of Ming architecture, this building was once owned by a wealthy merchant and showcases the high walls (for the "protection" of the womenfolk) and wooden frames of ancient Anhui homes. Chinese academics have lately speculated that Chen Qiong, a former resident, might have been the inspiration for Lin Daiyu, the tragic heroine of the Chinese classic, *Dream of the Red Chamber*. (Open daily 8am-5:30pm. Admission with guided tour in Chinese Y20, students Y10.)

▨ DAYTRIP FROM TUNXI: YIXIAN 黟县

47km from Tunxi. Yixian County consists of a dozen villages in the mountain basin, with the county government in Yixian township. Buses from Tunxi to Yixian (Y8) depart 7am-5pm. From the Yixian Bus Station (on the main road in Yixian), minibuses go to Tunxi (1½hr., 7:30am-5:30pm, Y8) via Yuting, and Tangkou (1½hr., 2 per day, Y13) via Xidi. Hongcun (10km north of Yixian) and Xidi (3km east of Yixian), the two main scenic spots, are accessible by minibus (Y2) and taxi (Hongcun Y20, Xidi Y5-10). Admission to Hongcun and Xidi are each Y55, students Y28. Foreigners require a travel permit to enter Yixian County (Y50), obtainable from the PSB offices in Tunxi and Tangkou.

Hidden in a tiny basin ringed by the Huangshan Mountains, Yixian (黟县) is one of the most isolated places in eastern China. Founded in 222 BC, the area was often a haven for refugees escaping conflicts on China's northern plains. During the Ming and Qing dynasties, residents of the county dominated commerce on the Yangzi delta and were often invited to perform opera for the emperors in Beijing. Devastating bouts of the plague in the 1800s put an end to the area's cultural and economic achievements and doomed Yixian to obscurity. Today, over 4000 well-preserved Ming- and Qing-era homes, shops, and bridges remain (all documented in Zhang Yimou's film *Judou*), a testament to Yixian's heyday and its ability to withstand the ravages of war and modernization.

　　While Yixian generally offers a quiet refuge from Huangshan's tour groups, those visitors mesmerized by the county's mist-shrouded mountains, sparkling streams, and bamboo groves should note that a PLA ballistic missile also lurks nearby. As a result, foreigners are not allowed to stay in any nearby accommodations. Local food specialties include "rock chicken," actually not chicken at all but a gray-colored frog (shíjī; 石鸡), salted pork (làròu; 腊肉), and egg cooked in a savory blend of spices and tea leaves (cháyè dàn; 茶叶蛋).

HONGCUN (hóngcūn; 红村). Locals claim that their village is built in the shape of a kneeling ox. From above, this may indeed be the case; from the ground, though, the image is less clear. According to legend, after several fires in the 1300s, local clan elders asked a *feng shui* master for advice. The master proposed giving the ox a "digestive system"—reservoirs and canals—to cleanse the village of "flammable spirits." As a result, water from a nearby stream was diverted to fill a pool in the center village. Narrow curbside aqueducts still run along every cobblestoned alleyway, carrying water from the pool throughout the village, eventually leading to South Lake. The constant flow of water past every doorstep lends a serene and picturesque quality to village life. Parts of Ang Lee's martial arts epic *Crouching Tiger, Hidden Dragon* were filmed here.

Only the **Inherit Dignity Hall** (chéngzhì táng; 承志堂) and a few smaller gardens are officially open to the public. Built by a Qing salt merchant in 1855, the Inherit Dignity Hall has 28 rooms in seven buildings. Dubbed the "Forbidden City for Civilians," it is the largest and most elaborate example of Yixian architecture. Yixian merchants spent most of their time abroad and feared that robbers would loot their homes. Thus, most of the plain, white walls have few windows. Inside, the open courtyards let in natural light and are known as "sky wells." The walls are covered with ornate wood relief carvings, including two panels that depict battle scenes from the *Romance of the Three Kingdoms* and a New Year's celebration featuring over 100 boys. Girlfriends take note: a carving in the master's parents' hall depicts a famous opera scene in which a daughter-in-law was beaten for not kowtowing to her mother-in-law during her birthday party.

XIDI (xīdì; 西递). In AD 904, the oldest son of the last Tang emperor fled to southern Anhui after the fall of the Tang Dynasty. Once there, he founded the Hu clan, now the biggest clan in town. Wealthy Xidi merchants, concerned about their social standing, donated generously to the imperial government. In return, the emperor awarded them various bureaucratic titles. Most of the houses display paintings of house masters dressed in mandarin attire, but few held any real power. Intricately carved window panes depict frost (symbolizing bitterness and hard work in winter) alongside bats and grapes (symbolizing good fortune) as a reminder that success and prosperity required sacrifice. At the village entrance sits the **Governor's Arch** (cìshǐ páifǎng; 刺使牌坊), a massive stone arch with 16 lions and six crocodiles commissioned by the Ming emperor Shenzong to honor a loyal subject from Xidi. More traditional homes and mansions are open to public viewing in Xidi than in Hongcun.

TANGKOU 汤口   ☎ 0559

As the final frontier before reaching the great craggy mountains, Tangkou captures an air of fresh excitement and anticipation. The small town wakes daily at dawn to a convoy of horn-tooting buses ferrying tour groups to the entrance of Huangshan. Quietening down by late morning, when the visiting hordes have all taken to the peaks, Tangkou comes back to life as evening approaches, when the innumerable eateries and hotels welcome back weary climbers. It's wise to spend a night here in order to get a head start on the yellow-hatted tour group brigade.

✦ 🛈 ORIENTATION AND PRACTICAL INFORMATION

Tangkou is a tiny cluster of hotels, shops, and restaurants spread out next to a stream that comes down from the mountain. **Yanxi Jie** (沿溪街) runs along **Spring Stream** (quán xī; 泉溪) until it dead-ends at **Shangye Jie** (商业街). The two-lane highway comes in from the southwest, drawing parallel to the stream as it heads north to the main gate into the Huangshan Scenic Area. Tangkou ends here, and the highway continues up to the **Hot Springs Area** and the cable car terminal, the starting point for most mountain hikes.

Buses: Huangshan Scenic Area Long-Distance Bus Station (huángshān fēngjǐng qū qìchē zhàn; 黄山风景区汽车站 ; ☎556 5291), at the main gate, about a 15min. walk from the center of Tangkou. Open daily 5:30am-7:30pm. To: **Hangzhou** (7hr., 8 per day 6:20am-5pm, Y56-76); **Hefei** (5hr., 2 per day, Y64); **Jiuhuashan** (4hr., 6am, Y27); **Jiujiang** (6hr., 7:40am, Y85); **Nanjing** (6hr., 4 per day 6am-2:30pm, Y76); **Wuhan** (9hr.; 9am, 6pm; Y154-Y178). In addition, minibuses to **Tunxi** ply the streets throughout the day (1hr., Y10-17).

Taxis: Taxis circle like sharks waiting for fresh tourist blood. Fares are negotiable; as always, bargain hard. From Tangkou to the base of the Eastern Steps about Y10; to the Hot Springs Area about Y5.

Tour Guides: 🔳 **Mr. Hu** (☎139 5626 4786), owner of **Mr. Hu's Restaurant** (p. 424), sells maps in English and should be every traveler's first stop for high quality information in English. He is happy to help book bus tickets and arrange tours at no cost. All he asks is that you eat at his restaurant once or twice.

Bank of China: (☎551 267 5330). Opposite the front gate of the Free and Unfettered Hotel. Exchanges currency and traveler's checks. Open daily 8am-5pm.

Hospital: A small hospital is located on Shangye Jie, on the left before you reach Tangkou Hotel. Open 8-11:30am and 2:30-5:30pm.

PSB: (☎556 2311). At the entrance to the town, on the eastern side of the river. Office is on the 3rd fl., to the right at the top of the staircase. Open daily 8am-5pm. Travel permits to Yixian (Y50) can be arranged here on the spot. Bring your passport. Also processes visa extensions.

Internet Access: Beetle Internet Cafe (jiǎkéchóng wǎngbā; 甲壳虫网吧), on the east side of the bisecting river. Look for a blue sign. Open daily 8am-9pm. Y3 per hr.

Post Office: Tangkou Post and Telecommunications Office (☎556 2017), on the highway toward the south end of town, north of the Tangkou Hotel. EMS. Open daily 8am-5:30pm.

Postal Code: 242708 for Tangkou. 242709 for Huangshan Scenic Area, including Hot Springs Area.

🏠 ACCOMMODATIONS

TANGKOU

Tangkou has no shortage of quality establishments. For cheaper quarters, ask around, since practically every local seems intent on feeding you or putting you up for the night. The best deals are often with private, family-run hotels. If you're overnighting on the mountain, ask to leave your luggage at a Tangkou hotel (Y2-5 per day). As in Tunxi, high season runs from Mar. 16 to Nov. 15.

Tiandu Mountain Villa Hotel (tiāndū shānzhuāng bīnguǎn; 天都山庄宾馆 ; ☎556 2998), on the highway, about half way between the bridge and the main gate to the mountains. Rooms are generally of good quality, with comfy carpets and clean baths.

The more expensive 4-person suites are a real treat, with wooden furniture, colorful rugs, 2 separate bedrooms and bathrooms, and a common living room. Doubles Y280; quads Y880, low-season Y240. ❹

Tangkou Hotel (tāngkǒu bīnguǎn; 汤口宾馆; ☎556 2400; fax 556 2687), 500m west of the Free and Unfettered Hotel on Shangye Jie, in a large white building with a blue tile roof. Clean, comfortable, well-decorated rooms with hot water and A/C make this hotel a popular spot, so book in advance. Doubles Y100; triples Y120. ❷

Free and Unfettered Hotel (xiāoyáo bīnguǎn; 逍遥宾馆; ☎556 2571; fax 556 1679). The shabby exterior is a good indication of what lies inside. Thinning carpets and somewhat grubby bathrooms. Try to get rooms on the lower 3 floors. Doubles Y80-120. ❷

Jade Screen Hotel (yùpíng fàndiàn; 玉屏饭店; ☎556 4111) on Shangye Jie. Large, perfectly clean rooms with tiled floors, TV, and A/C. 5am wake-up knock on the door if they suspect you're climbing the mountain. Curfew enforced at very irregular hours; make sure you know when the owners plan to lock up for the night. Singles Y60; doubles Y100; triples Y120. ❶

HOT SPRINGS

Don't expect a hot tub party—the "springs" gurgle, and that's about it. There's little to distinguish the "public springs" from a big swimming pool. The "private springs" are even sillier: they're just bathtubs in a bathroom. Both cost Y50 and are available at the Huangshan Hotel. The area's serenity and beauty do, however, make for a welcome respite from Tangkou's unwavering obsession with tourism.

Huangshan Spring Hotel (huángshān wēnquán dàjiǔdiàn; 黄山温泉大酒店; ☎558 5196; fax 558 5788), down the ramp from the road at the bridge, across the stream from the Huangshan Hotel. Foreigners can stay in all of the excitingly clean rooms and admire the private stream running in front of the hotel. Welcoming staff makes it feel like home. Doubles with A/C and private bath Y600, low-season Y200. ❺

Huangshan Hotel (huángshān fàndiàn; 黄山饭店; ☎558 5808), near Peach Flower Stream. Small, dark, standard rooms with A/C and tiny bathrooms. Hot springs swimming pool on site. Low-season singles Y140; doubles Y200. ❺

▣ FOOD

Many restaurant owners here aren't afraid to take the initiative: they find you, direct you to a table, and even choose menu items. If you do venture out on your own, billboards outside the many eateries advertise roughly the same food at about the same prices, so try your luck at wherever's most convenient.

An **open-air market** next to the stream sells everything from noodle and dumpling standbys to more exotic fare like eel, snake, and squirrel (each about Y3). Also here, tucked behind the first row of stalls, is ▨ **Mr. Hu's Restaurant ❶**. Look for the sign in English advertising coffee, toast, and advice. Sample crunchy bamboo shoots or sweet and sour potatoes from a menu of delicious home-made Chinese dishes in very hospitable surroundings. English translations let you know what you're eating. For those hankering for a taste of home, french fries (Y10) and French toast (Y4) beckon seductively. (☎139 5626 4786. Open daily 6am-11pm, or according to customers' wishes.)

HUANGSHAN MOUNTAIN 黄山

A trip to the jagged peaks of Huangshan should be first on every traveler's itinerary. The mountains are always high on the to-do lists of Chinese tourists, who, with all the centuries-old calligraphy scrolls and poetry dedicated to the place, practically breathe the Huangshan air before they've even been there. Not surprisingly, the trails along Huangshan are crowded. Only the luckiest low-season climbers manage to escape the aggravating inertia of loud Chinese tour groups. And, of course, the area's rooms and food are more expensive than in other parts of China, mostly because tourism is Huangshan's greatest cash cow.

But hike for a while amid the jagged peaks and delicately twisting spires of stone, up through caves and clusters of crooked pines, and you'll easily understand why travelers the world over come to Huangshan. Meander through dense woods of bamboo, clamber up Lotus Peak to see the mountains rise ghost-like from seas of swirling mist, or scramble on hands and knees over the treacherous ascents of Heavenly Capital Peak, and you'll see why emperors wanted to live here forever. While other mountain vistas elicit reverent sighs, Huangshan evokes breathless exclamations of disbelief.

AT A GLANCE

AREA: 154km²

CLIMATE: Even in summer, temperatures on the summit are much cooler.

FEATURES: Lotus Peak, Heavenly Capital Peak, Brightness Peak. Beihai Scenic Area.

HIGHLIGHTS: Scaling Lotus Peak, catching a sunrise from Brightness Peak.

GATEWAYS: Tunxi (p. 419), Tangkou (p. 422).

FEES: Y130, low-season Y86, children below 1.3m and students Y65.

TRANSPORTATION

Most travelers spend the night in **Tunxi** (p. 419) or **Tangkou** (p. 422), Huangshan's two gateway towns, before scaling the massive peaks. From Tunxi, minibuses go to Huangshan Scenic Area and Tangkou 6am-5pm (1hr., Y10-15). From Tangkou, minibuses and taxis (around Y10) make frequent trips to the Cloud Valley Cable Car Station (yúngǔ sì zhàn; 云谷寺站) at the base of the **Eastern Steps,** which marks the start of the climb for most hikers.

For those who choose to return via the Eastern Steps, the taxi fare from the Cloud Valley Temple to Tangkou is about Y10, although ridiculous fare hikes are common. Put your foot down (if your trembling muscles are in the condition to do so). A taxi from the Western Steps to the Hot Springs Area costs about Y10.

ORIENTATION AND PRACTICAL INFORMATION

Huangshan's myriad peaks, twisted rocks, and jutting fingers of stone can be simplified to three main peaks, which climbers can tackle once they've gone up the mountain proper. **Brightness Peak** (guāngmíng dǐng; 光明顶) is the most accessible, and the half-light of 4am often sees crowds of sleepy hikers scaling its height to catch the famed Huangshan sunrise. **Lotus Flower Peak** (liánhuā fēng; 莲花峰) is more difficult to reach and involves a trek through caves and up steep, irregular steps. **Heavenly Capital Peak** (tiān dū fēng; 天都峰) is frequently closed for safety reasons; the faint-hearted and safety-conscious may want to avoid it. In addition, new trails coiling down to the mountain valley have been opened and can be reached from the **Xihai Scenic Area.** Less frequented by tourists, this route involves some precarious descents and should not be attempted alone.

Services for travelers on the mountain are limited, so it's best to get your needs taken care of in Tunxi or Tangkou.

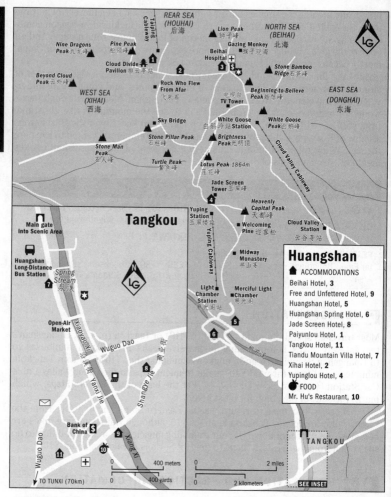

REAR SEA
(HOUHAI)
后海

Taiping
Cableway

Lion Peak
狮子峰

NORTH SEA
(BEIHAI)
北海

Nine Dragons
Peak 九龙峰

Pine Peak
松领峰

Gazing Monkey
猴子观海

Beihai
Hospital

Stone Bamboo
Ridge 石笋峰

Cloud Divide
Pavilion 排云亭站

Beyond Cloud
Peak 云外峰

WEST SEA
(XIHAI)
西海

Rock Who Flew
From Afar
飞来石

EAST SEA
(DONGHAI)
东海

TV Tower

Beginning-to-Believe
Peak 始信峰

Sky Bridge

White Goose
白鹅岭站 Station

White Goose
Peak 白鹅峰

Cloud Valley Cableway

Stone Man
Peak
石人峰

Stone Pillar Peak
石柱峰

Brightness
Peak 光明顶

Turtle Peak
鳌鱼峰

Lotus Peak 1864m
莲花峰

Jade Screen
Tower 玉屏峰

Tangkou

Yuping
Station
玉屏楼站

Heavenly
Capital Peak
天都峰

Cloud Valley
Station
云谷寺站

Main gate
into Scenic Area

Welcoming
Pine 迎客松

Huangshan
Long-Distance
Bus Station

Spring
Stream
泉溪

Yuping Cableway

Midway
Monastery
半山寺

Open-Air
Market

Light
Chamber
Station
慈光阁站

Merciful Light
Chamber
慈光阁

Huangshan

🏠 ACCOMMODATIONS
Beihai Hotel, **3**
Free and Unfettered Hotel, **9**
Huangshan Hotel, **5**
Huangshan Spring Hotel, **6**
Jade Screen Hotel, **8**
Paiyunlou Hotel, **1**
Tangkou Hotel, **11**
Tiandu Mountain Villa Hotel, **7**
Xihai Hotel, **2**
Yupinglou Hotel, **4**
⬤ FOOD
Mr. Hu's Restaurant, **10**

Wuguo Dao

Xiaolao Xi

Yanxi Jie

Shangye Jie

Open-Air
Market

Bank of
China

Xiang Xi

Wuguo Dao

0   400 meters
0   400 yards

0   2 miles

0   2 kilometers

TANGKOU

SEE INSET

TO TUNXI (70km)

Bank of China: (☎558 1396). Directly opposite Beihai Hotel. **24hr. ATM.** Exchanges currency and traveler's checks. Open daily 8-11am and 2:30-5:00pm.

Hospital: Medical Emergency Room of Beihai (☎558 5178, ext. 6128). To the left of the bank, opposite Beihai Hotel. Open daily 8:30-11:30am and 2-5pm.

Weather Conditions: ☎121. Weather is a crucial factor on Huangshan. Clear days can offer views of distant rock formations while cloudy weather creates seas of swirly mist. Rainy days are the worst, with slippery trails and poor visibility, but post-rain conditions are considered optimal, with fleeting cloud formation, sunshine, and the occasional rainbow. For more information, contact the **Huangshan Meteorological Observatory** (☎251 2411). Open daily 8-11am and 2-5pm. Or check www.huangshantour.com for the latest weather forecast in English.

PSB: (☎558 1388) opposite the Beihai Hotel. Accepts calls 24hr.

ACCOMMODATIONS AND FOOD

With the effort and cost of building in such an inaccessible location and of transporting all supplies by foot, prices for food and lodgings are accordingly expensive. The jovial hordes you encountered on the ascent are all planning to pile into the same, few, revoltingly overpriced mountaintop hotels. Overnighting on the summit is the only sane way to catch Huangshan at its early morning best, ethereal sunrises, mists, and all. If traveling in the high season, be sure to make reservations beforehand, especially for the cheaper options.

Up on the mountain, **snack stands** and **cookie** and **cucumber vendors** can be found at every turn; be prepared for Y10 bottles of water and exorbitantly priced instant noodles. Bargaining can work, but it's just not as effective when you're surrounded by tourists willing to fork over Y15 for a pack of beef jerky. If you don't mind lugging around some weight, it's best to stock up in Tangkou or Tunxi.

The following hotels are listed in the order in which they are positioned along the trail, assuming you walk from the Eastern Steps (White Goose Peak) toward the Western Steps.

Beihai Hotel (běihǎi bīnguǎn; 北海宾馆 ; ☎558 2555), in the Beihai Scenic Area, a 20min. walk from the White Goose Peak cable car. This is one of the nicer hotels, with convenient access to the popular summit route. Dorm rooms are pleasant and carpeted, with wooden bunk beds and cheerful curtains. High-season 6-bed dorms Y150; 5-bed dorms with bath Y250; doubles Y1080 and up. Low-season 5-bed dorms Y200; doubles Y850. MC/V. ❷

Xihai Hotel (xīhǎi fàndiàn; 西海饭店 ; ☎558 8888; fax 558 8988), Xihai Scenic Area, 20min. (2km) past the Beihai Hotel. This 2-building complex caters to all tastes, from luxurious doubles with majestic views to cramped 8-person dorms without baths. Even the cheapest rooms are cheerful, with purple and blue bedspreads, carpets, and wooden frame bunk beds. 8-bed dorms Y100, low-season Y80; 5-bed dorms with bath Y260/Y120; doubles from Y960/Y500; triples Y1170. AmEx/MC/V. ❷

Paiyunlou Hotel (páiyúnlóu bīnguǎn; 排云楼宾馆 ; ☎558 3999 or 558 1558), Xihai Scenic Area, about 2min. beyond the Xihai Hotel, near the fork to the Taiping cable car. Rooms are relatively plain; dorms have wooden floors. Decent, clean baths in all rooms. Doubles Y880, low season Y580; triples Y890/Y600; quads Y800/Y480. ❺

Yupinglou Hotel (yùpínglóu bīnguǎn; 玉屏楼宾馆; ☎558 2288), in the complex at Yuping Peak, site of the Welcoming Pine. One of the few options on the Western Steps, so it fills up quickly. A fun complex, nestled beside the hollow of the cliff, behind a rocky escarpment. You enter at the top floor and proceed downstairs to the bedrooms, making it feel more like a cruise-liner than a hotel. Rooms are in top condition, with thick carpets and clean baths. 4-bed dorms Y240, low season Y140; singles and doubles Y960/Y550; triples Y1080/Y900. ❸

CLIMBING HUANGSHAN

Clamber past the souvenir shops to reach the area's true gem: the mountain. Admission to **Huangshan Scenic Area** (huángshān fēngjǐng qū; 黄山风景区) is Y130, low-season Y86, children below 1.3m and students Y65.

Don't underestimate the physical toll of climbing several kilometers worth of steps, especially when you have to deal with maddening traffic jams of slow-moving crowds. Try to take advantage of the frequent stone benches or buy a walking stick to help you with the ascent. Do not, however, use them to swat at other tourists, no matter how much you may be tempted to do so.

Opt for the tried-and-true route: start at the base of the **Eastern Steps** and travel by foot to the top. At the **summit area**, a variety of trails loop through the main sights, with relatively little up-and-down terrain. The peak itself can very quickly become overcrowded with hordes of fearless, noisy photographers. These trails also offer access to **Brightness Peak, Lotus Peak,** and **Heavenly Capital Peak.** Then descend the Western Steps, the Eastern Steps' brutal compatriot, which is cartilage-crushing, knee-wrecking, and exhausting, even as a downhill run. The stairs can be hypnotizing so keep your head up and remember to admire the views.

There's no shame in taking the easy way out. Visitors can take the **Yungu Line** (Cloud Valley line, beginning at the Cloud Valley Cable Car Station) as an alternative to the Eastern Steps, or ride the **Yuping Line** instead of braving the endless stairs of the Western Steps, although the Yuping Line only goes halfway up the mountain, so Brightness Peak remains to be conquered. The **Taiping Line** starts from the north gate of Huangshan, an area much less frequented by travelers. Unless you come early enough to beat the tour groups (a difficult feat at best), expect long waits. The Taiping and Yungu cable cars run 6:30am-4:30pm, and the Yuping line runs 7am-4:30pm. All three lines charge the same fares. (Y65 each way, children Y35; low-season Y55/Y30.)

If you decide to walk, the trails are in great condition. However, some portions (particularly the route from Brightness Peak to Lotus Peak) are so steep that they're downright dangerous, especially when you add the menace of tour groups. Guides are available to lead the way for those who speak Chinese and want more detailed descriptions of the peaks and their legends. To help you find your way, signs are posted regularly along the trails. If all else fails, try pestering a Chinese tour group leader for information.

EASTERN STEPS

Much of the climb (ascent 1½-3hr., descent 2hr. or less) winds through forested areas. At the halfway point, hikers catch their first glimpses of the spectacular peaks, while various lookout points offer time for necessary water breaks. In general, the scenery is relatively plain until you near the top, where the path reaches the upper cable car station at **White Goose Peak** (bái é fēng; 白鹅峰) and the **Beihai Scenic Area** (běi hǎi; 北海; North Sea). The walk around the summit area is a popular and not-too-tiring route. On the sharp left, an obscure path leads toward the television towers and the Western Steps. If you're doing the east-west circuit, follow the main path past the structures down to the right.

From here, there are two paths. The path upwards leads past **Beginning-to-Believe Peak** (shǐxìn fēng; 始信峰) to **Stone Bamboo Ridge** (shísǔn fēng; 石笋峰). The path downward leads to the Beihai Hotel and the viewing area for the Beihai sunrise. Daily sunrise and sunset times and weather forecast are posted in the hotel lobby and at Brightness Peak. From here, it's a 20-30min. walk to the **Xihai Scenic Area** (xī hǎi; 西海; Western Sea), a well-known stop for watching the sunset as clouds drift by in the early evening sky. The super-long **Taiping cable car** (tàipíng suǒdào; 太平索道) runs from **Cloud Divide Pavilion** (páiyún tíng; 排云亭) to the distant **Pine Valley Nunnery** (sōng gǔ ān; 松谷庵), which leads to the North Gate. At 3km long with a 1km vertical drop, this cableway is supposedly the longest in Asia.

Beyond the Xihai Hotel, the path runs over **Lotus Ridge** (fúróng lǐng; 芙蓉岭), continuing past the **Rock Who Flew From Afar** (fēilái shí; 飞来石), a gigantic boulder precipitously balanced on a cliff, and Brightness Peak. From here, you can head toward the towers and loop back to the White Goose Peak cableway station or drop over the other side of the mountain for the long roller coaster hike that is the Western Steps.

WESTERN STEPS

From Brightness Peak, the path continues for five to six hours along the steep Western Steps down the mountain. From the rock formations of **Turtle Peak** (biēyú fēng; 鳖鱼峰), more steps lead to **Lotus Flower Peak** (liánhuā fēng; 莲花峰), the highest peak in the range. The two to three hour ascent up Lotus Flower Peak is steep and involves scrambling up irregular, twisting steps, but the sweat and adrenaline is more than redeemed by the exhilarating views at the top. For a short-cut, head down and to the right at the snack stand.

About halfway through the climb, the **Jade Screen Tower** (yù píng lóu; 玉屏楼) marks the terminus of the Yuping Line, which takes you to the bottom of the Western Steps. The cable car soars by the **Moon-Gazing Sky Dog** (tiān gǒu wàngyuè; 天狗望月) and the **Two Cats Capturing Mouse** (shuāng māo bǔ shǔ; 双猫捕鼠) rock formations en route to the **Merciful Light Chamber** (cíguāng gé; 慈光阁). From here, Tangkou is a short drive away. The Jade Screen Tower is near the solitary **Welcoming Pine** (yíngkè sōng; 迎客松), an eternal symbol of Huangshan. The long pine tree grows sideways out of the side of the mountain and hangs over the precipice below, awaiting photographers and painters who plaster its image in hotels and restaurants throughout the country. Just beyond the pine, at the top of an intimidating climb, looms **Heavenly Capital Peak** (tiāndū fēng; 天都峰). The bypass for this peak branches off at the Jade Screen Tower, but meets the main trail again at the Midway Monastery. The view from the top of Heavenly Capital Peak is fittingly divine—the best on the trail.

JIUHUASHAN MOUNTAIN 九华山 ☎0566

Jiuhuashan is famous for the soaring beauty of one of China's four sacred Buddhist mountains. Ever since a Korean prince chose these peaks as his place of meditation hundreds of years ago, the 1350m summit and its magnificent views have been infused with Buddhist serenity. Today, these hills are still alive with the sound of chanting *sutras* emanating from over 80 temples on the mountain, and journeying devotees do little to break the tranquil beauty. The village itself greets visitors with a brisk mountain freshness, a welcome change for those used to city grime. Wander the winding streets in the early morning or as the sun sets when Jiuhuashan's soothing charm is at its best.

▮ TRANSPORTATION

Trains: The nearest train station is the rather makeshift **Tongling Station** (tónglíng zhàn; 铜陵站), 2hr. away. From there, minibuses (Y18) and taxis (up to Y200) to Jiuhuashan line up outside the station.

Buses: Jiuhuashan Bus Station (jiǔhuáshān qìchē zhàn; 九华山汽车站 ; ☎555 3178), is 100m north of the main village gate. Open daily 6am-6pm. Buses run to: **Hangzhou** (6hr.; 6:30am, 7:10pm; Y70); **Hefei** (5hr., 7 per day 6:30am-2pm, Y50); **Nanjing** (5hr.; 6:30am, 1pm; Y54); **Shanghai** (9hr.; 6am, 1, 2:40pm; Y120); **Tangkou** (3hr.; 7am, 2:30pm; Y35). Many of the buses require you to transfer in Qingyang.

Local Transportation: Minibuses to various destinations depart throughout the day and can be found lined up along the main road, especially near the main gate. They regularly make the run to the Phoenix Tree and the cable car (Y5). Within Jiuhuashan, there isn't much need for taxis: the town takes about 20min. to cross on foot.

✖ ⚹ ORIENTATION AND PRACTICAL INFORMATION

Jiuhuashan is in the southern part of Anhui province, about 30km (1hr.) from **Qingyang** (青阳). The town sits cradled in a small valley, with the mountain wrapping around its south and east sides. To enter the village, buy a ticket at the main

TERROR ON THE MOUNTAIN

While brushing my teeth during my first night on Jiuhuashan, I noticed a suspicious, unsettling shadow lurking under the bathroom sink. Kneeling down cautiously, I saw the vague shape of an enormous insect, its hard, crusty shell curled up in a corner. Not entirely certain what this motionless object was, I ventured out into the hallway, toothbrush in hand, to seek a second opinion.

"*Xiēzi,*" snorted the landlady at a moment's glance, showing not the slightest bit of concern. She disappeared down the hall, presumably to fetch the *xiēzi* removal kit. "Just a *xiēzi,*" I muttered, reaching for the Chinese-English dictionary, more out of curiosity than anxiety. It was only when I read the translation that the real panic set in: scorpion.

The landlady returned wielding a large set of metal tongs, and went to work under the sink. There was some shuffling and sharp rasping before a final crunch. She emerged smiling, the offending crustacean firmly clamped, its back curled, legs flailing wildly, pincers chomping the air. "In China, we eat these," she added, as I cowered under the blanket. A narrow escape, I reflected, as I subjected my bedroom to a thorough inspection, lest there be a nest of them festering behind the TV set. It was a long time before I reluctantly snuffed out the light.

— *Gary Cooney*

gate, in the northeast corner of town. Admission from March 1 to November 30 is Y90, students Y70; winter admission is Y70, students Y50, but keep in mind that snow regularly renders the roads impassable. To check road conditions in advance, call any of the hotels. From the entrance, **Jiuhua Jie** (九华街) runs along the east side of the mountain, before turning right to curve along the front of the mountain. Small streets branch off from Jiuhua Jie, but none are particularly useful to tourists except the main square leading off the eastern stretch, where you will find the Bank of China, an Internet cafe, the post office, a pond full of small tortoises, as well as several hotels and restaurants. Few buildings have addresses, but most hotels are either found on, or are directly visible from, the main road.

Tourist Office: The official tourist office and the CTS have closed, but any of the friendly families that run the hotels will be happy to help visitors out. In this small village where everyone knows everyone, they can easily point you in the right direction, dispense advice, and even book accommodations for your next destination.

Bank of China: 65 Huacheng Lu (☎501 1270), about half a block west of the main square. Exchanges traveler's checks. Credit card advances. Open daily 8am-5:30pm.

PSB: (☎501 1331), in the main square. Toward the left corner, if one stands in the middle of the square, with the main road in front and the pond behind. Officers on call 24hr. a day.

Hospital: Jiuhuashan Red Cross Clinic (jiǔhuáshān hóngshízì yīyuàn; 九华山红十字会医院 ; ☎102) has a special examining room for tourists.

Internet: Nowhere is too remote for the world wide web. Log on in a small cafe in the main square, near the right-hand corner as you face the tortoise pond. It's not well-marked—look for dilapidated red wooden doors, covered on the inside with long drapes. Staff insists you present your passport. Y3 per hr. Open daily 8am-midnight.

Post and Telecommunications: The **post office** (☎502 1211), on the southwest corner of the main plaza, has EMS and Poste Restante. Open daily 8am-5:30pm. **China Telecom,** on Jiuhua Jie, on the right as you walk uphill, opposite the Construction Bank.

Postal Code: 242811.

ACCOMMODATIONS

Renting a room in smaller, family-run guesthouses is the best budget option available. In general, quality is high and prices are low, a good value for your *rénmínbì*. The personable, homey touch does have its drawbacks, however, as you'll wake soon after the children do, any time from 6am on. For a more professional atmosphere, turn to one of Jiuhuashan's many hotels that dot the main roadways. Travelers wishing to get in touch with their spiritual side may want to inquire about rooms at the mountain's many temples, particularly at the **Qiyuan Temple** just south of the bus station. These establishments rarely admit foreigners, though.

■ Hengfu Mountain Villa (héngfú shānzhuāng; 恒福山庄 ; ☎501 3031), in the main square, on the far right corner as you face the pond. Small, family-run guesthouse with attached restaurant and sweet shop. Large, comfy bedrooms, with nice decor and very clean baths. Wonderfully friendly family. Singles and doubles Y60; triples Y80. ❶

Dongya Hotel (dōngyà bīnguǎn; 东亚宾馆; ☎501 1370), a few blocks inside the main Jiuhuashan gate. Walk down the main road and turn right into a large parking lot; the hotel is at the very end. Pristine and well-kept, with strangely sweet-smelling air. The triples are in a separate, more run-down building within the hotel complex. Doubles and dorms include A/C, bath, and IDD phones. Doubles Y320; triples Y180. MC/V. ❸

Longquan Hotel (lóngquán fàndiàn; 龙泉饭店; ☎501 1323 or 501 1320), to the right side of the main road near its southwest corner, just before the street veers right. Attentive and perky staff. Rooms are small, with thin, well-worn carpets and tiled bathrooms. A/C, bath, 24hr. hot water in most rooms. Doubles Y120; triples Y180. ❷

Jiuhuashan Villa (jiǔhuá shānzhuāng; 九华山庄; ☎501 1036). Turn right past Furong bridge from the main road; it's near the end of the road. Shockingly posh and sparkling, with massive gardens and gleaming rooms. Cheerful, helpful staff. All rooms have A/C, bath, TV. Doubles Y580 and up. 20% discount possible. MC/V. ❺

■ FOOD

Numerous restaurants jostle for space with shops selling Buddhist paraphernalia on the main road. Many others are clustered on the southeast part of town. Prices here are significantly higher, and owners often try to steer customers toward the more expensive end of the menu. In just about every restaurant, you'll get to sample Jiuhuashan tea and *xiānggū* (香菇), a scrumptious dried mushroom cooked with tofu or vegetables. **Furong Food City** (fúróngzhuāng yǐnshíchéng; 芙蓉庄饮食城), on the corner before the road turns west, houses a large number of similar one-table restaurants. Pick your food from the refrigerator—the owner will disappear into the kitchen, returning moments later with a delicious meal. Prices can vary enormously (Y4-180), so it's best to agree on cost in advance. **Tu Specialties Restaurant ❷** (tèsè tǔ càiguǎn; 特色土菜馆), located toward the top of Jiuhua Jie just after it turns right, dishes up a wide selection of tasty, freshly-cooked food. (Noodles Y8, meat dishes Y25 and up. Open 24hr.) **Hengfu Mountain Villa ❷** (恒福山庄 ; ☎501 3031) cooks up the standard Chinese dishes with much good cheer. If there's room for dessert, take a tour of their homemade-sweet shop, attached to the restaurant. Also see **Accommodations,** above, about a night's stay. (Entrees Y8-Y30. Open daily 8am-10pm.)

◉ SIGHTS

Most visitors to Jiuhuashan come to worship at and admire the many Buddhist temples. The rich aroma of burning incense wafts through the town, and the low, muffled chanting of prayer, accompanied by the soft tapping on "wooden fish," sets a gentle rhythmic backdrop. Buddhists and non-Buddhists alike will appreciate the temples' intricate decoration and the creative energy that inspired their design. Friendly, smiling monks happily invite visitors inside, usually at no cost.

Take to the hills, however, if it's nature's spirit-shocking beauty that you seek. The two main trails, though long and arduous, reward hikers with truly magnificent views across the surrounding mountain range. For those who have no desire to make a sun-drenched uphill slog, both trails provide cable cars as an easy alternative. Look for the signs that direct you towards a "funicular."

Conveniently close to the gate is **Zhiyuan Temple** (zhǐyuán sì; 祇园寺), a yellow-walled, yellow-tiled building just inside the village, off to the left. A geographically easy point of reference, the distinctive temple hosts the Buddhist trinity inside the Mahavira Hall. (Open daily 6:30am-8:30pm. Y5.) As you leave the temple complex, head downhill and follow the signs that veer to the right, until you reach a long staircase. A hike up the steps leads to the **Hundred Year Palace** (bǎisuì gōng; 百岁宫), the white hilltop building visible from the village. (Open daily 5am-6pm. Y8.) Tread softly through the hushed palace, with its two large and separate halls. Monks meditating or chanting scripture occupy the entrance hall, which also contains the mummified, gilded body of Ming priest Wu Xia. Exceedingly friendly monks will happily tell the story of Wu Xia, who was known to use gold dust and his own blood in his work on the Huayan *sutras*. To the right is the **Five-Hundred Luohan Hall** (wǔbǎi luóhàn táng; 五百罗汉堂), where devotees gather to ask the arhats to grant their wishes or have their fortunes read by the monks. If the steps are too much, you can take the overpriced cable car, which runs from the village to the palace, and enjoy the view from the upper station. (Open daily 6:30am-6pm. Express up Y55, down Y40; regular Y40/35.)

Walk south along the ridge to the **Bell Tower** (zhōng lóu; 钟楼), another religious site, and the **East Peak Platform** (dōngyá yúnfáng; 东崖云舫). Watch out for the opportunistic monkeys waiting along the path—they're after your food and may latch onto your leg. Though the monkeys are generally not dangerous, it's still a good idea to travel with others. The platform, with its vast, sweeping views unfurling over mountains of rippling trees, is the perfect point to rest, catch your breath, and admire the heavenly beauty.

Continue south along the ridge for 10min. until you reach two more large temples, then begin your descent into the valley toward the **Phoenix Tree** (fēnghuáng sōng; 凤凰松), an ancient, jagged Huangshan pine thought to look like—surprise!—a phoenix. You may need to let your imagination run free to see the resemblance. Minibuses regularly bring visitors up to the Phoenix Tree. From here you can make your ascent to the **Heavenly Platform** (tiāntái; 天台) via one of two ways. To the left, a taxing 2hr. trail climbs steadily uphill. Very few people make this trek, taking into account the thin mountain air and searing midday sun. However, the trail is paved with stone steps all the way up, with no shortage of water stops along the way, making for a very safe climb. For the faint of heart, a **cable car** whisks travelers up to Mt. Jiuhua's 1342m summit. From the Phoenix Tree, follow the path upwards and to the right. (Open daily 7am-4:30pm. Up Y45, down Y40; children and Chinese students Y35/Y30.)

JIANGXI 江西

Jiangxi is a work in progress. China's famed vigorous development has been taken to a new extreme here, at times almost bordering upon the ridiculous. Cranes vie for air space, and forests of bamboo scaffolding stretch high into the sky. Such rapid growth spurts are not confined to the cities either—mountain villages like Jinggangshan are paving commercial avenues in one dizzying swoop, completely transforming their surroundings to make way for relentless progress.

Jiangxi's residents pride themselves on their Communist history, with monuments and museums spread liberally throughout the province. The 1920s brought fervent revolutionary spirit to Jiangxi, and many decisive battles took place on

IT'S AS EASY AS

one, two, three

uno, dos, tres

un, deux, trois

один, два, три

일 , 이 , 삼

Immerse yourself in a language.

Rosetta Stone° software is hands-down the fastest, easiest way to learn a new language — and that goes for any of the 27 we offer. The reason is our award-winning Dynamic Immersion™ method. Thousands of real-life images and the voices of native speakers teach you faster than you ever thought possible. And you'll amaze yourself at how effortlessly you learn.

Don't force-feed yourself endless grammar exercises and agonizing memory drills. Learn your next language the way you learned your first — the natural way. Order the language of your choice and get free overnight shipping in the United States!

Available for learning:
Arabic • Chinese • Danish • Dutch • English
French • German • Hebrew • Hindi • Indonesian
Italian • Japanese • Korean • Latin • Pashto
Polish • Portuguese • Russian • Swahili • Swedish
Spanish • Thai • Turkish • Vietnamese • Welsh

The guaranteed way to learn.

Rosetta Stone will teach you a language faster and easier than other language-learning methods. We guarantee it. If you are not satisfied for any reason, simply return the program within six months for a full refund!

Learn what NASA, the Peace Corps, thousands of schools, and millions around the world already know: Rosetta Stone is the most effective way to learn a new language!

FREE OVERNIGHT SHIPPING
In the United States
(Use promotion code lge005s)
1-800-788-0822
www.RosettaStone.com/lge005s

Personal Edition. Solutions for Organizations also available.

these lands, with far-reaching consequences for China's political trajectory. But there's far more to Jiangxi than Communism and construction. As the province dips south, a balmy warmth picks up and long-leafed lazy palms hint at the approaching tropics. The mountain scenery will leave none disappointed—a perfect blanket of evergreens enfolds the vast range of jagged peaks, promising beautiful, scenic bus journeys along mountain roads predictably beset by construction.

NANCHANG 南昌 ☎ 0791

Seventy kilometers south of Lake Poyang, on the Gan River between Shanghai and Changsha, the capital of Jiangxi province is a busy trade and commerce center. Its hotels are filled with businessmen making deals by day and frequenting flashy bars and shady massage parlors by night. Vendors crowd city streets lined with billboards, plying their wares to anyone who passes.

Yet this money-making, rat-race town is also cherished for its pivotal role in the birth of the Communist Party, and numerous monuments, museums, and souvenirs bear testimony to Nanchang's unique history. On August 1, 1927, Zhou Enlai and Zhu De, a pair of GMD officers with Communist inclinations, seized control of the city, sparking the chain of events that would eventually lead to the CCP's domination of China (see **The Long and Winding Road**, p. 79). The founding of the People's Liberation Army is celebrated each August 1, when visitors flood the city. Most foreign travelers, however, make only a brief pit-stop here, choosing to journey onward to the mountains of Lushan or Jinggangshan.

▐▀ TRANSPORTATION

Flights: Nanchang Airport (nánchāng jīchǎng; 南昌机场) is 30km away from the city. **China Eastern Airlines Ticket Offices** (zhōngguó dōngfāng hángkōng gōngsī; 中国东方航空公司) has 2 locations at 552 Nanjing Xi Lu (☎851 4195), and 87 Minde Lu (☎628 2654), just west of the Jiangxi (Binguan) Hotel. Both open daily 8am-9pm. To: **Beijing** (3-5 per day, Y700-1300); **Chengdu** (1-2 per day, Y960-120); **Guangzhou** (3 per day, Y365-730); **Haikou** (daily, Y600-1190); **Shanghai** (5 per day, Y426-710); **Xi'an** (daily, Y808-1010).

Trains: Nanchang is one of southern China's main rail hubs. **Nanchang Train Station** (nánchāng zhàn; 南昌站), on Zhanqian Lu, about 1km east of Fushan Traffic Circle, beneath a huge, square arch. There's also an unmarked ticket office (☎702 6099) to the right as you face the station. Open daily 7am-midnight. To: **Beijing** (14-17hr., 6 per day 1:30am-11pm, Y319-409); **Guangzhou** (12-14hr., 5 per day 1:40am-10pm, Y238); **Hefei** (6hr., 3 per day, Y64); **Jingdezhen** (4½hr., 2 per day, Y5.5-44); **Nanjing** (12hr., 2 per day, Y122); **Shanghai** (11½hr., 5 per day 12:30am-11pm, Y182-209); **Xiamen** (18hr., 4 per day 3am-5pm, Y181); **Xi'an** (22½hr., 2 per day, Y185).

Buses: Nanchang Long-Distance Bus Station (nánchāng chángtú qìchē zhàn; 南昌长途汽车站 ; ☎624 3217), in a long, shiny building on the east side of Bayi Dadao, a few blocks south of Bayi Sq. Open daily 5am-10:30pm. To: **Hefei** (6½hr., 2 per day, Y125); **Jingdezhen** (3½hr., every hr. 6:40am-7:10pm, Y65); **Jinggangshan** (6½hr., 3 per day, Y70); **Jiujiang** (2½hr., every 30min. 6am-7pm, Y26-36); **Lushan** (3½hr., 8 per day 7:10am-4:30pm, Y38).

Local Transportation: Most **buses** run 7am-8pm; major buses like #2 run 5am-10pm. Fare Y0.5-2. Bus #2 runs along Zhongshan Lu, stops at August 1 (Bayi) Museum, turns onto Bayi Dadao, stops at the post office and long-distance bus station, and terminates at the train station; #8 and 20 run along the river to the port and Tengwang Pavilion.

Taxis: Base fare Y6, each additional km Y1.4. Trips across town Y6. Fares are negotiable.

YANGZI BASIN

✦ ② ORIENTATION AND PRACTICAL INFORMATION

Nanchang is roughly oval-shaped with the **Gan River** (gàn jiāng; 赣江) stretching along its west side. **Bayi Square** (bāyī guǎngchǎng; 八一广场), though not the geographic center, is the spiritual and commercial heart of town. The major north-south thoroughfare **Bayi Dadao** (八一大道) runs along the west side of the square, and is lined with numerous hotels, restaurants, shops, and tourist-related services. Bayi Dadao heads south to the **Fushan Traffic Circle**, another service- and hotel-filled area. From here, **Zhanqian Lu** (站前路) extends east to the train station.

In the northwest part of town, **Bayi Bridge** (bāyī dàqiáo; 八一大桥) crosses the Gan River next to the ferry port on **Yanjiang Bei Lu** (沿江北路), from which **Minde Lu** (民德路), **Ruzi Lu**, and **Zhongshan Lu** (中山路) run east to Bayi Dadao. **Shengli Lu** (胜利路) and **Xiangshan Lu** (象山路) both run north-south through the district.

Travel Agencies: Jiangxi International Tour and Aviation Corporation, 169 Fuzhou Lu (☎621 5891), on the north side of the street, next door to Qingshang Hotel. Open daily 8am-9pm.

Bank of China: 1 Zhanqian Xi Lu (☎647 1688), on the west side of Fushan Traffic Circle, across from the Nanchang Hotel. Exchanges currency and traveler's checks. Credit card advances. Open daily summer 8am-6pm; winter 8am-5:30pm.

Bookstore: Xinhua Bookstore, 102 Bayi Dadao (☎630 1458), 3-4 blocks north of the Fushan Traffic Circle, on the west side of Bayi Dadao. The usual selection of dusty British classics. Open daily 8:30am-8pm. Another **branch**, 272 Bayi Dadao (☎626 2026), a few blocks north just past the bus station, has an impressive world music collection and a surprising range of dated Hollywood classics on DVD. Open daily 8:30am-8pm.

PSB: 66 Shengli Lu (☎674 2382), in an imposingly large gray building. **Visa extensions** and **Hong Kong** and **Macau** visas can be obtained here. Open daily 8am-6pm.

Hospital: No. 1 Hospital of Nanchang (nánchāng shì dìyī yīyuàn; 南昌市第一医院 ; ☎678 4813), to the left as you head north along Xiangshan Bei Lu. Open 24hr.

Pharmacy: Huangqing Renzhan Pharmacy, 197 Bayi Dadao (☎623 5990), on the left-hand side as you face the bus station. Mainly Chinese products; some Western medicine. Open 8am-9pm.

Internet Access: Xinhua Internet Cafe City (xīnhuá wǎngbā chéng; 新华网吧城), in an alleyway off Ruzi Lu directly opposite the entrance to China Telecom. Teens, computer games, and large rotating fans. Y1.5 per hr. Open 24hr. **Cultural Palace Internet Cafe** (wénhuá gōng wǎngbā; 文化宫网吧), to the right as you face the entrance to Cultural Palace Hotel, has dozens of whizzing terminals, sectioned off into tiny booths. Y1.5 per hr. Open 8am-midnight.

Post Office: China Post, 262 Bayi Dadao (☎640 0005). EMS, Poste Restante, and a "Philately" counter. Open daily summer 8am-7:30pm; winter 8am-6:30pm.

Postal Code: 330003.

▸ ACCOMMODATIONS

Nanchang hotels cater almost exclusively to business travelers. Most establishments offer bellhops, karaoke bars, and mysterious phone calls from even more mysterious women. The large number of rooms means that mid-range hotels often have openings, so try bargaining. All listed hotels have A/C, bath, and TV.

Ganjiang Hotel (gànjiāng bīnguǎn; 赣江宾馆), 138 Bayi Dadao (☎622 1159; fax 626 1968), opposite the bus station through a large archway. A large and innovative hotel complex, well worth the extra money. Wide corridors lead into pristine, elegant rooms with lovely interior decoration, although the shower in the more expensive standard room is somewhat exhibitionist. Doubles Y280-488. ❹

YANGZI BASIN

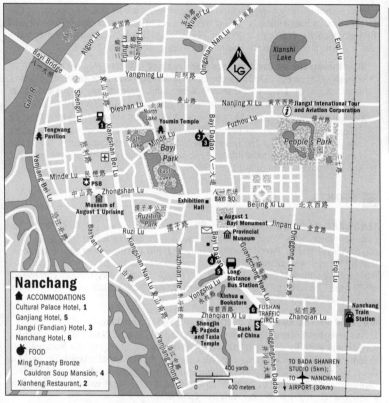

Nanchang

ACCOMMODATIONS
Cultural Palace Hotel, 1
Ganjiang Hotel, 5
Jiangxi (Fandian) Hotel, 3
Nanchang Hotel, 6

FOOD
Ming Dynasty Bronze
  Cauldron Soup Mansion, 4
Xianheng Restaurant, 2

Cultural Palace Hotel (wénhuá gōng bīnguǎn; 文化宫宾馆), 222 Xiangshan Bei Lu (☎679 5180), through a gate on the west side of Xiangshan Lu, 3 blocks north of Minde Lu. Spacious, tidy rooms with soft colors and wooden wardrobes. Singles Y100; doubles Y100-130; triples Y135. MC/V. ❷

Nanchang Hotel (nánchāng bīnguǎn; 南昌宾馆), 16 Bayi Dadao (☎622 3193), off Fushan Traffic Circle, between the bus and train stations. Friendly staff at this conveniently located hotel will help with bus and train tickets. Little differentiates the more expensive rooms from their cheaper counterparts. Doubles Y100-185; triples Y185. ❷

Jiangxi (Fandian) Hotel (jiāngxī fàndiàn; 江西饭店), 356 Bayi Dadao (☎885 8888; fax 885 8899), about 1 block south of Minde Lu, south of the other, nicer Jiangxi (Binguan) Hotel. The main hotel building keeps bright, clean, comfortable rooms with light wooden furniture. To the back, in a separate red building, are the cheaper rooms, with gaudy orange curtains, white walls, and thin carpets. Doubles Y260; doubles in red bldg. Y140, with Chinese toilet Y120. ❷

🛏 🎵 FOOD AND ENTERTAINMENT

Super-cheap eats are found on the south end of the railway plaza. A number of stands and restaurants offer **Chinese fast food**—pick and choose rice with one meat, two vegetable dishes, and soup for just Y3. Xiangshan Lu in the north and

YANGZI BASIN

the area around Tengwang Pavilion both have many **stir-fry stalls**. At night, hit **Cultural Palace** (wénhuà gōng; 文化宫), the giant entertainment complex just north of Renmin Square (rénmín guǎngchǎng; 人民广场). This self-contained center has a skating rink, a coffee and ice cream bar, a dance club, and a theater.

Ming Dynasty Bronze Cauldron Soup Mansion (míng cháo tóng dǐng wēi tāng fǔ; 明朝铜鼎煨汤府; ☎ 639 0283), directly opposite the long-distance bus station. Look for 2 large cauldrons. Frogs croak, snakes slither, and flames flicker in this cavernous kitchen—the resulting food is mouthwateringly good. Open daily 10am-10pm. ❷

Xianheng Restaurant (xián hēng jiǔdiàn; 咸亨酒店), 48 Mingde Lu (☎ 627 7777), a yellow building about a block beyond the parking lot on the left. Somewhat more expensive, though not without decorative flourish in both food and surroundings. The picture menu helps you make more informed decisions. Portions (Y15 and up) are small but strongly flavored. Open daily 11am-9:30pm. ❷

🅢 SIGHTS

TENGWANG PAVILION (téngwáng gé; 腾王阁). Overlooking the Gan River, this elaborate building is Nanchang's biggest attraction. Although first built in AD 653, the pavilion's ornate, eaved roofs are modern replicas. Numerous souvenir shops, a small theater, and a museum grace the premises, but the pavilions and gardens will probably interest the visitor more. *(38 Fanggu Jie, off Yanjiang Lu, north of Minde Lu. ☎ 670 4480. Open daily summer 7:30am-6:30pm, last admission 5:30pm; winter 8am-5:20pm, last admission 4:50pm. Y50.)*

MUSEUM OF THE AUGUST 1 UPRISING (bāyī qǐyì jìniànguǎn; 八一起义记念馆). It was here that Communist leaders planned the takeover of Nanchang. Trace their subsequent path to victory despite the knavish skullduggery of the Nationalists. Solemn meeting rooms, menacing rifles, and model fighter airplanes fill the first floor. Upstairs are largely photographic and written sources, with limited English captions. *(380 Zhongshan Lu, on the south side of the street, 3 blocks east of Yanjiang Lu, just after Shengli Lu. ☎ 661 3806. Open daily 8am-6pm. Y25.)*

BADA SHANREN STUDIO (qīngyún pǔ bādàshānrén jìniàntáng; 青云谱八大山人记念堂). This immaculate complex of gardens, courtyards, and various pavilions displays the work of the late-Ming/early-Qing painter Bada Shanren, also known as Zhu Da. Even if you're not into the art, the surroundings provide some fresh air away from the clatter of Nanchang. *(In Qingyun Pu, 5km south of Nanchang. Take bus #20 from along Yanjiang Lu to the Badashan stop. You'll see a large pond along the road; the studio is just across the footbridge. ☎ 527 3565. Open daily 8:30am-5:30pm. Y20.)*

JINGDEZHEN 景德镇   ☎ 0798

Jingdezhen put the "china" in China. In the Song Dynasty (AD 960-1127), Emperor Zhengzong first stumbled across Jingdezhen, a city that fashioned porcelain just the way he wanted: "White as jade, lustrous as mirror, thin as paper, resonant as a chime." With that, the city's destiny as the imperial porcelain factory was sealed.

Though an excellent place to stock up on high-quality, low-price crockery, teasets, and vases, the city is otherwise not really worth visiting. The streets are grimy, store fronts dusty and neglected, and even the parks could use a good scrubbing. Residents, however, predict a promising future for Jingdezhen. Lackluster streets are being rebuilt in styles inspired by traditional Chinese architecture, which lends some aesthetic appeal, despite being somewhat forced and incongruous. Luxury hotels are springing up, and their cheaper counterparts are busily renovating. Museums, too, have opted for facelifts. All in all, Jingdezhen looks like it's ready to leave the dust behind.

TRANSPORTATION

Flights: Luojia Airport (luójiā jīchǎng; 罗家机场), 10km northwest of the city, off the road to Jiujiang. **Jindezhen Staff and Workers Travel Service**, 16 Lianshe Bei Lu (☎/ fax 822 5258) is open daily 8am-5pm. To: **Beijing** (M, W, F, Su 9:10pm; Y1250); **Guangzhou** (Su, Th 11:40am; Y860); **Shanghai** (M-W, F-Su 8:40am; Y500).

Trains: Jingdezhen Train Station (jīngdézhèn huǒchē zhàn; 景德镇火车站 ; ☎702 2482), 1km southeast of the city center. The ticket office is on the left as you face the train station. Usually at least 1 window is open 24hr. To: **Beijing** (24hr., 7am, Y363); **Huangshan** (3-3½hr., 6 per day 5:30am-7:30pm, Y11-26); **Nanchang** (5hr., 2 per day, Y38-70); **Nanjing** (11hr., 6pm, Y30-214); **Xiamen** (17hr., 2 per day, Y55-85).

Buses: The **bus station** (☎820 8156), across from the train station, mainly serves destinations in Jiangxi, including **Jiujiang** (2hr., 8 per day 7am-3:30pm, Y30) and **Nanchang** (4hr., 13 per day 7:50am-5:15pm, Y65). Buses also go to **Fuzhou** (5hr., 9 per day 7am-3:10pm, Y38). Ticket office open daily 6am-5:30pm. Also buy tickets here for departures from the dingy, poorly organized station across the river on **Xinfeng Lu**. To: **Hangzhou** (6-7hr.; 8:30am, 7pm; Y110); **Hefei** (9hr., 6am, Y53).

Local Transportation: The **bus** system in Jingdezhen is fairly comprehensive, with 11 lines covering most of the city during daylight hours. #1 runs along Zhushan Zhong Lu; #11 and #12 run toward the train station; #4 plies Cidu Dadao, home to the Ceramics History Museum. **Minibus taxis** run across town for Y5; proper taxis charge Y10.

ORIENTATION AND PRACTICAL INFORMATION

The **Chang River** (chāng hé; 昌河) divides Jingdezhen into two. The old city in the eastern half has nearly everything a traveler needs. From the river, **Zhushan Lu** (珠 山路) runs east, through the middle of town, to the city center (a rotary with a large silver sculpture). **Ma'anshan Lu** (马鞍山路) runs southeast to the train station, and **Lianshe Bei Lu** (莲社北路), a stretch of road with some nightspots and many porcelain shops, branches up north.

Travel Agency: CITS (☎851 5888), on Zhushan Lu, just at the bridge on the western side. Open daily 8am-6pm. **Jindezhen Staff and Workers Travel Service** (jīngdézhèn zhígōng lǚxíngshè; 景德镇职工旅行社), 16 Lianshe Bei Lu (☎/fax 822 5258), offers full-day factory package tours in English (Y80-120). Open 8am-5pm.

Bank of China: (☎857 0586). On Cidu Dadao, next to the towering Kaimenzi Hotel. Open daily 8am-5:30pm.

PSB: (☎852 5354). In a tall building just north of the main Bank of China on Cidu Dadao, in the southwest part of town. Open 8:30-11:30am and 2:30-5:30pm.

Telephones: China Telecom, next to the post office on Zhushan Zhong Lu. 24hr. IDD service. Open daily summer 8am-6pm; winter 8am-5:30pm.

Internet Access: Internet cafes lurk behind shady curtains throughout the city, usually a block away from main thoroughfares. There are 2 on the right as you head south along Ma'anshan Lu toward the train station. Both Y2 per hour. Open daily 10am-midnight.

Post Office: Zhushan Post Office (☎856 7546), on the west side of the bridge on Zhushan Lu, next to CITS. EMS and Poste Restante. Open daily 8am-6pm.

Postal Code: 333000.

▚ ACCOMMODATIONS

Jingdezhen makes a nice daytrip, but the transportation gods have cursed the city, so chances are you're going to have to stay the night. Not surprisingly, a large collection of hotels line the streets leading to the train station. Further into the city, there are slightly more expensive options along Zhushan Lu, as well as some more luxurious establishments closer to the river.

Wenyuan Hotel (wényuàn dàfàndiàn; 文苑大饭店), 34 Tongzhan Lu (☎820 8888), half a block north of the train station. Recently renovated hotel has large doubles with exceptionally cozy beds. Train sirens blare late into the night. Singles Y80; doubles Y100; triples Y160. ❶

Jingdezhen Hotel (jǐngdézhèn bīnguǎn; 景德镇宾馆 ; ☎851 1888; fax 851 1999), on Zhongshan Lu, at the bridge on the eastern side. Excellent rooms with thick carpets, pristine bathrooms, a minibar, computer with Internet access, and large comfy beds. Doubles Y680-880. ❺

Gold Flourishing Hotel (jīnshèng bīnguǎn; 金盛宾馆 ; ☎827 1818; fax 827 1158), on Zhushan Lu. On the right as you head west, just after the intersection with Lianshe Lu. A great location at a very reasonable price, this hotel features blue-carpeted, white-walled rooms with wooden furniture and a small minibar. Singles Y100-138; doubles Y118-158; triples Y140-188. ❷

◖ FOOD

Along almost every sidewalk and in the narrow side streets, bristling, newly-washed greens peek out of red basins, a sure sign that Jindezhen takes its cooking seriously. The smallest unassuming eateries often whip up the tastiest meals—you'll find them throughout the city, but especially on the streets flanking the eastern river bank.

On Lianshe Bei Lu, the **Little Sparrow Seafood Restaurant** ❷ (xiǎo máquè hǎixiān lóu; 小麻雀海鲜楼) is to the left as you walk 100m north from the intersection with Zhushan Lu. When only the freshest fish will do, choose your dinner from a gurgling aquarium at the entrance. The menu deviates from seafood to include beef, chicken, and pork, but no small sparrows. (☎820 9907; entrees Y10-26. Open daily 9:30am-9pm.) **Half-Taste Restaurant** ❷ (bàn wèi jū; 半味居) is on the left as you head west on Zhushan Lu, a 3min. walk east of KFC, on the second floor. Look for the blinking strobe lights after dusk. The service is speedy, the tasty portions large and steaming hot. (☎821 1822. Open daily 10am-10pm.)

◉ SIGHTS

Jingdezhen has several factory tours and museums, all dedicated to the explanation and promotion of the region's tradition—churning out urn after urn's worth of smooth, shiny clay. CITS offers a **factory tour,** which features local porcelain factories, a porcelain-oriented research center, a 1000-year-old kiln site, and a museum. (Full-day tour Y160, 2 people Y240.)

If you're just in town to shop, head to **Jinchangli** (jīn chāng lì; 金昌利), a small cluster of porcelain stores at the eastern tip of Zhushan Lu, at its junction with Lianshe Bei Lu. Accident-prone people beware: these stores have an extensive range of vases, dishware, figurines, and every imaginable trinket that could possibly be made from clay. All are very high quality and surprisingly cheap. Vases of the man-sized variety sell for Y100-1500, bowls go for Y10 each, and complete teasets usually fall in the Y40-60 range. For more bargains, hop on a bus heading toward **Jiujiang**, just 3km outside the city, where you'll find a mind-boggling row of shops hawking plates, vases, and more.

JINDEZHEN MUSEUM OF PORCELAIN. Jindezhen is proud of its porcelain past, and this museum pays ample tribute to it. Displays in glass cabinets trace the tradition's thousand-year history with beautifully painted, ornate clay sculptures, culminating in a skillfully detailed dragon-ship piece. *(On Lianshe Bei Lu. ☎822 9784. Open daily 8am-5pm. Y15, students Y8.)*

CERAMIC HISTORY MUSEUM (táocí lìshǐ bówùguǎn; 陶瓷历史博物馆). More of a lazy man's garden than an exhibition space, the Ming- and Qing-era restored buildings bestow ample old-school charm. Walk past the pond and bridges toward the main display hall, which has examples of porcelain and pottery through the ages. *(On Fengshu Shan/Maple Tree Mountain, along Cidu Dadao, a 10min. walk from the main road. Accessible by bus #4. ☎852 1594. Open daily 8am-5pm. Combination ticket with the Ancient Porcelain Factory Y50, students Y25.)*

ANCIENT PORCELAIN FACTORY. Constructed in Ming and Qing styles, this factory is currently the only place in town that still employs traditional techniques. Wander along the long assembly lines guided by skilled human hands. Pieces are carefully shaped from raw clay (using a manual wheel driven by a cane), baked in the cavernous, multi-story wood kiln next door (into which you can walk), and finally honed and painted. *(Next door to the Ceramic History Museum. Open daily 8am-5pm. See above for admission fee.)*

LUSHAN 庐山   ☎0792

A Chinese saying states that Huangshan is *qí* (strange and magnificent), but Lushan is *xiù* (delicate and fair). Indeed, it's difficult not to be entranced by the cozy charm of this mountain resort town. Generations of Chinese political kingpins have felt the same, and the region was once famed as the "summer capital" of China's political movers and shakers. Even the Chairman himself left his mark on the mountain, in the form of everything from preserved villas to collections of poetry. But Lushan's illustrious past is not as important to visitors as the area's magical present. Gurgling streams run past paved walkways, tranquil, misty gardens lie in the heart of commercial activity, and English explanations of monuments and plants are everywhere. Foreigners aren't common here, but the generally mellow Lushan folk will provide you with a pleasant reception.

▐ TRANSPORTATION

Trains: The closest train station to Lushan is in **Jiujiang;** from here you can take bus #1 or 101 (Y1) to Jiujiang's long-distance bus station and catch a connecting bus to the mountain. To: **Beijing** (22hr., 6 per day 1-7:30pm, Y282); **Nanchang** (1½hr., many per day 1am-9:30pm, Y19-31); **Shanghai** (14hr., 8:01pm, Y50-351); **Wuhan** (5hr., 7 per day, Y16-155).

Buses: Buses may be more convenient than train. You can only buy long-distance bus tickets to **Nanchang** and **Jiujiang**. For Jiujiang, walk up Hexi Lu toward Guling Jie, through the tunnel, then turn left; the small ticket office (☎858 2369) is about 30m ahead on the left-hand side in the parking lot of the large bldg. that houses the tourist office. Open daily 7am-9pm. From **Jiujiang** (1hr., 8 per day 7:50am-4:30pm, Y7), you can catch buses to more distant places. The **Nanchang Bus Depot** (☎828 1983) is on the other side of the tunnel, just past the fork in Hexi Lu (2½hr., 2 per day, Y35).

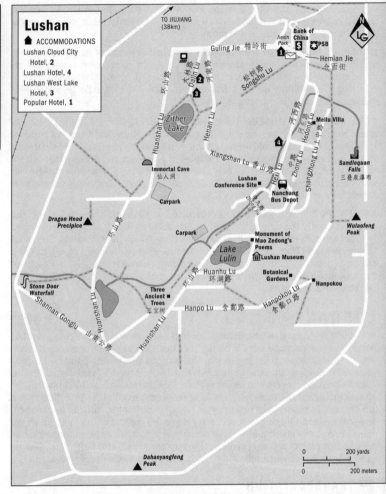

Lushan

▲ ACCOMMODATIONS

Lushan Cloud City Hotel, **2**
Lushan Hotel, **4**
Lushan West Lake Hotel, **3**
Popular Hotel, **1**

TO JIUJIANG (38km)

Jiexin Park
Bank of China
PSB
Guling Jie 牯岭街
Hemian Jie 含面街
Songshu Lu 松树路
Dalin Lu 大林路
Henan Lu 河南路
Huanshan Lu 环山路
Hexi Lu 河西路
Meilu Villa
Hedong 河东路
Zither Lake
Immortal Cave 仙人洞
Xiangshan Lu 香山路
Zhonglu 中路
Shangzhong Lu 上中路
Sandiequan Falls 三叠泉瀑布
Carpark
Dragon Head Precipice ▲
Lushan Conference Site
Nanchang Bus Depot
Wulaofeng Peak ▲
Carpark
Huanshan Lu 环山路
Jiulu 九路
Monument of Mao Zedong's Poems
Lake Lulin
Lushan Museum
Botanical Gardens
Hanpokou ■
Stone Door Waterfall
Shannan Gonglu 山南公路
Huanshan Lu 环山路
Huanhu Lu 环湖路
Three Ancient Trees 三宝树
Hanpo Lu 含鄱路
Hanpokou Lu 含鄱口路

Dahanyangfeng Peak ▲

| 0 | 200 yards |
| 0 | 200 meters |

Local Transportation: Taxi and **minibus** fare Y8 per 2km. Along Hexi Lu Y10; to other Guling sights Y15-25. They cluster in the parking lot opposite Jiexin Park at Guling Jie. **Minibuses** for other Lushan destinations leave frequently from outside Guling, on the road to Jiujiang.

✳ ℹ ORIENTATION AND PRACTICAL INFORMATION

The largest gateway to the Lushan area is **Jiujiang** (jiǔjiāng; 九江), a city on the mouth of Lake Poyang, which spreads to the north of the mountains. Between Jiujiang and **Guling** (gǔlǐng; 牯岭), the main town within the Lushan region, buses (Y7) cruise up a winding highway with fantastic views of the city and lake, right up to the entrance gate. (Open 24hr. ☎ 828 1734. Admission Y140, students Y80; plus Y10 taxi ride.) Guling is just a few kilometers beyond, wrapping around the mountain. Buses enter the town through a tunnel in the northeast. Those coming from Nanchang follow **Hexi Lu** (河西路), which heads south past hotels, restaurants, and sights. Branching off to the west, the pedestrian **Hemian Jie** (合面街) continues on to **Guling Jie** (牯岭街). Everything that a traveler would need can be found on these two streets. However, sights and scenic spots are farther from Guling.

Travel Agency: Lushan Tourist's Service Center (☎829 6565), in an imposingly large gray bldg., on the right just before you enter the tunnel as you head toward the town center. Very friendly staff members are ready to answer questions, dole out advice, and arrange tours of the local scenic points. 1-day tour including 10 of the main attractions Y120. All-inclusive 2-day tour Y240. Open daily 8am-10pm.

Bank of China: (☎828 1913), on Hemian Jie. Exchanges traveler's checks and foreign currency. Open daily 8am-6pm.

ATM: 24hr. ATM at the Bank of China on Hemian Jie.

PSB: 1 Hexi Lu (☎828 2952). A few doors downhill from the Tourist's Service Center. Open daily 8am-noon and 2:30-6pm.

Internet: 4 Internet cafes in Lushan, one of which is hidden in a very narrow alley, on Guling Jie, just past the intersection with Dalin Lu. Y2 per hr. Open 8am-midnight.

Weather Information: ☎121.

Post Office: The **post and telecommunications office** (☎828 1005), across from the Bank of China on pedestrian Hemian Jie. IDD service. Open daily summer 8am-6pm; winter 8am-5:30pm.

Postal Code: 332900.

ACCOMMODATIONS AND FOOD

Lushan is awash with middle-range hotels advertising top-end prices, but there's nothing here that a little bit of bargaining can't fix. That said, Lushan's residents have a few tricks up their own sleeves when it comes to striking accommodation deals. As a foreigner, you might find yourself conveniently dropped off at a hotel, where the driver and hotel management will implore you to take a look at the rooms and go to great lengths to convince you that Lushan, tourist magnet that it is, really doesn't often offer rooms this cheap. But in reality, beds can be found for as little as Y30 a night. More comfortable options are especially plentiful. Considering Guling's navigable size, you might be well served to shop around among neighboring hotels for thrifty deals. This is easier if you leave the bulk of your luggage in Jiujiang, taking only a day-pack to the mountain.

When it comes to dining, Lushan strives for a touch of class. Street vendors are nowhere to be found, and most meals have a higher price tag than elsewhere in China. The standard 1-2 Chinese stir-fried dishes with rice generally range from Y20 to Y30, but don't expect anything fancy unless you head to a hotel. Most restaurants that line Hexi Lu are family-run and, late in the evening, complement the tasty food with smiles, lively chat, and plenty of laughter.

Popular Hotel (dàzhòng fàndiàn; 大众饭店 ; ☎ 828 5918), through an archway under a red sign, where Hemian Jie and Guling Jie meet, at the heart of the town. Reasonable for budget accommodations, with 3 comfy beds to a room. Shared bathroom not the prettiest. Foreigners may be directed to more comfortable lodgings; explain that you prefer lower prices and you'll be welcomed. 3-bed dorms Y30. ❶

Lushan Cloud City Hotel (lúshān yúnchéng bīnguǎn; 庐山云城宾馆), 3 Dalin Lu (☎828 2727; fax 828 7888). 3min. walk downhill from Hexi Lu. A very comfortable hotel, with soft beds, glistening bathrooms, high ceilings, wooden flooring, and furniture to match. Curfew 11pm. Doubles Y120 and up. Discounts are possible. ❷

Lushan Hotel (lúshān bīnguǎn; 庐山宾馆), 446 Hexi Lu (☎829 5203), 1km south of the bus station. Rooms are in removed villas with nice views. Singles Y260; doubles Y350; triples Y400. MC/V. ❹

Lushan West Lake Hotel (xī hú bīnguǎn; 西湖宾馆), 113 Dalin Lu (☎828 5850; fax 828 5810), a 10min. walk downhill from Hexi Lu, where Dalin Lu first meets Ruqin Lake. A large domed building with tall flapping flags at the entrance. This newly built hotel embraces old world colonial decor. Rooms are comfortable and clean, with TV, A/ C, fridge, and bath. Pricier rooms have excellent views across the lake. Singles and doubles Y600-880 and up. ❺

◎ SIGHTS

Countless Chinese ancients have spent long, contemplative chunks of their lives in Lushan, resulting in some legend or gushing poem associated with every cave, tree, and waterfall on the mountain. No single sight really stands out. Wandering the trails and soaking in the oft-extolled surroundings is the best way to explore the area, whether for a day or a week. (See **Hiking Lushan,** p. 443.)

The expansive Lushan area stretches far beyond the trail. Some of the most spectacular waterfalls and cliffs are hours away from Guling. Getting to these places requires the better part of the day. The easiest option, unless you'd prefer to join a tour group, is to hire a **minibus** (found opposite Jiexin Park). Nearby Guling also has a number of historical and cultural sights.

SANDIEQUAN FALLS (sāndiéquán pùbù; 三叠泉瀑布). Sheets of water crash down three rock shelves through a cloud of mist at Sandiequan Falls, justifiably Lushan's most famous spot. Viewing the falls involves a hike up and down some very steep steps, jostling Chinese tour groups on narrow paths, and constant taunting by human porters trying to convince you that you can't make it without a guide. But Sandiequan is definitely worth the hassle, especially after (or during) rainy weather, when people stay inside and the fog and mists isolate the waterfall into a world of its own. *(Hike 3hr. Admission Y43.)*

LUSHAN MUSEUM (lúshān bówùguǎn; 庐山博物馆). This museum conveniently combines in one location all the elements that make the mountain interesting: culture, Communism, and natural history. Highlights include Buddhist paintings, a *papier maché* model of the Lushan region, Mao Zedong's bedroom with his original furniture (including a surprisingly large bed), photos of dignitaries who have visited Lushan, and a room full of impaled insects to help you identify that monstrous beetle in your bathroom. Limited English captions. *(1 Lulin Lu. On Huanhu Lu, southwest of Lake Lulin. ☎828 2341. Open daily 8am-6pm. Free.)*

MEILU VILLA (měilú biéshù; 美庐别墅). The villa comfortably showcases an unusual mix-and-match of political history. Built at the turn of the 20th century by a British lord, the complex was sold during the early 1930s to Song Meiling, the wife of Chiang Kai-shek. After the ruling couple's exile, the villa passed unscathed into the hands of Communists. Now it lies firmly in the grasp of the tour groups, who jostle loudly through the hallways, giving it the atmosphere of an over-crowded house party gone awry. Limited English captions. *(180 Hedong Lu. Across the stream from Hexi Lu. Open daily summer 7:30am-10pm; winter 8am-6pm. Y15, students Y8.)*

LUSHAN CONFERENCE SITE (lúshān huìyì huìzhǐ; 庐山会议会址). The Camelot camaraderie among Long March cadres wilted here. During a conference here in 1959, Chairman Mao overruled the objections of his defense minister Peng Dehuai and steamrolled ahead with the **Great Leap Forward** (p. 80). A large auditorium has a stage arranged as it might have been during party meetings, with videos (in Chinese) that feature Mao, in all his fleshy glory, enjoying a swim in the Lushan lakes. *(504 Hexi Lu. At a right fork in the road, in front of a pond. ☎ 828 2584. Open daily 10am-10pm. Y10, students Y5.)*

🔵 HIKING LUSHAN

Hiking along the mountain paths and taking in the sights as you pass is perhaps the most enjoyable and rewarding approach to Lushan's nearby scenic spots. Though the sights themselves are chock-full of tour groups, peace and solitude can easily be found along the quiet stretches of road separating them. As you walk the paths, the only disturbances you'll hear are the horn-tooting buses ferrying tourists around the mountain. The views along the mountain's western and southern face, from the Xianren Cave to the Ancient Trees and onto Lake Luling, make the hike well worth the effort.

With an early start, most of the nearby attractions can be covered comfortably in a day. Because the trek circles the mountain, the trail conveniently deposits you back at the starting point once you finish. From Guling town center, one option is to travel downhill along Dalin Lu for about 15min. until you reach the large and shadowy **Zither Lake** (rúqín hú; 如琴湖), supposedly shaped like a zither. Follow the lake's eastern shore to a small cluster of shops, which mark the arched entrance to the Xianren Cave pathway. After 20min. or so of skirting stone steps past some beautiful, expansive views, you'll arrive at **Immortal Cave** (xiānrén dòng; 仙人洞), where legendary folk hero Lu Dongbin gained immortality. The cave is somewhat anticlimactic, but still worth a visit, if only to soak in the surrounding spiritual atmosphere and smell the fragrant clouds of burning incense.

Continue downhill past the swarms of taxis and tour buses and follow the thickly-forested, winding mountain road with its long grasses and gurgling streams for about 45min. to the entrance of the **Star Dragon Ropeway** (xīnglóng suǒdào; 星龙索道), which leads to the **Stone Door Waterfall** (shímén pùbù;石门瀑布). (Ascent Y50, descent Y30, children Y10.) A small, discreet pathway, running behind the entrance to the ropeway, takes hikers to a short but steep uphill stretch through forests to the **Three Ancient Trees** (sān bǎo shù; 三宝树). Protected by fencing, these massive, towering giants are crowned kings of the forest, a status reinforced by the many visitors squinting in awe at the distant top-most branches. Of the three trees, two are said to be over 600 years old. The third, just beginning to show a few tell-tale signs of aging, has been around for about 1600 years. Down the hill from the Ancient Trees, two streams flow together to form the serene **Dragon Pools** (lóngchí; 龙池). Not far is the **Yellow Dragon Temple** (huáng lóng sì; 黄龙寺).

From here it's another 10min. of taxing forest steps. Continuing straight brings you to a parking lot, where you can stock up on water, or indulge in an ice-cream reward for getting through the toughest uphill slog. Plenty of taxis are available at this point for legs that refuse to walk farther.

A short and easy downhill road, leading left as you face out from the parking lot, brings you to the calming waters of **Lake Lulin** (lúlín hú; 庐林湖), set within mountains of swaying evergreens. The lake is an idyllic resting spot and the last point along the hike before you rejoin the noisy crowds.

Follow the perimeter of the lake, along Huanshan Lu (环山路), passing the **Monument to Mao Zedong's Poems,** and veer right to reach the **Lushan Museum,** also known as **Mao Zedong's Former Residence.** Taking a left at this junction will put you directly on the road back to Guling, though to reach **Lushan Conference Site,** you will need to turn left on Jiu Zhong Lu (九中路). A further 30min. of uphill walking, past **Meilu Villa,** will bring you safely back to your point of origin. (See **Sights,** p. 442, for more information on these.)

JINGGANGSHAN MOUNTAIN 井冈山 ☎0796

Dense, wet forests blanket most of the Jinggangshan mountain range, which sprawls nearly 700km between Hunan and Jiangxi provinces. Seemingly anything could hide in these forest valleys, which is precisely why the battered Communist army convened here before breaking through the GMD blockades and retreating on the Long March. Because of this brief but hugely significant historical congregation, Jinggangshan is known as "the cradle of the Chinese Revolution." Mao Zedong brought his Autumn Harvest Uprising troops here in 1927, joining forces with the remnants of Zhu De's troops from the Nanchang Uprising and Peng Dehuai's up-and-coming legion of soldiers. The leaders and their armies established residences in Jinggangshan's main village, Ciping, and other nearby towns. While most of their homes and outposts were subsequently destroyed by GMD reactionaries, the Chinese government has since resurrected the most important sites, turning Ciping into a scenic, orderly village.

Its remote, aesthetic appeal, however, is under threat from aggressive over-tourism. The village's infrastructure panders solely and unapologetically to the desires of packaged tour companies, ignoring, if not aggravating, those who try to foot it alone. Though the city may change, it clings fast to the unwavering Mao spirit. His portrait adorns the walls in most restaurants and hotels. It seems no matter where you turn in Jinggangshan, the Chairman is watching.

ORIENTATION AND PRACTICAL INFORMATION

The town of **Ciping** (茨坪), sometimes called **Jinggangshan City**, is small enough to be traversed in 30min. In the middle of the village, **Yicuihu Park** contains a large pond with an island pavilion and a pagoda on the south side. The large golden **Monument to the Jinggangshan Revolutionary Martyrs** sits atop a hill at the north end of town and is useful for getting your bearings, as long as the mist isn't too thick.

From the long-distance bus station in the northeast corner of town, the commercial **Tongmuling Lu** (桐木岭路) runs south down the hill, forking east and south along Yicuihu Park, becoming **Nanshan Lu** (南山路). On the other side of Nanshan Lu is **Nanshan Park** (nánshān gōng yuán; 南山公园), with a large pagoda in its center. **Hongjun Lu** (红军路) runs north-south along the west side of the parks. **Zhongxin Dajie** (中心大街) crosses Yicuihu Park from east to west and is parallel to **Wujing Lu** (五井路), which runs toward the bus station.

Trains: Jinggangshan Train Station (jīnggāngshān huǒchē zhàn; 井冈山火车站) is actually in Taihe, a 3hr. minibus ride from the mountain. From Taihe, buses leave for Jinggangshan approx. every hr. 6:30am-2 or 3pm; flag one down on the main street. From Jinggangshan, the last express bus leaves for Taihe around 12:30pm, the last regular bus around 2pm. Fare either way is Y25. Most visitors to Jinggangshan prefer to use the **Ji'an Train Station** (jí'ān huǒchē zhàn; 吉安火车站). Take a bus from Ciping bus station (3hr., every 30min. 6am-4 or 5pm, Y23) to Ji'an, and then take the #2 bus (45min., Y1) from the bus stop to the train station.

Buses: Jinggangshan Long-Distance Bus Station (jīnggāngshān chángtú qìchē zhàn; 井冈山长途汽车站), on the corner of Wujing Lu and Tongmuling Lu. To: **Changsha** (8-9hr., 12:15pm, Y76); **Nanchang** (5hr., 3 per day, Y61.5).

Local Transportation: As Ciping is quite a small town, anything local is within easy walking distance. For small groups or lone travelers, joining a tour group may be the only affordable, feasible option to access the mountain's more remote sights. No reliable, regular bus services to the outside attractions exist, and taxi fares tend to be steep.

Travel Agencies: Jinggangshan seems to have lost local tourist business to travel agents based in large cities, which forces visitors to make all travel arrangements for tour groups in advance. Helpful advice is available from the **ticket station** next to the Bank of China on Nanshan Lu.

Tourist Hotlines: Complaints ☎ 655 6108. **First aid** 655 2595. **Info** 655 2626.

Bank of China: 6 Nanshan Lu (☎ 655 2571), near the southwest tip of Yicuihu Park. Exchanges traveler's checks. **24hr. ATM.** Open M-F 8am-5:30pm.

PSB: (☎ 655 2360) in a pink building on Hongjun Nan Lu, 5min. south past the intersection with Nanshan Lu.

Hospital: Jiangxi Jinggangshan Chinese Medicine Hospital (jiāngxī jǐnggāngshān zhōngyīyuàn; 江西井冈山中医院), 47 Hongjun Nan Lu (daytime ☎ 655 2268, evening 655 3022).

Telephones: China Telecom, in a towering office about 100m south of Yicuihu Park. Open daily 8am-6:30pm.

Internet Access: Happiness E-Bar (kuàilè E-bā; 快乐 E吧), across the street from the bus station, facing out onto Tongmuling Lu. Speedy terminals. Quieter than most cafes. Y2 per hr. Open daily 8am-1am.

Post Office: (☎ 655 2896). On the left as you walk down south on Tongmuling Lu, where it becomes Nanshan Lu and meets Zhongxin Dajie. EMS and Poste Restante. Open daily 8am-5:30pm.

Postal Code: 343600.

ACCOMMODATIONS

If you've seen one hotel in Jinggangshan, you've pretty much seen them all. The variety is slim, with almost all hotels aiming for middle- to high-range comforts and prices. Unlike hotels elsewhere in China, Jinggangshan's otherwise identical establishments tend to fill up quickly, especially on weekends, so it is important to book in advance. This leaves the visitor in a weaker bargaining position, but strive for 20-30% discounts nonetheless.

Red Star Hotel (hóng xīng bīnguǎn; 红星宾馆), 18 Tongmuling Lu (☎ 655 9097). Around the corner from the bus station, about 5 doors down on the right. The 2nd fl. has the best deals in town. Very large, blue-carpeted, well-furnished rooms have fans instead of A/C. Doubles and triples Y150, but even on summer weekends, you can get 20-30% discounts. In winter, aim for 50% reductions. ❷

Minzheng Hotel (mín zhèng bīnguǎn; 民政宾馆 ; ☎ 655 2883), near Nanshan Park, next to a red-brick bldg., downhill behind China Telecom. Among the cheapest deals in town, but you get what you pay for. Basic and unattractive rooms. The cheapest "beds" (Y60) are in a large room full of mattresses on the floor. Midnight curfew. Book in advance. 8-bed dorms Y80; singles and doubles Y268. ❶

Gold Leaf Hotel (jīn yè dàshà; 金叶大厦), 30 Hongjun Bei Lu (☎ 655 8086). Bright and spacious rooms, a favorite among the tour groups. Doubles are comfortable and clean, but overpriced. Singles Y560; doubles Y470; triples Y660. ❺

Jinggangshan Guesthouse (jǐnggāngshān bīnguǎn; 景冈山宾馆), 10 Hongjun Bei Lu (☎ 655 2618 or 655 2272; fax 655 2551), above a long stone wall and accessible by a ramp leading up from the road. Light wooden furniture and thick, comfy carpets bring a cozy atmosphere to these rooms. Fridge, TV, A/C, and well-scrubbed baths. Very friendly staff. Singles Y400; doubles Y580. ❺

🍴 FOOD

Inexpensive restaurants can be found on nearly every corner. Those interested in an authentic Communist experience can live like the Red Army did and subsist on puny portions of the local specialty **red rice** (hóng mǐfàn; 红米饭) and **pumpkin soup** (nánguā tāng; 南瓜汤). Otherwise, a **fresh food market** down the hill to the left of the China Telecom office sells raw meat and veggies. The road leading downhill from the bus station has a few small places to eat, and a number of quick-fry stands congregate near the post office and at the east end of **Zhongyang Dajie.** The street that drops below and to the right at the north end of Hongjun Lu is crammed with outdoor eateries that cook up Jinggangshan specialties, including roasted pheasant (shānjī; 山鸡; Y60 per *jīn*), sautéed frog (qīngwā; 青蛙; Y60 per *jīn*), and just-picked **Red Army lettuce** (hóngjūn cài; 红军菜) with mint (Y15). Fresh vegetables and caged animals greet you at the entrance to the wonderfully warm, family-run ■ **Red Rice Restaurant ❷** (hóng mǐfàn dà jiǔdiàn; 红米饭大酒店), immediately left as you face the entrance to the bus stop. In the evenings, locals gather to share food and chat in the friendly atmosphere—if you're lucky they may even serenade you with revolutionary songs. Steep prices on the menu are quickly reduced for friendly customers. (☎655 5706. Most dishes Y20 and up. Open daily 8am-1am.)

👁 SIGHTS

Within Ciping, all the sights are easily accessible by foot. Unfortunately, much of Jinggangshan's most renowned scenery is outside the immediate area, beyond the reach of public transportation. To make matters worse, the sights are spread far apart, making cumulative **taxi** fares a complete budget burner. For larger groups, it might be worthwhile to charter one of the **minivans** near the ticket station on Nan Shan Lu and bargain for transport to distant sights. Prices vary according to season and destination, so it's a good idea to ask in advance at the ticket office for what a reasonable taxi fare should be. The only remaining option is joining a **tour group.** Find one before coming to Jinggangshan, as the local travel agencies and tour group services have all lost out to big companies based in major cities.

To gain entry to Jinggangshan's sights, you must first purchase a ticket at one of the four **ticket stations** (piàozhàn; 票站). Tickets are valid for three days and grant access to all of Jinggangshan's major attractions. There are ticket stations at the north, south, and west gates on the main roads approaching Ciping, and another centrally located on Nanshan Lu, next door to the Bank of China. (Open daily 8am-6pm. Entry Y100, students Y80; individual sights Y30 each.)

CITY SIGHTS

MONUMENT TO THE JINGGANGSHAN REVOLUTIONARY MARTYRS (jǐnggāngshān gémìng lièshì jìniàntǎ; 井冈山革命列士记念塔). In addition to the shimmering, angular sculpture representing a torch, the complex is also home to the **Revolutionary Martyrs' Cemetery,** a memorial hall inscribed with 15,744 names. The **Forest of Steles** has slabs of poetry inscribed with calligraphy by national leaders and celebrities, and the **sculpture garden** features 19 statues of early CCP leaders, including an especially virile-looking Mao Zedong. The site is not terribly interesting in its own right, but the views across the valley are worth the hike. The entrance to the monument is just up the hill to the west of the bus station; follow the loop trail to see all the sites. (*At the northern end of Ciping, towering atop a hill. Open daily 8am-5pm.*)

JINGGANGSHAN REVOLUTIONARY MUSEUM (jǐnggāngshān gémìng bówùguǎn; 井冈山革命博物馆). This museum houses an impressive collection of papers, photographs, maps, scale models, old uniforms, books, and weapons. English narrations are nowhere to be found, but the photos and relics speak for themselves. *(In the southwest part of Ciping.* ☎ *655 2449. Open daily 8am-5:30pm, last admission 5pm.)*

COMRADE MAO ZEDONG'S RESIDENCE (máo zédōng tóngzhì gùjū; 毛泽东同志 故居). Rebuilt after being burned down by the Nationalists, these former living quarters offer much insight into the primitive living conditions of the early revolutionaries, featuring luxuries like threadbare uniforms and rock-hard mattresses. The dimly lit caves seek to recapture the appropriate mood of stark solemnity. A plaque across from Mao's quarters explains the "traditions of Mt. Jinggang," a list of the CCP principles of toil and struggle. *(About 50m north of China Telecom; look for the yellow walls. Open daily 8am-6pm.)*

OUTSIDE JINGGANGSHAN

All listed sights are open during daylight hours and are among the sights accessible with the purchase of the Y100 common ticket.

HUANGYANGJIE (huángyáng jiè; 黄洋界). Originally an army post in the Mao era, this lookout point is now a favorite spot for sunrise-seekers and landscape-lovers. Perched 1343m above sea level, it offers spectacular views of the surrounding terrain. On foggy days the entire area is like a sea of clouds. *(A 20min. drive northwest of Jinggangshan.* ☎ *655 3520.)*

FIVE FINGERS PEAK (wǔzhǐ fēng; 五指峰). The Five Fingers Peak, most commonly seen plastered on the Y100 bill, can be seen life-sized here. On a clear day, the peak offers a magnificent panoramic view. *(At Huangyangjie.* ☎ *655 7667.)*

FIVE DRAGON POOLS (wǔlóng tán; 五龙潭). The Five Dragon Pools are a series of drooping valleys with five gushing waterfalls and winding paths through mystical water curtains. Poetic names like "fairy waterfall" and "rainbow curtain" grace spots in this mountainous and rocky area. Those short on time or eager to see everything can use the steep cable car ride (Y50) that goes past some main waterfalls and sights. *(7km from Jinggangshan City.* ☎ *655 3459.)*

HUNAN 湖南

Green fields, wandering cattle, farmers bent over paddy fields in the scalding sun—Hunan is the postcard image of China. Born in Shaoshan, Mao Zedong grew up in this iconic corner of China and learned the ABCs of Communism as a young revolutionary in Changsha, Hunan's capital. Apart from stops along the well-beaten Mao pilgrimage, this heartland province lays claim to the eerie, fog-enshrouded stone outcroppings of Zhangjiajie in the northwest, the lakeside city of Yueyang in the northeast, and the pine-forested peaks of Hengshan in the southeast. Several ethnic minorities, including Miao, Tujia, Dong, and Uighur (see **Peoples, Minority Nationalities,** p. 86), inhabit the border regions of the province.

CHANGSHA 长沙 ☎ 0731

The provincial capital of Changsha has had a long and intimate relationship with the ancient Chu Kingdom of the Warring States period (475-221 BC), building off both its literary richness and revolutionary fervor. Now, most people think of Mao Zedong when Changsha comes to mind, but the city has a smorgasbord of histori-

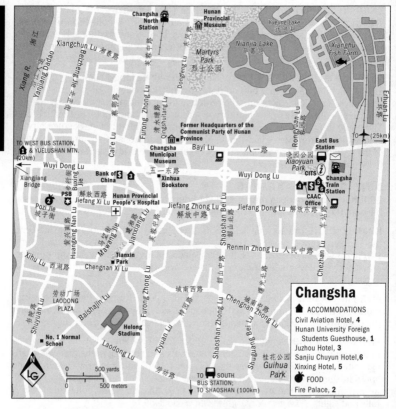

Changsha

🏠 ACCOMMODATIONS
Civil Aviation Hotel, **4**
Hunan University Foreign
  Students Guesthouse, **1**
Juzhou Hotel, **3**
Sanjiu Chuyun Hotel, **6**
Xinxing Hotel, **5**

🍴 FOOD
Fire Palace, **2**

cal delicacies, from the tomb of a 2100-year-old mummy to assorted Communist pilgrimage sites. Beyond Changsha's industrial facade, a pastoral side beckons under the scalding sun from the surrounding fields and Yuelu Mountain.

▣ TRANSPORTATION

Flights: Huanghua International Airport (chángshā huánghuā guójì jīchǎng; 长沙黄花 国际机场 ; ☎479 7255 or 411 9821), 25km east of Changsha. A taxi from the airport to town costs Y120. Buses (every 30min. 6am-8pm, Y13) shuttle between the airport and the **CAAC ticket office,** 75 Wuyi Dong Lu (☎411 2222 or 415 5777), next to the Aviation Hotel. Open daily 7:30am-10:30pm. **China Southern Airlines** (zhōngguó nán-fāng hángkōng gōngsī; 中国南方航空公司 ; ☎228 8320) has a ticket office outside the entrance to the train station. Open 8am-8pm. To: **Beijing** (7 per day, Y1210); **Chengdu** (4-5 per day, Y910); **Chongqing** (4-5 per day, Y740); **Guangzhou** (4-5 per day, Y690); **Kunming** (3 per day, Y650-980); **Nanjing** (1-2 per day, Y840); **Shanghai** (4-5 per day, Y890); **Xi'an** (3-4 per day, Y890).

Trains: Changsha Train Station (chángshā huǒchē zhàn; 长沙火车站 ; ☎229 6421), at Wuyi Dong Lu and Chezhan Lu, in the eastern part of town. Ticket window open 7am-10pm. To: **Beijing** (19-21hr., 10 per day, Y191); **Guangzhou** (9-11hr., 18-20 per day,

Y99); **Guilin** (9-11hr., 2 per day, Y76); **Kunming** (22-24hr., 5-6 per day, Y191); **Shanghai** (16-18hr., 9 per day, Y154); **Shenzhen** (12hr., 5 per day, Y147); **Tianjin** (10-12hr., daily, Y203); **Wuhan** (4-6hr., 5-6 per day, Y54); **Xi'an** (16-19hr., 2 per day, Y175); **Zhangjiajie** (6-7hr., 2 per day, Y41-99).

Buses: The **East Bus Station** (qìchē dōng zhàn; 汽车东站 ; ☎461 1731), on the east end of Bayi Lu. Accessible by bus #126 from the train station. To **Wuhan** (4hr., Y135) and **Yueyang** (2hr., Y55). The **South Bus Station** (qìchē nán zhàn; 汽车南站 ; ☎228 2816) is considerably south of the city on Shaoshan Nan Lu; take bus #7 or 107 from the train station. Open 5:30am-8:30pm. To **Guangzhou** (12hr., Y60) and **Hengyang** (3hr., every 30min. 7am-6pm, Y60). Buses to **Zhangjiajie** (6-7hr., 1:40pm, Y101) leave from the **West Bus Station** (qìchē xī zhàn; 汽车西站 ; ☎881 6553), on Fenglin Er Lu; take bus #312 from the train station.

Local Transportation: Most **buses** run 6am-8pm, but some minibuses and buses that serve the train station have extended hours. Fare Y1, with A/C Y2. Bus #202 runs from the train station to Yuelu Academy with stops near Hunan Teacher's College and Hunan University. The **Lishan Bus Line** (lìshān zhuān xiàn; 立珊专线) runs from the train station to Yuelu Academy via the Xiang River Bridge (xiāng jiāng dàqiáo; 湘江大桥).

Taxis: Base fare Y8, each additional km Y1.6.

✹ ⁊ ORIENTATION AND PRACTICAL INFORMATION

Most of Changsha lies on the eastern edge of the flood-prone **Xiang River.** The main train and bus stations are east of the city center. From the train station area, **Wuyi Lu** (五一路), also called **Wuyi Dadao** (五一大道), is the main east-west thoroughfare. West of the Xiang River, the road becomes **Fenglin Lu** (枫林路). **Cai'e Lu** (蔡鄂路) runs north-south and intersects Wuyi Lu. Apart from the Yuelu Mountains and Hunan University, most points of interest are in the city's eastern half.

Travel Agencies: CITS, Xiaoyuan Bldg., 8 Wuyi Dong Lu, 11th fl. (☎228 3610), near the train station. All-inclusive tour to Zhangjiajie Y720. Open daily 8am-6pm.

Bank of China: 43 Wuyi Dong Lu (☎417 2950), near the train station. Exchanges US$, euros, and traveler's checks. Open daily 8am-5:30pm.

Bookstore: Xinhua Bookstore, 338 Furong Lu (☎430 8590). Take bus #9 from the train station. Classic English novels. Open daily 8am-7:30pm.

PSB: 445 Huangxing Nan Lu (☎517 5620), at Jiefang Lu. Open daily 8am-noon and 2:30-6pm. Processes visa extensions.

Hospital: Hunan Provincial People's Hospital (húnánshěng rénmín yīyuàn; 湖南省人民医院), 28 Dongmao Jie (☎227 8071), on the southern side of Jiefang Xi Lu before reaching Cai'e Lu. Take bus #112 from the train station.

Internet Access: Golden Internet Cafe (jīnyīntè wǎngbā; 金因特网吧 ; ☎411 9278), on the 2nd fl. of the Sanjiu Chuyun Hotel (see **Accommodations and Food,** below), directly opposite the train station. Bright signs. Y3 per hr. Open 24hr.

Post Office: Changsha Post Office, on the north side of the train station square. EMS. Open daily 8am-8pm.

Postal Code: 410001.

⌂ ACCOMMODATIONS

Restrictions on foreigners are still imposed at many of Changsha's cheapest establishments; hotels open to foreigners tend to be of the upper-tier. Lodgings near the train station and around Wuyi Lu and Bayi Lu are convenient but expensive.

WHAT'S YOUR POISON?

What to do with all the snakes slithering around the mountains of China? Well, one solution is to chuck the slippery reptiles into a particularly potent alcoholic beverage. *Shé jiǔ* (蛇酒; snake wine) is easy to spot: look for large bottles with dubiously darkened glass. The giveaway feature is the large, perfectly preserved snake coiled inside the bottle.

After the snake is killed, various herbal ingredients are added, including angelica, wolfberry, and surprisingly—papaya. The resulting concoction is left to mature for three months to a year. If you're particularly lucky, you might find as many as three serpents squeezed into a bottle. Prices range from Y260 for smaller sizes to Y5000, which buys you a vat of the brew, complete with a sizeable constrictor wrapped up cozily inside. Cheaper snake wine is also available at Y30 per bottle, but sadly, at this price the snake is not included. Still, it might be a preferable alternative to explaining your bottle-preserved pythons to suspicious customs officials.

At 45% proof, the alcohol is strong enough to evaporate on your lips if you take tiny sips. Those who hazard a mouthful can expect a sharp burning sensation. Be warned—it delivers a powerful punch. The taste, of course, depends on the tongue. But if it's novelty you crave, snake wine will certainly quench your thirst.

Xinxing Hotel (xīnxīng dàjiǔdiàn; 新兴大酒店), 1 Wuyi Dong Lu (☎417 7288, ext. 2001; fax 411 0522), directly opposite the train station. Clean rooms with A/C and private bath tend to fill up by the early evening. Doubles 128-168. ❷

Sanjiu Chuyun Hotel (sānjiǔ chǔyún dàjiǔdiàn; 三九楚云大酒店), 239 Chezhan Zhong Lu (☎419 1999; fax 419 1399), directly across from the train station, facing the ticket office. Doubles Y128-138; triples Y168 and up. ❷

Civil Aviation Hotel (mínháng dàjiǔdiàn; 民航大酒店), 47 Wuyi Dong Lu (☎417 0288; fax 417 0388). CAAC office in the same building. A clean and spacious escape from the crowds at the eastern end of Wuyi Dong Lu. Call before noon if you want a guaranteed room on the same day. Doubles with A/C and private bath Y128-168. ❷

Hunan University Foreign Students Guesthouse (húnán dàxué wàibīn zhāodàisuǒ; 湖南大学外宾招待所 ; ☎882 3942). The well-furnished dorm offers a quiet stay west of the river near the base of Yuelu Mountain. Clean rooms and airy hallways. Price negotiable for extended stays. Doubles with A/C and private bath Y160. ❷

Juzhou Hotel (jùzhōu jiǔdiàn; 巨洲酒店), 1 Wuyi Xi Lu (☎268 0388), at Jianxiang Nan Lu. Take bus #9 from the train station to Wuyi Dadao. Rooms aren't spectacular, but the location is conveniently close to the city's commercial center. A/C, TV, private bath. Reservations recommended. Singles and doubles Y100-138; triples Y130. MC/V. ❷

🍴 🎵 FOOD AND ENTERTAINMENT

Visitors to Changsha should always be sure to have an ample supply of tissues and a gigantic jug of something cool to drink. The local cuisine is flavored with enough spice and hot pepper to make anyone's nose run; supposedly, Mao liked it that way. **Spicy chicken** (all parts included) and **stinky tofu** (chòu dòufǔ; 臭豆腐) are favorites, and every year in Changsha is the Year of the **Snake**—at least for more adventurous diners. These Hunanese treats can be found across the street west of the train station along Chezhan Zhong Lu and also one block farther west along Chaoyang Lu. Another hot spot for food is Yanshan Jie, one block south of Bayi Lu near Shaoshan Lu. The narrow lane has fruit stands and restaurants serving stir-fried vegetables and noodle dishes for rarely more than Y10 per meal. Farther west along Huangxing Lu, south of Wuyi Dong Lu, restaurants offer everything from wonton soup (húntun tāng; 馄饨汤) to stuffed bean crepes (dòupí;

豆皮). Local delicacies include just about anything that's edible—pig blood (zhūxuě; 猪血), duck liver (yāgān; 鸭肝), and various cow bits (niúbiān; 牛鞭) all make their way into the pot and onto the plate.

Perhaps the best Hunanese cuisine can be found at the **Fire Palace ❷** (huǒ gōngdiàn jiǔjiā; 火宫殿酒家), 78 Pozi Jie, guarded by a traditional red gate temple facade. Take bus #12 to Wuyi Guangchang (Wuyi Sq.), walk down Huangxing Lu, and turn right at the sign; Fire Palace is a block down toward the river. The smelly tofu here garnered praise from Mao during his historic visit in 1958. Its other branch is at 105 Wuyi Dong Lu. (☎581 4228. Appetizers Y4-10. Meals Y12-38. Open daily 7:30am-11:30pm.) Those less daring with their food can fall back on steaks and burgers at the **Mona Lisa Restaurant ❸** (méngnà lìshā zhōngxī cāntīng; 蒙娜丽莎中西餐厅), 458 Furong Zhong Lu, near Renmin Zhong Lu. Part of a five-store chain in Changsha, the Mona Lisa serves a wide variety of Western and Chinese cuisine, with live bands starting at 8pm. (☎516 3222. Entrees Y20-40. Set meals around Y60. Beer Y20-22. Cocktails Y28. Open daily 7am-2am.)

🜨 SIGHTS

🜨 HUNAN PROVINCIAL MUSEUM (húnánshěng bówùguǎn; 湖南省博物馆). Most people come here to check out the 2100-year-old corpse of a Han Dynasty woman that was unearthed in 1972. Evidence and observations regarding her final moments (she died soon after consuming a musk melon) decorate the walls. The faint-hearted might want to skip the large color photographs of the corpse as well as the glass jars carefully preserving her internal organs. The exhibition halls also hold other relics, including embroidered silk tapestries, paintings, early bronze vessels, lacquerware, and world-class collections of Ming and Qing paintings. English captions make this museum easily accessible. (28 Dongfeng Lu. Take bus #202 to Tianxin Park and transfer to bus #901; get off at the Bówùguǎn stop. ☎ 451 3123. Free English tours: call ☎453 5566, ext. 8605 to reserve a guide 3-4 days in advance. Open daily Apr.-Nov. 8am-6pm; Dec.-Mar. 8:30am-5:30pm. Y50, students Y25.)

NO. 1 NORMAL SCHOOL (dìyī shīfàn; 第一师范). Mao's old alma mater, the No. 1 Normal School, dates back to a major academy of the Southern Song Dynasty. Besides Mao, the teachers' college has witnessed many other famous revolutionaries and 20th-century intellectuals in its halls. Photographs of a college-age Mao fill the **Young Mao Zedong Museum** (qīngnián máozédōng jìniànguǎn; 青年毛泽东纪念馆). The large cluster of teaching buildings remain in use today. From classroom 8, where Mao studied, you might even catch snatches of traditional zither music from art students practicing in the adjacent building. (Take bus #1 from the train station to Diyi Shifan. ☎515 7430. Open 8am-5:30pm. Y6.)

YUELUSHAN MOUNTAIN (yuèlù shān; 岳麓山). A trip to this picturesque park is part nature hike and part cultural history lesson: famous ancient philosophers lived here, and modern revolutionaries are buried here. The "mountain" is really more of a large hill, scattered with the graves of notables. In his younger days Mao liked to hang out at **Aiwan Pavilion** (àiwǎn tíng; 爱晚亭); after he attained chairmanship, he came back and happily inscribed a stone tablet with his own poetry. (Take bus #202 or the Lishan bus from the train station to the Yuelu Gongyuan stop. Turn right from the bus stop and walk up the hill, past the Mao statue; keep left. Trolleys stopping here head into the park for Y5. ☎882 5011. Cable car up Y15, down Y13, round-trip Y23. Open daily 24hr. Y15.)

Just before the East Gate is **Yuelu Academy** (yuèlù shūyuàn; 岳麓书院), established in AD 976 as one of the four most outstanding institutions of the period. Although it's no longer a school, the traditional architecture and calligraphic inscriptions bear witness to its status. Stroll through the quiet bamboo-lined paths and find courtyard after courtyard of rooms where Chinese literati once studied. *(Take the Lishan bus to the Yuelu Academy Stop. ☎882 2316. Front door open daily 8am-7pm; back door 8am-5:30pm. Y30, students Y15.)*

CHANGSHA MUNICIPAL MUSEUM (chángshāshì bówùguǎn; 长沙市博物馆). A large, faded portrait of Mao marks the entrance to this small museum. The current exhibit displays photographs of Mao and his first wife, Yang Kaihui, along with the letters they exchanged. *(Exhibit continues until 2006. No English captions.)* The nearby **Former Headquarters of the Communist Party of Hunan Province** (zhōnggòng xiāngqū wěihuì jiùzhǐ; 中共湘区委会旧址) is also the former home of the subjects of the exhibits, Mao and Yang. *(480 Bayi Lu. Take bus #1 from the train station to Qingshuitang. ☎222 3498. Open daily 8am-5:30pm. Both sights Y10, students Y5.)*

OTHER SIGHTS. On the southeastern bank of the Xiang River, **Tianxin Park** (tiānxīn gōngyuán; 天心公园) contains one of the last remnants of the old city walls. Built during the Ming Dynasty, much of the wall was ruined during the Taiping Rebellion in Changsha in 1850. The 13m-tall wall you see today is partly rebuilt. *(On the corner of Jianxiang Nan Lu and Chengnan Xi Lu. Take bus #202 from the train station to Tianxin Gongyuan. ☎222 2404. Open daily 6am-10pm. Park Y2; pavilion Y8.)* The **Martyrs' Park** (lièshì gōngyuán; 烈士公园), with lakes, pagodas, and shaded walks, is the perfect place to get a breath of fresh air after visiting the macabre Hunan Provincial Museum. The Martyrs' Memorial pays homage to those who died for the Communist cause but may have little appeal for those whose Chinese is not up to task. *(The west entrance is a short walk from the Provincial Museum along Dongfeng Lu. From Tianxin Gongyuan take bus #901 to Lieshi Gongyuan. ☎451 3029. Open 6am-10:30pm. Free.)*

◤ DAYTRIPS FROM CHANGSHA

SHAOSHAN 韶山

*100km from Changsha. A **train** runs from Changsha daily (3-4hr.; departing 6:40am, returning 4:55pm; Y11). **Buses** leave from Changsha's South Bus Station (3hr.; every hr. 7am-6pm, last bus returns at 5pm; Y20). **Minibuses** (every 10min. or when full, Y1.5) leave from the Shaoshan train station to the sights area, in the village part of Shaoshan (gùjū; 故居). Staff at Mao's childhood home will provide free English tours of the small building and Nan'an school; enquire at entrance. Guides on the train and at the station may offer Y10 tours, but these are in Chinese. Area code: ☎0732.*

Shaoshan looks like the China you see in the movies. Green farmlands stretch as far as the eye can see in the quiet countryside, and terraced hillsides and rice paddies parade alongside the road to Shaoshan, the exalted birthplace of Mao Zedong. At the height of Mao's popularity in the 1960s, each day more than 8000 groupies paid homage to the Chairman's hometown, probably the most important Communist pilgrimage site in the country. As the fanaticism fizzled in the aftermath of the Cultural Revolution, so too did tourism to Shaoshan. Today, many new sights have been built, and vendors hawk plastic kitsch bearing the Chairman's beaming face.

While memorials and parks dedicated to you-know-who are seemingly everywhere, only three are original haunts of Mao in his sprightly youth. **Mao's childhood home** (máo zédōng tóngzhì gùjū; 毛泽东同志故居) is just outside the main village square. From the train station, take the road leading to the right after entering the village, past the souvenir market, or follow the signs in English and Chinese. The surprisingly roomy interior still has a couple of old threshing tools and beds. In summer, lotus flowers fill the pond in front of the house. (Open 8am-5:30pm. Free.) Climb up the wooden staircase of **Nan'an School** (nán'àn sīshú; 南岸私塾) to the second-floor classroom where Mao received his very first years of schooling. His seat is the second from the window, marked by a plaque. Downstairs is the headmaster's spacious room and wooden bed. (Open 8am-5:30pm. Y10.)

You can meet the mighty Mao clan at **Dripping Water Cave** (dīshuǐ dòng; 滴水洞). A steep 20min. hike to the top of Dragon Head Hill (lóngtóushān; 龙头山) arrives at the grave of Mao's great-grandfather; near the exit, a path on the right leads to Mao's ancestral tombs. The Chairman himself came here in June 1966 for a retreat. The park doesn't actually contain any caves, but it does provide a view of the surrounding countryside and an escape from Mao kitsch. *(Motorcycles make the trip for Y10 from the parking lot with the Mao statue. Open daily 8am-5:30pm. Y30.)*

If you just can't get enough of the Chairman, Shaoshan has more than enough museums and reproductions to satisfy your craving. A few hundred meters into the village, a large Mao statue marks the center of town. Directly opposite the statue, the **Mao Zedong Geneology Museum** (máo zédōng cí; 毛泽东祠) traces Mao's family history back to a Ming patriot who fought the Mongols. (Chinese captions only. Open daily 8am-5:30pm. Y10.) To the left is the **Museum of Comrade Mao** (máo zédōng tóngzhì jìniànguǎn; 毛泽东同志纪念馆). Though in Chinese, ample audiovisuals manage to keep all travelers interested. (Open summer daily 7:30am-5:30pm; winter 8am-5pm. Y10.) Southwest of the village area, the **Shaofeng Scenic Area** (sháofēng jǐngqū; 韶峰景区) contains the **Poetry of Mao Zedong Stele Park** (máo zédōng shīcí bēilín; 毛泽东诗词碑林), a large collection of Mao's poetry and calligraphy inscribed onto stone. (Motorcycles run from parking lot to scenic area for Y5-8. Cable car 8am-4:30pm; round-trip Y22. Open daily 8am-5pm. Y22.)

Tourists on organized tours of Shaoshan often visit **Liu Shaoqi's Childhood Home and Former Residence** (liúshàoqí jìniànguǎn; 刘少奇纪念馆), halfway between Changsha and Shaoshan. Another native of Hunan, Liu Shaoqi was the second-in-command under Mao in the 1950s and 60s, but was never as popular as his superior. This large park is architecturally more impressive than any of the Mao sights in Shaoshan and is also home to several museums. *(About a 50min. drive away. The only way to reach the park is by taxi or tour. Open daily 8am-6pm. Y28.)*

The main sights generally take 3-4hr. to see. Should you be stranded in this stronghold of Mao memorabilia, you'll find yourself at the mercy of pricey hotels. The **Shaofeng Hotel** (sháofēng bīnguǎn; 韶峰宾馆) is across from the Mao Zedong library next to Mao's childhood home. (☎568 5073. Singles with A/C and private bath Y130-298; doubles Y150-268.) To finish off your day with the Chairman, tuck into a plateful of his favorite food, roasted pork (hóngshāo ròu; 红烧肉), lovingly prepared by scores of restaurants along the streets near the Mao statue.

HENGSHAN 衡山

310km south of Changsha. Trains from Changsha (2hr., many per day, Y11-22) run to Hengshan Train Station. Frequent buses to Nanyue depart near the train station in Changsha (3hr., about Y30). To ascend, follow Zhurong Lu as it winds right onto Jinsha Lu to the main entrance; a taxi ride from the bottom of Zhurong Lu to the entrance is about Y5. The ticket office is farther up the road to the left, in the foothills past the Nanyue Great Temple (nányuè dà miào; 南岳大庙). Minibus to the summit Y12. Cable car to summit up Y30, down Y25, round-trip Y50. Open 24hr. Y80, students Y41.

It is no surprise that ancient Daoists made Hengshan Mountain (also known as *nányuè*; 南岳 ; "southern peak") a center for spiritual enlightenment. On the soaring cable-car approach to the summit, the mountain greets you with a breathless rush of awe, as the pine forest beneath your feet suddenly vanishes to reveal a dizzyingly deep valley. The mountain range stretches from Hengyang in the south all the way to Yuelushan Mountain in Changsha, but Hengshan (1290m) is the tallest and most famous of the 72 peaks. The mountain is known not only for its serene natural beauty, but also for the poetry and calligraphic engravings on its stelae.

Climbing the mountain is moderately difficult and takes about 4hr. The way up is dotted with a steady stream of Daoist and Buddhist temples. From the halfway point at **Xuandu Temple** (xuándū sì; 玄都寺), a major Daoist site, cable cars ascend to the base of the highest peak, providing not just an easy shortcut but also the best views of the valley. From here, a 30min. hike brings you to **Zhurong Palace** (zhùróng diàn; 祝融殿) at the peak. Those seeking an escape from the crowds should climb up the left side of the mountain to **Tianzhu Temple.** This hike is more strenuous and has fewer sights along the way, but the journey takes less time.

The ▨ **Water Curtain Cave** (shuǐpù dòng; 水瀑洞), near Zhunan Lu at the eastern edge of Nanyue village, can provide a refreshing post-climb break. Hungry hikers can refuel at the many restaurants on Jinsha Lu, just before the foothills that lead to the main gate. For a longer rest, Zhurong Lu has a wide selection of hotels, all with dorm beds for Y20-60 per night and singles and doubles for slightly more.

YUEYANG 岳阳   ☎ 0730

Many an eloquent poet has rhapsodized over Yueyang, overlooked by its famous tower on the shores of Dongting Lake. Lakeside pavilions and willows create a tranquil retreat from Wuhan's industrial clamor and the sultry Yangzi climate, while an otherworldly air pervades Junshan Island's rarely visited swampy marshes and ancient trees half-submerged by lake waters.

▛ TRANSPORTATION. The **Yueyang Train Station** (yuèyáng huǒchē zhàn; 岳阳火车站) is on Zhanqian Lu, in the northern part of the city. (Tickets sold 2:30am-midnight.) Trains run to Changsha (2hr., every hr. 6:30am-5:30pm, Y22) and Guangzhou (11½hr., 3 per day, soft seat Y113). Exit the train station, cross the street, and follow the rightmost path to cross under the highway to reach the **Yueyang Bus Station** (yuèyáng qìchēzhàn; 岳阳汽车站 ; ☎ 822 7458). Buses leave every hour 6am-6pm to Changsha (2½hr., Y30-55) and Wuhan (4hr., Y45-55). **Local bus** #10 goes from the train station to Yueyang Tower via the magnificent Dongting Bridge (Y5); #15 runs from the train station parking lot down Baling Lu and up Dongting Bei Lu, also passing the Yueyang Tower and dock areas to end at Yue Mountain Park (Y1). Bus #22 services the same route as bus #15 but ends at the paper factory (zhǐchǎng; 纸厂). **Taxis** charge a base fare of Y5 and Y2.5 for each additional km (Y1 to enter the station parking lot).

▧▨ ORIENTATION AND PRACTICAL INFORMATION. There are two main roads: **Baling Lu** (巴陵路) runs east-west past the bus station through the main part of the city and ends at the lakeside, where it intersects with Dongting Lu. **Dongting Lu** (洞庭路) runs north-south from the Yueyang Tower to the Old Town area. Bus #15 stops within walking distance of many major sights.

CITS, 25 Chengdong Lu, is next to the Yunmeng Hotel, on the second floor. Take bus #15 toward the lake and get off right before the Baling Bridge. Turn left down Chengdong Lu; the Yunmeng Hotel and CITS are on the right. English tours to Junshan Island and Yueyang Tower cost about Y120. (☎ 824 9936 or 823 2010. Open daily 8am-6pm.) **Bank of China,** 1 Zhanqian Lu, exchanges currency on weekdays. (☎ 826 4560. Open daily summer 8am-noon and 2-5:30pm; winter 8am-noon and 2:30-5pm.) Exiting from the train station, walk two blocks to the right to reach the **PSB.** (☎ 828 2864. Open 24hr.) There is also a hospital, **Yueyang Tower People's Hospital** (yuèyánglóu rénmín yīyuàn; 岳阳楼人民医院), 39 Dong Maoling Lu (☎ 822 1211). **Internet cafes** concentrate on the street across from the train station, inside **Full Goods Market** (fúrùnduō; 福润多) and the commercial building next door. (Y1.5-3. Most open 8am-midnight.) The main **post office** is on Zhanqian Lu. (EMS. Open 8:30am-noon and 2:30-6pm.) **China Telecom,** to the right as you exit from the train station has IDD. (Open daily 8am-8pm.) **Postal Code:** 414000.

⚑ ACCOMMODATIONS. As usual, the train station is the hub of a large number of hotels. **Zhongtian Hotel ❶** (zhōngtiān bīnguǎn; 中天宾馆), 100m to the right from the train station exit, next to the PSB, offers clean, furnished rooms. (A/C and TV. Singles with shared bath Y72-80, with private bath Y158-198; doubles Y120/Y158-198; triples Y168-208.) The best places to stay, however, are far removed from the bustle of the train station, near Dongting Lake and Yueyang Tower. **Snow Lily Hotel ❶** (xuělián bīnguǎn; 雪莲宾馆), on Dongting Bei Lu, across from the Yueyang Ferry Wharf, is one of the best bargains in town. Clean, slightly worn rooms all have A/C and private bath. (☎832 1633. Very friendly staff. Singles Y60; doubles Y100; triples Y120.) Take bus #15 to the Yueyang Tower stop, backtrack about 60m, and turn left onto a small side street; **Yueyang Tower Hotel ❷** (yuèyánglóu bīnguǎn; 岳阳楼宾馆), 57 Dongting Bei Lu, is on the right, just opposite the Yueyang Tower. This average hotel's main distinction is its location. (☎832 1288; fax 841 4000. A/C and private bath. Singles Y150-180; doubles Y120-180.) Bus #15 can also bring you to the **Yunmeng Hotel ❸** (yúnmèng bīnguǎn; 云梦宾馆), 25 Chengdong Nan Lu; heading toward the lake, get off just before Baling Bridge and turn left on Chengdong Lu. The hotel is a 10min. walk down, on the right. (☎822 1115. Standard amenities, including A/C and bath. Singles Y180 and up; doubles Y180-298; triples Y200-328.) The restaurant downstairs serves one of Yueyang's best **Baling Fish Feasts** (bālíng quān yúxí; 巴陵全鱼席 ; Y400 and up), 10-20 dishes all made with Dongting Lake's freshest catch, from fish to turtles to eel.

⚐ FOOD. Famous for its fish, Yueyang enjoys the bounty of more than 100 species of edibles swimming in Dongting Lake, the second-largest freshwater lake in China. Fill your belly with delicious catch like carp and eel (Y20-50) at the small restaurants along the street opposite the Yueyang Tower. Freshly caught and braised turtles go for Y200 each. Find more fishy options at the restaurants lining Dongting Bei Lu. For a less expensive meal, try *bāozǎi fàn* (煲仔饭), a variety of savory meats and veggies stewed with rice, served in palm-sized wooden plates kept hot and steamy in large iron pots at the many roadside eateries. About 200m west of Baling Bridge, the alleys of the Miaoqian Jie district are a popular place for a late-night dinner or snack, from roast duck to traditional fried sweets.

◪ SIGHTS. Built without a single nail, **Yueyang Tower** (yuèyáng lóu; 岳阳楼) was originally a naval watch station from the Three Kingdoms Period (AD 220-280). Several classical Chinese writers composed odes to the tower, including Song poet Fan Zhongyan's *Notes on the Yueyang Tower*. Today, the ascent up the tower is more a symbolic gesture in homage to literary masterpieces than a climb for inspiring views. Visitors unfamiliar with Chinese history or poetry may prefer to admire the structure from afar and skip the steep admission fee, paltry pavilions, and disconcerting wax museum. *(Inside Yueyang Tower Park, on Dongting Bei Lu, along the riverfront. Take bus #15 or 22 to Yueyang Tower. ☎831 9435. Open daily May-Sept. 7am-7pm; Oct.-Apr. 7:30am-6:30pm. Y46, students Y25.)*

A 30min. boat ride away lies **Junshan Park** (jūnshān gōngyuán; 君山公园), surrounded by tall reeds and marshes extending into the vast, sea-like expanse of Dongting Lake. Tang poet Liu Yuxi described the small "mountain" at the heart of Junshan Island as a sumptuous green conch on a silvery plate. Sample cups of the island's prized fragrant "silver needle" white tea. At **Monkey Mountain** (hóuzi shān; 猴子山), tucked away in the island's hilly interior, indigenous monkeys playfully vie for your attention. *(Speedboats every hr. or when full 7:30am-4pm from Yueyang Ferry Wharf, on Dongting Bei Lu, north of Yueyang Tower; Y20. Last boat departs Junshan Island 4:30-5pm. Or take bus #10 or 15 to last stop for Y5. ☎815 9066. Open 24hr. Y40, students Y20.)*

ZHANGJIAJIE 张家界 ☎0744

Situated in northwestern Hunan, sprawling Zhangjiajie encompasses some five scenic areas covering 264km² of forest, sandstone cliffs, rushing streams, and underground rivers wandering deep into enormous caverns. The mist hangs low, rising and vanishing like wisps of smoke, and in the silence of nighttime, the sinewy branches of gnarled pines and ghostly birdcalls take on a haunted life of their own. The park is named after Zhang Liang, a Han Dynasty general who lived in seclusion among the mountains, and Zhangjiajie is indeed a great place to hide from the world. Its steep drops and eerily beautiful peaks were ideal strongholds for the bands of outlaws that ravaged Hunan for centuries. Though the bandits were uprooted in the 1960s by the PLA, there is still something unnerving about the crags and the shadowy forests. Locals tell ghastly tales and warn of illicit activities and of supernatural phenomena sheltered deep within the park.

TRANSPORTATION AND PRACTICAL INFORMATION

Flights: Zhangjiajie Airport (zhāngjiājiè jīchǎng; 张家界机场; ☎823 1777 or 822 0128), southwest of the city center. Beware of frequent flight cancellations and massive delays. Taxi to the city costs Y20-25. To: **Beijing** (daily, Y1340); **Changsha** (2 per day, Y580); **Chengdu** (4-5 per week, Y800); **Chongqing** (3 per week; Y580); **Guangzhou** (2 per day, Y860); **Shanghai** (daily, Y1330).

Trains: Zhangjiajie Train Station (zhāngjiājiè huǒchē zhàn; 张家界火车站; ☎851 4442), outside of city center. Purchase tickets a week in advance. To: **Beijing** (27hr., daily, Y194); **Changsha** (8hr., 2 per day, Y71); **Guangzhou** (23hr., 2 per day, Y174).

Buses: Zhangjiajie Long-Distance Bus Station (zhāngjiājiè chángtú qìchē zhàn; 张家界长途汽车站), at the intersection of Renmin Lu and Huilong Lu. To: **Changsha** (11hr., 2-3 per day, Y120); **Guangzhou** (25hr., daily, Y370); **Guilin** (daily, Y150).

Local Transportation: Bus #2 (30min., Y1) shuttles from the train station to the long-distance bus station in Zhangjiajie city. From the bus station, transfer to one of the many **minibuses** (Y6) for a 1hr. ride to Forest Park (sēnlín gōngyuán; 森林公园). **Taxi** base fare Y5, each additional km Y1.8.

Travel Agencies: Zhangjiajie CITS, Wanjia Dept. Store, 9th fl., on Jiaochang Lu. 3-day tour from Changsha to Zhangjiajie Y700 per person, English-speaking guide additional Y100-200. Open daily 8:30am-6pm. **Dragon International Hotel** (xiánglóng guójì jiǔdiàn; 祥龙国际酒店), 46 Jiefang Lu (☎822 6888; fax 822 2935), arranges whitewater rafting trips and cave tours for a hefty surcharge (Y300). English-speaking staff.

Bank of China: 1 Xinmatou Jie (☎822 3383), in Zhangjiajie city. Currency exchange. Open daily 8am-6pm. There are no banks in the Zhangjiajie Park area.

PSB: ☎822 2334. On Ziwu Lu. Open daily 8am-6pm.

Internet Access: Park Internet Cafe (gōngyuán wǎngbā; 公园网吧), behind the Xiangdian International Hotel near the park entrance. Y2 per hr. Open 24hr.

Post Office: In Zhangjiajie city, the **post office** (☎822 4757) is on Huilong Lu, just east of the long-distance bus station. EMS. Another **branch** in Zhangjiajie Park, on the main street to the right of park entrance, 100m past Pipaxi Hotel. Both open daily 8am-6pm.

Postal Code: 427000.

ACCOMMODATIONS AND FOOD

Hotels are pricey both in Zhangjiajie city and near the park entrance. Most visitors head straight for the park, but if you arrive too late to make the 2hr. trip, try **New Capital Hotel** ❷ (xīn dū dàjiǔdiàn; 新都大酒店), to the right as you exit the train station. (☎851 8388 or 211 1888. A/C, private bath, and TV. Well-furnished doubles Y100-288; triples Y150.) Otherwise, a number of hotels border the main road leading to the park entrance. There are also some pricier establishments inside the park; reservations are essential in the summer. Bargaining is a possibility in most hotels, but more difficult in the high season. Dorms don't accept foreigners.

Although ethnic Miao people live in the area, **Tujia** (土家, another minority) restaurants dominate in Zhangjiajie. The eateries near the park entrance serve a variety of foods, from Mao's family tofu to capitalist dumplings. Buses to the park stop at the **Golden Rice Bowl Restaurant** ❷ (jīnfànwǎn jiǔlóu; 金饭碗酒楼), a two-story bamboo building overlooking a brook. The restaurant is permeated with the mouth-watering aromas of potato croquettes (tǔdòu bǐng; 土豆饼 ; Y15-20) and Tujia fried chicken (tǔjiā shāo jī; 土家烧鸡 ; Y60-90) with black fungus and peppers. (☎138 0744 6898. Entrees Y8-40. Open 8am-midnight.)

Golden Whip Crag Hotel (jīnbiānyán fàndiàn; 金鞭岩饭店 ; ☎571 2362). The hotel closest to the park entrance. Rooms are average, but it's the best deal near the park. Bath, A/C, and TV. Books rafting and sightseeing tours. Doubles Y150; triples Y180. ❷

Railway Hotel (tiělù bīnguǎn; 铁路宾馆 ; ☎571 2386), on the right side of the road, about 100m from the last bus stop. The building is worn and the carpets raggedy, but rooms still go quickly. Pool table in the common room. Doubles with A/C, bath, and TV Y120; luxury suites Y200 and up. ❷

Xiangdian International Hotel (xiāngdiàn guójì jiǔdiàn; 湘电国际酒店). Cross the street from the Railway Hotel and walk inside the lane. Books plane and train tickets (commission Y10-50). Luxurious singles and doubles Y100-420. ❷

Pipa Stream Hotel (pípa xī bīnguǎn; 琵琶溪宾馆 ; ☎571 8888; fax 571 2257), on the right side of the road as you enter the park area. Quieter and more comfortable than most other park options, with many luxuries. Singles and doubles Y300 and up. ❹

⚡ HIKING IN ZHANGJIAJIE

Zhangjiajie National Forest Park (zhāngjiājiè guójiā sēnlín gōngyuán; 张家界国家森林公园) marks the entrance to the vast scenic area, a forest of sandstone pillars towering above deep ravines and thundering rapids. The park can be hiked comfortably in about three days, but given its size and lack of signs, a tour guide is recommended. Most people come with a tour group, so the few well-touristed areas are crowded with people while the far-off places are completely empty. Even park management is limited to the main tourist spots. You can contact a travel agency for small tour groups (2-4 people), but this will be remarkably pricey (over Y1000 for 2-3 days), especially if you request an English-speaking tour guide. Less expensive and more knowledgeable local guides—suntanned farmers in sandals—seek out tourists at the bus and train stations. Beware where you are taken for food and lodging, as small family joints in the mountains are known to rip off unsuspecting tourists. Camping is not allowed in the park. Make sure to keep an eye out for wild animals, especially the lethal five-step snake. **Admission** costs Y158 and is valid for two days. Tickets can be purchased at four access points: Zhangjiajie Park, Yangjiajie, Tianzishan, and Wulongyuan in Suoxiyu. (☎829 5382. Open 24hr.)

While most people take to the trails, Zhangjiajie's rushing streams present little-known **white-water rafting** opportunities. Dubbed *piāoliú* (漂流 ; "drifting"), the two conventional routes ply the **Maoyan River**, flowing some 55km, and the farther **Mengdong River**, where the water is swifter and less predictable. Rafting is also possible in a part of **Suoxigu Stream** (running from Wulingyuan City to Tianzishan Scenic Area), the designated white-water rafting team training spot for the 2008 Olympics. Old women near the docks sell palm-sized water ladles and mysterious-looking water guns—a stick with a rubber end plugged into a foot-long bamboo section. If there is any doubt to the purpose of these souvenirs (Y1-2), the mystery is quickly cleared when little boys and even middle-aged couples throw water at you as you drift by. Expect to get very wet; bring a change of clothing. As there is no public transportation to the docks, it is easiest to join a hotel group (make arrangements the night before). Tours run about Y120-250 for Maoyan, more for Mengdong. The basic price gets you a spot on an eight-person raft, 3hr. of rafting, and transportation to and from the hotel. The first boat departs around 9am, and the last boat usually leaves the docks at 3pm, depending on demand.

ZHANGJIAJIE PARK 张家界公园

From Zhangjiajie Park, the typical route will touch down on Yellow Stone Village and Golden Whip Stream. **Yellow Stone Village** (huáng shí zhài; 黄石寨) is named after the wise old man who passed on the secrets of the art of war to Zhang Liang after the young man piously picked up the old man's shoes for him after they fell off the bridge, not once, but three times. The 990m-tall peak towers over the cliffs on the opposite side and, on sunny days, offers spectacular views of the forests blanketing the rugged landscape. A **cable car** runs to the top of Yellow Stone Village. (Open daily 8am-5pm. Up Y48, down Y38, round-trip Y68.) The park's largest stream, the **Golden Whip Stream** (jīn biān xī; 金鞭溪) flows 5.7km through forests and crags. Along the banks, strangely shaped sandstone pillars resemble deities and *Journey to the West* characters (or so locals claim). The stream's unique name comes from a tall whip-like crag that shines a golden hue in the last lights of dusk. If Yellow Stone Village is too crowded for your taste, you can visit the nearby **Sparrowhawk Village** (yàozi zhài; 鹞子寨) instead, with more breathtaking views and fewer tourists. There are no cable cars.

YANGJIAJIE 杨家界

From the Zhangjiajie Park area, hike northward into **Yuanjiajie** (袁家界), where a scenic bend, the **First Bridge Under Heaven** (tiān xià dìyī qiáo; 天下第一桥), overlooks one of the steepest drops in the entire forest of stony pillars. Nearby, **Lost Soul Terrace** (míhún tái; 迷魂台) and **Rear Garden** (hòu huāyuán; 后花园) offer ghostly views of peaks in the hazy distance. From the First Bridge Under Heaven, **buses** head to Tianzishan and further into Yuanjiajie, where you can hike to **Black Dragon Village** (wūlóng zhài; 乌龙寨), a former stronghold of outlaws near the very summit of Yangjiajie Scenic Area. The building is now a museum on Tujia marriage customs, but a large basket at the door harks back to darker days: it once confined kidnapped village girls. A climb up the steep stairs leads to **Tianbofu** (天波府), with misty panoramas on all sides and heartrending drops below.

Further northwest, a full 2hr. from Zhangjiajie Park, lies **Nine Heavens Cave** (jiǔ tiān dòng; 九天洞), a vast underground cavern spanning over 2.5km^2 with some 30 streams, 12 waterfalls, and 15 underground lakes. The area opened to tourism is barely a tenth of the cave, but it still takes 2-3hr. to follow the guide (mandatory with admission) around the immense stalagtites and terraced pools. Because of its distance from Zhangjiajie, few tour groups make it out here. Either book a tour at your hotel (around Y150) or take a bus from the long-distance bus station in Zhangjiajie city to **Cuiji** (1hr., Y20), where you will need to transfer to another bus or hire a motorcyle. (Open 9am-6pm. Y60.)

TIANZISHAN 天子山

The Tianzishan Scenic Area in the north, named for the area's highest peak, Tianzishan "Emperor Mountain," boasts yet more cliffs and crags for your climbing pleasure. Be sure not to miss **Commanding Troops Terrace** (diǎn jiàng tái; 点将台) and **Divine Altar Bend** (shén táng wān; 神堂湾), where a Tujia king, pursued by

Song troops, jumped to his death. Secluded and eerie, with sinister pines, the area is to this day the subject of warnings and ghostly stories told by locals. Supposedly, there are *other* things drifting around down there, especially in the forest under the bend. The tour groups that come to Tianzishan usually make a visit to **Helong Park** (hèlóng gōngyuán; 贺龙公园), a small mountaintop park with similar hazy views. You may want to lodge overnight at the Tianzishan Scenic Area entrance, from where it is easy to head out to Yellow Dragon Cave. A bus runs between First Bridge Under Heaven and Tianzishan.

SUOXIYU 索溪峪

About 1hr. east of Zhangjiajie Peak in Suoxiyu Nature Reserve, the palatial caverns of the **Yellow Dragon Cave** (huáng lóng dòng; 黄龙洞) are filled with stalagtites and fed by underground rivers and waterfalls. Despite the artificial lighting and clamoring crows magnified by cave acoustics, the natural wonder of the caves speaks for itself. There is no direct bus to the cave, so you must join a tour, hire a minivan, or take a local bus to **Wulongyuan** (武隆源) and transfer from there. (Y68. Open 9am-6pm.) Yellow Dragon Cave is fairly touristed, so if you're looking for a quieter experience (or have had your fair share of caves), you may want to skip it.

HUBEI 湖北

Hubei province has long been at the mercy of the Yangzi River and its many tributaries. But even as the river threatens yearly flooding and occasional disaster, it is also the source of livelihood for those living along its banks, bringing trade, industry, and tourists from the wealthier coastal provinces. The Yangzi meanders upstream through Wuhan, Hubei's capital and cultural center, and continues to the Three Gorges, forming a magnificent backdrop for the ferries cruising down the river. Much of the region south of the Yangzi is given over to industrial production and high-tech zones, but as one moves toward the northwest, the scenery turns wild and rugged. Known as the "Gateway to Nine Provinces," Hubei is central China's transportation hub, and tourists to the area are bound to spend some time here at one point or another. Summer weather can be brutal, but heaps of watermelon and a plentiful supply of local hospitality temper the stifling summer heat.

WUHAN 武汉   ☎027

Situated in the heart of China at the confluence of the Han and Yangzi rivers, Wuhan owes much of its development to its central position along the shipping lanes of the Yangzi. In 1842, the Treaty of Nanjing opened the district of Hankou to foreign trade. The city's European architecture is a visible reminder of its five foreign concessions. Since then, life in Wuhan has not been all peace and progress. During the 1911 Revolution, bombings and uprisings marred the city's prosperous facade, nearly leveling several parts of the city; periodic upheavals continued to wreak havoc until the end of the Cultural Revolution. Hot, humid summer months bring torrential rains that continuously threaten to flood this city of more than four million. Wuhan has not only survived, however, but also blossomed into a crucial regional hub. Wuhan's next challenge is to satisfy the rising number of foreign and Chinese visitors, but the city's sparkling commercial district and leisurely waterfront should prove that, once again, Wuhan will be up to the task at hand.

◪ TRANSPORTATION

Flights: Tianhe International Airport (tiānhé guójì jīchǎng; 天河国际机场; ☎8581 8658 or 8581 8413; www.whairport.com), 30km northwest of central Hankou.

Shuttles (☎8581 8309) to the airport stop at **Wuchang Fujiapo Long-Distance Bus Station** (6:40am, every hr. 7:30am-5:30pm, 7pm); **Wuchang Train Station** (6:50am, every hr. 7:40am-3:40pm, 5:40, 7:10pm); **Hankou Fanhu Tianhe Airport City Waiting Room** (6:30am, every hr. 7:20am-6:20pm, 7:50pm); **Hankou Minhang (Air China) District** (6:40am, every hr. 7:30am-6:30pm, 8pm). Shuttles from the airport stop at all the above places, except Wuchang Train Station, in addition to **Hankou Jinghan Dadao** and **Hanyang Changjiang Guangchang** (Yangzi Sq.). One-way shuttle fares to Hankou (Y15); Hanyang (Y20); Wuchang (Y30).

Tickets: China Southern Hubei Airlines office (zhōngguó nánfāng hángkōng húběi gōngsī; 中国南方航空湖北公司), 1 Hangkong Lu (☎8362 2000, 24hr. 8530 0000; fax 8363 2264). Open daily 8am-8pm. The **CAAC Booking Service Center** (wǔhàn tiānhé jīchǎng shòupiào fúwù zhōngxīn; 武汉天河机场售票服务中心), 96 Tanqing Lu, Hankou (☎8360 2228). Open 24hr. To: **Beijing** (7-8 per day, Y1080); **Chengdu** (5-6 per day, Y910); **Chongqing** (daily, Y790); **Guangzhou** (10 per day, Y930); **Guilin** (Tu, Th-Sa; Y780); **Kunming** (1-4 per day, Y1310); **Nanjing** (daily, Y730-800); **Shanghai** (11 per day, Y570-700); **Xi'an** (3-5 per day, Y690).

Trains: Most trains stop at both stations, though more pass through Wuchang.

Wuchang Train Station (wǔchāng huǒchē zhàn; 武昌火车站 ; 24hr. ☎8806 8888), on Zhongshan Lu, not far past Ziyang Lu. To: **Beijing** (12-16hr., 13 per day, Y272-558); **Chengdu** (17-24hr., 3 per day, Y300-491); **Chongqing** (24hr., 3 per day, Y247-433); **Fuzhou** (22hr., daily, Y140-247); **Guangzhou** (16hr., 14 per day, Y248); **Kunming** (44hr., 2 per day, Y385); **Nanchang** (9hr., 4 per day, Y106); **Shanghai** (19hr., 3 per day, Y271); **Xi'an** (14-16hr., 4 per day, Y209); **Xiangfan** (5-6hr., 4 per day, Y30).

Hankou Train Station (hànkǒu huǒchē zhàn; 汉口火车站 ; ☎6565 0666), at the intersection of Fazhan Dadao and Qingnian Lu. Luggage storage in the snack kiosk out front (Y4). Some trains passing through Wuchang also stop at Hankou; those going north or west from Wuhan stop first at Wuchang before passing through Hankou; those going south or east stop at Hankou before Wuchang. Prices are the same for trains stopping at both stations. Hankou also has trains to: **Harbin** (28hr., 4:05pm, Y631); **Hefei** (10hr., 9:26pm, Y89); **Lanzhou** (23hr., 6:55pm, Y528).

Buses: There are 2 bus stations in Wuchang and 1 in Hankou.

Wuchang: Hongji Passenger Transport Station (hóngjī kèyùn zhàn; 宏基客运站 ; ☎8807 4968), on Zhongshan Lu, 1 block from Ziyang Lu in the opposite direction from Wuchang Train Station. Tickets sold 24hr. To: **Changsha** (5hr., 2 per day, Y110-136); **Hefei** (6hr., 4 per day, Y90-140); **Nanjing** (8hr., 10 per day, Y100-193); **Yichang** (4-5hr., every hr. 7am-6pm, Y81); **Yueyang** (3hr., every hr., Y56). Wuchang's **Fujiapo Bus Station** (fùjiāpō qìchē zhàn; 傅家坡汽车站 ; ☎8712 2461), on Wuluo Lu near Da Dong Men and Zhongshan Lu. To: **Jiujiang** (every 40-50min. 7am-7:20pm; Y56, Y70); **Nanchang** (9 per day, Y105); **Shanghai** (20-22hr.; 9:10am, every hr. 6:40-9:40pm; Y305); **Xiangfan** (14 per day; Y65, Y90); **Yichang** (every 30-50min. 7am-7pm; Y65, Y105). Also many buses to towns and cities within Hubei province.

Hankou: Wuhan Port Long-Distance Bus Station (wǔhàn gǎng chángtú qìchē zhàn; 武汉港长途汽车站 ; ☎8285 7325), on Yanjiang Dadao, next to the passenger ferry terminal. Open daily 7am-7pm. To: **Jiujiang** (3½hr., 4-5 per day, Y55); **Nanjing** (14hr., 3 per day, Y192); **Shanghai** (13hr., 3 per day, Y268); **Yichang** (4hr., 5 per day, Y85).

Ferries: Wuhan Passenger Ferry Terminal (wǔhàn kèyùn gǎng; 武汉客运港 ; ☎8283 9546), on Yanjiang Dadao, Hankou. As you enter the ticket hall, the inquiry booth is on the right; timetables and ticket windows are against the back wall. Open daily 8:30am-8:30pm. Because the river often floods in the summer, ferry schedules and departures fluctuate frequently; boats going downstream are often cancelled, so call ahead. Price ranges are for 2nd- and 3rd-class. To: **Chongqing** (72hr., daily, Y309-580); **Jiujiang** (10hr., 8pm, Y78); **Nanjing** (33-36hr., Y193-333); **Shanghai** (43hr., Y298-538).

Local Transportation: Most buses run from around 6am to 9pm. Fare Y1.2-2. Bus #10 links the Wuchang and Hankou train stations; #209 goes from the ferry passenger terminal in Hankou to the Wuchang Train Station; #533 runs from the Hankou Train Station to the downtown area on Zhongshan Dadao. Tourist buses #401 and 413 connect sights and scenic areas in all 3 districts. **Ferries** link Hankou and Wuchang, with frequent departures from the **Hankou docks** along Yanjiang Lu and the **Zhonghua Lu** and **Hanyangmen docks** in Wuchang (10-15min., every 20min. 6am-11pm, Y1-4).

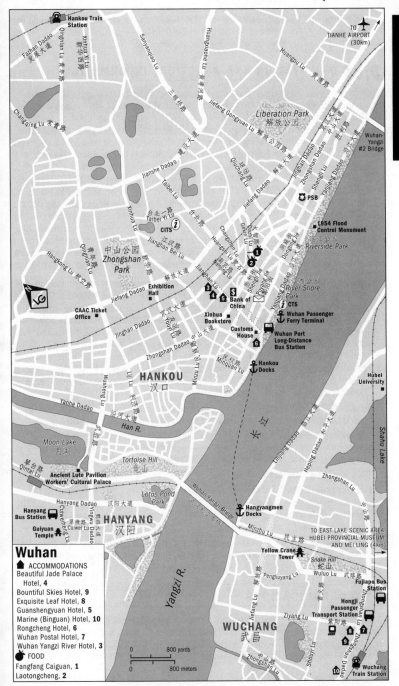

Wuhan

🏠 **ACCOMMODATIONS**
Beautiful Jade Palace
Hotel, **4**
Bountiful Skies Hotel, **9**
Exquisite Leaf Hotel, **8**
Guanshengyuan Hotel, **5**
Marine (Binguan) Hotel, **10**
Rongcheng Hotel, **6**
Wuhan Postal Hotel, **7**
Wuhan Yangzi River Hotel, **3**

🍎 **FOOD**
Fangfang Caiguan, **1**
Laotongcheng, **2**

Taxis: Base fare Y3, each additional km Y1.4. Ideal for short distances, considering the low base fare. From either train station to central Hankou around Zhongshan Dadao Y20-30. For sightseeing, buses are more economical.

ORIENTATION AND PRACTICAL INFORMATION

Wuhan is composed of three districts: **Hankou** (汉口) and **Hanyang** (汉阳), north of the Yangzi River, separated by the Han River, and **Wuchang** (武昌), southeast of the Yangzi. Hankou bustles with activity, while Hanyang, the smallest of the three, is a quiet center of light industry. Across the Yangzi, Wuchang has transformed from an ancient walled city into a sprawling urban settlement receding into green pastures out toward the East Lake Scenic Area. Bridges link all three districts.

Hankou is full of shops and offices, especially on **Zhongshan Dadao** (中山大道). Another important commercial thoroughfare is **Jiefang Dadao** (解放大道), which runs north of and parallel to Zhongshan Dadao. The train station is north of Hankou about 5km from the central business area. The main docks line the Yangzi along **Yanjiang Dadao** (沿江大道). Hanyang's main commercial streets are **Yingwu Dadao** (鹦鹉大道) and **Hanyang Dadao** (汉阳大道), which is roughly perpendicular to the Yangzi. In Wuchang, **Zhongshan Lu** (中山路) goes past the train station to intersect **Wuluo Lu** (武珞路), another important thoroughfare. The **East Lake Scenic Area** (东湖风景区) covers much of the southeast portion of Wuchang.

Travel Agencies: Travel agencies are everywhere, especially near the ferry passenger terminal, on Jiefang Dadao in Hankou, and around the train and bus stations in Wuchang. **Hubei CTS,** 909 Zhongshan Dadao, Hankou (☎8578 4125). English-, Japanese-, German-, French-, and Spanish-speaking staff. Open M-F 8:30am-5pm. **CTS,** 142 Yanjiang Dadao, Hankou (☎8284 4894; fax 8278 0820), specializes in air travel and river cruises. English-speaking staff. Take bus #527 from Jiefang Dadao to Nanning Lu. Open daily 8am-7pm. The **Hubei CITS Airplane Ticketing Center** (húběishěng zhōngguóguójìlǚxíngshè hángkōng fúwù zhōngxīn; 湖北省中国国际旅行社航空服务中心), 26 Jianghan Lu, Hankou (☎8586 6877), a few blocks toward the river from Yanjiang Dadao, can assist English-speaking travelers.

Bank of China: 593 Zhongshan Dadao, Hankou (☎8283 4891; fax 8283 5150), at Jianghan Lu. Exchanges currency and traveler's checks. Open M-F 8am-noon and 2-5:30pm.

Bookstore: Xinhua Bookstore, 896 Zhongshan Dadao, Hankou (☎8283 2761), a few doors down from Jianghan Lu. A large selection of books, including a decent stock of English-language novels and translations of Chinese classics. Open daily 9am-9pm.

PSB: Wuchang Train Station PSB (☎8807 6116), across from the station. Open 24hr.

Internet Access: Xinxin Internet Cafe (xīnxīn wǎngbā; 新欣网吧 ; ☎8283 3741). Next to the ticket booth at the Wuchang Train Station, 2nd fl. Y3 per hr. Open 24hr. **Youbang Internet Cafe** (yǒubāng wǎngbā; 友邦网吧), 268 Ziyang Lu (☎8807 6169), Wuchang, across from China Agricultural Bank. Y2 per hr. Open 24hr.

Post Office: Large branch on the pedestrian section of Jianghan Lu (Buxing Jie). EMS. Open 8:30am-10pm. Also branches outside the Hankou and Wudang train stations.

Postal Code: 430020.

ACCOMMODATIONS

Accommodations are plentiful in the Jianghan Lu area near Zhongshan Dadao in Hankou and near the Wuchang Train Station. Budget places abound, though few are open to foreigners. Wuhan is not a tourist city, but summer promotions and winter discounts help to bring the prices down at the larger hotels.

HANKOU

Wuhan Yangzi River Hotel (wǔhànshì yángzǐ jiāng jiǔdiàn; 武汉市扬子江酒店), 104 Jianghan Lu (☎8283 1193 or 8285 4962). Walk on Zhongshan Dadao, 1 block from the river. Good price and location. All rooms have A/C, attached bath, phone, and TV. Singles and doubles Y70; triples Y80; quads Y90. ❶

Guanshengyuan Hotel (guānshēngyuán dàjiūdiàn; 冠生园大酒店), 109 Jianghan Lu (☎8281 2658; fax 8282 5317), on the left, about 1 block past Zhongshan Dadao, heading away from the Yangzi. In the heart of Hankou's main shopping district. Rooms come with attached baths. 24hr. broadband Internet on 2nd fl. Y2 per hr. Singles Y128; doubles Y138; triples Y188. ❷

Beautiful Jade Palace Hotel (xuángōng fàndiàn; 璇宫饭店), 57 Jianghan Lu (☎6882 2588; fax 6882 2598). From Zhongshan Dadao, go 2 blocks up Jianghan Lu, away from the river; it's on the left. Classical European facade with dark, elegantly furnished rooms and chandeliers. Past guests include Zhou Enlai, Mao Zedong, and the British marshall Montgomery. 10% service charge. Singles Y308; doubles Y328. ❹

Rongcheng Hotel (róngchéng bīnguǎn; 戎城宾馆 ; ☎8283 7402), near the intersection of Yanjiang Dadao and Jianghan Lu. Tucked into a quiet corner, within a 5min. walk of the waterfront and nearby passenger ferry terminal. Doubles with A/C, TV, and bath Y138-268; triples Y160-298. ❷

WUCHANG

Bountiful Skies Hotel (tiānfēng bīnguǎn), 510 Zhongshan Lu (☎8832 5079 or 8832 5323), across from the train station. Clean singles Y48, with A/C and bath Y88; doubles Y68, with bath Y98; triples with bath Y108. ❶

Wuhan Postal Hotel (wǔhàn yóuzhèng bīnguǎn; 武汉邮政宾馆), 385 Zhongshan Lu (☎8808 4562; fax 8807 7375), next to the train station. Brightly lit on the outside, dimly lit on the inside. Long corridors with dark wood and red carpeting evoke a 1950s atmosphere. Singles with A/C and TV Y70; standard doubles with bath, A/C, phone, and TV Y118-170; triples Y220. ❶

Marine (Binguan) Hotel (hánghǎi bīnguǎn; 航海宾馆), 530 Zhongshan Lu (☎8874 0122; fax 8807 8717), near Ziyang Lu. Exit the train station and cross the street; it's a 10-15min. walk to the left. Pay attention to the characters: the nearby Marine Fandian (航海饭店) doesn't accept foreigners. Bright, spacious rooms and baths. Doubles Y138-170; triples Y168-190. ❷

Exquisite Leaf Hotel (jiāyè bīnguǎn; 嘉叶宾馆), 496 Zhongshan Lu (☎6888 6708; fax 6888 6670), at Ziyang Lu, near the train station. Neoclassical statues and chandeliers await you in the lobby, behind the European facade and wrought-iron gates. Dark rooms with few windows don't live up to their palatial introduction. Reservations recommended; rooms often fill up by 9 or 10pm, if not earlier. Singles with A/C and shared bath Y70, with attached bath Y148-208; doubles Y168-188; triples Y228-288. ❶

🔲 🎵 FOOD AND ENTERTAINMENT

Wuhan is known for its **Wuchang bream** (wǔchāng yú; 武昌鱼), a fish freshly caught from the East Lake. The waters around Wuhan also nourish light, crispy **lotus root** (ǒu; 藕), another local specialty that makes its way into stir-fried dishes, soups, and refreshingly sweet sticky rice. Look for pots or earthenware jars of slowly simmered **soups** (wēitāng; 煨汤) with lotus root, pork ribs, and sometimes mushrooms. Another local favorite, **sān xiān dòupí** (三鲜豆皮) is a thin crepe made of flour, bean flour, and egg, wrapped around sticky rice with scallions, sausage, mushrooms, and other ingredients, all fried to a golden crisp.

Floating restaurants line Bayi Lu, near East Lake. Also in Wuchang, several of the side streets off **Ziyang Lu** feature dense concentrations of street stalls. Hankou offers the most lively dinnertime choices, with its commercial centers and waterfront restaurants. On Dazhi Lu, near Zhongshan Dadao, the evening bustles with large sidewalk eateries and outdoor restaurants. A large archway marks the entrance to the **Jiqing Jie Food Street** (吉庆街).

Travelers nostalgic for a taste of home can stroll down the pedestrian section of **Jianghan (Buxing) Jie**, on the other end of Zhongshan Dadao. A block before the intersection with Dongfang Dadao, **Ejiaz ❶** (yījiāzi kuàicān; 伊家子快餐) serves Chinese-style fast food as well as a few Hubei specialties. (☎8281 0376. Dishes Y4-10. Open 9:30am-midnight.) Walk three more blocks toward the river to find the ambient dining of **Wankelai Steakhouse ❸** (wànkèlái niúpáiguǎn; 万客来牛排馆). Big, juicy European beef platters (Y33) come with sides and dessert. (☎8280 9390. Coffee Y12. Open until 1am.)

Nightlife in Wuhan takes the form of caffeine indulgence in the many cafes along the streets. A number of these classy hideaways are scattered among fancy bridal salons and clothing stores on Zhongshan Dadao. A stroll down **Xianggang Lu** leads to a few bars and clubs, and a walk up **Jianghan Lu** uncovers a karaoke lover's pot of gold. Locals while away their evenings at the **nightmarkets** around Jianghan Lu and Nanjing Lu. Vendors peddle clothing, footwear, food, jewelry, and more. You may see some locals heading to beauty parlors during late hours—note that many such establishments specialize in services other than beautification.

▨ **Fangfang Caiguan** (fāngfāng càiguǎn; 芳芳菜馆), 168 Dazhi Lu, Hankou (☎8281 0115), near the archway to Jiqing Jie. You can't miss the huge outdoor patio with bright yellow cushioned chairs. This popular eatery strives for the Chinese ideal in restaurant ambience: hot, noisy, and chaotic. Quieter seating with A/C available inside. Saxophones and traditional singers perform dueling serenades over the boisterous chatter (from 7pm on). Vegetable dishes Y6-12. Meat entrees Y20-30. Open daily 4pm-6am. ❷

Laotongcheng (lǎotōngchéng dòupí dàwáng; 老通城豆皮大王), 1 Dazhi Lu, 2nd and 3rd fl., Hankou (☎281 0616 or 283 4559), on the corner of Zhongshan Dadao across from Tianjin Lu. Proletarian fare in one of Mao's old haunts. Once *the* place in town to go for *sānxiān dòupí* (豆皮 ; Y3-6), the house specialty, this famous restaurant now thrives off the fat of its younger days. Dim sum Y0.5-5. Beijing duck Y40. Open daily 2nd fl. 6:30-8:30am; 3rd fl. 10am-2pm and 5-8:30pm. ❶

☞ SIGHTS

Wuhan first gained notoriety for its role in the novel *The Romance of the Three Kingdoms*, but most present-day sights relate to 20th-century events.

HANKOU 汉口

The center of Wuhan's modern commercial life, Hankou offers more atmosphere than official sights. The former hub of the foreign concessions of the early 20th century, **Zhongshang Dadao** now swarms with shoppers. A thicket of stores stretch up Jianghan Lu to Yanjiang Dadao near the Yangzi River, where glitzy malls and fast-food joints blast pop songs to lure patrons inside. In **River Shore Park** (jiāngtān gōngyuán; 江滩公园), European architecture lines the waterfront and shady willows create a quiet escape on summer evenings. Yanjiang Dadao, leading to the hulking Yangzi Ferry Terminal, is home to the old **Customs House** and several **open-air markets.** Farther north, **Riverside Park** (bīnjiāng gōngyuán; 滨江公园) is at the intersection of Yiyuan Lu and Yanjiang Dadao. The towering **1954 Flood Control Monument** marks the highest point in Wuhan's flooding history.

HANYANG 汉阳

ANCIENT LUTE PAVILION (gǔqíntái; 古琴台). Old engravings and gardens lined with bonsai make this a pleasant park, even if the intended attractions (an overgrown courtyard and a creepy waxworks display) leave you unimpressed. The part of the park that overlooks nearby **Moon Lake** is dedicated to two ancient lute enthusiasts who found friendship through their love of music. Nearby, **Tortoise Hill** (guī shān; 龟山) marks the spot where the heroic efforts of King Yu saved the city from flooding 4000 years ago. A **cable car** (Y15) from the "extreme sports" park on top of the hill makes the 800m crossing into Hankou, providing views of the city in the summer haze. *(At the intersection of Guishan Bei Lu, Qintai Lu, and Yingwu Dadao. Almost all buses passing through Hanyang stop at Ancient Lute Pavilion, including buses #401, 413, 507, and 701. Ancient Lute Pavilion ☎8483 4187. Both open daily 8am-6pm. Y10.)*

WUCHANG 武昌

EAST LAKE (dōng hú; 东湖). Six times the size of the West Lake in Hangzhou, Wuchang's own East Lake is a peaceful watery haven from the hurried pace of downtown Wuchang, surrounded by willows, Chinese redwoods and calm waters. Inside the lake area, **Moshan Hill Scenic Area** (móshān jǐngqū; 磨山景区) is studded with elegant pagodas and remains of the thousand-year-old city of Chu. A **cable car** goes to the top of Moshan Hill (one-way Y80). The lake is pleasant, and the vast stretches of water make for hours of rowing. *(In the eastern part of Wuchang. Tourist buses #401 and 413 stop at lake and Moshan Hill Scenic Area. Chu city ☎8751 0139; open 7:30am-8:30pm. Y40, students Y20. Rowboats Y15 per hr. Lake open 24hr.; free.)*

YELLOW CRANE TOWER (huánghè lóu; 黄鹤楼). Built in AD 223 and immortalized in Chinese poetry, the five-tiered tower today offers little except a hazy view of Wuchang. The cranes of old that soared from the tower, described in Li Bai's poems, have long vanished since the city's industrialization and the construction of the **Yangzi Bridge** (chángjiāng dàqiáo; 长江大桥) just beyond the tower. What comes in their place is a crane statue in front of the tower, a few gardens, touristy pavilions, and a faux Ming-Qing souvenir street. *(On Wuluo Lu. Bus #401 stops outside. ☎8283 2707. Open daily summer 7am-7pm; winter 7:30am-5:30pm. Y50, children Y25.)*

HUBEI PROVINCIAL MUSEUM (húběishěng bówùguǎn; 湖北省博物馆). With over 7000 artifacts on display from a 2400-year-old tomb, there's little room for other exhibits. Chime bells, zithers, and other musical instruments are among the finds, including one of the oldest excavated dynastic bronze bells. *(On Donghu Lu. The entrance is hard to miss if you backtrack from the East Lake entrance. Open daily 9am-5:30pm; tickets sold 9-11:30am and 1:30-5:30pm. Y30, students Y15.)*

YICHANG 宜昌   ☎0717

Sleepy little Yichang marks the end of the Yangzi canyonlands and the first disembarkment point for most river cruises. Despite the nearby Gezhou Dam and the gargantuan Three Gorges Dam construction project that looms farther upstream, there's nothing electric about Yichang. Most travelers pass through quickly and catch the first available train to Chongqing, Wuhan, or Wudangshan. For longer stays, the dams make for some fascinating sightseeing, and the city's welcoming atmosphere make visitors feel at home.

⌷ TRANSPORTATION

Flights: Three Gorges Airport (sānxiá jīchǎng; 三峡机场 ; ☎622 8915). Serves about 10 domestic cities. The airport bus (Y20) picks up passengers at the Three Gorges Hotel by the waterfront on Yanjiang Dadao. To: **Beijing** (3hr., 4pm, Y1300); **Chengdu** (1½hr., daily, Y790); **Chongqing** (1hr., daily, Y740); **Shanghai** (1½hr., daily, Y1080).

Trains: Yichang Train Station (yíchāng huǒchē zhàn; 宜昌火车站 ; ☎644 5242), at the intersection of Yunji Lu and Dongshan Dadao. Tickets sold on the left side of the station daily 5am-10pm. Be prepared to find that there are no sleepers available for trains within the next 2 days; travel agents in Yichang buy up sleeper tickets, making it nearly impossible to leave Yichang in a sleeper without paying a commission or waiting 3 days. Luggage storage 8am-2am (Y2). To: **Beijing** (19hr., 6:30am, Y175); **Guangzhou** (11hr.; 7, 10:40am; Y73); **Shanghai** (26hr., noon, Y208); **Taiyuan** (21hr., 3:10pm, Y78); **Xi'an** (18hr., daily, Y196-209).

Buses: Yichang has 3 bus stations, 2 of which are next to ferry terminals.

Yichang Bus Station (yíchāng qìchē zhàn; 宜昌汽车站 ; ☎644 5314), on Dongshan Dadao, 5min. from the train station. When facing the train station, turn right; the bus station is on your right. Open 24hr. Inquire about departure times and ticket prices at the "English and Dumbness Window." To: **Hefei** (9hr., 9am, Y186); **Wuhan** (every 30-60min. 7am-8pm, Y80-115); **Xiangfan** (4hr., every 40min., Y60); **Xingshan** (3hr., every 20-30min. 7am-late afternoon, Y30).

Yichang Port Bus Station (yíchāng gǎng qìché kèyùn zhàn; 宜昌港汽车客运站 ; ☎696 6157), near Dock 9. Next to and shares ticket windows with the Ferry Passenger Main Station.

A **bus station** is next to Dagongqiao Amphibious Passenger Terminal. To: **Maoping** (1-2hr., every 30min. 6:30am-6pm, Y13); **Wushan Scenic Area** (1:40pm, Y35), near Wu Gorge, via **Xingshan.**

Ferries: The most convenient place to purchase boat and bus tickets is at the **Ferry Passenger Main Station** (kèyùn zǒng zhàn; 客运总站 ; ☎622 4354), where most Three Gorges ships embark and disembark. Inquire at the "English and Dumbness" window. Passenger ships only to: **Chongqing** (45hr.+, Y125-785); **Nanjing** (50hr., Y129-1004); **Shanghai** (65hr., Y178-1248). **Dagongqiao Amphibious Passenger Terminal** (dàgōngqiáo shuǐlù kèyùn zhàn; 大公桥水陆客运站 ; ☎622 2144), on Yanjiang Dadao near Shengli Si Lu. Sells tickets to Chongqing via the Three Gorges. Passenger ships only (Y107-785). See **The Three Gorges,** p. 734, for details on prices and times.

Local Transportation: Buses run 6am-8pm. Fare Y1. Bus #2 zips from the dock along Yanjiang Dadao; #3, 4, and 29 go to the train station; #3 and 4 via Yunji Lu; #9 goes from the Yichang Bus Station to Gezhou Dam.

Taxis: Base fare Y5, each additional km Y1.2. Most trips Y5-10.

✦⁊ ORIENTATION AND PRACTICAL INFORMATION

Yichang's compact downtown area occupies the northeast Yangzi bank, bordered by **Yanjiang Dadao** (沿江大道). The docks are in the south, and the rail and bus stations in the north on **Dongshan Dadao** (东山大道), which runs roughly parallel to Yanjiang Dadao. **Jiefang Lu** (解放路), **Longkang Lu** (隆康路), and **Yiling Dadao** (夷陵大道) are parallel to Dongshan Dadao. Perpendicular to the river, **Yunji Lu** (云集路), the downtown street lined with stores, hotels, and entertainment options, extends for approximately 1km before intersecting with Dongshan Dadao at the train station. **Shengli Si Lu** (胜利四路) and **Shengli San Lu** (胜利三路) head away from the river farther east; **Huancheng Lu** (环城路) does so farther west. The blocks around Yunji Lu closest to the river share the main street's activity.

Travel Agencies: CITS, 21 Mingji Lu, Guoji Jinlong Dasha (International Golden Dragon Tower), 17th fl., Rm. 1708 (☎625 1737). Taxi from the docks Y5. English spoken. Offers group tours to the Three Gorges Dam and Three Gorges cruises (low season Y380, including dam Y480; doesn't include price of boat tickets or admissions). Train ticket commissions Y25. No air or cruise commissions. Open daily M-F 8:30am-6pm.

Bank of China: 10 Shengli Si Lu (☎623 6217), at Longkang Lu. Near Dagongqiao stop on bus #3 or 4. Exchanges currency and traveler's checks. Credit card advances. Open M-F 8-11:30am and 2-6pm. The **Taohualing Hotel** on Yunji Lu, north of Longkang Lu, exchange US dollars and euros for its lodgers.

PSB: Inside the Port Bus Station (☎622 4359) at Dock 9. Open 24hr.

Hospital: No. 2 People's Hospital (dì'èr rénmín yīyuàn; 第二人民医院 ; ☎673 2452), on Xiling Lu near Huancheng Lu.

Telephones: The main **China Telecom** is on Yunji Lu, at Yiling Dadao, next door to the post office. IDD service and pay phones available. Open daily 8am-5:30pm.

Internet Access: New Vista Internet Cafe (xīn shìyě wǎngbā; 新视野网吧 ; ☎622 9921). From the train station, walk 2 blocks toward the long-distance bus station and turn right on Guoyuan Yi Lu; it's another 2 blocks down. Y1.5 per hr. Open 24hr.

Post Office: On the corner of Yunji Lu and Yiling Dadao. EMS and Poste Restante. Open daily 8am-7pm.

Postal Code: 443000.

▮▮ ACCOMMODATIONS AND FOOD

Wealthy Three-Gorges-cruising clientele increase Yichang's hotel rates; the best deals are along Yunji Lu, near the docks, and near the train station.

The lively waterfront restaurants and nightmarket on **Taozhu Lu,** west of Yunji Lu, serve point-and-choose stir-fry platters for Y5-10 per person. A few hotpot restaurants also bubble up in the area. Around the train station, cheap food stands are strewn along **Dongshan Dadao,** near the base of the steps. The first street that runs toward the river from Longkang Lu (when coming from Yunji Lu) is filled with fruit and vegetable stands, meat shops, and steamers of *mántóu* (buns). Longkang Lu itself plays host to a few mouth-watering eateries. Try **KSB ❶** (KSB kǒu shuǐ bā; KSB 口水吧) for local delicacies and fried lamb chops on a stick for Y6 and up. (Open daily 10am-1:30am.) Next door, the cozy **A Walk in the Clouds Western Restaurant ❷** (yún zhōng mànbù xī cāntīng; 云中漫步西餐厅) appeases the homesick with spaghetti, omelettes (Y12-15), chef's salad (Y18), and a variety of Chinese teas and cocktails from Y18 to Y48. (☎624 3850. Open daily 9:30am-2am.)

Yijian Hostel (yíjiàn zhāodàisuǒ; 宜建招待所), 118 Dongshan Dadao (☎644 5127). Take bus #3 or 4 to the Huochezhan (train station) stop and make a right on Dongshan Dadao at its intersection with Yunji Lu. Convenient, clean, and friendly. Most rooms have color TV and a ceiling fan. 24hr. hot water. Singles and doubles with shared bath Y30, with A/C Y60; doubles with private bath and A/C Y80. ❶

Yichang Railway Hotel (yíchāng tiělù dàjiǔdiàn; 宜昌铁路大酒店 ; ☎646 3073), 107-9 Dongshan Dadao. In the train station square, just left of the station entrance, at the top of the steps to Dongshan Dadao. Rooms have A/C and some are quiet. 24hr. hot water. 5- and 6-bed dorms with shared bath and no A/C Y12; triples with shared bath Y120. Hourly stays Y35 for the 1st hr., each additional hr. Y15. ❶

Peaceful Holiday Hotel (hépíng jiàri jiǔdiàn; 和平假日酒店), 141 Yanjiang Dadao (☎625 4000; fax 625 4088), across from Dagongqiao Passenger Terminal, near the docks. Quiet waterfront stay, with view of the sleek bridge down Yanjiang Dadao. Well-furnished doubles Y198 and up; triples Y215-248. ❸

Taohualing Hotel (táohuālíng fàndiàn; 桃花岭饭店), 29 Yunji Lu (☎623 6666; fax 623 8888). Take bus #3 or 4. Tucked into a garden lane in a quiet, beautiful environment. Exchanges US dollars and euros for residents. Luxurious doubles Y280 and up. ❹

👁 SIGHTS

On hot days, locals use the riverbanks as an informal swimming hole, despite the questionable condition of the water. The riverside heights provide for leisurely strolls and vistas of the grand, murky Yangzi, laden with river traffic. Closer to the city center, the **Riverside Park** (bīnjiāng gōngyuán; 滨江公园) stretches along the waterfront from Shengli Lu to Xiling Lu, with a number of places to sit and watch the powerful Yangzi current. Yichang's main points of interest are the hydroelectric wonders that rumble upstream from town. The **Gezhou Dam** (gézhōu bà; 葛洲坝) squats on the Yangzi just north of the city. Finished in 1988 after 17 years of construction, the 2.6km-wide, 53m-high wall across the mouth of the Xiling Gorge has now been dwarfed by its larger, more famous cousin not far upstream. (Take Bus #9 from Dongshan Lu, or the Maoping-bound bus from the bus station next to Dagongqiao Passenger Terminal. Open daily 8am-late evening. Y20.) To visit the **Three Gorges Dam,** you must join a tour group, as transportation into the dam area is restricted. A typical tour package costs Y160 and includes only the tour guide fee and transportation to and from Yichang; try the Yijian Hostel for prices as low as Y100. For more information on the dam site, see the **Three Gorges**, p. 734.

SHENNONGJIA 神农架 ☎0719

Shennongjia National Natural Reserve sprawls over a vast wilderness of mountains, rivers, and virgin forest. Literally the "Trellis of Shennong," the reserve was named after the mythical god of medicine who discovered traditional Chinese herbal medicine, tasting hundreds of wild plants to test their medicinal properties. The region is among the most ecologically diverse in China, with some 2000 species of plants and rare animals like the golden monkey and crimson-bellied tragopan. Much of Shennongjia is still unexplored territory and closed to the public, but a small scenic area carved out from the larger expanse has been developed in recent years. Only specified sites within this scenic area, as well as the base town of Muyuping, 30km southeast of the reserve, are open to foreigners. Sheltered in one of China's most untouched natural landscapes, this tiny corner offers a glimpse into the whole of Shennongjia and its deep forests and stony mountains.

🚌 ℹ TRANSPORTATION AND PRACTICAL INFORMATION

Muyuping (mùyúpíng; 木鱼坪) serves as the base for daytrips into **Shennongjia National Natural Reserve** (shénnóngjià guójiā zìrán bǎohù qū; 神农架国家自然保护区). A main street lined with recently built hotels and restaurants runs east-west. Vans to the scenic area run up a smaller road that intersects with the main street at its midpoint. There are no official street names.

No foreigners are allowed beyond **Yazikou** (yāzikǒu; 鸭子口), a town past the scenic area en route to points farther north and east, where a huge military base is rumored to be stationed, a theory supported by the large number of soldiers wandering the area. Unless you have a permit or enjoy entanglements with the PSB, do not travel to **Songbai** (sōngbǎi; 松柏) or **Shiyan** (shí yàn; 十堰).

Buses: There is no official bus station in town; buses and minibuses rumble down the main street and its intersecting road. Most travelers arrive via **Xingshan** (1-2hr., every 30min. 6:30am-late afternoon) from **Yichang.** Minibuses to Xingshan (Y10) leave when full; price is the same going the opposite direction. **Taxis** Y30-40.

Local Transportation: Local minivans can be hired for the day to make the trip from Muyuping into the scenic area. You can also make arrangements with your driver from Xingshan. Minivan to **Shengnong Peak** area about Y150-200, **Yantian** area extra Y150.

Travel Agency: CYTS (24hr. ☎345 2879; snjcyts@chinaholiday.com), at the westernmost end of main road, past the bridge. Though little English is spoken, the extremely friendly staff do their best to help. Open daily summer 7am-10pm; winter 8am-9pm.

Bank: Agricultural Bank of China (☎333 3068). Open 8-11:30am and 2:30-5:30pm. It is very difficult to exchange foreign currency in town, so bring lots of *yuán*.

PSB: Muyu Police Station (☎345 2110). On the smaller road up the intersection with the main street. Open 24hr.

Hospital: Muyu Clinic (☎345 2244), on main road, west of intersection. Open 24hr.

Internet Access: Peace Internet Cafe (hépíng wǎng bā; 和平网吧 ; ☎345 2733). Just east of the intersection, on the main street. Y2 per hr. Open 24hr.

Post and Telecommunications: (☎345 2925), on small road intersecting with the main street, next to the Postal Hotel. No international mail service. Open daily 8am-noon and 2:30-5:30pm. **China Telecom,** next to the post office. Open daily 8am-5:30pm. Public phones available on adjacent street with IP/IC cards. International calls Y8.2 per min.

Postal Code: 442421.

ACCOMMODATIONS AND FOOD

No accommodations are allowed in the reserve area. Though small, hotels in Muyuping are all clean and furnished. Near the intersection, the **Xueyuan Hotel ●** (xuě yuán fàndiàn; 雪缘饭店) has the cheapest rooms in town open to foreigners. (☎345 2175. 3- and 4- bed dorms with shared bath Y10; doubles with private bath Y40-60.) On the left of the smaller road en route to Shennongjia scenic area, the **Postal Hotel ●** (yóuzhèng lǚyóu jiēdài zhōngxīn; 邮政旅游接待中心) offers rooms with bath and TV. (☎345 3477. Singles and doubles Y60-80.) Rooms at the **Big South Gate Hotel ●** (dà nán mén bīnguǎn; 大南门宾馆), across the street, are pretty much the same. (☎345 2292. Doubles Y70; triples Y110.) The most comfortable stay in town is at the **Shennongjia Mountain Villa ❷** (shénnóngjià shān zhuāng; 神农架山庄), west of the intersection on main street. Relax on the courtyard and spacious private patio overlooking trees and a brook. (☎345 3088; fax 345 3588. Private bath and TV. Doubles Y160; luxury suites Y400 and up.)

Small joints line the main street, serving noodles and dumplings (Y3-5). Many hotels also have a restaurant area on the first floor. The best place to find food is near the intersection or at either end of the main street.

SHENNONGJIA NATURE RESERVE

The scenic area now open to tourists is but a minute portion of the whole 700km^2 expanse. Much of the mountain ranges beyond, including those of Greater Shennongjia and Laojunshan, are yet untrodden except by a few expedition and research teams. Besides the thousands of species of flora and fauna inhabiting the wilds, rumors tell of the "Wild Man," a yeti-like creature that roams the area. To date, however, little supporting evidence has been found other than a few stray pinches of hair and local stories. The recently developed scenic area sees many Chinese tour groups, though few foreign travelers make it out to Shennong. Hiking trails are sparse outside the designated scenic spots, and camping inside the reserve is forbidden in order to preserve the environment. The only way to access the reserve is to charter a minivan in Muyuping (see **Local Transportation,** p. 469).

There are two scenic areas in opposite directions from Muyuping, and it's best to save two days for the trip. About 2hr. from Muyuping, **Shennong Peak** (shénnóng dǐng; 神农顶) is the highest point in the reserve at 3105m. The Y60 admission ticket includes four sights other than the summit: **Scenic Gorge** (fēngjǐng yà; 风景垭), a cliff overlooking seas of clouds, and, sometimes after summer storms, rainbows over the steeply plunging cliffs below; **Banbi Rock** (bǎnbì yán; 板壁岩), with a few trails leading into the forest and under mossy stones (about 1hr. of hiking); **Golden Monkey Cliff** (jīn hóu lǐng; 金猴岭), where golden monkeys once roamed beside a waterfall, though now they have moved deeper into the reserve; and an "Animal Healing Station" at **Little Dragon Lake** (xiǎolóng tán; 小龙潭). From the summit of Shennong Peak, visitors can find the best views, gazing from atop the watchtower to the mystic mountains of Greater Shennongjia on the horizon.

The second scenic region of **Yantian** lies near the town of Hongping (hóngpíng; 红坪), about an hour's drive from Muyu. This is the most hiking you'll be able to do in Shennongjia, from the picturesque "Hongping Art Corridor" (Y20), so named for its scenic stretch of forests and streams, to the stalagmite-studded Guxiniu Caves (Y30). Check on whether foreigners are permitted on the road to Songbai that runs through the Yantian scenic area. If passage is permitted, charter a van for your visit rather than taking the buses that run along this road.

XIANGFAN 襄樊 ☎ 0710

A place for travelers to spend the night, wash up, and make the appropriate transportation connections, Xiangfan devotes itself mainly to building cars and shuttling passengers throughout the country. If you're heading to Wudangshan, you'll probably spend a few hours or even a night in this pleasant, if unexciting, town.

✈ ? ORIENTATION AND PRACTICAL INFORMATION

The mid-sized city of Xiangfan is made smaller by the fact that most travelers don't need to venture very far away from the train or bus stations. The train station is in a large square just off **Qianjin Lu** (前进路), at the head of **Zhongyuan Lu** (中原路). Eateries and hotels cluster nearby. The long-distance bus station is about two blocks down Zhongyuan Lu from the train station; the local bus station is directly across from the train station.

Flights: CAAC ticket office, 44 Qianjin Lu (☎323 9213), at Zhongyuan Lu. Open daily 7am-7pm. The **Business Center of the Railway Grand Hotel** (☎322 0043, ext. 6205), on the right past the reception desk, also sells tickets, but for hotel lodgers only. Open daily 8am-7pm for airline tickets, 7:20am-11pm for train tickets. The **airport** has daily service to: **Beijing** (2hr., Y810); **Shanghai** (2hr., Y980); **Shenzhen** (2hr., Y990).

Trains: Xiangfan Train Station (xiāngfán huǒchē zhàn; 襄樊火车站) is off a square at the intersection of Zhongyuan Lu and Qianjin Lu. The main ticket hall is on the right, though it's currently under renovation; a temporary ticket station is outside. Buy tickets early; sleeper tickets can be extremely difficult to purchase, even in advance. Hard seat travelers be forewarned: passengers line up at the station gates 30min. before departure and then stampede to the trains at frightening speeds. To: **Beijing** (15-17hr., 5 per day, Y130-150) and **Wuhan** (3½-5hr., 3 per day, Y47).

Buses: Xiangfan Bus Station (xiāngfán qìchē zhàn; 襄樊汽车站 ; ☎322 3768) is on Zhongyuan Lu, 2 blocks from the train station. Ticket office open 24hr. Luggage storage in the ticket hall, just left of the entrance. Buses leave every hr. to: **Shiyan** (3½hr., Y45); **Wudangshan** (3hr., every hr. 7:30am-6pm, Y40); **Wuhan,** stopping at both **Hankou** and **Wuchang** (5hr., every hr. 7am-6pm, Y70); **Yichang** (4½hr., every 40min. 6am-6pm, Y60). **Minibuses** to Shiyan leave frequently from nearby depots.

Currency Exchange: None of the Bank of China branches exchanges foreign currency. The Railway Grand Hotel exchanges currency for lodgers only. Bring enough cash.

Telephones: China Unicom, at the end of Zhongyuan Lu, a block before the train station. Calls to the US Y2.4 per min., to Europe Y7.2 per min. Open daily 8am-9pm.

Post Office: Down the alley behind the train station, next to the luggage storage office. EMS. Open daily 8am-6pm.

Postal Code: 441003.

ACCOMMODATIONS AND FOOD

For the price of a meal, you can easily get a room for the night, but it might be less comfortable than a damp cardboard box. If you're coming from the train or the long-distance bus station, these super-cheap deals will find you in the form of over-eager women pulling weary passengers into their nearby hostels. Keep your eyes peeled for the bigger hotels and cleaner signs, where you'll find decent lodgings at budget prices.

The streets around the train stations are filled with a sprinkling of stalls with outside seating and small stores that sell ultra-convenient styrofoam-**boxed meals** (hé fàn; 盒饭 ; Y5) and ultra-inexpensive **dumplings** (Y1 for 7). It's easy to find both Chinese-style fast-food joints and pleasant sit-down restaurants. Two blocks from the train station, on Zhongyuan Lu, **Big Hong's Dumpling Restaurant ❶** (dà hóng jì jiǎozi guǎn; 大洪记饺子馆) serves not only a plethora of dumpling varieties (try the lotus root and pork meat for Y6), but also standard Hubei fare (Y8-30 per dish).

PSB Hotel (xiāngtiě gōng'ān zhāodàisuǒ; 襄铁公安招待所 ; ☎323 3877, ext. 0). Conveniently across from the long-distance bus station, on Zhongyuan Lu. As its name suggests, the brightly lit hotel is guarded by the PSB next door, and uniformed guards patrol the hallways, making it a safe place to stay if you don't have a guilty conscience. Rooms are clean, well-furnished, and quiet; even the standard rooms have TV, A/C, mirror, and desk. Dorms Y30; doubles Y50, with private bath Y100; triples Y80-120. ❶

Aeolus Hotel (fēngshén bīnguǎn; 风神宾馆), 36 Qianjin Lu (☎382 9299; fax 382 9000). From the train station, turn right on Qianjin Lu; look for the very tall building with the English name plastered on the side. Comfort for reasonable prices. All rooms have A/C, bath, phone, and TV. 24hr. hot water. Doubles Y200-288; 3hr. stay Y50-80. ❸

Railway Grand Hotel (tiělù dàjiǔdiàn; 铁路大酒店), 46 Qianjin Lu (☎322 0043; fax 322 1724), just across from the train station. Business center in lobby books plane and train tickets. Currency exchange. Laundry service. Doubles Y200-288; triples Y288-368. Major credit cards accepted. ❸

WUDANGSHAN MOUNTAIN 武当山 ☎0719

Long before *Crouching Tiger, Hidden Dragon* exposed this majestic mountain and its devotion to the martial arts to the Western world, Wudangshan figured prominently in the Chinese literary imagination, with its dark forests, lofty temples, and black-robed Daoist monks. Primarily famed as the birthplace of one of Daoism's deities, the Great Emperor Zhen Wu, the mountain is also known as the birthplace of Wudang boxing. This style of *wushu* is still practiced today by the mountaintop academy's long-haired masters, who use grace before strength and swiftness before power in the timeless art of self-defense. A stealthy beauty pervades the mountain, with temples and palaces scattered about more vertically

YANGZI BASIN

than horizontally, to accommodate the steep slopes. Clouds hang low, and the fog curls its way about craggy cliffs and slips around trees and rocks, creating an almost haunted atmosphere.

📷 ⁇ TRANSPORTATION AND PRACTICAL INFORMATION

The Wudangshan range stretches across northwestern Hubei province, between Xiangfan and Shiyan. Most travelers to Wudangshan stay in the city, about 25km from the main peak. One main street runs through town, going east to Xiangfan and west to Shiyan. The main entrance to the mountain is just past the bridge to the east. From there, a sharply curving road leads up to hotels, restaurants, and the mountain's main sights.

Trains: Wudangshan Train Station (wǔdàngshān huǒchē zhàn; 武当山火车站 ; ☎507 5782) is south of the main road, at the end of one of the side streets. If trains arrive early and no one is there, they often do not stick around, and if they're late, they tend to not stop at all. Ticket office open 11am-1pm, 4-6pm, and 10-11pm. To: **Beijing** (20hr., 5:50pm, Y165); **Wuhan** (7hr., 11pm, Y70); **Xiangfan** (2hr., 5:50pm, Y22).

Buses: There is a **bus station** on the main road, but it doesn't keep a regular schedule. Buses run along the main road, trolling for passengers (keep your eyes and ears open), and also stop to pick up people before entering the Xiang-Shi Highway (xiāngshí gāosù gōnglù; 襄十高速公路). Departures to **Shiyan** (1hr., Y6) are the most frequent. Buses to **Xiangfan** (Y30-40) are less frequent, so it may be better to take a minivan or cab to **Danjiang** (1hr., Y15) and then transfer onto a Xiangfan-bound bus (1hr., Y17).

Bank of China: (☎566 8668) Just west of the bridge, on the main road. Exchanges currency only. Open daily summer 8am-6pm; winter 8am-5:30pm.

PSB: Wudangshan Station (wǔdàngshān pàichūsuǒ; 武当山派出所 ; 24hr. ☎568 9195), on the mountain, about 1km downhill from Purple Heaven Hall.

Hospital: Wudangshan Hospital (wǔdàngshān yīyuàn; 武当山医院 ; ☎566 9120).

Internet Access: New Extremely Fast Internet Cafe (xīn jí sù wǎngbā; 新极速网吧), 2nd fl., on the main road opposite the Xuanwu Hotel. Y1.5 per hr. Open 8am-midnight.

Post Office (☎566 0414). From the bridge, walk 2 blocks from the main road and turn into the lane; look for a pagoda-topped building. EMS. Open daily summer 8am-6pm; winter 8am-5:30pm.

Postal Code: 442714.

🏠 ⁇ ACCOMMODATIONS AND FOOD

IN TOWN

Off the mountain, the main road is lined with newly furnished hotels of all tiers. The **Laoying Hotel** ❷ (lǎoyíng fàndiàn; 老营饭店), on the left side of the main road, across the bridge, is the best deal in town. Large rooms come with 24hr. hot water and A/C. (☎566 5349 or 566 5347. Doubles with bath Y100-200; triples Y140.) The **Xuanwu (Dajiudian) Hotel** ❷ (xuánwǔ dàjiǔdiàn; 玄武大酒店) is on the main road, across from the road leading to the train station. (☎566 5347. A/C, private bath, 24hr. hot water. Doubles Y128-180; triples Y100-148.)

Family-owned stalls fry several varieties of **scallion pancakes** (Y0.5) and golden, light-as-air dough (Y1 for a bagful). A handful of sit-down places (mostly in hotels) scatter along the main road. At night, go two blocks toward the main road from the train station to find a nearby street bustling with a lively **nightmarket**, where vendors wait with coals, frying pots, and colorful stands of fresh vegetables, meat, and seafood delicacies (dishes Y10-25).

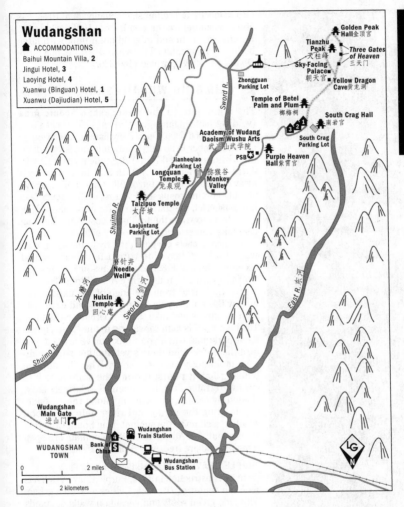

Wudangshan

ACCOMMODATIONS

Baihui Mountain Villa, **2**
Jingui Hotel, **3**
Laoying Hotel, **4**
Xuanwu (Binguan) Hotel, **1**
Xuanwu (Dajiudian) Hotel, **5**

Golden Peak Hall 金顶宫
Tianzhu Peak 天柱峰
Three Gates of Heaven 三天门
Sky-Facing Palace 朝天宫
Yellow Dragon Cave 黄龙洞
Zhongguan Parking Lot
Temple of Betel Palm and Plum 椰梅祠
South Crag Hall 南岩宫
South Crag Parking Lot
Academy of Wudang Daoism Wushu Arts 武当山武学院
PSB
Purple Heaven Hall 紫霄宫
Jianheqiao Parking Lot
Longquan Temple 龙泉观
Monkey Valley 猕猴谷
Taizipuo Temple 太子坡
Laojuntang Parking Lot
Needle Well 磨针井
Huixin Temple 回心庵
Sword R. 剑河
Shuimo R.
East R. 东河
Wudangshan Main Gate 进山门
Wudangshan Train Station
Bank of China
WUDANGSHAN TOWN
Wudangshan Bus Station

0   2 miles
0   2 kilometers

ON THE MOUNTAIN

Most accommodations lie along the main road leading up to the South Crag Hall parking lot halfway up the mountain. Family-run hotels charge lower prices for rooms of similar quality and often have restaurants on the first floor. The family-run **Jingui Hotel ❸** (jīnguì dàjiǔdiàn; 金贵大酒店), the first building on the left, has clean, bright rooms descending into the valley sloping off the road, in addition to a spacious patio for dining under the stars. Ordinary rooms (pǔjiān; 普间) lack a bath, but the owner will gladly let you enjoy the 24hr. hot water in the private bath attached to standard rooms (biāojiān; 标间). (☎568 9198. Singles Y45, with bath Y80-100; doubles Y60-80.) Near the end of the mountain road, the **Xuanwu (Binguan) Hotel ❷** (xuánwǔ bīnguǎn; 玄武宾馆) has 24hr. hot water and decent baths. (☎568 9175. Doubles Y120-240; triples Y160-320.) Right next to the Xuanwu, the **Baihui**

Mountain Villa ❷ (bǎihuì shānzhuāng; 百汇山庄) is about 500m before the South Crag Hall parking lot. Rooms are clean and in good condition, with large bathtubs, phone, and TV. (☎568 9191; fax 568 9088. Doubles Y140-280; triples Y160-320.)

🔼 CLIMBING WUDANGSHAN

The main gate to the **Wudangshan Scenic Area** (wǔdàngshān fēngjǐng qū; 武当山风景区) is just east of town. (☎566 5396. Open daily 6am to late evening; a staff member is on duty 24hr., but they stop admitting visitors around 6-7pm. Y70, students with ID Y35; extra Y1 for insurance.) With that in mind, speed away on a good 30min. terror-filled ride along narrow, sharply curving roads until you reach the **South Crag Hall parking lot,** the starting point for most hikers. Minivans from town to the trailhead cost Y10. They can also take you around to the other side of the mountain, where a **cable car** goes directly to the summit by way of a long, lazy ride with a few near-vertical ascents. (Open M-F 8:30am-4pm, Sa-Su 8:30am-5pm. Up Y45, down Y35; round-trip Y70, children Y35.)

Two trails lead from the edge of the parking lot. Follow the walkway on the right to South Crag Hall, then backtrack and take the left path to the summit. The hike itself is akin to waiting in line at an amusement park: just when you think you've arrived, you turn the corner and there's yet another steep staircase mocking your endurance. When it rains on Wudangshan it pours, turning the staircases into mini-waterfalls. Still, the ascent is relatively easy, shaded by foliage and winding along the cliffside, overlooking the valley and river below. In good weather, a climb to the summit from South Crag Hall takes about 2hr. All sights on the mountain are open 7am-6pm and are free, unless otherwise stated.

PURPLE HEAVEN HALL (zǐxiāo gōng; 紫霄宫). From its construction in 1413, Purple Heaven Hall has been the center of Daoist activities at Wudangshan. With jade green roofs and vermilion walls, it stands majestically at the lower part of the mountain. The daily Daoist chanting at 5pm, wafting incense, and occasional drifts of flute and *gǔqín* (a seven-stringed zither) floating from the quiet rear temples exude the air of a Daoist paradise. *(Open daily 7am-6pm. Y10.)*

SOUTH CRAG HALL (nányán gōng; 南岩宫). South Crag Hall is about a 15min. walk from the parking lot. From the large stone arch, go down the steps (heading up leads to a couple of uninteresting temples). According to legend, before Zhen Wu became a celestial being, he drank sacred water from the old hexagonal well within South Crag Hall. Take a left behind the main altar to **Tianyi Zhenqing Stone Palace** (tiānyǐ zhēnqìnggōng shídiàn; 天乙真庆宫石殿), where paths cling to the side of rocky cliffs. Here, **Dragon Head Rock** (lóngtóu shí; 龙头石) extends into the air beyond the mountain face. Incense burns at the end, as it has for centuries.

TEMPLE OF BETEL PALM AND PLUM (lángméi cí; 榔梅祠). The first major site on the way to the summit is a temple built during the Six Dynasties period to honor the Black Warriors, famous in Daoist legend for grafting a plum branch onto a betel palm. Much of the temple is devoted to Wudang boxing, developed by Zhang Sanfeng after he witnessed a fight between a magpie and a snake and understood their opposing natures.

YELLOW DRAGON CAVE (huánglóng dòng; 黄龙洞). As legend goes, the sage and medicine man Li Shizhen meditated here while completing his masterpiece *Materia Medica*, cataloguing Chinese plants and their medicinal uses. Go up the stairs to the left to see a grotesque statue of the mountain's dragon god, clad in a bright yellow cape. The Sacred Spring nearby is more a stagnant pool collected from water dripping off the stones above.

TO THE SUMMIT. From here, it's onward and upward to the summit. At **Sky-Facing Palace** (cháotiān gōng; 朝天宫), the path to the right leads to the **Three Gates of Heaven** (sāntiān mén; 三天门), where the view opens up after a steep ascent to a magnificent patio of rose gardens overlooking the valley below. Doves rise from the roofs of the brick-red temples, as Daoist monks float down the frighteningly steep staircases with uncanny ease. Pass through Harmony Palace and Lingguan Hall, dedicated to a Daoist god who punishes sinners by flinging them off the cliff. The top of the mountain (tiānzhù; 天柱) yields vistas of the rugged landscape. Provided your legs can manage the final walk, head to **Golden Peak Hall** (jīn dǐng gōng; 金顶宫) to check out a shiny, gilded brass statue of the balding Zhen Wu. *(Y10.)* To return to civilization, take the cable car down to the lower station or climb back via the less steep trails to **Purple-Gold Palace** and **Ancient Bronze Palace.**

SOUTH COAST

As the nation's gritty economic engine, the south coast throbs to a different beat than the rest of China, and likes it just fine that way. While much of the country struggles with growing pains, prosperity seems to be a given here. The coastal provinces of Guangdong and Fujian have long reaped the benefits of their prime locations, while impoverished but sunny Hainan Island basks in the sea breeze. From early trade with Arab merchants and European galleons to 20th-century commerce with nearby Hong Kong and Taiwan, the south coast has always raced ahead of the pack. It is no surprise then that China's first four Special Economic Zones—Shenzhen, Shantou, Xiamen, and Zhuhai—would all fall in the south coast. Subsequent SEZs followed, peppering the region with more than its share of slick commercial cities. What the south coast lacks in big-name sights, it makes up in character and cuisine. The tastes of Guangdong have spread to all corners of the world, and with Cantonese and Fujianese people making up the bulk of overseas Chinese, so have its people. From the balmy beach resorts of Hainan Island, to the gaudy theme parks of Shenzhen, to the heady nightlife of Guangzhou, this region creates its own attractions. Today's south coast inhabitants are proud of their roots and slightly disparaging of their snooty northern neighbors, preferring to revel in food, fun, and its favored status.

HIGHLIGHTS OF THE SOUTH COAST

DRIFT ON A BAMBOO RAFT down ethereal Nine-Bend River in **Wuyishan** (p. 486).

WALTZ DOWN THE STREETS of **Gulangyu** (p. 495), Xiamen's famous "Piano Isle," where classical music floats from colonial villa balconies.

SEE RED in Shaoguan at **Danxiashan Mountain** (p. 516), complete with red stones, green parks, and a phallic rock.

BITE BACK at man's best friend at **Guangzhou's** Qingping Market (p. 506) or at snakes in **Fujian,** where the scaly reptiles have slithered their way onto every menu.

FUJIAN 福建

Fujian province stares directly across the straits into Taiwan. While the province joins the rest of the mainland in expressing displeasure over Taiwan's "renegade" status, the flow of funds and friendship across the straits (most evident in the ostentatious riches of the provincial capital, Fuzhou) seems unlikely to slow because of mere politics—perhaps because Fujian has had a centuries-long practice of cavorting with outsiders. It first opened its ports to Arab and European traders hundreds of years ago, and Fujian's fabled mariners have been exploring the sea for even longer. In fact, many present-day Taiwanese have their roots in Fujian. Despite Fujian's delicate balancing act, the province seems blissfully unaware of the tension created by associating with the rest of the world. Instead, it prefers to dwell upon its splendid natural attributes, from its vibrant coasts to the craggy peaks and waterfalls of Wuyishan. In the bustling old-world port cities of Quanzhou and Xiamen, the patchwork of colonial facades and stately mosques spells out the intriguing fabric of cosmopolitan Fujian.

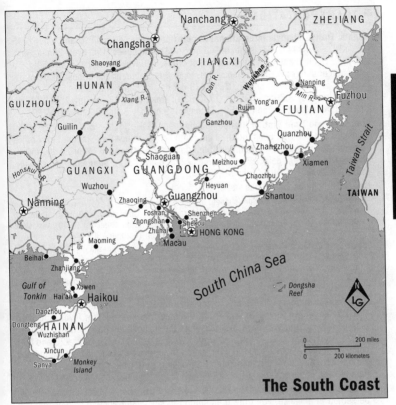

The South Coast

FUZHOU 福州 ☎ 0591

Though Fuzhou continues to expand upward and outward, it does so with a sense of image and class. The city frowns upon excess grime, tut-tuts at unsightly pollution, and positively balks at the din of superfluous traffic. Travelers are instead invited to admire the spanking new train station, a monument to modern architecture, sip fragrant brews in the city's exquisite tea houses, and reflect, as they breeze through the busy yet quiet streets on an air-conditioned bus, that there are therapeutic advantages to enforcing Y200 fines for the improper use of car horns.

Vibrant and eclectic, the city is a fascinating amalgam of *Mǐnnánhuà*-speaking locals of Portuguese descent, migrants from the poverty-stricken countryside eager to start anew in a wealthy provincial capital, Shanghainese expats peddling sticky rice cakes, and cell-phone-toting businessmen paying their respects at Buddhist temples. When the day's work is done, however, the community spirit of this unlikely blend comes alive as residents gather in parks, streets, and squares to chit-chat, fly kites, and line-dance the night away.

TRANSPORTATION

Flights: Fuzhou Changle International Airport (fúzhōu chánglè guójì jīchǎng; 福州长乐国际机场; ☎344 0664), south of Fuzhou city. **Shuttle buses** (1hr., every 25min. 6am-7pm, Y20) run to and from the **CAAC ticket office**, 185 Wuyi Zhong Lu (☎334 5988), a bit north of the South Long-Distance Passenger Bus Station on the opposite side of the street. Open daily 8am-8pm. To: **Beijing** (8 per day 8:25am-3pm, Y780-1559); **Guangzhou** (4 per day 9:20am-6:35pm, Y750-830); **Hong Kong** (5 per day 2:20-9:05pm, Y1300); **Nanchang** (3:45pm, Y450); **Shanghai** (9 per day 8am-8:20pm, Y390-780).

Trains: Fuzhou Train Station (fúzhōu huǒchē zhàn; 福州火车站; ☎705 0222), at the terminus of Hualin Lu, 5min. north of the North Long-Distance Bus Station. Ticket office open daily 6am-10pm. To: **Beijing** (35hr., daily, Y458); **Chengdu** (44hr., daily, Y424); **Nanchang** (11½hr., daily, Y96); **Nanjing** (22hr., daily, Y281); **Shanghai** (16hr., daily, Y250); **Wuyishan** (6½hr., 2 per day, Y47).

Buses: Fuzhou has 2 main bus stations.

North Long-Distance Bus Station (chángtú qìchē běi zhàn; 长途汽车北站; ☎758 0558), on Hualin Lu at Beihuan Lu, 5min. south of the train station. Open daily 5:30am-10:30pm. To: **Guangzhou** (21hr., 4 per day 5am-8pm, Y258); **Shanghai** (22hr., 2 per day, Y240); **Wuyishan** (7hr., 5:30pm, Y90); **Xiamen** (3½hr., every 10min. 5:50am-10:20pm, Y80).

South Long-Distance Passenger Bus Station (chángtú qìchē nán kèyùn zhàn; 长途汽车南客运站; ☎334 3446), on Wuyi Zhong Lu at Guohuo Xi Lu, in south Fuzhou, just south of the CAAC ticket office. Bus #51 runs here from the train station and the North Bus Station. Open daily 5:30am-9pm. To: **Guangzhou** (24hr., several per day 11am-8:20pm, Y218); **Hong Kong** (21hr., 4 per day 6:30-8pm, Y350-562); **Xiamen** (3½hr.; 6, 7am, 1pm; Y52-75).

Local Transportation: Fuzhou's **bus** routes run 5am-10 or 11pm. Fare Y1, with A/C Y2. Bus #1 runs down Bayiqi Lu and along the north bank of the Min River, and then crosses over to the south bank; #5 goes from the train station down Wusi Lu to Dong Jie; #8 heads up Wuyi Lu to the area around West Lake and Zuohai Park; #20 and 821 continue down Bayiqi Lu from the train station; #26 runs between the train station and airport; #51 runs from the train station to Taijiang Lu, traveling the length of the city from Wusi Lu to the end of Wuyi Lu; #949 runs from the train station to Drum Mountain.

Taxis: Base fare Y7-8, each additional km Y1.4-1.8. **Pedicabs** are plentiful; fares should be settled in advance. From the train station to city center about Y7. Pedicabs can sometimes cost as much as taxis, however.

ORIENTATION AND PRACTICAL INFORMATION

Fuzhou is a vast city, spanning from the train station in the northeast to the lower bank of the **Min River** (mǐn jiāng; 闽江) to the south. **Wusi Lu** (五四路), which becomes **Wuyi Lu** (五一路), runs north-south to the Min River and is chock-full of banks and luxurious hotels. Two other major north-south streets are **Bayiqi Lu** (八一七路) to the west and **Liuyi Lu** (六一路) to the east. **Hualin Lu** (华林路) curves northward to the train station and North Bus Station; **Dong Jie** (东街), between Bayiqi Lu and Wusi Lu, becomes **Dong Dalu** (东大路) east of Wusi Lu and is a large commercial street with many restaurants and department stores. **Gutian Lu** (古田路) roughly marks the heart of the city, sandwiched between **May First Square** (wǔyī guǎngchǎng; 五一广场) to the south and **Yushan Scenic Area** and a **Mao Zedong statue** to the north. The South Long-Distance Passenger Bus Station is at the intersection of Wuyi Zhong Lu and **Guohuo Xi Lu** (国货西路).

Travel Agencies: There are 2 CITS offices near the intersection of Wusi/Wuyi Lu and Dong Jie/Dong Dalu. **Tianma CITS** (☎334 0646; fax 331 3210) is on the 7th fl. of the large high-rise on the corner of Wuyi Bei Lu and Dong Dalu. English and Japanese interpreters available. 1-day tours of Fuzhou (Y70) are easier to book for groups. No com-

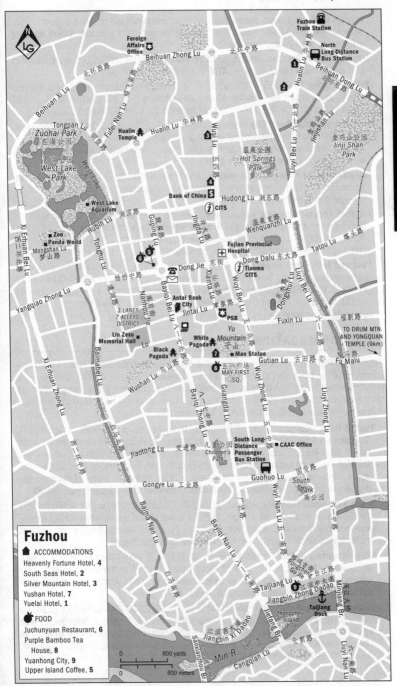

Fuzhou

🏠 ACCOMMODATIONS

Heavenly Fortune Hotel, **4**
South Seas Hotel, **2**
Silver Mountain Hotel, **3**
Yushan Hotel, **7**
Yuelai Hotel, **1**

🍴 FOOD

Juchunyuan Restaurant, **6**
Purple Bamboo Tea
 House, **8**
Yuanhong City, **9**
Upper Island Coffee, **5**

mission for plane tickets; commission for train tickets depend on price of ticket. Open daily summer 8am-6pm; winter 8am-5pm. Numerous plane and train **ticket booking offices** line Wuyi Lu and Wusi Lu.

Bank of China: The main branch is at 136 Wusi Lu (☎709 0821). Exchanges currency and issues credit card advances. **ATM.** Open daily 8am-5:45pm.

PSB: 1 Jingmen Lu (☎755 7705), off Jintai Lu. Open daily 8am-noon and 3-6pm. For visa extensions, contact the **Foreign Affairs Department** (wài guǎn kē; 外管科), 109 Beihuan Zhong Lu (☎782 1104), west of Wusi Bei Lu. Open M-F 8am-5:25pm.

Bookstores: Antai Book City (āntài shūchéng; 安泰书城 ; ☎752 7400), on the 1st fl. of the Antai Bldg., in a busy street vendor alley off the corner of Jintai Lu and Bayiqi Lu. A small but varied range of English books, mostly classics, but some contemporary works as well. Open daily 8:30am-10pm.

Hospital: Fujian Provincial Hospital (fújiàn shěnglì yīyuàn; 福建省立医院), 34 Dong Jie (☎755 7768), on the northwest corner of the intersection of Dong Jie and Wusi Lu. The emergency entrance is off Dong Jie.

Internet Access: Once you wander away from the main roads, you'll have no difficulty tracking down an Internet cafe. The **Scholar Internet Cafe** (zhuàngyuán wǎng bā; 状元 网吧), on Bayiqi Lu, on the left heading south, past Jintai Lu. Comfy seats in quiet surroundings perfectly suited for scholarly pursuits. Y2 per hr. Open 24hr.

Post and Telecommunications: 1 Dong Jie (☎752 2010), a high-rise on the southeast corner of Dong Jie and Bayiqi Bei Lu, opposite Juchunyuan Restaurant. EMS and Poste Restante. Open daily 7:30am-7:30pm. **DHL Worldwide Express,** 179 Tatou Jie (☎781 1111), off a small alley next to the Taiwan Hotel. Open daily 8am-6pm.

Postal Code: 350000 for city center, 350001 for Poste Restante.

ACCOMMODATIONS

Filthy-rich Fuzhou offers few options for dirt-poor backpackers. Many establishments near the train and bus stations have rooms for as little as Y30, but they are very reluctant to accept foreigners. Don't rule out high-end places altogether, as they sometimes lower their prices during the summer. The following listings, unless otherwise noted, all have A/C, bath, and TV.

Yushan Hotel (yūshān bīnguǎn; 于山宾馆), 10 Yushan Lu (☎335 1668 or 335 7694). Take bus #8 from South Bus Station to Yushan on Gutian Lu, or #51 from the train station to Wuyi Bei Lu (keep walking, then take the first right onto Gutian Lu). As you face the Mao statue on Gutian Lu, take the stairs to the left; the entrance is across a small street. Clean rooms exude an old-Orient feel, with low beds and a view of the inner garden. Breakfast included. Singles and doubles Y215-490. 20% discounts possible. ❸

South Seas Hotel (nányáng fàndiàn; 南洋饭店), 346 Hualin Lu (☎757 9699; fax 757 7085), where Hualin Lu veers east. Look for a red carpet. Plain, white-walled rooms, with minimal furnishing. Baths with tubs and 24hr. "hot" water. Singles and doubles Y159; triples Y220. Friendly staff is susceptible to bargaining. ❷

Silver Mountain Hotel (yínshān dàjiǔdiàn; 银山大酒店), 254 Wusi Lu (☎781 3688), at Hualin Lu. Accessible via bus #51 along Wusi Lu; get off at the Hualin Lu stop. Very spacious rooms, with large beds and extra tables and chairs. Admire your reflection in the bright, clean surfaces. Doubles Y80-Y128. ❶

Heavenly Fortune Hotel (tiānfú dàjiǔdiàn; 天福大酒店), 138 Wusi Lu (☎781 2328; fax 781 2308), just north of the Bank of China's main branch. Standard, clean rooms with colorful floral bedspreads. Climb to the higher floors for excellent city views. The cheaper rooms are very similar to their more expensive counterparts. Singles Y130-158; doubles Y178-190; extra bed Y80. ❷

Yuelai Hotel (yuèlái dàfàndiàn; 悦来大饭店), 376 Hualin Lu (☎757 2855; fax 310 681). 5min. walk south of the train station, on the right. Look for the large vertical sign running down the side of the building. Rooms are dark and lack windows, but at night you won't hear a sound. Singles and doubles Y60, with bath Y98-180. ❶

FOOD

Fuzhou's cannot-miss spot is the irresistible **Fuzhou Food Street** (róngchéng měishíjiē; 榕城美食街), a pedestrian street just off Taijiang Lu near the intersection with Wuyi Nan Lu. The street is designed to look like an endless row of traditional Chinese buildings, complete with eaved roofs and red lanterns. Shops sell everything from "real" VCDs to frivolous knick-knacks and luggage. On weekend nights, visiting opera troupes perform for free in the open-air stage at the end of the street among heaps of food, including all manners of *xiǎochī* (小吃; snacks), from steamed dumplings to noodles to skewered meat. One noteworthy stall is the award-winning **Fuzhou Fish Balls** ❶ (dàfúxīng yúwán; 大福星鱼丸). Fish-paste balls stuffed with meat (Y6 per bowl) are actually quite appetizing.

If you're still standing after this eating venture, behind Food St. is **Pedestrian Street** (bùxíng jiē; 步行街). At night, locals gather along this tree-lined, fountain-spangled boulevard and enjoy the lighted terraces and balmy breeze. The magnificent **Yuanhong City ❷** (yuánhóng chéng; 元洪城) dominates the street with its 1111 different kinds of foods served up in the food court on the sixth floor. (Take bus #51 or 951 from Wusi Lu to Taijiang Lu.) Savor crispy Beijing duck (Y35 for half), steamboat feasts (both regular and Sichuan-spicy seafood), Thai food, Southeast Asian delicacies, all manner of Chinese soups, Indian tandoori, Korean barbecue, and much—oh, so much—more.

For slightly more classy surroundings, wander across Liberation Bridge (jiěfàng qiáo; 解放桥), near the end of Wuyi Lu, to **Zhongzhou Island** (zhōng zhōu dǎo; 中洲岛), near the large, yellow Islamic-European-style building. Here you'll find a long line of bustling, cheerful restaurants, with seating looking out across the river. Most restaurants start serving around 5:30pm and close by 10pm.

Juchunyuan (jùchūnyuán cāntīng; 聚春园餐厅), Juchunyuan Hotel, 2 Dongjiekou, 3rd fl. (☎750 2328, ext. 8401), across from the post office. This 100-year-old establishment has garnered well-earned fame from its **Buddha Jumping Over the Wall** (fó tiào qiáng; 佛跳墙), a seafood concoction (Y200-5000 per person) served in

DANCIN' IN THE STREETS

The sun goes down, the lights go up—it's high time you got your groove on. Nightlife in Fuzhou is not confined to smoky bars and clubs. The city's best movers and shakers shuffle on down to May 1st Sq., where, from about 8pm, things start to heat up. A loud megaphone sets the beat with a thumping tune, and 200 or so locals form haphazard lines and begin line-dancing en masse.

Twist, kick, step, swivel, turn and repeat: it's very simple, and the more experienced dancers are always happy to assist newcomers. As a foreigner, you'll be particularly welcomed, though you can expect your every misstep to be a source of amusement and laughter. Some of the dances are a cinch for even the most awkward pair of feet. Others are more involved and may require strategically timed in-unison leaps. Sometimes, it's just best to stand back and admire.

The dancers themselves are a motley crew—teenagers keep the beat with grandmothers as a great community spirit is shared. Some take themselves very seriously, adding a flourish to each sequence to impress hordes of bystanders. But don't let them intimidate you. Whether you like line-dancing or not, this is a sight not to be missed. If the weather is good, the party continues to 10pm. And with no cover charge whatsoever, it's the best entertainment deal in town.

a traditional banquet-style setting and stuffed with such goodies as abalone, scallops, and shark's fin. For the non-fabulously wealthy, other specialties include the Eight Delicacies in a Pot (Y20), which features pig's stomach, scallops, and quail eggs, among other things. Juchunyuan is also famed for its fried jellyfish (Y35). Check the English menu to avoid accidentally eating pig tripe (zhūdù; 猪肚). Open daily 11am-1pm and 5-9pm. ❸

Purple Bamboo Tea House (zǐ zhú lín chálóu; 紫竹林茶楼), 18 Gutian Lu (☎333 0278), on the right as you approach Yushan Park, opposite the Yushan Hotel. Bamboo platforms, secluded compartments, delicate fans, and strumming zithers all create the perfect mood for tea tasting. A pot of the finest Iron Goddess (tiě guānyīn; 铁观音) comes at Y380. For those unwilling to fork over a fortune for a cuppa', fragrant jasmine (mòlìhuá chá; 茉莉花茶) is Y100, and green tea (lù chá; 绿茶) a mere Y80. Watch out for the china—delicate, oh-so-breakable works of art. Open daily 9am-1am. ❹

Upper Island Coffee (shàng dǎo kāfēi; 上岛咖啡; ☎750 2328, ext. 8302), downstairs upon entering Junchunyuan Hotel. Genuine relaxation here, with soft lights and a tinkling grand piano. Teas, coffee, and desserts are expensive but worth it for the aromas and artistic flair. Y20-43. Open daily 9am-1am. ❷

🄢 SIGHTS

Except for **Drum Mountain** to the east of the city, Fuzhou's sights are pleasant but not significant. Strolling through the city's various neighborhoods, particularly the ones that border the city center, is a much more worthwhile activity. West of Dongjiekou off Yangqiao Dong Lu, starting with Nanhou Jie, is the neighborhood of **"three lanes, seven alleys"** (sānfāng qīxiàng; 三坊七巷), a well-preserved cross section of old Fuzhou, with street stalls, festival lanterns, and *mahjong* groups. Among this maze of streets lie **Pagoda Alley** (tǎ jiē; 塔街) and **Literary Scholar Lane** (wénrú lù; 文儒路), both of which date back to the Ming and Qing Dynasties.

YU MOUNTAIN SCENIC AREA (yūshān fēngjǐng qū; 于山风景区). A gently sloping, curved path up the hill takes you past old buildings with stone archways and groups of elderly folk playing cards and *mahjong* to a rather insignificant **Fuzhou Municipal Museum** detailing the city's 700-year history. *(Open daily 8am-5pm. Y3.)* The nearby **flower nursery** (lánpǔ; 兰圃) houses hundreds of varieties of orchids. *(Admission Y3.)* The **White Pagoda** (bái tǎ; 白塔) marks the western edge and affords a bird's-eye view of the city. *(Open daily 8:30am-5:30pm. Y2.)* The crumbling remains of the old city walls still stand at the summit of Yushan. *(There are 2 entrances to the scenic area: one from a path to the left of and behind the Mao statue, the other off Wuyi Bei Lu, just north of its intersection with Gutian Lu. Free.)*

WEST LAKE PARK (xīhú gōngyuán; 西湖公园). It may not be Hangzhou's West Lake, but the park is worth a brief gander. Delicate garden paths surround the manmade lake, dotted with a few islands and a colony of paddle boats. The only other possible point of interest is the **West Lake Aquarium** (xīhú hǎiyáng shìjiè; 西湖海洋世界), which features a small selection of tropical fish. *(Main entrance on Hubin Lu. Park Y10, children Y5. Paddle boats available 5:30am-10pm for Y20-30 per hr. Aquarium open daily 8am-5:30pm. Y25, children under 1.2m Y15.)*

🄳 DAYTRIP FROM FUZHOU: DRUM MOUNTAIN 鼓山

*9km east of Fuzhou. Several public **buses** run regularly to the foot of the mountain: #36 or 37 from the Chating stop on Guangda Lu, west of the South Bus Station, next to the Children's Park; #949 from the train station; and #960 from West Lake. For #36 and 37 get off at the Xiayuan stop; for the other routes, the mountain is at the terminus (30-40min, Y1.5). **Minibuses** (Y5) go from the base up the mountain to Yongquan Temple. Minibuses from downtown Fuzhou (at the Nan Men stop, off Gutian Lu, 1 block east of*

Yushan to your left) also run directly to the summit (20-30min.; one-way Y5, round-trip Y8). **Cable car** *runs daily 7:30am-6pm (one-way Y25, round-trip Y30, children Y10/Y15). Eighteen View Park open daily 7am-5pm, Y10. Yongquan Temple open daily 6am-6pm, Y6.*

Rising 900m above sea level, Drum Mountain (gǔ shān; 鼓山) offers unbeatable panoramic views of Fuzhou and the outlying maze of rivers and mountains. The heart-pumping, sweat-pouring 1800m ascent along sloped stone steps, with markers every 200m, takes about an hour.

At the summit, the **Eighteen View Park** (shíbā jǐng gōngyuán; 十八景公园) is somewhat of a let-down. Trees often block the promised views, and you find yourself staring instead at large stones or peering into shallow caves. Alternatively, you can drop in to the far more impressive complex of the **Gushing Spring Temple** (yǒngquán sì; 涌泉寺) and its environs. In the temple, the 400-year-old, two-ton **Bell Tower** (zhōng lóu; 钟楼), facing the **Drum Tower** (gǔ lóu; 鼓楼), certainly warrants a visit. Monks have been carving scriptures into the **Depository of Buddhist Scriptures** (yìnjīng lóu; 印经楼) since the Song Dynasty, thus far producing a staggering 11,375 carving plates. The temple complex also houses a gigantic Goddess of Mercy statue, a vegetarian restaurant, and the **Hall of Heavenly Kings** (tiān wáng diàn; 天王殿). Wander down the path to the right of the entrance to the **Drinking Water Rock** (hēshuǐ shí; 喝水石). Formerly a place of repose frequented by the literati, as attested to by inscriptions on the surrounding rocks, this remains a serene, eerily shady spot seemingly untouched by tourism. Stay shadowed under whispering leaves, or make like a turtle and bask in the sun by the pond.

WUYISHAN 武夷山 ☎ 0599

There's something almost otherworldly about Wuyishan's natural splendor. A spellbinding wonderland of shadowy peaks fashioned into unlikely formations, the mountain captivates all those who wander its trails and float down its river. Though the main attractions—the Nine Bend River and its accompanying peaks—are undisputable highlights, meandering the mountain pathways past overhanging cliffs and hopping across stepping-stoned streams add immeasurably to the magical experience. Because of Wuyishan's secluded location, tour groups don't clutter the trails as they do in China's other more accessible scenic areas. Crowds do collect at the principal sights, but it's easy to escape the bustle and enjoy long stretches of unbroken tranquility. Stick to the clearly marked paths; Wuyishan's sizable population of poisonous snakes isn't quite so receptive to visitors. Few overseas tourists journey to Wuyishan, but those who do won't be disappointed.

▐ TRANSPORTATION

Flights: Wuyishan People's Airport (wǔyíshān mínháng zhàn; 武夷山民航站 ; ☎511 8114), on Wuyi Dadao, north of the resort town. Accessible by taxi van (15min., Y15) from the city center. Tickets available from **Wuyishan Airport Booking Office** (☎525 2102; fax 525 3897), 2 doors east of the Bank of China in the resort area. To: **Beijing** (7pm, Y1350); **Fuzhou** (7:30pm, Y310); **Guangzhou** (7:30am, Y890); **Shanghai** (1:50pm, Y660); **Xiamen** (1:50, 11:15pm; Y590).

Trains: Wuyishan Train Station (wǔyíshān huǒchē zhàn; 武夷山火车站 ; ☎510 2745), on the outskirts of Wuyishan city. From the resort area, take bus #6 to the city center, then take bus #2 or hop onto a taxi van. Open daily 8-11:30am and 2:30-6pm. To: **Fuzhou** (6hr., 11:28pm, Y47); **Quanzhou** (15hr., 4:06pm, Y82-155); **Xiamen** (15hr., 4:30pm, Y82-155).

Buses: Wuyishan Bus Station (wǔyíshān qìchē zhàn; 武夷山汽车站 ; ☎531 1446), in Wuyishan city, accessible by bus #6 from the city center or bus #2 from the train station. Open daily 5:30am-5:30pm. To: **Fuzhou** (7½hr.; 2:30, 6:50pm; Y88); **Xiamen** (13hr., 2:30pm, Y159); **Quanzhou** (10hr.; 2:30, 3:30pm; Y138).

Local Transportation: Two **bus** routes service the Wuyishan area. Bus #2 (Y1) shuttles passengers from the train station via the city center to the bus station and back; #6 (Y2) runs from the bus station, through the city, passing the train-station intersection before heading to the resort area. Both run daily 6am-9:30pm.

Taxis: Yellow **taxi vans** *(miàndī)* are very popular. From the resort town to Wuyishan city center Y3-5, or to Wuyishan Scenic Area Y1-2. Within Wuyishan Scenic Area, **scootered pedicabs** take tourists from sight to sight (each trip Y6-7, Y60-70 per day); some drivers may also informally serve as tour guides.

✦ 🛈 ORIENTATION AND PRACTICAL INFORMATION

Visitors arriving in Wuyishan should bypass the main city and head straight for the **Wuyishan National Tourist Resort Area** (wǔyíshān guójiā lǚyóu dùjià qū; 武夷山国家旅游度假区). Those arriving by bus can simply transfer to the local #6 bus, which goes down **Wuyi Dadao** (武夷大道), a long straight road that leads directly to the resort area. From the train station, travelers can catch a southbound bus #6 by walking straight down **Zhanqian Dadao** (站前大道) for 15min. to its intersection with Wuyi Dadao; bus #2 makes the same journey in 3min. With your back to the train station, the southbound bus #6 comes from your righthand side.

The main street of the surprisingly cheerful resort area, extending directly from Wuyi Dadao, is an endless row of middle-range hotels and souvenir stores. There is a palpable air of local charm, especially once you reach the area surrounding the **Huangbai** (黄柏) intersection, where bus #6 veers right and heads towards **Lantang Bridge** (lántāng dàqiáo; 兰汤大桥). There are no official street names in the resort area, and establishments do not use addresses.

Crossing Lantang Bridge brings you to the west side of the Chongyang Stream, into the **Wuyishan National Scenic Area** (wǔyíshān guójiā zhòngdiǎn fēngjǐng míng-shèng qū; 武夷山国家重点风景名胜区), which spans a whopping 60km². Easy access to transportation make the road flanking the west side of the river an ideal spot to begin your explorations of the sights.

Travel Agency: Wuyishan Travel Service (wǔyíshān lǚxíng shè; 武夷山旅行社 ; ☎525 5238), on the foot of the sloped path leading up to Wuyishan Mountain Villa. Cross Lantang Bridge to the Scenic Area; take a left onto the tree-lined path; walk straight for 5min., and turn right at the 2nd path toward the guard station. Although unaccustomed to individual travelers, staff are eager to help. Open M-F 8am-noon and 1:30-5pm.

Bank of China: ☎525 2890. A block east of Lantang bridge, to your left as you face the river. Exchanges currency and traveler's checks. **24hr. ATM.** Open daily 8am-noon and 2-5:30pm.

PSB: ☎525 2283. In the Wuyi Palace area of the resort town, in a small courtyard off to the right, about 50m before you reach the arch that marks the end of the main lane. Open daily 8am-6pm.

Hospitals: Municipal Clinic (shìlì yuàn; 市立院 ; ☎525 1990), to the right just before you reach Lantang Bridge on the resort area side. Follow the steps downhill and continue for a block. Open daily 8am-10pm.

Internet Access: As you face the post office, there is an **Internet cafe** about 2 doors left. Y3 per hr. Open daily 8am-midnight.

Post Office: Wuyishan Resort Town Post Office (☎525 2875), off the main road, marked by a large arched gate to the west of the Huangbai intersection. The office is 2 blocks down this road, in an alley on the left. EMS. Open daily 7:30am-6pm.

Postal Code: 354302.

▌ ACCOMMODATIONS

Wuyishan's resort town is full of near identical two- and three-star hotels, which generally puts travelers in a strong bargaining position. Ignore the listed prices and boldly ask for a room at the price you're willing to pay. This usually does the trick, but if not, you can always try next door.

Most of the budget options are directly across Lantang Bridge from the resort town. Unfortunately, proprietors of these mostly family-owned inns are unwilling to let foreigners stay in their hotels, which the tourist bureau has not approved. Overseas Chinese might be able to get the relatively basic rooms with rock-bottom prices beginning at Y10. The following rooms all come with A/C, bath, and TV.

▣ Wuyi Mountain Villa (wǔyí shānzhuāng; 武夷山庄 ; ☎525 1888; www.513villa.com). From Lantang Bridge, turn left and walk straight along the tree-lined path bordering the western bank of the river; the hotel is on the 2nd path to the right. Bus #6 stops in front. With an idyllic setting, award-winning landscaping, and large, comfortable rooms with a snazzy blue color scheme, this hotel is more than perfect. For cheaper rooms, ask for the underground economy doubles with standard amenities. Larger rooms have carpets and small balconies. Singles and doubles Y100-264; triples Y300. ❷

Three Flowers Hotel (sān huā jiǔdiàn; 三花酒店 ; ☎/fax 525 2889) on the eastern side of the river in the resort area, down a slight slope to the left, immediately before the bridge. Cheerful, spacious rooms with mountain and river views. Cheaper rooms have basic Chinese-style bathroom and no scenic views. Friendly staff can help you plan your visit. Singles and doubles Y60-100; triples Y80. ❶

Wuyishan Hotel (wǔyíshān jiǔdiàn; 武夷山酒店 ; ☎525 7888; fax 525 7866). Off the main street running through the resort area. As you head into the resort area, take a right after Chong Ange Hotel and follow the road to the end. High-quality, well-furnished rooms, especially the more expensive ones, which are a good deal larger and come with tea sets and extra furniture. Staff offer discounts on request. Singles and doubles Y160-580. Up to 60% reductions on more expensive suites in the low season. ❷

▐ FOOD

Visitors don't come to Wuyishan for the food, but lively street markets line the resort area. Wuyishan's culinary claim to fame is its **Snake Banquet,** not yellow eel or other snake-like creatures, but the real, slithering thing from Wuyishan's mountains. This delicacy should be sampled in large hotel restaurants rather than in small street shops: if handled improperly, the poisonous ones can be deadly. The going rate for a bowl of snake soup is Y300. Eaten separately, snake gall bladder and blood come free for your tasting pleasure. Most cheap options are on the road opposite a large archway, on your left just after you turn right off the main road to face the bridge. Liveliest from sunset to 2am, the street features small street dishes like tofu (Y6), noodle soups (Y10), and *bāozi* (Y3). Hotel restaurants and establishments with A/C tend to be more expensive, with prices hovering over Y30 for some basic dishes.

◉ SIGHTS

One of the best ways to explore breathtaking Wuyishan is to climb its peak and admire the sea of mountains set within an expansive ocean of clouds. The main trails are well maintained and safe. With glimmers of sunrise, early-morning dew, and respite from chaotic tour groups, dawn is the perfect time for solitary rambles. Almost all sights have admission fees; the Y111 all-inclusive ticket, available at all scenic spots, may be your best option.

NINE-BEND RIVER 九曲溪

Bamboo rafts (zhú fǎn; 竹泛) *are the most popular way to explore this winding creek, a mellow introduction to the famed peaks along the riverbanks. Rafts leave from* **Xingcun village,** *in the southwestern corner of Wuyishan Scenic Area. Each raft seats 6 people (5 when the water is high). The 1½hr. ride starts at the 9th bend of the stream and ends at the 1st. Boats leave daily 8am-6pm when full. Ticket office ☎526 1752.*

Winding through 9.5km of gorges and bends in the southern portion of Wuyishan, the Nine-Bend River (jiǔqū xī; 九曲溪) is one of the most justifiably hyped sights in the area. It zigzags through rugged canyons and peaks, its mirror-like waters and rushing rapids pristine and unspoiled. Bamboo chairs are bound to bamboo rafts, so that you can dip your feet into the water while floating downstream.

From **Xingcun Village** (xīngcūn zhèn; 星村镇) and the ninth bend, the raft drifts past **White Cloud Rock** (bái yún yán; 白云岩), a former gathering place for scholars and worshipping pilgrims. The eighth bend takes you past **Appreciating Calligraphy Rock** (pǐn zì yán; 品字岩), which is also known as **Wusha Rock,** named and shaped after the black gauze caps that imperial officers used to wear. Downstream at the sixth and fifth bends, the river flows by **Heavenly Tour Peak** (tiānyóu fēng; 天游峰), **Clouds' Nest,** and **Draper's Rock** (shàibù yán; 晒布岩), a cliff face named for its extraordinary fan-like folds. The second bend passes the oft photographed **Jade Goddess Peak** (yù nǚ fēng; 玉女峰). The first bend goes by the crown-shaped **King's Peak** (dàwáng fēng; 大王峰), one of the most spectacular of the 36 peaks.

The raft trip wraps up at **Wuyi Palace** (wǔyí gōng; 武夷宫), a small complex of hotels, souvenir shops, and restaurants. The area also houses the **Wuyishan Museum** (wǔyíshān bówùguǎn; 武夷山博物馆), a mostly archaeological museum featuring grizzly photographic displays on the nearby excavations of 3000-year-old hanging-coffins. (☎525 2729. Open daily 8am-5:30pm. Y5.)

OTHER SIGHTS

Just across from the Bamboo Raft Pier is the **Wuyishan Tea Research Center** (wǔyí běilín; 武夷碑林 ; ☎526 1997). At this flawlessly landscaped oasis of bridges, streams, and stone carvings, you can learn all about the different kinds of natural tea in Wuyishan and their famously curative qualities. Whether to taste or to heal, expect to pay Y30-100 for a pot. (Open daily 6am-5:30pm.)

A 5min. drive north past Lantang Bridge takes you to the **Big Red Robe Tea Mountain** (dà hóng páo; 大红袍), which houses the **Nine Dragons Nest,** a group of towering rock formations that resembles nine coiled dragons. Farther up the mountain, past myriad pools and waterfalls, a small pavilion overlooks the famous tea plantation that cultivates the prized Big Red Robe Tea. Visitors have the chance to sip the revered tea while admiring the view. (Open daily sunrise-sunset. Tea Y40-60 per pot. Y22.) Close to the summit is **Eternal Joy Temple** (yǒnglè chánsì; 永乐禅寺), the largest Buddhist temple in the area. (Open daily sunrise-sunset. Free.) A beautiful vista awaits those willing to clamber up (1½hr.) to the mist-enshrouded summit of **Heavenly Tour Peak.** (☎525 2827. Open daily sunrise-sunset.)

WATER CURTAIN CAVE (shuǐlián dòng; 水帘洞). This temperamental waterfall—a trickle on dry days and a gushing spout during the rainy season—forms a curtain over the entrance of a large, shallow, rocky cave. When the water flow is strong, the seemingly endless climb to the falls is well worth it. The shroud of mountain water cascading into the pond at the foot of the cave lends an almost sacred quality to the area. From the top of the first set of stairs leading to the cave, there is an excellent view of **Eagle's Peak** (yīngzuǐ yán; 鹰嘴岩), shaped like an eagle about to soar into flight. *(North of Lantang Bridge. Open daily 7am-6pm. Y20.)*

THREAD OF SKY (yī xiàn tiān; 一线天). South of the Nine-Bend River, this mind-bending, neck-craning work of nature far surpasses even the pleasant surrounding landscape of rolling hills and brooks. The highest and narrowest of its kind, the fissured cave was formed by a split in the stone linking the Fuxi and Feng Caves. At 0.3m wide, it lets in only a beam of light and a thread of sky. Look up to see bats flitting overhead. There is a short but steep climb through the seam. Rotund figures may have difficulty squeezing through. The ascent is dark and wet; a flashlight (Y5) can aid in maneuvering through the scarily narrow path. Admission also includes **Tiger Roaring Cliff.** (☎525 2577. Open daily 6:40am-6pm. Y30.)

MINYUE KINGDOM SCENIC AREA (mǐnyuè wángchéng jǐngqū; 闽越王城景区). The small museum gives a good introduction to the nearby archaeological excavation site, which, when discovered in the 1950s, helped to confirm the existence of Minyue, a lost Han-Dynasty-era civilization. The excavation itself is not terribly impressive, but the museum houses some rare examples of Han-era weapons, ceramics, and farming implements that are well worth a look. *(A 30km drive from the scenic area; round-trip taxis may cost Y200 and up, but ask around and you may find transport for Y100. ☎528 7695. With English captions. Open daily 8:00am-5:30pm. Y80, children Y40.)*

QUANZHOU 泉州   ☎0595

There is something markedly different about Quanzhou. Perhaps it's the solid Persian walls and the ruins of the grand Qingjing Mosque, or the eerie otherworldliness of the Islamic tombs tucked away on Qingyuan Mountain. The ease with which these rather out-of-place sights fit into Quanzhou is probably the best reminder of the city's all-embracing past. During the Song and Yuan Dynasties, Quanzhou was one of the largest ports in the world, shipping silk and porcelain to the Middle East in exchange for spices and ivory. Large merchant ships and a colorful mix of sailors, missionaries, and traders frequented the lively wharf neighborhood, where religions, languages, and architectural styles were exchanged as readily as teas and spices. Today, the port's significance lingers only in memory, and the Arab and Persian traders of yesteryear have either scattered to the winds or meshed into the local population. Although its status has diminished, Quanzhou's character remains unchanged. Thousand-year-old mosques straddle the same streets as Buddhist temples, and Western fast-food restaurants jostle for space with dime-a-dozen Chinese streetside stalls.

▮ TRANSPORTATION

Buses: Quanzhou Bus Station (quánzhōu qìchē zhàn; 泉州汽车站 ; ☎228 4141), at the intersection of Wenling Lu and Quanxiu Jie. Connects to north Quanzhou via bus #2. Ticket office open daily 6:30am-9:30pm. Like most buses that run on Fujian province's luxurious routes, Quanzhou's buses have restrooms and an attendant who serves tea and cookies. To **Fuzhou** (2½hr., approx. every 20min. 6:30am-7:30pm, Y52-60) and **Xiamen** (1½hr., every 20min. 6:20am-8:30pm, Y32-35). **Quanzhou China Travel Bus Station** (quánzhōu zhōnglǚ qìché zhàn; 泉州中旅汽车站 ; ☎228 7155), on Baiyuan Lu, just north of China Travel Service. Ticket office open daily 6:30am-9:30pm. To **Shenzhen** (7-8hr., 9am and 9:30pm, Y220).

Local Transportation: Many destinations within the city can be reached on foot, but most locals get around by **moped.** Quanzhou **buses** have comprehensive service, but some routes can get crowded—watch your belongings. Most routes run 6am-10pm. Fare Y1-2. Bus #2 runs from the bus station up Wenling Lu, past Dong Jie, Xi Jie, and Kaiyuan Temple; #3 runs from Guandi Temple and Qingjing Mosque to the Qingyuan Mountains; #15 travels Wenling Lu, continuing north to Qingyuan Mountain.

Taxis: Base fare Y8-10, each additional km Y1.4-1.8; *miàndí* taxis Y6, each additional km Y1.4 (but these pick up other passengers along the way). **Pedicabs** to most destinations within city center Y3-5, from bus station to Kaiyuan Temple Y8-10.

✈ 🛈 ORIENTATION AND PRACTICAL INFORMATION

Quanzhou is bordered by the **Jin River** (jìn jiāng; 晋江) to the west. The downtown area is bounded to the north by **Xi Jie** (西街) and **Dong Jie** (东街), both bisected by **Zhongshan Lu** (中山路), which runs north-south. Running parallel to and east of Zhongshan Lu is **Wenling Lu** (温陵路), which terminates in the south near the long-distance bus station, at the intersection with **Quanxiu Jie** (泉秀街). **Tumen Jie** (涂门街) and **Jiuyi Jie** (九一街) both run between Zhongshan Lu and Wenling Lu. Small alleys linking Zhongshan Lu and Tumen Jie, lively commercial streets lined with hotels, temples, and shops, are full of food stalls. Tumen Jie continues east of its intersection with Wenling Lu as **Fengze Jie** (丰泽街) into the newest part of town.

Travel Agency: China Travel Service Quanzhou, 1 Baiyuan Lu (☎298 6680; fax 228 5547), on the left as you head north. Look for the large sign in English over the door. Friendly, helpful staff speak a little English. Open daily 8am-6:30pm.

Bank of China: (☎215 2114 or 215 2100). On Fengze Jie, in a white skyscraper marked with the Bank of China logo. Exchanges currency and traveler's checks. Credit card advances. Open daily 8-11:30am and 3-6pm.

Bookstore: Xinhua Bookstore/Foreign Language Bookstore (wàiwén shūdiàn; 外文书店 ; ☎298 4631 or 228 2496), on Wenling Nan Lu, a few doors north of Jianfu Business Hotel. Small sample of English classics. Open daily 8:30am-10pm.

PSB: 62 Dong Jie (☎218 0318), a few minutes east of Zhongshan Zhong Lu. From the bus station or Wenling Lu, take bus #2 to the Bell Tower and backtrack a block. For visa extensions, the **Division of Entry and Exit** (chūrùjìng guǎnlǐ chù; 出入境管理处 ; ☎218 0308) has a separate entrance to the right. Open daily 8-11:30am and 3-6pm.

Hospital: Quanzhou No. 1 Hospital (quánzhōu dìyī yīyuàn; 泉州第一医院 ; ☎227 7300), just off Dong Jie, has English-speaking doctors. Open 8am-11:30pm and 3-6pm. 24hr. emergency section.

Internet Access: Zai Qian Internet Cafe, in the 1st alley off to the left when you enter Wenhua Jie from Tumen Jie. Look for a yellow awning. Speedy terminals, funky tunes, and chilled bottles of Coca-Cola for Y1. Y2.5 per hr. **Chichi Internet Cafe** (chíchí wǎngbā; 池池网吧), under a blue sign on Xianhou Lu, just off Dong Jie. Y3 per hr. Open daily 8am-2am.

Post Office: 213-217 Wenling Bei Lu (☎216 1401), on the corner of Jiuyi Jie and Wenling Bei Lu. EMS. Open daily 8am-8pm.

Postal Code: 362000.

⌂ ACCOMMODATIONS

Cheap living quarters are far easier to find in Quanzhou than in most Chinese cities its size. Surprisingly, it's the top end of the market that seems to have the fewest representatives. Unless you're a hardened budgeteer, it's wise to trade in the few extra *kuài* for A/C—even with a whirring fan, the nighttime heat can be suffocating. Mosquitoes find their way into most hotels, so if you don't have trusty netting or an arsenal of repellent, make sure the room comes with a *wén xiāng hé* (蚊香盒 ; "mosquito incense"), a plug-in device that keeps the pests at bay.

Bell Tower Hostel (zhōnglóu lǔshè;钟楼旅舍), 1 Zhongshan Bei Lu (☎237 3343), at Xi Jie. Take bus #2 from the long-distance bus station. Conveniently close to the Kaiyuan Temple and frequented by well-traveled backpackers. Rooms are basic. Seafood restaurant on 2nd fl. Safety deposit and 24hr. hot water. Singles Y50, with bath Y75; doubles Y70, with bath Y100; triples without A/C Y75, with bath and A/C Y150. ❶

Precious Jade Guesthouse (bǎoqí zhāodàisuǒ; 宝琦招待所; ☎282 2903), at the intersection of Wenling Nan Lu and Jinhuai Jie. A very small staircase entrance, to the left of the Kodak shop. Small, basic squarish rooms, but good value. Singles Y30, with A/C Y45, with bath Y60. ❶

Overseas Chinese Home (huáqiáo zhījiā;华侨之家), 147 Wenling Lu (☎217 5395; fax 217 5385), just north of the bus station. An aging hotel, with some signs of dilapidation, but kept reasonably clean nonetheless. Cheaper rooms are spacious, though bare. The more expensive option brings you wine-colored carpets and more comfortable bathrooms with bathtubs and Western-style toilets, plus an extra suite of comfy furniture. All rooms have A/C. Singles Y25, with bath Y50, with nicer bath Y100; doubles Y35/Y60/Y120; triples Y45/Y75/Y150. ❶

Business Hotel (shāngwù jiǔdiàn;商务酒店), 125-135 Wenling Lu (☎228 3511; fax 298 6041), on the south end of Wenling Lu, next to the Overseas Chinese Home. A nononsense hotel with high-quality rooms at very reasonable prices. Thickly carpeted, with fridges, mini-bars, and bathtubs. Singles Y138; doubles Y168; triples Y188. ❷

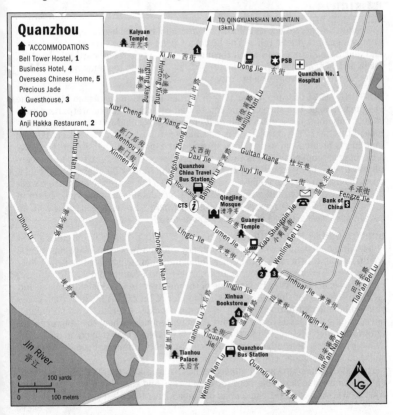

🍴 FOOD

Quanzhou might not have award-winning dishes of its own, but its streets are filled with restaurants and stalls selling perennial Chinese favorites. Try the **steamed sponge cakes,** snowy white rice cakes slightly fermented for a subtle sweet flavor. The **sticky rice** steamed with chicken, pork, or red bean paste and wrapped in bamboo or reed leaves in a pyramid shape (zòngzǐ; 粽子) is as fun to unravel as it is to eat. Colorful small streets in the older, northwest section of town—on and around Dong Jie, Xi Jie, and Zhongshan Bei Lu in particular—harbor a treasure of small eateries offering these snacks, as well as **Sha-style treats** (shā xiàn xiǎochī; 沙县小吃). Sha-style stalls can also be found in the small alleys linking Tumen Jie with Wenling Lu. Also try the *sānhé fàn* (三合饭), a concoction of three types of grain served in a small aluminum tin. At night, **Wenling Lu** is transformed into a sea of all-night street stalls selling barbecued kebabs (Y0.5 a stick), smelly tofu, and more. At the **Anji Hakka Restaurant ❶** (ānjì kèjiā wàng; 安记客家望 ; ☎ 228 0333), on the corner of Wenling Nan Lu and Tumen Jie, appetizing smells greet you at the door. The delicious crispy pork and vegetable dumplings (Y5) are particularly filling. Instead of menus, you select your food directly from sizzling woks and steaming carts. (Entrees Y3-6. Open daily 9am-3am.)

🔎 SIGHTS

Quanzhou's sights reflect its colorful religious and cultural heritage, with a wealth of Muslim and Buddhist relics. The best way to get a feel for Quanzhou's religious and maritime history is to stroll through the old city streets, particularly along **Jubao Jie** (聚宝街) and **Xiaomen Gang** (小门巷), home to the remains of the Maritime Administration of Foreign Trade.

QINGJING MOSQUE (qīngjìng sì; 清净寺). Also known as the **Ashab Mosque,** the Qingjing Mosque has survived the forces that destroyed its counterparts. Quanzhou's only mosque is but a shell of its former glory, and few visitors grace its halls. Still, the 1000-year-old site is fascinatingly un-Chinese. The stately Islamic building is located opposite a long, fortress-like medieval wall. From the eerily absorbing sarcophagus covers to the well-preserved stone engravings to the centuries-old well in the courtyard, an unnatural calm infuses the mosque and sets it apart from anything else you'll see in Quanzhou. To the left of the entrance a well-organized exhibition hall with English captions details the history of Islam in Quanzhou. *(On Tumen Jie, west of a minor Buddhist temple and near Baiyuan Lu. Take bus #5 from the bus station to Guandi Si. Open daily 8am-6pm. Y3.)*

QINGYUANSHAN MOUNTAIN (qīngyuán shān; 清源山). Rising 615m above sea-level, Qingyuanshan is often affectionately referred to as the Wuyishan of the south. Not quite as pretty as that other Fujian mountain, Qingyuanshan is infinitely holier, with Buddhist temples, Daoist shrines, and Islamic tombs. At the base, there is a shrine to Master Hongyi, one of the most revered Buddhist teachers, and an impressive stone statue of Laozi, the founder of Daoism. A farther climb takes you to **Mituo Rock** (mítuó shí; 弥陀石) and a delicate waterfall. A backbreaking, never-ending path leads to the summit. Another temple sits near the **Qingyuan Cave** (qīngyuán dòng; 清源洞), while the **Heavenly Clear Waters Lake** (qīngyuán tiānhú; 清源天湖) offers a heavenly and cool respite for weary climbers. From here, **motorcycles** can take you back down (Y5 per person).

Though the steep upward climb is at times nauseatingly tough, there are plenty of opportunities to scramble onto rocky outcrops and gaze down over the city as you catch your breath. Here upon one of China's least-touristed mountains, there's a real sense of winding your way through nature, with brilliantly colored butter-flies dancing alongside, teams of ants trailing the pathways, and the shrill chirps of cicadas reverberating through the air. *(3km north of the city. 15min. ride on bus #3 from Zhongshan Lu or #15 from Wenling Lu to the last stop, Y2. The Laozi and Qianshou Yan gates both lead to the scenic area. ☎ 279 7606. Open daily 5am until dark. Admission fee including all sights Y50, students Y40, children under 1.1m Y25.)*

KAIYUAN TEMPLE (kāiyuán sì; 开元寺). The largest of Quanzhou's Buddhist temples, Kaiyuan is also the city's primary tourist attraction. The temple has an airy, stone-paved courtyard flanked by the impressive **East** and **West Pagodas.** Surrounded by sculptures of Buddhist icons, the pagodas are unique for their Chinese and Indian artistic styles. Although the temple dates back to AD 686, the pagodas were not constructed until more than 500 years later. The ceiling of the main hall is lined with 24 flying *apsaras*, acrobatic figurines in the early Buddhist style.

To the right of the temple, just behind the garden containing the East Pagoda, is a small but worthwhile exhibit on the history of navigation and foreign contact in Quanzhou, focusing on the Song and Yuan Dynasties. The ancient boats here are strangely enticing, particularly the partially reconstructed 13th-century sailing ship, discovered in Quanzhou Bay in 1973 during the dredging of an irrigation channel. *(27 Xi Jie. In the northwest part of the city. Take bus #2 from the bus station or Wenling Lu to Kaiyuan Si. Maritime exhibition open 8am-6pm, Y2. Open daily 5am-6pm. Y10, children Y5.)*

XIAMEN 厦门   ☎ 0592

With its balmy climate, eclectic architecture, and fresh sea air, Xiamen is undoubt-edly one of China's showcase cities. Its air of tropical resort tranquility implores those seeking a fast-paced life to look elsewhere, and its gracious residents exude the slacker's charm, indulging in leisurely strolls, afternoon swims, and evening feasts. Over the past four centuries, the port city has seen a succession of foreign guests; Portuguese, British, French, and Japanese settlers have all exploited Xia-men's strategic trading location. Fortunately, Xiamen has adapted well to its cos-mopolitan influences. Even today, storefronts and residences in the western waterfront district proudly don renovated colonial facades, and restaurants throughout the city serve authentic international cuisine. Enjoying the benefits of foreign investment and its status as a Special Economic Zone, Xiamen has the same looming skyscrapers and conspicuous signs of consumer affluence as any frenetic south-coast city, but the city has made a point of laying the fruits of devel-opment *beside* the relics of its past, rather than bulldozing over them. If there is a method to the madness of China's development, it might turn out to be in Xiamen.

◧ TRANSPORTATION

Flights: Xiamen Gaoqi International Airport (xiàmén gāoqí guójì jīchǎng; 厦门高崎国际机场 ; ☎602 0033), about 10km northeast of downtown Xiamen, at the north end of the island, near the causeway to the mainland. Bus #37 goes from the airport to the train station. Taxis (Y40-50) take 30-40min. The **Xiamen Airlines Ticket Office** (xiàháng shòupiào zhōngxīn; 夏航售票中心), 219 Zhongshan Lu (☎205 8909; fax 205 8915), next door to the China Construction Bank. Open daily 8am-5:30pm. To: **Beijing** (7 per day, Y860-1710); **Guangzhou** (6 per day, Y500-660); **Hong Kong** (5 per day, Y1334); **Shanghai** (8 per day, Y380-960).

Trains: As with most cities in Fujian province, trains are not the best way to travel to and from Xiamen; buses are faster and more frequent. **Xiamen Train Station** (xiàmén huǒchē zhàn; 厦门火车站), 900 Xiahe Lu (☎398 8662), on the south end of Hubin Dong Lu, east of the waterfront. Buses #3, 4, and 28 connect to the pier. A taxi from the

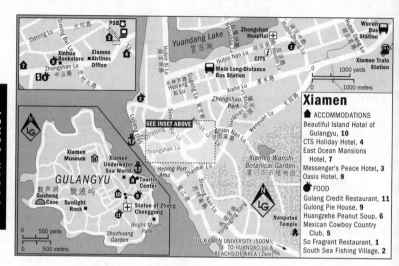

train station to the ferry pier costs about Y12-14. Open daily 7:40am-9:20pm. To:
Beijing (34hr., 9:22pm, Y458); **Guangzhou** (14hr., 5:15pm, Y254); **Hangzhou** (26hr.,
10am, Y224); **Nanchang** (18½hr., 2:02pm, Y181); **Shanghai** (26hr., 2:45pm, Y309);
Wuyishan (14½hr., 6:35pm, Y155).

Buses: Main Long-Distance Bus Station (xiàmén chángtú qìchē zhàn; 厦门长途汽车
站; ☎221 5238), on Hubin Nan Lu, sometimes called the **Hubin Long-Distance Bus
Station.** From here, bus #43 runs to the train station. Tickets sold daily 5:45am-10pm.
To: **Fuzhou** (4hr., every 10min. 5:55am-6:35pm, Y80); **Guangzhou** (9hr., many per day
6:55am-9:45pm, Y180); **Hong Kong** (10hr., 8:20am, Y350). **Wucun Bus Station**
(wúcūn qìchē zhàn; 梧村汽车站), 931 Xiahe Lu (☎581 5525). Turn right as you exit
from the train station and walk 2min. Open daily 6am-10pm. To: **Fuzhou** (3½hr., approx.
every 20min. 6:25am-10:30pm, Y80); **Guangzhou** (9hr., approx. every 1½hr. 7:15am-
10:30pm, Y180); **Quanzhou** (1½hr., every 30min. 6:20am-9pm, Y20).

Local Transportation: English transportation maps (Y5) are available at the Xinhua
Bookstore. Most **buses** run daily 6am-10pm. Fare Y1. Buses #1 and 21 go south
toward Nanputuo Temple and Xiamen University; #4 and 28 connect the train station to
the airport; #27 connects the airport to the ferry pier; #37 connects the train station to
the airport; #43 connects the main bus station to the train station.

Taxis: Base fare Y8, each additional km Y2. All taxis should be metered. Most western
district destinations (near the waterfront and Gulangyu) Y8-10; the waterfront from the
bus station Y10-12, from the train station Y12-14, and from the airport Y35-50.

✈🚌 ORIENTATION AND PRACTICAL INFORMATION

Xiamen city occupies the southwestern portion of **Xiamen Island,** connected to the
coast of southern Fujian by the **Xiamen Causeway.** The city's most visited spots are
around the waterfront, which faces **Gulangyu** (鼓浪屿), Xiamen's satellite islet and
biggest tourist attraction. This compact waterfront western district is dominated
by a 1km-long section of **Zhongshan Lu** (中山路), a bustling commercial street running east-west. Just north of Zhongshan Lu's western end, ferries depart for
Gulangyu. **Siming Lu** (思明路) runs north-south and intersects with Zhongshan Lu.

In the eastern part of the city, the main long-distance bus station is on **Hubin Nan Lu** (湖滨南路), and the train station is a 10min. bus ride farther east on **Xiahe Lu** (厦禾路). Xiamen's nicer night spots are also in the east, mainly along Hubin Dong Lu.

Travel Agency: Plane, train, and bus ticketing offices abound along Zhongshan Lu, Siming Lu, and near the waterfront. **CITS,** 334 Hexiang Xi Lu, 3rd fl. (☎223 1259; www.citsxm.com), west of the intersection of Hexiang Xi Lu (禾祥西路) and Bailuzhou Lu (白鹭洲路). Walk away from the intersection until a large arch leading to a red staircase is on your right. Make a left at the top of the stairs; continue toward the far left of complex to entrance marked with CITS banner. Helpful English-speaking staff, especially Nancy Chen. Arranges 1- and 2-day tours of major sights, books train and airline tickets, and provides English maps and brochures. Open M-F 9am-5pm. The **Gulangyu Tourist Center** (☎257 1226 or 206 3089),on Gulangyu, next to the Luzhou Hotel near the ferry port. Offers free maps, arranges tours, and stores luggage. Open daily 8am-6pm.

Bank of China: 4-10 Zhongshan Lu (☎298 7485), opposite the Lujiang and East Ocean Hotels, near the harbor. Exchanges currency and traveler's checks. Credit card advances. Open M-F 8:30am-6pm, Sa-Su 9am-5:30pm.

Bookstore: Xinhua Bookstore/Foreign-Language Bookstore (wàiwén shūdiàn; 外文书店), 151-153 Zhongshan Lu (☎202 4059), on the north side of the road, just west of Siming Bei Lu. Dictionaries, guidebooks, maps, and a fair selection of English classics. Check out *Amoy Magic* (Y30), by Dr. Bill Brown, for an English guide to Xiamen. Open daily 9:30am-9:30pm. More bookstores near Xiamen University, especially along its northwestern edge on Yanwu Lu.

PSB: 43 Xinhua Lu (☎202 5505), near Gongyuan Nan Lu, almost opposite the Xinhua Lu Post Office. Visa extensions at **Division of Exit and Entry** (chūrùjìng guǎnlǐ kē; 出入境管理科 ; ☎202 2329 or 226 2203), in a separate building in the far back corner of the compound, close to Gongyuan Nan Lu. Open daily 8am-noon and 3-6pm.

Hospitals: Xiamen Zhongshan Hospital (xiàmén zhōngshān yīyuàn; 厦门中山医院 ; ☎229 2139), on Hubin Nan Lu, 5min. east of long-distance bus station. Some English-speaking doctors. Open daily 8am-noon and 2:30-5:30pm. **Xiamen No. 2 Hospital** (xiàménshì dì'èr yīyuàn; 厦门市第二医院), 60 Fujian Lu (☎257 1723), on Gulangyu, off Longtou Lu, a 10min. walk from the ferry pier. Open daily 8am-noon and 2-5:30pm.

Internet Access: Electronic Reading Room (diànzǐ yuèlǎn shì; 电子阅览室), 3rd fl. of the Cultural Palace (wénhuà gōng; 文化宫), the large building at the eastern end of Zhongshan Lu, fronted by a cement plaza. Deposit Y10. Y3 per hr. Open 8am-midnight.

Post and Telecommunications: 54 Xinhua Lu (☎203 8277), north of Zhongshan Lu's eastern end. Open daily 7:30am-8pm. **Haihou Lu Post and Telecommunications Office** (hǎihòu lù yóudiàn jú; 海后路邮电局), 58 Haihou Lu (☎202 2360), on Lujiang Dao opposite the Gulangyu ferry pier, a short walk north of Zhongshan Lu's western end. Poste Restante. EMS and IDD service at both branches. Open daily 7:30am-7:30pm.

Postal Code: Western district and Poste Restante 361001, Gulangyu 361002.

ACCOMMODATIONS

When it comes to lodgings in Xiamen, luxury dominates the market, making even middle-range accommodations hard to come by. Precious few establishments will be impressed if you wave a crispy Y100 note, as most will be expecting at least triple that. On Gulangyu, however, hotels are not only affordable, but beautiful as well—especially if they overlook the beach area. A few aging colonial villas along Gulangyu's shores are now inhabited by families or retirees, who rent out these gorgeous, if spartan, rooms for a small fee; this option may take time, patience, and Chinese-language skills. The low season is from September to June (excluding national holidays), when prices fall by as much as 50%. Quality is generally high, with even the cheapest beds promising a cozy night's sleep. In Xiamen city, the hotels around the train station are inexpensive (around Y100), but far from scenic.

XIAMEN CITY

Xiamen Messengers' Peace Hotel (xiàmén yì ān jiǔdiàn; 厦门驿安酒店), 30-32 Xinhua Lu (☎266 2666). Turn left at the top of Zhongshan Lu and continue for 3min. downhill past the post office on Xinhua Lu. Look for the large red lanterns at the entrance. Large, clean rooms with faded yellow carpets and pokey bathrooms with tubs. A/C and TV. Singles Y100; doubles Y130; triples Y180. ❷

Xiamen CTS Holiday Hotel (xiàmén zhōnglǚ jiàrì jiǔdiàn; 厦门中旅假日酒店), 70-74 Xinhua Lu (☎266 0888; fax 202 4709). From the top of Zhongshan Lu, turn right and walk half a block; it's on the right just before a parking lot. Classy, well-lit rooms with plenty of furniture and fluffy bedspreads. TV, A/C, kettle, and powerful showers. Singles Y156; doubles Y187; triples Y218. ❷

East Ocean Mansions Hotel (dōng hǎi dàshà jiǔdiàn; 东海大厦酒店), 1 Zhongshan Lu (☎202 1111; fax 203 3264). Entrance on 1st side-road on the left as you walk up Zhongshan Lu, facing away from the sea. Comfy rooms, with patterned blue carpets, high-quality furniture, and bathtubs. Harbor views in more expensive rooms. Singles Y240-290; doubles Y270-290; triples Y350. ❸

GULANGYU

Beautiful Island Hotel of Gulangyu (lìzhīdǎo jiǔdiàn; 丽之岛酒店), 133 Longtou Lu (☎206 3309; www.lzd-hotel.com). From the ferry pier, head toward McDonald's and follow Longtou Lu to the right. Bear left at the crossroads; it's on the right, in the heart of the shopping district. No glistening sea views here. Wallpaper is cracking in places, but rooms are generally in good condition, all with A/C, bath, and TV. Singles Y208-218; doubles Y120, with windows Y168-218; triples Y210. 15% low-season discounts. ❷

Oasis Hotel (lǜzhōu bīnguǎn; 绿洲宾馆), 1 Longtou Lu (☎266 5390; fax 206 843), immediately opposite the main ferry port. Spotless tiled rooms with colorful drapes and new wooden furniture. Nice views of the nearby park and the sea. All rooms have A/C, bath, and TV. Singles Y228; doubles Y268; triples Y298. Expect at least 20% discount. ❸

◨ ◲ FOOD AND ENTERTAINMENT

Xiamen's every corner and every street overflow with local, national, and international cuisine. The northern end of Xiamen University, south of Nanputuo Temple, is one of the best places for variety. There are restaurants specializing in **northwestern-style noodles** (xīběi lāmiàn; 西北拉面), **Taiwanese** eateries around the corner from a McDonald's, and **Korean** restaurants farther away. Near the waterfront, the wharf and western districts teem with cosmopolitan cuisine. A few eateries on Siming Dong Lu serve up Fujian **Sha-style** (shā xiàn fēngwèi; 沙县风味) dishes.

Halal Northwestern Pulled Noodles ❶, 26 Zhongshan Lu, serves Xinjiang food. Its windows look in upon hard-working chefs pounding dough and molding perfect stringlets of noodles (bàn miàn; 拌面) for Y5. (☎203 1985. Open daily 9am-10pm.) Along Zhongshan Lu, streetside vendors sell skewers of Korean-style barbecue (Y2). For a more enlightened culinary experience, try the Buddhist vegetarian food (Y50 per set meal) at **Nanputuo Temple.**

Seafood tops the list of local favorites, especially on Gulangyu. The adventurous can seek out **turtle soup** and **grilled crayfish**. Seafood restaurants line Longtou Lu, the commercial market road leading inland from the pier. For Y40, you get soup and three dishes; for Y250, you get soup and a diet-busting eight dishes. Xiamen's specialty snacks, including sweet fried **pastries** stuffed with peanut crumblies, a sweet **peanut soup** (huāshēng tāng; 花生汤), and savory chive pastries (jiǔcài hé; 韭菜盒), can be found along the road leading from the ferry pier on Gulangyu or in specialty bakeries on Zhongshan Lu. Two other Xiamen treats are paper-thin **rice noodles** with vegetable and seafood (miànxiàn hú; 面线糊) and, most tempting of all, *tǔsǔndòng* (土笋冻), a gelatinous blend of boiled sea worm and jellyfish.

Youthful, energetic Xiamen is no newcomer to the night scene either. **Clubs** and **pubs** liberally dot the city. A particularly vibrant stretch along Hubin Dong Lu has at least four establishments lined up one after another.

XIAMEN CITY

▨ **Huangzehe Peanut Soup** (huángzéhé huāshēngtāng diàn; 黄则和花生汤店), 22-24 Zhongshan Lu (☎212 5825 or 202 4670), between McDonald's and the Bank of China. This wildly popular family restaurant and bakery serves the famous *miànxiàn hú* (Y4) and other noodle and dumpling dishes (Y3-5). Peanut soup Y1.5. Sesame buns Y2. Green bean shaved ice Y3. Open daily 6:30am-10:30pm. ❶

So Fragrant (hǎo qīngxiāng dà jiǔlóu; 好清香大酒楼), 59 Hubin Zhong Lu (☎220 9178), at its intersection with Hubin Nan Lu. The best place to savor local flavors, including *miànxiànhú*, meat-filled *zòngzi* (sticky rice wrapped in reed leaves), *tǔsǔndòng*, and tasty spring rolls. Try "5 spices pork" (wǔ xiāng ròu; 五香肉), stuffed with onions and water chestnuts (Y5). Open daily 10:30am-2pm and 5-9:30pm. ❶

South Sea Fishing Village (nán hǎi yú cūn; 南海渔村), on Lujiang Dao close to the waterfront, across from the COSCO building. A very popular seafood restaurant, with outdoor seating by the sea. Bubbling tanks full of unidentifiable sea creatures with a disturbing number of limbs. More familiar faces such as squid (Y20-28 per *jīn*), frogs (Y22 per *jīn*), and a vast range of fish, crabs, and lobsters. Open daily 7:30am-3am. ❷

Mexican Cowboy Country Club, 69 Zhongshan Lu (☎204 0687). If your tummy rumbles for tastes closer to home, this restaurant serves up a great variety of delicious Western dishes (Y10-50), including steak, pizza, burgers, and pasta. Servers sport nifty cowboy costumes. Open daily 10am-11pm. ❷

GULANGYU

▨ **Gulong Pie House** (gǔlóng bǐngjiā; 鼓龙饼家), 21 Longtou Lu (☎206 0721). From the pier, 1 block down and on the left. Paris has its croissant, New York its bagel, and Gulangyu its *xiànbǐng* (馅饼), a pastry with sweet green bean paste filling (Y1), made fresh at this longtime establishment. Available in boxes of 8 (Y6). Also has fruit-flavored, peanut-paste, and yam pastries. Open daily 8am-9pm. ❶

Gulang Credit Restaurant (gǔlàng xìnyù jiǔlóu; 鼓浪信誉酒楼), 4 Zhonghua Lu (☎206 3073). From Sunlight Rock, go down Huangyan Lu past the turf area; take a right and walk for half a block; it's on the left. The food doesn't come cheap, but your taste buds will thank you. Seafood dominates the menu, but there are plenty of land options too. Try the pearl fish (jīnzhū yú; 金珠鱼 ; Y90 per kg, average dish Y120), steamed to tender perfection, and sip eight-treasures tea (Y10), made from 8 ingredients, including dried chrysanthemum. Dishes Y20-50. Open daily 8am-10:30pm. ❸

☉ SIGHTS

Xiamen's biggest draw is **Gulangyu,** but Xiamen city is also full of interesting diversions. The neighborhoods along the southwestern shore of Xiamen Island (including some renovated colonial facades along Zhongshan Lu) are worth a peek. The beach area in southern Xiamen city along the stretch of Huandao Lu (环岛路) provides mile upon mile of rollicking, frolicking fun, with an uninterrupted, swimmable coastline, bike rental shops, and rows of vendors selling everything from fruit drinks to Pokemon life jackets. Perhaps more sobering is the view of Taiwan-controlled **Jinmen Island** (金门岛), only 2km from shore.

GULANGYU 鼓浪屿

*Ferry boats to Gulangyu leave from the busy **passenger terminal** (xiàgŭ lúndù mătóu; 厦鼓轮渡码头), north of the western end of Zhongshan Lu (every 10-20min. 7am-6:30pm and 9-11:20pm; last boats at 11:50pm and 12:30am). Purchase round-trip ticket (Y3) at the ferry port on Gulangyu; no ticket needed to board boats to the island. The upper deck has the best views and plenty of seating but costs an extra Y1, paid during the 10min. trip. **Speedboats** (seating 6) offer island cruises for Y100; tickets available from the small fishing pier opposite the Underwater World or outside Shuzhuang Garden. Available at entrances to all sights, all-inclusive ticket (with exception of aquarium) Y80, children Y40.*

Those who set foot on the multicolored cobblestoned streets of Gulangyu may come away convinced that this tiny island is the stuff of which legends are made. Gulangyu's grand assembly of colonial-style European architecture, winding gardens, and rocky, windswept beaches have all made the island a must-see for resort-seeking vacationers and culture-craving aesthetes alike. Even cars can't mar the pristine streets, which are reserved for pedestrians and the occasional electric golf cart (Y10-50). Hidden speakers spill the twinkling notes of Bohemian rhapsodies and Viennese waltzes into the streets, setting the slow, rolling rhythm of Gulangyu, long known as the "Garden on the Sea" and the "Piano Isle."

Sensuous pleasures aside, Gulangyu's sunny shores carry a great deal of historical significance. From the Xiamen waterfront, two of Gulangyu's most recognizable sights are clearly visible. At the island's southern end, the colossal **Statue of Zheng Chenggong** (郑成功) honors the national military hero and Fujian native. Near the center of the island, military battlements cap the stark grey **Sunlight Rock** (rìguāng yán; 日光岩). The island not only served as a base for Zheng Chenggong's resistance *against* foreign invaders during the 17th century, but it has also been the concession area *for* foreigners—Portuguese, British, French, and Japanese—who came to Xiamen to capitalize on its strategic commercial location. Ghosts from this checkered past survive in an eclectic jumble of **colonial architecture,** ranging from terraced patios and red brick structures to stone mansions with yellow-shuttered windows. Many of these buildings still serve as residences; a stroll along **Fujian Lu** (福建路) is a showcase for these crumbling but still impressive villas. Many families are willing to open their doors and let visitors look around. Gulangyu has also produced many of China's greatest pianists, and the ratio of pianos to families here is the highest in the nation. The music school on the island strives to keep up the tradition, and the melodies of students hard at practice drift through open kitchen doors and windows. To best sample Gulangyu's many delights, take a couple days to wander through its streets, leaving China, civilization, and your cares behind.

▓ SUNLIGHT ROCK (rìguāng yán; 日光岩). From the 100m boulder, admire views of the entire island, the shores of mainland China, and the distant East China Sea. Supposedly the first spot on Gulangyu to catch glimmers of the sun, the summit is a great place to watch the sunrise and join groups of *tai chi* practitioners. *(Open daily 5am-8:30pm. Y30, children Y15.)* Zheng Chenggong stationed troops on this "peak" to fight the Dutch colonialists who occupied Taiwan in 1612. Beyond a Buddhist temple near the base of the hill and near the Zheng Chenggong Memorial Hall, several paths head upward toward the peak; climb the last steep steps to the "naval command post" at the top for a bird's-eye view. The **Zheng Chenggong Memorial Hall** (zhèng chénggōng jìniànguǎn; 郑成功纪念馆), in a stately three-story colonial building, is dedicated to the national hero. *(Open daily 8am-5pm. Free.)*

From the foot of the wrought-iron stairs leading to the summit, a cable car brings you to **Hundred Bird Park** (bǎi niǎo yuán; 百鸟园), a massive net-enclosed area where rare birds roam somewhat freely. Hourly shows feature parrots grooving to disco tunes. *(Off Huangyan Lu, in the interior of the island beyond Gulangyu Guesthouse. Signs, some in English, will direct you from the ferry pier. Open daily 8am-6pm. Y40, children Y20; includes cable car and entrance to Hundred Bird Park.)*

SHUZHUANG GARDEN (shūzhuāng huāyuán; 菽庄花园). Shuzhuang Garden sits on the far southeast side of the island, past rows of dried seafood, trinkets, and photo vendors, next to a pristine beach. Meticulously crafted in classical Chinese fashion, the garden has immaculate little pavilions alongside lakes full of floating lotus flowers. Also worth a gander is **Twelve Cave Hill** (shí'èr dòngtiān; 十二洞天), a grotto filled with looming, oddly shaped rocks. Emerge to enjoy the evening from beachside tables. On Tianwei Lu at the end of Nine-Bend Bridge, the **Gulangyu Piano Museum** (gǔlàngyǔ gāngqín bówùguǎn; 鼓浪屿钢琴博物馆) features over 80 different pianos from all periods and countries. *(Follow signs that lead off to the left from the main road after you disembark from the ferry. ☎ 206 3680. Open daily 8:15am-6pm. Y20.)*

BRIGHT MOON PARK (hào yuè yuán; 皓月园). From this point, visitors can view the **Statue of Zheng Chenggong** (zhèng chénggōng shídiāoxiàng; 郑成功石雕像) up close and personal—all 16m, 1400 tons, and 625 granite pieces of it. According to legend, Zheng threw his sword into the sea before departing for battle, and he was subsequently transformed into a huge rock to guard the motherland he loved so dearly. Designed to withstand scale-12 typhoons and 8.0 earthquakes, Zheng won't be going anywhere anytime soon. The 150 peacocks in the **Peacock Park** (kǒngquè yuán; 孔雀园) aren't shy about begging visitors for food. *(From Shuzhuang Garden, follow the coastline east until you reach the park. Open daily sunrise-sunset. Y15.)*

XIAMEN UNDERWATER SEA WORLD (xiàmén hǎidǐ shìjiè; 厦门海底世界). This compact aquarium features over 10,000 denizens of the deep. Several hundred fresh- and sea-water species are represented, including paddlefish, penguins, and piranhas. Four daily shows feature dolphins and seals doing tricks and stunts. *(2 Longtou Lu. On the main road leading off to the right from the ferry pier, after a grassy park; look for a golden octopus statue. ☎ 206 7668; fax 206 7825. Open daily 8am-6:30pm. Y70; seniors over 60, children, and students Y40.)*

XIAMEN CITY SIGHTS

NANPUTUO TEMPLE (nánpǔtuó sì; 南普陀寺). Nanputuo Temple, a huge complex with multicolored halls, a golden Buddha statue, ponds, and pavilions, is perhaps one of the most beautifully kept and heavily touristed monasteries in China. Built in the Tang Dynasty, the temple is now the site of the **Buddhism College of South Fujian** (mǐnnán fóxué yuàn; 闽南佛学院). Like its namesake, Putuoshan (p. 406), an island off the coast of Zhejiang province, Nanputuo Temple is dedicated to Guanyin, the Bodhisattva of Mercy. The Guanyin statues here are perhaps the most impressive aspect of the temple, particularly the three **thousand-hand golden Guanyin statues** in an elevated rotunda behind the main hall. *(On the southwestern edge of the city, north of Xiamen University. The eastern gate and entrance is next to the bus station at the terminus for buses #1 and 21, both of which run south along Siming Nan Lu. The entrance is marked by a large pond. Open daily 4am-8pm. Y3, children under 1m free.)*

XIAMEN UNIVERSITY (xiàmén dàxué; 厦门大学). Xiamen University's lovely campus contains buildings that manage to be both modern and tasteful. To the left of the main Yanwu Lu entrance is the **Lu Xun Memorial Hall** (lǔxùn jìniànguǎn; 鲁迅

纪念馆）, built in honor of the scholar and author who used to be a professor at the university. At the very center of the campus is a large and lovely lake. *(South of Nanputuo Temple. Buses #1 and 21 run south along Siming Nan Lu and terminate at a parking lot outside of the north entrance on Yanwu Lu; there is an entrance on your right.)*

GUANGDONG 广东

Tell anyone you're traveling to Guangdong, home to three of the country's four first SEZs, and they're likely to raise their eyebrows and mention money. Bus rides through the region reveal fields guarded by factory after factory and road signs pointing to endless golf courses and vacation resorts. Guangdong is pressing ahead in the race to modernize, mesmerize, and make money, all in the same breath. Despite the seemingly one-track mind of the province, the green spaces stay green year-round and people haven't forgotten to save time (and money) for beautiful national parks and natural spaces. Even as Guangzhou obsessively expands its metro system, mountain streams continue to flow serenely down Dinghushan Mountain outside Zhaoqing.

GUANGZHOU 广洲 ☎ 020

Beijing is China's political and cultural heart and Shanghai is the new economic powerhouse, so where does that leave Guangzhou, the last of the country's "Big Three"? The bewildered tourist who arrives at Guangzhou's chaotic train station may initially disagree, but Guangzhou is a city where the inhabitants are comfortable with themselves and their hectic surroundings. Perhaps this can be attributed to Guangzhou's history of prosperity. While many cities have just recently come into their own, Guangzhou has long reaped the benefits of its proximity to SEZs like Shenzhen and Zhuhai, not to mention Hong Kong. Though bigger and faster than any of its neighbors in the province, Guangzhou can't compare to the cultured glamour of its now-mature siblings up north or the cosmopolitan glitz of Hong Kong. Nonetheless this urban giant is perfectly content to take a breather and move ever-so-slightly out of the spotlight it once monopolized.

▓ ORIENTATION

Guangzhou seems to lack any apparent city planning. Fortunately, most major streets are labeled according to direction, and the new subway system helps with orientation. **Huanshi Lu** (环市路), the city's busiest road, runs west from the city center, intersecting **Tianhe Lu** (天河路) in Tianhe district. **Zhongshan Lu** (中山路) also runs east-west, bisecting the city. The subway follows most of the length of this street, before making an abrupt turn northward at Tiyu Dong Lu and continuing northward until it terminates at Guangzhou East Train Station. Four-lane **Dongfeng Lu** (东风路) runs parallel to Zhongshan Lu. North of the Pearl River, the more organized **Tianhe district** makes up the eastern part of Guangzhou. **Guangzhou Dadao** (广洲大道) divides Tianhe district and Dongshan district. Backpacker headquarters, **Shamian Island** (shāmiàn dǎo; 沙面岛)—no longer an island due to land reclamation—sits at the southwest fork in the **Pearl River** (zhū jiāng; 珠江).

Each of the large thoroughfares, as well as many of the smaller streets, are divided into north (běi; 北), central (zhōng; 中), and south (nán; 南) sections, or east (dōng; 东), central, and west (xī; 西) sections. Streets are numbered as well; Zhongshan Lu is divided into eight numbered sections from east to west.

▛ TRANSPORTATION

Flights: Guangzhou's **Baiyun Airport** (báiyún jīchǎng; 白云机场 ; ☎8612 0000) is west of White Cloud Mountain. A taxi from central Guangzhou to the airport costs Y40-50. A **shuttle bus** leaves from the gray building next to CITS on 179 Huanshi Xi Lu (30min., every 30min. 7am-7pm, Y3-4). The city is planning construction on a new airport within the next year. The following major airlines fly to Guangzhou:

Air China (zhōngguó mínháng gōngsī; 中国民航公司), 300 Dongfeng Zhong Lu (☎8363 7523), in the Jin'an Commercial Bldg. Open daily 8am-5pm.

China Southwest Airlines (zhōngguó xīnán hángkōng gōngsī; 中国西南航空公司), 181 Huanshi Xi Lu (☎8612 0449, ext. 477). Open daily 8am-5:30pm. To: **Chengdu** (8-9 per day, Y1300); **Chongqing** (3 per day, Y1150); **Guilin** (7-8 per day, Y530); **Harbin** (1-2 per day, Y2580); **Kunming** (3-4 per day, Y1200); **Xiamen** (2-3 per day, Y630).

Hainan Airlines (hǎinán hángkōng gōngsī; 海南航空公司), 371 Huanshi Dong Lu, World Trade Center South Tower, Rm. 905 (☎8760 9037). Open M-F 8:30am-6pm, Sa-Su 8:30am-5:30pm. To **Haikou** (5 per day, Y560).

Malaysian Airlines (mǎláixīyà hángkōng gōngsī; 马来西亚航空公司), 368 Huanshi Dong Lu, 2nd fl. (☎8335 8838). In the Garden Hotel. Open M-F 8:30am-5:30pm, Sa 8:30am-12:30pm. To **Kuala Lumpur, Malaysia** (Tu-Th; Y2500, round-trip Y3550).

Shanghai Airlines (shànghǎi hángkōng gōngsī; 上海航空公司), Baiyun Airport (☎8668 1149), in the northern wing of the Liuhua Hotel. Open daily 8am-8pm. To **Shanghai** (Y1020, but ask for a Y200 discount).

Trains: The enormous **Guangzhou Train Station** (guǎngzhōu zhàn; 广州站 ; ☎8715 7222) is on the western end of Huanshi Lu. The **Guangzhou East Train Station** (guǎngzhōu dōngzhàn; 广州东站 ; ☎8755 0917 or 8755 8714) is considerably cleaner, safer, and less harrowing than the notorious main station. Easily accessible by subway line #1, it is just outside the last subway stop (also named Guangzhou Dongzhan). **Tourist information center** (☎8714 6164 or 8714 6222) open daily 6:10am-10pm. Fast and efficient service to the Kowloon KCR station in **Hong Kong** (1½-2hr., 12 per day 8:30am-8:45pm, Y240) and **Shenzhen** (1hr., every 25-45min. 7am-11:20pm, Y70). Trains to other destinations are listed in the table below; all run from the main station, although many also stop at Guangzhou East.

TO	TRAVEL TIME	PER DAY	PRICE
Beijing	24hr.	2	Y258
Changsha	8-10¼hr.	at least 10	Y183
Chengdu	44hr.	1	Y480
Chongqing	46-47hr.	2	Y399
Guilin	12-13hr.	3	Y215
Guiyang	33hr.	5	Y301
Hangzhou	25½hr.	1	Y330
Hefei	24hr.	1	Y323
Hengyang	4-5hr.	at least 20	Y122
Ji'nan	34½hr.	1	Y409
Kunming	44hr.	1	Y313
Lanzhou	44hr.	3	Y528
Liuzhou	16¼hr.	1	Y249
Luoyang	28½hr.	1	Y123

TO	TRAVEL TIME	PER DAY	PRICE
Nanchang	15½-18hr.	4	Y208
Nanjing	33½hr.	1	Y372
Nanning	17½hr.	5	Y185
Ningbo	30hr.	1	Y345
Shanghai	24-27hr.	3	Y355
Shantou	7-10hr.	3	Y168
Shaoguan	3hr.	at least 20	Y92
Shenyang	35hr.	1	Y552
Tianjin	33¼hr.	1	Y480
Wuhan	14-14½hr.	9	Y257
Xi'an	28hr.	2	Y430
Yueyang	12hr.	at least 10	Y209
Zhangjiajie	23hr.	1	Y277
Zhengzhou	20hr.	3	Y313

Buses:

Municipal Bus Passenger Station (shì qìchē kèyùn zhàn; 市汽车客运站; ☎8227 9825), down Huanshi Xi Lu from the train station, on the left at the pedestrian overpass. To **Foshan** (1hr., every 15min. 5am-10:30pm, Y12) and **Zhaoqing** (2hr., every 20min. 6am-7:30pm, Y30).

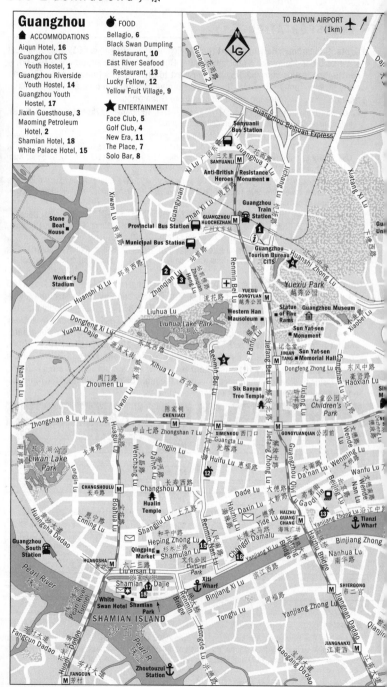

Guangzhou

⌂ ACCOMMODATIONS
Aiqun Hotel, **16**
Guangzhou CITS
    Youth Hostel, **1**
Guangzhou Riverside
    Youth Hostel, **14**
Guangzhou Youth
    Hostel, **17**
Jiaxin Guesthouse, **3**
Maoming Petroleum
    Hotel, **2**
Shamian Hotel, **18**
White Palace Hotel, **15**

● FOOD
Bellagio, **6**
Black Swan Dumpling
    Restaurant, **10**
East River Seafood
    Restaurant, **13**
Lucky Fellow, **12**
Yellow Fruit Village, **9**

★ ENTERTAINMENT
Face Club, **5**
Golf Club, **4**
New Era, **11**
The Place, **7**
Solo Bar, **8**

TO BAIYUN AIRPORT
(1km)

SOUTH COAST

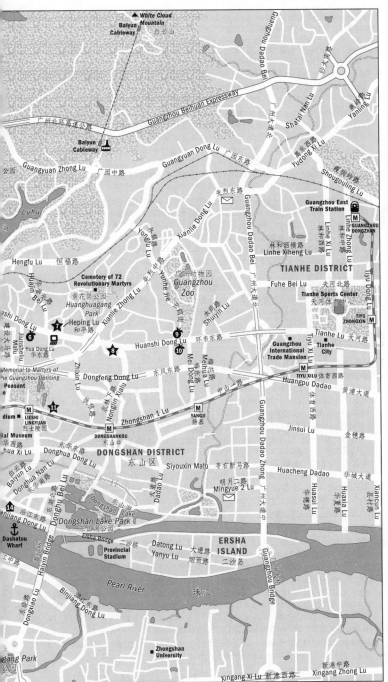

Provincial Bus Station (shěng qìchē kèyùn zhàn; 省汽车客运站), 145 Huanshi Xi Lu (☎8666 1297), opposite the Municipal Station. To **Guilin** (8hr., 1pm, Y150) and **Haikou** (12hr., several per day 9:45am-6pm, Y255). Buses to **Hong Kong** and **Macau** board from major hotels, including the Garden Hotel (☎8333 8989), China Hotel (☎8666 6888), Hotel Landmark (☎8335 5988), and Liuhua Hotel (☎8666 8800).

Ferries: Turbo Jet (☎8222 2555) offers 4hr. boat trips from the **East River Guangzhou Ferry Terminal** (dōngjiāng suìkèlián mǎtóu; 东江穗客连马头) to the **Hong Kong China Ferry Terminal** (10am and 4:30pm, HK$189-284).

Subway: The newly opened subway system (☎8755 3460, inquiries 8667 3366, ext. 1703) has 2 lines. Line 1 runs along Zhongshan Lu between Xilang Lu in the southwest and the Guangzhou East Train Station in the northeast; line 2 runs north-south, from the main train station across the river to Jiangnan Dong Lu. Stops are marked by a yellow sign with two red stripes. Single-ride tickets available from dispensers (accepting only Y1 coins) at every stop. The subway runs approximately 6am-11pm. Fare Y2 per 3 stops, Y1 per additional 3 stops, with a maximum of Y6 per ride.

City Buses: The bus system is Guangzhou's most common and convenient method of travel and one of China's most comprehensive city transportation systems. Double-digit buses scour the city center (Y1, A/C Y2), while triple-digits travel to the far ends of the city (Y1-2). To board a bus, wave one down at a stop and pay exact change. Route signs are in Chinese. The most important bus routes for travelers, buses #5 and 31, shuttle between Shamian Island and the main train station (30-60min., Y1).

Taxis: Base fare Y7 for the 1st 2.6km, each additional km Y2.2. Taxis are not allowed to stop on Huanshi Xi Lu opposite the bus and train stations; to hail a taxi, walk onto a side street off the main road. **Motorbike** drivers provide short rides for around Y5 and usually hang around the train and bus stations.

▌ PRACTICAL INFORMATION

TOURIST AND FINANCIAL SERVICES

Tourist Office: Guangzhou Tourism Bureau (guǎngzhōushì lǚyóu jú; 广洲市旅游局), 180 Huanshi Xi Lu (☎8668 7051 or 8669 8043), to the left as you exit the train station. English-speaking staff of recent college graduates is knowledgeable and enthusiastic. Free maps, brochures, pamphlets, and advice. Open daily 8am-5:30pm.

Travel Agencies: CITS, inside the Guangzhou Tourism Bureau (☎8666 6889). Books train and air tickets and offers 1-day city bus tours with Chinese-speaking guides for Y98. Extremely helpful and professional English-speaking staff. In the same office, there is also an **STA Travel** branch (☎8667 1455) with staff members who speak excellent English and can book air tickets. The **White Swan Hotel Ticketing Office** (☎8188 6968, ext. 14), on Shamian Nan Jie, Shamian Island, is intended for guests only, but the office rarely asks for identification. English speakers. Open daily 7:30am-10pm.

Tourist Complaint Hotline: ☎8668 7042.

Bank of China: Almost all city branches exchange currency and traveler's checks and issue credit card advances. Main branch ☎8190 7077. The branch on Shamian Dajie between Shamian Yi Jie and Shamian Er Jie, on Shamian Island, has English-speaking staff members. Exchanges traveler's checks M-F. Open M-F 9am-6pm, Sa-Su 9am-5pm.

ATM: Bank of China, 91 Chandi Damalu, opposite McDonald's, has an indoor ATM that accepts international cards. Open M-F 9am-6pm, Sa-Su 9am-noon and 2-5pm. Near the bus and train stations, another Bank of China branch in Guangdong International Hotel (guǎngdōng guójì dàjiǔdiàn; 广东国际大酒店), 339 Huanshi Dong Lu, has 2 ATMs. Open M-F 9am-noon and 2-5pm, Sa 9am-6pm.

Western Union: 153 Huanshi Xi Lu (☎8667 3866), to the right as you exit the train station, next to the post office. Open 9am-5pm.

LOCAL SERVICES

Bookstores: Foreign Language Bookstore (wàiwén shūdiàn; 外文书店), 326 Beijing Lu, near the pedestrian street; entrance is down a small alley that serves as a bike parking lot—the sign is in Chinese. The store has 2 floors, but English-language books are limited to a paltry selection of classics on the top floor. Open daily 9am-8pm.

Libraries: Zhongshan Library (zhōngshān túshūguǎn; 中山图书馆 ; ☎8382 5710), on Wenming Lu near Dezheng Lu, has a relatively large English section on the 3rd fl. The bigger **Guangzhou Library** (guǎngzhōu túshūguǎn; 广州图书馆), on Zhongshan Si Lu, is to the north up Dezheng Lu. Foreigners with ID or passport can obtain library cards and borrow for free at both libraries. Refundable deposit Guangzhou Y200, Zhongshan Y20. Open Su-W and F-Sa 8:30am-9pm.

Supermarkets: JUSCO, on the 2nd fl. of the shopping mall **China Plaza.** Take the subway to Leishi Lingyuan and follow the signs for China Plaza. This huge supermarket sells produce, prepared foods, and sushi. Open daily 10am-10pm.

EMERGENCY AND COMMUNICATIONS

Hospital: Guangzhou No. 1 People's Hospital (guǎngzhōu shì dìyī rénmín yīyuàn; 广州市第一人民医院), 602 Renmin Bei Lu (☎8108 3090). Some English-speaking staff members. Open M-F 8am-noon and 2-5pm, Sa 8am-noon, Su emergencies only.

PSB: 20 Shamian Dajie (☎8121 9119). Open 24hr.

Internet Access: Internet Tea House (qīngshuǐ jū; 清水居; ☎8318 1680), at the end of the side street, just to the left of East River Seafood Restaurant. Y6 per hr. Open 9am-2am. **Henan Webmail**, on Shamian San Jie next to the Henan Hotel. Y10 per hr. Open 9am-11pm. **e-Dragon Internet Bar,** 376 Huanshi Dong Lu, 3rd fl. (☎8386 2888, ext. 0418). Y3 or Y4 per hr., depending on connection speed.

Post Offices: Liuhua Post Office, on the right side of the main train station's parking lot. EMS and Poste Restante. Open daily 8am-8pm. On Shamian Island, **Shamian Post Office** is on Shamian San Jie. EMS. Open M-F 9am-5pm. **Xidi Post Office** (guǎngzhōushì xīdī yóujú; 广州市西堤邮局), just east of Shamian Island, across the street from Cultural Park. EMS and Poste Restante. Open daily 8:30am-7pm.

Postal Code: 510010 and 510130.

▚ ACCOMMODATIONS

Most budget establishments are in the Shamian Island area or near the train station. During the two trade fairs (the end of April and September), prices rise and rooms are scarce. Bargaining is expected in the vast majority of hotels, including five-star establishments. A standard discount is typically available on weekdays. Most hotels accept major credit cards and have a 5-10% service charge.

SHAMIAN ISLAND AND PEARL RIVER

Two buses go to Shamian Island. From Huanshi Lu near the train station, take the southbound bus #5 to the end; go left out of the parking lot and cross over the canal. Or take bus #31 to its last stop at Culture Park. The eastern edge of Shamian Island is across Liu'ersan Lu and to the right.

Guangzhou Youth Hostel (guǎngzhōu qīngnián zhāodàisuǒ; 广州青年招待所), 2 Shamian Si Jie (☎8188 4298 or 8188 7912, ext. 3102). 8-bed dorms on the ground fl. face a small courtyard. Standard bunk beds with decent communal baths. Call ahead. Deposit Y50. 8-bed dorms with A/C Y45; singles Y100; doubles Y170, with bath Y190-210. Cash only. ❶

Guangzhou Riverside Youth Hostel (HI) (guǎngzhōu bīnjiāng guójì qīngnián lǚguǎn; 广 洲滨江国际青年旅馆), 405 Yanjiang Dong Lu (☎8382 4110). Many buses run down Yanjiang Lu from Shamian Island; metro stop Lieshi Lingyuan is 10min. away up Baiyun Lu. Rooms are clean and uncluttered. Free lockers in dorms. Gymnasium and ping pong available. A/C and TV. 4-bed dorms Y40; singles and doubles Y130. ❶

White Palace Hotel (báigōng jiǔdiàn; 白宫酒店), 13-17 Renmin Nan Lu (☎8188 2313; fax 8188 9161). Clean, charming rooms have A/C, lovely attached bath, phone, and TV. Personable, English-speaking staff just might give you an impressive discount. Singles and doubles Y180-230. ❸

Shamian Hotel (shāmiàn jiǔdiàn; 沙面酒店), 52 Shamian Nan Jie (☎8191 2288, ext. 3123). Very friendly, English-speaking staff. Well-maintained rooms have A/C, bath, phones, and TVs. A little more upscale than other Shamian budget options, with an excellent restaurant right next door. Singles Y170; doubles Y215. ❷

Aiqun Hotel (àiqún dàjiǔdiàn; 爱群大酒店), 113 Yanjiang Xi Lu (☎8186 6668), a 15min. walk east along the river. Somewhat upscale and pricey, Aiqun is for those who want to avoid Shamian Island without straying too far. Well-furnished rooms and spotless baths. Rooms spread over 2 wings; try to get a room in east wing, which faces the river. Singles Y180; doubles Y260-320. 20% weekday discount possible. ❷

ZHANQIAN LU (NEAR THE TRAIN STATION)

Amid the chaos of the station area, touts claiming to have special hotel discounts approach anyone with a suitcase or backpack. Many work with larger hotels that give them a small commission, and they sometimes offer discounts of up to 50%. Ask for a business card and insist on paying the hotel, not the tout.

Guangzhou CITS Youth Hostel (HI) (guǎngzhōu guójì qīngnián lǚguǎn; 广州国际青年 旅馆), 179 Huanshi Xi Lu (☎8666 6889; fax 8667 9787), inside the Guangdong Tourist Hotel, next to the long-distance train station. Despite outside frenzy, well-kept rooms are serene, with decent shared baths. Meets all your basic wants including a restaurant with dim sum breakfast and Internet downstairs for Y20 per hr. Deposit Y50. 2- and 4-bed dorms and singles Y50-75 for HI members. ❶

Jiaxin Guesthouse (jiāxìn bīnguǎn; 嘉信宾馆), 92 Zhanqian Lu (☎8666 7888), right of the Overseas Chinese Hotel. Large, clean rooms. Attached baths are a bit worn. Busy restaurant on the 2nd fl. Elevator runs only to the 4th and 5th. Singles and doubles Y148, extra beds Y80. ❷

Maoming Petroleum Hotel (màomíng shíhuà bīnguǎn; 茂名石化宾馆), 101 Zhanqian Lu (☎8622 0388, ext. 2128). Very friendly English-speaking staff. Very clean rooms. Very powerful A/C. Singles and doubles Y238. 30% discount possible. ❸

🗋 FOOD

It may be hotly disputed in China, but overseas, Guangzhou is the seat of Chinese cuisine. Residents often quote the Chinese saying that a perfect life is "to be born in Suzhou, live in Hangzhou, eat in Guangzhou, and die in Liuzhou." Guangzhou's world-famous dim sum and snake dishes make dining an adventure, and those who enjoy unusual fare will delight in delicious, exquisitely prepared meals for a pittance. Government-owned food stalls on every street corner boast the best deals: Y4-7 buys rice, a choice of three or four side dishes, and even soup.

SHAMIAN ISLAND AND PEARL RIVER

Kiumei Restaurant (qiáoměi shíjiā; 侨美食家), 52 Shamian Nan Jie (☎8188 4168), dishes up a culinary menagerie of Cantonese delicacies. Spiced pig ears (Y28), a wide assortment of vegetable offerings (Y10-25), fried frog (Y68), and sliced snake. The double-boiled crocodile with sea coconut (Y188) may not be available the day you visit, but the food here is so well prepared that you'll have forgotten all about the crocodile by the time your dish hits the table. Extremely friendly English-speaking staff and English menu—but don't be fooled, there's hardly a foreigner in the place. Open daily 11:30am-3pm and 5:30pm-4am. ❷

🔳 **Lan Kwai Fong** (lán guì fáng; 兰桂坊), 5 Shamian Nan Jie, Shamian Island (☎8191 9733 or 8192 1523). Hard to find, but not to worry—staff wait on Shamian Nan Jie to escort customers to this delicious Thai restaurant and bar. The food ranges from green curry (Y28) to braised eel (Y48) to fried prawns and fruit in whole coconut (Y33). Try the *roti* with either pineapples or bananas. Even on weeknights, this place overflows with customers. Reservations recommended. Open daily 11am-3pm and 5pm-4am. ❸

Shamian Coffee Shop (shāmiàn kāfēi wū; 沙面咖啡屋 ; ☎8190 7062), at the intersection of Shamian Nan Jie and Shamian Xi Jie, behind the White Swan Hotel. Look for glass windows plastered with large red characters. Plain food, but a quick and easy option for travelers. Most backpackers in Shamian stop here at least once for some pig heart and intestines congee (Y6), steamed claws (Y8), deep-fried tentacles (Y10), or the much more exotic pan-fried Italian noodles (Y6.5). English menu available. Open daily 7:30am-1am. ❶

Guangzhou East River Seafood Restaurant (guǎngzhōu dōng jiāng hǎixiān jiǔjiā; 广州东江海鲜酒家), 2 Yan-jiang Lu (☎8333 0283). Across the bridge from Shamian Island, this is the big poppa of Guangzhou's big seafood restaurants. The 1st fl. of this bustling 5-floor establishment is filled with tanks holding everything from snapping turtles to snakes. Before ordering, patrons walk the floor pointing to the animals they'd like to eat. Food is expensive (entrees Y30-60), especially if you order the alligator (Y148 for ½kg), but walking around is free. ❸

DOWNTOWN GUANGZHOU

🔳 **Bellagio** (lù gǎng xiǎozhèn; 鹿港小镇), 360 Huangshi Zhong Lu (☎8376 6106), in the Zhujiang Bldg. Despite the Italian name, Bellagio is billed as a Taiwanese restaurant, but actually serves a wide variety of Cantonese, Sichuan, and Hakka offerings, each more delicious than the last. Calm and quiet (a rarity for Guangzhou) with a hip mirror, glass, and mosaic decor. The claypot-simmered tofu (Y24) and the pineapple and shrimp stuffed in crullers (Y38) are delicious. Open 11am-4am. ❸

Lucky Fellow (yángchéng xìngyùn lóu hǎixiān jiǔjiā; 羊城幸运楼海鲜酒家), 322 Renmin Zhong Lu (☎8188 8318). Popular with local families, this restaurant will

THE LOCAL STORY

ROYAL RAMS

Cooks and chefs can take as much credit as they want, but Guangzhou's world-famous cuisine has its roots elsewhere—in simple stems of rice and the clattering hooves of our humble friend the goat. Legend has it that over 2500 years ago a terrible drought hit the land where Guangzhou is now, causing hunger and famine for the region's people. They prayed and prayed, but for years rain would not fall. Finally, five celestial beings appeared in the city riding on rams, each carrying a stem of rice. They gave the rice to the city's residents, forever blessing them with abundant food. The otherworldly beings departed, but their rams remained, turning to stone and staying forever in what would eventually become Guangzhou. In 1959, the city erected a statue in honor of the legend, and the happy goats stand atop a hill in Yuexiu Park.

Famine aside, Guangzhou has developed some of the most famously delicious food in the world. Yet 'delicious' doesn't always convey the distinction of Cantonese food. Goats are well known for eating everything, from farmer's clothes to tin cans. Similarly, there is a saying that Cantonese people will eat anything with wings except airplanes and anything with four legs except tables and chairs. It seems the goats have affected the city in more ways than one.

make a lucky fellow out of you if it's an excellent Cantonese dish you desire. Choose from the one tattered English menu and the live seafood tanks, or ask for a recommendation. The sliced goose (Y38) is delicious. Seafood dishes Y25-40. ❸

Black Swan Dumpling Restaurant (hēi tiān'é jiǎozǐ guǎn; 黑天鹅饺子馆 ; ☎8767 5687) has branches in the Guiguan Bldg., 786 Jiefang Bei Lu, 2nd and 3rd fl. (☎8354 8305), and at 486 Huanshi Lu, 2nd fl. (☎8757 5687). Hot, plump *jiǎozi* are dished up by the dozen to happy customers. Y8-15 for a heaping plateful. Vegetarian dumplings and non-dumpling dishes available. English menu. Open daily 9am-11pm. ❶

Yellow Fruit Village (huáng guǒ cūn; 黄果村), 475 Huanshi Dong Lu, 2nd fl. (☎8769 6459). This restaurant specializes in Guizhou cuisine, and almost every dish is guaranteed to knock your socks off—with hot peppers, that is. Bring some tissues for your running nose and watering eyes. No English menu, but Chinese menu has pictures, and the staff is happy to make recommendations. Entrees Y20-35. ❷

🅖 SIGHTS

🅖 SHAMIAN ISLAND (shāmiàn dǎo; 沙面岛). At the beginning of the century, Shamian housed all of Guangzhou's foreigners and their European-style customs and government buildings. These days, Shamian's wide, shaded streets are free from the incessant traffic that plagues the rest of Guangzhou. You wouldn't believe you're in the same city: the hectic crowds are gone, and even the air seems fresher. **Shamian Park** (shāmiàn gōngyuán; 沙面公园) overlooks the river. Especially popular at night, the park twinkles with electric lights along the river's edge, where old men and women play dominoes, chess, and *mahjong. (Take the bus down to Shamian Island from the train station.)*

PEARL RIVER (zhū jiāng; 珠江). Pearl River was beautiful once, before industrialization and pollution set in, or so the locals claim. In any case, Guangzhou residents still flock here to escape the grime and noise of the much more polluted city. In the morning, elderly men and women intently practice *tai chi.* In the evening, fishermen doze or wait beside their lines, and at night, the river lights up with neon, China's favorite architectural accessory. The **Guangzhou Passenger Ship Tourism Company** (guǎngzhōu shì kèlún lǚyóu fēngōngsī; 广州市客轮旅游分公司) at Xidi Wharf (☎8190 8190 or 8188 8932) and at Tianzi Wharf (tiānzì mǎtóu; 天字马头; ☎8333 0397) on Yanjiang Lu sells cruise tickets for river tours. *(Open 6:30am-10:45pm. 1hr. cruise at 3pm daily from both wharves, Y38. Dinner cruise from Tianzi Wharf daily at 7:05, 7:15, 7:30, 8, 9pm, Y38-Y68.)* Tickets sell out fast and can also be purchased from most travel agencies.

Shangjiu Lu (上九路), which becomes **Xiajiu Lu** (下九路), is lined with shops selling stationery, souvenirs, jewelry, shoes, and clothes. Companies hand out samples, hold contests for prizes, and put on zany shows. Pedestrians visit on weekends when the street is closed to traffic. From Shamian Island, head north past Qingping Market, away from the river for about 10-15min.

QINGPING MARKET (qīngpíng shìchǎng; 清平市场). This market might as well be an edible zoo; a walk through it takes extreme patience and morbid curiosity. The innocuous herb and root section closes in the late afternoon, but the poultry, fish, and meat markets farther north rage against the dying light. Every day, 60,000 patrons visit this 2000-stall testament to the inclusive nature of Cantonese cuisine—snails, roaches, beetles, fish heads and guts, freshly killed chickens, and meat carcasses are all up for grabs. Also check out the strange interpretations of pet stores, which feature caged squirrels, chipmunks, and small dogs as far as the eye can see. *(A small collection of streets just north of Shamian Island. From Shamian, walk over the canal via the footbridge. The medicine section is at the outer fringe; the meat section lies farther in, along Shanmulan, Shibafu Nan Lu, and Tiyun Dong Lu. The wild game section is opposite the poultry street.)*

WHITE CLOUD MOUNTAIN (báiyún shān; 白云山). A popular sight for pollution-weary travelers and locals, this tidy hill draws nearly 1000 visitors per day, who make the strenuous 2hr. climb to the top. From the **radio tower** at the top, visitors can wheeze their way past bamboo groves, fragrant foliage, and the tombs of Qing Dynasty officials. A concrete road leads to the entrance of a **mountaintop park** (Y5), with views of the airport, amusement park, and surrounding countryside. Side attractions include a **temple** (Y5), **Mingchun Bird Valley** (Y10), and a mountain **toboggan ride** (Y20-30) at the foot of the mountain. *(Bus #24 will take you to the south side of the mountain, where you can take a cable car to the top for Y30. Bus #11 will take you to the north side, where you can begin your ascent if you're interested in walking.)*

YUEXIU PARK (yuèxiù gōngyuán; 越秀公园). The park guards the **Statue of the Five Rams** (wǔ yáng shíxiàng; 五羊石像), long seen by Guangzhou residents as an emblem of their city. A closer look costs Y3. **Guangzhou Museum** (guǎngzhōu bówùguǎn; 广洲博物馆 ; ☎ 8354 5253 or 8666 2357) is housed in the beautiful **Zhenhai Tower**, which dates to 1380. The jungle-like Yuexiu has quite a few natural attractions, some blessed with names like "Elegant and Intelligent Waterfall." *(Open daily 9am-5pm. Y10, children Y5.)* In the northwest corner of the park, the **Orchid Garden** (lán pǔ; 兰圃) is filled with over 10,000 pots and 200 varieties of orchids. The flowers bloom in fall and spring, but in the dead of winter or in summer, you may end up staring at pots of dirt. *(On Huifu Xi Lu, near the main train station. Take bus #202 or 219 from the bus stop opposite the Xidi Wharf on Yanjiang Lu to the stop nearest to the huge crag or boulder on Jiefang Lu. Open daily 9am-11pm. Y4-10, depending on time of day; get there after 7pm for cheapest entrance fee. Price includes tea in the central house near the ponds.)* You may also want to check out the nearby **Sun Yat-sen Memorial Hall**. The building itself is impressive, but don't expect a history lesson. *(Open 8am-4:30pm. Y10.)*

ZHONGSHAN LU. A walk along the route of the subway east on Zhongshan Lu (中山路) leads to a few interesting sights in the heart of Guangzhou. **Six Banyan Tree Temple** (liùróng tǎ; 六榕塔) houses a multi-tiered pagoda surrounded by temples. *(Park Y1, pagoda Y6.)* The next stop, Gongyuanqian, is surrounded by a shopping bonanza that centers around **Beijing Lu** (北京路). Every night at 7pm, hundreds of stalls appear on **Xihu Lu** (西湖路) and the neighboring streets.

At the **Site of the Former Peasant Movement Institute** (nóngjiǎng suǒ jiùzhǐ; 农讲所旧址 ; ☎ 8333 3936), on Zhongshan Lu next to the Guangzhou Library, Mao Zedong instructed trainees on the theories and methods of peasant uprising. Now a museum with limited English captions, the compound once witnessed the peasants' strict military training; the pull-up bar they used remains in the yard. *(Open daily 9am-4:30pm. Y5.)* The **Memorial to the Martyrs of the Guangzhou Uprising** (guǎngzhōu qǐyì lièshì língyuán; 广洲起义烈士陵园) commemorates those who died in the revolt against the GMD on December 11, 1927. A giant statue of a hand clenching a machine gun casts a shadow over tourists. *(On Zhongshan Er Lu. Take the subway to Lieshi Lingyuan. Open daily 6am-9pm. Y3, but visible from outside the gate.)*

NIGHTLIFE

Nightlife is taken seriously in Guangzhou, one of the few cities in Guangdong where you'll find more than just a few token clubs and bars. Locals, weekend revelers from Hong Kong and Macau, foreign businessmen, and tourists come out in full force at night. Yanjiang Lu, on the Pearl River, has larger venues with live **shows** and the biggest of Guangzhou's **discos**. Popular **dance clubs** and **bars** line Huanshi, Dongfeng, and Zhongshan Lu. Heping Lu, or Peace Road, is off Huanshi Lu next to the Holiday Inn and home to many tourist-heavy bars and dance floors. From Shamian Island, cross Renmin Qiao (People's Bridge) and turn right; impromptu **riverside stalls** sell beer and sodas to customers lucky enough to grab a table. The more **karaoke**-oriented Panfu Lu scene, dominated by **D&D Disco Two**, keeps 'em singing all night long. The free English magazine *That's Guangzhou*, available at hotels and kiosks, has extensive nightlife listings.

Golf Club (gāoěrfū jiǔbā; 高尔夫酒吧; ☎8666 6708), on Huanshi Zhong Lu, near the north gate of Yuexiu Park. A 10min. walk east from the train station, on the opposite side of the street. This former mini-golf course is now a club with something for everyone: packed dance floor and bar complemented by outdoor seating by the pond, VIP and karaoke rooms, and a quieter indoor bar removed from the incessant bass. A local favorite, it's busy nearly every night of the week. No cover makes it accessible to everyone. Beer Y38 and up. Karaoke room Y300 and up. Open 9pm-3am.

Solo Bar, 420 Huanshi Dong Lu (☎8769 5229). This small bar is a welcome change from the huge and hectic discos of Huanshi Lu and Yanjiang Lu. Booth and table seating fills up with chatting local youth playing drinking games or just taking in the live music (daily at 10pm). Beer Y20 and up. Open 8pm-3am.

New Era (xīnyī qū; 新î区), 2 Zhongshan San Lu (☎8381 3327). Proving that youth culture is alive and kicking in Guangzhou, New Era packs 2 floors with dancing bodies and 3 more with VIP and karaoke rooms. Patrons are not only hip, but enthusiastic. Be ready to walk in and get swept up in the action. Beer and cocktails from Y40. Open 8pm until the last customer leaves.

The Place (lùdiǎn; 路点), 2 Heping Lu (☎8357 5833), part of the Overseas Chinese Village. Tiny white lights strung over the path to the entrance lead you to a small but crowded bar frequented by both locals and expats. Live music every Friday or Saturday night provides a change from the bass-heavy musical offerings on the rest of Heping Lu. Beer Y30. Open 7:30pm-2am.

Face Club, 191 Dongfeng Xi Lu (☎8388 0688), in the basement of the International Bank Tower. The dance floor gets pretty crowded, but this is still one of the best places in Guangzhou to strut your stuff, especially late at night after many other venues have closed. Music changes according to the whims of guest DJs. Drinks Y40 and up. Karaoke rooms Y380 and up. Open daily 8:30pm-2am.

ET Space (wàixīngrén kōngjiān; 外星人空间), 183 Yanjiang Lu (☎8339 6088). Easily the weirdest way to spend your Saturday night, ET Space features the (fairly amateur) live shows of Yanjiang Lu's clubs amid terrifying statues of aliens and monsters. Never gets really crowded, but worth a visit for surreal value. Western and Chinese food served in the early evening. Beer Y30 and up. Open 7:30pm-2am.

FOSHAN 佛山

☎**0757**

The quiet little town of Foshan, the famed birthplace of Cantonese opera and martial arts master Huang Fei Hong, is a great place for visitors to take a breather after surviving overcrowded Guangzhou.

TRANSPORTATION. Most train transportation to and from Foshan is via Guangzhou. **Trains** run from the Foshan Train Station (fóshān huǒchē zhàn; 佛山火车站), in the north, to Guangzhou (Y10-25); Hong Kong (3hr., daily, Y240); and Zhaoqing (Y20-30). The CTS, 14 Zumiao Lu, next to the Overseas Chinese Hotel, can book train tickets for a Y5 commission but will in most cases encourage you to take a bus to get a train in Guangzhou. **Buses** from the Foshan Bus Station (fóshān qìchē zhàn; 佛山汽

车站；☎228 6700), on Fenjiang Lu, at the north end of town, run to: Guangzhou (1hr., every 20min. 6:50am-6:25pm, Y13); Huizhou (3hr., 8 per day 7:20am-5:50pm, Y85); Shenzhen (every 30min. 6:40am-8:50pm, Y88); and Zhongshan (20 per day 6:30am-8:10pm, Y36). From the Zumiao Bus Station (zǔmiào qìchē zhàn; 祖庙汽车站 ；☎222 0557 or 225 5409), on Chengmentou Lu, buses go to Guangzhou (1hr., every 15-20min. 7am-9pm, Y13). **Local buses** #1, 4, 6, 9, 11, 12, and 16 connect the Foshan Train Station, Foshan Bus Station, and the Ancestral Temple. Another major local bus station is on Zumiao Lu, just opposite the Ancestral Temple. Base fare for **taxis** is Y7, and each additional km costs Y2.2-2.6. **Pedicabs** or **motorbikes** cost about Y5.

⌨▐ ORIENTATION AND PRACTICAL INFORMATION. Visitors to Foshan will find almost all of their daily needs satisfied within a two-block commercial quadrangle bordered by **Qinren Lu** (亲人路) in the north, **Zumiao Lu** (祖庙路) in the east, **Chengmentou Lu** (城门头路) in the south, and **Fenjiang Lu** (纷江路) in the west. The main branch of **Bank of China** (☎224 3761) is on the corner of Renmin Xi Lu and Fenjiang Zhong Lu, where it becomes Zumiao Lu, and exchanges currency and traveler's checks. (Open M-F 8am-5:30pm, Sa-Su 9am-5pm.) Another branch on Zumiao Lu exchanges currency. (Open M-F 8am-5:30pm, Sa-Su 9am-5pm.) Internet access is available at **Receivers of Kindness Internet Cafe** (shòu huì zhě wǎngbā; 受惠者网吧). Take your first left walking away from the Foshan Bus Station toward Baihua Square. (☎8228 7872. Y2 per hr.) The **post office**, 4 Qinren Lu, has EMS and Poste Restante. (Open daily 8:30am-9pm.) Another branch (☎8333 9157) in Baihua Square on Jiaxin Lu has EMS and Western Union. **Postal Code:** 528000.

▐▐ ACCOMMODATIONS AND FOOD. For those who fall in love with Foshan (or miss the last bus), the cheapest and most convenient place to stay is the **Foshan City Huasheng Hotel ❶** (fóshān shì huáshèng jiǔdiàn; 佛山市华盛酒店) , 3 Fenjiang Lu, to the right of the Foshan Bus Station. It's old but all the bang you'll need for your buck. (☎228 7950. Communal bath. Windowless rooms with fan Y60; rooms facing the street with A/C Y83; singles and doubles Y60-150.) Another slightly more upscale option is the **Jiayue Hotel ❷** (jiāyuè jiǔdiàn; 嘉悦酒店), 2 Chengmentou Lu, in the midst of the action of Baihua Square, next to Pizza Hut. (☎222 2868. Doubles Y160.) A collection of restaurants and *dà pái dàng* (street stalls; 大排挡) present fried foods, meats, and pastry snacks. Standard Chinese entrees go for Y6-15 at the **Scholar Passes the Imperial Exam Rice Porridge ❶** (zhuàngyuán jídì zhōu; 状元及第粥), diagonal from the Ancestral Temple. (☎8228 6438. Open 9am-10pm.) The romantically lit **Rose Garden Coffee Shop ❷** (méiguì yuán kāfēitīng; 玫瑰园咖啡厅), 32 Zumiao Lu, serves small portions of everything from fried rice (Y15-18) to fresh fruit salad (Y15). Ask for the daily buffet special or the four-course lunch set. (English menus available. Open daily 10am-midnight.)

◎ SIGHTS. Foshan myth holds that a Daoist god, the Northern Emperor, rules the world's waters and holds sway over the denizens of the flood-prone Pearl River region. Inside the serene, shady grounds of the **Ancestral Temple** (zǔmiào; 祖庙), a weapons collection guards the altar of this important deity. The temple grounds are replete with gift shops and the sounds of "mood music," but there are some worthwhile sights. Across from the temple, the **Wanfu Stage** is famed as the birthplace of Cantonese opera. Halls of musical instruments and carved steles are worth a look. Perhaps the real reason to visit this temple, however, is the ▨ **Huang Fei Hong Memorial Museum,** to the left once inside the temple. Huang Fei Hong, born in Foshan in 1856, is a famous Cantonese folk hero. The museum's exhibits, all with English captions, chronicle his legacy, from his beginnings as a hired protector of market workers to his larger-than-life status as a patriotic martial arts master, doctor, and philosopher. The museum has instructions on how to perform some of his moves, but don't expect to become a martial arts master in a day. (21 Zumiao Lu. Temple open daily 8:30am-7pm; last admission 6:30pm. Museum open daily 9:30am-4:30pm. Temple admission including museum Y20.)

The tiny **Renshou Temple** (rénshòu sì; 仁寿寺), on Zumiao Lu, welcomes worshippers to pray at its three towers. Traditional Chinese-style walkways surround a small but attractive tower. A pleasant collection of bonsai trees sits in the courtyard. The complex is in the process of slow renovation and accepts donations. (Take bus #1, 5, or 11. ☎225 3053. Open daily 8am-5pm.) Just north of the temple, the **Folk Art Research Institute** (mínjiān yìshù yánjiū shè; 民间艺术研究社), set up by the government to promote and develop folk art, offers a chance to view and buy pricey hand-crafted items from all over China, including clothes, scarves, intricate paper cuttings, and carvings on jade, stone, and bone. (Open daily 9am-5pm.)

ZHONGSHAN 中山 ☎0760

Yet another rapidly developing city, Zhongshan's attempts to emulate its bigger and brighter neighbors aren't entirely convincing. The city has adorned itself with neon lights, flashy shops, and big hotels, but it can't quite forget its friendly, small-town feel. Crowds hang out by the river rather than in the stores, and traffic circles remain quiet and relatively empty. No more than a brief stop for most travelers, Zhongshan is famed as the birthplace of its namesake, early-20th century reformist leader Sun Yat-sen (Sun Zhongshan), and it's here that the city's passion can really be felt. Every visitor should make trip to see the museum built in his honor.

◨? TRANSPORTATION AND PRACTICAL INFORMATION

On the west side of the **Shiqi River** (shíqí hé; 石歧河), **Zhongshan Lu** (中山路) runs north-south; on the east side it runs east-west. **Fuhua Dadao** (富华大道) intersects Zhongshan Lu near the Zhongshan International Hotel. On the east side of the river, Fuhua Dadao becomes **Sunwen Xi Lu** (孙文西路), a beautifully paved pedestrian street winding past pastel buildings, glossy shops, and pinewood benches. East of the pedestrian street, **Sunwen Zhong Lu** (孙文中路) continues to the commercial center of Zhongshan.

Buses: Zhongshan International Hotel Bus Station (zhōngshān guójì jiǔdiàn chē zhàn; 中山国际酒店车站; ☎863 2149), in the parking lot of Zhongshan International Hotel, on the corner of Zhongshan Yi Lu and Fuhua Dadao. To: **Guangzhou** (2hr., every 25min. 6am-6:30pm, Y30); **Hong Kong** (3hr., 4 per day, Y130); **Shenzhen** (2hr., every 30min. 7:40am-7:40pm, Y70); **Zhuhai** (50min., every 20min. 7am-7:20pm, Y15). The **Zhongshan Bus Station** (☎866 9145) is a 10min. ride out of town, east down Fuhua Dao, but there's no real reason to make the trek; smaller bus stations with identical prices abound around the hotels on Zhongshan Lu.

Local Transportation: The main bus stop (☎183 9831 or 183 9811) is on Sunwen Lu. Most **buses** run roughly 6am-10pm. Fare Y2-5. Aggressive **sampan** and **motorbike** drivers also wait impatiently to grab tourists. Fare Y5 and up.

Taxis: Base fare Y7-8, each additional km Y0.5.

Travel Agencies: CTS (☎888 0888), in the Fuhua Hotel, doesn't provide many services, but can give information about local sights. Open daily 8am-5:30pm.

Bank of China: On the 1st fl. of **Zhongshan International Hotel** (zhōngshān guójì jiǔdiàn; 中山国际酒店), on Zhongshan Yi Lu. Exchanges traveler's checks. Open daily 8:30am-5:30pm.

ATM: The Bank of China across the river, at the intersection of Anlan Lu and Lai'an Lu, has **24hr. ATMs.** Open 8am-noon and 2:30-9pm.

Bookstore: Harvard In Bookstore (hànlín shūyuàn; 翰林书苑 ; ☎884 6966), opposite the Bank of China on Anlan Lu, sells maps.

Internet Access: Glinton Cafe (gélíntè wǎngluó cāntīng; 格林特网络餐厅 ; ☎882 2788), on the 3rd fl. A 5min. walk from the river on Sunwen Lu. Y6 per hr.

Post and Telecommunications: On Sunwen Lu (☎882 3405), 7min. walk from the Shiqi River. EMS and IDD service. Open daily 8am-10pm.

Postal Code: 528400.

ACCOMMODATIONS AND FOOD

Zhongshan's accommodations tend to ignore budget travelers. Prices vary for weekday and weekend stays—a standard discount of at least 20% is given on weekdays. Most hotels accept major credit cards.

Most hotels offer reasonably priced breakfast buffets, but don't expect later meals to be such good deals. A walk down **Sunwen Lu,** across the river, will bring you past more fast-food and noodle shops, restaurants, and food stalls than you could possibly need, all for meals under Y20. Eateries become less fast-food oriented and more like restaurants once you get out of the pedestrian-only section. The **Fuzhou Hotel ❷** (fùzhōu jiǔdiàn; 富洲酒店), 131 Fuhua Dadao, 14th fl., serves the best dim sum breakfast (7:30-11am) in Zhongshan for Y8-12. (Open daily 7:30am-1am.) Large windows overlooking the street let an abundance of light into the **I Love You Cafe ❷**, 139 Fuhua Dadao (☎862 6970). Pine tables, tie-dyed bench covers, and a fresh atmosphere complement the 40 kinds of tea, coffee, and floats. (Tea Y15-18 per set. Open 10am-1am.)

Zhongshan Zhuhai Airlines Hotel (zhōngshān zhūhǎi hángkōng dàjiǔdiàn; 中山珠海航空大酒店), 133 Fuhua Dadao (☎862 1788), a block west of the Fuzhou Hotel. This hotel takes its affiliation with Zhuhai Airlines seriously: there's a 30ft. model and an equally large golden mural of a plane in the lobby, and slightly smaller models in each room. Unlike a plane ride, rooms are comfortable, well furnished, and spacious, with A/C, TV, and attached bath. Singles and doubles Y148 and up. ❷

Xiangshan Hotel (xiāngshān jiǔdiàn; 香山酒店), 113 Zhongshan Yi Lu (☎863 4567). Rooms are more than comfortable with standard amenities. Ask for a room with a view. Doubles Y160-260; triples Y350 and up. ❷

Zhongshan Jinyue Hotel (zhōngshān jīnyuè jiǔdiàn; 中山金悦酒店), 111 Zhongshan Yi Lu (☎862 2888), across the street from the Zhongshan International Hotel. Clean, perfumed rooms and service like you're paying Y300 to stay there—because you are. English-speaking staff. Doubles Y460 and up. "Special offer" rooms begin at Y268 but may be unavailable. ❺

⊙ SIGHTS

MUSEUM OF THE FORMER SUN YAT-SEN RESIDENCE (sūn zhōngshān gùjū; 孙中山故居). No trip to Zhongshan is complete without a visit here. Born in Cuiheng, a nearby village, in 1866, Sun Yat-sen went on to head the movement that overthrew the last remnants of the Qing Dynasty in 1912 (see **Birth of a Nation,** p. 78). An exhibition hall proudly and meticulously details his childhood in Cuiheng, his early work as a pharmacist in Guangzhou and doctor in Macau, and his revolutionary career fighting The Man. English and Chinese captions, photographs, and small recreative exhibitions abound, in addition to multimedia presentations on the second floor. Outside, the museum features a not-to-scale recreation of the village as it was during Sun Yat-sen's childhood, including the watchtower his father used to man, the house of the bean curd maker (whose son bullied Sun Yat-sen), and various explications of traditional foods and festivals. *(In Cuiheng* 翠亨 *. Bus #12 from the Fuzhou Hotel stop outside, approx. 1hr., Y3.5. Taxi 45 min., Y50-80. Admission Y20. Free tours in English and Chinese available at the visitor center.)*

OTHER SIGHTS. Great for a relaxing stroll, the sidewalks along the river near the bridge leading to Sunwen Lu are always full of people. The riverbank area opposite the Fuhua Hotel becomes an impromptu **nightmarket** from 8 to 11pm each night. A little farther east on Sunwen Lu, **Sun Yat-sen Memorial Hall** (zhōngshān jìniàn guǎn; 中山纪念馆) pays homage to the city's most famous Sun. The hall hosts a number of local and international dance and music performances. (☎882 2014. Open daily 8am-5pm. Free.) **Zhongshang Park,** accessible by a left turn off Sunwen Lu, is home to a small temple and the **Fufeng Pagoda,** which affords nice views of the city from its hilltop perch. *(Open sunrise to sunset. Free.)*

ZHAOQING 肇庆 ☎0758

According to legend, the Seven Star Crags, Zhaoqing's primary attraction, formed when seven stars fell to earth. For hundreds of years, these dramatic peaks inspired moving poems and essays, but the once-natural mountains are now exorbitantly priced and dressed in flashing light bulbs. Mt. Dinghu, Zhaoqing's other major sight, suffers from similar prices and tourist clogs, but the air is too clear and the trees too dense for even the Chinese tourism industry to blight its wilds. Nightly light shows attract a gathering by the lake, and friendly residents offer help to travelers that look the least bit lost. A quiet city with a sense of community, Zhaoqing is a worthwhile stop for anyone fed up with Western backpackers or the breakneck speed of Guangdong's life.

⏸ ▐ TRANSPORTATION AND PRACTICAL INFORMATION

Zhaoqing is fairly small. Seven Star Crags and the train tracks define Zhaoqing's north border, and the **Xi River** (xī hé; 西河) marks its southern end. **Tianning Lu** (天宁路) houses tourists and their hotels, and **Gongnong Lu** (工农路) houses locals and their shops. These two streets are connected by **Jianshe Lu** (建设路) and **Duanzhou Lu** (端州路).

Trains: Zhaoqing Train Station (zhàoqìng huǒchē zhàn; 肇庆火车站, ☎283 5114), north of town, a Y15 taxi ride from Duanzhou Lu. Bus #1 also runs from the train station to the city center. Ticket office open 24hr.; travel agents don't sell tickets. To **Guangzhou** (2hr., 9 per day, Y15-25) and **Hong Kong** (4hr., 9:30am, Y235).

Buses: Zhaoqing City Bus Station (zhàoqìng shì qìchē zhàn; 肇庆市汽车站, ☎223 3629), on Duanzhou Lu, between Wenming Lu and Gongnong Lu. To: **Guangzhou** (2hr., at least every 30min. 6:20am-8pm, Y30); **Shenzhen** (3½hr., every 1-2hr. 8:20am-6:30pm, Y85); **Zhongshan** (2½hr., 5 per day 7am-5:35pm, Y38); **Zhuhai** (3½hr., 2 per day, Y36-50).

Local Transportation: Bus fare Y1-2 within the city center, Y3 on the outskirts. **Taxi** base fare Y7, each additional km Y2.2-2.6. Aggressive **motorbike** drivers are always on hand; look for their colored helmets. Short trips approx. Y5.

Travel Agencies: CITS, 46 Renmin Nan Lu (☎228 6038). On the corner of Duanzhou Lu and Tianning Lu is the **Star Lake International Travel Service** (xīnghú guójì lǚxíngshè; 星湖国际旅行社, ☎223 5813), not to be confused with the Star Lake Travel Service opposite the memorial arch. Very helpful English-speaking service selling bus tickets to Guangzhou and Shenzhen (no commission). Open daily 8am-8pm.

Bank of China: Next to Texboy on Duanzhou Lu (☎222 0314). Changes currency. Open M-F 8:30am-5:30pm, Sa-Su 9am-5pm. Another branch inside the lobby of the **Star Lake Hotel** (xīnghú dàjiǔdiàn; 星湖大酒店), 37 Duanzhou Lu, has an international **ATM** and exchanges traveler's checks. Open daily 7:30am-midnight.

Bookstore: Xinhua Bookstore, 69 Tianning Lu (☎231 8382), at the corner of Songcheng Lu and Tianning Lu, in the New World Commercial Bldg. Assorted maps.

Hospital: People's Hospital (rénmín yīyuàn; 人民医院 ; ☎283 3612), near the intersection of Songcheng Xi Lu and Renmin Nan Lu.

PSB: On Lianhu Xi Lu (☎2231 4882), 2 blocks east of the memorial arch.

Internet: Tianzhi Jiaozi Internet Cafe (tiān zhī jiāozǐ wǎngbā; 天之娇子网吧), 76 Tianning Lu (☎223 8438), in the same building as Precious Big World Hotel. Enter the shopping mall to the left of the hotel's entrance and take the stairs on your left. Y2 per hr. **Sunday Cafe** (xīngqīrì wǎngbā; 星期日网吧), a 5min. walk up Xinghu Xi Lu to the left of the memorial arch. Look for the big orange sign on your right. Y2 per hr.

Post Office: On Jianshe Lu, near its intersection with Wenming Lu. EMS. Open daily 7:30am-9:30pm.

Postal Code: 526040.

▛▟ ACCOMMODATIONS AND FOOD

Zhaoqing has plenty of hotels with fancy amenities. Most offer discounts, but many also increase prices during the summer and on weekends and holidays.

Bakeries and tiny **rice** and **noodle shops** line Gongnong Lu and Jianghe Lu. The end of Wenming Lu near the bus station is the best place to find dinner in Zhaoqing. Small restaurants line this half of the street and offer standard Chinese dishes (Y8-15) and outdoor seating. At the northwest corner of Duanzhou Lu and Tianning Lu, ▨ **Texboy ❶** (dézhōu niúzǎi kuàicān; 德州牛仔快餐; ☎223 2952 or 223 3328) has swing-and-barrel seating, Western and Chinese fast food, and a ball set for kids. Staff members wear cowboy hats, plaid shirts, and bandanas and attempt southern accents. (Noodle soups Y7. Pizza Y6.5 per slice. Chinese set meals with rice and vegetable and meat dish Y9.5. Open daily 9am-11pm.)

Mount Dinghu International Youth Hostel (dīnghúshān guójì qīngnián lǚxíngguǎn; 鼎湖山国际青年旅行馆; ☎262 1668; fax 262 1665), at Dinghushan. Take bus #21 to Mt. Dinghu's parking lot and entrance. Pay the park admission fee, hop on a park bus (Y3), and ask to be let off near the hostel. The hostel is on the right, but you must enquire about rooms in the hotel opposite the hostel. Staff is extremely friendly. Dorms have wooden bunk beds, A/C, and shared hall baths. Every time you leave the park, you must buy another ticket (Y50) to re-enter, making the stay deceptively expensive and best suited for those who wish to explore the park extensively. 4-bed dorms Y55, HI members Y38, groups Y50. ❶

Jiangshan Hotel (jiāngshān dàjiǔdiàn; 江山大酒店), 40 Jianshe San Lu (☎223 2088), between Tianning Lu and Wenming Lu. Building has no 4th wall, so hallways look out into a courtyard and over the city's roofs. Singles and doubles are spare but clean. A/C and attached bath. Singles and doubles Y80; standard luxury room Y100. ❶

Precious Big World Hotel (zhēnbǎo dà shìjiè jiǔdiàn; 珍宝大世界酒店), 76 Tianning Lu (☎229 0168). Look for an Italian chef outside this hotel. Don't be put off by the sculptures of small boys peeing in the lobby's fountain. Clean rooms, with bathroom and balcony as an added bonus. Singles and doubles Y120-150. ❷

👁 SIGHTS

The **Seven Star Crags** (qīxīng yán; 七星岩) is said to mirror the pattern of the Big Dipper. The center of the crags has been made into a park with fishing and spelunking opportunities. Despite the unfortunate amount of kitsch, the park allows for strolls along, and even hikes up, the crags. Romantics can hire a pedicab (Y10) for a turn around the park. (Take bus #19 from the stop near the memorial arch, right below the Star Lake International Travel Service sign. ☎227 7724. Open 24hr. Tickets sold 7:30am-6pm. Y30.) Boats (Y4-8) speed across **Star Lake** (xīnghú; 星湖) between the park and the dock, near **Seven Star Crags Memorial Arch.** On the corner of Duanzhou Lu and Tianning Lu, the arch frames the mountains from afar. Around 8pm every night, Zhaoqing's residents emerge from their homes to watch a water-and-light show. Fountains spurt water as high as 100m into the sky, while patriotic music plays in the background. Around 8:20pm, the show ends and the nightly community gathering disperses.

🧗 CLIMBING DINGHUSHAN MOUNTAIN 鼎湖山

18km east of Zhaoqing. Bus #21 (30-60min., every 20min., Y3) leaves from the bus stop up the small road to the right of the Memorial Arch Plaza. Buses drop off in the parking lot near the entrance; catch a return bus here. Avoid going on weekends, when the park is crowded and bus tickets hard to come by. Tourist office sells maps (Y5). Buses (Y3) and smaller open cars (Y10) drive up to the summit every 5-10min. Open daily 8am-5pm. Y50.

Dinghushan Mountain (dǐnghú shān; 鼎湖山) draws crowds every day of the week, and makes for a very pleasant daytrip from Zhaoqing. Inside **Dinghushan Park** (dǐng-húshān gōngyuán; 鼎湖山公园), a concrete path winds up the mountain, leading past spectacular views of the farmland. For those who want to avoid the crowds and buses, it takes about two hours to hike the loop, past Qingyun Temple and Baoding Park. Follow side routes along one of the mountain streams for a glimpse of the Flying Waterpool and Two Rainbows Over the Chasm Bridge and the chance to dip your feet in the cool waters. Qingyun Temple is fairly unremarkable, but **Baoding Park** is home to China's largest ancient cauldron (dǐng; 鼎), an admittedly huge, dragon-engraved bronze pot. Dinghushan's other attraction, the **White Cloud Temple,** is now part of a nature reserve and inaccessible to park visitors. Those who tire halfway up the route can always hop on a motorbike (Y5-10). Some travelers, enthralled by the clean air and forested scenery, stay a little longer at Dinghushan. There are several restaurants surrounding the area near the youth hostel, in the hotel opposite and down the road to the left. Pricey hotel meals cost Y30 and up, but smaller outdoor eateries provide food for Y10 to 20.

SHAOGUAN 韶关

☎0751

The select few who choose to stop in Shaoguan on their way out of Guangdong will find a comfortable and welcoming city, if only for a few nights. Shaoguan, the site of heavy Japanese saturation bombing in the 1930s, has rebuilt itself to a city of roughly three million, with the bustling shopping streets of many other Chinese cities, but without the self-consciousness of a major tourist destination. The mountains of Danxiashan National Park draw a few crowds, but for the most part Shaoguan exists independently from the international travel crowd. Often the holiday spot for Chinese tourists from nearby cities, the city gamely ignores them and cranks on at its own pace.

TRANSPORTATION AND PRACTICAL INFORMATION

Shaoguan straddles a peninsula at the confluence of the **Wu River** (wǔ jiāng; 武江) and the **Zhen River** (zhēn jiāng; 浈江). **Fengdu Lu** (风度路) runs north-south and divides the city in half. It's also closed to cars and full of boutiques, food stalls, and restaurants. **Xunfeng Lu** and **Jiefang Lu** (解放路) form a cross at the southern part of the bottom of Fengdu Lu. **Jiefang Lu** (解方路) leads to the train station just off the peninsula to the east, across the bridge. **Fengcai Lu** (风采路) forms the northern border of the pedestrian-only section of Fengdu Lu. The sprawling **Zhongshan Park** makes up the southernmost part of the peninsula.

Trains: Shaoguan Train Station (sháoguān huǒchē zhàn; 韶关火车站 ; ☎617 2794), on Nanshao Lu at the Qujiang Bridge, just across from the terminus of Jiefang Lu on the peninsula. To: **Foshan** (3hr., daily, Y41); **Guangzhou** (2½-3hr., 6 per day, Y36); **Guilin** (11hr., 8:30pm, Y92-156); **Shantou** (14½hr., 2 per day, sleeper Y102-129); **Shenzhen** (4hr., daily, Y70).

Buses: Xihe Coach Station (xīhé kèyùn zhàn; 西河客运站 ; ☎857 4176), on Gongye Xi Lu, just east of the peninsula. Ticket office open daily 5:30am-6pm. To: **Guangzhou** (4hr., daily, Y62); **Shenzhen** (5 per day, Y112); **Zhuhai** (8hr., daily, Y90). **Shaoguan Coach Station** (☎822 1669), on the right side of the train station plaza as you exit the station. To: **Guangzhou** (3hr., many per day, Y70); **Shenzhen** (6 per day, Y97); **Zhuhai** (3 per day, Y100).

Local Transportation: Most **buses** stop at the train station square. **Taxi** base fare Y4, but not all taxis are metered. **Motorbike** and **sampan** drivers charge about Y3.

Travel Agency: Shaoguan Tourist Corporation, 12 Xunfeng Lu (☎889 5941), near the intersection with Jiefang Lu. Doesn't provide any services for travelers within China, but helpful staff can provide train and bus timetables. Open daily 9-11:30am and 2-5pm.

Bank of China: 160 Jiefang Lu (☎888 8338, ext. 212). Exchanges traveler's checks daily 3-5pm. The branch to the right of the train station exchanges currency only. Open M-Sa 8am-5:30pm, Su 10am-3pm.

Bookstore: Xinhua Bookstore, at the intersection of Xunfeng Lu and Jiefang Lu (☎888 5741), sells bilingual maps of cities all over China. Open 8am-9pm.

PSB: 76 Heping Lu (☎846 9405), between Fengcai Lu and Fuxing Lu.

Hospital: Yuebei No. 2 People's Hospital (yuebĕi dièr rénmín yīyuàn; 粤北第二人民医院), 117 Fengdu Lu (☎888 5661), just below Fuxing Lu.

Internet Access: Dong Fang Wang Ba (东方网吧), 7 Fuxing Lu, down a small alley. 40 computers. Y2 per hr. Open 8am-midnight. There are several Internet cafes in the lobby of the building to the left of the **Jin Yuan Hotel**, 66 Fengcai Lu; walk in and look to your left. Y4 per hr.

Post and Telecommunications: To the right when you exit the train station. EMS and Poste Restante. Open daily 8am-9:30pm. **China Telecom** has IDD service. Open daily 8am-10:30pm.

Postal Code: 512000.

ACCOMMODATIONS AND FOOD

Finding good, cheap food in Shaoguan is relatively easy. The ubiquitous Y5 *dà pái dàng* (streetside food stalls; 大排挡) are out in full force around the peninsula and north of the train station. **Shaoguan Restaurant Fast Food ❶** (sháoguān jiŭjiā kuàicān; 韶关酒家快餐), 2 Xunfeng Lu, just off Jiefang Lu, serves dishes for Y5-13. (Open daily 10:30am-8:30pm.) Fast-food joints as well as smaller, pricier restaurants crowd around the mall on Fengcai Lu and on Fuxing Lu and Heping Lu. Many hotel restaurants offer surprisingly good deals in the form of all-you-can-eat buffets (usually Y15-40). Check out the third floor of the **Shaohua Hotel** for a delicious lunch buffet. For some delectable foods of the sea in style, **Bei Jiang Fengqing ❷** (北江风情) floats on the Wu River, west of the peninsula. At night, walk down Yunqian Xi Lu to the river and look for the neon lights glowing on the water. (☎886 8668. Seafood entrees Y15-25.)

Shaohua Hotel (shàohuá jiǔdiàn; 韶华酒店), 162 Jiefang Lu (☎888 1870, ext. 3888), across the bridge from the train station on the peninsula. A warm welcome to Shaoguan, with English-speaking staff. Clean, well-kept rooms have A/C, bath, refrigerator, and TV. An excellent Cantonese restaurant and gym on premises. Singles Y260; triples Y350. 15% discount available. Major credit cards accepted. **❸**

Hualin Hotel (huálín dàshà; 华林大厦), 81 Jiefang Lu, near Fuxing Lu. Large, cheap rooms with shower, but no A/C. Friendly staff. Internet available on the 6th fl. for Y3 per hr. Singles Y68; doubles Y88-130. **❶**

Yue Lai Hotel (☎822 2333), to the left as you exit the station. Obliging staff will show you to fairly clean rooms with A/C and TV. Nothing special, but a fine way to spend a night. Singles Y250; doubles Y360. 40% discount. **❷**

👁 SIGHTS

Shaoguan's sights can be seen in a day or two. Travel agencies organize one- or two-day tours, but it's easier and cheaper to rely on public transportation.

🏔 DANXIASHAN MOUNTAIN (dānxiá shān; 丹霞山). Danxiashan Mountain is just one part of a national park known as the "Red Stone Park of China." It'll take you a full day (or more) to see the whole park, but Danxiashan Mountain itself is worth the trip. Whether you ride the cable car (Y35), hike to the top, or admire the peak from the bottom, you'll be rewarded with views of endless green growth and towering, dusty red stone. The carefully tended crops of the park's residents preface the lovely scenery within. Extensive trails lead to such sights as the **Yangyuanyi Stone,** which park literature refers to as the "Stone Penis." *(1hr. north of Shaoguan. Take an immediate left as you exit the train station and walk down the road for a minute before reaching a bus station on the right. Bus Y15. The last minibus back to Shaoguan leaves around 6pm; if you miss it, take a minibus to Yunhe city and negotiate a Y50-100 taxi ride back to Shaoguan. Y27-43, depending on which part of the park you visit.)*

LION CRAG (shīzì yán; 狮子岩). **Maba Man,** the bones of an early *Homo sapien* that date to 600,000 BC, is the crag's claim to fame—which may not be saying much. Admission includes a brief walking tour of the caves and a guide who describes Maba Man's use of tools and division of labor among his family. If you don't know Chinese, good luck stumbling around the caves by yourself. The bones and artifacts have been moved from the caves to a run-down museum to the right of the path that leads to the crag, and all that remains in the cave are poorly positioned fluorescent lights, some rope, and tacky statues of Maba Man and family. Beware of bats on your climb, although they may provide a welcome distraction from the cave itself. *(South of Shaoguan, outside the town of Qujiang, 曲江 , known as Maba. From the Shaoguan Train Station, cross the bridge to the peninsula; the bus stop is past the pedestrian overpass on the left. Blue buses cost Y3 and leave every 15min. for the 30min. drive to Maba. Open daily 8am-7:30pm, last admission 5:30pm. Y10, museum Y5.)*

NANHUA TEMPLE (nánhuá sì; 南华寺). This rather enormous temple at the base of Baolin Mountain is famous as the nexus of Zen Buddhism. Built in AD 502, the temple has acquired a rather impressive collection of relics, including the 2m-wide "Thousand Man Pot," cast in AD 19, and a 1.2m-wide drum, which causes the enormous 10,000kg bronze bell in the bell tower to resonate. The monks' residences flank the temple's numerous halls, which lead to the back of the temple. Behind the temple, the Zhuoxi Spring flows past nine ancient cypress trees, creating a quiet and beautiful spot. The fairly low traffic of visitors may actually allow you to enjoy the temple as a site of religious worship. *(Minibuses take 30min. and cost Y10, while taxis cost around Y50 and leave from Shaoguan Train Station. Buses return to Shaoguan daily until 6pm. Open daily 8am-5pm. Y20.)*

ZHUHAI 珠海 ☎ 0756

For many tourists crossing the China-Macau border at Zhuhai, the city is but a brief stopover. Those who stay longer come to understand why it is the stomping ground of choice for wheelers and dealers at work or at play. The SEZ privileges bestowed on Zhuhai have made it a hub of free enterprise of all kinds—the streets are filled with bargain-basement electronics, food stands, and young women hoping to catch the eyes of visiting businessmen. With restaurants, karaoke bars, and hotels fielding a steady stream of customers all night long, few residents seem to notice the setting of the sun amid the glare of flashing neon lights.

TRANSPORTATION

Flights: Zhuhai Airport (zhūhǎi jīchǎng; 珠海机场 ; ☎ 889 5494), on the peninsula southwest of Gongbei. Airport buses leave from the Zhangzhou Bldg., near Gongbei Market, or the Xiangzhou Bus Station (40min., every 30min., Y20). Taxi to the airport Y100; ask for a flat rate. **Zhuhai Airlines** (zhūhǎi hángkōng gōngsī; 珠海航空公司), 34 Yuehai Dong Lu (☎ 889 7881). Open 24hr.; call first if visiting after 10pm. To: **Beijing** (1-2 per day, Y1760); **Kunming** (1-3 per day, Y1115); **Shanghai** (1-3 per day, Y840).

Buses: The best way to leave Zhuhai is by bus.

Gongbei Bus Station (gōngběi qìchē zhàn; 拱北汽车站), 1 Lianhua Lu or 1 Shuiwan Lu (☎ 888 8887), adjacent to the Yongtong Hotel. To: **Guangzhou** (2hr., every 20min. 6am-9:30pm, Y35-60); **Guilin** (13hr., 6:30pm, Y200); **Huizhou** (4hr., 5 per day, Y85); **Xiamen** (12hr., 1:30pm, Y210); **Zhongshan** (1hr.; every 30min. 9:10am-7pm; Y16, Sa-Su Y18).

Xiangzhou Long-Distance Bus Station (xiāngzhōu chángtú qìchē zhàn; 香洲长途汽车站 ; ☎ 222 5345), on Shuiwan Lu, next to the Gongbei Palace Hotel. To: **Guangzhou** (3hr.; every 30min. 7am-7pm; Y35, A/C minibus approx. Y50); **Guilin** (12:30pm, Y80); **Haikou** (2 per day, Y165); **Xiamen** (2pm, Y200).

Ferries: Jiuzhou Ferry Terminal (jiǔzhōu gǎng kèyùn zhàn; 九州港客运站), on Jiuzhou Lu in Jida. Take bus #4 from the border crossing to the Jiuzhou Gang stop. Info on boats to Hong Kong ☎ 333 2113, to Shenzhen ☎ 333 3359. To: **Hong Kong** (70min., 5 per day 8am-5pm, Y150); **Jiuzhou Island** (1½-2hr., 1-2 per day, Y70); **Shenzhen** (1hr., approx. every 30min. 7:50am-6pm, Y70).

Local Transportation: Buses are cream-colored with red lettering. Stops are marked by signs or a large orange pagoda roof. Fare Y1, with A/C Y2. Most routes serve Gongbei Bus Station near the Macau border. Bus #2 runs along Yingbin Nan Lu and Jingshan Lu, from Xiangzhou to Lianhuashan to Gongbei; #4 runs from the Xiangzhou bus station to the Gongbei bus station, passing the Gongbei Market and the Jiuzhou Ferry Terminal; #26 runs from the Zhuhai Holiday Resort to Shijingshan; #99 runs from the intersection of Linhua Lu and Yuehai Lu along the water past the Fishing Girl statue.

Taxis: Base fare Y10, each additional km Y2.4. Complaints ☎ 226 2628.

ORIENTATION AND PRACTICAL INFORMATION

Zhuhai is divided into three districts: **Gongbei** (拱北), the main tourist district, bordering Macau; **Jida** (吉大), the site of the ferry terminal and the Fishing Girl statue; and **Xiangzhou** (香洲), to the north. **Shuiwan Lu** (水湾路) and **Yingbin Nan Lu** (迎宾南路) pass through Gongbei and Jida. Two very good bilingual maps (about Y5 each), the *Zhuhai Tourist Map* and the *Tour and Transportation Map of Zhuhai*, are available at the border crossing and in most hotels and bookstores.

> To reach the border crossing into Macau, walk south down Yingbin Lu to the very end. Foreign travelers to Zhuhai need **Chinese visas**. Visas can be obtained abroad before departure (p. 12), in Hong Kong (p. 551), or Macau (p. 584).

Travel Agency: CTS (☎888 5777), on the corner of Yingbin Lu and Lian'an Lu, next to the Overseas Chinese Hotel. More a ticket office than a travel agency, selling plane tickets but not tours. Open daily 8am-7pm. **Zhuhai Holiday International Travel Service** (zhūhǎi guójì dùjià lǚxíng shè; 珠海国际度假旅行社; ☎333 3838), on Shihua Dong Lu, just east of the Zhuhai Holiday Resort Hotel, has an extremely helpful English-speaking staff. In addition to providing information about the city's sights and transportation, they book plane tickets and offer day-tours for Y100 or more.

Bank of China: 1148 Yuehai Dong Lu (☎888 3333), on the corner of Yingbin Lu and Yuehai Dong Lu. US or Hong Kong dollars are easiest to exchange. Also exchanges traveler's checks. Open M-F 8:30am-noon and 2-5pm, Sa-Su 9am-noon and 1:30-4pm. Another branch, on Shihua Dong Lu, just east of the entrance to the Zhuhai Holiday Resort Hotel, has currency exchange and an **ATM**. Open M-F 8:30am-5pm and Sa-Su 10am-4pm. Hotels usually charge exorbitant exchange fees.

Bookstore: Xinhua Bookstore, on Yingbin Dadao in Gongbei, sells maps of Zhuhai and a limited selection of highly abridged English classics. Open daily 9am-9:15pm.

Hospitals: People's Hospital (rénmín yīyuàn; 人民医院; ☎222 2571), on Kangling Lu. **Gongbei Hospital** (gǒngběi yīyuàn; 拱北医院), 2 Lianhua Lu (☎888 5463), next to the Lianhua Hotel. Both have some English-speaking staff members and are open 24hr.

Internet Access: e-Bar (e-bà wǎngbā; e- 霸网吧; ☎822 1759), at the intersection of Yuehua Lu and Yingbin Lu, on the 2nd fl. Over 50 computers. Y3 per hr.

Post and Telecommunications: 1043 Yuehai Dong Lu (☎887 1821), a few blocks east of the Guangdong Hotel. EMS and IDD service. Open daily 8am-8pm.

Postal Code: 519020.

ACCOMMODATIONS

Most accommodations in Zhuhai cater to wealthy tourists and businesspeople. Discounts of 10-40% are often available to anyone who asks. Unless otherwise noted, major credit cards are accepted. Most hotels demand a deposit of at least twice the price of the room.

Zhuhai International Youth Hostel (HI) (zhūhǎi guójì xuéshēng lǚguǎn; 珠海国际学生旅馆; ☎333 3838, toll-free reservation hotline 800 830 8000; www.zhuhai-holitel.com). On the luxuriant grounds of the Zhuhai Holiday Resort Hotel (zhūhǎi dùjià cūn jiǔdiàn; 珠海度假村酒店) on Shihua Mountain. Take bus #4 from central Zhuhai to the hotel and inquire at hotel reception. A free shuttle runs from the hotel to the hostel. Luxury hotel treatment at a budget price. 10-bed dorms with wooden bunk beds, free lockers, attached bath, and A/C Y60, HI members Y50. ❶

Overseas Chinese Hotel (huá qiáo bīnguǎn; 华侨宾馆 ; ☎888 6288), on Yingbin Nan Lu, past Lian'an Lu. Clean, comfortable rooms with gigantic beds, plus a friendly staff, "Tang Dynasty" restaurant, gym, and CTS office next door. If you can squeeze out a discount, this is certainly the best value for your money. 13% service charge. Singles Y286-338; doubles Y438. 10% increase on weekends, 30% on holidays. ❹

Friendship Hotel (yǒuyì jiǔdiàn; 友谊酒店), 46 Changsheng Lu (☎813 1818). Nothing beats this hotel's location, just a few steps from the gate to Macau. Rooms with standard amenities are more than comfortable enough for a night's stay. A/C, TV, and attached bath. Staff speaks excellent English. Singles and doubles Y150. ❷

🍴 FOOD

Most hotel restaurants serve dim sum and house Western-style cafes or coffee houses. At night, food vendors set up makeshift tables and chairs and serve simple but tasty meals (Y10-20, beer Y7-10). Street **food stalls** (dà pái dǎng; 大排挡) are numerous, particularly along the Xiangzhou coastline and in Gongbei on **Yuehai Dong Lu** and **Yingbin Lu.** In the evening, cooks wheel carts down the streets, dishing out tea and snacks for Y2-3. Stall owners are friendly, but most don't speak English. The **Haili Seafood Restaurant ❷** (hǎilì hǎixiān cāntīng; 海利海鲜餐厅 ; ☎888 9813) is diagonally opposite the Overseas Chinese Hotel. Around 6pm, plastic tables and chairs come out to transform the sidewalk into a crowded outdoor restaurant. (English menu available. Eel casserole Y23. Goose feet with mushroom Y30. Fish head with tofu Y18. Chicken and pineapple Y20. Open 24hr.) The **Chinese Food Street ❷** (zhōngguó dàshí jiē; 中国大食街), on the 2nd fl. of the Overseas Chinese Hotel, has an extensive array of Cantonese dishes at surprisingly affordable prices. (Beef with peppers Y12. Beijing duck Y15. Open daily 11am-9:30pm.)

📷 🎭 SIGHTS AND ENTERTAINMENT

Zhuhai is more for visitors on business trips, but there are a few things to do if you have some time to spare en route to Macau. Bus #9 from Gongbei Station or #99 from the intersection of Yuehai Lu and Lianhua Lu breeze along the river, passing **Lingjiaozui Beach** (líng jiǎo zuǐ; 棱角咀), a popular swimming spot, and the famed **Fishing Girl statue** (yú nǚ; 渔女), which doesn't necessarily warrant getting off the bus. Bus #4 from the city center or bus #26 from the Zhuhai Holiday Resort Hotel will take you to **Shijingshan** (石景山), a mountain and activity park. There's go-kart racing for Y30 and paddleboating for Y15, but hiking (roughly 30-45min.) is free. (Cable car up Y30. Toboggan ride down Y50. Entrance free.) The **New Yuan Ming Palace** (yuán míng xīn yuán; 园明新园), accessible by bus #13, is a recreation of the Old Summer Palace in Beijing, destroyed by the Europeans during the Second Opium War, featuring daily kitschy cultural performances, such as the "Qing Dynasty Bells Dance Performance" and the "Emperor's Wedding Ceremony." The attached **Lost City Water Park** (mènghuàn shuǐ chéng; 梦幻水城) has a wave pool, waterfall, and river. (Open daily noon-9pm. Admission to both parks Y100.)

Zhuhai almost never sleeps. Most of the night action is contained in the triangular region of Gongbei, between Yingbin Lu and Shuiwan Lu, where a generous selection of discos and clubs thrill revelers from nearby Macau. Every night around 6pm, **Gongbei Market** (gǒngběi shìchǎng; 拱北市场) appears out of nowhere to hawk everything from watches to lingerie. (Take bus #4 to Gongbei Shichang.) When the market shuts down around 10pm, business picks up at the numerous karaoke clubs on the 2nd floor of almost every hotel in town.

SHENZHEN 深圳 ☎0755

Other Chinese cities enjoy Special Economic Zone (SEZ) status, but none takes the title quite as seriously as Shenzhen. This well-tended city jets ahead of the rest of China in the quest to be just like Singapore, Seoul, Tokyo, and, most of all, its neighbor Hong Kong. All tourist maps point west, to the colossal parks where miniaturization and multiculturalism are the contrived themes of the day. But once back in downtown Shenzhen, it's money and what it can buy that matters. The city's visitors stroll amidst a steel and glass forest of hotels and skyscrapers on short trips away from home. Shenzhen is rarely more than a brief stopover on the way to or from Hong Kong, but on the weekends thrill (and kitsch) seekers come flocking to the parks and glitzy nightlife offerings.

▐ TRANSPORTATION

Flights: Shenzhen International Airport (shēnzhèn guójì jīchǎng; 深圳国际机场; ☎2777 6789; hotline 2777 2000), in the northwestern Bao'an district. Take bus #330 from Hualian Bldg., or minibus #507. **Hualian Ticket Center** (☎965788), Hualian Bldg., Shennan Zhong Lu, 1st fl., west of Lizhi Park. **CAAC ticket office**, on Shangbu Lu, Nanfang Daily Bldg., Rm. 609 (☎8328 4315), sells domestic tickets. Open M-F 8am-6pm, Sa-Su 9am-4:30pm. To: **Beijing** (many per day, Y1600); **Chengdu** (11 per day, Y1290); **Guilin** (6 per day; Y600); **Tianjin** (3-4 per day, Y1400). **Shanghai Airlines**, 18 Shangbu Zhong Lu (☎324 1431), is open daily 8am-5pm. To **Shanghai** (several per day, Y1270). **Eastern Airlines** (zhōngguó dōngfāng hángkōng gōngsī; 中国东方航空公司; ☎8322 7740), in the Chinese Airlines Bldg., 1st fl., at Huaqian Bei Lu and Hongli Lu. Open daily 8:30am-5pm. Several flights per day to: **Shanghai** (Y1270); **Kunming** (Y1130); **Nanjing** (Y1250).

Trains: (See also **Border Crossing into Hong Kong: Shenzhen,** p. 524.) **Shenzhen Train Station** (shēnzhèn huǒchē zhàn; 深圳火车站; ☎232 8647, tickets 232 5043), on Jianshe Lu, a giant building connected to the customs and immigration office and the bus station by covered walkways. Schedules are all in Chinese; find out the characters for your destination and preferred type of seat before you go. Lockers available 6:30am-10:30pm (Y5-30, depending on size). Open daily 5:50am-11pm. To: **Beijing** (24hr., 2 per day, Y452); **Changsha** (12½hr., daily, Y287); **Guangzhou** (1hr., every 10-35min. 6am-9pm, Y40-70); **Guilin** (14½hr., daily, Y225); **Shaoguan** (4hr., 2 per day, Y112); **Shantou** (9¾hr., daily, Y155).

Buses: (See also **Border Crossing into Hong Kong: Shenzhen,** p. 524.)

Luohu Bus Terminus (luóhú qìchē zhàn; 罗湖汽车站; ☎233 7378 or 232 1670), in the same complex as the train station, across the raised walkway, and in the same building as the Luohu Commercial Plaza. Most buses to Guangzhou depart from the basement level of the station. Tickets sold on the 2nd fl. Open daily 7am-6pm. To: **Chaozhou** (4½hr., 3 per day, Y160); **Foshan** (2½hr., every 30min. 8am-7pm, Y75); **Guangzhou** (2hr., every 4min. 6am-10pm, Y60); **Huizhou** (1½hr., every 15min. 7am-8pm, Y40); **Shantou** (4hr., every 30min. 8am-8pm, Y150); **Xiamen** (9½hr., 8 per day, Y187); **Zhaoqing** (3hr., every 30min. 7:10am-9:30pm, Y95).

Qiaoshe Bus Station, on Heping Lu, between the Overseas Chinese Building and the Regency Overseas Chinese Hotel. Open daily 7am-9pm. Buses to Fuzhou, Xiamen, and Quanzhou. Long-distance A/C luxury coach buses to most destinations in Guangdong (but not Guangzhou). Check prices, as they very well may be cheaper than the buses leaving from **Luohu Bus Terminus**.

Shenzhen Bay Hotel bus stop, near the theme parks. A/C double-decker bus to **Shangri-La Hotel,** near the border crossing (every hr. 6:30am-8pm) and **China's Hong Kong City** (3:45, 4:45, 5:15pm). Ticket prices vary (M-F HK$65-180, children HK$45-110, depending on starting point; weekend prices rise HK$20). Credit cards accepted.

Ferries: Shekou Port (shékǒu gǎng; 蛇口港; ☎669 5600). Take bus #113 (Y6), heading west on Shennan Lu, or bus #204 or 217. For those who value scenery over convenience. The **ticket office** (☎669 1213), in the domestic ferry bldg., sells tickets 10

SOUTH COAST

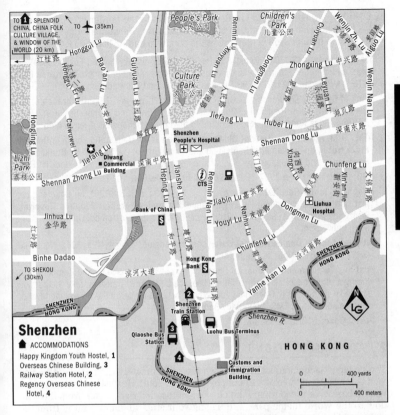

Shenzhen

⬤ ACCOMMODATIONS

Happy Kingdom Youth Hostel, **1**
Overseas Chinese Building, **3**
Railway Station Hotel, **2**
Regency Overseas Chinese
Hotel, **4**

days in advance for Hong Kong and Macau. To: **Haikou** (16hr., Su-F 4pm, Y218-458); **Hong Kong** (50min., 10 per day 7:45am-9:30pm, HK$90-125); **Macau** (1½hr., 11am, HK$87); **Zhuhai** (1hr., every 15-30min. 7:30am-6pm, Y70).

Local Transportation: Many local A/C **buses** stop at the parking lot just south of the train station on Huping Lu. Bus fares are based on the number of stops—tell the fare collector your destination. Buses within the city usually bear single- or double-digit numbers (Y1-3); buses with triple-digit numbers go far from the center (Y2-12). Bus #3 runs down Shennan Lu; #101 and 113 (7am-7pm) follow Shennan Lu past the theme parks to Shekou. **Minibuses** (Y2-5) post the destination in the front window. Red minibuses stay within the SEZ; green minibuses go beyond the border. Minibus #455, which you can catch next to the train station, will take you to the theme parks for Y4.

Taxis: Possibly the priciest taxis in China. Base fare Y12.5, each additional 250m or 45 seconds of waiting time Y0.6. 30% surcharge 11pm-6am. Complaints ☎ 322 8111.

ORIENTATION AND PRACTICAL INFORMATION

Shenzhen county covers a broad area, the southeastern corner of which is Shenzhen proper. Most theme parks and other tourist attractions lie a few kilometers west of the city center along **Shennan Lu** (深南路), which runs east-west past many of Shenzhen's hotels. **Renmin Lu** (人民路) is perpendicular to Shennan Lu. **Jianshe**

Lu (建设路), roughly parallel to Renmin Lu, leads to the border crossing (see p. 524). The Shenzhen Train Station and the Luohu Bus Terminus, adjacent to the customs and immigration center, are at the southern end of Jianshe Lu.

Travel Agency: CTS, 3023 Renmin Lu (☎225 5888), usually has an English-speaking staff member. Sells train tickets. Open daily 9am-6pm. Another branch, **Shenzhen Port CTS,** 11 Guiyuan Lu (☎2558 9323), has a friendly and knowledgeable staff.

Bank of China: 2023 Jianshe Lu. Open daily 8:30am-12pm and 2-5pm. A **branch** at the train station, 1009 Renmin Lu. Open M-F 8:30-11:30am and 2-5pm, Sa-Su 9:30am-3:30pm. Hong Kong dollars are accepted in the city, but change is given in RMB.

ATM: 24hr. ATMs at the **Bank of China** on Jianshe Lu; the train station branch; **Century Plaza Hotel,** on the corner of Renmin Lu and Chunfeng Lu; the **Hong Kong Bank,** 1015 Renmin Lu; and throughout the city. Most bank ATMs service Cirrus, Plus, and NYCE.

PSB: On Jiefang Lu (☎2557 3611). **Shekou** branch (☎669 1011).

Hospital: Liuhua Hospital (liúhuā yīyuàn; 流花医院 ; ☎223 8826), on Chunfeng Lu, just northeast of Dongmen Lu. English-speaking staff. **Shenzhen People's Hospital,** 3046 Shennan Dong Lu (☎8217 7591), right next to the post office. Open daily 8am-noon and 2-5pm.

Internet Access: Damao Internet Cafe (dàmào wǎngluò; 大茂网络), 3015 Nanhu Lu (☎8225 7295). Y4 per hr. Open 24hr.

Post and Telecommunications: On Shennan Lu, between Jianshe Lu and Renmin Lu, to the right of the hospital. For international service and money transfers, take the outside staircase to the 2nd fl. Open daily 8am-7pm. The post office on the mezzanine level of the bus station has EMS. Open daily 8am-8pm.

Postal Code: 518000 or 518001.

🏠 ACCOMMODATIONS

The cheapest accommodations in town are unfortunately the farthest afield as well. A long trek out of town, the Happy Kingdom Youth Hostel lives up to its name with inexpensive, clean rooms and convenient location right across from the Window to the World theme park. If dragging your stuff 40 minutes away from the train and bus stations doesn't sound ideal, the Overseas Chinese Building has rooms for comparable prices. In the more expensive hotels, a few minutes of bargaining can usually bring "deluxe" rooms prices down to the "standard" rates.

Happy Kingdom Youth Hostel (HI) (☎694 9443; fax 694 9046). Across the street from the theme park, a large rainbow-colored sign marks the entrance to the Happy Kingdom Plaza. Enter, bear right, and walk up the road for about 5min. Turn left into the plaza parking lot and walk another 5min.; the hostel will be on your right. From the train station, take minibus #473 (Y4) to the last stop; or take bus #101 or 223 (40min., Y4) to Window of the World theme park. Plain, sunny dorms face the street off very long corridors. Internet jacks, A/C, baths, and lockers in every room. Laundry Y5. Hot water 5:30pm-midnight. Reservations recommended in summer. Entrance to the theme parks discounted to Y114 with a coupon from the front desk. 12-bed dorms Y50, 6-bed dorms Y55; doubles Y180-240. Y5 discount for HI members. ❶

Overseas Chinese Building (huáqiáo dàshà; 华侨大厦), 1043 Heping Lu (☎556 4762), across from the Regency Overseas Chinese Hotel on the same side of the street. This place is nothing special, but if you're only staying for a night, it can be just right. Singles (sometimes in two-bed rooms) have clean sheets. Random scrawlings on the headboards or water marks on the walls decorate a few choice rooms. Friendly, animated staff doesn't speak a word of English. Shared bath, TV, A/C. Singles Y238; doubles Y138-268. Singles can be argued down to Y100 without much effort. ❶

Railway Station Hotel (huǒchē zhàn dàjiǔdiàn; 火车站大酒店 ; ☎232 1168), in the silver New Railway Station Bldg. on Jianshe Lu, just north of the train station. If you're willing to spend a little more, this is the place, with art on the walls and real bathtubs. Rooms on the higher floors have great views. 10% service charge. Singles HK$238; doubles HK$268. Don't forget to ask for discounts. ❹

Regency Overseas Chinese Hotel (huáqiáo jiǔdiàn; 华侨酒店), 1009 Heping Lu (☎559 6688; fax 558 3779). As you exit the train station, take the escalator up the pedestrian overpass to your left; the hotel is just across the street. A busy and inviting lobby and fairly standard luxury rooms upstairs. A "deluxe single" will get you a nice view, bathtub, and bed, but no frills beyond that. 10% service charge. Singles Y258; doubles Y298. Discounts vary according to starting price. Credit cards accepted. ❹

FOOD

Exotic dining at exorbitant rates await those visitors who pay the equally exorbitant tickets to the **theme parks**. In the city center, most establishments are either fast-food joints or pricey restaurants, although the diligent budget traveler can find food stalls scattered about, especially off the major streets. Try the "french frices" (Y18) or steaks (Y30-48) at the Asian-style Western food chain restaurant, **Sandra** ❷ (xiānlè dū; 仙乐都), 1068 Heping Lu. (Open daily 8am-2am.) **Diwang Commercial Building,** on Shennan Zhong Lu, midway between Jianshe Lu and Hongling Lu, brings together several fast-food and Western restaurants. The tallest building in Shenzhen (and green!), Diwang has a viewing room on the top floor, and, for Y60, you can ascend and meet the advertised "robot guide worth RMB one million." Cheap **eateries** and **cafeterias** abound at the train station and in the city's busiest shopping area at the intersection of Dongmeng Lu and Chunfeng Lu.

SIGHTS AND ENTERTAINMENT

Shenzhen, with no natural attractions of its own, usurps those of the rest of the world. Theme parks Splendid China, China Folk Culture Village, and Window of the World are all within walking distance of one another, but try the **Happy Line** anyway: the monorail circles the three sights and the Shenzhen Bay Hotel (Y35 between any 2 of its 7 stops). Nightlife in Shenzhen leaves the budget traveler in the dust; although there's no shortage of discos and karaoke bars, these pricey joints often cater to vice-seeking businessmen rather than common travelers.

CHINA FOLK CULTURE VILLAGE (zhōngguó mínsú wénhuà cūn; 中国民俗文化村). This village was set up to teach visitors about China's many minority nationalities, and the result is definitely engaging, if not particularly informative. It highlights the different dwellings and handicrafts made by the Bai, Dai, Dong, Mongolian, and other ethnic minorities. There's a lot thrown into this park, and certain displays, such as the bejewelled seven-foot lion head, are not quite as educationally relevant. Mini-cars with drivers run between villages (20min., Y20). Frequent minority drumming and dancing shows culminate in a large evening performance on the stage with the lion head (7:30 and 8:30pm, Y15-20). Don't miss the twice-daily "Great Horse Battle," complete with 20-plus riders, tricks, flames, and musically coordinated whips. Visitors can dress up in ethnic costumes (Y10-20), participate in staged wedding rituals, or create their own handicrafts. A food street (Y5-10) offers a taste of Sichuanese, Dai, Cantonese, and Northern Chinese cuisines. (*Accessible by bus #101 or 113. ☎660 0626, ext. 2020. Free wheelchairs and baby carriages. Open M-F 10:30am-9pm, Sa-Su 10:30am-11pm. Combination ticket with Splendid China Y120, children 1.1-1.4m tall and seniors 65-69 half price. No separate admission.*)

WINDOW OF THE WORLD (shìjiè zhī chuāng; 世界之窗). Wildly popular among Hong Kong and Chinese tourists, this theme park seeks to unite the world under the global banner of kitsch. A walk through the well-landscaped park will bring you past the world's most famous landmarks in wide variations of scale—the Eiffel Tower is impressively tall (ride to the top for Y20), but be careful not to trip over Notre Dame. Stop by (and step over) the Taj Mahal, the Golden Gate Bridge, the Louvre, the Pyramids, and the Grand Canyon. The International Street to the right of the entrance is crowded with restaurants offering everything from Viennese coffee to German sauerkraut to Turkish kebabs. Several rides compliment the worldly attractions, from the Grand Canyon Flume to the Amazon Bob-cart Ride. *(From Shekou or Shenzhen, take bus #101 or 113; Y4, 45min. Get off near the Eiffel Tower or the Golden Gate Bridge. Open daily 9am-10:30pm, last admission 9pm. Y120, children 1.1-1.4m tall and seniors age 65-69 Y60.)*

SPLENDID CHINA (jǐnxiù zhōnghuá; 锦绣中华). In the words of former President Jiang Zemin, Splendid China hopes "to make the world get close with China." Unfortunately, miniature versions of the Great Wall, Terracotta Warriors, Forbidden City, Seven Star Crags, and the Three Gorges leave a little too much to the imagination. Once you hand over the hefty price for the combination ticket with **China Folk Culture Village,** do enjoy taking a snapshot of your towering frame next to a guard tower on the impenetrable Great Wall. Good luck recognizing any names in the "Trees Planted By The Most Famous People In The World" section of the park. *(Take bus #101 or 113 from the train station to Shenzhen Bay Hotel for the Happy Line, or all the way to the park. Open daily 8:30am-6pm. Combination ticket with China Folk Culture Village Y120, children 1.1-1.4m tall and seniors age 65-69 Y60.)*

BORDER CROSSING INTO HONG KONG: SHENZHEN

The border is open daily 6:30am-11:30pm. To enter **Hong Kong** (p. 542), take a train from Shenzhen (p. 520) to Kowloon Tong (in Tsim Sha Tsui East, see p. 561), Hung Hom Station (p. 547), or cities in the New Territories (p. 575). The customs office abuts the Lo Wu KCR station on the Hong Kong side.

Entrance into **Shenzhen** or any mainland destination requires a valid Chinese visa; get one at the Hong Kong CTS office for a hefty commission or at the Chinese Visa office in Hong Kong (p. 551). When entering Shenzhen County by **bus,** visitors must show valid travel documents. Chinese citizens may have to disembark briefly to go through inspections. Foreign passport holders usually stay on the bus and show their passports to an official, but sometimes they, too, must accompany the official to the inspection counter. In Hong Kong, **trains** depart for Shenzhen from Hung Hom Station (daily 5:45am-10:19pm) or the Lo Wu KCR Station (daily 6:01am-12:20am).

SHANTOU 汕头 ☎ 0754

Shantou today is the vision of China's dreams for the future. The country's first Special Economic Zone, this city is rich, and it shows. Monstrous, gleaming skyscrapers and condominiums pop up at an alarming rate, Western fast-food restaurants are a dime a dozen, and Mercedes-Benzes cruise down the wide, tree-lined streets. The ultra-modern appeal of street after street of stores and commercial buildings may be lost on some, but the nearby old city area revives memories of Shantou's rough past. As a former frontier and British trading port, the old city still bears all the raggedness of its rowdy youth. Decaying colonial buildings, complete with Grecian columns and elaborate carvings, fight for space with rows of stalls in the chaotic, jam-packed narrow streets. But with all of Shantou's casual, comfortable wealth, the city has nothing much for travelers beyond the glitter of storefronts and a watered-down remnant of wilder days.

TRANSPORTATION

Flights: Shantou Airport (shàntóu guójì jīchǎng; 汕头国际机场 ; ☎862 6678), 15km northeast of central Shantou. From the airport, a shuttle bus takes you to the city (30min., 2-3 per day, Y10). Taxi to city about Y50. **CAAC ticket office,** 83 Jinsha Lu (☎825 1915), 3 blocks west of the main Bank of China. Tickets can also be purchased from the CTS office on the 1st floor of the Overseas Chinese Bldg. To: **Beijing** (3hr., 2 per day, Y1830); **Guangzhou** (50min., many per day, Y660); **Hong Kong** (2 per day, Y1334); **Shanghai** (1¾hr., many per day, Y990).

Trains: Shantou Train Station (shàntóu huǒchē zhàn; 汕头火车站 ; ☎881 6487), on Taishan Lu, at the eastern edge of city. Accessible by buses #2, 8, 11, and 12 (Y2). Taxis to the station from western Shantou costs about Y35. Open daily 5am-midnight. To **Guangzhou** (10hr., 9:30am, Y92) and **Shenzhen** (9hr., 9:15pm, Y160).

Buses:

Shantou Passenger Transit Station (shàntóu qìchē kèyùn zhàn; 汕头汽车客运站 ; ☎810 2757), on Chaoshan Lu, north of Huoche Lu, 7km from the train station. Accessible by bus #30 from the Overseas Chinese Hotel. Connects to Jinsha Lu by bus #4 and to Zhongshan Lu by bus #7. Open daily 6am-1am. To: **Fuzhou** (many per day 8:40am-10pm, Y120-140); **Guangzhou** (6hr.; every 20min. 6:30am-1am; Y85-110, express Y150); **Xiamen** (every 2hr. 7am-9pm; Y45-85, express Y90).

East Bus Station (☎836 8470), on Jinsha Lu, 1 block from the Bank of China on the other side of the street. Accessible by buses #1, 2, and 11 from the old city. Open daily 6:30am-11pm. To: **Fuzhou** (7 per day 9am-9pm, Y140); **Guangzhou** (every 20 min. 7am-2am, Y150); **Xiamen** (every 40 min. 7:30am-11:30pm, Y90). Buses to **Chaozhou** leave from the Overseas Chinese Hotel bus station (every 20min., Y10).

Local Transportation: Most **buses** run approx. 6am-10:30pm. Fare Y2. Buses #2, 4, 6, 8, 11, and 12 terminate at the train station in the far east of the city. Bus #1 goes up and down Wai Malu from Xiti Lu and the old city to the Bank of China on Jinsha Lu; #2, 4, 6, and 18 run along Jinsha Lu; #11 runs from the old city dock area and along Jinsha Lu. Private **minibuses** run the same routes (Y2) but are often in worse condition.

Taxis: Base fare Y8, each additional km Y2.6; with A/C base fare Y9, each additional km Y2.8. **Pedicabs** to most destinations within city center Y5-8. Motorcycle taxis are also common, but take the seat at your own risk—helmets not included.

ORIENTATION AND PRACTICAL INFORMATION

Shantou is vast, sprawling on the northern bank of its **harbor** (shàntóu gǎng; 汕头港) in the far east of Guangdong province. The old town center is in the southwestern end around a tiny peninsula and consists of several small streets that converge at traffic circles. The most important of these is fed by **Shengping Lu** (升平路), **Minzu Lu** (民族路), and **Anping Lu** (安平路). From the old town, the larger streets of **Wai Malu** (外马路) and **Zhongshan Lu** (中山路) run eastward into the newer parts of town. The new areas seem to have spread north and east at such a rapid pace that there is no well-defined city center. **Jinsha Lu** (金沙路) runs east-west through the city and is a major commercial thoroughfare with many hotels, fast-food restaurants, and banking services.

Travel Agency: Shantou Travel Agency, 41 Shanzhang Lu (☎862 9888), in the same complex as the Overseas Chinese Hotel. 1st fl. office books local tours and tickets. An extremely friendly staff will help guide you around the city. Tours Y108 per day, but without any sights to speak of, it's unclear what you're paying for. No commission for air tickets. Y10-30 fee per train ticket.

Bank of China: 98 Jinsha Lu (☎826 2955), just east of the Golden Gulf Hotel. Take buses #1, 2, 4, or 6 to Jinhaiwan Dajiudian. Exchanges currency and traveler's checks (counters #8 and 9). Credit card advances on Cirrus/MC/Plus/V. Counters open M-F 8:30-11:30am and 3-5:30pm; bank open M-F 8:30am-noon and 2:30-5pm.

ATM: Various Bank of China branches along Wai Malu between Shanzhang Lu and Shengping Lu have 24hr. ATMs.

Bookstore: Xinhua Bookstore, 26 Lian Lu (☎827 7021), opposite the Xinhua Hotel. A limited selection of classics and a wide selection of maps. Open 8:30am-10pm.

PSB: 11 Yuejing Lu (☎827 2275), off Nanhai Lu, south of Wai Malu, west of the No. 2 Hospital in the old part of town.

Hospital: No. 2 People's Hospital (dì'èr rénmín yīyuàn; 第二人民医院), 28 Wai Malu (☎827 2765), east of Shengping Lu. Take bus #1 to Shengping Lu. **Shantou Center Hospital,** 114 Wai Malu (☎855 0450). Take bus #1. Open 24hr.

Post and Telecommunications: 147 Wai Malu, 1st fl. (☎828 9495), in a massive building 1 block from the Xinhua Hotel. EMS and Western Union. Open 8am-11pm.

Postal Code: 515031.

ACCOMMODATIONS

Accommodations are easy enough to find, but there shouldn't be much to keep you in Shantou more than a night or two. Chaozhou, a 1hr. bus ride away, provides comparable prices and a calmer-paced city in which to take a couple days' break.

Qiaolian Hotel (qiáolián dàshà; 侨联大厦), 39 Shanzhang Lu (☎825 9109 or 825 0108). The nondescript building just around the corner from the Overseas Chinese Hotel. The most basic singles have TVs and clean, well-kept communal baths, but beware hot rooms without A/C and with bugs. The convenient location near the bus station and CTS, sunny rooms, and friendly staff make it all worthwhile. Singles Y60-65; doubles Y115-270; rooms with bath from Y125, with A/C additional Y5. ❶

Swatow Peninsula Hotel, 36 Jinsha Lu (☎831 6668; www.pihotel.com). Take bus #4 or 11 from the bus station or #2, 4, 6, or 11 from the train station to Jinsha Gongyuan. Beautiful rooms, with mini-bars, glass cabinets, and complimentary decks of cards. Ask the eager and attentive staff for a room with a view of Jinsha Park (they cost the same anyway). Doubles Y388 and up; suites Y788. Except during the national holidays in May and Oct., singles and doubles are more likely to be Y160-200. AmEx/DC/MC/V. ❸

Xinhua Hotel (xīnhuá jiǔdiàn; 新华酒店), 121 Wai Malu (☎827 6734), accessible by buses #10, 11, and 12. For those here to take in Shantou's ramshackle past, the Xinhua is well situated just outside the old city on Wai Malu. Singles and doubles are the standard double bed-bath-TV combo, but are clean and comfortable. Hot water 6am-9am and 6pm-10pm. A/C, TV, and bath. Singles Y120-180; doubles Y220-280. 20-30% discounts possible. ❷

FOOD

Shantou, urban city-with-a-mission, has no official sights, and even the local CTS seems to have resigned itself to that fact. To escape from the city's commercialism, take a 20min. bus ride to the old town area, an interesting, aging neighborhood with small streets crammed with tatami mat vendors, vegetable stalls, and an entirely different feel from unabashedly modern Shantou. From the train or bus stations or anywhere on Jinsha Lu, take bus #11 to Xiti Harbor (xītí gǎng; 西堤港). **Xiti Lu** (西堤路) runs north and is lined with crumbling, wooden European buildings left over from the British treaty days. **Anping Lu** and **Shengping Lu** run east off

Xiti Lu and are brimming with local markets that sell fresh cilantro and bamboo shoots. Any of the little streets around here are good places to sniff out small restaurants that serve flat white rice noodles and delicious boiled pork and cabbage dumplings. For dessert, an absolute must-try is the ▧ **yam paste with gingko nuts,** a thick, ultra-sweet concoction that will put a smile on your face.

CHAOZHOU 潮州 ☎ 0768

Just 39km north of Shantou, Chaozhou takes commerce considerably less seriously than its business-like neighbor. Lacking Shantou's gleam and *nouveau riche* glamor, Chaozhou's shady streets fill with schoolchildren each day around noon, and more than enough food stalls and small-time vendors stay open until dawn. Attempts at developing tourist attractions have fallen somewhat by the wayside, but if you're spending any time in Chaozhou, that time would be best spent at rest anyway. Chaozhou is at its best in the maze of streets near the ancient city and Kaiyuan Temple. Intimate and crammed with Buddhist paraphernalia, these sleepy streets provide a welcome change of pace.

▛▜ TRANSPORTATION AND PRACTICAL INFORMATION

Chaozhou's old city walls stretch along the city's eastern border along the **Han River** (hán jiāng; 韩江), between **Huancheng Bei Lu** (环城北路) in the north and **Huancheng Nan Lu** (环城南路) in the south. **Kaiyuan Lu** (开元路) runs west from the wall, about halfway between Huancheng Bei and Nan Lu. **Xi Malu** (西马路) runs just north of and parallel to Kaiyuan Lu. **West Lake** (xī hú; 西湖) and the sprawling **West Lake Park** (西湖公园) are not far west of the northern portion of the wall, bordered to the east by **Huancheng Xi Lu** (环城西路). From Huancheng Xi Lu, **Xihe Lu** (西河路) branches southwest and **Yonghu Lu** (永护路) branches off Xihe Lu. These two roads have many hotels and streetside stalls.

Trains: Chaozhou Train Station (cháozhōu huǒchē zhàn; 潮州火车站 ; ☎685 3708), off Xinfeng Lu, 7km southwest of the city. Pedicab rides to the old city Y10. Ticket office open daily 7:30-11:30am and 2-8pm. Train ticket stands throughout the city and the CITS on Chaofeng Lu sell tickets for a Y5 commission. To: **Guangzhou** (9hr., 2 per day, Y160); **Meizhou** (2hr., 3 per day, Y30); **Shenzhen** (9hr., daily, Y160).

Buses: Chaozhou Long-Distance Bus Station (cháozhōu chángtú qìchē zhàn; 潮州长途汽车站 ; ☎220 6052), on Chaofeng Lu, southwest of West Lake and 1km west of the city wall. Open daily 6:30am-12:30am. To: **Guangzhou** (5hr., 8 per day 8am-11:55pm, Y50-190); **Shantou** (1hr., every 30min. 6:30am-7:30pm, Y10); **Zhuhai** (10hr., daily, Y100).

Local Transportation: Pedicabs are the norm here; professional drivers wear yellow helmets and vests. Most places in the old city Y5-Y10.

Travel Agency: CITS, 77 Chaofeng Lu (☎228 4177), 2 blocks west of the bus station. Train tickets available for a Y5 commission, but tours are scarce. Open M-F 8-11:30am and 2:30-6pm. Private travel agencies can be found in most hotels; several are located along Chaofeng Lu, near the CITS.

Bank of China (☎286 3121), at the intersection of Chaofeng Lu and Chaozhou Jie. Exchanges US and Hong Kong dollars and traveler's checks. Open daily 8-11:30am and 2:30-5pm. Pedicab rides to the bank Y4.

PSB: 81 Cheng Xin Xi Lu (☎235 5572). Cheng Xin Lu is at the other end of Yonghu Lu from the bus station; the PSB station is further towards Chaozhou Jie. Open 8-11am and 2:30-5:30pm.

HIGH-KICKIN' TEA

No beverage has attained the status tea enjoys in Chinese cups everywhere. Few take it as seriously, however, as Chaozhou's residents. Chances are, if you've taken an amble around the streets of Chaozhou, you've noticed people congregating around sets of tiny tea cups, especially near meal times. These tea cups contain "kung fu tea" gōngfū chá; 功夫茶), which refers not to a specific tea but to a style of preparation.

To prepare the tea, one must have a small teapot, three tiny tea cups arranged in a triangle, and a draining tray. First, the teapot and cups are rinsed in boiling water. Once the teapot has been purified, the leaves are placed in the pot and quickly rinsed with hot water to open the aroma of the leaves. Next, the pot is filled to the top with water. Water is poured over the lid until water spills out of the spout. After allowing time to steep, the tea is poured into the three cups at once in equal amounts. At this point, the tea can finally be enjoyed. Before pouring more, however, the cups must be washed again. While this preparation style might seem a bit much—a lot of water wasted and not much tea enjoyed—gongfu cha is the norm for most homes, especially when a guest is present. Be sure to share some before you leave the city: the delicate group affair is said to aid digestion.

Pinkies out!

Hospital: Central Hospital (zhōngxīn yīyuàn; 中心医院), 84 Huancheng Xi Lu (☎222 4092, emergency 222 4868), just north of Xi Malu. Open 24hr.

Internet Access: 43 Shenzheng Lu (☎832 5175), north from the Qiaolian Hotel. Y2 per hr. Open 8am-12am.

Post Office: China Post, 3 Feng Chun Wan Lu (☎228 5100, 5min. walk from Yonghu Lu. Open 8am-9pm. An **EMS** office (☎226 1111) is just next door at the intersection of Feng Chun Wan Lu and Cheng Xin Xi Lu. Open 8am-5:30pm.

Postal Code: 521011.

🏠🍴 ACCOMMODATIONS AND FOOD

Variety is not one of Chaozhou's strong suits in terms of accommodation, but the good news is that they're all comfortable. Discounts and bargaining are possible at virtually all establishments year-round (except during the national holidays in May and October). It may be possible to convince the hostels near the bus station to accept foreigners. All establishments listed have A/C, bath, and TV.

Chaozhou, home to one of China's famed regional flavors, gets creative with its cuisine. The flour-and-vegetable staples of the north have been traded for the tasty tripe and cow-tongue exoticisms of the coast. Chaozhou also serves up delicacies like smoked pigeon and lake-grown vegetables, local specialties gathered from the neighboring mountain area. Two items certainly worth experiencing are the **goose with plum sauce** and **kung fu tea**, a post-meal tea served in tiny porcelain tea cups. Chaozhou is most famous, however, for its **braised meats**. Side streets between **Huangcheng Nan Lu** and **Yonghu Lu** are full of street stalls that dish up liberal doses of vegetable soups and flat rice noodle dishes. Chaozhou has few big restaurants that aren't working from a Western theme, but that's just fine because the street food and smaller local restaurants are delicious and cheap.

Chunguang Hotel (chūnguāng dàjiǔdiàn; 春光大酒店; ☎226 1211), opposite the Yunhe Hotel, diagonally opposite the bus station. Don't be alarmed if the windows are open and the A/C off in your room when you arrive—they'll turn it on once you book a room. Singles Y110; doubles Y168; triples Y195. ❷

Chaozhou Yunhe Hotel (cháozhōu shì yúnhé dàjiǔdiàn; 潮州市大酒店), 26 Xihe Dadao (☎213 6128). Across the street from the Chunguang Hotel; look for the stone elephants out front. Slightly more modern rooms feature electronic water boilers and powerful A/C. The friendly staff can advise you on dining options throughout the city. Singles Y120; doubles Y140. Y20 discounts available. ❷

Overseas Chinese Building Mansions, 34 Huangchang Nan Lu (☎222 8899), 5min. south of Kaiyuan Lu. The Overseas Chinese Building puts you closer to Kaiyuan Temple, the old city, and the street's many schools. Rooms are as nice as any, if a bit dark. Singles Y100; doubles Y140. ❷

🌀 SIGHTS

The city would have you believe that **West Lake Park** (xī hú gongyuan; 西湖公园) is full of tourist sights. But if you pay the Y8 to get in you'll find that there's not much to see or do, unless you're interested in taking a load off with local students, senior citizens, and young children. A paddleboat around the water (Y15) is always an option, and a nice walk on the public side of the river leads past many food stalls and small-time merchants.

At the southern tip of the West Lake, Huancheng Xi Lu leads south to **Kaiyuan Lu,** where shoppers can rummage to their heart's content. Electronics stores sit comfortably alongside merchants selling Buddhist silk brocades, banners, wooden and gilded sculptures, and precious jewelry and jade. **Kaiyuan Temple** (kāiyuán sì; 开元 寺), 32 Kaiyuan Lu, 200m down the road, marks the transition from new city to old—the old city walls are only a five-minute walk further west. Monks, worshippers, and tourists alike throng the main courtyard of this active temple. There isn't anything distinctive about Kaiyuan Temple, but its beautiful big trees and greenery make it a nice place to sit down and relax. As you approach the temple on Kaiyuan Lu, the stores blaring techno music fade away; go inside to join the old men seated throughout the temple for a quiet break from Chaozhou. (Open daily 8am-6pm. Y5.)

MEIZHOU 梅洲   ☎0753

Meizhou has yet to suffer the indignities of a tourist boom, and residents continue to chatter in their distinctive Hakka dialect, a strangely melodious tune that Mandarin speakers have difficulty understanding. Originally one of Guangdong's poorest regions, today's Meizhou has come into its own quietly and gracefully. Everything in the city is accessible on foot or by pedicab, but to see the surrounding sights you'll have to stray further afield. There are no compelling reasons to stop here for a day or two, other than to get away from the frenzy. Meizhou is simply a city ready to accept you as its guest.

▣ TRANSPORTATION

Flights: Meizhou Airport (méixiàn jīchǎng; 梅县机场 ; ☎224 2666), at Sanjiao Di Lu, 2km south of the city center. Purchase tickets at the **CAAC office** (☎224 2716) or the **Meizhou Tourism Bureau.** To: **Guangzhou** (M, W, F; Y350) and **Hong Kong** (M, F 3pm; Y1184).

Trains: Meizhou Railway Station (méizhōu huǒchē zhàn; 梅洲火车站 ; ☎231 1742), on Binfang Dadao at the southernmost edge of the city. Accessible by bus #6 from Jiangnan Lu. Ticket window open daily 8am-10pm. To: **Chaozhou** (3hr., 3 per day, Y20-35); **Guangzhou** (10hr., 2 per day, Y78-209); **Nanchang** (5-8hr., many per day 8:45am-10pm, Y117-350); **Shenzhen** (7 hr., 3 per day, Y73-193); **Xiamen** (8hr., 2 per day, Y58-73).

Buses: Meizhou Main Bus Station (méizhōu qìchē zǒngzhàn; 梅洲汽车总站), 1 Meishe Lu, Jiangbei (☎222 2137). Accessible by buses #2 and 3. Tickets sold daily 8am-6:30pm. To: **Dongguan** (2 per day, Y85-100); **Guangzhou** (many per day 6:40am-10pm, Y45-110); **Shenzhen** (many per day 8:40am-7:40pm, Y45-110).

Local Transportation: Meizhou's **bus** service is erratic, with buses running roughly every 30min. on most routes. If you manage to find them, buses #4 and 6 run down Binfang Dadao toward the train station; #1, 3, and 6 run along Jiangnan Lu; #3 and 4 navigate the old city area of Jiangbei. It's often more convenient to hop on the **pedicabs** that whiz through the city (most destinations Y1-3 for bicycles, Y5 or less for scooters; to outlying sights Y20 or less). **Taxis** are few and far between. Base fare Y4, each additional km Y1.6. More common than taxis are the white, air-conditioned minibuses that will take you to the train station (Y30), or to more far-flung sights (Y200 and up).

✳ 🛈 ORIENTATION AND PRACTICAL INFORMATION

Meizhou city is fairly large, but the areas of interest to the travelers are the districts of the city directly north and south of the **Mei River** (méi jiāng; 梅江), which separates **Jiangnan** (江南) from the old city district of **Jiangbei** (江北). Jiangnan's major commercial avenue, **Jiangnan Lu** (江南路), is perpendicular to **Meijiang Dadao** (梅江大道) and **Binfang Dadao** (彬芳大道), which run north-south from the city center to the train station. Along Jiangnan Lu and Meijiang Dadao lie numerous eateries, shops, and tourist-related services. North of Meijiang Dadao, the pedestrian **Mei River Bridge** (méi jiāng qiáo; 梅江桥) connects the two districts. **Yuancheng Lu** (元城路) and **Taikang Lu** (泰康路), which run west of **Cultural Park** (wénhuà gōngyuán; 文化公园), forms the center of Jiangbei; these areas are markedly more tranquil, with upscale hotels, dozing shopping streets, and bicycles peacefully roaming wide, empty spaces. The spanking new commercial **Jiangbian Lu** (江边路) branches east toward the development area.

Tourist Office: Meizhou Tourism Bureau (méizhōu lǚyóu jú; 梅洲旅游局), 28 Binfang Dadao (tickets ☎225 5777, tours 224 2751), 2 blocks south of Jiangnan Lu. 1st floor ticket sales, 2nd floor tours. Friendly staff can help arrange transportation to and from Meizhou, but day tours are mainly limited to setting you up with a taxi driver and guide for more than what it's worth (Y360). Open daily 8-11:30am and 2-5:30pm.

Travel Agency: CTS, 105 Jiangnan Lu (☎226 1089), near Dongshan Daqiao. The staff can book tours to nearby sites, but if you're traveling alone or in a small group, it might be cheaper to bargain with taxi drivers on your own. Tours Y200 and up. Open M-F 8:30-11:30am and 2:30-5:30pm.

Bank of China: 53 Meijiang Dadao (☎218 9287), north of Jiangnan Lu. Exchanges currency and traveler's checks. Credit card advances. Open M-F 8-11:30am and 2:30-5:30pm. Another Bank of China (☎218 9210), across from the post office on Gongyuan Lu, has a **24hr. ATM.** Open M-F 8am-5pm and Sa-Su 9am-4pm.

PSB: 1 Fazheng Lu (☎216 9332), the 1st street off Meijiang Dadao, as you backtrack south from the river. The **Division of Exit and Entry** (chūrùjìng guǎnlǐ chù; 出入境管理处), to the left as you walk in, handles visa extensions. Open daily 8-11:30am and 2-5:30pm.

Hospital: Meizhou No. 3 People's Hospital (méizhōu shì dì sān rénmín yīyuàn; 梅洲市第三人民医院; ☎235 4244), at the end of Dalangkou Lu. Take bus #8.

Internet Access: Spare Time Fast Food Restaurant (huāshíjiān kuàicāntīng; 花时间快餐厅), 11 Meijiang Dadao (☎225 0866), opposite the Bank of China. Y2 per hr. Open daily 8:30am-11pm. **Gongyuan Lu Fantasy Internet Cafe** (gōngyuán lù mènghuàn wǎng bā; 公园路梦幻网吧) is down the road to the right of the Cultural Park; look for it on the left. Y2 per hr.

Post Office: 5 Gongyuan Lu (☎223 7586), off Jiangbian Lu, near Cultural Park. EMS and Poste Restante. Open daily 7:30am-7:30pm.

Postal Code: 514021 for Jiangnan; 514011 for Jiangbei.

![] ACCOMMODATIONS

There's a surprising lack of range and quantity in Meizhou's accommodation options. For relatively low prices, you can stay at one of the city's better hotels, which suffer from a depressing lack of business and are usually willing (after some seasoned wheeling and dealing) to rent out rooms for as little as half the list price. All listings have rooms with A/C, bath, and TV.

Xinnan Hotel (xīnnán jiŭdiàn; 新南酒店), 41 Binfang Dadao (☎224 2489), across from the Meizhou Tourism Bureau, 2 blocks south of Jiangnan Lu. In addition to its cheaper prices, the Xinnan gives you something a little different to work with: sprawling rooms, polished stone floors, and balconies. Entertain yourself with the high-tech paraphernalia in the bathrooms. No separate shower space beyond the bathroom floor. Singles Y118; doubles Y128. ❷

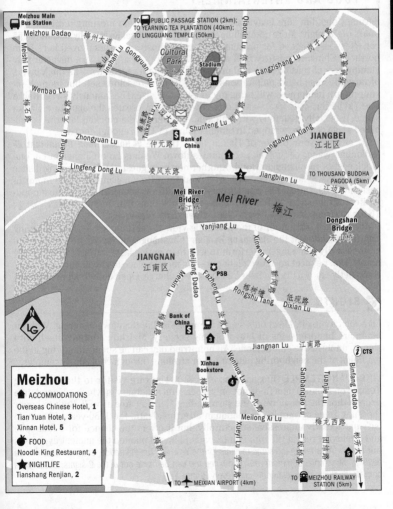

SOUTH COAST

Tian Yuan Hotel (tián yuán dàjiǔdiàn; 田园大酒店), 35 Jiangnan Lu (☎216 3888), at Meijiang Dadao. Located centrally along Jiangnan Lu, this hotel should make it high on the list of anyone willing to spend a little more. A garden in the lobby courtyard, complimentary items (snacks, teeth whitener) in the beautiful rooms, and an extremely friendly hotel manager show you where your money's going. Singles Y300; doubles Y368 and up; "Presidential Suite" Y9888. 30-50% discounts possible. ❹

Overseas Chinese Hotel (huá qiáo dàshà; 华侨大厦), 12 Jiangbian Lu (☎219 2388), just east of Meijiang Bridge. This former hostel turned 3-star hotel is the stuff that dreams are made of: lovely, clean rooms, a staff that will bend over backwards to make you feel welcome, and a fabulous location. Lack of keys can be bothersome—ask the floor attendants to be let in. Doubles Y300; suites Y380. 10% service charge. 50% discounts very possible. AmEx/MC/V. ❹

🍴 FOOD AND ENTERTAINMENT

Scrumptious dim sum is available in most eateries from morning until the wee hours of the night. More compelling, however, is the local **Ke Minority Cuisine** (kèjiā cài; 客家菜), named for present-day locals whose ancestors moved here from northern China. A must-try is ▨ *méicài kòuròu* (梅菜扣肉), a devastatingly yummy dish of roasted pork and preserved mountain vegetables. The thick layers of fat will cause heart palpitations for the health-conscious set, but its melt-in-your-mouth tenderness will bring joy to everyone else. The famously sweet **Hakka wine** (kèjiā jiǔ; 客家酒), when mixed with ginger, creates the signature Hakka sauce, especially delicious with chicken. Another Hakka chicken favorite is **salt-baked whole chicken,** wrapped in butcher paper (Y25-30; enough for two).

To cleanse your palate of Hakka food, try the ▨ **Noodle King Restaurant** ❶ (miàndiàn wáng; 面店王), two minutes down Wenhua Lu off Jiangnan Lu, one block east of the Jiangnan Hotel. Another northern guest, the Noodle King dishes up an extensive selection of authentic food from Heilongjiang province in northeastern China. Dumplings range from goat meat to vegetarian, but the most popular item is the pork-filled *xiǎolóngbāo* (steamed buns with juicy fillings; 小笼包); Y5 for 10) from Shanghai. (☎226 7861. Open daily 8am-9pm.)

At night, the sixth floor of the Riverside View Hotel Complex features grooving Canto-pop action at the **Tianshang Renjian** (tiānshàng rénjiān; 天上人间) dance club. Scantily clad singers perform to less than enthusiastic crowds from nearby hotels. Don't expect an active night out—it's more a place to check out local talent and quietly enjoy a drink. (Beer Y20. No cover charge. Open daily 7:30pm-1:30am.)

📷 SIGHTS

Like the city itself, Meizhou's sights are more idyllic than awe-inspiring. Without landmark historic ruins or jaw-dropping scenery, Meizhou contents itself with sleepy, unobtrusive charm alone. An unhurried day can be spent wandering in the tea fields of the neighboring plantation, or strolling through cool, shady temples.

LINGGUANG TEMPLE (língguāng sì; 灵光寺). The rare visitor to the Lingguang Temple on Mount Yinna finds not only a peaceful sanctuary in which to spend time deep in thought, but views of the surrounding Meizhou area as well. Built to honor the Tang Dynasty monk Pan Liaoquan after his death, the 1150-year-old temple isn't particularly impressive structurally, but it offers the chance for a nice hike and a relaxing rest at the top. Pan Liaoquan himself planted the ancient cypresses out front. (*After taking the same minibus for the Yearning Tea Plantation, continue past the tea fields to the temple. 50min. drive. A combined trip can be made out of the 2 sights. Buses pass both destinations going either direction every 30min. Y5.*)

YEARNING TEA PLANTATION (yànnánfēi chátián; 雁南飞茶田). A testament to the ancient Chinese art of tea-growing and tea culture, immaculate rows of tea fields rise up on mountains surrounding this plantation and resort. The numerous tea houses at the entrance serve up constant (free) feasts of China's favorite beverage and sell elaborate (and expensive) packets of tea leaves (Y120-450). Meander leisurely around the trimmed lawns, hedges, and pigeon aviaries, but don't expect to *do* anything in particular. *(About 40km from the city center. Take the #4 bus from the Cultural Park to Yue Mei Public Passage Station, the last stop, and hop on a Y8 minibus to the Tea Plantation. Buses return or move on to Lingguang Temple every 30min.; last bus 6pm. Taxi Y250 round-trip. ☎ 282 8888; fax 282 6898. Open daily 8am-10pm. Y30. Visitors can spend the cost of their admission ticket at the restaurants and tea houses, or toward defraying the cost of the villas, Y1980-7000 per night.)*

THOUSAND BUDDHA PAGODA (qiānfó tǎ; 千佛塔). A Thai expatriate donated mind-boggling amounts of money to this temple, resulting in a crazed frenzy of building and rebuilding that overshadows the real draw of the place: a Tang Dynasty steel pagoda (engraved with 1000 steel Buddhas), which has weathered wars, revolutions, and even a stint in a water-pumping factory. A climb to the top rewards visitors with views of Meizhou, the surrounding area, and a stone pagoda that now overshadows its older sibling. The entire gaudy complex may be only worth seeing if you have time to spare. *(Take bus #6 from Binfang Dadao or the Cultural Park to the end of Dongshan Dadao and ask the driver to drive you the extra few minutes to the pagoda. Bus Y2. Taxi Y50-100. Open daily 8am-6pm. Y5.)*

HAINAN 海南

Praised for its legendary beauty, Hainan is China's smallest, southernmost, and newest province, boasting dense tropical forests, hot springs, and gorgeous beaches. Part of Guangdong until it became a Special Economic Zone (SEZ) in 1988, Hainan province officially encompasses the isle of Hainan and the South China Sea archipelagos of Nansha (Spratly), Xisha (Paracel), and Zhongsha—although China's territorial claims on all but Hainan's main island are hotly disputed. But why bother with those reef bed islands when you have Hainan Dao and its some 1500km of glittering beaches stretching as far as the eye can see? Sanya—so far south that its southernmost point is dubbed "the End of the Earth"—attracts countless tourists with its promise of sandy bliss and turquoise waters.

While most of Hainan's residents are Han Chinese, the island is home to three other large minority groups, the Li, Hui, and Miao. Many Li continue to live in the thatch-roofed, mud-walled cottages that dot the highlands around Wuzhishan, formerly known as Tongzha. With such diverse cultures and natural splendor, it's no wonder some people call Hainan an island paradise.

HAIKOU 海口 ☎ 0898

Poised on its northern coast, Haikou is the unofficial gateway to Hainan. The port became a center for international trade after the area was opened to foreign ships in 1876 under the Treaty of Tianjin. Most people pass through Haikou on their way to and from the mainland, and few stay for very long. The amiable, breezy attitude and lifestyle that visitors from Hong Kong and Guangzhou find so soothing conceal a rash of crime. Prostitution and local gangs thrive, and tourists are often the targets of pickpockets, especially along Haixiu Lu in Haikou's shopping district. Although Haikou is pleasant for a couple of days, the island's better beaches are nearer Sanya, on the southern tip of Hainan, where the sands are white, the people care free, and the living easy.

TRANSPORTATION

Flights: Haikou Meilan International Airport (hǎikǒu měilán guójì jīchǎng; 海口美兰国际机场; enquiries ☎ 130 9898 8001), 20km southwest of the city. Shuttle buses (Y15) run from the airport to the China Southern Office and the ticket office from 7am until the last flight of the day. Buses from the airport to the city wait outside the lower level of the airport terminal (30min.; free with a plane ticket, Y15 without). Taxis cost about Y30. **China Southern** (zhōngguó nánfāng hángkōng; 中国南方航空), 9 Haixiu Lu (☎ 6652 5581; fax 6652 5580), just to the right of the Civil Aviation Hotel. Open daily 8am-8:30pm. To: **Beihai** (daily, Y380); **Beijing** (4 per day, Y700); **Guangzhou** (daily, Y280-300); **Guilin** (daily, Y780); **Hong Kong** (daily); **Shanghai** (daily, Y700); **Xi'an** (daily, Y800).

Buses: Hainan has 3 main bus stations.

Hainan Province General Bus Station (hǎinán shěng qìchē zōng zhàn; 海南省汽车总站; ☎ 6677 2791), on Nanbao Lu, behind the Pearl Plaza. Open daily 6:30am-6:30pm. To: **Fuzhou** (46hr., daily, Y350-400); **Guangzhou** (24hr., 3 per day, Y185); **Guilin** (10hr., daily, Y195); **Shenzhen** (30hr., daily, Y236); **Wuhan** (2:30pm, Y335).

East Bus Station (qìchē dōng zhàn; 汽车东站; ☎ 6534 0753), on Haifu Lu, is accessible by bus #217 heading toward the Five Figures Temple. Hainan buses only. Open daily 6am-11pm. To **Sanya** (Luxury bus: 3hr.; every 20min. 7am-6pm, every hr. 6-11pm; Y78. Standard bus: 5hr., every 30min. 6:45am-9:30pm, Y49) and **Wenchang** (1hr., every 20min. 7am-8pm, Y12-16).

West Bus Station (qìchē xī zhàn; 汽车西站; ☎ 6865 7306), on Haixiu Lu, is also on the route of bus #217, but toward Xiuying. Open daily 5:30am-8pm. To **Ledong** (6hr., every hr. 7am-6:30pm, Y45) and **Wuzhishan** (6hr., every hr. 6am-4pm, Y40-67).

Boats: Haikou Xiuying Port (hǎikǒu xiùyīng gǎng; 海口秀英港), on Binhai Dadao, east of the city, is accessible by bus #217. Buy tickets at the port. To: **Beihai** (12hr., 6pm, Y57-115); **Guangzhou** (19hr.; M, W, F 4pm; Y145-450); **Hai'an** (1½hr., every 1-1½hr., Y26); **Shenzhen** (19½hr.; Tu, Th, Su 3:30pm; Y113); **Zhanjiang** (10hr., daily, Y65-175).

Local Transportation: The ubiquitous yellow and white **bus #217,** a cross between a minibus and a full-sized bus, covers all tourist destinations, including CAAC, CITS, the main hotel strip, the International Commercial Center, the Five Lords Temple, Hai Rui's Tomb, the port, and East and West Bus Stations (Y2).

ORIENTATION AND PRACTICAL INFORMATION

Haikou sits at the northern tip of Hainan Island, across the Qiongzhou Strait from Hai'an on the Leizhou peninsula in Guangdong province. **Haikou Park** (hǎikǒu gōngyuán; 海口公园) marks the central reference point in the city: from here, **Haixiu Lu** (海秀路) runs to the southwest; **Datong Lu** (大同路) runs to the northwest; **Haifu Dadao** (海府大道) runs to the southeast. One of the most important landmarks is the **Hainan International Commercial Center** (hǎinán guójì shāngyè dàshà; 海南国际商业大厦), 38 Haixiu Lu (☎ 6679 2778 or 6677 4840). Pearl Plaza (míngzhū guǎngchǎng; 明珠广场), at 16 Haixiu Lu, and the Rainbow Bridge at the junction of Haixiu Lu and Lantian Lu are also highly visible reference points.

Travel Agency: CITS, 8 Haifu Lu (☎ 535 7999 or 537 9966). Books flights and organizes tour groups. English service usually available. Open daily 8:30am-10pm.

Bank of China: 33 Datong Lu (☎ 6677 7800), in the International Commercial Center behind the International Commerce Mansion. Exchanges currency and traveler's checks and handles credit card advances (windows 2 and 3). AmEx/Cirrus/MC/Plus/V **ATM.** Another branch at 10 Datong Lu (☎ 6671 8697), close to the shops on Jiefang Xi Lu, offers the same services. Both open daily 8:30am-noon and 2:30-5pm.

Bookstore: Hainan Creative Bookstore (hǎinán chuàngxīn shūdiàn; 海南创新书店), 11 Jiefang Xi Lu, 2nd and 3rd fl. (☎ 6621 3699). Novels, reference books, and English travel guides. Open daily 9am-10:30pm. Credit cards accepted.

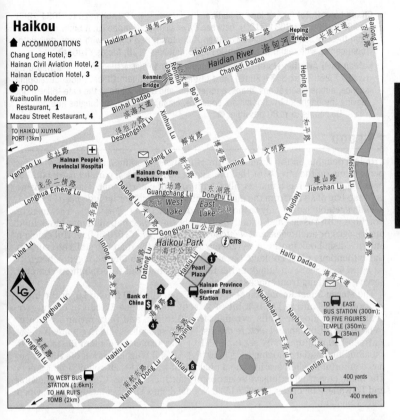

Haikou

▲ ACCOMMODATIONS
Chang Long Hotel, **5**
Hainan Civil Aviation Hotel, **2**
Hainan Education Hotel, **3**

🍴 FOOD
Kuaihuolin Modern
  Restaurant, **1**
Macau Street Restaurant, **4**

SOUTH COAST

Hospital: Hainan People's Provincial Hospital (hǎinán shěng rénmín yīyuàn; 海南省
人民医院; ☎6622 6666), corner of Yanzhao Lu and Datong Lu. Open 24hr.

Post and Telecommunications: 28 Haifu Dadao (☎6533 8840), in the China Telecom
Building. Open daily 8am-9pm. Branch at 16 Jiefang Xi Jie (☎6622 6323) is open
24hr. EMS, IDD service, and Poste Restante available at both offices. No English speakers. Another branch (☎6622 5706) is at the intersection of Datong Lu and Gongyuan
Lu, just across from Haikou Park. Open 8am-6pm.

Postal Code: 570102, 570203, or 570206.

🏠 ACCOMMODATIONS

Budget accommodations in Haikou are scarce. Bargain for cheaper rates, especially during the summer. Phone, 24hr. hot water, A/C, and TV are standard at all
hotels officially allowed to house foreigners.

Hainan Education Hotel (hǎinán jiàoyuàn dàshà; 海南教苑大厦), 18 Haixiu Lu
(☎6677 2998; fax 6677 2107), on the block past and opposite the International Commerce Mansion. Excellent location amid shops and restaurants. Compact, bright, and
newly refurbished rooms. Discounted singles Y80; doubles Y150. ❷

Chang Long Hotel (chāng lóng dàjiǔdiàn; 昌隆大酒店), 19 Lantian Lu (☎ 3631 2888 or 3631 2666; fax 3631 2100), between Daying Lu and Nanbao Lu. A 5min. walk away from the city center in a quieter quarter of the town. Bed comes with comforter. Bathroom comes with real bathtub. Singles Y100; doubles Y120; triples Y140. ❷

Hainan Civil Aviation Hotel (hǎinán mínháng bīnguǎn; 海南民航宾馆), 9 Haixiu Lu (☎ 6677 2608; fax 6677 2610), next to the China Southern Office. Photo developing service, airline reservations, maps, phonecards, and a quick bite at the cafe—all without leaving the bright lobby. Rooms are spacious, clean, and modern. Singles and doubles Y488. Discounts to Y180 possible. ❺

🍴 FOOD

Tropical delights, in the luscious form of mangos, coconuts, and bananas, tempt pedestrians on the streets of Haikou. Yilong Lu (义龙路), parallel to Haixiu Lu, near Longkun Lu, has a market filled with rows of colorful **fruit**. The local cuisine is a grab-bag of styles from the mainland. Hainan specialties include *yěcài* (野菜), a wild vegetable native only to the island, *hǎinán xīfàn* (海南稀饭), a set meal of porridge with rustic (and usually extremely salty) accompaniments like salted duck's eggs or anchovies, and *wénchāng jī fàn* (文昌鸡饭), a flavorful chicken and rice dish. Look for the 正宗 (zhèngzōng) sign at the roadside stalls attesting to the authenticity of its cooking. Locals recommend **China City** (zhōngguó chéng; 中国城 ; ☎ 6588 8888) on Lungkun Bei Lu, a large food and entertainment complex serving everything from snacks to seafood.

The **Macau Street Restaurant** ❷ (àomén jiē; 澳门街), 20 Haixiu Lu, at the intersection with Lantian Lu, is a bit of kitschy Portuguese Macau in downtown Haikou, with mosaic walls, wrought-iron fixtures, and faux rattan furniture. (☎ 6670 5857. English and picture menus. Macau specialties and rice plates Y15-25. Entrees Y20 and up. Daily set lunch Y10.) The **Kuaihuolin Modern Restaurant** ❶ (kuàihuólín xiàndài xiǎochú; 快活林现代小厨), 2 Wuzhishan Lu, off Haixiu Lu, has comfortable, slick seating and a phalanx of waitresses attired in bright green. The menu covers an extensive selection of Hainanese dishes, Cantonese dim sum, and Taiwanese favorites. (☎ 6677 4539. Noodle dishes Y3-8. Set meals Y10-18. Open daily 7am-2am.)

👁 SIGHTS

HAI RUI'S TOMB (hǎi ruì mù; 海瑞墓). Local Hainan boy Hai Rui (1514-1587), revered as an honest and well-loved Ming statesman, is interred here. A famous play by contemporary writer Wu Han about Hai Rui's dismissal by a tyrannical emperor provoked the wrath of Mao Zedong, who saw it as veiled criticism of his own purges. The Chairman unleashed the nation's youth to purge "corrupting elements" from Chinese culture, and the tomb became a prime target for the Red Guards during the Cultural Revolution. Now restored, Hai Rui's resting place has its original stone tablets once more. Everything else, however, is a warning against recreated period architecture. Nonetheless, the surrounding greenery, insulated from Haikou's frantic traffic and crowds, is a peaceful throwback to earlier, more cultured times. (*On Shugang Dadao. Take bus #1 or 217 towards Xiuying Port to Hai Rui Bridge and walk over. Open daily 8am-6pm. Y10.*)

FIVE FIGURES TEMPLE (wǔgōng cí; 五公祠). Erected in 1889, this temple houses life-like stone sculptures of five Tang and Song Dynasty officials who were banished to Hainan Island. The derelict exhibition hall displays local artifacts, but tends toward the dry, historical side of things. An amble through the "Historical

Relics Area" is more interesting, with opportunities to admire displays of bronze artifacts and calligraphy by Su Dongpo, a Song Dynasty poet and literati. *(Take bus #1 or 217, get off after the East Station, and cross the road. Open daily 8am-6pm. Y25.)*

SANYA 三亚 ☎ 0898

Known as the "Hawaii of the Orient," Sanya fully deserves its moniker, with its endless shores of white sand fading into a crystalline, azure ocean. All the trappings of resort living are here: golf courses, tennis courts, saunas, and swimming pools, as well as scuba diving, deep-sea fishing, windsurfing, and parasailing—not to mention the heavy prices that come with them. Several sights are slathered with high entrance fees and swarming with enterprising vendors, but there are humbler and cheaper pleasures to be had, once you flee the obvious tourist magnets. Heavy, fierce showers from May to October may surprise vacationers, but these short-lived storms shouldn't dampen vacations plans too much. Beware of September, when the rainy season hits full swing and turns the toasty sand between your toes into sodden clumps. But come on a clear day, and Sanya just might be the perfect place to float in the balmy waters, soaking up the sunshine.

■? TRANSPORTATION AND PRACTICAL INFORMATION

Sanya is divided into two main sections: **Sanya City** (三亚市) and **Dadonghai** (大东海), the beach resort area just east of the city. **Yuya Dadao** (榆亚大道) runs through Dadonghai, turns into **Gangmen Lu** (港门路) as it crosses the Sanya river, then finally veers right to the main thoroughfare, **Jiefang Lu** (解放路). Jiefang Lu is divided into four sections, starting from the stretch closest to Dadonghai, to past the city limits. Street numbers are functionally nonexistent.

Flights: Sanya Phoenix International Airport (sānyà fènghuáng guójì jīchǎng; 三亚凤凰国际机场), is 16km northwest of town. **Sanya Phoenix International Airport (SYPIA) Ticket Offices,** on Jiefang Er Lu (☎8827 7820, bookings 8829 0315), deliver tickets for free within the city. To: **Beijing** (4hr., 3 per day, Y880); **Guangzhou** (1hr., 3-5 per day, Y200-320); **Hong Kong** (1½hr., every 2 days, Y1000); **Shanghai** (3hr., 3 per day, Y1660); **Shenzhen** (1½hr., Y360).

Buses: Sanya Bus Station (sānyà qìchē zhàn; 三亚汽车站 ; ☎8827 2440), on Jiefang Lu. Take any bus or minibus up Jiefang Lu; the station is on the left. Open 6am-11pm. To: **Haikou** (Luxury bus: 3hr., every 20min. 7am-11pm, Y78. Standard bus: 5hr., runs irregularly, Y50.); **Lingshui** (1½hr., every hr. 7am-6pm, Y13); **Wuzhishan** (2½hr., every 30min. 7am-3pm, Y13).

Local Transportation: Taxis, motorcabs, pedicabs, and a rickety selection of **minibuses** relentlessly troll the main thoroughfares and attractions and stop just about anywhere upon request. Fare Y1-5. **Bus #202** runs from Dong Lu to Xi Lu, roughly from Dadonghai to Sanya City. Minibus #2 runs up and down all of Jiefang Lu (Y1).

Travel Agency: Sanya Spring-Autumn Travel Service (sānyà chūnqiū lǚshè; 三亚春秋旅社 ; ☎8826 5249; fax 8825 7242), 12th fl., Xiangtai Dept. Store on Xihe Xi Lu. Has English-speaking tour guides. Open daily 9am-10pm.

Bank of China: 31 Yuya Lu, Dadonghai, next to Northeast King. Exchanges traveler's checks. Credit card advances. Open daily 8am-5:30pm. A 2nd branch is across from the bus station on Jiefang Er Lu. Open daily 8:30am-5:30pm, holidays 9am-5pm.

Bookstores and Internet Access: Hainan Creative Bookstore (hǎinán chuàngxīn shūdiàn; 海南创新书店 ; ☎8826 9983), on Jiefang Er Lu and Xinfeng Jie. Open daily 9am-10:30pm. **Ocean Sky Bookstore** (hǎitiān shūdiàn; 海天书店), on Jiefang Er Lu across from the Sanya Hotel, has **Internet** access for Y2 per hr. Open daily 9am-1:30am. Both offer a small selection of English-language books.

Post Office: Jiefang San Lu (☎8827 2049), across from the People's Hospital. EMS and Poste Restante on the 2nd fl. Open M and W-Su 7:30am-9pm, Tu 7:30am-6pm.

Postal Code: 572000.

ACCOMMODATIONS

Even in China, beachfront property doesn't come cheap. Skip the budget-busting luxury resorts and hotels of Yalong Bay and Dadonghai and stay in Sanya City instead. High season (Oct.-May) and low season rates are indicated for the places listed below. Lodgings are almost impossible to get during national holidays.

Sanya Jingbeiqu Guesthouse (sānyà jǐngbèiqū yíngbīnlóu; 三亚警备区迎宾楼 ; ☎8821 2345; fax 8821 2345, ext.18004), on Yuya Lu about 500m east of Dadonghai. Drag yourself out of your bright, breezy, spacious room and catch a minibus in front of the hotel right to the beach or into Sanya city. Doubles Y600, low-season Y80. ❺/❶

Heng Sheng Hotel (héng shèng bīnguǎn; 恒盛宾馆 ; ☎8825 1391 or 8827 5089), on Jiefang Er Lu, just opposite the bus station. Smack in the thronging action of Sanya City and conveniently near the bus station and a supermarket. Comfortable beds with thick comforters and buoyant pillows. Amiable staff. Singles Y70; doubles Y80-100. ❷

Precious Stone Hotel (huábǎoshí dàjiǔdiàn; 华宝石大酒店 ; 10 Jiefang Er Lu (☎8825 6588; fax 8825 7018). Convenient location 5min. from the bus station and a panoramic view of the city shoreline are redeeming factors for the generic, slightly worn but spacious rooms. Doubles Y380, low-season Y198. ❺/❸

FOOD

Sanya is justifiably famous for its seafood. Bustling **seafood** and **hotpot restaurants** serving up denizens of the deep crowd Yuya Dadao and Binhai Lu along the city shore. Seafood is typically sold by weight; the standard unit of measurement is the *jīn* (斤), about half a kilogram. At night, seafood **stalls** (dishes Y5-10) fill the area around China City and Xinfeng Qiao (an island in the Sanya river). Guitar-strumming troubadours add an extra flair to streetside dining with a song or story, in return for a few *yuán* or a seat at the table. Another local specialty is **yellow oil old duck** (huángliú lǎoyā; 黄流老鸭 ; Y30-35 per bird), an inexplicably chewy and flavorful duck. Exercise your jaws at any of the stands on Shengli Lu behind the bus station. Vendors on the street offer the best meal at the best price, but those wanting a sit-down meal can slurp up some rice porridge at the **Northeast Porridge King** ❶ (dōngběi zhōuwáng; 东北粥王), 3 Xi Hedong Lu. This shop makes even porridge sexy—and you can try all 18 varieties if you please. The all-you-can-eat buffet will have you coming back for seconds. Porridge haters, don't despair: dumplings and vegetable dishes abound. (☎826 3684. Buffet breakfast Y6, lunch and dinner Y12. Open daily 7am-9pm.)

SIGHTS AND BEACHES

The non-sandy parts of Sanya are an afterthought for most visitors. **Deer Look Back Park** (lù huítóu gōngyuán; 鹿回头公园) is on the peninsula between Sanya City and Dadonghai. Though they may not justify the hefty admission fee, views from the nearby mountain are indeed spectacular, especially at sunset or at night when the city lights twinkle at your feet. Try to ignore the gaudy laser lights and loud, synthesized classical music. *(Open daily 7am-11:30pm. Y50-60.)*

YALONG BAY (yàlóng wān; 亚龙湾). Sanya has big plans for this 7km stretch of beachfront resort complexes and the sand and surf that fringe them. An official poster announces the ambitious goal of taking on Australia's Great Barrier Reef and Indonesia's Bali as their direct competitors. Yet Yalong remains unmistakably Chinese. Tourists garbed in starfish and coral motif attire madly click photos of the ocean. The water itself is not absolutely pristine, but the waves are respectable (although no one's surfing). Wander along the shores until the tourists and resorts fade from view and enjoy the company of verdant mist-swirled hills instead. The **Hainan Yalong Bay Underwater World** (hǎinán yàlóng wān hǎidǐ shìjiè; 海南亚龙湾海底世界 ; ☎8856 5588) offers a slew of aquatic activities. *(25km east of Sanya. Catch #202 to East Bus Station, and then switch to the #102 bus for a 30min. ride to the Yalong Bay Waterfront. Open daily 8am-4:30pm. Parasailing Y320 per 5min., deep sea fishing Y350 per hr., boating Y130 per hr., scuba diving Y247 per hr., underwater excursions in a submerged viewing deck Y200 per 30min. Swimming, of course, is always free.)*

DADONGHAI (dàdōng hǎi; 大东海). Dadonghai's 2km of angel dust may not be Sanya's best beach, but it is undoubtedly the most crowded and convenient. Water sports are cheaper here than at Yalong Bay. Try bargaining a scuba diving trip down to Y250. The usual beachy merchandise and enterprising stalls, including even a designer coffee bar, saturate the meticulously landscaped beachfront plaza. Shaded by beach umbrellas, the ample deckchairs are comfortable and usually unoccupied, mainly because you'll be charged for using them. *(3km southeast of Sanya. Accessible by numerous minibuses including #202. Minibuses Y1.)*

TIANYA HAIJIAO (tiānyá hǎijiǎo; 天涯海角). Dubbed the "End of the Earth," the southernmost point of China is a popular destination for tourists and appears on the back of the Y2 note. Its romantic name signifies a love that knows no bounds, and as a result, Tianya Haijiao witnesses the weddings of over 100 couples from around the world every November during the Sanya International Wedding Ceremony (sānyà guójì hūnlǐ jié; 三亚国际婚礼节). Festivities include a parade through Sanya City with elephants and dances, followed by a mass wedding. *(23km west of Sanya. Take any bus or minibus labeled 天涯海角 going up Jiefang Lu. Y60.)*

▸ DAYTRIP FROM SANYA: XINCUN AND MONKEY ISLAND

About 62km northeast of Sanya City. Take the bus to Lingshui from the Sanya Bus Station (Y13). Then catch a minibus labeled 光坡 - 新村 across the road from the Lingshui Bus Station for a ride to Xincun (25min., Y2). The last bus back from Lingshui to Sanya leaves at 5:40pm. In Xincun, a side car (Y1) will bring you to the waterfront, where you can take a motorboat to Monkey Island (Y30) and Mountain Lake Island. The Visitors Center and ticket office is 2km down the road, walkable or reachable by motorcab. Open daily 8am-5pm. Monkey Island Nature Reserve Y30.

Xincun (xīncūn; 新村) provides access to nearby **South Gulf Monkey Island** (nánwān hóu dǎo; 南湾猴岛), a small peninsula that juts out into the ocean. This small green crag is home to over 300 wild macaques, personable golden-brown monkeys with red behinds. Legend has it that during the Tang Dynasty, a plague left residents of this seaside port blind and near death. Local hero Yan'an set sail in search of black pearls that would cure the disease, but the young boy was shipwrecked during a fierce storm. A group of compassionate monkeys saved him and returned with the boy and the black pearls, saving the town and finding a new home, which the grateful villagers vowed to protect forever. Legend is strangely silent on how the monkeys' rumps turned crimson.

Folklore aside, Monkey Island offers a great chance to see these wild animals up close. The boat ride to Monkey Island weaves through the floating matrix of houseboats, bound by makeshift boardwalks and nets and posts marking each family's fishery. Monkey Island's main attraction, the nature reserve, is home to tropical macaques (some allowed to frolic freely, some enlisted into amusing stunt performances). The "Monkey Vaudevilles" and "Comedic Performance" both run every hour or so, from 8am-4:30pm. Visitors can buy a pack of peanuts (Y10) and watch monkeys frolic around their feet, or undertake the 30min. climb to the highest point on the island for an impressive view of the surrounding countryside.

If this is too much institutionalized entertainment, the adjacent **Mountain Lake Island** (shānhú dǎo; 山湖岛), also accessible from Xincun, offers natural, untrammeled scenery. Xincun itself is populated by the Hakka and Danjia minorities, many of whom earn their living from fishing.

WUZHISHAN 五指山 ☎ 0898

Formerly called Tongzha, this small, laid-back Li and Miao village is best known for its museum. Aside from this attraction, the city rarely transcends its ethnic heritage. To best appreciate Wuzhishan's hidden treasures, visit the minority villages that dot the surrounding countryside.

■ ■ ORIENTATION AND PRACTICAL INFORMATION.

Wuzhishan is bisected by the **Nansheng River** (nánshèng hé; 南圣河), with the downtown area to the south and the museum and bus station to the north. The **Wuzhishan Bus Station** (wǔzhǐshān qìchē zhàn; 五指山汽车站) is on Haiyu Bei Lu. Cross the bridge and turn left; the station is 50m ahead on the right. Luxury **buses** run to Haikou (4hr., 5 per day, Y67). Regular buses make the same trip in 4½hr. (Y41-47) and also service Lingshui (2½hr., 3 per day, Y13) and Sanya (2½hr., every 30min. 6:30am-5:30pm, Y13). (☎8662 2419. Open daily 5:30am-5pm.) The **Bank of China,** 8 Jiefang Lu, near Xinhua Lu, exchanges traveler's checks and offers credit card advances. (☎662 3642. Open daily 8am-6:30pm.) The **Telecom Internet Bar** (wǔzhǐshān diànxìn yīntè wǎngbā; 五指山电信因特网吧 ; ☎8662 7773), on Hong Qi Lu, has Internet access for Y2 per hr. (Open M-Th 8:30am-midnight, F-Su 24hr.) The **Main Communications Post Office,** at Haiyu Nan Lu and Hebei Xi Lu, provides IDD service. (☎8663 2782. Open daily 7:30am-9pm.) **Postal Code:** 572200.

■ ■ ACCOMMODATIONS AND FOOD.

Wuzhishan has few accommodations and restaurants. Most budget accommodations are south of the river, clustered around Jiefang Lu. The **Wuzhishan International Hotel** ❶ (wǔzhǐshān guólǚ bīnguǎn; 五指山国旅宾馆) is on 1 Haiyu Bei Lu. Leaving the bus station, make a left, and then a right. It's next to the river on your right, conveniently located near the museum. Rooms have A/C, TV, and bath. (☎8663 3368. Singles Y50; doubles Y60-80.) The best places to grab a bite are the **food stalls** (dishes Y3-8) near the bus station and along the river. Li specialties like **bamboo-steamed rice** and **rice wine** are served in some of the minority restaurants in the Li villages surrounding Wuzhishan. For java junkies, **Green Island Coffee** ❶ (lǜ dǎo kāfēi; 绿岛咖啡 ; ☎8663 9866) on Haiyu Bei Lu, just opposite the bus station, brews Colombian, Brazilian, French, and "Left Bank" blends (Y6-20). Groups of locals gather here on rainy mornings to chat loudly in animated Hainanese, smoke, and enjoy steaming porridge with pigeon, eel, or pork and egg (Y5). The atmosphere is placidly domestic with low-rise chairs, perfect for lolling around and puffing away a sodden day.

◉ **SIGHTS.** The main sight in Wuzhishan is the **Hainan Provincial Minority National-ities Museum** (hǎinán shěng mínzú bówùguǎn; 海南省民族博物馆), just past the bus station, if heading north from the town center. Turn right at the sign and climb up the steep hill. The museum has an impressive collection of Li and Miao cloth-ing, tools, and handwoven tapestries, but the most beautiful part is probably the view of the surrounding countryside and its green hills topped with seeping mist. (☎ 8662 2336. Open daily 8am-5:30pm. Y10.) **Qiongzhou University** (qióngzhōu dàxué; 琼州大学) is a fine example of traditional Li architecture. From the bus station, go up the steep slope to its left and then up the long flight of steps. The **Fanmao Li Vil-lage** (fānmáo lízhài; 番茅黎寨), 2km north of Wuzhishan, has numerous traditional boot-shaped houses with pyramidal huts. (Accessible by motorcab, Y3.)

HONG KONG
AND MACAU

In July 1997, Hong Kong returned to Chinese rule after being under British control for nearly a century. Macau soon followed suit, with the Portuguese relinquishing control in December of 1999. Although both areas interacted with mainland China during their colonial years due to geographical and cultural proximity, socially and economically they could not have been farther apart. Cosmopolitan, commercialized, and thoroughly capitalist Hong Kong is among the most open ports in the world, with a per capita income that greatly exceeds that of China (and indeed that of Britain). Tiny Macau revolves around its affectionate vice—the casino industry that supplements its livelihood. Anyone who lives in either city is reluctant to call their home "China," and a few days in either of the former colonies will show you why. Whether it's street fashion or high-stakes poker, Hong Kong and Macau set themselves apart from their motherland. Both regions balance bustling, money-obsessed city centers with island escapes and beautiful natural spaces, and both struggle in their own ways with their return to China.

HIGHLIGHTS OF HONG KONG AND MACAU

MARKET HOPPING in **Kowloon**'s hectic outdoor markets (p. 563), where anything and everything is for sale.

ISLAND HOPPING through **Hong Kong**'s outlying islands (p. 579), reveling in secluded beaches, natural parks, and Lantau's very own **Big Buddha** (p. 581).

CASINO HOPPING in **Macau** (p. 583), living it up, and then gambling it all away.

LANGUAGE

Chinese and English are the official languages of Hong Kong. Since the handover, the use of English in the official domain (such as education and civil service) has markedly decreased, while the use of Mandarin is on the rise, but **Cantonese** is still by far the primary spoken dialect in Hong Kong. Cantonese, like Mandarin, is a tonal dialect, but it has at least seven different tones compared to Mandarin's four (see **China: Language,** p. 87). Tones in Cantonese are also more difficult to distinguish than their Mandarin counterparts—even native speakers have trouble telling them apart from one another. Cantonese speakers have the habit of adding a lagging "ah" sound to the end of phrases and will tell you a sentence feels incomplete without it. English words and phrases are generously scattered into daily speech, and many have been completely integrated into the dialect, such that you might take a "dik si" (taxi) or a "ba si" (bus) from the airport.

Chinese language skills are not necessary to comfortably navigate Hong Kong, as almost all signs are in both English and Chinese. Most people who work in the tourist and service industries speak English; many small shopkeepers, vendors, and eatery owners may not speak English or Mandarin, but will be accustomed to dealing with foreigners. Learning to count and say a few key phrases in Cantonese can prove very useful (see **Cantonese Phrasebook,** p. 878).

Unlike Mandarin pinyin, there is no universal standardized romanization system for Cantonese, and it is more difficult to represent the sounds with Roman letters. Because Hong Kong and Macau were under British and Portuguese rule, respectively, when the Chinese government introduced simplified characters (see **China: Writing,** p. 88), the former colonies continue to use **traditional characters.** Wherever possible and deemed helpful, *Let's Go* includes traditional characters and simple Cantonese pronunciation in parentheses for this chapter.

MONEY

Hong Kong uses a separate currency from the rest of China. The **Hong Kong dollar** (HK$) is divided into 100 **cents.** Bronze-colored government-issued coins come in 10¢, 20¢, and 50¢ denominations; silver-colored coins come in $1, $2, and $5; silver- and bronze-colored coins come in $10. Three private banks issue notes in denominations of $10, $20, $50, $100, $500, and $1000. The Hong Kong dollar fluctuates around HK$7.8 to US$1. Currency and traveler's checks can be easily exchanged at banks and there are **ATMs** throughout the city. All major **credit cards** are generally accepted in Hong Kong, but some shops may apply a surcharge.

Tipping is discretionary, so don't feel obligated to tip waiters, bellhops, or other attendants, although a small tip is expected for taxis and room service. Most restaurants automatically levy a 10% service charge and expect to keep the change; a 10% tip is appropriate if the service charge is not included.

HONG KONG DOLLAR		
AUS$1=HK$5.48	HK$1=AUS$0.18
CDN$1=HK$5.94	HK$1=CDN$0.17
NZ$1=HK$5.09	HK$1=NZ$0.20
EUR€1=HK$9.38	HK$1=EUR€0.11
UK£1=HK$13.97	HK$1=UK£0.07
US$1=HK$7.80	HK$1=US$0.13
Y1=HK$0.94	HK$1=Y1.06
MOP1=HK$0.97	HK$1=MOP1.03

HONG KONG, SAR 香港 ☎852

Despite Britain's flight from Victoria Harbour and Hong Kong's status as a Special Administrative Region (SAR) of China, on the surface it's business as usual in the former colony—lightning-fast and devil-may-care. The cultural contrasts and unabashed urban decadence that encapsulate Hong Kong's raw appeal still resonate as strongly as ever. Chinese junks glide in Victoria Harbour under the glow of neon lights and the all-too-ubiquitous golden arches, over a backdrop of glossy building exteriors punctuating the sky. Chic socialites towing the latest LV bag and Armani-clad moguls sporting requisite Rolexes wander the same sleepless streets as everyday Hong Kongers who aspire to be one or the other. Vibrant markets sell everything from seahorse aphrodiasics to pirated goods of all colors and grades, while the sounds of Chinese opera and Canto-pop duke it out in the streets with the Beatles and the latest American pop ballad. A city in search of free-trade nirvana, Hong Kong works hard and plays harder, leaving many invigorated visitors stunned and slightly out of breath.

Beneath the shine of gilded commerce, however, Hong Kong has struggled in the last few years. The gates came crashing down on the city's giddiness in 1997, not so much in the form of political handover as in the form of financial recession.

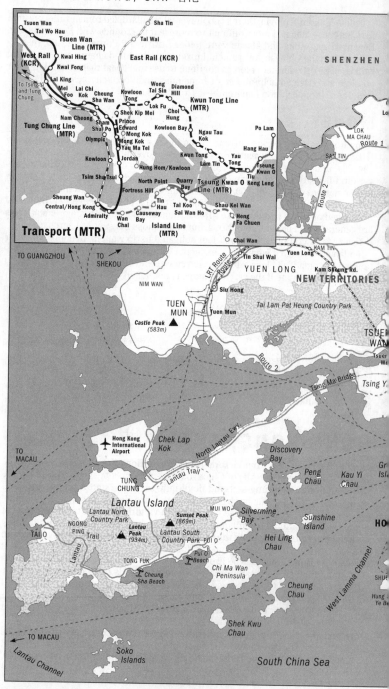

Transport (MTR)

Tsuen Wan
Tai Wo Hau
Sha Tin
Tsuen Wan Line (MTR)
Tai Wai
West Rail (KCR)
East Rail (KCR)
SHENZHEN
Kwai Hing
Kwai Fong
To Tsing Yi and Tung Chung
Lai King
Mei Foo
Lai Chi Kok
Cheung Sha Wan
Wong Tai Sin
Diamond Hill
Kowloon Tong
Kwun Tong Line (MTR)
Nam Cheong
Sham Shui Po
Shek Kip Mei
Lok Fu
Choi Hung
Tung Chung Line (MTR)
Prince Edward
Mong Kok
Kowloon Bay
Ngau Tau Kok
Po Lam
LOK MA CHAU Route 1
Olympic
Mong Kok
Yau Ma Tei
Hang Hau
SAN TIN
Kowloon
Jordan
Kwun Tong
Lam Tin
Yau Tong
Tseung Kwan O
Route 1
Tsim Sha Tsui
Hung Hom/Kowloon
Tiu Keng Leng
Sheung Wan
North Point
Quarry Bay
Tseung Kwan O Line (MTR)
Route 2
Central/Hong Kong
Fortress Hill
Tin Hau
Tai Koo
Shau Kei Wan
Admiralty
Causeway Bay
Sai Wan Ho
Heng Fa Chuen
Wan Chai
Island Line (MTR)
Chai Wan

TO GUANGZHOU
TO SHEKOU
Tin Shui Wai
Yuen Long
KAM TIN
LRT Route
Route 3
YUEN LONG
Kam Sheung Rd.
NEW TERRITORIES
NIM WAN
Siu Hong
Tai Lam Pat Heung Country Park
TUEN MUN
Tuen Mun
Castle Peak (583m)
TSUEN WAN
Tsuen Wan
Route 2
Tsing Ma Bridge
Tsing Yi

TO MACAU
Hong Kong International Airport
Chek Lap Kok
North Lantau Expy.
Lantau Trail
Discovery Bay
Peng Chau
Kau Yi Chau
Great Island
TUNG CHUNG
Lantau Island
Lantau North Country Park
Sunset Peak (869m)
MUI WO
Silvermine Bay
Sunshine Island
HONG
TAI O
NGONG PING Trail
Lantau Peak (934m)
Lantau South Country Park
PUI O
Hei Ling Chau
Lantau Trail
PUI O
Pui O Beach
TONG FUK
Cheung Sha Beach
Chi Ma Wan Peninsula
West Lamma Channel
SHE
Hung Ye Be
Cheung Chau

TO MACAU
Lantau Channel
Soko Islands
Shek Kwu Chau
South China Sea

HONG KONG

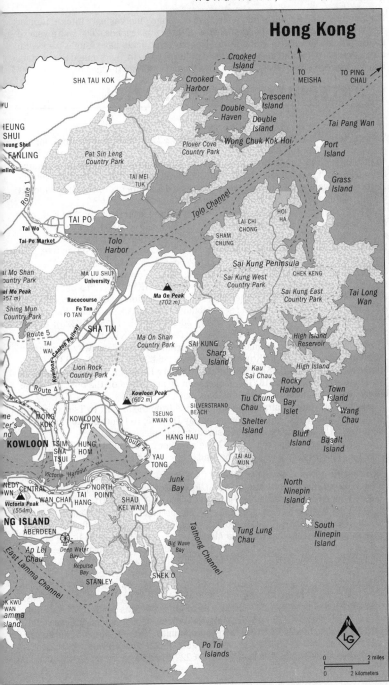

Hong Kong

SHA TAU KOK

Crooked
Island

Crooked
Harbor

TO
MEISHA

TO PING
CHAU

HEUNG
SHUI
heung Shui
FANLING
nling

Double
Haven

Crescent
Island

Double
Island

Wong Chuk Kok Hoi

Tai Pang Wan

Port
Island

Route 1

Pat Sin Leng
Country Park

Plover Cove
Country Park

Grass
Island

TAI MEI
TUK

Tolo Channel

HOI
HA

TAI PO

LAI CHI
CHONG

Tai Wo

Tai Po Market

Tolo
Harbor

SHAM
CHUNG

Sai Kung Peninsula

ai Mo Shan
ountry Park

MA LIU SHUI
University

Sai Kung West
Country Park

CHEK KENG

ai Mo Peak
157 m)

Racecourse

Fo Tan

Ma On Peak
(702 m)

Sai Kung East
Country Park

Tai Long
Wan

Shing Mun
Country Park

FO TAN

Route 5

SHA TIN

TAI
WAI

Ma On Shan
Country Park

SAI KUNG

High Island
Reservoir

Kowloon-Canton Railway

Sharp
Island

High Island

Lion Rock
Country Park

Kau
Sai Chau

Rocky
Harbor

Town
Island

Route A

Kowloon Peak
(602 m)

TSEUNG
KWAN O

SILVERSTRAND
BEACH

Tiu Chung
Chau

Bay
Islet

Wang
Chau

ne
ter's
nd

MONG
KOK

KOWLOON
CITY

Route 4

HANG HAU

Shelter
Island

Bluff
Island

Basalt
Island

KOWLOON

TSIM
SHA
TSUI

HUNG
HOM

YAU
TONG

TAI AU
MUN

Victoria Harbour

NEDY
WN

CENTRAL

WAN CHAI

NORTH
POINT

TAI
HANG

SHAU
KEI WAN

Junk
Bay

North
Ninepin
Island

Victoria Peak
(554m)

NG ISLAND

ABERDEEN

Tung Lung
Chau

South
Ninepin
Island

East Lamma Channel

Ap Lei
Chau

Deep Water
Bay

Big Wave
Bay

Tathong Channel

Repulse
Bay

STANLEY

SHEK O

K KWU
WAN
amma
sland

Po Toi
Islands

N
LG

0   2 miles
0   2 kilometers

Shaken by the SARS outbreak, a sluggish economy, increasingly interventionist mainland policies, and the sudden deaths of three pop legends, 2003 was a year of memorable mourning for Hong Kong. The city's residents have fought back with characteristic vigor and uncharacteristic political passion, determined to maintain its civil and economic freedoms and to reclaim its tourism throne.

✈ INTERCITY TRANSPORTATION

BY AIR

The modern **Hong Kong International Airport** (☎2181 0000; www.hongkongairport.com) at **Chek Lap Kok** sits just off Lantau Island's northern rim, some 30km from central Hong Kong. New arrivals enjoy all the latest airport perks, including 54 moving walkways, a mall, and a high-speed rail linking the airport and Victoria Harbour. Travelers ages 12 and over must pay a departure tax of HK$120, which is usually included in the price of the plane ticket.

A direct **Airport Express Line (AEL)** jets every 12min. from the airport to Kowloon (20min.; one-way or same-day return HK$90, children 3-11 HK$45, round-trip valid for 1 month HK$160) and Hong Kong Island (23min.; one-way or same-day return HK$100, children 3-11 HK$50, round-trip HK$180). Children under 3 ride free. The trains run 5:45am-12:48am.

Airbuses run from the airport to Hong Kong Island, Kowloon, and the New Territories. A11 goes to Causeway Bay (every 15min., HK$40); A12 to Siu Sai Wan (every 15min., HK$45); A21 to the Hung Hom KCR Station (every 10min., HK$33); A22 to the Lam Tin MTR Station (every 15min., HK$39); A31 to Tsuen Wan (every 15-20min., HK$17); A35 to Mui Wo (every 30-40min.; HK$14, Su HK$23); A41 to Shatin (every 20min., HK$20); A43 to Fanling (every hr., HK$28).

Less expensive, conventional **bus** routes include E11 to Causeway Bay (every 10-20min., HK$21), E22 to Kowloon City (every 6-20min., HK$18), E33 to Tuen Mun (every 11-20min., HK$13), E41 to Tai Po (every 12-20min., HK$13), and E42 to Sha Tin (every 15-20min., HK$13). Tickets can be purchased on the buses or at the booths across the lobby from the customs exit.

Taxis wait outside the airport terminal. A ride from the airport to Tsim Sha Tsui (TST) costs about HK$270; to Causeway Bay HK$345; to Central HK$340; and to Tsuen Wan HK$240. There is a HK$5 surcharge per piece of luggage.

Numerous carriers fly from Hong Kong to other major Chinese cities, destinations in Southeast Asia, and points beyond.

Asia-Pacific Airlines: Air China (CAAC), CAAC Bldg., 10 Queen's Rd., 2nd fl., Central (☎3102 3030); 54-64B Nathan Rd., Mirador Mansions, ground fl., TST (☎2739 0022). **Air New Zealand,** Jardine House, 1 Connaught Pl., Ste. 1701, Central (☎2862 8988). **All Nippon,** Int'l Finance Centre, 1 Harbourview St., Rm. 501, Central (☎2810 7332). **Cathay Pacific,** Peninsula Office Tower, 18 Middle Rd., 10th fl., TST (☎2747 1888, ticketing 2747 1577). **China Airlines,** St. George's Bldg., 2 Ice House St., 3rd fl., #2, Central (☎2843 9800, ticketing 2843 9800). **Qantas,** Jardine House, 1 Connaught Pl., 24th fl., Ste. 3701, Central (☎2822 9000, ticketing 2822 9090). **Dragon Air,** Cosco Tower, 183 Queen's Rd., 46th fl., Sheung Wan (☎2868 6777). **Garuda Indonesia,** Dah Sing Financial Bldg., 108 Gloucester Rd., Rm. 1501-1505, Wan Chai (☎2840 0000). **Japan Airlines,** Harbour City, Tower 6, 9 Canton Rd., Rm. 304, TST (☎2523 0081, ticketing 2847 4573). **Korean Air,** South Seas Centre II, 75 Mody Rd., 11th fl., TST East (☎2733 1577). **Malaysia Airlines,** Central Tower, 28 Queen's Rd., 23rd fl., Central (☎2521 8181). **Singapore Airlines,** United Centre, 95 Queensway, 17th fl., Admiralty (☎2520 2233, ticketing 2529 6821). **Thai Airways,** United Centre, 95 Queensway, 24th fl., Admiralty (☎2876 6222).

European Airlines: Air France, Jardine House, 1 Connaught Pl., 25th fl., Central (☎2216 1088, ticketing 2501 9433). **British Airways,** Jardine House, 1 Connaught Pl., 24th fl. (☎2822 9000). **KLM Royal Dutch,** World Trade Centre, 280 Gloucester Rd., Rm. 2201, Causeway Bay (☎2808 2111). **Lufthansa,** Schenker International, Nanfung Tower, 173 Des Voeux Rd., 11th fl., Rm. 9, Central (☎2868 2313). **Virgin Atlantic,** Alexander House, 16-20 Trader Rd., 8th fl., Rm. 801, Central (☎2532 6060).

North American Airlines: Air Canada, New World Tower, Tower 1, 18 Queen's Rd., Rm. 1612, Central (☎2876 8111). **American Airlines,** Peninsula Office Tower, 10th fl., 18 Middle Rd., TST (☎2826 9269, ticketing 2826 9102). **Northwest Airlines,** Alexandra House, 20 Chater Rd., 29th fl., Central (☎2810 4288). **United Airlines,** Gloucester Tower, 11 Pedder St., Landmark, 29th fl., Central (☎2810 4888).

Flights from Hong Kong to major Chinese destinations include:

DESTINATION	FREQUENCY	PRICE (HK$)	DESTINATION	FREQUENCY	PRICE (HK$)
Beijing	many per day	1870	Kunming	2-3 per day	1390
Changsha	daily	1340	Nanchang	Tu, F, Su	1180
Chengdu	2-3 per day	1660	Nanjing	3-4 per day	1290
Chongqing	1-2 per day	1660	Ningbo	2-3 per day	1290
Dalian	daily	1880	Qingdao	2-3 per day	1560
Fuzhou	5 per day	1130	Shanghai	many per day	1290
Guilin	2 per day	1190	Shenyang	Th and Su	2370
Guiyang	Tu, F	1450	Tianjin	daily	2190
Haikou	1-2 per day	1020	Wuhan	1-2 per day	1120
Hangzhou	4-5 per day	1290	Xiamen	3-4 per day	1020
Ji'nan	daily	1180	Xi'an	1-2 per day	1900

BY LAND

TRAINS. Hong Kong is connected to the mainland by the **Kowloon-Canton Railway (KCR)** (☎2947 7888 or 2602 7799), which runs from **Hung Hom (Kowloon) Station** to **Lo Wu Station** (every 3-10min.; HK$33, ages 3-12 and 65 and over HK$17). Passengers can cross the Chinese border at Lo Wu into **Shenzhen** (p. 524). Trains leave from Hung Hom Station 5:45am-10:19pm and return from Lo Wu Station 6:01am-12:20am. The KCR also has direct service to the mainland. Tickets can be purchased at any KCR station or from **CTS** (p. 551). Trains depart from Hung Hom Station to: Beijing West (24hr., every other day 3pm, HK$574); Dongguan (1hr., 8 per day, 1st class HK$135-145); Foshan (3hr., 2:20pm, HK$210); Guangzhou (1½-2hr., roughly every hr. 7:30am-7:15pm, premium class HK$180-230); Shanghai (29¼hr., 3pm, HK$508); Zhaoqing (4¼hr., 2:20pm, HK$235). Children ages 5-9 travel for half-price. Prices rise during high season and on holidays and festivals.

Overland routes from Hong Kong reach destinations as distant as London or Moscow via China, Mongolia, and the **Trans-Siberian Railroad** (p. 39). **Moonsky Star,** 36-44 Nathan Rd., Chungking Mansions, Block E, 4th fl., Flat 6 (☎2723 1376; www.monkeyshrine.com), is the best place to book packages and tickets. (Open M-Sa 10am-6pm.) Moonsky Star can arrange passage from Hong Kong, Guangzhou, or Beijing to **Moscow, St. Petersburg,** and beyond. Russian and Mongolian visas are available to those who book with them. Prices vary depending on stopovers, train, and point of origin. Visit their website for up-to-date information.

BUSES. Buses journey between Hong Kong and Guangdong province. **CTS** (p. 551) can arrange bus tickets in advance to Shenzhen and Guangzhou through a variety of agencies at no commission. Buses depart from Hung Hom station to

Guangzhou (4hr.; every hr. 6:45am-12:45am; HK$100, round-trip HK$160) and Shenzhen (1hr., every 15-20min. 6am-midnight, HK$30). Expect a 1hr. delay when crossing the border on holidays. Bus reservations are recommended on holidays.

BY SEA

Independent companies run ferries to **Guangzhou** and **Shenzhen. CTS** (p. 551) arranges passage to Shantou (14hr., W and Sa 5pm, HK$202-212), Xiamen (18hr., Tu 2pm, HK$428-478), and Zhuhai (1¼hr., 10 per day, HK$176-186).

Travel from Hong Kong to **Macau** is easiest by boat. Most boats depart from the **Macau Ferry Terminal**, Shun Tak Centre, 200 Connaught Rd., Sheung Wan (MTR: Sheung Wan), but some leave from the **China Ferry Terminal**, 33 Canton Rd., TST, behind Kowloon Park. The **Macau Government Tourist Office** and the **Hong Kong Tourist Board** (p. 551) provide detailed schedules and fare information. All ferries from Hong Kong arrive at the **Macau Maritime Ferry Terminal**. A HK$26 departure tax is included in all tickets, and prices are HK$5-10 more on the return trip from Macau.

First Ferry (☎2131 8181; www.nwff.com.hk). Ferry service from China Ferry Terminal to **Macau** (1hr.; every 30min. 7am-5pm, every hr. 5-9pm, 10pm (subject to demand); M-F HK$140, Sa-Su HK$155, after 5pm HK$175).

TurboJet (☎2859 3333, booking 2921 6688; www.turbojet.com.hk). Tickets can be purchased at the CTS at the China Ferry Terminal or in the Shun Tak Centre, 3rd fl., 200 Connaught Rd., Central (MTR: Sheung Wan, exit D). To **Macau** (1hr.; every 15min., less frequent in the early morning; M-F HK$141, Sa-Su HK$153, after 6pm HK$175) and **Shenzhen** (1hr., 6-8 per day 7:30am-5:30pm, HK$189).

Far East Jetfoil Company (☎2859 3333), Shun Tak Centre, Macau Ferry Terminal. From the Macau Ferry Terminal to **Macau** (1hr.; every 15min., less frequent at night; economy HK$141, after 6pm HK$161).

❄ ORIENTATION

A small dot on the southeastern coast of China, Hong Kong squeezes in approximately seven million residents into a mere 1100km², spread out over a surprisingly varied terrain of islands, mountains, beaches, and urban spaces. The compact and overcrowded **Kowloon peninsula,** where Hong Kong's tourist hub Tsim Sha Tsui is located, juts out into **Victoria Harbour.** Situated across the harbor from Kowloon, **Hong Kong Island** and its many skyscrapers are accessible by three tunnels, the MTR, and the Star Ferry. The more rural and residential **New Territories** sprawl all the way to the border with mainland China. The other **outlying islands** that make up the Hong Kong archipelago are distributed throughout the South China Sea. Of the over 260 islands, **Lantau Island,** the site of the Hong Kong International Airport, **Lamma Island, Cheung Chau,** and **Peng Chau** are easily accessible by ferry and make pleasant retreats.

▣ LOCAL TRANSPORTATION

OCTOPUS CARD (baat daat tung; 八達通 ; ☎2266 2266; www.octopuscard.com). Visitors may want to invest in an all-purpose Octopus card, accepted by all major public transports including the MTR, KCR, buses, the tram, most ferries, and many coach and maxicab companies. More than just a metro pass, the Octopus card is actually a comprehensive **smart card** system that can also be used at many retail outlets, such as supermarkets, convenience stores, and fast-food restaurants, not to mention pay phones, photo booths, and vending machines. Just touch the card—or the bag, wallet, or pocket holding your card—onto the scanner. Cards can be purchased at MTR, KCR, and bus customer service centers. (HK$150, students HK$100, ages 3-12 and elderly HK$70.) The price covers a refundable HK$50 deposit and the initial stored value. A **Tourist Octopus card** entitles you to an Airport Express ride and three days of unlimited MTR (Airport Express HK$220, round-trip HK$300). Money can be added at Add-Value machines, transport counters, and participating retail outlets. The deposit and remaining value can be refunded at a customer service center.

MASS TRANSIT RAILWAY (MTR). The MTR (☎ 2881 8888; www.mtr.com.hk) is Hong Kong in a nutshell: super-efficient, automated, and lightning-fast. It's also the most expensive of Hong Kong's public transport options. Five MTR lines connect Kowloon, Hong Kong Island, the New Territories, Chek Lap Kok Airport, and most points in between. Tickets (HK$4-13, max. HK$26) are valid for 1½hr. of travel on the day of issue. Most tickets cost more during **rush hour** (7:30-9:30am and 5:30-7:30pm). A **one-day pass** costs HK$50. The MTR runs 6am-1am, although a few stations are open 7am-midnight.

KOWLOON-CANTON RAILWAY (KCR) AND LIGHT RAIL (LR). An older version of the MTR, the KCR (☎ 2602 7799; www.kcrc.hk) ventures further outside the city. The **East Rail** runs from Hung Hom Station in TST East, through the New Territories, and to the Chinese border at Lo Wu (HK$3.5-9, children and seniors half-price). Passengers can change from the MTR to the KCR at Kowloon Tong Station. Trains run every 3min. 5:30am-12:20am. The KCR also operates direct service to the mainland (p. 547). The **Light Rail** or **West Rail** (☎ 2929 3399) joins the towns of Yuen Long and Tuen Mun in the New Territories. Tickets are HK$4-5.8 and can be purchased at ticket dispensers along the route. Trains run daily 5:40am-12:30am. Another two lines are under construction: one extends northeast from Tai Wai station towards Wu Kai Sha and is due to open in late 2004; the other runs west from Sheung Shui to Lok Ma Chau and will open by 2007.

BUSES. Hong Kong's five-star bus system ventures into any area worth visiting. Schedules and fares are posted at bus stops and available at tourist offices. Fares run HK$1.2-45; it usually costs under HK$10 to travel within the city and under HK$20 to travel to the New Territories. Double-decker buses with numbers followed by an "M" run to MTR stations, by a "K" to KCR stations; those followed by "X" indicate express routes. The four major bus companies are **New World First Bus** (☎ 2136 8888; www.nwfb.com.hk) and **Citybus** (☎ 2873 0818; www.citybus.com.hk) on Hong Kong Island, **Kowloon Motor Bus** (☎ 2745 4466; www.kmb.com.hk) in Kowloon, and **New Lantau Bus** (☎ 2984 9848) on Lantau Island.

Red-and-cream **minibuses** barrel down the streets; they will stop anywhere along their routes except busy intersections and restricted areas. Wave them down, tell the driver your stop, and pay as you disembark. Green-and-cream minibuses called **maxicabs** follow fixed routes and only stop at marked maxicab stops; pay once on board. In both cases, destinations are on the front of the bus, but the English is often small and hard to read. Minibuses accept only exact fare (HK$1.5-20) and only as many passengers as there are seats (14-16).

TAXIS. Taxis are red in Kowloon and Hong Kong Island, blue on Lantau Island, and green in the New Territories. Base fare for **red** (Kowloon and Hong Kong Island) taxis is HK$15, each additional 200m or minute of waiting time HK$1.4. Red taxis will take you to Hong Kong Island and vice versa, but there are surcharges for the Cross-Harbour Tunnel (HK$20), the Eastern Harbour Tunnel

HONG KONG

(HK$30), and the Western Harbour Tunnel (HK$45) to cover the round-trip tunnel toll. Base fare for **green** taxis is HK$12.5, each additional 200m or minute of waiting time HK$1.2. Green taxis only pick up and drop off passengers within the New Territories. Base fare for **blue** (Lantau) taxis is HK$12, each additional 200m or minute of waiting time HK$1.2. Taxi drivers may charge HK$5 per piece of luggage. Some drivers will only take passengers to specific destinations. Most major thoroughfares have taxi stands. Taxis are not allowed to pick up or set down passengers in areas marked with yellow lines. To file a complaint against a driver, copy down the taxi number on the dashboard and call the police hotline (☎2527 7177).

TRAMS. Aging trams have lumbered along northern Hong Kong Island since 1904 and are an inexpensive way to see the island. The double-decker trams follow routes from Kennedy Town or Western Market to Shau Kei Wan, Happy Valley, or Causeway Bay; all trams pass through Central, Admiralty, Wan Chai, and Causeway Bay. Trams run 6am-midnight. Fare is only HK$2, children and seniors HK$1. Board at the rear and pay with exact change as you exit. The tram's last stop is written in English on the front. Contact **Hong Kong Tramways** (☎2118 6338; www.hktramways.com) for more information.

FERRIES. The ■**Star Ferry** (☎2367 7065; www.starferry.com) has been gliding ferries between TST and **Central** (every 5-10min. 6:30am-11:30pm; lower deck HK$1.7, upper deck HK$2.2) and between TST and **Wan Chai** (every 8-20min. 7:30am-11pm, HK$2.2) for over 100 years. The Star Ferry Terminal in TST is at the end of Salisbury Rd. Ferries to **Hung Hom** (7am-7pm, HK$5.3) leave from the Star Ferry pier in Central, in front of Jardine House in Exchange Sq.

Ferries to the outlying islands leave from the **New Ferry Piers,** off Exchange Sq. in Central, to **Lamma Island** from Pier 4 (30min.; every hr. 6:30am-12:30am; M-Sa HK$10, Su HK$14); **Cheung Chau** from Pier 5 (regular 1hr.; every hr. 6:30am-11:30pm; M-Sa HK$10.5, Su HK$15.7; express 40min.; every hr. 8:45am-11:45pm, 4 per day 12:30-7am; M-Sa HK$21, Su HK$31); **Lantau Island** from Pier 6 (regular 1hr.; every 2hr. 8:30am-4:30pm, 7 per day 5:20pm-6:10am; M-Sa HK$10.5, Su HK$15.7; express 40min.; 12:30, 3am, 2 every 2hr. 7:10am-11:50pm; M-Sa HK$21, Su HK$31); and **Peng Chau** from Pier 6 (regular 45min.; about every 1½hr. 7am-11:30pm; M-Sa HK$10.5, Su HK$15.7; express 30min.; about every 2hr. 8am-10:45pm; M-Sa HK$21, Su HK$31). For schedules and fares, contact **First Ferry Customer Service Hotline** (☎2131 8181; www.nwff.com.hk).

TRANSPORTATION INFORMATION

For up-to-date information, contact one of the following companies or visit www.info.gov.hk online. If all else fails, try the **HKTB hotline** (☎2508 1234).
Hong Kong International Airport (☎2181 0000).
To and From the Airport: Airbus Coach (☎2745 4466). **Airport Express** (☎2881 8888).
Trains: MTR (☎2881 8888). **KCR: East Rail** (☎2602 7799); **West Rail** and **Light Rail** (2929 3399).
Buses: City Bus (☎2873 0818). **Kowloon Motor Bus** (☎2745 4466). **New Lantau Bus Co.** (☎2984 9848). **New World First Bus** (☎2136 8888).
Taxis: Hong Kong Island (☎2861 1008), Kowloon/New Territories (☎2397 0922). **Taxi Union Loss Report Hotline** (☎2385 8288).
Trams: Hong Kong Tramway (☎2548 7102). **Peak Tramway** (☎2522 0922).
Ferries: First Ferry (☎2131 8181). **HK & Kowloon Ferry** (☎2815 6063). **Star Ferry** (☎2367 7065).

⑦ PRACTICAL INFORMATION

TOURIST SERVICES

TOURIST OFFICES

▓ **Hong Kong Tourist Board (HKTB),** The Center, 99 Queen's Rd. Central, Ground fl., Central (☎2807 6543; www.discoverhongkong.com). MTR: Central, exit D. Turn left on Pedder St., and then turn left onto Des Voeux Rd. Central. Walk 10min. until you reach a set of escalators on your left; take the escalator up 1 level; walk through the maze of steel mirrors between the water pools until you reach another set of escalators. Take the escalator down to the basement, turn left, and voilà! Extremely professional staff and scores of useful, glossy brochures and pamphlets for the taking. Visitors can request a **Hong Kong VIP card** that offers special discounts at many upscale stores or a complimentary guide to one of Hong Kong's 18 districts. *Exploring Hong Kong's Countryside* by Edwards Stokes (HK$80) serves as an excellent reference for walks and hikes on Hong Kong Island, Lamma, Lantau, and New Territories. Self-guided **walking tour** guides with portable CD-ROM player and headphone HK$50, deposit HK$500. Open daily 8am-6pm. Other offices: **Hong Kong International Airport,** Buffer Halls A and B and the E2 transit area (open daily 7am-11pm); **Lo Wu Terminal Building,** 2nd fl., Lo Wu (open daily 8am-6pm); **Star Ferry Concourse,** TST (open daily 8am-6pm).

Macau Government Tourism Office (MGTO), Macau Ferry Terminal Bldg., 3rd. fl., Sheung Wan (☎2857 2287 or 2559 0147; www.macautourism.gov.mo). MTR: Sheung Wan, D exit. Maps, a comprehensive *Macau Guide Book*, and information about museums, walking tours, and accommodations. Open daily 9am-1pm and 2:30-5:30pm.

Multilingual HKTB Visitor Hotline (☎2508 1234). Open daily 8am-6pm.

TRAVEL AGENCIES

CTS, CTS House, 78-83 Connaught Rd., 4th fl., Central (☎2853 3888; ctsdmd@hkstar.com). Open M-Sa 9am-5pm. Branch offices in **Alpha House** (☎2315 7188), 27-33 Nathan Rd., 1st fl.; **Central** (☎2522 0450), China Travel Bldg., 77 Queen's Rd., Mezzanine; **Mong Kok** (☎278 9582), 62-72 Sai Yee St., 2nd fl.; **Wan Chai** (☎283 2388), 138 Hennessy Rd., Southorn Centre, 1st fl.

Traveller Services, Silvercord Tower 1, 30 Canton Rd., 10th fl., Rm. 1012 (☎2375 2222; www.taketraveller.com). Originally started in Chungking Mansions for backpackers. Inquire about cheap air and boat tickets. Also offers tours of Hong Kong and visas to China. Open M-F 9am-1pm and 2-6pm, Sa 9am-1pm.

Sincerity Travel, 835A Star House East Block (☎2730 3269), next to the Star Ferry pier. Discounts for ISIC holders (ISIC HK$100). Open M-F 10am-7:30pm, Sa 10am-6:30pm.

Travel-Net Services, Sands Bldg., 17 Hankow Rd., Rm. 9894 (☎2723 7138; trvlnet@navigator.com). Visas to Burma, Cambodia, Nepal, Taiwan, Thailand, and Vietnam. Open M-F 9am-6pm, Sa 9am-1pm.

Sunflower Travel Service, Alpha House, 27-33 Nathan Rd., 1st fl. (☎2721 1682, ticketing 2881 1788). Tours into mainland China by bus, train, car, ferry, and air. Specify if you're looking for low prices. Open daily 8am-9pm.

Armaan Travel Service, Alpha House, 27-33 Nathan Rd., 5th fl., Flat C (☎2723 3330; atsl@armaantravel.com). Mostly deals with air travel. Arranges visas to China. Open M-F 9:30am-6pm, Sa 9:30am-1pm.

CONSULATES, VISAS, AND IMMIGRATION

The **Chinese consulate** is on 26 Harbour Rd., Lower Block, 7th fl., Wan Chai (☎2827 1881 or 2106 6304). For an extensive listing of other consular offices in Hong Kong, see **Essentials: Consular Services in China** (p. 10). British citizens can stay in Hong

Kong visa-free for 180 days; US, Canadian, Australian, New Zealand, Western European, and most Central and South American citizens can stay for 90 days. Eastern European and African citizens usually require a visa, although some can stay visa-free for 40 days. Most travel agencies can arrange **Chinese visas** (p. 12). This may take up to five days, and prices vary (HK$100-200 for single-entry, 1-month tourist visa). Photo machines in every subway station (HK$35) and CTS office (HK$30) provide fast visa and passport photos.

Hong Kong Immigration Department, Immigration Tower, 7 Gloucester Rd., 5th fl., Wan Chai (☎2824 6111; www.immd.gov.hk). For **visa extensions,** bring HK$135, passport, airplane ticket or other proof that you must extend your stay, and fill out form ID91. Work and study visas extensions require an ID card, passport, completed ID91 form, and a letter from the company or school. Open M-F 8:45am-4:30pm, Sa 9-11:30am.

Visa Office of the Ministry of Foreign Affairs of the P.R. of China in Hong Kong, China Resources Bldg., 26 Harbour Rd., Lower Block, 7th fl., Wan Chai (☎3413 2424, 24hr. 3413 2300). Entrance is off Gloucester Rd., in the red-and-white building. Issues single-entry tourist visas (1-month HK$150); double-entry visas (1-month HK$220); multi-ple-entry visas (6-month HK$420; 1-year HK$600). The Chinese government sets prices on a reciprocal basis for certain countries, including Brazil, Chile, Netherlands, the UK, and the US; call first for prices. Visa processing takes 1 working day. Express 1hr. service HK$250; 2nd-day service HK$150. Photos HK$35 for 4. Open M-F 9am-noon and 2-5pm. Prepare to wait; the office gets very busy, especially in the afternoon.

CTS (p. 551). Bring HK$210, a passport, and a recent photo to fill out a visa application at the office. Citizens of the Netherlands, UK, and the US may have to pay more; call ahead to ask. 3-month single-entry visitor visa in 3 days, express visas (HK$580) in 1 working day. Apply before 1pm. Open daily 9am-5pm.

FINANCIAL SERVICES

Banks: Anyone with a passport can open a bank account in Hong Kong. For a basic ATM account, **Hang Seng Bank** (☎2825 5111, hotline 2822 0228) has no service fees or balance requirement. Other major banks: **Bank of China** (☎2826 6888), **Citibank** (www.citibank.com.hk), **HongkongBank** (☎2822 1111, hotline 2749 3322), **HSBC** (☎2748 3322), **Wing Lung Bank** (☎2826 8333). Most banks open M-F 9am-4:30pm, Sa 9am-12:30pm.

ATM: ATMs connected to international money networks like Cirrus, Plus, Mondex, and NYCE can be found throughout the city and in **MTR** stations. All **HongkongBank** "Electronic Money" ATMs accept Cirrus, MC, Plus, and Visa. In general, look for machines marked "For International Cards."

Currency Exchange: Currency can be exchanged at banks, hotels, moneychangers, various major retail outlets, and 24hr. automatic currency exchange machines called **EA$YXCHANGE.** In **Chungking Mansions,** stalls on the 1st fl. (not the very 1st booth) have competitive rates and are usually open daily 9:30am-6pm. AmEx cardholders can use **Jetco** ATMs for cash advances in HK$. Banks usually offer the best rates.

American Express: Henley Bldg., 5 Queen's Rd., 1st fl., **Central** (☎2277 1010). MTR: Central Station, Landmark exit. Exchanges currency and AmEx Traveler's Cheques (no fee) and handles credit card payments. China Insurance Bldg., 48 Cameron Rd., 1st fl., **TST** (☎2926 1606). Exchanges Traveler's Cheques. Taikoo Place, Somerset House, 979 King's Rd., 18th fl., **Quarry** Branch (☎2811 6888). Offers client mail services; mail held 30 days at no fee for members and holders of AmEx Traveler's Cheques. All open M-F 9am-5pm, Sa 9am-12:30pm.

Western Union: United Centre, 95 Guinsway St., 2nd fl., Rm. 2038, Admiralty (☎2528 5631). **Thomas Cook:** ☎2854 4938.

Lost or Stolen Credit Cards: American Express ☎2811 6122. Citibank ☎2823 2323. JCB ☎2366 7211. Mastercard ☎2511 6387. Visa ☎2810 8033.

LOCAL SERVICES

Bookstores: PageOne, Harbour City, 3rd fl., Shop 3002, TST (☎2730 6080). Use the entrance near the Star Ferry Concourse. Wide selection of art and culture books, novels, bestsellers, magazines. Open 10:30am-9:30pm. Times, Pacific Mansion, 172 Nathan Rd., TST (☎2730 8899). Opposite the TST Police Station. Writing supplies, maps, and discounted fiction. Open daily 11am-9pm. Branches in Central and Causeway Bay.

Library: Hong Kong Central Library, 66 Causeway Rd. (☎2921 0372, hotline 3150 1234; www.hkpl.gov.hk). MTR: Causeway Bay. Major branch libraries in Kowloon, Hong Kong Island, Sha Tin, Tuen Mun, Tsuen Wan, Kwai Tsing, Tai Po, and Cheung Chau. Visitors can check out a max. of 5 books for a refundable deposit of HK$130 per book. Free Internet access at all libraries; the giant Central Library has over 500 computers. Open M-Th 10am-7pm, F 10am-9pm, Sa-Su 10am-5pm.

Weather and Local Information: Time and Temperature in English (☎18501). Weather Conditions in English (☎187 8066). Typhoon Hotline (☎2835 1473). English Newsline (☎2272 0000).

Gay Organizations: HORIZONS, Winning Commercial Bldg., 46-48 Hillwood Rd., TST (☎2815 9268; www.horizons.org.hk). Information on gay nightlife and events around town, as well as support and counseling. Open Tu and Th 7:30am-10:30pm.

EMERGENCY AND COMMUNICATIONS

Emergency: ☎999.

Police: General enquiries ☎2527 7177, nearest police station ☎2860 2000.

Medical Services: Hong Kong Island: Queen Mary Hospital (☎2855 3111). Kowloon: Queen Elizabeth Hospital (☎2958 8888). New Territories: Prince of Wales Hospital (☎2632 2211). Free ambulance service: Hong Kong Island ☎2576 6555, Kowloon and New Territories ☎2713 5555.

Telecommunications: PCCW-HKT phonecards are sold at MTR stations, HKTB offices, 7-Eleven and Circle K stores, and street kiosks. English-language service access number (☎2808 8081). Pay phone surcharge 15%. Local calls HK$1 per 5min. For home country operators, call your HCD number: Telstra Australia (☎800 96 0161); British Telecom (☎800 96 0044); Canada Direct (☎800 96 1100); Telecom Eireann (☎800 96 0353); New Zealand Telecom (☎800 96 0064); AT&T (☎800 96 1111); MCI (☎800 96 1121); Sprint (☎800 96 1877).

Telephone Information: Directory Assistance English ☎1081, Cantonese 1083, Mandarin 1088. Operator assistance for collect calls ☎10010, for IDD ☎10013.

Internet Access: All public libraries have free Internet access, with enough computers that you usually don't have to wait too long, especially on weekdays. Universities, such as the Hong Kong Polytechnic University, on Yuk Choi Rd., Hung Hom, often have many computers with Internet access.

Cyber Clan, Golden Crown Court, 66-70 Nathan Rd., South Basement, TST (☎2723 2821). Enter from Carnarvon Rd., just around the corner from Nathan Rd. HK$10 per hr. Refundable deposit for nonmembers HK$40. Printing HK$2 per page.

Pacific Coffee House Company, Queensway Plaza, 1st fl., Shop C34 (☎2861 2302). MTR: Admiralty. Free access for 15-20min. with purchase of coffee (HK$20). Open daily 7:30am-9pm. Numerous other branches around Hong Kong. The New Territories branch is at Festival Walk, Kowloon Tong exit (☎2265 8600). MTR: Kowloon Tong. Open M-Sa 7am-10pm, Su 9am-9pm.

Grand Central Plaza, Customer Service Centre, 2nd fl., Sha Tin. Exit the station directly into the mall and walk straight to the stairs going down to the food court; take the escalator behind the stairs. Service desk and computers in the main hall.

Post Offices: General Post Office, 2 Connaught Pl., **Central** (☎2921 2332, enquiry hotline 2921 2222; www.hongkongpost.com). MTR: Central, Jardine House exit. To the right of Star Ferry and in front of the Jardine House. EMS. Poste Restante held for 2 weeks. **TST Post Office,** Hermes House, 10 Middle Rd., ground fl., TST (☎2366 4111). MTR: TST, Nathan Rd. exit. Walk past Chungking Mansions toward the harbor, and turn left onto Middle Rd.; Hermes House is at the end of the street on the left. Poste Restante held for 3 months. All post offices open M-F and Su 8am-6pm, Sa 8am-2pm.

ENTERTAINMENT INFORMATION

There's *always* something going on in Hong Kong. Pick up a copy of *HK Magazine* or *bc magazine* for the latest events and arts and entertainment listings. Here are some additional resources:

HKTB events calendar (☎2508 1234; www.discoverhongkong.com).

bc Magazine event listings (☎2976 0876; www.bcmagazine.net).

HK Magazine event listings (☎2850 5065; asiacity@asia-city.com.hk).

Leisure and Cultural Services Department (☎2415 5555; www.lcsd.gov.hk).

Hong Kong Arts Centre (☎2582 0200; www.hkac.org.hk).

URBTIX (☎2111 5999; www.urbtix.gov.hk).

Hong Kong Academy for Performing Arts (☎2584 8514).

Hong Kong Coliseum box office (☎2895 1347). Open daily 10am-6:30pm.

Hong Kong Cultural Centre (☎2734 2009; www.hkculturalcentre.gov.hk).

Hong Kong Stadium box office (☎2895 7895). Open daily 10am-6pm.

KOWLOON 九龍

Kowloon (*gau long* in Cantonese), the jam-packed peninsula off the New Territories, is the quintessential picture of Hong Kong. Literally "nine dragons," Kowloon is named for the mythical dragons said to inhabit the peninsula—one for each of the peninsula's eight mountain peaks and one more for Ping, an ancient child-emperor. Today, the color and fury of these legendary winged beasts linger in the natural beauty of the area, but endless apartment blocks, hotels, restaurants, and plazas encroach on their original turf. Crowds along the perpetually busy Nathan Road collect in front of jewelry stores, inhale the subtle hue of saffron in restaurants, or don three-inch dancing shoes at night to paint the town red. All the while, the dragon's fiery breath still blows throughout the land—a pulsing heat that travelers to Hong Kong simply cannot avoid.

 ORIENTATION

At the southernmost tip of the Kowloon peninsula, **Tsim Sha Tsui (TST)** and **Tsim Sha Tsui East (TST East)** are separated by **Chatham Road South** and bounded in the south by **Salisbury Road.** Along the waterfront are some of Kowloon's most recognizable landmarks, including the Star Ferry Concourse, the Cultural Centre, Hong Kong Space Museum, and the New World Centre. **Nathan Road.** begins at Salisbury Rd. and runs north into the smaller districts of **Yau Ma Tei** (油麻地) and **Mong Kok** (旺角) both of which are famous for their crowded street markets. The red line of the MTR subway system runs along Nathan Rd. and under the harbor to Hong Kong Island. To the east, past the **terminus of the KCR** and the **Hong Kong Coliseum,** lies quiet **Hung Hom.** In the north, **Boundary Street** in **New Kowloon** marks the frontier between the waterfront districts and the New Territories.

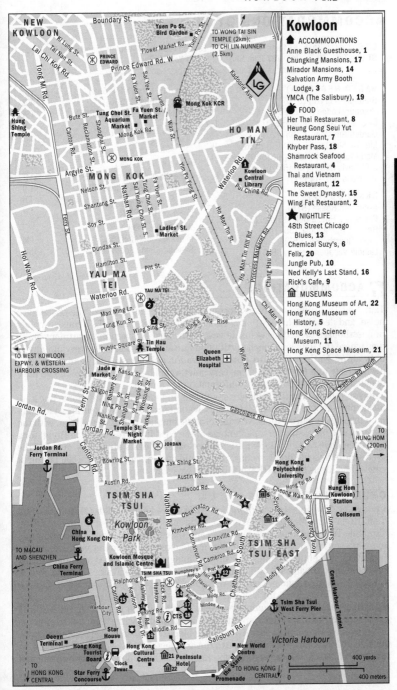

Kowloon

▲ **ACCOMMODATIONS**
Anne Black Guesthouse, **1**
Chungking Mansions, **17**
Mirador Mansions, **14**
Salvation Army Booth
  Lodge, **3**
YMCA (The Salisbury), **19**

🍴 **FOOD**
Her Thai Restaurant, **8**
Heung Gong Seui Yut
  Restaurant, **7**
Khyber Pass, **18**
Shamrock Seafood
  Restaurant, **4**
Thai and Vietnam
  Restaurant, **12**
The Sweet Dynasty, **15**
Wing Fat Restaurant, **2**

★ **NIGHTLIFE**
48th Street Chicago
  Blues, **13**
Chemical Suzy's, **6**
Felix, **20**
Jungle Pub, **10**
Ned Kelly's Last Stand, **16**
Rick's Cafe, **9**

🏛 **MUSEUMS**
Hong Kong Museum of Art, **22**
Hong Kong Museum of
  History, **5**
Hong Kong Science
  Museum, **11**
Hong Kong Space Museum, **21**

HONG KONG

ACCOMMODATIONS BY PRICE

CB Causeway Bay **KT** Kennedy Town **LM** Lamma Island **LT** Lantau Island **SK** Sai Kung **ST** Sha Tin **TP** Tai Po **TST** Tsim Sha Tsui **YMT** Yau Ma Tei

UNDER HK$80 (❶)			
Bradbury Hall (HI) (576)	TP	Man Hing Lung Hotel (558)	TST
Bradbury Lodge (HI) (575)	SK	Wang Fat Hostel (566)	CB
▨ Cosmic Guesthouse (557)	TST	▨ Welcome Guesthouse (557)	TST
Garden Guesthouse (557)	TST		
Ma Wui Mt. Davis Hostel (HI) (566)	KT	**HK$181-250 (❸)**	
Mong Tung Wan Hostel (HI) (580)	LT	YMCA (558)	TST
S.G. Davis Hostel (HI) (580)	LT		
Traveler's Hostel (557)	TST	**HK$250-350(❹)**	
		Anne Black Guesthouse (558)	YMT
HK$81-80 (❷)		Jetvan Traveller's House (566)	CB
Ascension House (575)	ST	Mui Wo Inn (580)	LTI
Chungking House Deluxe Hotel (557)	TST	Noble Hostel (566)	CB
Harbour Guesthouse (557)	TST		
Kyoto Guesthouse (557)	TST	**HK$350+ (❺)**	
Lamma Vacation House (582)	LM	Man Lai Wah Hotel (582)	LM
		Salvation Army Booth Lodge (558)	YMT

🏠 ACCOMMODATIONS

Tsim Sha Tsui offers numerous accommodations in the center of the chaos, dirt, noise, and decadent luxury that is Hong Kong. Budget digs in TST consist mainly of guesthouses tucked away inside vast "mansions"—cavernous apartment buildings where the flats have been partitioned into smaller rooms. Be wary of individuals along Nathan Rd. and outside Mirador and Chungking Mansions who aggressively tout their "very clean, very quiet, very cheap" rooms. Also, if you have decided where to stay, keep this information to yourself.

Beyond the Nathan Rd. mansions, you can find more hotel-like rooms in establishments run by the YMCA, YWCA, or Salvation Army. These hotels aren't as commercial as their more expensive counterparts, but they're just as well run, with the benefits of a hotel stay for a percentage of the cost. If you're staying in Hong Kong for seven days or more, look for excellent package deals offered by many of the area's more upscale hotels; rooms that would cost upwards of HK$1000 per night can be had for as little as HK$3500 for a week's stay.

CHUNGKING MANSIONS 重慶大廈

Chungking Mansions (or *chunghing daiha*), 36-44 Nathan Rd. (MTR: Tsim Sha Tsui, Hong Kong Museum of Art exit), is far and away the most notorious of the Tsim Sha Tsui mansions. The building's apartments, guesthouses, and restaurants leave no square foot unoccupied, serving backpackers, immigrants, small-time importers, and entire families of visitors. Chungking Mansions is legendary for its dim labyrinth of hallways and dank staircases, crowded elevators, and disreputable inhabitants, as romanticized in Wong Kar Wai's *Chungking Express*. Its also *the* place in Hong Kong for a cheap room. Despite its reputation for shady clientele, there are some very quiet and clean rooms hidden in its caverns, but it is unlikely that the touts on the ground floor are affiliated with them.

Chungking Mansions is divided into five blocks, unimaginatively called A, B, C, D, and E blocks. From the entrance to the arcade, the A, B, and C elevators are on the left, while D and E are on the right. Each block has a pair of elevators: one services even-numbered floors, the other odd-numbered ones. Quality varies more than price, so choose guesthouses carefully; ask to look at a room before agreeing to spend the night. All guesthouses accept cash only.

Women traveling alone should take particular care: they may find themselves the object of unwanted attention from some long-term Chungking residents.

Welcome Guesthouse, A5, 7th fl. (☎2721 7793 or 2721 7436; gloriak@netvigator.com). It might not seem likely, but a warm welcome is possible in Chungking Mansions. This guesthouse doesn't provide nicer rooms or more space than its competitors, but after a long day battling the crowds on Nathan Rd., you might be cheered up by a friendly face, a pulled-out chair, and a cup of tea. The father-son owners give out free travel advice, tell stories, and seem to enjoy their guests' company. Singles HK$100, with bath HK$130-150; doubles with twin beds and bath HK$200-220. In July prices rise 10-20%. 10-15% student discount available. ❷

Kyoto Guesthouse, A8, 15th fl. (☎2721 3574 or 9077 8297). Clean, colorful rooms and a warm and cheerful staff. Singles and doubles are of average size, but prices are good and negotiable. Singles HK$80-100, with bath and A/C HK$120; doubles with bath and A/C HK$150-160. HK$10 discount for individual travelers. ❷

Harbour Guesthouse, B8, 4th fl. (☎2721 2207 or 2367 2777). All rooms have A/C and TV, and many have fairly large windows. A smaller and quieter establishment: the staff seems less harried and the reception area isn't bursting at the seams with people. Singles HK$100, with bath HK$110; doubles HK$160, with bath HK$200. Discounts for longer stays. Rates increase by about HK$10 in summer. ❷

Travelers Hostel, A Block, 16th fl. (☎2368 2505 or 2368 7710; digand@hotmail.com). Dimly lit dorms are small and spare with cement floors, but popular with backpackers. Cable TV in common room. Free lockers but no padlocks provided. Luggage storage HK$5-10 per day. Internet access HK$10 per 15min. IDD service. Single-sex 6-bed dorms with A/C HK$65; singles HK$100, with A/C HK$130. ❶

Chungking House Deluxe Hotel, A Block, reception on 4th fl. (☎2366 5362). While hardly living up to its name, the Deluxe Hotel is the most hotel-like of Chungking's guesthouses, complete with a makeshift lobby. The most spacious rooms in the building, with A/C, TV, and phone. Singles HK$150; doubles HK$200 and up. Expect to pay more for sunlight and a view of the street. ❷

MIRADOR MANSIONS

These days, many backpackers seem to be moving from the Chungking to Mirador Mansions, a few doors down at 54-64 Nathan Rd. The change is most likely in their best interest—Mirador Mansions is quieter, cleaner, and less crowded than its infamous neighbor. There are fewer guesthouses, interspersed with private residences. Elevators are to the right as you enter the arcade.

Cosmic Guesthouse, A1, A2, and F1, 12th fl. (☎2721 3077 or 2369 6669). Open for just over 3 years and run by a very friendly family, the Cosmic Guesthouse is out of this world. The whole place seems cleaner, brighter, and more homey than the average Mansion establishment. A/C, phone, and TV in every room. Communal fridge and hot water dispenser in the hallway. IDD service. Check-out 11am. Deposit HK$100. For singles, doubles, and triples, there are 2 tiers of quality: luxury rooms tend to be about HK$50 more. 8-bed dorms HK$60; singles HK$110-130, with bath HK$150; doubles with bath HK$200-220; triples with bath HK$240-270. Discounts for *Let's Go* users. ❶

Garden Guesthouse, F4, 3rd fl. (☎2311 1183). Very popular with backpackers for its dorm rooms, but its best feature is the large outdoor balcony. Friendly owners speak excellent English. Free small lockers; bring your own lock. A/C, phone, and TV in the common room. 6-bed single-sex dorms HK$60; doubles with bath HK$200. ❶

HAPPY HEARTS

Dim sum (點心) is translated as "a little bit of heart" or, more romantically, as "to touch the heart." Either way, when it comes to touching our little heart with delicious food, Hong Kong pulls ahead of the pack. Dim sum emerged as a Cantonese custom when tea houses started serving small snacks to accompany that ever-important cup of tea. The dim sum seems to take center stage these days, but its origins are clear: in Cantonese, you don't go to eat dim sum, you go to *yum cha* ("drink tea").

Although dim sum has become an internationally popular cuisine, the average Hong Kong dim sum experience can still be rather intimidating to an outsider. The crowds get quite intense, racing for tables and vying for the attention of the waiters, and there are many conventions involved. A common pre-food routine is to wash the chopsticks in a cup of tea. If you notice people tapping their fingers against the table when tea is being poured by a companion, this actually represents a silent thank you. When a pot of tea is finished, remove the lid and balance it on the top of the pot, and a waiter will refill it.

To order dim sum, catch the attention of the cart-pusher, who loudly recites the contents of the cart as she snakes around the tables. Pointing at the desired delicacies will suffice, and your order card will be stamped to keep tally of the dishes. In recent

Man Hing Lung Hotel, F2, 14th fl. (☎2311 8807 or 2722 0678; mhlhotel@hkstar.com). This clean guesthouse offers a wide variety of rooms; shop around before committing. The most basic rooms are tiny (and cheap); more expensive ones have their own small showers and are more carefully kept. A/C, phone, and TV. Singles HK$100, with private bath HK$150; doubles HK$150-220; triples HK$220-270. ❷

BEYOND THE MANSIONS

YMCA (The Salisbury), 41 Salisbury Rd., TST (☎2268 7000; room@ymcahk.org.hk), next to the Peninsula Hotel and opposite the Hong Kong Cultural Centre. MTR: Tsim Sha Tsui. Definitely not what the Village People were singing about—this posh establishment boasts a swimming pool, squash courts, and indoor climbing walls. IDD service and Internet access. Closet-sized lockers with personal safes. 7-night max. stay in the dorm rooms; guests must show a visa proving that they've been in Hong Kong for 10 days or fewer. Reservations recommended, especially during summer and holidays. Wheelchair-accessible. Deposit HK$150. 4-bed dorms with A/C and bath HK$210; singles and doubles HK$680-800; package rates for longer stays. 10% service charge. 10% discount for YMCA associates. Credit cards accepted. ❸

Anne Black Guesthouse (YWCA), 5 Man Fuk Rd., Waterloo Hill, Ho Man Tin (☎2713 9211). MTR: Yau Ma Tei. Walk east up Waterloo Rd. for 10min. and take a right onto Pui Ching Rd.; Man Fuk Rd. is the 1st street on the left. Like the Salisbury, this is much more hotel-like than your average YWCA. The location is a bit removed from the action, but rooms are extremely clean and well kept. All rooms have A/C, TV, and phone. Singles and doubles with clean communal bath HK$270-300, with attached bath HK$420-480. Great discount packages for stays of 7 days or more. ❹

Salvation Army Booth Lodge, 11 Wing Sing Ln., Yau Ma Tei (☎2771 9266), just south of the Yau Ma Tei MTR exit on Nathan Rd. Take a left onto Wing Sing Ln.; the lodge is on your left. Even the Salvation Army can be upscale. Typical hotel standards, with TV, A/C, phone, fridge, and bathtub. Restaurant and reception on 7th fl. Breakfast included. Singles and doubles HK$460-620. Discount for stays of more than 7 days. ❺

🍴 FOOD

Hong Kong is a self-acclaimed culinary heaven, with restaurants and food stalls lining every road. The *Official Dining and Entertainment Guide* (available at HKTB offices), the *HK Magazine*, and *bc Magazine* all list and rank restaurants and are free and widely available at most hotels and restaurants.

You'll find the range of any major metropolitan city in Kowloon, from steaks and apple crumble to Vietnamese spring rolls and peanut soups. Many restaurants presuppose a hefty budget, but that doesn't mean there aren't good deals to be found. Restaurants serving the typical budget traveler staples (such as noodle soups and dumplings) are as numerous as those serving HK$800 shark fin. Inexpensive set menus and dim sum provide good lunch options. If price is not an issue, then Hong Kong is your oyster; food here is seriously delicious.

Some of the best culinary bargains are found in **no-name shops** and **stalls.** Food vendors come out in the late evening (after 11pm) to refuel eager shoppers along **Nathan, Carnarvon,** and **Mody Road.** Also, try the small streets west of Nathan Rd. While many Indian restaurants have members-only rules, **Chungking Mansions** hosts a number of jam-packed but dirt-cheap stalls and small restaurants serving delectable South Asian dishes (often under HK$20).

Small cafes along **Haiphong** and **Canton Road** are popular for their cheap but well-prepared Chinese and Western dishes (HK$30-40); most leave copies of their menu outside. For those seeking Western food, **Ashley Road** features restaurants and pubs that serve up hearty portions of Australian, Italian, and British food at mid-range prices. **Kimberley Road,** which branches off Nathan Rd. farther inland, is packed to the brim with restaurants. The area bounded by **Hart Avenue** and **Prat Avenue,** on the opposite side of Nathan Rd. to Kowloon Park, has an exciting selection of both Western and Asian establishments, as well as nightlife venues to help sated diners work away the extra calories.

Most malls in the city have **food courts,** which usually offer a great selection of cheap Asian and Western fast food. **City's Super ❷,** inside Harbour City Mall on Canton Rd. in TST, has a dizzying selection of international fast-food cuisine a little more upscale than most food-court fare. Set meals run about HK$26-60. (Open Su-Th 10:30am-9:30pm, F-Sa and public holidays 10:30am-10pm.)

FOOD BY TYPE

▨ **The Sweet Dynasty,** 88 Canton Rd., TST (☎2375 9119), opposite the Harbour City shopping plaza. Famed for its *tong sui,* sweet soups traditionally served after meals. A wonderful range of sweet concoctions, from pudding soups and sticky rice balls with peanut

years, many restaurants have eliminated the carts altogether and transitioned to a menu-ordering system, making for a less chaotic, but also less fun and authentic, experience.

Dim sum is supposed to be consumed in a certain order. Lighter, steamed dishes like dumplings, including the perennial favorite *ha gau* (shrimp dumpling), are first. More "exotic" items, such as chicken feet (*fung jau;* "phoenix claws"), come next. Third are the heavier, often deep-fried dishes, such as sesame-seed balls filled with red bean paste. Last comes dessert, like mango pudding. In practice, you tend to eat whatever arrives first.

On weekends, restaurants fill with families, with the men reading newspapers and the children playing hand-held video games. When it gets busy, restaurants will put patrons into any available seat, but they usually ask beforehand if you mind sharing a table. Ideal for breakfast or brunch, dim sum begins as early as 6:30am, and is rarely served past 4 or 5pm. It is the quintessential, time-consuming beginning to a lazy morning in Hong Kong. For those unaccustomed to the loud atmosphere and elbowing crowds, dim sum may not be the most relaxing way to start the day, but your stomach will definitely leave happy. When you've eaten to your heart's content, catch a waiter's eye and say *mai daan.*

filling to more exotic and curiously named options. You may want to start off with a delicious bowl of almond soup (HK$15). Menu extends beyond desserts to include dishes such as sauteed prawn with walnut (HK$70) and noodle with shrimp dumpling (HK$36). Open Su-Th 7:30am-midnight, F-Sa 7:30am-1am. ❷

Khyber Pass, Chungking Mansions, 36-44 Nathan Rd., E-2, 7th fl., TST (☎2721 2786). Indian food isn't hard to find in the Mansions, but quality varies quite a bit. Khyber Pass is popular for its authentic taste and fresh preparation. Chicken, mutton, and beef entrees HK$42-68. Rice and vegetables HK$30-45. Open 6-11:30pm daily. ❸

Shamrock Seafood Restaurant, 223 Nathan Rd., TST (☎2735 6722). Despite the name, there's nothing Irish about this joint. Delicious and affordable dim sum (7am-4:30pm; HK$8-22), but don't neglect the extensive menu, ranging from sliced conch with shrimp (HK$40) to roast goose (HK$68). Open daily 7am-2am. ❸

Thai and Vietnam Restaurant, Wardley Centre, 9-11 Prat Ave., TST (☎2368 6181). This small, homey restaurant offers free red-bean-and-sweet-rice dessert. Although the menu is not the most extensive, consider the delicious soups of sliced beef or peanut curry (HK$32-48) or the fresh Vietnamese spring rolls (HK$24). Open noon-1am. ❸

Wing Fat Restaurant, 448 Nathan Rd., 1st fl., Yau Ma Tei (☎2359 4885). The unpretentious fare, low prices, long hours, and plastic-vinyl decor are as down-to-earth as you can get. Dishes HK$18-45. French toast HK$15. Open 24hr. ❷

Heung Gong Seui Yut Restaurant (香江歲月粥麵名家), 182 Nathan Rd., TST (☎2735 5332). The extensive menu seems to have been conveniently designed with the budget traveler in mind. Congee, noodles, and rice dishes HK$20-30. Pig intestine, cabbage rolls, shrimp dumplings in soup HK$20. Open 11am-1am. ❷

Her Thai Restaurant, Shop 1, Promenade Level Tower 1, on Canton Rd. (☎2735 8898), in China Hong Kong City, TST. At the top of a 3-story escalator. Outdoor tables and a stunning view of the harbor. The *longan* drink is a sweet refreshment. Stick with the less expensive set menus (lunch HK$55, dinner HK$138-298). Entrees HK$50-70. Seafood HK$100-120. Drinks HK$27-30. Happy hour 3-7pm. Open daily noon-11pm. ❹

CHINESE
Heung Gong Seui Yut (560) Tsim Sha Tsui ❷
🦀 Happy Bean (567) Central ❷
🦀 Sweet Dynasty (559) Tsim Sha Tsui ❷
Tsim Chai Kee Noodle (567) Central ❶
Wing Fat Restaurant (567) Wan Chai ❸
Wing Fat Restaurant (560) Yau Ma Tei ❷

FOOD COURTS/FAST FOOD
City's Super (559) Tsim Sha Tsui ❷
Grand Central Plaza (576) Sha Tin ❷
Maxim's Fast Food (576) Sha Tin ❷

GOURMET
Lucy's (568) Stanley ❺

INDIAN
Deli Lamma (582) Lamma Island ❹
Khyber Pass (560) Tsim Sha Tsui ❸

ITALIAN
Pepperoni's (576) Sai Kung ❸

MEXICAN
El Taco Loco (567) Sheung Wan ❷

MIDDLE EASTERN
Bahce Turkish (580) Lantau Island ❸
Morocco's Restaurant (583) Cheung Chau ❹
🦀 Sonthra Kebab (567) Wan Chai ❷

SEAFOOD
Hung Kee Seafood (576) Sai Kung ❸
Lamma Seaview (582) Lamma Island ❹
Shamrock Seafood (560) Tsim Sha Tsui ❸

SOUTHEAST ASIAN
Her Thai Restaurant (560) Tsim Sha Tsui ❹
Nha Trang (567) Central ❸
Thai and Vietnam (560) Tsim Sha Tsui ❸

VARIETY
🦀 Bookworm Cafe (582) Lamma Island ❸
🦀 Catstreet Cafe (580) Lantau Island ❸
Friend's Cafe (567) Causeway Bay ❸
Golden Leaf (567) Sheung Wan ❸
New Star Restaurant (568) Stanley ❷

VEGETARIAN
Fantasy Vegetarian (568) Causeway Bay ❷
Po Lin Vegetarian (580) Lantau Island ❷

HONG KONG

⊙ SIGHTS

TSIM SHA TSUI 尖沙咀

NATHAN ROAD. Nathan Rd. is as crazy, chaotic, and hectic as Hong Kong gets. TST's most important thoroughfare is also its greatest tourist attraction. The distinguished **Peninsula Hotel** marks one end of the boutique-packed road. Covering the vast area between Nathan and Canton Rd., **Kowloon Park** (MTR: Tsim Sha Tsui, A1 exit) is a green oasis amid Hong Kong's endless stretches of concrete. The park features leafy foliage, postmodern sculptures, a small soccer pitch often used for local pick-up games, and exotic wildlife. Toucans and rare Asian birds share an open-air aviary while flamingos crowd a nearby lake. The footbridge to the Royal Pacific Hotel offers great views of the harbor. *(Open daily 6am-midnight.)* The majestic **Kowloon Mosque and Islamic Centre** sits near the park's entrance on Nathan Rd. *(105 Nathan Rd. ☎2724 0095. Visitors must wear pants or long skirts. Open daily 4:30am-10pm. Free.)* The tiny **Tin Hau Temple,** a 10min. walk north to the intersection with Public Square St., has a small but colorful main courtyard. The rafters are crowded with long-burning incense coils, scenting the air with lovely-smelling smoke. *(Open daily 8am-6pm. Free, but donations accepted.)*

ON THE WATERFRONT. Many of TST's ultra-modern museums and landmark attractions cluster along the waterfront near the Star Ferry Concourse, far from the neon lights and bargain-bonanza commotion of Nathan Rd. From the **Clock Tower,** a lonely remnant of the old KCR station, a concrete walkway known as the **Promenade** stretches along the northern banks of Victoria Harbour into TST East. The Promenade passes by the **Hong Kong Cultural Centre,** the city's prime venue for Cantonese opera, Andrew Lloyd Webber musicals, and symphony concerts.

Directly adjacent to the Cultural Centre is the golf-ball-shaped **Hong Kong Space Museum.** The museum halls aren't particularly exciting, but the hands-on exhibits are popular among kids and kids at heart. You can ride the Multi-Axis Chair, a machine used to train astronauts, or strap yourself into the Moonwalk Machine, which simulates a walk on the moon. The **planetarium** doubles as an **Omnimax Theater** and has several shows per day; at least one is presented in English, usually in the evening. *(10 Salisbury Rd. ☎2734 2722. Shows usually every hr. 11:30am-8:30pm. Shows M-F HK$15, students and seniors HK$10; Sa-Su HK$24/HK$12. Cantonese, English, Japanese, and Mandarin audio tours HK$10/HK$5; free W. Open M, W-F 1-9pm, Sa-Su 10am-9pm. Admission HK$32/HK$16.)* Behind the Space Museum, the **Hong Kong Museum of Art** has limited but well-maintained collections of ancient and modern Chinese art, ranging from traditional landscapes to old pottery. *(☎2721 0116. Open daily 10am-6pm. HK$10, students and seniors HK$5; W free.)*

TSIM SHA TSUI EAST 尖沙咀東部

The Promenade begins in TST and ends in TST East, more commonly called *tsim dung* (尖東). Fishermen dangle makeshift lines in the harbor, but they seem to catch more rubbish than fish, while couples cuddle on the second-level walkway (open daily 7am-11pm) behind the Cultural Centre. Farther down, the Promenade runs past the **New World Centre,** near an artificial waterfall and a gigantic watch embedded in a rock. Behind the New World Centre, the newly created **Avenue of Stars** pays rather dubious homage to Hong Kong's biggest celebrities. Modeled after Hollywood's Walk of Fame, this stretch is dotted with stars for Chow Yun-Fat, Jackie Chan, Jet Li, Michelle Yeoh, and Wong Kar-wai, among others.

HONG KONG

Chatham Road South, the boundary between the two TSTs, veers off Salisbury Rd., away from the waterfront, just after the New World Centre. Noodle, rice, and dim sum restaurants line one side of the street, while parks and covered rest areas have benches for tired sightseers on the other. At the intersection of Chatham Rd. and Austin Rd., the new 🌐**Hong Kong Museum of History** showcases six years and HK$190 million in the making. If you can make it to only one of Kowloon's museums, this should be it. Engaging exhibits chronicle the history of the city, from its ancient natural environment (complete with real plants and bubbling water) to the cultures of the current population. Explore a Boat Dweller's boat or peek backstage at a Chinese opera hall. (☎ 2724 9042. Open M and W-Sa 10am-6pm, Su 10am-7pm. HK$10; students, seniors, and disabled HK$5; W free.) Just next to the Museum of History is the **Hong Kong Science Museum.** All four floors are filled with interactive exhibits best suited for kids. "Betsy the DC-3," a passenger and cargo plane from WWII, hangs above the transportation exhibit. Check out the 22m-high Energy Tower, a perpetual motion machine. (2 Science Museum Rd., TST East. ☎ 2732 3232. Open M-W and F 1-9pm, Sa-Su 10am-9pm. HK$25; students, seniors, and disabled HK$12.50; W free.)

NEW KOWLOON 新九龍

Squeezed between Mong Kok and the New Territories, New Kowloon has neither the glamour of Kowloon nor the seclusion of the New Territories.

CHI LIN NUNNERY. Reputedly built without a single nail over the course of 10 years, the nunnery is the latest architectural wonder of Hong Kong. This newly opened Tang Dynasty-style Buddhist complex is visually impressive, with 16 halls and a beautiful rock garden. Such elegant grandeur in the midst of an urban setting is rather bizarre—as is the aura of newness for a building constructed with the same technique as a monastery built 1000 years ago. (5 Chi Lin Dr. MTR: Diamond Hall, C exit. Follow the yellow signs. Bus 11c from Wong Tai Sin Temple Complex. ☎ 2354 1604 or 2354 1882. Open daily 9am-4:30pm. Western Lotus Pond Garden open daily 6:30am-7pm.)

WONG TAI SIN TEMPLE COMPLEX. Named after a legendary healer, the complex is dedicated to Daoist and Buddhist deities and Confucius. The courtyard in front of the popular main temple is often crowded with worshippers, shaking divination sticks and lighting incense. Quieter halls and gardens, including the beautiful **Good Wish Garden,** make up the rest of the complex. Donations go to support education and temple maintenance. (2 Chuk Yuen Village. MTR: Wong Tai Sin, B exit. Or bus 11c from Chi Lin Nunnery. ☎ 2327 8141. Good Wish Garden open Tu-Su 9am-4pm. HK$2. Complex open daily 7am-5pm. Free.)

📷 SHOPPING

There is no need to go looking for good shopping in Hong Kong—it's everywhere and it's hard to resist. Serious shoppers may want to pick up *The Official Shopping Guide* from HKTB offices (p. 551). It features shipping and insurance advice, bargaining and bargain-hunting hints, and the hours and addresses of almost every store in the city. HKTB also offers a free VIP card, which lists discounts available for tourists using upscale tours. **Bargaining** is inappropriate in boutiques and department stores. In many smaller shops and especially in street markets, it's expected—don't hesitate to ask for a "special price."

For short shopping sojourns near any of TST's "mansions," head to Nathan Rd.'s **Golden Mile,** the road's final stretch on the way to Victoria Harbour. Shops selling clothing at incredible discounts line **Granville Road** and **Kimberley Road,** off Nathan

Rd. A few good secondhand shops and trendy boutiques are on Hillwood Rd., across Nathan Rd. from the northern border of Kowloon Park. **Streetside vendors** emerge with their carts along Salisbury Rd., Nathan Rd., and beside major hotels most evenings. Watches and shirts (from "Rolax" to "Tammy Hillfinger") cost about half what they do in the more crowded street markets. Electronics along Nathan Rd. may be tempting but are risky, as vendors usually don't include the packaging, prices vary wildly, and there is no assurance of quality.

OUTDOOR MARKETS. Outdoor markets are perhaps the ideal Hong Kong shopping environment. Prices are low and vendors are willing to bargain. For those who just want to take a look around, there's no pressure to buy and a lot to see. A good walking tour of the markets in Kowloon begins at the Prince Edward MTR station. Walk north up Nathan Rd. to Boundary St., and go east 10min. to the **Yuen Po Street Bird Garden.** Recently built to replace the old Bird Street Market on Hong Lok St., the Bird Garden houses vendors selling birds, cages, and live grasshoppers. Elderly men come here daily to "walk" their birds. (Open daily 10am-6pm.) The Bird Garden leads to **Flower Market Road,** Hong Kong's best-smelling street.

Walk south across Prince Edward Rd. West to two streets of markets running parallel to each other. The **Fa Yuen Street Market** is a great place to pick up cheap sporting goods and apparel. Parallel to Fa Yuen St., starting a block from Prince Edward St., the **Tung Choi Street Aquarium Market** is more of a collection of shops than an actual market. Pet store after pet store lines its facades with fish in little plastic bags. Don't forget to look up, as there are many more stores on the second floors of these buildings, many selling exotic reptiles. (Open daily 10am-6pm.) Further south, Tung Choi St. becomes the **Ladies' Street Market,** filled with stalls selling T-shirts, hair accessories, sunglasses, sandals, toys, and backpacks (for both the ladies *and* the gentlemen among you). The market ends at Dundas St. To reach the **Jade Market,** walk west along Dundas St. to Nathan Rd. and south past the Yau Ma Tei MTR station until you hit Public Square St. Take a right, passing the **Tin Hau Temple** on your left, until you reach a covered square full of vendors perched next to their tables. Merchants display real and fake jade necklaces, pendants, and trinkets of every hue. Think twice before paying more than HK$50 for a piece of jade, unless you are quite sure that it is the real thing. (Open daily 10am-4:30pm.)

From the south end of the Jade Market, walk east along Kansu St. until you hit Temple St.—you'll know when you do, as the ▨**Temple Street Night Market** is one of Hong Kong's unmistakable spots. Palm readers (most of whom speak English) and small groups performing Cantonese opera fill the open area at the north end of the market, but the street soon gives way to a bustling overabundance of vendors and their crowded stalls, filled with imitation everything—clothes, handbags, watches, toys, and then some. (Open daily approximately 6pm-midnight.)

MALLS. Kowloon has several huge malls, each one bigger (and easier to get lost in) than the last. The massive **Harbour City** stretches up Canton Rd., from the Star Ferry Concourse past Haiphong Rd. You can find anything here except a bargain. Electronics stores, upscale boutiques, and cosmetics stores fill the labyrinth of halls. (Open daily 10:30am-9:30pm.) **China Hong Kong City,** a slightly smaller but similar option, is just north of Harbour City on Canton Rd. (Open 10:30am-9pm.) Signs at the Kowloon Tong KCR station direct you toward **Festival Walk,** a mall complete with an AMC Cinema and an ice skating rink, in addition to the many stores. (Open daily 10:30am-8pm. Rink open M-F 1:30-10pm, Sa 8:30am-10pm, Su 1-5:30pm. Skate rental HK$60.) **Rise Commercial Building,** 5-11 Granville Circuit, is home to the latest in young and hip fashions, from secondhand T-shirts to trendy sneaker shops. (Open daily 11am-10pm.)

NIGHTLIFE

Bars and pubs pack the odd quadrilateral formed by Carnarvon, Cameron, Chatham, and Mody Rd. and the area bounded by Hart Ave. and Prat Ave.

Chemical Suzy's, 2 Austin Ave. (☎2736 0087). Surrounded by noisy and characterless karaoke lounges between Austin Ave. and Kimberley Rd., this small bar is a great find. Drinks are moderately priced (HK$30-45) and the music is more listenable than what the other bars spin; nightly DJ stays far away from top-40 hits and cheesy pop. Mixed local and backpacker crowd. Open daily M-Sa 6pm-4am, Su 9pm-4am.

48th Street Chicago Blues, 2A Hart Ave. (☎2723 7633). This tiny bar squeezed in a stage for some of the best local bands in Hong Kong. The crowd is young and hip, and there's a wide range of performing acts. Drinks HK$40 and up. Music starts nightly at 10pm, Su 8:30pm. Cover HK$15-60, depending on band. Open daily 5pm-3am.

Rick's Cafe, 53-59 Kimberley Rd. (☎2367 2939 or 2311 2255). Sharp dress code: shorts (for men) and sandals are not allowed inside. Dark and comfortable seating surrounds a packed dance floor. Happy hour 5-10pm (mixed drinks and bottled beer HK$22). Open M-Th 5pm-3am, F-Sa 5pm-5am.

Jungle Pub, 80 Kimberley Rd. (☎2730 9230). At this classically constructed pub, you've got your booths, your bar, and your beer, with a bustling crowd to boot. There's not much to be had except a nice chat over a quiet drink, but if that's what you're looking for, the Jungle Pub works quite nicely. Open daily 3:30pm-4am.

Felix, Peninsula Hotel, Salisbury Rd., TST (☎2315 3188). The uppity Felix is worth a stop for one reason only: the bathroom. By which we mean: the view. On the 28th fl., Felix dishes out exclusivity at HK$80 a pop, but there is no charge to use the facilities, which boast the best view of Hong Kong Island in Tsim Sha Tsui. Open daily 6pm-1am.

Ned Kelly's Last Stand, 11A Ashley Rd. (☎2376 0562). This touristy Aussie saloon immortalizes a famed outlaw. For jazz lovers, this is the place to be. Live jazz band 9pm-2am. Happy hour 11:30am-10pm. Menu items HK$48-130. Fried eggs, bacon, sausages, chips, toast, and coffee HK$64. Open daily 11:30am-2am.

HONG KONG ISLAND 香港島

When viewed from across the harbor, Hong Kong Island's impressive skyline is an unbroken string of high-rises, adorned with unflickering neon as soon as the sun begins to set. The island reaches to the skies in more ways than one—from the high-profile international corporations that hold office in Central, to the astronomically priced Mid-Level mansions that house Hong Kong's movers and shakers, it's all about prime real estate. For those who can afford to play, Hong Kong Island, with its chic boutiques, yuppie coffee shops, and bawdy nightlife, is the place to be. Breaking away from the lure of the lights, there is also a simpler side to the island. Mountains and public parks, most of which remain pristine and undeveloped, dominate its center, and southern Hong Kong still remains relatively rustic. Hong Kong Island is much like its famed Victoria Peak—the view from the top is tinged by commercialism but fabulous nonetheless.

ORIENTATION

NORTHERN HONG KONG ISLAND. The north side of Hong Kong Island facing Kowloon is divided east-to-west into the districts of Causeway Bay, Wan Chai, Admiralty, Central, and Sheung Wan, all connected by the MTR Island line. The area's main thoroughfare follows the edge of the harbor. Starting out as **Connaught**

Northern Hong Kong Island

▲ ACCOMMODATIONS
Jetvan Traveller's House, 2
Noble Hostel, 4
Wang Fat Hostel, 3

● FOOD
El Taco Loco, 19
Fantasy Vegetarian Restaurant, 5
Friends' Cafe, 6
Golden Leaf Restaurant, 22
Happy Bean Restaurant, 18
Sonthra Kebab, 7
Tsim Chai Kee Noodle, 20
Wing Fat Restaurant, 9

★ NIGHTLIFE
C-Plus, 16
Carnegie's, 8
Cinta-J, 11
Club 64, 17
Dickens, 1
Edge, 15
Fringe Club, 13
Joe Bananas, 10
Propaganda, 21
The Wanch, 14
Yumla, 12

Victoria Harbour

HONG KONG

TO MACAU
Macau Ferry Terminal
TO LAMMA CHAU ISLAND
TO CHEUNG CHAU
TO LANTAU ISLAND AND PENG CHAU

Pier 1
Pier 2
Pier 3
Pier 4
Pier 5
Pier 6
Pier 7
NEW FERRY PIERS

HONG KONG ISLAND

SHEUNG WAN
Man Wan Rd.
Connaught Rd. C.
Des Voeux Rd. C.
Bonham Strand E.

TO WESTERN MARKET
Western Market
TO MAN MO TEMPLE
MAN MO TEMPLE

The Center

CENTRAL
Queen's Pier
Star Ferry Pier
City Hall
STATUE SQ.
Jardine House
Two IFC
Harbour View St.
Exchange Square
CENTRAL
Legislative Council Building
The Landmark
Chater Garden
Chater Rd.
Murray Rd.
Jackson Rd.
Bank of China Tower
Cheung Kong Centre

SOHO
LAN KWAI FONG
Wellington St.
Hollywood Rd.
Old Bailey St.
Wyndham St.
Staunton St.
Elgin St.
Wing Wah Ln.
D'Aguilar St.
Wo On Ln.
Shelley St.
Queen's Rd. C.
Mid-Levels Escalator
Lower Albert Rd.
Upper Albert Rd.
Cotton Tree Dr.
Garden Rd.
Kennedy Rd.

Zoological and Botanical Gardens
Hong Kong Park
Flagstaff Museum of Teaware

ADMIRALTY
Lung Wui Rd.
Harcourt Rd.
Queensway
Queen's Rd. E.
Queensway Plaza
Pacific Place
Tamar St.
Justice Dr.

Victoria Peak Tram
US 5
TO VICTORIA PEAK TOWER (300 m)
Old Peak Rd.

WAN CHAI
Wan Chai Sports Ground
Wan Chai Swimming Pool
China Resources Building
Central Plaza
Hong Kong Convention and Exhibition Centre
HKCEC Extension
Hong Kong Arts Centre
Hong Kong Academy for Performing Arts
Immigration Tower
Harbour Rd.
Expo Dr.
Expo Dr. C.
Hung Hing Rd.
Fleming Rd.
Tonochy Rd.
Stewart Rd.
Marsh Rd.
O'Brien Rd.
Lockhart Rd.
Hennessy Rd.
Jaffe Rd.
Gloucester Rd.
Luard Rd.
Fenwick St.
Fenwick Pier St.
Arsenal St.
Ship St.
Johnston Rd.
Wan Chai Rd.
Wood Rd.
Tin Lok Ln.

CAUSEWAY BAY
Victoria Park
Victoria Park Rd.
Gloucester Rd.
Leighton Rd.
Paterson St.
Yee Wo St.
Caroline Hill Rd.
Pennington St.
Jardine's Bazaar
Yun Ping Rd.
Lee Garden Rd.
Percival St.
Russell St.
Canal Rd.
Wong Nai Chung Rd.
Tin Tau
Excelsior Hotel
Noon Day Gun
Cross Harbour Tunnel
Times Square
Happy Valley Racecourse
TO TIN HAU TEMPLE & 5 (400m)

WAN CHAI-HUNG HOM FERRY
WAN CHAI-TSIM SHA TSUI FERRY
CENTRAL-TSIM SHA TSUI EAST HOVERFERRY
CENTRAL-HUNG HOM FERRY
HIGH SPEED STAR FERRY TO DISCOVERY BAY

TRAMS

0   500 yards
0   500 meters

Road Central from Sheung Wan, it becomes **Harcourt Road** as it passes through Central and Admiralty, morphs into **Gloucester Road** in Wan Chai, and finally takes a sharp right-angle turn when it hits **Victoria Park** in Causeway Bay.

In **Sheung Wan** (上環), Des Voeux Rd. Central and Queen's Rd. Central run parallel to Connaught Rd. Central. Roughly three blocks south of Queen's Rd. Central, Hollywood Rd. marks the edge of the **Soho** ("South of Hollywood Rd.") district, with the **Mid-Level** district further south and **Lan Kwai Fong** further east. In **Central** (jung waan; 中環) and **Admiralty** (gam jung; 金鐘), Des Voeux Rd. Central and Queen's Rd. Central merge to become **Queensway.** Most Central landmarks are easy to find using the **Star Ferry Pier** as a reference point. Queensway continues eastward into **Wan Chai** (灣仔) as Hennessy Rd. and intersects with Fleming Rd., which runs north-south from the tram tracks to the waterfront. Hennessy Rd., which turns into Yee Wo. St., roughly divides the **Causeway Bay** (tung lo waan; 銅鑼灣) area into two sections, with **Times Square** and **Happy Valley** to the south and Victoria Park to the north.

SOUTHERN HONG KONG ISLAND. The southern side of Hong Kong Island is separated from the north by vast stretches of public parks. Most attractions in **Stanley** (chek chyu; 赤柱), including its famous market, are on Stanley Main St., an intricate thread of connected lanes. **Aberdeen** (heung gong jai; 香港仔) is a short skip to the west. Between Stanley and Aberdeen, **Deep Water Bay** (sam seui waan; 深水灣) and **Repulse Bay** (chin seui waan; 淺水灣) have the island's most famous beaches. In the southeastern peninsula, **Shek O** (石澳) is a rural respite.

ACCOMMODATIONS

Accommodations on Hong Kong Island, apart from a few semi-affordable options in Causeway Bay, are usually at least twice as expensive as the guesthouses on Kowloon peninsula.

Ma Wui Mt. Davis Youth Hostel (HI) (☎2817 5715 or 2788 1638) is far, far away on top of Mt. Davis Path, off Victoria Rd., in Kennedy Town. A shuttle runs to the hostel from the Macau Ferry Terminal in Sheung Wan (20min.; 9:30am, 4:30, 7, 9, 10:30pm; HK$10). If you miss the shuttle, be warned: a 50min. uphill walk to the only inexpensive option on Hong Kong Island awaits. Large, clean dorm rooms and an upbeat communal atmosphere. Great views of the ocean from an open yard and picnic area. Common kitchen, bath, phone, A/C, linen. Simple chores required daily. Lights out 11pm. Curfew midnight. Call ahead. Single-sex dorms HK$65; doubles HK$150; quads HK$300. ❶

Wang Fat Hostel, Paterson Bldg., 47 Paterson St., 3rd fl., Flat A2, Causeway Bay (☎2895 1015; WangFath@netvigator.com). MTR: Causeway Bay. Expensive anywhere else, but it's a good deal on Hong Kong Island. If you don't want to sacrifice your legs to Ma Wui, Wang Fat is the next-best budget option. Clean standard rooms popular with backpackers. A/C, TV, phone, free Internet. 4-bed single-sex dorms HK$150; singles HK$220, with bath HK$250; doubles HK$250/HK$300. ❷

Jetvan Traveller's House, Fairview Mansion, 51 Paterson St., Flat 4A, Causeway Bay (☎2890 8133 or 2984 8539). MTR: Causeway Bay. Welcoming proprietors and clean rooms make this guesthouse well worth the few extra bucks. Rooms come with A/C, phone, towels, linen, and TV. Shared fridge and microwave in the reception area. Singles HK$250, with bath HK$300; doubles with bath HK$350; triples HK$450. ❹

Noble Hostel, Great George Bldg., 27 Paterson St., Flat A3, 17/F, Causeway Bay (☎2576 6148). MTR: Causeway Bay. Steps away from the station. Rooms smell slightly of smoke, but are otherwise perfectly acceptable. All your standard amenities, with space to breathe and windows letting in quite a bit of light. A/C, phone, and TV. Some rooms come with fridges. Singles HK$270 and up; doubles HK$320 and up. ❹

🍴 FOOD

Hankering for a taste of Russian caviar, Japanese *sashimi*, or Argentinian steak? Hong Kong Island caters to all tastes, though not all pockets. In Soho, candle-lit bistros sit next to modern home-furnishings shops, each one more expensive and stylish than the last. Coffee shops and cafes catering to lunching yuppies and shoppers abound in Central and Admiralty. The only thing you might have trouble finding is a decent, affordable Chinese meal.

SHEUNG WAN

El Taco Loco, 7-9 Staunton St. (☎2522 1239), just off the Mid-Level Escalators. One of Soho's more down-to-earth options. A crispy pork taco with chili sauce, cilantro, and onions is only HK$16. Vegetarian burrito HK$28. Open daily 10am-10pm. ❷

Golden Leaf Restaurant, Alliance Bldg., 130-131 Connaught Rd. (☎2121 0506). An extensive selection of European, Chinese, and Malaysian food at low prices. The menu includes chicken satay (HK$45), Indonesian fried rice (HK$38), and set meals (all under HK$70). Open daily 8am-10:30pm. ❸

CENTRAL

🍴 Happy Bean Restaurant, 48 Cochrane St. (☎3184 0213). The Happy Bean sits as a beacon of hope for budget travelers in search of delicious local food. In addition to classic dishes like braised tofu with diced chicken and mushrooms on rice (HK$27), Happy Bean offers daily set menus (breakfast HK$18; afternoon tea HK$20; dinner including rice, soup, and vegetables HK$38). Open daily M-Sa 10am-10pm. ❷

Tsim Chai Kee Noodle, 98 Wellington St. (☎2850 6471). Known by locals as the "10-dollar noodle shop," Tsim Chai Kee is famous for its cheap and hearty portions of noodles and vegetables. Variety is not their strong suit, and tables are tiny and often shared, but with these prices, no one seems to care. Prawn dumpling, fish ball, or sliced beef noodle soup HK$10. Chinese vegetables HK$5. Open 9am-9pm. ❷

Nha Trang Vietnamese Cuisine, 88-90 Wellington St. (☎2581 9992). Delicious food in a hip, chic setting and prices that won't break the bank. Thin-sliced beef noodle soup HK$34. Vietnamese spring rolls HK$40. Open daily noon-10:30pm. ❸

WAN CHAI

🍴 Sonthra Kebab, Yeu On Bldg., 146-148 Lockhart Rd., Shop C2. MTR: Wan Chai, exit A1 or A2; entrance is just around the corner from Lockhart Rd. on O'Brien Rd. This hole-in-the-wall might not look like much, but the food is delicious and fresh, and the proprietors friendly and helpful. An excellent stop for a quick meal. They've managed to squeeze in a couple tables. Try the vegetable falafel (HK$35) or samosa (HK$25). Open daily 11:30am-midnight. ❷

Wing Fat Restaurant, 117 Hennessy Rd. (☎2865 5987), across from the soccer pitch and basketball courts. Chinese dishes in an area otherwise packed with restaurants cooking items like "fried steak with cheese sauce." Wing Fat offers great set meals like fried spicy squid or eggplant with salted fish for HK$35. ❸

CAUSEWAY BAY

Friends' Cafe, Percival House, 83 Percival St., 2nd fl. (☎2890 6799). The perfect place to escape the noise and clamor of Times Sq., this small restaurant looks out onto the bustle below from a 2nd fl. remove. In addition to inexpensive noodle and rice dishes (HK$30 and up), the cozy and stylish restaurant serves a different HK$56 set meal every day. Open M-Th noon-midnight, F-Su noon-2am. ❸

Fantasy Vegetarian Restaurant, 66 Electric Rd. (☎2887 3886 or 2807 0569). MTR: Tin Hau, Electric Rd. exit. One of the few vegetarian places in town features an English menu and friendly English-speaking staff members. The line-up includes noodles (HK$17-29); soups (HK$30-40); vegetables with mock kidney (HK$52); and zucchini, black fungus, and mock meat (HK$48). The mock meat is not only novel—it's actually good! Open daily 10am-10pm; dim sum stalls 9am-11:30pm. ❸

STANLEY

New Star Restaurant, 40-42 Stanley Main St. (☎2813 9982). From the bus station, walk down toward the waterfront, take a left at the Delifrance, and walk 5min. up Stanley Main St. The New Star has a small fishing-town feel, which suits the seafood dishes (HK$38) just fine. The menu will surprise you with its low prices and variety—oatmeal with ham for HK$18, anyone? Open daily 8am-8pm. ❷

Lucy's, 64 Stanley Main St. (☎2813 9055). Your wallet will not appreciate Lucy's, but wallets don't actually have feelings; it'd be hard to find food this good (or gourmet) anywhere else. Avocado and mozzarella salad HK$75. Lamb shank with cinnamon and lemon served with mashed potato HK$190. Eggplant with mixed herbs and feta cheese in a filo pastry HK$170. Open daily noon-3pm and 7-10pm. ❺

⊙ SIGHTS

SHEUNG WAN 上環

It was here in Sheung Wan that the Royal Navy first raised the Union Jack in 1841. A testament to Hong Kong's composite culture, this area is rich in local character and overflows with little shops, streetside markets, and mildewing apartments. The **Macau Ferry Terminal** sits on the northern edge of the district. Farther south, on the corner of Ladder St. and Hollywood Rd., looms **Man Mo Temple,** where the lovelorn shake divination sticks to check on the state of their star-crossed destinies. Dedicated to the ancient gods of *Man* (文 ; "literature") and *Mo* (武 ; "warfare"), the temple also houses shrines to the city god and the 10 divine judges. *Feng shui* advice and palm-reading are available. (☎2540 0350. Open daily 8am-6pm. Free.)

Hollywood Road curves across the center of Sheung Wan, lined by shops selling antiques and Chinese artwork. (Open daily 10am-6pm.) The **Central Mid-Level Escalators,** the longest covered escalator in the world, follow Hollywood Rd. to the eastern edge of Sheung Wan, on Cochrane St. and Shelley St. A series of over 800m of moving stairs (and a total of 20 exits) transport residents down the hill (6-10am) and up again (10am-11pm). Bars and restaurants constantly sprout up on the hillside along the escalators, and toward the top is Hong Kong's own **SoHo.**

CENTRAL 中環

VICTORIA PEAK. The quintessential Hong Kong experience is a trip to Victoria Peak, or so all the brochures claim. At 396m above sea level, the Peak provides a spectacular view of Hong Kong, but the expensive shops and restaurants and dubious entertainment options in the mall adjacent to the viewing platforms are a bit off-putting. Nevertheless, as Hong Kong's skyscrapers are all owned by big companies and off-limits to laypeople, this is your best chance to get a great view of the city. Sitting quietly and absorbing the panoramic view from the Level Four terrace is free, as is walking the trails at the top. Binoculars are available on levels two, four, and five of the Peak Tower. The slow **Peak Tram** passes trees and buildings, which largely obscure any view to be had on the way up. *(33 Garden Rd., behind the Murray Bldg. A double-decker bus departs from the Central Star Ferry pier to the tram station daily* *every 15min. 7am-midnight. Alternatively, walk the 600m by following Garden Rd. away from the harbour. ☎ 2522 0922. Binoculars HK$2 per 5min. Tram departs every 10-15min. 7am-midnight; HK$20, round-trip HK$30; children 3-11 HK$6/HK$9; seniors over 65 HK$7/HK$14.)*

HONG KONG PARK. This park does its best to construct a pleasant green space, but it seems next to impossible to inspire serenity with busy Cotton Tree Drive, Citibank Plaza, and Hong Kong's tallest buildings only steps away. Still, the park is definitely worth a visit. A raised walkway allows visitors to walk through the **Edward Youde Aviary** and come eye-to-eye with the over 800 birds upon their tree-top perches. The view up through the aviary's netted roof sets tree branches against skyscrapers, placing the soaring parrot upon a backdrop of rooftops and corporate logos. *(Aviary open daily 9am-5pm. Pelican feeding 3 times per day.)* The park's other attractions include a **gallery**, the **Visual Arts Centre**, and the **Flagstaff Museum of Teaware,** which offers a comprehensive and innovative study of British and Chinese tea and tea customs. *(☎ 2869 0690. Video at noon, 2, 4pm; groups of 10 or more can inquire about additional screenings. Open M and W-Su 10am-5pm.)* The **Sports Centre** at the entrance near the Peak Tram has squash courts (HK$27 per hr.), badminton courts (HK$59 per hr.), and ping pong tables (HK$21 per hr.). *(Park ☎ 2521 5041. Open daily 6:30am-11pm. Gallery ☎ 2869 6690. Open M-Tu and Th-Su 10am-5pm. Visual Arts Centre ☎ 2521 3008. Open M and W-Su 10am-9pm. Wheelchair accessible. All free.)*

ZOOLOGICAL AND BOTANICAL GARDENS. Both flora and fauna enthusiasts and primate lovers will take pleasure in the Zoological and Botanical Gardens. In addition to energetic gibbons and big orange orangutans, there's a jaguar enclosure, a reptile house, and an aviary. The gardens are fairly uncrowded on weekdays, which is surprising given the vast array of animals and plants. The herb garden is less than thrilling. *(Just off Garden Rd., a 10min. walk from the Hilton past St. John's Cathedral. The main entrance is at the intersection of Garden Rd. and Upper Albert Rd. Stick to the maze of pedestrian walkways and keep your eyes alert for signs pointing to the gardens. ☎ 2530 0153. Open daily 6am-7pm; greenhouse open 9am-4:30pm.)*

TWO INTERNATIONAL FINANCE CENTER. Completed in 2003, Two International Finance Center is Hong Kong's tallest building—at least for now. Its 420m and 88 stories, constructed by over 3500 workers from around the world, will be surpassed by another skyscraper due to be finished in 2007. Unfortunately, you can't ascend the IFC, but you can get a sense of how the other half lives by wandering through the shiny line-up of brand-name stores in the IFC luxury mall. *(Between the Star Ferry Concourse and the New Ferry Piers in Central. www.ifc.com.hk.)*

WAN CHAI 灣仔

CENTRAL PLAZA. The second-tallest building in Hong Kong, Central Plaza is easily spotted from most locations on the island. Its color beams serve as a clock; the color of the bottom light indicates the hour: red 6pm, white 7, purple 8, yellow 9, pink 10, and green 11pm. If the top light is a different color, it's a quarter past; if the top two and bottom two lights differ, it's half past; if the top three match, the time is 45min. past the hour; and when all four lights match, it is on the hour.

HONG KONG CONVENTION AND EXHIBITION CENTRE (HKCEC). This grandiose waterfront building stands as an impressive testament to Hong Kong's ability to put on a good show. Opened in 1997 for the handover ceremonies, the Centre is a sprawling marvel of glass, sunlight, and expansive floor-to-ceiling windows. The convention space is mainly used for trade shows and occasional concerts, but the constant buzz of business and commerce fills the center's numerous offices and conference rooms. The building was supposedly designed to look like a bird on the brink of flight, though many claim it resembles the Sydney Opera House.

Exhibits, cafes, and restaurants keep the HKCEC active at night. (☎ 2582 8888. No slippers or shorts. Open 24hr.) The outdoor garden and waterfront promenade come as a welcome surprise in this urban desert. The **Hong Kong Arts Centre,** to the right as you leave the HKCEC, hosts events ranging from independent film screenings to Shakespeare performances. Students' artwork, interactive poetry exhibits, or contemporary art shows hang in the exhibition space. (Program inquiries ☎ 2582 0202, URBTIX hotline 2734 9009. Box office open daily 10am-6pm.)

CAUSEWAY BAY 銅鑼灣

VICTORIA PARK. At dawn and dusk, this haven of sprawling green lawns and leafy boulevards is peppered with *tai chi* devotees, some wielding swords, moving in extremely slow motion. Sports facilities include tennis courts, a roller-skating rink, a bowling green, and a swimming pool. Jogging trails wind through spacious lawns, an aviary, and a topiary garden. (Enter on Gloucester Rd., opposite the Park Lane Hotel. ☎ 2890 5824. Park open 24hr. Roller-skating rink open daily 9am-11pm; HK$16 per hr. Swimming pool open daily 6:30am-noon and 1-10pm; HK$19, children HK$9.)

NEAR VICTORIA PARK. A single footbridge in the northwest corner of the park, along the path from the Model Boat Pool, leads to **Causeway Bay Typhoon Shelter,** where floating homes bob next to sleek yachts. Northeast of the park, an amble down Victoria Park Rd. leads to the famous **Noon Day Gun,** featured in Noel Coward's 1924 satire *Mad Dogs and Englishmen.* In the 19th century, the Jardine Matheson Company, Hong Kong's oldest British trading company, angered naval officers by obtaining its own private artillery. The navy punished this unlicensed show of military might by making Matheson fire the gun every day at noon—a tradition that continues to this day. (MTR: Causeway Bay. Go down into the carpark right of the entrance to the Excelsior Hotel on Gloucester Rd.; signs direct you through a tunnel, which goes under the road to the gun. Open daily 7am-midnight.)

HAPPY VALLEY RACECOURSE. Built in the mid-1840s when horseracing first became popular among wealthy residents, horseracing (or more specifically, horse gambling) has since become a pastime for the masses. The racecourse lends its name to the **Pau Ma Tei** (跑馬地) area, which literally means "racing horse grounds," although the English name of "Happy Valley" may be equally revealing. Horseracing is so steeped in Hong Kong culture that a tagline for continuity after the handover promised that "the horses would keep on racing." Besides the 14-lane track, the complex pays homage to itself with the **Hong Kong Racing Museum** on the second floor, which tells the story behind one of Hong Kong's greatest passions with lots of hands-on exhibits. (MTR: Causeway Bay, exit A. 20min. walk via Leighton Rd. and Morrison Hill Rd. Racecourse ☎ 2966 8111. Museum ☎ 2966 806. Museum open Su and Tu-Sa 10am-5pm; race days 10am-12:30pm. Races Sept.-June W nights and Sa-Su. HK$10.)

ABERDEEN 香港仔

PROMENADE. The Aberdeen Promenade, a very small version of the TST walkway, passes junks, *sampan,* and teenagers fishing in waters clearly marked with pollution warnings. The iconic **Jumbo Floating Restaurant,** the self-proclaimed "most luxurious floating restaurant in the world," offers overpriced seafood. Little old ladies waylay tourists near the bus stop for *sampan* cruises (HK$40-50 per 30min.) around the harbor. (Bus #70 runs every 6-15min. 6am-midnight between Central and Aberdeen; HK$4.7.)

OCEAN PARK (hoi yeung gung yun; 海洋公園). Hong Kong's premier amusement park (at least until Disneyland opens) has an "upper" and "lower" section, connected by a cable car that offers excellent views of the sea. In the highlands, check out the shark aquarium and **Atoll Reef,** where 400 species of fish stare at visitors from behind a glass gallery. Other than some nerve-wracking roller coasters, most rides don't live up to expectations, unless you're looking for something calming. In the lowlands, the most worthwhile sights are the **Goldfish Pagoda,** with some seriously strange-looking fish, and Hong Kong's beloved **giant pandas,** An An (安安) and Jia Jia (佳佳). To exit the park, you must either descend by cable car to the main entrance, or take extremely long escalators (an experience in and of itself) down the hill to the **Middle Kingdom,** the section of the park that recreates "imperial China." *(A Citybus shuttle runs from the Aberdeen bus terminal to Ocean Park for HK$12. Take bus #70 from Exchange Sq. in Central or bus #72 from Causeway Bay; get off at the stop after the Aberdeen Tunnel and follow the blue signs. A Citybus runs directly to the park gate from Admiralty. ☎ 2552 0291; www.oceanpark.com.hk. Open daily 10am-6pm. HK$140, 1st child ages 3-11 free with purchase of adult ticket, additional children ages 3-11 HK$70.)*

STANLEY 赤柱

Stanley's main attraction is **Stanley Market.** Stanley Main St. runs through clean stalls and petite shops full of every garment known to man, from snake-skin boots to the street's specialty, silk pajamas. The frenzied clusters of stalls and restaurants that line this street make it nearly impossible to use addresses to navigate. **Stanley Main Beach,** just east of the market along Stanley Beach Rd., is often packed on weekends. **St. Stephen Beach** is a 10min. walk south along Wong Ma Kok Rd., away from the market and toward the hills. From the bus station terminus on Stanley Village St., turn left and follow the signs in pink print. The road to the right of the market, as you approach from the bus station, leads to a shopping center. Follow the water to a tiny **Tin Hau Temple,** removed from it all, above waves crashing on the rocks. (To get to Stanley, take bus #973 from the Star Ferry Pier in TST or Express Bus #260 from the Star Ferry Pier in Central. Market open daily 9am-6:30pm. Shower facilities available at Stanley Beach. Beaches open 24hr.)

▓DEEP WATER BAY 深水灣 AND REPULSE BAY 淺水灣

Deep Water Bay beach has a long coast, a beautiful view, and powdery soft sand. (Bus #6 runs every 10-30min. from Central Exchange Sq. to the Deep Water Bay stop.; HK$5.3.) **Repulse Bay** (literally, "Shallow Water Bay") has warm, swimmable waters, with resort-style apartments inhabited by rich businessmen looming on the shores. Sturdy nets anchored offshore keep out unwanted sea creatures, and two large statues of Gwan Tum and Tin Mau, traditional protectors of local fishermen, guard the shores. There's a **golf course** behind the beach and a scenic **promenade** stretching off to the left, facing the water. (Bus #6 to Repulse Bay Beach. Bus Bus #73 connects Aberdeen, Repulse Bay, and Stanley; every 15-25min., HK$5.8.)

SHEK O 石澳

On the southeast coast of Hong Kong Island, not far from Stanley, lies the lovely **Shek O Beach.** Crowded with oiled-up sun-worshippers and fanned by breezes filtering down from the mountains, this long, well-maintained stretch of shore is one of the most popular and beautiful beaches on Hong Kong Island. The small array of shops behind the beach has various services and cheap food. (Dishes HK$25 and up.) Stake out a spot and rent an umbrella tent (HK$30 per day). Several shops rent bikes for exploring the nearby hills. (HK$15-20 per hr., HK$35-40 per day.) Wander around the markets in **Shau Kei Wan** if you have time. Allow at least 2hr. to get to the beach if you're going this way. *(From Central, bus #309 runs Su every 30min.; 50min., HK$11. On weekdays, ride the tram to its last stop and board bus #9 at the Shau Kei Wan MTR Station, A1 or A2 exits; every 15-30min. 6am-11pm; HK$4.2, A/C HK$6.20.)*

🏛 MUSEUMS

Hong Kong Museum of Coastal Defense, 175 Tung Hei Rd., Shau Kei Wan (☎2569 1500). MTR: Shau Kei Wan. Open M-W and F-Su 10am-5pm. HK$10, students and seniors HK$5; W free.

Police Museum, 27 Coome Rd., Mid-Level (☎2849 7019). Take bus #15 from Exchange Sq. in Central to the intersection of Stubbs Rd. and Peak Rd.; follow the signs to the Mid-Level Escalators. Open Su 9am-5pm, Tu 2-5pm, W-Sa 9am-5pm. Free.

Hong Kong Correctional Services Museum, 45 Tung Tau Wan Rd., Stanley (☎2147 3199). Take bus #260 from Central and get off in Stanley on Tung Tau Wan Rd. Open Tu-Su 10am-5pm. Free.

University of HK Museum and Art Gallery, University of Hong Kong, 94 Bonham Rd. (☎2975 5600). Take bus #23 from Pacific Place in Admiralty to the university main gate on Bonham Rd.

🛍 SHOPPING

Whereas Kowloon shopping is all about chaotic markets and bargain buys, shopping on Hong Kong Island is a more refined brand of designer boutiques and marbled atriums for the dedicated followers of Vuitton and Versace. Luxury shopping centers such as **Pacific Place** in Admiralty, the IFC mall (p. 569), and the almost clichéd **Landmark** in Central, favored by celebrities and fashion-conscious "OLs" (office ladies) alike, are tried-and-true odes to conspicuous consumption. For more varied and down-to-earth options, neon-lit **Causeway Bay,** one of Hong Kong Island's premier shopping areas, has a hectic **Times Square** and giant Japanese department stores like **Sogo** and **Mitsukoshi,** both on Hennessy Rd. The best time for intense wallet-bleeding is during the summer **"shopping festival"** season (July-Aug.), when hours are extended, prices are slashed, and even high-end stores sport large gaudy sale signs.

Hong Kong Island only has a few cheap markets where customers can bargain. The **Li Yuen Street Market** in Central is split into two sections. **Li Yuen Street East,** between Des Voeux Rd. and Queen's Rd., has excellent bargains for traditional Chinese dresses. **Li Yuen Street West,** parallel to and one block down from Li Yuen St. East, has more shops than its sister street and a selection of shoes that will make footwear fans delirious. (Open daily 7am-10pm.) The **Graham Street Fruit and Vegetable Market,** off Queen's Rd. between the Union Bank and the V. Heun Building, is a fruit connoisseur's fantasy. If Soho's trendiness starts to make your head spin, take a walk down Graham St. and return to the real world of fresh tofu and corn on the cob. (Open daily 6am-8pm.) Farther west, the indoor **Western Market** is a cloth alley of experienced traditional tailors. For a more uncanny experience, **Dried Seafood Street,** the stretch of Des Voeux Rd. West between Sheung Wan and Kennedy Town, consists of rows of shops, all selling dried seafood. Pungent smells abound, and you're likely to spy some pretty unusual-looking creatures of the sea (or parts of them), from seahorses to shark's fin. (Open daily 9am-6pm.)

🎵 NIGHTLIFE

Before heading out for a night on the town, stop by a restaurant, hotel, coffee shop, or newsstand and pick up a free copy of *HK Magazine* or *bc magazine,* two English-language weeklies with up-to-date entertainment and event listings.

CENTRAL AND ADMIRALTY

The L-shaped **Lan Kwai Fong** (蘭桂坊) area overflows with trendy restaurants and bars, filled to saturation with expats, businessmen, socialites, and the odd backpacker or prep school kid. From Thursday to Sunday, the neighborhood is a veritable sea of people milling about in the streets, paying the exclusive cover charges and bar tabs at posh establishments. It's certainly a buzzing scene, but even locals complain that the infamous Lan Kwai Fong is losing its edge. Most bars and clubs blare the same bland music and pour the same expensive drinks to drunk, bored expats. For a less stifling atmosphere, some of the best nightlife options can actually be found just outside of Lan Kwai Fong.

Fringe Club, 2 Lower Albert Rd. (☎2521 7485; www.hkfringeclub.com). The Fringe is one of Hong Kong's best live music venues and cultural centers. Local bands and indie artists play on the bar's small stage most F-Sa nights. Also houses the popular **M at the Fringe** restaurant and 2 contemporary art galleries. Pick up a calendar to find out about special events. Vegetarian lunch buffet (HK$75) M-F noon-2:30pm. Drinks HK$35-55. Happy hour M-Sa 4-9pm. Open M-Th noon-midnight, F-Sa noon-2am.

Yumla, Harilela House, 79 Wyndham St., lower basement (☎2147 2382). Live DJ Th-Sa nights, and, what's more, it's usually a *good* DJ. No top-40 hits here, just eminently danceable funk, techno, reggae, and electronica. The crowd is young and energetic, and there's no one parked at the front door waiting to turn people away. Outdoor patio provides a nice break from the action.

C-Plus, 27-29 Wellington St., basement. (☎2869 9990), down a small alley connecting Wellington St. and Stanley St. C-Plus revels in its removed location, creating a chilled-out and friendly atmosphere for its young and trendy patrons. Nice lighting, plush seating, friendly waitstaff, and occasional special events. Drinks HK$48-58. Open M-F 5:30pm-2am, Sa-Su 5:30pm-3am.

Propaganda, 1 Hollywood Rd., lower ground fl. (☎2868 1316). Hong Kong's highest-profile gay club has equally high cover charges to match. The fun doesn't really get started on weekend nights until after 2am, but once the dancing fervor picks up, especially on Saturday's "Boy's Night," this is a happening place to be. Beer HK$50-56.

Edge, The Centrium, 60 Wyndham St. (☎2523 6690). If you just want to dance, the Edge is for you: the large dance floor is completely packed on weekend nights. A cheesy band playing cheesy pop brings you back to the early- and mid-90s. Live music every night. Happy hour 6-10pm (beer HK$31); after 10pm, beer becomes a pricey HK$61. Open M-Th until 2am, F-Su until 6am.

THE LOCAL STORY

KOOL KULU

DJ Kulu, a well-known Hong Kong personality, is immediately recognizable by his long beard. After spending decades as a photographer, club owner, and DJ in the UK, he returned to his native Hong Kong in 1999. He now spins every weekend at Hong Kong's most happening clubs.

LG: How does it feel to be such a different age from most DJs?

A: Sometimes I say, "Kulu, you're 60, what are you doing?" But I feel like I'm 20. I feel like I get along with young people better than with people my age.

LG: Does Hong Kong have a distinct musical style?

A: Hong Kong people like their pop music and they make their own pop music. It basically caters to the karaoke market, which Hong Kong also loves. It's a part of the local color. It was hard at first, coming from London, but I realize that I'm in a place with a totally different culture.

LG: How has Hong Kong changed since you've gotten back?

A: Things are gradually changing. Hong Kong is a business center and before, it was very much about money and material, full on, non-stop, 365 days a year. Now Hong Kong has mellowed out a bit. Hong Kong had a bad time after 1997—the property and stock markets weren't good. People were given a chance to slow down and once they got that space, they started to think of alternative lifestyles.

Club 64, 12-14 Wing Wah Ln., ground fl. (☎2523 2801), off D'Aguilar St. Popular with both expats and backpackers, this laid-back bar is normally filled to the brim on weekends. Happy hour daily noon-9pm (beer HK$22). Drinks HK$40-60. Open M-Th noon-2am, F-Sa 10am-3am, Su 6pm-1am.

WAN CHAI

As the famed setting of Richard Mason's novel *The World of Suzie Wong*, Wan Chai will never quite shake its image as a seedy, dissolute area filled with brothels, bars, and furloughed sailors. Though Wan Chai has largely shed its sordid past, at night it's still hard to not notice the strip clubs, the beckoning females in extremely short skirts, and the unsavory-looking characters standing outside brightly lit hostess establishments. Many bars and clubs do work hard to put forth a cleaner, polished facade, and a "ladies' night"—for better or worse—is almost ubiquitous in Wan Chai's bars. Wan Chai can be fun, but be prepared to see it all go down.

🏶 The Wanch, 54 Jaffe Rd. (☎2861 1621). MTR: Wan Chai, Lockhart Rd. exit. A tiny upbeat place that managed to squeeze in a stage, making it look even tinier. The Wanch gives local bands a place to play. The bands aren't always good, but they're always happy to be there. Join in the fun and try your hand at rocking out on stage on Jam Night (Th). Happy hour M-Th noon-10pm, F noon-9pm (drinks HK$24-30). Open M-Th 11am-2am, F-Sa 11am-3am, Su noon-late.

Joe Bananas, 23 Luard Rd. (☎2529 1811), at Jaffe Rd. Despite the many rules—no furs, t-shirts, or shorts—this swinging spot is a Hong Kong landmark. Kitschy tropical decor with palm trees and tin-foil-covered walls. Asian, European, and New World food served until midnight. F unplugged; W popular ladies' night. Happy hour 7-10pm (2 for 1 drinks). 21+ after 6pm, but not ardently enforced. Open M-Sa noon-6am, Su 3pm-6am.

Carnegie's, 53-55 Lockhart Rd. (☎2866 6289). Leather, polished wood, musician posters, and a DJ that plays non-stop rock. This popular pub has specials on drinks every night. "Power Hour" on Sa night (drinks HK$20). Happy hour M-Sa 11am-10pm. Cocktails HK$40-150. Open M-Sa 11am-5am, Su 5pm-2am.

Cinta-J, 69 Jaffe Rd., Shop G-4, Malaysia Bldg. (☎2529 6622). A Southeast Asian restaurant and lounge with tasty food and jammin' cover band. Beware a strict dress code—no t-shirts or sandals. Live music M-Sa 5pm-1am, Su 11am-1am. Happy hour M-F 3-9pm (half-pints HK$15-16, pints HK$25-27). Open daily 11am-5am. Major credit cards accepted (HK$200 min. charge).

CAUSEWAY BAY

Causeway Bay isn't as happening as its nearby neighborhoods, but if small, relaxed bars are your scene, look to **Yiu Wa Street** and the streets running parallel off Matheson St., south of **Times Square,** for local hangouts. Be prepared to do more than one double-take: bars on these streets are almost identical, but can be comfortable enough for a quiet night out. Hotel bars and lounges provide little more variety. Die-hard sports fan should check out **Dickens,** 281 Gloucester Rd., downstairs and to the right of the Excelsior Hotel entrance. Autographed pictures of tennis, soccer, and marathon champions adorn the walls, and TVs broadcast the latest big sports event. (Beer HK$50. Happy hour 5-8pm. Dinner 6-10pm. Open Su-Th 11am-1:30am, F-Sa 11am-2:30am.)

🏶 WALKS ON HONG KONG ISLAND

Hong Kong's dense urban fabric is intriguingly nestled between sweeping, unspoiled hills and mountains. Over 40% of the territory has been preserved in public parks, most of which have intricate networks of extremely well-maintained trails. The "Magic Walks" series (HK$45-85), available in major bookstores and at

HKTB offices, cover most hiking options. The HKTB (p. 551) also distributes pamphlets about specific trails. The **Wilson Trail,** named after an ex-governor and inveterate hiker, starts in Stanley and ends in the New Territories; the **Shing Mun Jogging Trail,** the **Sai Kung Coddle Stones** path, and the southern valley of **Mount Butler** are some of the trail's highlights. The entire route takes 27hr. The **Wan Chai Green Trail** begins at the Wan Chai Old Post Office on Queen's Rd. East and ends at Stubbs Rd. Eleven educational stations along the trail point out plants of interest. The **Hong Kong Trail** passes through five country parks on Hong Kong Island, passing scenic views of some of the island's most beautiful areas.

NEW TERRITORIES 新界

Though most people associate Hong Kong with Kowloon and Hong Kong Island, the New Territories actually cover over two-thirds of the landmass. The quiet, somewhat rural, and somewhat reserved region stretches over 794km² of rugged mountains, country parks, unexplored beaches, and burgeoning cities. Home to almost half of Hong Kong's population, the area is rich in temples, rock carvings, hiking trails, cultural relics, and of course, housing developments. HKTB has free booklets that outline sights and hiking trails for the New Territories' nine districts.

◪ TRANSPORTATION

The best way to get around the New Territories is to use the KCR and MTR. Each stop has buses, minibuses, and taxis. The KCR East Rail runs south-north, beginning at Hung Hom and zigzagging through **Mong Kok, Sha Tin, Fotan,** the **Chinese University,** and **Tai Po,** ending at **Lo Wu** on the Chinese border. From Central, the MTR red line runs north, finishing at **Tsuen Wan.** Accessible by ferry or bus, **Tuen Mun,** a residential center in the far west, is connected to **Yuen Long** in the northeast by Light and West Rails. The beaches of **Sai Kung Peninsula** and **Clearwater Bay,** in the southeast corner, are accessible by bus #299 from University KCR Station.

◪ ACCOMMODATIONS

If you're headed to the New Territories to enjoy the beautiful parks or secluded natural spaces, staying overnight is definitely an option. Otherwise, the New Territories are also well connected to Kowloon by KCR and can make for a more peaceful and calming stay away from Hong Kong's urban congestion.

Ascension House, 33 Tao Fong Shan Rd., Sha Tin (☎2691 4196 or 9348 9776; ascend@netvigator.com). KCR: Sha Tin. Exit from station to the minibus terminus and take the pedestrian ramp to the left down to street level. Then do an about-face and walk with the ramp on your left toward some houses. Hike up the small stairs between 2 houses for about 15min. until you reach a small rotary and a road. Take the road to your right; you'll see a sign on the right directing you to the guesthouse. Taxi from station HK$25. Despite the long climb and less-than-central location, Ascension House is one of the best deals in Hong Kong. HK$125 gets you a comfortable dorm bed, 3 sit-down meals per day, free laundry, and Internet access. Run by 4 young, friendly Scandinavians who offer travel advice and organize free daytrips every Saturday. Affiliated with the local Christian Center, but participation in religious activities is optional. ❷

Bradbury Lodge (HI), 66 Tai Mei Tuk Rd., Tai Mei Tuk, Tai Po (☎2662 5123). KCR: Tai Po Market. Look for the sign and trail at the back of the bus terminal. Puts up guests who wish to stay at the Plover Cove Reservoir for the night. The lodge has a rustic and communal atmosphere with A/C, a large kitchen and dining area, TV, and a rooftop balcony with a splendid view of Plover Cove. Drawbacks include the 6 shared showers, squat toilets for up to 48 guests, and cleaning duties. Reception daily 7-10am and 3-11pm. Lockout 10am-noon. Lights-out 11pm. Reservations recommended on weekends. 8- and 12-bed dorms HK$55; doubles HK$150. ❶

Bradbury Hall (HI), 8 Tai Fong Rd., Chek Keng, Sai Kung (☎2328 2458). MTR: Choi Hung. Take a green minibus to Sai Kung, and bus #94 to Pak Tam Au bus station (ask the driver to drop you off). Look for signs directing you to Bradbury Hall; it's a scenic 45min. hike to the hostel. Mostly houses travelers interested in hiking around Sai Kung for multiple days. You can sleep out on the beaches all you want, but if sand pillows and mosquito attacks aren't your cup of tea, Bradbury Hall provides a clean, friendly alternative. Shared kitchen and barbecue pits. Reservations are essential. 6-, 8-, and 24-bed dorms with A/C, shared bath, and 24hr. hot water HK$45. Camping grounds HK$25. HI members only. ❶

🍴 FOOD

Sai Kung town overflows with **seafood** restaurants, many of which face the water on the boulevard near the bus terminus. Small junks pull up to the docks and unload their catch straight into restaurant tanks. The fare doesn't differ greatly from place to place; it might be better to choose a restaurant for a perfect ocean view. On the water's edge, dishes like prawns sauteed with chili run from HK$60, but farther inland you'll find cheaper options down the narrow alleys and streets. A good bet for a delicious meal is **Hung Kee Seafood Restaurant ❸**, 4-8 Sai Kung Hoi Pong Sq., where you can sit outside by the water or venture upstairs for dim sum (served until 4:30pm). In town, the original **Pepperoni's ❸**, 1592 Po Tung Rd., is probably the only reason to not eat seafood in Sai Kung. With additional locations in Stanley, Wan Chai, and Central, Pepperoni's makes a mean, if pricey, pie. Go at lunchtime for a cheaper set meal (HK$43) of tomato soup, a drink, and an 8-inch pizza. (☎2792 2083. Open daily 9am-11pm.)

Sha Tin isn't particularly welcoming to the budget traveler, but the delicious **food court ❷** in Grand Central Plaza is surprisingly cheap and varied. Most of the chains here are local ones, serving traditional Chinese dishes among the ubiquitous McDonald's and KFCs. The Sha Tin KCR has an exit directly into the mall; walk straight until you reach a set of stairs and walk down to the food court. If you take the escalator behind the stairs up one flight, you'll find **Maxim's Fast Food ❷**, Shop 240-244, phase 1, a very popular local chain with branches all over Hong Kong. (☎2697 3405. Chinese dishes HK$20 and up. Open daily 7am-10:30pm.)

🔆 SIGHTS

SAI KUNG 西貢

On a lazy Sunday afternoon, **Sai Kung** town feels like an old fishing village. Relaxed, foreigner-friendly, and filled with hikers, campers, and beach lovers, Sai Kung is a completely different world from the hustle, bustle, and heat of Kowloon and Hong Kong Island. The **country park** offers many hikes, some of which lead out to beautiful secluded beaches, the best in Hong Kong (according to proud locals and the tourist office).

For a convenient and enjoyable trek, start from Pak Tam Chung and follow Sai Wan Rd. The entire walk takes around 2½hr. and passes the **Sheung Yiu Folk Museum**, a recreation of rural life in a 19th-century Hakka village. (☎2792 6365. Open M and W-Su 9am-4pm. Free.) The paved road winds out toward **Sai Wan Beach**, whose isolated stretches of sand and warm, clear waters are the stuff dreams are made of. You can also take a taxi out, leaving you with a mere 30min. walk through a mangrove to get to the beach. Signs on the trail point to other secluded beaches along the coast. Just up from the beach, a few tiny restaurants can serve you dinner or furnish you with candy bars as reward for your long hike. You can also rent a room in a nearby house for around HK$250 a night. (MTR: Choi Hung, exit A2. Cross the street using the pedestrian overpass and walk away from the station until Lung Cheung Rd. Take green minibus #1A to Sai Kung Hoi Pong Sq., the bus terminus. The last minibus to Choi Hung or Mong Kok leaves Sai Kung around midnight. Bus #94 takes you to various destinations including Pak Tam Chung.) Built in honor of the Goddess of the Sea, the **Tin Hau Temple** is a popular place of worship for fishermen whose lives are inextricably bound to her will. (With the waterfront behind you, walk left from the bus station.)

If seclusion isn't your thing, the popular **Clearwater Bay Beaches No. 1** and **2** (ching sui waan; 清水灣), famed for pristine sands and clean turquoise waters, attract quite a crowd on weekends. Clearwater Bay comes fully equipped with showers, changing rooms, a first aid station, lifeguards, and a disturbingly high number of shark warning signs. Contact the **Chong Hing Water Sports Centre** (☎2792 6810) to windsurf, canoe, row a *sampan*, or kayak. (MTR: Diamond Hill. Bus #91 runs every 12-18min. 6am-10pm; HK$4.7, with A/C HK$6.5. Beach open 9am-6pm.)

SHA TIN 沙田

Sha Tin's **Shing Man River** is a popular venue for dragon boat racing during the **Dragon Boat Festival**. The **Bo Fook Ancestral Worship Halls** on Tai Po Rd. also count among Sha Tin's attractions. Situated in the mountains, these halls have a pristine tranquility that contrasts dramatically with the industrial sprawl below. Use the escalator at the base of the building for easy access.

■HONG KONG HERITAGE MUSEUM. This large and well-run museum has informative and creative exhibits on Hong Kong history, culture, and art. Permanent displays include Cantonese opera, contemporary Chinese painting, and ancient local rocks, while rotating exhibits focus on topics like the history of public housing. *(1 Man Lam Rd. KCR: Sha Tin. Free shuttle bus every 15min. from station on weekends and public holidays. ☎2180 8188. Open M and W-Sa 10am-6pm, Su 10am-7pm. HK$10, students and seniors HK$5; W free.)*

TEN THOUSAND BUDDHAS TEMPLE. A slightly unusual foray into the world of Buddhism, the Ten Thousand Buddhas Temple forgoes traditional austerity in favor of bizarre and surreal life-size statues of monks and deities. Visitors ascending the 450-odd steps will notice widely grinning or grimacing gold-enameled monks, many with brightly painted lips and bulging eyes. The main hall is home to an admittedly impressive number of small Buddha statues, but they pale in comparison to the gargantuan statue of a mysterious blue dog outside. *(KCR: Sha Tin. Exit through the left station entrance and follow the yellow signs. Open daily 9am-5pm.)*

SHA TIN RACECOURSE. Hong Kong's second horseracing mecca draws thousands of spectators on race days. In the center of the track sits **Penfold Park** and a bird sanctuary. *(KCR: Sha Tin. Take bus #888 from the station. Races W evenings and Sa-Su afternoons late Sept. to late June. Park open Su and Tu-Sa 9am-5pm. Closed on race days.)*

CHINESE UNIVERSITY (香港中文大學). Built into the side of a mountain in Ma Liu Shui, the lovely campus with surrounding green parks and peaceful lakes is also prime landslide territory during the monsoon season. The on-campus **art museum**, next to the university library and miniature hedge maze, has an extensive collection of modern and ancient Chinese art, including painting and ceramics. Exhibits change about every two months. *(KCR: University. A shuttle bus runs from the station to the center of campus every 30min. M-F 9am-5:15pm, Sa 9am-1am; HK$1. Shuttle ☎2609 7990. Art museum ☎2609 7416. Open M-Sa 10am-4:30pm, Su 12:30-5:30pm; closed on public holidays. Free admission and audio tour.)*

TSUEN WAN 荃灣

A bit of a spiritual and cultural center, temples in Tsuen Wan see more prayer and incense than any others in Hong Kong. Not surprisingly, the ever-expanding city has capitalized on its spiritual popularity and is the most expensive place to deposit the ashes of the departed. **Tai Mo Shan,** Hong Kong's tallest mountain at 958m, is also in Tsuen Wan.

WESTERN MONASTERY. The monastery, along with its neighbor, the famous **Yuen Yuen Institute,** is a colorful, sprawling temple complex dedicated to Confucianism, Buddhism, and Daoism. In the center, a large building contains 60 statues of deities, one for each year in the Chinese calendar cycle. Outside, a birthday chart helps determine which deity corresponds to your birth year. The complex is also home to a bonsai garden, a bronze statue of Confucius, and three of Hong Kong's largest "Precious Buddha" statues. On the second floor, the Western Monastery holds religious ceremonies that are sometimes open to tourists. *(MTR: Tsuen Wan, exit B. Follow the pedestrian overpass until the end; once on the street below, with your back to the station, take a left; make a right at Chung On St. Walk up the block, turn right at the corner, and the green minibus #81 to Lo Wai Village will be on your right. Monastery ☎ 2411 5111. Institute ☎ 2429 2220. Both open daily 9am-5pm. Free.)*

OTHER SIGHTS. A restored walled Hakka village dating back to 1786, **Sam Tung Uk Museum** now houses a variety of exhibits replicating Hakka cooking, living spaces, dress, and rice-harvesting techniques. A larger hall hosts exhibits on issues of local interest. *(2 Kwu Uk Ln. A 5min. walk from the Tsuen Wan station. ☎ 2411 2001. Open M and W-Su 9am-5pm. Free.)* From the Museum, follow the signs through **Tai Ming Ling Square** to **Man Mo Temple,** passing many interesting markets. The rafters of this small temple are filled with long-burning incense coils. According to *feng shui* tenets, the water gate just inside the main door opens on the first day of every month and during the full moon. Friendly English-speaking temple attendants can show you around and explain the temple's features. *(Open daily 8am-6pm. Free.)*

TAI PO 大浦

Tai Po is a typical New Territories town: a mess of construction, a marvel of identical apartments, and a stone's throw from stunning panoramic views of land and sea. **Plover Clove Reservoir** is a favorite for both hikers and picnickers. Just outside the bus terminus is an area for barbecuing and picnicking, a hostel (see **Accommodations,** p. 575), and a water sports center. The picnic area is open to everyone. The sports center requires guests to complete an instructional class before renting equipment. The reservoir itself offers a scenic vista of the water and both relaxing and challenging walks through the surrounding area. A nice low-key path begins next to the Bradbury Lodge, touring the reservoir in under 1hr. *(KCR: Tai Po Market, Uptown Plaza exit. Take the pedestrian underpass; hop on bus #75K at the far back corner of the bus station for a 50min. ride to the last stop, HK$3.6.)*

The **Hong Kong Railway Museum,** 13 Shung Tak St., in the old Tai Po Market Station Building erected in 1913, houses several historical railway carriages. *(KCR: Tai Wo. ☎ 2653 3455. Open M and W-Su 9am-5pm. Free.)*

KWAI TSING 葵青

The **Kwai Tsing** district, in the southwestern corner of the New Territories, consists of **Tsing Yi Island** and **Kwai Chung.** This unpretentious urban and industrial area has some worthwhile sights, including Hong Kong's pride and the world's longest road and rail suspension bridge, **Tsing Ma Bridge** (青馬大僑), connecting Tsing Yi, Lantau Islands, and the **Lantau Link View Point,** which overlooks Tsing Ma, Ting Kau Bridge, and the Ma Wan Channel. (MTR: Tsing Yi, exit 1A to Maritime Sq. Take minibus 304M to View Point. Open M-F 10am-5pm, Sa-Su 10am-6:30pm.) Another way to see the area is a hike along the **Kwai Tsing Reunification Health Trail,** which winds through Liuto Valley on Tsing Yi Island. (Take bus 248M from Maritime Sq.)

LANTAU ISLAND 大嶼山

Lantau Island's craggy mountains, isolated monasteries, giant Buddha statue, and wide open skies give Hong Kong's largest island an otherworldly feel. But even on the island it's hard to get away from city life entirely, and Lantau's days of serenity may be numbered. The new airport on Chek Lap Kok has made the island a required stop for most travelers, and the new Disneyland under construction in Penny's Bay in northwest Lantau is sure to bring in hordes of tourists upon its completion. On weekends, city dwellers come in droves to indulge in fresh seafood, visit temples, and picnic in the mountains. After daytrippers go home, quiet descends, leaving residents and hikers to marvel at the beautiful night sky.

TRANSPORTATION

Trains: Trains travel along the orange **Tung Chung line,** beginning at Hong Kong station and ending at Tung Chung MTR Station (HK$23).

Buses: E31 leaves from Tsuen Wan and Discovery Park to **Tung Chung MTR;** E32 leaves from Kwai Fong MTR via Tung Chung MTR to the **Chek Lap Kok** airport terminus. Both buses run every 10-20min. and cost HK$10.

Ferries: Ferries depart from **Pier 6** at the New Ferry Piers off Exchange Sq., west of the Star Ferry Concourse to **Mui Wo port.** Free schedules available from HKTB offices and the First Ferry ticket office. **Regular ferry** (1hr.; 6:10, 6:50am, every 2hr. 8:30am-4:30pm, 5:40, 6:30, 8, 8:30, 10:30pm; M-Sa HK$10.5, Su HK$15.7); **express ferry** (40min.; 12:30am, 3am, 2 every 2hr. 7:10am-11:50pm; M-Sa HK$21, Su HK$23).

Local Transportation: Mui Wo, Tung Chung, Pui O, Tong Fuk, Tai O, and Ngong Ping each have conspicuous bus stations with fares and schedules listed in English. Buses are run by the New Lantau Bus Co. (☎2984 9848). **Bus #1** goes from Mui O to Tai O (M-Sa HK$8, Su HK$11.8); 2 from Mui Wo to the Po Lin Monastery (HK$16); 3M from Mui Wo to Tung Chung (HK$10); 4 from Mui Wo to Tung Fuk (HK$5.8); 7P from Mui Wo to Pui O (HK$3.4); 23 from Tung Chung to the Po Lin Monastery (HK$16).

Taxis: Blue **taxis** are available at all bus stations, but because all the major roads spiral up the mountains in a leisurely fashion, taking a taxi is not recommended. Base fare HK$12 for the 1st 2km, HK$1.2 each additional 0.2km or 1min. of waiting time. Luggage HK$5 per piece.

Bike Rental: Friendly Bicycle Shop (☎2984 2278), behind McDonald's in Mui Wo. HK$10 per hr.; standard bike HK$25 per day, excellent bike HK$50. Students HK$5 discount on weekdays. Open M and W-Su 10am-8pm. **Bike Shop** (☎2984 2002), in the Silver Centre Bldg. facing the ferry terminal in Mui Wo. Provides free maps of the area. HK$10 per hr., HK$25 per day.

ORIENTATION AND PRACTICAL INFORMATION

Lantau Island is comprised of small towns that span the island's coast. On the northeast coast, **Discovery Bay** is a tight-knit community of high-income individuals who can afford to maintain a picture-perfect neighborhood. Along the eastern coast is Lantau's ferry port, **Mui Wo** (梅窩), also known as **Silvermine Bay.** A residential area along the southern coast, **Pui O** (貝澳) eventually leads to the famous beaches of **Tong Fuk Village.** On the west coast, **Tai O** (大澳) is an old fishing village.

Ngong Ping (昂坪), in the inner Western region of Lantau, is overlooked by the immense Tian Tan Buddha atop Po Lin Monastery. The quickly developing central town, **Tung Chung** (東涌), was previously the remote site of an old fort built to keep out opium traders. Now the site of the shiny new airport, **Chek Lap Kok** was once an insignificant appendage on the northwest coast hanging onto Lantau by a thin thread of land. The 2.2km-long **Tsing Ma Bridge** effectively links Chek Lap Kok, Lantau Island, and Hong Kong.

Government and financial services are concentrated in **Mui Wo** and **Tung Chung.** In Mui Wo, banks, **ATMs,** chain grocery stores, and 7-Elevens cluster around the square surrounding the bus station. Tung Chung MTR Station has a small bank with **ATM** machines. Mui Wo's police station, clinic, and post office are all in the same government complex. Walk toward Silvermine Bay beach on **Ngan Kwong Wan Road;** just after the bridge to the beach branches off Ngan Kwong Wan Rd., you will see a gray complex on the left labeled "Government Offices." Citygate Mall, attached to the MTR station, has a large **grocery store** on the bottom floor. The **police** (☎2984 1270) are in Rm. 215. A **clinic** (☎2984 2178) and **post office** are on the ground floor. (Open M-F 9am-4:30pm, Sa 9am-12:30pm.)

ACCOMMODATIONS

S.G. Davis Hostel (HI), Ngong Ping (☎2985 5610). From the Mui Wo bus station at the ferry port, take bus #2 to Po Lin Monastery, Ngong Ping. Follow the sign to the left of the Buddha statue; the hostel is a 7min. walk away. Extremely convenient for visits to the Big Buddha and hikes around the countryside (the trail up to Lantau Peak begins right outside the door). Rooms are as sparse as they get, with bare bunk beds and shared baths. Simple chores required. Curfew 11pm. Office open 7-10am and 4-11pm; the gate to the hostel is locked at all other times. Reservations recommended on weekends. Dorms HK$75, HI members HK$45; doubles HK$150. ❶

Jockey Club Mong Tung Wan Hostel (HI), Pui O (☎2984 1389). From the Mui Wo bus station, take bus #7 to Pui O. Follow the signs for the hostel on Chi Ma Wan Rd., which loops around the bus station; it's a 20min. walk on a paved road, followed by a 25min. walk on a hiking path—this is not the place to be lugging your 60lb. pack. Alternatively, take the ferry from Pier 6 (in Central) to Cheung Chau and hire a *sampan* (HK$100) to the jetty at Mong Tung Wan; the hostel is a few min. away. Within walking distance (45min.) of Pui O beach. Very basic single-sex 25-bed dorms, with bunk beds, thin mattresses, and serene environment. A pretty and secluded beach just steps away. Prices and curfew times same as at the S.G. Davis Hostel. ❶

Mui Wo Inn, 24 Tung Wan Tau Rd., Silvermine Bay/Mui Wo (☎2984 8597). From the Mui Wo bus station, walk toward Silvermine Bay beach; Tung Wan Tau Rd. runs along the beach. Well-equipped rooms have beach views, bathtub, refrigerator, TV, VCR, and A/C. There's a hot tub in front, but the (somewhat trash-ridden) beach is just steps away. Singles HK$280, waterfront singles HK$400; weekends HK$480/HK$600. ❹

FOOD

Mui Wo Square surrounding the bus station has a few Chinese restaurants tucked between the stores and many restaurants with excellent Middle-Eastern and Indian cuisine. The **Bahçe Turkish Restaurant** ❸ complements its tasteful Persian rugs and seat cushions with excellent and reasonably priced fare. Try the Turkish Ploughman's lunch (HK$40), an onion-, pepper-, and olive-omelette sandwich. The **Mui Wo Cooked Food Market,** also by the ferry terminal, consists of small blocks of restaurants that share an outdoor seating area. (Open daily 6am-midnight.)

Apart from Mui Wo, **Pui O** is your best bet for good food in the midst of rural Lantau. From Mui Wo bus station, take bus #7 to the Pui O bus terminus. A string of mostly Chinese restaurants lines the street opposite the bus station. If you want to eat as the Chinese do, take bus #1 from Mui Wo bus station and get off at **Tai O.** This small, densely populated fishing village is famous for its **seafood** restaurants.

For vegans, **Po Lin Monastery** in Ngong Ping is the place to eat. Walk away from the Big Buddha towards the Welto Temple; the **vegetarian restaurant ❷** is on your left. A standard meal ticket (combined with museum admission) costs HK$60, while a VIP ticket costs HK$120. The HK$23 snack ticket gets you a plate of fried noodles and two pieces of dim sum. (☎ 2985 5248. Noodles or tofu HK$20. Dim sum HK$10. Open daily 11:30am-5pm.)

The **Tung Chung** MTR station exits into the new Citygate Mall. On the other side of a Delifrance is the ▦**Catstreet Cafe ❸,** with outdoor seating, upscale decor, and decent prices. The menu includes both Western and Chinese dishes, like ox tongue with spiced salt for a mere HK$28. (☎ 2109 1131. Breakfast sets HK$18. Fried noodle lunch sets HK$34. Open daily 11am-10pm. MC/V.)

◉ SIGHTS

▦**TIAN TAN BUDDHA** (天壇大佛) **AND PO LIN MONASTERY** (寶蓮寺). Lantau Island's most popular sight, the giant Tian Tan Buddha statue is the largest outdoor seated bronze Buddha in the world. Opened to the public in 1993, the 220-ton statue is 26.4m tall, with a base that covers 3284m². Be prepared to walk up some 260 steps to view Big Buddha up close. High atop his altar, Buddha raises his majestic right hand, as if greeting his visitors, while peacefully watching over the lives of those below at the Po Lin Monastery. Every feature of the statue is symbolic: its broad forehead and elongated ears signify virtue, wisdom, and perfection. The museum inside the Buddha isn't particularly exciting, but has relics and informative exhibits. Purchase tickets at the foot of the statue and at souvenir stands next to the restaurant; tickets also entitle you to entrance to the museum and food from the restaurant. (In Ngong Ping. Take bus #2 from Mui Wo station at the pier. ☎ 2985 5248. Admission with snack ticket HK$23, meal ticket HK$60. Open daily 10am-6pm.)

SILVERMINE WATERFALL. A short walk from the ferry terminal in Mui Wo, Silvermine Waterfall is unknown even to many locals. A small pagoda is set up to view the crashing waters, and a path winds past small fields and clusters of homes. (Take a right out of the ferry terminal; continue down the road and turn right on Ngen Shek St. Follow Ngen Shek St. as it curves to the right, and then turn left onto Wong Tong Rd. Keep to the left at the 2 forks, and you'll soon hear the falls in the distance. The walk takes about 35min.)

▣ **BEACHES.** Accessible by bus #1, 2, and 7P on weekends, **Pui O beach** is popular with locals and equipped with showers, a snack stand, and bathrooms, but it's not exactly the cleanest beach on the island. The **Cheung Sha Upper beach,** accessible via bus #4 (specify to the driver that you're going to Cheung Sha *Upper* beach), has lovely views and good water quality. (Beach hotline ☎ 2414 5555. All beaches in Lantau open daily 9am-6pm.)

◪ HIKING LANTAU ISLAND

Lantau is rich in country parks and hiking terrain. A large map pointing out walking trails, campsites, and country parks often greets visitors to each town. For the dedicated hiker, E. Stokes's *Exploring Hong Kong's Countryside* is highly recommended (HK$80, available at HKTB main office and major bookstores). The

HKTB (p. 551) also publishes a free guide to five walking trails, one of which is on Lantau. **Mui Wo** is a good starting point, with a **Country Parks Information Post** in the ferry station. (Open M-F 8:30am-noon, Sa-Su 8:30am-4pm.) You should see signs behind the Po Lin Monastery leading you to various hiking trails.

The beauty of the surrounding misty mountains makes for inspirational hiking. The **Lantau Trail** passes **Sunset Peak** (869m), the second-highest mountain on Lantau. Early birds can catch the unforgettable sunrise from the top. Although the path can be dangerous when wet, the climb to **Po Lam Zen Monastery** (45min. from Po Lin Monastery) is manageable and winds through incredible scenery. The hike up **Lantau Peak** (934m) begins near Po Lin Monastery. Follow the path leading to the youth hostel and signs will direct you toward the peak. At the base of the climb, the cement pathway becomes an endless staircase of huge stones passing for steps—this 2hr. hike is not for the weak of knee. The view from the top is often not a view at all—you may be standing in the middle of a cloud. Nonetheless, the jungle-like vegetation and seemingly ancient path make this climb worthwhile.

🏞 LAMMA ISLAND 南丫島

Though Hong Kong and Lamma Islands are separated only by a few miles of water, Lamma might as well be an entire planet away. On one island, life never stands still; on the other, life is in a perpetually languorous state. Lamma shuns cars, business suits, and stress, glorying instead in the beach. Needless to say, Lamma is an escapist haven for expats in search of a more bohemian atmosphere.

🚍 TRANSPORTATION AND PRACTICAL INFORMATION. Lamma has a northern and a southern half held together by a strip of land. The port of arrival in the north is **Yung Shue Wan** (榕樹灣); in the south, **Sok Kwu Wan** (素罟灣). A **ferry** shuttles from Pier 4 at the **New Ferry Piers** in Central to Lamma (30min.; every hr. 6:30am-12:30am; M-Sa HK$10, Su HK$14). Lamma is so small that a walk from Yung Shue Wan to Sok Kwu Wan takes under 1hr. There are no cars on the island, and most people walk or bike. **Bikes** can be rented at **Hoi Nam** bicycle store in front of the Shai Po New Village street sign. (☎2982 2500. HK$15 per hr. Open daily 7am-11pm.) The **Bookworm Cafe** has free **Internet** for customers.

🏨 ACCOMMODATIONS AND FOOD. The **Man Lai Wah Hotel ❺**, right off the ferry terminal at Yung Shue Wan, has very comfortable and spacious rooms, many with balconies overlooking the bay. (☎2982 0220 or 2982 0600. A/C, bath, phone, and TV. Doubles HK$350, weekends HK$500 and up.) Don't be put off by the dingy linoleum floor and sleepy service at the **Lamma Vacation House ❷**, 29 Yung Shue Wan Main St., 1st fl. Cheaper rooms are hard to come by on Lamma, especially in such a convenient location. Standard rooms have A/C, bath, fridge, and TV. (☎2982 0427. Singles HK$150; doubles HK$200; weekends HK$500 and up.)

Lamma's undisputed culinary specialty is **seafood.** Restaurants showcasing entire aquariums of fish line the docks and walkways along the bay in **Sok Kwu Wan.** In **Yung Shue Wan,** they cluster around the ferry terminal. A reliable option is **Lamma Seaview Man Fung Restaurant ❹**, 5 Main St., your standard fresh-from-the-sea restaurant with giant groupers in the windows, outdoor seating, and, as promised, a view of the sea. (☎5982 0719. Seafood HK$55-100. Open daily 11am-10pm.)

For an alternative to seafood, you can cool your body with a pineapple smoothie (HK$30) at 📖**Bookworm Cafe ❸**, 70 Yung Shue Wan Main St., or warm your heart by chatting with the friendly proprietor. In addition to healthy sandwiches and salads (HK$40 and up), this hippie restaurant offers Internet, cheap secondhand books, and "a venue for spiritual and political discourse." (☎2982 4838. Open M, W, Sa-Su

10am-10pm, Tu and Th-F 10am-6pm.) **Deli Lamma** ❹, 36 Main St., serves hefty and high-quality portions of both Western and Indian delights and occasionally hosts typhoon-watching parties. (☎2982 1583. Veggie dishes HK$75-80. Open daily 9am-11pm.)

■ **HIKING.** The trail from **Yung Shue Wan** to **Sok Kwu Wan** passes breathtaking beaches and caves before emerging near the ferries bound for Central. From Yung Shue Wan, turn onto Yung Shue Wan Back St. and follow the concrete path through tiny villages until you hit the countryside. The trail veers past the full equipped and staffed **Hung Shing Ye Beach,** a 25min. walk away, before continuing over and around the isolated **Kamikaze Caves.** During WWII, Japanese occupiers dug two large grottoes into the hillside, where they hid kamikaze speedboats intended to blast the Allied Navy. In Sok Kwu Wan, you can catch a ferry back to Central or continue on to **Mo Tat Wan** or **Lo So Shing** beaches. From Sok Kwu Wan, the trail follows the curve of the mini-bay. Walking the entire trail takes under 1hr.; watch for signs for the trail in both cities.

■ CHEUNG CHAU 長州

Tiny in landmass but teeming with character, Cheung Chau Island is perhaps the most buoyant of the outlying islands. It boasts quite a list of flamboyant characters, from Lee Lai Shan, Hong Kong's first Olympic gold medalist, to Cheung Po Tsai, a legendary pirate who supposedly hid in a cave that now bears his name. When things gets too hectic in Hong Kong, locals gleefully escape to Cheung Chau for weekend excursions.

If you like Cheung Chau so much you decide to stay overnight, finding **accommodations** is easy. Proprietors set up stands in front of the ferry pier, waiting for travelers to disembark. Many of them are willing to bargain far below their already reasonable starting prices. Ask to see the rooms before handing over any cash. A 10min. walk to your left from the ferry will bring you to a row of **seafood restaurants** with copious outdoor seating and heaps of fresh, tasty food; dinner entrees run from HK$45. Lots of tiny restaurants can be found in the streets behind the promenade, serving standard Chinese dishes and rather unappetizing attempts at Western food. For alternative fare, try **Morocco's Restaurant and Bar** ❹, 71 San Hing Praya St. (☎2986 9767. Vegetable samosa HK$25. Set dinners HK$70 and up. Happy hour 4-9pm. Open daily 11:30am-1am.)

Ride the regular **ferry** from Pier 5 at the New Ferry Piers in Central (1hr.; every hr. 6:30am-11:30pm; M-Sa HK$10.5, Su HK$15.7) or opt for the **express ferry** (40min.; every hr. 8:45am-11:45pm, 12:30, 1:30, 4:15, 7am; M-Sa HK$21, Su HK$31). Both will take you on a cruise through stunning visions of mountain and sea. The promenade, **San Hing Praya Street,** stretching 10min. in either direction away from the ferry pier, is home to all the grocery stores, **ATMs,** restaurants, and little fruit stands that you'll ever need, in addition to the **police station.** Visible from the ferry pier, the large, cream-colored **Cheung Chau Library** has computers available for **Internet** access. (Open daily 9am-7:30pm.)

MACAU 澳門 ☎853

Portuguese traders first dropped anchor in Macau in 1513, transforming this tiny peninsula into the first European colony in Asia and a flourishing center for the silk and spice trade. Today, every pastel colonial building or crumbling Tin Hau temple tells a story of conquest, trade, and hybridization. A scattering of elegant and aging churches recalls the origin of Macau's given name, "City of the Name of God, Macau." These days, however, Macau's visitors are a very different kind of devout. Portuguese tourists and giddy Hong Kong weekenders come to gamble religiously at Macau's famed casinos or partake of the city's racy nightlife. Round-the-clock jet foils ensure a bustling tourism industry, which brings in over half of Macau's yearly revenue. After more than 400 years of colonial rule, Macau returned to China on December 19, 1999 as the second SAR, but the dice continue to roll without skipping a beat in this Portuguese city in Chinese guise.

MONEY

Gambler-friendly Macau takes its money seriously. The **pataca** (MOP), divided into 100 **avos,** is the official unit of currency of Macau. Coins come in 10, 20, and 50 avos and 1, 5, and 10 patacas; bills come in 10, 20, 50, 100, 500, and 1000 patacas. All Macau businesses accept HK$, but public pay phones only take patacas. **Banks** exchange currency and traveler's checks; **ATMs** hooked up to Cirrus, Jetco, Plus, and Visa networks are everywhere in Macau. Most hotels and restaurants accept credit cards, but some may add a 10% service charge and 5% government tax to all bills. **Tipping** is usually not expected.

MACAU PATACA	
AUS$1=MOP5.55	MOP1=AUS$0.18
CDN$1=MOP6.12	MOP1=CDN$0.16
EUR€1=MOP9.66	MOP1=EUR€0.10
HK$1=MOP1.03	MOP1=HK$0.97
NZ$1=MOP5.25	MOP1=NZ$.19
UK£1=MOP14.39	MOP1=UK£0.07
US$1=MOP8.03	MOP1=US$0.12
Y1=MOP0.97	MOP1=Y1.03

✈ INTERCITY TRANSPORTATION

VISAS AND CUSTOMS. Citizens of Australia, Canada, Israel, New Zealand, South Africa, and the US can enter Macau with a passport or travel document and stay for 30 days. Citizens of EU countries can stay for 90 days. Permanent Hong Kong residents and Portuguese passport holders can stay visa-free for one year. Single-entry individual visas are available at any Portuguese consulate or at the Macau Ferry Terminal. 20-day visas cost HK$100, for families with children under age 12 HK$200, and for members of a group of 10 or more HK$50.

Macau does not levy export duties, but Hong Kong limits the quantities of duty-free cigarettes (200) and wine (1 liter) that travelers can carry back with them.

BY AIR. Completed in 1995, **Macau International Airport** (☎861 111; www.macau-airport.gov.mo), on the eastern coast of Taipa Island, has regular flights to Beijing, Shanghai, and other cities in China, as well as to Bangkok, Brussels, Kaohsiung, Kuala Lumpur, Lisbon, Seoul, Singapore, and Taipei. More flights and carriers will be added in coming years. There is a departure tax on all flights (destinations in China MOP80, children ages 2-12 MOP50; all other destinations MOP130, children ages 2-12 MOP80), except for stays under 24hr. The AP1 bus (every 15min., MOP6) runs from the airport to major hotels. Taxis are also available.

BY SEA. In Hong Kong, boats depart from the **Macau Ferry Terminal,** 200 Connaught Rd., Shun Tak Centre, Sheung Wan (MTR: Sheung Wan) and the **China Ferry Terminal,** 33 Canton Rd., TST (☎2516 9581), behind Kowloon Park. A departure tax (to Macau HK$26, to Hong Kong MOP25) is included in the price of ferry tickets.

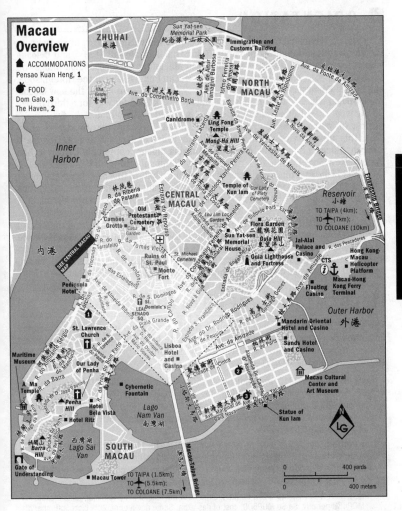

Macau Overview

♠ ACCOMMODATIONS
Pensao Kuan Heng, **1**

♦ FOOD
Dom Galo, **3**
The Haven, **2**

HONG KONG

First Ferry (☎ 2131 8181; www.nwff.com.hk). Ferry service to China Ferry Terminal in TST, **Hong Kong** (1hr.; every ½hr. 6:30am–5:30pm, 6:30, 7:30, 8:30pm; M-F HK$140, Sa-Su HK$155, after 5pm HK$175).

Turbojet (Macau ☎ 285 9333, Hong Kong 790 7039) has boats to Macau Ferry Terminal in Sheung Wan, **Hong Kong** (1hr.; every 15min., less frequent in early morning; HK$142, Sa-Su HK$154, after 6pm HK$176). Make advance reservations for weekend tickets from Hong Kong to Macau. Also goes to **Shenzhen** (1hr.; 10:30am, 12:30, 3:30, 6:45pm; HK$171).

Yuet Tung Shipping Company. Daily ferry from Macau Pier 14, beside the Peninsula Hotel, to Shekou in **Shenzhen** (2:30pm; MOP100, children MOP57).

✸ ORIENTATION

Tiny Macau Peninsula (ou mun; 澳門) occupies the western Pearl River Delta, at the gateway to Guangdong province. **Taipa Island** (taam jai; 氹仔) and **Coloane Island** (lo waan dou; 路環島) are linked to Macau by the **Macau-Taipa Bridge** (ou taam daikiu; 澳氹大橋), which leaves the Macau Peninsula near the Hotel Lisboa, and by the **Friendship Bridge** (yauyi daikiu; 友誼大橋), also called the **New Macau-Taipa Bridge,** which leaves from North Macau. Work is under way for a third bridge on the west side. Taipa and Coloane are connected by an isthmus.

Most of Macau's casinos are in **central Macau.** Twisting, narrow streets criss-cross this area, curving around Guia Hill, the Ruins of St. Paul, and St. Dominic's Church. Macau's main road, **Avenida de Almeida Ribeiro,** commonly known as **San Ma Lo** ("New Street"; 新馬路), runs from the Peninsula Hotel on the west coast to the Hotel Lisboa on the south coast. The southern half of this road bears the name **Avenida do Infante D. Henrique. Avenida de Amizade** (yauyi daimalo;友誼大馬路) runs from the Macau-Hong Kong ferry terminal to the Hotel Lisboa. **North Macau,** bordering Zhuhai, has few casinos but enough bars and clubs for a lively nightlife.

In hilly **south Macau,** Our Lady of Penha Church, A Ma Temple, and the Macau Maritime Museum huddle together. The large thoroughfare **Avenida da Praia Grande** (laam wan daimalo; 南灣大馬路) becomes **Rua da Praia do Bom Parto,** passing historic Hotel Bela Vista and Hotel Ritz before changing again (as roads in Macau are apt to do) into **Avenida da República** (munguo daimalo;民國大馬路) near Barra Hill.

HONG KONG

⧉ LOCAL TRANSPORTATION

The Macau Peninsula is small enough to walk across in under an hour. **Transportes Colectivos de Macau (TCM)** and **Transmac** operate frequent air-conditioned buses. Prices are posted next to the turnstiles (within Macau proper MOP2.5, to Taipa MOP3.3, to Coloane MOP5).

Taxis: Base fare MOP10, each additional 250m MOP1; waiting time MOP1 per min.; luggage MOP3. Surcharges for trips from the airport (MOP5), as well as to, but not from, the islands (to Coloane MOP5, from Taipa to Coloane MOP2). **Pedicabs** wait near the ferry terminal and Hotel Lisboa; rates are negotiable (about MOP100 per hr., a ride around the bay MOP15-20).

Car Rental: The only reason to rent anything might be to drive a *moke*—a cute, small cousin of the jeep. Drivers must be at least age 21, with a valid driver's license. All Hong Kong, Canadian, Japanese, Indian, and Singaporean citizens need an IDP (see **Essentials: By Car,** p. 48), valid for at least 2 years.

Happy Rent A Car (☎726 868), on the ground fl. of the Macau Ferry Terminal, rents *mokes*. M-F MOP480 per day, Sa-Su MOP500; cost of gas extra. Same-day returns 20% discount; other discounts available upon request. Credit card deposit MOP4000. Open daily 9am-5:30pm.

Avis (☎726 571), also in the ferry terminal. ID for customers not from Australia, the US, or UK. Several options, including automatic transmission. M-F from MOP300 per day, Sa-Su MOP350. Same-day returns 20% discount. Credit card deposit MOP2000. Open daily 9am-5:30pm.

▨ PRACTICAL INFORMATION

TOURIST AND FINANCIAL SERVICES

Tourist Offices: The **Macau Government Tourism Office (MGTO),** 9 Largo de Senado (☎315 566, daily 9am-6pm hotline 333 000; www.macautourism.gov.mo), provides information in Chinese, English, Japanese, and Portuguese. Make sure to pick up a

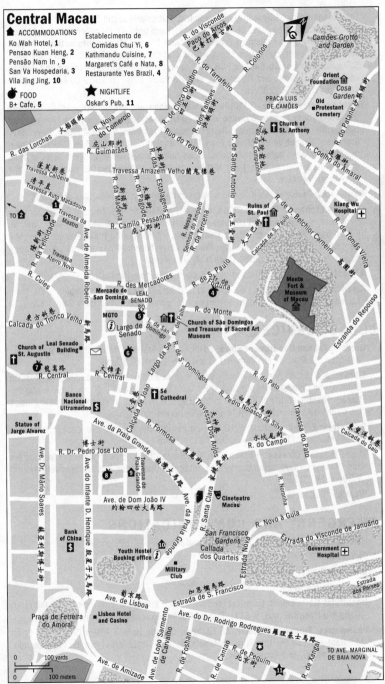

Central Macau

ACCOMMODATIONS
Ko Wah Hotel, **1**
Pensao Kuan Heng, **2**
Pensão Nam In , **9**
San Va Hospedaria, **3**
Vila Jing Jing, **10**

Establecimento de
Comidas Chui Yi, **6**
Kathmandu Cuisine, **7**
Margaret's Café e Nata, **8**
Restaurante Yes Brazil, **4**

FOOD
B+ Cafe, **5**

★ **NIGHTLIFE**
Oskar's Pub, **11**

HONG KONG

copy of the *Official Map and Guide,* which is particularly useful for the islands and bus routes. Provides free local calls. Open daily 9am-6pm. Other offices: at the **Macau Ferry Terminal,** near customs (open daily 9am-10pm); **Macau International Airport** (☎861 436; open daily 9am-10pm); **Guia Lighthouse** (☎569 808; open daily 9am-5:30pm); **Ruins of St. Paul** (☎358 444; open daily 9am-6pm); in **Hong Kong,** Macau Ferry Terminal Bldg., 3rd fl., Sheung Wan (☎2857 2287 or 2559 0147; open daily 9am 1pm and 2:30-5:30pm).

Travel Agencies: CTS (☎700 888), on Rua de Nagasaki, Xinhua Bldg., 1st fl., opposite the World Trade Centre. **Chinese single-entry visas** MOP150; arrive before noon for pickup after noon the next day. Bring a photo or take one there (MOP30). Open daily 9am-9pm. **Branch** at the Macau Ferry Terminal, 3rd fl., shop 1027 (☎726 756), near the MGTO. Makes hotel reservations. Open daily 9am-8:30pm. 2 agencies offer tours through the MGTO; various 1-day highlight tours all under MOP100. Book tours at the Ferry Terminal office.

Consulates: Portugal, 45 Rua Pedro Nolasco da Silva (☎356 660; fax 356 658).

Currency Exchange: Bank of China, on Ave. Dr. Mário Soares. Open M-F 9am-5pm, Sa 9am-1pm. **Banco Nacional Ultramarino (BNU),** 22 Ave. de Almeida Ribeiro. Open M-F 9am-5pm, Sa 9am-noon. **Hong Kong Bank,** 73-75 Rua da Praia Grande. Open M-F 9am-5pm, Sa 9am-12:30pm. The **Macau Ferry Terminal** has a currency exchange counter near the tourist office. Open daily 9am-6pm.

ATM: Many international ATMs in the city center and near the casinos.

American Express: 23B Rua de S. Paulo R/C (☎363 262), near the Ruins of St. Paul. Traveler's Cheques, credit card advances, AmEx payments. Open daily 9am-5:30pm.

LOCAL SERVICES

Grocery: Yaohan Department Store, 1579 Ave. da Amizade. Follow the pedestrian walkway from the Macau Ferry Terminal. Open daily 11am-10:30pm.

Library: A freestanding one-room library sits at Jardine de S. Francisco on Rua Do Campo, in a Chinese-style building. Open daily 9am-noon and 7-10pm. There is another **library** near the statue of Kun Iam in the UNESCO building, in the middle of the Parque Dr. Carlos d'Assumpção. Open M and W-Su noon-8pm.

Bookstore: Elite Bookstore, 8-10 Rua de Palha. International and local maps and a good selection of English books. Open daily 10am-10pm.

Movie Theater: Cineteatro Macau, on Rua Santa Clara. Screens Western blockbusters and Chinese movies, some dubbed in Cantonese. Open 1pm; last movie usually around 9:30pm. MOP30.

Weather: English ☎1311.

EMERGENCY AND COMMUNICATIONS

Emergency: ☎999. **Fire:** ☎572 222. **Ambulance:** ☎577 199 or 378 311.

Police: ☎919 or 573 333.

Maritime Police: ☎559 944.

Judicial Police: ☎993.

Hospitals: Government Hospital (☎313 731), Estrada do Visconde de S. Januário. **Kiang Wu Hospital** (☎378 311), Rua de Coelho do Amaral. Both open 24hr.

Pharmacies: Farmacia Popular, 16 Largo de Senado (☎573 739 or 566 568). Open M-F 9am-9pm, Sa-Su 9am-8pm. **Watson's,** at the intersection of Ave. da Praia Grande, Rua do Campo, and Rua de Santa Clara.

HONG KONG

Telephones: Companhia de Telecomunicações de Macau (CTM) offices and snack shops on the 2nd fl. of the Macau Ferry Terminal sell MOP70 and MOP100 phone cards. For international calls, dial 00 and then the country code. For Hong Kong, dial 01. **International Directory Assistance:** ☎ 101. **Collect Calls:** ☎ 191. **Local Directory:** English and Cantonese ☎ 181, Portuguese 185.

Internet Access: Institute for Civic and Municipal Affairs, on the 4th fl. of Domingo's Market near Leal Senado Sq., has free Internet. Get there early, as computers book up quickly and are only available in 30min. increments. The UNESCO **library** in Parque Dr. Carlos d'Assumpção offers Internet for MOP10 per hr. **Team Spirit,** 102 Rua Dos Mercadores (☎ 355 859), near Leal Senado Sq. MOP10 per hr. Open noon until late.

Post Office: CTT de Macau, Largo do Senado, in Leal Senado Sq. EMS and Poste Restante (counter #1; mail is held for 1 month). Open M-F 9am-6pm, Sa 9am-1pm.

CANTO-SAVVY. Bus and taxi drivers are most likely to know your destination by its Cantonese name. While certain places like Leal Senado Square or Hac Sa Beach are universally known, you'll have a hard time getting to Maritime Museum if you don't know how to give directions in Chinese. And *everyone* calls Ave. de Almeida Ribeiro "San Ma Lo." Many tourists carry a map and point to their destinations; you can also use your copy of *Let's Go,* which includes characters and pronunciations for major roads and sights.

HONG KONG

⌂ ACCOMMODATIONS

Almost all accommodations are located in central Macau, clustered on side streets branching off **Avenida de Almeida Ribeiro,** near the harbor, or off **Avenida do Infante D. Henrique.** Many budget rooms are carved out of a single apartment and let in little natural light. Consider yourself lucky to have a room with a view.

Anyone planning to spend more than MOP200 should first check out the travel agencies at the ferry terminal; they typically offer up to 50% discounts on larger hotels. Some packages include ferry tickets to or from Hong Kong. Advance reservations are almost universally recommended for weekend stays, when hotels are packed full of Hong Kong weekenders.

Ko Wah Hotel (高華酒店), 71 Rua da Felicidade (☎ 375 599 or 930 755). Rooms are larger, cleaner, and sunnier than almost every other hotel at this price. Spacious hallways creatively decorated with flowers. A/C, bath, and TV. Reception on 3rd fl. Singles MOP150; doubles and triples MOP186. Bargain hard—it should be possible to get the price down to MOP120. Discounts for long-term stays. ❷

Pensao Kuan Heng (群興賓館), 4 Rua de Ponte e Horta (☎ 573 629), past the Sun Sun Hotel on the opposite side of the street. Rooms are small but clean, and the bathrooms are cheery and filled with light. Proximity to a quiet square is an added plus—join the locals gathering there around dusk. Standard amenities include A/C, TV, phone, and attached bath. Singles MOP120; doubles MOP160. ❷

San Va Hospedaria (新華大旅店), 67 Rua da Felicidade (☎ 573 701; sanva@hongkong.com), off Rua dos Mercadores from Ave. de Almeida Ribeiro. Nowhere is the strategy of making a hotel out of an apartment more apparent. Rooms aren't separated so much by walls as by partitions—you may be more aware of your neighbor's activities than you'd like. Nevertheless, many backpackers call the balcony and 2 semi-outdoor toilets and showers home. Best price in Macau. Singles and doubles with fan and shared bath MOP60, with A/C and attached bath MOP80. ❶

Hac Sa Beach Youth Hostel (☎882 701), on Estrada Nova de Hac Sa, off the main road on the way to the beach, Coloane Island. Take bus #26 or 26a from Almeida Ribiero and get off at the 1st stop off the main road. This government-owned hostel is in the gray building on the right labeled Pousada de Juventud. Dorm rooms are clean and homey, with couch, locker, TV, and colorful sheets. Shared bathrooms are spotless. Fairly comprehensive list of regulations: HI members only, midnight curfew, no cooking, and beds made by 10am. Must pay in advance at the **Youth Hostel Booking Office** (☎344 340), on Ave. de Praia Grande across from the Military Club in Central Macau. Booking office open M-F 9am-5:45pm. Often fully booked by Hong Kong youth groups in the summer. 10-bed dorms MOP40-100 for foreigners, MOP20-80 for locals. ❶

Vila Jing Jing (晶晶賓館), 998 Ave. da Praia Grande (☎715 037), across from the pink colonial building known as the Military Club. Pretty, carpeted rooms (albeit slightly musty), with A/C, TV, rooftop balcony, and plenty of sunlight. Discounts for stays over 1 week. Singles MOP100, with bath MOP130; triples MOP230. ❷

Pensão Nam In (南苑賓館), 3 Travessa da Praia Grande (☎710 024 or 710 008). Make sure you are on Travessa da Praia Grande, not Rua da Praia Grande, and that you're at Nam In, not Nam Tin (just across the street). Clean, airy rooms with A/C, couch, phone, TV, and natural light. Singles with A/C and bathroom MOP150. ❷

🍴 FOOD

Macau is home to more *establicimentos de comida* than you can shake a stick at, and many of them serve their fascinating hybrid Chinese-Portuguese cuisine at very reasonable prices. Around the city, you'll find Chinese noodles and dim sum with German pig *knöchel, caldo verde* soup, *tiramisu,* and Portuguese egg tarts. The city's bakeries also sell their own creations unique to Macau. Lining the streets off Almeida Ribiero, tiny shops offer free samples of their delicious tiny almond cookies and snippets of beef jerky. As you pass these shops, hover for a moment, look interested, and you are likely to receive a complimentary snack.

Rua do Almirante Sérgio, running past A Ma Temple and the Macau Maritime Museum in South Macau, is home to cheap Chinese eateries and slightly more expensive Portuguese restaurants. A combination of cheap *establicimentos de comida* and more upscale Portuguese and international restaurants crowd the block of streets formed by **Alameda Dr. Carlos D'Assumção, Avenida Dr. Sun Yat-sen, Avenida da Amizade,** and **Avenida de Sagres** to the right of the **Kun Iam statue.** Coffee shops and stores offering Western and international food fill the streets around **Leal Senado Square.** West of the **Lisboa Hotel and Casino,** numerous upscale (or just expensive) Chinese restaurants cluster amid the hotels and casinos. **Rua Com. Mata e Oliveira,** off Ave. de Dom João IV, has colorful outdoor seating and many cafes.

CENTRAL MACAU

Establecimento de Comidas Chui Yi (翠怡咖啡美食), 13 Travessa de São Domingos (☎550 017). Surrounded by more upscale coffee shops and restaurants, Chui Yi is the quintessential *establicimento de comida*. For cheap and delicious Macanese cuisine, this is the place to go. Try the sole with vegetables (MOP25) or the Portuguese fried rice with seafood (MOP20). Open daily 7:30am-9:30pm. ❷

Kathmandu Cuisine (加德満都美食), 8-G Rua Central (☎372 750). The city's only Nepalese restaurant showcases a delicious and affordable menu of vegetarian and meat dishes adapted for the Macanese palate. A lovely atmosphere of warm colors, warm food, and warm people. Vegetable curry MOP25. Prawn masala MOP38. ❷

Dom Galo (公鷄葡國餐廳), on Ave. Sir Anders Ljung Stedt (☎751 383). With Portuguese owners, Portuguese food, and a regular Portuguese clientele, Dom Galo serves up all the right dishes without breaking the bank. Octopus salad MOP28. Portuguese-style clams MOP40. Open daily 11:30am-11:30pm. ❷

Margaret's Café e Nata (瑪嘉烈蛋撻店 ; ☎527 791), on Rua Alm. Costa Cabral. Walking toward the Lisboa on Ave. de Infante D. Henrique, take a left onto Ave. de Dom João IV; look for sign to Margaret's. A great place to grab a pastry (MOP5-10), sandwich (MOP10-20), or homemade yogurt with fresh fruit (MOP9). Open 9am-8pm. ❷

The Haven (海雲軒), 101 Rua Franciso H. Fernandes, Walorly Bldg. (☎335 080). Large portions of wickedly good food. Try the Thai-style clams (MOP40), Mexican salad (MOP34), chicken cordon bleu (MOP45), or New England clam chowder in a bread bowl (MOP26). Open 11:30am-11:30pm. ❸

Restaurante Yes Brazil (巴西美食), 6-A Travessa Fortuna (☎358 097). One of the city's few Brazilian restaurants, Yes Brazil makes up for a less-than-extensive menu with one of the friendliest owners you'll meet in Macau. Stop in for a tall glass of real milk (MOP5) or set lunch of Brazilian food (MOP38). Open 10am-8pm. ❸

B+ Cafe, Edf. Kai Fu Centro Comercial, 3/5 A Rua Leste Mercs Domingos (☎356 778). With 2 floors of seating and a central location near Leal Senado Sq., this joint draws the crowds. Sichuan-style filet of fish with rice noodles MOP10. Ham and cheese sandwich special (3-6pm) MOP5. Open M-F 11am-10pm, Sa-Su 11am-midnight. ❶

TAIPA ISLAND

Rua da Cunha ("Food Street") cuts through the village and is chock-full of places to grab a bite. **Panda Portuguese Restaurant** ❹ (熊猫葡國餐廳), 4-8 Rua Carlos Eugenio, in Taipa Village, cooks up charcoal eel (MOP78), African chicken (MOP48), and other Portuguese and Macanese favorites. (☎827 338. Open daily 11am-11pm.) **Cafe Luso II** (露素餐廳), 18 Rua do Sol (☎825 580), off Rua da Cunha, cooks up Mediterranean dishes like Portuguese-style clams (MOP40) and spinach soup with scallops (MOP30). **Ka Li Man** ❶ (咖喱文), 3 Largo Dos Bomberos, near the tourist information booth at the western edge of Taipa village, dishes up its famous rice noodles for MOP10-15. (☎822 801. Open daily 6am-6:30pm.)

COLOANE ISLAND

Restaurant selections in Coloane village are rather limited. **◪Nga Tim Cafe** ❸ (路環雅憩花園葡國餐), 8 Rue Caetano, in front of the Chapel of St. Francis Xavier, is an excellent local favorite that serves up Portuguese and Chinese fare for under MOP50. (☎882 086. Delicious fresh-squeezed juice MOP15. Open daily 1pm-1am. MC/V.) **Fernando's Restaurant** ❹, 9 Praia de Hac Sa, next to the main bus stop, is famous for its clams (MOP98). You may have to wait an hour for a table, but it's worth it. (☎882 264. Open daily noon-9:30pm.)

🆂 SIGHTS

CENTRAL MACAU

LEAL SENADO SQUARE. Named for the gray Municipal Council Building (known as Leal Senado) across Ave. de Almeida Ribiero, the square and the surrounding streets have become the city's center for tourism, shopping, performances, and general passing of time under shady trees and the overhangs of the square's beautiful pastel buildings. The Municipal Council Building, which houses the Senate Chamber and library, received its name (meaning "Loyal Senate") for keeping close ties to its mother country when Spain occupied Portugal in the 17th century. Once a powerful oligarchy, the Senate now functions as a conventional political body with limited powers. *(Take bus #3 or 10a from the ferry terminal, or walk 10min. from either the Hotel Lisboa or the Floating Casino on Ave. de Almeida Ribeiro. Open Tu-Su 9am-9pm. Municipal Council Bldg. open Tu-Su 10am-7pm. Free.)* White stucco moldings and green shutters adorn the nearby **Church of São Domingos,** belying the building's long history. Built at the turn of the 16th century by Dominican friars, the church has a graceful and airy interior. Some of the works in the **Treasure of Sacred Art Museum** (including gold and silver religious objects) date back to the 17th century. *(On Largo de São Domingos in Leal Senado Sq. Open daily 10am-6pm. Donations accepted.)*

RUINS OF ST. PAUL. The winding path behind the Church of São Domingos leads to Rua da Palha and the Ruins of St. Paul, once dubbed the "greatest monument to Christianity in all the Eastern lands." A devastating fire in 1835 destroyed all but the front facade and a few cornerstones. The **Museum of Sacred Art,** under the site of the old church, contains the bones of Japanese and Vietnamese Christian martyrs. A side hall of relics adds to the store of curiosities. *(Open daily 9am-6pm. Free.)*

MONTE FORT (dai paau toi; 大炮台). Monte Fort, a stone's throw from the Ruins of St. Paul, once repelled a Dutch invasion in 1622. The newly opened **Museum of Macau,** built into the excavated citadel, aims to educate visitors on Macau's cultural history with exhibits on the customs and practices of the city's diverse communities. The inside is nothing exceptional, but old fort cannons stand outside. *(☎ 357 911. Museum entrances at the top and bottom of the fort; open daily 10am-6pm. Fort open daily 7am-6:30pm. MOP15, children under 11 and seniors MOP8, students MOP7.5.)*

CAMÕES GROTTO AND GARDEN. Away from the Ruins of St. Paul, this park sprawls behind the intersection of Rua de Terrafeiro, Rua de Tomás Vieira, and Rua de Santo Antonio. Named after the Portuguese poet Luis de Camões, the park features cool, shady trails and relaxing pavilions, in addition to stone engravings of several of the poet's sonnets. A public library is at the back of the park. The **Old Protestant Cemetery** to the right of the entrance is the final resting place of 150 residents of old Macau. *(On Praça Luís de Camões. Buses #8A, 17, 18, 19, and 26 stop at the garden. Garden open daily sunrise-sunset. Cemetery gates usually open during the day; if not, knock or ring the bell. Both free.)* Between the Camões Garden and the cemetery lies the **Cosa Garden.** The old headquarters of the British East India Company, it now houses the **Orient Foundation,** which sponsors one-month rotating art exhibits. *(The entrance is hidden to the right of the building's stairs. Open daily 10am-7pm. Free.)*

GUIA LIGHTHOUSE AND FORTRESS (dung mong yeung dang taap; 東望洋燈塔). Built in 1638, Guia Fort hosts a lighthouse and a small chapel, both visible at the top of leafy Guia Hill from most of the Macau Peninsula. The best vantage point from which to see the two structures is Ave. de Amizade. Before 8am and after 5pm, joggers, *tai chi* practitioners, and old ladies walking backwards up the hill all take to the trails and stairs. There's a pleasant community feel, and views to justify the 20min. walk up. For the less athletically-inclined, a cable car leaves from the Flora Garden. *(Take the #9 bus to the Flora Garden or walk up Estrada do Engelheiro Trigo from the Guia Hotel. Cable car MOP20. Open daily 5am-sunset. Free.)*

MACAU ART MUSEUM. Part of the Cultural Center complex, the museum is home to two floors of permanent exhibits and one rotating gallery. The small collection strikes an interesting balance between contemporary and ancient arts, and reflects the struggle of Macanese artists between European and Eastern artistic traditions. *(☎791 9800. Ave. Xian Xing Hai, near Ave. Dr. Sun Yat-sen. Take bus 1A from the ferry, #23 from the Lisboa, or #17 from Camões Gardens. Open daily Su, Tu-Sa 10am-7pm; last admission 6:30pm. MOP10; students, children, seniors MOP5; Su free.)*

NORTH MACAU

In the spirit of Macau gambling, watch greyhounds race and chase metal bunnies at the **Canidrome,** at the foot of Mong-Há hill on Ave. General Castelo Branco. (☎ 221 199. Races M-Tu and Th-Sa starting at 7:30pm.) For something more pious, the **Buddhist Temple of Kun Iam,** on Ave. do Coronel Mesquita, is dedicated to the Goddess of Mercy. One of Macau's biggest and wealthiest temples, it boasts many halls separated by open courtyards. Fortune-tellers and joss-stick vendors surround the three altars to the Precious Buddhas, the Buddha of Longevity, and Kun Iam, whose embroidered silk dress is changed every year. The table where the Chinese government and US Ambassador Cushing signed their 1844 friendship treaty is on display in a side room. (Open daily 7am-6pm. Free.)

SOUTH MACAU

A MA TEMPLE (ma jou gok; 媽祖閣). Macau's most famous temple pays tribute to the goddess of the sea A Ma (more commonly known as Tian Hou, Tin Hau, or Mazu in other parts of China). According to legend, A Ma led a group of storm-tossed, weary sailors to what was to become Macau. The grateful survivors named the place A Ma. A Ma became A Ma Gao (Bay of A Ma), which the Portuguese changed to Macau upon their arrival. Shrines to A Ma and rock paintings of the first fateful ship dot the landscape of the temple. *(Open daily sunrise-sunset. Free.)*

MACAU MARITIME MUSEUM (hoi si bok mat gun; 海事博物館). Devoted to the long maritime history of Macau, this waterfront museum includes a special exhibit on the A Ma Temple. Definitely worth a look for maritime enthusiasts, but if knotting and tide changes don't interest you, the aquarium, boat models, and junk tours might. Intercoms and telephones give audio descriptions in Cantonese, English, Mandarin, and Portuguese. *(1 Largo do Pogode da Barra, at the northern end of Rua de S. Tiago de Barro. ☎ 595 481. 30min. junk tours M-Tu and Th-Su 10:30, 11, 11:30am, noon, and 2pm; MOP10, children under 10 free. Open M and W-Su 10am-5:30pm. M and W-Sa MOP10, ages 10-17 MOP5, under 10 and over 65 free; Su MOP5, ages 10-17 MOP3.)*

AVENIDA DA PRAIA GRANDE. For a walking tour of southern Macau, start on Ave. da Praia Grande at the **Statue of Jorge Alvares,** which honors the first Portuguese man to set foot on Chinese lands. Continuing along the street brings you to the pink, colonial **Government House,** a masterpiece of architect Thomaz de Aquino. Travessa do Padre Narciso, off Ave. da Praia Grande, leads to **St. Lawrence Church,** constructed in the 1560s. Walk through a side entrance to view the stained-glass windows and intricate artwork of the main and side altars. *(On Rua de St. Lourenço. Open M 10am-1pm and 2-6pm, Tu-Su 10am-6pm. Donations accepted.)* Avenida da Praia Grande becomes Rua da Praia do Bom Parto, and a side street off the main thoroughfare splits into two. To the left, the road leads to Bela Vista and Hotel Ritz; to the right, Calcada da Penha takes a steep climb to Penha Church. Compared to its sister church, São Domingos in Senado Sq., the **Chapel of Our Lady of Penha Church** is unremarkable, but the grounds offer a lovely view of nearby bridges and Taipa Island. *(Open daily 9am-5:30pm. Free.)*

MACAU TOWER AND CYBERNETIC FOUNTAIN. Opened to the public in 2002, the Macau Tower is 338m of excitement. For most people, that just means an elevator ride to an outstanding view from both indoor and outdoor viewing platforms, but for the daring few, it can mean the chance to participate in X-treme activities, such as a thrilling walk around the outer rim of the tower at 233m, or even the chance to climb the 10th-tallest tower in the world from the bottom to the top. The Tower complex is also home to shops, a movie theater, and several expensive restaurants and cafes. *(☎ 888 858; www.macautower.com.mo. Take bus #23 or 32 from the Hotel Lisboa. Elevator ride MOP70; children, local students, seniors MOP30. Walk around outer rim M-Th*

MOP160, F-Su MOP190. Tower climb 2hr.; M-Th MOP800, F-Su MOP900; advance booking required. Open M-F 10am-9pm, Sa-Su 9am-9pm.) The **Cybernetic Fountain** in Nam Van Lake, one of two artificial reservoirs on the peninsula, is the largest manmade fountain in Asia, shooting water 70m into the air. There is a free laser show every night 8-10pm. *(Take bus #18, 9A, or 28B from the bus stop near the Jorge Alvares statue.)*

TAIPA ISLAND 冰仔

Buses #11, 22, and 33 traverse Taipa from the Hotel Lisboa (10min., MOP3.3). Tourist information booth on Rua Direita de Carlos Eugenio, at the western edge of Taipa village. (☎827 882. Open M-F 9am-1pm and 2:30-5:30 or 5:45pm.) Bike rental (MOP12-16 per hr.) is available from the shops at the western end of Taipa Village.

Just across the Macau-Taipa Bridge you'll find the pink Taipa Stadium and the **Macau Jockey Club.** (18+. Races June W 9:30pm, July W and Sa 7:30pm. Proper clothing required. Cell phones prohibited. 1st fl. free, 2nd fl. MOP20.) On race days, the area buzzes with excitement, and people boost their luck by lighting incense to the **Four Faces Buddha** down the street.

The large, white **Taipa Monument** on the hillside greets visitors. Once in Taipa Village, signs will direct you towards **Our Lady of Carmel,** a lovely small church and square accented by the tiny **Carmel Garden.** Down the steps from the square is the **Taipa Houses Museum,** a series of five houses built in different cultural styles native to Macau. (☎827 103. Open Tu-Su 10am-6pm. Tu-Sa MOP5, under 10 and over 60 free, Su free.) Several colorful temples cluster around the main bus station in Taipa village. The 170-year-old **Tin Hau Temple** stands on Rua Governador Tamagnini Barbosa, while the slightly larger **Pou Tai Un Temple** is close by on Rua do Legedo.

COLOANE ISLAND 路環島

From A Ma Temple or Hotel Lisboa on Macau proper, bus #21 runs through Taipa to Coloane village (MOP4). Buses #21A and 25 travel to Cheoc Van and Hac Sa Beaches (MOP5). Trips take 10-15min.

Most visitors head to the beaches of this sleepy holiday island to soak in the sun and frolic in the water. The thin string of the **Taipa-Coloane Bridge** becomes a road winding along the coastline, changing from Estrada de Seac Pai Van, to Estrada de Cheoc Van, to Estrada de Hac Sa, to Estrada do Altinho de Ka-Ho. The first stop past the Kartódromo Karting Track is **Seac Pai Van Park,** on the island's western side, home to a large walk-in aviary, a small zoo, and a children's playground. The park also provides access to the 25km **Trilho de Coloane hiking trail,** which leads to **Alto de Coloane,** the island's highest point. A white marble statue of the goddess A Ma stands at the top. (Open daily 9am-7pm. Aviary open Tu-Sa 10am-4pm. Free.)

The next stop for buses on the island is tiny **Coloane village,** in the southwest. The **Chapel of St. Francis Xavier** is the town's claim to fame, and its tiny meeting hall and folk-art decorations exude warmth and community. Street stalls and cafes line the picturesque square. Giant trees grow in the middle of eating areas and stretch through the canopy roofs. Near the pier, right of the chapel, is the very red and very tiny **Sam Seng Temple.** To the left is **Tin Hau Temple;** beyond it on Ave. de Cinco de Outubro, the larger **Tam Kung Temple** boasts a dragon boat carved from a whale bone. (Chapel and temples open daily sunrise-sunset. Donations accepted.)

Buses stop last at the beaches. There are three stops for **Cheoc Van Beach** (竹灣 海灘), the slightly smaller and less-populated of the two beaches. It features a swimming pool, snack bar and yacht club. Get off at the first stop for the pool and the second or third for the beach. Past Cheoc Van is **Hac Sa Beach** (黑沙海灘), famous for its black-tinted sands and popular for its sports complex and barbecue and picnic facilities. The water is often slightly brown-colored, but don't worry—it's perfectly clean for swimming.

◪ CASINOS

If you arrived in Macau's old city and never walked down to the water, you'd have a hard time believing that Macau is home to 14 casinos that pull in more than half the city's revenue. Casinos and gambling in Macau vary wildly depending on where you are and who you're with. At some tables, dealers will chat with players or even laugh; elsewhere, stakes are high and stony faces don't break. VIP doesn't mean much in Macau—almost all "VIP rooms" are open to the public. Macau residents under 21 and visitors under 18 are prohibited from gambling. **Slot machines,** dubbed "hungry tigers" by the locals, devour HK$/MOP1 and HK$/MOP2 coins. Other ways to get rich quick include **baccarat** and **blackjack.** An easy and popular game is **Big and Small** (dai siu; 大小), in which players try to predict the numbers that show up on three dice. You can bet on specific combinations of numbers, or simply "big" (sum of dice will be 11 or more) and "small" (sum will be 10 or less). Minimum bets are MOP100-500 at most casinos.

Sands (金沙娛樂場 ; ☎883 388), on Ave. de Amizade, Outer Harbor. Next to the Macau Museum of Art. The newest, biggest, and most popular of Macau's casinos (for the moment), Sands was the first to unseat Lisboa as the reigning casino champ. Humming crowds descend on 405 slot machines and 277 tables spread out over one huge floor under a towering ceiling. Dealers are all business, money flows like water, and everything seems a little more Las-Vegas-like, complete with regular table-dancing shows, a live (and cheesy) band, and the largest chandelier in the world. Tables and slots on the 2nd fl. Open 24hr.

Lisboa (葡京娛樂場), 2-4 Ave. de Amizade (☎375 111), part of the Lisboa Hotel. Lisboa is the forefather of all that is to come for Macau, but its worn carpets and less-than-majestic atmosphere give it a nostalgic air. Still very popular with gamblers and home to 150 table games each night, Lisboa hasn't given up by any means. Its central location makes it hard to pass up a chance to check it out. Baccarat in the basement, slot machines and table games (MOP$2) on the 1st and 2nd floors, VIP rooms on the 5th.

Casino Macau Palace (皇宮娛樂場 ; ☎727 988), on Ave. de Amizade, Outer Harbour, by the ferry terminal. Better known as the **Floating Casino** since it actually does float. In fact, it recently floated over from its previous location in the Inner Harbour. No match for

IN RECENT NEWS

LAS VEGAS, MACAU?

Sixty percent of Macau's tax revenue comes from its casinos, and for nearly 40 years, all of it was pulled in by a single man. Legendary Hong Kong mogul Stanley Ho owned all 12 of Macau's casinos, but his monopoly ended in 2002, when the Macau government decided to open the industry to competition. It issued two new operating licenses, chosen from a field of over 20 bidders. Sheldon Adelson, the man behind the Venetian Resort Hotel Casino in Las Vegas, took his new license and ran with it, opening the city's newest casino, Sands, on May 18, 2004. The glitzy Sands was an immediate and frenzied success, with people injuring themselves as they broke through glass doors on opening day.

The second license was issued to another American businessman, Steve Wynn, who began building his US$750 million casino in late June of 2004. It is expected to open in September 2006, right around the time that Adelson's second casino, a replica of Las Vegas's Venetian, will be unveiled on the strip of reclaimed land between Coloane and Taipa Islands. Adelson reportedly hopes to develop this area into Macau's Las Vegas. There's been no mention of making changes to the crowded old city as of yet, but the government seems eager to bring more business to the region, and more players are looking to get in the game.

Macau's bigger guns, but the novelty of its watery location draws a faithful crowd. Adorned in red velvet from head to toe. An entire floor devoted to slot machines and several smaller rooms of table games. Open 24hr.

Jai-Alai Palace and Casino (回力娛樂場 ; ☎726 262), Outer Harbour, near the ferry terminal. Signs warning of pickpockets welcome visitors. Everything feels a little more rough-and-tumble in Jai-Alai, but for some it only adds to the allure. To avoid the thick layer of smoke coating the air, visit the health spa. Open 24hr.

Mandarin Oriental (☎567 888), on Ave. de Amizade, next to the World Trade Centre. Dwarfed by its new neighbor Sands, the Mandarin Oriental is still an old standby for those seeking a more personal atmosphere. Patrons and dealers know each other and aren't afraid to make a little noise when things don't go their way. Open noon-4am.

NIGHTLIFE

After emptying your pockets at the casinos, head to one of Macau's happening **nightclubs** and **bars**. A copy of *Macau Travel Talk* (available at many restaurants, hotels, and newsstands) has weekly entertainment listings. Many locals opt to go to Zhuhai for a wild weekend in search of newer dance clubs.

Macau's nightlife comes in two main varieties: seedy live shows and discos, or bars popular with tourists and local expats. For the former, hit up the **Crazy Paris Show** at the Hotel Lisboa. (18+. MOP300. Shows at 8 and 9:30pm.) Also try the popular and massive **DD Disco**, on the corner of Ave. do Infante D. Henrique and Ave. de Dom João IV. (☎711 800. Open daily 10pm-7am. No cover.) On weekends, the disco parties rage past dawn, but you may find yourself in questionable company if you stay into the wee hours. The bar scene centers mostly around the block of streets west of the Kun Iam statue and below **Avenida de Amizade**. A line of bars on **Avenida Marginal de Baia Nova** look out onto **Avenida Dr. Sun Yat-sen** and the water, drawing crowds of locals, tourists, and expats. In **Taipa**, bars across from the racing track are the stomping grounds of faithful expats.

Café Farol (燈塔 ; ☎751 104), on Ave. Marginal de Baia Nova. Ample outdoor seating makes this bar popular with large groups and people-watchers. Live music F-Su 10:30pm-midnight. Beer from MOP28. Cocktails from MOP38. Open daily 6pm-3am.

Oskar's Pub, 82-86 Rua de Pequim, on the ground fl. of the Holiday Inn. Popular with local expats for its live music and relaxed, jovial atmosphere. Comfortable seating and romantic lighting. Drink prices a bit inflated at MOP40 and up.

Moonwalker, on Ave. Marginal de Baia Nova (☎751 327). Live acts belt out pop hits to varying degrees of success. A lively atmosphere and loyal regulars. Beer MOP20 and up. Live music 10:30pm-1:30am. Open daily 4pm-4am.

Irish Bar, on Jardim Nam San, Taipa. Neon shamrocks, black leather couches, and an almost exclusively expat crowd. Feels like a country club with an Irish identity crisis. Drinks from MOP20. Happy hour (buy 1, get 1 free) 6-8pm. Open daily 5:30pm-3am.

Hugo's Pub, across from the Jockey Club, Taipa. Hugo's a cool guy, and his bar makes up for its relative lack of patrons with a graffiti wall and tiger sharks in the fish tank. Drinks MOP30-40. Happy hour (half-priced drinks) 5-8pm. Open daily 5pm-2am

Casablanca (☎751 281), on Ave. Marginal de Baia Nova. Patrons at Casablanca can play pool or enjoy their drink, reveling in the fact that they are quieter and more refined than their neighbors. Beer from MOP30. Cocktails from MOP40.

THE SOUTHWEST

The landscape of southwest China soars up to the alpine highlands of northwestern Yunnan and plunges down to steeply carved gorges. Rivers wind their way through limestone pinnacles in Guangxi, and backpackers weave their way through steamy jungles in Xishuangbanna. Natural variety aside, the southwest is also a patchwork of cultures, with at least three dozen ethnic groups (see **Southwestern Minorities,** p. 87), including the **Bai, Dai, Dong, Miao,** and **Naxi.** Some of these groups, such as the **Zhuang,** have assimilated completely. Others, aware of the revenue to be earned from cultural tourism, market themselves to visitors in contrived settings, uncharitably dubbed "ethnic circuses" and "human zoos." Still others abide by tradition in isolated mountain villages and are surprised to discover travelers interested in their lifestyles.

The government's apparent tolerance of minority peoples today hides a long history of discrimination and programs designed to force assimilation. The region was long dismissed by rulers as the home of fractious "southern barbarians," but a closer peek at the history of the southwest reveals a unique and sophisticated cultural dynamism arising from the arrival of Miao-Yao peoples from the Yangzi region, Tibetans from the west, the Burmese, Thai, Khmer, and Vietnamese from the south, and Hui Muslim traders, lured by the promise of riches from the silk and spice trade along the ancient Southern Silk Road. Caravans no longer journey down the well-trodden roads of the southwest, but countless tourists follow in their wake. Visitors to rowdy backpacker enclaves like Dali and Yangshuo may enjoy rare banana pancakes, espresso, and English conversation, but ultimately, they come for the natural splendor and eclectic culture.

HIGHLIGHTS OF THE SOUTHWEST

TREK THROUGH THE TROPICS of **Xishuangbanna** (p. 652) amid minority villages, primeval forests, and flooded rice paddies.

CHEER ON THE DRAGON boats racing down the Li River in **Guilin** (p. 605) during the Dragon Boat Festival around May-June.

SOAR INTO SHANGRI-LA in **Zhongdian** (p. 682) and **Deqin** (p. 686), where Tibetan villages nestle in valleys, and mountains rear up impossibly high.

GUANGXI 广西

Mention "Guangxi" and you're more than likely to hear something about "karst." The distinctive limestone pinnacles, arches, bridges, and caverns of Guilin and Yangshuo are undoubtedly and justifiably Guangxi's biggest tourist draws, but this region's beautiful topography also boasts stunning terraced rice fields, winding rivers, misty mountains, and even a few seaside resorts. Other than picturesque landscapes, much of the area's character derives from its diverse peoples. Renamed Guangxi Zhuang Autonomous Region in 1958, the region takes its name from its largest minority group. The Zhuang are well assimilated into the Han population, but the Guangxi's other minority groups like the Yao and the Miao retain traditional lifestyles in villages far from the glare of mainstream tourism.

The Southwest

Traveling in Guangxi is a constant negotiation between the highly touristed and the road less traveled, the hostel owner who speaks perfect English and the small-town local perplexed by the presence of foreigners. Guangxi offers the best of both worlds, and with a little initiative, you can easily find yourself lost in a natural wonderland or in a cafe surrounded by friendly travelers from your home country.

NANNING 南宁 ☎0771

Formerly a derelict market town called *Yōng* (邕), Nanning, only a few hundred kilometers from the Vietnam border, is a booming metropolis with lofty ambitions. The changes wrought in its recent past seem to reprise an earlier period of accelerated growth. After opening itself to foreign trade in 1907, the city quickly outgrew its old city walls. Today, Nanning is similarly extending its boundaries with rapid, orderly expansion to the north and southeast, past the Yong River. As a result of this development drive, Nanning has won several awards, including the Dubai International Award for Best Practices in Improving the Living Environment (DIABP), that have in turn further fueled its self-improvement project.

TRANSPORTATION

Flights: CAAC ticket office, 82 Chaoyang Lu (☎243 1459). Tickets go on sale a week in advance. Book early for discounts, especially for the popular Hanoi flights. Buses shuttle between Nanning and the airport (40min., every hr. 8am-7pm, Y15) and meet flights at the arrivals terminal. Taxis to the airport Y90 and up. Open 8am-8pm. To: **Beijing** (2 per day, Y1870); **Chengdu** (daily, Y930); **Guangzhou** (at least 3 per day, Y660); **Guiyang** (Tu, Th-Su; Y570); **Hong Kong** (Tu, Th, F, Sa 11:40am; Y1831); **Kunming** (daily, Y570); **Shanghai** (daily, Y1520); **Xi'an** (daily, Y1310). International flights to **Hanoi, Vietnam** (M, Th; Y800).

Trains: Nanning Train Station (nánníng huǒchē zhàn; 南宁火车站), on Zhonghua Lu at the north end of Chaoyang Lu. Open 24hr. To: **Beijing** (28hr., daily, Y276-770); **Changsha** (12½hr., daily, Y62-216); **Guangzhou** (12hr., daily, Y94-286); **Guilin** (8hr., daily, Y60-75); **Kunming** (19hr., daily, Y105-113); **Shanghai** (36hr., daily, Y206-570); **Xi'an** (36hr., daily, Y223-625). International trains to **Pingxiang** on the Vietnam border (4hr., daily, Y30).

Buses: Nanning Bus Station (nánníng qìchē zhàn; 南宁汽车站), 80 Chaoyang Lu (☎242 4529). Tickets go on sale 2 days before departure. Open daily 5:30am-12:30am. To: **Beihai** (3hr., many per day 7:30am-4:30pm, Y50); **Fancheng** (2½hr., 12 per day, Y30); **Guangzhou** (9½hr., 3 per day, Y180); **Guilin** (4½hr., every 30min. 7am-11:30pm, Y80); **Pingxiang** (4½hr., 4 per day, Y50); **Wuzhou** (6hr., 6 per day, Y180). Buses also depart at irregular intervals from Chaoyang Gardens (cháoyáng huāyuán; 朝阳花园), at the intersection of Chaoyang Lu and Renmin Lu, to **Wuming** and **Yiling Cave.** Due to the reorganization of Nanning's bus route systems, **Anji Passenger Transport Center** (ānjí kèyùn zhàn; 安吉客运站), 42 Anji Lu, is the main terminus for buses going to **Wuming** and **Yiling Cave,** as well as the cities of **Beihai, Haikou, Shenzhen,** and **Guangzhou.** Take bus #2 from Chaoyang Gardens.

Local Transportation: Fare Y1-2. Buses #6 and 10 both head down Chaoyang Lu to the train station; #6 then travels east on Minzu Dadao, while #10 heads southeast down Taoyuan Lu, passing Nanhu Lake on its way to the Blue Mountain Scenic Area; #2 travels north from Chaoyang Gardens to Anji Passenger Transport Center or south across the Yong River Bridge (yōng jiāng qiáo; 邕江桥) to Jiangnan Passenger Transport Center. **Minibuses** from Chaoyang Gardens go directly to destinations such as Nanhu Park and the Blue Mountain Scenic Area. Fare Y1-3.

Taxis: Base fare Y7. **Pedicab** and **motorcab** rides average Y3-5.

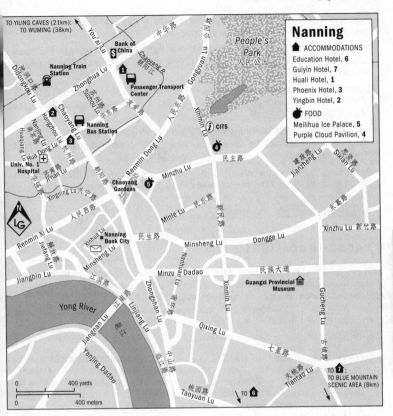

Nanning

🏠 ACCOMMODATIONS
Education Hotel, **6**
Guiyin Hotel, **7**
Huali Hotel, **1**
Phoenix Hotel, **3**
Yingbin Hotel, **2**

🍴 FOOD
Meilihua Ice Palace, **5**
Purple Cloud Pavilion, **4**

✦ 🛈 ORIENTATION AND PRACTICAL INFORMATION

Not too long ago, the area north of Nanning's railroad tracks was the crumbling, unkempt quarter of the city, with roads studded with potholes and military personnel performing exercises on the street. Much of that has now disappeared, as Nanning expands relentlessly to its northern, eastern, and southeastern frontiers. Immaculate new civic and commercial buildings rise up at astonishing rates and wide, extensive roads devour new distances everyday. The area north of the Yong River remains the frantic commercial core of the city, bounded by the railroad to the north and east, department-store-drag **Chaoyang Lu** (朝阳路) to the west, and the **Yong River** (邕江) to the south. The sprawling multi-lane boulevard **Minzu Dadao** (民族大道) runs east-west through the city center.

Travel Agency: CITS, 40 Xinmin Lu (tours ☎281 6062, visas 282 2527, tickets 285 3764; citsbusiness@163.com). Tours and great suggestions for local tourist sights. Vietnamese visas are Y450 (3 working days processing time) or Y600 for a same-day rush visa; get one in Hong Kong, Guangzhou, or Bangkok ahead of time if possible. Open daily 8am-noon and 3-6pm.

Bank of China: At the corner of Zhonghua Lu and You'ai Lu. Open M-F 8:30am-6:30pm, winter until 6pm; Sa-Su and holidays 9am-5pm.

PSB: Temporarily housed to the north on the outskirts of the city while its new building is being completed. For enquiries, call ☎110.

Hospital: Guangxi Medicine and Science University No.1 Hospital (guǎngxī yīkē dàxué dìyī fùshǔ yīyuàn; 广西医科大学第一附属医院), 6 Binhu Lu (☎535 3266). English speakers available. 24hr. pharmacy.

Bookstore: Nanning Book City (nánníng shū chéng; 南宁书城), 15 Xinhua Lu (☎281 0296). Another entrance on Minsheng Lu. Has a large English-language section on the 4th fl. Open daily 9am-9pm.

Internet Access: Great South Internet Cafe (wěi nán wǎngbā; 伟南网吧), next to Nan-fang Hotel on Chaoyang Lu. Look for the blue sign with white characters. Go right through the video game arcade. Y1 per hr. Open 24hr.

Post Office: 4-2 Suzhou Lu (☎241 8976), near the bus station. EMS, IDD service, and Poste Restante. Open 24hr. Another **branch** is near the city center at 96 Minsheng Lu. Open 8am-9pm.

Postal Code: 530012.

ACCOMMODATIONS

Few foreigners spend the night in Nanning unless they're en route to Vietnam. Those that do prefer to hide out in huge luxury palaces armed with all the modern conveniences. Budget options are available but tend to be smack in the middle of the noisy, maddening crowd, especially along Chaoyang Lu near the train station. Try the numerous guesthouses on Taoyuan Lu for more congenial surroundings.

Yingbin Hotel (yíngbīn fàndiàn; 迎宾饭店), 71 Chaoyang Lu (☎211 6288); www.ybfd.com). Exit the train station, cross the street, and bear right. Comfortable and clean rooms. Chinese- and Western-style restaurants. No key: lodgers get a pass to show the floor attendant, who unlocks your room; key deposit Y10. 24hr. hot water. Noon check-out. Dorms Y40; singles with TV, A/C, bath, and towels Y70, with Internet, bath, and A/C Y98; doubles Y45, with Internet, bath, and A/C Y108; triples Y48. ❶

Phoenix Hotel (fènghuáng bīnguǎn; 凤凰宾馆), 63 Chaoyang Lu (☎211 9888); www.fhhotel.com.cn). The main Golden Phoenix building is a grand, peculiar Chinese interpretation of Western-style glamor, attractively kitschy with extensive business facilities and a Chinese restaurant. Standard twin discounted Y268; suites Y840+. ❹ The smaller South Chaoyang building offers cheaper rooms in a slightly decrepit setting, but rooms are clean and come with TV, A/C, and bath. Singles Y68; doubles Y88. ❶

Huali Hotel (huálì bīnguǎn; 华丽宾馆), 12 You'ai Lu (☎210 2211). Close to the Passenger Transport Center. Probably the cheapest spot in town to bed down. Noon check-out. "Economical big mattress" Y5. 8-bed dorm Y10, 2-bed Y20; singles with bath, TV, and fan Y50; standard double with summer discount Y60; "suite" Y85. ❶

Education Hotel (jiàoyù bīnguǎn; 教育宾馆), 64 Taoyuan Lu (☎280 6056, ext. 6001; fax 284 0822), at the end of the alley next to Everbright Bank. At the intersection of Taoyuan Lu and Jiaoyu Lu, just left of the "Happy Space" entertainment center. A bit removed from the main thoroughfare, and therefore quieter. Renovated rooms include A/C, phone, bath, and TV. 24hr. hot water. Singles Y110-150; doubles Y110-280. ❷

Guiyin Hotel (guìyín dàjiǔdiàn; 桂银大酒店), 15 Jiaoyu Lu (☎283 2833; fax 281 1018). A fair option in a less frantic section of Nanning, with great views of the city from the 20th fl. With bath, TV, and A/C. Singles Y238; doubles Y268. ❸

🔋 📊 FOOD AND ENTERTAINMENT

Though it borrows much of its food from the venerable Yue (粤) cuisine of neighboring Guangdong province, Nanning nonetheless has its specialties, such as the sour and spicy **"Old Friend Noodles"** (lǎo yǒu miàn; 老友面), **rolled rice noodles** (juàn tǒng fěn; 卷筒粉), **fried snails** (chǎo tiánluó;炒田螺), and pyramid-shaped **glutinous rice wrapped in reed leaves** (zòng zi; 粽子). The **Zhongshan Lu nightmarket,** near the train station around Zhonghua Lu and Chaoyang Lu, is a veritable emporium of seafood, especially **shellfish,** readily displayed and barbecued to order. Grilled oysters on the half-shell with a garlicky chili sauce are only Y9 for a half dozen. (Open daily approx. 7:30pm-midnight.) Look for cheap, homemade noodle stands (zhèng zǒng lā miàn; 正宗拉面 ; Y3 per bowl). For a more thrilling fix, a little hideaway on Taoyuan Lu offers an anatomized catalog of various **horse** bits. Try the horsemeat rice noodle broth (huí mǎ qiāng ròu fěn; 回马枪肉粉). Look for a picture of a running horse, to the left while facing the Happy Space Complex. (Open 24hr.)

Meilihua Ice Palace (měilìhuá bīngchéng;美丽华冰城), 51 Minzhu Lu, at Xinhua Lu. A 2nd location named **Meijie Ice Palace** (méijié bīng chéng; 梅姐冰城), 12 Jiaoxu Lu (☎531 1280). Simple, homestyle cooking and a prime opportunity to people-watch at the busy intersection near Chaoyang Gardens. English menu and a few Western-style options. Less suitable for vegetarians, or those who detest Taiwanese pop songs. A/C. Assorted juices, shakes, and bubble teas Y6-9. Shaved ice Y5-12. Small dishes Y5-15. Open daily 9:30am-2:30am. ❶

Tianhong Northeastern Dumplings (tiān hóng dōngběi jiǎozǐ;天宏东北饺子), 65 Chaoyang Lu (☎242 8868). An alarming variety of dumplings (Y2.5-5 for 6), from lamb and onion to vegetarian fillings. Try the crunchy pork and water chestnut (zhūròu mǎtí; 猪肉马蹄), or sample the pretty smorgasbord of cold dishes on display (Y7). Open 24hr. ❶

Purple Cloud Pavilion (zǐyúnxuān; 紫云轩), 38 Xinmin Lu (☎211 8290), by the Mingyuan Xindu Hotel. Rustic wooden chairs and tables belong more in a tea house (or a pavilion) than a food court. Dim sum, pastries, juices, fries, sushi. Picture menu in English. Dishes Y4-35. Open daily lunch 11am-2:30pm, dinner 5pm-midnight. ❶

🔘 SIGHTS

BLUE MOUNTAIN SCENIC AREA (qīngxiù shān fēngjǐng qū; 青秀山风景区). A subtropical oasis to the southeast of the city center, this park sprawls across the surrounding hills. Hikers can tackle the surprisingly steep climbs to reach invigorating panoramas. Otherwise, take the yellow minibus shuttle (Y2) from the main entrance on Qingxiu Lu to the center of the park. Those who make the trek entirely on foot, however, will be rewarded by the opportunity to pick fruit in gardens (zìxuǎn guǒ yuán; 自选果园) lining the long path near the start of the route. Take time to feed the overly eager goldfish in the pond at the base of the **Dragon Pagoda** (lóngxiàng tǎ;龙象塔), or venture to the **Phoenix Pagoda** (fènghuáng tǎ;凤凰塔) at the other end of the park. **Lion Forest Temple** (shī lín; 狮林), one of several temples on the mountainside, is not far from the cable car to the **Monument to Martyrs of the Sino-Japanese War.** *(8km southeast of Nanning. Take bus #10 along Chaoyang Lu to the West Gate. A minibus leaves irregularly 8am-5pm from Chaoyang Gardens for Y3. ☎530 7280. Open 6am-1am. Y15.)*

GUANGXI MUSEUM (guǎngxī bówùguǎn; 广西博物馆). This museum is positively obsessed with bronze drums, displaying them in the museum proper as well as in the form of a giant drum-shaped restaurant (tóng gǔ lóu; 铜鼓楼). The second floor is dedicated to traditional handicrafts and costumes of Guangxi's 12 minority peoples, including weaving machines and the *lúshēng*, a reed instrument of the Miao people. Behind the museum, bridges and open-air pavilions in the style of minority architecture adorn **Nanning Cultural Park** (nánníng wénwù yuàn; 南宁文物 苑). There is also a somewhat derelict stage for performances and a crafts shop. *(On Minzu Dadao. Bus #6 runs from the train station and stops in front of the museum. ☎281 0907. Open 8:30am-noon and 2:30-5:30pm; summer 8:30am-noon and 3-6pm; holidays 9am-5pm. Last admission 1hr. before closing.)*

PARKS. The early mornings and evenings see Nanning residents congregating in the city's well-kept parks, filled with shapely rock formations and ample shade from thick foliage. **People's Park** (rénmín gōngyuán; 人民公园) lies a short distance northeast of the city center and also has a small children's amusement park, a sea lion show, and an underwater world, as well as sculpted gardens, rocks, pavilions, and a lake. Joggers, lovers, and *tai chi* practitioners take to the dense woods and boulevard-like paths. *(Main entrance is on Gongyuan Lu, near where Renmin Lu branches off to the right. Side entrance is on Xinmin Lu. Open 24hr. Paddle boats Y12 per hr.)* The Nanning skyline forms an impressive backdrop for **Nanhu Park**. *(Accessible by buses #3, 8, and 10. Open 24hr. Y2.)*

■ DAYTRIPS FROM NANNING

YILING CAVE AND WUMING

Yiling and Wuming are 21km and 38km north of Nanning, respectively. Bus #2 runs to Yiling from Chaoyang Gardens, at Chaoyang Lu and Renmin Lu. Alternatively, take bus #36 to the Anji Passenger Transport Center or #41 to Anji Da Lu; a taxi from the train station is about Y15. Buses (every 40min. 7am-7pm; Yiling Y6, Wuming Y10) leave from the transport center. ☎602 0420. Guided tours in Chinese every hr. 8am-5pm. Open daily 8am-5pm. Gate entrance Y15, cave fee Y25; students half-price, ages 70 and up free.

Yiling Cave (yīlǐng yán; 伊岭岩) and the village of **Wuming** (武鸣) are the biggest tourist draws around Nanning. A million-year-old karst cave known as an "underground palace," Yiling adds artificial fun to its attractions with a reconstructed Zhuang (壮) minority village. Join in the bamboo pole dancing and folk song sessions, or sample traditional confectionery and glutinous rice wine (included in the entrance fee). Within the cave, red, blue, and green spotlights are slightly kitschy accessories to an otherwise intricate array of rock structures, many of which are named after elements of Chinese mythology. Beware the monkeys in the grounds outside, as they are known to grab and attack humans carrying food or colorful objects. North of the caves, the village of **Wuming** is known for its natural springs swimming pool. **Lingshui** (líng shuǐ; 灵水), the size of a small lake, has a gate fee of Y6 per day; inner tubes are Y5 per day. There are no lifeguards or closing hours.

ZUO RIVER SCENIC AREA

To reach the Zuo River Scenic Area (zuǒjiāng fēngjǐngqū; 左江风景区), take a bus or train bound for Pingxiang (凭祥) from Jiangnan Bus Station or Nanning Train Station. (Both take about 3hr. Train Y26. Bus Y50.) Once at the town of Ningming (宁明), a 2½hr. train ride away from the Vietnamese border, take a cruise down the Zuo River (boat ride Y30) to view karst rock formations and tour the neighboring minority villages. Take a 40min. boat ride from Ningming to see the **Huashan wall paintings,** emblazoned on the cliff rocks by Zhuang minority people (Y15).

GUILIN 桂林 ☎ 0773

Cradled by dramatic limestone hills known as karst formations, Guilin enjoys its reputation as one of China's most beautiful natural settings. The jagged peaks and the Li River's gentle green bends attract visitors from throughout China and the world. Nearly everywhere in the busy, modern city, you're only minutes away from a quiet and beautiful park, a respite you'll appreciate given Guilin's apparent love affair with neon lights and monolithic department stores. Guilin is one of China's celebrity cities and, like any celebrity, it loves the limelight (and the limestone).

⌐ TRANSPORTATION

Flights: Lijiang International Airport (líjiāng guójì jīchǎng; 漓江国际机场 ; ☎284 5304). Taxis from downtown Guilin to the airport cost Y80-100. A shuttle bus (6:30am-7:30pm, Y20) runs from the airport to the train station (follow the signs to the minivan, right outside the baggage area), and also shuttles between the airport and the **CAAC ticket office** (☎384 3918, 384 7208, or 384 7209; fax 380 6463), on Shanghai Lu and Minzhu Lu, which can book domestic tickets. Open daily 7:30am-10:30pm. To: **Beijing** (3 per day, Y1790); **Guangzhou** (5 per day, Y660); **Hong Kong** (1-2 per day, Y1744); **Wuhan** (2 per week, Y780).

Trains: Guilin Railway Station (guìlín huǒchē zhàn; 桂林火车站 ; ☎383 2904), at the intersection of Zhongshan Nan Lu and Shanghai Lu. The ticket office is on the 1st fl., on the left when facing the station. Tickets go on sale 3 days in advance and frequently sell out in summer, especially hard sleeper tickets, so arrive at 8am when the ticket office opens. Luggage storage. To: **Beijing** (27hr., 3 per day, Y401-420); **Guangzhou** (14hr., 6pm, Y201-215); **Kunming** (23hr., 3 per day, Y251-277); **Nanning** (5hr., many per day, Y50); **Shanghai** (27hr., 3 per day, Y330-353); **Xi'an** (28hr., 5:25pm, Y323-346). Most trains through Guilin also pass through the **Guilin North Train Station** (guìlín běi huǒchē zhàn; 桂林北火车站), on Zhongshan Bei Lu, north of the city center.

Buses: Guilin Long-Distance Bus Station (guìlín chángtú qìchē zhàn; 桂林长途汽车站 ; ☎382 0600), on the northern section of Zhongshan Nan Lu, between Yinding Lu and Nanhuan Lu, a 10min. walk north of the train station. To: **Longsheng** (2hr., 20 per day 7am-8pm, Y15); **Nanning** (8hr.; 3, 8pm; Y94); **Sanjiang** (6hr., 5 per day, Y22); **Yangshuo** (1½hr., every 20min., Y6-10). Direct buses to Guangzhou, Longsheng, and Nanning are a bit more expensive but twice as fast. **Minibuses** to Yangshuo (Y10) leave from the Guilin Train Station parking lot; verify price and destination before boarding.

Local Transportation: Most **buses** leave from Zhongshan Nan Lu, outside the train station. Fare Y1-2. Maps at the bus stop indicate routes. Bus frequency within the city is every 5-10min. Bus #1 runs from the intersection of Shanghai Lu and Zhongshan Nan Lu to the North Train Station; #2 from Guilin Railway Station, past Nanmen Bridge, Elephant Trunk Hill, Fubo Hill, and Folded Brocade Hill; #3 from Guilin Railway Station through the rice fields at the edge of town to Reed Flute Park toward Yangshuo; #5 from Guilin Railway Station, past Wayan Crossroad and Yanshan Zhen, to Yangshuo; #8 and 27 from Guilin Railway Station down Cuizhu Lu to Xiongsen Bear and Tiger Village; #11 from Seven Star Park, past Crossroad Circle, the Guilin Railway Station, and South Stream Park, to Pingshan; #13 from Seven Star Park, up Zhongshan Zhong Lu past Solitary Peak Park and Folded Brocade Hill, to Reed Flute Park; #14 from West Hill Park, past Jiefang Bridge and Sanlidian Circle, to Wulidian.

Taxis: Taxis cluster around bus and train stations from early morning to past 11pm.

Bicycle Rental: Inquire at the **Overseas Chinese Mansions**, 39 Zhongshan Nan Lu. An old man down the block rents bikes for Y15 per day. Deposit Y150 or passport: opt for the cash. Bikes due back at 7pm on the day of rental. Bikes from the **Universal Hotel** are significantly more expensive at Y8 per hr.

＊ 🔏 ORIENTATION AND PRACTICAL INFORMATION

Guilin's four urban districts, one suburban district, and two counties cover 4195km² of parks, karst pinnacles, and lakes. The city center lies between **Zhongshan Lu** (中山路), which runs north-south, and the **Li River** (漓江), which runs parallel in the east. **Binjiang Lu** (滨江路) runs along the river's western shore, with **Chuanshan Lu** (穿山路) along its eastern shore. **Jiefang Lu** (解放路), **Nanhuan Lu** (南环路), and **Shanghai Lu** (上海路) run east-west and intersect Zhongshan Lu. **Seven Star Park** (qīxīng gōngyuán; 七星公园) is in a residential area east of the river.

Travel Agency: CITS, 41 Binjiang Lu (☎286 1801, English 282 8314 or 282 8304; fax 280 5303), north from where Nanhuan Lu hits Li River. Books tours, Li River cruises (Y450 to Yangshuo), and flights. Also has an Individual Travelers Department, but go to them for information rather than for overpriced tours. Open daily 8:30am-noon and 3-6:30pm, international services M-F only.

Bank of China: 5 Shanhu Bei Lu (☎283 1147). Exchanges traveler's checks. Credit card advances. Open daily 8am-noon and 3-6pm. A branch on the corner of Yinding Lu and Zhongshan Nan Lu, near the train station, exchanges currency, as does a branch on Zhongshan Zhong Lu, near the post office on the corner of Lequn Lu. The **Lijiang Hotel,** 1 Shanhu Bei Lu, and the **Sheraton Guilin Hotel,** 9 Binjiang Nan Lu, exchange currency for non-guests.

Bookstore: Xinhua Bookstore (☎280 2868) in Guilin Book City has a small selection of English-language books, including an extensive "Chicken Soup for the Soul" collection. Books in Russian, Italian, and Spanish also available. Music and VCDs in the basement. Open daily 8am-10pm.

Department Stores: Guilin Niko Niko Do Plaza (guìlín wēixiào táng; 桂林微笑堂), 187 Zhongshan Zhong Lu (☎281 5390), at Jiefang Lu. A behemoth 6-floor department store with a pharmacy, grocery store, and selection of English-language books. Open daily 7am-10pm. Credit cards accepted. Department stores abound on this section of Zhongshan Lu, most of them just south of Niko Niko Do.

Hospital: People's Hospital (shìrénmín yīyuàn; 市人民医院 ; ☎282 3767), on Wenming Lu, which curves off Zhongshan Zhong Lu and Nanhuan Lu.

Pharmacy: On Zhongshan Nan Lu, south of the bus station, under a sign saying "medicine."

Internet Access: Purple Fate Internet Bar (zǐyuán wǎng bā; 紫缘网吧 ; ☎288 3049) is on the northern section of Zhengyang Lu. Walking north, look for it on your left. Y2 per hr. Another **Internet cafe,** on Wenming Lu, is just around the corner from Nanhuan Lu toward the hospital. Y6 per hr.

Post and Telecommunications: 249 Zhongshan Lu (☎281 4339), 2 blocks north of Jiefang Lu, toward Solitary Peak Park. EMS, IDD service, and Poste Restante. The only place in town to make collect calls. There are 2 other post offices along Zhongshan Lu. All open daily 8am-8pm.

Postal Code: 541000.

🔏 ACCOMMODATIONS

Guilin is packed with hotels for ritzy tour groups, but a handful of budget accommodations cater to independent travelers. Zhongshan Nan Lu has the widest selection. Many budget travelers opt to head directly to Yangshuo for the night.

Overseas Chinese Mansions (huáqiáo dàshà; 华侨大厦), 39 Zhongshan Nan Lu (☎383 5753; fax 383 5614). From the station, take bus #4 or 11 to Nanxi Park, and backtrack a few minutes; or turn right as you exit the train station, and walk down

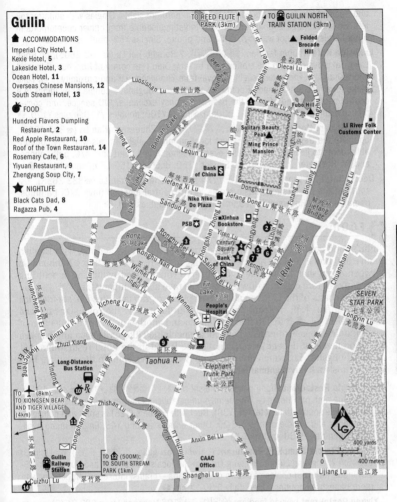

Guilin

▲ ACCOMMODATIONS

Imperial City Hotel, 1
Kexie Hotel, 5
Lakeside Hotel, 3
Ocean Hotel, 11
Overseas Chinese Mansions, 12
South Stream Hotel, 13

● FOOD

Hundred Flavors Dumpling
   Restaurant, 2
Red Apple Restaurant, 10
Roof of the Town Restaurant, 14
Rosemary Cafe, 6
Yiyuan Restaurant, 9
Zhengyang Soup City, 7

■ NIGHTLIFE

Black Cats Dad, 8
Ragazza Pub, 4

Zhongshan Lu. Clean, well-furnished rooms away from the commotion, but within walking distance of the city center. Friendly staff. 24hr. hot water, A/C, bath, phone, and TV. 10% service charge. Dorms Y60; doubles Y120-250; triples Y300. ❶

Kexie Hotel (kēxié zhāodàisuǒ; 科协招待所), 3 Yiren Lu (☎282 5237). From the station, take the #1 to Century Sq. and walk down Yiren Lu past Zhengyang Lu. The hotel is on your right, opposite the Yiren Hotel. Clean rooms provide all the basic amenities (A/C, TV, phone, and bath) and look out into a pleasant open courtyard filled with plants. Singles are a bit small, but doubles are larger than average to compensate. Singles Y90; doubles Y100; triples Y120. ❷

Imperial City Hotel (huángchéng fàndiàn; 皇城饭店), 4 Feng Bei Lu (☎282 9453). North of the post office, right around the corner from Solitary Beauty Peak, on the corner of Feng Bei and Zhongshan Zhong Lu. The location may be more removed from the train and bus stations, but it puts you closer to the northern sights. Singles with squatter toilets are small; large doubles are virtually indistinguishable from pricier counterparts in other hotels. 24hr. hot water, A/C, TV, and phone. Singles Y50; doubles Y90. ❶

Lakeside Hotel (húbīn fàndiàn; 湖滨饭店), 2 Ronghu Bei Lu (☎282 2665), on Rong Lake. Take bus #2 from the station area to Yang Qiao (the corner of Ronghu Bei Lu and Zhongshan Lu). The hotel's slight removal from Zhongshan Lu and proximity to Fir Lake make for a nice atmosphere. Rooms are scattered throughout a couple of buildings in a central courtyard and offer all the basics. Currency exchange, IDD service, and convenience counter. Hot water 7:30-11:30pm. Singles Y100; doubles Y110; triples Y120. ❷

South Stream Hotel (nánxī fàndiàn; 南溪饭店), 84 Zhongshan Nan Lu (☎383 4943), opposite the train station. Convenient location for late-night arrivals with very comfortable rooms to justify the price, and even a bellhop if you need one. A/C, bath, phone, and TV. Hot water 7:30-11:30pm. Singles Y150; doubles Y150-180; triples Y150. ❷

Ocean Hotel (hǎiyáng fàndiàn; 海洋饭店), 95 Zhongshan Nan Lu (☎383 3688), just south of the bus station. Basic rooms in this central location have A/C, bathtubs, phone, and TV. Hot water 7am-9pm. Singles and doubles Y80. ❶

🍴 FOOD

Guilin's food comes in two varieties: tourist fare in swanky settings with English menus, and home cooking at sidewalk stalls. In the restaurants lining Nanhuan Lu between Zhongshan Lu and the river, observe your **seafood** swimming or scuttling in the tanks before chowing down. The locals rave about Linjiang Lu (临江路), on the eastern bank of the Li River, as the best place to grab favorites like **stir-fried rice noodles** (mǐfěn; 米粉). From Zhongshan Nan Lu, follow the road signs to **Food Street** (měishí jiē; 美食街) to find Yinding Lu and another impressive collection of local noodle shops. Both areas have local specialties like **turtle soup** and **bamboo rat**. Good meals at decent prices can also be found in the hotel restaurants that crowd Zhongshan Lu, which are surprisingly busy after 7pm. In the evening, Binjiang Lu hosts a lively **nightmarket**.

Red Apple Restaurant (hóng píngguǒ měishí zhījiā; 红苹果美食之家 ; ☎382 4678), under the arch on Yinding Lu. This family-run establishment prepares great local dishes like tortoise soup with vegetables (Y38). Beef with peppers (Y28) is spicy and delicious. Dumplings and noodle dishes Y15-20. Other entrees around Y48. English menu available. Open daily 9:30am-11pm. ❷

Hundred Flavors Dumpling Restaurant (bǎiwèi jiǎozi guǎn; 百味饺子馆), on Libin Lu between Zhengyang Lu and Binjiang Lu. Join the locals for noodles and dumplings (Y5-15) made with your choice of bizarre chicken parts—brains, intestines, or feet—or with more pedestrian options. Open daily 6:30-11pm. ❶

Yiyuan Restaurant (yíyuán fàndiàn; 怡园饭店), 106 Nanhuan Lu (☎282 0470), serves up tasty Sichuanese dishes in a lively setting. Huge windows, a humming evening crowd, and fresh, spicy food make up for the lack of live food displays. Try the spicy pickles, if you dare. Carp with hot bean sauce (Y35) is a house specialty. English menu available. Entrees Y6-60. Open daily 11:30am-2:30pm and 4:30-9:30pm. ❷

Roof of the Town Restaurant at Hong Kong Hotel (xiāngjiāng fàndiàn; 香江饭店 ; ☎383 3889; fax 383 8575), on the 19th fl. of the Hong Kong Hotel, down Cuizhu Lu, 1 block west of the train station. Tasty standard Chinese dishes play 2nd fiddle to the outstanding view and rotating windows. The Cantonese breakfast buffet, served 7:30-10am, is a delicious bargain at Y22. Entrees Y30-80. Open daily 7:30am-10:30pm. ❸

Rosemary Cafe (bǐsàdiàn; 比萨店), 1-3 Yiren Lu (☎281 0063), west of the pedestrian street. The owner of this cafe took her cues from the thriving backpacker culture of her native Yangshuo to create a haven that caters to the backpacker's every need. The free maps, book swap, friendly English-speaking company, and food ranging from yogurt with muesli (Y10) to vegetable pizza (Y19) and cappucino (Y15) may be just what you're looking for. Open daily 10am-midnight. ❷

Zhengyang Soup City (zhèngyáng tāng chéng; 正杨汤城), 60 Zhengyang Lu (☎285 8553), between Yiren Lu and Renmin Lu. Terrific English menu has standard favorites like sweet-and-sour pork (Y30) and fried Guilin rice noodles (Y20), in addition to its namesake soups, ranging from double boiled mushroom (Y30) to turtle (Y120). Open daily 11:30am-2:30pm and 5-10pm. ❷

🧭 SIGHTS

Guilin's parks, misty caves, and river vistas attract visitors from far and wide. At times, especially during the summer, the city swarms with camera-toting tourists on a mission to see it all in one afternoon. Taxis offer full-day city tours for about Y100, usually bargainable to about half-price for those willing to tail tour buses, but everything is easily accessible by public transportation. Travelers with a few days to spare will be rewarded with time to discover the relaxing, quieter parks outside the downtown area.

Guilin's biggest party is the annual **Dragon Boat Festival** (duānwǔ jié; 端午节), which falls on the fifth day of the fifth lunar month on the Chinese calendar. During the festival, the Li River churns with Dragon Boat Races, while spectators and old Chinese drums line the shores to cheer on the rowers.

REED FLUTE PARK (lúdí gōngyuán; 芦笛公园). Reed Flute Park is famed as home to Guilin's best scenery, both above and below ground. The park's main attraction is **Reed Flute Cave** (lúdí yán; 芦笛岩), an enormous cavern filled with elaborate rock formations, formed nearly 1 million years ago. To control the flow of people through the subterranean wonderland, Guilin has built a 500m-long paved trail with garish neon lights, at times making the cave appear more like a movie set than anything else. English tours are available upon request, but you may want to convince the staff to let you skip the tour in favor of freedom to move around on your own. The rest of the park provides the rare opportunity to commune with Guilin's karst hills without paying admission. Climb the peak across from the cave entrance to admire the karst-studded landscape. Nearby **Fragrant Lotus Pool** (fāng lián chí; 芳莲池) has bamboo rafts available for rental. (*A 25min. ride from the center of Guilin. Accessible by bus #3. Park open daily sunrise to sunset. Free. Pond open daily Apr.-Nov. 7:30am-6pm; Dec.-Mar. 8am-5:30pm. Y45, Dec.-Mar. Y40; bamboo rafts Y5 per hr. Cave open 8am-6pm. Y60.*)

ELEPHANT TRUNK PARK (xiàng shān gōngyuán; 象山公园). Knee-deep in the water, **Elephant Trunk Hill** (xiàng bí shān; 象鼻山) stands at the meeting point of the Li River and the **Peach Blossom River** (táohuā jiāng; 桃花江). As the most famous karst pinnacle of Guilin, the leafy limestone elephant pokes up its trunk in photographs and postcards everywhere. On its back, it carries the **Puxian Pagoda** (pǔxián tǎ; 普贤塔), built during the Song Dynasty as an offering to calm the flood-prone river. Visitors can also climb to the **Elephant Eye Cave** (xiàng yǎn yán; 象眼岩), watch cormorant fishing from a boat, pose with a monkey for a souvenir photo, or simply relax on the **Three Star Island** (sānxīng dǎo; 三星岛) across the crooked bridge. (*On Nanhuan Lu, across from CITS. Open daily 6:30am-10:30pm. Cormorant fishing Y10, monkey photo Y3. Y25, but some get in free around twilight when there are fewer visitors.*)

SEVEN STAR PARK (qī xīng gōngyuán; 七星公园). Guilin's largest park boasts **Seven Star Cave** (qī xīng yán; 七星岩) and the appropriately named **Camel Hill** (luò-tuó shān; 骆驼山) among its attractions, but attractions aren't the most important thing here. The expansive park's relative seclusion from the tour group circuit makes it a peaceful place to wander and rest. *(Across the Li River from the city center. Open daily 6am-11pm. Cave open 8am-5:30pm. Park Y25; cave Y30.)*

XIONGSEN BEAR AND TIGER VILLAGE (xióngsēn xiónghǔ shānzhuāng; 雄森熊虎山庄). Giant tiger and bear statues welcome visitors to this "village" (don't be fooled, it's actually a zoo), which cares for some of the most endangered animals in Asia, including the South China and Siberian tigers and the black bear. An assortment of crocodiles, monkeys, and ostriches is added to the mix. Skip the guided 3hr. Chinese tour to roam the premises on your own. *(On Cuizhu Lu, halfway to the airport. To get there, get a minibus from the train station, or take the #8 or 27 bus down Cuizhu Lu. Y2-3. ☎280 9257. Open daily 9am-5pm. Y80.)*

SOUTH STREAM PARK (nánxī shān gōngyuán; 南溪山公园). This park is far less heavily touristed than its northern counterparts, though less well tended and without the breathtaking vistas. The **Buddha Cave** and **White Dragon Cave,** which house Buddha statues and stalactite and stalagmite formations, respectively, can be skipped. Frequented by local families and seniors, the park's community atmosphere provides a perfect place to relax at the end of the day. You should be able to get in free near sunset. *(On Zhongshan Nan Lu, a 15min. walk south of the train station. ☎280 9217. Open daily sunrise to sunset. Park Y6, Buddha Cave Y6, White Dragon Cave Y15.)*

LI RIVER FOLK CUSTOMS CENTER (guìlín líjiāng mínsú fēngqíng yuán; 桂林漓江民俗风情园). The province's largest venue showcases the culture, architecture, and art of Guangxi's minorities in a predictably cheesy and overdone manner. Admission includes educational demonstrations and minority dancing and singing performances throughout the day. *(On Linjiang Lu, at Linjiang Kou. ☎581 5678. Open daily 8:30am-11pm. Y45, after 7pm Y60.)*

OTHER SIGHTS. In the center of Guilin, sharing the **Ming Prince Mansion** with Guangxi Normal University, the monolith-like **Solitary Beauty Peak** (dú xiù fēng; 独秀峰) rises over 150m and offers a stunning panoramic view. *(On Zhongshan Zhong Lu, north of Jiefang Lu. ☎280 9217. Y15.)* **Fubo Hill** (fúbō shān; 伏波山), on the Li River's western bank near Solitary Beauty Peak, rises to a slightly lesser height above the Li River at the point where Binjiang Lu turns into Longzhu Lu. The Tang and Song Dynasties left their mark in **Thousand Buddha Cave** (qiānfó dòng; 千佛洞), where sculptors carved and artists painted (significantly fewer than 1000) Buddhist statues and frescoes into the walls. *(Open daily sunrise-sunset. Y15.)* To visit **Folded Brocade Hill** (dié cǎi shān; 叠彩山), continue north on Longzhu Lu, take a left at Diecai Lu, and then a right. The hill is down the long tree-lined path. Skip the creepy butterfly museum pagodas and Fantastic Stones Museum, and head for the top to gaze at the sprawling city and the misty crags beyond. *(Open daily sunrise-sunset. Y13.)*

♫ 🍸 ENTERTAINMENT AND NIGHTLIFE

The city lights up at nightfall; lasers slice the sky, neon floods over buildings, and music pulses from every storefront. The **nightmarket** on Binjiang Lu is always crowded and worth a visit. Coffee shops on Zhengyang Lu are open until 11pm or later, and outdoor seating offers a place to relax and chat. Bars crowd the downtown area, but most are primarily frequented by karaoke-seeking businessmen. To live up to the ambitious sign proclaiming itself the "Best Bar in Town," **Ragazza Pub,** on Yiren Lu at Zhengyang Lu, blasts live music most nights to a lively young crowd, while karaoke rooms fill the 2nd floor. (No cover. Local draft beer Y20. Open daily 8pm-2am.) For some chest-thumping bass and a chance to groove with local youth, head to **Black Cats Dad,** a club you'll hear long before you see, off Zhengyang Lu just south of the Ragazza Pub. (No cover. Beer Y30. Open nightly 9pm-2am.)

YANGSHUO 阳朔 ☎0773

Like Guilin, Yangshuo is home to some of the country's most beautiful scenery, and provides ample opportunity to explore the craggy limestone pinnacles that are the region's hallmark. The Li River snakes its way between the two cities, and many expensive package tours cruise to Yangshuo from Guilin, stopping only long enough to let passengers load up on cheap trinkets. When the tour boats go, the backpackers remain—often longer than they ever intended—captivated by Yangshuo's curving river, misty green peaks, and traveler-friendly atmosphere. The main streets are an oasis of faux familiarity to visitors who chuckle at its "Fawlty Towers Hotel," "Hard Seat Cafe," and "Planet Yangshuo." Travelers pass the days exploring the natural wonders of the nearby countryside and spend the evenings in the eateries along Xi Jie, sipping coffee and swapping stories to the sounds of Jimi Hendrix and Britney Spears. Yangshuo might be right in the midst of things in Guangxi province, but you'll have trouble convincing yourself that this is actually China. More a backpacker enclave than a Chinese city, it seems to exist almost solely for the travelers who pack its hotels and guesthouses.

▐▌ TRANSPORTATION

Buses: The **bus station,** on Pantao Lu across from Yangshuo Park gate, services both long-distance and local traffic. Buses not going toward the Li River region usually depart from Guilin. Tickets sold daily 8am-5:30pm, but booking window is often unmanned in the middle and end of the day. Tickets also available from travel agents and hostel owners. Bus to **Guangzhou** (14hr., 2 per day, Y98), express overnight (9, 10, 11pm; Y150).

Minibuses: Minibuses make the trip to **Guilin** (1½hr., every 10-15min. or when bus fills to 110% capacity, Y6-10), leaving from or around the bus station. Beware of being overcharged. Minibuses go to **Xingping** (1hr., every 20min., Y5) via **Fuli** (15min., Y5).

Ferries: See the Li River description in **Sights,** p. 614.

Bike Rental: Many hotels and vendors along Xi Jie rent mountain bikes for Y10-15 per day. Make sure you test your bike out before you leave—not all of them are in the best condition. Bikes are due back between 6 and 7pm the same day.

SOUTHWEST

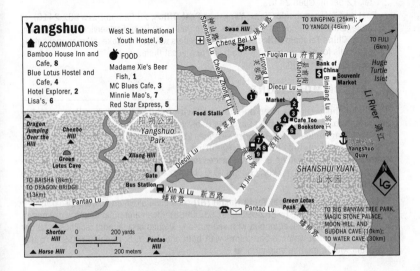

Yangshuo

⌂ ACCOMMODATIONS
Bamboo House Inn and Cafe, **8**
Blue Lotus Hostel and Cafe, **4**
Hotel Explorer, **2**
Lisa's, **6**
West St. International Youth Hostel, **9**

♥ FOOD
Madame Xie's Beer Fish, **1**
MC Blues Cafe, **3**
Minnie Mao's, **7**
Red Star Express, **5**

■ ☷ ORIENTATION AND PRACTICAL INFORMATION

Southeast of Guilin, central Yangshuo lies between **Yangshuo Park** to the west and the **Li River** and **Green Lotus Peak** to the east. Across the street from the park gate, the bus station sits on the town's main road **Pantao Lu** (蟠桃路). From the bus station, Pantao Lu runs east toward the city center and the river. The post office is at the intersection of Pantao Lu and **Xi Jie** (西街), where you'll find Yangshuo's guesthouses, cafes, and restaurants. Visitors who arrive by boat at the **Yangshuo Quay** (yángshuò mǎtóu; 阳朔码头) on **Binjiang Lu** (滨江路) should walk along the river toward Green Lotus Peak. Xi Jie runs away from the river, on the right.

Travel Agencies: Travel agencies, backpacker cafes, and self-proclaimed tour guides crowd Xi Jie and Pantao Lu. Don't expect the guides to give you a good deal, but many can be approached for information and advice. **Light Travels** (làngmàn zhī lǚ; 浪漫之旅; ☎881 1939; www.yangshuo-light-travels.com) on Xi Jie, run by a friendly husband and wife team (Bill and Kathy), can give you free information about tours and daytrip options and offer numerous tours.

Bank of China: 11 Binjiang Lu (☎882 2329). Walk to the end of Xi Jie, and turn left at the river; it's 100m down on the left. Exchanges currency and traveler's checks. Another branch is on Xi Jie, near Pantao Lu. Credit card advances. Open daily summer 9am-noon and 2:30-5pm; winter 9am-noon and 3-5pm.

PSB: 39 Cheng Bei Lu (☎882 0778), on the right side of the building. Officer Zhang Jianyuan handles crimes against foreigners. Open daily 8:30am-5:30pm.

Hospital: People's Hospital (rénmín yīyuàn; 人民医院), on Shenshan Lu, at the intersection with Cheng Bei Lu. Dr. Lee (☎882 0472; pager 127 159 8929) is **SOS International's** Yangshuo doctor.

Bookstore: Cafe Too (zìyóurén cāntīng; 自游人餐厅), 56 Xi Jie (☎882 8342). English books available for trade or purchase line the walls of this small establishment.

Internet Access: Many restaurants on Xi Jie will let you use their Internet for free if you buy food, and some hostels provide free Internet for guests. Otherwise, the best deal in town is **Red Sun Computer Training** (hóngrì jìsuàn péixùn; 红日计算机培训; ☎881 1886), accessible by the tiny alley to the left of the West Street International Youth Hostel. Y2 per hr. Open 24hr.

Post and Telecommunications: Yangshuo Post Office, 28 Pantao Lu (☎882 2416), at Xi Jie. EMS, IDD, and Poste Restante. Open daily 8am-9pm. Fax service 2 doors down, in the **China Telecom Office.** Some hostel owners will let you make international calling card calls for Y2-5, or even for free if you're a guest there.

Postal Code: 541900.

⌂ ACCOMMODATIONS

Finding a cheap room—even one outfitted with toilet seats—is usually no trouble in Yangshuo. Many of the best bargains boast not only a place to lay your head, but also travel agencies, cafes, laundry services (Y1-3 per piece), and more. Bargaining hard may yield savings of up to 50% during colder months, and, as always, don't take the first price you hear. Room prices may double or triple during national holidays and Chinese New Year. Guests who stay for extended periods of time may be eligible for discounts.

▨ **West Street International Youth Hostel (HI)** (xījiē guójì qīngnián lǚguǎn; 西街国际青年旅馆), 102 Xi Jie (☎882 0933; fax 882 0988). Clean and quiet rooms with wooden bunk beds. Very well-equipped with self-catering kitchen and laundry facilities (Y10 per load). 24hr. hot water. 8-bed dorms with bath and A/C Y25; doubles Y80-90. Y5 discount with HI membership card. ❶

Bamboo House Inn and Cafe (zhúlín fàndiàn; 竹林饭店), 23 Guihua Lu (☎882 3222; bamboohouse23@hotmail.com). This popular establishment provides cheap dorm rooms that are very basic, but you'll have trouble finding a better deal on Xi Jie. Look for recruiters approaching you right off the bus. 4-bed dorms Y15; doubles and triples Y20-25, with A/C Y35-60. ❶

Lisa's (lǐshā jiǔdiàn; 李莎酒店), 71 Xi Jie (☎882 0217; lisa@public.glptt.gx.cn). The grande dame of this establishment freely dispenses travel advice and tips, but Lisa may want to get involved with every aspect of your stay: she offers it all, tours, ticket book-ings, the works. Rooms are well-kept and comfortable. 24hr. hot water. Dorms with bath Y30; singles and doubles with A/C Y50; triples Y60. Prices negotiable. ❶

Blue Lotus Hostel and Cafe (dīngdīng fàndiàn; 丁丁饭店), 62 Xi Jie (☎882 7873). Cozy rooms create a homey feel, and the tasty cafe is popular both with those staying in the hostel and others. 24hr. hot water in shared baths. Dorms Y15; singles Y20; dou-bles Y30; triples Y45. ❶

Nature House, 2 Diecui Lu (☎881 1121). Listen for bubbling streams and chirping birds. Nature House takes its name seriously, with unusual rocks in the lobby and recorded nature sounds emanating from the building. Rooms are fairly plain, but cheap. Tiny rooms only slightly bigger than a closet are the cheapest in Yangshuo at Y10. Sin-gles and doubles Y25-40. ❶

Hotel Explorer (wénhuà fàndiàn; 文化饭店), 40 Xianqian Jie (☎882 8116; fax 883 7816). This sparklingly clean establishment escapes the hubbub of Xi Jie. Slightly more upscale accommodations than what you'll find in the guesthouses. 24hr. hot water. 3-bed dorms with shared bath and A/C Y50; singles, doubles, and triples Y110-125. ❶

🄵🄵 FOOD AND NIGHTLIFE

Apart from the surrounding countryside, Yangshuo's main attraction for indepen-dent travelers is its abundant supply of Western food and company. Visitors typi-cally pass the evening hours and an occasional rainy day in the small cafes and restaurants lining **Xi Jie.** These establishments are the heart of Yangshuo's nightlife and a handy forum for trading information. Several cafes have nightly double-fea-ture showings of recent American blockbusters, and the crowd stick around until 1am or later. Make arrangements for the week's excursions, get free advice, sip coffee, knock back a few beers, play some pool, or boogie to disco.

If Western food and tourists aren't what you're looking for, you'll be hard pressed to find Chinese fare (and often, Chinese people) on Xi Jie, which appropri-ately means "West Street." To get away from the backpacker scene, look for res-taurants filled with locals on **Diecui Lu,** or the line of food stalls on **Cheng Zhong Lu,** just north of Diecui Lu.

Red Star Express (hóng xīng tèkuài; 红星特快), 66 Xi Jie (☎882 2699), has the best pizza in town, and the most variety too. The owner keeps the joint open into the wee hours. A mixed crowd of backpackers and locals makes for great socializing and story swapping. Pizza Y15-20. Chocolate cake and ice cream Y15. Beer and cocktails Y8-20. Open daily 8am-midnight (or whenever the last straggler wanders home). ❷

Minnie Mao's, 83 Xi Jie (☎882 6484). Despite the address, actually around the corner on Guihua Lu. The oldest restaurant on Xi Jie is still one of the most popular, with an extensive menu of local cuisine as well as the typical Western food offerings. Nightly movies and occasional live music. Try the stuffed tomatoes (Y6) or the steamed dump-lings (Y8-12). Entrees Y8-20. Open daily 6:30am-late. ❶

Madame Xie's Beer Fish (xiè dàjiě; 谢大姐; ☎485 5112), on Diecui Lu, just east of the intersection of Diecui Lu and Xianqian Jie. Away from Xi Jie, Yangshuo restaurants bub-ble with locals and Chinese tourists in search of beer fish (Y18-30 depending on the portion), a Yangshuo specialty. Besides fish fried in beer, this particularly popular restaurant offers an array of other standard Chinese dishes. Vegetables Y6-10. Meat and poultry Y15-25. Open daily 10am-11pm. ❷

MC Blues Cafe (lìshì jiǔdiàn; 黎士酒店), 40 Xianqian Jie (☎882 0746; fax 882 7816), a few steps from Xi Jie. Whistle while you work, listen while you eat. Food selection is typical, but MC Blues's real draw is the best selection of music around. The small book swap collection (give 1, get 2) and many copies of English publications attract Anglophones from far and wide. Soups Y8. Pizza Y12-25. Roasted bamboo rat Y80. Open daily 7am-midnight. ❷

👁 SIGHTS

Yangshuo is easily explored on foot, by bike, or by boat. The countryside overflows with routes for lazy bike rides, and the more independent biker can take to the hills and roads without a map or guide. Even visiting couch potatoes can hop on a bus to experience Yangshuo's fantastic slice of the great outdoors.

LI RIVER 漓江

Marking the eastern border of town, the Li River (líjiāng; 漓江) is Yangshuo's main attraction. It winds for miles around fantastically shaped limestone peaks bearing names like Camel Crossing the River (luòtuó guòjiāng; 骆驼过江) and Waiting for Husband Rock (wàngfū shí; 望夫石). Most travelers explore the river by boat or by bike. The most popular method is to take a one-way **boat** ride and return by **bike** to Yangshuo. You can buy boat tickets at travel agencies, guesthouses, or from the guides who will approach you on the street—but remember, always bargain.

The most popular nearby destinations along the Li River are **Xingping** (xīngpíng; 兴坪) and **Yangdi** (yángdī; 杨堤). Between Xingping (boat 3hr.; bike 2hr.) and Yangdi (boat 5hr.; bike 1½hr.) is the area's most impressive scenery. Boats float leisurely down the river with more than enough time for you to relax, take in the view, and perhaps build up an interest for the faster bike ride back. Since 2001, tour operators in Yangshuo have not been allowed to run boats to these destinations because of tourist traffic in the river and near the destination cities. A common (although still technically illegal) alternative is to take a **minibus** to Xingping (30min., departs daily around 6:30am or 3pm, Y5), where it is possible to take a round-trip cruise to **Yangdi** (3hr., Y50). Travelers usually leave early in the morning or late in the afternoon to avoid officials. Travel agents warn that a more forceful crackdown could begin at any time. To return to Yangshuo, **buses** make the trip every 15min. For those who prefer biking, bicycles can be left for safekeeping in Xingping for the return trip. Those wishing to make a day-long trip to Xingping should visit on **market days**—the 3rd, 6th, 9th, 13th, 16th, 19th, 23rd, 26th, and 29th of each month—just like in Yangshuo. From Yangshuo, you can also rent a sidecar to Xingping (round-trip Y90-100) or Fuli (round-trip Y30).

Fuli (fúlì; 福利) is the only destination available to Yangshuo boats. Most people find that the scenery on this stretch of river does not justify the inflated price, and even travel guides will admit that it may not be worth the money. But the shorter trip to Fuli (1hr. by boat, 40min. back by bike) can be a good choice for travelers with only a few days in Yangshuo. **Boat tickets** can be purchased at the **Yangshuo Dock** on Binjiang Lu for Y150, but better deals can be negotiated with travel agents. You can bike to Fuli from Xingping by taking a right on the main road. Fuli has markets like those in Xingping, with an assortment of goods, including frogs, snakes, firecrackers, fishing baskets, and woven hats. Fuli specializes in fans and calligraphy: visit any of the calligraphy shops lining the street perpendicular to the river. **Markets** are on the 2nd, 5th, 8th, 12th, 15th, 18th, 22nd, 25th, and 28th of each month.

If boat rides seem too structured for your exploration of the Li River, **kayaks** and **inner tubes** can be rented from travel agencies on Xi Jie or Pantao Lu. Li River fishermen have long trained **cormorants** to dive into the river and catch fish by the light of a flaming torch, and some enterprising locals now allow tourist boats to tag along and watch them practice their trade. (1-1½hr., daily around 8pm, Y30.) The whole experience feels contrived, but it's interesting nonetheless. Ask around at your hostel or nearby travel agent.

Opinions vary as to the quality of the Li River's water for **swimming,** but many travelers take a dip at some point. To find the favored swimming spots, take a left off Xi Jie and walk along the river upstream towards Guilin for about 30min. Water is supposedly cleaner outside and upstream from the city.

MOON HILL 月亮山

Bike for 40min. along Pantao Lu past Green Lotus Peak; take Kangzhan Lu to your right when the road forks and look for the English sign. Or take a 1-2hr. bamboo raft down the Yulong River (Y50-80). Minibuses or small trucks (Y2) from around the Yangshuo Bus Station heading to Gaotian also stop at the entrance. Open daily sunrise-sunset. Y9, with a bike Y10. Buddha Cave is down the road from Moon Hill, in the direction of Yangshuo. Water Cave is a 20min. drive past Moon Hill, in the opposite direction from Yangshuo.

Nine hundred steep steps are no leisurely stroll, but they do bring you to the top of Moon Hill (yuèliàng shān; 月亮山), named for the crescent-shaped hole through its center. The truly outstanding panorama of the countryside at the top is definitely worth the sweat. Take the short path to the top of the arch for the highest lookout. Some people advise against taking to the stairs alone: pickpockets use Moon Hill as a convenient base to target tourists admiring the scenery or struggling to the top. Tours of the hill and parts of the surrounding villages cost about Y50. Touts will look for you along Xi Jie and at other major tourist sights, but guides aren't necessary. Bike tours through the countryside (Y20-50) that bring you to Moon Hill are also popular, and can be arranged in almost any guesthouse or tourist office.

The trip to Moon Hill is best combined with visits to the Buddha Cave and the Water Cave. Try to arrange your price for the caves with a guide or ticket agent on Xi Jie before you actually reach the entrance. Bargaining can be attempted, but usually not at the ticket window.

BUDDHA CAVE (fó dòng; 佛洞). Local villagers used the cave as a shelter from the invading Japanese army during WWII. It draws its name from a tiny stalagmite inside the cave that resembles the Maitreya, or Future Buddha. The hike down through the caves is no walk in the park and can be dangerous, especially with the shoes they provide (bringing your own waterproof sandals is advisable). You'll have to duck your head, shimmy along a wall, and even crawl several times. A guide and flashlight (included in the ticket price) are required, as many parts of the massive cave system are closed to visitors. The hike will bring you past intricate rock formations, underground pools, and even a waterfall. Visitors can lie weightless in the popular **Muddy Bath,** a huge pool of mud in the depths of the caves, and emerge for a shower back at the entrance. Bargain to include the Muddy Bath as part of the half-tour. *(Half-tour Y80, full-tour Y120; both prices are negotiable.)*

WATER CAVE (shuǐ dòng; 水洞). One of the newer sights available in Yangshuo, Water Cave aims to challenge Buddha Cave's reputation as the most extensive, unaltered subterranean microcosm in the area. Tours enter the cave by boat, and pass attractions such as a 100m waterfall. Bargaining may be easier at this slightly less touristed site. *(2hr. tour Y78; 4-6hr. tour Y108; both prices are negotiable.)*

SOUTHWEST

OTHER SIGHTS

Dragon Bridge (yùlóng qiáo; 玉龙桥) lies 13km from Yangshuo, 3min. beyond the town of **Baisha.** From the bridge, built in 1412, travelers can catch a glimpse of the Li River winding through Yangshuo's rice fields and karst hills. *(Sidecar to Baisha Y5; sidecar from Baisha to Dragon Bridge Y2.)* To get up close and personal with a karst hill without parting with a single *yuán*, try **Green Lotus Peak.** The steep and often slippery 20min. trek rewards hearty hikers with a panoramic view. Follow Pantao Lu south to the end of the buildings and take the stairway from the end of the sidewalk to the beginning of the trail. Halfway up the road to Moon Hill, **Big Banyan Tree Park** is home to a tree over 1500 years old and a Zhuang minority cultural showcase. Those who balk at the Y18 admission just to see a tree may content themselves with a good glimpse as they pass by on bicycle. *(30min. bike ride, or take a Y2 minibus to Gaotian.)* A little farther across the street stands the **Magic Stone Palace** (qí shí gōng; 奇石宫), showcasing over 1000 odd geological formations found in nearby **Dragon Cave.** *(Open daily 9:30am-6pm. Y23.)*

SHOPPING

Yangshuo is the best place in China to fill your pack with priceless treasures for the folks back home. An endless variety of silk scarves, batiks, jade chopsticks, and Mao memorabilia fill the stalls along **Binjiang Lu.** Many visitors come for custom-made silk clothing, and tailors along **Xi Jie** can accommodate unusual requests (like brocade overalls) and are quick with custom orders (same-day to one-day service). Prices run about Y50 for a skirt, Y35-40 for a shirt, and Y80 for pants. Bargain when shopping in Yangshuo; the first price you hear should never be the last.

LONGSHENG 龙胜 ☎ 0773

Near karst-obsessed Guilin and Yangshuo, Longsheng provides a refreshing change of scenery. The city itself is small and unremarkable, and no rival to its backpacker-heavy neighbors, but a short bus ride away are the terraced rice fields for which Longsheng is becoming more and more heavily traveled. Longji Titian ("The Backbone of the Dragon") draws both Chinese and overseas visitors, who hike up to see the expanses of narrow ribbons of green and silver carved into the rolling hillsides and spend a night at the surrounding small villages. Clustered on either side of the Sang River, Longsheng is still unaccustomed to its sudden popularity, but it's equipped with everything you need for a comfortable stay.

TRANSPORTATION AND PRACTICAL INFORMATION

Everything relevant to a traveler lies on either side of the Heping River, a subsidiary of the **Sang River** (sāng jiāng; 桑江), and the **White Dragon Bridge** (bái lóng qiáo; 白龙桥). On the west side of the bridge, **Xi Lu** (西路) continues west to Guilin, and **Guilong Lu** (桂龙路) runs south, parallel to the river. Across the river, **Xinglong Lu** (兴龙路) and **Gulong Lu** (古龙路) are also parallel to the river. Xi Lu crosses the river to bisect these two streets and form the town center. Pedestrian paths follow the river and pass under the bridge on the eastern side.

Buses: Longsheng Long-Distance Bus Station (☎ 751 6047), on Xi Lu, just up the road from the bridge. To: **Guangzhou** (2pm, Y57-90); **Guilin** (2hr., every 20min., Y12-18); **Sanjiang** (21 per day 6:30am-6pm, Y6.5-10).

Local Transportation: Bus #1 goes along Xinglong Lu; #2 goes up Xi Lu towards Guilin. Sporadically numbered **minibuses** go to more far-flung destinations. Everything in the city is within walking distance. **Pedicabs** are Y2 and up.

Travel Agency: CITS (☎ 751 9028), on the corner of Xi Lu and Guilong Lu, just before the bridge, can organize tours to Ping'an Village and surrounding sights, but you're far better off taking public transportation.

Bank: There is no Bank of China, and no ATM that serves any major international networks. The post office doesn't have Western Union, and the fanciest hotel in town won't change money, so make sure you take out enough money for your trip.

PSB: (☎ 751 2211), on Gulong Lu, down the street from the post office, on the opposite side of the street. Open 8am-noon and 3-5pm.

Hospital: Longsheng Town Hospital (☎ 751 5675), on Gulong Lu, north of the bridge. Open 8am-9:30pm.

Bookstore: Xinhua Bookstore, on the corner of Xi Lu and Gulong Lu, on your 2nd right once over the bridge from the bus station. Limited selection of maps. Open 8am-6pm.

Internet Access: Guilin Global Internet Cafe (guìlín huánqiú wǎngbā; 桂林环球网吧; ☎ 751 4445), in a small alley behind the Xinhua Bookstore's building. An **Internet cafe** above the Xinhua Bookstore always seems to be fully occupied. Both Y2 per hr.

Post and Telecommunications: China Post (☎ 751 2316), on Gulong Lu. Down the street from the Xinhua Bookstore, on the 2nd right once across the bridge from the bus station. EMS and IDD service. Open 8am-6pm.

Postal Code: 541700.

ACCOMMODATIONS

Longsheng's accommodations are a mix of standard hotels with the usual amenities and cheaper guesthouses with plainer rooms and more limited services. If you've come to Longsheng to see Ping'an, you might be better off spending the night in the village, where rooms are cheaper and in a truly picturesque location.

Riverside Guesthouse (kǎikǎi lǚshè; 凯凯旅社), 5 Guilong Lu (☎ 751 1335). From the bus station, approach the bridge and take the last available right turn before crossing. It's down the street, on your left. Run by an English teacher, the hotel is brightened by her students, who are always eager to provide maps and help plan trips. Rooms are clean and well-kept. No A/C or phones in rooms, but TV and 24hr. hot water. Singles with squatter toilets Y20; singles and doubles with bath Y30; triples Y50. ❶

Wang Wang Guesthouse (wàng wàng zhāodàisuǒ; 旺旺招待所), 24 Zhongxin Jie (☎ 751 7045). Once across the bridge, take the 1st left and look for the English sign on the left. Wang Wang provides clean

NO WORK, ALL PLAY

KING FOR A DAY

Being a cow might seem like it's all fun and games, but in China it's hard work. Plowing, hauling and pulling in rice field after rice field, oxen are an integral part of labor (and at the end of the day in danger of becoming dinner) While these animals get few official awards for the grueling work they do, there comes a time every year when the cow becomes king The eighth day of the fourth Lunar month is the birthday of the King of Oxen, and one of the traditional festivals of the **Zhuang** people Unfortunately for the cows, the Zhuang are one of the most assimilated minority groups in Guangxi, and the festival is practiced only in rural areas where traditional culture still thrives. Where it is celebrated, the festival is a happy relief from work and much food is prepared—for the cows.

During **Ox Soul Festival,** oxen are relieved of their yokes washed, and put out to pasture with abundant water and grass The ox fence is cleaned and covered with dry rice stalks, and working or whipping the animals is strictly forbidden. The cows are fed steamed black rice, and their coats are carefully brushed. Folk songs are sung thanking the oxen for their work. In 2005, keep your eyes peeled on May 15 (May 5 2006) as you pass the rice fields the cows will be sitting back with shiny coats and mouths full of rice. The next day, of course, it's back to the yoke—birthdays come but once a year.

rooms with no frills: a bed and bathroom with squatter toilets are all you get. Singles and doubles Y50, with A/C Y80. ❶

Suifeng Hotel (suìfēng bīnguǎn; 穗丰宾馆), Xinglong Bei Lu (☎751 4598). Opposite and down the street from the Longsheng Green Food Restaurant, about a 5min. walk from the bridge. Higher prices buy you all the standard amenities (A/C, TV, phone, and free room snacks), but toilets are still squatters. Rooms are clean, staff is friendly, and the hotel is always bubbling with people. Singles Y100; doubles Y120. ❷

Tourism Guesthouse (lǚyóu zhāodàisuǒ; 旅游招待所), 1 Shengyuan Lu (☎751 2501). Take the 2nd left onto Gulong Lu once across the bridge, then the 1st right. Not the "Tourism Hotel" on Gulong Lu; this is around the corner. Dark, somewhat damp hallways lead to slightly brighter and cleaner rooms. Marks on the walls and floors. No A/C, but mosquito nets provided. Tiny balconies. Small bathrooms with squat toilets. They also run the fairly popular restaurant next door. Singles Y20; doubles Y40; triples Y30. ❶

◧ FOOD

Food, in the form of made-to-order dishes from stalls crowding the main streets, is easy to come by in Longsheng. Restaurant fare is harder to find. **Longsheng Green Food Restaurant ❷**, on Xinglong Bei Lu, has an English menu and standard Chinese selections in a congenial setting. Across the bridge from the bus station, take the first left; the restaurant is 5min. up on your left, diagonally opposite a small square. Nothing too crazy is attempted with the entrees, but what you ask for is what you get. (☎751 2473. Soups Y12-18. Meat and poultry Y15-20. Vegetables Y5-10.) **Riverside Hotel ❷** has an English menu with items like french fries (Y10) and pancakes (Y10). On Shengyuan Lu, the **Tourism Hotel** has a **restaurant ❷** next door, often full of people. Look for the **nightmarket** beneath the bridge on the side opposite the bus station for a plethora of street food, ranging from a handful of snails (Y3) to *jiǎozi* (Y5 for 20), and numerous fruit, nut, and dried fish stalls.

◉ SIGHTS

Sights in Longsheng tend to be less structured and tour-group-oriented than in other Chinese cities, and it's relatively easy to see them on your own with public transportation. Most visitors come with the intention of seeing Longji Titian. For those with more time, exploring the smaller sights and villages surrounding Longsheng can be a rewarding experience.

LONGSHENG HOT SPRINGS NATIONAL FOREST (lóngshèng wēnquán guójiā sēnlín gōngyuán; 龙胜温泉国家森林公园). The awe-inspiring view from the roughly 100 ft. wide bridge across the Sang River is a fitting entrance to the park. A path takes you into the depths of the forest, right into the middle of the beautiful trees that you gaped at on the ride here. Butterflies explode out of the foliage with every step. The forest has a prominent picture of a monkey on its sign for good reason. You very well might catch a monkey staring at you from the treetops, but don't stare back! *(The forest is a 1hr. ride away. At the train station, ask for the minibus to Senlin Gongyuan, which also goes in the same direction as Baimian, Red Yao Village, and the Hot Springs. Y5. Admission Y20.)*

DONG VILLAGES OF YINGSHUI (yínshuǐ dòng zhài; 银水侗寨). The Dong peoples are one of the many minority groups inhabiting rural Guangxi, and this village welcomes those who'd like to take a look around. Be aware though—visiting a village doesn't guarantee that residents will be eager to discuss or display their culture. The Dong have a thriving tradition of song, and you may walk in on a group singing in the village center. Take the stone path to the right of the waterfall for a nice, short climb. *(Bus #2 picks up in front of the Agricultural Bank across the bridge from the train station. The village is around 20min. away. Y10.)*

OTHER SIGHTS. The bus that goes to the National Forest also goes to several villages and other places of interest. **Red Yao Village** (zhōu jiā; 周家), a collection of beautiful traditional wooden houses at the base of a hikable slope, offers a peek into Yao culture. Yao men and women are known for their long hair and may offer to perform their hair combing ritual for you for a fee. *(40min. from Longsheng. Y10.)* Longsheng is known for its unusual rocks, and the claim to fame of the **Strange Rock of Baimian** (báimiàn qí shí; 白面奇石) is its size. This attraction centered around a stone (which admittedly is rather large) is only worth the trek if you're heading to other sights on the same route. *(45min. from Longsheng, just past Red Yao Village. Y10.)* Past the forest, the fairly commercial **Hot Springs** (wēn quán; 温泉) is aimed mainly at Chinese tourists, but still provides the chance for a nice dip in the two large hot springs pools. *(1¼hr. from Longsheng. Admission Y10, swimming Y20.)*

DAYTRIP: LONGJI TITIAN AND PING'AN VILLAGE

*About 1hr. from Longsheng. To get to Longji Titian, take the tour **buses** (Y6.5) that leave Longsheng daily at 7:40, 11am, 1, and 3pm from the bus station or in front of the Riverside Hotel. Buses drop off at Ping'an Village. Last bus from Longji Titian at 5:40pm. To reach the viewing points, a hike up a stone path from the main road takes 1½hr. Minibuses also bring visitors up. Hiking between viewing points No. 1 and 2 takes 45min. Y50.*

High up in the mountains, **Longji Titian** (龙脊梯田; "Backbone of the Dragon Terraces") is named for the contoured row after row of perfectly terraced rice paddies. Impressive for its sheer beauty and the work that must go into its upkeep, this is arguably the real reason to come to Longsheng. There are two viewing points set up, named No. 1 and 2, but the hike up the stone path is just as picturesque. From this lofty height, the terraces unfurl into the distance as far as the eye can see, radiating down the steep hillside. Paths link the viewing points to nearby minority villages and a reservoir, both of which take about one hour to walk to (ask for a map or directions at the entrance). The nearby **Old Zhuang Village** is skippable, if only because the base for all these hikes is a Zhuang Village itself, Ping'an.

The lovely **Ping'an Village** (píngān cūn; 平安村) is home to the Zhuang people, the largest minority group in China. The Longji Titian is the product of hundreds of years of toil from the Zhuang people. As the entrance point to the terraces, the village has grown used to the influx of travelers and supplies cheap overnight accommodations, restaurants, and even a one-computer **Internet cafe** for Y12 per hr. **Ping'an Hotel ❷** (píngān jiǔdiàn; 平安酒店), which sits below viewing point No. 2, is the only guesthouse with A/C and private bath. (☎758 3198. Singles Y100; doubles Y120.) Most other guesthouses have singles for Y20, doubles for Y30, and triples for Y40, give or take Y10. Housed in beautiful wooden buildings with floors connected by ladders, rooms have shared baths and no A/C, but are generally well-kept. **Countryside Inn** (xiāngcūn lǚguǎn; 乡村旅馆; ☎758 3020), where the friendly owners speak English, is a good bet. Their blue sign is visible as you walk into the village. Just around the corner, **Flying Dragon Pavilion Hotel** (lóngténg gé; 龙腾阁; ☎758 3008) is run by a neighborly father-daughter team.

BEIHAI 北海   ☎0779

Poised at the breezy edge of the southern coast of Guangxi, Beihai and its residents measure out their days by the languid waves that lap at its shores. Along the northern coastline, weather-beaten canoes and small *shānbǎn*, light wooden Chinese sailboats, nestle quietly alongside rows of sleepy shophouses, while tourists on the southern shore move to a quicker pulse—the noisy uproar of beachgoers and the heady thrum of motorboat engines.

⌐ TRANSPORTATION

Flights: Beihai International Airport (běihǎi guójì jīchǎng; 北海国际机场 ; ☎207 2511), 25km northeast of the city. **Buses** (Y10) depart for the airport 1½-2hr. before flights from the **CAAC ticket office,** 7 Beibuwan Lu (☎303 3757). Open daily 8:30am-10pm. To: **Beijing** (daily, Y2060); **Changsha** (2 per day, Y830); **Chengdu** (M, W, Su; Y1080); **Guangzhou** (2 per day, Y690); **Guilin** (1-2 per day, Y480); **Haikou** (M, T, Th-F; Y380); **Kunming** (Tu, Th, Sa; Y710); **Shanghai** (Sa-Th, Y1690).

Trains: Beihai Train Station (běihǎi huǒchē zhàn; 北海火车站 ; ☎320 9898), at the southern end of Beijing Lu. All destinations via **Nanning:** express (3hr., 7am and 4pm, Y40), regular (4¼hr., 1:48pm, Y22).

Buses: Beihai Main Bus Station (běihǎi qìchē zǒngzhàn; 北海汽车总站 ; ☎202 2094), on Beibuwan Lu. Open daily 6am-9pm. Express buses to: **Fangcheng** (2hr., 8 per day, Y30); **Guangzhou** (10hr.; 8:45, 1:10am, 8:50, 9:40pm; Y180); **Guilin** (7hr.; 8, 9am; 9:10, 10pm; Y150); **Liuzhou** (5½hr., 3 per day, Y108); **Nanning** (3hr., every 30min.-1hr. 6:50am-9pm, Y65-71).

Beihai International Passenger Dock (běihǎi guójì kèyùn mǎtóu; 北海国际客运码头), 4 Yintan Lu (☎388 1963). Open daily 7:30am-6pm. **Beihai Marine Transportation Co. (Passenger) Ticket Hall** (běihǎi hǎiyùn zǒnggōngsī kèyùn shòupiào dàtīng; 北海海运总公司客运售票大厅 ; ☎306 6829), on Sichuan Bei Lu, 100m north of Beibuwan Plaza, on the opposite side of the street. Open daily 7am-10pm. To: **Haikou** (12hr., 6pm, Y90-230); **Weizhou** (2hr., 8am, Y40-50; express 1¼hr., Y62-100). For Haikou trips only, a free bus to the dock leaves from the ticket office daily at 5:20pm.

Local Transportation: Bus stops are clearly labeled with route numbers and directions. Bus #2 runs along Haijiao Lu, Sichuan Lu, Beibuwan Lu, and Beijing Lu toward the train station; #3 runs from Haibin Park past Beibuwan Plaza to Silver Beach; #8 starts from Beibuwan Plaza and circles the entire downtown area. Y1-2.

Taxis: Base fare Y5. Pedicabs also available.

▌ PRACTICAL INFORMATION

Beihai is on a peninsula that juts into Beibuwan (literally "North Bay"; běibùwān; 北部湾). **Beibuwan Lu,** the main thoroughfare, runs from the southwest to the northeast of town. The major streets that intersect Beibuwan Lu are, from west to east, **Yunnan Lu, Guizhou Lu, Sichuan Lu, Beijing Lu,** and **Guangdong Lu.** Get directions at **Beibuwan Plaza** (běibùwān guǎngcháng; 北部湾广场) in the city center.

Travel Agency: CITS, 33 Chating Lu (☎207 8060; fax 206 2929), on the 3rd fl. of the Shangri-La Hotel, past Haibin Park. Service in English available. The **ticket center** (☎207 8030 or 207 9030; fax 207 8029) on the 1st fl. books plane, train, and bus tickets. Open daily 9am-6pm. A more accessible **branch** (☎308 5288; fax 308 5266) is on the 1st fl. of Yinhui International Hotel (yínhuī guójì dàjiǔdiàn; 银晖国际大酒店) on Beihai Dadao Xi.

Bank of China: On Beibuwan Xi Lu, to the right of Qidong Shopping Center. Open summer M-F 8:30am-6:30pm, Sa-Su and holidays 9am-5pm; winter M-F 8:30am-5pm, Sa-Su and holidays 9am-5pm. Another branch is located on Sichuan Lu, just south of the intersection with Beibuwan Lu.

ATM: Available at both Bank of China branches. DC/MC/V.

Hospital: People's Municipal Hospital (rénmín yīyuàn; 人民医院), 84 Heping Lu (☎202 2245). 24hr. pharmacy.

PSB: 213 Zhongshan Dong Lu (☎209 1114 or 209 1811). Processes visa extensions. Open daily 8:30am-noon and 3-5:30pm.

Internet Access: Healthy Internet Cafe (jiànkāng wǎng bā; 健康网吧), on the 3rd fl. of the Qidong Shopping Center on Beibuwan Lu, in the computer department. Look for the blue sign with white characters. Y2 per hr.

Post and Telecommunications: On Sichuan Lu, about 300m south of Beibuwan Sq., on the opposite side of the street. EMS and Poste Restante. Open daily 8am-8pm. The Business Services Center next door offers 24hr. fax and IDD service.

Postal Code: 536000.

■ ACCOMMODATIONS

Both no-name hostels and big-name hotels line Silver Beach, but some are uncomfortably close to nearby karaoke restaurants. The hotels within Beihai city are your best bet for a good night's sleep.

▓**Taoyuan Hotel** (táoyuán dàjiǔdiàn; 桃源大酒店; ☎202 0919; fax 202 0520) on Beibuwan Zhong Lu, opposite the bus station. Look for a bright yellow sign advertising rooms for Y68. Friendly service, cheesy paintings, and potted plants grace this homely 5-fl. guesthouse. Bright rooms come with a small snack/drink bar and mineral water dispenser. Singles Y68 and Y88; doubles Y138; triples Y168. ❶

Golden Garden Hotel (jīn yuán bīnguǎn; 金园宾馆; ☎306 8188; fax 303 5795), on Beibuwan Xi Lu opposite Qidong Shopping Center. Just a few minutes walk from Beibuwan Plaza. Surreal blue light in bathroom is a bizarre touch. TV, A/C, carpet, squat toilet, mineral water dispenser. Discounted singles Y100. ❷

Ocean Hostel (hǎiyáng zhāodàisuǒ; 海洋招待所), 224 Haijiao Lu (☎390 2014). Dirt cheap and don't expect a sandy beach. Off the beaten path near mechanical and automotive industries in a gritty area. 4-bed dorms Y18. With private bath, doubles Y70; triples Y90; quads Y100. With A/C and bath, singles Y60; doubles Y100; triples Y120. ❶

Hualian Hotel (huálián jiǔdiàn; 华联酒店), 1 Beibuwan Xi Lu (☎308 7888; fax 308 7889). Excellent location near major shopping centers and a few minutes' walk from Beibuwan Sq. All standard amenities. Singles, doubles, and triples Y280. ❹

▐ FOOD

Beihai residents seem to have a predilection for chewy sea critters like **cuttlefish** (yóuyú; 鱿鱼), **octopus** (zhāngyú; 章鱼), and **tube worm** (shā chóng; 沙虫), an innocuous, blubbery white cylinder the size of a french fry consumed more for texture than flavor. More typical aquatic fare include fish of all kinds. From its north end, Sichuan Lu leads onto the small islet Waisha Dao (外沙岛), an assembly of palatial seafood restaurants with prime waterfront seating and floating pavilions. For cheaper eats, the **nightmarket** on Changqing Lu (长青路) is strewn with hawkers selling **Sichuan stinky tofu** (sìchuān chòu dòufǔ; 四川臭豆腐) and other grilled and barbecued foods.

Waisha Danjia Restaurant (☎202 6889), on the far right side of the row of restaurants on Waisha Islet. A large, glittering, wooden barn of a restaurant, this flagship location of the Guangxi chain has the usual live seafood scampering about in tanks, plus prime oceanside seating in an open-air cabana. Live performances nightly. Seafood mostly Y20 and up. Other dishes Y5-15. Open daily 9am-2am. ❷

Danjia Food Plaza, 4 Beibuwan Lu (☎207 4168), the 2nd of 3 restaurants in the same chain, has more non-seafood dishes. An elaborate and extensive buffet display makes the menu superfluous—select your sea critter of choice from large tanks. Open daily 7:30am-2am. ❷

Guangdong Restaurant (guǎngdōng shíjiē; 广东食街 ; ☎306 3488), on Guizhou Lu about 50m north of Beibuwan Lu, just a little removed from the main thoroughfare. A popular spot for congregating locals, though the fluorescent white does nothing for the appearance of your food. Serves Beihai specialties like cuttlefish, octopus, and tube worm. Entrees Y10-30. Open daily 7am-midnight. ❷

Dexing Restaurant (déxīng jiǔlóu; 得兴酒楼), 1 Sichuan Lu, behind Beibuwan Sq. (☎303 3199). Conveniently adjacent to Beibuwan Sq. Predominantly Cantonese menu with all-day dim sum (Y2-8) and double-boiled herbal preparations (individual portion Y8). Most entrees Y8-20. English menu available. Open daily 7am-2am. ❷

👁 SIGHTS

MARINE MARKET (shuǐchǎn shìchǎng;水产市场). See all the ocean's magnificent creatures: dried, bagged, and on sale. **Pearl City,** on the market's second floor, sells pearls, shells, and derivative products, many with arcane medicinal uses that are probably opaque to the casual observer. *(On Yunnan Bei Lu at Haijiao Lu. Take bus #8 to the Marine Market stop. ☎390 8333. Pearl City open daily 9am-5:30pm; downstairs market open for indefinite hours. Free.)*

SILVER BEACH (yín tān;银滩). At Beihai's main attraction, tourists are as ubiquitous as sandcrabs, basking in droves beneath multicolored umbrellas. The best way to enjoy Silver Beach is to cruise away from the crowds by motorboat (Y8 per 10min.), or to plop down in a relatively secluded spot. *(Take minibus #3 from Beibuwan Plaza along Sichuan Lu for the 15min. ride from the city center. Taxi Y20-25. Open 24hr. Y25.)*

BEIHAI UNDERWATER WORLD (běihǎi hǎidǐ shìjiè;北海海底世界). Although it offers some entertaining diversions like fish-feeding and diving shows, as well as the usual array of fresh-water and marine life viewed through a glass tunnel, the aquarium charges a hefty fee. Not even Fei-fei (literally, Fat-fat), the biggest turtle in China, makes this sight worthwhile. The park in which the aquarium sits has no admission free. Check out the "dodgems." *(27 Chating Lu. Take bus #3 or 9 to the Seaside Park (hǎibīn gōngyuán; 海滨公园). ☎206 9973; www.seashow.org. Open daily 8am-5:30pm. Adults Y60, children Y30.)*

🚩 DAYTRIP FROM BEIHAI: WEIZHOU ISLAND 涠洲岛

Ferries leave from the Beihai Marine Transportation Co. at 8:15am. 2hr. ferry Y40-50, 1¼hr. express ferry Y62-100. Ferries return to Beihai daily at 3:30pm; same duration and prices. Pedicab chauffeur Y25 per day; 8-person minivan Y50. Motorboat rides Y20. Diving excursions with qualified instructor, no experience required, Y150.

A little rustic retreat away from Beihai, China's youngest and largest volcanic island is graced by jagged rock outcroppings and natural erosion features. A little packed by eager Chinese tourists in awkward beachwear, Weizhou Island (wéizhōu dǎo;涠洲岛) nonetheless offers all the regular beach resort activities, including diving, coral-viewing, motorboats, and camping. A walk on the rocky shores, however, will soon lead you away from the crowds to isolated hideaways of rugged beauty. A short ferry ride away, **Xieyang Island** (xiéyáng dǎo;斜阳岛), a smaller islet off the coast of Weizhou, promises more seclusion and unique volcanic rock formations. Try the small, green, unripe-looking bananas: they're surprisingly sweet. Those who can't get enough of the island's charms can overnight in one of several hotels and guesthouses.

GUIZHOU 贵州

As the saying goes, "In Guizhou, the sky is never three days clear, the land does not have three feet that are flat, and the people haven't three cents' worth of money." In other words, Guizhou is drizzly, hilly, and poor. More accurately, the landscape, strewn with jagged and soft-peaked karst hills, is undeniably evocative, but Guizhou's defiant beauty is also its sorrow: the mountainous topography and low-grade soils have always hindered agriculture yields. In many ways, the province is something of a Chinese Appalachia, with its wretched material poverty, gentle mountain beauty, and great cultural wealth.

Today, 30 distinct minority groups make up 30% of Guizhou's population. Historically, the province has always resisted Chinese control—not until the Ming Dynasty did Guizhou become part of the empire. Unrest continued during the Qing period, when major ethnic conflicts broke out between the Miao and the Chinese, who were then ironically also led by another minority group, the ruling Manchu. In the infamous Battle of Mount Leikong in 1726, more than 10,000 Miao were beheaded, and another 40,000 starved to death. Tensions surged again in 1856 when Guizhou Miao joined the Taiping Rebellion (p. 56), but they were defeated in 1871. Even in the 20th century, relations between minorities and Han were tense. Only recently has the government begun to make efforts to protect minority cultures and set up autonomous regions and prefectures.

Many tourists visit Guizhou with two things in mind: the famed caves and waterfalls near the town of Anshun (p. 627) and the province's most acclaimed export, *máotái* liquor (buyer beware: much of the liquor sold in markets is fake). Yet Guizhou has much more to offer—the peaceful, welcoming hamlets of Miao, Dong, and other minorities snuggle in mountain valleys and by riversides, offering glimpses into a life both difficult and enchanting, much like the province itself.

GUIYANG 贵阳 ☎ 0851

Guiyang, the capital of Guizhou, is a curious beast: a wealthy urban center in an overwhelmingly rural, impoverished province. Like most of the province, the city was originally populated entirely by non-Chinese peoples, until the Mongol invasion of southwest China in 1279 brought in displaced Han Chinese settlers. Today, Guizhou's minority culture still makes its presence felt in the surrounding villages, spicy food, and local festivals. As a result of recent economic development, buoyant commercial districts gradually replace the crumbling buildings typical of much of the rest of Guizhou. While pollution and a naturally overcast climate means Guiyang sees little of the "precious sunshine" promised by its name, continued development predicts a bright future for this gateway to Guizhou's countryside.

▐ TRANSPORTATION

Flights: An airport bus (Y10) runs to and from the city center, stopping several times along the way; board at the airport entrance. **China Southern Airlines** (zhōngguó nán-fāng hángkōng gōngsī; 中国南方航空公司), 70 Zunyi Lu (☎582 8429). Open daily 8am-8pm. To: **Beijing** (5 per day, Y1730); **Chengdu** (3 per day, Y630); **Chongqing** (3 per day, Y490); **Guangzhou** (5 per day, Y250); **Guilin** (daily, Y630); **Kunming** (3-4 per day, Y440); **Shanghai** (2-4 per day, Y1600).

Trains: Guiyang Train Station (guìyáng huǒchē zhàn; 贵阳火车站; ☎698 1222), at the south end of Zunyi Lu. The ticket booth is slightly to the right of the train station center. Few trains originate here, making tickets difficult to obtain; express tickets are easier to get but more expensive. Advance purchase is advised during the summer. Luggage storage 6am-midnight; Y2 per bag. To: **Beijing** (33hr., 2 per day, Y490); **Chengdu** (18hr., 4 per day, Y193); **Chongqing** (15½hr., 9 per day, Y78-180); **Guangzhou** (33hr., 7 per day, Y301); **Kaili** (3-4½hr., 5 per day, Y73); **Kunming** (12-14hr., 10 per day, Y131); **Shanghai** (32hr., 4 per day, Y362); **Zunyi** (4½hr., several per day, Y12-30).

Buses: There are 2 main bus stations in Guiyang.

Guiyang Long-Distance Bus Station (guìyáng chángtú kèyùn zhàn; 贵阳长途客运站 ; ☎682 4224), to the front left of the train station. Buy tickets once on board. To: **Anshun** (1½hr., departs when full 7am-7pm, Y14); **Kaili** (2½hr., Y30-35); **Zunyi** (2½-3½hr., departs when full 7am-7pm, Y21-34).

Another **bus station** (kè zhàn; 客站 ; ☎687 1116) is on Yan'an Xi Lu. Walking north up Ruijin Lu, turn left at Yan'an Lu. The station is 10min. down the road, on the right. Open daily 5:30am-9pm. To: **Anshun** (1½hr., every 20min. 6:30am-8pm, Y13); **Huangguoshu Falls** (5 per day, Y40); **Kunming** (15hr., daily, Y120); **Zunyi** (2½-3½hr., every 30min. 7am-9pm, Y25-40).

Local Transportation: The most useful **buses** are #1 and 2, which run in opposite circular routes up Zunyi Lu, along Ruijin Lu, Beijing Lu, and Zhonghua Lu. Fare Y1. Guiyang also has an extensive and complex system of **minibuses** (Y0.5-2).

Taxis: Base fare Y10.

✸❼ ORIENTATION AND PRACTICAL INFORMATION

The city sits along the **Nanming River** (nánmíng hé; 南明河), a tributary of the Wu River. **Yan'an Lu** (延安路), Guiyang's main shopping thoroughfare, runs east-west through the city center. **Beijing Lu** (北京路) runs parallel to and north of Yan'an Lu; **Zhongshan Lu** (中山路) runs parallel to and south of it. **Zhonghua Lu** (中华路) runs north-south, intersects Yan'an Lu, becomes **Zunyi Lu** (遵义路), and then terminates at the train station. Other north-south thoroughfares include **Ruijin Lu** (瑞金路), which is west of Zhonghua Lu and home to several budget accommodations, and **Baoshan Bei Lu,** which intersects Yan'an Lu at the entrance to Guizhou University, east of the city center, and also has several affordable hostels.

Travel Agencies: CITS, 20 Yan'an Zhong Lu (☎690 1660; fax 690 1600), opposite the large ICBC Bank. Books airplane and train tickets and arranges tours. Knowledgeable English-speaking staff members available upon request. Be persistent: many private offices on the 2nd fl. may offer assistance. Open daily 8:15am-noon and 2:30-6pm.

Bank of China: 30 Dusi Lu (☎586 9790), a 10min. walk from Yan'an Lu down Zhonghua Lu; turn right on Dusi Lu. Exchanges currency and traveler's checks. Credit card advances. Open M-F 8am-noon and 2:30-6pm, Sa-Su 9am-5pm.

Bookstores: Foreign-Language Bookstore (wài wén shūdiàn; 外文书店), 62 Yan'an Dong Lu (☎525 4328), has English-language classics. Open daily 8:30am-6pm.

PSB: (☎676 5230). A foreign affairs officer handles visa extension requests daily 8:30am-5:30pm.

Telephones: China Telecom, 68 Zhonghua Nan Lu (☎585 0330), across from the intersection of Zunyi Lu and off Zhonghua Nan Lu. IDD in central hall. Open daily 8am-6pm.

Internet Access: Several Internet bars line the 1st 2 blocks of Hequn Lu, off Yan'an Lu. Take a right on Yan'an Lu to find the **Xinya Internet Cafe** (xīnyǎ wǎngbā; 新雅网吧) and **Yiwang Internet Cafe** (yīwǎng qíngyuán wǎngluò; 伊网情缘网络). Both have 20+ computers with average connection speeds and charge Y2 per hr. Personal ID cards, which can be purchased throughout the city, are required to use computers, but you may be able to talk owners into allowing you access without a card. Both open 24hr.

Post Office: China Post, 1 Zhonghua Bei Lu (☎686 0891), at Yan'an Lu. EMS and Poste Restante. Open daily 8am-7:30pm.

Postal Code: 550001.

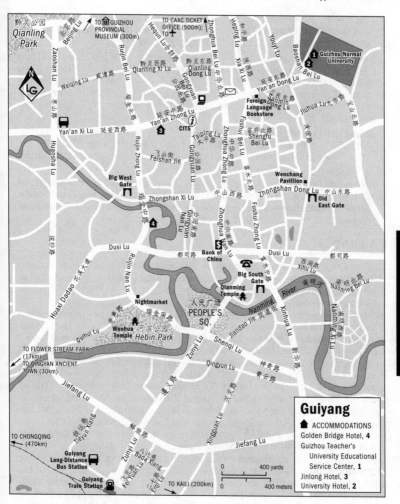

Guiyang

<table>
<tr><td colspan="2">▲ ACCOMMODATIONS</td></tr>
<tr><td>Golden Bridge Hotel,</td><td>4</td></tr>
<tr><td>Guizhou Teacher's
University Educational
Service Center,</td><td>1</td></tr>
<tr><td>Jinlong Hotel,</td><td>3</td></tr>
<tr><td>University Hotel,</td><td>2</td></tr>
</table>

▐ ACCOMMODATIONS

Guiyang's hotels cater mainly to upscale tour groups, and budget choices are few. Call ahead to find affordable beds June through August. During the rest of the year, most hotels offer up to 20% discounts. All hotels listed have 24hr. hot water unless otherwise noted.

Guizhou Teacher's University Educational Service Center (guìzhōu shīfàn dàxué jiàoyù fúwù zhōngxīn; 贵州师范大学教育服务中心), 180 Baoshan Bei Lu (☎670 2582). From the end of Yan'an Dong Lu, enter the front gate of Guizhou Teacher's University and follow the road. It's on the right side of the street. Guiyang's cheapest rooms are in this crowded but well-kept guest dorm next to Guizhou University. College dorm decor and atmosphere. Check your wit and sobriety at the door. Hot water until 10pm. 4-bed dorms Y20; singles Y110; doubles Y120; triples Y130. ❶

University Hotel (dàxué lǚguǎn; 大学旅馆), 180 Baoshan Lu (☎670 2348). Part of the **Guizhou Teacher's University Academic Exchange Center** (guìzhōu shīfàn dàxué xuéshù jiāoliú zhōngxīn; 贵州师范大学学术交流中心), just before the Education Service Center on the path from the University's entrance. Book well in advance for a summer stay in this cheap, if spartan, establishment. 4-bed dorms Y22; doubles Y130; triples Y300. ❶

Jinlong Hotel (jīnlóng dàjiŭdiàn; 金龙大酒店), 62 Yan'an Zhong Lu (☎528 2321; fax 528 1507), set back from the road 1 block toward Ruijin Lu from CITS on the left. Clean, newly furnished rooms have A/C, bath, and TV. Economy singles Y109, singles Y128; doubles Y168; triples Y188. ❷

Golden Bridge Hotel (jīnqiáo bīnguǎn; 金桥宾馆), 2 Ruijin Zhong Lu (☎581 3867; fax 581 3867). Take bus #2 from the train or main bus stations. Come here to see how the richer half lives. Currency exchange and complimentary airport pick-up. Singles and doubles Y200; triples Y233. ❸

◖ FOOD

Most of Guiyang's culinary offerings are very spicy. Those faint of tongue might want to order less throat-burning versions of the local fare. Say *"qǐng shǎo fàng làjiāo"* (请少放辣椒) to request less chili pepper.

Guiyang overflows with snacks of all varieties: meals are best taken as a series of small courses spread out over several blocks. The city's culinary diversity stems from its position at the crossroads of a multicultural province. Look for men selling delectable **kebabs** (shāokǎo; 烧烤) of spiced lamb (Y1). Guizhou is also known for its very sour dishes. Pickled vegetables, such as **sour radish** (suān luóbù; 酸萝卜), which looks like a tongue on a stick, turn up by the bushel. Miao minority vendors contribute to the mix with grilled tofu (Y2) and deliciously sweet steamed bread speckled with candied fruits (Y5). All these treats (and many more) can be found on Ruijin Lu, between Yan'an Lu and the Golden Bridge Hotel, or on the food-infested Feishan Jie, which branches off Ruijin Lu nearby. The stalls that line the road leading to Qianling Park provide another good grazing area during the day. No matter where you find yourself, vendors offer do-it-yourself spring rolls and crepe-like meals of noodles and vegetables.

After dark, try the **nightmarket** on Ruijin Nan Lu in front of Hebin Park. Other nightmarkets offering the same delicious edibles line Yan'an Lu and Hequn Lu. Those hungering for a real meal can try the hotpot sold at stalls opposite the nightmarket on Ruijin Nan Lu or on Feishan Jie. The base price for hotpot tends to be Y2-3, with each additional ingredient Y3-8. **Dog hotpot** (gǒuròu huǒguō; 狗肉火锅) is quite common but more expensive than other meats. Other restaurants and bars cluster around Baoshan Bei Lu, near the Guizhou University campus.

◉ SIGHTS

While you might arrive in Guiyang with other Guizhou sights in mind, the city and its outlying area have a few attractions. In town, the city's street life and active parks provide ample entertainment. Visits to towns like Qingyan reveal mazes of old houses and narrow paths that are prime for exploration.

QIANLING PARK (qiánlíng gōngyuán; 黔灵公园). Guiyang's biggest park combines forested seclusion, religious solemnity, and amusement park tackiness. The 383 steps to the top of Mt. Qianling, known as the "nine-winding path" for its steep switchbacks, lead to views of the city's uninspiring skyline and the park's lakes and gardens below. Wild Rhesus monkeys lining park paths won't try to sell you souvenirs, but some can be aggressive (particularly those with newborns). If you're packing a picnic, bring along some snacks for the monkeys. The more hungry ones will snatch food out of your hands!

The park's main attraction is **Hongfu Temple** (hóngfú sì; 弘福寺), at the top of Mt. Qianling. Built in 1672, Hongfu was an important regional center for Buddhists. During the Cultural Revolution, Red Guards evicted the monks and damaged the temple, but many monks have since returned, including a few from Shaolin Monastery (p. 289). The tea house just outside the temple gate is a good place to rejuvenate after the climb. *(Temple and tea house open daily 6:30am-5:30pm. Park Y1.)*

Family-oriented diversions pepper the rest of the park and draw a steady stream of locals and tourists. Near the entrance, the new **aquarium**'s displays of tropical fish pucker at visitors. *(Open daily 9am-5pm. Y30.)* Some people choose to swim in **Qianling Lake** (qiánlíng hú; 黔灵湖) even though it's not exactly the cleanest place to take a dip. Beyond Hongfu Temple, on the far side of Mt. Qianling, a **zoo** features some of China's endangered species as well as more common animals. *(Take bus #1 or 2 to the corner of Beijing Lu and Zaoshan Lu, or walk all the way up Ruijin Lu, past Yan'an Lu, and turn left onto Beijing Lu. The park is up a shaded road leading away from the city. Park open daily 6:30am-10pm; zoo daily 9am-6:30pm. Park Y5, zoo Y20.)*

QINGYAN ANCIENT TOWN (qíngyán gǔ zhèn; 青岩古镇). Known to locals simply as Qingyan, this bustling village contains a number of well-preserved Ming Dynasty buildings. On market days (ask at Guiyang CITS for the schedule), traditional architecture is overrun by throngs of buyers and sellers. For a more relaxing visit, wander away from the main streets. Residents will happily point you in the direction of the local temple and church and other simple sights like the Ancient West Gate and Longevity Palace. *(Bus from Guiyang Long-Distance Bus Station 1hr., Y6. Alternatively, catch a minibus from the parking lot across from Flower Stream Park.)*

FLOWER STREAM PARK (huāxī gōngyuán; 花溪公园). The park, 17km southwest of Guiyang, is a popular afternoon outing from the city. In the summer, visitors swim in the fairly clean river or the nearby water reservoir. *(Bus from the Guiyang Long-Distance Bus Station 30min., Y2-4. Open daily 7am-9pm. Y6, free outside of park hours.)*

OTHER SIGHTS. The **Guizhou Provincial Museum** (guìzhōu shěng bówùguǎn; 贵州省博物馆) focuses most of its exhibitions on Guizhou's 48 minority peoples, featuring displays of festivals, traditional dress, and minority art. Permanent exhibits are on the second floor. *(On Beijing Lu. Take bus #1 or 2 and ask to stop at the museum; or walk up Zhonghua Bei Lu from Yan'an Lu, turn left onto Beijing Lu; museum is 10min. down on the right. Open Su, Tu-Sa 9am-5pm. Y10, students Y5.)* Locals head for the swimming pool at **Hebin Park** (hébīn gōngyuán; 河滨公园), on Ruijin Nan Lu near Zunyi Lu, to escape the sweltering summer heat. Several restaurants and a tea garden are hidden in the foliage around the park. *(Open daily 5am-midnight. Paddle-boats Y20 per hr. Free.)*

ANSHUN 安顺 ☎ 0853

On the rail line between Guiyang and Kunming in Guizhou's western frontier, Anshun serves as an ideal base city from which to explore the several attractions in the nearby countryside. Once plagued by ramshackled buildings and undeveloped infrastructure, the city now offers all the practical necessities (and a few luxuries) for the weary traveler. You'll need at least a couple of days here to catch the spray of the thundering Huangguoshu Falls and drift down Longgong Caves' winding underground river. Farther away, the Zhijin Caves, Asia's largest system of karst caves, beckon from its inky depths.

SOUTHWEST

▣ TRANSPORTATION

Trains: Anshun Train Station (ānshùn huǒchē zhàn; 安顺火车站 ; ☎329 3295), at the south end of Nanhua Lu. Sleeper tickets require a reservation slip from office on the 2nd fl. to the left of the stairs (open daily 9am-6pm); actual purchase completed at window #2 (open 8:10-11am, 12:30-6:30pm, 9:30pm-3am). Luggage storage open 24hr. (Y2). To: **Chongqing** (12hr., 2 per day, Y130); **Guiyang** (1½hr.; 3 per day, last train at 7:50pm; Y14); **Kunming** (11hr., 8 per day, Y86-130); **Shanghai** (39hr., daily, Y440).

Buses: Prices and destinations are similar at the 2 bus stations. Buy tickets on board. **Anshun Passenger Bus Station** (ānshùn kèchē zhàn; 安顺客车站 ; ☎322 3111), at the intersection of Nanhua Lu and Guihuang Lu. Open daily 7am-7pm. To: **Guiyang** (1½hr., every 20-30min. 6:30am-7pm, Y13.5); **Huangguoshu Falls** (1½hr., when full 8am-6pm, Y6); **Kunming** (12hr., 2 per day, Y134). A small van goes to **Longgong Caves** (1hr., when 5-7 people show up, Y10). **Anshun West Bus Station** (ānshùn xī zhàn; 安顺西站 ; ☎322 3839), on Tashan Xi Lu. From the train or passenger bus station, head toward the large buildings on Nanhua Lu and turn left at the Bank of China; the station is 5min. down on the left. Open daily 6:30am-5:40pm. To: **Guiyang** (1½hr., every 20min. 7am-7pm, Y9); **Huangguoshu Falls** (1½hr., every 20min. 8am-5:40pm, Y4); **Longgong Caves** (1hr., 2 per day, Y6).

Local Transportation: Fare Y0.8. **Buses** #3 and 4 go up Nanhua Lu and turn right on Tashan Dong Lu; #2 runs from the train station up Nanhua Lu and turns left on Tashan Xi Lu; #12 travels the length of Tashan Lu.

Taxi: Y3-5 gets you to most destinations in town.

▣ ▣ ORIENTATION AND PRACTICAL INFORMATION

Nanhua Lu (南华路) runs north-south from the train station in the southeast through two traffic circles at **Guihuang Lu** (贵黄路) and **Tashan Lu** (塔山路). Anshun's largest modern buildings, including the Bank of China, the post office, and China Telecom, all sit at the intersection of Tashan Lu and Nanhua Lu. With only 2km separating the train station and the town center at Tashan Lu, Anshun is small enough to navigate easily on foot.

Travel Agencies: CITS (☎323 4662 or 323 4661), on Tashan Dong Lu. Turn right off Nanhua Lu; CITS is on the left, near the end of the road, 15min. on foot. Open M-F 8am-6:30pm. **CPITS** (jīng'ān zhígōng lǚxíng shè; 京安职工旅行社), 48 Nanhua Lu (☎322 5525; fax 322 4377), to the right of Ruofei Hotel, is a friendly place to buy tickets for the day tour to Huangguoshu and Longgong (Y270). Open daily 8:30am-6pm.

Bank of China: 1 Tashan Xi Lu (☎/fax 322 9684), at Nanhua Lu. Exchanges currency and traveler's checks. Credit card advances. Open M-F May-Oct. 8:30-11:30am and 2-6:30pm; Nov.-Apr. 8:30-11:30am and 2-6pm.

PSB: On Tashan Xi Lu (☎322 2391). From the train station, turn left off Nanhua Lu at the Bank of China, and walk ahead for 10min; the PSB is on the left. For visa extensions, go to the Foreigners' Bureau on the 5th fl. Open M-F 8am-noon and 2:30-6pm.

Internet Access: High Speed Internet Cafe (jísù wǎngbā; 极速网吧), 10min. down Tashan Dong Lu, on the right, is cleaner and less crowded than most. **Xinxin Internet Cafe** (xīnxīn wǎngbā; 欣欣网吧), across from Ruofei Hotel. Follow the side street 5min. down; it's on the left. 20 computers. Both open 24hr. Y2 per hr.

Post and Telecommunications: China Post and Telecom, 2 Nanhua Lu (☎332 1288), at Tashan Lu, opposite the Bank of China. EMS and Poste Restante. Open daily 8:30am-6:30pm. **China Telecom** (☎853 3001). Open daily 8:30am-6pm.

Postal Code: 561000.

ACCOMMODATIONS AND FOOD

Those looking for gourmet thrills in Anshun are barking up the wrong tree. **Dog** (gǒu; 狗), known as a hearty, warming staple, is immensely popular here, as in most of Guizhou. Restaurants can be found on or near all of the major roads and their side streets. For **fish in sour soup** (suāntāng yú; 酸汤鱼), head to the alley across from the Ruofei Hotel. The main **markets** are near the intersection of Nanhua Lu and Tashan Lu. **Fruit** sellers, snack stalls, **meat-on-a-stick** vendors, and **dumpling** houses are all over the city, clustered on Nanhua Lu in the markets just up from the post office and between the train and bus stations.

Anshun's few cheap accommodations tend to be a little rough around the edges. Hotels listed have 24hr. hot water.

Wholesale Market Hotel (làrǎn shìcháng zhāodàisuǒ; 蜡染市场招待所 ; ☎334 0954), located just to the right of the "Wholesale Market of Small Goods in Anshun" gate. Walk through street stalls under the hostel's sign and take the 1st left; it's on the 3rd fl. Very bright and clean rooms with new furniture, including a couch. Well-maintained public baths. Singles Y20; doubles Y50. ❶

Ruofei Hotel (ruòfēi bīnguǎn; 若飞宾馆), 48 Nanhua Lu (☎/fax 322 5374), halfway between Tashan Lu and Guihuang Lu, next to the Wholesale Market. Renovations haven't yet extended to the cheaper rooms, but quarters are clean, with fans, attached baths, and lots of light. 3-bed dorms Y40; singles and doubles Y70-120. ❶

Huayou Hotel (huáyóu bīnguǎn; 华油宾馆), 15 Tashan Lu (☎322 6020). Turn left off Nanhua Lu, 2min. down on the left. Equivalent rooms to the pricier Xixiu Mountain, but less posh. Singles Y120; doubles Y180. ❷

Xixiu Mountain Hotel (xīxiù shān bīnguǎn; 西秀山宾馆), 63 Nanhua Lu (☎221 1888), opposite the Ruofei Hotel and toward Guihuang Lu. Very friendly staff greets you in the ritzy lobby. Luxurious rooms with attached bath. Singles Y170; doubles Y200. ❷

SIGHTS

Most people visit Anshun for the roaring waters of nearby Huangguoshu Falls and the subterranean wonders of Longgong Caves, but Anshun has enough diversions for a pleasant afternoon in town as well. Tours to sights like Huangguoshu Falls, Longgong Caves, and Heavenly Star Bridge Scenic Area cost about Y270, including admission to all three sights. **CPITS** (see **Travel Agencies,** p. 628) sells tickets for a tour bus that leaves from the Ruofei Hotel (departs 7am, returns 5-6pm).

Anshun is famous for its **batik.** While batik sellers clog the tourist sights, the best prices are usually in town. Shops line Nanhua Lu between the traffic circle and the Bank of China. Bargain hard; start at slightly less than half of the first price.

HUANGGUOSHU FALLS (huángguǒshù pùbù; 黄果树瀑布). At a whopping 81m wide and 74m high, Huangguoshu Falls is Guizhou's biggest tourist attraction, and one imposing wall of water. At their most thunderous after the summer's heavy rains, the falls cascade in all directions, throwing off misty spray that gives rise to rainbows and cools down tourists in the summer heat. Bring a slicker if you plan to get close, particularly with a camera. Get an early start to beat the late-morning and early-afternoon crowd of tour groups. Signs point the way to several viewing platforms around the crashing waters. Follow the English signs to **Water Veil Cave** for the opportunity to walk behind the falls and hear and feel the force of the water's descent. It's worth getting a little wet just to see the rainbows that frequently arch over **Rhinoceros Pool** at the foot of the falls.

Huangguoshu Falls are not the only monumental falls inside the park. A 15min. walk in either direction will bring you to a more secluded waterfall, where you can idle in quiet contemplation or take a little dip. **Luositan Falls** (luósītán pùbù; 螺丝滩瀑布) lies 1km downstream along the path by the river. *(Bus from Anshun 1½hr., Y6-10; from Guiyang 3hr., Y65. Open daily 6am-7:30pm. Mar.-Oct. Y90; Nov.-Feb. Y70.)*

HEAVENLY STAR BRIDGE SCENIC DISTRICT (tiānxīng qiáo fēngjǐng qū; 天星桥风景区). A long and winding stone path strings together the four "sights" that comprise the Heavenly Star Bridge Scenic Area. Plan for at least an hour of walking to see the park, more if you want to savor the scenery. It begins with a series of ponds dotted by stepping stones and a pavilion lovely enough to be a prime target for assembly-line picture-taking. Be prepared to bump elbows with throngs of tourists, all sporting the brightly-colored hats of their tour groups. Most guides end their Y10 tour here, leading less-daring travelers out of the area. The remaining area is left undisturbed and celestial for those who strike out on their own. If you don't continue on, you're missing the park's most peaceful and rewarding sights.

From here, the path twists and turns past clusters of tree roots and a lovely series of waterfalls, caves, and rock formations. After entering the cave area, cross the bridge and climb up the path to the right for a brilliant view of the rocky pools of water below. Continue down the path to the bridge's left for more caves and a closer view of the pool and rapids. Farther on awaits the **Heavenly Star Bridge**, formed when a boulder just happened to drop between two stone outcroppings to span a 10m ravine. The rock has since been hollowed to allow visitors to walk through the holy boulder. A cable car (Y8) goes to the exit from this area; the car operator will also point you in the right direction for the short walk out.

The park path, clear and well marked in Chinese signs, includes enough off-shoots and alternative routes for exploration, and many pleasant and peaceful spots can be found by leaving the main path. If in doubt about where to go, one of the strategically placed souvenir sellers will point you in the right direction. *(6km downstream from Huangguoshu Falls. Motorcycle taxis or pedicabs ply the route from the falls; don't pay more than Y10 one-way. To return to Anshun or Guiyang, you must first return to the Huangguoshu Falls area or the nearby town. Open daily 6am-7:30pm. Y60.)*

LONGGONG CAVES (lónggōng dòng; 龙宫洞). Along with Huangguoshu Falls, the Longgong Caves form the backbone of any jaunt through the area. China's longest underground river flows through these caverns, among the most extensive karst caves yet discovered. All visitors must set sail on small yellow boats that glide into the caves (traffic jams permitting) accompanied by a Chinese-speaking guide. The 30min. trip is something like wandering through the haunted house of a third-rate carnival, passing bits of cave lit up by red, green, and purple lights to highlight the prominent karst features. Bats rest peacefully (not to worry!) in nooks and crannies high above. All in all, the caves are magnificent, with stalactites and stalagmites sharp enough to put out an eye. For a more secluded setting, check out the **Guanyin Caves** (guānyīn dòng; 观音洞), also within the park. The viewing platform in the large park near the entrance allows visitors to look down into the thundering waters of **Guanputai Waterfall** (guānpùtái pùbù; 观瀑台瀑布) and grin in the face of watery death. While many tours try to sweep quickly through Longgong in the same day as Huangguoshu Falls and Heavenly Star Bridge, the park doesn't deserve to be rushed through, and four hours easily fly past as you explore. As excavation work continues, more and more caves will be open to visitors. *(2 buses depart daily from Anshun West Bus Station, Y6. Minibuses from Anshun Passenger Bus Station depart when full, Y5-10. 30min. drive. Y95.)*

OTHER SIGHTS. The same **Xixiu Mountain Pagoda** (xīxiù shān tǎ; 西秀山塔) that lends its name to so many local institutions sits on a small hill overlooking Tashan Lu. *(Turn left at the intersection of Nanhua Lu and Tashan Lu, if coming from the train or bus sta-*

tion area. The entrance is opposite Anshun West Bus Station.) Peddlers trying to eke out a living stake out the smaller streets in this part of town. During the week, sellers seem to outnumber buyers, but the neighborhood becomes the liveliest trade center during Anshun's **Sunday Market.**

Wen Temple (wénmiào; 文庙), off Qianjin Lu, in the northeast corner of town, was built in the early Ming years and still contains many original structure pieces. The staff, several of whom speak a little English, love the temple and revel in showing visitors its nooks and crannies. Though not as well maintained as many ancient Chinese temples, the cracked steps and vine-covered stones add a feel of authenticity—that, combined with fewer tourists, makes this a worthy stop on a lazy afternoon in town. *(Taxi from center of town is easiest, Y5. Open daily 8am-6pm. Y3.)*

⚡ DAYTRIP FROM ANSHUN: ZHIJIN CAVES

About 150km (3hr.) from Anshun. **Buses** *from Anshun's North Gate (北门); take bus #2 from Tashan Lu Y18, from Guiyang Long-Distance Bus Station Y60. Buses may frequently leave at unscheduled times. Inquire the day before you visit the caves. Once in Zhijin, take the public bus (Y3) to the caves. Minibus drivers will take you for Y5-30, depending on the number of passengers. Last bus back to Anshun leaves at 6pm. CITS in Anshun can arrange daytrips (Y300-4500 per vehicle). Open daily 8am-5pm. Y100.*

The spectacular ■ Zhijin Caves (zhījīn dòng; 织金洞), the largest series of karst caves in Asia, are touted with increasing fervor as the "number one cave in the world." Over 15 "halls," one the size of a soccer field, are open to the public. The sheer immensity of the caves and the awe-inspiring formations of stalactites and stalagmites are mind-boggling. Unlike at the Longgong Caves, park authorities have installed normal lighting, leaving only natural beauty to impress spelunkers. While some might think a trip to Zhijin redundant after Longgong, the monumental scope of the caverns (traversed by foot, not boat), combined with remarkable forests of jagged karst and contorted rock formations, make this sight a must-see.

KAILI 凯里   ☎ 0855

Although its residents are mostly Han Chinese, the little town of Kaili in eastern Guizhou is nestled among numerous minority villages and serves as a great jumping-off point for exploration. Even a short trip out of town quickly exchanges the somewhat drab and dusty city interior for spiky karst pinnacles and rice paddies steeply terraced on the green hillsides. Visitors usually alternate daytrips and overnight rambles in the countryside with peaceful evenings in Kaili, where convenient accommodations and good restaurants make for an ideal base town.

One of the most ethnically diverse regions in China, eastern Guizhou is mainly known for the Miao and Dong minority peoples, but the area is also home to the Yao, Shui, Buyi, Mulao, and Gelao peoples. Miao villages surround Kaili, and an hour's journey in any direction will bring you to at least one cluster of low wooden houses built in the traditional Miao fashion. Dong villages cluster in the province's southeastern corner, six hours by bus from Kaili. In both areas, some villages have only recently opened to non-Chinese visitors, and Westerners may be met with as much curiosity as they bring.

⬛ TRANSPORTATION

Trains: Kaili Train Station (kǎilǐ huǒchē zhàn; 凯里火车站 ; ☎855 2222), on Qingjiang Lu, at the far northern end of town. Take bus #2 or a taxi (Y10-15). The ticket office is on the left. Although officially open 24hr., the office is more consistently staffed 8am-

8pm. Because few trains originate in Kaili, sleeper tickets are easier to buy in Guiyang, where you'll find trains to destinations outside of Guizhou province. To: **Guiyang** (4hr., 15 per day, Y25); **Shibing** (1hr., 2 per day, Y10); **Zhenyuan** (2hr., 9 per day, Y14).

Buses: 2 bus stations offer transportation to and from Kaili.

Kaili Long-Distance Bus Station (kǎilǐ qìchē kèyùn zhàn; 凯里汽车客运站 ; ☎822 3794), on Wenhua Bei Lu. From Dashizi, go east on Beijing Dong Lu and take the 2nd left up Wenhua Lu. The station is on the left, past Yingpan Dong Lu. Ticket office open daily 6am-10:30pm, but most tickets are bought on board. To: **Duyun** (every 25min. 6:30am-4:20pm, Y21); **Guiyang** (2½hr., every 20min. 6:30am-10:30pm, Y30-40); **Huangping** (3hr., every hr. 6am-6pm, Y25-35); **Leishan** (1½hr.-2½hr., every 30min. 7am-6pm, Y7); **Rongjiang** (5-6hr., every hr. 6am-4pm, Y35-45); **Sanhui** (3-4hr., every 40min. 6am-6pm, Y25-30).

Kaili Society Bus Station (kǎilǐ shèhuì kèyùn zhàn; 凯里社会客运站), next to the Kaili Hotel, in the south of town, mainly offers southbound buses. Sleeper buses to **Guangzhou** (24hr., 1-2 per day, Y200) and comparably priced buses to **Guiyang**.

Local Transportation: Bus #2 runs from the train station to Dashizi. Bus #6 will take you to and from the bus station, traveling on the city's major roads. Fare Y0.5.

Taxi: Base fare Y5.

✦❷ ORIENTATION AND PRACTICAL INFORMATION

Kaili is easy to navigate. With the exception of the train station, most important places and attractions lie within a walkable small area around the city center. **Beijing Lu** (北京路) runs east-west and intersects **Shaoshan Lu** (韶山路), which runs north-south at **Dashizi** ("Big Cross"; 大十字). North of and parallel to Beijing Lu is **Yingpan Lu** (营盘路), lined with restaurants and budget accommodations. **Wenhua Lu** (文化路) runs east of and parallel to Shaoshan Lu.

Travel Agencies: CITS, 53 Yingpan Dong Lu (☎822 2506), on the grounds of the Yingpan Hotel, next to the tennis court. Friendly and helpful staff members speak excellent English (ask for Wu Zengou), Japanese, and French, and can provide information on local events. 1-day trips to **Langde** start at Y400 per person; prices drop significantly for larger groups. Open M-F 9am-6pm; staff is sometimes there on weekends.

Bank of China: 6 Shaoshan Nan Lu (☎/fax 822 6304). Exchanges traveler's checks. Credit card advances. Open daily 8am-noon and 2:30-5:30pm.

PSB: 7 Yonghua Lu. Follow Beijing Dong Lu until Yonghua Lu forks to the left. It's on the left. Handles visa extension requests. Open M-F 8:30am-5:30pm.

Internet Access: Lianxun Internet Cafe (liánxùn wǎngbā; 联讯网吧 ; ☎826 4395), on Shaoshan Bei Lu, just before the Grand Pavilion. 68 computers. Y2 per hr. Open 24hr. The **CITS** also provides Internet access for Y3 per hr. (see above).

Post and Telecommunications: 1 Beijing Lu (☎/fax 822 3542), at Shaoshan Lu. EMS and Poste Restante. **China Telecom** is on the 2nd fl. Both open daily 8am-6pm.

Postal Code: 556000.

▟ ACCOMMODATIONS

The days of dirt-cheap accommodations in Kaili are gone. Several hotels, however, still offer reasonable rates; the best deals are on **Beijing Lu** and **Yingpan Dong Lu**. For travelers who choose to visit the surrounding villages, all listed hotels store luggage; most have 24hr. hot water.

Longfen Hotel (lóngfēng jiǔdiàn; 隆丰酒店), on Wenhua Lu (☎822 1650). Turn left as you exit the bus station; it's on the left before the next corner. Some rooms have A/C and bath; others share well-maintained baths. TV in all rooms. Singles Y30; doubles and triples Y60. ❶

Cloud Springs Hotel (yúnquán bīnguǎn; 云泉宾馆), 54 Beijing Dong Lu (☎827 1138). Just to the right after crossing Wenhua Lu. This budget hotel offers huge rooms, including separate sitting rooms, A/C, TV, and bath. Many rooms have patios overlooking a quiet garden. Singles and doubles Y80; triples Y90. ❶

Petroleum Guesthouse (shíyóu bīnguǎn; 石油宾馆), 44 Yingpan Dong Lu (☎823 4331), near Wenhua Lu. From the bus station, walk toward town on Wenhua Lu and turn right on Yingpan Lu; it's on the left. Kaili's cheapest rooms in a dilapidated old building with green astroturf-like carpeting. Spartan rooms have baths, Chinese-style toilets, fans, and TVs. 5-bed dorms Y23; 2-bed with bath Y34; singles Y68. ❶

▌ FOOD

Cuisine in Kaili is standard Chinese fare, but with a mouth-puckering twist: sour is the flavor *du jour* every day. Kaili's pride and joy is **sour soup** (suān tāng; 酸汤), a hotpot concoction made with a choice of meats and flavored with lemongrass, and known throughout China as a regional treat. The **Bright Joy Village** ❷ (liàng huān zhài; 亮欢寨), 54 Huancheng Lu, serves some of the city's best sour soup (Y12-30) in an elegant dining area.

Those craving puppy chow can head to the row of **dog hotpot** restaurants on Beijing Dong Lu, on the left, just past Wenhua Lu. The pick of the litter is the **Zhangjia Dog Restaurant** ❷ (zhāngjiā gǒuròu diàn; 张家狗肉店), which serves hotpot for Y30 per person. (Open daily until 10pm.) There is a small **nightmarket** on Beijing Lu near Dashizi, and restaurants and food stalls line the alleys off both sides of Beijing Dong Lu. For something sweet, head to Bejing Lu for some *bīngfēn* (冰芬), a type of **jello** with ice, pickled fruits, and nuts (Y1-3 per bowl).

◎ SIGHTS

Most visitors to Kaili head elsewhere to sightsee. In town, the **Grand Pavilion** (dà gé; 大阁) is a small temple perched atop a hill, an active site of worship and an attractive spot from which to observe local life. On special occasions, the temple is open at night. (*Walk to the end of Shaoshan Bei Lu, turn right, and then take the first left up Dage Xiang, which leads to the base of the hill. Open daily 8am-6:30pm. Y5.*)

For a view of daily life in Kaili, turn onto a side street near the base of the Grand Pavilion Hill. This area, between Dongmen Lu and Yingpan Lu to the east of Shaoshan Bei Lu, is known as **Old Town** because it includes Kaili's first street. Many traditional wooden homes from Kaili's days as a Miao village still remain.

At the opposite end of town, Shaoshan Nan Lu leads to the **Minorities Museum,** which is set back from the road behind the Kaili Society Bus Station. The museum occupies the second and third floors of an imposing building but falls short of its potential with only four display halls. There are a few interesting examples of Dong and Miao handiwork, but not enough to justify the admission price. For the best exhibits head to—where else?—the countryside. (*Buy tickets at the souvenir shop on the stairway to the entrance. Open daily 8:30-noon and 2-6pm. Y10.*)

▌ SHOPPING

Every Sunday, the **Kaili Market** sets up along Dongmen Lu, north of and parallel to Beijing Lu. Some serious mercantile action happens here, but it pales in comparison to the spectacular Sunday markets in the minority villages throughout the region (see **Markets,** p. 635). Head to Yingpan Lu for Miao and Dong crafts, mainly colorfully embroidered cloths and bags, sold in shops near the Yingpan Hotel.

⚡ DAYTRIP FROM KAILI: LANGDE

*South of Kaili, on the road into the Leigong Hills. Take the Leishan-bound **bus** (45min., every 30min., Y7) from the long-distance bus station. Remind the driver 30-40min. into the drive that you want to get off (xiàchē; 下车) at Langde—sometimes they forget. There is a small guesthouse (zhāodàisuǒ; 招待所) in Langde and one in Upper Langde (both Y10 per person). Every villager knows the way and will happily show you; you're unlikely to find it on your own in the twists and turns of identical-looking streets.*

Langde (lǎngdé; 郎德), one of Guizhou's most accessible Miao villages (pop. 500), is a picturesque labyrinth of wooden houses and narrow cobblestone streets. For the most part, village life goes on as usual here. Pigs and chickens rummage for lunch, children play, and adults carry out their domestic chores in the streets. A slow-moving river urges the town's waterwheels forward and cools the water buffalo that linger in its deeper spots. Unfortunately, it's becoming more difficult to visit Langde and simply observe; visitors often arrive to a flurry of activity as local residents rush from their houses to sell handicrafts, especially in the afternoon. Despite the commercial twist on traditional Miao hospitality, the reception is still extremely warm. Families offer lodgings in the form of wooden beds with thin mattresses. Guest bath is in the male- and female-designated parts of the river.

Upper Langde (lǎngdé shàng; 郎德上) lies 1km up the path from Langde, across the river but on the same side of the road from Kaili. The villages look and feel quite similar, but the walk between them, especially across the double-tiered wooden bridge above Upper Langde, justifies the effort. The views of the village, river, and nearby mountains at Upper Langde provide further incentive to hike up and down the undulating hills. Tour groups from Kaili frequently visit Upper Langde, and it's easy for independent explorers to join in the scheduled festivities. Men bring out reed flutes (lúshēng; 芦笙) to greet guests, and women toast visitors with small bowls of homemade liquor. Traditional dancing and festivities follow. Because tour groups usually pay for all performances, individual visitors standing with the villagers (instead of sitting at the wooden tables with the guests) do not have to pay. However, if a villager approaches you for payment, Y50 is appropriate.

KAILI MINORITY VILLAGES

The area around Kaili may well contain the single most diverse concentration of minority peoples in all of China. The two dominant groups are the Miao (to the north, south, and west of Kaili) and the Dong (to the southeast), but a scattering of Gelao, Mulao, Gejia, Yao, and Shui peoples supplies cultural contrast at every turn. Thanks to the slow growth of tourist traffic through the region, villages are still just villages in this part of the world, and the sights and smells of everyday life have not yet been sterilized or forced to conform to tourist expectations. These are some of China's poorest villages, but you wouldn't know it given the extreme warmth with which locals greet their far richer visitors. Travelers should take care to be respectful of local culture and customs.

Between the towns, roads wind around spiky green karst peaks, and the natural beauty compensates for the long, bone-rattling bus rides along ill-kept roads. Trips require planning and patience—don't expect to whip through three villages in a day. Kaili is the point from which most roads radiate, so it's easiest to approach your exploration as a series of one- or two-night trips from Kaili. Most buses back to Kaili stop running by mid-afternoon, and bus trips often take longer than expected. **Langde** (see **Daytrips from Kaili**, p. 634), **Leishan**, and **Xijiang** form a small cluster to the southeast of the city, manageable with an overnight stay in Xijiang. **Chong'an, Shibing,** and **Zhenyuan** work as a circuit to the north of Kaili. And the **Dong villages** in far southeast Guizhou provide ample material for a third itinerary.

Along the way, many other villages tempt visitors to linger longer. If you venture far, remember that some towns have only recently been opened to foreign tourists and may not yet have approved accommodations for non-Chinese guests. If you announce your presence by walking around town, the PSB may just announce its presence with a midnight visit to your hotel room. Travelers report a fine of Y200-300 for staying in unapproved lodging.

MARKETS

Part grocery, part mall, and part livestock fair, eastern Guizhou's markets bring together buyers and sellers from around the region. Souvenir hunters should expect to find intricately embroidered goods from the minority villages (without the mark-up of minority craft stores throughout the southwest). The Miao are known for their work with silver, and good bargainers can get small pieces for under Y20, though some sellers might try a higher price. The presence of both Miao and Gejia craftsmen makes the Chong'an market the best in the region. Most markets open very early in the day and wind down by noon. On Sunday, markets are held in **Kaili** (p. 631) and **Shibing** (p. 637). Markets are held every five days in **Chong'an** (p. 636) and every six days in the villages of **Leishan** (p. 635), **Xijiang** (p. 636), and **Zhouxi,** according to the lunar calendar. For more comprehensive listings and date information, check with the Kaili CITS.

FESTIVALS

Eastern Guizhou's ethnic diversity results in a nearly non-stop calendar of festivals, with at least 135 every year. Local festivals are occasions for mass gatherings, singing, dancing, reed flute performances, and horseracing, as well as opportunities to meet potential spouses. Locals generally welcome visitors to participate in festivities. Most festivals are annual events, but some are far rarer: the **Miao Guzang** festival is held every 13 years. Kaili CITS has a full schedule of regional festivals, which follow the lunar calendar. Here is a small selection: the **Dong Ancestor Worship** (dòngzú jìsàsuì; 侗族祭萨岁) in Longtu and Conjiang (Feb. 9, 2005 and Jan. 29, 2006); **Miao Reed Flute Festival** (miáozú lúshēnghuì; 苗族芦笙会) in different towns every two to three days in the first month of the lunar calendar (approx. Feb. 2005 and 2006); the **Miao Hill-Leaping Festival** (miáozú tiào pápō jié; 苗族爬坡节) in Kaili (July 24, 2005 and July 14, 2006); the **Miao Dragon Boat Festival** (miáozú lóngchuán jié; 苗族龙船节) in Shidong (July 1, 2005 and June 20, 2006); the **Miao Sisters' Meal Festival** (miáozú zǐmèi jié; 苗族姊妹节) in Shidong (Apr. 24-25, 2005 and Apr. 13-14, 2006); and the **Shui Dragon Boat Festival** (shuǐzú duān jié; 水族端节).

LEISHAN 雷山 ☎ 0855

Leishan (south of Kaili) is little more than a useful mini-hub for travel farther south or northwest of Xijiang. Leishan has three roads. The bus stops at one end of town; from here, the main road runs through town and across the river. Two-thirds of the way to the river, the main road intersects the second street. At the far end of town, the third street branches right off the main road and runs parallel to it on the opposite riverbank.

Pretty hardwood floors add to the otherwise standard budget accommodations at the **Supply and Marketing Hotel ❶** (gōngxiāo bīnguǎn; 供销宾馆). From the bus station, turn left and follow Yongle Lu until it hits the bridge; the hotel is on the corner on the left. (☎333 3188. Singles and doubles Y45, with A/C Y65.) The **Xinhe Hotel ❶** (xìnhé bīnguǎn; 信合宾馆) has clean, quiet, and newly-renovated rooms across the river from the street to the right of the bus station, on the intersecting street 200m down to the right. (☎333 4448. Singles and doubles Y68, with A/C Y88.) Street stalls, small restaurants, and fruit vendors cluster around the post office.

Buses go to Leishan from **Kaili** (1½hr., every 30min. 7am-6pm, Y9), returning to Kaili when full; last bus leaves from Leishan for Kaili at 4pm. Buses from Leishan depart from the bus station on Yongle Lu. Buses to **Xijiang** (1½hr., every 1½hr. 8:30am-4pm, Y8) leave earlier and sometimes more frequently on market days (see **Markets,** p. 635).

XIJIANG 西江   ☎0855

Xijiang, southwest of Kaili, is the largest Miao village in the region. Nestled in the Longgong Hills, Xijiang snakes along steep passes, cut in two by a shallow river where villagers pass hot days. The village is also an ideal place to spend the Miao New Year (mid-Oct.), when locals pile on their finest silver and enjoy a good bull-fight or two. Unlike many countryside villages in Guizhou and other provinces like Yunnan, Xijiang has yet to experience the changes wrought by tourism. Visitors need not worry about aggressive vendors or heavy mark-ups.

The entire village is a sight to be seen, but a walk along the terraced fields above and to the sides can be a relaxing half-day trek. From anywhere in the village, walk up the hill until you reach the terraces. A forest and a small graveyard are just two of the things you may see on the way. Staying the night is usually necessary and, fortunately, in endearing Xijiang, this should be no hardship. Extremely warm staff will take care of you at the **Nationalities Guesthouse ❶** (mínzú zhāodàisuǒ; 民族招待所), and may even invite you to dinner (Y10). Communal bathrooms and showers look dirtier than they actually are. (☎334 8688. Singles Y30; doubles Y40; triples Y30.) Or spend the night in a villager's home—no PSB to worry about in this peaceful village. (Y15, dinner Y7.)

To get to Xijiang, take the **bus** from Kaili to Leishan, where you hop on another bus to Xijiang (1½hr., every 30min. 7am-6pm, Y6). Two **buses** each day return to Kaili (1½hr.; 8am, 1pm; Y11), and the last bus leaves for Leishan at 4pm.

CHONG'AN JIANG 重安江   ☎0855

Tiny Chong'an is the place to be when the local **market** comes to life by the river every five days. Drawing mostly Miao and a few Dong traders, the market sprawls into local alleyways and creates human traffic jams. Snorting pigs and screaming chickens join the pandemonium of buying, selling, auctioning, and haggling.

If you're unlucky enough to miss the area's wildest market, the scenery around Chong'an makes for some wonderful hiking options. A short walk along the river offers some good views of the lazy waterway. To venture out of Chong'an, walk up the main road with the river to your left and turn right at the end; the path leads to a **Gejia minority village** several hours away. A hike across the river leads to **Xinzai,** another Gejia village, across from the Chong'an River Holiday Resort Hotel. Cross the river by boat or bridge. The hike should take 1-1½hr. round-trip. Guides (Y15) can be arranged at area hotels. The **Xiaojiangnan Guesthouse** (☎245 1208) has a list of suggested routes, including a 10hr. trip through **Mulao minority villages.** The guesthouse can also arrange **bus tours** (6-10 people, Y100 per day), 10km trips by **horse cart** (3-4 people, Y30), 10km outings in a **fishtail boat** (10-15 people, Y80), and, for the proud and brave, 5km trips in an **"armored wooden boat"** (Y30).

Take the direct **bus** (2hr., Y11) to Chong'an from Kaili or get off on the way to Huangping (黄平) or Shibing (施秉). ■ **Chong'an River Holiday Resort ❶** (chóng'ān jiāng lǚyóu tíngcūn; 重安江旅游停村) is 10min. down the road from the bus drop-off, with the river on your left. The staff here will bend over backwards for you, even if it means rowing you across the river in torrential downpours and lightning storms. All rooms have views of the river. (Communal baths. Dinner included. Singles Y30; doubles Y60.) The **Xiao Jiangnan Guesthouse ❶** (xiǎojiāngnán zhāodàisuǒ; 小江南招待所) is in a two-story brick building just before the Chong'an Jiang Holiday Resort. Helpful English map of the area provided with spartan rooms. (No showers. Singles Y20; doubles Y30).

SHIBING 施秉
☎ 0855

Shibing, a small city northeast of Chong'an, is more of a crossroads than a destination. Most travelers use the town as a base from which to explore the **Wuyang River** (wǔyáng hé; 舞阳河) and **Shamu River** (shāmù hé; 杉木河). CITS (☎ 422 1177), in the Shamu River Hotel on Dong Jie, can arrange **cruises, rafting,** and **tubing** trips.

Smaller than the Wuyang, the Shamu River flows at a calmer pace, flanked by relatively less spectacular scenery. But the Shamu's slow-paced meandering does make swimming in the deeper pools possible. As you drift, be sure to pull your raft to shore occasionally to savor the enticing barbecued fish, chicken, corn, frog, or crab that locals serve up. (Try to join a CITS group already heading out to the Yantai Mountains. Round-trip bus from town Y15, from the train station Y100. River admission Y120. Raft rental Y100.)

Between Shibing and Zhenyuan, the Wuyang River runs through a remarkable array of gorges and rock formations. To explore the area, take a Zhenyuan-bound bus from Shibing (Y6) and ask to be let off at **Lower Wuyang River** (xià wǔyáng hé; 下舞阳河). From the drop-off point, walk down the hill. At the river ticket office, you can ask for several different 2-hr. tours (Y55), one of which will bring you back to the starting point. The other will leave you 17km from Zhenyuan, near the **Buddhist Green Dragon Temple** (Y10). To get to Zhenyuan, walk up the hill and wait for the bus. Buses to Zhenyuan (Y6) will be going in the direction that leads uphill.

ZHENYUAN 镇远

Zhenyuan, a small city east of Shibing, provides a quieter hub for travelers than its neighbor, though most villages are within a day's striking distance from both towns. Cobblestone roads wind through the city's Old Town, and a pleasant evening stroll along the Wuyang River passes elegant white-walled, red-trimmed buildings dating back hundreds of years.

From the bus station, go right and take a right onto the main road to reach the **Business Savings Guesthouse ❶** (shāng chǔ zhāodàisuǒ; 商储招待所), 12 Xinzhong Jie, 10min. down the road and 50m after the bridge. Small rooms have fans and a view of the river. (Singles Y30; doubles Y40.) Two guesthouses vie for the prestigious title of **Bus Station Guesthouse ❶** (qìchē zhàn zhāodàisuǒ; 汽车站招待所) along the flanks of the bus station. One is just to the left as you leave through the station's front entrance, and the other is to the right from the side entrance on the main road. The small rooms at both are more spare than those at the Business Savings Guesthouse. (Singles Y20; doubles Y30.)

DONG VILLAGES 侗村
☎ 0855

This region, on the formidable road between Guizhou and Guangxi province, is said to be one of the most breathtaking wildernesses in China. Roads are bad, transport links spotty, and tourists rare indeed, but the outlay of time and patience will be rewarded many times over by the chance to experience, amid blindingly beautiful scenery, a culture virtually unknown to most Westerners. The Dong villages' most distinguishing feature is their architecture, most easily seen in engineering feats such as their drum towers and flower bridges.

Buses (5hr., every hr. 6am-5:30pm, Y35-45) go from Kaili to **Rongjiang** (榕江). From Rongjiang, more buses go on to **Xiajiang** (下江) via **Tingdong** (停洞). Some buses go directly from Rongjiang to **Congjiang** (从江), at the Guangxi border; others terminate at Xiajiang, making it necessary to take another bus to reach Congjiang. Westbound travelers should keep in mind that the last bus from Congjiang to Xiajiang leaves in the early afternoon. If you miss it, taking a taxi to Xiajiang may be worthwhile, since no one who puts forth the effort to get to Dong county should even think of missing this remarkable town.

A manageable two-day itinerary from Kaili begins with a bus trip to Rongjiang. From there, **Chejiang** (车江), with its large drum tower (Y5), is an excellent spot to spend the day. Tall, leafy banyan trees become useful sun shades for a walk alongside the Rong River (rōng jiāng; 榕江) flowing past the village. For the night, return to Rongjiang, which offers several good accommodations. The budget traveler can find a room for about Y60, while a more comfortable stay runs Y130. The next day, take a bus from Rongjiang to Congjiang (2hr., Y20), then catch another bus to **Zhaoxing** (肇兴), the largest Dong village in the region with 800 families (1½hr., Y15-20). Spend the night in a villager's home or one of the hotels.

ZUNYI 遵义 ☎ 0852

In 1935, this backwater-to-end-all-backwaters made its way onto the map when the desperate, bedraggled Red Army staggered into town during the Long March (see p. 79). It was here that the central committee of the CCP made the fateful decision to hand the chairmanship to a Hunanese peasant by the name of Mao Zedong. Zunyi's only worthwhile attraction is the historic site where the famous agreement was made. The city itself offers the pollution and congestion characteristic of rapid development. As with other semi-major towns in Guizhou, Zunyi best serves as a base from which to explore the marvelous countryside.

TRANSPORTATION AND PRACTICAL INFORMATION

The train and bus stations cluster off **Beijing Lu** (北京路), which leads to the main shopping street **Zhonghua Lu** (中华路). **Zijun Lu** (子君路), the fabled conference site, and the entrances to the city park are on the other side of **Phoenix Hill** (fènghuáng shān; 凤凰山), which marks the center of town. **Daxing Lu** (大兴路) is another major street on the route of bus #1.

Trains: Zunyi Train Station (zūnyì huǒchē zhàn; 遵义火车站 ; ☎883 2074), just off Beijing Lu. The ticket office is in the middle facing the station; an information window is inside on the left. To: **Chengdu** (14½hr., 4 per day, Y91); **Chongqing** (10hr., 12 per day, Y24-40); **Guiyang** (2½-4hr., 13 per day, Y12-22); **Guangzhou** (35hr., 5 per day, Y93-200); **Kunming** (17hr., 2 per day, Y106).

Buses: A faster and more comfortable way to get to Guiyang than taking the train. **Zunyi Bus Station** (zūnyì qìchē zhàn; 遵义汽车站 ; ☎885 8084), just off Beijing Lu, in front and to the left of the train station. Purchase tickets in the parking lot or once on board the bus. To: **Chishui** (10-12hr., 2 per day, Y68); **Guangzhou** (34hr., daily, Y220); **Guiyang** (2½hr., every 30min. 5am-7pm, Y20-30).

Local Transportation: Bus #1 leaves from Beijing Lu, runs along the edge of town, and then heads down Zhonghua Lu and Daxing Lu. Fare Y0.5.

Taxi: Base fare Y5.

Bank of China: 1 Minzhi Lu, at Honghua Gang (红花岗). Take bus #1 and ask to get off at the Bank of China. Exchanges traveler's checks, though staff must first call a central office, so the wait is longer than usual. Credit card advances. Open daily 8am-6pm.

Internet Access: Jinyu Internet Cafe (jīnyǔ wǎngbā; 金宇网吧), 62 Beijing Lu (☎882 2449), on the 2nd fl. of a computer store 10min. from the train station. You must buy a pre-paid Internet card, but you may be able to pay as you go with a little negotiating.

Post and Telecommunications: 26 Daxing Lu (☎825 7560), at a bend in the road across from a pedestrian bridge. EMS and Poste Restante. **China Telecom** (☎825 0800) is in the huge building to the left when facing China Post. Open daily 8am-6pm.

Postal Code: 563000.

▚▐ ACCOMMODATIONS AND FOOD

Zunyi offers an array of accommodations, most of which are scattered along Beijing Lu and Zhonghua Lu. The few budget options are very budget indeed. All hotels have 24hr. hot water unless otherwise noted.

Restaurants, snack stalls, and **fruit vendors** congregate around the train and bus stations and in alleys off Zhongshan Lu. **Hotpot** is available in restaurants just up the road from the train station, as well as along Zunyi Lu near the conference site.

Golden Rainbow Hotel (jīnhóng dàjiǔdiàn; 金虹大酒店 ; ☎319 1188), directly across and to the left of the train station. Though the dark hallways give an air of seediness, this hotel is clean, safe, and highly affordable. Rooms come with full bath, TV, and telephone. Biggest plus is its proximity to the train and bus stations, though this leads to noise at night. Singles Y60; doubles Y70; triples Y128. ❶

Home Under Heaven Hotel (jiā tiān xià bīnguǎn; 家天下宾馆), 18 Xinhua Lu (☎822 0380), across the river from China Telecom. Take bus #1 and get off at Honghua Gang. Newly built hotel in the city center offers slightly nicer rooms with A/C and water boiler. Singles Y126; doubles Y135; triples Y218. ❷

Zunyi Guesthouse (zūnyì bīnguǎn; 遵义宾馆), 3 Shilong Lu (☎822 4902, ext. 8001 or 8003), just up the street from the Red Army monument. By far Zunyi's nicest and most expensive hotel, the guesthouse is divided into 2 buildings (1 brand new) and provides difficult-to-find seclusion from the noisy downtown. Singles Y326; doubles Y388; triples in the old building Y166. ❷

◉ SIGHTS

ZUNYI CONFERENCE SITE (zūnyì huìyìzhǐ; 遵义会议址). After the GMD drove the Red Army out of their guerrilla stronghold in Jinggangshan (p. 444) in Jiangxi province, the rapidly dwindling forces played a deadly game of hide-and-seek with the GMD as they fled through the Guizhou countryside. When the Army stopped off in Zunyi midway through their Long March, the top CCP leaders spent three days and nights (Jan. 15-17, 1935) engaged in acrimonious arguments over their future strategy. At the end of the meeting, a popular vote handed the chairmanship of the party to Mao Zedong.

The conference site is a mansion that originally belonged to a GMD-affiliated warlord. The house itself is nothing much, but just picturing Zhou Enlai, Zhu De, and other soon-to-be CCP big shots settling down in the various rooms is exciting enough if you have the slightest interest in modern Chinese history. If you've come to Zunyi and decide to not visit this conference site, why, may we ask, have you come? *(On Zijun Lu. 8am-5:30pm. Y20.)*

MONUMENT TO THE MARTYRS OF THE RED ARMY (hóng jūn lièshì língyuán; 红军烈士陵园). This masterpiece of Soviet-style revolutionary art dates back to the days when Sino-Soviet relations were more friendly, and is markedly different from many other martyrs' monuments. It is also particularly poignant since three-quarters of the 80,000 Long March participants did not survive. In front of the wall lies a quiet park with interlocking streams and bamboo trees. (*Just off Fenghuang Lu. From Zunyi Park, proceed up the road and turn left at the end. Free.*)

OTHER SIGHTS. The **Military Fortress** (jūnshì chéngbǎo; 军事城堡) was built in the Ming Dynasty by a rebellious general who liked to stage Roman-style gladiatorial contests. The hike to the top is grueling and takes 2-3hr., but it does offer some spectacular views. (*Free.*) The small but dense **Xiangshan Temple Complex** (xiāngshān sì; 湘山寺), off Zhonghua Nan Lu, sits on a hill that affords an impressive view of the city, factories, and TV towers. (*Continue from the traffic circle at the base of the street and turn left up a small winding alley; the temple is a few minutes up ahead. Open daily 7am-9pm. Y2.*) The smaller **White Cloud Temple** (báiyún sì; 白云寺), also off Zhonghua Nan Lu, is near a slightly more interesting covered market. (*Free.*)

CHISHUI 赤水

☎ 0852

The little-visited but beautiful town of Chishui lies on the Guizhou-Sichuan border, about 300km northwest of Zunyi, in the middle of an isolated and untrampled subtropical forest. Chishui's landscape, cityscape, and cuisine have a distinct Sichuanese flavor, and the surrounding scenery is utterly stunning and virtually tourist-free. For those traveling from Guizhou to Chongqing and the Three Gorges, Chishui can provide a quiet and enchanting rest.

The two main attractions in the area are the **Shizhangdong Falls** (shízhàngdòng pùbù; 十丈洞瀑布), 40km south of Chishui, and the **Four Caves and Gorges** (sìdòng gōu; 四洞沟), just a few kilometers southwest of the town center. The falls may not be as high as the Huangguoshu Falls near Anshun, but they are far less touristed and an equally pleasant get-away. The cave and gorges, with four smaller waterfalls and a famous "sea of bamboo and ferns," are also worth a visit. Public buses and *miàndī* (minivan) taxis run from the main **bus station** (chíshuǐ kèyùn zhàn; 赤水客运站) in the southwest corner of town to both of these areas (to Shizhangdong Falls Y8-10; to the Four Caves and Gorges Y3-5); return transportation is available until dusk.

Buses travel from the main bus station to **Zunyi** (14hr.; 6:30am Y70, 5pm Y80). Just across the bridge that separates Sichuan from Chishui, the **Jiuzhi Bus Station** (jiǔzhī chēzhàn; 九支车站) has buses to **Luzhou** (3hr., every 30min. 5am-5pm). At Luzhou, you can take a Y5 taxi to the **Xiaoshi Bus Station** to transfer to **Yibin** (2.5hr., Y15) or **Chongqing** (6hr., 2 per day, Y45). **Taxis** to sites within Chishui cost Y2-3.

YUNNAN 云南

It would take very little to convince the blissful backpackers in Yunnan that they've died and gone to heaven. And indeed, the province's dreamy name, "south of the clouds," evokes the celestial attractions awaiting. Tucked away in the far southwest, China's fourth-largest province has few, if any, unpleasant destinations. From the chilly mountain passes and snow-capped peaks of the north, to the upbeat urbanity of the south, to the dormant volcanoes and luxuriant tropical rainforests of the south, Yunnan has something for everyone. The province's allure does not end with its scenic splendor, however—Yunnan is almost always spoken of in the same breath as the names of its many minority peoples. A trip through the province from north to south passes nomadic Tibetan herders, the Bai, the Mosuo, the matriarchal Naxi, the Lahu, Dai, Yi, and Bulang minorities of Xishuangbanna, and the Myanmese of Ruili, offering glimpses of distinctive ways of life fast disappearing elsewhere.

KUNMING 昆明 ☎ 0871

Kunming, the "city of eternal spring," lives up to its name, with year-round blooms and mild weather. As a leader in China's determined march through the 21st century, the city maintains a precarious balance between development and natural beauty with surprising grace. The Han, Dai, and Muslim influences in local architecture and cuisine, however, only hint at the cultural clash that has shaped the surrounding area for centuries.

The 1999 International Horticultural Exposition, coupled with domestic and international investment, has transformed the city's infrastructure, including many of Kunming's historic neighborhoods and narrow *hútòng*. Fortunately, Kunming's push for modernization is bedecked more with flowers than with the dreary pollution and congestion that plagues other cities. The city is lively, clean, free of population crunch, and bursting at the seams with character—a fleeting visit makes you wish for a longer one, and a longer one makes you wonder what it would be like to call this place home.

▟ TRANSPORTATION

Flights: Kunming Airport (kūnmíng jīchǎng; 昆明机场 ; ☎ 717 9113 or 711 3229) is a few kilometers outside town. Accessible via buses #52 from Huguo Bridge, 78 from Qingnian Lu, and 67 from North Train Station. A shuttle bus (Y5) from the airport to the Worker's Palace usually takes passengers to any central destination they request. Different airlines sometimes offer different "discount" prices to the same destination. Any of the listed travel agencies can book tickets for no added fees. Regional flights to: **Baoshan** (daily, Y550); **Dali** (4 per day, Y430); **Jinghong** (15 per day, Y650); **Lijiang** (8 per day, Y530); **Mangshi** (4 per day, Y660). Other domestic flights to: **Beijing** (7 per day, Y1810); **Chengdu** (10 per day, Y700); **Chongqing** (10 per day, Y710); **Guangzhou** (6 per day, Y1260); **Guilin** (2 per day, Y840); **Guiyang** (4 per day, Y440); **Hong Kong** (2 per day, Y1310-1540); **Shanghai** (6 per day, Y1900). International flights to **Bangkok, Thailand** (1hr., daily, Y1240).

Air China (zhōngguó mínháng; 中国民航 ; ☎ 351 1591), by the main train station, left of the main ticket office. Open daily 8am-8pm.

China Southern Airlines (zhōngguó nánfāng hángkōng gōngsī; 中国南方航空公司), 433 Beijing Lu (☎ 310 1831 or 310 1832), near Dongfeng Lu. Open daily 8am-8pm. Credit cards accepted.

China Southwestern Airlines (zhōngguó xīnán hángkōng gōngsī; 中国西南航空公司 ; ☎ 353 1222), on Huancheng Nan Lu opposite the Bank of China. Open daily 8am-6:30pm.

China Yunnan Airlines (zhōngguó yúnnán hángkōng gōngsī; 中国云南航空公司), 24-28 Tuodong Lu (☎ 316 4270, reconfirmation 316 4415). Open 24hr. Credit cards accepted (4% surcharge).

Shanghai Airlines (shànghǎi hángkōng gōngsī; 上海航空公司), 46 Dongfeng Dong Lu (☎ 351 1534), east of Beijing Lu.

Trains: Kunming Train Station (kūnmíng zhàn; 昆明站 ; ☎ 351 1534 or 302 2122) is at the southern end of Beijing Lu. The ticket office is on the left of the station. Open daily 6am-11:30pm. Tickets are sold 3 days to 1 week in advance, beginning at 8:15am. To: **Beijing** (42hr., daily, Y539-578); **Chengdu** (24hr., 3 per day, Y240-274); **Chongqing** (22hr., 2 per day, Y246-263); **Dali** (8hr., daily, Y30); **Guangzhou** (30hr., daily, Y171-330); **Guiyang** (13hr., daily, Y54-193); **Shanghai** (57hr., 2 per day, Y326-519); **Xi'an** (35hr., daily, Y287-369). No direct train to **Guilin; go to Nanning** (16hr., 2 per day, Y160-174) first.

Buses: Kunming has 3 main bus stations.

Kunming Passenger Station (qìchē kèyùn zhàn; 汽车客运站 ; ☎ 354 3325), to the right as you face the train station. Ticket office is inside the gate to the left. Open daily 7am-10pm. To: **Jinghong** (24hr., 16 per day, Y165); **Lijiang** (10hr., 2 per day, Y119); **Ruili** (24hr., 8 per day, Y178); **Xiaguan/Dali** (5hr., 30+ per day, Y64-81); **Zhongdian** (16hr., 2 per day, Y142).

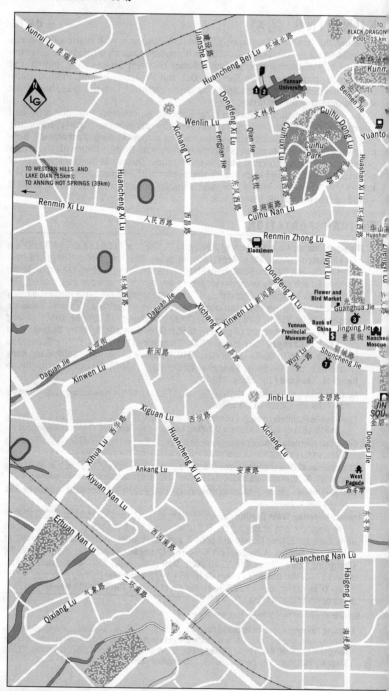

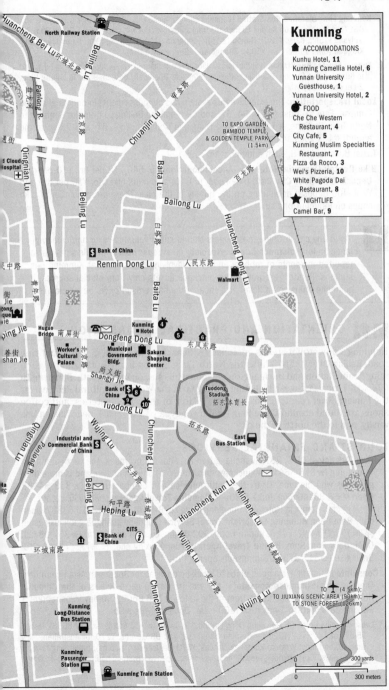

SOUTHWEST

Kunming

ACCOMMODATIONS

Kunhu Hotel, **11**
Kunming Camellia Hotel, **6**
Yunnan University
 Guesthouse, **1**
Yunnan University Hotel, **2**

FOOD

Che Che Western
 Restaurant, **4**
City Cafe, **5**
Kunming Muslim Specialties
 Restaurant, **7**
Pizza da Rocco, **3**
Wei's Pizzeria, **10**
White Pagoda Dai
 Restaurant, **8**

★ NIGHTLIFE

Camel Bar, **9**

Kunming Long-Distance Bus Station (kūnmíng chángtú qìchē zhàn; 昆明长途汽车站; ☎351 0617), a 5min. walk up Beijing Lu from the train station, on the left. Open daily 6:30am-9pm. To: **Guiyang** (15hr., daily, Y130); **Hekou** (8-10hr., 2 per day, Y112); **Lijiang** (9hr., 6 per day, Y151); **Xiaguan** (6hr., 11 per day, Y103); **Zhongdian** (12hr., daily, Y197).

Yunnan Express Bus Station (yúnnán gāosù gōnglù kèyùn zhàn; 云南高速公路客运站), next to Kunming Bus Station. The ticket office is to the left. Open daily 6:30am-9pm. To **Lijiang** (8hr., 2 per day, Y130).

Local Transportation: The extensive **bus** system has announcements in both English and Chinese. Fare Y1. Buses #50, 64, 67, and 68 run along Beijing Lu from the Kunming to North Train Stations; #5 travels along Dongfeng Dong Lu; #52, 67, and 78 go to the airport; #101 goes around Cuihu Park.

Taxis: Base fare Y7-8, each additional km Y1.6-1.8.

Bike Rental: Camellia Hotel (see **Accommodations**, p. 646). Y2 per hr., Y10 per day. Deposit Y200-300. **City Cafe** (see **Food**, p. 646) also rents bikes for Y10 per day and Y200-400 deposit, depending on the quality of the bike. There are a number of bike shops on Renmin Dong Lu.

As in any city in China, passengers should guard valuables with particular vigilance on **long-distance buses,** especially on **sleeper buses.** Travelers have also reported incidents of robbery and fraud involving tickets sold at Kunming bus stations. Readers are advised to purchase tickets only from official sources; if someone offers you a ticket at a cheaper-than-advertised price, be suspicious.

ORIENTATION AND PRACTICAL INFORMATION

Kunming's downtown area is encircled by **Huancheng Lu** (环城路), the first ring road. **Beijing Lu** (北京路) links the North Train Station in the north and the Kunming Train Station and the main long-distance bus station in the south. **Dongfeng Lu** (东风路) runs east-west, bisecting Beijing Lu at the Worker's Cultural Palace near the **Panlong River** (pánlóng hé; 盘龙河). Most of the parks, eateries, and coffee shops are found around **Cuihu Park** (cuìhú gōngyuán; 翠湖公园), near **Yunnan University,** and to the north of the city.

TOURIST AND FINANCIAL SERVICES

Travel Agencies: CITS, 287 Huancheng Nan Lu, after the overpass. The very helpful Ma Tongchung (☎356 6644; makmcits@public.km.yn.cn) speaks English and is more than generous with his time. Or try the North America and Europe bureau (☎353 5448). Open M-F 8:30am-noon and 2-5:30pm. **Camellia Travel Agency** (cháhuā lǚxíng shè; 茶花旅行社), Camellia Hotel, 96 Dongfeng Dong Lu, Bldg. 1, 1st fl. (☎316 6388). Open daily 8am-8pm. **Kunming Everbright Travel Service** (kūnmíng guāngdà guójì lǚxíngshè; 昆明光大国际旅行社), Kunhu Hotel, 202 Beijing Lu, 2nd and 3rd fl. (☎357 0871). Open daily 8am-8pm. **Kunhu Travel Agency** (kūnhú lǚxíng shè; 昆湖旅行社), 202 Beijing Lu (☎313 3737). Supposedly open 24hr.

Consulates: Kunming is a good place to stock up on visas for Southeast Asian countries. There is no **Vietnamese consulate;** the easiest way to get a visa is at the Camellia Hotel, in the ticket office at the front of the hotel (☎316 6600). 30-day visas require 3 working days (Y400); 1-day rush Y100 extra. Open daily 8am-9pm.

Laos, Camellia Hotel, 96 Dongfeng Dong Lu, Bldg. 1, 1st fl. (☎317 6624; fax 317 8556). Issues 15-day transit visas (Y320 for German, Japanese, and US citizens; Y270 for Australian, New Zealand, and most Western European citizens; Y370 for Canadian citizens); processing takes 3 working days. Visas are not issued at the Laos border. Open M-F 8:30am-noon and 1:30-4:30pm.

Myanmar, Camellia Hotel, 96 Dongfeng Dong Lu, Bldg. 1, 2nd fl. (☎317 6609; fax 317 6309). Issues 28-day tourist visas (Y185; no extensions). Processing takes 3 working days (3hr. rush fee Y185). Open M-F 8:30am-noon and 1-4:30pm.

Thailand, Kunming Hotel, 145 Dongfeng Dong Lu, South Bldg., 1st fl. (☎316 8916 or 314 9296; fax 316 6891). Citizens of Australia, Canada, Ireland, New Zealand, the UK, and the US do not need to apply for visas. 60-day tourist visas (Y200; up to 1-month extension permitted). Processing takes 2 working days. Open M-F 9-11:30am.

Banks: Bank of China, 515 Beijing Lu (☎318 8974), at Renmin Dong Lu. Open daily 9-11:45am and 1:30-4:45pm. **Industrial and Commercial Bank of China** (zhōngguó gōngshāng yínháng; 中国工商银行), 275 Beijing Lu (☎317 0614). Exchanges traveler's checks. MC/V **ATM.** Open daily 9am-5:30pm. Major hotels may also exchange currency and traveler's checks.

LOCAL SERVICES

Bookstores: Mandarin Books (kūnmíng mànlín shūyuàn; 昆明曼林书苑), 52 Wenhua Xiang (☎220 6575). From the Jouney to the East Cafe, walk straight; it's 2min. on the left. One of the most interesting and eclectic collections of English books you'll encounter. Current and classic fiction and non-fiction books, as well as German and French selections. The imported books are expensive (Y96-310), but the store is worth browsing even if you're not buying. Open daily 9am-10pm. **Foreign Language Bookstore** (wàiwén shūdiàn; 外文书店), on Shulin Jie. Take a left off Jinbi Lu; it's 20m on the right. Small selection of English-language classics and current fiction. Open 9:30am-6pm. **Journey to the East Cafe** (p. 647) has book rentals (Y1 per day); Y10-20 for purchase after bargaining. Try also **Wei's Pizzeria** (p. 647).

EMERGENCY AND COMMUNICATIONS

Markets: Sakura Shopping Center (yīnghuā gòuwù zhōngxīn; 樱花购物中心), 27 Dongfeng Dong Lu (☎314 0429), across from the Kunming Hotel. An expensive **grocery section** is on the 1st fl. Open daily 9:30am-10pm. Credit cards accepted. **Paul's Shop** (bǎolì shāngdiàn; 保利商店), 40 Wenlin Jie (☎535 4210), stocks imported foods and drinks. Open daily 8:30am-9pm.

PSB: (☎571 7001). In Jinxing Garden on Jinxing Lu, east of Beijing Lu. Take bus #3, 25, or 57 and get off at Jinjiang Lu; make a left onto Jinxing Lu; it's 5min. down on the right. Processes visa extensions. Open M-F 9-11:30am and 1-5pm.

Internets: Aofeisi Internet Cafe (àofēisī wǎngbā; 澳菲斯网吧), 5min. east on Dongfeng Dong Lu from the Camellia Hotel, on the left corner at the intersection with Huancheng Lu. 50+ computers of above-average speed. Y2-5 per hr. Open 8am-midnight. **Tailong Internet Cafe** (tàilóng wǎngbā; 泰龙网吧), in the Kunming Worker's Cultural Palace, on the southwest corner of Beijing Lu and Dongfeng Lu. Walk south on Beijing Lu and turn right at the market gate 2min. down; the gate is in the alley just to the left. Less crowded than most Internet cafes. Y2 per hr. Open 8am-midnight. **Feiyunda Internet Cafe** (fēiyùndá wǎngbā; 飞运达网吧 ; ☎640 8230), on Beimen Jie. From the east gate of Cuihu Park, walk left up the hill and take the 1st left onto Beimen Jie. The cafe is just down on the right. Y2 per hr. Open 8am-11pm. Internet is also available at most hotels and Western restaurants, but expect to pay more for the added convenience.

Post and Telecommunications: Post Office, 231 Beijing Lu (☎318 4132), just above Heping Lu. EMS and Poste Restante. Open daily 8am-8pm. **China Telecom** (☎316 4187), on the northeast corner of Beijing Lu and Dongfeng Lu. Open M-F 8:30am-5:30pm, Sa-Su 9am-5:30pm.

Postal Code: 650011.

SOUTHWEST

ACCOMMODATIONS

Hotels and hostels in Kunming are plentiful and available at reasonable rates. All hotels provide 24hr. hot water unless otherwise specified.

Kunming Camellia Hotel (kūnmíng cháhuā bīnguǎn; 昆明茶花宾馆), 96 Dongfeng Dong Lu (☎316 3000 or 316 2918; www.kmcamelliahotel.com). Bus #63 will take you right near the hotel on Dongfeng Dong Lu; pick it up on Yongping Lu, the 1st right off Beijing Lu after the train station. The undisputed favorite of Kunming backpackers, with cheap beds, clean facilities, good service, and a lovely garden. On-site travel agency, 2 consulates, Internet access (Y10 per hr.), currency exchange, and free airport shuttles. 4- and 8-bed dorms Y30; doubles with bath Y200. Credit cards accepted. ❶

Yunnan University Guesthouse (yúnnán dàxué zhāodàisuǒ; 云南大学招待所 ; ☎505 3557; ccfs@ynu.edu.cn), on Tianjundian Xiang, off Yieryi Dajie, on the western edge of campus. Take bus #10, 22, 55, 64, 65, 84, or 111 to the university's west gate (xīmén; 西门). Guesthouse is just up the hill on the right. A good alternative to the Camellia. Spartan rooms are clean and have full baths. Beautiful campus surroundings in funky neighborhood. Singles and doubles Y60; triples Y100. ❶

Kunhu Hotel (kūnhú fàndiàn; 昆湖饭店), 202 Beijing Lu (☎313 3737), by Huancheng Lu. Dim corridors, but clean rooms and facilities. Next to 3 cafes, with travel agencies on the 2nd and 3rd fl. 3-bed dorms Y25; singles Y40; doubles Y50, with bath Y80. ❶

Yunnan University Hotel (yún dà bīnguǎn; 云大宾馆 ; ☎503 1481), just up from the Yunnan University Guesthouse on Tianjundian Xiang, on the left. Bright new lobby and rooms offer a more luxurious option at reasonable rates. Singles and doubles Y120. ❷

FOOD

Kunming offers a wide array of local, national, and Western cuisine to make your tastebuds tingle. Cheap snacks and more expensive tea houses and coffee shops surround **Cuihu Park.** Just north of the park, near **Yunnan University,** restaurants dish up heartier fare and ask only Y2-5 for everything from dumplings to Muslim entrees. Another prime place for cheap food is **Beijing Lu,** near the long-distance bus station and Kunming Train Station. Try **Shuncheng Jie** (顺城街) in the Muslim district for quick, tasty, and inexpensive meals.

KUNMING SPECIALTIES

Kunming is most famous for its **Across-the-Bridge Noodles.** To sample this local treat at a fair price, try **The Jiang Brothers' Fragrant Bridge Garden** ❶ (jiāng shì xiōngdì qiáo xiāng yuán; 江氏兄弟桥香园), a chain with many locations throughout the city, including one on Wuyi Lu, across from the museum, and another on the north side of Dongfeng Dong Lu right before Beijing Lu. Noodles cost Y5-60. Hours vary by location. Most restaurants serve another local Kunming dish, **steampot chicken** (qìguō jī; 气锅鸡), chunks of tender, flavorful chicken cooked with broth in brown earthenware pots. Expect to pay Y10-40, depending on the size of the pot.

MUSLIM CUISINE

Parallel to Dongfeng Xi Lu, **Shuncheng Jie** is a bustling alley filled with Hui restaurants sporting green store fronts and Arabic inscriptions. From Dongfeng Xi Lu, turn left onto Wuyi Lu at their intersection by the Yunnan Provincial Museum, and take the first left. Many stalls serve up spicy noodle soups (Y2-3) and pastries filled with nuts and cream (Y10-20 per kg). The **Kunming Muslim Specialties Restaurant** ❷ (kūnmíng qīngzhēn fēngwèi'er chéng; 昆明清真风味儿城), 76 Shuncheng Jie, near Wuyi Lu, is the only restaurant in the area with an English menu, though it may be difficult to distinguish Muslim specialties from Chinese fare. Skinned white duck (Y18), spiced lamb kebabs (Y20), and flaky, round, sesame-covered sweet pastries (Y4) are favorites. (☎316 8806 or 313 0898. Most entrees Y10-30. Open daily 11:30am-2pm and 5-9pm.)

DAI CUISINE

One of the few Dai restaurants in town, the **White Pagoda Dai Restaurant ❷** (bái tǎ dǎi wèitīng; 白塔傣味厅), 127 Shangyi Jie, showcases heavily spiced food, often wrapped in banana leaves, grass, or bamboo. Go south on Baita Lu from the intersection with Dongfeng Dong Lu and take the first right; the restaurant is a 3min. walk on the left. Try the house favorite, sticky black rice cooked in pineapple for Y10. (☎317 2932. Open daily 8:30am-9pm.)

WESTERN FOOD AND BACKPACKER HANGOUTS

🦟 **Pizza da Rocco** (☎362 7951), in the Flower and Bird Market. Turn left at the market entrance; continue into the market until you see a sign for Rocco's Pizza on the right. Rocco dishes out Italian food so good you'll forget you're in China. The quality of home-made pasta, cheese, and imported wine makes waits (20-30min.) worthwhile. Try the tiramisu (Y10). Entrees and appetizers Y15-60. Open daily 11am-10pm. ❷

Wei's Pizzeria (hāhā fàndiàn; 哈哈饭店), 400 Tuodong Lu (☎316 6189), a 10min. walk from Beijing Lu. From the Camellia Hotel, turn right. Then take a left at the Holiday Inn, walk down Baita Lu, and turn right onto Tuodong Lu; it's up the road, on the right. Good pizza (Y20-30), with Western music and a refreshing mix of locals and foreigners. Try the goat with onions, a local favorite. Open daily 7:30am-midnight. ❷

City Cafe, on Dongfeng Dong Lu, 2min. west of the Camellia. Friendly staff, English menu, and a wide selection of Chinese and Western favorites (Y5-20). Try the chocolate, banana, or apple pancakes (Y8). Open 7am until the last customers leave. ❷

Che Che Western Restaurant (chēchē xī cāntīng; 车车西餐厅), 233 Baita Lu (☎316 9868), 2min. north from Dongfeng Dong Lu on the right. Standard Western and Chinese fare (Y5-25). Foreigners get a free beer or coffee with their meal. English menu with pictures. 10% discount if you return for a 2nd meal; ask for a card. Open 7am-11pm. ❷

Journey to the East Cafe (dōngfāng zhīlǚ; 东方之旅), 15 Tianjundian Xiang (☎531 7451), near the Yunnan University (Yunda) Hotel. Turn right out of Yunnan University Guesthouse and walk up the slope. A decent international book collection (see **Practical Information,** p. 645) redeems the below-average food. Internet access Y5 per hr. Entrees Y5-15. Open 9am-11pm. ❶

🎐 SIGHTS

Too many misguided travelers assume that Kunming is just another dull provincial capital, choosing to stop only for a night or two. Little do they know that Kunming is one of China's most remarkable cities, with enough attractions to merit much longer stays. The city's charm stems as much from its laidback atmosphere as from specific sights. In preparation for the 1999 International Horticultural Exposition, much of the city was razed, including many of the older *hútòng* neighborhoods and large portions of the Vietnamese and Cantonese commercial centers. The remaining traditional architecture, however, still provides an intriguing contrast to the dizzying scale of Kunming's latest additions.

GOLDEN TEMPLE PARK (jīndiàn míngshèng qū; 金殿名胜区). The main attractions here are the **Bell Tower,** which contains China's largest ancient bell, and the **Golden Temple** itself—the largest bronze temple in China. Over 300 years old, the temple was commissioned by Wu Sangui, a military genius later named the King of

Yunnan. Extensive gardens and hilly grounds provide plenty of quiet territory to explore, while a climb up the Bell Tower culminates in an excellent panoramic view of the city and its surroundings. *(Take bus #10 or 71 to the end of the line. Alternatively, walk toward the Expo Garden and turn left when Bailong Lu forks; turn right at Cuanjin Lu. The park is 15min. away, on the right. From the Expo Garden, you can also enter via cable car: one-way Y10, round-trip Y25. Open daily 7am-7pm. Y15.)*

MUSLIM NEIGHBORHOOD. Approximately 40,000 Hui Muslims live in Kunming, primarily in the neighborhood bounded by **Wuyi Lu, Dongfeng Xi Lu**, and **Jinbi Lu.** The best remaining examples of Islamic architecture line **Shuncheng Jie.** Most older mosques are no longer standing. Among the new places of worship, **Nancheng Mosque** (nánchéng qīngzhēn gǔsi; 南城清真古寺) is the most impressive, located on the corner of Zhengyi Lu and Chongyun Jie. Go north at the large intersection with Zhengyi Lu; the mosque is in an alley just past the Giordano shop. The green minarets and gold Arabic rooftop blaze bright and clear from afar. The first floor is occupied by a canteen; the prayer hall is upstairs. Devotees arrive each day around 1:30pm, particularly on Fridays. The **Yixigong Mosque** (yǐxīgōng qīngzhēn sì; 迤西公清真寺), near the corner of Huguo Lu and Dongfeng Xi Lu, just opposite the Bank of Communications, is larger, if less visually stunning.

CUIHU PARK (cuìhú yuán; 翠湖园). Four lakes link together to form Cuihu, "Jade-Green Lake," the remnants of a swampland drained in the 17th century. Today, sculpted gardens, restaurants, and an amusement park gracefully share the lake shores. Even on weekdays, elderly *mahjong* players fill the tree-shaded stone benches, while many locals fly kites high in the blue sky above. More tranquil grounds are near the entrance or directly to the north, across Wenling Jie, on the beautiful campus of **Yunnan University.** *(Take bus #5 up Dongfeng Lu and get off at Xiaoxi Gate. Continue walking in the same direction north; turn right on Cuihu Nan Lu and walk for 10min. to the south entrance. There are also entrances on the east, north, and west sides. ☎363 2081. Open daily 8:30am-10:30pm. Free.)*

EAST AND WEST PAGODAS (dōng xī sì tǎ; 东西寺塔). The oldest standing structures in Kunming, these twin relics date back to the Tang Dynasty. The time-worn gray towers, surrounded by small parks, provide pleasant grounds for the timeless art of relaxation. The West Pagoda is easily visible on a street flanked by old red walls. *Mahjong* players and other gamblers frequent its courtyard. Unfortunately, visitors may not climb the pagodas. *(The East Pagoda is on Shulin Jie, halfway between Jinbi Lu and Huancheng Nan Lu. The West Pagoda is directly opposite the East Pagoda on Dongsi Jie, parallel to Shulin Jie. Both open daily 7am-7pm. Y0.5 each.)*

YUNNAN PROVINCIAL MUSEUM (yúnnán shěng bówùguǎn; 云南省博物馆). An extravagant testament to provincial pride and ethnic diversity, this museum houses exhibits on textiles, costumes, handicrafts, and artifacts, with life-size mannequins of minority people in costume. The second floor has Neolithic Yunnan bronzeware and Buddhist art. *(At the intersection of Dongfeng Xi Lu and Wuyi Lu. Take bus #5 along Dongfeng Lu to Jinri Gongyuan, 近日公园. Continue walking in the same direction; the museum is on the left. ☎361 1551. Open daily 9:30am-5:30pm. Y10, students Y5.)*

BAMBOO TEMPLE (qióngzhú sì; 筇竹寺). This Zen Buddhist temple, dating from the late 13th century, is famous for its art and architecture. Legend has it that a magical rhinoceros led two princes to a group of strange monks on the site of the future temple. The monks left behind walking sticks that managed to arrange themselves into a bamboo grove. The temple's 500 quirky, life-sized depictions of *luohan* are to the right of the colorful gardens in the main courtyard. *(12km northwest of Kunming. Take bus #1 to the end of the line; change to a minibus, Y5-10. Y4.)*

WORLD HORTICULTURAL EXPOSITION GARDEN (shìjiè yuányì bólǎnhuì; 世界园艺博览会). Kunming's 1999 International Horticultural Exposition closed over three years ago, but the grounds remain a prime tourist attraction. Small gardens represent Chinese provinces, Taiwan, and 34 foreign countries (the US garden is a "Texas ranch," complete with cacti). Unless you really enjoy specimens of unusually large garlic, squash, and plums, among other horticultural oddities, the steep entrance fee is probably not worth it. *(In the northeast part of Kunming. Take bus #47, 68, 69, or 71. From Beijing Lu, you can also walk up to the intersection with Renmin Dong Lu and make a right, then a left on Baita Lu, and follow Baita Lu around to the right as it becomes Bailong Lu. Go to the end of Bailong Lu; the entrance is on the right where the road forks. ☎501 2367. Open daily 8am-9pm. Y100.)*

OTHER SIGHTS. A restored Ming-Dynasty Daoist temple, the **Black Dragon Pool** (hēi lóng tān; 黑龙滩) is named for a legendary black dragon whose life was spared by a Daoist immortal in return for its promise to aid mankind. The grounds contain cypresses and flowering trees that bloom in April and May. *(16km from Kunming. Accessible by bus #9 or 79 from North Train Station. Open daily sunrise-sunset. Free.)*

Underground waters of around 38°C (100°F) flow up from **Anning Hot Springs** (ānníng wēnquán; 安宁温泉), a favored bathing spot since its discovery in the Han Dynasty. *(Take bus #5 to Xiao Ximen and change to a minibus to Anning for a 45min. ride. Open 9am-11pm. Entrance fee including all sights Y88.)* Across the river and 2km south of the hot springs is **Caoxi Temple** (cáoxī sì; 曹溪寺), a Song-era monastery. Another ancient Buddhist temple, **Yuantong Temple** (yuántōng sì; 圆通寺) was built over 1000 years ago and represents the Mahayana, Theravada, and Tibetan sects. The best time to go is in the early morning or late afternoon, when tourists are scarce. *(30 Yuantong Jie, about a 10min. walk from Qingnian Lu away from the stream. ☎517 2881. Open daily 8am-5:20pm. Y4.)*

Stalls in the sprawling **Flower and Bird Market** (huāniǎo shìchǎng; 花鸟市场) peddle much more than flowers and birds. You can buy practically anything, from carved wooden animals to gerbils, maggots, and plastic cockroaches. *(Between Jingxing Jie and Guanghua Jie. Walk north up Zhengyi Lu from the large intersection with Dongfeng Xi Lu, and turn left on Guanghua Jie. The market begins with plants 5min. down on the left.)*

🎵 ENTERTAINMENT

Looking for nighttime entertainment in Kunming can, at times, be a lost cause. In order to make the city more "presentable" for the 1999 International Horticultural Exposition, local police shut down many of the city's nightspots. Currently, locals favor the discos in a few major hotels. Most party-goers are in their late teens or early 20s, though expats of all ages frequent the Western hangouts.

The **Camel Bar** (luòtuó jiǔbā; 骆驼酒吧), 274 Baita Lu, is a long trek down Baita Lu, but there's live music and plenty of revelers. Drink up (Y12-15) before moving onto the hot dance floor—they don't call this the camel bar for nothing. (☎317 6255. Open 24hr.) For larger crowds and better dancing, try the Camel's second location, 65 Tuodong Lu (☎319 5841), though both provide an entertaining ride. From Dongfeng Dong Lu, go south down Baita Lu before turning right onto Tuodong Lu; it's 3min. down on the right. **The Speakeasy** (shuōbā; 说吧) is on Dongfeng Xi Lu, 10min. down on the right after walking north from Xiao Ximen. Pool tables and classic rock complement the eclectic mix of locals and foreigners. (☎532 7047. Drinks Y8-15. Open daily 11am-late.)

S O U T H W E S T

⚡ DAYTRIPS FROM KUNMING

STONE FOREST 路南石林

*In Lunan Yi Autonomous County, 126km outside Kunming. **Minibuses** from the Camellia Hotel (round-trip Y40) depart at 8:30am, stop several times along the way, and return at 3pm; you won't actually arrive at the forest until 1-1:30pm. Minibuses also depart from the Long-Distance Bus Station (one-way Y20). From the forest, minibuses (Y20) return to Kunming frequently. Open 24hr. Admission Y80, students Y55.*

Yunnan's Stone Forest (lùnán shílín; 路南石林) lives up to its self-designated moniker as a "wonder of the world," with rock formations spiking up high above like redwoods or Scottish pines. Only the Big and Little Stone Forests portion is open to visitors. The forest is a gigantic labyrinth of jagged karst (limestone) pillars, some over 30m high, lashed and split by eons of ice and rain, and eroded to their present form. Formed more than 200 million years ago, some rocks were miraculously distorted into shapes that resemble "a 1000-year-old tortoise," "a baby elephant," or "a stone buffalo." Don't be frustrated if you can't see the resemblance— sometimes a rock is just a rock.

While the overcrowding characteristic of Yunnan's tourism sometimes plagues the forest, it's certainly possible to strike out and wander on your own. From the Sword Pool, turn right and go right at the next fork; you'll have to crouch a bit to enter this hidden path. From there, choose your own route to the top, where brilliant vistas await, undisturbed by the crowds that climb to the park's pavilion. Of course, for those wary of heights, the stairs and railings of the pavilion provide equally rewarding views for less effort.

After expending your energy on the climb up, head to the tea house in the rest area up the hill from the path that exits the pavilion. There, the local Yi (彝) minority leads free tea tastings. At the tasting's conclusion, don't feel obligated to buy anything; the many fragrant teas are tempting, but their prices are not—even the cheapest go for over Y100 per kilogram.

LAKE DIAN AND THE WESTERN HILLS

*A **minibus** (8am, Y10) runs from the Yunnan Hotel, 128 Dongfeng Xi Lu; to get to the Hotel, take bus #5 along Dongfeng Lu to the stop after the Yunnan Provincial Museum. Or, take bus #5 all the way to the end of the line, where you can squeeze onto the crowded #6 bus to the base of the hills; from here, minibuses run to the Tomb of Nie Er (Y3). **Buses** also run back down the hill (Y5); many of these will go all the way to the beginning of bus #5. To **bike** to the Western Hills (1½-2hr.), take Renmin Xi Lu; bear left when the road forks. The road leads directly to the Western Hills. Take the cable car up (Y30), and the ride down should be a breeze. Chairlift from Tomb of Nie Er to summit (8:30am-3:30pm, Y15). Western Hills Dragon Gate area open daily 7am-8pm. Admission Y20.*

Lined with small fishing hamlets, **Lake Dian** (diān chí; 滇池) is the largest lake in Yunnan and the sixth largest in China. Many of the sights around Kunming are in fact spots to view the lake, which is unfortunately tinged green with pollution from the overdevelopment nearby. Thankfully, a trip to the **Western Hills** (xī shān; 西山), nicknamed **Sleeping Beauty Mountain** because it resembles a woman reclining, offers many other diversions. A convoluted network of paths coils over the hills, offering fine views and a chance to stretch your legs. Carved into the craggy cliff faces are Yuan, Ming, and Qing Dynasty temples, with a series of grottoes thrown in for good measure.

The area between the Tomb of Nie Er and the top of the mountain is officially known as **Dragon Gate** (lóng mén; 龙门). A chairlift runs from the tomb to the top. In 1781, the Daoist monk Wu Laiqing, armed only with a hammer, a chisel, and sheer determination, chipped a long corridor up the face of the mountain. Legend has it that the tip of his chisel broke as he neared the end of his work (a good 14 years later). In a fit of despair, he threw himself into the waters below. Over 50 years later, the monk's followers finally reached a natural cliff-top platform, now called Dragon Gate. Over 2400m high, it commands a breathtaking vista of Lake Dian, as do the many platforms above. A 15min. climb from Dragon Gate leads to a rock-strewn hilltop, known as the Small Stone Forest (xiǎo shílín; 小石林), with a large pagoda. A 10min. descent from the forest leads to **Sanqing Pavilion** (sānqīng gé; 三清阁). Built in the 14th century as a country retreat for a Yuan Dynasty prince, the pavilion was later reincarnated as a Daoist shrine.

Further down the hills from Sanqing pavilion is the **Tomb of Nie Er** (niè ěr mù; 聂耳墓). A native of Yunnan, Nie Er (1912-1936) composed China's national anthem before drowning en route to the Soviet Union. From the Tomb of Nie Er, buses run to the base of the hills or back to Kunming. However, those who choose to walk can see two more temples. Thirty minutes down the mountain from Nie Er's tomb, **Taihua Temple** (tàihuá sì; 太华寺) is known for its camellia blossoms and dates from the Yuan Dynasty, though it was rebuilt during Qing Emperor Kangxi's reign. (Open daily sunrise-sunset. Y5.) Beyond the ornamental lake and garden, **Huating Temple** (huátíng sì; 华亭寺), 30min. down the main road from Taihuai Temple, boasts lavishly painted Buddha statues. (Open daily sunrise-sunset. Y5.) The mountain base is yet another 30min. walk away.

JIUXIANG SCENIC AREA 九乡风景区

*The East Bus Station, accessible by buses #11, 50, and 63, has **minibuses** that leave when full (Y20). Renting a minibus costs approximately Y220 round-trip. Y50.*

Not nearly as well known as the Stone Forest but definitely just as impressive a natural wonder, Jiuxiang Scenic Area (jiǔxiāng fēngjǐng qū; 九乡风景区) contains 66 caves, of which only a few have been opened to the public. Human and other mammalian remains from the Paleolithic Age were discovered in the 1980s, and the caves became a scenic spot in 1989. Despite a heavy human presence (camera toting vendors and the tacky neon lights that plague many a Chinese cave), the Jiuxiang caves still retain a number of untouched natural wonders, including a 1km wide canyon, a series of rock terraces, and a thundering underground waterfall. We recommend that you discover this place before tour groups do.

BORDER CROSSING INTO VIETNAM. Hekou (hékǒu; 河口) is the small town at the Chinese border with Vietnam; on the other side of the border is **Sapa**, an old French hill station populated by Hmong people. The border crossing is actually a small bridge across a river, and border formalities take place on either side. Border officials rarely speak much English, but tend to be friendly on the Chinese side, though many travelers have to pay a small "handling fee" on the Vietnamese side. **The border crossing does not process Vietnamese visas;** visas can be obtained at the Camellia Hotel Ticket Agency in Kunming (p. 644). **Buses** to Kunming run from the Long-Distance Bus Station (10-12hr.; 9:45am, 7:30pm; daybus Y122, sleeper Y90). Chinese time is 1hr. ahead of Vietnamese—be careful to not the miss the bus. The first thing most people need to do once in China is change money. The **Bank of China** is at the end of the main road, on the left side on the corner. The bank will not exchange Vietnamese currency for Chinese, but many locals will do so. Hekou has plenty of **hotels.** One cluster is up the main road, and another cluster is left out of the border office and left again. Dorms go for Y10-40, but many places only have standard rooms (Y100 and up). Key deposits tend to be high. Both the **Tourism Administration of Hekou County** (☎/fax 0873 342 1259) and the **CITS** (☎0873 342 2256; fax 342 1252) are at 9 Renmin Lu.

XISHUANGBANNA 西双版纳

Bordering Laos and Myanmar, Xishuangbanna Dai Autonomous Prefecture (xīshuāngbǎnnà; "Bǎnnà" for short), with its old-growth tropical rain forests, is one of China's most diverse regions, both ethnically and ecologically. The Dai minority group makes up one-third of Banna's population, which also includes the Lahu, Hani, Bulong, Yao, and Jinuo minorities. Most of the local people are Buddhists of the Southeast Asian Theravada school, and local Buddhist art and architecture closely resemble that of Thailand and Laos. The prefecture is composed of three counties: Jinghong, Menghai, and Mengla. Jinghong, the capital and largest city, is the base from which most travelers explore this fascinating region.

While an onslaught of Chinese tour groups in the mid- to late-1990s scared off many Western travelers from exploring Banna, the last two years have seen a decline in domestic tourism, reflected in the closing of hotels and travel agencies and the shortening of many attractions' opening hours. The result is a more laid-back atmosphere, with all the conveniences of modern infrastructure still in place. Xishuangbanna will not disappoint, whether you choose to vegetate in Jinghong's many backpacker hangouts or rough it on a trek into the gorgeous countryside.

◪ TREKKING IN XISHUANGBANNA

Trekking is certainly the single best way to experience Xishuangbanna's most unique attractions. Many travelers arrange for **guides** (usually in Jinghong); this option is more expensive than traveling alone, but guides can be invaluable on the twisting country roads hemmed in by dense jungle. They often speak both Mandarin and Dai, an important skill in a region where English speakers are almost nonexistent and a striking number of adults do not speak standard Mandarin. Guides can also scout out less-traversed routes and are almost always more effective diplomats in isolated villages than the average foreigner. If you decide to venture out on your own, try to find traveling companions. Pick up a few Dai phrases beforehand; younger people are more likely to know Mandarin than older ones.

Many people spend the night in villagers' homes along the way, but don't assume that you and your party are welcome unless you have what is indisputably an invitation. If possible, try to arrange a price before you eat or spend the night, and aim for slightly higher than the market price. Most guides advise paying Y10-15 per person for an overnight stay; food costs about Y5 per meal. Some villagers won't accept money for their hospitality; in these cases, bringing gifts, Western or Chinese, is a nice touch. One other etiquette point to note: always ask (or pantomime) before taking a photograph of anyone, especially with monks and in temples.

When packing, bring **food** and **bottled water** or **iodine tablets,** as well as a sizable stash of **toilet paper.** Take care to dispose of plastic and paper waste as responsibly as possible. You may need to ford a few small rivers; use **matches** to rid yourself of leeches. Before setting off, scour **travelers' notebooks** for advice and anecdotes. Those at Mei Mei's and Forest Cafe in Jinghong are the most useful, including maps in some cases. Consider bringing a **compass** if you're going on a particularly confusing route.

 WATER, WATER, EVERYWHERE. While bottled water is available in many of Xishuangbanna's villages, some areas have not yet adopted this modern "convenience." Bring a hot water container (Y5-15) and a supply of tea leaves to improve the taste of boiled water, which the villagers will offer you. Also, be wary of tap water in disguise as suspiciously packaged bottled water.

JINGHONG 景洪 ☎0691

While Xishuangbanna's beautiful forests and quiet villages are the region's most obvious attractions, this central city provides an ideal base for preparation and relaxation before and after treks. Several local sights, as well as a number of excellent backpacker cafes, make a stay here perfectly enjoyable.

▐ TRANSPORTATION

Flights: A bus (Y4) goes from the **airport** to the Xishuangbanna Hotel; ask to be dropped off near your destination. To get to the airport, take bus #1 (Y2) diagonally across from the booking office. Taxis cost Y10-15 after negotiation. **Xishuangbanna Booking Office** (xīshuāngbǎnnà shòupiào tīng; 西双版纳售票厅; ☎212 4781), on the southeast corner of Jingde Xi Lu and Minhang Lu. Open daily 8am-9pm. To **Kunming** (12-13 per day, Y390-650) and **Xiaguan** (F 9pm, Y650).

Buses: Long trips, like those to Dali and Kunming, can take up to 14hr. longer than usual, especially if roads are washed out during the rainy season. The prices below all apply to the trip out of Jinghong; return trips along the same routes vary in price.

Jinghong Banna Main Bus Station (jīnghóng bānnà kèyùn zhàn; 景洪版纳客运站), 5 Minzu Bei Lu (☎212 4427 or 212 3348), at Jinghong Bei Lu. Also known as **Fantai Chang** (fāntài chǎng; 翻胎厂). Open daily 6am-8pm. To: **Hekou** (26hr., daily, Y155); **Kunming** (12hr., 6 per day, Y145-169); **Xiaguan/Dali** (18hr., daily, Y150). Minibuses run to: **Menghai** (1hr., every 20min. 7am-6pm, Y8); **Menghan/Galanba** (45min., every 20min. 7am-7pm, Y7); **Mengla** (5hr., every hr. 7:20am-5:30pm, Y27); **Menglong** (2hr., every 10min. 6:30am-7pm, Y14); **Menglun** (2hr., every 30min., Y12); **Mengyang** (1½hr., every 40min. 8am-6:30pm, Y6); **Puer** (5hr., 6 per day, Y40); **Simao** (4hr., every 20min., Y29).

Jinghong Long-Distance Bus Station (jīnghóng qìchē kèyùn zhàn; 景洪汽车客运站), 23 Jinghong Bei Lu (☎212 3570). Stay on Jinghong Lu as it turns from Jinghong Nan Lu into Jinghong Bei Lu; the station is 10min. down on the right. Open daily 6am-9pm. Sleeper buses to **Kunming** (18hr., about 5 per day or whenever there are 15 passengers, Y146) and **Xiaguan/Dali** (16hr., daily, Y152). Minibuses to: **Menghai** (Y9); **Menghan** (Y7); **Mengla** (Y27); **Menglun** (Y13); **Mengyang** (Y7).

Local Transportation: Bus #3 (Y1) runs along Manting Lu. **Pedicabs** will go anywhere; Y2 is normally enough within the city, but arrange the price before embarking. **Taxis** to destinations within the city Y5-7.

Bike Rental: Mei Mei's (☎212 7324; see **Food**, p. 655) rents the city's best mountain bikes (Y20 per day, Y200 deposit), but beware the charges they may levy for breakdowns from routine use.

✈🚲 ORIENTATION AND PRACTICAL INFORMATION

Jinghong lies southwest of the **Lancang River** (láncāng jiāng; 澜沧江), which flows into Laos and Vietnam; the new **Lancang Bridge** (láncāng qiáo; 澜沧桥) is just east of town. The city is centered on **Peacock Lake** (kǒngquè hú; 孔雀湖), from which **Jinghong Lu** (景洪路) stretches in the four cardinal directions. **Jingde Lu** (景德路) runs south of the lake, parallel to **Jinghong Xi Lu** and **Jinghong Dong Lu**. Most restaurants and some backpacker accommodations are on **Manting Lu** (曼听路), at one end of Jingde Dong Lu. The town is easily navigable on foot, but the sweltering, muggy summers can leave travelers in a sweat in no time flat.

Travel Agencies: The English-speaking staff of **Mei Mei's, Forest Cafe,** and **Mekong Cafe** are much more helpful for backpackers than travel agencies. Sarah at the Forest Cafe is known as the city's best trek-guide (Y200 per person per day). James of **James' Cafe** is also very knowledgeable (Y250 per person per day). **CITS** (☎212 6783), on Luandian Lu (峦滇路), caters more to those looking for tours. From Jingde Lu, turn left onto Jinghong Lu. At the next intersection, take the street that branches off diagonally to the southwest; CITS is 10min. down on the left in the tall building on the corner.

Banks: Bank of China, 1 Jinghong Nan Lu, on the corner opposite Peacock Lake. Exchanges traveler's checks. Credit card advances. **ATM.** Open M-F 8am-5:30pm, Sa-Su 8-11:30am and 3-5:30pm. **Agricultural Bank of China** (zhōngguó nóngyè yínháng; 中国农业银行), 15 Jinghong Dong Lu, opposite the Jingyong Hotel. Exchanges traveler's checks. Open daily 8am-8pm.

PSB: 5 Jinghong Dong Lu (☎212 2676), with an English sign. Visa extensions on 2nd fl. Open M-F 8-11:30am and 3-5:30pm.

Bookstore: Mei Mei's, Mekong Cafe, and **Forest Cafe** have book exchanges.

Internet Access: Intellect Internet Cafe (zhìnéng wǎngbā; 智能网吧), on Manting Lu, 2min. before Mekong Cafe. Y2 per hr. Open 24hr. Other Internet cafes cluster nearby.

Post and Telecommunications: 2 Jinghong Xi Lu, opposite Peacock Lake. EMS and Poste Restante. Next door, **China Telecom** has IDD service. Both open daily 8am-8:30pm.

Postal Code: 666100.

ACCOMMODATIONS

Jinghong's lodgings provide welcome reprieve from rough village nights.

Xishuangbanna Technical College Hotel (xīshuāngbǎnnà zhíyè jìshù xuéyuàn bīnguǎn; 西双版纳职业技术学院宾馆 ; ☎881 9691), just after the botanical gardens on Jinghong Xi Lu. The best bargain beds in Jinghong are just within the gates of the city's technical college. Full baths. A/C available for Y25-50 extra. Singles Y20-25; doubles Y40-50; triples Y45. ❶

Dai Garden Hotel (dǎijiā huāyuàn xiǎolóu; 傣家花苑小楼), 57 Manting Lu (☎213 2592). From Peacock Lake, go down Jinghong Nan Lu, turn left onto Jingde Dong Lu, and turn right at the end of the road; the hotel is 5min. ahead, on the right, just past the Mekong Cafe. Small, clean Dai-style bamboo huts on stilts, each with a narrow balcony and charm to spare. Fans and mosquito nets. Solar-heated water approx. 10am-midnight depending on the weather. Luggage storage Y1 per day. Deposit Y5. 2- to 4-bed dorms Y25; doubles Y50. ❶

Banna Hotel (bǎnnà jiǔdiàn; 版纳酒店 ; ☎213 2052), on Ganlanba Lu, to the right of the Forest Cafe across the street. Clean rooms with A/C, TV, and full bath at reasonable prices. Singles and doubles Y50. ❶

Jingyong Hotel (jǐngyǒng fàndiàn;景永饭店), 12 Jinghong Dong Lu (☎/fax 214 5701), just to the right of Peacock Lake. Clean, comfortable rooms with attached bath. Singles and doubles Y60; triples Y70. ❶

FOOD AND ENTERTAINMENT

Dai cuisine is a strong presence in Jinghong, set apart by its emphasis on vegetables and unusual ingredients like oil-fried river moss. Restaurants serve dishes like the vaguely labeled "pungent vegetables with egg," which tastes far better than it sounds. Pineapple often combines with more savory foods, such as tomatoes, potatoes, or rice, which is eaten off one's hands. Mint leaves, cilantro, and lemongrass make frequent appearances. The Dai version of *shāo kǎo* (Chinese barbecue; 烧烤) consists of fish and chicken drenched in a delicious spicy sour sauce.

Dai restaurants along Manting Lu and its side alleys are instantly recognizable by the brightly clad women standing in front. These restaurants are a main source of Jinghong's evening entertainment, as Dai dancers perform (approximately 6-9pm) while guests enjoy their food. **Mekong Cafe** and **James' Cafe** serve similar Dai cuisine with helpful English menus, but their dishes (Y10-20) are less of a bargain. Many small restaurants serve **Thai-style noodles** (Y5-8). Stalls by the bus stations and along Galanba Lu and Jingde Lu dish up standard Chinese fare. **Pastry shops** cluster on northern Jinghong Bei Lu (Y1-2 per several buns).

For imported goods and trekking supplies, try the **supermarkets** on Jinghong Nan Lu, just before Peacock Lake. Mouth-watering fruits like mango, melon, and jackfruit are sold everywhere (Y2-5 per *jīn*, or 500g). Don't miss the sweet, abundant, and obscenely cheap fresh pineapples (Y0.5-1 each). Jinghong's main **produce market** (jímào shìchǎng; 集贸市场), between Jingde Xi Lu and Nonglin Lu, sells food, household items, and other local products. The listings below are for those with a hankering for Western flavors.

Mekong Cafe, 111 Manting Lu (☎216 2395), 5min. down from Mei Mei's, on the right. The youngest and prettiest of Jinghong's backpacker cafes. Don't miss the fish with lemongrass (Y2) for Dai food, or the chicken burger (Y10) for good Western fare. Trekking info, limited book collection, and the city's most eclectic music. 2 British expats serve as the cafe's unofficial advisors and consultants. Open daily 8:30am-late. ❶

GOT RICE?

n Jinghong, guides and treks
seem to be a dime a dozen, but
Sarah at the **Forest Cafe** runs a
particularly unique trek for more
than twice the going rate. About
200km from Jinghong, the **Ailao
Terrace Fields** are some of
China's most beautifully cultivated rice paddies. While mere
rice fields may not sound like the
most astounding natural scenery
n Yunnan, the Ailao terraces are
truly one-of-a-kind. Over centu-
ies, the Hani people painstak-
ngly carved the terraces' freeform
contour patterns into the moun-
ains. With every change of the
seasons, the terraces take on a
palette of myriad colors. Ask
Sarah to show you pictures if
you're not convinced.

Sarah recommends going on
he adventure November-April,
when the water-filled terraces
hine like gold in the rays of the
setting sun and glow a luminous
silver at sunrise. Other than the
rice terraces, highlights of the
seven-day trek include a night at
he Qing-era estate of a wealthy
country noble and a visit to the
hird-largest Confucian Temple in
China.

The Ailao Terraces (āiláo tītián;
哀牢梯田 *), also known as the*
Yuanyang Terraced Fields
(yuányáng tītián; 元阳梯田), are
east of Xishuangbanna, in south-
ern Yunnan. Forest Cafe ☎*213*
6957. Groups of 2-5 people.
¥3500 includes all transportation
and lodgings.

Mei Mei's (měiměi kāfēidiàn; 美美咖啡店 ; ☎212
7324), on Jinde Xi Lu, near the top left corner of the
traffic triangle as you walk away from Manting Lu. Good
Western and Chinese food (Y6-18) and a great BLT
(Y9). Those with a sweet tooth should dig into the
brownie with ice cream (Y7). English book collection
(deposit Y100). Slow but free Internet and DVDs
upstairs. Open daily 9am-1am. ❶

The Forest Cafe (sēnlín kāfēi; 森林咖啡 ; ☎213
6957), on Galanba Nan Lu diagonally opposite Mei
Mei's. Loaves of homemade bread (Y13-17; order a
half-day in advance), Western and Chinese dishes (Y5-
18), and a good vegetarian selection. Best fruit shakes
(Y6) of any of the cafes; try the passionfruit and pineapple mix. A surprisingly large English book collection
(deposit Y200), as well as guidebooks (Y100-200) and
phrasebooks (Y85) to most Southeast Asia destinations for sale. Tampons also available. Open daily
8:30am-10pm. ❶

James' Cafe (jiémǔsī kāfēi; 杰姆斯咖啡 ; ☎216
1462), on Manting Lu, 2min. left of the traffic triangle.
One of the few places that attract both Chinese and foreigners. Good Dai, Chinese, and Western food (Y10-
20). Try the *peroda* (Y6), a sweet drink made of jello,
bread, ice, milk, and *peroda* (a type of fruit) juice.
Open daily 8am-10:30pm. ❷

SIGHTS

Many visitors' first impulse is to ignore Jinghong in
favor of Xishuangbanna's surrounding villages. While
the region's best attractions undoubtedly lie in the
countryside, there are several sights within the city.

XISHUANGBANNA TROPICAL FLOWERS AND
PLANTS GARDEN (xīshuāngbǎnnà rèdài huā huì
yuàn; 西双版纳热带花卉苑). This garden, organized around a chain of lakes and ponds, provides
ample opportunity to ramble freely. One thousand
species of flowers live here, enough to make any bot-
anist green with envy. *(28 Jinghong Xi Lu. The main
entrance is just past the Yilan Resort; walk under the arch and
toward the end of the road. Open daily 7:30am-6:30pm. Y40,
students Y20.)*

MANTING PARK (màntīng gōngyuán; 曼听公园).
Originally known as Chunhuang Park ("Garden of the
Soul"), this park is the oldest in Xishuangbanna.
When the beloved companion of one of Banna's
ancient rulers fell ill and died after spending a day
here, the court physician concluded that the lady
must have left her soul in the garden. The vast area
includes a Bodhi tree, 400 peacocks, and a garishly
painted temple. Every day, locals perform death-

defying tightrope maneuvers across the Lancang River and the **Dai Water Splashing Dance,** traditionally part of the Dai New Year celebrations in April. *(1 Manting Lu, a 10min. walk from town; Manting Park is on the right, marked by English signs. Water Splashing Dance 10am, 1:30pm. Open daily 8am-7pm. Y35, students with ISIC Y15.)*

NATIONALITIES PARK (mínzú fēngguāng yuán; 民族风光园). Somewhat informative despite its contrived nature, this is Jinghong's dubious tribute to the minority peoples of Xishuangbanna. Six small houses are dedicated to the Dai, Jinuo, Hani, Lahu, Yao, and Buan peoples. Cock-fights, dancing, music, and elephant performances are staged throughout the day. *(4 Minhang Lu. Follow Jingde Lu to Minhang Lu and turn left; the park is on the right. Open daily 8am-6pm. Y30.)*

XISHUANGBANNA PRIMEVAL FOREST PARK (xīshuāngbǎnnà yuánshǐ sēnlín gōngyuán; 西双版纳原始森林公园). The closest tropical rain forest to Jinghong offers a glimpse of what the region was like before the invasion of construction and tourism. Parts of the forest are extremely slippery; be especially careful on the bamboo paths and bridges. The park also hosts ethnic dances and stages "marriage ceremonies" between audience members and blushing—or at least heavily rouged—minority brides. *(8km north of Jinghong. Bike along the highway from Jinghong to Mengyang and then turn left into the park's very visible entrance after about 1hr. Bus from long-distance bus station 30min., Y3. Animal shows featuring tigers and elephants daily at 1, 5:10pm. Open daily 7:30am-5:30pm. Y60, students Y35.)*

MONASTERIES. Young boys come to the cool, dark, and wonderfully ornate interiors of the two largest active Buddhist monasteries to study Buddhism and learn the Dai language and script. Respectful observers are also welcome; shoes should be removed before entering the prayer hall, and photography is not permitted. Even outside the prayer hall, ask first before taking any pictures, as many monks dislike being photographed. Known in Dai as *Wat Chienglarn,* the **Manjing Temple** (mànjǐng fósì; 曼景佛寺) is just left past the Dai Garden Hotel on Manting Lu, guarded by golden dragons and lions. *(Open daily sunrise-sunset. Free.)* A 10min. walk down the road toward Manting Park leads to the similarly dragon-guarded **Manting Temple** (màntīng fósì; 曼听佛寺), or *Manting Wat. (Y30, students Y15.)*

▶ DAYTRIP FROM JINGHONG: MANDIAN WATERFALLS

The **Mandian Waterfalls** (màndiǎn pùbù; 曼典瀑布) are an hour's hike from Mandian village, 1hr. north of Jinghong by bumpy road. Take a taxi to Gadong village, near Jinghong, to try to catch an infrequent bus (Y6-7) or hire a minibus (round-trip Y80-120 after negotation). The easiest option is to ask the Mekong Cafe to charter a minibus for a day; pick-up is at the cafe in the morning.

At the village, walk up the steps and take a left immediately past a rubber plantation to a small path with the river on your left. After 10min., cross the second bamboo bridge; if you're walking uphill, you've gone too far. Follow the river on your right, continuing into the rain forest until the falls appear through the greenery. The water tumbles down more than 20m in the midst of the rain forest. This trip is only feasible in the dry season. In April you may be able to swim in the waters below the falls. Admission is Y5.

 BIKES ON BUSES. It often makes more sense to rent bikes in a hub town, like Jinghong or Dali, where there's a greater selection of models. If you don't want to bike all the way to your destination, most buses will take bikes on the roof for an extra Y2. If the driver makes you tie the bike down yourself, act helpless and they will normally take over.

MENGHAN 勐罕

Menghan, also known by its Dai name, **Galanba** (gǎnlǎnbà; 橄榄坝), is 27km southeast of Jinghong, encircled by fields overflowing with rice, palms, and flowers. The town itself is very small and has few sights, but the flat roads that radiate from it make for leisurely biking through the countryside and its emerald backdrop of rubber plantations and rice fields. Don't worry about staying on any particular route; those who stray are sure to stumble upon something quite marvelous.

The **Xishuangbanna Dai Garden** (xīshuāngbǎnnà dǎizú yuán; 西双版纳傣族园) combines many negatives of China's tourist sights—throngs of tour groups, manufactured displays of indigenous minority culture, and tacky remodelings of ancient relics. Still, the cluster of centuries-old temples and monasteries within the park does offer some authentic sights. A pedicab (Y1) will take you into the park and leave you at the **Menghan Chunman Temple** (mànchūnmǎn gǔ fósì; 曼春满古佛寺), also known as *Wat Ban Suan Men*. A resplendent golden *stupa* sits at the center of the temple's courtyard, surrounded by smaller *stupas*. From the temple, continue along the main road to the center square. Walk through the Dai Song and Dance Show Grounds and follow the English signs right to **Manzha Village** (mànzhà; 曼乍), across from a humble wooden monastery. Turn left before the village and walk 10min. down, following the path left to the **Manting Buddhist Temple** (màntīng fósì; 曼听佛寺), the last monastery in the park, set apart by an enormous white *stupa*. From the temple, you can walk back to town in 30min., longer if you choose to explore the surrounding villages in the park's undeveloped areas. From the minibus drop-off, go down the sloping road and take the 1st left; the park is 10min. down at the end of the road. (☎250 4099. Dai shows daily at 3:30 and 4:30pm. Open 24hr. Y50, students Y25.)

Buses stop just off the main road, near a small office. Tickets to Jinghong (45min., every 20min. 7am-6pm, Y6) can be bought inside. To go to Mengla (5hr., every 20min., Y25) or Menglun (1hr., every 20min., Y10), stand on the road and hail down any bus traveling from Jinghong. To **bike** to Menghan from Jinghong, go north up Ganlanba Lu and take the first right at the traffic circle. Continue riding straight across the river over the new bridge and go right at the traffic circle to the road to Ganlanba along the Mekong River. The ride takes about 2½hr. In Galanba, **rent a bicycle** opposite the Dai Bamboo House; bikes are kept in the courtyard at the end of the path. (Standard bikes Y10 per day, mountain bikes Y20. Deposit Y300.) You can't exchange currency anywhere in town, so bring sufficient cash.

The **Dai Bamboo House ❶** (dǎijiā zhúlóu; 傣家竹楼), in the middle of the Dai minority Park, near the center square, has thin mattresses on a bamboo floor and cold showers. (6- to 7-bed dorms Y10.) The **Galanba Guesthouse ❶** (gǎnlǎnbà bīnguǎn; 橄榄坝宾馆) is just before the park on the right. Spartan rooms are clean and cheap. (Doubles, triples, and quads Y15-20 per person after bargaining.) Fruit sellers line the road. A **market,** off and halfway down the main road, joins the two largest streets in town.

MENGLUN 勐仑

Southeast of Jinghong, Menglun is another lazy village whose biggest draw are its luscious natural attractions. Sure to fulfill any botany buff's floral fantasies, the enormous **Chinese Academy of Science Tropical Botanical Gardens** (zhōngguó kēxuéyuàn xīshuāngbǎnnà rèdài zhíwùyuán; 中国科学院西双版纳热带植物园) sets this town apart from the rest. Even the less horticulturally savvy should be humbled by the presence of over 10,000 species of tropical and subtropical plants, many native to Xishuangbanna. Especially famous are the "stranglers," parasites that cling on to other trees and grow over their trunks before squeezing the life out of their prey, and the friendlier "dancing plant," which moves its tender leaves when you sing to it. It's advisable to get to the gardens before the midday influx of tour groups, though the sheer size of the park—the largest botanical garden in China, sprawling over 900 hectares—makes for plenty of breathing room. Continue walking in the direction the bus travels and turn right at the market; the gardens are at the end of the road. To return to Menglun, backtrack through the park; a much longer 5-6hr. route on foot leads out of the East Gate, through the countryside, and back into town. (☎871 5404. Open 24hr. Y60, students Y40.)

The **Xishuangbanna Biosphere Reserve** (xīshuāngbǎnnà yǔlínqǔ; 西双版纳雨林谷) is 7km before Menglun, off the main road on the left. Recently opened and granted the highest level of state protection, this reserve shelters China's largest stretch of tropical rainforest and 90% of the country's wild elephant population. Many minority groups also traditionally make their homes within the reserve. The park offers several canopy walks through the rain forest. Ask the bus coming from or going to Jinghong to drop you off at the park. (Open 8am-sunset.)

Buses go to Menglun from Jinghong (1½hr., every 30min., Y13), Menghan (1hr., every 20min., Y12), and Mengla (5hr., when full). From Jinghong or Menghan, take the bus heading to Mengla and ask to be dropped off at Menglun; vice versa coming from Mengla. In Menglun, the bus station is on the right side of the main road, 50m after the road to the botanical gardens.

The **Botanical Gardens Hotel ❷** (zhíwù yuán bīnguǎn; 植物园宾馆) offers a quiet alternative to Banna's bustling towns. Follow signs within the botanical gardens to the Shade Plant Collection; the hotel is further down on the left. All rooms have a terrace overlooking the garden's grounds. (☎871 7008. Singles and doubles start at Y140 and go much higher.) For more affordable accommodations, try the **Spring Forest Guesthouse ❶** (chūnlín lǚshè; 春林旅舍), right before the gate to the botanical gardens, on the right. Rooms are spartan but clean. (☎871 5816. No hot water. Singles Y10; doubles Y20; triples Y30.) Small, bland **restaurants** line the main street. There are also snack stalls within the garden.

MENGHAI 勐海

Normally only visited en route to more interesting nearby destinations, Menghai is the largest town in western Xishuangbanna. The region is prime tea-growing country and an important source of **pu-erh tea,** a black, earthy brew favored by dieters but few others. The town also has a sizable Muslim population, rare in Xishuangbanna; the mosque (qīngzhēn sì; 清真寺) is on the main street, a 10min. walk left from the bus station. About 10min. outside the city are some small **Dai villages** and a golden **pagoda.** A path to the left leads to another small hilltop **pagoda** and attached **temple,** with sweeping views of vast tea fields.

Menghai's **Sunday market** is particularly popular, drawing crowds from throughout Xishuangbanna. The Sunday market in nearby **Menghun** (měnghùn; 勐混), a tiny town southwest of Menghai, is even busier. A lively mix of Dai, Bulang, and Ahe people live in the surrounding area. It is best to stay in Menghun or nearby Menghai the night before; the market is at its most active in the early morning, around 7-9am. Activity is more subdued during the wet season and the summer holidays. **Buses** overflowing with people, animals, and goods run from Jinghong (2-2½hr., Y8) and Menghai (30min., Y4-6) to Menghun.

Just about everything a visitor could need in Menghai is on the main street, **Xiangshan Xin Jie** (香山新街). The newly renovated **Menghai Bus Station** (měnghǎi kèyùn zhàn; 勐海客运站) sits in the center of town on Xiangshan Xin Jie, just off its intersection with another main road. Buses run to Jinghong (2hr., Y8), Kunming (24hr., 4 per day, Y142), and Ruili (28hr., daily, Y120).

MAKING A SPLASH

Dai legend tells of an evil demon who set his sights on a beautiful princess. After kidnapping her, he forced the princess to be his wife and "invited" her to celebrate the new year festival with him. The princess drank, danced, and flattered the demon shamelessly, until he revealed to her his one weakness: if one wrapped a single hair from his head around his neck, he would be decapitated. The stealthy princess proceeded to use the trick to slay the monster. After this bloody deed, she promptly returned to the human world, where the first item on her to-do list was to wash the demon blood from her hands.

Every April 13 to 15, the Dai reenact this cleansing at their annual **Water Splashing Festival** (泼水节) in celebration of the Dai New Year. The first day represents the last of the old year, the second is a transition day between years that does not exist on the Dai calendar, and the third welcomes the new year. Dragon boat racing and the throwing of love pouches are also part of the festivities, but water splashing is the main event. The Dai believe that the splashing symbolically washes away sins, purifies the spirit, and brings good fortune and new life for the coming year. Accordingly, the **Water Splashing Down Dance** involves huge amounts of water, filling Jinghong's streets with soaked revellers—bring a raincoat if you want to stay dry.

The **Grain Trade Guesthouse ❶** (liáng mào lǔshè; 粮贸旅社), on the third floor, is on Xiangshan Xin Jie, 5min. on the left from the train station, in the direction of the mosque. Clean rooms overlook the noisy main street. (☎512 2274. Singles and doubles Y20; triples Y30; quads Y40.) For a bit of luxury, try the **Menghai Transportation Hotel ❶** (měnghǎi jiāotōng bīnguǎn; 勐海交通宾馆), just opposite the bus station. Rooms with clean, new facilities rise above the hubbub below. (☎512 6851. Full baths. A/C Y10 extra. Singles and doubles Y60; triples Y70.)

The **Sichuan Flavor Restaurant ❷** (chuān wèi dà quān; 川味大全), on the same block as the Grain Trade Guesthouse, serves very spicy food. (☎665 4409. Chinese entrees and local fare Y8-25.) For **Muslim food,** try the side streets near the mosque; look for green signs and Arabic script.

DAMENGLONG 大勐龙

Damenglong, listed on bus timetables as **Menglong** (měnglóng; 勐龙), is basically just a single bustling street, but it serves as a fine base for trekking. Two marvelous temples stand at either end of town. The **Manfeilong Bamboo Temple** (mànfēilóng sǔn tǎ; 曼飞龙笋塔) lies at the base of a hill, several kilometers back toward Jinghong. To reach the *stupa*, walk 15min. up the hill, through the village streets lined with jackfruit trees and beautiful architecture; when the road forks, go to the right and up the stairs instead of continuing on the path. Built in AD 1204, the pagoda was named for the resemblance of its slender white spires to bamboo shoots. While the moss-covered steps leading to the temple betray its lack of visitors, the slightly unkempt feel is a refreshing change from the touristy temples ubiquitous in the region. The whole complex is awash with carvings of plants, animals, and Buddhas, as well as a variety of vegetation more befitting of Banna's many botanical gardens. (Open 24hr. Y5 when the attendant is actually attending.)

At the other end of town, just before the road bends to the left, a street branches off to the right, leading to the **Black Pagoda** (hēi tǎ; 黑塔). This monastery, fronted by a silver *stupa*, sits 50m up the hill. Another 10min. of scrambling brings you to the main shining golden *stupa*. (Open 24hr. Free.) Food stalls line the street before the pagoda, while a few restaurants are scattered along the main road. The town's market is off the same street as the pagoda, in the opposite, downhill direction from the main road.

Buses to Damenglong depart from Jinghong Banna Main Bus Station (3hr., every 20min., Y13). The **Lai Lai Hotel ❶**, right at the bus drop-off, has decent beds, mosquito nets, and a friendly staff that speaks some English. (Hot water in dirty public baths based on solar power. Singles and doubles Y25; triples Y30; quads Y40.)

⚑ TREKKING AROUND DAMENGLONG

The 50km stretch between Damenglong and **Bulangshan** (布朗山) usually takes two to four days. This route is fairly populated; if you have walked more than two hours without seeing any structures or people, chances are you're lost. The road covers some steep terrain and is definitely more rigorous than the Menghan-to-Menglun circuit. Most villages between Manpo (the first true village heading out from Damenglong) and Bulangshan sell **water** and snacks, but it's best to carry provisions with you regardless. Beware of dogs; some travelers have reported vicious canines roaming the villages. Be extra observant during the rainy season, as the geography can look different and the route becomes more difficult. It is also possible to do this trek on a **mountain bike,** though you may have to push the bike up steep hills and through river fords. Do not attempt to bike during the rainy season.

DAMENGLONG TO BULANGSHAN. Rough **maps** for the trek are available in Jinghong, from both Mei Mei's (make a photocopy next door) and the Forest Cafe, which provides photocopies for free (see **Jinghong: Food,** p. 655). Also check traveler's notebooks in Jinghong for more updated information.

The following is a rough description of the trek. The first village after Damenglong is **Manguanghan** (3hr. trek). Follow the road south toward Myanmar and turn right onto the lower path where the concrete on the sides of the road ends. It is also possible to grab rides in motorbike sidecars. After Manguanghan, follow the tractor trail for 30min. to **Guanmin,** a small Hani village. From there, it's a 5km walk to **Manpo,** a Bulang minority village. Accustomed to trekkers, Manpo is an excellent place to spend the night. Plan to spend about Y10 per night and Y5 per meal.

Leave Manpo for the walk to **Nula** (1½-2hr.) from the trail starting at the back of the town. After crossing the newly built steel bridge just past Nula, take the trail to the left that runs along the edge of some rice paddies. Within 20-25min. you'll see a somewhat trodden path that descends to a makeshift bridge across the river. The winding path may make it seem like you're backtracking, but you're actually on your way to **Songer** (1hr.), a Lahu village. Songer is the poorest of the villages along the route, which may mean that villagers are more aggressive in promoting a night's stay or a mid-day meal. Don't leave your belongings unattended.

From Songer, take the path that heads down for about 30min., until you descend a steep hill to a clearing near some fields. During the dry season, take a sharp left on the short path toward the stream. Shallow water will allow you to ford the river and walk to Weidong in 30-60min. In the wet season, take the more obvious path uphill to the right. This path leads to **Weidong,** a Hani village, in 2hr. The latter half of the walk passes through a beautiful valley filled with immaculate rice paddies. From Weidong, follow the broad tractor trail to **Bulangshan** (3½hr.). During the wet season, there is only one **bus** back to Menghun (4hr., Y14) and Menghai (4½hr., Y16) from Bulangshan, leaving at 8:30am. In the dry season, a second bus runs in the early afternoon. For this reason, it makes more sense to push on from Weidong to the end of the trek. If you have time, ask the villagers at Weidong to take you to the **waterfalls** (pùbù; 瀑布).

In Bulangshan, the only accommodation available is the **Bulangshan Guesthouse ❶** (bùlángshān zhāodàisuǒ; 布朗山招待所), on the left side of the main road coming from the trek. The rooms are clean and new, but the bathroom is off-site, 50m away. (☎815 8237. Singles and doubles Y50.)

MENGLA 勐腊

Mengla's main draw is its proximity to **Mohan,** site of the border crossing into Laos. Due to the increasing flow of people and goods across the border, Mengla is growing fast, but most tourists pass through quickly. **Buses** run to Jinghong (5hr., Y27) and Menghan (5hr., Y26) from the bus station (qìchē zhàn; 汽车站 ; ☎812 2773). **Bank of China,** outside the bus station, on the left corner of the next intersection, exchanges currency and traveler's checks. **Postal Code:** 666300.

BORDER CROSSING INTO LAOS: MOHAN. Buses (2hr., Y10-15) go from Mengla to Mohan (磨憨), the small town where China ends and Laos begins. Minibuses (Y60) also ply the route. To leave Jinghong and cross the border in the same day, travelers must leave early in the morning (before 8am), as the border is normally only open 8am-5pm. There is no Bank of China in Mohan; other banks will change US dollars, but usually only in amounts over US$100. Notes of any amount can be changed on the black market. Laos visas are not issued at the border. All visas must be obtained at the embassy in Beijing (p. 11) or the consulate in Kunming (p. 644). The Laos entry checkpoint is a 20min. walk from the border.

BAOSHAN 保山 AND DEHONG 德宏

Baoshan Prefecture and Dehong Dai Jinpo Autonomous County, in far southwestern Yunnan, have a reputation as the province's wildest regions. A large number of Dai, Jinpo, Achang, and other ethnic minorities live in the area, and Dehong County's long border with Myanmar adds a strong international flavor to the already colorful ethnic mix. A crucial stretch of the ancient Southern Silk Road connecting China, Southeast Asia, and India, the region continues to serve as an important hub for trade, both legal and otherwise. A rise in prostitution, drug trade, and disease has only further entrenched the image of Baoshan and Dehong as Yunnan's "Wild West." Nevertheless, the area does have plenty of attractions, whether seen on their own or en route to or from Myanmar. Despite the aura of danger given off by these recent trends, travelers need not worry—the sights are well-maintained and the people warm and generous.

BAOSHAN 保山   ☎0875

In the 4th and 5th centuries, silk, gold, precious stones, and elephants journeyed through Baoshan city on their way to India and Southeast Asia. Though remnants of this glorious past are hardly apparent, the seat of Baoshan Prefecture is still a convenient stopping point on the way to the livelier towns of Tengchong and Ruili and the rest of the southwestern frontier.

☐ TRANSPORTATION. Baoshan Airport (bǎoshān jīchǎng; 保山机场 ; ☎223 2222) is not far out of town. **Yunnan Baoshan CAAC Ticket Office** (yúnnán bǎoshān mínháng shòupiào chù; 云南保山民航售票) is in the Landu Hotel, the largest hotel on Baoxiu Xi Lu. (☎212 1888, ext. 660. Open daily 8-11:30am and 2-5:30pm.) Flights go to Kunming daily (7:30pm, Y550). **Buses** depart from the **Baoshan Passenger Transport Station** (bǎoshān kèyùn zhàn; 保山客运站), at the intersection of Baoxiu Dong Lu and Huancheng Bei Lu. It's also the best place to buy maps. (☎212 2311. Open daily 6am-9pm.) The station sends buses to Ruili (4hr., every

40min. 6:30am-2:20pm, Y47); Tengchong (5hr., every 40min., Y27-35); Xiaguan (2½hr., every 40min., Y40); Yingjiang (7hr., 4 per day, Y39). Sleeper buses go to Kunming (10hr., 7 per day, Y122-150).

▓ ♂ ORIENTATION AND PRACTICAL INFORMATION. Most hotels and many high-end shops are on Baoxiu Lu (保岫路) and Xiang Jie (巷街), the latter of which is divided into upper and lower reaches, Shangxiang Jie (上巷街) and Xiaxi-ang Jie (下巷街), respectively. Baoxiu Lu and Xiang Jie run parallel to one another, a block apart. These two thoroughfares are bounded by the long-distance bus station on one side and Taibao Park on the other.

The **Bank of China,** 1 Baoxiu Dong Lu, next to the Yindu Hotel, exchanges trav-eler's checks and processes credit card advances. (Open daily M-F 8-11:30am and 2:30-6pm.) A block before the bank, turn right onto Zhuzi Jie from Baoxiu Lu; the **PSB** (☎214 0397 or 212 2445) is on the right. Turn left from the bank and walk down to reach the more than 50 computers at **Heavenly Dragon Internet City** (tiān-lóng wǎngchéng; 天龙网城), on the second floor. (Y2 per hr. Open 8am-midnight.) Walk south on Huancheng Lu from its intersection with Baoxiu Lu and take the first right onto Xiaxiang Jie; continue to the next intersection to find **China Post,** 21 Xiaxiang Jie. (EMS and Poste Restante. Open daily 8am-8pm.) **Postal Code:** 678000.

♂ ♄ ACCOMMODATIONS AND FOOD. Hotels here are fairly basic. The main distinguishing factor is the friendliness of the staff. All the establishments listed below are within a 15min. walk of the bus station and have 24hr. hot water. Turn right out of the bus station and left at the traffic circle and walk down to the **Rising Sun Hotel ❶** (shēngyáng bīnguǎn; 升阳宾馆), on the right. Rooms are clean and comfortable, but may be slightly noisy, with karaoke outside lasting late into the night. (☎216 0660. Singles and doubles Y30, with bath Y60; triples Y45/Y70.) A right at the same traffic circle leads you to **Yongchang Hotel ❶** (yǒngchāng bīnguǎn; 永昌 宾馆), 11 Baoxiu Xi Lu, 10min. up the road on the left. Relax on the soft beds and enjoy the hardwood floors. (☎212 2802. Singles Y30, with bath Y60; doubles Y30/ Y50.) Next to the Yongchang, the **Blue Flower Hotel ❶** (lánhuā bīnguǎn; 兰花宾馆), 23 Baoxiu Xi Lu, attempts chandeliered grandeur, but only manages to set a chintzy tone for the rest of the hotel. (☎212 0835. Clean and functional rooms. Sin-gles Y30, with bath Y80; doubles Y60/Y80; triples with bath Y60.) Across the street from the bus station, **Flower City Hotel ❶** (huāchéng bīnguǎn; 花城宾馆), 16 Hua-ncheng Dong Lu, features clean new rooms and luxury at a reasonable price. (☎220 3999. Singles Y80; doubles Y90.)

Food vendors lay out their edible bonanza for inspection, clustering around the passenger transport station, the market on **Xiashuihe,** and along Shangxiang Jie.

◎ SIGHTS. The countryside around Baoshan is beautiful and tempting, but unfortunately, there is no bike rental in town. Within the city, all sights are concen-trated on the western edge. Walk along Baoxiu Lu away from the bus station, past the Bank of China and the Landu Hotel, to the end of the road. **Taibao Park** (tàibǎo gōngyuán; 太保公园), a wooded area interspersed with pagodas, has a number of quiet places to relax, including the Yuhuang Pavilion, from which you can get a good view of the city, especially at night. (Open 24hr. Free.) From the paths that run through the park, the 13-tiered **Wenbi Pagoda** (wénbǐ tǎ; 文笔塔) is visible just to the south. There is no need to go any closer: it looks best from a distance. **Yiluo Pond** (yìluó chí; 易罗池) is just below the hill on which the Wenbi Pagoda rests. Relax at the pagoda at the center of the pond and breathe some fresh Baoshan air.

SOUTHWEST

TENGCHONG 腾冲 ☎ 0875

With its green mountains, extinct volcanoes, and bubbling hot springs, Tengchong boasts wilder and rougher surroundings than Baoshan. The main streets, unlike those of Baoshan, are dismal thoroughfares filled with scurrying vehicles and dirty mechanics' shops. The side streets, however, are delightfully labyrinthine, lined with traditional architecture inviting independent exploration.

☐☑ TRANSPORTATION AND PRACTICAL INFORMATION

Although there is no distinction between an old town and a new town, Tengchong certainly seems divided between the maze of narrow side streets and their encircling wide main roads. Stretching vaguely northeast-southwest, **Huancheng Dong Lu** (环城东路), also named **Dongfang Dong Lu** (东方东路), passes Tengchong's two bus stations. Parallel to it is **Fengshan Jie** (风山街). Intersecting those two streets are **Yingjiang Lu** (盈江路), the larger **Guanghua Lu** (光华路), and **Huancheng Nan Lu** (环城南路), also known as **Feicui Lu** (翡翠路).

Buses: Tengchong has 2 bus stations serving different destinations. The **Old Passenger Transport Station** (lǎo kèyùn zhàn; 老客运站 ; ☎515 2363), on Huancheng Dong Lu, across from the Tonglida Hotel. Open daily 6:30am-9pm. To Ruili (6-7hr., 6 per day, Y36) and **Yingjiang** (3hr., every 40min., Y19). The **New Bus Station** (xīn kèyùn zhàn; 新客运站 ; ☎516 1526), south of the city on Rehai Lu, a 15min. pedicab ride from the old station. From Feicui Lu, turn left at the traffic circle; the station is 20min. down on the right. Open daily 6:30am-8pm. To: **Baoshan** (4hr., 10 or more per day, Y29-36); **Kunming** (12hr., 7-8 per day, Y158); **Xiaguan/Dali** (6-7hr., 2 per day, Y83).

Bike Rental: Go right from the Jixing Hotel; take the 1st right onto Guanghua Lu. A shop with a "Bikes for Hire" sign (in English) is 5min. on the right. Y10 per day, deposit Y100.

Bank of China: At the intersection of Fengshan Lu and Yingjiang Lu. Exchanges traveler's checks. Credit card advances. Open daily 8-11:30am and 2:30-6pm.

PSB: ☎513 1146. Go west on Guanghua Lu at Fengshan Lu; after 5min. turn left down an alley. The PSB is in a yellow building a few min. down on the right. **Foreign Bureau** for visa extensions open M-Sa 8-11:30am and 2:30-5:30pm. It's better to take care of visa problems in Xiaguan, where PSB officials are more accustomed to such requests.

Internet Access: Great Asia Computing (hóngyà diànnǎo; 鸿亚电脑), on Rehai Lu, just to the right after the traffic circle. Average connection speeds. Y2 per hr. Open 9am-midnight. **Shunyuan Internet Cafe** (shùnyuán wǎngbā; 顺源网吧), on Huancheng Dong Lu, just north of Feicui Lu. Y2 per hr. Open 8am-midnight.

Post Office: China Post (☎512 3192), a 3min. walk down Fengshan Lu, before Bank of China on the left. Open daily 8am-6pm.

Postal Code: 679100.

☐☐ ACCOMMODATIONS AND FOOD

Hotels in Tengchong cluster along Huancheng Dong Lu, Feicui Lu, and Rehai Lu near the bus stations. While all hotels listed claim to have 24hr. hot water, your best bet for a hot shower is in the evening (6pm-midnight).

Good, cheap Chinese fare is available in many restaurants on **Guihua Dong Lu,** between Fengshan Lu and Huangcheng Dong Lu, as well as **Yingjiang Lu.**

Tonglida Hotel (tōnglìdá bīnguǎn; 通利达宾馆), 50 Huancheng Dong Lu (☎518 7871), in a prominent white building. Proximity to bus station makes Tonglida a good, if somewhat noisy, stop. Singles and doubles Y20, with bath Y50; triples Y30/Y70. ❶

Jixing Hotel (jíxīng bīnguǎn; 吉兴宾馆), 21 Huancheng Dong Lu (☎516 8039), 5min. south of the old bus station on the right. Clean, brightly lit rooms. Singles and doubles Y20, with bath Y40; triples Y60. ❶

Tengchong Guesthouse (téngchōng bīnguǎn; 腾冲宾馆), 3 Fanjia Xiaoqu (☎515 5044), a Y5 pedicab ride or a 20min. walk from the bus station. Take Huancheng Dong Lu toward Tonglida Hotel; at the crossroads turn right on Huancheng Nan Lu; the hotel is 10min. on the left with an English sign. Old rooms are clean and functional. Singles and doubles with bath Y50; triples Y60. ❶

Linye Hotel (línyè dàshà; 林业大厦 ; ☎516 4058), on Huancheng Dong Lu on the left, 2min. before the intersection with Feicui Lu. New, luxurious rooms with full amenities, including bath. Singles and doubles Y80-140. ❷

👁 SIGHTS

🏯 **HESHUN VILLAGE** (héshùn xiāng; 和顺乡). Narrow cobblestone streets wind through Heshun, set amid undulating hills and rice fields. A half-day or more in this well-preserved, charming Qing Dynasty village promises ample relaxation and therapy for those frazzled by Tengchong's bustle. Most come to soak up the atmosphere, but there are a few noteworthy sights: the **ancient library** (túshūguǎn; 图书馆), opposite the arch that serves as the village entrance; **Yuanlong Pavilion** (yuánlóng gé; 元龙阁), a small lakeside temple; and the **House of Ai Siqi** (ài sīqí gùjū; 艾思奇故居), a museum memorializing one of Communism's great educational reformers. The museum has an extensive collection of pictures documenting Ai's life, but have no English captions. The latter two are on the path running from the entrance around the left edge of the village, a 15min. walk past a manmade lake on the left. (*5km southwest of Tengchong. Bus #3 takes 10min., and costs Y1.5; it leaves every 20min. from Huancheng Nan Lu at Fengshan Lu, heading away from the Tongchang Hotel. A minibus goes there for the same price. All sights open daily 7:30am-7:30pm. Admission to the village Y30, students Y15. Some travelers have reported backtracking and then crossing the fields in order to enter the village from the side.*)

SEA OF HEAT (rè hǎi; 热海). In the middle of a once-active tectonic region, Tengchong can claim as its neighbors some 60 volcanoes and 80 geysers, most of which cluster in the "Sea of Heat." Geyser names conjure up images of nightmarish amusement park rides ("Toad Mouth Spring," "Pregnant Spring," "Big Boiler"), and a naturally heated pool lures Buddha-bellied local men into bathing suits to test the waters. Sometimes it's hard to tell whether the fragrant smell of sulfur comes from the boiled eggs sold by vendors or the springs themselves. Despite all the absurdity, the geysers still manage to impress. The waters are rumored to have healing qualities, and it's not hard to believe that dips in the steaming pool might cure a stress-induced ailment or two. (*12km south of Tengchong. Minibuses to Rehai leave 8am-6pm from the traffic circle on Rehai Lu; the 15min. ride costs Y5 per person for groups, Y10 for individuals. Taxis cost Y20-30. www.chinaspa.cn. Open 24hr. Admission Y30, students Y20.*)

TENGCHONG VOLCANOES (téngchōng huǒshān; 腾冲火山). Along with the hot springs, another remnant of Tengchong's explosive past lives on in more than 60 extinct volcanoes nearby. The most accessible are north of the town of **Mazhan** (mǎzhàn; 马站). These fire-mountains-no-more have most definitely belched their last: thick tufts of grass run rampant over any residue of ash or rock. Steep steps climb to the top for views of a typical countryside landscape; the crater is more worth a peek. (*25km north of Tengchong. Minibuses run to Mazhan (马站) from Tengchong. Follow Guanghua Lu around the corner to the right and up Huancheng Xi Lu to the West Gate. At* *the traffic circle, turn right. The West Gate Bus Station is 5min. down on the left. Take the bus labeled 滇滩 to Diantan which runs 7:30am-7:30pm and goes through Mazhan; it takes 40min. and costs Y5. In Mazhan, continue down the main road and turn right onto a flat road. 15min. walk leads to the ticket counter. Open 8:30am-5:30pm. Y30, students Y20.)*

OTHER SIGHTS. About 2km west of town, **Laifeng Temple** (láifēng sì; 来凤寺) is set inside **Laifeng Mountain National Park** (láifēng shān guójiā gōngyuán; 来凤山国家公园). The attraction here is more the journey than the destination. From Tengchong, walk along Fengshan Lu toward Guanghua Lu to Yinjiang Lu; when the road forks, bear right. (Open daily sunrise-sunset. Y10.)

RUILI 瑞丽 ☎ 0692

Ruili is the last major town in Yunnan before the border with Myanmar. This famous stronghold of free (and sometimes illicit) trade is dedicated to its mega-lithic markets and slightly racy nightlife. Like towns in the rest of Yunnan and other southwest provinces, the city has seen a recent rise in heroin addiction, HIV/AIDS infection, and prostitution. Irrepressible Ruili, however, seems to be recovering in fine form. While the city has few conventional sights, Myanmese and Chinese cultures mix and match within busy shops and markets, coloring Ruili with all the life and grit of a border town.

TRANSPORTATION AND PRACTICAL INFORMATION

Ruili's major street, **Nanmao Jie** (南卯街), runs east-west through town. The street's eastern portion, **Ruihong Lu** (瑞宏路), forks into two highways; the left road leads to Wangding and the right to Nongdao. Two blocks west of the bus station, **Renmin Lu** (人民路) intersects Nanmao Jie; north of this intersection, **Mengmao Lu** (勐卯路) parallels Nanmao Jie. **Bianmao Market** (biānmào shìchǎng; 边贸市场) runs parallel to and a block from Nanmao Jie.

Flights: Flights leave from **Mangshi Airport** (mángshì jīchǎng; 芒市机场). A shuttle (Y25) leaves 3hr. before the 1st flight of the day from **Yongchang Travel Agency** (yǒngchāng lǚxíngshè; 永昌旅行社 ; ☎414 2699), on Renmin Lu, next to the Yongchang Hotel. Or take the minibus to Mangshi and ask the driver to drop you off at the airport. Open daily 8:30am-5:30pm. To **Kunming** (2-3 per day, Y360).

Buses: Ruili Bus Station (ruìlì kèyùn zhàn; 瑞丽客运站), 9 Nanmao Lu (☎414 1423). **Luggage storage** small bags Y2, big bags Y3. Open daily 5:30am-9pm. To: **Baoshan** (6hr., 10 or more per day, Y49); **Kunming** (20hr., 4 per day, Y181); **Tengchong** (6hr., every 40min., Y36); **Xiaguan** (8hr., 5 per day 4-8pm, Y100). **Minibuses** gather opposite the bus station, leaving when full for: **Jiegao** (15min., Y5); **Mangshi** (1½hr., Y25); **Wanding** (20min., Y5).

Bike Rental: The **Limin Hotel** rents bikes for Y10 per day; deposit Y200 if not a guest.

Travel Agency: South of the Border, inside the Taihe Hotel, across from the bus station. Ask for the very helpful, English-speaking Min Min Zaw (minminzawjones@163.com.cn).

Bank of China: On Nanmao Jie, 1 block right of and opposite the bus station. Exchanges traveler's checks. Credit card advances. Open M-F 8-11:30am and 2:30-6pm.

PSB: 10 Jinshe Lu (☎414 1282). Pass the Ruili Guesthouse and take the 1st right up the hill; bear left when the road forks. Issues **visa extensions.** Not surprisingly (given the flourishing local heroin and smuggling trade), the officers are a suspicious crowd; non-emergency affairs are probably best handled in **Mangshi**. Visas to **Myanmar** must be obtained in Kunming (p. 644).

Internet Access: Prosperous City Internet Cafe (wàngchéng wǎngbā; 旺城网吧), on Nanmao Jie after it intersects Renmin Lu, on the right. Y2 per hr. Open 8am-midnight.

Post and Telecommunications: China Post, on Mengmao Lu, just off the corner with Renmin Lu. Open daily 8am-7:30pm. **China Telecom,** on Mengmao Lu, past the post office on the left. IDD service. Open daily 8am-7pm.

Postal Code: 678600.

ACCOMMODATIONS AND FOOD

There are several good budget establishments in Ruili. Most have 24hr. hot water.

Food stalls and restaurants serve a combination of Chinese, Burmese, and Dai cuisine. Signs in Burmese exist for the benefit of the sizeable Burmese population and do not necessarily indicate Burmese fare. Several **nightmarkets** come alive after 8pm, including one just off Ruili Market, north of Nanmao Jie.

Taihe Hotel (tàihé bīnguǎn; 泰和宾馆 ; ☎414 4666), off Nanmao Jie, across from the bus station and up the 1st alley to the left. Nice hardwood floors and a convenient location make Taihe a good choice. All rooms have A/C and bath. On-site travel agency (see **Practical Information,** above). Singles and doubles Y60; triples Y90. ❶

Limin Hotel (lìmín bīnguǎn; 利民宾馆), 2 Nanmao Jie (☎414 2249). From the bus station, turn left; the hotel is 500m away, a block down on the left. Simple, clean rooms. Bike rental Y10 per day. Hot water 6am-midnight. 3-bed dorms Y20; 2-bed Y25; doubles with A/C and bath Y120; triples with bath Y150. ❶

Heavenly Capital Hotel (tiān dū jiǔdiàn; 天都酒店 ; ☎414 4835), on Mengmao Lu across from China Telecom. Spartan dorm beds. Solar-heated showers. 4-bed dorms Y15; doubles Y25; triples Y20. ❶

Qiaorui Hotel (qiáoruì fàndiàn; 乔瑞饭店 ; ☎415 6666). Luxurious rooms come with all the bells, whistles, and even blow dryers. Singles and doubles Y100; triples Y150. ❷

SIGHTS

Ruili has few sights of note; this town is more about doing (or buying, selling, or partying) than looking. Day and night, the town's life revolves around the markets.

RUILI MARKET. Part mall, part outdoor bazaar—the heart of Ruili is its colossal market. Buyers beware: not all products are what they seem. Mango jam is probably genuine; "jade" bracelets (Y200-Y10,000 per pair) often are not. Colorful Burmese sarongs (Y20-35) are sure bets. At night, drinks (Y20-35) are stiff and the stage is set for virtual orgies of karaoke. (Between the minibus station and Jianshe Lu.)

TEMPLES. Biking through the countryside is perhaps the best way to escape the commercial fray of Ruili. If you prefer specific destinations, the surrounding area has several worthwhile temples. Despite reports 10 years ago that a gold Buddha had fallen from the sky and landed nearby, **Leixian Zhuang Temple** (léixiānzhuàng sì; 雷仙奘寺) remains out of the way and rarely frequented. To get to Leixian, take the minibus to Nongdao and ask to be dropped off at *léixiān zhàn.* From the road, walk toward the fields to the Dai village, where anyone can lead you to the temple. On the left side of the road to Nongdao, heading away from Ruili, a mud trail veers left toward **Denghannongzhuang Temple** (děnghǎnnòngzhuāng sì; 等喊弄 奘寺), a wooden edifice painted red with yellow markings to distinguish it from local residences. After you get off at the stop for the temple, walk a few minutes toward a small bridge, after which you'll see the temple; a sign points the way.

SOUTHWEST

The **Nong'an Golden Duck Temple** (nòng'ān jīn yā tǎ; 弄安金鸭塔) complex is just southwest of town. One of the temples has elaborate white decorations and golden duck carvings on its red roof; the other has two blue dragons etched onto its walls. Past Ruili, on the way to Wanding and just past the village of Jiele, lies the popular **Jiele Golden Pagoda** (jiělè jīn tǎ; 姐勒金塔), whose name comes from the gold paint on its central *stupa*. Seven smaller *stupas* represent the seven days of the week. *(Pedicab takes 15min. and costs Y3, leaving from the minibus station. Y10.)*

BORDER CROSSING INTO MYANMAR. Ruili is close to 2 checkpoints on the Myanmar border: **Jiegao** (15min., Y4) and **Wanding** (20min., Y10), both accessible by minibus from Ruili. In Jiegao (jiēgào; 姐告), a huge jade market sets up next to the bus stop. The border crossing into Myanmar is now open to foreigners; obtain visas in advance (see **Kunming: Consulates**, p. 644). Wanding (wǎndīng; 畹町) is China's smallest open border town, distinguished by the bridge to Myanmar. For current info on border crossings, contact the PSB (☎466 0359) in Jiegao. Border open daily 8am-11:30pm.

DALI 大理 ☎ 0872

Lying between Erhai Lake and the Cangshan mountain range at 1940m above sea level, the charming old town of Dali sits on the Yunnan-Myanmar and Yunnan-Tibet trade routes. The Bai people, a branch of the Yi minority, once led the Nanzhao Kingdom (AD 739 to 937) and ruled Yunnan with Dali as their capital, but today, much of the prefecture's economic and political hustle and bustle centers around the city of Xiaguan. Fortunately, Dali has none of the chaos and pollution of many other Chinese cities. The relaxing atmosphere and laid-back pace have turned Dali into a backpacker mecca of sorts, where days mysteriously turn into weeks and weeks into months. While the city often clads itself in contrived "tradition" for the nearly constant influx of tourists, authentic history, winding backroads, and scenic landscapes are only a few minutes away. Travelers eager for the "real" China, a mythical place free of the "damages" of tourism, may be disappointed by Dali's easy expatriate air and keen interest in colorful pieces of *yuán*.

▣ TRANSPORTATION

Because Dali's airport, train station, and three major bus stations are all located in **Xiaguan** (下关), sometimes referred to as **Dali City** (dàlǐ shì; 大理市), this somewhat dull transportation hub is generally unavoidable en route to the much more charming old city of Dali (gǔchéng; 古城).

Flights: Dali Airport (dàlǐ jīchǎng; 大理机场; ☎231 5335), 16km outside Xiaguan. Accessible only by taxi (Y30-50). To **Kunming** (2-3 per day, Y430). Purchase tickets in one of Dali's many travel agencies.

Trains: Dali Train Station (dàlǐ zhàn; 大理站; ☎219 1660), in Xiaguan, 2km from the intersection of Jianshe Xi Lu and Renmin Lu. From Dali, take bus #8 all the way to the train station (huǒchē zhàn), the last stop. To **Kunming** (9hr., 2-3 per day, Y69).

Buses: Xiaguan has 3 major bus terminals, all accessible by buses #4 and 8 from Dali. A 4th station is in Dali itself, but serves fewer destinations.

Dali Old City Long-Distance Bus Station (dàlǐ gǔchéng chángtú qìchē zhàn; 大理古城长途汽车站; ☎267 9287), on Dianzang Lu, about 30m from Huguo Lu, just past the No. 4 Guesthouse. Most travel agencies, guesthouses, and restaurants sell tickets with little or no commission. Open daily 7am-7:30pm. To: **Kunming** (7hr., 5 per day, Y65-105); **Lijiang** (3hr., every 30min., Y35-50); **Zhongdian** (8hr., every 30min. until 11am, Y50).

Dali Long-Distance Bus Station (dàlǐ qìchē kèyùn zhàn; 大理汽车客运站 ; ☎218 9330), near the intersection of Jianshe and Renmin Lu. To **Kunming** (7hr., every 25min., Y68-105).

Bus Station of Dali Prefecture (dàlǐzhōu kèyùn zhàn; 大理州客运站 ; ☎212 3436), also called *gāosù kèyùn zhàn* (高速客运站). The only station with an English sign, diagonally across from the Dali Long-Distance Bus Station, near Jianshe Lu at Renmin Lu. Open daily 6am-11pm. To: **Baoshan** (2½hr., every 40min., Y40); **Jinghong** (10-11hr., 2 per day, Y100); **Kunming** (7hr., every hr., Y68-105); **Lijiang** (3hr., 5 per day, Y50); **Ruili** (10-11hr., 2 per day, Y100).

North Road Station (běi lù qìchē kèyùn zhàn; 北路汽车客运站 ; ☎225 8724), on Dali Lu, a block from its intersection with Renmin Lu. Open daily 6am-8pm. To **Lijiang** (3hr., every 10min. Y38) and **Zhongdian** (8hr., every 30min. 7:20am-11pm, Y51).

Local Transportation: While the old town of Dali can be navigated entirely on foot, local **buses** and **minibuses** cover the distance to nearby Xiaguan. The #4 bus (30min., every 5min., Y1) stops frequently along Bo'ai Lu, as do minibuses charging similar rates. The #8 bus (Y1) runs to Xiaguan, terminating at the train station; flag it down on Yu'er Lu, just north of Huguo Lu. Buses and minibuses also traverse Dianzang Lu.

Bike Rental: Available at the majority of guesthouses as well as in many shops along Bo'ai Lu. The **No. 4** and **No. 5 Guesthouses** both charge Y10 per day.

✴ 🖪 ORIENTATION AND PRACTICAL INFORMATION

Dali's historical role as a defense-worthy administrative center is evident from the remnants of stone walls marking the outer boundaries of the old, square-shaped town. **Fuxing Lu** (复兴路) runs between the **North City Gate** (běi mén; 北门) and the **South City Gate** (nán mén; 南门). **Bo'ai Lu** (博爱路) and **Dianzang Lu** (滇藏路) are west of and parallel to Fuxing Lu, with Dianzang Lu outside the city walls. **Renmin Lu** (人民路) and **Huguo Lu** (护国路), the coffee- and pizza-laden "foreigner street" (yángrén jiē; 洋人街), branch off from Fuxing Lu.

Travel Agencies: It's easy to find travel advice or information in Dali. **Dali Travel Information Service Bureau** (dàlǐ lǚyóu xìnxī zīxún fúwù bù; 大理旅游信息咨询服务部 ; ☎266 4266 or 689 5611), on Huguo Lu before the Tibetan Cafe. Open daily 8am-9pm. Friendly, helpful Dong Yuepin speaks English. **Dali Travel Center** (dàlǐ gǔchéng kèchē zhōngxīn; 大理古城客车中心 ; ☎267 1282 or 689 4978), on the corner of Fuxing Lu and Huguo Lu. Open daily 7:30am-10:30pm. Most agencies can arrange travel to local destinations or to Kunming, Lijiang, and Zhongdian; many also provide maps.

Bank: Bank of China, 304 Fuxing Lu (☎267 0171). Exchanges traveler's checks. **ATM.** Credit card advances. Open daily 8am-6pm. The **Industrial Bank of China** (zhōngguó gōngshāng yínháng; 中国工商银行 ; ☎267 0281), on Huguo Lu just before Fuxing Lu on the right. Exchanges US currency and traveler's checks. Open daily 8am-5pm.

Bookstore: Mandarin Books, 285 Fuxing Lu (☎267 9014), 5min. south of Huguo Lu. Quite a few good books, though the Kunming branch (p. 645) has a larger selection.

PSB: 4 Huguo Lu (☎267 0016), next to the No. 4 Guesthouse. Open M-F 2-5:30pm. Visa extensions available from **Dali PSB Foreign Affairs Office** (☎220 2800 or 220 2900), on Renmin Lu in Xiaguan. Open daily 8am-5pm.

Internet Access: China Telecom, on the northeast corner of Fuxing Lu and Huguo Lu. 20 computers of average speed. Y2 per hr. Open daily 9am-11pm. **Internet Friend** (wǎng yǒu; 网友), 2 blocks north on Fuxing Lu from Huguo Lu. Y1-1.5 per hr. depending on time of day. Open 9am-midnight. Most guesthouses also offer free Internet for guests.

Post and Telecommunications: On the corner of Fuxing Lu and Huguo Lu (☎267 0142). With the mountains behind you, the post office is on the left, and China Telecom is on the right. EMS and IDD service. Open daily 8am-9pm.

Postal Code: 671003.

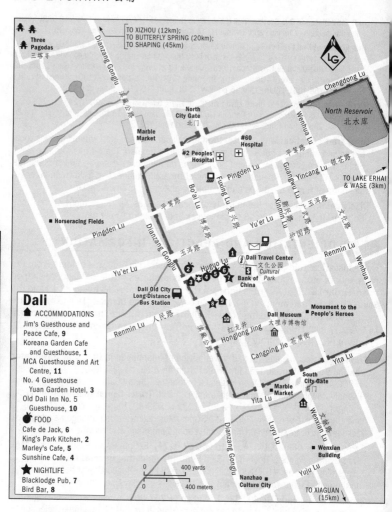

Dali

▲ ACCOMMODATIONS

Jim's Guesthouse and
  Peace Cafe, **9**
Koreana Garden Cafe
  and Guesthouse, **1**
MCA Guesthouse and Art
  Centre, **11**
No. 4 Guesthouse
  Yuan Garden Hotel, **3**
Old Dali Inn No. 5
  Guesthouse, **10**

● FOOD

Cafe de Jack, **6**
King's Park Kitchen, **2**
Marley's Cafe, **5**
Sunshine Cafe, **4**

★ NIGHTLIFE

Blacklodge Pub, **7**
Bird Bar, **8**

● ACCOMMODATIONS

Most of the cheapest places in backpacker-friendly Dali cluster around Huguo Lu
and Bo'ai Lu, near the tourist cafes. All have dormitories (often co-ed), individual
rooms, laundry service, luggage storage, and possibly Internet access.

▨ **Old Dali Inn No. 5 Guesthouse** (dàlĭ sìjì kèzhàn; 大理四季客栈), 51 Bo'ai Lu (☎267
0382). Attractive rooms and a garden courtyard create an inviting atmosphere. Newly
renovated restroom facilities feature some blissful Western-style toilets. Bike rental Y10
per day. Free Internet for guests. 24hr. hot water. 4-bed dorms Y10-15; 3-bed Y20; singles Y30; doubles Y50, with TV and bath Y110-115; triples Y20. ●

■ **No. 4 Guesthouse Yuan Garden Hotel** (yú'ān yuán huāyuán lǚshè; 榆安园花园旅舍), 4 Huguo Lu (☎267 2093), past Bo'ai Lu and steps before the intersection with Dian-zang Lu, a common stop for minibuses. Backpackers loll about in the pretty courtyard and cafe. 24hr. hot water. Free laundry machines. Bikes Y10 per day. 5- to 6-bed dorms Y10; 3- to 4-bed Y15; singles Y30, with bath Y100; doubles Y50/Y100. ❶

■ **MCA Guesthouse and Art Centre**, 7000 Wenxian Lu (☎267 3666 or 267 1999), 5min. walk out of Dali from the South Gate, 10min. from the town center. No Chinese name; ask for "MC" if you need directions. Run by artists affiliated with the Yunnan School of Art. Although the remote location may be inconvenient, the MCA has it all, including outdoor pool, cafe, book rental (Y2 per day), pool tables, Internet, and bike rental (Y10 with deposit). 4- to 5-bed dorms Y10; singles and doubles with bath Y100-120. ❶

Jim's Guesthouse and Peace Cafe (jímǔ hépíng kèzhàn; 吉姆和平客栈), 63 Bo'ai Lu (☎267 1822; jimsguesthouse@hotmail.com), on the right just after crossing Renmin Lu. Guesthouse is on the 2nd and 3rd fl. above the cafe. A good place to rest if you're sick of crowded backpacker hostels. Nice hardwood floors and spotless facilities. Staff can arrange treks to nearby Bai and Yi villages as well as more distant locations, includ-ing Tibet. 3-bed dorms Y15; doubles Y30, with bath Y50. ❶

Koreana Garden Cafe and Guesthouse (dàlǐ gāolìtíng cānyǐn; 大理高丽亭餐饮), 115 Huguo Lu (☎266 5083). The Koreana has a prime location, a decent Korean restau-rant, and a relaxed atmosphere. Friendly staff offer travel advice. Dorms Y20. ❶

🍴 FOOD

Most Chinese restaurants cluster on Renmin Lu and Yu'er Lu. Locals sell melted goat cheese on sticks all along Huguo Lu and Fuxing Lu, as well as sweet or salty fried pancakes. Most foreigners pounce on the chance to enjoy good Western food and head to the hard-to-miss cafes and restaurants, with colorful English signs and menus, clustered around **Huguo Lu.** Many Chinese tourists see Western cafes as part of the Dali attraction, a place to observe the *lǎowài* in their native habitat. To avoid feeling like an animal at the zoo, try the restaurants off Huguo Lu.

■ **Sunshine Cafe** (yángguāng kāfēi; 阳光咖啡), 16 Huguo Lu (☎267 0712). Comfy chairs, great location, and a friendly staff. The main attraction here is the wide array of delicious, spicy Indian food (Y10-25)—almost anything is a treat. The Western food is also quite good; try the chocolate brownie (Y8). Open daily 8:30am-midnight. ❷

■ **King's Park Kitchen**, 5 Huguo Lu (☎266 4082). Coming from Huguo Lu, turn right at the alley just before the No. 4 Guesthouse. No sign. Well-hidden from the street and with a lovely outdoor beer garden, King's Park is the perfect place to escape the tourism of Huguo Lu and enjoy some delicious Cantonese cuisine. Watch movies while you munch in the room opposite the main dining area across the courtyard. King, the owner, loves to talk movies with customers. Black mushrooms with spring vegetables Y12. Stewed beef in *chu-hau* paste Y15. Homemade wines Y5 per glass. ❷

Marley's Cafe (mǎlì kāfēi guǎn; 马丽咖啡馆 ; ☎267 6651), on the southwest corner of Bo'ai Lu and Huguo Lu. Try the buffet Su night for 8-10 courses of Bai cuisine with a glass of wine (Y20). Western, Chinese, and Bai food Y5-25. Open 8am-12:30am. ❷

Cafe de Jack (yīnghuā yuán xī cāntīng; 樱花园西餐厅), 46 Bo'ai Lu (☎267 1572), just left off Huguo Lu. The atmosphere *de* Jack is warm and welcoming, particularly upstairs. Customers are encouraged not to order "complicated dishes" when the place is busy. Dishes Y6-14. Open daily 8am-1am or whenever the last customer leaves. ❶

Koreana Restaurant (☎266 5083), run in conjunction with the Koreana Guesthouse on Huguo Lu. Authentic Korean food is a bit pricey (Y20-50). Try the *bi bim bap* (Y20), rice topped with veggies. ❸

👁 SIGHTS

Dali's relaxed atmosphere, unique architecture, and people-watching opportunities are far more impressive than its actual sights. For some non-law-abiding tourists, a certain locally grown herb (dàmá; 大麻) is one of the greatest attractions of Dali. Possession of marijuana is illegal in China. *Let's Go* does not recommend getting wacky with the tabacky, though it's certainly something readily peddled by Huguo Lu's old ladies. Most spend no more than Y50 on these illicit smokes. The **North** or **South City Gate** along the Old Town Wall affords good views of the town and Lake Erhai. (Open daily 9am-7pm. Y2.) From here, a visitor can get a sense of what it was like back when Dali's strategic importance was not so dependent on Internet cafes and pizza joints. The **Dali Museum** (dàlǐshì bówùguǎn; 大理市博物馆), 111 Fuxing Lu, is not at all dedicated to Surrealism. The Bai-style building is far more interesting than its exceedingly bland collection of historical relics. (☎267 0196. Open daily 8:30am-6:30pm. Y10.)

THREE PAGODAS (sān tǎ sì; 三塔寺). The oldest standing structures in Yunnan, these pagodas have come to symbolize Dali. With Cangshan in the background, the majestic towers rise from a hill a few kilometers beyond the North Gate and are visible from almost any vantage point within Dali and the surrounding area. In many ways, they're the most scenic when seen from a distance. Constructed over 42 years during the Nanzhao era, the original pagodas were destroyed in a fire in the 19th century and rebuilt in 1997. From the nearby **Reflection Park** (dàoyìng gōngyuán; 倒映公园), you can see the pagodas reflected in the lake. West of the pagodas, the **Guanyin Palace of Copper Rain** has an impressive golden *stupa*. Unfortunately, the original was destroyed during the Cultural Revolution, but the current *stupa* tastefully recreates the original, which dates back to AD 899. *(Turn right off Huguo Lu onto Dianzang Lu; follow Dianzang Lu for approx. 30min. Horse carts will take you for Y5, but it's a bumpy ride. ☎267 0179 or 267 1847. Open daily 7am-8pm. Y52.)*

OTHER SIGHTS. Legend tells the tale of star-crossed lovers who threw themselves into the waters of **Butterfly Spring** (húdié quán; 蝴蝶泉) in despair. Their spirits turned into butterflies and return each spring to frolic (as lovers are wont to do) at the site of their last union. Despite the romantic legend and the beautiful ride to reach the sight, the spring itself is not terribly inspiring. *(Buses make the 35min. trip every 20min. starting at 7:30am for Y4. By bicycle, follow Dianzang Lu all the way to the spring, taking about 2½hr. each way. Y32.)* For those who want to go shopping in **Shaping** (沙坪), the market takes place every Monday 8am-1pm. *(By bike, the trip takes about 2½hr. each way; turn right off Huguo Lu onto Dianzang Lu. Public buses leave Dali Bus Station on Dianzang Lu to Shaping; 20min., every 20min., Y6. Travelers can also book tickets on a tour bus; departure 9am, return 1:30pm, Y15.)*

🛍 SHOPPING

Shopping is the Dali pastime of choice, with a bonanza of knick-knacks of varying levels of charm and uselessness to tantalize the traveler. Most **batik** (blue wax-dyed or colorfully painted clothes) are made in Guizhou, but Dali is one of the best places in Yunnan to buy them. Along **Huguo Lu,** tailors sell all manner of striped or batik clothing. If you don't like what they have, many will fill a custom order. Peddlers at street stalls hawk jewelry and small potteries, while Bai women selling silver and embroidery often follow people from restaurant to restaurant. Fortunately, Dali's vendors are not overly aggressive, save for shoe-shiners and little old ladies. Just outside the city's South and North Gates, many shops offer Dali's famous **marble,** fashioned into all forms and shapes. In fact, the Chinese word for marble, *dàlǐshí* (大理石), literally means "stone of Dali."

ENTERTAINMENT

With a steady stream of backpackers and travelers, Dali promises laid-back evenings of beer and conversation. A lively mix of locals and foreigners bask in the relaxed atmosphere at **Bird Bar** (niǎo bā; 鸟吧), complete with brick fireplace, hardwood floors, courtyard, and an occasionally used dance floor. Walk south on Bai Lu and turn right onto Renmin Lu; the bar is just on the left. Don't be put off by the locked door: simply knock and you'll be warmly welcomed in at almost all hours of the night. (☎ 266 1843; birdbar@hotmail.com. Beer starts at Y6. Open 8am-late.) The **Blacklodge Pub** (fǎguó hóng; 法国红), 80 Bo'ai Lu, is just up Bo'ai Lu from Huguo Lu on the left. The hip, friendly staff play good music. (☎ 266 3518. Beer Y6 and up. Imported liquor Y15-40. Open 10am-1am.)

DAYTRIPS FROM DALI

Half the joy of the sights around Dali is in getting to them. Cycling, taking the bus, walking, or horseback riding are all good ways to take in the mesmerizing scenery.

CANGSHAN MOUNTAINS 苍山

Take bus #4 (Y5) on Bo'ai Lu toward Xiaguan to Gantong Temple. From there, cable cars go to Cangshan Temple (Y52, round-trip Y82). Horse carriages or small vans to the foot of the mountain 30min., Y5. Horseback riding to Cangshan Temple about Y70. Cheapest to hike (6-8hr.) from Gantong to Zhonghe Temple. The path is not clearly marked; ask at a travel agency in Dali for a more detailed map. Temple admission free; other sights Y6-10.

The Cangshan Mountains (cāng shān; 苍山) surrounding Dali offer more than just pleasant scenery. For the many monks and nuns residing on these hills, they are also a place for religious worship and retreat. **Cangshan Temple,** the most touristy sight, offers an expansive view of Lake Erhai and the surrounding area. From Cangshan, walk along a flat road north (the left, facing away from the mountains) to **Zhonghe Temple** (zhōnghé sì; 中和寺), or head off in the opposite direction to **Gantong Temple** (gǎntōng sì; 感通寺). Arrive around noon and you can join the residents for a vegetarian meal. A 10min. trek from Gantong leads to **Jizhao Monastery** (jìzhào ān; 寂照庵). Wandering the various paths up and down the mountain leads to many small gorges and equally beautiful vistas without the temple crowds.

WASE 挖色

Boats shuttle frequently between Dali and Wase (30min., Y30). Many local Dali street merchants will offer to take you for at least Y50 one-way. The market is best in the afternoon, when there are fewer tourists. For tourist boats exploring other parts of Lake Erhai, inquire at the Yuxing Tourist Office. Most trips take 6hr. and cost Y20-50.

The **market** in Wase (wāsè; 挖色), held every five days from the 5th to the 25th of each month, is your "typical" Bai market—teeming with life and confusion. In the the market square, near the shores of Lake Erhai, Bai merchants in traditional dress ply their peaches, rice noodles, household goods (including rat poison), and live fowl. Walk into the town to explore the small streets and local architecture. Those who wish to stay a night in the village can try the **Wase Hotel ❶** (wāsè bīnguǎn; 挖色宾馆), along the main road to Wase. From the market square, return to the main road and backtrack 15min. past some cornfields; the hotel is on the right as the road bends. Beautiful hardwood floors and reasonably priced rooms make a stay here easy. (☎246 8688. Singles and doubles Y50-60; triples Y80; 2-bedroom suites, easily sleeping 5 with living room and 2 full baths, Y160.)

Tourist boats ply the route across Lake Erhai, usually taking in sights such as **Minor Putuo Island** (xiǎo pǔtuó; 小普陀 ; Y1 boat from shore), **Tianjing Pavilion** (tiān-jìng gé; 天镜阁 ; Y10), and **Sea Island** (hǎi dǎo; 海岛). Biking to Wase (just over 4hr.) allows the opportunity to meander through lakeside Bai villages. If you go to Wase by car, ask to stop in **Shuanglang** (双廊), a fishing village along the way. Here you can see ancient Bai architecture without the normal deluge of tourists. Even if it's not a market day, you can still take a trip on **Lake Erhai** to visit some of the major sites around the lake; inquire at local travel agencies.

XIZHOU VILLAGE 喜州镇

Buses and minibuses (30min., Y3) frequently make the trip to Xizhou on Dianzang Lu. Ask to be dropped at Xizhou when you get on the bus or when buying your ticket. There are 2 attractive routes for biking to Xizhou (one-way 2hr.). To take the low road, follow Fuxing Lu out through North Gate. Take the high road along Dianzang Lu if it's hot; the road is a little uneven, but trees are shady. Traveling on Dianzang Lu will land you at a large sign (in English) pointing to Xizhou. Arrows direct you all the way to the main square.

Xizhou (xǐzhōu zhèn; 喜州镇), a military stronghold during the Nanzhao Kingdom, retained enough wealth to build huge houses, whose crumbling remains harken back to the town's glorious past. The road to Xizhou, lined by green rice paddies with the Cangshan Mountains in the background, is perhaps more of an attraction than the rather contrived display of Bai culture in the town itself. The special sight here is **Yan Family's Big Courtyard** (yánjiā dàyuàn; 严家大院), in the main square, a massive house owned by rich industrialists who left China during the Cultural Revolution. Traditionally clad dancers and singers perform while Bai bread and the "trilogy tea of the Bai clan" (named for its three flavors: bitter, sweet, and spicy) are served. Performances start once enough people show up. (Open daily 7:30am-7pm. Y10, students Y5; meal and performance Y20.) For a more authentic village, head to **Shuanglang** instead (see above).

LIJIANG 丽江   ☎0888

Lijiang Naxi Autonomous Prefecture claims flat plains, the highest mountain ranges south of the Yangzi, and the first bend of the Yangzi itself. With 22 ethnic minority groups, from the matriarchal Mosuo and Naxi to the Tibetan, the region's inhabitants are just as varied. Activity centers around the prefectural seat of Lijiang, a city latticed by an intricate maze of narrow waterways and canals set at an elevation of 2400m. In 1996, an earthquake measuring 7.0 on the Richter scale devastated Lijiang, leveling the old part of town. Since then, for better or worse, a replica of the original old town has been built, and Lijiang has become a UNESCO World Heritage Site. Some decry the faux antique, tourist-trap atmosphere, but off the main drags, the tourist shops dwindle, the well-worn cobblestone back alleys take on the musty air of centuries past, and the traditional Naxi-style architecture of wood and stone remains untouched. Along narrow streets and tiny bridges, the mysterious force of the Naxi's Dongba religion, with its synthesis of sorcery, medicine, and philosophy, can still be felt.

▆ TRANSPORTATION

Flights: Lijiang Airport (lìjiāng jīchǎng; 丽江机场 ; ☎517 0987 or 512 8088), 26km from the city. Buses leave from the **Lijiang CAAC Blue Sky Ticket Office** (丽江民航蓝天机票代理处 ; ☎516 1289), at Shangri La Dadao and Fuhui Lu. Tickets can also be purchased at the **branch** on the corner of Xin Dajie just after exiting the old city. Open daily 8:30am-noon and 2:30-5:30pm. Most interprovincial flights go through Kunming. To: **Chengdu** (M, W, Sa 9:30pm; Y880); **Jinghong/Xishuangbanna** (daily, Y760); **Kunming** (10 per day, Y530).

Buses: None of the 3 main bus stations has service to Baoshan or Chengdu. To get to **Baoshan,** take the bus to Xiaguan and catch another bus there. To get to **Chengdu,** take the bus to the railhead of Jinjiang/Panzhihua and then take a train.

Main Long-Distance Bus Station (lìjiāng kèyùn zhàn; 丽江客运站 ; ☎512 1106), at the far end of Minzhu Lu. Turn left out of the old town and follow the road left as it turns into Minzhu Lu. Open 6:30am-10pm. To: **Jinjiang/Panzhihua** (8hr., 4 per day, Y48-62); **Kunming** (10hr., 12 per day, Y122-154); **Xiaguan** (3hr., 26 per day, Y38-53); **Zhongdian** (5hr., 11 per day, Y30).

Guluwan Bus Station (gǔlùwān qìchē zhàn; 古路湾汽车站 ; ☎512 2929), on Xin Dajie, just past Mao Square, on the same side as the Lijiang International Ethnic Cultural Exchange Center. Also called **North Bus Station** (běi qìchē zhàn; 北汽车站), but buses are marked "Guluwan." Open daily 6:30am-8pm. To: **Daju** (3-4hr., 2 per day, Y23); **Jinjiang/Panzhihua** (8hr., 3 per day, Y45); **Kunming** (10hr., 12 per day, Y119-150); **Qiaotou** (2hr., 2 per day, Y12); **Xiaguan** (3hr., every 30min., Y34-53); **Zhongdian** (5hr., 4 per day, Y27).

Local Transportation: Several local **buses** crisscross the new city. From Xin Dajie, near Mao Sq., bus #7 (every hr. 8am-6pm) heads to Baisha (Y3) and Jade Dragon Mountain (Y8). Bus #1 (every 15min. 7am-9 or 10pm, Y1) stops at the South Bus Station, Fuhui Lu, and Xin Dajie, near the entrance to the Old Town.

Bike Rental: Best bikes in the city at the **Ancient Town International Youth Hostel** (Y20 per day; deposit for non-guests Y200).

Taxis: A flat fare of Y6 can usually get you anywhere in the city.

ORIENTATION AND PRACTICAL INFORMATION

Lijiang is divided into two very distinct entities: the New and Old Towns. The **New Town** (xīn chéng; 新城) is still under construction. Most visitors encounter the stretch of **Xin Dajie** (新大街) from the entrance of the Old Town to Black Dragon Fountain Park, via **Mao Square** and the bus station. Just west of the Old Town entrance, Xin Dajie becomes **Minzhu Lu** (民主路), which extends to the South Bus Station. The **Old Town** (gǔ chéng; 古城) tries just as hard to preserve (and, in some cases, commercialize) history as the New Town tries to disregard it. Wandering the Old Town will likely lead to many moments of confusion, as winding cobblestone streets seem to twist and turn without rhyme or reason. Use the **Old Market Square** (sìfāng jiē; 四方街) as a point of reference. Most hostels and restaurants are located north of the Square (toward the Old Town entrance).

Travel Agencies: There is certainly no dearth of travel agencies or travel advice in Lijiang. **Lijiang CITS Reception Center** (☎516 0369), on Shangri La Dadao, just opposite the airplane ticket office. Ask for Wang Jiali, who speaks some English and Japanese. Very friendly staff can help arrange travel to just about anywhere in the area. Open daily 8:30am-5:30pm. **Three Rivers Tourist Reception Center** (☎510 9118 or 510 7668), on Dong Dajie, 2 shops down from the Naxi Music Association. Staff speak little English but can arrange tickets and travel.

Bank: Bank of China, on Xin Dajie at Fuhui Lu, opposite the Chinese Construction Bank. Exchanges traveler's checks. **ATMs.** Open daily 8:30am-7pm. Another **branch,** opposite and left of South Bus Station, exchanges traveler's checks. Open daily 8am-5:30pm. **Industrial Bank,** on Dong Dajie, near the Market Sq. entrance, exchanges traveler's checks and US, Hong Kong, and Japanese currencies. **ATM.** Open daily 8am-5:30pm.

Bookstore: Mandarin Books (☎510 2956), across the canal from Sakura Cafe. Smaller selection of English, German, and French books than its comrades in Kunming and Dali, but certainly the best foreign-language bookstore in Lijiang. Open daily 9am-midnight.

SOUTHWEST

PSB: ☎518 8437. Located on Fuhui Lu, 5min. down from Xin Dajie on the left. Grants up to 2 1-month visa extensions. Open daily 8-11:30am and 2-5:30pm.

Hospitals: Lijiang People's Hospital (lìjiāngshì rénmín yīyuàn; 丽江市人民医院; ☎512 1545, emergency 512 2393 or 512 2335), on Fuhui Lu. Minimal English.

Internet Access: The city government prohibits Internet cafes within the Old Town. Most Western restaurants offer access for Y6 per hr., and some accommodations have free Internet for guests. There are several cafes within a 10min. walk of Old Town. **Vanguard Internet Cafe** (xiānfēng wǎngbā; 先锋网吧), on Fuhui Lu, 2min. on the left from Minzhu Lu, on the 2nd fl. Very fast connection speeds for Y2 per hr. Open 8am-midnight. **Destined Sky Internet Cafe** (yuánfèn tiānkōng wǎngbā; 缘分天空网吧), on Minzhu Lu, 3min. south of the Old Town entrance. Y2 per hr. Open 7:30am-midnight.

Post and Telecommunications: The main **post office** is on Minzhu Lu. Turn left out of the Old Town, and then left again; the post office is on the right. EMS. IDD service. Open daily 8am-8pm. The **branch** on Dong Dajie also offers EMS and IDD service. Facing the Old Town entrance, take the middle of the 3 roads, Dong Dajie; the post office is 5min. down on the left, opposite the Industrial Bank. Open daily 8am-8pm.

Postal Code: 674100.

ACCOMMODATIONS

Prices are roughly the same in the Old and New Towns; most travelers prefer to stay in the Naxi-style Old Town, 5min. from the North Bus Station. Most guesthouses have 24hr. hot water and prices usually begin around Y10-15 per bed.

■ **Xiangge Yun Guesthouse** (gǔchéng xiānggé yùn kèzhàn; 古城香格韵客栈), 78 Wenhua Xiang (☎518 5930 or 510 0700; qinyn@yahoo.com.cn), from Wuyi Jie. With Mama Fu's on your right, continue along the canal and turn left at the bridge. Walk 5min. down Wuyi Jie past a blue and white "hotel" sign; turn right at a red-lettered sign for "A Liang Inn." Take the next left and follow the river around the bend to the right; the guesthouse is 2min. down on the right. One of the most difficult guesthouses to find amid the Old Town's maze-like alleys, Xiangge Yun is also easily the city's most worthwhile accommodation. Run by Mama—part cook, part tour guide, and part motherly figure—the guesthouse offers peace and quiet from Old Town's oft overwhelming main streets. Mama cooks a feast (Y8) every night at 6:30pm and prepares breakfast and lunch as well (Y2 each). Free use of laundry machine with soap provided. A single moody computer for your Internet needs. With every perk at dirt-cheap prices, it's no wonder satisfied backpackers hang out in the courtyard day and night, sharing the space with Mama's 9 cats and 3 dogs. Dorms Y15; doubles Y50-80 depending on season. ❶

First Bend Inn (dìyīwān jiǔdiàn; 第一湾酒店), 43 Mishi Xiang (☎518 1688 or 518 1073), off Xinyi Jie. As you go into the Old Town, veer left onto Xinyi Jie and keep going past Lamu's House of Tibet and go right as the road curves. A peaceful courtyard and comfortable beds, along with excellent maps and information for Tiger Leaping Gorge trekkers. Free luggage storage for 4 days. Hot water 8-10am and 7-10pm. Laundry Y1-6 per item. 4-bed dorms Y20; 3-bed Y30; singles and doubles Y80. ❶

Ancient Town International Youth Hostel (HI) (gǔchéng guójì qīngnián lǚguǎn; 古城国际青年旅馆), 44 Mishi Xiang, to the left of First Bend Inn. This popular backpacker stop has a cafe with book exchange, bike rentals (Y20 per day; no deposit for guests), and a laundry machine (Y10 per hr.). Hot water 8am-noon and 7pm-midnight. 8-bed dorms Y20, with bath Y30; singles and doubles Y120. ❶

Dongba House Inn (dōngbā háosī kèlóu; 东巴豪斯客楼), 16 Jishan Xiang (☎518 7630; dongbahouse@hotmail.com), off Xinyi Jie, 3min. past Lamu's House of Tibet, but before First Bend Inn. Standard rooms, bike rentals (Y15 per day), and free Internet (Y6 if you're not staying here). 8-bed dorms Y20; 3-bed Y30; singles Y50. ❶

Tea and Horses Naxi Family Guesthouse (chámǎ kèzhàn; 茶马客栈), 9 Jishan Xiang (☎512 0351), just before Dongba House, with a blue and white English sign. The friendly English-speaking staff book air, train, and bus tickets. Standard doubles Y120, low-season Y80; triples Y150/Y100. ❶

🎏 FOOD

Vendors in the Old Town steam, fry, and grill an inviting selection of local delicacies, including **bābā** (fried Naxi flatbreads; 粑粑), noodle soups, hotpot pork, fresh corn, and rice dishes. Anyone craving travel advice, the company of foreigners, or just some steak and chocolate cake can head to the gaily marked cafes that line **Jishan Xiang**, **Mishi Xiang**, and **Market Square**.

🏯 **Lamu's House of Tibet** (xīzàng wū; 西藏屋), 56 Jishan Xiang (☎518 9000 or 139 8704 9750), off Xinyi Jie, not far past the entrance to the Old Town. A favorite with many travelers for its relaxing atmosphere and readily available travel advice. Fabulous Tibetan food (Y8-15), especially the *momo* (Y10), served in a lovely bamboo structure with a garden. Free Internet, a rarity in the Old Town, upstairs. Open daily summer 7am-midnight; winter 8:30am-midnight. ❷

Sakura Cafe (yīnghuā kāfēi; 樱花咖啡; ☎312 6766), on Xinhua Jie. From the Old Town entrance, take the road on the right, to the right of the waterwheel; it's 5min. down on the left. Run by an amiable Lijiang resident and his Korean wife, this comfy spot has great Korean and Japanese food (Y10-30), apple pie (Y10), and Naxi food (Y6-20). Crowds of nearby tourists are often intense. Free movies. Open daily 8am-3am. ❷

Blue Page Vegetarian Restaurant, 69 Mishi Xiang (☎518 5206), down the street from First Bend Inn, toward Market Sq. A favorite of Lijiang vegetarians, with friendly, English-speaking staff, and Internet for Y6 per hr. According to some travelers, the vegetable burger (Y12) is perhaps the best in China. Open daily 8am-midnight. ❷

Well Bistro (☎518 6431), on Mishi Xiang, up from Blue Page. Brightly decorated interior adds to the otherwise standard fare. Claims to serve "China's best pizza" (Y15-25), but most travelers beg to differ. Try the apple strudel (Y10). Open 8am-midnight. ❷

Mama Fu's Restaurant (māmāfù cāntīng; 妈妈傅餐厅), 76 Xinyi Jie, Mishi Xiang (☎512 2285), with outdoor tables overlooking the canal. The Chinese food tends to taste better than the Western food, though both are often cheaper than what Western cafes serve. Try the kungpao chicken (gōngbǎo jīdīng; 宫保鸡丁 ; Y15) and the chrysanthemum tea (Y3). Open daily 9am-11pm. ❷

👁 🎵 SIGHTS AND ENTERTAINMENT

The old town's winding cobbled streets, traditional Naxi houses with intricate wooden facades, and women in Naxi dress make aimless wandering perhaps Lijiang's most appealing activity. Head away from the main streets to escape the gift shops. Getting lost in the narrow back alleys is quite rewarding (and almost inevitable), at least in the daytime. Due to the recent tourism boom, the price of admission to tourist sights is ever-growing.

THE LOCAL STORY

PARADISE LOST

"Shangri-La," in a Zhongdian dia-
ect of Tibetan, means "the slope
eading to the land of the sun and
noon in my heart." British author
James Hilton based his novel *Lost
Horizon* (1933) on this hidden
paradise in southwest China. The
anciful have long sought this surreal town of eternal youth, supposedly in the mountains
between Tibet and Yunnan.

In 1997, a team of investiga-
ors sent by the Chinese government officially declared Deqin
Prefecture (encompassing Zhongdian) to be Hilton's Eden. Their
argument relied on a plane crash
n Zhongdian, involving four Amer-
cans trying to escape 1930s
China. Hilton's novel described
just such a crash involving four
Westerners. With such a clean fit
between factual glove and fic-
ional hand, the tourism-savvy
Yunnan government didn't hesi-
ate to make its claim.

Debate has ensued between
cynics and romantics: the former
search for physical evidence,
while the latter insist that Shangri-
La is not a real place, but rather a
paradise in the heart that could
exist nowhere and everywhere.

A visit to modern Zhongdian
will likely satisfy the doubts of
cynics and ease the romantics.
Like most Chinese towns, Zhongdian shows eternal bustle, but a
survey of the city's elderly will
yield few who claim eternal youth.
Either way, the beautiful landscapes of northern Yunnan merit
a visit from travelers of any belief.

◪ DAYAN NAXI MUSIC ASSOCIATION (dàyánnàxī
gǔyuèhuì; 大研纳西古乐会). Word has it that Naxi
music is actually very similar to ancient Han music,
brought from the north during the Yuan and Ming
Dynasties. Indeed, the Naxi minority has historically
appropriated Han styles. The music is haunting and
often called "a musical fossil," as it preserves elements from ancient Daoist music and now-lost court
music. The charismatic director of this association,
Xuan Ke, spices up his introduction of the orchestra,
the music, and himself with provocative social com-
mentary. Though he translates important details into
English, Xuan Ke often talks as much as the orchestra performs. The performance also features wonderful displays of folk songs. *(On Dong Dajie. Don't worry
about missing the place—there's a large sign right outside the
door, and every night you'll see countless people waiting there.
☎ 512 7971 or 4559. Performances nightly 8pm. Y50-100.)*

LION HILL (shīzi shān; 狮子山). Both the hill and
the wooden **Wangu Tower** (wàngǔ lóu; 万古楼) provide excellent views of the Old Town and the surrounding countryside. The 15min. hike is well
rewarded by a respite from the tourist madness in
the streets below. *(Stroll up the street to the right of CC's
Bar and look for signs to take a left to Wangulou. The round-trip
walk takes under 45min. Open daily 6am-11pm. Climbing Lion
Hill is free; Wangu Tower Y15, students Y8.)*

BLACK DRAGON POOL PARK (hēi lóng tán
gōngyuán; 黑龙潭公园). Here you will find numerous Dongba art galleries, temples, and gardens along
with the small lake that is the park's namesake. Most
pictures of Jade Dragon Snow Mountain are taken
from here. For a little adventure, make the 1hr. climb
up **Elephant Hill** (xiàng shān; 象山), where a spectacular view awaits. Women may want to exercise particular caution in this area. *(Take a left out of the Old Town,
and then a right on Xin Dajie and follow it 15min. to its end. For
a more scenic route, follow the stream out of the Old Town.
Cross the bridge on your left just before the small waterfall;
bear left when the road forks, and follow it to the end. The
museum entrance is 20m to the right. Open daily 6:30am-
8pm. Y20, students Y10; some travelers report being able to
get in free before 7am.)*

▶ DAYTRIPS FROM LIJIANG

BAISHA

*About 10km north of Lijiang. From Fuhui Lu or from the
market right outside Old Town, take bus #7 (every hr.,
Y1). To bike to Baisha, cycle north along Xin Dajie and go
left where the road forks; if you hit Black Dragon Pool
Park, you've gone too far. Continue straight through 2*

traffic circles onto the road out of town. Follow this road until you see a green sign with white lettering that says "Baisha," just after the 8km road marker. Turn left and ride straight into town.

The small village of Baisha (báishā; 白沙) is best known for its frescoes of Tibetan-Buddhist, Daoist, and Han origins. Follow the road into town until you see red lettering directing you to turn right for the frescoes. Go through the parking lot to the entrance. A cheesy song and dance performance requiring "voluntary" donations may also be tacked on. (Open 8am-8pm. Y8.)

Perhaps more famous than the frescoes, Dr. Ho, the "Daoist physician" and herbal medicine man made famous by travel writer Bruce Chatwin, also calls Baisha home. You may encounter him near his office, strolling in a slightly dirtied white coat. Go along the next road past the fresco sign to reach his office. Be prepared for an onslaught of newspaper clippings documenting the doctor's fame, though Dr. Ho is certainly a memorable character to sketch in your travel diary.

To reach the **Dragon Springs** (lóng quán; 龙泉) or **Fuguo Monastery** (fùguó sì; 福国寺) and explore a typical Naxi village along the way, continue straight through Baisha down the main road and across some fields; cross the river and look for a collection of houses where the road ends. Go left to reach Dragon Springs, 5km away, or right to Fuguo Monastery, 3km away. For a good biking map of the nearby area and a bite to eat, stop by **Cafe Buena Vista ❶,** just before Dr. Ho's office. Service can be slow. (☎ 131 7078 0719. Dishes Y6-15. Open 8:30am-6pm.)

JADE DRAGON SNOW MOUNTAIN

35km north of Lijiang. Take bus #7 (30min., every hr., Y8) from Mao Sq. on Xinda Jie. Open daily 8:30am-4:30pm. Admission Y80, mandatory maintenance fee additional Y40.

Jade Dragon Snow Mountain (yùlóng xuěshān; 玉龙雪山) is the dramatic 5596m peak that appears in virtually every postcard of the area. After staring at the peak every day in Lijiang, it would be a shame to miss the chance to see the mountain up close, though with the long lines and pricey admissions, no one would blame you. Two cable cars ascend the mountain: the shorter lift (Y40) ends at **Donkey Meadow,** where you get to see pretty shrubbery and Naxi dancing; the longer, more worthwhile lift (Y160) is one of China's longest cable-car rides. At the top is a short but exhausting walk to a viewing platform; those who suck up the financial and physical abuse of the trip are rewarded with breathtaking views. It is perhaps a bit alarming that hawkers at the peak sell oxygen pillows (Y30) instead of the usual tacky trinkets, but some climbers have no difficulty with the altitude, and even manage to get some mileage out of the karaoke machine in the teahouse, where they at least have an excuse for sounding like strangled monkeys. Vendors also rent winter coats. For great views of the mountain without the steep fees and long lines, we recommend instead the spectacular Tiger Leaping Gorge (see below).

TIGER LEAPING GORGE 虎跳峡

Tiger Leaping Gorge (hǔ tiào xiá), named for the legend of a hunted tiger that leapt across the stone abyss to escape its pursuer, has become a backpacker's rite of passage—a ready source of conversation and the topic of innumerable entries in travelers' notebooks. This 35km-long and 12km-wide gorge deserves all the adulation it gets. The gorge lies at the point where **Haba Snow Peak** (hābā xuěshān; 哈巴雪山) shoots up to face the Jade Dragon Snow Mountain over the swift waters of the fledgling Yangzi River. Known as the Jinsha (Gold Sand) River along its upper streams, it has chiseled out one of the deepest and most awe-inspiring gorges in the country and, indeed, the world. Adding to its splendor, Shanzidou, the highest

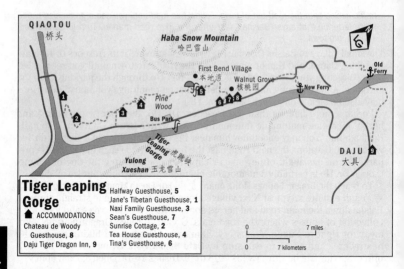

QIAOTOU
桥头

Haba Snow Mountain
哈巴雪山

First Bend Village
本地湾

Walnut Grove
核桃园

Old Ferry

New Ferry

Pine Wood

Bus Park

Tiger Leaping Gorge 虎跳峡

Yulong Xueshan 玉龙雪山

DAJU 大具

Tiger Leaping Gorge

⌂ ACCOMMODATIONS
Chateau de Woody Guesthouse, 8
Daju Tiger Dragon Inn, 9

Halfway Guesthouse, 5
Jane's Tibetan Guesthouse, 1
Naxi Family Guesthouse, 3
Sean's Guesthouse, 7
Sunrise Cottage, 2
Tea House Guesthouse, 4
Tina's Guesthouse, 6

0   7 miles
0   7 kilometers

of the peaks looming over the gorge, rises up at a lofty 5600m above sea level and also makes up the southernmost glacial mountains. No trip to northern Yunnan, long or short, would be complete without a jaunt to Tiger Leaping Gorge.

◪ TREKKING AROUND TIGER LEAPING GORGE

The hike is extremely challenging and not for the faint of heart, out-of-shape, or wary-of-heights. During the rainy season, the trek can be particularly treacherous; flooding and mudslides are not uncommon, and sometimes particularly nasty rains force travelers to spend more time in the gorge than they had originally anticipated. Plan wisely, but remain flexible; the situation for gorge trekkers is constantly changing. Leave large packs behind in Lijiang. Ask other travelers what they have done and talk to locals in cafes before setting off. Many local guesthouses and restaurants may underestimate the length of time it will take to get to the next stopping point. The best places to get information include **Lamu's House of Tibet** and **First Bend Inn** (see **Lijiang**, p. 674). The best **trekking map** of the gorge, by the Scottish engineering mapper Neil McLean, is available at First Bend Inn (Y1). With or without a map, it is difficult to get lost; friendly locals and endless colored arrows will point the way.

Tiger Leaping Gorge is bounded on one side by the town of **Qiaotou** (qiáotóu; 桥头) and on the other by **Daju** (dàjù; 大具). **First Bend Village** (běndìwān; 本地湾) and **Walnut Grove** (hétáo yuán; 核桃园) lie in between. Admission to the gorge is Y30 from Qiaotou. If you enter from Daju, you must pay an additional Y40 to the Zhongdian Prefecture ticket office. Some travelers have reported that the ticket-takers are more lax near dawn.

QIAOTOU TO TWENTY-FOUR BENDS. Buses to Qiaotou (2hr., 2 per day, Y12-19) and Daju (3-4hr., 2 per day, Y23) leave from Lijiang's North Station. If you can't get a direct ticket to Qiaotou, buy a ticket to Zhongdian (Y35) and ask to get off at Qiaotou. Alternatively, hire a **minibus** (Y100-120). Once in Qiaotou, you can head to **Jane's Tibetan Guesthouse** ❶ (xiágǔ xíng kèzhàn; 峡谷行客栈) for lodgings and meals. (☎880 6570. Food Y8-15. Dorms Y10; singles Y20; doubles Y30.) The trek begins after a 10min. walk up the road away from Qiaotou, on a gravel path up the hill on the left. **Sunrise Cottage ❶**, the first guesthouse from Qiaotou, is 30min. down. (Dorms Y10.) Another hour along the moderately uphill trail leads to **Naxi Family Guesthouse ❶** (nàxī yǎ gé; 纳西雅阁 ; ☎130 8742 2492), a good place to stop for lunch if your schedule allows. From here, the hardest part of the trail lies ahead.

TWENTY-FOUR BENDS TO HALFWAY. The 24 Bends (marked "28" on some Chinese maps) is a grueling and winding 2hr. stretch that leads to the highest point of the trek at 2670m. Those unwilling to brave the bends on foot can rent a horse at the Naxi Family Guesthouse or along the way for Y50. Another 30min. of downhill walking will restore your breath and bring you to **Tea House Guesthouse ❶**. (☎139 8870 7922. Dorms Y10.) It's another 1½hr., past a cave and a small waterfall, to **Halfway Guesthouse ❶** (zhōngtú kèzhàn; 中途客栈 ; ☎139 8870 0522), the preferred stop for many travelers at the end of the first day's trek. The kitchen serves up nourishing Chinese and Western food (Y6-20) and the patio overlooks the gargantuan Jade Dragon Snow Mountain across the gorge.

HALFWAY TO WALNUT GROVE. From Halfway Guesthouse, another 1½hr. along the trail leads to **Tina's Guesthouse ❶** (zhōng xiá lǚdiàn; 中峡旅店), just off the main road. (☎139 8871 7693 or 880 6079. 24hr. hot water.) From here there are several routes to Walnut Grove: the high path above Tina's (2½hr.), the main road (30min.), or the path along the river. The first two options are straightforward and well marked by ever-present arrows, but the more grueling river trek is by far the most rewarding and beautiful leg of the trip. You may want to consider hiring a guide at Tina's (individuals Y20, groups Y5 per person). At Walnut's Grove, **Sean's Guesthouse ❶** and **Chateau de Woody Guesthouse ❶** (shān báiliǎn lǚguǎn; 山白脸旅馆 ; ☎880 6628) both have patios, Chinese and Western food, and dorms (Y10-15).

WALNUT GROVE TO DAJU. The low road is the only route to Daju from Walnut Grove. Three to four hours along the main road brings you to the ferry crossing (Y10). The last ferry runs at 6pm, so plan accordingly. From the other side it's a 1hr. walk or a 10min. cab ride to Daju (Y5-10). Buses (Y25) back to Lijiang leave daily at 7am and 1:30pm. If you miss the last bus, **Daju Tiger Dragon Inn ❶** (dàjù lóng hǔ kèzhàn; 大具龙虎客栈 ; ☎888 532 6040) provides clean beds (Y15) and a convenient departure point—the bus leaves directly from here. For those trekking Tiger Leaping Gorge in the reverse direction, this would be your starting point.

LUGU LAKE 泸沽湖   ☎0888

The lengthy bus ride from Lijiang unwittingly discourages many potential visitors to Lugu Lake, a (less and less) quiet getaway on the Yunnan-Sichuan border. Once there, however, the warmth and hospitality of the people in the Tibetan, Yi, Pumi, and Mosuo villages and the laidback atmosphere on the lake make it difficult for travelers to leave. The Lugu Lake area is best known as home of the Mosuo, a matrilineal society whose members participate in traditional "walking marriages," in which husband and wife remain in their respective maternal homes and often have more than one partner. According to locals, the lake is gorgeous in all seasons, but most visitors prefer to visit in late spring or fall when the sky is a clear blue and the weather is more mild. In the winter, Lugu Lake is very cold and often snowy, with wild geese and sea gulls flocking on its icy shores; in late summer, rains are frequent and visibility is limited.

TRANSPORTATION. The easiest way to get to Lugu Lake is from Lijiang. A **bus** (6-7hr., 9am, Y46) runs to the lake via Ninglang, making several stops along the way. A **minibus** (8:30am; one-way Y60, round-trip Y100) leaves from the Lijiang Old Town parking lot, a 3min. walk left from the town entrance, to the village of **Lige**, the second stop on the lake from the main road. **Buses** (3hr.; 7am, 2pm; Y26) leave from Lijiang South Station for Ninglang (p. 675). It is fairly easy to get a bus from Ninglang Bus Station or the main street to Lugu Lake. Buses from Lugu to Ninglang leave from the **Mosuo Hotel** (7:30, 8am; Y20). From Ninglang, buses go to Kunming (1pm, Y105); Lijiang (every hr. 7am-1pm, Y26); and Xiaguan (7am, Y48).

ACCOMMODATIONS AND FOOD. Every year, development extends a bit further along the lake, making it more and more difficult to find tranquil spots to stay. Luoshui is the first village from the road to Lugu Lake. The bus will drop you off here, but most travelers prefer to push on to Lige (30min.) or Dazu (1hr.). All along the lake, **dorm** beds go for Y15. In Lige, **Guangyin Guesthouse ❶** (guāngmíng yīnyuè dōng kèzhàn; 光明音乐客栈 ; ☎588 1218) has a nice if expensive bar and free Internet (non-guests Y6). Cold showers, however, may make you seek other rooms, like **Dadu's Hostel ❶** (☎588 1006) and **Lige First Guesthouse ❶** (lǐgé dìyī jiā; 里格第一家 ; ☎588 1159). In **Dazu**, spend the night in **local homes** (Y15-20 includes meals). Most travelers eat where they stay. All guesthouses on the lake serve Chinese dishes, and some offer a small selection of Western food (Y10-20).

SIGHTS AND HIKING. The key to visiting Lugu Lake is to get away from inn-cluttered and tourist-laden **Luoshui** (落水) village. **Boats** (one island Y25, both islands Y35) go from the Luoshui Dock to **Tusi** and **Liwubi**, two small islands with lamaseries. There's not much to see on the islands, but the boat ride across the lake is worthwhile. The boatsmen and Chinese tourists may be inclined to sing at times; more often, though, they're inclined to wail. At the dock area, you can also hire a guide (best to arrive 7-8am to arrange this; about Y100 per day) or a **horse** (Y60) that stops at a nearby meadow, where travelers can wrestle local champions. Beware: a "tradition" is to split the opponent's pants in these matches.

Mosuo culture is at its most fascinating in the smaller, more tranquil villages of **Lige** (里格), **Xiao Luoshui** (小落水), and **Dazui** (大咀), which have remained relatively untouched by the ever-expanding mass-marketing of the region. It takes over 12hr. to walk around the lake, and about 7hr. to get to the three villages. Hiring a minibus for the day costs Y30-35 per person. For further insight into Mosuo culture, the majority of the Mosuo live in **Yongning** (永宁), about a 1hr. bus ride from Lugu Lake. The **bus** from Ninglang to Yongning (Y5) passes by Luoshui daily at 10am; ask the manager at **Husi Tea House** to take you to the bus or arrange for transportation. **Accommodations** in Yongning are available in village homes.

The **trek** from Yongning to Lijiang is said to be gorgeous, and some backpackers do it by camping or staying at villagers' homes along the way. It is difficult to get information about this trek once in Lugu Lake. While in Lijiang, ask other backpackers, check out travelers' notebooks, or talk to travel agencies. The folks at the **Lamu's House of Tibet** in Lijiang (p. 677) are particularly helpful.

ZHONGDIAN 中甸 ☎0887

Zhongdian, the name of both the county and its capital, is part of Diqing Tibetan Autonomous Prefecture (known as *Gyelthang* in Tibetan) in the far north of Yunnan province. Because travel from Tibet from Zhongdian is now possible, droves of backpackers flock to the town that many believe was once the fabled Shangri-La. Even if you don't continue on to Tibet, a stay in the area can give you a fascinating glimpse into Tibetan life. Tibetan villages dot the valleys, and saffron-robed monks walk the streets. With elevation ranging from 1480m to 6740m, the prefecture encompasses mystical scenery at nearly every turn, and buses teeter along precarious but exhilirating mountain roads.

Like many Chinese towns of regional import, Zhongdian seems to endure a constant frenzy of construction and a continual haze of dust, making it one of Yunnan's grimier cities—considerably detracting from the whole Shangri-La hoopla. Even the old section of town has been invaded by impersonal masses of concrete and faux-traditional buildings. Despite its dwindling structural character, Zhongdian's multicultural spirit—a mosaic of Han Chinese, Tibetan, Bai, and Naxi minorities—and natural scenery continue to bring Zhongdian to life.

▐▘ TRANSPORTATION

Flights: Diqing Airport (díqìng jīchǎng; 迪庆机场 ; ☎822 9916) is 3km out of town. No airport shuttles. A taxi from town costs Y15-20. The **Qingnan Airlines ticket office** (☎822 9901) is open daily 8:30am-noon and 2-5:30pm. From Long Life Tibetan Hotel, walk toward Changzhong Lu and take the 1st right onto Heping Lu; the office is to the left from the 2nd intersection. To: **Chengdu** (Sept.-June every Sa; Y980, via Kunming Y1400); **Kunming** (2-4 per day, Y700); **Lhasa** (M-Tu, F; Y1380).

Bus: Zhongdian Central Bus Station (zhōngdiàn kèyùn fúwù zhōngxīn zhàn; 中甸客运服务中心站 ; ☎822 3501), on Zhongxiang Lu (中乡路). From Changzheng Lu, walk away from the old town and turn right at the traffic circle; it's 10min. away on the right. The ticket office is inside the waiting room. Luggage storage Y2 per bag per day. Open daily 6:30am-7:20pm. To: **Deqin** (6hr., 4 per day, Y37); **Kunming** (15hr., 6 per day, Y147); **Lijiang** (6hr., every hr., Y20); **Sanba** (4hr., 2 per day, Y22) via **Baishuitai; Xiaguan** (8hr., every 30min., Y45-65). Travel from Yunnan to Sichuan is easiest between Zhongdian and Xiangzheng. There are no travel restrictions and the route features some wonderful scenery to brighten the long, bumpy bus rides.

Local Transportation: Bus #2 travels the length of Changzheng Lu; #3 runs every 5min. from the Long Life Tibetan Hotel down Changzheng Lu, past the bus station and bank, going toward Songzanlin Lamasery. Fare Y1. For shorter distances, you can also take a **pedicab** (Y2-3) or **taxi** (Y5 within the city proper).

Bicycle Rental: Tibet Cafe is the only place with mountain bikes. Y3 per hr., Y25 per day. **Long Life Tibetan Hotel** has old, single-gear clunkers. Y15 per day.

▉▓ ▌ ORIENTATION AND PRACTICAL INFORMATION

There are two distinct areas within Zhongdian. The rough-hewn, construction-crazed area around **Changzheng Lu** (长征路), the main shopping street, constitutes the modern part of Zhongdian. **Heping Lu** (和平路) parallels it just to the east. The **old town,** on the other hand, is a muddled series of dusty lanes and dilapidated houses, complete with barking dogs and wandering pigs. **Tuanjie Jie** (团结街) flanks the old town to the north, intersecting the southern end of Changzheng Lu.

Travel Agencies: The **Long Life Tibetan Travel Service** (yǒng shēng lǚxíng shè; 永生旅行社 ; ☎823 0110), at the Long Life Tibetan Hotel. Arranges trips to nearby sights. Overland trips to Tibet Y5000 (driver and permit), by air Y2450 (ticket and permit). **Shangri-La County Service Center** (xiānggélǐlā xiàn lǚyóu fúwù zhōngxīn; 香格里拉县旅游服务中心 ; ☎828 8781) sells tickets to sights throughout the region.

Bank: Agricultural Bank of China (☎822 2567), on Changzheng Lu, across from China Post. Exchanges traveler's checks. Credit card advances. Open M-F 8:30am-12:30pm and 1:30-5pm.

PSB: ☎822 6834. On Heping Lu, 3rd fl., 5min. from the plane ticket office, toward the bus station on the right. Visa extensions. Open M-F 8:30am-noon and 2:30-5pm.

Internet Access: Many Internet cafes are on Changzheng Lu. **Q Q Internet Cafe,** 3 blocks down Changzheng Lu from Tuanjie Jie on the right. Very fast connections. **Snowlands Bright Pearl Internet Cafe** (xuěyù míngzhū wǎngbā; 雪域明珠网吧), next to the Agricultural Bank of China, toward old town. Both Y2 per hr. Open 8am-midnight.

Post and Telecommunications: China Post, on Changzheng Lu, 2 blocks toward the old town. EMS and Poste Restante. Open daily summer 8:30am-8:30pm; winter 9am-8pm. **China Telecom** (☎822 6141), next to China Post. IDD service. Open daily summer 8:30am-10pm; winter 9am-8pm.

Postal Code: 674400.

TIP

SUMMER FREEZE! While Yunnan's year-round weather might normally beg shorts, sandals, and a handy umbrella, a trip to the high-altitude north can be chilly even in the dog days of summer. Be sure to bring a pull-over. Long underwear (miánmáokù; 棉毛裤) is available at many local stores for Y20-60.

■ ACCOMMODATIONS

As Zhongdian grows as a backpacker hangout, more and more budget options are becoming available. At times, there seems to be more guesthouses than guests.

Guanglin Guesthouse (guǎng lín kèzhàn; 广林客栈 ; ☎822 2100), on Beimen Jie (北门街), in the old town. From Changzheng Lu and Tuanjie Jie, continue into the old town and take the 1st left; it's 5min. on the left. In an old wooden building, this charming guesthouse has the feel of a cabin and oozes character. Laid-back staff play good music and will go out of their way to accommodate you. Free Internet on sole computer. 24hr. hot water. Dinner Y8. Dorm beds Y15. ❶

Long Life Tibetan Hotel (yǒng shēng fàndiàn; 永生饭店), 106 Tuanjie Jie (☎822 2448). Follow Changzheng Lu away from the station and turn left on Tuanjie Jie; hotel is 10min. on the right. From Changzheng Lu, taxi Y5, bus Y1. If there are any foreigners in Zhongdian, you'll likely find them here. Staff are friendly and offer good travel advice. Rooms are clean and usually quiet. Travel agency, bike rental (Y3 per hr., Y15 per day), cafe with English menu, Internet access (Y3 per hr.), and IDD service. Hot water 6pm-8am. Deposit Y100. 6-bed dorms Y15; doubles Y30. ❶

Diqing Tibetan Area International Youth Hostel (HI) (díqìng zàngdì guójì qīngnián-lǚshè; 迪庆藏地国际青年旅舍 ; ☎822 8671), on the corner of Tuanjie Jie at Heping Lu. Popular backpacker hangout with cafe, bike rental (Y15 per day), and 24hr. hot water. 9-bed dorms Y15; singles and doubles Y50. ❶

Paradise Hotel (tiān jiè shénchuān dàjiǔdiàn; 天界神川大酒店 ; ☎822 8008), on Changzheng Lu, opposite the People's Bank. By far the most luxurious and expensive hotel in Zhongdian, the Paradise's most heavenly characteristic is its beautiful atrium and gardens. For those looking to splurge, this is the place to unload your wallet. Every amenity imaginable from 24hr. room service to tennis courts to massages. Rooms start at Y600-800, but bargain hard to get to Y400. ❺

FOOD AND ENTERTAINMENT

Food in Zhongdian consists mostly of Chinese staples flavored with heavy Sichuanese spices. Local favorites include **hotpot** and **cured beef**. Restaurant stalls line Changzheng Lu and Heping Lu (dishes Y5-8), and there are some **dumpling** stalls along Hongqi Lu. More and more **Western** restaurants are opening, with most clustering along Tuanjie Jie. At night, head to **Cow Pub** (niú péng jiǔbā; 牛棚酒吧), 101 Jinlong Jie, in the old town. Keep walking past Big Turtle Park to the end of the road. Creaky wood and Tibetan crafts create a unique atmosphere in this hard-to-find waterhole. The Swedish owners play an eclectic range of Western music. (Beer Y10 and up. Open nightly 7:30pm-1am.)

Yak Bar (yăkè bā; 雅客吧; ☎828 8665), on the corner of Tuanjie Jie at Changzheng Lu. This cozy restaurant offers a little bit of everything: Tibetan "meatballs" (more like fried batter with meat inside; Y15), tasty Korean and Japanese fare (Y10-20), and decent Western food (pizza Y20-30). ❷

White Temple Book Cafe (bái tă shū bā; 白塔书吧; ☎139 887 8211), just before Yak Bar on Tuanjie Jie. A range of Tibetan specialties that go beyond the dishes listed on the English menu. Get a group of starving backpackers together for delicious Tibetan hotpot featuring meatballs (real ones this time) and yak meat (Y80 feeds 4 or more). ❷

Tibet Cafe (xīzàng kāfēi guǎn; 西藏咖啡馆; ☎823 0019), on Changzheng Lu just before the old town. Atmosphere and music make up for mediocre food. Popular place to grab a late night beer (Y7) or dessert (Y10-15). Rents out the best bikes in town. ❷

◧ SIGHTS

Although Zhongdian itself may not be much to look at, it serves as a useful base from which to explore the more scenic surroundings. The old town's part-cobblestone, part-dirt roads can make for interesting walks, but be wary of mud during the rainy season. Exploring the countryside in the direction of Lijiang can also be rewarding. **Big Turtle Park** (dà guīshān gōngyuán; 大龟山公园) provides a good view of the old town. From Changzheng Lu, go straight, then turn left onto Beimen Jie; follow it to the end and turn right. From here you should be able to see the base of the small hill and a monastery. Toward the end of April or beginning of May, Tibetan families trek up to the monastery to burn incense and pray for a good harvest. (Open daily 24hr. Y2.) There are also two small **monasteries** near the upper end of the old town. (Open daily sunrise-sunset. Y3 and Y5.)

■**SONGZANLIN MONASTERY** (sōngzànlín sì; 松赞林寺). This monastery alone justifies a trip to Zhongdian. Affiliated with the Gelug school and built by the fifth Dalai Lama, Songzanlin is the largest Tibetan Buddhist monastery in Yunnan. Perched on a hill, the temple feels like a fort, with tall walls and commanding views of the sloping countryside. Songzanlin was first established in 1679, but was almost completely demolished during the Cultural Revolution. It has since been beautifully reconstructed and has many lamas in residence. The main hall contains some stunning Tibetan artwork. Musical entertainment awaits early morning visitors. (5km northwest of Zhongdian. Bus #3 runs every 5-10min. from outside the Long Life Tibetan Hotel for a 15min. drive. Open daily sunrise-sunset. Monastery free, main hall Y10.)

NAPA LAKE (nàpà hǎi; 纳帕海). This "lake" only exists from July to September, and even then it's rather underwhelming. At other times of the year, it is a large, boring meadow. Patches of wild blossoms blanket the encircling hills in May and June, creating a relaxing place for a picnic and a nap. In the winter, rare black-neck cranes visit. There is a small temple nearby. (5km from Songzanlin Lamasery. Take

SOUTHWEST

bus #2 from Changzheng Lu for Y5; ask before you board, as not all of them go to Napa Lake. You can also bike to the lake by riding straight through the traffic circle on Changzheng Lu and continuing all the way up the winding road. This grueling 1hr. ride is best done on Tibet Cafe's mountain bikes. Lake Y10. Horse rides Y30.)

BITA LAKE (bìtǎ hǎi; 碧塔海). Bita Lake is 3540m above sea level, 3km from the west entrance to the scenic area. For those interested in a more equine experience, it is also possible to rent a horse (about Y30). From the south entrance, it's a 2km hike down a log-covered path. Most of the hike around the lake is not grueling, and the woods around the lake are lovely, with long strands of mosses hanging from trees and wildflowers bursting forth from the most surprising places. Accommodation is available in white-shingled wood cabins (Y15-30 per person) or in campgrounds on the premises. Bring plenty of water. A visit to **Shudu Lake** (shǔdū hǎi; 属都海), also west of Zhongdian, costs as much as one to Bita Lake. *(About 1hr. west of Zhongdian. No regular public transportation. Taxi from Zhongdian round-trip Y250 for 3-4 people. Canoe rental Y20; speedboat Y25 per person. Bita Lake Y30. Shudu Lake Y10.)*

WHITE WATER TERRACE (báishuǐ tái; 白水台). Baishui's terraces of limestone form the second-largest natural terrace of its kind in the world. In the fall, red and pink wildflowers carpet the valley, thought to be fed by a holy spring. Crowds can be intimidating at certain times of the year, especially in March, when it becomes a pilgrimage site. *(Bus to Sanba from Zhongdian costs Y22 and takes 3½hr.; it leaves at 8:30am in summer and 6:30am in winter. Buses return to Zhongdian the next morning. Unless you hire a vehicle, a trip to Baishui Terrace requires an overnight stay. Beds available in guesthouses by the road for Y15-30. Also possible to hire horses in Baishuitai and trek to Tiger Leaping Gorge; Y400-500 per day. Ask at the Long Life Tibetan Hotel for details. Admission Y30.)*

DEQIN 德钦   ☎ 0887

For those disappointed with less-than-romantic Zhongdian, Deqin Tibetan Autonomous County just might restore the promise of a mythical Shangri-La. Nestled in the Hengduanshan Mountains on the southern edge of the Tibetan plateau, Deqin hosts a population of just 55,000 souls, 80% of whom are Tibetan. While the nearby glacier is Deqin's most compelling sight, the road from Zhongdian bumps and twists by no shortage of awe-inspiring passes, snow-capped peaks, and rushing river rapids. Those who aren't fond of heights should choose an aisle seat on the bus to avoid stomach-wrenching views of the steep drops from the road's edge. Travelers should also be prepared for road closures during winter months.

🚌 TRANSPORTATION AND PRACTICAL INFORMATION

Deqin is a one-street town: **Nanping Jie** (南平街) has good hotels, the bus station, bank, the post and telecommunications offices, and many small eateries. The town is laid out on a hillside. Aimless wandering leads to many good views of the surrounding mountains. From the **Deqin Bus Station** (déqīn kèyùn fúwù zhàn; 德钦客运服务站 ; ☎ 841 2115), buses run to Zhongdian (6hr., 3-4 per day, Y33). It is difficult to cross into Sichuan from Deqin without going through Tibet, which requires a permit. Another option is to go to **Benzilan,** halfway between Zhongdian and Deqin, and take a **ferry** across the river to Sichuan. From here, you can travel to Derong and on to Xiancheng, via a frequently traveled backpacker route.

The owners of the **Dexin Hotel** are very helpful when it comes to sightseeing: if they can't arrange the trip for you, they know someone who can. **Internet cafes** are located on nearly every block and offer similar connection speeds for Y3 per hr. The **China Telecom** office is just next to the bus station, and the **post office** is another 30m up the hill. **Postal Code:** 674500.

ACCOMMODATIONS AND FOOD

Although the main street has several "tourist-designated restaurants," none of these—in fact, no restaurant in town—has an English menu. Go into the kitchen of your chosen restaurant and pick the ingredients of your meal yourself (usually around Y5-12 per dish). Food is standard Chinese cuisine. You can stock up on fresh fruit for the long rides at **produce** and **meat markets** at the end of Nanping Jie.

Dexin Tibetan Hotel (déxīn bīnguǎn; 德薪宾馆), 86 Nanping Jie (☎841 2031). Walk downhill from the bus station; it's on the right. Graceful Tibetan-style floral patterns on the walls, a glassed-in patio, and a friendly Tibetan family make this a relaxing spot to rest up after a jarring bus ride. The owner's son is an excellent tour guide. Thin dorm mattresses don't provide much comfort, but 2nd-fl. rooms sport comfy mattresses, TV, and newly renovated bath. 24hr. warm showers are sometimes spotty. Dorms Y20; singles Y30, with bath Y80; doubles Y60/Y80; triples with bath Y90. ❶

Meili Hotel (méilĭ jiǔdiàn; 梅里酒店 ; ☎841 3998), uphill from the bus station on the right. Clean, spartan singles and doubles Y50, with bath Y140. ❶

Adunzi Hotel (ādūnzi jiǔdiàn; 阿墩子酒店 ; ☎841 3378), on Nanping Jie. Turn right out of the bus station. Rooms are clean but somewhat noisy. Travel agency. Newly renovated doubles with full Western bath start at Y110. ❷

SIGHTS

Deqin's beauty and charm beg for stays much longer than a few days. If you have more time, consider an extended daytrip to **Yubeng Village** (yǔbēng cūn; 雨崩村). A 75km ride from Deqin or a 3-4hr. drive away, even more tranquil mountain scenery awaits for those willing to spend a night or two in Yubeng Village. A 2hr. hike from Yubeng leads to a waterfall, which tumbles down over 30m and is worth the visit alone. A bus (Y20) leaves Deqin at irregular times in the afternoon and returns the next morning. Local Tibetan homes offer a night's sleep for Y10 per person.

MEILIXUESHAN MOUNTAINS (méilĭxuě shān; 梅里雪山). The Meili Snow Mountains lie just beyond the banks of the Mekong River on the Yunnan-Tibet border, counting among its lofty ranks the 6740m **Mount Kagebo,** Yunnan's highest peak. The mountain is a magnificent sight, with its piercingly white peaks ascending defiantly toward the sky. The closest most travelers come to Kagebo is the fantastic hike up to **Mingyong Glacier** (míngyǒng bīngchuān; 明永冰川), which at 2700m is the world's lowest-altitude glacier. If you're lucky, you might see and hear some ice slides as the glacier grinds its way down the mountain. *(West of Deqin. A bus to Mingyong Glacier leaves daily at 3pm from Nanping Jie near the bus station and returns the next day at 8 or 9am; one-way Y15, round-trip Y30. A taxi to Mingyong costs Y200 round-trip. Accommodations are available in the hotel near the glacier for Y20 per person. Hike up to glacier 2hr. Horses one-way Y70, round-trip Y85. Admission Y60, students Y33.)*

FEILAI MONASTERY (fēilái sì; 飞来寺). Feilai Monastery is the name given to both the small monastery and a viewing area 1km away; ask to have the prayer hall opened for you. The viewing terrace is a sight in itself, with a line of nine bright white *stupas* and row after row of colorful Tibetan prayer flags. On clear days, the terrace offers stunning panoramas (best in the afternoon) that no postcard could ever properly convey. *(11km from Deqin. A bus leaves daily around 7am from Nanping Jie near the bus station for Y6. You can also walk. Taxi Y30-50. Roads are almost deserted, making other means of transportation almost impossible. If you've rented a car to the glacier, ask the driver to stop here along the way. Terrace open daily sunrise-sunset. Y10.)*

China's New Ecotourism Industry

The concept and implementation of ecotourism in China is still an entirely new endeavor, despite the fact that 2002 was named the International Year of Ecotourism by the United Nations. Since China is currently the world's number one tourist destination (with 31.2 million visitors according to Newsweek July 22, 2000/July 29, 2002), it is imperative to illustrate China's potential for ecotourism. Ecotourism is travel to fragile, pristine, and usually protected areas that strives to be low-impact and small-scale. Such travel is educational and fosters respect for different cultures as well as for human rights (Martha Honey in *Ecotourism & Sustainable Development*, 1999, Island Press).

Yunnan Province, in southwest China, is a wonderful place for ecotourism. Roughly the size of France or California (at 5% of China's total land mass), it is the sixth-largest of China's 27 provinces and has towering, icy mountains, as well as lush jungles. Of the approximately 56 recognized nationalities found in China, 24 exist only in Yunnan. The province also has abundant natural resources and the highest level of biodiversity in China (half of all China's animal and plant species can be found somewhere in Yunnan). Yet the province also has one of the most poorly developed infrastructures in the country.

Geologically, Yunnan is an offshoot of Tibet, whose soaring tableland spreads eastward, creating a plateau over a mile high. In Western Yunnan, the ranges of the eastern Himalayas spread south from Tibet's border, channeling some of southern Asia's greatest rivers through deep canyons. The Nu-Salween, the Lancang (Mekong), and the Yangzi Rivers race side by side far below the snow capped peaks, barely 50 mi. apart, cutting plunging gorges and watering fertile valleys.

Movements in the earth's unstable crust subject Yunnan to periodic earthquakes. In the province's southwestern tip, the Tengchong Volcano system is regarded as one of the densest clusters of volcanoes in the world. Together with hot springs, the 90 pot-like volcanoes produce "terrestrial heat" of over 98°C. In far northern Yunnan, the mountains rear up to form the southern foot of the Tibetan Plateau.

Fertile lake basins lie in the geological fault on the plateau. Among these, Kunming's Dianc Lake is the largest. These form the agricultural, political, and cultural heart of the province. Th red soil produces rice in abundance, along wi year-round vegetable crops and teas that are co sidered among the best in China.

Botanical gardens in Kunming and in tropic Xishuangbanna display an astonishing array plant species. Botanists come to see the came lias and rhododendrons, the province's speci pride, as all species of these shrubs trace the ancestry to Yunnan. Wild animals and birds exi in great variety. Species of elephants, tiger bears, snow leopards, takin, slow loris, golde monkeys, and gibbons can all be found in Yu nan, thus making it an unparalleled natural bi logical museum.

Though ecotourism is new to China, Yunnan the most fertile ground for its beginnings. In 199 the Chinese Minstry of Forestry allotted tho sands of acres in the Gaoligongshan Nation Nature Reserve for tourism development. Th estimated total carrying capacity for the area 215,000 visitors per year. Since then, there hav been several attempts at surveying and identif ing eco- and heritage-tourism sites within th area, but none have been implemented. In 200 the Reserve revised its approach and delineate six areas for tourism development, including th Baihualing Area.

There are few locations in the world that po sess the biodiversiy and unique character of th Gaoligongshan National Nature Reserve. Locate just north of the Tropic of Cancer, it has a unusual seven climate zones, which results i Yunnan's astounding variety of plants and an mals. Take this along with its diverse geologic formations, and it becomes clear why Yunna appeals to travelers.

Though the seeds for ecotourism in China ar just starting to be planted, it can be expected tha they will blossom fruitfully. With provinces suc as Yunnan, and reserves such as Gaoligongsha China seems well on its way to achieving the sta tus of not only the most touristed nation, but th most ecotouristed as well.

Victoria Drake has worked for the Smithsonian Institute and The Great Lakes Conservation Fund. She started IUCN-US in Washington, DC, and was the first program director for Global Alliance for Africa in Chicago.

SICHUAN AND CHONGQING

Blessed with vigorous rivers, a mild climate, and endlessly green valleys, Sichuan province and the municipality of Chongqing are justifiably known as China's "Heaven on Earth." The major breadbasket of the southwest, the area is home to a whopping 123 million people. Most live in the flat and fertile Sichuan basin, centered around the bustling provincial capital of Chengdu, which once served as the seat of Sichuan's Kingdom of Shu in the 3rd century AD. Formerly the region's largest city, Chengdu's rival Chongqing was penciled in as a municipality in 1997, instantly becoming the largest "city" in the world, with a population of over 32 million. In contrast, the western and northern hinterlands of Sichuan, sparsely populated with Tibetan, Qiang, and Yi minorities, paint an entirely different landscape of glacier-fed rivers, snowy peaks, and horizon-wide grasslands scattered with yaks and splashes of wildflowers.

HIGHLIGHTS OF SICHUAN AND CHONGQING

COUNT THE COLORS sparkling in Jiuzhaigou's brilliant mineral lakes (p. 734).

WAKE UP IN THE CLOUDS to the chanting of monks high in the mist-wreathed peaks of **Emeishan** (p. 706).

SPICE UP YOUR LIFE with peppers galore and sample the famed **hotpot** of **Chongqing** (p. 727) and **Chengdu** (p. 706).

SICHUAN 四川

Sichuan's rugged mountainous terrain, death-defying rapids, and fortress towns girded by ancient battlefields have long inspired the Chinese imagination. With thousands of years of history set against a majestic landscape, Sichuan is heavy with legends and redolent with fresh air from its richly green forests and valleys. Historically a border region between the civilized Central Plains and the "western barbarians," the province has always been a little wilder and a little more free-spirited than the rest of China, with a stark beauty mirrored in its knife-cut peaks, highland plateaus, and a hell-fire spicy cuisine to boot.

Today, contact with "barbaric" foreigners continues in the form of eager backpackers in search of adventure, whether in Sichuan itself or in Tibet, for which Chengdu serves as an official jump-off point. North of Chengdu, tiny villages nestle deep in valleys and beside mountain lakes, while Tibetan, Hui Muslim, and Qiang minorities continue to lead nomadic and farming lives on the grasslands bordering Gansu. Emeishan and Qingchengshan welcome visitors behind their veils of mist and jungly foliage, and those in search of a high, clear air trek west to the Tibetan town of Kangding and the snow mountains beyond.

CHENGDU 成都   ☎028

With its tree-lined streets, lazy rivers, soaring skyscrapers, and glitzy department stores, Chengdu is at once stimulating and mellow. Known for its spicy food—hot enough to be cathartic—and prolific tea gardens, this fast-expanding metropolis is the perfect stop for the travel-weary to slow down and take a deep breath. After days of touring and nights spent dancing, Chengdu lures travelers into the great outdoors with trips to gorgeous, mountain-in-the-clouds nature parks—notably Four Maiden Mountains and Qingcheng Mountains, and the much farther Jiuzhaigou and Emeishan—for which the city serves as an ideal base.

Chengdu is steeped in more than 3000 years of history, relics, and legends, from as early as the mythical Shang Dynasty (1600-1066 BC). The Qin Dynasty (221-206 BC) followed up with an amazing feat of engineering, the remarkably successful Dujiangyan irrigation system, which can still be seen today. But when most people think of ancient Sichuan, they think of the short-lived Shu Kingdom (AD 221-263) and its heroes, immortalized by the ancient epic *Romance of the Three Kingdoms*. In the Tang Dynasty, China's literary golden age, Chengdu was graced with the master poet Du Fu (AD 712-770), who penned poems in his thatched cottage in the western part of the city. Today, communism is just the latest in Chengdu's long stream of dynasties and empires. Despite the giant statue of Mao overlooking the main plaza, what *Chéngdūrén* like best at the end of the day is the historical drama series currently airing on TV, the latest pop star and newest disco, or better yet, another pot of tea and another game of *mahjong* in one of Chengdu's parks.

▐ TRANSPORTATION

Flights: Shuangliu Airport (shuāngliú jīchǎng; 双流机场; ☎8520 5333), 16km southwest of the central districts. Mainly served by China Southwest Airlines, Dragon Air, and Sichuan Airlines. Public buses run between Minshan Hotel and the airport (approx. every 30min. 4:30am-9pm, Y8). Taxis (40min., Y40-80) also make the trip. Airport tax Y90. To: **Beijing** (many per day, Y1440); **Guangzhou** (several per day, Y1300); **Guiyang** (many per day, Y630); **Kunming** (several per day, Y700); **Lanzhou** (several per day, Y940); **Lhasa** (several per day, Y1500); **Shanghai** (many per day, Y1610); **Xi'an** (several per day, Y630); **Xining** (several per day, Y990).

Trains: Chengdu North Train Station (chéngdū běi huǒchēzhàn; 成都北火车站; ☎8444 5111; inquiries 8317 0324; www.chengdustation.com), at the northernmost end of Renmin Bei Lu, at the intersection with Erhuan Lu. To: **Beijing** (26-33hr., 3-5 per day, Y232-405); **Chongqing** (10-11hr., 2-4 per day, Y63-179); **Emeishan** (2hr., 7 per day, Y9-19); **Guangzhou** (39hr., 1-2 per day, Y271-754); **Guiyang** (17hr., 4 per day, Y117-352); **Kunming** (18-23hr., 4 per day, Y70-338); **Lanzhou** (22hr., 1 per day, Y73-389); **Nanjing** (37hr., 1 per day, Y113-705); **Shanghai** (36-42hr., 4 per day, Y126-770); **Taiyuan** (42hr., daily, Y88-304); **Xi'an** (16-40½hr., 3 per day, Y55-316).

Buses: Chengdu has bus stations in every direction. The most important ones are Chadianzi and New South Gate. Nearly all service nearby attractions like Dujiangyan.

New South Gate Bus Station (xīnnánmén qìchē zhan; 新南门汽车站; ☎543 3609), on Linjiang Zhong Lu, next to the Traffic Hotel on the south bank of the river. Chengdu's main bus station. Open daily 8am-6pm. To: **Chongqing** (4½hr., Y110); **Emeishan** (2hr., every 20min. 7am-7pm, Y33); **Jiuzhaigou** (12-14hr., 8am, Y94) via **Dujiangyan** (1-2hr., Y16); **Kangding** (every hr. 7am-3pm, Y98); **Leshan** (every 20min. 7:50am-7:35pm, Y33-38); **Moxi** (6-8hr., 9am, Y104 plus an additional Y20 insurance fee); **Qingchengshan** (2hr., every 30min. 8:30-11am, Y26). Buses to Moxi are also marked **Hailuogou** (海螺沟).

Chadianzi Bus Station (chádiànzǐ kèyùn zhàn; 茶店子客运站). Northwest of the city, accessible by bus #82. To: **Dujiangyan** (every 5min. from 6:40am on, Y8.5); **Jiuzhaigou** (7:20, 8am, 4pm; Y63-86); **Songpan** (6:30, 7, 7:30am; Y45-49); **Wolong** (11:40am, Y23); **Four Maidens Mountain** (8:20am, Y66).

Chengdu North Bus Station (chéngdū běi mén zhōngxīn kèyùn zhàn; 成都北门中心客运站; ☎8317 5758, info 8317 5992), next to the train station. Exit North Train Station and stay on the right side of the square. Make a right on the 1st street from the square and go straight; follow

signs until the street ends and enter the large gate. Buses #2, 16, 25, 28, 44, 64, and 65 stop nearby. Open daily 6:30am-9pm. To: **Chongqing** (4hr., every 30min., Y85); **Dujiangyan** (1hr., every 20min., Y8-9); **Kangding** (at least 12hr.; 8:30am, 4:30pm; Y101).

Local Transportation: The **Chengdu North Bus Station** also has a local station (☎317 6210). Exit the North Train Station and stay on the right side of the square; take the first right and the local bus station is 100m away, on the left. **Buses** #55 and 64 go to the city center; #16 runs from the North Train Station through the city center to the South Train Station. Fare Y1, with A/C Y2.

Taxis: Most taxis charge a base fee of Y5, each additional km Y1.4. **Tricycles** are a cheaper alternative, but only for intrepid negotiators.

ORIENTATION AND PRACTICAL INFORMATION

Nestled at the intersection of the **Fu** (fǔ hé; 府河) and **Nan Rivers** (nán hé; 南河), Chengdu's city center is surrounded by three concentric ring roads, though most visitor rarely even make it to the second one. **Renmin Lu** (人民路) extends north-south from **Tianfu Plaza** (天府广场) in the center of town to bisect the two ring roads that encircle the city. Major streets are divided into north (北), south (南),

SICHUAN

Chengdu

ACCOMMODATIONS
Holly's Hostel, **16**
Sam's Backpacker
Guesthouse, **7**
Shunhe Hotel, **1**
Soma Hostel, **9**
Riverside Hotel, **10**
Traffic Hotel, **15**

FOOD
Chen Mapo Doufu, **4**
Gesar Tibetan Cafe, **17**
High Fly Cafe, **14**
Jade Forest Tasty Kebabs, **18**
Paul and Dave's Oasis, **12**
Vegetarian Restaurant, **3**
Yixiang Shunhe Cafe, **2**

ENTERTAINMENT
Carol's by the River, **13**
Chengdu Soccer, **5**
Companions Island, **11**
Elegant Rhythm, **6**
The Little Bar, **19**
MGM, **8**

TO GIANT PANDA
BREEDING RESEARCH
CENTER (16km)

TO WOLONG NATURE
RESERVE (100km);

Shahe River 沙河

North Train Station

Chengdu
Local Bus
Station

Rongbeishangliu
Dadao

Chengdu
North Bus
Station

Zhan Si Lu 占四路

Erhuan Lu Bei Sanduan

Erhuan Lu Bei Erduan

Beizhan Xi Yi Lu

Beizhan Xi Er Lu 北站西二段

赵家村西一巷 Xiaojiacun Si Xiang
赵家村西二巷 Beizhan Xi Yi Xiang
赵家村西一巷 Xiaojiacun San Xiang
赵家村西二巷 Beizhan Xi Er Xiang
赵家村三巷 Beizhan Xi San Xiang
赵家村三巷 Xiaojiacun Er Xiang

Yihuan Lu Bei Erduan

二环路北二段

二环路北一段

Yihuan Lu Bei Sanduan
Xinghui Zhong Lu Xinghui Dong Lu

Hongxing Bei Lu

Jianshe Bei Lu

East Suburb
Stadium

Sanyou Lu

Xinzhu Lu
聚菊路

Jiefang Bei Lu

Gymnastics
Park

Chenghua Jie
成华街

Da'an Lu

Wenshu
Monastery
文殊院

Renmin Bei Lu

Madao Jie

Tongshun Jie
Yuquan Jie
玉泉街

Desheng Lu

Fangzheng Jie

Renmin Zhong Lu

Wenwu Lu 文武路

Zhenghu
Bank
of China

CYTS

Tourism
Bureau

Xi Yulong Jie

Renmin Zho

Renmin Zhong Lu

Qinglong Jie

Jianghan Jie

Wangjiatang
Ningxia Jie

Babao Jie

Dongchenggen

West Suburb
Stadium

Jiaoda Lu 交大路

Shawan Lu 沙湾路

TO CHADIANZI
BUS STATION (2.3km);
TO DUJIANGYAN (56km);
TO QINGCHENGSHAN
MOUNTAIN (50km);
TO FOUR MAIDENS
MOUNTAINS (160km)

Yingmenkou Lu 营门口路

Yihuan Lu Bei Yiduan

Xi Dao Dajie

Shihui Jie 石灰街

Xi Dao Dajie

Tomb of
Wang Jian

Huaihu Jie

Yongling Lu 永陵路

Yihuan Lu Xi Sanduan

Fuqin Xi Lu 抚琴西路

Qingjiang Dong Lu 清江东路

Modi River

Tomb of
Wang Jian

Hospital of Chengdu
Medical College

Yihuan Lu Xi Sanduan

Liao River

Modi River

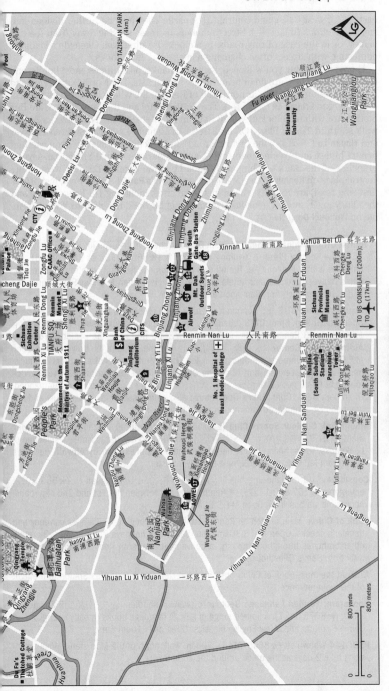

TO TAZISHAN PARK (4km)

Shunjiang Lu 顺江路

Wangjianglou Park 望江楼公园

Fu River

Sichuan University 四川大学

Yihuan Lu Dong Wuduan 一环路东五段

Dongfeng Lu 东风路

Dong'an Bei Jie 东安北街

Pool

Xshengti Bei Jie

Wangping Jie 望平街

Dong'an Nan Jie

Fu River

Shengli Dong Lu 胜利东路

Qinglong Zhengjie 青龙正街

Zhongdong

Hongxing Zhong Lu 红星中路

Fuxing Jie 复兴街

Fuyu Jie 福宇街

Daci Si Lu 大慈寺路

Shanqi Jie 商启街

Kangshi Jie 康石街

Dong Dajie 东大街

Tianmaoqiao Lu

Shijie Jie

Shulin Jie 书林街

Zhimin Lu 致民路

Qingjianshang Jie

Yihuan Nan Lu Yiduan 一环南路一段

Palace

Xinglongjie

Zongfu Lu 总府路

Zongfu Jie 总府街

Tidu Jie 提督街

cheng Dajie

CAAC Office

CITY (i)

Xiping Jie 西平街

Chunxi Lu 春熙路

Zhanqian Lu 占前路

Xinnan Lu 新南路

Kehua Bei Lu 科华北路

Binjiang Dong Lu 滨江东路

Linjiang Dong Lu 临江东路

Longjiang Xi Lu 龙江西路

Yuanyuan Nan Lu 园园南路

Renmin Dong Lu 人民东路

Renmin Xi Lu 人民西路

Renmin Nan Lu 人民南路

Renmin Nan Lu 人民南路

Sichuan Exhibition Center 四川展览馆

Renmin Market

Shengli Xi Lu 胜利西路

Lihua Jie 利华街

Xinguanghua Jie 新光华街

Bank of China 中国银行

CITS (i)

TIANFU SQ. 天府广场

Guangda Hang 光大行

Qingshi Qiao 青石桥

Fu Lu 府路

Binjiang Zhong Lu 滨江中路

Linjiang Zhong Lu 临江中路

New South Gate Bus Station 新南门汽车站

Mt. Dak Outdoor Sports

Airwolf

Jianzhu Lu 建筑路

Daxue Lu 大学路

Daxue Lu 大学路

Sichuan Provincial Museum 四川省博物馆

Yihuan Lu Nan Erduan 一环路南二段

Kehua Xi Lu 科华西路

Chenghe Xi Lu

Chenghe Dong Lu 成河东路

TO US CONSULATE (200m); (17km)

S I C H U A N

Sichuan

Monument to the Martyrs of Autumn 1911

Binjiang Auditorium

Shaanxi Jie 陕西街

Dongsheng Jie 东升街

People's Park 人民公园

Fangchi Lu 方池路

Xidong Dajie

Wenmiao Houjie 文庙后街

Wenmiao Qianjie 文庙前街

Tunbing Jie 屯兵街

Jinjiang Binjiang Yi Lu

Binjiang Xi Lu 滨江西路

Linjiang Xi Lu 临江西路

Nan Dong Jie 南东街

Xiao

Huaxing Jie 华兴街

Jinjiang Dong Lu 锦江东路

Jianchi Jie 建池街

No. 1 Hospital of Huaxi Medical College 华西医科大学第一医院

Nanjiao (South Suburb) Stadium 南郊体育场

Parachute Tower

Yulin Dong Lu 玉林东路

Yulin Dong Jie 玉林东街

Yulin Bei Lu 玉林北路

Niijiaqiao Lu 倪家桥路

Fangcao Jie 芳草街

Yihuan Lu Nan Sanduan 一环路南三段

Yulin Xi Lu 玉林西路

Ximingqiao Jie 西珉桥街

Jinjiang Nanpu Dong Lu 锦江南浦东路

Wuhouci Dajie 武侯祠大街

Nanpu Dong Jie 南浦东街

Wuhouci Heng Jie 武侯祠横街

Xiaotianzhu Jie

Nanpu Zhong Lu

Wenhui Qianjie 文汇前街

Wenhui Houjie 文汇后街

Nanpu Zhong Jie 南浦中街

Nanjiao Park 南郊公园

Wuhou Temple 武侯祠

AOWEI

Wuhou Dong Jie 武侯东街

Yihuan Lu Nan Siduan 一环路南四段

Qingyang Temple 青羊宫

Baihuatan Park 百花潭公园

Du Fu's Thatched Cottage 杜甫草堂

Qingyang Zhengjie 青羊正街

Huanhua Creek 浣花溪

Nanpu Xi Lu 南浦西路

Yihuan Lu Xi Yiduan 一环路西一段

Yongfeng Lu 永丰路

800 yards

800 meters

east (东), west (西), and central (中) parts. They may be further divided into smaller sections (duàn; 段). Street numbers increase moving away from the city center, or in the case of ring roads, in a clockwise direction. Chengdu's layout is confusing, with streets often changing names every few blocks.

Almost everything you will need, including banks, post offices, most hotels, and transportation hubs, are on or near the city's main axis. The North Bus Station and the train station sit at the far north end of Renmin Lu, where it intersects the second ring road **Erhuan Lu** (二环路). The Traffic Hotel and the New South Gate Bus Station are within a block of where Renmin Lu intersects the Nan River, a 20min. walk south of Tianfu Plaza. On the stretch of Renmin Lu between the Nan River and **Yihuan Lu** (一环路 ; the first ring road), near Sichuan University, you can find many Chinese and Western bars, cafes, and restaurants. Inside Yihuan Lu, several branches of the Bank of China and China Post line Renmin Lu. Just west of the central plaza on **Renmin Xi Lu** (人民西路) is **People's Park.** Farther west, just off the first ring road, are the city's main historical sites, including Du Fu's cottage and the Qingyang Temple. Chengdu's Tibetan neighborhood lies next to Wuhou Temple on **Wuhouci Dong Jie** (武侯祠东街).

Tourist Office: China Chengdu Tourism Bureau (chéngdūshì lǚyóu jú; 成都市旅游局), 267 New Century Plaza, 6 Xiyulong Jie, 26th fl. (☎8658 2358 or 8662 2065). The entrance is at 2 Xiyulong Jie. The office's main purpose is quality control; it settles disputes between tourists and hotels or travel agencies. Open M-F May-Sept. 8am-noon and 2:30-6pm; Oct.-Apr. 8am-noon and 2-5:30pm.

Travel Agencies: CITS, 65 Renmin Nan Lu, Er Duan (☎8666 9111). Open M-F 8:30am-8pm, Sa-Su 9am-6pm. **CYTS** (chéngdū zhōngguó qīngnián lǚxíngshè; 成都中国青年旅行社), 43 Renmin Zhong Lu, Er Duan (☎8606 6633), in the corner of **Yongxing Airline Tickets Center** (永兴航空售票中心) on the 7th fl. of the Baiyun Hotel. Open M-F 9am-6pm. Three travel agencies in the **Traffic Hotel** specialize in tours to Emeishan, Jiuzhaigou, Leshan, and Tibet. The **Chengdu Tianfu International Travel Service** (chéngdū tiānfǔ guójì lǚxíngshè; 成都天府国际旅行社) is especially recommended. Open daily 8am-10pm. **Sam's Guesthouse** also arranges similarly priced tours and is a great source of unbiased information about travel in Tibet.

Mount Dak Outdoor Sports Club (gāoshān hùwài tànxiǎn lǚyóu zhuāngbèi zhuānyíng diàn; 高山户外探险旅游装备专营店), next door to the Traffic Hotel. A selection of backpacks, tents, hiking boots, fleece, and other supplies. Also try **Airwolf,** down the street from Mt. Dak, or **AOWEI,** next to Holly's Hostel.

Consulates: US (měiguó lǐngshìguǎn; 美国领事馆), 4 Lingshiguan Lu (☎558 3992, emergency ☎137 800 1422), off Renmin Nan Lu, between the 1st and 2nd ring roads. Accessible via bus #16. Open M-F 8:30am-6pm.

Bank of China: Main branch on Renmin Lu, near Qinglong Jie. Exchanges currency and traveler's checks. Open M-F 8:30am-6pm, Sa-Su and holidays 8:30am-5pm. There are other branches throughout the city; a convenient one is on Renmin Nan Lu, a 5min. walk from Sam's Guesthouse.

ATM: At the main Bank of China branch and at New South Gate Bus Station to the right of the main entrance.

Bookstore: Foreign Language Bookstore (wàiwén shūdiàn; 外文书店), 5 Zongfu Lu, 3rd fl. (☎8675 0437). A limited range of foreign language books (mostly in English) on Chinese culture and a few English classics. Open daily 10am-6pm.

PSB: 144 Wenwu Lu (☎8640 7114), 20min. walk north of the Mao statue. Visa extensions take 2 days at the office around the corner.

Hospitals: Sichuan People's Hospital (sìchuān shěng rénmín yīyuàn; 四川省人民医院), 32 Yihuan Xi Lu, Er Duan (☎8776 9982). **No. 1 Hospital of Huaxi Medical College** (huáxī yīkēdàxué fùshǔ dìyī yīyuàn; 华西医科大学附属第一医院), 37 Guoxue Xiang (☎8555 1255). **Hospital of Chengdu Chinese Traditional Medical College,** 17 Shi'erqiao Lu (☎8776 9902).

Pharmacy: Tongrentang Pharmacy (tóngréntáng yàodiàn; 同仁堂药店), 1 Zongfu Lu (☎8675 7454), 3min. from the Holiday Inn Crowne Plaza. Mostly Chinese medicine, with some Western medicine and supplies. Chinese doctor upstairs. Open daily 8:30am-9:30pm.

Internet Access: The **Traffic Hotel** has 5 terminals. Y10 per hr. **Sam's** (Y6 per hr.) and **High Fly Cafe's** Linjiang Lu location (1st 30min. free, Y10 per hr. after that) each have 1 terminal. Otherwise, look for the characters 网吧 (wǎngbā; "Internet cafe").

Post and Telecommunications: Chengdu Post Office, 80 Renmin Nan Lu, on the 2nd fl. of Jinjiang Hotel. Offers EMS. Open 8am-6pm. The branch on Shawan Lu has both EMS and Poste Restante.

Postal Code: 610000.

ACCOMMODATIONS

Two establishments have become backpacker favorites in Chengdu: the Traffic Hotel and Sam's. Holly's Hostel is a close third. Several other hotels and guesthouses in the area offer low- to mid-range rooms but lack comprehensive tour services and easy access to travel information.

■ **Traffic Hotel** (jiāotōng fàndiàn; 交通饭店), 6 Linjiang Zhong Lu (☎8545 1017; fax 8544 0977). On the south bank of Nan River, near Renmin Nan Lu, a 20min. walk south of Tianfu Plaza. From the North Train Station, take bus #55 or 28 to the New South Gate Bus Station; the hotel is next door. Clean rooms with A/C and TV. Most of the friendly staff speak English. Along with a central location, Traffic Hotel offers 4 travel agencies, Internet access (Y10 per hr.), bike rental (Y15 per day), self-service laundry (Y10 per load), and the chance to meet many other travelers. 3-bed dorms Y40; standard rooms with breakfast included Y200. MC/V. ❶

■ **Sam's Backpacker Guesthouse** (chéngdū róngchéng fàndiàn; 成都蓉城饭店), 130 Shanxi Jie (☎8615 4179; www.samtourchina.com). Attached to the Rongcheng Hotel, near People's Park. Look for "Sam's Guesthouse registration" to the left of the Rongcheng Hotel. Rooms are spacious and clean. Popular among travelers for both its price and comprehensive tour services. Cafe and currency exchange. 2-bed dorms with attached bath and A/C Y40. ❶

Holly's Hostel (chéngdū jiǔ lóng dǐng qīngnián kèzhàn; 成都九龙鼎青年客栈), 246 Wuhouci Dajie (☎8554 8131 or 8554 0492; fax 8554 8131), a little bit down and across the street from Wuhou Temple. Feels like a college student center, complete with billiard tables and fish tanks. Run by the same people as Sam's, Holly's Hostel offers cheaper and more basic rooms, with the same tour services, English-speaking staff, laundry, and bike rental (Y100 deposit, Y15 per day). 8-bed dorms Y20; 4-bed Y30. ❶

Shunhe Hotel (shùnhé jiǔdiàn; 顺和酒店 ; ☎8317 2886; fax 8317 5509), Erhuan Bei Lu, Er Duan. A 2-star hotel west of the North Train Station. Pristine rooms with private baths, Western toilets, and beautiful carpeting. A/C, IDD phones, refrigerators, and TVs. 2 travel agents inside. Popular hotpot and barbecue eatery and a Sichuanese restaurant next door. Breakfast included. Doubles Y180. Student discounts available. ❷

SICHUAN

Riverside Hotel (bīnjiāng fàndiàn; 滨江饭店), 16 Binjiang Zhong Lu (☎8665 1565; fax 8665 6009). From the North Train Station, take bus #16 to Jinjiang Hotel; walk 3min. to the left. More spacious than the Shunhe Hotel. Rooms have A/C; private baths have Western-style toilets. Breakfast included. Doubles Y180. MC/V, but cash preferred. ❷

Soma Hostel (suǒmǎhuā jiǔdiàn; 索玛花酒店), 81 Nan Dajie, 6th fl. (☎8611 3500). Take bus #16 to Jinjiang Hotel, go to the right along Binjiang Lu, and turn right onto Nan Dajie. Rooms are very basic but clean. 24hr. hot water, free Internet. 3-bed dorms Y25; standard rooms Y98. Students Y10 discount. ❶

🍴 FOOD

A Chengdu policy that outlaws all forms of street vending has tamed the busy open-air scene common to Chinese cities. With street markets on Chunxi Lu and near the People's Park quieted, people must take their empty stomachs to excellent but less exciting restaurants. Various kinds of sweet dumplings and porridge are available in many shops along the downtown shopping strips.

Sichuan is famous for its spicy **hotpot** (huǒguō; 火锅), a cook-it-yourself meal over a pot of soup, frothing red with peppers. Although Chongqing's hotpot is better known, Chengdu's hotpot scene can hold its own. Sichuan's peppers are as flavorful as they are hot, and many tastes are available, often listed on menus next to the name of the dish. Streetside restaurants will generally cook meals for Y20 per person, or sell food grilled on a stick for Y2-4 each. There is also a strip of more upscale establishments in the Sichuan Opera district along **Qintai Lu**, on the eastern edge of Cultural Park.

Other famous plates include *mápó dòufǔ* (麻婆豆腐), a spicy tofu and pork dish, and *fūqī fèi piàn* (夫妻肺片), beef slices and tripe lathered in spices and hot oil. Most regional specialties have their own original stores, including **Dan Dan Noodles** (dāndān miàn; 担担面), on the first section of Renmin Zhong Lu. **Lai Tang Yuan** (lài tāngyuán; 赖汤圆 ; ☎8662 9976), on Zongfu Jie, right next to the Holiday Inn Crowne Plaza Hotel and Parkson Shopping Center, specializes in *tāngyuán*, sweet, sticky balls of dough, with sugary, ground black sesame filling (Y2 for 6). At **Zhangcha Duck Restaurant** (zhāngchá yāzi; 樟茶鸭子), next door to Lai Tang Yuan, a plate of their famous duck costs Y10-15.

🏠 **Paul and Dave's Oasis**, 21/1 Binjiang Zhong Lu (☎8950 0646; dave_oasis@163.com), across the river from the Traffic Hotel. With graffiti-covered walls, plush couches, and Western music from breakbeat to flamenco, the Oasis is a watering hole in a desert of spices. The owner is an affable former professor of Chinese philosophy who cooks up a mean pizza (Y20-30) as well as delicious Chinese dishes. A great place to meet other travelers (Paul is keen on introducing them to each other) and get advice on daytrips. Open daily 10am until the last customer leaves. ❷

Vegetarian Restaurant (sùcài cānguǎn; 素菜餐馆), 15 Wenshuyuan Jie (☎8693 2018). This delicious vegetarian restaurant is inside Chengdu's largest Buddhist monastery, Wenshu Monastery, and to the right. Plenty of excellent vegetarian specialties skillfully disguised as Sichuanese meat dishes (Y10-50 per dish). English menu. Open daily 10:30am-8:30pm. ❷

Yixiang Shunhe Cafe (yìxiāng shùnhè cāntīng; 溢香顺和餐厅), 6 Erhuan Lu, Er Duan (☎8317 5006), left of Shunhe Hotel. Cool and calm next to the madness of Chengdu North Station. Basic Sichuanese menu, with snacks available. Friendly proprietor. ❶

High Fly Cafe (gāofēi kāfēi; 高飞咖啡), 18 Linjiang Zhong Lu (☎8544 2820). Down the street from Traffic Hotel. After dinner, stuff down a brownie à la mode (Y10). Western and Chinese food. Imported beer and Internet. High Fly throws Saturday night parties with dancing and live music that run until morning. New branch at 18 Binjiang Lu, just east of Renmin Lu along the river, across from the Traffic Hotel. Specializes in pizza (Y15-32; delivery available) and Italian food. Pink decor and jazz music. English spoken. Open daily 8:30am-1am. ❷

Jade Forest Tasty Kebabs (yù lín chuànchuàn xiāng; 玉林串串香) on Xinnan Lu behind New South Gate Bus Station and a block down the street. This little hotpot place is a big favorite with locals, boasting a wide selection of animal organs and meat and vegetables for the less daring. Pot Y10, additional Y0.1 per kebab. Open 8:30am-10pm. ❶

Chen Mapo Doufu (chén mápó dòufū diàn; 陈麻婆豆腐店), 197 Xi Yulong Jie (☎8662 7005; www.chenmapo.com), right smack in the city center, north of the Chengdu Stadium; take bus #16. Chen Mapo Doufu is famous around Chengdu for its delicious spicy tofu (mápó dòufū, Y6) and other Sichuan specialties. Other location at 141 Qingyang Zheng Jie. Open daily 10:30am-9pm. ❶

Gesar Tibetan Cafe (gésà'ěr zàng cānbā; 格萨尔藏餐吧), 5 Wuhouci Heng Jie (☎8994 8369), at its corner with Ximianqiao Heng Jie. In the center of Chengdu's Tibetan neighborhood, Gesar offers a simple menu of Tibetan fare. Try the famous Tibetan dumplings (Y10) while you catch up on the latest Himalayan VCDs. Open 7am-midnight. ❷

🍵 TEA GARDENS

Tea-drinking, accompanied by card-playing, *mahjong*, and gossiping, ranks among the favorite pastimes of Chengdu's residents. The city's endless cacophony of bicycle bells and car horns fade away in the tea gardens found in virtually every park. Just Y3-8 can buy a little peace of mind.

One of Chengdu's most attractive tea gardens is in secluded **Wangjianglou Park** (wàngjiānglóu yuán; 望江楼园), near Sichuan Union University. (Entrance Y2. Tea Y4.) For a more buzzing and energetic tea garden, crowds gather at **People's Park** (rénmín gōngyuán; 人民公园), along Jinhe Lu, in the early afternoon and evening in a tea pavilion by a lake shaded by willow trees. (Entrance free. Tea Y5.) For a more secluded and introspective sipping experience, check out the park surrounding the **Tomb of Wang Jian** (wángjiànmù; 王建墓), in the northwest of the city. Enjoy your beverage in a pavilion over a lily pond. (Entrance Y3. Tea Y3.) Or, when running around town, look for the big character *chá* (茶).

👁 SIGHTS

▨DU FU'S THATCHED COTTAGE (dùfū cǎotáng; 杜甫草堂). Chengdu's most famous cultural relic is only a few blocks west of Qingyang Temple. During the chaotic An Lushan Rebellion that divided the Tang and Late Tang Dynasties, Du Fu (AD 712-770), also known as the "Poet Saint," escaped to Chengdu and wrote about his harsh life in exile during his four-year stay. The legendary poet produced roughly 240 poems, including the famous "verse for the destruction of my thatched-roof cabin by the autumn windstorm." The cottage today is a replica, and most of the majestic present-day buildings were built after Du Fu's time here. However, the sheer beauty and mystique of the maze-like grounds makes this site a very worthwhile visit. (Entrances on Qinghua Lu and Caotang Lu. Open daily summer 7am-7pm; winter 7:30am-6:30pm. Y30, young children and disabled travelers free.)

QINGYANG TEMPLE (qīngyáng gōng; 青羊宫). Qingyang Temple, or the Green Ram Monastery, is one of China's most famous Daoist temples and an active center of worship for Chengdu and the surrounding region. The giant "Hall of Hunyuan Originator" houses a deified Laozi, who holds a large golden ring representing the state of chaos before creation. In the central courtyard sits the

remarkable "Eight Diagrams Pavilion," a wooden structure built entirely without nails. Dragon lovers will appreciate the 81 carvings of the mythical creature surrounding the pavilion. The main building, the "Hall of Three Purities," contains statues of the supreme Daoist deities and the 12 golden immortals. Vegetarian food (Y10-30), tea (Y5), and accommodations are all available on the temple grounds. *(9 Yihuan Lu, near the West Gate. Open daily 7:30am-8:30pm. Y5.)*

PEOPLE'S PARK (rénmín gōngyuán; 人民公园). Near the city center, People's Park is—as its name suggests—heavily populated by Chengdu urbanites. The bustling park is no quieter than the city just outside its gates, but it makes for delightful people watching. Sectioned-off gardens shelter plums, flowers, crabapples, bonsai, and of course, a tea house. Families take small boats out on the lake at the center of the park. A 31m tall monument honors those who perished during the Xinhai Revolution in 1911, when Chengdu residents fought imperial powers to build the Chengdu-Chongqing railway. *(From Tianfu Plaza, walk 5min. east along Renmin Dong Lu. Open daily summer 6am-10:30pm; winter 6:30am-10pm. Boat rental Y20 per 30min. Free admission, except during flower exhibitions.)*

GIANT PANDA BREEDING RESEARCH CENTER (dàxióngmāo fánzhí zhōngxīn; 大熊猫繁殖中心). The breeding center contains 12 to 13 adorable giant and red pandas housed in a pseudo-natural environment where, besides lounging, sleeping, and napping, the pandas enjoy climbing trees and eating. Come between 8:30 and 10:30am to see them while they are being fed and are most active. Otherwise, it's hard to catch a glimpse of them in their large forested arenas. For a much more intimate encounter with the pandas, head for the **Wolong Research Center** (p. 702), where smaller pens bring you closer to the animals. The **Giant Panda Museum** also features life-size dioramas and detailed information on the evolution, feeding, and mating behavior of pandas, not to mention an exhibit displaying one lucky panda's carefully preserved reproductive organs. Bird-lovers can stroll by **Swan Lake** to check out the black-necked crane enclosure, which also has peacocks. *(About 16km northeast of the city center. No buses. Taxis Y40-90. Bike ride to the center 3-4hr. Or take bus #9 to the zoo; from there a taxi is Y10 and a pedicab Y5-10. Traffic Hotel runs tours for Y50, including admission and transportation. ☎8351 6748. Open daily 8am-8pm. Y30.)*

WUHOU TEMPLE (wǔhòu cí; 武侯祠). Over 1500 years old, Wuhou Temple is holy ground to Chinese people who have grown up with the stories from *Romance of the Three Kingdoms*, whether as a history lesson, novel, or TV series. To those unfamiliar with the story, it may be less interesting. The famous sight honors Zhuge Liang (诸葛亮 , AD 181-234), the outstanding prime minister of Shu who briefly set up Chengdu as the capital city. Surrounded by manicured gardens, green lawns, and a large red wall, the Wuhou Temple houses over 40 stone tablets, the most valuable of which is **The Tablet of Three Wonders,** carved during the Tang Dynasty (AD 618-907). The 41 clay statues, each 1.7 to 3m high, are the temple's most captivating aspects. Apart from gold-coated statues and traditional paintings, Liu Bei's tomb can be also found here. Be sure to check out the **Display Hall of Three Kingdoms Culture,** with a collection of sculptures, ink rubbings, and maps. *(231 Wuhouci Jie, in the southwest, across the Nan River from the downtown area. Accessible by buses #1, 10, 26, 53, and 59. ☎8555 2397. Open daily 7am-7:30pm. Admission includes Nanjiao Park next door. Y30, young children and seniors 70+ free.)*

WENSHU MONASTERY (wénshū yuàn; 文殊院). Founded in the Sui Dynasty (AD 589-618), Wenshu is a maze of gardens, shrines, and some 400 Buddhist statues gazing upon incense-filled courtyards. Some, like the fine iron figures of the 10 *bodhisattvas*, are recognized as great works of art. To overdose on buddhas, check out the **Thousand Buddha Pagoda** and **Hall of 500 Arhats**. The monastery is an ideal place to have a cup of tea (Y2-3) if you enjoy watching card-playing locals. Come earlier to dine at the vegetarian restaurant (p. 696), or catch the monks chanting at 5pm daily. *(On Wenshuyuan Jie, close to Renmin Zhong Lu, north of the city center. Accessible by buses #16, 55, and 64. ☎693 2375. Main gate open daily 8am-5:40pm. Y1.)*

WANGJIANGLOU PARK (wàngjiānglóu; 望江楼). Wangjianglou Park (also called River-Viewing Park) is dedicated to the famous Tang poet Xue Tao, one of the few women in the classical Chinese literary pantheon. The park is a peaceful, less-crowded alternative to People's Park. Climb to the top of its elegant pagoda (Y3) for a wonderful view of the Fu River and the surrounding area. The park also offers visitors a serene tea garden, a famous well, Xue Tao's tomb, and Qing Dynasty architecture. Over 150 species of bamboo, some rare, have earned the park the name "Kingdom of Bamboo of Endless Charms." *(On Wangjiang Lu, near Sichuan University. Accessible by bus #35 and #19. Open daily 6am-9pm. Y2.)*

TOMB OF WANG JIAN (wángjiàn mù; 王建墓). Revered for his bravery, wisdom, and kindness, Wang Jian (AD 847-918) climbed the military ranks to become emperor of the Shu Kingdom. Originally built into a small hill, his mausoleum is reputed to be the largest of the royal tombs from the Five Dynasties and Ten Kingdoms Period (AD 907-979). Today, only the stone platform upon which Wang Jian's coffin once rested still remains. Exquisite stone reliefs depicting ancient Chinese musical instruments decorate the platform. The mausoleum isn't much of an attraction, but follow the narrow bamboo-lined paths to well-kept gardens, collections of bonsai trees, and pavilions where you can enjoy a cup of tea. *(5 Fuqin Dong Jie, inside the 1st ring road and northwest of downtown. Accessible by bus #48. ☎8778 8888. Open daily 8am-5pm. Park Y3, tomb Y15.)*

🎵 🍷 ENTERTAINMENT AND NIGHTLIFE

From Sichuan opera to soccer matches, from bass-thumping discos to laid-back folk and rock venues, Chengdu's nights are always busy. A number of **Western-style bars** and **cafes** light up Linjiang Zhong Lu, along the Nan River. Students crowd a strip of bars along Renmin Nan Lu, Si Duan, just south of the first ring road. For the club scene, be sure to check out the newly renovated **Red Generation** (hóng sè niándài; 红色年代), on the corner of Renmin Nan Lu and Nijia Qiao. The cafes at Sam's Guesthouse and Paul's Cafe are also tried-and-true standbys, if you feel like kicking back with other travelers over cheap beer and VCDs. Of course, no one should overlook a pleasant walk by the river or a lazy cup of tea in one of Chengdu's many parks.

Elegant Rhythm of the Shu Wind (shǔ fēng yǎyùn; 蜀风雅韵), 23 Qintai Lu (www.shufengyayun.com), in Qingyang Temple. Although expressly for tourists, the nightly Sichuan opera (sì jù; 四剧) provides a colorful sampling of Sichuan's traditional performing arts. Acrobatics, face-changing, fire-breathing, puppetry, *erhu* (Chinese 2-string violin), and hand-shadow performances, accompanied by tea and peanuts, round out the evening. The Traffic Hotel offers a discounted package of Y80 for admission and transportation. Shows 8pm nightly.

MGM (měi gāo měi; 美高美), Yanshikou Guangchang, Lihuai Jie, 5th fl. (☎8666 6618; www.scmgm.com), just south of Tianfu Sq. and east of Renmin Nan Lu. A bevy of hostesses in orange dresses welcomes you to this posh and pumping nightclub. Chengdu's young and hip come here for casual encounters at the face bar, American hip-hop karaoke, and dancing to Chinese pop disco. Live, international DJs attract a full house Friday and Saturday nights. Beer Y20 and up. Open daily 8pm-2am.

SICHUAN

Companions Island on Jin River (jīnjiāng bàn dǎo; 锦江伴岛), Binjiang Zhong Lu, along the river bank. Cross the street, but not the river, from Paul and Dave's Oasis. Sip imported beers (Y25) and specialty coffees (Y20-30) on the riverside patio of this pleasant cafe with full bar. Don't miss the multi-colored banana ice-cream boat, if only for its presentation (Y18). Open daily 8am-1:30am.

The Little Bar (xiǎo jiǔguǎn; 小酒馆), 55 Yulin Xi Lu (☎8556 8552; www.littlebar.org). From Renmin Nan Lu, turn west onto Yulin Dong Lu and continue straight. Having just celebrated its 7th anniversary, The Little Bar, though small, is a well-established stop in the city's nightlife. With live rock shows on the weekends, this spot gives a taste of local up-and-coming stars, set amid intimate decor. Beer Y10 and up. Open daily 2pm-late.

Carol's by the River (kǎluó xīcāntīng; 卡罗西餐厅), 2 Linjiang Zhong Lu (☎8544 9639; www.carolsbytheriver.com), off Renmin Nan Lu. Mexican food (burritos Y30), homemade cheesecake (Y12), and all night jazz and blues make Carol's a favorite among homesick backpackers. American BBQ on Friday nights and disco parties on Saturdays. Beer Y20 and up. Open daily 9:30am-midnight.

Chengdu Soccer (zúqiú bǐsài; 足球比赛). The Chengdu or Sichuan soccer teams play other cities or provinces every Saturday and Sunday evening. Season runs from Apr.-Nov. The provincial-level games have better attendance and play quality than the city games, but any match is still a blast. Games are held in the main Chengdu People's Stadium, just northeast of Tianfu Plaza, and usually start at 7pm. Tickets Y10.

▶ DAYTRIPS FROM CHENGDU

DUJIANGYAN IRRIGATION SYSTEM 都江堰水利工程

56km west of Chengdu. Buses run from the Chadianzi Bus Station (1hr., every 5min. from 6:40am on, Y8.5) or from New South Gate Bus Station (1hr., 8:30am, Y17) to Dujiangyan. From Dujiangyan Transportation, cross the street and take bus #4 (every 10min., Y1) to the Lidui Park (离堆公园) stop. Buses returning to Chengdu run until 6-7pm. Open daily 8am-6pm. Y60, children under 1.3m Y30, under 1m free.

Thousands of years ago, Li Bing, the governor of the Shu prefecture, constructed the Dujiangyan Irrigation System (dūjiāngyàn shuǐlì gōngchéng) to control the yearly flooding of the Min River, a tributary of the Yangzi. His ingenious system diverted the Min into a manmade channel through Mount Yulei, dividing it into an inner and outer river with two spillways to control flooding and collect silt. Perhaps most impressively, Li Bing engineered all this in BC 256, and since then, the region has become a land of abundance, with a yearly bumper crop.

Dujiangyan is divided into three parts: the **Fishmouth Pier** (yúzuǐ; 鱼嘴) splits the river in two; the **Flying Sands Spillway** (fēishàyàn; 飞沙堰) drains flood water and flushes out sediment deposits; and the **Mouth of the Precious Jar** (bǎopíng kǒu; 宝瓶口), or the trunk canal, cuts through Mount Yulei and diverts water to irrigate nearby farmlands. A typical tour starts at the left main gate and winds through the exhibition center and main dyke structures before crossing the beautiful **Anlan Bridge** (ānlán qiáo; 安澜桥), suspended (at least outwardly) by woven bamboo cables. Once called Fuqi (Husband and Wife) Bridge, Anla was built by a devoted couple. The locks that hold together the chain railing symbolize the pair's never-ending devotion. From the bridge, the trail heads into the hills and returns along the far bank. Up the hill and overlooking the irrigation project are temples and pavilions separated by forest and gardens, the most important of which is **Two Kings Temple** (èrwáng sì; 二王寺), built as a tribute to Li Bing and his son. The **Chenghuang Temple** is easily the most impressive structure on the hillside, with 10 levels of flying-eaved temples. You may also run into the **oldest tree in China,** measuring 3.6m across and dating back to the Yin Shang Dynasty (1700-1100 BC). Get a bird's-eye view of the whole system by continuing up to the five-story-high **Qinyan Tower** (qínyàn lóu; 秦堰楼). Buses run from Flying Sands Spillway to Fishmouth Pier (Y10 one way; Y15 roundtrip). Cable cars (Y25 per stop) run from Mount Yulei Park to Erwang Temple and Lidui Park.

Several cheap **eateries** (Y5-15 a meal) serving basic Sichuanese food line the street close to the entrance and riverfront. Although pure scenery-seekers may find Dujiangyan disappointing, the sheer ingenuity and history surrounding the ancient complex compensate for its rather drab appearance.

QINGCHENGSHAN MOUNTAIN 青城山

About 50km from Chengdu. Buses depart daily from the New South Gate Bus Station (2hr., 8:30-11am, Y26). You can also take a bus from Dujiangyan (1hr.; every 20-30min. 8am-5pm; to Qingcheng Front Mountain Y4, to Rear Mountain Y6.5). Last bus to Chengdu departs around 6pm from the main gate (Y22). ☎8728 8159. Minibuses run frequently from Front Mountain to the Rear Mountain (30min., Y5). Cable car one-way Y30, round-trip Y50. Ferry one-way Y5. Admission Y60, children under 1.3m Y30, under 1m free.

Immersed in a sea of green trees and veiled in layers of chiffon mist, Qingcheng (Green City) Mountain is so named with good reason. Qingcheng has much of the same captivating beauty as Emeishan, but without the rigorous climb. The south face of the mountain, known as **Qingcheng Front Mountain** (qīngchéng qiánshān; 青城前山) is home to many Daoist temples. The best preserved of these, **Jianfu Temple** (jiànfú gōng; 建福宫), lies at the foot of the mountain and dates back to the Tang Dynasty, when it was known as Zhangren Temple. According to myth, an immortal spirit once lived on Zhangren Mountain, practicing Daoism in seclusion. For good fortune, a king visited the Daoist Superbeing before heading into battle. He returned victorious, and built Zhangren in the immortal's honor. Today, the temple's pavilions hold ancient relics.

Halfway up Qingcheng, lies **Tianshi Cave** (tiānshī dòng; 天师洞), a mazelike temple dedicated to the Daoist master Zhang Ling. Built up on the mountainside, it eventually dips into the cave where Zhang once lived. Tianshi houses a giant gingko tree planted by Zhang Ling in the Han Dynasty and a colossal boulder that supposedly split when a sky demon hurled a lightning bolt.

The **Shangqing Temple** (shàngqīng gōng; 上清宫), a multi-layered pavilion, dominates the mountain's first peak. Among its relics, the temple counts a wood carving of the Daoist scriptures and the consecrations of three Daoist deities—the High Lord Li Laojun and Daoism's founders, Lu Chunyang and Zhang Sanfeng. From the rear of the temple, visitors can walk farther up the mountain to the six-story **Laojun Pavilion** (lǎojūn gé; 老君阁). This massive structure, the highest point on the mountain, offers a sweeping panorama of the green-clad mountains and mist below.

Stands offering water, noodles, cucumbers, and film are at each rest stop. Jianfu Temple, Tianfu Temple (entrance Y10-20), and Shangqing Temple, near the exit of the second cable car, all offer **food** and **accommodation** (Y50-80). Qingcheng Front Mountain can be done as a long daytrip out of Chengdu, or can be shortened by taking the cable car one way. Another option is to stay a night on the mountain, perhaps at Shangqing Temple, to catch the sunrise.

About 30km from Qingcheng Front Mountain is **Qingcheng Rear Mountain** (qīngchéng hòushān; 青城后山), the north face of Qingcheng. Tranquil and unspoiled, Qingcheng Rear Mountain is a more secluded and less touristed alternative to the Front Mountain. While visitors hike up the south face for its Daoist temples, the north face is better known for its natural scenery, caverns, waterfalls, gardens, and ancient graves. At the main gate of Rear Mountain, a trail winds up through **Qinan Temple** before reaching a cable car, which goes about halfway up the mountain to a small village. From here the trail continues up to **White Cloud Temple**

SICHUAN

(báiyún sì; 白云寺) near the summit. Alternatively, hike up the **Flying Springs Gorge** (fēiquán gōu; 飞泉沟) from the bottom of the cable car, passing a small lake before reaching the **Heavenly Bridge** (tiān qiáo; 天桥), which goes over a small waterfall and up to the **Cloud-Gazing Pavilion** (wàngyún tíng; 望云亭). Continue up the trail to the White Cloud Temple, passing a series of caves on the way.

WOLONG NATURE RESERVE 卧龙自然保护区

100km northwest of Chengdu. Buses go from Chengdu's Chadianzi Bus Station (3½-4hr., 11:40am, Y23) and Dujiangyan (2-3hr., 2pm, Y12). From Jiuzhaigou, take a return bus heading toward Chengdu and get off at the town of Yinxin; then take a taxi van (Y20 per person) to the town of Wolong. Take a bus to Xiaojin if you plan on hiking, since you can ask them to let you off at the trailhead for the Valley of Heroes, about 10km from the Dujiangyan bus stop. Otherwise, a ride from Wolong town can cost Y20. 2 direct buses return to Chengdu in the morning, the last at 8am (Y23). Buses return to Dujiangyan at 11am (Y12). Hail returning buses anywhere along the road through Wolong. ☎837 624 6615. Ticket center sells maps (Y5). Admission to the Giant Panda Research Center Y30.

Established by the Chinese government in the late 1970s, the Wolong Nature Reserve seeks to protect the highly endangered—and highly adorable—giant panda. The panda lives in some of the most stunning and dramatic wilderness in Sichuan, and you may find your face pressed against the glass during the entire last hour of the bus ride to the reserve.

Your chances of catching a glimpse of a panda while hiking in the wilds are extremely slim. The furry creatures are best seen in the **Giant Panda Research Center** (dàxióngmāo guǎn; 大熊猫馆), halfway up the mountain, where they can be observed in zoo-like enclosures. Many a lucky visitor can pet and even shake hands with young panda cubs, who curiously rear up to poke their muzzles and paws out through the bars. The best time to visit is 8am-3pm, when the pandas are active and more likely to take an interest in visitors. The **Red Panda Center** (xiǎoxióngmāo guǎn; 小熊猫馆), 25km farther up the mountain, is home to the less rare and more raccoon-like, but still adorable, red pandas.

Up in the mountains, pandas, golden monkeys, takins, and pheasants can be observed in their natural habitat. Even if no animals make an appearance, visitors can still find solace in Sichuan's immense forests and wilds. Wolong lacks major tourist facilities, and as a result, it offers the only real pristine hiking around Chengdu. Two of the best hikes in the area start from a bridge about 10km past the town of Wolong, which is itself about 7km past the Panda Center. Cross the bridge and hike up to the **Valley of the Heroes** (yīngxióng gōu; 英雄沟 ; 3hr.), through a beautiful gorge. To reach the second hike, head in the other direction from the roadside trailhead up to the **Yinchang Valley** (4-5hr.).

Wolong is a long haul from Chengdu, and transportation is limited, so plan on two days for this trip. Consider visiting the Panda Center on the evening of arrival and the museum next morning; then add another day for hiking. The **Panda Inn ❹** (xióngmāo shānzhuāng; 熊猫山庄 ; ☎837 624 6628) has doubles for Y320, but discounts of over 50% are possible. Alternatively, cheaper rooms can be found at the **Sitong Hotel** (sìtōng bīnguǎn; 四通宾馆 ; ☎837 624 6772) near the museum. Lodging is also available in the town of Wolong (Y30 per bed). If your only intention is to see a panda, you may want to opt to stay in Chengdu and visit the Giant Panda Breeding Research Center instead (p. 698).

FOUR MAIDENS MOUNTAINS 四姑娘山

From Chengdu, take a bus (5hr., 8:20am, Y66) to Four Maidens Mountains (sì gūniáng shān) from Chadianzi. The Traffic Hotel runs 3-day tours with transportation, accommodations, admission, and guides for Y480.

About 100km past the town of Wolong, the Four Maidens Mountains offers pristine, virtually untouristed hiking and camping opportunities. Higher in elevation than Wolong, the mountains are traversed by three main hiking trails, beginning in Rilong, where hostels have dorm beds for Y20 to 30. The hikes ascend through wildflower-filled meadows and alpine forests, all dominated by the glittering majesty of the four jagged snow-mantled peaks. The tallest crag juts up at 6240m, while the lowest of the mountain looms more gently, with a slope that can be climbed in several days. Though food and accommodations are available, expect to camp while you are scaling any significant distances, or stay on the lower trails and make day hikes.

LESHAN MOUNTAIN 乐山   ☎0833

The bustling city of Leshan, with a population of six million, becomes even more crowded each summer, when hordes of tourists descend upon the city to visit the celebrated Big Buddha—the tallest stone statue in the world. Once a scholarly center that produced several members of the Chinese literati, Leshan today has caught the building bug. Massive construction efforts have turned parts of the town into busy commercial centers, complete with neon signs, highrises, and glittering advertisements. In spite of these modern disturbances, Big Buddha sits serenely on a cliff face on the far shore, overlooking the city at the confluence of three major rivers. In the early morning, *tai chi* and *wushu* practitioners fill the parks and plazas along the river banks, and in the late afternoon, the young and old come to sip tea and relax with the setting sun.

⌐ TRANSPORTATION

Buses: Coming from Yibin or Zigong, you may be dropped off at **Changjiang Bus Station** (chángjiāng kèyùn zhàn; 长江客运站), just off the old Leshan bridge farther west on Jiading Lu. There are also **tour buses** coming from Emeishan which you can negotiate to hop on; most of them are heading to Zigong and Yibin. Many locals hail these buses down near Big Buddha Park, when there are no police around.

Leshan Long-Distance Bus Station (lèshān zhōngxīn chángtú qìchē zhàn; 乐山中心长途汽车站), 165 Jiading Zhong Lu (☎245 0177). Buses run roughly 7am-5pm. Luggage storage in the main lobby (6:30am-6:30pm, Y2 per day). To: **Chengdu** (1½hr., every 20min. 6:30am-7pm, Y36); **Chongqing** (6hr., every 50min. 7:10am-5:10pm, Y79-83); **Emeishan** (1hr., every 15min. 7am-6pm, Y7); **Kangding** (8-10hr., 9:30am, Y80-90); **Yibin** (6hr., 5 per day 7am-3pm, Y52); **Zigong** (4hr., every 30min. 6:30am-4pm, Y25-30).

Emeishan-Giant Buddha Bus Ticket Office (lǚyóu zhídá chē shòupiàochù; 旅游直达车售票处 ; ☎559 1549 or 280 5319), just outside of the north gate entrance to the Big Buddha park. Departs for Emeishan every 30min. 8:30am-5pm.

Local Transportation:

Buses run between Leshan's 2 ferry piers along Binjiang Lu. Local bus #3 runs from the back gate of the Wuyou Temple to Leshan, stopping at the long-distance bus station just before the end of the route; #13 runs between the Big Buddha Park and the dock area near Taoyuan Hotel, where you can catch boats to see the Big Buddha across the river.

Ferry: The cheapest and most common way to go to the Buddha from the **Leshan Dock** (lèshān gǎng; 乐山港) if you're staying in Leshan city. Y1. You can also opt for the more expensive cruise (Y30), a quick drift past the Big Buddha. After heavy rains, the boats cease operation. Minimum 10 passengers, so you may have to wait as long as 30min. Dock hours daily May-Sept. 7:30am-7:30pm; Oct.-Apr. 8am-6pm.

Speedboats: Dock on the Big Buddha side of the river, about 300km outside of the north gate entrance. 30min. tours of the Buddha and the island 8am-6pm. Y30.

Taxis: Base fare Y3, each additional km Y1. **Tricycles** charge Y1-2 every 300-500m. Most convenient if you're going from one gate to another at the Big Buddha Park, but for longer distances the local bus or taxi is suggested.

✦♦ ORIENTATION AND PRACTICAL INFORMATION

About 166km southwest of Chengdu, Leshan occupies the flat northwestern shores of the T-shaped intersection formed by the **Min** and **Dadu Rivers.** Most of Leshan's attractions are carved on or built atop the rocky embankment on the far shore facing the city. The **Leshan Bridge** (乐山大桥) farther upstream and the **Minjiang Bridge** (岷江大桥) closer to the docks connect the island banks with the city bank of the river. On the city side, **Binjiang Jie** (滨江街) runs along the waterfront, while **Jiading Lu** (嘉定路), also parallel to the Min River, flows farther inland, connecting the bus station in the north with the waterfront in the east. Farther inland still, **Renmin Lu** (人民路) crosses **Daqiao Xi Jie** (大桥西街), the road across the Minjiang Bridge.

Tourist Office: Leshan Tourism Bureau (lèshānshì lǚyóu jú; 乐山市旅游局 ; ☎213 6926, 24hr. complaints 230 2121), on Binhe Lu, in the city government's office. Open M-F 8am-6pm.

Bank of China: 36 Renmin Nan Lu, Huangjia Shan (☎212 5121). Exchanges currency and traveler's checks. Credit card advances. Open daily 8am-6pm.

ATM: At the Bank of China on Renmin Nan Lu and at another branch on Jiading Bei Lu.

PSB: On Xian Jie (☎219 3718), at Zhanggong Qiao. Open daily 9am-noon and 3-6pm.

Hospitals: Leshan People's Hospital (lèshānshì rénmín yīyuàn; 乐山市人民医院), 76 Baita Jie (☎211 9328), up the street from the Jiazhou Hotel. **Leshan City Red Cross Hospital** (lèshānshì hóng shízì yīyuàn; 乐山市红十字医院), 45 Xincun Jie (☎213 9082), appears slightly cleaner and newer than the People's Hospital. Both open 24hr.

Post Office: Post and Telecommunications Market (yóudiàn shāngchǎng; 邮电商场 ; ☎211 8384), on Yutang Jie. EMS and IDD service. Open daily 8:30am-6pm.

Postal Code: 614000.

♠ ACCOMMODATIONS

With most tourists arriving in high-rolling tour groups, individual and budget travelers are often left stranded. It is best to make Leshan a daytrip from Chengdu or Emeishan and continue on to the next destination, as it takes at most 5-6hr. to see the entire park. If you must stay overnight, your best bet is to arrive early in the day and stay across the river from the Big Buddha park in Leshan city.

The **Peach Springs Hotel** ❷ (táoyuán bīnguǎn; 桃源宾馆), 12 Binjiang Jie, near the ferry pier at Leshan dock and across from the main parking lot, is the most conveniently located for a boat ride across the river to the park. Not far from the last stop of bus #13, the hotel offers clean, bright, carpeted rooms with attached bath. (☎210 1188. Doubles Y100 and up.) Next best in terms of location and quality, the **Postal Hotel** ❷ (yóudiàn bīnguǎn; 邮电宾馆) is only a 5min. walk from the waterfront, next to the Post and Telecommunications office on Yutang Jie. (☎213 5450. Standard doubles Y130; clean triples with bath Y100.) For those who wish to stay near the Big Buddha on the opposite side of the river, try the **Jifenglou Hotel** ❷ (jífēnglóu bīnguǎn; 集凤楼宾馆), next to Lingyun Temple, near the east entrance. Though you miss out on the lively atmosphere and good food in Leshan city, the Jifenglou offers a quiet stay, a gorgeous setting, and easy access to the park. But you'll have to shell out Y35 for admission to the Eastern Buddha Capital (dōngfāng fódū; 东方佛都) every time you enter. For next day's transportation, ask any tricycle owner to take you to an informal bus stop about five minutes away on the main road outside the park. There you can hop on buses to Zigong, Yibin, and a number of other destinations, saving a trip to the city. (☎230 2807. Clean bathrooms, A/C, IDD, TV, and 24hr. hot water. Doubles with attached bath Y150.)

🍴 FOOD

Leshan is renowned for its **xiba tofu** (*xībà dòufǔ;* 西坝豆腐), said to be especially delicious because of the waters used to prepare it. Near the Peach Springs Hotel, tofu restaurants along the streets serve many variations of xiba tofu. If you're looking for an upscale environment, try **Old and Trusted Name Tofu Fishing Boat ❷** (lǎozìhào dòufǔ yúchuán; 老字号豆腐渔船), set on a quaint ship near the docks overlooking the river. For a cozy environment bubbling with the chatter of locals, head to **Xiba Tofu Restaurant ❷** (xībà dòufǔ dà jiǔdiàn; 西坝豆腐大酒店), 121 Binjiang Lu (☎210 0848), a block over from the Peach Springs Hotel.

Roasted meat, veggies and dumplings (Y2-4 per bowl) can be found on the strip along the river from the pier to the Jiazhou Hotel. Visitors dine outside at the restaurants and tea houses that pack the strip (dishes Y5-15). **Leshan Dock** is busy in the late afternoon and early evening, but the waterfront is quieter.

🔆 SIGHTS

All the sights are on the two hills across the Min River, which locals say resemble a reclining Buddha, with the smaller **Wuyou Hill** as the head and **Linyun Hill** as the body. The **Big Buddha** stands where the chest would be, facing the river. Higher on Linyun Hill nestles a series of other smaller temples, quiet and undisturbed, as the hordes of tourists all descend to gawk at Big Buddha. Tricycles at the entrance will also carry you to any destination on the two hills for Y5-15. Head to **Leshan Dock** (lèshān gǎng; 乐山港) for the **ferry** (Y1) across the river.

BIG BUDDHA 大佛

Make a right off the ferry dock and walk 200m to the entrance of Lingyun Temple. Tour boats (Y30) from the Leshan pier (see Practical Information, p. 704) drift by the Big Buddha for a quick view. Ticket office open 7:30am-7:30pm. Big Buddha and Lingyun Temple including smaller temples on Linyun Hill Y40, students Y20.

The 71m-tall statue carved into red sandstone is the world's largest (and least imaginatively named) stone Buddha. Originally designed by the monk Haitong in order to control the menacing waters of the Min, Dadu, and Qingyi rivers that wreaked havoc on the people of Leshan, construction on the Big Buddha (dà fó; 大佛) began in AD 713 and was not completed until 90 years later. Despite his serene expression, untouched by wear and tear, time has taken its toll on other parts of the Enlightened One, and curious patches of body hair have sprouted up in the form of green vegetation. At the top, visitors can stick a finger into the Buddha's ear or pat his nose for good luck. Doing both at the same time is not recommended. On the way down the flight of steps from his head to his manicured toes, a white scar can be detected on the Buddha's chest, where a thief dug out a book of Buddhist scriptures and a jade statue of Avalokiteshvara.

OTHER SIGHTS

LINGYUN TEMPLE (língyún sì; 凌云寺). Built in the 7th century and also called Big Buddha Temple, Lingyun Temple pays tribute to the three famous figures who contributed to the taming of rivers—Haitong, Li Bing, and Zhao Yu. Legend has it that Haitong dug out his eyes to convey his sincerity and good faith, as well as to blind himself to the corruption of the age. Accordingly, his statue stares out empty-eyed into the hall. Li Bing built Dujiangyan reservoir (p. 700), and the mythical hero Zhao Yu slew a ferocious flood-causing river dragon. Off the main courtyard, corridors depict the history of the Big Buddha and other large Buddha statues. The small chapel next door, dedicated to a Sakyamuni statue, is carved out of just one piece of wood. *(On Lingyun Hill. Enter from the Big Buddha entrance.)*

WUYOU TEMPLE (wūyóu sì; 乌尤寺). Wuyou Hill and Lingyun Hill were attached 2000 years ago, until Li Bing, the Dujiangyan engineer, cut a waterway between them to stop the annual floods. A steep climb to the top brings you to the entrance to Wuyou Temple, guarded by four giant gods. Inside the main chapel stand gold-plated statues of the Buddha of Boundless Life, Sakyamuni, Puxian, Bodhisattva of Wisdom, and Wenshu, Bodhisattva of Behavior. The temple's best-regarded statues, Song Dynasty iron casts of the three **Saints of the West,** are further back. While in the Wuyou Temple complex, you may want to check out **Arhat Hall,** which has contemporary, life-like sculptures of the 500 *arhats. (Accessible by bridge from Lingyun Hill, or by ferry from the main pier, Y2-3. Open daily 8:30am-6pm. Y8.)*

MAHAO CAVE TOMBS (máhào yámù; 麻浩崖墓). Cave tombs were popular in Sichuan during the Han Dynasty, when people believed in ghosts and the afterlife. Along with the tombs, the museums that are interspersed throughout the compound display a number of beautiful stone carvings and various funerary objects. *(At the foot of Lingyun Hill, left of the Haoshang Bridge. Open daily May-Sept. 8:30am-6pm; Oct.-Apr. 8:30am-5:30pm. Y5.)*

EASTERN BUDDHA CAPITAL (dōngfāng fódū; 东方佛都). The museum is constructed in an Indian architectural style, complete with red earth and stylized domes. The Eastern Buddha Capital has a collection of replicated buddhas, ranging from the huge, 173m-long reclining Buddha on the hill to modern copies of statues taken from China by foreign powers. The naked *bodhisattvas* may be the most erotic sculptures in Leshan. With authentic statues all over the island, you may find that this site is not worth the price or time. *(Behind Linyun Hill, near the east gate. Either enter from Wuyou Temple and walk toward the Big Buddha, or from Linyun Temple near the north gate and walk to Wuyou Temple. Open daily 8:30am-6pm. Y35, students Y20.)*

EMEISHAN MOUNTAIN 峨眉山 ☎ 0833

Legend has it that the first monk traveled as early as AD 100 to Emeishan, one of the four holy Buddhist mountains in China. In the past, worshippers impatient to become Buddhist deities believed one could compensate for not leading a life of self-sacrifice and abstinence by leaping off Sheshen Cliff near the Golden Summit onto a rocky platform resembling Buddha's outstretched palm. Today, the devout prove their faith by fending off ferocious monkeys and chattering tour groups on their way to the various temples that are scattered throughout the peaks.

The number of temples that dot Emeishan may be impressive, but the dense forests and monumental peaks steal the show. Narrow, stone-paved trails thread through valleys latticed by waterfalls and mineral pools, ascend towering cliff faces, and unfurl vistas of layered peaks receding into the mist. In the early morning, while gazing at the rising sun over a sea of clouds, very lucky visitors may witness the phenomenon known as **Buddha's Light** (fóguāng; 佛光), when their shadows are cast from the peak into the mists before, and a colorfully glowing halo encircles the shadows. You will more likely be enveloped in Emeishan's frequent thick fog and drizzle, but the trailside scenery of jungle forest and ancient, gnarled trees will still make you feel like a mystical wanderer.

▶ TRANSPORTATION

Trains: Emeishan Train Station (éméishān huǒchē zhàn; 峨眉山火车站 ; ☎547 0699), on Mingshan Dong Lu, Shengli Town, about 4km east of Emeishan. Inconveniently located, so buses may be a better, albeit more expensive, option. To: **Chengdu** (2½hr.; 9, 10am, noon; Y22); **Chongqing** (14hr., 4am, Y79); **Kunming** (18hr.; 3, 5, 6pm; Y109) via **Panzhihua** (14hr., Y41-71); **Xi'an** (21hr., 10am, Y113).

Buses: Buses from Chengdu arrive at the Long-Distance Bus Station, but the most convenient way to depart Emeishan is from the Emeishan Passenger Transport Center, which saves you a trip into Emeishan city.

Long-Distance Bus Station (éméishān kèyùn zhàn; 峨眉山客运站 ; ☎553 6498), on Mingshan Dong Lu. To: **Chengdu** (2hr., every 10min. 7am-6:30pm, Y31); **Chongqing** (7:20, 9am; Y90); **Leshan** (30-40min., every 5min. 7am-7pm, Y7); **Yibin** (4hr.; 7:10, 10am, 1pm; Y49); **Zigong** (8 per day 7:50am-2:30pm, Y31).

Emeishan Passenger Transport Center (éméishān lǚyóu kèyùn zhōngxīn; 峨眉山旅游客运中心; ☎559 2404), 1km up the main road at the base of the mountain, near the Teddy Bear Hotel. To: **Chengdu** (2½hr., every 30min.-60min. 7:10am-6pm, Y35); **Chongqing** (7hr., 8:30am, Y95); **Leshan** (50min., every hr. 9am-5pm, Y8).

Local Transportation:

Buses from the Emeishan Passenger Transport Center leave every 30min. from 6am until the early afternoon (exact times depend on season). To: **Wannian Cable Car Station** (Y16); **Wuxiangang** and **Qingyin Pavilion** (Y11); **Leidongping Parking Lot** (1½-2hr.; Y30, Y20 down).

Cable Car: Between **Wannian Cable Car Station** and **Wannian Temple** (8-10min.); between **Leidongping Parking Lot** and **Jinding Peak** (5-8min.). Up Y40, down Y30, round-trip Y60.

Monorail: Runs between **Jinding Peak** and **Wanfo Peak,** the highest point of Emeishan at 3099m above sea level. Open 7am-6pm. Y50.

Taxis: Unmetered taxis within the city Y10. To the foot of Emeishan (past the toll booth) and the Baoguo Monastery Y10-20. Bargain.

✵ ? ORIENTATION AND PRACTICAL INFORMATION

There is little reason to stay long in Emeishan city (not to be confused with the city of Meishan), as the **Baoguo Monastery Scenic Area,** about 1.5km up the mountain along the main road, can provide lodgings and most services. **Foguang Lu** (佛光路) forms a ring around the city. Both **Wannian Lu** (万年路) and **Mingshan Lu** (明山路) run parallel to the Bowen River and intersect **Jinding Lu** (金顶路).

After the bus drops you off at the Long-Distance Bus Station in the city, take a taxi or get on a bus near the station to the Penshuichi stop (喷水池 ; Y0.5) and transfer to another bus (Y1) to reach the scenic area.

Entrance fee to Emeishan park is Y120, Y60 for students with ID and seniors over 60. Some temples charge additional admissions: **Wannian Temple,** Y10; **Fuhu Temple,** Y6; **Baoguo Monastery,** Y8; **Huazang Temple,** Y10. Plan two to three days for climbing the mountain by foot, with overnight stays in the monasteries. You can also cheat by taking advantage of buses and cable cars and complete the visit in one day.

Travel Agency: Emeishan Travel Service (éméishān lǚxíng shè; 峨眉山旅行社 ; ☎559 0528) is located in the same building as **Mount Emei Golden Journey Network Tourism Company** (jīnpài wǎngluò lǚyóu gōngsī; 金派网络旅游公司 ; www.ems517.com). Next to the Emeishan Passenger Transport Center, the government-run **Mount Emei Tourist Service Center** (lǚyóu sǎnkè fúwù zhōngxīn; 旅游散客服务中心 ; ☎559 2404) can provide the most reliable information and bus schedules. Open 6am-10pm. At the **Emeishan Passenger Transport Center,** you can directly book plane and train tickets from Chengdu without going to a travel agency.

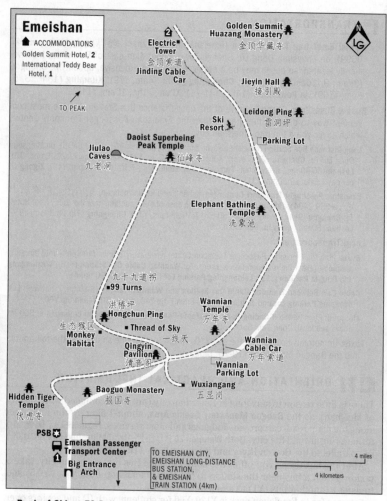

Emeishan

⌂ ACCOMMODATIONS
Golden Summit Hotel, **2**
International Teddy Bear
Hotel, **1**

↗ TO PEAK

Golden Summit ♣
Huazang Monastery ♣
金顶华藏寺

Electric ■
Tower
金顶索道
Jinding Cable
Car

Jieyin Hall ♣
接引殿

Leidong Ping ♣
雷洞坪

Ski ↙
Resort

Parking Lot

Daoist Superbeing
Peak Temple
♣ 仙峰寺

Jiulao
Caves
九老洞

Elephant Bathing
Temple ♣
洗象池

九十九道拐
■ 99 Turns

洪椿坪
♣ Hongchun Ping
■ Thread of Sky

生态猴区
Monkey ■
Habitat

Qingyin
Pavilion
清音阁

一线天

Wannian
Temple
万年寺
♣

Wannian
Cable Car
万年索道

Wannian
Parking Lot

■ Wuxiangang
五显岗

Hidden Tiger ♣
Temple
伏虎寺

♣ Baoguo Monastery
报国寺

PSB ⊞
🚌 Emeishan Passenger
Transport Center
⌂ Big Entrance
☐ Arch
↓

TO EMEISHAN CITY,
EMEISHAN LONG-DISTANCE
BUS STATION,
& EMEISHAN
TRAIN STATION (4km)

0 _____ 4 miles
0 _____ 4 kilometers

Bank of China: 73 Bailong Nan Lu (☎552 0142 or 552 3737). The only bank in town
that exchanges currency and traveler's checks. English spoken. Open daily 8am-6pm.
You can also exchange currency at a number of 4-star hotels at the base of Emeishan.

PSB: Baoguo Monastery Local Police Station (éméishān gōngānjú bàoguó sì pàichūsuǒ; 峨眉山公安局报国寺派出所; ☎559 3398). On the main road, next to the
Emeishan Passenger Transport Center. Open 24hr.

Hospital: Emeishan People's Hospital (éméishān rénmín yīyuàn; 峨眉山人民医院),
81 Santaishan Jie (☎552 2408), off Jinding Nan Lu in Emeishan city. There is also a
Dressing Station for Emergency Medical Treatment (jiēyǐn diàn yīliáo jíjiù zhàn; 接引
殿医急救站; ☎509 8074) at Jieyin Hall, near the summit.

Internet Access: The **Teddy Bear Hotel** (see **Accommodations,** below) has 2 computers
in the reception area. Y2 per 30min., Y5 per hr. Open daily 8am-10pm.

Post and Telecommunications: Post and Telecommunications Office (☎553 7217), on Suishan Zhong Lu. EMS and IDD. Open daily 8:30am-8:30pm. Another branch in the Post and Telecommunication Hotel.

Postal Code: 614200.

📷📷 ACCOMMODATIONS AND FOOD

BAOGUO MONASTERY SCENIC AREA

On the drive from Emeishan city, look for the huge archway that marks the entrance to Baoguo Monastery Scenic Area (bàoguó fēngjǐng qū; 报国寺风景区), the most convenient place to rest up and plan your hike. A strip of restaurants and hotels along the main road lead up to the temple. Six or seven blocks down after turning in at the entrance, on the left, the **International Teddy Bear Hotel ❶** (wánjù xióng jiǔdiàn; 玩具熊酒店) is tucked into a small lane. Owners Andy and Shirley, both English speakers, will provide free hiking advice, as well as a hiking stick. **Luggage storage** is free for guests; non-residents can pay a small fee. (☎559 0135 or 296 0586; teddybearcafe@yahoo.com.cn. 24hr. hot water. Free laundry machine. Dorm beds with clean shared bath Y15-30; doubles and triples with A/C, TV, and private bath Y30-60 per bed.) A number of other small guesthouses (cāntīng zhùsù; 餐厅住宿) line the same street.

The **Teddy Bear Cafe ❷**, affiliated with the hotel of the same name, is popular among foreigners for both standard Sichuanese fare (Y6-15 per dish) and Western dishes like pancakes with chocolate and banana (Y10) and Israeli salad (Y5). An English menu and an Israeli menu are available. Farther up the road from the Teddy Bear Cafe, **Climbing Moon Restaurant ❶** (dēngyuè jiǔlóu; 登月酒楼) also has an English menu and serves noodles (Y4), veggie dishes (Y6-10), and Sichuanese offerings. (☎559 0085. Open daily 6:30am-9:30pm.)

ON EMEISHAN

Almost every monastery and temple on the mountain provides lodgings with dorm beds and vegetarian refectories in large, incense-scented woodhouses. Because of the growing number of tourists in recent years, monasteries have begun charging higher prices (Y20-40 per bed), which climb with the elevation. At the same time, this has brought about better conditions, with hot showers, later hours, and private rooms (in addition to dorms) at most temples. The experience is peaceful and unique: fall asleep to the monks' soft drumming and chanting in the early evening, and wake up the next morning at 4am to the same lulling voices and birds warbling in the woods. Prices are set—no bargaining! The temples provide vegetarian meals for modest prices (Y4-7 per dish). The refectories serve breakfast 6-7am, lunch 11:30am-12:30pm, and dinner 5-6pm. Miss the meal times and you'll be left at the mercy of roadside vendors, who may charge Y7-10 for a simple bowl of noodles.

There are also a number of hotels at the summit, all of which are within a 5-10min. walk from the Huazang Monastery platform, where people gather to watch the sunrise. Prices vary from Y20-30 for dorm beds to Y200 for comfortable rooms at 4- and 5-star hotels set amid the clouds. Because the number of tourists varies greatly, low season is prime time for bargaining.

Baoguo Monastery Guesthouse (bàoguó sì sùshè; 报国寺宿舍). One of the largest monasteries on Emeishan, Baoguo, with its round archways, bonsai trees, and chanting ceremonies, is a beautiful place to begin your journey. Luggage storage. Open daily summer 6:30am-8pm; winter 7:30am-7pm. Beds Y4-6, with public showers Y10-40; doubles with private bath Y50. ❶

Hongchunping (hóngchūnpíng; 洪椿坪). The best place to stay midway up the mountain. According to one poet, the dew on the trees surrounding this quiet woodhouse collects on the passerby's coat like early morning rain. In the evening, relax by the fish pond or watch monks play chess under the trees. Clean public showers. Open 6am-10pm. Triples Y40 per bed; quads Y35 per bed. ❶

Golden Summit Huazang Monastery (jīndǐng huázàng sì; 金顶华藏寺). At the very summit of the mountain, this majestic temple stands at the center of an immense plaza, enveloped by seas of clouds on all 4 sides. The best place to stay to watch the sunrise, but expensive. No showers. Doubles Y100; triples Y120. ❷

Golden Summit Hotel (jīndǐng dà jiǔdiàn; 金顶大酒店; ☎509 8077). Walk along a path among trees from the main road to the summit to reach this quiet, well-furnished hotel, which has its own platform from which to watch the sunrise. A/C and 24hr. hot water. Doubles Y300 and up. ❹

 CLIMBING EMEISHAN

The Emeishan mountains, 7km southeast of Emeishan city, cover some 300km². In addition to the three dozen historical sites connected by 100km of trails, the 60km² park area is also a nature reserve home to red pandas, bearded frogs, and hundreds of kinds of butterflies, not to mention the bands of semi-domesticated monkey-devils that roam the trails. There are also over 3000 species of plants, including 60 varieties of Indian azaleas.

> **TIP** **WHEN MONKEYS ATTACK.** Hikers and worshippers on Emeishan have had varying experiences with the mountain's most famous residents, from being the object of their unwavering beady stare to being surrounded by monkey packs and robbed of food and camera. Roaming bands of wild monkeys are known to haunt **Xianfeng Temple,** near the summit. The **Monkey Habitat** area, past Thread of Sky, is another favorite. Bring a wooden cane (Y5) to scare off these wily creatures. Tuck into a bag all food, small bags, detachable goods, and shiny objects to attract less attention. When possible, traverse the monkey-prone areas in groups, as lone travelers are especially vulnerable.

HIKING

The traditional pilgrimage up the mountain begins at Baoguo Monastery and winds along the Emeishan foothills through terraced farmland and bamboo forest, passing Fuitu Leiyin and Shenshui temples before reaching the **Qingyin Pavilion** (qīngyīn gé; 清音阁), named after the clear sound of water cascading down the ebony stones in front of the pavilion. From here, the main trail up the mountain diverges. The left branch leads up a scenic gorge. Although this is a difficult route, including the "99 switchbacks" and greedy-monkey roadblocks, it is by far the more beautiful and awe-inspiring of the two routes, following a coursing waterfall through towering cliffs and misty jungle valleys. If you arrive in the afternoon, a quicker way to reach Qingyin Pavilion is to take the bus and cable car to **Wannian Temple** (see **Local Transportation,** p. 707) and hike back down past the White Dragon Cave (bái lóng dòng; 白龙洞) to Qingyin Pavilion. Where the path divides, take the left branch and climb past the narrow Thread of Sky (yī xiàn tiān; 一线天) and the Natural Monkey Reserve to Hongchunping. Spend the night here and wake up bright and bushy-tailed for a full-day hike to the summit. Sights along the way include the **Elephant-Bathing Pool** (xǐxiàng chí; 洗象池) and **Jieyin Hall** (jiēyǐn diàn; 接引殿), with vermilion walls and gold-tressed lanterns. From there, the ascent to the Golden Summit takes about two hours.

The right path, enclosed by forest on all sides and lacking the expansive views of the left path, passes through several important historical sites, including **Wannian Temple** (wàn nián sì; 万年寺), which dates back to the Jin Dynasty. From Wannian Temple, the hike to the peak takes two days. The left and right trails eventually converge near Jiuling Gang (Nine Peak Hill) and lead past the Elephant-Bathing Pool, Leidongping, and the Jieyin Hall to the **Golden Summit**. At the peak, the plaza surrounding **Huazang Monastery** (huázàng sì; 华藏寺) opens to a majestic panorama of cloud seas and steep drops into the mists. For those wishing a time- and knee-saving alternative, take the bus all the way up, and catch a cable car from Jieyin Hall (a 20min. walk from the bus drop-off) to the Golden Summit.

To return to Baoguo Monastery Scenic Area at the foot of the mountain, the weary can bus back down from the peak (1½-2hr.), but not before catching the sunrise at the Huazang platform. Hiking back down via Wannian Temple takes one to two days. If you have the time (4-6hr.) and energy, from Qingyin Pavilion, hike all the way back to Baoguo via the oft-neglected lowland path that passes the **Shenshui Pavilion** and **Fuitu Leiyin Temple**. As you continue down the mountain, stop to visit the **Hidden Tiger Temple** (fúhǔ sì; 伏虎寺), with pavilion after pavilion concealed under the foliage and shadows of ancient trees.

Due to the 2500m elevation difference, mountain weather can be unpredictable and much cooler (7-10°C lower) than city temperatures. The rainy season, which lasts from June to August, is the best time to visit Emeishan, when fast-fleeing clouds are accompanied by rainbows and, sometimes, the rare Buddha's Light. Make sure to bring a raincoat or an umbrella, and take special care when descending the steep steps after (or during) a rainstorm. If you wish to watch the sunrise (summer 5:30-6am, winter 7am) dress properly, as temperatures at the summit average 9°C, even in late June. You can rent parkas (Y10) at Huazang Monastery or many of the hotels near the summit.

SIGHTS

BAOGUO MONASTERY (bàoguó sì; 报国寺). Built in 1615, Baoguo, along with Fuhu, is the largest monastery on Emeishan, sitting 550m above sea level at the foot of the mountain. Originally known as the **Assembled Religions Hall,** it united the three popular belief systems of Buddhism, Daoism, and Confucianism. *Bàoguó* ("dedication to one's country") is considered one of the four acts of benevolence. The monastery's main historical relic is the 25-ton bronze **Shengji Bell,** reputedly the second-largest bell in China (after Beijing's Great Bell), and cast in 1564. During the Great Leap Forward, the bell was damaged and rendered unusable. *(Open daily summer 6:30am-8pm; winter 7:30am-7pm. Y8.)*

FUHU MONASTERY (fúhǔ sì; 伏虎寺). Named for a tiger that harassed the monastery's inhabitants, Fuhu (Hidden Tiger) Monastery is the best-kept secret on Emeishan, due to its inconvenient location for most treks. It's easily the most gorgeous monastery on the mountain, with pavilions set amid groves of ancient trees and bamboo, as well as majestic stairways leading to its temples and the Hall of Arhats. After a long trek, while away a couple of hours here, sipping tea and silently taking in the scenery. *(Open daily 6:30am-8pm. Y6.)*

WANNIAN TEMPLE (wànnián sì; 万年寺). The mountain's oldest building, dating back to the Jin Dynasty (AD 280-316), was consumed by fire in 1945, leaving only one brick chapel unscathed. Once known as Baishui Puxian Monastery, it was named after the famous *bodhisattva* Puxian (Samantabhadra), the main deity worshipped at Emeishan. In AD 980, Tang Emperor Taizong commissioned the most important statue in the temple—a bronze 7.4m statue of Bodhisattva Puxian riding atop his white elephant. Today the statue sits in **Wuliang Hall,** guarded by 1000 small copper statues of Buddha. Wannian Temple is also famous for its melodious musical frogs. Arrive early in the morning to catch these creatures in concert. *(Open daily 11am-7pm. Y10.)*

ELEPHANT-BATHING TEMPLE (xǐxiàng sì; 洗象寺). At 2100m, seated upon a small precipice with tremendous drops on both sides, Xixiang Temple used to be known as Lotus Flower Temple, because of a large rock resembling a lotus flower found there. Some years later, a medicine man reported seeing Bodhisattva Puxian bathing his white elephant in the small hexagonal pond in front of the temple. It seems doubtful that this miniscule pool could accommodate the girth of Puxian's trusty friend, but we won't argue. *(Open daily 7am-8pm. Y1.)*

GOLDEN SUMMIT HUAZANG MONASTERY (jīndǐng huázàng sì; 金顶华藏寺). First constructed during the Eastern Han, the Golden Summit Huazang Temple is a simple structure and not terribly interesting, but it provides a platform from which to admire the mystical scenery, from the distant mountains veiled with mists to the deep gorges below. All it takes to witness a dazzling sunrise over a sea of clouds is the determination to wake up at 5am, the patience to wait around in the chilly dawn, and a little luck. The starry skies to the east above the summit occasionally yield a phenomenon that the locals call the **Buddha's Lamp** (fó dēng; 佛灯), supposedly similar to the *aurora borealis.* From here, you can take the monorail to **Wanfo Peak,** Emeishan's highest point. *(Open daily 6am-7pm. Y10.)*

MOXI 磨西   ☎ 0836

Tucked in the snowy Daxueshan Mountains, about 40km away from Luding, the town of Moxi is battling growing pains. Travelers often compare Hailuogou Glacier, the sole reason for visiting Moxi, to the pristine natural scenery of Jiuzhaigou (p. 716), but, unlike its northern Sichuan neighbor (which sees nearly half a million tourists each year), little Moxi remains largely undiscovered. Plans for the future are well underway, but the town still retains its time-worn charm. Away from the frenzy and tangle of construction, old men smoke pipes, women knit furiously, and children scramble on dirt roads after chickens and ducks wandering at will. This juxtaposition of tradition and manic change makes Moxi a fascinating stop, but most travelers don't stick around for long, instead using this hilltop town as a base for trips into Hailuogou Glacier Park.

▟▞ TRANSPORTATION AND PRACTICAL INFORMATION. The town of Moxi sits on the slope of a hill and consists of three main streets, all of which run from the bottom to the top of the hill. Closest to the river is **Guojing Lu** (过境路). The central road is **Laojie Dao** (老街道), and **Buxing Jie** (步行街) is on the mountain side. There are no street signs and most residents do not use street names, as the town is small enough to navigate without them. All three roads are connected by crossroads at the top and bottom of the hill, as well as by footpaths.

Moxi is accessible only by **bus,** though there is no official bus station. The bus to **Chengdu** is the only direct transportation out of Moxi and leaves from the front of the Haiyun Hotel (6-8hr., 8:30am, Y100). For all other destinations, it is necessary first to take a taxi to **Luding** or **Kangding** and transfer from there. **Taxis** and **minibuses** wait at the top of the hill on Laojie Dao to depart for Luding (1-2hr., 7:30am on, about Y20) and Kangding (2-3hr., 7:30am on, Y40). Buses from Chengdu drop off in front of the Haiyun Hotel, up the hill on the farthest street away from the river. Buses from Luding drop off either at the Haiyun Hotel or near the Catholic Church, up the hill on the middle road.

Little Moxi hasn't quite yet made the jump to the ranks of tourist hotspots, and there are no travel agencies. Staff at the Haiyun Hotel or at one of the shops at the park entrance can help hire **guides** for two- to six-day **treks** in Hailuogou Glacier Park. Moxi has a small **clinic**, about halfway down Laojie Dao. **Golden City Pharmacy** (jīn chéng yàofáng; 金成药房), on the crossroad at the top of the hill between Buxing Jie and Laojie Dao, has very limited offerings. The **PSB** is on the middle road, set slightly off the street one-third of the way up the hill. (24hr. emergency. ☎326 6271. Open M-Sa 9am-5pm.) The **post office**, across the street from the PSB, has EMS. (☎326 6268. Open M-Sa 9am-5pm.)

⌐⌐ ACCOMMODATIONS AND FOOD. Moxi has more rooms than visitors. Hotels desperate for lodgers often offer deep discounts. Restaurants on Buxing Jie and Laojie Dao also provide rooms upstairs. These tend to be cheap (Y15) and clean, but lack attached bathrooms. Basic hotels go for Y30-50 a night.

For a special treat, stay at the colorful Tibetan-style **Kangba Hotel ❷** (kāngbā fēngqíng yuán; 康巴风情园), just next to Haiyun Hotel, on Buxing Jie. Rooms are spotless and elegant with attached bathrooms and TV. (☎/fax 326 8267. Doubles Y100, with A/C Y120.) The **Hailin Hotel ❶** (hǎilín bīnguǎn; 海林宾馆) is conveniently located at the top of the middle street, near the park entrance and taxi stand. Rooms are clean, with TV and 24hr. hot water. (☎326 6390; fax 326 6086. Y50.) **Haiyun Hotel ❶** (hǎiyùn fàndiàn; 海运饭店), is on the road farthest from the river, just before the Kangba Hotel. Rooms are spotless and cozy, though the plumbing leaves something to be desired. Ask for a room overlooking the mountains. (☎326 6503. Doubles Y75.) Halfway down the middle street, the **Golden Sea Conch Hotel ❶** (jīn hǎiluó bīnguǎn; 金海螺宾馆) has standard furnishings, beautiful views, and bathtubs. (☎326 6348; fax 326 6349. Doubles Y50.) To reach the **Glacier Restaurant and Hotel ❶** (bīngchuān fàndiàn; 冰川饭店), go up the middle road after the fork with the right road; the hotel is 100m ahead on the left. Do not confuse this hotel with the 4-star Bingchuan Fandian up the hill from Haiyun Hotel. Clean, attractive rooms and a quiet location make the Glacier Hotel a relaxing place to spend a day or two. (☎326 6266. Doubles with TV Y50.)

A number of small, cheap restaurants serve up the best and spiciest of Sichuanese cuisine. Hotpot eateries line the middle street. **Yak meat** is readily available; look for *máoniúròu* (牦牛肉). Try **Tibetan Snowlands** (xuěyù xīzàng; 雪域西藏) at the top of Buxing Jie for Tibetan food in a colorful setting.

THE LOCAL STORY

MAO IN MOXI

Mr. Yao, caretaker of Moxi's Catholic church, recalls the taking of Luding, when soldiers crawled hand over hand over a chain bridge under heavy fire—immortalized in Long March history.

In 1935, after the Zunyi Conference, Chairman Mao led the Red Army [to Moxi]. On May 28, seven or eight people came inside. One of them yelled, "Quickly prepare a bed! Chairman Mao needs to rest." On the next day Mao went to work, right here in this building. In the afternoon they met and discussed taking Luding Bridge, 60km away. The GMD were right across the bridge. The Communists had a force of 18, and lost one on the first day. After the Chairman heard this, he urged them to press on and overwhelm the GMD with fire power. Then 17 soldiers charged over the chain-links and killed the GMD. Afterwards, the Chairman and his soldiers crossed the river and over the snowy mountains to Yan'an.

During the Cultural Revolution, they destroyed things in this church, including chairs and a table used by Mao. They took away other things. We can't get them back. They said these were foreign and must be destroyed. In the 80s we restored the church to the way it used to be, but the old chairs were better.

But we should still thank the Party and Chairman Mao for liberating us, for giving us the happiness we have today.

◙ **SIGHTS.** Moxi's claim to fame is far and away Hailuogou Glacier Park, but those with extra time can visit (for novelty's sake alone) **Golden Flower Temple** (jīnhuá sì; 金花寺), back from the road in between Kampa Hotel and Haiyun Hotel. Though claiming a history of more than 1000 years, it was actually constructed in 2003 in a delightful blend of Tibetan and Chinese Buddhist traditions. A third of the way up the middle road, on the left and past the PSB, the more authentic **Catholic Church** (tiānzhǔ táng; 天主堂) has a room that Mao Zedong slept in during the Long March, just before the storming of the Luding Bridge in 1935. (Y3.) For more on the account of Mao's historic visit, see p. 713

▨ **HAILUOGOU GLACIER PARK** (hǎiluógōu bīngchuān gōngyuán; 海螺沟冰川公园). The lowest glacier in Asia, Hailuogou lies at the foot of the legendary, 7556m-tall **Gonggashan Mountain** (gònggāshān; 贡嘎山). The best way to see the park with limited time is to take the bus from the park entrance up to **Camp No. 3.** From here, catch the cable cars for a breathtaking but pricey ride up to the glacier viewing area. Because of frequent, heavy rainfall in the summer, pesky clouds and fog often obscure the peaks of the mountain. On a clear day, however, the view stretches for miles, from the ice- and snow-sealed Gonggashan, to the glittering ice cascade, where the glacier plunges 1500m, to the lower glacier, to the town of Moxi itself. Coming back down, the bus will usually sidetrack to a hotel for lunch, and then head to Camp No. 2 for the **hot springs.** Channeled into manmade pools, the hot springs are quite pleasant and free of crowds. Plan about seven hours for a complete trip. Accommodations are available inside the park but at expensive rates. It is also possible to continue down into the glacier itself if the weather is good. At this time, no trails exist within the park for independent exploration. Trekkers should inquire at the shops around the park entrance about hiring a guide. *(At the top of the hill in Moxi, turn left and walk straight for about 300m until you reach the park entrance. Tourist Service Center ☎ 326 6321. Buses from entrance to Camp No. 3 1½hr., 7:30am-6pm, Y50. Cable cars 20min., 8:30am-4pm, round-trip Y160. Those planning to visit the hot springs should bring a swimsuit with them or buy one from the shops outside the park entrance. Maps Y2. Hot springs Y65. Entrance ticket Y80, students Y60.)*

KANGDING 康定　　　　　　　　　　　　　☎0836

Tibetan nomads once traded their horses for Chinese teas in Kangding, historically the easternmost outpost of the Tibetan world. Its Tibetan name, *Dartsendo* or *Dardo*, means "at the meeting place of three mountains and two rivers." Famed in Tibet for its savvy merchants and in China for the catchy folk song, *Kangding Love Song,* today the town usually serves as a stopover point for travelers on their way to sights farther west. Though Kangding's population is predominantly Han Chinese, scents of yak butter tea and Tibetan herbs still waft through the narrow side streets. With the city's scattered temples and refreshing atmosphere and Paomashan Mountain's flowing grasslands overlooked by daunting, snow-topped peaks, Kangding deserves a few days of exploration before you barrel off along the Sichuan-Tibetan highway.

✺ ⁊ ORIENTATION AND PRACTICAL INFORMATION

The town straddles the **Zheduo River** (zhéduō hé; 折多河) and has four main bridges starting at the bottom of the hill. Most of Kangding's daily grind occurs along **Yanhe Dong Lu** (沿河东路) and **Yanhe Xi Lu** (沿河西路), running parallel to the river. Looping behind Yanhe Xi Lu from the third to the fourth bridges is **Guangming Lu** (光明路) and the greatest number of hotels. **Dong Dajie** (东大街) parallels

Yanhe Dong Lu and features many small restaurants. **Xi Dajie** (西大街) is parallel to Yanhe Xi Lu from the first to second bridge. The bus station is about a 10min. walk north from the first bridge.

Buses: The only way to get to Kangding is by bus. The **Kangding Bus Station** (kāngdìng qìchē zhàn; 康定汽车站 ; ☎283 7914), 10min. from the 1st bridge, teems with activity. To: **Chengdu** (8hr., every hr. 6am-4pm, Y112-122); **Ganzi** (12hr., 6am, Y105); **Leshan** (7hr., 6am, Y72-90); **Litang** (8hr., 7am, Y80); **Xiangcheng** (16hr. excluding overnight stop in Litang, 7:15am, Y110); **Ya'an** (6hr.; 6:30, 8:30, 10:30am; Y62-72). **Taxis** (2hr.) to **Luding** costs Y20 and wait by the 1st bridge.

Tourist Information: The best source for travel information is the **Knapsack Inn.** They also arrange tours to Tagong Grasslands and Mugecuo Lake. For package tours of the Tibetan regions in Sichuan, try **Ganzi Prefecture Youth Travel Company** (gānzī zhōu qīngnián lǚxíng shè; 甘孜洲青年旅行社 ; ☎2813779; fax 281 3777) inside the Love Song Hotel, directly opposite the 3rd bridge.

Bank of China: On Yanhe Xi Lu between the 1st and 2nd bridges. Open daily 8:30am-5:30pm. No banks in Kangding exchange currency; try the **Knapsack Inn** instead.

PSB: (☎281 1415, ext. 5035.) On Dong Dajie, past the 4th bridge, on the left side of the street. Open M-F 8:30am-noon and 2:30-5:30pm.

Pharmacies: There are a number of pharmacies scattered around town, on Xi Dajie, Dong Dajie, and by the bus station. **Fixed Point Pharmacy** (dìngdiǎnlíng shòuyàodiàn; 定点零售药店 ; ☎283 4785), halfway down Xi Dajie. Open daily 9am-10pm.

Internet Access: 2 **Internet cafes** are both down alleyways and on the 2nd fl., located off Xi Dajie and Dong Dajie, respectively. Look for the characters 网巴 (wǎngbā) and follow the signs. Both Y3 per hr. **Sally's Cafe** has 1 terminal for Y3 per hr.

Post Office: (☎283 2037). Just to the left of the town square, on the west side of the 2nd bridge. Open daily 8am-noon, and 2:30-5pm.

Postal Code: 626000.

ACCOMMODATIONS AND FOOD

Given the Tibetan influences at work in Kangding, you would expect to find a lot of Tibetan food around town. In fact, only **Sally's Cafe**, at the Knapsack Inn, serves Tibetan meals. Small restaurants serve spicy **Sichuanese** food along Yanhe Dong Lu and Dong Dajie. At sunset, stalls spring up out of nowhere to sell **kebabs** smeared with tasty spices. **Spring rolls** (chūn juàn; 春卷) are Y2 per plate.

Black Tent Guesthouse (hēi zhàngpéng zhùsù; 黑帐篷住宿 ; ☎886 2907), on Yanhe Xi Lu. From the bus station, turn right; veer right at the fork in the road. Turn left, walk along the river, and cross the 4th bridge; it's the building on the corner with the porch. The family-run Black Tent offers cozy and clean rooms, all with electric blankets (necessary for Kangding's chilly nights—even in the summer). Downstairs, a tea house serves up fortifying Tibetan teas (Y10-40). The only drawback is the pungent, open-stall common bathrooms. 4-bed dorms Y20; doubles with TV and carpet Y50. ❶

Knapsack Inn and Sally's Cafe (☎283 8377; sally51010677@yahoo.com), directly left of Jingang Si, a 20-30min. walk from town. The Knapsack Inn has clean, delightful rooms with Tibetan beds, as well as Internet access, currency exchange, travel services, and good food. 3-bed dorm Y20. ❶

Paomashan Hotel (pǎomǎshān bīnguǎn; 跑马山宾馆 ; ☎283 5888), on Guangming Lu. Cross the river at the 3rd bridge. Turn left onto Yanhe Xi Lu, and make the 1st right onto Guangming Lu; it's about 150m ahead on the right. If you're after Western amenities, Paomashan is the place to go. Spotless rooms all have TV and attached Western bath. 3-bed dorms must be booked in advance. Standard room Y120. ❷

Traffic Hotel (kāngdìng jiāotōng dàjiǔdiàn; 康定交通大酒店 ; ☎282 2840; fax 282 2492), on Binhe Lu, behind the bus station, along the river. Near the edge of town. Nice rooms at a fair price, with pristine bathrooms and large beds. Doubles Y120. ❷

Kangding Hotel (kāngdìng bīnguǎn; 康定宾馆) 25 Guangming Lu (☎283 3081; fax 283 3442). Cross the 4th bridge; the Kangding Hotel is at the top of the small hill in front of you. Built for Chinese tour groups, the building is rather grandiose, and is often fully booked. Enclosed shower stalls may just make your day. 3-bed dorms with common bath Y110, doubles Y140. ❷

🄶 SIGHTS

Although most of the more interesting sights are outside town, there are also a few peaceful places of interest that don't require a substantial time commitment. Sandwiched between the Black Tent Hotel and the Kangding Hotel, the **Ngachö Gompa Temple** (ānjué sì; 安觉寺) belongs to the Gelug school of Tibetan Buddhism and had more than 300 monks in residence in its heyday.

Paomashan Mountain (pǎomǎ shān; 跑马山 ; "running horse mountain") rears up in the east, named for the annual horse racing festival held here every year on the 8th day of the 4th lunar month (May 15, 2005 and May 5, 2006). Hike up the mountain for about 45min. for rewarding views and a respite from the crowds. From town, turn right just before the bus station and continue until you reach a temple and the stairs up the hill. To take the cable car up, walk up the hill, past the fourth bridge, until you come to a traffic circle. Turn left and follow the signs to the cable car. (Open 8:30am-5:30pm. One-way Y20, round-trip Y30.) Across the town square at the second bridge is **Gyundrang Chumik Spring** (shuǐjǐngzǐ jì; 水井子记), whose water flows down from the peaks of Paomashan. Just outside of town, next to the Knapsack Inn, are two Tibetan temples, **Dorje Dra Gompa** (jīn gāng sì; 金刚寺 ; "Diamond Temple") and **Nanjiao Temple** (nánjiāo sì; 南郊寺).

For transportation to the **Tagong Grasslands** (tǎgōng cǎoyuán; 塔公草原), surrounded by snowy mountains, **minibuses** leave from Yanhe Dong Lu each morning, near the second bridge.

Hire a private car and drive approximately 25km to reach **Mugecuo Lake** (mùgécuò; 木格措), a natural hot spring lake high up in the alpine mountains. Admire the reflection of the frosty peaks towering above and mirrored below in the clear cold waters, and hike through the verdant forests and wildflower-spangled grasslands along its shores. (Y35.) For more information on transportation to **Gongga Temple** (gònggā sì; 贡嘎寺), and **trekking** around Gonggashan Mountain, ask around town. Locals advise that travelers should not attempt this trip unless they have proper equipment and hiking experience.

JIUZHAIGOU 九寨沟 ☎0837

Set against a backdrop of thundering waterfalls, snow-capped peaks, and forests, 108 iridescent turquoise lakes fan out across mountains valleys like a peacock unfurling its plumage. Legend tells of a Tibetan goddess who dropped her mirror, whose broken shards became the shimmering pools which the locals call "little seas" (hǎizi; 海子). The best time to visit is late October to mid-November, when the leaves blaze fiery red and gold against the brilliant waters. Even in early summer, the lakes and streams paint a vivid palette of greens and blues, illuminated by sunlight to hint at fallen logs strewn within its depths.

Named after the nine Tibetan villages in the gully, Jiuzhaigou has grown to a full-blown tourist attraction in the last decade. Behind dusty banners fluttering in the wind and incense-scented Tibetan wood houses, satellite dishes bring in the latest news. Old women clad in traditional clothing may still offer you yak butter tea or, more likely, fur hats for sale. The government's attempt at eco-conscious tourism has resulted in a string of "environmentally friendly" shuttle buses and regulations prohibiting tourists from staying in the park overnight. Despite the over 10,000 visitors that swarm the reserve daily in high season, the trails are well-maintained, the wilds litter-free, and the water as clear as ever.

Trails wind into beautiful and isolated stretches of forest and meadow, providing an escape from tour bus stops bubbling with photo-snapping tourists. Beyond the southernmost bus stop, untrammeled forest and grassy mountain peaks promise undisturbed day hikes and serene vistas of the radiant pools below.

▐▐ TRANSPORTATION AND PRACTICAL INFORMATION

Jiuzhaigou is tucked into the Minshan Mountain Range in Nanping County, part of the Aba and Qiang Autonomous Prefecture near the Gansu border. The 450km of road north from Chengdu is a bumpy ride, running next to the silty waters and rapids of the Min River. Winter snow, summer rain, and mudslides may render Jiuzhaigou inaccessible or prolong the ride from the listed 10hr. to as long as 14hr. But look out the window at the surrounding mountains, summer-green valleys, and tiny villages, and it will at least be a breathtaking 14 hours.

Jiuzhaigou Scenic Park is Y-shaped, with three gullies forming each branch of the Y. Entrance is at the bottom of the Y, off the highway that connects Jiuzhaigou to Chengdu. At the terminus of the 80km scenic area, the elevation rises to 3060m in the primeval forest at the right branch of the Y. A dense thicket of hotels, restaurants, and other tourist services lines the highway to each side of the entrance.

Buses: Long-Distance Bus Station (jiǔzhàigōu qìchē zhàn; 九寨沟汽车站 ; ☎773 2030), in the parking lot of the Jiutong Hotel (jiǔtōng bīnguǎn; 九通宾馆), about 200m along the road toward Jiuzhaigou city; keep right as you exit the park gates across from the gas station. Insurance fee Y2. To: **Chengdu** (12-14hr.; 6:30, 7, 8am, 2pm; morning Y92, afternoon Y86); **Huanglong; Songpan** (2-3hr., 7:10am, Y41). You can also fill a taxi van to **Huanglong** for about Y250, but you may want to stop at Songpan first, as the drive to Huanglong takes you within 10km of Songpan.

Local Transportation: Inside Jiuzhaigou, buses run up and down the main road. A bus pass (Y90) gives you unlimited rides. The last bus from Long Lake and Arrow Bamboo Lake leaves at 4pm, from Nuorilang Falls 5-5:30pm.

PSB: Inside the main Visitors Center facing the park entrance, on the 1st fl. Some English spoken. Open daily 8:30am-5:30pm; someone is on duty 24hr.

Hospitals: Jiuzhaigou County Hospital (jiǔzhàigōuxiàn yīyuàn; 九寨沟县医院 ; ☎773 2146), 43km past the turn-off to the Jiuzhaigou entrance, down the road to Nanping County, on the right. Ambulance service. Open 24hr. 5km up the road in the other direction is the **Jiuzhaigou County Clinic** (jiǔzhàigōu xiàn yīyuàn zhàngzhá fēnyuàn; 九寨沟县医院障扎分院 ; ☎773 4007). Open 24hr.

Internet Access: Grand Jiuzhaigou Hotel (xīngyǔ guójì dàjiǔdiàn; 星宇国际大酒店), about a 25min. walk along the highway to the left of the park entrance. Y5-8 per hr.

Post and Telecommunications: On the right (coming from Chengdu) in a 3-story building, 5-6km from the entrance to Jiuzhaigou. The Visitors Center offers international mail service for postcards and small packages. IDD service. Open daily 10am-5pm.

▐ ACCOMMODATIONS

In an effort to preserve a degree of tranquility and ecological balance, the Jiuzhaigou Tourism Bureau regularly informs tour groups that no accommodations are available inside the park. As a result, the strip of road outside the park gates has become a breeding ground for mid- to high-end hotels, the cheapest of which charges Y80-90 per room in the low season and Y200 and up in the high season. Walk a little farther along the road in either direction from the park entrance, and you'll find smaller guesthouses which charge Y20-30 per bed in the low season and Y40-50 in the high season. Tibetan families inside the park are also willing to host tourists, although this is illegal and not recommended. Travelers who do so usually ask families in the early afternoon, when the majority of visitors and guides are busy sightseeing.

Jiutong Binguan (jiǔtōng bīnguǎn; 九通宾馆; ☎773 9400), just left of the bus station, about a 15min. walk from the park entrance. Clean and functional. Public showers. The adjacent telephone room provides phone service (domestic Y0.3 per min., international Y4.5). Open 6am-11pm. Beds Y30; singles with private bath Y190, but can be bargained down to Y80. ❶

Jiuzhaigou Grand Hotel (guìbīnlóu fàndiàn; 贵宾楼饭店; ☎773 4163; fax 773 9000), just to the right of the Visitors Center. Run by the Jiuzhaigou Administration, this is the most convenient of the lot. Luxury doubles start at Y260. ❸

Heye Guesthouse (héyè yíng bīnguǎn; 荷叶迎宾馆; ☎773 5555; fax 773 5688), just to the left of the park entrance. Luxury doubles start at Y290. ❸

🍴 FOOD

Jiuzhaigou's best culinary options are wild vegetable dishes, like the **sliced pork with tree fungus** (mùěr ròupiàn; 木耳肉片; Y18-30) and the **walnut flower dish** (hétáohuā; 核桃花; Y18-30). **Yak** (máoniú; 牦牛; Y28-45) is also worth trying if you have money to spare. Outside the park, make a right turn in the lane before the Grand Jiuzhaigou Hotel (not to be confused with the Jiuzhaigou Grand Hotel) onto **Huoba Jie** (火坝街), a small street clustered with restaurants serving local delicacies. The **Dazhong Restaurant** ❷ (dàzhòng cāntīng; 大众餐厅; ☎889 8080) serves wild mushrooms for Y10 and yak meat for Y28.

Be forewarned: food prices are greatly inflated within Jiuzhaigou. Vendors have no qualms about asking Y5-8 for instant noodles and Y5 for bottles of water. To save money, bring your own snacks and drinks into the park. The **Nuorilang Restaurant** ❷ (nuòrìláng cāntīng; 诺日郎餐厅), the only restaurant within the park, offers a buffet lunch for Y25 (with drinks Y40). The menu changes every day, and usually there are over 10 dishes to choose from.

👁 SIGHTS

Jiuzhaigou's beauty is as legendary as its origins. According to a local tale, the warrior-god Dage presented a magic mirror, painstakingly crafted from clouds and winds, to his beloved goddess Wunosemo. One day, a meddling devil, envious of the couple's love and happiness, made Wunosemo drop her treasured mirror. It fell to Earth, where it shattered and formed the glittering lakes of Jiuzhaigou.

The park gates are open daily 7am-7pm. A ticket costs Y145; students and seniors over 60 pay Y115. If you plan to spend two days in the park, the second day you receive two tickets for the price of one. The shuttle pass is Y90. Buses stop at several points along the park roads, and most tourists who visit Jiuzhaigou jump from bus stop to bus stop, congregating around demarcated scenic vistas that provide easy access photo-ops. Time allowing, it is far more pleasant and rewarding to walk and admire the lakes and rivers that spangle the forests along the way.

Once through the gates, the park road passes the quiet village of **Heye** (héyè zhài; 荷叶寨), about 4km up, before reaching the more touristed **Shuzheng Village** (shùzhèng zhài; 树正寨), about 8km up the road. Two kilometers farther is the **Nuorilang** area, site of the Nuorilang Falls, where the road forks to form the two branches of the Y. The left branch passes through **Zhechawa Village** (zéchāwā zhài; 则查洼寨) before heading to the Long Lake. The right branch passes through the Pearl Shoal Falls, near Panda Lake, and up to the currently closed section through the Rize Gully and Swan Lake.

SHUZHENG GULLY. From the entrance, along Shuzheng Gully (shùzhèng gōu; 树正沟), the lowest branch of the Y, the first pool you encounter is **Reed Lake** (lúwěi hǎi; 芦苇海). Watch the sunrise over **Sparkle Lake** (huǒhuá hǎi; 火花海), the next lake in the gully. In the same cluster of lakes, two waterfalls form the two dragons of **Twin Dragon Lake** (shuāng lóng hǎi; 双龙海). Farther along the valley, **Tiger Lake** (lǎohǔ hǎi; 老虎海) is named for the roaring waters of **Shuzheng Waterfall** (shùzhèng pùbù; 树正瀑布), the sound of which the locals say is like the bellow of a tiger. Beneath the waters, branching calcium formations create a series of multi-colored terraces that step up the mountainside.

NUORILANG FALLS AND RIZE GULLY. Midway up the gorge, Nuorilang Falls (nuòrìláng pùbù; 诺日郎瀑布), over 30m tall and 320m wide, cascade down. Just above Nuorilang Falls, the main road forks. The right path follows the **Rize Gully** (rìzé gōu; 日则沟). At **Pearl Shoals** (zhēnzhū tān; 珍珠滩), a long series of water-falls rushes between trees and flowering bushes, dividing the broad **Peacock River** (kǒngquè hédào; 孔雀河道; 孔雀河道) into thousands of tiny latticed streams before cascading over the Pearl Shoal Falls. Continuing up this path, the pure, intense blues of **Five Flower Lake** (wǔ huā hǎi; 五花海) extend indefinitely into the pristine depths. Locals say that pandas once roamed through the bamboo forests surrounding **Panda Lake** (xióngmāo hǎi; 熊猫海). The final bus stop along the right fork is **Arrow Bamboo Lake** (jiànzhú hǎi; 箭竹海), near the primeval forest. From here, the road continues up through quiet meadows, following the mountain stream past forested peaks overshadowed by the majestic snowcaps in the far distance.

LONG LAKE (cháng hǎi; 长海). Along the left branch of the road, the sights are scattered farther apart, so take a bus from **Zechawa Village** (zécháwā zhài; 则查洼寨) up to Long Lake, 18km from Nuorilang Falls. Crystal clear and strikingly deep, the azure blue waters of this tranquil lake attract migratory wild swans. Although jagged cliffs make hiking around the lake virtually impossible, simply walk left down from the parking lot along a small path that leads to a boat dock. Here, a boulder-strewn beach provides shelter from both the visual and auditory intrusions of the fray of visitors above. From the Long Lake parking lot, walk 1.5km down a small, paved footpath to the **Five Color Pool** (wǔcǎi chí; 五彩池), a radiant gem enclosed by steep, forested hills on all sides. It fades from reddish yellow through the color spectrum to a vibrant deep blue violet at the center point. Most tourists arrive at Long Lake and descend to the Five Color Pool between 2 and 5pm, so head up the left branch route in the morning to avoid the crowds.

ZARU TEMPLE (zárú sì; 扎如寺). Near the entrance, this small Tibetan monastery is equally happy to accept visitors and their donations. At the center of the main assembly hall is a prominent statue of Sakyamuni, and over 1000 smaller Sakyamunis line its side walls. *(At the end of a small road branching left about 1km up from the main trail. Open daily 8am-7pm.)*

◪ HIKING IN JIUZHAIGOU

It's easy to avoid the swarming masses in this spacious reserve. Many **horse** and **foot trails** weave through the park, with long interludes of quiet and solitude between major tourist sights. The park can be hiked comfortably in three days, two days if in a hurry. Because the reserve does not allow camping, hikers must exit the park between hikes, which makes multi-day hikes expensive.

Hiking the entire circuit from the entrance to **Arrow Bamboo Lake,** at the end of Rize Gully, to **Peacock River** takes about an entire day. Descend the footpath along the left side of the main road into wooded forest and green meadows to **Heye Village** and wander to the cluster of gorgeous lakes along Shuzheng Gully. Near Sparkle Lake, the path brings you down to eye-level with the water. Follow the trail on to the main road and walk upwards past **Tiger Lake** and **Rhinoceros Lake.** Take the bus to the **primeval forest,** where lichen and honeysuckle abound in the virgin cedar and spruce forest. The trail winds down to **Swan Lake.** The vast distance to **Grass Lake** and **Arrow Bamboo Lake** can be done by bus or on foot. Once there, descend to the most gorgeous sections of the park (Panda Lake, Five Flower Lake, Peacock River, and the Pearl Shoals Waterfall). If you're lucky, you may catch a glimpse of the expanse of turquoise and blue waters touched by gold under the setting sun.

One of the best ways to go from the **Pearl Shoals Waterfall** back to the **Nuorilang** area is to hike along the shores of **Mirror Lake** opposite the major road. Instead of crossing the last bridge back to the road at the bottom of the Pearl Shoals Waterfall walkway, go through an opening in the shrubbery and walk along a well-trod horse trail that leads through several wildflower meadows, past brilliant green marshland and through pine forests, eventually hitting the road just below the Nuorilang Falls. If you're hiking up to the Pearl Shoals, walk down the road from Nuorilang and head upstream on a small path just after the first bridge.

In **Shuzheng,** reach another nice unmarked trail by crossing the small footbridge on Tiger Lake and then either heading right toward Nuorilang Falls or left toward Sleeping Dragon Lake. Another longer, more strenuous hike starts above the last bus stop at **Arrow Bamboo Lake.** Walk up the road from the parking lot for about 20min. At the first cluster of buildings, the **Rize Protection Center** (rìzé bǎohù zhàn; 日则保护站), walk through the compound and up the grassy pastures behind it. Follow well-defined horse and yak trails up the mountainside on your right to reach the summit in about 3-4hr. From this brilliant vantage point, the iridescent lakes fan out to the north and south, framed by distant snow-frosted peaks.

SONGPAN 松潘   ☎ 0837

Surrounded by terraced grasslands and bright fields of yellow mountain flowers, Songpan's ancient city walls guard the entry into this vibrant community of Tibetan, Hui Muslim, and Han Chinese, who live and work together in a way rarely seen in other Chinese towns. A dense network of cobblestone paths and canals weaves through the neighborhoods of traditional wooden houses, courtyard gardens, and local mosques and temples nestled into the surrounding hills.

Songpan, situated at the intersection of the northwest road to Gansu and the southern road to Chengdu, has had a long history of contact with foreigners and non-Han ethnicities. Fueled by a rapidly growing tourist industry, the town sports several modern hotels, Internet cafes, and backpacker hangouts.

▐▋ TRANSPORTATION AND PRACTICAL INFORMATION

Songpan is centered on the intersection of four roads. Each road leads to a large gate tower, with the exception of the west road, which quickly branches into alleyways and market streets as you move away from the center intersection. The town center is a wide road that runs between the north and south gate towers and is filled with restaurants, Tibetan souvenir shops, and cafes.

Songpan's **bus station** is half a kilometer outside the north gate, about two blocks north of the horse trek companies, and in the parking lot of Songzhou Traffic Hotel. Buses run to: Chengdu (6-7hr.; 6, 6:30, 7am; Y50); Dujiangyan (6hr.,

10am, Y45); Huanglong (2hr., 7am, Y25); Jiuzhaigou (3hr.; 7, 11am, 1:30pm; Y20); Zöigê (6hr., 7am, Y46). The road to Zöigê is currently under construction and the bus detours through Hongyuan (红原) on a dirt road.

There are no locations in Songpan to exchange currency or traveler's checks. If you're in dire straits, you can **exchange US dollars** on the black market relatively easily; ask at any backpacker information center. The **PSB** (☎723 2735) is across from the Pancake House between the north gate and the city center, but does not process visa extensions. (Open M-F 8am-noon and 3-6pm.) **Songzhou County Hospital** (sōngzhōu xiàn rénmín yīyuàn; 松州县人民医院) is to the east of the main crossroads. (☎723 3300. Open 8am-6pm.) **Snowlands Happiness Internet Cafe,** west of the main crossroads and a block before the ancient Gusong Bridge, has the cheapest Internet access in town (Y3 per hr.). Several Internet cafes also line the road between the city center and the north gate and charge Y5-6 per hr. A **post and telecommunications** office, south of the Pancake House, has IDD service. (Open summer 8:30am-6pm; winter 9am-5:30pm.) You can also make calls at a small **telephone station** just outside of the north gate. (Domestic calls Y0.3 per min., international calls Y2-3 per min.)

🏠 FOOD AND ACCOMMODATIONS

Prices may jump Y10-20 during peak season (July-Oct.) and Chinese New Year. Most foreigners who come horseback riding stay at the **Shunjiang Guesthouse ❶** (shùnjiāng zìzhù lǚguǎn; 顺江自助旅馆), conveniently adjacent to the horse trek companies. (Clean 2-bed and 3-bed dorms Y20. Public showers a block down Y3.) **Songzhou Hotel ❶** (sōngzhōu bīnguǎn; 松州宾馆), near the south gate, has decent dorm rooms. (Y15-20 per bed. Adjacent public showers Y3.) The **Traffic Hotel ❷** (jiāotōng bīnguǎn; 交通宾馆) is up the street from the horse trek companies and in the same parking lot as the bus station. (Hot water 1-5pm and in the evenings upon request. Singles with bath Y150.) **Deyang Restaurant and Guesthouse ❶** (déyáng cāntīng zhùsù; 德阳餐厅住宿) is a newly opened bed and breakfast. (Y10 per bed. Free shower with stay.)

Many good restaurants are clustered near the central intersection. A large fruit and vegetable market lies west of the center. **Sarah Yang's ❶** (shānyě zhī gē fàndiàn; 山野之歌饭店), right next door to the horse trek company, is a favorite among backpackers who arrive late (after 10pm) or depart early (before 6:30am). (Oatmeal Y3. Hamburgers Y5.) The **Pancake House ❶** (yùlán fàndiàn; 玉兰饭店), halfway between the north gate and the central crossroads, gets you going in the morning with coffee (Y5) and pancakes (Y6). Heartier fare includes hamburgers (Y5) and fried egg sandwiches (Y5). An English menu takes the guesswork out of ordering. **Star Moon Restaurant ❷** (xīngyuèlóu cāntīng; 星月楼餐厅), just south of the main crossroads on the west side, has green moons in the windows and a green sign overhead. Although these Muslim dishes are rather expensive (Y15-20), they are well worth the price. Lunch specials for Y10 include one meat and one vegetable dish. Friendly cooks let you come into the kitchen to see how it's done.

🐎 HORSE TREKS

Many claim that the horse treks out of Songpan are the highlights of their Sichuan travels. The price (Y100 per day) includes meals, tents, bedding, cold water gear, and lovable guides. What used to be two competing companies, **Happy Trails Horse Treks** (kuàilè de xiǎolù qímǎ lǚyóu; 快乐的小路骑马旅游 ; ☎723 1064) and **Shunjiang Horse Treks** (shùnjiāng lǚyóu mǎduì; 顺江旅游马队 ; ☎723 1201), now share a desk in the same office under the Shunjiang banner, just outside of the north gate, and offer the same tours with the same high quality. Treks to **Munigou** and the **Hot Springs** at **Er Dao Hai** take two days; a detour to the **Zhaya** waterfall takes an extra day. The Hot Springs are actually rather cold (21°C), and the mineral pools that form the area's main attraction don't compare in the least to Huanglong's or Jiuzhaigou's, even if the 100m Zhaya Waterfall is quite beautiful. (Entrance fee to Munigou and Er Dao Hai Y70. Zhaya Waterfall another Y70. Hot springs extra Y10.) Two-day trips to the **Leaping Stone Cliff** (kuà shí yá; 跨石崖) are highly recommended, especially for those short on time.

Treks to **Ice Mountain** (bīng shān; 冰山 , or xuě bǎo dǐng; 雪宝顶) take four days of riding (5-6hr. per day), ascending the majestic snowy peaks that you can only gaze at from a distance on other trails. (Entrance fee to Ice Mountain Y10, expected to climb to Y20 in the next few years.) For even longer stays in the wild, go on a six-day trek to **Qizang Valley** (qīzàng gōu; 七藏沟) and **Red Star Cliff** (hóng xīng yán; 红星岩), a yet undeveloped expanse of sandstone. Treks to the **Zöigë** (ruòěrgài; 若尔盖) grasslands last 12 days, including the return journey. You can also trek to **Huanglong** (2 long days of riding, 1 day hiking in the park), passing close to the snowline, but since bus service is convenient and several hours of riding must be done on the public highway, this trek is not very popular.

▓ DAYTRIP FROM SONGPAN: HUANGLONG

*About 17km north of Songpan, the main road branches north toward Jiuzhaigou and east to Huanglong (56km). **Buses** leave the Songpan Bus Station for the park gates daily at 7am (2hr., Y25) and cross a breathtaking pass just below the snowline. **Horse treks** from Songpan (p. 721) involve a 1-day ride to Huanglong through the same pass, 1-day hike in the park, and 1-day return. From Jiuzhaigou and Songpan, you can also get to Huanglong by taking a **minibus** (Y200-300 for a 4- to 5-seater). The round-trip **hike** to Huanglong Temple and the Five Colored Pool is 7.5km and takes 3-4hr. From the park gates, buses return to Songpan at approximately 2:30pm. There are many small restaurants along the main road in front of the park, but there are no vendors inside, so bring food and drink. Park opens daily 7:30am to approximately 8pm. Mar.-Oct. Y110, students and seniors over 60 Y80; Nov.-Feb. Y70/Y50.*

Guarded by 10 majestic peaks, the Huanglong Scenic Reserve is famous for its radiant turquoise pools and breathtaking alpine scenery. Unlike Jiuzhaigou's crashing waterfalls and deep lakes, Huanglong consists of a long, narrow cascade of pearly white calcium terraces, which fan out into myriad small pools of luminous blue and green. On a sunny day, the mineral deposits at the bottom glisten through the water. These deposits, with their distinctive yellow shade, led locals to name the region Huanglong ("Yellow Dragon"; huánglóng; 黄龙) because it reminded them of a dragon leaping down from the mountains.

Walking up the boardwalk through the narrow gorge, the snowline is just a few hundred meters up the mountain, and the air is thin and pure. The highest viewing point in the park is at the **Five-Colored Pool.** From the veranda of the nearby **Huanglong Temple,** the gem-like terraces of yellow, red, and blue glitter under a formidable frozen peak. Ensconced high above, just below the temple, a cave shelters rock formations said to resemble the local god. Behind the pool, a footpath leads to grassy hills and boulder-strewn fields, from which the more energetic hiker can admire the immensity of the entire Huanglong Gorge unfurled below.

While Huanglong is indeed beautiful, it is designed for easy access and convenient photo-ops. Every day, swarms of tourists tread the paved and wood-plank paths that traverse the park. Because of the fragility of the calcium formations that cover the narrow gorge, it is nearly impossible to strike off on your own. Ordinarily, visitors ascend to the Five-Colored Pool along the main boardwalk path and descend along an uninteresting stone path through the woods to avoid congestion on the narrow boardwalk path. You may want to return along the same path and brave the mass of tourists for better views of the pool.

Huanglong is located at an exhaustive 3000m elevation, and guides frequently warn the infirm not to attempt the ascent. Oxygen pillows (Y50) are available for purchase, and there are free "oxygen stations" every kilometer or so up the mountain. Local porters dressed in blue will also gladly carry you up to the Five-Colored Pool in a bamboo seat for an exorbitant Y250.

Huanglong is at its best in fall, when plentiful rainfall ensures that none of the many terraced pools run dry. The most secluded time to visit is in the late afternoon, as the majority of tourists leave on the 2:30pm bus. Joining up with a group of people helps to minimize the cost of hiring a private car or taxi. Three to four hours should be sufficient for the round-trip hike to the Five-Colored Pool.

Accommodation in Huanglong is generally very expensive, hovering around Y200 per night, so it's probably best to make only a daytrip out of the excursion.

ZÖIGÊ 若尔盖

Pronounced *ruòěrgài* in Mandarin, Zöigê serves mainly as a stopover point for north- or southbound bus riders. Because there are no direct buses between Langmusi and Songpan, you will have to spend the night here and catch a connection bus early the next morning. This dusty waystop is somewhat inhospitable: the uniform, cement buildings block the views of the beautiful surrounding hills, and few hotels offer showers. However, the town is gradually being revamped as a tourist destination in its own right, with vast expanses of grasslands nearby and the Zöigê Everglades midway between Zöigê and Langmusi. Souvenir shops selling Tibetan handicrafts and tiny family restaurants dishing up homemade Sichuan food line the streets. Get a glimpse of local life in the small lane branching off the main roads, where venders peddle daily local necessities and Tibetan men gather around for a friendly game of pool.

Buses leave from the main bus station (kèyùn zhàn; 客运站), on a small lane on Maixi Jie (麦溪街) to: Chengdu (12hr., 6am, Y90); Hezuo (4-5hr., 6am, Y39); Langmusi (5-6hr., 2:30pm, Y16); Linxia (6am, Y51); Songpan (5-7hr., 6am, Y51). From Songpan, buses leave at 6am for Zöigê. Note that while it is possible to get from Songpan to Langmusi in one day via Zöigê, it is not possible the other way around.

On the same side of the street as the bus station, about a block down, the **Red Star Hotel ❶** (hóngxīng bīnguǎn; 红星宾馆) has hot water until late evening and shower stalls and bathrooms on the 1st fl. (☎ 229 1882. Doubles with TV Y20 per bed, 3rd fl. doubles without TV Y15.) Directly across from the bus station, the **Liyuan Hotel ❶** (líyuán bīnguǎn; 丽源宾馆 ; ☎ 229 1885) offers clean doubles (Y20 per bed), though showers are lacking. The newly built **Ruoergai Hotel ❶** (ruòěrgài xiàn bīnguǎn; 若尔盖县宾馆) is the best hotel in town, with the most amenities for the road-weary. Located at the far end of Business St. from its intersection with Maixi Jie, the hotel is inconvenient, unless you're planning an extended stay or absolutely dislike pungent bathrooms. (☎ 229 1998 or 229 8888. Hot water 8am-12pm. Beds Y48; doubles Y180.)

Hungry travelers' best bet for food is at one of the small local **restaurants.** Lack of English menus makes ordering an adventure. Dishes are priced Y8-20.

LANGMUSI 郎木寺   ☎ 0941

If it weren't for the mountains surrounding this tiny town, you'd think you were on the Tibetan Plateau: the streets are filled with robed Tibetan monks and women clad in the ornate costumes of Tibetan herders. Langmusi is also one of the last places in which a tourist can witness a traditional **sky-burial** atop the northern hills overlooking the town and the nearby Dacang Langmusaichi Temple.

7 PRACTICAL INFORMATION. The town's main street runs east-west and branches to the **Gansu Dacang Langmusaichi Temple** (gānsū dácāng lángmùsàichì sì; 甘肃达仓郎木赛赤寺) to the northeast and the **Taktsang Lhamo Kirti Monastery** (gé'ěrdēng sì; 格尔登寺) to the south. **Buses** stop at the intersection of the three roads, leaving for Diebu (30min., Y5) and Hezuo (5-6hr.; 7, 8am; Y20). A direct bus to Zöigê (8am, Y20) leaves daily in front of the Langmusaichi Temple. You can also take the 7am bus to Diebu and hop off midway at Rediba (热地坝), and stay the night to transfer to the Zöigê bus (4-6hr., 8am, Y20). From Hezuo, you can transfer to Xiahe (2-3hr.) in Gansu province. **Internet access** is across the street from the Hotel Restaurant. (Y3 per hr. Open until last customers leave.)

▮▯ ACCOMMODATIONS AND FOOD. A few minutes' walk down the main road, west of the intersection, the new ▨ **Sana Hotel ❶** (sànà bīnguǎn; 萨娜宾馆) is run by a friendly Hui Muslim family. With 24hr. hot water and a free laundry machine, this cleanly furnished hotel makes for a pleasant stay. (☎667 1062. Doubles Y20 per bed; triples Y15 per bed.) The **Langmusi Hotel ❶** (lángmù sì bīnguǎn; 郎木寺宾馆) is conveniently located at the intersection where buses stop. It offers clean beds with communal showers and doubles with private bath. The English-speaking manager can give a guided tour of the town for a small fee. (☎667 1086. Hot water 8-11pm. Payphone in the hall. Beds Y15; doubles Y25 per person.) Across the street from the Langmusi Hotel, the sizeable **Gansu Dacang Langmu Hotel ❶** (gānsū dácāng lángmù bīnguǎn; 甘肃达仓郎木宾馆) provides clean beds. (☎667 1388. Hot water 7-9am and 8-11pm. 3-bed dorms Y10; 2-bed Y20; standard doubles with bath Y70.)

A few restaurants with English menus dot the Langmusi streets. **Lesha's Cafe ❷** (líshā fànguǎn; 丽莎饭馆 ; ☎667 1179) has become a Langmusi tradition for foreign backpackers. The English-speaking manager, Ding Xuewen, and his wife Lesha serve frisbee-sized yak burgers (Y12) and delicious apple, peach, or apricot pie (Y8 per slice). Be forewarned: portions are huge. Have a homemade cappuccino (Y15) at **Talo's Friends Cafe and Restaurant ❶** (dálǎo kāfēi xī cāntīng; 达老咖啡西餐厅), on the 2nd floor of a small building on the west side of the main road. Dimly lit and ambient with quiet conversations in Tibetan, this small cafe tucked cozily behind Tibetan curtains cooks up specialties like wild sweet *toma* with rice (Y8) and Dhuma (Y6). Omelettes with onion (Y8), and pancakes (Y15) revive the spirits of homesick Westerners. (☎139 0941 9881. Beers Y8-12. Yak butter tea Y5. Espresso Y12. Open 8am-10pm.) The **Hotel Restaurant ❷** (bīnguǎn cāntīng; 宾馆餐厅 ; ☎667 1164), just under the Langmusi Hotel, offers a nice break from potatoes and yak at Lesha's with tasty fried rice and vegetable dishes (Y10-12).

◪ SIGHTS. The town's main attractions are its two temples. The **Taktsang Lhamo Kirti Monastery** (gé'ěrdēng sì; 格尔登寺) is in the south of town. (Admission Y15.) To the northeast, the **Dacang Langmusaichi Temple** (dácāng lángmùsàichì sì; 达仓郎木赛赤寺) is divided into two complexes: the one upstream nestles into the valley, and the other, smaller complex on the high hill flanks the town to the east.

From the muddy gate at the bottom of the hill, follow dirt paths up past pine trees and a dusty cabin with giant prayer wheels, and walk to the highest temple structure on the eastern hill to reach the open grasslands. There, find a majestic view of the hills and the temples below. Gaze up to the **sky-burial** grounds, decked with prayer flags. Man-sized vultures perch on the flag poles in the early morning, and human remains and bone fragments litter the ground.

A great hike starts from the sky burial site, winding up through the grasslands to a row of orange cliffs that tower above the town below (3-4hr. to the highest prayer flags and back to the valley town). On the opposite side of the valley, head north along a horse trail by the river and up into the rockier and more barren mountain crags to the west (5-6hr. to the first main rock group and back to town).

YIBIN 宜宾 ☎831

Situated at the confluence of the Min and Jinsha tributaries of the Yangzi River in southeastern Sichuan, the bustling city of Yibin is a transfer point for travelers heading to Bamboo Sea or south to Yunnan. The industrial town has far more than just industry—nightlife keeps the docks busy and bright after dark, and the many bridges are peaceful spots to sip tea and watch the sunset.

Yibin is home to **Wuliangye** (wǔliángyè; 五粮液), one of China's largest beer companies. To take a tour of the factory and sample some Chinese alcohol, take bus #4 from the Nan'an Bus Station to Nanmen Bridge (nánmén dàqiáo; 南门大桥) and transfer to bus #2 to the last stop. Taking Bus #4 to Zhongshan Jie brings you to **Cuiping Hill** (cuìpíng shān; 翠坪山), with a temple at the top and its share of natural scenery. In the evening, relax in one of many teahouses and waterfront bars by the Min River, where a tall stone archway marks the entrance to the docks.

Yibin is laid along a rough grid with a crossroads at the center. Renmin Lu (人民路) runs east-west and becomes Zhongshan Jie (中山街) east of the crossroads, dead-ending on the banks of the Min River. South of the crossroads, Minzhu Lu (民主路) passes the post office and becomes Nan Jie (南街) before crossing the Jinsha River in the south. Cuiping Lu (翠屏路) winds from the train station in the southwest to the **North Bus Station**, intersecting Renmin Lu at the entrance to the Cuiping City Park at the western end of the city.

Across the Jinsha River from the city, **Nan'an Bus Station** (nán'àn kèyùn zhàn; 南岸客运站; ☎233 3724) sends buses to **Bamboo Sea** (2-3hr.; 7:30, 8:30am; Y21); **Chengdu** (4-5hr., every hr. 8am-4pm, Y80); and **Chongqing** (4-5hr., every hr. 8:30am-4:30pm, Y70). Buses also leave more frequently for Changning, where local buses depart for Bamboo Sea. The **North Bus Station** (běi kèzhàn; 北客站; ☎822 6000) has buses to similar destinations. The Bank of China on Renmin Lu and Nan Jie has an international **ATM**. (Open 8am-noon and 2-6pm.) **China Post,** 1 Nan Jie, has EMS service but not IDD. **Postal Code:** 600000.

If going to Bamboo Sea, it's best to arrive early and go directly from Nan'an Bus Station. If you have to stay the night, the **Passenger Station Guesthouse ➊** (kèyùn zhàn zhāodàisuǒ; 客运站招待所) is right at the bus station. (☎233 3724. Public bath, TV, luggage storage. 4-bed dorms Y10; 2-bed Y20.) Or take a cab to **Electricity Hotel ➊** (diànlì bīnguǎn; 电力宾馆) nearby. (☎233 4999. 24hr. security and phones. Doubles with A/C, TV, and shared bath Y60; singles and doubles with attached bath Y120-150.) To sample the city nightlife across the river, take bus #4 to Renmin Lu. The **Xufu Hotel ➋** (xùfǔ bīnguǎn; 叙府宾馆) lands you in the middle of the busy shopping district, conveniently close to hotpot restaurants and Internet cafes. (☎818 9999. Well-furnished doubles with bath, A/C, TV, and Internet Y168.)

For traditional, cheap Chinese delicacies and snacks, cross Nan Jie and walk up the small street on the opposite side to find hotpot restaurants and roasted meat vendors. In the downtown and western areas, small alleys off Renmin Lu offer an assortment of noodle dishes (Y1-2) and **grilled foods** (xiǎokǎo; 小烤). Try the lamb kebabs (Y0.5 per stick) and grilled eggplant or cucumber (Y2 for 15 or so skewers), drizzled with spicy Sichuan sauce and ground peanuts. In the mornings, look for meat-filled sticky buns to start the day as it should be started: with sweet goo and nourishing meat. Dockside dining creates a more upscale experience, near Shuidongmen Gate (shuǐdōngmén; 水东门), two blocks down from Zhongshan Jie.

THE HIDDEN DEAL

FLYING OVER THE BAMBOO SEA

Remember the majestic scene in *Crouching Tiger, Hidden Dragon*, when Master Li Mubai (Chow Yun Fat) leapt over a sea of bamboo to chase the beautiful sword thief played by Zhang Ziyi? They soared across the screen, lightly brushing the tops of the delicate bamboo and walking atop the rustling leaves in an elegant feat of martial arts. Not all of that was due to creative cinematography or special effects. It was filmed here in Sichuan's **Bamboo Sea,** and you too can have the experience of flying over the bamboo. Though the experience won't be quite as romantic—a glider and a pilot will help you wing your way across—it will only cost you Y200 for 1-2hr. of gravity-free exhilaration above a gently waving sea of green. You'll have to supply the martial arts moves yourself, however. For the truly thrifty or those with a fear of heights, head to the nearest street market and browse the DVD selections—for an unbeatable Y10 you can recapture the soaring experience over and over again, right from the comfort of your own room.

Inquire at any hotel near the entrance to the trails of the Bamboo Sea, or ask a motorbike driver, who will take you straight to the glider field, located halfway between the base of the mountain and Sea-Gazing Tower (guānhǎi lóu; 观海楼).

Try the dimly-lit **Sanlitun Bar** (sānlǐtún; 三里屯), quite a ways from its namesake in Beijing, or the number of hotpot restaurants on both sides of the street.

BAMBOO SEA 蜀南竹海   ☎831

About 60km southeast of Yibin, one of China's largest expanses of bamboo forest stretches over 120km² of mountain peaks, towering cliffs, and deep, secluded valleys. A network of stone-paved trails weaves through the park, ascending steep rock faces, ducking behind waterfalls, and passing by traditional houses. Swarms of tourists often inundate the main lower-elevation trails, especially on weekends and holidays, but seclusion and silence is just a hike away, high up into the hills and untrammeled backcountry.

▣ TRANSPORTATION. From Yibin, take local bus #4 or 5 or a taxi (Y5) south across the Jinsha River bridge to the **Nan'an Bus Station** (see **Yibin,** p. 725). Buses go directly to **Bamboo Sea** (zhúhǎi; 竹海) every day (7:30, 8:30am; Y21). Another bus travels to **Wanling** (wànlíng; 万岭), the base town for Bamboo Sea (1:25pm, Y16). Don't worry if you miss these; hop on a bus to **Changning** (chángníng; 长宁) instead (1hr., every 12min. 6:30am-7pm, Y8.5) and transfer to a local bus to Bamboo Sea (1½hr., every 15-20min. 6am-5pm, Y4). The bus stops at the west gate of the park to purchase **entrance tickets** (Y67, students Y35), then continues up a few kilometers to the base of the scenic area. If you miss the 6am bus back to **Yibin,** buses to Changning are frequent and run as late as 5pm, allowing for more time in the park.

▐ ACCOMMODATIONS. At the base of the scenic area, you can lodge in one of the small bamboo-decorated hotels or take a motorbike to one of the scenic points inside the park and find a hotel there. The best bet for accommodations inside the park is one of the mountain-top hotels, which range from Y50 to Y300 per night. In addition, a night on the mountain is the best way to see the sunrise and the early morning seas of clouds drifting over the valleys. The bamboo **▨ Fairy Dwelling Mountain Villa ❶** (xiānyù shānzhuàng; 仙寓山庄 ; ☎497 0218), just off the mountain-top parking lot near Fairy Lake, offers high-season doubles for Y80 and low-season doubles for Y40. Across from the pleasant bamboo house, the more upscale **Guanxian Lou Hotel ❸** (guānxiān lóu bīnguǎn; 观仙楼宾馆) has well-furnished standard doubles with A/C, TV, and bath for Y200 and up. Lodging can also be found on the main street near the entrance to the trails. A number of small-run family hotels, some with clean bamboo-house facades, charge as little as Y10-40 per bed. The **Chengbin Hotel ❶** (chéngbīn lóu; 承宾楼 ; ☎8608 0803) has a good Y40 per bed deal and Y100 for doubles with bath and A/C.

◪ BAMBOO SEA. The Bamboo Sea is divided into three main sights: **Forgetting Melancholy Valley** (wàngyōu gǔ; 忘忧谷), **Fairy Lake** (xiānnǔ hú; 仙女湖), and the three-layered **Seven-Colors Waterfall** (qīcǎi pùbù; 七彩瀑布), near Dragon Lake (lóng tán; 龙潭). The same curved path connects them all. While you can follow brick-red trails through the towering bamboo woods to the sights, they are few and far apart. A time-saving strategy is to hop on a motorbike (one destination Y10, from Wanling to Seven-Colors Waterfall Y20).

At Fairy Lake and the nearby **Sea Among Seas** lake, drift on a bamboo raft (Y20, time unlimited). From there, follow the trail to **Fairy Cave** and continue to **Echo Valley,** where, from high up on the sandstone cliffs, you can hear your voice resonate in the valley below, over fields and waterfalls. A sporadically operating cable car (Y30 one-way) leads to **Sea-Gazing Tower** (guānhǎi lóu; 观海楼), the main sight before Fairy Cave. Ascend the seven-story pagoda-shaped building to take in the boundless expanse of green ocean waving gently in the wind.

CHONGQING 重庆　　　　　☎023

Over the years, some have come to see Chongqing (meaning "Doubly Blessed") as a lackluster interior city, but nothing could be further from the truth. The landscape of this attractive Yangzi River-side city is uniquely serene, given the city's sweltering sub-tropical climate and spicy food. Even the streets are mellow, thanks to a city ordinance against car horns. At the same time, air raid tunnels and Guomindang prison camps hint at a turbulent past. This thriving Yangzi port first opened to British trade in 1890 and then to the Japanese in 1895. After the Japanese departure at the onset of the Sino-Japanese War in 1937 (see p. 79) and the fall of Nanjing, the GMD chose Chongqing as the site of their new capital due to its strategic position straddling two rivers and the heavy fogs, which frequently frustrated aerial attacks. In the final days of the civil war between the CCP and the GMD, Chongqing saw intense fighting memorialized in chilling pictures and artifacts at Red Cliff Village and Gele Mountain.

Since 1997, Chongqing has enjoyed the special status of independent municipality, a title it shares with Beijing, Tianjin, and Shanghai. These days, this booming industrial city, seething with the humidity and dust of the sultry Yangzi Valley, is best known as the starting-off point for cruises through the Three Gorges. Walk near the Liberation Monument at night and feel the city pulsing with booming techno beats and flashing neon lights. With its well-dressed young crowds and trendy nightlife, Chongqing has come to acquire a cosmopolitan glamor of its own.

▎ TRANSPORTATION

Flights: Jiangbei Airport (jiāngběi jīchǎng; 江北机场 ; ☎6715 2336), 35km north of the city center. **Shuttle buses** (40-50min., every 30min. 6am-6:30pm, Y15) connect the airport to the CAAC office near the intersection of Renmin Lu and Zhongshan Lu, in Shangqi Si. Chongqing is mainly served by **China Southwest Airlines** (xīnán hángkōng gōngsī; 西南航空公司 ; ☎6382 5926) and **Sichuan Airlines** (sìchuān hángkōng gōngsī; 四川航空公司), 17 Minquan Lu (☎6370 7070 or 6383 9999; fax 6370 0818), just beyond the post office when coming from the Liberation Monument. Open daily 8:30am-10pm. To: **Beijing** (6-7 per day, Y1500); **Guangzhou** (6 per day, Y180); **Kunming** (10 per day, Y710); **Shanghai** (7-8 per day, Y1440); **Xi'an** (4 per day, Y700).

Trains: Caiyuanba Train Station (càiyuánbà huǒchē zhàn; 菜园坝火车站), 4 Caiyuan Lu (☎6168 1111), in Yuzhong district's southwestern corner. Also called **Chongqing (Main) Train Station** (chóngqìng huǒchē zhàn; 重庆火车站). Ticket office open daily 8:30-11:30am, 2:30-5:30pm, and 6:30-10pm. The official taxi stand is on the right as you walk out of the station; taxis opposite the exit may not use meters. To: **Beijing** (25-33hr.; 2 per day; Y181-337, express Y238-430); **Chengdu** (9-10hr., 3 per day, Y67-120); **Guangzhou** (34-43hr.; 5 per day; Y121-256, express Y220-380) via **Nanning**; **Guiyang** (9-10hr., 2 per day, Y34-75); **Kunming** (23-24hr., 2 per day, Y122-216); **Shanghai** (41-42hr., 5:42pm, Y271-475); **Yibin** (8hr., daily, Y25-57).

Buses: Chongqing Long-Distance Bus Station (chóngqìng chángtú qìchē zhàn; 重庆长途汽车站), 6 Caiyuan Lu (☎8903 3877), next to the train station. Open daily 5:30am-midnight. To: **Chengdu** (4hr., every 30min. 6:30am-8:30pm, Y78); **Dazu** (2hr., 6am, Y39). **Chaotianmen Bus Station** (cháotiānmén qìchē zhàn; 朝天门汽车站 ; ☎6373 6788). To **Chengdu** (4hr., every hr. 8am-5pm, Y73) and **Yichang** (12hr., noon, Y197).

Ferries: See the **Three Gorges,** p. 734.

Local Transportation: Buses are cheap and efficient, but the number of routes can make the system overwhelming. If you don't see the bus you're looking for, listen for your destination (each bus has someone yelling out its route at major stops) or ask the driver. Fare Y1-2. Buses #102, 120, and 130 run along Jiefang Lu between Chaotianmen Dock and the Caiyuanba Train Station; #210 runs between Caiyuanba and Bai Mansion via Red Cliff Village; #271 and 462 link the Liberation Monument (Jiefang Bei) and Chongqing University (Chongqing Daxue), with 271 continuing on to Red Cliff Village; #429 runs from Caiyuanba to the Liberation Monument. Stops are far apart; ask drivers to let you off close to your destination.

Taxis: Base fare Y5, each additional km Y1.2.

✷7 ORIENTATION AND PRACTICAL INFORMATION

Situated at the confluence of the **Yangzi** (长江) and **Jialing** (嘉陵) rivers, Chongqing municipality is divided into five central districts. Of these, **Yuzhong** (渝中) juts out, peninsula-like into the junction of the two rivers, and contains the most conveniently located hotels, shops, and transport facilities. **Jiangbei** (江北) to the north, across the Jialing River, and **Shapingba** (沙坪坝) to the west are important gateways to sights in the outer reaches of the city. Steep and narrow winding streets make Chongqing difficult to navigate, and Yuzhong alone is too big to cover on foot. The district, bounded to the southwest by the train and bus stations on Caiyuan Lu and to the northeast by the **Chaotianmen Dock** (cháotiānmén mǎtóu; 朝天门码头), is best navigated by bus or taxi. Hotels, restaurants, nightlife, and most services cluster in a compact, convenient area near the **Liberation Monument** (jiěfàng bēi; 解放碑), a 15min. walk from the docks at the intersection of **Zourong Lu** (邹容路) and **Minzu Lu** (民族路), which turns into **Minquan Lu** (民权路).

Travel Agencies: CITS, at 120 Zaozi Lanya Zheng Jie (☎6385 0693 or 6385 2490; fax 6385 0693). Open daily 9am-6pm. Another **branch** (☎8903 7560; fax 8937 559) is more conveniently located in Zourong Plaza (邹容广场) near the Liberation Monument. Open daily 9am-6pm. **China Youth Travel Service** (zhōngguó qīngnián lǚxíngshè; 中国青年旅行社), 125 Renmin Lu (☎6386 0814), near the intersection with Zhongshan Lu. Open M-F 9am-6pm. A 2nd **branch** (☎6370 9621) is in the Liberation Monument area on the 3rd fl. of the Commerce Bldg. (shāngyè dàshà; 商业大厦). Open M-F 9am-6:30pm, Sa-Su 10am-5:30pm.

Chongqing

ACCOMMODATIONS
Bayi Hotel, 8
Chongqing
Chaotianmen Hotel, 1
Fuyuan Hotel, 11
Huixianlou Hotel, 2
Opera House
Guesthouse, 9

FOOD
Bayi Duck, 7
Old Sichuan
Chongqing
Restaurant, 3

NIGHTLIFE
Havana Club, 10
Newcastle Bar, 5
Oceanus, 6
Reunion Club, 4

Yangzi R. 长江

JIANGBEI 江北

Jialing R. 嘉陵江

Jialingjiang Binjiang Lu 嘉陵江滨江路

Huanhua Yuan Bridge

TO NORTH HOT SPRINGS
(30km)

Cable Car

Chaotianmen Docks
Chaotianmen Bus Station
Port Ticket Office
To Red Cliff Village
Carrefour
Luohan Temple
Chaodong Lu 朝东路
Changjiang Binjiang Lu
Shaanxi Lu 陕西路
Xinhua Lu 新华路
No. 1 Hospital

Bank of China
Food Street
Zhonghua Lu
Bayi Lu
Xinhua Lu

Bank of China
Wuyi Lu 五一路
Metropolitan Plaza
Liberation Monument
Linjiang Lu
Zourong Lu
SEE INSET
Minquan Lu 民权路
Minzu Lu 民族路
Bayi Lu 八一路
Zhonghua Lu
Zhongshan Yi Lu 中山一路
Minsheng Lu 民生路
LINJIANGMEN
Jiefang Dong Lu 解放东路

Beiqu Lu 北区路
Shangqing Si 上清寺
Hanwei Lu
Huayi Lu
Zhongshan Yi Lu 中山一路
Xinmin Lu 新民路
Zhongshan Er Lu 中山二路
Zhongqing Lu
Changjiang Binjiang Lu
Jiefang Xi Lu 解放西路

Yangzi R. Bridge
Coral Reef Island 珊瑚坝

Chongqing Natural History Museum
Pipa Hill Park
Pipashan Zheng Jie 枇杷山正街

CYTS
Renmin Lu
Renmin Jie 人民街
Qingli Xiang
Huang Xiang
Zaozi Lanya Zheng Jie 枣子岚垭正街
Great Hall of the People
PEOPLE'S SQ
CITS
Buses to Gele Mountain

YUZHONG 渝中

Zhongshan San Lu 中山三路
Zhongshan Si Lu 中山四路
Nandu Lu
Nanqu Lu 南区路

Caiyuanba Train Station
Chongqing Long-Distance Bus Station
Chongqing Emergency Center

Sixin Lu
Shangqing Si Si Lu 上清寺四路
TO SHAPINGBA;
TO RED CLIFF VILLAGE (4km);
TO GELE MOUNTAIN
MARTYRS MEMORIAL
Zhongshan San Lu 中山三路

TO (35km)
TO DAZU
(80km)

Caiyuan Lu
Eling Park 鹅岭公园

0   400 yards
0   400 meters

N
S
W
E

SICHUAN

Consulates: Canada: Metropolitan Tower, Ste. 1705, Wuyi Lu (☎6373 8007). **UK:** in Ste. 2801 of the same building (☎6381 0321). Both open M-F 9am-noon and 1-5pm.

Bank of China: 104 Minzu Lu (☎6380 0654; fax 6370 1294), beyond the Huixianlou Hotel if coming from the Liberation Monument. Exchanges currency and traveler's checks. Credit card advances. Open daily 9am-noon and 2-5:30pm.

Market: Carrefour (jiālèfú; 家乐福), 2 Cangbai Lu (☎6378 8415), with an entrance around the corner at 14 Minzu Lu, seems to offer more dairy products than anywhere else in China. Open daily 9am-10pm.

PSB: 48 Wusi Lu (☎6384 3641; fax 6383 1830), in the Liberation Monument area. Serves foreigners and processes visa requests. Another **branch** (☎6384 2238) is on Cangbai Lu, opposite Carrefour. Both open 9am-5pm.

Hospitals: Chongqing Emergency Center (chóngqìngshì jíjiù yīliáo zhōngxīn; 重庆市救医疗中心), 1 Jiankang Lu (☎6387 4000; http://chongqing.emss.cn). English-speaking doctors and "baby friendly." Emergency room open 24hr. **Chongqing No. 1 People's Hospital** (chóngqìngshì dìyī rénmín yīyuàn; 重庆市第一人民医院), 40 Damen Kou (☎6384 1324). Open 24hr. Both are in the Yuzhong district.

Internet Access: Reader's Club (dúzhě jùlèbù; 读者俱乐部), 181 Minsheng Lu, 3rd fl. (☎6371 6367 or 6371 6347). From the Huixianlou Hotel, turn right at the Liberation Monument and then left on Zhonghua Lu. Stay right until the street ends; turn right and enter next to the Xinhua Bookstore. A sea of fast computers. Y2-8 per hr. Open 24hr. Internet room at the **Bayi Hotel** (see **Accommodations**, p. 730). Y2 per hr. Open 24hr.

Post Offices: Each district has a main post office. **Yuzhong central office,** 3 Mingnan Lu (☎6386 2200), is half a block from the Liberation Monument, on the left. Now under the China Mobile sign; walk past the cell phone counters to the back. EMS, IDD service. Open daily 8:30am-9:30pm. **Western Union** is next door.

Postal Code: 400014.

ACCOMMODATIONS

Accommodations in Chongqing are all about skyscrapers and sky-scraping prices. Foreigners hoping for budget hotels will have to look far and wide. Fortunately, the cheapest district, Yuzhong, is also the most convenient. All listed hotels have 24hr. hot water unless otherwise noted.

Opera House Guesthouse (gējù yuàn zhāodàisuǒ; 歌剧院招待所), 263 Bayi Lu (☎6383 3770; fax 6371 1216), 2 blocks from the Liberation Monument. Inconspicuous entrance opposite Bayi Hotel. One of the few places in the city that will let you pay per bed, it's also the only place with free Communist-era opera for your listening pleasure. Don't expect velvet curtains and chandeliers; do expect clean beds, private baths, and security gates that lock at 11pm. Triples with A/C, bath, and TV Y45 per bed. ❶

Bayi Hotel (bāyī bīnguǎn; 八一宾馆; ☎6380 5400 or 6381 4210), on Bayi Lu, parallel to Minquan Lu, off Food St. in the Liberation Monument area. Internet in basement Y2 per hr. Well-furnished doubles Y100-160, low season Y80. ❷

Huixianlou Hotel (huìxiānlóu fàndiàn; 会仙楼饭店), 186 Minzu Lu (☎6383 7495; fax 6384 4234), 2 blocks from the Liberation Monument. The best deal in town. This place is plush: even dorms have A/C, carpets, and TV. Books river cruises, plane tickets, and tours. 6-bed dorms Y50; doubles and singles Y240-260, low season Y138. ❶

Fuyuan Hotel (fùyuàn bīnguǎn; 富苑宾馆), 38 Caiyuan Lu (☎6903 3111; fax 6903 3922), around the corner from the bus and train stations toward the river. Fine, clean rooms with central A/C and TV. Close to loud transportation hubs, but not much else. Hot water 7pm-10am. Singles and doubles Y180-260; triples Y260. ❸

Chongqing Chaotianmen Hotel (chóngqìng cháotiānmén dàjiǔdiàn; 重庆朝天门大酒店; ☎6310 1666 or 6310 0370), across the street from the ticket office at Chaotianmen Dock. Convenient for hopping on a cruise ship, this classy 3-star hotel has rooms with gorgeous waterfront views. Books cruises, arranges daytrips, and exchanges currency. Singles Y328; doubles Y400 and up. ❹

🍴 FOOD

Superhuman chili-eaters will be right at home in Chongqing. The local specialty **Sichuanese hotpot** (sìchuān huǒguō; 四川火锅) is said to have originated near Minzu Lu in the family-run joints of Xiaomishi (xiǎomíshì; 小米市), now a street of flashy, high-end malls. Unlike the clear Mongolian variety, Chongqing hotpot broth is an ultra-spicy psychedelic-red concoction that used to be laced with opium for added "flavor." The ubiquitous hotpot joints are easily recognized by the rows of tables with holes in the middle. Ranging from Y70-80 at a street-side family-run place to hundreds of *yuán* at a high-end restaurant, a typical hotpot meal for a table of four consists of plates of raw meat, vegetables, and seafood delicacies cooked in the bubbling soup. In the Liberation Monument area, the cheapest stalls are in the alleys, near the Huixianlou Hotel; from the hotel, walk toward the monument, take the first right, and then turn into an alley to the left. A small **nightmarket** on Cangbai Lu features hotpot; walk in the opposite direction on Minzu Lu for 7-10min. and simply turn right at the Carrefour. Further on Cangbai Lu, **Canglong Hotpot** ❸ (cānglóng huǒguō; 沧龙火锅 ; ☎6371 2301) and a number of restaurants in traditional architecture line the street, serving up plates of beef, mushrooms, kidney slices, and tofu (Y150-200 per table of 4).

There's more to Sichuanese food than just hotpot. Next to the Huixianlou Hotel in the Liberation Monument area, the **Old Sichuan Restaurant** ❷ (lǎo sìchuān dà jiǔlóu; 老四川大酒楼) specializes in beef dishes (Y15-28), but doesn't neglect herbivores with its veggie concoctions (Y6-15). The yummy *ǒubǐng* (藕饼), a pastry made from starchy lotus root, is only Y8. (☎6382 6644. Open until 10pm.) McDonald's lurks across from **Bayi Duck** ❷ (bāyī zuì jī cháng; 八一醉鸡肠), envying its rival's delicous platters of drunken duck and other poultry. (☎5381 1792. Entrees Y12 and up. Open until 11pm.)

When you're ready to give your blistered taste buds a rest, indulge in Chongqing's sweet delicacies. In the Liberation Monument plaza, **Food Street** ❶ (hǎochī jiē; 好吃街), parallel to Minquan Lu, teems with vendors selling *bōzǎi gāo* (钵仔糕), a round, glutinous cake studded with sweet red beans on a stick (Y0.5), and sticky rice balls with sweet filling (shānchéng tāngyuán; 山城汤园) for Y2 per bowl. Food Street's *dàpáidàng* (outdoor eateries) overflow with clear noodle and hot dishes. (Y4-Y8. Open until 10pm.) On Bayi Lu, **Blue and White** ❶ (lán hé bái; 蓝和白) offers a chic, air-conditioned space for pick-as-you-point dishes and late-night munchies. (☎6370 2616. Dishes Y5-8. Rice congee Y1. Open 10am-3am.)

👁 SIGHTS

It's easy to lose a day walking among Chongqing's attractive architecture and steep winding streets. Not a city for natural scenery or ancient relics, Chongqing focuses largely on the grim and not-so-ancient past of the 1947-49 civil war with the GMD. These political sights offer a glimpse at some of the founding facts and perceptions behind the Chinese worldview.

LIBERATION MONUMENT (jiěfàng bēi; 解放碑). This short tower, built to commemorate the Communist liberation of Chongqing from GMD control, is now the most prominent meeting point in Yuzhong district. Surrounded by flashing neon lights, fast-food joints, and billboards, the monument looks like it's celebrating Chongqing's "liberation" from socialist austerity. The monument area is a great place to watch fashion-conscious children strutting by with new clothes from the huge **Metropolitan Plaza** (dàdūhuì guǎngchǎng; 大都会广场), the city's largest mall.

PEOPLE'S SQUARE (rénmín guǎngchǎng; 人民广场). The massive People's Square is dominated by the **Great Hall of the People** (rénmín dàlǐtáng; 人民大礼堂), designed by the famous Chinese architect Zhang Jiade and completed in 1954. The building was modeled after the Temple of Heaven in Beijing (p. 148), but the interior is fairly uninteresting. In 1981, "the people" sacrificed their access to the south and north wings and turned them into the palatial Chongqing People's Hotel. *(Open daily 8am-6:30pm. Y5.)* Visit People's Square at night, when the plaza becomes a massive dance floor, with hundreds of people spinning and whirling to music blasted over giant loudspeakers. The mixed crowd includes a good number of young people intent on learning steps from the elegant older women who rule this community dance hall. The finale is an over-the-top feel-good musical bonanza. *(Accessible by bus #103 from the Liberation Monument area. Dancing daily 8-9:30pm.)*

GELE MOUNTAIN MARTYRS MEMORIAL (gēlè shān lièshì língyuán; 歌乐山烈士陵园). Gele Mountain encompasses three sites, all documenting GMD violence during the Chinese Civil War. Also known as the **Site of Sino-American Special Technical Cooperation Organization (SACO)** (zhōngměi hézùosuǒ; 中美合作所), the complex takes its name from the alliance that lent US support to the GMD against the CCP. Some 300 Communist Party members were held for questioning and later executed at the larger camp known as **Refuse Pit Prison** (zhāzǐ dòng; 渣滓洞). The interrogation room, with its faintly blood-stained rope and torture apparatus, has been kept just the way it was, as have some of the prison cells. On November 27, 1949, after the Communist Party proclaimed the People's Republic of China, the GMD commander in charge of Chongqing ordered the massacre of the prisoners. Only 15 people managed to escape.

Three kilometers down the hill, the **Bai Mansion** (bái gōngguǎn; 白公馆) relates some of the same gruesome past, albeit on a smaller scale. Exhibits tell the stories of individual prisoners. The interrogation room is in a small cave at the back of the mansion. Cool, damp air and red lights enhance the eeriness of the chamber, which still contains various 50-year-old tools.

Another 3-4km away, down the hill back toward the road, the **Martyrs' Tomb** (lièshì mù; 烈士墓) commemorates the members of the Communist Party who died at Gele Mountain. A museum displays photographs, clothes (most bearing marks of suffering), and writings of the deceased, as well as a larger collection of tools used during interrogation sessions. For visitors who can't read Chinese, the Martyrs' Tomb is the least moving piece in the trio of sights. *(On Gele Mtn., 50min. from the city center. Take bus #215 from the Liberation Monument area, Renmin Lu at Zhongshan Lu, or People's Sq., to Shapingba and change to #210, which runs to Bai Mansion via Martyrs' Tomb. Taxi from Bai Mansion to Refuse Pit Prison Y5. ☎6363 0300. 2hr. interrogation reenactments at Refuse Pit Prison 7pm, Y40. Refuse Pit Prison and Bai Mansion open daily 8am-7pm. Martyr's Tomb open daily 8am-late evening. Combined admission to all sights and museum Y25, includes Chinese tour guide and buses to all 3 sights. Individual sights Y2-5.)*

RED CLIFF VILLAGE (hóngyán cūn; 红岩村). The Communist Party built this modest complex to serve as its headquarters during the shaky Communist-Nationalist alliance against the Japanese. A newly renovated museum near the entrance displays revolutionary photographs and essays. Slightly farther away are the southern headquarters and living quarters of the Communist Party and the 8th

Route Army (which later grew into the People's Liberation Army); Zhou Enlai lived here for several years during the war with Japan. Despite Chongqing's scorching summers, Mao's room is the only one with an electric fan. *(30-45min. ride on bus #104 from Cangbai Lu. Red Cliff Village is at the terminus, on the opposite side of the road. ☎6330 0192. No English captions. Open daily 8:30am-5pm. Y18.)*

NORTH HOT SPRINGS (běi wēnquán; 北温泉). Kiss those unsightly rashes goodbye; a dip in these three pools can reputedly cure skin ailments. Private baths and showers are also available for those who fear that the water's healing powers may be diluted by the itchy crowds. The grounds of North Hot Springs Park invite aimless wanderings or a trip to a deep mountain cave, where stalactites, stalagmites, and bats prove amiable company. *(1hr. bus ride away. Bus #502 runs every hr. 10am-11:30pm from Chongqing Guesthouse on Mingshen Lu for Y11; get off at the last stop, Beipei, and transfer to bus #518 to the springs. Open 24hr. Y10.)*

OTHER SIGHTS. Built over 1000 years ago, **Luohan Temple** (luóhàn sì; 罗汉寺) contains 500 carved and painted terracotta figures guarded by a large golden Buddha. *(7 Minzu Lu. Open daily 9am-6:30pm. Y5.)* **Pipa Hill Park** (pípá shān gōngyuán; 枇杷山公园) stretches between Zhongshan Er Lu and Pipashan Zhenjie. The central pavilion provides views of Chongqing that glitter brightly after dark. *(Open daily 7am-11pm. Y5.)* On the path from the road on the south side of the park, the tiny **Chongqing Natural History Museum** (zìrán bówùguǎn; 自然博物馆) houses two dinosaur skeletons and other fossil remains. *(Open daily 8:30am-5:30pm. Y2.)*

🎵 NIGHTLIFE

In the world of Chongqing nightlife, any pub or club that's been around for a year must be on the downswing. Word of mouth should always be your first guide to this booming scene (just ask the city's hip young English speakers). If nobody's talking, follow the packs of glittering night owls who prowl the blocks around the Liberation Monument, Yuzhong's most happening area.

Reunion Club (huíguī jiǔláng; 回归酒廊 ; ☎6376 2882), in the Yutian Bldg., 8th fl. From the Huixianlou Hotel, turn left at the monument; the building is a block ahead on the right—the one with the McDonald's inside. Chongqing's best-dressed come here to see and be seen. The Reunion's throbbing techno and exuberant crowd keep the place moving until closing time. Corona Y25. Open daily 8pm-3am.

Newcastle Bar (niŭkǎqî'ěr jiǔbā; 纽卡斯尔酒吧 ; ☎6373 1488), 3rd fl. of bldg. directly across from the Reunion. The sleek tables and barfront are cleared at midnight for a massive dance floor. Margaritas Y25-30. Guinness Y40. Open until 2am.

Havana Club (hāwǎnà jùlèbù; 哈瓦那俱乐部 ; ☎6371 1916). Heading away from the Liberation Monument, go 1 block past Newcastle Bar and Reunion Club; look for signs on Bayi Lu. Posh interiors and live jazz bands give this place a Caribbean feel. A slightly older crowd. Themed parties and ladies specials Sa-Su. Corona Y25. Open 8pm-2am.

Oceanus International Entertainment Club (hǎi zhī dū; 海之都 ; ☎6373 9388), 3rd fl. of the cone-shaped bldg. next to McDonald's; look for the flashy entrance. Watch out for the fish swimming under your feet while dancing on the transparent glass floor. Budweiser Y15. Open until 2am.

Linglong Bar and Teahouse (línglóng bā; 玲珑吧 ; ☎6669 6990). Tucked into a quiet corner on Cangbai Lu, off Mingzu Lu. A low-key alternative for those who prefer to kick back in wicker chairs, admire folk-dyed art, and quietly enjoy a drink at the dimly lit wooden bar. Tea Y10. Drinks Y20 and up. Open 9am-11pm.

▶ DAYTRIP: DAZU STONE CARVINGS 大足石刻

80km east of Chongqing in the town of Dazu. Buses head to Dazu from the long-distance bus station in Caiyuanba, next to the train station (2hr., 6am, Y39). Holy Summit, North Mtn., and South Mtn. are all in different directions from Dazu, requiring a return to town in between destinations. Buses go to Holy Summit (15-20min., Y2); cab to North and South Mtns. Y5-10. All 3 sites open 8:30am-6pm. Holy Summit Y50; students and seniors over 70 Y25. North Mtn. Y40/Y20. South Mtn. Y5. Combined admission Y85.

Though not quite Dunhuang, the Dazu Stone Carvings (dàzú shíkè; 大足石刻) encompass more than 50,000 clifftop Buddhist sculptures, scattered at 75 sites throughout the region. Dating from the Tang and Song Dynasties, these fine examples of late-period Chinese grotto artwork have aged eerily well—some still glint with tinges of their original blue and gold pigments.

The best-preserved and largest collection of carvings can be seen at **Holy Summit** (bǎodǐng shān; 宝顶山), 15km northeast of Dazu. Dozens of tiny stone figures encircle a 31m-long statue of the reclining Sakyamuni, built in the Southern Song (1127-1279). A nearby temple is home to the magnificent gold-coated Avalokitesvara of a Thousand Hands—if in doubt, simply count the dazzling array of fingers and hands fanning out on the main temple wall. The less well-preserved **North Mountain** (běi shān; 北山) contains older works from the late Tang Dynasty (AD 618-907) and the Sutrapitaka Cave. The sculptures on the **South Mountain** (nán shān; 南山) are among the few Daoist relics in the region, revealing a rich history of contact between the two major Chinese traditions.

THREE GORGES 三峡

From the White Emperor City (446km downstream from Chongqing) to Nanjingguan (6km west of Yichang), the mighty Yangzi rolls through 196km of death-defying rapids and imposing peaks known as the Three Gorges (sānxiá). Immortalized

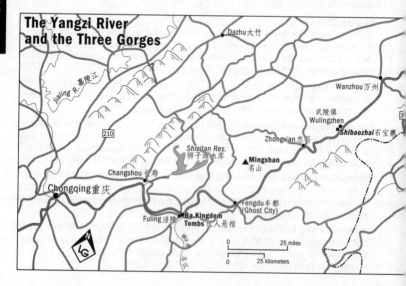

The Yangzi River and the Three Gorges

Dazhu 大竹

Jialing R. 嘉陵江

210

Wanzhou 万州

武陵镇 Wulingzhen

Shizitan Res. 狮子滩水库

Zhongxian 忠县

Shibaozhai 石宝寨

▲Mingshan 名山

Changshou 长寿

Chongqing 重庆

Fengdu 丰都 (Ghost City)

Fuling 涪陵

Ba Kingdom Tombs 巴人悬棺

0   25 miles

0   25 kilometers

in poetry and literature, these gorges have captivated the imagination of everyone from Li Bai to Bill Gates. However, the construction of the Three Gorges Dam, due to be completed in 2009, has already raised the water by 135m, marring the landscape irrevocably, with more changes to come. While the main sights—Mingshan, Shibaozhai, and White Emperor City—will still be visible behind thick, long walls blocking the water, historical landmarks such as Zhang Fei Temple have been relocated to higher elevations. The gorges themselves will undergo the most transformation, and what remains after dam's completion will be a mockery of the original. Already, the steep, shadowy peaks that once menaced the narrow river dwindle in height, their grandeur and mystery swallowed by the rising river.

Yet, however altered, the gorges remain an undeniable attraction of the river, drawing travelers both foreign and domestic. The cruise is steeped in Chinese tourist culture, and passengers expecting a peaceful ride down the Yangzi may come away disappointed by how packaged the experience is. An army of tour guides narrate the trip, and the river churns a disappointing shade of yellow. The souvenir frenzy awaiting at each stop and the overpriced, manmade attractions diminish the sense of wonder that the trip promises. In the near future, passengers may be required to purchase the tickets to all the sights along with the cruise, making it impossible to skip over uninteresting places with wallet unscathed. Be prepared to shell out a few hundred *yuán* for the admissions alone.

TRANSPORTATION AND PRACTICAL INFORMATION

Most tourists make the downstream journey from Chongqing and disembark at either **Yichang** (p. 465) or **Wuhan** (p. 459) in Hubei province. Some cruises go as far as **Jiujiang** in Jiangxi province or all the way to **Shanghai.** The increased numbers of ships have made it easy to find a ticket, but advance purchase is a wise move. The **Official Port Ticket Office** (chóngqìng gǎng shòupiào chù; 重庆港售票处), under the Chaotianmen Hotel at the Chaotianmen Dock (cháotiānmén mǎtóu; 朝天门码头) is perhaps the most trustworthy place to buy tickets. (☎6310 0680;

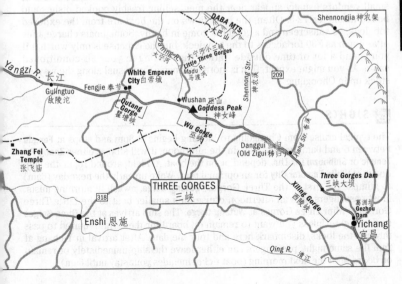

www.cqpits.com.cn. Open daily 6am-8pm.) Most reputable companies have a booth here and all offer the same fixed prices. CQG ("Chongqing Port") officials, recognizable by their blue shirts, black pants/skirts, and small red pins, monitor the goings-on. Questions or concerns can be addressed at the CQG desks in the back. Next to the ticket windows, the friendly staff at **Chongqing Port International Travel Service** (chóngqìng gǎng guójì lǚxíngshè; 重庆港国际旅行社) provide free English consultations. (☎6310 0314 or 6310 0866. Open 9am-6pm.)

Going **downstream** from Chongqing to Yichang, there are several options. **Speedboats,** used mainly for transportation purposes, traverse the entire stretch without stopping (12hr., Y402). Higher-end cruises with small tours cost considerably more (Y1600-3000). These are usually both run and frequented by foreigners. The most common options are the **Chinese cruise ships,** which stop around 1-3hr. at the sights, and **passenger ships,** which only stop for 30min. at the sights. There are different classes of **berths:** 1st class (2 beds, A/C, TV, and bath); 2nd class (2-4 beds, A/C, TV, and sometimes bath); 3rd class (6-8 beds, A/C, TV, and sometimes a washbasin); 4th class (8-12 beds, sometimes TV); and 5th class (any space you can find on the deck). The Chinese cruise ships going to **Yichang** offer only 1st- to 3rd-class cabins. (50+hr., or 3 days; 1st-class Y1022, 2nd Y578-636, 3rd Y270-297). Passenger ships are slightly cheaper and have all five classes, but the conditions are more cramped. (1st-class Y976, 2nd Y530, 3rd Y248, 4th Y176, 5th Y96.) Children pay 5th-class fare. Most departures are 5-8pm, so a three-day cruise is really one evening, two days, and two nights.

Going **upstream,** from Yichang to Chongqing, is slightly cheaper and cuts back a few hours of travel time. However, these are passenger ships only, and to take the Chinese cruise ship, you must join a tour group, which requires extra money for middlemen and tour guide fees.

There is no pre-paid board option on the regular tourist boats, and the cruise experience varies significantly from boat to boat. Most ships have one or two restaurants on board selling overpriced food. Many passengers bring groceries aboard and supplement their stash of instant noodles with cheap snacks from the stalls at the stops. With the boats often docking at meal times, a number of small vendors usually appear near the pier, selling freshly cooked dishes and boxed meals for Y2-5. Often, the best views on the boat are from the exposed top deck, so sunscreen and a good hat come in handy. Some boats charge a fee of as much as Y30 for access to the top deck, but the expense is only worth it if you spend a lot of time outside, rather than hiding in your air-conditioned cabin. As you might expect, film is more expensive than usual along the way, so stock up in Chongqing.

🔘 SIGHTS

The typical cruise from Chongqing to Yichang begins at 8pm and stops at **Fengdu** between 6 and 9am the next day. In the afternoon, it will stop at either **Zhang Fei Temple** or **Shibaozai** for 1hr., depending on the boat. At night, around 10pm, the ship docks at **White Emperor City** for an optional tour. Wake up early the next day (6am) to glimpse the first of the Three Gorges, **Qutang Gorge,** awash in morning mists. Most passengers take an afternoon cruise on a smaller boat to the Little Three Gorges or Mini Three Gorges at **Wutang Gorge.** The ship arrives at the **Three Gorges Dam** at night. Unless you want to remain on board for the 4-7hr. required to pass through the locks, disembark here and tour the dam. After arrival in Yichang at 2am the same night, passengers can either leave the ship immediately or remain on board until the next morning (boat ticket includes your stay until 6am).

FENGDU 丰都

The surrounding riverbank of this "City of Ghosts" (guǐ chéng; 鬼城) is fabled to be home to demonic spirits, and the tourist town feeds off the legend with a kitschy, carnival atmosphere. Appreciate it while you can. Once they open the floodgates of the Three Gorges Dam, the entire city of Fengdu will be an underwater ghost town, leaving only (a much shorter) Mingshan Mountain above the water. The visit usually lasts 3hr. and is designed to funnel tourists directly to Mingshan.

MINGSHAN MOUNTAIN (míng shān; 名山). Said to be the capital of a ghost kingdom, Mingshan Mountain now sees just enough activity to wake the dead—and empty your wallet. From the docks, follow the crowd of visor-wearing tourists straight ahead. If arriving at Dock #4, head left on **Dongmen Lu** (东门路) and **Beimen Lu** (北门路) before turning right on **Zhongshan Lu** (中山路). The massive stone head on the hill indicates the route. The mountain has been collecting ghost-ornamented temples since the Tang Dynasty. Today, the garish **God Palace** (guǐguó shéngōng; 鬼国神宫) is overrun with palm readers (Y60), photographers (Y10), tea houses (Y20), and trinket sellers (Y10-100). The suspension bridge leading to the mountain is said to determine the soul's destination in the afterlife, whether it be nirvana or hell. (☎ 7062 3235. Open daily 6am-6pm. Y60, students Y42. Chairlift Y20.)

SHIBAOZHAI (shíbǎozhài; 石宝寨). Three hours and 106km downstream from Fengdu, the "Stone Treasure Stronghold" of Shibaozhai is a 12-storied, red-walled, green-eaved pagoda built against a sheer cliff. While some boats just cruise by Shibaozhai for a passing view, others stop for an entire hour. The short visit is just enough time to scramble up the ramp, through the vendor-crammed streets, and up the "Stairs to the Clouds" of the 56m Ming-era tower dedicated to the Jade Emperor, the omnipotent ruler of heaven in folk religion. According to legend, Shibaozhai is the elaborately colored jade shard left behind by the goddess Nü Wa when she mended the broken sky. (Open daily 8am-4pm. Y15.)

ZHANG FEI TEMPLE (zhāngfēi miào; 张飞庙). Originally marking the site where Zhang Fei, a famous general of the Three Kingdoms period, met his end, the temple has now been relocated to higher ground on the opposite side of the river. Two of Zhang Fei's men, who had been on the receiving end of their commander's wrath, decapitated him and supposedly threw his head into the Yangzi. Rebuilt in 1870 after a flood destroyed an earlier version, the current temple contains statues of Zhang Fei and several noteworthy tablets and woodcuts. Boats that stop here typically arrive 6-8pm and stay for just under 1hr. Despite the temple's excellent view of the sunset over the Yangzi, the brief visit is perhaps best spent getting dinner from one of the vendors crowding the path from the boat; there is little inside the temple to warrant its steep admission charge. (Open daily 9am-9pm. Y20.)

FENGJIE 奉节

The small, history-laden town of Fengjie (fèng jié) guards the entrance to Qutang Gorge, at the confluence of the Yangzi River and Plum Creek. Two 1000-year-old coffins discovered in the exposed valley wall confirm Fengjie as the capital of the Kui Kingdom of the Ba people, ancestors of today's Tujia minority. Kuizhou, the Tang-era name of Fengjie, was a hotspot for itinerant Tang poets like Li Bai, Du Fu, and Lu You, all of whom braved the gorges.

About 1hr. away from town, unusual geological formations cover the ground. The 500m-wide, 600m-deep crater-like funnel called the **Heavenly Pit** (tiāngēn dìfèng; 天根地缝) leads to myriad caverns fed by underground rivers. Because

DAM IT

At Sandouping, some 40km from Yichang, is an overwhelming sight: the Three Gorges Project, the world's largest dam. The sheer scale of the structure makes bull-dozers, drills, and other machinery look like sandbox toys. Due for completion in 2009, this 185m-tall, 2km-wide wall across the Yangzi and its 28 superturbines will harness more energy than 18 nuclear power plants. The price tag? A mere US$10 billion according to official figures, but outside sources pin it at two to five times that amount.

The project has sparked controversy since its very conception. Proponents argue that China has a serious shortage of electricity, and that the reservoir would aid in controlling the Yangzi's infamous floods. Official figures estimate that the dam will generate more than 10% of China's electricity 84 billion kw). The flood reservoir will hold some 22 billion liters, and the entire reservoir will hold 40 billion liters.

The dam has been operating since 2002, and opponents point to its negative effects, including deteriorating water quality, increasing sedimentation, possible extinction of endangered species, and rock slides. The project will also relocate 1.3 million people in three stages and submerge the unexcavated treasures of some 8000 archaeological sites, many of which date back to the earliest days of Chinese civiliza-

many boats drop anchor for the night outside Fengjie and enter the Three Gorges early the next morning, it is more advisable to visit the on-site **White Emperor City** (báidì chéng; 白帝城), Fengjie's greatest claim to fame and the site of some *Romance of the Three Kingdoms* episodes.

Just outside Fengjie, White Emperor City is a cluster of temples built during the Han Dynasty by Gongsun Zan, the ruler of Sichuan. One day, some white vapors escaping from a well appeared to Gongsun as a white imperial dragon, which he took as a sign that he should assume the title of White Emperor. About 450 years ago, *Romance of the Three Kingdoms* buffs tossed out Gong's altar and replaced it with one for their hero, **Liu Bei.** According to the novel, in AD 221 Liu Bei, the King of Shu, launched a 750,000-man invasion against a former ally to avenge the decapitation of his blood brother (the aforementioned Zhang Fei). Against the better judgment of his advisor Zhuge Liang, Liu stationed his enormous army in the forests of Yichang, which were promptly burned by enemy troops. Zhuge Liang's ingenious **Eight Diagram Formation** helped Liu Bei to escape, but he died of illness soon after, leaving his son A'dou in Zhuge's care. Many visitors feel that the sights in White Emperor City don't necessarily justify the steep admission; some choose to stay aboard at this stop to rest up for their visit to the Three Gorges the next morning. *(Open daily with no set admission hours. Chairlift one-way Y17. Boat fee Y3-5. Y55.)*

QUTANG GORGE 瞿塘峡

Qutang Gorge (qútáng xiá), just east of Fengjie, is the shortest and narrowest of the Three Gorges at 8km long and only 50m wide at its narrowest point. Much of the majesty of **Kuimen** (kuí mén; 夔门), the steep, knife-sharp gateway cliffs, has been diminished by the rising water level, at 135m in 2004 and slated to be another 40m higher by 2009. Already submerged areas include the original north bank site of the now relocated **Red Armor Cliff,** named after a battalion outfitted with red armor in the Spring and Autumn Period (722-481 BC), and part of the **White Salt Cliffs ancient plankway,** built by the Ba people by placing wooden planks into the sheer rock face. Despite these changes (with more to come), vividly named rock formations like Phoenix Drinking Spring, Upside-Down Monk, and Rhinoceros Gazing at the Moon still remain, along the sides of what used to be the most dangerous and spectacular stretch of the river.

LITTLE THREE GORGES 小三峡

Qutang Gorge ends at the town of Wushan, located at the confluence of the Daning and Yangzi Rivers. From here, the Little Three Gorges (xiǎo sān xiá) spans 50km north along the Daning and its tributary, the Madu River. These narrower passes may not boast the imposing austerity of their counterparts, but the 6hr. tour to see them is widely considered to be the most rewarding part of the Yangzi trip. Smaller boats provide a more intimate experience, and more time allows for visits to river caves and the archaeological site where a two-million-year-old ape-man was unearthed. As it winds through the Longmen, Bawu, and Dicui Gorges, the Daning river turns into a splendid stream spindling through uninhabited limestone ravines, now known as the **Mini Three Gorges** (xiǎoxiǎo sānxiǎ; 小小三峡). Monkeys call and egrets karr in the dense forests high above as boatsmen propel wooden *sampan* by thrusting bamboo poles into the clear creek bed full of smooth, iridescent pebbles. *(Flood status uncertain. Passengers must join a tour group to see this sight. Purchase tickets on board, Y150-180, including all boat rides, tour guide fee, and admission ticket. Do not pay more than Y190.)*

WU GORGE 巫峡

Once passengers return from the Little Three Gorges, boats continue from Wushan into Wu Gorge (wū xiá), the "gorge of witches," generally considered to be the most enchanting of the Three Gorges. What used to be 2000m-high canyon walls still overshadow the river below, creating a surreal atmosphere complemented by dappled sunlight and occasional misty showers. The western section of the 40km-long gorge, called **Gold-Helmet Silver-Armor Gorge**, and the eastern section, called the **Iron Coffin Gorge**, are both partially submerged. However, the famed **Goddess Peak** (shénnǔ xiá; 神女峡) still juts up in stony serenity, gazing at the endless stream of passing ships from her lofty height. Legend has it that a goddess waited for her lover by the gorge until she turned into stone. At the western end of the gorge, the 12 peaks of the Wushan Mountains tower over the river, six on either side.

SHENNONG STREAM 神农溪

A stop on the upstream journey from Yichang to Chongqing, the Shennong Stream (shénnóng xī) is one of the last places on the Yangzi River where boatmen still work, sweat trickling down their bare torsos as they tow boats by the netting strung to their backs. Passengers disembark on a small boat and

tion. Of the 170,000 people already relocated, many have not received the full amount of the promised compensation.

Similarities between the Three Gorges Dam and the earlier Sanmenxia Dam on the Yellow River are another cause for concern. When the government admitted that the over-silted reservoir of the Sanmenxia Dam was responsible for the massive flooding that killed or relocated thousands in 2003, it confirmed disregarded warnings voiced by scientists during the construction of the dam. These same scientists also criticized the engineering and design of the Three Gorges Dam, but were ignored again.

When this project reaches its final stage in five years, the Three Gorges will vanish forever. In its place will be stunted peaks, destroyed cultural sites, and civilians without homes. Analysts are finally facing up to the extent of damage inflicted on the Yellow River, which has withered into a trickle along much of its length. Even one of the chief engineers of Sanmenxia, Zhang Guangdou, has called for the closing of Mao's pet project. Most believe, though, that too much money has been spent for the project to stop, and construction forges ahead. Meanwhile, China, which already has some 22,000 big dams, has 87 other dams currently under construction and is planning another 36. The proposed dams include 13 on the Nu-Salween River, a pristine jungle river flowing from Yunnan into Thailand.

descend into quiet valleys of shallow water and verdant cliff-side forests. The Shennong Stream leads to **Shennongjia** (shénnóngjià; 神农架), a wildly pristine natural reserve between the Yangzi and Wudangshan in northern Hubei. *(Inquire on board: you may be asked to join a tour. Y120, including boat costs.)*

XILING GORGE 西陵峡

The longest and last of the Three Gorges, the 80km-long Xiling Gorge (xīlíng xiá) is no lazy homestretch. Most of this canyon's hidden shoals have been blasted clear. Once known as a ship graveyard, the treacherous 42km stretch that includes the Art-of-War, Cow-Liver-Horse-Lung (supposedly named after the cliffside imagery) and Yellow Cow and Yellow Cat Gorges are now mostly harmless and submerged. Some relics from the gorge were moved to the new Three Gorges Museum in Chongqing, which is still in the midst of construction.

THREE GORGES DAM 三峡大坝

The nemesis of the Gorges, the **Three Gorges Dam** (sānxiá dà bà), lies just 1hr. beyond the end of Xiling Gorge. Despite all the skepticism and controversy, the dam itself is surprisingly impressive. The massive site is a surreal world of gigantic machinery, with a valley of cranes, engines, and construction poles. Eight of the 30 or so turbines scheduled to be completed in 2009 are already generating power. If all goes as planned, in less than a decade the reservoir will reach a storage level of 175m, and the dam will generate a tenth of all China's power. Tourists on the cruise must join a tour group on board to see the dam, as non-construction-related traffic at the site is limited to a few big coach buses. The usual price of the tour is Y150-170 per person, including admission (Y75) and bus transport to and from the ship and sightseeing fees. As the cruise ship passes through the locks, passengers can expect a few hours of entertainment in the form of a nearby aquarium and re-enacted scenes from the *Romance of the Three Kingdoms*. Those visiting from **Yichang** must also join a tour (see p. 468).

Another hour away, past the Nanjin Gate, boats line up in the placid **Gezhou Dam** lake to await their turn at the Gezhou Dam lock. The opening of the lock's massive doors marks the end of the trip for Yichang-bound passengers.

THE NORTHWEST

Vast, sparsely populated, and blanketed by deserts, plateaus, mountains, and inland salt seas, China's far northwest is often dismissed as an inhospitable back-water frontier. The area has historically lagged behind its coastal counterparts in economic development, but a long history of contact with "outsiders" along the famed Silk Road has left a lasting legacy of imperial tombs, Buddhist grottoes, city ruins, and desert mummies. Just as it did a thousand years ago, the region—Xin-jiang in particular—serves as a gateway to Central Asia and Pakistan.

A trip in the northwest can often feel hauntingly surreal. Angry red rock forma-tions jut out from the hot desert floor, as the Taklimakan Desert gradually buckles north into the long Tianshan mountain range. Coupled with the peculiar black rocks of the Gobi Desert, north of Jiayuguan and Dunhuang, you could be forgiven for imagining that you've been transported to Mars. The area's geographic diver-sity does not stop here. Within an hour or two, the landscape can change from soft sand dunes to alpine forest to sweeping grasslands to snow-white mountain peaks. A colorful collage of faces, hats, and costumes whirls by in Uighur bazaars, Tibetan monasteries, Mongolian yurts, Kazakh log cabin villages, and Hui mosques. The northwest is also a fantastic place to delve into the great outdoors, with sheepskin-rafting down the Yellow River, traveling by camel through the desert, or hiking through unexplored alpine valleys.

HIGHLIGHTS OF THE NORTHWEST

CAVE IN to the wonder of Dunhuang's **Mogao** (p. 781), Zhangye's Matisi **33rd Heaven** (p. 751), and Tianshui's **Maijishan** (p. 768) grottoes.

WADE THROUGH WILDFLOWERS by the shores of **Hanas Lake** (p. 792).

PEDDLE YOUR WAY down the fabled Silk Road, with stops in **Zhongwei** (p. 748), **Tianshui** (p. 765), **Turpan** (p. 765), **Kuqa** (p. 804), and **Kashgar** (p. 807).

SHOP UNTIL YOUR DONKEY DROPS at the **Hotan Bazaar** (p. 815).

NINGXIA 宁夏

China's smallest province at just over 66,000km², the Ningxia Hui Autonomous Region is quietly wedged between Shaanxi and Gansu provinces. The terrain here seems to be an anomaly, incredibly green and bountiful for a land so far north-west, with desert nipping at its sides. The Helan Mountains looming at the region's edge add yet another visual piece to the geographical puzzle. With the help of an extensive irrigation system, local peasants scratch out fields of corn, wheat, millet, and sorghum, visible for miles from the winding country roads. Zhongwei herds-men, meanwhile, follow their stock of high-quality, cashmere-producing sheep as they graze lazily across the grassy hillsides.

Although the majority of the region's 5.6 million non-sheep inhabitants are actu-ally Han Chinese, the Hui people, who make up a third of the population, leave a strong print on Ningxia's architectural and religious landscape. For travelers to northwestern China, Ningxia is a transitional province, where Han slowly gives way to Islamic influences farther west. With its multicultural history and natural beauty, there are more than enough reasons to visit laidback, welcoming Ningxia.

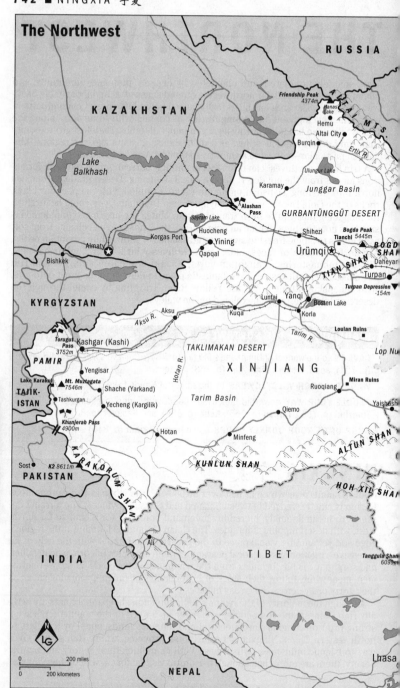

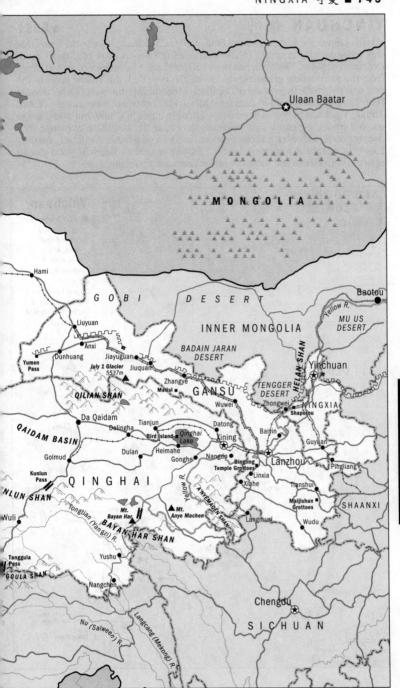

YINCHUAN 银川 ☎ 0951

Strolling down the wide, tree-lined boulevards of Yinchuan, it's easy to forget that this leisurely city is smack in the middle of the desert. One of China's more dynamic outposts, Yinchuan has seen its fair share of conquerors swoop down from the surrounding grasslands to invade the city. With the Yellow River to the east and the protective ranges of the Helan Mountains to the west, it's no wonder Han, Tangut, and Mongol leaders have all vied for control of this strategic center. Today, Yinchuan is one of the fastest growing cities in China, but you'd never guess it from the clean air, uncongested streets, and beautiful parks replete with fishing ponds, alabaster bridges, pagodas, and lounging locals. Genuinely friendly hawkers, plentiful accommodations, and an overabundance of good dining options, both formal and roadside, make Yinchuan a pleasant stop.

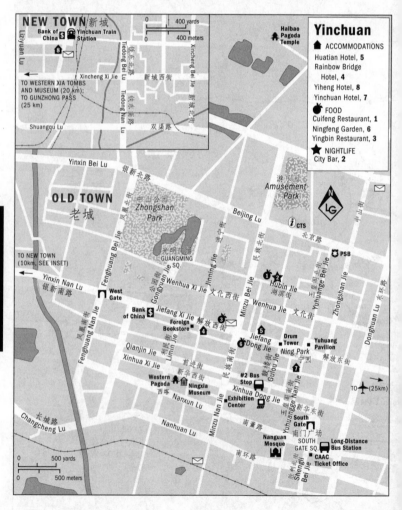

Yinchuan

🏠 ACCOMMODATIONS
Huatian Hotel, **5**
Rainbow Bridge
 Hotel, **4**
Yiheng Hotel, **8**
Yinchuan Hotel, **7**

🍴 FOOD
Cuifeng Restaurant, **1**
Ningfeng Garden, **6**
Yingbin Restaurant, **3**

★ NIGHTLIFE
City Bar, **2**

▐ TRANSPORTATION

Flights: Yinchuan's **People's Airport** (yínchuān mínháng jīchǎng; 银川民航机场；☎691 2218) is 25km east of Old Town. Frequent minibuses (Y40) make the 30min. trip to the Old Town center. Shuttle buses (Y15) leave from the **CAAC ticket office** (☎691 3456), near the South Gate. From this gate, walk 5min. south on Yuhuangge Nan Jie; the office is on the left in Minhang Dasha (民航大厦). Open M-F 8am-6:30pm. To: **Beijing** (at least 5 per day, Y1090); **Chengdu** (daily, Y1110); **Dunhuang** (Tu-W and F-Sa; Y890); **Guangzhou** (at least 2 per day, Y1890); **Shanghai** (daily, Y1080); **Taiyuan** (daily, Y450); **Xi'an** (6 per day, Y600).

Trains: Yinchuan Train Station (yínchuān huǒchē zhàn; 银川火车站; ☎504 6271), on Xingzhou Lu, in the eastern quarter of New Town. The train schedules posted and sold in the station are deceptively incomplete—ask before assuming that there is no convenient train to your next destination. To: **Baotou** (7-8hr., 3 per day, Y63-82); **Beijing** (19hr., 2 per day, Y262); **Lanzhou** (9hr., daily, Y46-97); **Pingliang** (11hr., 2 per day, Y29-34); **Shanghai** (36hr., daily, Y436); **Xi'an** (14-15hr., 2 per day, Y122-195); **Xining** (13hr., daily, Y128); **Zhongwei** (2½-4hr., 4 per day, Y11-24).

Buses: Yinchuan Long-Distance Bus Station (yínchuān chángtú qìchē zhàn; 银川长途汽车站 ; ☎603 2902), in the southeastern corner of Old Town, on the east side of South Gate Sq. Posted timetable may be outdated. To: **Baotou** (14hr., daily, Y70); **Lanzhou** (6½hr., 3 per day, Y89); **Taiyuan** (15hr., 2:30pm, Y150); **Xi'an** (12hr., 8 per day, Y114); **Zhongwei** (4hr., every 30min. 8am-5:40pm, Y13).

Local Transportation: Buses #1, 2, 4, 11, 17, 18, and 24 make the 15min. commute between New Town and Old Town. Fare Y1. Bus #1 leaves from the train station in New Town and heads east on Yinxin Bei Lu, passing the Old Drum Tower and Yuhuang Pavilion on Jiefang Xi Jie; 2 departs from the train station and heads east on Yinxin Nan Lu past the Western Pagoda, before terminating at Old Town's South Gate, next to the long-distance bus station.

Taxis: Trips between Old Town and New Town cost Y15-20.

◀▷ ▐ ORIENTATION AND PRACTICAL INFORMATION

Yinchuan is divided into two distinct communities that lie 11km apart: **Old Town** (lǎo chéng; 老城) in the east and **New Town** (xīn chéng; 新城) in the west. The two towns are connected by three main roads. **Yinxin Nan Lu** (银新南路) is sandwiched between **Yinxin Bei Lu** (银新北路) to the north and **Changcheng Lu** (长城路) to the south. The vast majority of hotels and attractions are liberally dispersed throughout the paradoxically more modern Old Town. Old Town's bustling main road, **Jiefang Xi Jie** (解放西街), becomes Yinxin Nan Lu in New Town. Jiefang Xi Jie and **Jiefang Dong Jie** (解放东街) intersect with **Minzu Jie** (民族街) to form the backbone of Old Town. The **Drum Tower** (gǔ lóu; 鼓楼), just east of Minzu Jie, is at the intersection of Jiefang Jie and the pedestrian street **Gulou Jie** (鼓楼街).

Travel Agency: CTS, on Beijing Dong Lu, in the Ningxia Tourism Bldg., south of the amusement park. English-speaking staff member. Organizes tours of Sand Lake (shā hú; 沙湖) for Y300 per person, the Xia tombs and Gunzhong Pass for Y218 per person, and other famous destinations in Ningxia. Good resource for planning group excursions along the Silk Road and into Qinghai. Open M-F 8:30am-6:30pm.

Bookstore: Foreign Bookstore (wàiwén shūdiàn; 外文书店), 46 Jiefang Xi Jie. Selection limited to the usual dictionaries and English classics. Open daily 9am-6:30pm.

NORTHWEST

Bank of China: In **New Town,** on the southwest corner across from the train station. Exchanges traveler's checks. MC/V **ATM.** Open M-F 6am-6pm, Sa-Su 9am-5pm. In **Old Town,** on the left side of Jiefang Jie, 10min. walk west of the Foreign Bookstore. Exchanges traveler's checks. Open M-F summer 9am-noon and 2:30-6pm; winter 9am-noon and 2-5:30pm.

PSB: ☎691 5080. on the northern end of Yuhuangge Bei Jie. Take bus #3 north from the South Gate stop. **Visa extensions** available M-F 2:30-6pm. Open M-F 8am-6pm.

Hospital: Yinchuan's best hospital is **Medical University Hospital** (yīxuéyuàn fùshǔ yīyuàn; 医学院附属医院; ☎409 1488), 2km south of Old Town.

Internet Access: Dragon Internet Cafe (lóng wǎngbā; 龙网吧), on the south side of Xinhua Jie, just west of the intersection with Gulou Jie. Y2 per hr.

Post and Telecommunications: In **Old Town,** at the northwestern corner of Minzu Jie at Jiefang Jie. EMS and IDD. Open M-F 8am-8:30pm. A **New Town branch,** directly east of the train station, has EMS. Open daily summer 8am-6:30pm; winter 8am-6pm.

Postal Code: 750001.

ACCOMMODATIONS

Other than proximity to the train station, there is no reason to stay in New Town. Most accommodations in Old Town are on or around Jiefang Xi Jie.

OLD TOWN

Yinchuan Hotel (yínchuān bīnguǎn; 银川宾馆), 28 Yuhuangge Nan Jie (☎607 1401), south of Yuhuang Pavilion. Grand faux-marble entrance leads to carpeted rooms with spic-and-span baths. South Bldg. has A/C, elevator, and bigger rooms, some with bay windows. Doubles in the North Bldg. Y158, in the South Bldg. Y228; triples Y188. ❷

Huatian Hotel (huátiān bīnguǎn; 华天宾馆), 75 Jiefang Dong Jie (☎602 5555), a 5min. walk east of Minzu Jie. Good value with a central location, but don't expect to be blown away. Rooms have linoleum or cement floors. Some only offer small windows that face the courtyard. Be sure to look at several rooms. Those in the rear building are cheaper. Singles and doubles Y80-105; triples Y150. ❶

Rainbow Bridge Hotel (hóng qiáo dàjiǔdiàn; 虹桥大酒店 ; ☎691 8888), at the corner of Jiefang Xi Jie at Jinning Jie. Weary travelers will delight at the range of services, the impressive rooms, and the staff's impeccable English. CAAC booking office, mini-golf, sauna, bar, and coffee shop. All rooms equipped with ethernet, and most come with computers. Singles with computer Y382; doubles with Internet jack Y339. ❹

NEW TOWN

Yiheng Hotel (yìhéng bīnguǎn; 颐恒宾馆 ; ☎396 5366), on Xingzhou Bei Jie, at the southeastern corner across from the train station. Carpeted rooms are clean and moderately sized, complete with bathtubs. 3-bed dorms with spotless communal squat toilets and showers Y40; doubles Y150 and up. ❶

FOOD AND ENTERTAINMENT

While not renowned for any culinary specialties of its own, Yinchuan benefits from its proximity to the sheep herds of Ürümqi and the hotpot of Inner Mongolia, and joins the two to make delicious **lamb hotpot.** Locals take advantage of the pleasant summer nights to sip yogurt from ceramic jars on street corners and enjoy all varieties of hole-in-the-wall restaurants. Establishments along Jiefang Xi Jie, Zhongxin Qiao (one block east of Minzu Nan Jie), and Xinhua Dong Jie serve up tasty **lamb kebabs** (yángròu chuàn; 羊肉串). Rampant ice cream stands are a welcome relief from the summer heat, while plenty of **nightmarkets** open daily from about 7pm to midnight. Yinchuan also hosts a large number of **Muslim restaurants,** especially near Nanguan Mosque and along bustling side streets.

In **Ning Park** (níng yuán; 宁园), just south of the Yuhuang Pavilion, locals fish, play cards, or sip tea under gazebos and low-hanging trees. South of Zhongshan Park is the lively, festive **Guangming Square** (guāngmíng guǎngchǎng; 光明广场). Those not willing to call it a night can head for the laidback **City Bar** on Hubin Jie, next to Cuifeng Restaurant, or the **bars** lining Xinhua Dong Jie. Down a beer at the rather un-Latin **Havana Club** or rock the stainless steel boat of **9+9 Disco Club.**

> **Cuifeng Restaurant** (cuìfēng xiǎojiǔlóu; 璀丰小酒楼), 139 Hubin Dong Jie (☎673 2008), next to City Bar. It's always a good sign when a restaurant is packed to the gills with happy locals. Cuifeng serves nearly everything at reasonable prices (under Y20) on its 2 small floors. Asking for local specialties will get you lamb dishes, or you can always point to tasty dishes at nearby tables. Open daily 11am-10pm. ❷
>
> **Ningfeng Garden** (níngfēng yuàn; 宁丰苑 ; ☎602 2007), attached to the Ningfeng Hotel at Jiefang Jie at Minzu Jie. As Yinchuan's best-loved breakfast spot, this restaurant sees most of its activity from 7 to 9:30am. It turns into a veritable hotpot festival at lunch and dinner. Buy Y3 tickets and choose from the selection of noodles, steamed buns, omelettes, porridge, and fruit juices at the counters. Most items Y2-5. ❶
>
> **Yingbin Restaurant** (yíngbīn lóu; 迎宾楼 ; ☎602 2339), west of the Post and Telecommunications, at the corner of Jiefang Jie and Minzu Jie. This Muslim restaurant serves Mongolian- and Sichuan-style hotpots, with an abundant selection of vegetables and delicacies (around Y40). ❸

🧭 SIGHTS

OLD TOWN

HAIBAO PAGODA TEMPLE (hǎi bǎo tǎsì; 海宝塔寺). Also known as the **North Pagoda** (běi tǎ; 北塔), Haibao Pagoda was built in the early 5th century and reinforced in the late 18th century. This nine-story pagoda is part of an active (both for prayer and construction) temple complex just beyond the northern edge of Old Town. After chatting with the friendly monk at the first shrine, climb up the pagoda for a bird's-eye view of the surrounding farmland and quickly approaching estate construction. *(Take bus #20 north from the intersection between Jinning Jie and Jiefang Xi Jie and get off as it turns east. Walk up the road, take a left at the dead end. A taxi from the Old Town center is Y5. Open daily sunrise-sunset. Y5.)*

NANGUAN MOSQUE (nánguān qīngzhēn sì; 南关清真寺). This grand mosque is a surprising white-tile architectural respite from typical Chinese temples and mosques. Erected in the late Ming Dynasty, the mosque was destroyed during the Cultural Revolution and rebuilt in 1981 with Middle Eastern cooperation. Nanguan has lost some of its splendor over the years, but it's still worth a visit. The main dome is over 25m tall, surrounded by four turquoise domes symbolizing the four sects of Islam. The pleasant sound of running water greets visitors in the main courtyard, while pheasants, peacocks, and parakeets chatter in the aviary that wraps around the garden. Visitors are asked to remove their shoes before entering the back of the mosque. *(15min. walk south of the Yuhuang Pavilion on Yuhuangge Nan Jie, at Nanhuan Dong Lu. ☎410 6714. Open daily 7am-8pm. Y8.)*

NINGXIA MUSEUM (níngxià bówùguǎn; 宁夏博物馆). Though dusty and poorly maintained, this regional museum's extensive collection of Northern Zhou and Western Xia objects is still worth a quick peek. In the center of the courtyard, the **Western Pagoda** extends a commanding view of the city after an exhausting 12-

story climb. Morning visitors still standing after the climb are often invited to join the group of locals in the courtyard for some popular workout routines. *(32 Jinning Jie. Walk west along Xinhua Xi Jie; take a left onto Jinning Nan Jie; entrance is on the right. ☎503 6497. Open summer 8:30am-6pm; winter 9am-6pm. Museum and pagoda Y22, students Y12.)*

NEAR YINCHUAN

The Western Xia Tombs and Museum and Gunzhong Pass can be visited together in one day. Take a taxi van from Old Town (round-trip Y130). Or take bus #2 west from the depot on Xinhua Jie (across from Dragon Internet Cafe) to **Xi Xia Square** (xī xià guǎngchǎng; 西夏广场); from here a taxi to the Western Xia Tombs and Gunzhong Pass should be no more than Y10 one-way. A taxi from the tombs to Gunzhong and back to the bus stop should be about Y50. CITS also runs tours.

WESTERN XIA TOMBS (xī xià wánglíng; 西夏王陵). Undoubtedly the best sight in Yinchuan, the Western Xia Tombs pay silent tribute to an empire that ruled for 190 years, before being completely obliterated in 1227 by Mongol hordes avenging the death of Genghis Khan, who died in battle against the Xia. Described by proud Yinchuan residents as the Egypt of China, these towering mounds of earth require visitors to have an active imagination, as only a museum accompanies the desolate tombs of the Western Xia kings. Nine windswept heaps of soil, said to house the remains of the nine emperors, are scattered across the rocky plains, while the 200 smaller structures scattered in the distance may have been raised for various nobles. When visiting the tombs, take the time to wander out into the desert scenery and discover the lonelier tombs on the horizons. *(20km west of New Town. A 30min. ride. Open daily sunrise-sunset. Tombs and museum Y36, students Y20.)*

WESTERN XIA MUSEUM (xī xià bówùguǎn; 西夏博物馆). The first floor displays well-preserved relics of the Western Xia, ranging from 800-year-old leather shoes to imperial seals. On the second floor, massive horse, ox, and dog figures in bronze, gold, and stone maintain their ancient vigilance in modern glass displays. Both floors have a number of large maps showing the territory of the Western Xia, spanning Ningxia, Gansu, western Inner Mongolia, northern Shaanxi, and eastern Qinghai. The museum is a good warm-up to the tombs themselves and the barren Helan Mountains rising in the distance. *(Next to the parking lot, a short distance from the largest tombs. Open daily sunrise-sunset. Admission included in tombs ticket.)*

GUNZHONG PASS (gǔnzhōng kǒu; 滚钟口). Several paved trails winding along the red foothills of the Helanshan mountain range make up this secluded hiking reserve, which offers majestic vistas of the Yellow River valley. The greener rock faces near the pass fade into barren clay and sand farther south toward the Western Xia Tombs. There are also possibilities for longer day hikes into the craggy peaks looming above, some rising over 5000 ft. The none-too-taxing trails are suitable for all ages and abilities. *(Open daily sunrise-sunset. Y20.)*

ZHONGWEI 中卫   ☎0953

A mere 160km southwest of Yinchuan, Zhongwei has the low-key atmosphere of a beach town—but without the beach. Instead, sand dunes offer their own surf-able slopes, and the Yellow River rushes past, perfect for a sheepskin raft. For the full desert experience, travelers can explore the Tengger Desert atop occasionally cranky camels. These activities—all less than 40min. from town—are a welcome relief from the endless temples, tombs, and grottoes of central and northwestern China. Zhongwei's take on life at a more fun-loving and markedly slower pace than the rest of China doesn't stop there. Multitudes of card games litter the sidewalks, women gossip the day away under the shade of tree-lined avenues, and tempting markets fill the town every Thursday. Sleepy Zhongwei wakes up at night, when families, couples, and groups of old women stroll through the streets in search of lamb kebabs, fresh ears of corn, and ice cream cones.

📠 🔋 TRANSPORTATION AND PRACTICAL INFORMATION

Zhongwei's simple grid-like layout makes navigation easy. Radiating from the **Drum Tower** (gǔ lóu; 鼓楼) in the city center, **Bei Dajie** (北大街), **Nan Dajie** (南大街), **Dong Dajie** (东大街), and **Xi Dajie** (西大街) mark the town's northern, southern, eastern, and western neighborhoods, respectively. The train station is at the northern end of Bei Dajie, and the bus station is at the eastern end of Dong Dajie. China Telecom, the PSB, and the hospital are all on Xi Dajie. Taxis and bikes are unnecessary as most points of interest are within a 10min. walk of the Drum Tower.

Trains: Zhongwei Train Station (zhōngwèi huǒchē zhàn; 中卫火车站; ☎709 5222), on Bei Dajie, 15min. north of the Drum Tower. Open 24hr. To: **Beijing** (24hr., 9:28pm, Y163); **Guyuan** (4hr., daily, Y15-17); **Lanzhou** (6hr., Y34-48); **Ürümqi** (20hr., 9:44am, Y168); **Xi'an** (13hr., 2 per day, Y46-76); **Yinchuan** (2½hr., 2 per day, Y11-13).

Buses: Zhongwei Long-Distance Bus Station (zhōngwèi chángtú qìchē zhàn; 中卫长途汽车站 ; ☎701 2775), on Dong Dajie, a 15min. walk east of the Drum Tower. While buses to Zhongwei may require a transfer in Zhongning, buses leaving Zhongwei for large cities are direct. To **Lanzhou** (6-7hr., 10:30pm, Y50) and **Yinchuan** (2-3hr., approx. every 30min. 6am-6pm, Y28).

Travel Agency: Ningxia Shapotou Travel Service (níngxià shāpōtóu lǚxíngshè; 宁夏沙坡头旅行社), 33 Xi Dajie (☎701 2961), at the entrance to the Zhongwei Hotel. Arranges Shapotou group tours, Yellow River rafting tours (Y120 per 1hr.), and Tengger Desert camping trips (1-day Y300, 3-day Y800). English-speaking guides and staff.

Bank of China: 1 Dong Dajie, next to the Drum Tower. Exchanges traveler's checks M-F. **ATM** (MC/V). Open daily summer 8am-6:30pm; winter 8am-6pm.

PSB: ☎701 2914, ext. 8830. On the north side of Xi Dajie, just past its intersection with Shangye Jie. Open daily 8am-6:30pm.

Pharmacy: North Street Chemist's Shop (běi jiē yàodiàn; 北街药店 ; ☎701 1191), on Bei Dajie, just south of the train station. Western medicine. Open daily 8am-9:30pm.

Hospital: Kangfu Hospital (☎701 1632), on Xi Dajie, just west of the intersection with Shangye Jie, on the south side of the street.

Internet Access: An **Internet cafe** (wǎngbā; 网吧), 4th fl., on the south side of Xi Dajie, west of the large supermarket at the Drum Tower. Enter through the alleyway. Y2 per hr.

Post and Telecommunications: 30 Xi Dajie (☎855 6850), the large glass-faced building 15min. walk west of the Drum Tower, on the left side of the road. EMS. **China Telecom,** on Zhongshan Nan Jie, at Xi Dajie. IDD service. Both open daily 8am-7pm.

Postal Code: 751700.

🔋 📳 ACCOMMODATIONS AND FOOD

Zhongwei has many hotels, but reservations are recommended during the **Shapotou Festival** (dàmò huánghé guójì lǚyóu jié; 大漠黄河国际旅游节) in late July.

From noodle shops and kebab stands along **Bei Dajie** to the sparkling restaurant in the Yixing Hotel, tasty options abound in Zhongwei. Lamb dishes, stir-fried beef in oyster sauce (Y10), and *hāozi miàn* (spicy noodles in soup; 蒿子面 ; Y3) are popular. In the summer, apricots and other fresh fruit are sold everywhere.

NORTHWEST

Zhongwei Hotel (zhōngwèi bīnguǎn; 中卫宾馆), 33 Xi Dajie (☎ 701 2609), part of the government complex. Bright, quiet rooms with possibly Zhongwei's most comfortable beds. The front building, *qiánlóu* (or *dōnglóu*), is cement-floored and clean, but spartan. Breakfast included. 3-bed dorms Y25; doubles in front building Y88, in main building with bath, fan, and phone Y120. ❶

Longhui Hotel (lóng huì dàjiǔdiàn; 龙汇大酒店 ; ☎ 709 5254), to the right as you exit the train station. This glitzy hotel provides luxury rooms for businessmen and tourists, but the dorms maintain the same high quality (and comfortable beds) at a lower cost. Closets, clean carpet, immaculate bath, weight room (Y5 per hr.), and bowling alley (Y5-8 per game). 3-bed dorms Y75, with bath Y150; standard doubles Y186-298. ❶

Yixing Hotel (yìxīng dàjiǔdiàn; 逸兴大酒店 ; ☎ 701 7666; fax 701 9993), in a large, modern building at the northeast corner of the Drum Tower intersection. Rooms are spacious and clean, though slightly worn, with bath, A/C, and 24hr. hot water. Good but slightly overpriced restaurant on the 2nd fl. Business center. Doubles and triples Y120-240, depending on size and view of Drum Tower. ❷

Railway Hotel (tiělù bīnguǎn; 铁路宾馆 ; ☎ 703 1948). Take a left out of the train station; the hotel is across the street on the right. The wallpaper is new, the rooms quiet, and the prices unbeatable, but the bathrooms aren't so great. 4-bed dorms Y15, with bath Y25; 3-bed Y28; singles Y66; doubles Y120. ❶

◉ SIGHTS

▨ **SHAPOTOU** (shāpōtóu; 沙坡头). Sandwiched between the stark, arid Tengger Desert and the loess-filled Yellow River, Shapotou is Zhongwei's prime destination, worth the visit for its natural beauty alone. For outdoors enthusiasts, a day at Shapotou begins at the top, with a heart-stopping toboggan ride down the 100m dune. From there on, the options are numerous and exciting. Fly across the Yellow River on China's first zipline, raft down the Yellow River in inflated sheepskin rafts, or take a 6hr. motorboat cruise to an ancient waterwheel. You can also ride camels in the desert, across the railroad from the main entrance.

To escape the tour groups that usually overrun the resort's riverbanks, take the chairlift to the top of the sand cliff and hike along a small path wandering through flowering shrubs and textured dunes, skirting the high bank of the Yellow River below. The world-famous **Desert Research Center,** next to the Yellow River, carries out desert reclamation work to protect the important Lanzhou-Yinchuan rail line, but it's not open to the public. *(Minibus leaves opposite the bus station; approx. every hr. from 9am, Y3.5. Taxi from Zhongwei 35min., round-trip Y50. No tours necessary. Except for the dune ride, all activities are down at the riverbank. Purchase tickets for individual activities from the kiosks at each site. Toboggan ride Y20. Zipline Y60. Rafting Y50-60. Motorboat Y110. Camel ride Y50 per hr., entrance Y20. All prices include chairlift when necessary. Admission Y30.)*

GAO TEMPLE (gāo miào; 高庙). Built between AD 1403 and 1424, the Gao Temple is an intriguing architectural and spiritual conglomeration, housing Confucian, Buddhist, and Daoist religious figures. The temple complex has many courtyards with spiraling towers, open-air walkways, and elegant pavilions. Each feature is painstakingly unique: intricate latticework, carved faces on the end roofing tiles, flowers engraved upon boughs, and magnificent paintings and calligraphy on every partition. Although many visitors come for the serenity and beauty of the prayer halls, an equal number come for the bizarrely fascinating, haunted-house-like netherworld underground. Black lights, neon paint, styrofoam, and eerie music set the mood for 18 jails displaying unlucky souls in various stages of decapitation, disembowelment, and other forms of punishment that words simply fail to adequately convey. *(On Bei Dajie, halfway between the Drum Tower and train station. ☎ 701 2164. Open daily sunrise-sunset. Y15.)*

GUYUAN 固原
☎0954

Drab, dusty, and small, this southern Ningxia town serves only as a convenient staging post for a trip to the Xumishan Grottoes, 55km to the northwest. Inexpensive accommodations and a lively street scene—often including fireworks on summer nights—can make for a pleasant short stay in Guyuan.

⌗🔃 TRANSPORTATION AND PRACTICAL INFORMATION. Guyuan's **train station** (☎392 7222) is 3km east of the town center, an 8min. ride (Y3) on a *bèngbèng chē* (motorized 3-wheeled cab; 蹦蹦车). Buying tickets in advance is challenging; an attendant is only available 1½hr. before each train departure. Trains go to: Lanzhou (11hr., daily, Y32), Xi'an (7½hr., 2 per day, Y34), and Yinchuan (6hr., 3 per day, Y27). The **bus station** is 5min. west of the town's major north-south axis, **Zhongshan Jie** (中山街). Buses go to: Lanzhou (8hr., daily, Y45); Xi'an (7hr.; 7, 9:30, 10:40am; Y48); Yinchuan (4½hr., every hr. 8am-5:30pm, Y50). All attractions are within walking distance of the bus station.

The **hospital** is on Renmin Jie; from the bus station, turn right onto Wenhua Jie, walk through the intersection, and take the first right. **China Telecom** is across from the post office. (Open daily 7:30am-10pm.) **Internet** access is available in the post office branch across from the main building on Zhengfu Jie; from the bus station, take the first left and turn right onto Zhengfu Jie, the first main cross street. (Y5 per hr.) On Zhongshan Nan Jie, a block south of Wenhua Jie, the newly renovated **post office** has EMS. (Open daily 7:30am-6pm.) **Postal Code:** 756000.

▐▐ ACCOMMODATIONS AND FOOD. Guyuan has only a few options for food and lodgings. Fortunately, most are cheap and cluster around the bus station and Zhongshan Jie. Muslim restaurants are scattered along Wenhua Jie; hotel restaurants also serve inexpensive fare. The bright and modern **Guyuan Post and Telecommunications Hotel ❷** (gùyuán yóudiàn bīnguǎn; 固原邮电宾馆), 12 Zhengfu Lu, is just a 5min. walk east of Zhongshan Nan Jie, or 10min. south of Wenhua Jie. Spacious, carpeted rooms and modern baths are complemented by a friendly and polite staff. (☎203 1784. Singles and doubles Y128-168.)

◙ SIGHTS. Guyuan's main claim to fame are the **Xumishan Grottoes** (xūmíshān shíkū; 须弥山石窟), set among beautiful red sandstone cliffs, although the entire experience is not particularly impressive. Tucked into the folds of a massive rock face, Xumishan consists of eight cliff art sites, 70 Buddhist statues, 130 Buddhist relief carvings, and 350 caverns. The expansive array of sculptures and temples were originally built by the rulers of the Northern Wei (AD 386-534) and Northern Zhou (AD 557-584) Dynasties. The most commanding of the statues, a 22m-high Tang-era **Maitreya Buddha,** maintains silent watch over both the riverbed below and delinquent tourists snapping pictures in this camera-forbidden zone. Unfortunately, most of the caves are empty, making for a rather underwhelming experience. *(Direct buses from Guyuan bus station leave daily at 1:30pm. Frequent minibuses, Y3, from a small bus station opposite the main bus station travel in the direction of Xumishan, stopping at a dirt road about 16km away. From here, local taxis go the rest of the way; round-trip Y50, waiting time Y5 per hr. Minibuses return to Guyuan in late evening. Walking around Xumishan can take up to 2hr. Open daily sunrise-sunset. Y20.)*

The **Guyuan Museum** (gùyuán bówùguǎn; 固原博物馆) contains artifacts ranging from the Stone Age to the Qin Dynasty, a spectacular set of regional history exhibits, and an electronic map showing routes along the Silk Road. Bronze, clay, and jade works mingle with ancient fishing weapons, musical instruments, and stone axes. The tour guide may speak only a little English, but the tour is still recommended. All posted signs and explanations are in Chinese. *(On the east end of Zhengfu Jie. Open Tu-Sa 8am-noon and 2:30-6pm. Y20, students Y10.)*

GANSU 甘肃

Gansu is by no means China's largest province, but its irregular and distinctive shape gives it one of the longest provincial borders in the country. Bounded by the Qilian and Zoulan mountains to the south and the Gobi Desert to the north, the province sprawls through grasslands and rugged landscape, reaching northwest along the Hexi Corridor. The Silk Road once carved its path through this foreboding valley passage, leaving behind a string of outpost ruins and frontier towns. Long one of China's poorest regions, Gansu has seen the revitalizing return of traders and travelers with the building of the Lanzhou-Ürümqi railroad in 1963.

No surprise, then, that the province is a lively crossroads of Han, Mongolian, Tibetan, and Turkic cultures. A sizable Tibetan population make its home in the wooded foothills, centered around the town of Xiahe in the southwest corner of the province. Relentless deserts hem in the leafy avenues, poplar-lined parks, and fresh springs of oases like Dunhuang and Jiayuguan. Recent excavations suggest that the Great Wall may in fact extend past Jiayuguan, the wall's traditional terminus, and reach farther west into Xinjiang province. Where these two provinces merge, the predominant Han and Hui presence fades into the Uighur and Yughur cultures, while the pebbled flats give way to wind-ruffled sand dunes.

LANZHOU 兰州 ☎ 0931

Although it's the geographical center of the country, Lanzhou (pop. 3 million) has long been considered a peripheral outpost. Initially a pit stop along the Silk Road, the city was elevated to the status of provincial capital in 1666. Today, massive skyscrapers, wide boulevards, shopping centers, and fantastic restaurants complement the stark natural scenery of the surrounding mountains and the Yellow River. Its most popular attraction, the cave art at Bingling Temple, is just a few hours away. The province-renowned beef noodles, locally brewed beer, rapidly developing Western district, and nightlife seven days a week make the city an exciting destination. Universally friendly, the people of Lanzhou create a relaxed, welcoming atmosphere. On an evening in Dongfang Square, sitting locals drink beer with army members on the steps of the giant department store, while science-fiction flicks play on a big screen. On the other side of the square, the young and old busy themselves with games, exercise, and dancing until late in the evening. A mere outpost no longer, Lanzhou is a bastion of modern convenience en route to China's otherwise underdeveloped western frontier.

▐▀ TRANSPORTATION

Insurance, compulsory for a stay within Gansu province, costs Y40, is valid for 20 days, and can be purchased at any hotel, travel agency, or bus station. An additional **life insurance** policy, also costing Y40 and valid for 20 days, is required for traveling to tourist sights such as Bingling Temple. Both policies are sold by the **PICC** (zhōngguó rénmín bǎoxiǎn gōngsī; 中国人民保险公司). Buying both policies before you leave is generally cheaper than purchasing them en route.

> **Flights: Zhongchuan Airport** (lánzhōu zhōngchuān jīchǎng; 兰州中川机场), 73km north of the city. Bus #80 (Y30) shuttles between the airport and the **China Northwest Airlines ticket office** (xīběi hángkōng gōngsī shòupiào chù; 西北航空公司售票处), 512 Donggang Xi Lu (24hr. ☎882 1964, free ticket delivery 883 9064). Turn left with your back to Legend Hotel and walk 5min.; the office is on the right. Open daily 8am-9pm. To: **Beijing** (3 per day, Y1340); **Chengdu** (2 per day, Y940); **Dunhuang** (4 per week, Y1050); **Shanghai** (1 per day, Y1720); **Ürümqi** (Th and Su, Y1140); **Xi'an** (1-3 per day, Y580).

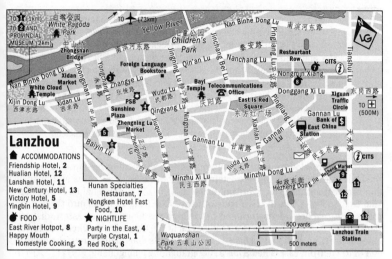

Trains: Lanzhou Train Station (lánzhōu huǒchē zhàn; 兰州火车站 ; ☎882 2142), at the southern end of Tianshui Lu at Pingliang Lu, in Lanzhou's eastern district. Tickets sold 2-5 days in advance. Buying tickets (especially hard sleepers) for trains not originating in Lanzhou is extremely difficult, particularly in the summer. To: **Beijing** (25hr., 3 per day, Y215); **Golmud** (20hr., 1 per day, Y78); **Guangzhou** (35hr., 1 per day, Y293); **Shanghai** (31hr., 2 per day, Y242); **Ürümqi** (32hr., 6 per day, Y185); **Xi'an** (13hr., 10 per day, Y94); **Xining** (5hr., every 30min. 9am-5pm, Y33).

Buses: Besides the East and West Stations, a much smaller bus station is on Pingliang Lu across from the train station, but departures are sporadic and prices erratic.

East Station (lánzhōu dōng zhàn; 兰州东站 ; ☎841 8411), on Pingliang Lu, a 20min. walk north of the train station. To: **Dunhuang** (24hr., 2:30 and 6pm, Y140); **Jiayuguan** (17hr., 2:30 and 6pm, Y95); **Pingliang** (4½-8hr., every 30min. 6:30am-7:30pm, Y48-62); **Ürümqi** (38hr., 6pm, Y246); **Xi'an** (16hr., 6:30pm, Y86-130); **Yinchuan** (12hr., 7am and 7pm, Y68).

West Station (lánzhōu xī zhàn; 兰州西站 ; ☎233 3285), on Xijin Dong Lu. To: **Linxia** (3hr., every 30min. 7am-4:30pm, Y27); **Xiahe** (6hr., 7:30 and 8:30am, Y32-44); **Xining** (5hr., every 30min. 9am-5pm, Y31).

Local Transportaion: The extensive and convenient public **bus** system makes the crosstown commute almost enjoyable. Fare Y1. Buses #1, 7, 10, and 31 travel north from the train station. Bus #1 goes to the Lanzhou Hotel and the intersection of Donggang Xi Lu and Tianshui Lu before proceeding westward along Zhongshan Lu. Bus #6 heads toward the east of the town to the intersection of Pingliang Lu and Minzhu Dong Lu, where you must change to bus #33 to carry on traveling east. Catch any of the yellow buses to Guangchang Xikou. From the same junction, change to bus #34 to get to Zhongshan Bridge. The newest buses are equipped with a TV.

Taxis: A ride around town should rarely cost more than Y10. Be sure to always use the registered green taxis to avoid being overcharged.

✈ 🛈 ORIENTATION AND PRACTICAL INFORMATION

Lanzhou sits on the southern shores of the Yellow River and is divided into two distinct districts. Visitors usually enter Lanzhou from the **eastern district.** The part of the city that radiates out from the train station in the south contains dozens of street markets, cheap accommodations, and bustling restaurants. In contrast, the glitzy Shanghai-like **western district** boasts fashion stores and upscale dim sum restaurants. The riverfront **Binhe Lu** (滨河路) and the main thoroughfare **Xijin Lu** (西津路) link the two ends of town. **Xijin Dong Lu** forks into three main roads as it reaches the eastern end of town. In the heart of the eastern district, **Tianshui Lu** (天水路) bisects Donggang Xi Lu at the **Xiguan Traffic Circle** and terminates at the train station. **Pingliang Lu** (平凉路) cuts diagonally across the eastern end of town, from **East is Red Square** (dōngfānghóng guǎngchǎng; 东方红广场) to the train station. The main Yellow River crossing is the **Zhongshan Bridge** (zhōngshān qiáo; 中山桥).

Travel Agencies: CITS, 10 Nongmin Xiang (☎841 6164 or 886 1333), directly behind the Lanzhou Hotel. Another location at 290 Tianshui Lu (☎862 5678), a 20min. walk north from the train station. No tours for individual travelers. Both branches open daily 9am-6pm. **Yingbin Travel Agency** (yíngbīn lǚxíngshè; 迎宾旅行社 ; ☎888 1272), next to the Yingbin Hotel. Full-day tours to Bingling Temple Y280 per person. Some English spoken. **Gansu Western Tour Service** (gānsù xībù lǚxíngshè; 甘肃西部旅行社; ☎885 2929, 24hr. 908 9110), in the Lanzhou Hotel. Open daily 8am-noon and 2:30-6pm.

Bank of China: The main branch is at 589 Tianshui Lu (☎888 9942), a 20min. walk from the train station. Exchanges traveler's checks at counter #42. Credit card advances (4% commission) at counter #47. Open M-F 8:30am-5:30pm. More than 20 other branches around the city.

Bookstore: Foreign Language Bookstore (wài wén shūdiàn; 外文书店 ; ☎843 8844), on Zhangye Lu, between Jingning Lu and Jiuquan Lu. A large selection of English classics. Open daily 8am-6:30pm.

PSB: 310 Wudu Lu (☎846 2851, ext. 8550). From Zhongshan Lu, go north on Jiuquan Lu, then turn left on Wudu Lu. A sign points you down a small street to the right, but the branch that deals with foreigners faces Wudu Lu. **Visa extensions** for UK citizens Y320, US citizens Y250. Open M-F 8am-noon and 2:30-6pm.

Hospital: People's Hospital of Gansu Province (gānsù shěng rénmín yīyuàn; 甘肃省人民医院), 160 Donggang Xi Lu (ambulance ☎812 0120). A 10min. walk east of the Lanzhou Hotel.

Internet Access: (☎841 4238 or 886 9196). This little **Internet cafe** tucked away on the 2nd fl. is easy to miss. Walk toward the post office from the train station on Pingliang Lu. It's the blue and yellow sign, on the right after Hezheng Market. Y2 per hr.

Post Office: (☎878 9692). On the corner of Minzhu Dong Lu and Pingliang Lu, a 15min. walk northwest of the train station. Parcel pickup on the left. EMS and Poste Restante. Open daily 8am-7pm; telecommunications office open daily 8am-11pm.

Postal Code: 730000.

ACCOMMODATIONS

Most budget accommodations are in the city's eastern district along Tianshui Lu, within a 20min. walk of the train station. A few cheap lodgings can also be found amid the pricy real estate in the western district.

EASTERN DISTRICT

Hualian Hotel (huálián bīnguǎn; 华联宾馆), 9 Tianshui Lu (☎499 2000), opposite the train station. By far the best value in town, but proximity to train station may land you close to noisy street performers. Although the pricier doubles are nothing short of beautiful, it's not worth the extra *yuan*, as the Y88 rooms are better than many of the Y160 doubles in other hotels. Clean sheets, bathtub, and TV. Hot water 8am-midnight. Haircuts in the lobby Y10. Breakfast included with singles and doubles. Deposit Y100. 3-bed dorms Y58; singles Y88-138; doubles Y88-240; deluxe room Y188. ❶

Yingbin Hotel (yíngbīn fàndiàn; 迎宾饭店), 37 Tianshui Lu (☎888 6552), just around the corner from Hualian Hotel on the left. Main building on the street front. Smaller building in the back has a courtyard entrance at the side of the main building and a shiny new lobby with brown leather sofas. Very friendly staff. 24hr. hot water. Deposit Y100. Singles Y98; doubles Y112; triples Y78, with bath Y183. ❷

Lanshan Hotel (lánshān bīnguǎn; 兰山宾馆), 6 Tianshui Lu (☎861 7211), a 2min. walk from the train station, on the right. With concrete floors and green walls, this 18-year-old establishment feels oddly like a hospital or school inside. In spite of its sterile appearance, this hotel actually oozes character. Baths are tiny, but rooms are clean and very affordable. Hot water 7pm-midnight. Deposit Y20. Singles Y40, with bath Y86; doubles Y52/Y88; triples Y60/Y135. ❶

New Century Hotel (xīn shìjì jiǔdiàn; 新世纪酒店 ; ☎861 5888), right next to the train station. Illuminated from top to bottom in Las-Vegas-style lights, this 5-year-old hotel has mid-range rooms, an enormous lobby, and wide corridor windows gazing down at the square below. Breakfast included. 24hr. hot water. Singles, doubles, and triples all priced at Y258-268 are a little anticlimactic. ❹

WESTERN DISTRICT

Friendship Hotel (lánzhōu yǒuyì bīnguǎn; 兰州友谊宾馆), 16 Xijing Xi Lu (☎263 9999), opposite the Provincial Museum in the western district. Take bus #1 from the train station. An excellent option for anyone planning to explore the west end, this huge hotel has a wide variety of rooms. Cheaper rooms available in the somewhat dilapidated East Building (dōnglóu; 东楼). Deposit double the room rate, Y100 minimum. Doubles Y104-360; triples Y160. Credit cards accepted. ❷

Victory Hotel (shènglì bīnguǎn; 胜利宾馆), 43 Zhongshan Lu (☎846 5221, ext. 2500). Take bus #1 from the train station. Rooms are pristinely kept, with spotless showers and bathrooms. The staff is helpful and down-to-earth, and a few speak English. The best rooms are on the 5th through 8th fl. Deposit double the room rate. Doubles with bath Y280-420; triples Y150, with bath Y380. ❹

FOOD

A trip to Lanzhou is incomplete without a taste of its **honeydew melon** (báilánguā; 白兰瓜). Another local delight is the famed **eight-treasures tea** (bābǎo chá; 八宝茶 ; Y1), steeped from a selection of herbs and dried fruit. The best quality and best value on food in Lanzhou can be found at a **street market** tucked away beneath a busy little tunnel in Xidan (西单). Just around the corner on the north part of Yongcheng Lu, locals enjoy delicious meals in dirt-cheap restaurants. Numerous eateries line **Tianshui Lu** between the train station and Xiguan Traffic Circle. **Nong-**

NORTHWEST

min Xiang (农民巷), a small street near the Xiguan Traffic Circle, has nothing but posh restaurants. Just south of Minzhu Dong Lu, running between Pingliang Lu and Tianshui Lu, is **Hezheng Market** (hézhèng shìchǎng; 和政市场). Vendors sell lamb kebabs (yángròu chuàn; 羊肉串 ; Y0.4), fried dishes for under Y5, fruits and nuts, and all kinds of animal parts, from pigs' trotters to lamb heads. Dozens of **hotpot** restaurants cluster around the Pingliang Lu gate. **Zhongshan Jie,** near the Victory Hotel, has many excellent cafes and dim sum spots, with some staying open well past midnight. Outdoor cafes abound on **Donggang Xi Lu.** For a lively **nightmarket,** visit Zhengning Lu, which joins the west side of Qingyang Lu to Baiyin Lu. Vendors show off huge bowls of fruit, nuts, and shellfish. The usual lamb kebabs are available, but experiment with a wider variety of barbecued delicacies, including tasty lamb's kidney. With roast chickens, noodle dishes, and even hotpot, the Zhengning Lu nightmarket has it all.

Happy Mouth Homestyle Cooking (kǒu fúlè jīngpǐn jiācháng cài; 口福乐精品家常菜), 284 Yongchang Lu (☎840 3224). You can't go wrong at this eatery serving the best in Lanzhou cuisine. The friendly owner is also a professional wrestler. Try the pan-fried beef with rice noodle chunks (fěn kuài shāo niúròu; 粉块烧牛肉) and the stir-fried crunchy hot and sour potatoes (suān là tǔdòusī; 酸辣土豆丝). 4 dishes and rice only Y50. Open daily 11am-10pm. ❷

East River Hotpot (dōngchuān huǒguō; 东川火锅 ; ☎888 1713), on west Nongmin Xiang. One of the best hotpot stops in town. Thinly sliced meats, vegetables, noodles, and dumplings are cooked on the table in front of your eyes in a bubbling pot of hot, spicy soup, then dipped into sesame oil and garlic sauce. 4 people can eat their fill twice over for Y70. Open late. ❷

Nongken Hotel Fast Food (nóng kěn bīnguǎn kuàicāntīng; 农垦宾馆快餐厅). Just around the corner from the Hualian Hotel on Pingliang Lu. This fast food eatery serves an authentic Chinese breakfast of hot fried dough (yóutiáo; 油条) and warm, sugary soy milk (dòujiāng; 豆浆) for Y3. Come back for lunch and choose from 4 vegetable dishes and 3 meat dishes. You'll do well to spend more than Y6. ❶

Hunan Specialties Restaurant (húnán tǔcài guǎn; 湖南土菜馆 ; ☎887 1892), on central Nongmin Xiang, 150m west of the Northwestern Hotel. Slightly more upscale, this popular restaurant serves up some mean pork ribs (Y28). Open 11am-9:30pm. ❷

🄖 SIGHTS

The provincial museum and a smattering of city parks aside, the **Bingling Temple Grottoes** outside the city are Lanzhou's most famous tourist attractions. Those with a bit of extra time may want to visit the **White Cloud Temple** (báiyún guǎn; 白云关), a 10min. walk west of Zhongshan Bridge along the river. The most important Daoist temple in Lanzhou remains serene, despite the street noise that manages to penetrate the darkest recesses. *(Open daily sunrise-sunset. Free.)*

GANSU PROVINCIAL MUSEUM (gānsùshěng bówùguǎn; 甘肃省博物馆). This splendid museum is a fountain of information on the 3000-year history of Gansu civilization. One of the most interesting sights in Lanzhou, it is a must-see for all travelers, history junkies or not. Be warned, however, that the museum is undergoing a multi-year renovation, making some galleries inaccessible. The second-floor gallery displays art and tools dating back to the Neolithic period, including bronze and jade ritual objects, Han wooden horses, and beautiful pottery artifacts from before 2000 BC. The world-renowned **Han Horse of Wuwei,** a marvelous bronze sculpture of a divine prancing horse, takes center stage in the second room. A massive electronic map shows the various branches of the Silk Road. The final room of the front hall displays a Tang Dynasty camel driver's woolen expense log. *(On Xijin Xi Lu, directly across from the Friendship Hotel, in the western district. Open Tu-Sa 9am-noon and 2:30-5:30pm. Y25, students Y15.)*

WUQUANSHAN PARK (wǔquánshān gōngyuán; 五泉山公园). Far less touristed than the White Pagoda Park across town, this park features a series of small temples, pavilions, and tea houses terraced into the steep, rocky hills south of the city. Sheltered by towering cypress trees, the park's courtyards offer an expansive view of Lanzhou's skyline and a perfect spot to lounge and enjoy a cup of eight-treasures tea. *(South of town, at the terminus of bus #8. Taxi from the main train station Y7. Also accessible via bus #141 from Lanzhou West Train Station. Open daily sunrise to sunset. Y5.)*

WHITE PAGODA PARK (báitǎ gōngyuán; 白塔公园). A barrage of circus games, neon lights, foodhawkers, and animated afternoon karaoke greets visitors after they climb the stairs to the right of the park entrance. The pagoda at the top rewards persistent visitors with a more serene view of Lanzhou. During the summer, locals gather around tables on the covered terrace that surrounds the site to play card games, drink tea, and nibble sunflower seeds. *(At the end of Zhongshan Lu, on the north bank of the Yellow River, near Zhongshan Bridge. Open daily 7:30am-7:30pm. Y5.)*

▣ NIGHTLIFE

Don't look down upon Lanzhou's nightlife: despite its remote location in the frontier region of China, the town has a surprisingly lively and trendy club scene. The music here is far from stale, with energizing techno and house beats keeping dance floors busy. Chilled beers are lovely in the baking heat.

Red Rock Nightclub (xīn hóng shí; 新红石 ; ☎847 2888), between Baiyin Lu and Gannan Lu. This busy nightclub is pumping 7 nights a week. You'll find a loud and friendly crowd of Lanzhou locals being entertained from 10pm to midnight by an amusingly diverse selection of performances. Acts range from boy-band-esque dance duos to child acrobats and costume drama excerpts. Later in the night, the action evolves into on-stage drinking games, with the winner receiving 10 bottles of beer for the evening. As the entertainment dies down, the crowd moves to an adjoining dance floor to groove to classic Chinese hard house. Beers Y20, cocktails Y40. No cover. Open 10pm-late.

Party in the East Nightclub (dōng fāng huì; 东方会 ; ☎460 1888), at the intersection of Qingyang Lu and Jiuquan Lu. A rich, young, and trendy Lanzhou crowd dances with glowsticks to uplifting house and garage. Performances include a short and extremely energetic singer/martial artist who sets his pants on fire. In the more relaxed outer room, clientele play drinking games with dice and shakers. Around the corner from a corridor with monsters and gargoyles hanging off the walls, tipsy patrons test out their vocal cords in lavishly furnished karaoke booths. Beers Y20-25 (4 minimum!), bottle of whiskey Y380. Open 10pm-late.

Purple Crystal (zǐ shuǐjīng; 紫水晶), on Xijin Dong Lu. This gay-friendly, "alternative" (lìnglèi; 另类) bar provides some raucous fun, featuring a hilarious drag fashion parade followed by a farcical Beijing Opera skit. Beers only Y5. Open 10pm-late.

▶ DAYTRIP FROM LANZHOU: BINGLING TEMPLE GROTTOES

From the West Bus Station, take a **bus** *(3hr., every 20min. starting at 7am, Y12) to Liujiaxia Dam (liújiāxiá; 刘家峡), and ask to get off at Bingling Temple. The bus takes at least 1½hr. just to leave the city, picking up passengers along the way. Another 2hr. later, the bus drops you at a ticket office along the main road. If traveling on your own, walk to*

TEMPLE TALK

Our researcher met up with a monk of Bingling Si Temple (p. 757) over cups of tea and talked about everything from Buddhism to beef noodles.

LG: Are you lonely living here?

Monk: No. I became a monk out of my own choice. I like being alone. Life is short—when you're on earth, you should do the thing you want to do, the thing you care about, so you won't have any regrets. I really like being a monk.

LG: How many hours of TV do you watch every day?

M: Four hours every day. But it's not a fixed time. In the mornings I wake up at 5:30am and pray. I usually watch some TV at noon. Sometimes in the afternoon I watch TV. At night I watch TV before bed as a way to relax.

LG: Do you watch American movies?

M: Yes. I saw an American movie once, with animals, like dogs, pig, chickens. It featured a little pig who could talk. At the time, Linxia's Muslims accused Tibetans of making up this movie—they didn't eat pork. They were offended and said, "You made this up." This was during the time when there were lots of conflicts and ethnic clashes between Muslims and Tibetans in Linxia. The Tibetans said, "No, we didn't do it, the Americans made the movie." And now they don't show that film anymore.

the dock without buying the boat fare. It's only 150m away. Take the 1st left after the ticket office, and walk straight in the direction the bus just came in until you reach the dock. If the water level is too low, you may be forced to take a **speedboat** (70min.) rather than the ferry. A speedboat without roof Y300, half-covered Y400, luxury Y525; you may be able to haggle a roofless boat down to Y230, but bring a jacket along. Solo travelers may want to wait for fellow passengers to split the cost. Regular admission Y30; admission to locked caves additional Y60-300 per cave (caves #140, 144, 169, and 182 are the most expensive). After passing the statue of Matreiya, you can take a **jeep** (Y30) through the gorge to a tiny monastery, hidden away in the rock. **Admission** Y10. To return to Lanzhou, take a bus from the first ticket booth along the main road (last bus leaves around 5:30-6pm), or share a taxi to the far west end of town (Y10-20 per person) and then take bus #41 (1hr., Y1.1) into the center of town. Depending on whether you take the speedboat or the ferry, the whole trip includes a 6-7hr. bus ride and a 2-6hr. boat ride. If you set off early and don't join a tour, you can spend as long as 5hr. at the caves, if your boat waits for you. Consider taking an all-inclusive tour (Y180 and up) through a travel agency to save transit time.

Although hailed as one of the best-preserved collections of Buddhist cave art in China, the **Bingling Temple Grottoes** (bǐnglíng sì shíkū; 炳灵寺石窟) are becoming famous in traveling circles for not quite living up to expectations. Despite the complaints, however, the grotto art still merits a visit. The ride from Lanzhou takes you through vast corn fields and distinctive red-clay banks. The upriver cruise from the dam crosses a wide expanse of water, shielded on both sides by a mountainous desertscape. As the boats snake through a narrow rocky gorge, the site appears after a bend in the river, sheltering the caves in a horseshoe-shaped ring of finger-like stone spires, rising 30-50m above the rushing waters.

Reality, in the form of a pastel billboard and exorbitant prices, rudely awakens travelers upon their arrival at the caves. The extra money to visit locked caves buys the chance to climb bamboo ladders to trapdoors leading four stories up into the cliffs, an experience hardly worth the steep price. Compared to the caves included in the basic admission, these caves are rather dull.

Construction on the first of the 183 caves, 694 stone statues, and 82 clay figures began in AD 366 and continued for 1000 years. Most of the best preserved cave art dates from the Tang Dynasty. Caves #69, 82, 134, 136, and the curiously black-and-white 28 (all visible when you pass to the left of the Maitreya) are in good condition, with murals and calligraphic *sutras* adorning the inner caverns. The 27m tall Tang-era Maitreya, future Buddha, sits at the far end of the access bridge. Legend has it that the upper body, carved out of the rock cliff, symbolizes the internal realm, and the lower body, molded out of excavated stone and clay, symbolizes the external. The Buddha is said to sit equally mindful of both.

LINXIA 临夏 ☎ 0930

The most memorable image you'll take away from this small town, mostly populated by the Huí minority, will be of Linxia eyeglasses. Think Audrey Hepburn, then double the frame size. Handmade on the streets, these famous glasses range from Y140 for a more conservative look to Y1200 for a really enormous pair.

Mornings and evenings remain cold in Linxia well into the summer. As early as 4am, the haunting voices of Muslim worshippers can be heard, echoing around the town. On the main street, Jiefang Nan Lu, a bright array of shops and stalls sell anything from vividly-hued wools and silks to daggers, leopard pelts, and even VCDs. Spice vendors can be seen pouring sacks of kernels and grains into huge grinding machines. The resulting rare and pungent aroma wafts through the streets. Locals chat in the *Línxià* dialect, a unique form of Mandarin with striking differences in intonation as well as pronunciation, that even those with a considerable knowledge of Chinese will find virtually impossible to understand. Luckily, residents can switch effortlessly between the two to help hapless *lǎowài*. Travelers are rare, and foreigners can expect to be the center of attention.

⊞ TRANSPORTATION AND PRACTICAL INFORMATION. The main bus station in Linxia is the **South Bus Station** (qìchē nánzhàn; 汽车南站) on Jiefang Lu (解放路), the town's main street. To: Lanzhou (3½hr., every 20min. 6am-6pm, Y27); Menda Tianchi (3½hr., 6:30am, Y15); Xiahe (2½hr., every 30min. 7am-5pm, Y14); Xining (9hr., 6am, Y38); Xunhua (3½hr., every 30min. 6am-8:30am, Y15). Note that competition among private operators, particularly on the Lanzhou route, is fierce; it is not uncommon for people to be manhandled into buses. Foreigners are rarely subjected to such physical treatment, but it never hurts to be careful. The much smaller **West Station** on Minzhu Xi Lu is accessible by taxi.

The **Bank of China,** 157 Jiefang Nan Lu, just after the first intersection on the left, exchanges traveler's checks. (Open M-F 8am-noon and 2:30-6pm.) The **PSB** office (☎ 621 7525) is located in the city government building (gōngzhèngchù; 公证处), on Jiefang Nan Lu, before the traffic circle on the left. The **post office** is also on Jiefang Nan Lu, just next to the city government building. **Postal Code:** 730010.

⊠ ACCOMMODATIONS. Budget accommodations can be found near the bus station and on or near Jiefang Nan Lu. **Shuiquan Hotel ❶** (shuǐquán bīnguǎn; 水泉宾馆) has two distinct buildings and entrances. The first building (yī bù; 一部) is on Jiefang Nan Lu, near the South Bus Station. The second building (èr bù; 二部) is a little further down the street from the station at the intersection with Sandao Qiao. The conditions and prices of rooms in each of the two buildings are nearly identical. Rooms are basic, but comfortable and clean. (☎ 621 4968. Hot water 6pm-midnight. 3-bed dorms Y10; doubles Y36, with bath Y50.) **Nationalities Hotel ❷** (mínzú bīnguǎn; 民族宾馆), also on Jiefang Nan Lu, is a more upscale option. The triples and quads are designated for Chinese guests only; the Y160 doubles with bathrooms are spacious with shiny wooden benches in the reception rooms. The comical manager's playful rapport with the cleaning staff, plus his occasional skip in the air, adds to the pleasant atmosphere. (☎ 621 5472. Doubles Y130 or Y160.) **Eight Mills Hotel ❶** (bā fáng bīnguǎn; 八坊宾馆) is a 5min. cab ride from Jiefang Nan Lu, on Guanli Zhan, off Huancheng Xi Lu. The hotel is in a quiet courtyard, with a cafe next door that dishes up delicious Huí fried noodles. (☎628 0638. Hot water 6pm-midnight. Haircuts on 2nd fl. Y10. Deposit Y100. Doubles Y55, newer rooms Y68.)

🖸 **FOOD.** The most popular Huí dish in Linxia is locally named *chǎo cài* (炒菜 ; elsewhere in China the term simply means stir-fry), a soup of fried, flat noodles, beef, vegetables, hot spices, and lashings of garlic. Locals love this dish for breakfast, but it's also delicious washed down with a Yellow River Beer in the evening. From 7pm until midnight, the **nightmarket** dishes up local treats at the end of Jiefang Nan Lu, on the traffic circle. While all manner of breads, dumplings, noodles, and chicken parts are available, nothing quite compares to China's favorite meat-on-a-stick, 🖾 **lamb kebab** (yángròuchuàn; 羊肉串 ; Y0.5). The lamb is seasoned with *cǎo guǒ* (草果 ; amomum seed), a spice believed to have medicinal benefits for the spleen and stomach. Most food stands have small seating areas and serve free tea. Muslim restaurants (denoted by 清真 ; qīngzhēn) abound on Jiefang Nan Lu.

If a stroll around Red Park leaves you feeling peckish, try **Hotpot City ❷** (rén jù dé huǒguō chéng; 仁聚德火锅城), on the left as you leave the park. While you wait for the food, crunch on a complimentary dish of winter melon (*dōngguā; 冬瓜*), a delicious melon with a light, crisp cucumber-like texture and a subtle, orange-like sweetness. (Appetizers Y8, main courses Y20-30).

🖬 **SIGHTS.** On Jiefang Nan Lu, just before the traffic circle, stands **Nanguan Mosque** (nánguān qīngzhēn dàsì; 南关清真大寺), the largest in Linxia. A succession of mosques have stood on the site for more than 800 years, but the current building is just a decade old. On a warm day, groups of worshippers spill out onto the steps of the mosque to sit and read the Koran. Visitors are allowed to walk into the main gate, but not inside the mosque itself. Peeking inside the open doors is also permitted, and some of the more relaxed worshippers reclining on prayer mats may smile, wave, and offer a friendly hello.

Red Park (hóngyuán; 红园) is a pleasant retreat on Hongyuan Lu. Take the second left from Tuanjie Lu; bypass the first, smaller park and continue on the road to the right. The park is a fine place to spend an afternoon in the shade of a pondside gazebo. It offers amusement rides, including bumper cars...on water. You can purchase a cup of eight-treasures tea for Y40 and relax under one of the pavilions, or watch the locals fish in the suspiciously green pond. (Admission Y2.) Across the street from Red Park, **Silver Star Muslim Cafe** (línxià yín xīng qīngzhēn cāntīng; 临夏银星清真餐厅 ; ☎621 6737) is next to a driveway lined with flowers, leading to a group of pavilions. This area is in better condition than Red Park, with outdoor tables and chairs positioned beside a small peach blossom grove.

Around the corner from the Shuiquan Hotel on Sandao Qiao is **Zhelin Market-place** (zhé lín shāngchǎng; 浙临商场), an outdoor bazaar selling clothes, shoes, and various knick-knacks. Almost half the stalls sell only ties, hundreds of them.

XIAHE 夏河   ☎0941

Home to the Labrang Monastery, the largest center of Tibetan Buddhism outside of Tibet, Xiahe is rapidly becoming a mecca for budget travelers. Still, the influx of tourist buses has done little to diminish the charm of this quiet, spiritual town in the middle of nowhere. Just outside the monastery, locals fill the balconies of second-floor cafes, which perch above tiny shops selling Labrang Buddhist handicrafts. After a short walk into the surrounding mountains and grasslands, you are likely to encounter few people other than grizzled nomads tending their flocks. The town remains a fascinating mix of monks, devout pilgrims, and traders.

📳 TRANSPORTATION AND PRACTICAL INFORMATION

Xiahe lies along a single road that runs from the bus station and administrative buildings in the east to the Labrang Monastery in the west. Unless otherwise indicated, all the listings for Xiahe are along this nameless strip.

Buses: Xiahe is accessible only by bus. **Xiahe Bus Station** (xiàhé chángtú qìchē zhàn; 夏河长途汽车站 ; ☎712 1462) is on the eastern edge of town. To: **Langmusi** via **Hezuo** (2hr., every 30min. 6:10am-5:30pm, Y9); **Lanzhou** (5-7hr., 4 per day 6:30am-2:30pm, Y32-44); **Linxia** (3hr., every 30min. 6am-6pm, Y13).

PSB: (☎712 1526). Take a right out of the bus station. The building is offset from the street in a courtyard just 3 buildings down. Open M-F 8am-noon and 2:30-6pm.

Bank: Be mindful not to arrive in Xiahe with no cash on you. No banks in Xiahe exchange traveler's checks. Some hotels may convert US dollars; try the Overseas Tibetan Hotel or Golden Wheel Hotel. The nearest Bank of China is in **Linxia.**

Internet Access: In the **Overseas Tibetan Hotel** and the **Snowlands Hotel.** Both establishments charge Y5 per hr. Open daily approximately 8am-10pm.

Post Office: (☎712 2225). Take a right out of the bus station and walk 3min. up the road. The office is on the opposite side of the street, split into two by the **telecommunications office,** which offers IDD service. Both open daily 8am-6pm.

Postal Code: 747100.

📍 ACCOMMODATIONS

Xiahe has several pleasant and inexpensive accommodations, all run by friendly managers used to dealing with foreigners.

▩ Snowlands Hotel (xuěyù bīnguǎn; 雪域宾馆 ; ☎712 2866), opposite the Tara Guesthouse, next to the Labrang Monastery. Built in 2003, this spotless hotel is easily the nicest place to stay in Xiahe. The interior is simple and tasteful, with beautiful bathrooms. Fresh rooms illuminated by plentiful windows. 4 computers in lobby with Internet access. 24hr. hot water. 3-bed dorms Y30; doubles Y160; deluxe suite Y200. ❶

Tara Guesthouse (zhuōmǎ lǚshè; 卓玛旅舍 ; ☎712 1274). The closest hotel to the Monastery, on the left of the main street. Head to the sun terrace on the 3rd fl. for the best elevated views of the monastery's east side in town. Travelers congregate in several stylishly fitted common rooms with leather sofas. All rooms have common baths. Bike rental Y10 per day. Hot water 7am-noon and 6-10pm. 2nd fl.: 5-bed dorms Y20-25; doubles Y60; triples Y60-75. 3rd fl.: 5-bed dorms Y30; doubles Y70. ❶

Overseas Tibetan Hotel (huáqiáo fàndiàn; 华侨饭店 ; ☎712 2642; othotel@public.lz.gs.cn), next to the Tara Guesthouse, is the most popular choice for Western travelers. The chief of staff, Cai Wang, speaks excellent English and goes all out to make your stay as smooth as possible. 4-bed dorms have lockers, but the beds are hard, and the stuffy rooms don't get much light. New doubles have ceilings painted with ornate Tibetan pattern-work. Hotel taxi (to Lanzhou Y600, Ganjia Y300), laundry service, bike rental (Y10 per day), IDD, and book exchange. 24hr. hot water. Dorms Y20; doubles Y80, with bath Y160-200. ❶

White Conch Hotel (bái hǎiluó bīnguǎn; 白海螺宾馆 ; ☎712 2486), halfway up the main street on the left, just after the Agricultural Bank of China. Guests can fall asleep listening to the soothing sounds of the Daxia River. Rooms to the right of the staircase are closest to the water. English-speaking staff. Fairly new rooms have white sheets, heavy blankets, clean carpets, and well-kept baths. Hot water 8-11pm. 3-bed dorms Y30 or Y40; doubles with bath Y160; suites Y240. ❶

📋 FOOD

Han, Hui, and Tibetan cuisines are all widely available in their respective sections of town. A dozen or so restaurants display outdoor English menus. For genuine Tibetan food, steer clear of the "Yak Restaurant" or similar imitation restaurants in the east of town that serve indifferent faux-Tibetan food. Instead, continue past the Tara Guesthouse and cross the little bridge into the west of town. On the right side of the road, just before the monastery, the **Labrang Monastery Restaurant ❶** (lābǔlèng sì fànguǎn; 拉卜楞寺饭馆) is a backpacker's dream, with an English menu, with fried beef noodles (Y5) and particularly delicious breakfast foods, including piping hot Tibetan bread (Y2). Just across the street, **Snowlands Restaurant ❶** (xuěyù cāntīng; 雪域餐厅) serves up Tibetan, Han, and creative Western cuisine. The extensive Chinese menu has the best food. On the Western side of the menu, the banana or apple pancakes with honey are excellent. **Everest Cafe ❷** (☎712 2642), attached to the Overseas Tibetan Hotel, serves a full English breakfast (Y15). Lunch and dinner fall under a Han Chinese menu. Aside from a pricey shrimp and cashew dish at Y40, all other main courses are under Y20. Across the street from the Golden Wheel Hotel, half-way up the main street and on the right, is the **Labrang Crystal Hotel** (lābǔlèng shuǐjīng dàjiǔdiàn; 拉卜楞水晶大酒店; ☎712 1223). The **restaurant ❷** on the first floor serves 10 large Tibetan dumplings for just Y8. A pot of yak-butter tea at Y8 completes an authentic Tibetan experience.

🔵 SIGHTS

Labrang Monastery alone is reason enough to visit Xiahe. The surrounding grasslands offer the chance to escape into some of the most peaceful and remote regions of China. If your schedule permits only one day for exploring the grasslands, choose Ganjia Grasslands over Sanke. For some strenuous exercise, take a right onto the dirt track just before the monastery and follow it up into the mountains for about 20min. You just might witness a sky burial, which is still occasionally performed in Xiahe.

LABRANG MONASTERY (lābǔlèng sì; 拉卜楞寺). The largest Tibetan Buddhist institution outside Tibet, Labrang Monastery was founded in 1709 by Eang Zongahe, a monk who was named the first *Jiamuyang*, or "living Buddha." The monastery, which belongs to the Gelug School, is still active today. In its prime, Labrang housed some 4000 monks, but large-scale, bloody disputes between Tibetan and local Hui rulers in the 1920s and ravages of the Cultural Revolution vastly reduced the monastery's population. Today, about 2000 monks attend the six colleges within the monastery complex, studying philosophy, Tibetan medicine, geography, Sanskrit, and astrology.

Each morning at 5am, the monks gather in a giant prayer hall at the heart of the complex. The prayer hall was rebuilt in 1990 after an electrical fire in 1985. Inside, yak-butter lamps illuminate the statues of Buddhas from the past, present, and future. In the afternoon, the monks gather together for a Tibetan Buddhist ritual, creating melodic sounds that travel far into the surrounding grasslands. Some clang on steel percussion or deep, resonant brass instruments, while others chant in booming bass voices.

A leisurely walk around the exterior of the monastery lasts about 1½hr. If you set off around six in the morning, you can buy a fresh loaf of hot bread on the street. At this early hour, the people of Xiahe begin their ritualistic circuit of the Labrang. Each on their own independent journey, they circumambulate the complex in single file, spinning each of the 2500 prayer wheels and whispering prayers under their breath. The prayer wheels are identically painted six-sided cylinders, about three ft. tall, with wooden bars on every edge for spinning. Periodically, a doorway will interrupt the long line of wheels and lead into a small room with a giant prayer wheel. The villagers circle the wheel once, then exit the room and continue on. Following the prayer circuit to the end in a counterclockwise direction brings you to the **Gongtang Pagoda** (gòngtáng bǎotǎ; 贡唐宝塔).

To appreciate all that the monastery has to offer, be sure to take a tour, after which you may wander about the entire complex on your own. From the exit, take the first left and follow the right wall to a small garden. At certain times of the day, you may be able to view lamas exercising or practicing meditative gymnastics. *(The main entrance is a 3min. walk up the road, which continues on from the main street. Tours leave daily at 10am and 3pm from the ticket office, which is to the right of the entrance, through the center of the monastery complex. Office open daily 8:15am-noon and 2-6pm; monastery open daily 9am-5pm. Admission free. Tours Y21.)*

SANGKE GRASSLANDS (sāngkē cǎoyuán; 桑科草原). The best way to experience the grasslands is on a bike, which you can rent for Y10 per day at the Tara Guesthouse or the Overseas Tibetan Hotel (see **Accommodations,** p. 761). Otherwise, the round-trip journey costs Y25 by taxi. Cross any of the bridges over the Daxia River and turn right. You'll reach the first gate into the grasslands in about 30min. Passing through the gate, you enter a mountain panorama with an artificial lake on the right. The main attraction here is pony riding, with five Tibetan pony ranches with maypoles dotting a stretch of about 10km. Beware the touristy yurt village to the right of the road. The bike ride back from Sangke may be the most exciting part of the trip. The road slopes down gradually, allowing bikers to ease off pedaling and breathe in the fresh mountain air. Watch out for falling rocks on the right side of the road just before the first gate of entrance into the grasslands. *(Horses Y20 per hr. Entry to grasslands Y3.)*

GANJIA GRASSLANDS (gānjiā cǎoyuán; 甘加草原). Ganjia is vaster, more starkly beautiful, and far more isolated than Sangke. Although it's only about 35km from Xiahe, it takes nearly 1hr. to drive there on a primitive, winding, mountain road. At the top of the climb, the expanses of the Ganjia grasslands stretch out as far as the eye can see. Tibetan nomads live in small scattered villages along the track. They survive almost entirely on the sheep they herd and whizz around on motorbikes, familiar with every bump in the road.

Pilgrims and tourists often visit a holy cave at **White Rock Cliff** (*takker* in Tibetan; báishíyá in Chinese; 白石崖), 34km away from Xiahe. Monks will guide you through the caves for 1hr., past allegorical rock formations, underground pools, and a handprint made by the 10th Panchen Lama. Much of the fun is in the descent, as the cave extends deep into the mountain. This is not for the faint-hearted, the claustrophobic, or those wishing to stay clean. Balancing a candle, visitors rappel down a slippery rock face in pitch darkness, with candle wax dripping down (that is, if you don't set yourself on fire). Even normally brash travelers might find some parts downright terrifying, as they peer down into seemingly bottomless chasms on either side. Be very careful, and if the thought of clutching a candle while crawling about on all fours makes you nervous, bring a flashlight. *(Ganjia is accessible by private vehicle only. Driving east out of Xiahe, 2min. past the bus station, a left turn leads to a bumpy road that reaches up into the mountains. The grasslands are at the top of the climb. If you don't mind forking out Y150, Cai Wang at the Overseas Tibetan Hotel will take you there on his motorbike, stopping along the way for tea with his brother-in-law in a Ganjia countryside village. Alternatively, he will drive a miàndì, a small van, for Y200. A full van holds about 5-6 people, approximately Y40 per person. The Tara Guesthouse offers the same deal for Y30 each with a full van. The White Conch Hotel also arranges tours. On a motorbike, the cave can be reached in about 2hr.; a little longer in the miàndì. White Rock Cliff Y15.)*

PINGLIANG 平谅 ☎0933

A growing industrial town in Gansu just across the Ningxia border, Pingliang is most famous—and with good reason—for nearby Kongtongshan, a craggy Daoist mountain. Like most other cities in central China, Pingliang is on the fast-track to modernization and can claim as many newly built hospitals as watermelon vendors. This young city is handling its growing pains relatively well, pleasantly surprising visitors with its festive markets and lively town square. The beautiful surrounding countryside of rocky cliffs topped by rambling greenery and high ridges of terraced farmlands make Pingliang an enjoyable stop.

🚊 TRANSPORTATION. The **Pingliang Train Station** (píngliàng huǒchē zhàn; 平谅 火车站) is at the end of Jiefang Bei Lu, north of the city center. (☎862 9978. Open daily 6-6:45am, 8:30am-noon, 2-5pm, and 6:30pm-4:25am.) Trains go to: Chengdu (18hr., daily, Y88); Lanzhou (11hr., daily, Y36); Ürümqi (26hr., daily, Y184); Xi'an (7hr., 2 per day, Y27); Yinchuan (8hr., 2 per day, Y34). The **Pingliang East Bus Station** (píngliàng qìchē dōng zhàn; 平谅汽车东站) is on Jiefang Bei Lu, 10min. north of the city center. (☎863 1271. Open daily 6am-7pm.) Buses head to: Lanzhou (4-5hr., every 40min. 7:50am-9pm, Y62); Xi'an (58hr., every 30min. 6:30am-4pm, Y50); Yinchuan (8hr.; 6am, 7pm; Y44). The **West Bus Station** (xī qìchē zhàn; 西汽车站) is also known as **Pingliang Bus Station** (píngliàng qìchē zhàn; 平谅汽车站), 2.5km west of the town center on National Hwy. 312. Buses run to: Guyuan (2hr., every 30min. 8am-4pm, Y13); Lanzhou (5hr., many per day 7am-6pm, Y52-80); Xi'an (5hr., every 30min. 9am-6pm, Y35). **Local bus** #1 stops at the train station and West Bus Station; 2 cruises down Zhongshan Jie to the Panxuan Lu traffic circle. (Fare Y1.) **Bèngbèng chē** (motorized three-wheeled cabs; 蹦蹦车) to most destinations cost Y2.

🧭 ORIENTATION AND PRACTICAL INFORMATION. Pingliang is built on a grid, with **National Highway 312** (sānyāo'èr guódào; 312 国道) running east-west, north of the city center and south of the East Bus Station and the train station. **Jiefang Bei Lu** (解放北路) runs north from the city past the East Bus Station and dead-ends at the train station. The other major road, **Dong Dajie** (东大街), becomes **Xi Dajie** (西大街) farther west, parallel to and south of National Highway 312.

A **Bank of China,** 17 Xi Dajie, about 5min. west of the post office, exchanges currency and traveler's checks, and also has an **ATM.** (Open M-F 8:30am-6pm.) The **District Hospital** (dìqū yīyuàn; 地区医院) is on Kongtong Dong Lu, 10min. east of Panxuan Lu traffic circle; turn north at the first intersection, at the large blue sign. Surf the net at **Century Internet City** (shìjì wǎngchéng; 世纪网城), across from the post office and slightly east, on the second floor. (Y2 per hr.) EMS can be found at the **Pingliang Post Office,** on Dong Dajie, 5min. east of the Bank of China. (Open daily 8am-7pm.) **Postal Code:** 744000.

🍴 ACCOMMODATIONS AND FOOD. Cheap and relatively clean accommodations are available for about Y10 per bed in the many hostels near the train and bus stations. The **Yuanheng Hotel ❷** (yuánhēng bīnguǎn; 元亨宾馆), on the southeast side of the Panxuan Lu traffic circle, south of the East Bus Station, has clean, though worn, rooms with full baths. The courteous staff and sparkling glass-lined lobby contribute to a welcoming stay. (☎822 6831, ext. 8999. Doubles Y100; triples with bath Y156.) The **Blue Star Hotel ❶** (lánxīng fàndiàn; 蓝星饭店), on the left side of Jiefang Nan Lu, south of the traffic circle, has linoleum-tiled floors, bright white walls, clean sheets, and sanitary common baths, but no showers. (☎862 4419. Singles and doubles Y25-50.) The downtown area offers a lively atmosphere to walk off an evening meal. Standard, inexpensive Chinese cuisine can be found at any of the street vendors clustering in the area.

◎ SIGHTS. One of China's most famous Daoist mountains, **Kongtongshan Mountain** (kōngtóng shān; 崆峒山) is undoubtedly the best reason to visit Pingliang. If the number of art students is any indication of a place's aesthetic appeal, Kongtongshan is off the charts, with hordes of easel-wielding beauty seekers making the pilgrimage. Formerly the realm of the Eight Immortals and the hermitage of ascetic priests, the mountain has 42 Qin- and Han-Dynasty temples and pavilions built on high, forested cliffs. Once accessible only by chiseled steps and dangling chains, the area is now marked by a newly opened road and parking lot, though climbing to the small temples is still a rather precarious affair. The spectacular view of the surrounding terraced farmland and the bright smiles of the mountain priests are more than enough to restore the calm sense of spirituality once so central to the mountain. Visitors seeking to follow the traditional pilgrimage route can start at **Qiánshān** ("Front Mountain"; 前山) and ascend the roughly 4km of steps, stopping at smaller temples along the way to burn incense. For less athletic visitors, a cable car traverses the emerald lake, and taxis can ascend to **Middle Peak** (zhōngtái; 中台) via **Hòushān** ("Rear Mountain"; 后山). *(15km west of Pingliang. A taxi to Houshan or Qianshan costs about Y25 one-way. Y60, students Y31.)*

A post-dinner stroll through the nightmarkets of Pingliang brings visitors to the **Bao Pagoda** (bǎo tǎ; 宝塔). Southeast of the Panxuan Lu traffic circle, this seven-story Ming structure houses bronze Buddha statues on each level. *(Walk south on Jiefang Nan Lu and turn left on Zhongshan Lu, which becomes Baota Lu after several blocks. Bao Pagoda is on the left.)* **Willow Lake Park** (liǔ hú gōngyuán; 柳湖公园) has meandering garden paths, a small zoo, paddle boat rentals (Y10), and frequent music performances. *(Near the old bus station on National Hwy. 312, about 10min. east of the West Bus Station. Open daily until sunset. Y2.)*

TIANSHUI 天水 ☎0938

When travelers talk of their latest expedition to Tianshui, this industrial city usually takes an uninspired backseat to discussions of the nearby Maijishan Grottoes. These caverns house amazingly well-preserved Buddhist sculptures in over 200 cliff caves dating back more than 1500 years. Tianshui also puts travelers within easy reach of several other sights, most notably the Immortals' Cliff, a great hiking spot made more enjoyable by the breezy and dry climate. Surprisingly green considering the deserts are not far off, the natural beauty of these sights can be appreciated when contrasted with the parched yellow cliffs of Gangu and the Great Statue Mountain. An ideal two- or three-day stop for those traveling the southern route of the Silk Road, Tianshui is a vibrant, wonderfully clean modern-day oasis, playing welcoming host to cave-loving tourists.

NORTHWEST

▆ TRANSPORTATION

Trains: Tianshui Train Station (tiānshuǐ huǒchē zhàn; 天水火车站 ; ☎492 2222), in Beidao, facing a large square, is the departure point for Qincheng- and Maijishan-bound minibuses. Ticket office open daily 24hr. Information desk directly inside the front door. To: **Lanzhou** (4hr., 19 per day, Y52); **Ürümqi** (28-35hr., 10 per day, Y120-240); **Xi'an** (4hr., 16 per day, Y51); **Xining** (8hr., 3 per day, Y39-79); **Yinchuan** (14hr., daily, Y53).

Buses: Tianshui Long-Distance Bus Station (tiānshuǐ chángtú qìchē zhàn; 天水长途汽车站 ; ☎821 4028), on Xinhua Lu, in the northern part of Qincheng. From Central Sq., walk 3 blocks east on Minzhu Lu and turn left on Hezuo Bei Lu. Walk 5min. and make a right at the 1st major intersection; the station is on the left. Both local and long-distance buses are rarely crowded; 30min. is enough time to buy a ticket and find the bus. Departure times vary by day and season. To: **Gangu** (2hr., many per day 8am-6pm, Y10); **Lanzhou** (4hr., every 20min. 6:50am-7pm, Y50); **Linxia** (10hr., 6:30am, Y47); **Pingliang** (8hr., 4 per day, Y45); **Xi'an** (5-6hr., every hr. 7am-4:30pm, Y60).

Local Transportation: Buses #1 and 6 shuttle between Central Sq. in Qincheng and the train station in Beidao, leaving every 10-15min. Bus #1 takes about 45min. (Y2); 6 is an express bus (approx. 30min., Y2.4). Private **minibuses,** which often look very similar to city buses, also travel between these 2 points, but take much longer. City buses clearly display their numbers in the front windshield.

Taxis: Base fare Y4, each additional km Y1. Taxi to Jade Springs Park Y3-10. Taxi between Beidao and Qincheng Y20.

■✈❶ ORIENTATION AND PRACTICAL INFORMATION

Tianshui is comprised of two main sections, separated by 18km of industrial development and several small, rural communities. In the eastern section of **Beidao** (北道), several large avenues radiate out from the train station. **Longchang Lu** (龙昌路) runs east-west, passing directly in front of the train station. Public buses and minibuses make the 45min. trip every 10min. to the modern and lively **Qincheng** district (秦城) in the west; they drop passengers off at bus stops on **Dazhong Lu** (大众路), just southwest of **Central Square** (zhōngxīn guǎngchǎng; 中心广场). **Minzhu Lu** (民主路) follows the north edge of the square, and **Jiefang Lu** (解放路) borders the south side, extending to the western end of the city. For the most part, walking is a good way to get around within each district.

Travel Agency: CITS (☎828 7337 or 821 3621), on the northwest corner of Minzhu Lu and Hezuo Lu, Qincheng. Walk 10min. east from Central Sq.; the office is on the left. Although the staff is friendly to individual travelers, the office specializes in group package tours—including high-priced tours of Maijishan and Immortals' Cliffs (Y150 per group including English-speaking guide and excluding transportation; guides not available in July). English-speaking staff member. Open daily 8:30am-6pm.

Bank of China: In **Qincheng,** on Minzhu Lu. From the city square, walk east for 8min.; the bank is on the left, in a clearly visible glass high-rise, several minutes before CITS. Exchanges currency and traveler's checks. **ATM** (MC/V). Open daily 7:30am-6pm. In **Beidao,** on Longchang Lu, across the street and slightly east of the train station. Exchanges cash only. Open daily 8:30am-5:30pm.

Hospital: In Qincheng, **No. 1 Hospital,** 105 Jianshe Lu (☎821 3722), out of town past CITS. In Beidao, **No. 2 People's Hospital,** 26 Weibin Bei Lu (☎261 6052).

Internet Access: Internet Plaza, in Qincheng, on the south side of Central Sq., on the 2nd fl. Y2 per hr. Open 24hr.

Post and Telecommunications: A **post office** is in Qincheng, on the corner of Dazhong Lu and Minzhu Lu, on the north side of Central Sq. EMS. Open daily 8am-6pm. **China Telecom** is next door. No IDD service. In Beidao, a post office is on Longchang Lu, a 2min. walk west of the train station.

Postal Code: Beidao 741020. Qincheng 741000.

❏❒ ACCOMMODATIONS AND FOOD

BEIDAO

Most of Beidao's hotels are within minutes of the noisy train station. Travelers usually only stay in Beidao if they need to catch an early morning train or are heading to Maijishan. Dining options are limited to a few restaurants across from the train station. A good pick is **Zhonghua Fast Food ❷** (zhōnghuá kuàicān; 中华快餐),

on the southwest corner across from the train station. Friendly staff give out free watermelon and readily help travelers choose dishes, like the house specialty Sichuan *làmèizi* (辣妹子). The first floor is a canteen and hides the stairs to the second-floor restaurant. (Open daily 1st fl. 10am-11pm, 2nd fl. 10am-9pm.)

Silver Capital Guesthouse (yíndū zhāodàisuǒ; 银都招待所 ; ☎261 6246), on Longchang Lu, across from and slightly east of the train station. Courteous staff. Well-maintained spacious rooms. Common baths have open showers and squat toilets. Singles and doubles Y60, with bath Y120; triples without bath Y90. ❶

Raibow Bridge Hotel (hóngqiáo bīnguǎn; 虹桥宾馆 ; ☎261 8882) borders the eastern edge of the train station parking lot. Rooms are carpeted and bathrooms are one step toward luxury. The large rooms are a very good deal. Standard rooms without A/C Y106-Y126 depending on size. Prices are negotiable. ❷

Maiji Hotel (màijī dàjiǔdiàn; 麦积大酒店 ; ☎492 0000). On the right side of the train station square as you exit the station. Large rooms have electric fan, TV, and bathtub. Singles and doubles Y180; triples Y200. Feel free to bargain. ❷

QINCHENG

Qincheng offers centrally located and inexpensive lodging with easy access to major city sights. For dinner, the bustling **nightmarket** at the southeast corner of Central Sq. dispenses noodle stand-bys and numerous more exciting delicacies. A number of **Muslim eateries** gather one block west of Central Sq.

Hualian Hotel (huálián dàjiǔdiàn; 华联大酒店 ; ☎821 5356). From the Qincheng bus stop, walk straight with Central Sq. on your left and cross Minzhu Lu at the 1st intersection; the hotel entrance is around the corner to the left. Bright and airy modern rooms with new beds and all the amenities. Rooms on higher floors have great balcony views. Hospitable staff. Singles Y120; doubles Y130. ❷

Tianyao Guesthouse (tiānyào zhāodàisuǒ; 天药招待所 ; ☎828 7503), on Minzhu Lu, 1 block east of the post office, down the 1st alley on the south side of the street. Quiet and away from Central Sq. Worn but clean rooms are good budget options, but may lack windows. Bathrooms are old. Common showers 3-11pm. Windowless doubles without showers Y48; singles and doubles with shower and linoleum tiles Y88; triples Y70, with bath Y90; 6-bed rooms without bath Y90. ❶

Post Hotel (yóujú bīnguǎn; 邮局宾馆 ; ☎829 8866), directly east of the post office, overlooking Central Sq. from the north. Great views of the square on summer nights come with the accompanying noise. Clean but slightly cramped rooms. Shared bathrooms are passable. 3-bed dorms Y40; doubles Y140-160. ❶

🅖 SIGHTS

The several worthwhile spots around Qincheng can all be seen in one day. For outdoors enthusiasts and grotto-lovers, the Majishan Grottoes and Immortals' Cliffs, south of Beidao, and the Great Statue Mountain in nearby Gangu make a great pair of daytrips through contrasting landscapes.

🅘**IMMORTALS' CLIFFS** (xiānrén yá; 仙人崖). Surrounded by forested ridges and cultivated fields, this area is best known for the Buddhist and Daoist temples built under the shelter of an enormous overhanging cliff. A short but strenuous 10min. hike is necessary to reach the cliffs' breathtaking peaks and emerald lake. Over 50 prayer halls are tucked into this cave-like niche, each housing evocative sculptures and murals dating back over 1600 years. To get a good look at the recessed figures, approach an altar at the front of the prayer hall. As you do so, it is appropriate to burn a stick of incense and donate some small change as a sign of respect. Hiking to the isolated temples dotting the surrounding hills may be the most rewarding part of the trip, as you wind through a network of small dirt trails, crisscrossing fragrant farmland and gorgeous dark green pine forests. A small floating gazebo in the lake next to the main parking lot is perfect for picnicking; paddle boats (Y30) can also be rented. *(For greater time flexibility, groups can arrange a minibus at Beidao Train Station for both the cliffs and Maijishan; round-trip Y40. Bus to Maijishan also stops at the cliffs after the grottoes. A taxi for a full day costs Y130-150. Admission Y22.)*

MAIJISHAN GROTTOES (màijīshān shíkū; 麦积山石窟). Named for their resemblance to stacks of harvested wheat, the sheer rock cliffs of Maijishan rise dramatically from the deep forests below. Nearly 1000m^2 of preserved murals still exist in 194 grotto niches. Scurry up the scaffolding to the caves on the rock face to see the intricacy of the carvings and paintings.

A central figure, some over 16m tall, dominates each cave. Their expressions and gestures depict a particular realm of the Buddhist cosmos, reflected in the surrounding sculpture and murals. Fortunately for tourists with short attention spans, the sculpture styles and spatial arrangements continually change, progressing 1600 years from late Qin- to Qing-Dynasty traditions. Although Maijishan's caves are closed off, visitors can peer inside through the metal screens. Guided tours allow guests to step inside some of these locked areas. *(Minibuses make the 2hr. trip from Tianshui Train Station in the morning; Y10, round-trip Y20-25. Bus will wait several hours at both Maijishan and Immortals' Cliffs. For information on tours, check with the tourist office to the left of the museum. Park admission Y23; caves Y32, with English guide Y40.)*

JADE SPRINGS DAOIST TEMPLE (yùquánguān gōngyuán; 玉泉观公园). First built during the Yuan Dynasty, this temple in the dusty hills northwest of the Qincheng city center has embarrassingly young 700-year-old cypress trees. Relax here and sip tea on a long hot afternoon, or wait till evening to watch dusk fall over the city from this sweeping vantage point. If you go right before sunset, you can catch a glimpse of monks performing Daoist prayer rituals. *(From Fuxi Temple, turn left on Jiefang Lu, take the 1st left on Shuangqiao Bei Lu, and turn right onto Renmin Xi Lu. Walk for 5min.; the temple will be visible up a small street to the left. Open daily sunrise-sunset. Y10.)*

FUXI TEMPLE (fúxī miào; 伏羲庙). This beautiful and expansive Ming-Dynasty temple is devoted to Fuxi, the chief of a southeastern Gansu Neolithic clan society said to be one of the original ancestors of the Chinese people. In the courtyard, 1000-year-old cypress trees and a pair of enormous phoenix and dragon reliefs—reputed to be carved from a single piece of wood—frame the intricate temple facade. The **Tianshui Museum** (tiānshuǐ bówùguǎn; 天水博物馆), on the left as you enter, houses an impressive collection of Neolithic pottery, ritual vessels, and even some prized sculptures taken from Maijishan. As you walk around the temple complex, take a peek into the rooms bordering the courtyard, many of which are studios for local painters and calligraphers. *(On Jiefang Lu. From the Qincheng central square, walk west for 20min.; the temple is on the right. Open daily sunrise-sunset. Y30.)*

NANGUO TEMPLE. This large park sits in a mountain valley and wraps around a pond brightened with colored lights at night. Two 2000-year-old cypress trees, each 3m in diameter, guard the temple's main gate, admitting strolling couples and small families. In AD 759, the Tang Dynasty poet Du Fu visited the temple while in exile and wrote a poem singing its praise. The cypress in the courtyard, verified to be over 1600 years old, is reputed to be the very tree that caught Du Fu's fancy. *(2km south of Qincheng. Taxi from Central Sq. Y20. Open daily 6am-6pm. Y15.)*

ANTIQUE MARKET (gǔwán chéng; 古玩城). Collectors and artists run this veritable market of fascinating art studios and antique shops, selling everything from Ming-Dynasty furniture and model architecture to contemporary sculptures (gēndiāo; 根雕), using gnarled roots and branches. *(On Jiefang Lu, underneath Central Sq. in Qincheng. Enter across the street from a small mosque. Open daily 8:30am-5:30pm. Free.)*

◪ DAYTRIP: GANGU AND GREAT STATUE MOUNTAIN

2hr. west of Tianshui. Buses to Gangu (every hr., Y10) run from the Qincheng local bus station on Dazhong Lu. Return buses to Tianshui depart every hr. until 6pm. A taxi costs approx. Y100. Temple open daily sunrise-sunset. Y10.

Gangu's rolling wheat fields stretch out beneath **Great Statue Mountain** (dàxiàng shān; 大像山), a temple complex that hugs a high ridge above the small, tourist-free town. It takes no more than a few hours to explore the temple, perched along an often narrow path, but the climb is more than worthwhile. If welcoming locals and monks aren't enough, the views of the surrounding countryside and the large Buddha statue at the end of the hike are icing on the cake. At over 1300 years old, the surprisingly well-preserved 23.3m tall statue is Gansu's second-largest Buddha. West of Tianshui, Gangu's landscape is much drier than that of Maijishan, a reminder of the deserts only hours away at Lanzhou's backdoor.

ZHANGYE 张掖 ☎0936

Zhangye was once one of the most important Silk Road outposts along the Hexi Corridor, a narrow strip of fertile land running between the Qilian Mountains to the south and the Gobi and Budain Jaran Deserts to the north. In typical Chinese fashion, the town today has become a fascinating blend of the old and the new. The streets are lit with lanterns, and a 6th-century wooden pagoda rises above the entirely modern Central Square. Zhangye is perhaps most famous for the Big Buddha Temple, with the largest reclining Buddha in China. For travelers in a hurry, the town is a useful jumping-off point to the temple town of Matisi, which lies in the foothills of the Qilian Mountains, towering in the distance.

◪ TRANSPORTATION AND PRACTICAL INFORMATION

The city is centered around the **Drum Tower** (zhōnggǔ lóu; 钟鼓楼). From here, **Bei** (北), **Nan** (南), **Dong** (东), and **Xi** (西) **Dajie** (大街)—or, North, South, East, and West Streets—emanate. **Xianfu Nan Jie** (县府南街) connects to the city's major sights, running north from **Huancheng Nan Lu** (环城南路) to **Xi Dajie.**

Trains: Zhangye Train Station (zhāngyē huǒchē zhàn; 张掖火车站; ☎597 2222), 8km northwest of the town center, is accessible by bus #1. Open 24hr. All trains running between **Lanzhou** and **Ürümqi** stop here.

Buses: 2 main bus stations service Zhangye.

South Bus Station (qìchē nán zhàn; 汽车南站; ☎824 0019), on Huancheng Nan Lu, a 5min. walk from the Zhangye Hotel. Open daily 6:10am-7:30pm. To: **Dunhuang** (12hr., 5:30pm, Y120); **Jiayuguan** (4hr.; every hr. 8:20am-4:20pm, last bus at 5:30pm; Y31.5); **Lanzhou** (10hr., 8am, Y80); **Matisi** (1hr. 40min.; M-F 8am and 3:40pm, Sa-Su 3:40pm; Y8.5); **Xining** (12hr.; 7:10am, 6:10pm; Y45.5).

East Bus Station (qìchē dōng zhàn; 汽车东站; ☎821 4073) is accessible via bus #9. Open daily 7am-10pm. To: **Lanzhou** (11hr.; 7:15, 8:30, 9:20, 10:20, 11:10am, 12:20, 1:50pm; Y70); **Wuwei** (6hr., every hr. 7:40am-5:30pm, Y43). Both stations clearly service more buses than the official schedule claims.

Local Buses: Bus #1 connects the South Bus Station, Zhangye Hotel, Drum Tower, and train station; **#9** circles the south and east bus stations as well as the Drum Tower.

Travel Agency: CITS, 60 Xianfu Nan Jie (☎824 3445). Upon exiting the Zhangye Hotel, turn right. The CITS is 3 doors down on the right.

Bank of China: ☎821 5844. On Dong Dajie, a 5min. walk from the Drum Tower, on the left side of the street. Exchanges traveler's checks. A more convenient option is a smaller **branch** on Xianfu Nan Jie. Exit the Zhangye Hotel, turn right; bank is 2 doors down on the right. Exchanges currency. Both open M-F 8am-6pm, Sa-Su 9am-5pm.

Internet Access: Rendezvous Internet Cafe (xiāngyuē wǎngbā; 相约网吧 ; ☎823 6400), on Xi Dajie, opposite the post office. Y2 per hr. Open 24hr.

Post Office: (☎821 5135). On Xi Dajie, a 3min. walk west of the Drum Tower, on the right side of the street. Open daily 8am-8pm.

Postal Code: 734000.

🏔🏯 ACCOMMODATIONS AND FOOD

Zhangye has fairly limited but decent budget lodgings for foreigners. Small restaurants and vendors serve up tasty treats at the **pedestrian mall,** north of the intersection of Xianfu Nanjie at Xi Dajie. **Sun's Chaopao ❶** (sūn jì chǎopào; 孙记炒炮 ; ☎821 1608), on the left on Xi Dajie, 5min. from the Drum Tower, serves a Zhangye specialty, pork fried with chopped noodles (chǎopào; 炒炮).

Goldroom Hotel (jīnfáng bīnguǎn; 金房宾馆 ; ☎824 2111), on Nan Jie, inside Jinfang Tower. Walk past Jinfang Shopping Center on Nan Dajie; the hotel entrance can be found in a small courtyard on the left. Renovated in summer of 2004, all rooms are spotlessly clean. Singles have bigger beds. 24hr. hot water. After bargaining down a little, singles and doubles Y88; triples with shared bath Y58. ❶

Zhangye Hotel (zhāngyē bīnguǎn; 张掖宾馆), 56 Xianfu Nan Jie (☎821 2601, ext. 6289). From the South Bus Station, turn right on Huancheng Nan Lu; take the first right onto Xianfu Nan Jie; the lobby is 2min. ahead on the right. Bright, clean dorms with mopped linoleum floors that overlook a garden. High-class rooms with drink decanter units and power showers. Helpful bellhops. Deposit 150% of room price. Singles in rear building Y210, singles with bath Y266; doubles with bath Y380. ❸

Ganzhou Hotel (gānzhōu bīnguǎn; 甘州宾馆), 11 Nan Dajie, 5min. south of the Drum Tower, on the right. Rooms in the South Bldg. (nán lóu; 南楼) have small adjoining tea rooms with sliding doors. Cheaper North Bldg. (běilóu; 北楼) has very basic rooms. All rooms have TV and soft beds with spotless sheets, though no towels. Hot water 6am-2pm and 5pm-midnight. 3-bed dorms Y25; doubles Y80-380; quads Y160. ❶

👁 SIGHTS

BIG BUDDHA TEMPLE (dàfó sì; 大佛寺). Built in 1098 and restored during the Qing Dynasty, this temple houses China's largest reclining Buddha, guarded by a host of sinister-looking arhats. Shrouded in darkness and seated in various poses, they seem to follow you across the hall with their many eyes. The Buddha himself stretches a massive 34.5m long and 7.5m high; his ears alone are 2m long. Just behind the main temple hall, an art gallery exhibits handscrolls of landscape paintings and calligraphy. Behind the gallery, there is a palace of Buddhist sculptures that doesn't quite live up to its name—the intricately painted wooden beams on the ceiling are far more eye-catching than any of the items on display. The **Earth Pavilion** (tǔ tǎ; 土塔) at the very back of the complex mixes Indo-Tibetan *stupa* structures with traditional flying-eaved Chinese pagoda styles. Don't be fooled into thinking you can enter the base of the tower. On the south edge of the court-yard, an archaeological survey of Zhangye's dynastic history features bronze kettles, weaponry, and iron armor. A brightly painted statue of Guan Yu, the famous warrior from the Three Kingdoms period, sits in the Shanxi Guild Hall, framed by two golden dragons snaking around the pillars and rafters above. (On Minzhu Xi Jie, around the corner from Central Sq. Open daily 7:30am-6:30pm. Y21.)

WOOD PAGODA (mù tǎ; 木塔). Towering over the east side of Central Square, this 31m-tall pagoda was built in the 6th century and restored in 1925. Now it shares the city air space with the futuristic China Telecom building and an abandoned church sporting a distinctive red dome. Take care on the way down, particularly near the bottom, where the steps are extremely narrow. The small **Wanshou Temple** (wànshòu sì; 万寿寺) is tucked away behind the pagoda. If approaching from the east side, the view of the pagoda may be blocked; look for the swallows circling above. (Open daily 8am-6pm. Y5.)

XILAI TEMPLE (xīlái sì; 西来寺). Perhaps because there is no entry fee, this temple has a genuinely humble and authentic feel. Three golden Buddhas sit in the main room, with a reclining Buddha in a side room. Handcrafted drapes of hundreds of patchwork circles hang from the ceilings. With incense burning at all hours, this temple provides a spiritual space for the people here. (From the Wooden Pagoda complex, turn right on Minzhu Xi Jie; make the 1st left onto a small umarked alley called Xilaisi Jie; the temple is on the right. Open daily sunrise-sunset. Free.)

◪ DAYTRIP FROM ZHANGYE: MATISI 马蹄寺

Buses (2hr.; 8am, 3pm; Y17) go from Zhangye South Station to Mati countryside. Buses run more frequently to Nangu (nángǔ; 南古 ; every 30-45min. 7am-3pm) and stop near Matisi. Regardless, you're likely to be let off about 8km from the temple area. Taxis cost Y15 to go the rest of the way. Buses return to Zhangye every 30min. until 5:30pm. Taxis back to Zhangye Y100. Y25, compulsory Y10 to view performances of Tibetan music and Yugu minority dancing. The 33rd Heaven Grottoes will be closed until 2006 because of cave damage caused by earthquakes.

Matisi ("Horse Hoof Temple"; mǎtí sì; 马蹄寺) is the area's main attraction. The 33rd Heaven Grottoes and other smaller temples are built into a vein of sheer cliffs at the foothills of the 2300m-high **Qilian Mountains.** Several large waterfalls cascade from the ice-capped peaks above, lacing through cool pine forests and expanses of valley wildflowers. An easy 1hr. hike up the valley to the side of the 33rd Heaven Grottoes ends at the largest waterfall in the area, **Pine Mountain Waterfall** (línsōng-shān pùbù; 临松山瀑布). Many of the Tibetan villagers in the area eagerly wait with horses for rent to speed up the journey to the most beautiful spots. A 10min. pony ride (Y13) takes you to Sword-Split Stone (jiàn pī shí; 剑劈石), a 12-ft. rock with a sharp narrow crack down the middle. For those skinny enough, it's believed that sliding through the tiny gap brings good luck.

The **33rd Heaven Grottoes** (sānshísān tiān shíkū; 三十三天石窟) are fine examples of Tibetan art. Richly detailed tapestries and sculptures depict peaceful, smiling Buddhas as well as the frightening guardians of the Southern Sea Realm. The name of the grottoes refers to the highest level of heavenly existence short of enlightenment and Buddhahood. Narrow, tunnel-like passages through the rock connect to the five levels of caves, which overlook two white *stupas* to the west. Look for the horse hoof imprint in stone that gives the temple its name, proudly displayed in a glass case on the floor of the first temple.

For those wishing to spend the night in the Matisi area, the best bet is the **Horse's Hoof Travel Lodge ❶** (mǎ tí sì lǚyóu qū; 马蹄寺旅游区). Rooms have fantastic views of the mountains. (☎889 1694. No hot water. Doubles can be bargained down to

Y80. 4-bed dorms Y15; triples with shared baths Y70.) The hotel is just below the Tibetan dining tents, which offer reasonable Tibetan food for under Y10. The best place to eat, however, is across the road from the Matisi Travel Lodge, at **Reclining Dragon Mountain Shack ❶** (wòlóng shānzhuāng; 卧龙山庄). The small restaurant serves up delicious spicy pork noodles (chǎopào; 炒炮).

JIAYUGUAN 嘉峪关   ☎ 0937

Squeezed by the Heishan (Black Mountains) to the north and the Qilian Mountains to the south, Jiayuguan guards the strategic Hexi Corridor at its narrowest point. In ancient China, the city stood as one of the last gates on the Silk Road before travelers and traders passed beyond the known Han empire into the uncertain deserts beyond. Years later, the Ming Dynasty extended the western end of the Great Wall here and built its last bastion, marked by Jiayuguan Fort, the Overhanging Great Wall, and the First Beacon Tower.

Today, the small city enjoys a slow pace of life, with a refreshingly low population density. Its distant location from industry makes it one of the few places in China where you can kick back and relax in uninterrupted sunshine. Or, journey into the Qilian Mountains to hike upon the icy splendor of the July 1st Glacier.

▐ TRANSPORTATION

Flights: Jiayuguan Airport (jiāyùguān jīchǎng; 嘉峪关机场), 11km northeast of town. CAAC shuttle buses (20min.; Y10, don't let them over-charge) depart 1½hr. before flights from the **CAAC ticket office,** 1 Xinhua Nan Lu (☎ 622 6237), about 50m before the central traffic circle, opposite the post office. Flights are less frequent in winter. Open M-Sa 8:30am-noon and 2:30-5:30pm. To: **Xi'an** (M, W, F, Su 5pm; Y1010) via **Lanzhou** (Y730).

Trains: Jiayuguan Train Station (jiāyùguān huǒchē zhàn; 嘉峪关火车站 ; ☎ 631 5074), on Yingbin Xi Lu, several km southwest of town, accessible by pedicab or minibus #1. Purchase tickets 3-5 days in advance if possible. To: **Beijing** (33hr., 1-2 per day, Y509); **Chengdu** (26hr., daily, Y314); **Shanghai** (28hr., daily, Y507); **Xi'an** (20hr., 6 per day, Y198). All westbound trains (12 per day) stop at: **Liuyuan** (6hr.; Y20, with A/C Y44); **Turpan** (17hr., Y109); and **Ürümqi** (13hr.; Y326, with A/C Y519).

Buses: A **Gansu PICC insurance ticket** (Y30) is required to purchase bus tickets in Gansu. The **PICC office** (zhōngguó rénmín bǎoxiǎn; 中国人民保险 ; ☎ 622 6362), 36 Xinhua Nan Lu, is about 100m to the right of the Bank of China; look for the "PICC LIFE" sign. Open M-F 8:30am-12:30pm and 2:30-6:30pm. **Jiayuguan Bus Station** (jiāyùguān qìchē zhàn; 嘉峪关汽车站; ☎ 622 5528), on the corner of Jingtie Xi Lu and Shengli Nan Lu. To: **Dunhuang** (M-F 5hr., 5 per day 9am-2:30pm, Y66; Sa-Su 8hr., 9am, Y45.5); **Lanzhou** (14hr., 5 per day 2:30-6:30pm, sleeper Y135); **Zhangye** (4-5hr., 5 per day, Y30.5-37.5).

Local Transportation: There are 4 **minibus** routes. Bus fare Y0.5-1. Minibuses #1 and 2 run along Xinhua Lu, from the train station to the center of town; #3 runs west from the Jiayuguan Hotel along the Gansu Highway; #4 runs southeast-northwest.

Taxis: Base fare Y7 (should be metered within the city). **Pedicabs** cost about Y3 around town.

Bike Rental: A stand outside Great Wall Hotel rents bikes for Y3 per hr., deposit Y40.

✳ ⏷ ORIENTATION AND PRACTICAL INFORMATION

The small city of Jiayuguan lies on a tilted grid sliced horizontally by the **Gansu Highway** (National Route 312; sānyāo'èr guódào; 312国道), also called **Lanxin Lu** (兰 新路), which heads to Jiayuguan Fort in the west. **Xinhua Lu** (新华路) runs from

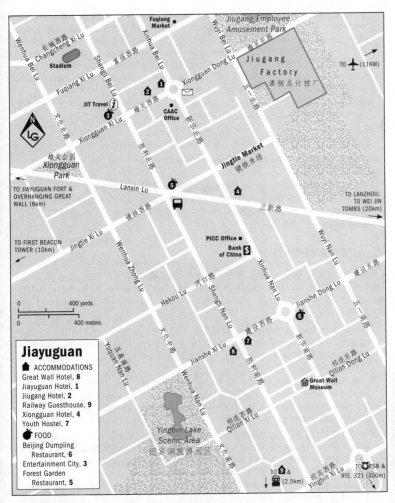

Jiayuguan

▲ ACCOMMODATIONS
Great Wall Hotel, **8**
Jiayuguan Hotel, **1**
Jiugang Hotel, **2**
Railway Guesthouse, **9**
Xiongguan Hotel, **4**
Youth Hostel, **7**

● FOOD
Beijing Dumpling
　Restaurant, **6**
Entertainment City, **3**
Forest Garden
　Restaurant, **5**

northwest to southeast, meeting **Xiongguan Lu** (雄关路) at the main traffic circle. Then it proceeds south to intersect **Jingtie Lu** (镜铁路), **Jianshe Lu** (建设路), and **Yingbin Lu** (迎宾路) at another small traffic circle. The bus station is at the intersection of Route 312, **Jingtie Xi Lu,** and **Shengli Lu** (胜利路). The train station is in the southwest corner of town, at the west end of Yingbin Xi Lu. Almost all services are within a 10min. walk of the hotels; none of the far-flung sights are accessible by public transportation.

Travel Agencies: Tours are offered through 2 travel agencies, most large hotels, and any taxi driver; ask at your hotel for the best rates. **Great Wall Travel Service** (gānsū jiāyùguān chángchéng lǚxíngshè; 甘肃嘉峪关长城旅行社) has branches at the Xiongguan (☎628 2226) and Great Wall Hotels (☎622 6568). Friendly, English-speaking staff arranges 1-day tours of Jiayuguan's sights for Y100 per person, and 1-day trips to the July 1st Glacier (from Y150, depending on demand). Open daily 8:30am-10pm; low-season 8:30am-6pm. **Gansu Jiayuguan International Travel Service (JIT)** (gānsù jiāyùguān guójì lǚxíngshè; 甘肃嘉峪关国际旅行社 ; ☎622 6598), 2 Shengli Bei Lu, 2nd fl., a 5min. walk west of the Jiayuguan Hotel. Pass the government building on Xiongguan Xi Lu and turn right on Shengli Bei Lu; it's to the right of the CITS restaurant. Knowledgeable staff arranges tours of local sights (Y100) and trips to July 1st Glacier (1 person Y500, 10 people Y150 each). Open 8:30am-noon and 2:30-6pm.

Bank of China: (☎628 0643). On Xinhua Nan Lu, just south of the PICC building. Exchanges traveler's checks. Open M-F 9am-5:30pm, Sa-Su 9:30am-4:30pm.

PSB: (☎139 9379 2815). At the intesection of Xinhua Nan Lu and National Rte. 312. Visa extensions available. Open M-F 8:30am-noon and 2:30-6pm.

Internet Access: In the **China Telecom** building to the left of the post office. Y2 per hr. Open 24hr.

Post and Telecommunications: The **post office** (☎622 7774) is opposite Jiayuguan Hotel, on the central traffic circle. EMS and Poste Restante. IDD service to left of post office counters. Open M-F 8:30am-7pm, Sa 10am-6pm, holidays 10am-4pm.

Postal Code: 735100.

ACCOMMODATIONS

Unlike the rest of China, regulations on accommodations for foreigners seem to have clamped down rather than loosened up. Only a few relatively high-end hotels accept foreigners. Per city regulations, hotels charge an extra service fee of Y1 per person per day.

Railway Guesthouse (tiědào bīnguǎn; 铁道宾馆), 1 Yingbin Xi Lu (☎631 1234), across from the train station, 5min. from town center in a cab. Tiled floors keep the whole building cool in the summer months. All rooms with clean but small bathrooms. Singles Y130; doubles Y200. ❷

Youth Hostel (qīngnián bīnguǎn; 青年宾馆), 3 Jianshe Xi Lu (☎620 1088). The only hotel in town that allows foreigners to pay by the bed. Make sure to ask for everything: room key, towels, and toilet paper. Communal baths. Deposit Y100. 3-bed dorms Y30; doubles with private baths Y140. ❶

Xiongguan Hotel (xióngguān bīnguǎn; 雄关宾馆 ; ☎620 1166), at the intersection of Xinhua Lu and Lanxin Lu. Accommodating staff (some speak English) and an excellent Sichuanese restaurant in back. Hot water 7am-noon and 6pm-2am. Deposit Y100. Doubles with baths Y160; triples Y78; quads Y100. ❶

Jiugang Hotel (jiǔgāng bīnguǎn; 酒钢宾馆 ; front building ☎671 3662, back building 671 4425), around the corner from the Jiayuguan Hotel. Foreigners permitted to stay in the main (back) building only. IDD service and private baths. Deposit twice room rate. Singles with large beds and green leather sofas Y200; doubles Y160. ❷

Great Wall Hotel (chángchéng bīnguǎn; 长城宾馆), 6 Jianshe Xi Lu (☎622 5288). Modeled on Jiayuguan Fort, this monster of a hotel comes with business center, rooms looking out onto a garden, and a health and fitness center complete with gym, sauna, and massage parlor. Unless you're staying in the luxury suite, the rooms are no better than those of other hotels in town. Deposit 30% room rate. Doubles Y380; triples Y300; suites Y780-980. 10-20% discounts possible for students, seniors, and groups. ❹

Jiayuguan Hotel (jiāyùguān bīnguǎn; 嘉峪关宾馆 ; ☎622 6983, 622 5406, or 620 1588), on the corner of Xiongguan Xi Lu at Xinhua Bei Lu. Jiayuguan's most luxurious hotel, with the highest quality rooms to boot. Enormous lobby with giant pillars draped in crushed gold material. Doubles Y280; triples Y300. Prices are after bargaining. ❹

🆗 FOOD

Restaurants and vendors serve up Han and Hui foods at **Jingtie Market** (jìngtiě shìchǎng; 镜铁市场) and its larger counterpart, **Fuqiang Market** (fùqiáng shìchǎng; 富强市场), above the post office off Xinhua Bei Lu. Sample everything from hot noodles to excellent roast meat (Y8-10) to sizzling pots of beef noodle broth (shāguō; 砂锅). At night, the small block between Qilian Dong Lu and Jianshe Dong Lu also fills up with street vendors selling lamb kebabs, skewered and drizzled with a variety of sauces and seasonings, grilled to tender perfection. Jiayuguan's lamb kebabs are especially tasty and famous throughout Gansu province. Locals claim that the meat is so good because the sheep are grazed in the Qilian Mountains, where the grass is uniquely sweet and succulent.

🍲 **Forest Garden Restaurant** (línyuán jiǔdiàn;林苑酒店 ; ☎628 2699). At the Liupin Kou intersection, opposite the bus station on Lanxin Lu. Shiny, bright interior, with big windows overlooking the street. Outstanding Chinese food at very reasonable prices. Delicious *shāguō* (hot soups) Y10. Try the stir-fried pork tenderloin with crispy rice (guōbā ròupiàn; 锅粑肉片) for Y20, or the incredible deep-fried sweet and sour carp (tāngcù lǐyú; 糖醋鲤鱼) for Y35. Most dishes under Y35. ❷

🍲 **Beijing Dumpling Restaurant** (běijīng jiǎozi guǎn;北京饺子馆), at the intersection of Xinhua Nan Lu and Jianshe Lu. This tiny spot, part of a local chain, serves up 30 choices of delicious dumplings at dirt cheap prices—most cost Y1-2 per *liǎng* (half-dozen); one person can eat about 3-6 *liǎng*. Try the pork with Chinese cilantro (xiāngcài; 香菜). ❶

Entertainment City (dàshìjiè yúlè měishíchéng; 大世界娱乐美食城; ☎628 5237). On the corner of Xiongguan Xi Lu and Shengli Bei Lu. Great place to eat any time of day. Huge eating area on the east side of the entertainment complex. Canteen-style restaurant with food out on display. Hot milk, breads, and dumplings for breakfast, and noodle soups and rice dishes later on. Breakfast about Y6, dinner no more than Y30. ❷

🅾 SIGHTS

Because no public transportation runs to the sights, most travelers hire a taxi or join a tour run by one of Jiayuguan's travel agencies (see **Practical Information,** p. 773). JIT, 2 Shengli Bei Lu, arranges daytrips to the four major sights, with driver and Chinese-speaking guide for Y155. With ticket prices adding up to Y111, this makes a total cost of Y266 for the day. The **Great Wall Travel Service** quotes Y310 for the same deal, entrance fees included, but will match JIT's cheaper price if you call them on it. If a Chinese guide is no use to you, knock off Y50 from the total price. Remember, all taxi hire fees are negotiable.

🏯 **JIAYUGUAN FORT** (jiāyùguān chénglóu;嘉峪关城楼). One of the most photographed spots in northwest China, Jiayuguan Fort stands in a desert against a backdrop of snow-capped peaks and sunset views. Built in 1372, the fort traditionally marks the end of the 2000km Great Wall, although at various times the wall extended several hundred kilometers farther west. A 10m-high, 733m-long outer wall surrounds Jiayuguan Fort. Past a small gate in the east, watchtowers guard a further set of inner walls. Here, an "entrapping rampart" once trapped and annihilated raiders. Today, those who force their way into the inner stronghold find a walkway through a tiny oasis of trees. A group of horse and camel owners offers rides into the great beyond. The ramps on the north side of each gate once allowed teams of horses onto the wall, enabling mounted archers to speed about. The masons conscripted to build the fort were of such high caliber that they calculated in advance the exact number of bricks needed for the entire structure. Somehow, one brick was left unused. The odd-brick-out still rests on the ledge, taunting the math whiz who forgot to carry the one. *(If you're planning an independent trip, you can bike here in 30-45min. on the Gansu Hwy., which extends from Lanxin Lu; turn right at the posted sign and then left at the next posted sign. Pedicab or taxi is a better option for the 6km trip; one-way Y20-25, round-trip Y45-50. The ticket office is opposite the souvenir stalls. Open daily 9am-9pm; winter 8am-7pm. Y60, students with valid ID Y30.)*

OVERHANGING GREAT WALL (xuánbì chángchéng; 悬壁长城). A 750m peripheral defense wall extending from Jiayuguan Fort along the cliffs of the Heishan Gorge, the Overhanging Great Wall would like to claim hundreds of years of history, but it was in fact restored in 1987 and looks hardly a day over 10 years old. The wall snakes over the ridges of the lifeless black mountains. The steep climb to the top takes about 20min., where a view of the Gobi Desert, a surreal dark wasteland, extends hundreds of kilometers to the north. *(From the Jiayuguan Fort parking lot, exit left; make your 1st left onto a small paved road. You should see the wall to your left as you bike 30min. toward the entrance. Taxi round-trip Y15. Open daily 8:30am-8pm. Y8.)*

FIRST BEACON TOWER (dìyī fēnghuǒ tái; 第一烽火台). The only surviving portion of the original Jiayuguan Fort is the beacon tower, once used to relay warnings with windborne smoke signals. Fragments of the wall are scattered in the surrounding area. Below the Beacon Tower, the newest attempt to lure tourists (and make money) has resulted in a somewhat tacky reconstruction of a Ming Dynasty frontier town. Steps leading down to the Taolai River Gorge (tǎolài hé dàxiágǔ; 讨赖河大峡谷) bring visitors to a commander's tent, complete with reconstructed suits of armor. To the left, you can cross a suspension bridge that hangs over the rushing waters below. Other period creations include a military podium, civilian housing, war-drum platforms, and a weaponry exhibit, featuring scaling ladders, boulder launchers, and cannon artillery. Crossing the suspension bridge may be the most fun and semi-thrilling adventure in this part-tourist trap, part-history lesson. *(7km southwest of Jiayuguan Fort. Y11.)*

WEI AND JIN TOMBS (wèijìn mù; 魏晋墓). Thousands of these tombs, dating from AD 220-420, dot the desert surrounding Jiayuguan, but only one is open to the public. There are three chambers inside the tomb, each progressively smaller than the last. The first served as an "office" for the tomb's occupants, and paintings of hunting scenes adorned the walls. The second chamber represents domestic life, with one side devoted to male images and the other to female ones. The final chamber, known as "the bedroom," holds the coffins themselves. While the outside of the tomb has been slightly fixed up to allow for easy access, the vibrant paintings inside are said not to have been tampered with. *(20km east of Jiayuguan. A taxi costs Y40 each way or Y60 round-trip by meter. The folks living in the ticket office claim to welcome visitors 24hr. a day, but you might want to visit during daylight hours. Admission Y31, guides Y25.)*

▶ DAYTRIP FROM JIAYUGUAN: JULY 1ST GLACIER

Generally accessible Apr.-Sept., but best visited Jun.-Aug., when clouds are least likely to obscure the peak. Foreigners can arrive via private van or taxi (round-trip Y260-500 with the driver waiting at the glacier). Taxis generally cost more than private vans. Also check with travel agencies for tour groups. If you leave around 7am, you can spend as long as 6hr. at the glacier, not including 6hr. of traveling on some of the worst roads in Gansu.

The July 1st Glacier (qīyī bīngchuān; 七一冰川), 120km south of Jiayuguan, rests at an altitude of 4700m in the Qilian Mtns. It's possible to climb to the top of the enormous 500m glacier from midway up the mountain and walk about on the lowest segment, which slopes gently into the mountain valley like a giant teardrop. From the parking area below, the climb to the glacier is only about 2.5km long but takes at least two hours due to the high altitude. Except for the final 200m, the change in elevation is gradual, though dizziness can lead to unexpected missteps. There are only a few spots where climbers should take extra care, passing steep drops on the left side. About 45min. into the climb, a pure white slice of the glacier finally peeks out between the gap in the mountains. When the sun is shining, it's hard to believe that anything could be whiter. Even in the summer, take warm clothes and some food, as both hiking and road conditions can change quickly.

DUNHUANG 敦煌 ☎ 0937

At the parting of the southern and northern trade routes that curve around the Tarim Basin, Dunhuang gazes west into the vast deserts and harsh expanses that once marked the outer limits of China. In the 2nd century BC, the ambitious Han Emperor Wudi incorporated the frontier town into the empire. Hungry for more territory, he sent General Zhang Qian west to exploit tribal rivalries and forge allies for his next offensive. After eight years, the general returned and reported that local leaders were reluctant to make war but eager to trade. Caravans laden with precious silk set out from Xi'an with thousands of miles ahead of them, across the unimaginably treacherous terrain that became known as the trans-Eur-

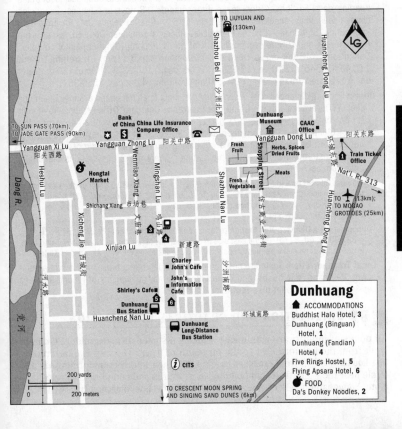

asian Silk Road. The Huns, Jie, Xianbei, Qiang, Tubo (Tibetan), Tangut, Mongols, and Uighurs all tried wresting the strategic outpost from Han control, and the sands of Dunhuang saw many a bleak battle, remembered in haunting poems written by the ancient Chinese.

Lately, Dunhuang has profited from its past by promoting its sweeping deserts and the Mogao Grottoes' unparalleled Buddhist cave art, sculpted and painted over the course of a thousand years. The city itself is a relaxing, beautiful area, with beer gardens and markets around every corner. An evening spent in the dunes and by the Crescent Moon Springs is an experience not easily forgotten.

⬛ TRANSPORTATION

Flights: Dunhuang Airport (dūnhuáng fēijīchǎng; 敦煌飞机场), 13km east of the city. CAAC advises travelers to take a taxi (15min., Y15-20). Beware that many Dunhuang hotels pay drivers to bring them potential guests. **CAAC ticket office** (☎882 2389), on Yangguan Dong Lu, near Xinhua Bookstore. Open daily 8am-6pm. To: **Beijing** (2 per day; 10:40am, Y1500; 9:15pm, Y1320) via **Lanzhou** (Y1030); **Ürümqi** (M-Sa, Y710); **Xi'an** (daily, Y1680).

Trains: Dunhuang Train Station (dūnhuáng huǒchē zhàn; 敦煌火车站 ; ☎0937 557 2995), 2½hr. north of Dunhuang in **Liuyuan**. Frequent buses, taxis, and minibuses leave from the Dunhuang Bus Station. It's usually more difficult to book tickets for trains heading east. For longer trips, make arrangements 2-3 days in advance. Schedules change seasonally; check with John's Cafe, CITS, or Charley John's Cafe for up-to-date information. Station fee Y25. The main ticket office, 14 Yangguan Dong Lu, just past the Huancheng Dong Lu intersection, is part of the Dunhuang (Binguan) Hotel complex. Commission Y40 per ticket. Open daily 7am-noon and 3-11pm. To: **Beijing** (38hr., 11:14am, Y545); **Lanzhou** (13-18hr., 10 per day, Y150-230); **Ürümqi** (13hr., 9 per day, Y175) via **Turpan** (11hr., Y146); **Xi'an** (30-38hr., 4 per day, Y210-357).

Buses: For long-distance travel beyond Liuyuan, most foreigners need a Gansu Insurance Ticket (Y30), available at the **China Life Insurance Company Office** (zhōngguó rénmín bǎoxiǎn gōngsī; 中国人民保险公司), 12 Yangguan Zhong Lu (☎882 7469), near the Bank of China. Open M-F 8am-noon and 3-6:30pm. Most buses have a side luggage compartment; be prepared to have a wet pack if you leave it on the roof, as short but furious rainstorms are frequent in the summer. There are 2 bus stations diagonally across from each other on Mingshan Lu.

Dunhuang Bus Station (dūnhuáng qìchē zhàn;敦煌汽车站 ; ☎882 2174), on the west side of the intersection. Open daily 7am-10:30pm. To: **Golmud** (8hr., 2 per day, Y78-91); **Jiayuguan** (4-5hr., 2 per day, Y44-77); **Lanzhou** (17hr., 2 per day, Y214); **Liuyuan** (2hr., 8 per day, Y15); **Zhangye** (13hr., 6pm, Y117).

Dunhuang Long-Distance Bus Station (dūnhuáng chángtú qìchē zhàn; 敦煌长途汽车站 ; ☎882 3072, ext. 8115), on the east side of the road, has slower buses. Open daily 7am-10pm. Buses to **Lanzhou** make frequent stops in all major towns along the way. Also serves **Xining.**

Local Transportation: Taxis are not metered. Don't pay more than Y5 for a ride around town. **Pedicabs, minibuses,** and **motorbikes** abound, but walking or renting a bike is easier. Most hotels offer **bike rental** for Y1 per hr.

⬛⬛ ORIENTATION AND PRACTICAL INFORMATION

All points of interest are within easy walking distance. It takes under 20min. to walk from the far northeast to the far south of town. The city is quartered by **Shazhou Lu** (沙州路) and **Yangguan Lu** (阳关路), their intersection forming a traffic circle near the China Telecom building. Most tourist and commercial services are along Yangguan Lu, while budget lodgings and cafes line **Mingshan Lu** (鸣山路).

Travel Agencies: Dunhuang's 3 main sights (Mogao Grottoes, Crescent Moon Lake, and the Singing Sand Dunes) can all be seen without the aid of a travel agency. Charley at **Charley John's Cafe** helps individuals arrange trips to distant Yangguan and Yumenguan. **John's Information Cafe** offers 1-day (Y30) and 2-day (Y80) tours of the area. Larger hotels, several tourist-oriented restaurants, and John's Information Cafe offer ticket booking and travel information. **CITS,** 32 Mingshan Lu (☎882 3312), has English-, French-, German-, and Japanese-speaking staff. Commission Y30-50. Open M-F 8am-6pm, Sa-Su 9am-noon and 3-5pm. Similar "CITS" travel services in various hotels are in-house operations and not branches of the national agency.

Bank of China: On Yangguan Zhong Lu, a 2min. walk west from Mingshan Lu. Exchanges traveler's checks. Credit card advances. Open M-F summer 8am-noon and 3-6:30pm; winter 8:30am-noon and 2:30-6pm. A smaller branch across the street also exchanges traveler's checks. Open M-Sa 8:30am-6pm, Su 9am-5pm.

ATM: Bank of China ATM on Yangguan Dong Lu, across from the Dunhuang museum.

PSB: 18 Xuanguan Lu (☎882 2660), just west of the intersection between Yangguan Lu and Mingshan Lu. Visa extension office just right of the main gate. Open M-F 7:30am-noon and 3-6:30pm.

Internet Access: A new **Internet cafe** has opened on Mingshan Zhong Lu. Y3 per hr. Open daily 8am-midnight. A few doors down, **Charley John's Cafe** has incredibly slow Internet for Y10 per hr.

Post and Telecommunications: (☎882 2446), on the corner of Shazhou Bei Lu and Yangguan Zhong Lu, on the west side of the traffic circle. EMS and Poste Restante. **China Telecom** is on the 2nd fl. IDD service. Both open daily 8am-7pm.

Postal Code: 736200.

▙ ACCOMMODATIONS

Most affordable hotels here are on **Mingshan Lu.** Like almost everything here, accommodation costs are inflated. Prices are negotiable when visitors are rare. Most hotels in Dunhuang have 24hr. hot water.

▨ **Dunhuang (Fandian) Hotel** (dūnhuáng fàndiàn; 敦煌饭店), 16 Mingshan Lu (☎882 7588), not to be confused with the more upscale Dunhuang (Binguan) Hotel. Smart, breezy, and colorful rooms. Bathrooms have enormous mirrors. Singles can be bargained down to Y100; doubles Y180; triples Y120, Y180, or Y270. ❷

Five Rings Hostel (wǔhuán bīnguǎn; 五环宾馆), 20 Mingshan Lu (☎883 2147), a few strides north of Dunhuang Bus Station. This is about as cheap as it gets in Dunhuang. With low-season doubles at Y60, you can't grumble, though rooms may be a little dark and dingy. Hot water 7pm-midnight. Prices increase after the end of June. In low season, solo travelers can get a double for Y30. Dorms Y15-30 per bed; doubles Y80-120; triples Y120-180, low-season Y90-120. ❶

Flying Apsara Hotel (fēitiān bīnguǎn; 飞天宾馆; ☎882 2337), 22 Mingshan Lu, behind John's Information Cafe. Clean, basic dorms and smiling staff. Shop in the lobby sells Chinese paintings for decent prices. Dorms Y20; doubles with small bath Y130, with large bath Y160. Prices are slightly higher July-Aug. ❶

Buddhist Halo Hotel (fóguāng dàjiǔdiàn; 佛光大酒店), 15 Mingshan Lu (☎882 5040), opposite the Dunhuang Hotel. English-speaking staff. A/C and telephone in all rooms except dorms. Deposit Y100-300. Dorms Y20; doubles Y160; triples Y200. ❶

Dunhuang (Binguan) Hotel (dūnhuáng bīnguǎn; 敦煌宾馆 ; ☎885 9268). This gorgeous hotel is Dunhuang's finest. Brand new garden has a "beer square" (píjiǔ guǎngchǎng; 啤酒广场) and seating area under shady pavilions. If you're feeling decadent, luxury suites come with leather thrones in the living room, a love seat in the bed-

room, and perhaps the best views of the Singing Sand Dunes and Sanwei Mountains from town. Business center, souvenir shop, and Japanese and Chinese restaurants in the lobby. Doubles in old building Y488; new building Y688; quads Y600. ❺

❸ FOOD

Chinese, Muslim, Western, and fusion restaurants are everywhere in Dunhuang, and signs indicating "cafes" are ubiquitous. Fruit yogurt shakes (Y5), coffee (Y5), scrambled eggs on toast (Y7), and french fries (Y6) park alongside your regular Chinese staples. Places that serve Western food, though, are mostly tourist traps.

Perhaps the liveliest center for food is the **nightmarket** to the south of Yangguan Dong Lu, in a rather grand open-air courtyard roughly opposite the Dunhuang Museum. The market brims with stalls selling roasted chickens (dàpán jī; 大盘鸡 ; Y50), Chinese-style hamburgers, dumplings, hotpot, pastries, beer, and assorted teas. Market activity peaks around 7:30pm and lasts until 12:30am; some stalls are open during the day as well. For an unusual culinary experience, try the **yellow noodles with donkey meat** (lǘròu huángmiàn; 驴肉黄面 ; Y4), a local specialty. Another Dunhuang treat is the *lǐguǎng xìng* (李广杏), a plum-apricot hybrid.

Da's Donkey Noodles (dájì lǘròu huángmiàn; 达记驴肉黄面), on Xicheng Jie, tucked away behind Hongtai Market. The restaurant has its own sign, carved into an archway at the far end of the market; passing under the sign, walk toward Yangguan Xi Lu. Daji is the 1st on the right. A popular local hangout, this lively restaurant serves a unique selection of donkey meat dishes, and as those who know Dunhuang well will tell you, the best yellow noodles with donkey meat in town. ❶

Charley John's Cafe (☎883 3039), a 5min. walk from the post office down Mingshan Lu, on the left. Owner Charley serves up excellent Chinese and fusion food at reasonable prices. Try the Sichuan specialties (Y10). Bike rental Y1 per hr., Y2 for newer bikes. Organizes cabs or minibuses to sights. His sister runs **Shirley's Cafe** across the street (☎351 1019). Same prices, hours, and services. Both places have a warm, hospitable atmosphere and quite a local following. Open daily 7am-midnight. ❶

John's Information Cafe (☎882 7000), opposite the Five Rings Hotel on Mingshan Lu. A modern Silk Road refueling stop for travelers, with franchises in Kashgar and Turpan. The food is acceptable, though a bit overpriced. Manager Jian Junwang can procure bus tickets for no commission, and air and train tickets for Y25-30 per ticket. Internet Y5 per hr. Bike rental Y1 per hr. Open 7am-midnight. ❶

SIGHTS

There is little to see in Dunhuang itself. The delapidated **Dunhuang Museum** (dūn-huáng bówùguǎn; 敦煌博物馆 ; ☎ 882 2981), on Yangguan Dong Lu, is not the most exciting place in the world and could use a facelift. The most memorable items on display are the three-dimensional models of Dunhuang's topography, the ancient Silk Road, and the Han Dynasty Great Wall. (Open daily 8am-6:30pm. Y10.)

MOGAO GROTTOES 莫高石窟

*25km southeast of Dunhuang. **Minibuses** cruise to the grottoes along Mingshan Lu (daily 7:30-10:30am, Y60). For return trip, minibuses wait around the parking lot area next to the hotel until 6pm or so. John's Cafe has a daily bus (8am, returns at noon; one-way Y10), as does the Five Rings Hotel if enough people are interested (8am, round-trip Y10). Grottoes open daily 8am-5pm. Arrange at the front ticket office for access and tours (English tours daily 9:10am and 2pm). Chinese guide Y100, English-speaking guides Y120. Expect to see 8-10 caves. Caves open to the public rotated periodically. Best-preserved caves require Y100-500 per person surcharge to enter. The bright and colorful caves #45 (Y120) and 57 (Y500) are most worthwhile. Photography prohibited. Admission Y100.*

According to legend, in AD 366 an Eastern Jin Dynasty monk, Le Zun, saw thousands of Buddhas—manifested as rays of light—glimmering from the cliff shafts of the Sanwei Mountain gully one night. He immediately decided to create artwork in a cave in the cliffs to honor the Buddhas. A few years later, another monk passed by and, seeing the first monk hard at work, began a second cave. Eventually, everyone from the local nobility to the Tang court joined in, investing small fortunes and decades of labor on single cave designs.

The clay of Mogao, unlike the cliff boulders of grottoes farther east, is ill-suited to large carvings, so artists created stucco figurines and frescoes. Over the course of the next 11 dynasties, more than 1000 caves were created. Today, nearly 500 remain, containing an astounding 2150 statues and 45,000m² of artwork spanning a row of caves 1.6km long. Most of the original reds, greens, ochres, and blues have ionized to a dark black, lending the murals an austere appearance. The themes are primarily Buddhist, but scenes also illustrate Confucian virtues, historical events, landscapes, and daily life. In addition to its endless numbers of Buddhas, *arhats*, and *bodhisattvas*, the Mogao Caves (mògāo shíkū) are unique for their *apsaras* (fēitiān; 飞天), hovering angelic Buddhas with fluttering drapery. This trademark has even made its way onto the tails of China Northwest Airlines' jets. In the 1900s, a Buddhist monk discovered a hidden library in Cave 16 that had been covered over with clay and disguised behind a mural. In the 20th century, European, Japanese, Russian, and American expeditions looted the majority of the library's contents, a fact which the Mogao Caves Museum still bitterly remembers in exhibits. Cave 96 contains a 35m high Buddha, the third-tallest Buddha statue in the world. Built under the orders of the powerful empress Wu Zetian of the Tang Dynasty, the Mogao Buddha is said to resemble her own figure. During the Cultural Revolution, the caves escaped unharmed, thanks to the protection of Premier Zhou Enlai. In 1987, Mogao was named a UNESCO World Heritage Site.

Today, Dunhuang artwork in China and around the world (the result of more thievery!) has created a field in art history and religion known as **Dunhuangology.** The **Dunhuang Research Institute,** past the entrance, on the left, presents six hand-painted, professionally replicated caves, brightly lit but less memorable than the originals. (☎ 886 9050. Open daily 8:20am-5:30pm. Free with Mogao Grottoes.)

NORTHWEST

OTHER SIGHTS

CRESCENT MOON SPRING AND SINGING SAND DUNES (yuèyá quán; 月牙泉; and míngshā shān; 鸣沙山).

In the summer, the sun sets around 9 or 9:30pm, casting an amber glow over the sands. Easily the most beautiful spot to spend an evening in Dunhuang, this expanse of sunburnt desert, with its camel rides, sand-dune-sledding, parasailing, and engine-powered glides, also gives the chance to have the most sandy fun you'll have since you outgrew the sandbox. A paradise for children, the young-at-heart, and the adventurous, the limitless sands stretch as far as the eye can see. The harsh red rocks of the Triple Threat Mountains (sānwēi shān; 三危山) to the southeast jut up in striking contrast to the soft, billowing dunes surging up from the oasis frontier in the southwest. The Crescent Moon Spring glimmers at the lowest point of a valley, walled in by 300ft. dunes on every side. Legend has it that the pool, fed by an eternal spring, has been in the same location for more than 2000 years. A temple built just five years ago by the side of the springs has a free exhibit of photographs of the majestic Dunhuang scenery. Although the sands are scalding before 5pm, the dunes can be scaled by climbing some 600 steps or following one of the narrow ridges sloping gradually to the top. Depending on your bargaining skills, camel rides cost Y40-60, parasailing Y30-60, unlimited sand-sledding Y10, and gliding Y120-150. *(An easy 30min. bike ride from Dunhuang. Ride south on Mingshan Lu and follow the road for 6km to the gate. Due to the summer heat, departing Dunhuang around 5pm is best. Y80.)*

JADE GATE PASS AND SUN PASS (yùmén guān; 玉门关; and yángguāndào; 阳关 道).

The ruins of Jade Gate Pass and Sun Pass would likely interest history buffs more for their historical significance than for their current state. The Jade Gate Pass and Sun Pass were the last Han outposts on the northern and southern Silk Roads, and for ancient Chinese, these gates opened onto exile and wilderness. Quickly deteriorating under the relentless heat and wind, these once-great gateways are nothing more than fading mounds in the desert, although the surrounding scenery isn't bad. A trip consumes the better part of a day and should probably be considered only by those who have time and money to burn. For better ruins, head west to Turpan. *(80km west of Dunhuang. Taxi Y300, minibus Y270-280. Organized tours generally also include a military storage facility (hé cān chéng; 河仓城) and the Han Dynasty Great Wall relics (hàn cháng chéng; 汉长城). Jade Gate Pass Y30. Sun Pass Y10.)*

WHITE HORSE PAGODA (báimǎ tǎ; 白马塔).

Legend says that an emperor of the Sixteen Dynasties (439-304 BC) invited a monk from India to come and teach in China. The monk answered the summons and made the long journey east. When he came to Dunhuang, the white horse he was riding appeared to him in a dream, telling the priest that he was no ordinary horse but the incarnation of the white dragon of the western seas, sent by the Buddha to help the monk reach China. Now that he had brought his rider through the Sun Pass, the horse had finished his task. In the morning, the monk awoke to discover that the horse passed away during the night, and he built this pagoda in memory of his faithful steed. The pagoda has since been rebuilt during the Ming Dynasty and is in the style of a Ming-era Tibetan pagoda. *(2km from town. Entrance Y15.)*

XINJIANG 新疆

The Xinjiang Uighur Autonomous Region stretches over 1.66 million km², about a sixth of China's total landmass, or 10 times the size of England. In this land of extremes, freezing peaks rise 7600m while deep basins plunge well below sea level. Once known as *Xīyù* (西域), or "The Western Borderlands," Xinjiang is a world unto itself, with a little of everything, whether you're looking for ancient ruins, vineyards, glaciers, or just some sunshine. Inhabited by people of varied nationalities and conflicting religions throughout history, today the region counts Uighurs, Kazakhs, Uzbeks, Mongols, Hui, and Han among its ranks. Though the cultural and ideological diversity of the region's inhabitants is one of its many charms, it has also created myriad difficulties.

The region's recent political history has been a tangled web of violence and unrest. The first half of the 20th century saw a succession of tyrannical warlords resisting the GMD government. Political backstabbings and makeshift coalitions led to a series of military coups, assassinations, and mysterious disappearances. Only the arrival of the PLA in 1949 imposed some stability on the region, but the Cultural Revolution ushered in a new age of chaos. Heavy state-sponsored Han immigration has dramatically altered Xinjiang's ethnic composition, and animosity between Han Chinese and Uighurs flares up from time to time, spurred by legal injustices, unequal opportunities, and mutual distrust. Ethnic riots rocked Kashgar in 1992 and 1997, while car bombs set by Uighur extremists shook Ürümqi and Beijing. A September 2000 bombing in Ürümqi, allegedly the act of Islamic fundamentalists, killed over 100 people. Although things have calmed down since, hope for autonomy from China lives on in the Uighur population.

In Xinjiang, time is generally told in **Beijing time** (běijīng shíjiān; 北京时间). However, informally, many people go according to Xinjiang time (xīnjiāng shíjiān; 新疆时间), 2 or 3hr. behind Beijing time. Anything official like trains, buses, planes, banks, etc., operates under Beijing time. Many government offices compensate by opening as late as 10am and staying open until 8pm. Some hotels push back their check-out time to 2pm. In Xinjiang more so than in many other parts of China, **money** can be an issue. As of yet, no ATMs in Xinjiang accept international credit cards; bring plenty of credit cards. Do not pay for tours before you return and are satisfied that the conditions have been met. If you charter a taxi or minibus, do not pay in advance. Many men in Xinjiang carry knives, so above all, handle disagreements as calmly as possible.

ÜRÜMQI 乌鲁木齐 ☎0991

Ironically, the capital of the Xinjiang Uighur Autonomous Region is very much a Han city, in both urban appearance and ethnic composition. Of the two million inhabitants, a comparatively small number of Uighur, Xibo, Hui, and Kazakh people live here, creating an unusual mix that makes it just the slightest bit easier for Westerners to blend in amid the air of foreignness. The flashing stripes of color in Uighur skirts, the bob of the *fez* in the crowd, and the rich tapestry of Uighur, Cyrillic, and Chinese scripts adorning virtually every street facade create a virtual 21st-century Silk Road, a vibrant confluence of people and cultures on the move. Ürümqi comes alive after sunset, disregarding the cues of Beijing time as it pulses deep into the night. The scents of freshly baked bread, roasting meat from night bazaars and smoky, vibrant back alleys waft through the streets.

Occupying a strategic point in the Tianshan Mountain range, Ürümqi has seen its share of power struggles. The 1955 discovery of oil in nearby Karamay kick-started the economy, and now Ürümqi oil executives compete with investors in Texas and Tokyo in the rush to cash in on the petroleum reserves around the Caspian Sea. For tourists, though, the city is a crucial link to China, Russia, and Central Asia, and a network of backpackers and travel agencies dispense advice about further travel in Xinjiang.

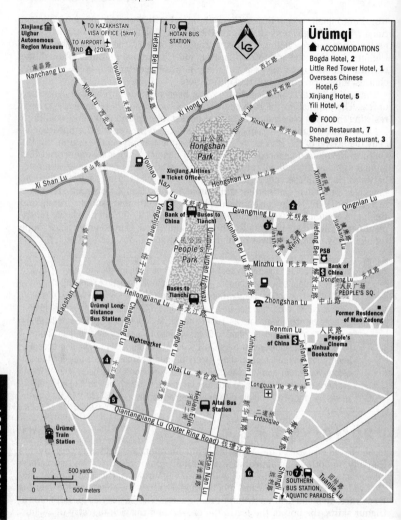

Ürümqi

ACCOMMODATIONS
Bogda Hotel, **2**
Little Red Tower Hotel, **1**
Overseas Chinese
  Hotel, **6**
Xinjiang Hotel, **5**
Yili Hotel, **4**

FOOD
Donar Restaurant, **7**
Shengyuan Restaurant, **3**

NORTHWEST

🗐 TRANSPORTATION

Flights: Ürümqi Airport (wūlǔmùqí jīchǎng; 乌鲁木齐机场; ☎371 9511, ext. 113) is 20km from town. Taxis from the city center cost about Y80. Local bus #51 from the center of town (40min., Y1). Shuttle buses (40min., Y8) leave the **Xinjiang Airlines Ticket Office** (xīnjiāng hángkōng shòupiào chù; 新疆航空售票处), 62 Youhao Nan Lu (☎950 333), 2hr. before plane departure. Open daily 9:30am-7pm. **Xinjiang Century IATA Ticket Office** (xīnjiāng shìjì tóngchén mínháng shòupiào chù; 新疆世纪同辰民航售票处), 22 Beijing Nan Lu (24hr. ☎385 9322, international 380 1493, ticketing 878 0570). To: **Altai** (1hr., 6-8 per day, Y500); **Hotan** (1hr.; 1:20, 7:35pm; Y1260); **Kashgar** (1½hr., 8:15am, Y1230); **Kuqa** (1hr., 3:20pm, Y590); **Yining** (1-1½hr., 7 per day 8:30am-9pm, Y740). Other domestic flights to: **Beijing** (3½hr., 5 per day 10am-8:30pm, Y2410); **Dunhuang** (2hr., 9:40am, Y710); **Guangzhou** (4½hr., 2 per day, Y2840); **Lanzhou** (2hr., 2-4 per day, Y1300); **Shanghai** (4hr., 3 per day, Y2800); **Xi'an** (4 per day 9:20am-4pm, Y1660); **Xining** (2hr., Sa 11:35am, Y1130). International flights to: **Almaty, Kazakhstan** (M, W, F; Y1720); **Islamabad, Pakistan** (Tu-W, Sa-Su; Y2270); **Moscow, Russia** (Tu, Su; Y2490); **Novosibirsk, Russia** (F, Y1310).

Trains: Ürümqi Train Station (wūlǔmùqí huǒchézhàn; 乌鲁木齐火车站), on Qingfeng Lu. To: **Beijing** (45hr., 2:19pm, Y631); **Dunhuang** (13hr., 7:44pm, Y201); **Hami** (9hr., 8:54am, Y145); **Jiayuguan** (24hr., 2:34pm, Y254); **Kashgar** (23hr., 3:51pm, Y177); **Korla** (11hr., 9:41am, Y83); **Lanzhou** (24hr., 6:47am, Y377); **Shanghai** (52hr., 8:20am, Y675); **Turpan** (12hr., 2:06pm, Y67); **Xi'an** (25hr., 2:55pm, Y483); **Zhangye** (17hr., 12:15am, Y291). Train also to **Almaty, Kazakhstan** (48hr., 10pm, Y491).

Buses: Ürümqi has several bus stations. International buses depart from the Long-Distance Bus Station.

Ürümqi Long-Distance Bus Station (wūlǔmùqí chángtú qìchē zhàn; 乌鲁木齐长途汽车站 ; ☎587 8898), on Heilongjiang Lu, west of Yangzijiang Lu. To: **Burqin** (15hr., 11am, Y120); **Kashgar** (24hr., several per day 8am-8pm, Y170); **Lanzhou** (40hr., 3pm, Y130); **Yining** (16hr., several per day 9am-9pm, Y140). International buses to **Almaty, Kazakhstan** (16hr., 7-8pm, Y450).

Southern Bus Station (nánjiāo qìchē zhàn; 南郊汽车站 ; ☎286 6635), the biggest and most organized station in town, on the south side of Xinhua Lu and Shengli Lu. Serves destinations to the south and west and Turpan in the east. Accessible via bus #109 from across Changjiang Lu from the Xinjiang Hotel or by taxi (Y8). Most buses leave from the back of the station, where the waiting room is, except for the bus to Korla, which leaves from the front. Open daily 8:30am-8:30pm. To: **Kashgar** (24hr., express 20hr.; every hr. 10:40am-5:20pm; Y155-174); **Korla** (10hr.; 1:30, 8pm; Y64-74); **Kuqa** (16hr., every hr. 2-8pm, Y86-96); **Turpan** (2½hr.; 8:40am, every 15min. until 8pm; Y30).

Altai Bus Station (ālètài bànshìchù; 阿勒泰办事处), 89 Hetian Er Jie. Frequent departures to the Altai region are erratically scheduled and priced. This is the place to find a shared taxi, which can cut travel times nearly in half (about Y300 to Burqin).

Hotan Bus Station (hétián bànshìchù; 和田办事处), on Hetan Bei Lu, near the northern terminus of bus #109. The place to find buses going to and arriving from Hotan.

Local Transportation: Buses lumber along Xinhua Lu: #7 and 28 are the most frequent. #1 runs south from the Hongshan Hotel to the Main Bus Station; #2 runs from the train station northwest to the Kazakh Consulate; #101 cuts through the Uighur area of Erdaoqiao. Fare Y0.5-0.8.

Taxis: Base fare Y6. Trips around town around Y10. Gray-bottomed, natural-gas-powered cabs can go anywhere. Other taxis may face pollution and movement restrictions.

◼ ❼ ORIENTATION AND PRACTICAL INFORMATION

Ürümqi lacks any discernible city center. **Xinhua Lu** (新华路) cuts north-south through the sprawl, running past most budget hotels and tourist services. The main shopping and business districts are between **Jiefang Lu** (解放路) and Xinhua Bei Lu. **Heilongjiang Lu** (黑龙江路) leads to the main bus station, and **Qiantangjiang Lu** (钱塘江路) leads to the train station farther south. **Guangming Lu** (光明路), dividing People's and Hongshan Parks, absorbs the north end of Xinhua Lu and leads to a number of tourist and financial services. The Uighur quarter of the city is in the southern neighborhood of **Erdaoqiao** (二道桥).

Travel Agencies: Xinjiang Snow Lily Travel Agency (xīnjiāng xuělián lǔxíngshè; 新疆雪莲旅行社; ☎585 1299), in the lobby of the Xinjiang Hotel. 1-day Y120 tours to Tianchi include meals, tolls, and admission. Also sells tickets on tourist buses to Tianchi (Y30-50, depending on bus quality). Open daily 24hr.

Adventure Travel: Some agencies offer more rigorous activities like mountain climbing, wilderness backpacking tours, and guided desert excursions. **Ürümqi Mountain Climbing Club** leads one of the most reputable and hard-core guided trips, a 2- to 3-week ascent of the 5445m Bogda Peak near Tianchi, for experienced climbers only (Y5800). Contact Wang Tienan, the head of the club (☎ 130 0968 1695; pager 127 103 1177). Other 3-day trips cost Y500, including tents, gear, cooks, and pack animals.

Bank of China: 2 Dongfeng Lu, just south of the PSB. Exchanges traveler's checks. Credit card advances on the 2nd fl. **Branches** at 343 Jiefang Nan Lu, at Renmin Lu, and 1 Yangzijiang Lu, opposite the post office. All open M-F 9:30am-1:30pm and 4-7:30pm, Sa-Su 11am-4:30pm. No international ATMs in Ürümqi, or anywhere else in Xinjiang.

Bookstore: Xinhua Bookstore (☎ 281 8136). A good selection of English-Uighur phrasebooks and maps of Xinjiang. Open daily 10am-10pm.

PSB: Foreigner Reception Office (wàiguórén jiēdàishì; 外国人接待室 ; ☎ 281 0452, ext. 3646), on the corner of Minzhu Lu and Jiankang Lu. Processes visa extensions (US citizens Y440). Open M-Tu, Th-F 9:30am-1pm and 4-8pm.

Internet Access: There are several hundred Internet cafes in the city, some with names like Cool Bear and Green Apple. Tucked away in a narrow side street, **Network the World Internet Cafe** (wǎngluò tiānxià yī fēndiàn; 网络天下一分店), 100 Zhongshan Lu, is in the center of town. Y2 per hr. Open 24hr. The **Fashionable Internet Cafe** (shíshàng wǎngbā; 时尚网吧), 107 Youhao Nan Lu, is a 5min. walk north of the post office. Open 24hr.

Post and Telecommuncations: China Post (☎ 585 7329), on Yangzijiang Lu, opposite the Bank of China, on the south side of the Youhao Nan Lu roundabout. Descend the underground walkway in front of the bank and re-emerge at the post office. EMS, Poste Restante, and Western Union. Open daily 9:30am-8:30pm. **China Telecom,** 157 Zhongshan Lu, at Xinhua Bei Lu. Helpful staff. IDD service. Open daily 9:30am-8pm.

Postal Code: 830000.

ACCOMMODATIONS

Budget hotels gather around the train station to the southeast, but they're inconveniently located for exploration of the city. Newer and better buildings constantly replace their somewhat new counterparts. Though beneficial from an economic standpoint, this also means that budget options for foreigners are dwindling fast.

Bogda Hotel (bógédá bīnguǎn; 博格达宾馆), 10 Guangming Lu (☎ 886 3910, ext. 2119), a 10min. walk east of the Hongshan Hotel, in the "First Guesthouse of the Xinjiang Military Region" compound. This privatized ex-military hostel has bargain dorms but pricey rooms and no showers. With a guard at the front, the Bogda is possibly the safest hotel in Ürümqi. 6-bed dorms Y20; doubles with bath Y280-388. Low-season discounts possible. ❶

Xinjiang Hotel (xīnjiāng fàndiàn; 新疆饭店), 107 Changjiang Lu (☎ 585 2511, ext. 2000), facing the traffic circle at Qiantangjiang Lu and Changjiang Lu. Rooms have clean sheets and clotheslines to hang laundry. TV, phone, and A/C in all rooms except dorms. Deposit Y20-200. 3- to 6-bed dorms Y15; 2-bed dorms Y30; doubles with bath Y50-680; quads Y80. ❶

Little Red Tower Hotel (xiǎo hóng lóu jiǔdiàn; 小红楼酒店), 38 Yingbin Lu (☎ 796 0537), 5min. from the airport. This is as close as it gets to a budget hotel in the vicinity of the airport. Extremely warm staff. Independent water boilers in baths ensure 24hr. piping hot water. Excellent, reasonably priced restaurant next to the lobby. Manager can find airplane tickets, sometimes for as low as half the listed price. Bright, clean rooms Y160, or Y120 after resolute bargaining. ❷

Overseas Chinese Hotel (huáqiáo bīnguǎn; 华侨宾馆), 51 Xinhua Nan Lu (☎852 1888), in the south of town, past Qiantangjiang Lu. This favorite among Russian merchants has a variety of pleasant rooms. The east building has cheaper rooms. Attached to the Troika Restaurant/Disco. Deposit Y500. Singles Y260; doubles Y200-280. ❸

Yili Hotel (yīlí dàjiǔdiàn; 伊梨大酒店), 80 Changjiang Lu (☎585 6888), near the night-market. Shiny marble entrance. Stylish rooms with red, embroidered silk cushions and large windows. Dorms Y100; doubles Y340; triples Y240; luxury suites Y680. ❷

🗋 FOOD

The thousands of little eateries along Xinhua Lu and in the Erdaoqiao Muslim district can always satisfy a hungry traveler. **Nightmarkets** abound in the train station area, starting around 8:30pm. The best is on Changjiang Lu, about a 5min. walk from the Xinjiang Hotel. Try the lamb kebabs (yángròu chuàn; 羊肉串 ; Y1). Cold **Xinjiang beer** is served up at nearly every stand (Y2.5-3 per bottle).

Donar Restaurant (duōnà'ěr; 多那尔), 120 Xinhua Nan Lu (☎285 0099), next to the zoo. Take bus #7, 51, 68, 109, 910, or 915 to the Dongwuyuan (动物园) stop. Specializes in Uighur and Turkish specialties. Outdoor seating and grill. Lamb kebabs served in pita bread with a variety of sauces (Y18). Open daily 10am-2:30am. ❷

Muslim Specialties Restaurant (qīngzhēn fēngwèi cāntīng; 清真风味餐厅), 7 Jian-kang Lu (☎281 5182). A wide selection of Muslim rice and noodle dishes (Y15). Frozen fruit and yogurt shaved ice (suānnǎi shuǐguǒ bàobīng; 酸奶水果刨冰). Wacky German comic strips printed along the tables. Open daily 24hr. ❷

Shengyuan Restaurant (shèngyuán cāntīng; 盛源餐厅), on Jianshe Lu, a 3min. walk from the Bogda Hotel. If you like spicy food, try the "Flying Nights Beef" (piāoxiāo niúròu; 飘宵牛肉), a bubbling pot of beef, vegetables, and red chilis. ❷

👁 SIGHTS

XINJIANG UIGHUR AUTONOMOUS REGION MUSEUM (xīnjiāng wéiwú'ěr zú zìzhì qū bówùguǎn; 新疆维吾尔族自治区). Like many things in Ürümqi, the highly regarded Xinjiang Museum was recently torn down to make way for a bigger, better, and glitzier version, expected to open in October 2005. Many of the best exhibits are on display in a temporary building behind the former museum. Particularly noteworthy is a creepy but fantastic collection of mummies, including an infant who died 3800 years ago and the "Loulan Beauty," the corpse of a 45-year-old woman of Indo-European ethnicity reputed to be 4000 years old. In the backroom are the remains of Zhang Xiong, a general and minister of defense in the Gaochang Kingdom. The gift shop sells spectacular Uighur rugs. *(132 Aletai Lu. In the north part of town, a 25min. walk along Xibei Lu from the post office, or a 5min. ride on bus #52. ☎453 6436. Free tours in Mandarin; most exhibits have English captions. Open M-F 9:30am-7:30pm, Sa-Su 10:30am-5:30pm; last admission 1hr. before closing. Y25, students Y16. Be adamant: ticket sellers will try to tell you that the student ticket is only for those in middle school.)*

AQUATIC PARADISE (shuǐshàng lèyuán; 水上乐园). Ürümqi's fame as the farthest inland city in the world explains this bizarre amusement park. The main attraction is the city reservoir, where speedboats churn up the waters, watched over by the mighty Tianshan mountains. Climbing along the imitation Great Wall (Y2) reveals a great view of the city. *(Next to the Southern Bus Station. Take bus #7 or 109. Admission Y5. Log flume Y5. Rollercoasters and ferris wheel Y20 each.)*

ERDAOQIAO MARKET (èrdàoqiáo shìchǎng; 二道桥市场). One of the best stops in town, this market sits in the heart of Ürümqi's Uighur quarter. On weekends, shops selling textiles and crafts spread out over an area almost one-fourth the size of Kashgar's famous Sunday bazaar (p. 811). The main market is on Shengli Lu, stretching for several blocks south of where it turns into Jiefang Lu. A large gateway leads to a back alley full of rugs, silk, and food.

▐ NIGHTLIFE

Chinatown (zhōngguó chéng; 中国城), 9 Kelamayi Dong Lu, off Youhao Lu. A young crowd dances to high-energy house and garage on the packed dance floor 7 nights a week. Sexy, smart casual dress. Beer Y20. Cover Y20, women free. Open 9pm-4am.

House (hàosī; 浩斯), 26 Xinshi Jie (☎885 4493). The largest and glitziest nightclub in Ürümqi. Scantily clad gogo dancers writhe on stage while the dance floor below gyrates to electro-house. Beer Y15-20. Cover Y20, women free. Open 10pm-4am.

Red Tomato (hóng fānqié; 红番茄), 26 Jianguo Lu (☎883 5787). Live traditional Uighur dance performances over a techno beat, featuring women balancing vessels on their heads. Ever-present smell of a steady supply of microwave popcorn in the relaxed and friendly atmosphere. Young, laidback Uighur crowd. Cover Y10. Open 8:30pm-3am.

Space Disco Club (kōngjiān; 空间), 40 Minzhu Lu (☎231 1889). If dancing to techno remixes of Bryan Adams is your idea of fun, this is the place to be, 7 nights a week. Live DJ likes to chirp down the microphone with "Oooh, baby" and "Yeah, come on." Last 30min. devoted to hip hop. Cover Y20, women free. Open 9:30pm-3:30am.

▐ DAYTRIP FROM ÜRÜMQI: TIANCHI LAKE 天池

*Buses (2-2½hr.; 9-9:30am; same-day round-trip Y30, with A/C Y35) leave for Tianchi daily from the south and north ends of People's Park. Buy tickets the day before or in the morning. Be sure to ask whether fare includes a highway toll fee, which may be tacked on at the last minute by drivers. If you plan to spend the night at Tianchi, buy another ticket the next day. Buses go to Ürümqi daily 4:30-5:30pm, stopping mid-mountain as well as at the bottom parking lot before returning. **Public buses** leave Tianchi every 30min. 8:30-10:30am and return to Ürümqi 3-6pm; you will need to change buses at Fukang (Y10) and Ermao (Y9); delays and complications are common. Bring warm clothes for overnight stays. Cable car up Y10, down Y5. Electric cars to the top Y5, minivans Y5. Speed boats Y25, ferry Y20. Horseback riding Y70 per 1½hr.*

Nestled high in the Tianshan range, 115km east of Ürümqi, the mountain lake of Tianchi (tiānchí; 天池) lies 1950m above sea level, guarded by the stately 6000m Bogda peak. Tianchi rewards visitors with unforgettable experiences, including alpine hiking, star-gazing, and camping in Kazakh yurts. According to myth, the Mother of the Western Skies held a feast at this lake whenever a local peach tree bore fruit. As this only happened about once every 3000 years, the banquets were understandably grand affairs. All the immortals would gather together for this long-awaited festival, converting the lake area into something of a Little Heaven—hence its name, the "Heavenly Pool."

While immortals are hard to come by these days, Tianchi's natural beauty attracts hordes of worldly tourists. Breaking away from the paved lakeside paths and up into the surrounding hills will put plenty of distance between you and them. Several horse trails wind up into the high ridges overlooking the snowy mountains in the distance. Small Kazakh encampments scatter in pockets of grassland at high altitudes. In the summer, a refreshing dip in the lake hits the spot.

Overnight stays are highly recommended, as Tianchi regains its heavenly tranquility only after the majority of daytrippers leave around 5pm. Finding lodging in the many lakeside yurts is simple: just ask or, more likely, you will be asked. Three meals and lodging cost about Y40; agree on the price early on. **Rashit**, an endearing Kazakh guide, has been hosting guests in his nine-yurt camp on the southwest bank of the lake for over 15 years. He speaks Mandarin and English, and is a great cook. While many backpackers go to Tianchi in search of solitude, they usually find their way to Rashit's, attracted by the warm food and convivial atmosphere.

ALTAI PREFECTURE 阿勒泰地区

In the northernmost corner of Xinjiang, near the Kazakh, Mongolian, and Russian borders, Altai is a sharp contrast to the deserts of the south. Here, rivers thunder past thick pine and birch forests, while Kazakh and Mongol herders tend their sheep and cattle on fertile grasslands overlooked by rocky peaks. Snow falls regularly nine months of the year, but temperatures in July and August can be as warm as 38°C. The Ertix, the main river in the region, is the only one in China to empty into the Arctic Ocean. Beautiful beyond compare, the blue waters of Hanas Lake are more than enough reason for a trip up to distant Altai, but the region's pristine wilderness and remote villages are equally worthy of exploration.

BORDER CROSSINGS INTO KAZAKHSTAN AND MONGO-LIA. For those looking to skip the country, Altai is fertile ground for border crossings. To Kazakhstan, the main crossing is at **Jimunai** (吉木乃), near Burqin. To Mongolia, there are crossings at **Hongshanzui** (红山嘴) and **Takeshiken** (塔克什肯), both accessible from Altai City. Traveling to any of those border towns requires a permit from the PSB. There is currently no legal way to cross into Russia from Altai. Visas for travel to Kazakhstan are now handled in the **Kazakh Airlines Visa Office** (hāsàkèsītǎn mínhánggōngsī zhùwū bànqiānzhèngchù; 哈萨克斯坦民航公司驻乌办签证处), 31 Kunming Lu (☎383 2324), off Beijing Lu, behind the Torch Mansions (huǒjù dàshà; 火炬大厦); look for the flame sign on Beijing Lu. Accessible by bus #2 or taxis (Y20). 30-day **tourist visas** cost Y30. A letter of invitation from the Kazakhstan Foreign Ministry is no longer required for tourist visas, but those without the letter must pay an extra Y45. You will need both your passport and a photocopy of the passport. Processing time 3 days. The helpful visa officer speaks fluent English. Open M-Th 10am-1pm, new applications accepted before 1pm.

ALTAI CITY 阿勒泰市   ☎0906

Altai City, the prefectural capital, is set amid dramatic charcoal-gray hills and split by the roaring Kelan River, a tributary of the Ertix, with lovely birch forests stretching miles upon miles on its shores. "Altai" means "gold" in Kazakh and Mongolian, and the city is renowned for its jewelry industry. While swimming in the river in the summertime, sift a handful of sand from the riverbed through your finers to see tiny flecks of gold.

◧ TRANSPORTATION. The **Altai City Airport** (ālètàishì jīchǎng; 阿勒泰市机场) is 17km from the city. A 20min. taxi from the city costs about Y20. The **CAAC Ticket Office** is just right of the Xinhua bookstore. Look for a blue sign with an airplane on it. (☎212 8686; pager 126 8374094. Open M-F 9:30am-8pm, Sa 11am-6pm.) All flights go through Ürümqi (many per day M-F, Su 8:30pm; Y450, with 10-15 days advance purchase Y350). Walk 25min. south of the city center or take bus #1 or 101 to the **Altai Passenger Station** (ālètàishì kèyùnzhàn; 阿勒泰市客运站), on Tuanjie Lu. Sleeper buses arriving in Altai tend to continue north into town and should be happy to drop you off wherever you're staying. Beware of taxi drivers around the entrance who will tell you there are no more buses running: it probably won't be true. **Buses** depart to Burqin (1½hr., frequent buses approx. 9am-8pm, Y14); Ürümqi (12hr.; 10am, 7pm; Y116-122); and Yining (2 days, 11am, Y142-162).

🔲🔼 ORIENTATION AND PRACTICAL INFORMATION. Altai City is built along the banks of the **Kelan River** (kèlán hé; 克兰河), flowing north-south through the city. There are two main roads, also running north-south: **Tuanjie Lu** (团结路) runs from the bus station in the far south before becoming **Gongyuan Lu** (公园路) and winding north out of town to **Birch Forest Park; Jiefang Lu** (解放路) branches off Tuanjie Lu near the bus station and is home to the Bank of China, Xinhua Bookstore, and Golden Bridge Hotel. The center of the city is at **Golden Mountain Square** (jīnshān guǎngchǎng; 金山广场) on Jiefang Lu, where the **Camel Hump Bridge** (tuófēngqiáo; 驼峰桥) links the two main roads.

A number of travel agencies in town market expensive tours to Hanas Lake (Y1150-1400). It's far kinder to your wallet to take the public bus to Burqin and arrange a taxi to Hanas (Y50). The **Bank of China,** on Jiefang Nan Lu, a 5min. walk south of the Kelan Bridge, exchanges traveler's checks. (☎212 1032. Open M-F 9:30am-1pm and 4-7:30pm, Sa-Su 11am-3pm.) The **Xinhua Bookstore,** on Jiefang Lu, north of Golden Mountain Sq., sells handy city and regional maps (Y3) on the third floor. (☎212 2032. Open daily 9:30am-8pm.) Take a left onto Wenhua Lu just north of Xinhua Bookstore; the **PSB** is at the end of this dead-end road. There is a visa department on the second floor. Foreigners no longer need permits to travel to Hanas Lake; simply register at the lake upon arrival. (☎212 2624. Open M-F 9:30am-1:30pm and 4-8pm.) **China Telecom** is on the second floor of the building right of the post office. (Open daily 9:30am-8pm.) The **post office** (☎213 3482) is on the second floor, on Jiefang Lu across from the bookstore. **Postal Code:** 836500.

🔳🔲 ACCOMMODATIONS AND FOOD. Budget options for foreigners, like the foreigners themselves, are pretty scarce. Still, the **Sunshine Hotel ❶** (yángguāng dàjiǔdiàn; 阳光大酒店), 234 Tuanjie Lu, just before the Kelan Bridge, has well-priced rooms and a convenient location. Small, colorful rooms have all the amenities of more expensive hotels at less than a third of the price. Adjoining dining hall and several private karaoke rooms serve excellent food at dirt-cheap prices. (☎212 9688. Doubles with bath Y70. Luxury suites with 2 rooms, 1 of which has a double bed and the other 3 single beds Y120.) The **Altai Tourist Hotel ❷** (ālètài dìqū lǚyóu bīnguǎn;阿勒泰地区旅游宾馆) is on Gongyuan Lu, just across the Camel Hump Bridge from Golden Mountain Sq. Token goats graze on the lawn of this large, pleasant complex. (☎212 3804. Clean sheets, big windows, TV, and a water dispenser. Basic but functional attached baths. 24hr. hot water. Individual beds Y100; doubles Y240; triples Y270.) The **Golden Bridge Hotel ❺** (jīnqiáo dàjiǔdiàn; 金桥大酒店), 1 Jiefang Lu, is opposite Golden Mountain Sq. Foreign tour groups usually stay at the Golden Bridge, which has the comforts to cater to their rarefied tastes, with the high prices to match. (☎212 7566. Doubles and triples Y360.)

Some of the best beef noodles in the northwest can be found at 🔳 **Gansu Beef Noodles Restaurant ❶** (gānsū niúròu miàn fànguǎn; 甘肃牛肉面饭馆), on Jiefang Nan Lu, just south of the Kelan Bridge. Slightly more expensive, the **Haiyun Restaurant ❷** (hǎiyùn fànguǎn; 海酝饭馆 ; ☎212 1966) serves enormous portions. A mere Y30 buys two dishes and rice, ample food for two bellies. A **nightmarket** comes alive around 8pm next to the Golden Bridge Hotel, selling lamb kebabs (Y1), lamb pastries (Y1), and lamb dumplings (Y0.4).

◙ **SIGHTS.** Altai City's most famous sight is the vast, thick **Birch Forest Park** (huálín gōngyuán; 桦林公园) along the Kelan River, north of town. Known among Chinese tourists as a prime bird-watching spot, the birch groves are also well-endowed with wildflowers. A paved road circumnavigates the park, with count-less small dirt paths leading into the woods and along the river. One could easily spend the better part of a day exploring or just taking in the sights and smells. A few scattered tea houses serve up snacks and Kazakh milk tea. (On Gongyuan Lu, north of town. Y1 ride in a taxi or bus #101. Open daily sunrise-sunset. Y5.)

BURQIN 布尔津 ☎0906

A sleepy town with mostly Kazakh residents, Burqin is named for the Burqin River, a vast, lazy stream that empties into the Ertix. With the winding riverbank so sparsely populated, the water remains clean and home to enormous, leaping fish. The drive from Altai to Burqin, and then on to Hanas Lake and Hemu, weaves through a vast, dry wilderness, past miles and miles of sunflower fields, planted with the help of the river's clear waters.

✈️ 🛈 ORIENTATION AND PRACTICAL INFORMATION

Burqin is small enough to navigate on foot. The main road, **Wenming Lu** (文明路), runs roughly north to south through town and is home to the bus station, main square, and several nightmarkets. Taking a left out of the bus station on Wenming Lu brings you to **Xingfu Lu** (幸福路), where you can find the PSB and the Jinhe Hotel. Wenming Lu runs past **Huancheng Nan Lu** (环城南路) before exiting town, crossing the Ertix River, and extending toward Ürümqi.

Buses: The **Passenger Terminal** (kèyùn zhàn; 客运站) is on Wenming Lu, in the north-ern part of town. To **Altai City** (1½hr., frequent buses 9am-8pm, Y14) and **Ürümqi** (12hr., 6pm, Y98-112). July-Aug., tickets to Altai run like hotcakes, usually sold out 2hr. in advance. July-Aug., **tourist buses** leave for **Hanas Lake.**

Travel Agency: Xinjiang Round World Tourism Co. (xīnjiāng huányóu lǚxíngshè; 新疆环游旅行社; ☎625 5531 or 139 9945 9722). From the Tourist Hotel, turn left, and walk 2min. down Huancheng Nan Xi Lu. The agency is on the right, inside the Kanas Hotel. Gives sound advice and reasonable prices for trips to Hanas Lake, though it might be simpler to find a driver at the bus station. Offers overnight stays in Mongolian yurts for just Y20, but those showing up on the spot may be charged Y30.

PSB: On the corner of Xingfu Lu and Xiangyang Lu (☎652 2161, ext. 2009; beeper 126 837 7212), west of Wenming Lu. Permits no longer needed to travel beyond Burqin. Open M-F 9:30am-1:30pm and 4-8pm.

Post and Telecommunications: On Huancheng Zhong Nan Lu, near Wenming Lu. Open daily 9:30am-8pm.

🏠 🍴 ACCOMMODATIONS AND FOOD

You haven't tasted fish until you've tried the freshly caught fish from the Burqin River. The place to go is the ◙ **Fish Stew Restaurant** ❸ (āo yú guǎn; 熬鱼馆), on Huan Nan Zhong Lu. If you're not averse to hot spices, try the chef's specialty, country fish stew (xiāngcūn āo yú; 乡村熬鱼 ; Y48 per kg). The stew arrives bub-bling over a small burner and is more than enough to fill one person. (☎652 2117. Open daily 10am until last customers leave.)

Jinhe Hotel (jīnhé bīnguǎn; 津河宾馆 ; ☎652 3170), on Xingfu Lu, next to the PSB. From the bus station, turn left on Wenming Lu, then right on Xingfu Lu. This breezy hotel has an old and homey feel, with wood-panelled walls and doorways. Corridors softly scented with perfume make it possibly the nicest-smelling hotel in China. Hot water 4pm-midnight. 3- to 4-bed dorms Y35-40; doubles with bath Y120; suites Y180. ❶

Traffic Hotel (jiāotōng bīnguǎn; 交通宾馆 ; ☎652 2643), at the bus station. Conveniently located. This Traffic Hotel actually lives up to its name with pictures of traffic jams decorating its walls. 2- to 4-bed dorms Y20-40; singles Y90. ❶

Burqin Tourist Hotel (bù'ěrjīn lǚyóu bīnguǎn; 布尔津旅游宾馆), 4 Huancheng Nan Xi Lu (☎652 1325), by the intersection with Wenming Lu. The large complex is off the street, behind a sunny flower garden with a seating area, a bridge leading over a pond, and a dinky little pavilion. 24hr. hot water and A/C. Doubles Y240-300; triples with bath in red-roofed wood cabins Y180. ❶

📷 DAYTRIPS FROM BURQIN

After jaunts to Hanas Lake and Hemu, or on some lazy evening in town, head to the **Burqin River** (bù'ěrjīn hé; 布尔津河), northwest of town, to unwind and relax. The river can swell to a width of 100m after heavy rains, which are frequent during the summer. Birch trees shade the bank, making a perfect retreat by the slowly flowing water. A bit upstream from the road bridge is an island park frequented by locals, where visitors can sample regional fare at numerous yurt-restaurants. *(Round-trip taxi should cost about Y10.)*

📷 HANAS LAKE 哈纳斯湖

About 150km north of Burqin (a 3hr. drive). A taxi from Burqin is the best option; one-way Y50 per person (fixed price). Drivers and prospective passengers alike hang out at the Burqin bus station. Even though foreigners no longer need permits, they still must register at the police station at the lake; bring your passport. Entry to Hanas Lake area Y100.

Set in a pristine alpine valley, Hanas Lake (hǎnàsī hú, 哈纳斯湖 ; also called Kanas Lake, 喀纳斯湖) is one of the crown jewels of Xinjiang's tourist attractions. Long and narrow, the lake shines vivid hues of emerald and turquoise, reflecting its surrounding forests of tall pines and steep, rocky mountains. To the north, the icy 4374m **Friendship Peak** (yǒuyì fēng; 友谊峰) rears up at the meeting of the borders of China, Kazakhstan, Mongolia, and Russia. Climb up a neighboring hill for the best views of the lake. A popular day hike leads to **Fish-Watching Pavilion** (guānyú tíng; 观鱼亭), up a short, steep trail on the west bank. From the pavilion, the vista encompasses the lake, Friendship Peak, the valley, and eagles circling overhead. Keep an eye out for the **giant lake monster** (húguài; 湖怪) rumored to live in the depths below. Early mornings are the best time for hikes, when the still water mirrors the sky, and mist drifts over the lake and mountains. In July and August, wildflowers bloom, and by September, the leaves burst into brilliant reds and yellows.

Rafting at the lake costs Y150 for 45min., during which you can cover about 15km. Trekking to **Hemu,** 23km away, with an overnight stay at **Black Lake,** 7km away, costs Y400. For more information about Hanas Lake's adventure opportunities, call Lily, also named Free Girl (☎131 9979 5649). She speaks excellent English, and her husband owns a yurt.

Spending at least one night at Hanas is necessary due to the long drive from Burqin. A **tourist village** has sprung up about 2km south of the lake, where the taxi will most likely leave you. A night's stay in a **yurt** only costs Y30. If you're looking for more standard shelter, a good bet is the **Linhai Mountain Villa** ❶ (línhǎi shānzhuāng; 林海山庄), a scattering of wood houses alongside the Hanas River. Take the first left off the main road and cross the river; the Linhai is the second guesthouse on the left. (3-bed dorms without bath Y30; doubles Y200.) Expect to pay at least double the usual prices for food in Hanas.

The area's designation as a national nature reserve and the Y100 admission have yet to mar the isolated loveliness of the lake, which remains untouched by pollution. Boardwalks and well-groomed trails are the only evidence of a tourism industry. You'll be hard-pressed to find a more beautiful spot in the whole of China.

TIP **DON'T LET IT RAIN ON YOUR YURT.** When sleeping in a yurt, especially around Hanas Lake, be sure to keep your clothes, bags, and other belongings well away from the sides of the yurt. A surprise downpour in the night will soak everything close to the outer edges.

HEMU 禾木

About 30km southeast of Hanas Lake. Accessible only by jeep (about Y150) over a very bumpy road in poor condition. Best visited on the way back from Hanas Lake to Burqin. Drivers wait at the Hanas/Hemu intersection for you to switch cars.

The tiny village of Hemu (hémù), sometimes called **Hemu Kanas** (hémù kānàsī, 禾木喀纳斯), is idyllic beyond imagination. A few hundred families live here in log cabins, beneath towering peaks rising out of shreds of mist. Snow lingers on parts of the ground throughout the summer. Adorable miniature cows wander about the river picking fights with each other and searching for prime grazing opportunities in the high grass. Wild strawberries ramble over the hillsides, and in July and August wildflowers transform the hills and valleys outside town into seas of purple and yellow. Hemu is home to a small community of the isolated Tuwa minority, a tiny branch of the Mongolian people, but with their own distinctive language. There are around 2000 surviving Tuwa people today, mostly living in the Hemu and Kanas Lake areas in northern Altai. The tourist industry in Hemu is almost nonexistent, as the muddy, bumpy road keeps most visitors away. Foreigners are required to stay at a simple guesthouse run by the village government (about Y30 per person, with bargaining); your driver will most likely drop you off there.

YINING 伊宁 ☎ 0999

Nestled in a peaceful valley and surrounded by flower-blanketed grasslands and the towering Tianshan mountain range, Yining is very much on the fringes of China. Strategically located and populated by an eclectic mix of Kazakhs, Uighurs, Xibo, and Han Chinese, the city has often been a focal point for conflict, most recently in 1997, when Uighur separatists took to rioting in the streets. Although Yining itself has little of interest, the surrounding area is home to some of Xinjiang's most pristine wildernesses, the most accessible of which is the breathtaking Sayram Lake. The bus routes to Yining from both Ürümqi and Korla pass through barren deserts, alpine river valleys, and distant snow-capped mountains. Stopping along the way between Yining and Ürümqi is quite feasible; buses are frequent and often pick up passengers along the way.

TRANSPORTATION AND PRACTICAL INFORMATION

Jiefang Lu (解放路) leads from the bus station in the northwest down to the post office near the southern limits of the city. **Sidalin Jie** (斯大林街) runs east-west, crossing **Qingnian Square** (qīngnián guǎngchǎng; 青年广场) and Jiefang Lu at the post office. Hotels are clustered near the bus station in the west and around Qingnian Sq. in the southeast.

NORTHWEST

Flights: The **airport** is a 15min. taxi ride north of the city (Y10; drivers might try to charge Y20). **CAAC ticket office** (☎804 4328, 24hr. 804 4000), in the Yilite Hotel on Sidalin Jie, on the corner of People's Sq. Cancellations and delays are extremely common; check in advance with the CAAC ticket office or the travel agency. To: **Ürümqi** (1-3 per day; morning flights Y410, evening Y590).

Buses: Yining Long-Distance Bus Station (yīníng chángtú qìchē zhàn; 伊宁长途汽车站; ☎802 3413), on the northwest end of Jiefang Lu, near Ahemaitijiang Lu. Open daily 8am-8pm. To: **Almaty, Kazakhstan** (M, W-Th, Sa 8am; US$30); **Altai City** (48hr.; noon; sleeper bus top bunk Y130, bottom Y150) via **Burqin; Kashgar** (48hr.; daily; hardseat Y116, sleeper Y226); **Korla** (18-30hr., 12:30pm, Y105); **Ürümqi** (15hr., many per day 3-9pm, Y80-150).

Local Transportation: Bus #1 (Y0.5) runs east along Jiefang Lu from the bus station to Qingnian Sq.; #2 (Y1.2) runs from the northwest end of Qingnian Sq. west along Sidalin Jie before going south to Yili River Park along Yilihe Lu. **Pedicabs** are Y3 within the city.

Travel Agencies: Yili International Travel Agency (yīlí guójì lǚxíngshè; 伊梨国际旅行社; ☎802 4939), on Yilihe Lu, in the southeast part of town. Accessible by pedicab (Y3) from the bus station or downtown. Open daily 9:30am-1:30pm and 4-8pm. **Yining International Travel Agency** (yīníng guójì lǚxíng shè; 伊宁国际旅行社; ☎812 0298), on Ahemaitijiang Lu, in Jianyin Mansion (jiànyín dàshà; 建银大厦), a 5min. walk south of Jiefang Lu. Both agencies offer 1- to 3-day package tours of Sayram Lake, Nalati Grasslands, and other Yili Valley sites (Y50-600 per day), depending on the group numbers; single travelers may have to wait to tag along with a larger tour group. Ticket commission Y20 at both agencies.

Bank of China: ☎822 3350. On Jiefang Lu, just east of and across the street from the bus station. Exchange traveler's checks. Open summer M-F 9:30am-1:30pm and 4-8pm; winter M-F 10am-2pm and 3:30-7:30pm; year-round Sa-Su 11am-5pm.

PSB: ☎802 2491, ext. 3026. On Sidalin Jie, across from Qingnian Park. The unhelpful visa office is in the squat building on the left side of the complex. Staff are a bit secretive—office is appropriately located on Stalin St. Open M-F 9:30am-1:30pm and 4-8pm.

Internet Access: Yaxiya Internet Cafe (yàxìyà wǎngbā; 亚细亚网吧; ☎803 1505), on Jiefang Xi Lu, next to the Yaxiya Hotel. Y2 per hr. Open daily 24hr.

Post and Telecommunications: On Xinhua Lu, near Qingnian Lu. EMS and Poste Restante. **China Telecom,** on the corner on Sidalin Lu and Jiefang Lu. IDD. Both open daily summer 9:30am-8pm; winter 10am-7:30pm.

Postal Code: 835000.

ACCOMMODATIONS AND FOOD

Yining has limited budget options. Dorm beds are not open to foreigners; many hotels require single travelers to pay for an entire room, a policy almost impossible to get around. Luckily, mid-range doubles are available in the conveniently located Yaxiya Hotel.

The charming Uighur **Weisa'er Fast Food ❶** (wéisà'ěr kuàicān; 维萨尔快餐; ☎809 8035), first floor of Halisi'aji Bldg., opposite People's Park, has a welcoming staff and a romantic atmosphere. The small rectangular tables are fit for a meal for two, or a very squashed four. Delicious noodle dishes come at remarkably cheap prices. Try the *guòyóu ròumiàn* (过油肉面), fried noodles with lamb and red and green peppers (Y7). Eat as much as you like at the Muslim buffet of **Pindeju ❶** (pǐn dé jū fànguǎn; 品居居饭馆; ☎803 8655), 11 Sidalin Jie, east of China Telecom. Choose from over 10 different hot dishes, including seafood, tender chicken on the bone, and various vegetarian options. Best of all, it's only Y8. Another place to eat ridic-

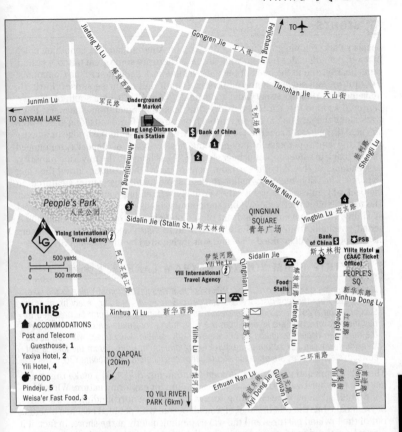

Yining

ACCOMMODATIONS
Post and Telecom
  Guesthouse, 1
Yaxiya Hotel, 2
Yili Hotel, 4

FOOD
Pindeju, 5
Weisa'er Fast Food, 3

ulously cheap yet tasty food is near the intersection of Jiefang Nan Lu and Xinhua Dong Lu, just south of China Telecom. A number of eateries serving **yellow fried rice** dishes (zhuā fàn; 抓饭; Y5) are popular among the locals.

Yaxiya Hotel (yàxìyà bīnguǎn; 亚细亚宾馆; ☎803 1800, ext. 5100). From the bus station, turn right on Jiefang Lu, then turn right on the street directly across from the Bank of China; it's on the left. The friendly staff speak a bit of English and are happy to bargain, although breakfast is not included if you get a discount. Cheapest doubles on 5-7th fl. Y90, with A/C Y100 (although A/C is never absolutely necessary in Yining). ❷

Post and Telecommunications Guesthouse (yóudiàn bīnguǎn; 邮电宾馆), 162 Jiefang Lu (☎822 3844), a short walk east of the Bank of China. Many of the bright, cheery rooms have an inspiring view of the trash-strewn roof of the building next door. Lovely double beds in the single rooms, if the view doesn't bother you. Bath. Front building: singles Y158; doubles Y158-600. Back building: doubles Y138; triples Y135. ❷

Yili Hotel (yīlí bīnguǎn; 伊梨宾馆), 22 Yingbin Lu (☎802 2794 or 802 3799), a 5min. walk north of Qingnian Sq., at the end of Hongqi Lu. A beige gate leads to the forest-like grounds of the complex. Rooms in the west wing (bldg. #4) have large breezy baths. The main building is more modern and sterile. Frequent evening music and dance performances. Russian-style restaurants. Standard doubles Y160, nicer ones Y228-488. ❷

NORTHWEST

⊙ SIGHTS

People's Park (rénmín gōngyuán; 人民公园), on Ahetoutijiang Lu, is nothing much in itself, but still a nice place to walk around. There are some great outdoor restaurants nearby, and in the back of the park, a mini-park dedicated to the Communist Revolution has several martyrs' tombs. (Open daily sunrise-sunset. Park Y3; museum Y2.) **Yili River Park** (yīlíhé gōngyuán; 伊犁河公园), 6km south of the city, centered around the Yili River Bridge, has less than outstanding scenery, but a walk along the far bank takes you through picturesque farmland along grassy poplar-lined dirt paths. (From the Yili Hotel, take either bus #2 to the bridge or a taxi.)

For the anthropologically inclined, the nearby town of **Qapqal** (pronounced tshap-tshael; in Chinese chábùcháěr, 察布查尔), is home to the tiny Xibo minority, descendents of the Manchu garrisons sent to guard the frontier during the Qing Dynasty. The Xibo zealously maintain their spoken language, script (featured on the back of Chinese money—it's the vertically written one), and archery prowess. The town itself is pretty sleepy, but the countryside is pleasant. (20km southwest of Yining. Buses leave from the front of the long-distance bus station when full. A **permit,** available from Yining PSB, is required to visit Qapqal county. Foreigners lacking permits will be fined Y500 and sternly lectured by the Qapqal PSB.)

▶ DAYTRIP FROM YINING: SAYRAM LAKE 赛里木湖

*Just off the main Ürümqi-Yining Hwy., 90km north of Yining. To go from Yining to the lake, take a **bus** from the long-distance bus station to **Bole** (博乐 ; 2hr., every hr. approx. 9:30am-noon, Y25). Frequent buses return to Yining approx. 8am-5pm; be prepared to hail them down. If you are coming from the east, take a long-distance bus from **Ürümqi;** the road is in decent condition and buses are fairly reliable. Most buses will stop at the lakeside town, but ask before to be sure. Going directly to Ürümqi from the lake is not advised; sleeper buses are often full and ticket prices inflated. Speedboats Y30.*

The still waters and isolation of Sayram (sàilǐmù hú; 赛里木湖) make this unforgettable lake northwestern Xinjiang's best option for exploring nature. While Tianchi's small size encourages hiking forays up into the surrounding alpine cliffs, Sayram Lake has the relaxing feel of a small ocean, with pebbled beaches bleeding out of the lowland pastures and the waves lapping quietly at the shore. In fact, if it weren't for the ring of mountains in the distance, you just might believe that you are indeed by the ocean. Although the stretch of highway alongside the lake has become a dizzying tourist center (complete with food stands, cinder block housing, and pestering horse owners), you only have to walk along a small dirt road clockwise around the lake from the bus stop to ramble through lakeside wildflower meadows and grazing pastures. The grasslands and wildflower coves are home to a few hundred scattered Mongol and Kazakh family yurts, many of which offer a night's sleep with meals (Y30; more for lamb). More isolated yurts may also take you in if you bear a simple gift (and payment). Bring warm clothes, as evenings can get cold, even in the summer. Indeed, visiting anytime other than June to September is not advised, as most local families spend the low season in Yili Valley, making it difficult to find lodgings.

TURPAN 吐鲁番　　　　　　　　　　☎0995

Turpan is hot—very hot. Nicknamed "The Oven," the town gamely endures the sun's harsh rays in the Turpan Depression, the second-lowest depression in the world, on the fringe of Xinjiang's starkly beautiful terrain. Summer temperatures hover around 40°C (100°F), while in the nearby Flaming Mountains, they can

Turpan

⌂ ACCOMMODATIONS
Gaochang Hotel, 1
Grain Trade Hotel, 8
Oasis Hotel, 2
Traffic Hotel, 5
Turpan Hotel, 9
Western Lands Hotel, 3

🍖 FOOD
Nuoruzi Local Specialties
  Restaurant, 4
Qianbai He Restaurant, 6
Xi'an Dumpling
  Restaurant, 7

exceed 50°C (120°F). Famous for its grapes, Turpan's central pedestrian alleyway, Qingnian Lu, provides a relaxing escape from the blistering heat, under the shade of a long corridor of hanging vines. During the warmest months, thousands and thousands of white grapes dangle from the trellises, while kids cycle, old men play Chinese chess, and lovers stroll the marble walkway beneath the dappled sun and shadows. The Turpan folk are a musical bunch, quite unafraid to share their talents with the public. Drummers and horn players often give impromptu performances in the backs of trucks or on street corners, with elderly women dancing away to the music. Tombs and ruins in the nearby valleys have attracted archaeologists for decades, but two days in the stifling heat is more than enough for most visitors. Travelers can always avoid the toasty weather by coming during the winter months, when Turpan's extreme temperatures drop to around -25°C (-13°F).

▐ TRANSPORTATION

Trains: Turpan Train Station (tǔlǔfān zhàn; 吐鲁番站) is actually in the town of **Daheyan** (dàhéyán; 大河沿), 50km northwest of Turpan. Minibuses go to Daheyan every 30min. or when full (7am-7pm, Y7.5). To: **Dunhuang/Liuyuan** (14hr.; 10, 11pm; Y151); **Kashgar** (25hr.; 5:30, 6:30pm; Y191); **Korla** (8hr.; 5:30, 6:30pm, midnight; Y82); **Xi'an** (40-45hr.; 9:40, 11pm; Y270) via **Lanzhou** (25hr., Y242).

NORTHWEST

Bus: The **long-distance bus station** (☎852 2325) on Laocheng Lu resembles a white-and green-tiled mosque. Roads to Hami aren't great; take the train instead. Open daily 6:30am-9pm. To: **Kashgar** (32hr., 10am, Y152) via **Korla** (6-7hr., Y46); **Kuqa** (13-14hr., Y90); **Ürümqi** (2½hr., every 30min. 7:30am-7:30pm, Y30).

Local Transportation: Minibus fare Y0.5. Minibus #1 travels east-west along Xincheng Lu, Laocheng Lu, and Muna'er Lu; #2 runs north-south along Gaocheng Lu; #5 goes north on Gaocheng Lu before heading east; #6 runs south on Gaocheng Lu, before heading east (at the Turpan Hotel) and continuing to Emin Minaret. **Taxis** Y5 in the city.

✹ ❓ ORIENTATION AND PRACTICAL INFORMATION

Turpan can be crossed in 20min. on foot. **Gaochang Lu** (高昌路), the central thoroughfare, runs north-south, parallel to **Qingnian Lu** (青年路) and **Bozikelike Lu** (柏孜克里克路). The busiest street is **Laocheng Lu** (老城路), which intersects all of the above streets, becoming **Muna'er Lu** (木纳尔路) in the east and **Xincheng Lu** (新城路) in the west of town. The long-distance bus station and many tourist offices are along Laocheng Lu. The Turpan Museum is on Gaochang Lu. Hotels are spread rather evenly throughout the area. The center for nightlife and entertainment is the **Cultural Square** (wénhuà yóu guǎngchǎng; 文化游广场), sandwiched between Qingnian Lu and Gaochang Lu.

Travel Agency: CITS, 41 Qingnian Lu (☎852 1352), in the Oasis Hotel, to the right of the gated entrance. A 2nd branch in the Turpan Hotel is open only during the summer. Commission Y30-50. The English-speaking staff at the main office is more efficient, but both offices provide tours of Turpan for Y60 per person if a minibus can be reasonably filled; otherwise, it's Y300 for a car for 1 day. The **Traffic Hotel** offers the same Y60 per person deal, with minibuses leaving from the front of the hotel at 9am and returning from the Jiaohe ruins as late as 8pm. Private car Y350. Ask for Mamat (☎133 1995 0839). Or try bargaining with taxi drivers, worthwhile if the price can be shared by 4 people; you also avoid the hassles of a larger tour group. Expect to pay between Y250-350 for 1 car. Ticket prices not included in the above prices. A guide at John's Information Cafe, also named Mamat, runs trips out to the Gobi Desert for Y500 per car.

Bank of China: 18 Laocheng Lu (☎852 3067), across from the bus station. Exchanges traveler's checks. Open summer M-F 9:30am-1pm and 4:30-8pm; winter M-F 10am-2pm and 4-8pm.

Bookstore: Xinhua Bookstore, 130 Laocheng Lu (☎852 2709), on the south side of the street. Locally published Xinjiang guidebooks in English and Chinese (Y15 and up).

PSB: 47 Gaochang Lu (☎130 9504 3356 or 098 9975 3512), opposite the Victory Hotel, in the north part of town. The **Foreign Affairs Office** for visa extensions is on the 2nd fl. of the building to the right, inside the compound gate. Open M-F 9:30am-1pm and 4:30-7:30pm.

Internet Access: There are over 30 Internet cafes in town. **John's Information Cafe** has IDD service and Internet access for Y5 per hr.

Post and Telecommunications: China Post (☎852 2731 or 133 4542 1906), on Laocheng Lu, west of the bus station. EMS and Poste Restante. Open daily 9am-8pm. **China Telecom,** 570 Laocheng Lu (☎852 3070), 50m west of the post office. Also Internet for Y10 per hr. Open daily summer 9:30am-7:30pm; winter 10am-8pm.

Postal Code: 838000.

🏠 ACCOMMODATIONS

All hotels in Turpan are within walking distance of the central square and the night bazaar, although the Turpan Hotel is closest. Almost all hotel rooms, except for some of the cheap dorms, have air-conditioning.

Turpan Hotel (tǔlǔfān bīnguǎn; 吐鲁番宾馆), 2 Qingnian Lu (☎852 2301; fax 852 3262). A huge, indoor swimming pool, massage/sauna center, beauty salon, billiard hall, and Muslim restaurant are in the surrounding buildings. Nightly Uighur song and dance shows in the summer. Hot water 7am-2am, common showers 3:30-9pm. Deposit Y120. Dorms in a remarkably cool subterranean location Y25, with A/C Y27; doubles Y270; triples Y300. AmEx/MC/V. ❶

Traffic Hotel (jiāotōng bīnguǎn; 交通宾馆), 125 Laocheng Lu (☎853 1320), close to the bustle of town, is one of Turpan's cheapest options. Cool, tiled floors, but thin mattresses. Rooms look out onto the bus station. Helpful manager speaks English well. Hot water 7:30pm-midnight. See **Travel Agency,** p. 798, for tour information. 6- to 10-bed dorms Y15; 4-bed dorms Y25; 3-bed dorms Y35; doubles with bath Y120. ❶

Gaochang Hotel (gāochāng bīnguǎn; 高昌宾馆), 22 Gaochang Lu (☎852 3229), just south of the museum. If you tell them you don't mind sharing the room, they give you a double with bath for Y50 and leave you on your own. Some rooms have balconies. Amiable staff, 24hr. lukewarm water, and somewhat aged A/C. Singles Y100; doubles on the 1st fl. Y120, on the 2nd fl. Y100; triples Y120; suites with king-sized bed Y160. ❷

Grain Trade Hotel (liángmào bīnguǎn; 粮贸宾馆), 7 Laocheng Lu (☎856 7449), across the street from the local CCP headquarters. Rooms are bright, clean, and spacious. Stalls selling Uighur hand-crafted knives with white copper and ox-horn handles, traditional Uighur clothing, fish fossils, and jade trinkets fill the lobby. Deposit Y50. Doubles Y100; triples and quads Y40 per bed. ❶

Western Lands Hotel (xīzhōu dàjiǔdiàn; 西州大酒店 ; ☎855 4000), on the corner of Qingnian Lu and Wenhua Lu. Built in 2004, this spanking new luxury hotel has beautiful rooms at affordable prices. Crisp, white sheets and the best A/C in town. Gymnasium, ping pong hall, and Western and Muslim restaurants. Singles Y180; doubles Y240. ❷

Oasis Hotel (lǜzhōu bīnguǎn; 绿洲宾馆) 815 Qingnian Lu (☎852 2491), a 15min. walk north from the Turpan Hotel, along Qingnian Lu. Authentic and classy, 22 beautiful rooms feature traditional *khan* beds, carved wooden beams, and *kilim* (woven rugs). 24hr. hot water, flower gardens, terraced walkways, and Muslim and Han Chinese restaurants. Bazaar sells paintings (Y800) and giant tapestries (US$6000). Doubles Y280, in VIP building Y680. MC/V. ❹

🍴 FOOD

Opposite the post office on Laocheng Lu, the lively indoor **Turpan Market** (tǔlǔfān shāngchéng; 吐鲁番商城) features rows of stalls selling Uighur, Hui, and Han foods. Falafel, kidney beans, and sliced egg all swim in a bowl of Uighur beef noodle soup. The city square, Cultural Sq., and surrounding **nightmarkets** are the best options for a cheap meal and a cold beer, with lamb kebabs going for Y1. The **Xi'an Dumpling Restaurant** ❶ (xī'ān jiǎozi guǎn; 西安饺子馆), on the south side of Cultural Sq., serves up tasty lamb and cabbage dumplings (Y6 for 20). Point to the filling you want, and watch the dumplings get made. On the same side of the square, the Xi'an's archrival, **Northeast Flavor Dumpling Restaurant** ❶ (dōngběi fēngwèi jiǎozi guǎn; 东北风味饺子馆) offers more variations on the lamb theme.

Nuoruzi Local Specialties Restaurant (nuòrúzī fēngwèi kuàicāntīng; 诺茹孜风味快餐厅 ; ☎859 2223), on Bozikelike Lu, just south of the Wenhua Lu intersection, on the east side of the street. Hearty lamb kebabs (Y2) and delicious lamb-dumpling tomato soup (Y5), a regional Uighur specialty. Extensive Han Chinese menu is exceptionally tasty. Live Uighur entertainment downstairs. ❶

NORTHWEST

Qianbai He Restaurant (qiānbǎi hé qīngzhēn cāntīng; 千百和清真餐厅), 170 Laocheng Lu (☎852 8912). Conveniently positioned on the corner of Laocheng Lu and Gaochang Lu, this popular Han Chinese restaurant makes for an ideal pit-stop before getting on a bus at the station next door. The Japanese tofu (rìběn dòufǔ; 日本豆腐; Y15) is to die for. A big meal for 3 comes to Y40-60. ❷

👁 SIGHTS

Turpan's sights are best visited in one busy day, especially during the blistering summer months. Taxis average Y250-350 for the day; admission is extra. Although there is no need to hire a guide to the sights in and around Turpan, they can help you make arrangements for further travel within Xinjiang. Most private Uighur guides speak fluent Japanese and English; drivers usually speak Uighur and Mandarin only. For a local tour, go to the Traffic Hotel on Laocheng Lu or John's Information Cafe across from the Turpan Hotel. It's cheapest to join a group and hire a guide (Y60), but you won't be able to pick and choose the places to visit.

TURPAN CITY

EMIN MINARET (émǐn tǎ; 额敏塔). Also known as **Sugong Minaret** (sūgōng tǎ; 苏公塔), this active mosque was built by Emin Hoja, the prefecture governor of Turpan, and his son Suleimon in 1777 during the Qing Dynasty. Climb the spiral staircase for a view of the surrounding vineyards, or simply admire the geometric patterns on the outer walls of the tower. *(2km east of town center. Included in most tours. Open daily sunrise-sunset. Y20, students Y10.)*

TURPAN MUSEUM (tǔlǔfān bówùguǎn; 吐鲁番博物馆). This recently renovated complex is well lit and well financed, but lacks English captions. Colorful models of prehistoric animals, fossilized remains, and 1500-year-old mummies, unearthed in Turpan, remind you just how ancient the desert is. *(On Gaochang Lu, just north of the Gaochang Hotel. ☎852 3774. Open daily 9am-8pm. Y20, students Y10.)*

NEAR TURPAN

▓ JIAOHE RUINS (jiāohé gùchéng; 交河故城). A long time ago, the twin branches of a once-powerful, gushing river carved out a 30m-high plateau, the site of this fascinating abandoned city. But for a trickling spring, the two rivers have dried up into ravines, which are paradoxically home to flourishing vineyards. High above, the 2000-year-old ruins of the desolate city drowse in the dry, scorching heat. Han records indicate that in 109 BC, Jiaohe contained 700 families, 6050 citizens, and 1856 soldiers. It served as the capital of the Kingdom of Cheshi in AD 450 but was eventually abandoned, perhaps due to a lack of water. At the demise of the Yuan Dynasty, war gutted what remained of the city. You can still lose your way wandering through the small rooms, temples, courtyards, and graveyards extending for kilometers toward the barren, infinite desert. Inside the monastery ruins, there are even the remains of tiny Buddha statues carved into the bare white rock. In 1994, archaeologists found the graves of more than 200 infants northwest of the site. The reason for their burial is still a mystery. During the summer, try to visit around twilight, when the heat lets up a little and the setting sun casts long shadows upon the silent streets. *(7km west of town. Open daily sunrise-sunset. Y30.)*

GAOCHANG RUINS (gāochāng gùchéng; 高昌故城). The center of the Uighur empire in the 9th century, Gaochang has largely crumbled away, leaving dusty ruins in its wake. Founded in the Liang Dynasty (AD 397-439), Gaochang was conquered by Tang Emperor Taizong in 640. Later, the famous monk Xuan Zang taught Buddhism here during his 18-year epic journey to obtain Indian scriptures.

Like Jiaohe, Gaochang met its end by fire in the turbulent transition from the Yuan to the Ming Dynasty. Today, donkey carts filled with tourists speed up and down the road through the outer section that joins the entrance to the palace. The cart drivers will tell you the distance is 3km, but it's closer to 1km, making walking a simpler and more rewarding experience. Take the opportunity to wander the streets of the ancient city freely. Travelers can poke into cracks and explore places that had formerly been building interiors. The palace walls have been reinforced in recent years to retain the structure's original shape. The only other identifiable structure is the city's massive outer wall, beyond which the distant Flaming Mountains loom in the northeast. (*A good 40km east of Turpan. Donkey cart round-trip Y7-10. Open daily sunrise-sunset. Y20, students Y10.*)

BEZEKLIK CAVES (bózīkèlǐkè qiānfó dòng; 柏孜克里克千佛洞). Burrowed into a cliff on the west bank of the Mutou Valley in the Flaming Mountains, the 88 caves once displayed 1200m^2 of frescoes. Today, many of the walls are bare, thanks to prestige-hungry foreign archaeologists like Aurel Stein and Albert von Le Coq, who stripped the caves of all their best artwork in the 20th century. Many of these frescoes were subsequently lost in the bombing of Berlin during WWII. You can actually see where the frescoes have been carved off the wall and carted off whole, leaving massive holes three inches deep. What remains has been heavily vandalized by Islamic fundamentalists, who scratched out the eyes of most of the images. Many of the caves open to the public (between 10 and 20) date to the Buddhist kingdom of Gaochang. The vivid landscape—deep green valleys set against red-gold cliffs and mountains—will make up for the minimal caves, however. An overpriced 5min. camel ride (Y40) up a nearby hill allows for a photo-op of the rare mountain scenery. Expect to pay extra if your camel leader offers to take photographs for you. (*40km east of Turpan. Y20, students Y10.*)

GRAPE VALLEY (pútáo gōu; 葡萄沟). Most of Turpan's grapes are grown in Grape Valley. With thousands of bunches of grapes dangling overhead, the lush green vineyards create a shady retreat from the sun-baked desert outside. The valley was originally called "Peach Valley" due to the peach groves that once grew naturally here. However, the Qing Emperor Guangxu, deciding that he preferred grapes, replaced the trees with vines and renamed the gully in 1886. Beware of picking fruit from any of the vines hanging to the right of the entrance: those caught red-handed are fined. Sample a wide selection of raisins, made from myriad varieties of grapes, to the left of the entrance. Vendors will try to sell you a large bag for Y15, but that many raisins would keep you going for a week. A Y5 bag is enough for two people. (*Open daily sunrise-sunset. Y20.*)

FLAMING MOUNTAINS (huǒyàn shān; 火焰山). Aptly named, these russet slopes often blaze at temperatures of over 55°C. According to the famous novel *Journey to the West*, when the Tang Dynasty monk Xuan Zang came here, fires raged for hundreds of miles. His companion, the Monkey King, had to extinguish the flames with a magical palm fan whisked from the ever-protective Iron Fan Princess. Fortunately, you don't have to cross these mountains (no longer on fire but still pretty hot). Your driver will stop just outside the Xinjiang Desert Pottery Art Museum, which contains reconstructions of frescoes taken by German archaeologists from the nearby Bezeklik caves. Skip the pricey museum and instead admire the charred red peaks jutting up from the sands. (*Flaming Mountain free. Museum Y25.*)

KAREZ IRRIGATION SYSTEM. An exposed section of the ancient Persian-style underground irrigation tunnels, Karez is visible elsewhere in Turpan. Hordes of tourists and more trinket vendors than you can count crowd into a tiny section of the original baked earthen wall canals. (*6km to the northwest of Turpan. Wine tasting by the entrance. Open daily sunrise-sunset. Y20.*)

KORLA 库尔勒 ☎0996

This predominantly Han Chinese city is one of Xinjiang's most important economic centers, but sight-seeking tourists who can't tell their supply from their demand will probably find little of interest in Korla. The bus ride into the city, however, features incredible views of the desert's barren canyons and black and red rock formations. At night, the city streets teem with food bazaars, live music, and fashionable young women. The Vegas-style fountain and music display in People's Square keep the kids occupied (and more importantly, cooled down), while the adults get serious with high-speed outdoor aerobics. There are less visible extremes of poverty here than in other cities of similar size, and the neon-lit streets, trees, and lawns are all kept neat and tidy. Nearby lie the largest lake in Xinjiang and a handful of ruins. Half-way down the road to Kuqa, an ancient poplar forest makes for a startling sight upon the rippling dunes.

▣ TRANSPORTATION

Flights: Korla Airport (kù'ěrlè fēijīchǎng; 库尔勒飞机场), in the south of town, a Y20 cab ride away. To: **Ürümqi** (Y320, 1 week advance booking Y220).

Trains: Korla Train Station (kù'ěrlè huǒchē zhàn; 库尔勒火车站), in the southeast corner of the city. Take bus #1 from People's Sq. or a taxi (Y10). Booking sleeper tickets to **Kashgar** is virtually impossible here, but you may be able to upgrade to a sleeper once onboard. To **Kashgar** (14hr.; 2 per day; hard seat Y100-130, hard sleeper Y196-239) and **Ürümqi** (10hr.; 4 per day; hard seat Y82, hard sleeper Y145-155).

Buses: Bus Station (kèyùn zhōngxīn; 客运中心 ; ☎207 6390), on Beishan Lu, in the north of the city. Accessible by bus #2 from People's Sq. Roads are often in terrible condition (especially those heading west); buses are the most convenient way to travel to Kuqa and Ürümqi. To: **Hotan** (26hr., daily, Y188-208); **Kashgar** (18hr., 3 per day, Y146-166); **Kuqa** (4hr., 6 per day, Y33-44); **Ruoqiang** (6hr., 4 per day, Y63); **Ürümqi** (8hr., several per day 9:30am-9:30pm, Y65-110); **Yining** (30hr., daily, Y73-107).

Shuttle Taxis: Immediately to the right of the bus station, a stand sells tickets for high-speed transport; these shuttles travel about twice as fast as buses. The rates apply to full cars (4 passengers); you must either wait or pay for the empty seats. To: **Kuqa** (Y85); **Lotus Lake** or **Western Bosten Lake** (Y15); **Luntai** (Y30); **Ürümqi** (Y150).

Local Transportation: Bus fare Y1. Bus #1 runs along Renmin Lu; #2 runs north to the long-distance bus station and west to the Bosten Hotel.

Taxi: Base fare Y5. From People's Sq. to the train station Y10, to most other points Y5.

✴ ❓ ORIENTATION AND PRACTICAL INFORMATION

The downtown area clusters around **People's Square** (rénmín guǎngchǎng; 人民广场). Most tourist services and accommodations are within a 20min. walk of the square. **Renmin Lu** (人民路) runs east-west, south of the square. The bus station is to the north on **Beishan Lu** (北山路), which runs south into **Jiaotong Lu** (交通路). **Jianshe Lu** (建设路) passes People's Sq. and connects Renmin Lu and Beishan Lu.

The **Xinjiang Korla Desert Travel Agency** (xīnjiāng kù'ěrlè dàmò lǚxíngshè; 新疆库尔勒大漠旅行社) is in the Silver Star Hotel, opposite the Kaide Hotel on Renmin Lu. The **Bazhou Bositeng Travel Agency** (bāzhōu bósīténg lǚxíngshè; 巴州博斯腾旅行社) is in the Bosten Hotel. Both offer package tours of various sights in and around Korla. (Poplar Forest Park Y1160, including car, driver, and guide.) The **Bank of China,** on Renmin Lu, a 10min. walk east of People's Sq., on the left, exchanges traveler's checks on weekdays only. (☎202 5086. Open daily 9:30am-1:30pm and 4-8pm.) The **China Telecom** in People's Sq., on Renmin Lu, has free **Inter-**

net access. (☎202 3788. Open daily past midnight.) The large neon sign only says "China Telecom," but the **post office** is also inside. (EMS, Poste Restante, Western Union. Open daily 9:30am-1:30pm and 4:30-7:30pm.) **Postal Code:** 841000.

ACCOMMODATIONS AND FOOD

Korla's fledgling tourism industry is not taking its first steps in a budget-friendly direction. None of the hotels allow foreigners to stay in cheap dorm beds.

A former underground parking lot, the **Well-Off City Food Street** (xiǎokāng chéng měishí jiē; 小康城美食街), on Qingnian Lu, now has plenty of flavorful options in its food court. Try the *chǎobǐng* (炒饼), a bowl of crispy fried beef noodles, shredded tofu, bean sprouts, and green beans, served at **Yifengzhai Crispy Meats** (yìfēngzhāi sū ròu guǎn; 益丰斋酥肉馆 ; ☎226 2506).

Campus Hotel (jiàoyuán bīnguǎn; 教园宾馆 ; ☎222 5743), on Tianshan Dong Lu. Rooms have water dispenser, TV, showers, and 24hr. hot water. On the 5th fl. water pressure is a weak trickle. Restaurant next to lobby serves a breakfast buffet (Y3). Only rooms open to foreigners are triples with bath Y75, with A/C Y84. ❶

Kaide Hotel (kǎidé jiǔdiàn; 凯德酒店), 12 Renmin Dong Lu (☎209 2188), a 15min. walk east of People's Sq. Rooms in this modern glass tower are relatively good bargains despite the high prices. Business center, smiling receptionists, and excellent on-site restaurant. Singles and doubles on the 5th fl. Y198, 6th fl. Y268. MC/V. ❸

Bazhou Hotel (bāzhōu bīnguǎn; 巴州宾馆 ; ☎202 4441), on Renmin Dong Lu, a 15min. walk east of People's Sq. Look for the enormous flying goose by the entrance. Rooms with A/C, TV, wooden decor, and sparkling tile floors. Doubles Y198. ❸

Bosten Hotel (bósīténg bīnguǎn; 博斯腾宾馆 ; ☎202 2118), on Renmin Lu, pretty far west from People's Sq. and the night bazaars. English speaker and on-site travel agency (☎203 3444). Singles and doubles Y160; triples Y70 per person. ❶

SIGHTS

Korla's biggest tourist draw is the nearby Bosten Lake, but the best reason to come to Korla is to see the northern fringe of the **Taklimakan Desert** (tǎkèlāmǎgān shāmò; 塔克拉玛干沙漠), a fascinating ecosystem filled with flowering bushes, white sands, and ancient poplar trees. The tiny streams and rivulets of the **Tarim River** (tǎlǐmù hé; 塔里木河) branch through the desert during brief rainy periods.

POPLAR FOREST PARK (húyáng sēnlín gōngyuán; 胡杨森林公园). About 40km south of **Lunnan** (轮南), the highway winding through the Taklimakan Desert en route to Hotan encounters a surreal landscape of ancient poplar trees. Gnarled and weathered trunks emerge from seemingly barren white sands high above basins of water. A quiet, solemn atmosphere pervades this dusty forest. Swans circle brown silty pools, looking somehow lost as the water slowly dries up. Oblivious sheep graze in the heat. The park itself is of little interest and is 15min. from the groves along the road that feature the older, more impressive spots. To simplify things, tell the driver that you want to go to the park and ask him to stop at the roadside groves along the way. Hiking the dunes can easily fill an entire afternoon. *(Morning shuttle taxi from Korla to Lunnan 2hr., Y40. From Lunnan, a hired taxi to the forest costs Y100 round-trip, more if you want to do some hiking. Make sure the driver understands that you will be gone a long time; pay him once you return to Lunnan. 4-5hr. bus from Lunnan to Korla Y20. Shuttle taxis also go to Korla. Alternatively, if Kuqa is your next destination, take a shuttle taxi from Lunnan to Luntai; Y10 per person, but it's hard to fill seats. Buses from Luntai to Kuqa Y15. Total traveling time 2½hr. Or take an overnight train from Ürümqi to Luntai. Park Y10.)*

NORTHWEST

BOSTEN LAKE (bósīténg hú; 博斯腾湖). Though touted as Korla's premier attraction, Bosten Lake is a resounding disappointment. Only two spots on the lake are accessible by public transportation: the Golden Sands Resort and the Lotus Pond. **Golden Sands** (jīn shātān; 金沙滩) is a tacky beach resort with inflatable air mattresses and plastic umbrellas to spare. If you want to shell out Y200-250, you can hire a boat to explore the reed-covered marshes and small fishing towns nearby. If you really want to see the lake, a better option is to visit **Lotus Pond** (liánhuā chí; 莲花池), where you can spend a few hours strolling next to thickly growing lotuses and water lilies. In summer, however, you may not be able to see anything more than the tips of rushes peeking out through the seasonally high water. *(Buses to the Golden Sands leave daily 9am-1pm from the south side of People's Sq., across from the PICC Bldg.; 1hr., round-trip Y50. Buses return betwen 4 and 7pm. Golden Sands Y20. Lotus Pond is best reached by taxi; about Y100 round-trip. Lotus Pond Y10.)*

KUQA 库车   ☎ 0996

Kuqa is a good place to break up the long journey between Ürümqi and Kashgar. Tucked into the foothills of the Tianshan mountains, the town helped spread Buddhism into China via the Northern Silk Road. Grottoes and ancient ruins are scattered to the north of the city, a testament to the rich 1500-year history of Kuqa that the remarkable desert climate has preserved so well. The divide between Han and Uighur is far less apparent in Kuqa than in most other towns in Xinjiang. The compact New Town quickly fades into an entrancing network of small dirt roads weaving through traditional mud-brick Uighur architecture, colorful archways, shady grape trellises, mosques, and food markets. Young men walk around with their shirts off, eating the town's famous Kuqa apricots. A stroll through this area is a great way to immerse yourself in Uighur culture and traditional living without the glare of tour bus glass. Chatting to the locals, you may find that you might be the first foreigner they've met. Their inquisitive yet unintrusive willingness to help will easily make travelers feel quite welcome.

■ ⁊ ORIENTATION AND PRACTICAL INFORMATION

Kuqa is divided into two sections. To the east is the predominantly Han Chinese **New Town** (xīn chéng; 新城), a relatively modern area containing foreigner-friendly hotels, tourist services, and the bus and train stations. To the west is the predominantly Uighur section of the city known as the **Old Town** (lǎo chéng; 老城), with bustling market streets in the south and residential areas in the north, which are connected by small farm plots and poplar-lined dirt roads. **Wenhua Lu** (文化路) runs through the center of town, parallel to **Tianshan Lu** (天山路), which passes the bus station and the Traffic and Kuqa Hotels before intersecting with the two main north-south thoroughfares: **Youyi Lu** (友谊路) and **Jiefang Lu** (解放路). Tianshan Lu branches north just past the western limits of the new city before it enters the Uighur residential district. The southern fork becomes **Renmin Lu** (人民路), crosses a large bridge (the effective center of the Friday bazaar), and then heads into the heart of the Old Town, passing the Kuqa Mosque on the right.

Trains: Kuqa Train Station (kùchē huǒchē zhàn; 库车火车站 ; ☎293 6462), 7km southeast of New Town, accessible by taxi (Y10) or bus #2 or 6. Tickets for westbound trains can only be purchased at the station no more than 1hr. before departure. In July-Aug., all sleepers and seats are often filled before the train gets to Kuqa. To avoid sitting in the toilet cubicle, buy your ticket in Ürümqi or Kashgar if possible. To: **Kashgar** (Express 9hr.; 5:43am, but may be 1hr. late; Y99. Regular 11hr., 11:20am, Y41); **Ürümqi** (Express 12hr., 1:40am, Y116. Regular 17-18hr.; 7:50, 10:40pm; Y48).

Buses: Kuqa Long-Distance Bus Station (kùchē chángtú qìchē zhàn; 库车长途汽车站 ; ☎712 2379), in the southeast of New Town. Take any bus going east on Tianshan Lu or a Y6 taxi from most hotels. Open daily 8am-8:30pm. Buses to Kashgar originate in Korla or Ürümqi. Departure times from Kuqa are irregular, and seats or sleepers are not guaranteed. To: **Kashgar** (20hr., morning and afternoon departures, Y74-116); **Korla** (8hr., every hr. 9:30am-2:30pm, Y25); **Ürümqi** (18hr., 2 per day, sleeper Y80-90); **Yining** (48hr., 8am, Y77).

Local Transportation: Taxis are unmetered; within the city usually Y5-10. **Pedicab** Y3.

Travel Agency: Kuqa's only travel agency (☎713 6016) is on Tianshan Lu, in the main lobby of the Qiuci Hotel. Rates for private tours of the Kuqa area slightly more expensive than arrangements with drivers associated with hotels. Staff are accommodating and can help single travelers link up with others to share expenses. Be sure to specify which of Kuqa's sights you want to see, as there are too many to see in 1 day. Standard 1-day tours of Kuqa Y300 per car. 1-day tours to Big Dragon Lake (dàlóng chí; 大龙池), 140km to the north, Y400-500 per car. Open daily 9:30am-1:30pm and 4-8:30pm.

Bank of China: On Tianshan Lu (☎712 1922), a 10min. walk west of the bus station. Credit card advances. Open daily summer 9:30am-8pm; winter 10am-7:30pm.

Bookstore: Xinhua Bookstore (☎712 2765), on the corner of Youyi Lu and Wenhua Lu, in the center of New Town. Sells maps of Kuqa and surrounding tourist sights for Y3.

PSB: 25 Jiefang Bei Lu (☎797 5080). Open 9:30am-8pm.

Hospital: People's Hospital of Kuqa County (kùchē xiàn rénmín yīyuàn; 库车县人民医院) 36 Jiefang Lu (☎712 1573). Open 24hr.

Post and Telecommunications: On the central downtown corner of Wenhua Lu and Youyi Lu. **Post office** (☎712 2644) is on the left, **China Telecom** (☎712 5113) a few doors down on the right. IDD. Both open daily summer 9:30am-8pm; winter 10am-7:30pm.

ACCOMMODATIONS AND FOOD

When staying in Kuqa, decide how much you care about being in the center of town, as the out-of-the-way Traffic and Kuqa Hotels are great values.

The best **nightmarkets** are in the Uighur quarter. The Kuqa Hotel has top-notch Sichuanese and Muslim restaurants. If you're staying at the Traffic Hotel, a string of Chinese restaurants line the same side of the street as the bus station, leading toward the center of town. The corner of Tianshan Lu and Wuyi Lu is a good place to hang out with the locals in the evening while munching on lamb kebabs.

Qiuci Hotel (qiūcí bīnguǎn; 龟兹宾馆), 93 Tianshan Lu (☎712 2005), a good 3km west of the bus station. The closest hotel to the Uighur Old Town is also Kuqa's most attractive option. Most rooms have spring water dispenser, bath, 24hr. hot water, telephone, TV, A/C, and views of the lush arbors and flower gardens. Restaurant has a romantic setting and outdoor seating under a trellis. Most dishes Y20-30. Kuqa's only travel service is down a corridor right of the main lobby. Singles Y240; doubles Y220. ❸

Kuqa Hotel (kùchē fàndiàn; 库车饭店 ; ☎713 1156), on Tianshan Lu. From the bus station, take a left and walk 10min.; the hotel is on the right. The reception area is reached by walking past a rose garden with willow trees over a lotus pond. Down a corridor to the left of the lobby is one of the cleanest public bathrooms you're likely to see in China, with Western-style toilets, soap, and even toilet paper! Restaurant in a separate building to the right of the main reception building. All rooms come with A/C, bath, water dispenser, TV, and 24hr. hot water. Breakfast included. Business center books eastbound train tickets. Singles and doubles Y280; triples Y320. ❹

Traffic Hotel (jiāotōng bīnguǎn; 交通宾馆 ; ☎712 2682), facing the parking lot on the right side as you exit the bus station. Doubles have decent sheets, concrete floors, hostel-green paint, and sometimes even a TV. Hot water 8:30pm-2am. Singles and doubles with bath Y120; quads without bath Y60. ❶

Minmao Hotel (mínmào bīnguǎn; 民贸宾馆), 16 Wenhua Lu (☎712 2999), at Jiefang Lu, in the heart of New Town. This hotel has dark and dingy corridors, but surprisingly pleasant rooms with clean carpet, tiled bath, and A/C. Doubles Y120; triples Y165. ❷

◉ SIGHTS

The mountains around Kuqa are filled with Buddhist grottoes and remnants of Silk Road-era cities, but there is no public transportation available and roads are often in poor condition. Check with the travel agency in **Qiuci Hotel** to plan out your day in advance. Normally, a standard one-day tour (Y300) includes the Kizil Grottoes, Kizilgaha Beacon Tower, Subashi Temple Ruins, and the Kuqa Mosque. Independent **taxi** drivers will take you to these four sights for Y150, but they often set off without knowing how to get to three of the four places. To avoid potential hapless breakdowns in the middle of the desert or wandering around aimless for several hours, it's best to stick with the travel agency. Perhaps the best part of the tour is the ride to the Kizil Grottoes on a desolate highway as it winds through the red canyons of the Tianshan foothills. Known as **Tianshan Mai** (天山脉 ; "the veins of the Tianshan mountains"), the landscape resembles the set of a science-fiction movie and is a great photo-op stop, although the rough terrain makes hiking extremely difficult. If you have time and money, you can charter a taxi to the less-known but more interesting nearby areas, such as the **Sall Water Passage.**

DON'T GO HUNGRY. If you decide to hire an independent taxi to visit Kuqa's sights, be sure to bring along an emergency suppy of food and water in case of breakdowns. Once you're stranded on the highway, there's nothing but you, miles upon miles of desert, and the ruthless sun.

KIZIL GROTTOES (kèzǐ'ěr qiān fó dòng; 克孜尔千佛洞). Even though it's supposedly the richest and best-preserved Buddhist grotto site in the Kuqa area, this cliffside network of caves is actually in poor condition. Dating from the third through ninth centuries AD, the caves have been vandalized several times by Islamic fundamentalists, who gouged out the painted eyes of the Buddhas and scraped away their hand *mudra*s (teaching gestures). To top it off, the caves were also looted by German archaeologist Albert Von Le Coq in the beginning of the 20th century. Le Coq gave his collection to the Berlin Museum, where almost everything was destroyed in WWII by Allied bombing. Today, hardly any murals and sculptures remain intact. Many of the caves included in the 10-cave tour are sadly bare, with only a few holes in the walls and a story of what once was. Foreigners will likely be shown cave #110, which is entirely empty except for an inscription describing the plundering of the area by Le Coq and Hungarian Aurel Stein.

Like those at Dunhuang's Mogao Grottoes, the best-preserved caves require a special ticket (Y100 and up), but many visitors feel that these aren't worth the extra cash. Photos of caves #38 and 67 grace the gate's tourist board, but don't indicate what you'll actually see. Before leaving, check out the **Gurgling Spring** (gǔquán; 泪泉), a 20min. walk past the caves through a shallow, reed-covered canyon. *(Guides are expensive at Y30-100. At the main gate, you must buy a ticket for either the slightly closer west caves or the east caves, both similar in content. Y35.)*

SUBASHI TEMPLE RUINS (sūbāshí gùchéng; 苏巴什故城). These ruins of a Buddhist temple complex date back to the Wei and Jin Dynasties (third century AD). Set against the backdrop of the 2000m Tianshan Mountains, the amorphous mudbrick shapes rising from the barren scrubland hint at the scope of the original construction while remaining hauntingly similar to the textures of the surrounding landscape. This is quite a spectacular spot to see the sun set if you can convince the driver to head out in the late afternoon. It is also the post-lunch destination for most tours, as there are no roads connecting the site to the nearby Beacon Tower. *(50km north of the old city, accessible only by a small dirt road.)*

KIZILGAHA BEACON TOWER (kèzī'ěrgāhā fēnghuǒ tái; 克孜尔尕哈烽火台). During the Han, soldiers lit signal fires upon this 13m-high watchtower of packed earth when enemies approached, sparking a chain of similar towers strung out along the ancient Silk Road over the inhospitable desert. *(13km from Kuqa.)* You may want to ask the driver to take you to the nearby Kizilgaha Grottoes (kèzī'ěrgāhā qiān fó dòng; 克孜尔尕哈千佛洞), which are much closer to Kuqa than the Kizil Grottoes, though smaller in number and with a higher admission fee (Y40).

KUQA OLD TOWN MOSQUE (kùchē dàsì; 库车大寺). Built in 1923, the mosque's intricately masoned brick dome and minaret-flanked facade overlook a bustling neighborhood of grape-covered courtyards and trodding donkey carts full of fruits and breads. *(In the old Uighur quarter, 4km northwest of New Town. You may have to yell for the gatekeeper to let you in. Y10.)*

OTHER SIGHTS. After Kizil, the most famous grottoes in the area are at **Kumtura** (kùmùtǔlā; 库木吐拉) and **Simsem** (sēnmùsāimǔ; 森木塞姆); locals particularly recommend Simsem, about 80km east of Kuqa. To the north, deep in the Tianshan Mountain Range, you can find **Big Dragon Lake** (dàlóng chí; 大龙池) and **Small Dragon Lake** (xiǎolóng chí; 小龙池), with scenery similar to that of Tianchi (p. 788) but less touristy. On the way, you'll pass through the **Kiziliya Grand Canyon** (kèzīlìyà dà xiágǔ; 克孜力亚大峡谷), another spot about which locals rave.

KASHGAR 喀什   ☎ 0998

Kashgar's relative inaccessibility sets it a world apart from China and even Xinjiang province. This predominantly Uighur city has developed rapidly over the past 10 years but still retains hints of its Silk Road trading post character. Bustling markets teem with animated Central Asian traders, wizened Uighurs, and veiled Muslim women. Mosques rise above mud-thatched houses, and donkey carts trundle down narrow alleyways. The completion of the Ürümqi-Kashgar rail line in late 1999 has increased Chinese influence, breaching the expanse of the Taklimakan Desert that had long protected Kashgar from the whims of the CCP. Since then, Kashgar's Han population has steadily increased, and like most of Xinjiang's cities, there continues to be a severe polarization of Uighur and Han. With a small Pakistani community emerging and a steady flow of foreigners, Kashgar is a truly international city and an essential stop for travelers and traders alike before they plunge into the even more remote regions of Pakistan and Central Asia.

NORTHWEST

◼ TRANSPORTATION

Flights: Kashgar Airport (kāshí jīchǎng; 喀什机场), 18km north of the city. Take a taxi (25min., Y20) or bus #2 from People's Sq. **CAAC ticket office** (mínháng shòupiàochù; 民航售票处), 95 Jiefang Nan Lu (☎ 282 2113). Open daily summer 9:30am-8pm; winter 10am-7:20pm. **Xinjiang Airlines** (xīnjiāng hángkōng gōngsī; 新疆航空公司 ;

☎284 1186), on the right side of the People's Hotel lobby. Open daily 9:30am-8pm. All flights out of Kashgar go through **Ürümqi** (summer 4-6 per day, winter 2 per day; CAAC Y550-860 depending on demand, Xinjiang Airlines Y1230).

Trains: Kashgar Train Station (kāshí huǒchē zhàn; 喀什火车站), on Renmin Dong Lu, about 15km east of the city. Accessible by bus (Y0.5) from Renmin Dong Lu, or by taxi (Y10). Tickets can be difficult to book on short notice; CITS, John's Cafe, and most hotels have connections with the station and charge about Y50 commission for sleeper tickets. The Ürümqi express uses double-decker sleeper cars. To **Ürümqi** (express 27hr., 4:45am, Y335; slow 31hr., 9:25am, Y177) via **Kuqa** (express 9hr., Y177; slow 11hr., Y96) and **Korla** (express 13hr., Y232; slow 16hr., Y125).

Buses:

International Bus Station (kāshí guójì qìchē zhàn; 喀什国际汽车站), 5 Jichang Lu (☎296 1351). Follow Jiefang Lu north across the river; the ticket office is to the right of the Tuman River Hotel, in the same building. Open daily 8:30am-9pm. To **Korla** (16hr., 4 per day 11am-9pm, Y108-118) via **Kuqa** (11hr., Y78-85) and **Ürümqi** (24hr., every hr. 9am-9pm, Y185-213). Buses to **Sost, Pakistan** (around noon, Y270) on the Karakorum Highway have an overnight stay in **Tashkurgan** (10hr., Y63) and stop at **Karakul Lake** (6hr., Y43) and the **Khunjerab Pass** (around noon the 2nd day, Y270). For the bus to **Bishkek, Kyrgyzstan** via the **Torugut Pass** (16hr. including overnight stop, M, US$50), you need a transit **permit** (pīzhèng; 批证) to cross the border; only a travel agency can obtain the permit (Y500 for groups smaller than 10), but most require you to take their tour. Make sure you have a valid entry **visa** to Kyrgyzstan; they can only be obtained in Beijing or Hong Kong (see **Consulate Services in China,** p. 10).

Kashgar Bus Station (kèyùn zhàn; 客运站 ; ☎282 9673), on Tiannan Lu, off Renmin Dong Lu. Open daily 7:30am-8pm. To: **Hotan** (10hr.; every 1½hr. 9:30am-9:30pm; seat Y54, sleeper Y88); **Tashkurgan** (8hr., 10am, Y44); **Yecheng** (4hr., every 30min. 9am-9:30pm, Y30).

Local Transportation: Kashgar is best navigated by bike or mototaxi. Look for motorcyclists in metallic red hard hats and flag them down. They'll whisk you wherever you want to go for Y1-3. **Taxis** are Y5 within the city. Local **buses** are unreliable; #9 goes from the Seman Lu area to the mosque area and #10 runs east toward the Abokh Hoja Tomb.

Bike Rental: The **Qinibagh Hotel** has bike rental for Y3 per hr., though sometimes only after 4pm. **John's Information Cafe** charges Y10 per 6hr., deposit Y200.

■★🛈 ORIENTATION AND PRACTICAL INFORMATION

The geographical and commercial center of Kashgar is the intersection of **Jiefang Lu** (解放路) and **Renmin Lu** (人民路); the religious, cultural, and culinary center is the **Id Kah Mosque** and **Id Kah Square**, on Jiefang Bei Lu, north of Renmin Lu. The Great Sunday Bazaar is east of the **Tuman River** (tǔmàn hé; 吐曼河), on the south side of **Yizirete Lu** (艾孜热特路). The area of most use to foreigners is near the Seman Hotel off **Seman Lu** (色满路), in the far west.

Travel Agencies:

John's Information Cafe (☎/fax 258 1186, mobile 139 0998 1722; johncafe@hotmail.com), in the Seman Hotel. John speaks fluent English and organizes trips around **Kashgar** (1 day, Y200 per car); **Lake Karakul** (1 day, Y800-1000 per car); **Taklimakan Desert** (1 day, Y1000 per car). For trips to the **Torugut Pass** (4-5 people max., US$200-240 total), fax or email your name, passport number, nationality, and itinerary, and John will obtain the border patrol permit, jeep, and driver. He can also arrange transport to **Bishkek, Kyrgyzstan** from the border (US$280).

CITS: Main branch to the left of the Qinibagh Hotel has unreliable hours. Smaller branch at the hotel gate has regular hours and a manager who speaks excellent English. (☎298 0473; wjo9985801@sina.com). Tours include: **Lake Karakul** (1 day Y700, 2 days Y1000); **Kashgar** (Y300 per car, English-speaking guide Y100); **Taklimakan Desert** (1 day, Y800); **Torugut Pass** (1-2 days; Y500 permit for 1-5 people; small car Y900, minibus Y1000; guide Y200). Extra US$100 per person to **Bishkek** from the border. Commission for hard seats or sleepers Y30, soft seats or sleepers Y50; purchase 3 days in advance. Open daily 9:30am-1:30pm and 4-8pm.

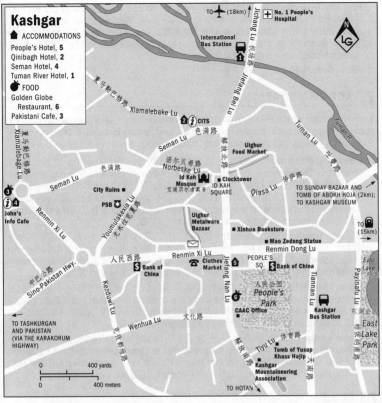

Kashgar

🛏 ACCOMMODATIONS

People's Hotel, **5**
Qinibagh Hotel, **2**
Seman Hotel, **4**
Tuman River Hotel, **1**

🍎 FOOD

Golden Globe
  Restaurant, **6**
Pakistani Cafe, **3**

TO ✈ (18km)
Jichang Lu 机场路

✚ No. 1 People's
Hospital

International
Bus Station

Jiefang Bei Lu

Tuman Lu 吐曼路

Tuman R.

CITS

Xiamalebake Lu
色满路

夏马勒巴特路

Seman Lu 色满路

Uighur
Food Market

诺尔贝希路
Norbeske Lu

Id Kah
Mosque
艾堤尕尔清真寺

Clocktower
ID KAH
SQUARE

恰萨路
Qiasa Lu

TO SUNDAY BAZAAR AND
TOMB OF ABOKH HOJA (2km);
TO KASHGAR MUSEUM

City Ruins ■

John's
Info Cafe

Xiamalebage Lu
夏马勒巴格路

Seman Lu

PSB ✚

Renmin Xi Lu

Youmulakexia Lu
尤木拉克夏路

Uighur
Metalware
Bazaar

■ Xinhua Bookstore

■ Mao Zedong Statue
Renmin Dong Lu

TO 🚉
(15km)

East
Lake

中巴公路
Sino-Pakistan Hwy.

Keziduwi Lu
克孜都维路

人民西路
Renmin Xi Lu

Jiefang Nan Lu

$ Bank of
China

Clothes
Market

PEOPLE'S
SQ.

$ Bank of China

Tiannan Lu

人民公园
People's
Park

Payinatu Lu 帕依纳提路

East
Lake
Park

东湖公园

TO TASHKURGAN
AND PAKISTAN
(VIA THE KARAKORUM
HIGHWAY)

Wenhua Lu
文华路

文化路

CAAC Office

Kashgar
Bus Station

Tiyu Lu
体育路

Tomb of Yusup
Khass Hajip

Kashgar
Mountaineering
Association

解放南路

0 ___ 400 yards
0 ___ 400 meters

TO HOTAN

不甫路

NORTHWEST

Kashgar Mountaineering Association (kāshí dēngshān xiéhuì; 喀什登山协会) 45 Tiyu Lu
(☎252 3680, mobile 131 9998 2966), near the Yusup Khass Hajib Tomb. Experienced guides
take you to the top of **K2** (8611m), the world's second-tallest and most dangerous peak (60 days,
including 1 week of camel-trekking each way to reach the base camp; US$6000). More manage-
able is the 7546m **Mount Muztagata** (12 days trekking, US$1500), near Lake Karakul. If near-
death experiences on icy crags aren't your cup of tea, the Association also arranges all sorts of
guided trekking in the remote areas of the **Pamirs** (1 week, US$1000), the **Karakorum Range** (15
days, US$2000), and the **Taklimakan Desert** (10 days US$2000, 20 days US$3000).

Bookstore: Xinhua Bookstore, 21 Jiefang Bei Lu (☎282 2318). Kashgar maps (Y6),
regional tourist maps (Y6), and Xinjiang province maps (Y5). Open daily 8am-8pm.

Bank of China: People's Sq. branch (☎282 5668). Exchanges traveler's checks. Credit
card advances M-F. Open daily 9:30am-7:30pm.

PSB: 139 Yunmulakexia Lu (☎282 2814), just south of Seman Lu. Visa office on the left
before the main entrance. European and US **visa** extensions Y160. Open M-F 9:30am-
1:30pm and 4-8pm.

Hospital: No. 1 People's Hospital (dìyī rénmín yīyuàn; 第一人民医院 ; ☎296 2750),
on Jichang Lu, just north of the International Bus Station.

Internet Access: Business center in the **Seman Hotel** is the only reasonable option for
Internet (1st 30min. free, then Y3 per hr.) The **International Hotel** next to the Qinibagh
Hotel charges Y16 per hr. Most Internet cafes in Kashgar do not allow foreigners in.

Post and Telecommunications: 7 Renmin Xi Lu (☎282 5007), west of the People's Hotel. EMS and Poste Restante on 2nd fl. (M-F only). Western Union on 1st fl. Open daily 9:30am-8pm. **China Telecom** (☎282 8006), across the street. IDD service. Open daily 9:30am-10pm. Plenty of street booths with English signs reading "IDD" or "long-distance calls" open until around 2am.

Postal Code: 844000.

ACCOMMODATIONS

Kashgar is a great place to kick back for a week. Budget rooms are easy to find. On summer days, the area around the Qinibagh and Seman Hotels becomes a bizarre foreigner's village, as backpackers and package-tour types converge on the city.

Seman Hotel (sèmǎn bīnguǎn; 色满宾馆), 170 Seman Lu (☎255 2129), has 2 branches. The foreigner-oriented, showier branch houses John's Cafe and is easily recognizable by its colorful tiled minarets. Deposit Y100. 3-bed dorms Y15; 5-bed dorms with bath and A/C Y30; doubles Y120. The 2nd branch on the opposite side of the roundabout has Internet in the business center and bike rental (Y10 per 6hr., deposit Y200). Tiny but comfortable doubles with bath Y80. ❶

Qinibagh Hotel (qíníwǎkè bīnguǎn; 其尼瓦克宾馆), 93 Seman Lu (☎284 2299). Clean rooms and dorms have fans and attached bath. Newly renovated rooms cost more. Laundry, IDD service, English-speaking staff, and 2 travel agencies right outside. 4-bed dorms Y20; 3-bed Y25; doubles Y80; with reliable shower Y120. ❶

Tuman River Hotel (tǔmànhé dàfàndiàn; 吐曼河大饭店 ; ☎296 1336), 5 Jichang Lu, at the International Bus Station. The lobby and corridors have seen better days, but the doubles are well maintained with spring water dispenser and TV. Singles with bath and A/C Y140; doubles with bath and A/C Y120; triples Y50. ❶

People's Hotel (rénmín fàndiàn; 人民饭店), 1 Jiefang Nan Lu (☎282 3373), at Renmin Lu at Jiefang Lu. Ask to see the rooms first as some have delapidated balconies. The best rooms have tiled floors that keep the place cool, but all have A/C and bath and overlook the busy street. Singles Y90; doubles Y130. ❷

FOOD

Kashgar's street food is not for the faint of heart. Markets overflow with ant-head stew, carcasses and intestines hang from massive hooks, and the pungent scent of barbecue smoke fills the air. The delicious Uighur *laghman* (拉面 ; Y3), noodles with tomatoes, onions, garlic, and meats, is readily available in streetside shops. Kebabs are everywhere, with liver, heart, and other skewered treats on offer. The small, square meat- or vegetable-packed pastries (*samsa*, Y0.5) are excellent. For breakfast or lunch, a big bowl of rice, carrot, and squash (zhuā fàn; 抓饭) costs Y2, Y7 with hunks of lamb meat thrown on top. Other street delights include hot sweet milk (Y1), deep-fried raisin, walnut, and sugar pastries (Y0.5), bagel-like creations (Y0.5), and sweet breads (Y0.5-1).

Golden Globe Restaurant (jīn qiú kuài cāntīng; 金球快餐厅), 71 Jiefang Nan Lu (☎282 9011). This lively Uighur restaurant is a local favorite, with Uighur music VCDs playing on the corner TV. *Dàpánjī* (大盘鸡), a delicious stew of tender chicken, potatoes, peppers, red chili, and thick chunks of ginger served over noodles Y20. Portions are huge: a small *pánjī* (Y12) can still serve 2. Lamb *laghman* Y3.5, with chicken Y5. ❶

Pakistani Cafe (☎222 4479), on Seman Lu, across the street from John's Information Cafe on Seman Lu. Friendly crowd of Pakistani travelers and traders may invite you to join their tables. Excellent lamb and chicken curries (Y8) with fresh *naan* (bread). Side order of *daal* (lentils) Y3. Tasty, creamy Pakistani tea Y1. ❶

Light and Fragrant Noodle Shop (qīng xiāng liángpí gǎn miànpí diàn; 清香凉皮擀面皮店 ; ☎282 2733), on the corner of Renmin Xi Lu at Yunmulakexia Lu. A wide variety of the highest-quality cold noodle dishes. Instant service, no nonsense. *Liángpí* (凉皮), rice noodles with shredded tofu in a refreshing vinegary sauce, just Y1.5. ❶

Open-Mouthed Dumplings (kāikǒu lùxiàn shuǐjiǎo; 开口露馅水饺), 113 Yunmulakexia Lu (☎284 1899). Your traditional hotpot restaurant, but with a variety of fresh "open-mouthed" dumplings (so you can see the filling peeking out) to chuck into the pot, as well as a vast selection of the usual meats and veggies. 2 can eat for Y50. ❷

John's Information Cafe, 170 Seman Lu (☎258 1186), in the Seman Hotel. Western and Chinese food at double the price you would pay anywhere else. The money goes to the information and clean toilets, but otherwise this is just a rip-off tourist hang-out. ❷

👁 SIGHTS

SUNDAY BAZAAR (kāshí xīngqī tiān shìchǎng; 喀什星期天市场). Nothing can prepare visitors for the grandeur and exoticism of the Sunday Bazaar. With an impressive green-tiled dome and a multilingual sign proclaiming "Kashgar International Trade Market of Central and Western Asia," the bazaar is hard to miss. Every Sunday, a bubbling cauldron of human activity descends upon the lot. A wild reminder of the days when Kashgar was a major crossroads on the Silk Road, the bazaar hosts a colorful mix of Uighurs, Tajiks, Kyrgyz, Uzbeks, Han Chinese, Russians, and tourists. Livestock and other creatures are held within a vast pen; vegetables and other foodstuffs are sequestered in a separate section. The fragrance of rare spices on one side fades into the sharp tang of leather from the shoes on the other side. The market tantalizes passersby with silks, knives, clothes, and more; bargain for 60-70% off the stated price. All sorts of tasty treats are also available in the alleys: just point and you shall receive. *(About 1 mi. east down Yizirete Lu on the right, in the northeast of town. Guard your cash and belongings carefully. The bazaar begins about 9am, peaks noon-2pm, and ends around 6pm.)*

TOMB OF YUSUP KHASS HAJIP (yùsùfú hāsī hājífú mù; 玉素甫哈斯哈吉甫墓). Locals love the fact that visitors stop by to see the city's much-beloved 11th-century poet and philosopher, who wrote the "Widsom of Happiness and Pleasure," a poem with a whopping 13,290 lines in the ancient Uighur language. The tomb is a beautifully detailed structure with a main dome decorated with intricate lattices and high minarets. *(From Id Kah Sq., follow Jiefang Bei Lu through the main intersection until it turns into Jiefang Nan Lu; after about 1.8km, take a left on the small Tiyu Lu, just after the stadium. Y10. Photo and video usage Y100.)*

TOMB OF ABOKH HOJA (āpàkè huòjiā língmù; 阿帕克霍加陵墓). Built around 1635 by Abokh Hoja, this stately tomb also houses five generations of his family. Abokh Hoja was the king of the Hoja regime in Kashgar and leader of the Baishan sect in 1640, as well as the great-uncle of Emperor Qianlong's favorite concubine. Born of Uighur descent, the girl is said to have possessed a rare and exotic bodily aroma since childhood and was nicknamed *Ikparhan*, or "fragrant maid." Accepted into the palace in 1760 at the age of 14, she was known as *Xiāngfēi*, the Fragrant Concubine, and later elevated to a mythological status, the subject of many Chinese literary works. She is buried here in this tomb, also known as the **Tomb of Xiangfei** (xiāngfēi mù; 香妃), featuring domed turrets and intricate multi-colored mosaics. *(About 2km northeast of town on a road off Yizirete Lu. Bus #20 stops right outside. Cab from city center Y15. Bike ride 45min.; turn at a small English sign on the left; continue 700m, through an alley on the right. Bike parking Y0.5. Open daily 8am-8pm. Abohk tomb Y15, museum Y5, Abokh Hoja family residence exhibition Y5.)*

OTHER SIGHTS. Id Kah Mosque (yìtígǎ'ěr qīngzhēn sì; 艾提尕尔清真寺), on Jiefang Bei Lu north of Renmin Lu, was built in 1442 and is still the religious center of Xinjiang's Uighur community. On festival days, it packs a crowd of 21,000. Please respect worshippers by remaining silent. *(Y10.)* The **Kashgar Museum** (kāshí bówùguǎn; 喀什博物馆) is not terribly thrilling, especially if you've seen Ürümqi's museum, but the Early Iron Age corpses may be of interest. *(Returning to town along Yizirete Lu from the Tomb of Abokh Hoja, take a left at Taukuz Lu and continue for 1km; it's on the right before Renmin Dong Lu. Open daily 9:30am-1:30pm and 4-8pm. Y8, students Y4.)*

THE KARAKORUM HIGHWAY

Running beneath some of the highest mountains in the world and connecting Kashgar to **Sost, Pakistan** via the 4733m **Khunjerab Pass** (hóngqílāfù shānkǒu; 红其拉甫山口), the **Karkorum Highway** (kālǎkūnlún gōnglù; 喀喇昆仑公路) has long appealed to adventure-seekers, backpackers, and the Pakistani traders who regularly ply the route. Even if you're not going to Pakistan, the highway is a fascinating trip to the border at **Tashkurgan** (tǎshíkù'ěrgān; 塔什库尔干), especially if you stop at the breathtaking **Karakul Lake**. From the lake, the highway circles the west side of the 7546m-high Mt. Muztagata. With the highway elevation already at 3600m, it's hard to imagine that the white mound of rock to the side of the bus is reaching 4km into the sky. The sheer magnitude of Mutztagata only begins to register as the mountain refuses to diminish, unimaginably huge even after an hour's worth of driving toward its beckoning height on the horizon. Buses run daily May-October. Otherwise, transportation options are limited and the road often impassable. Even during the summer, closures are common, as mudslides can demolish the road in seconds. Generally, buses eventually find some way through, or travelers can walk across the obstacle and switch buses; be prepared for long delays.

KARAKUL LAKE 卡拉库力湖

200km south of Kashgar, a 6hr. drive along the Karakorum Highway. Buses between Kashgar and Tashkurgan all pass by the lake. Bus from the Kashgar Bus Station (9:30am, Y32) is often full; buy tickets the day before. Pakistan-bound bus from the International Bus Station (noon, Y43 to Karakul) is easier to book at short notice. Buses from Tashkurgan go to Lake Karakul (2½hr., 9:30am). To leave the lake, buses to Kashgar pass by at about noon, to Tashkurgan at about 3 and 6pm. It is often possible to catch a ride with travel agency buses that stop at Karakul. Lake admission Y20.

With towering glaciers and the "Father of Ice Mountains" **Mount Muztagata** (7546m) looming on the far side, **Lake Karakul** (kǎlākùlì hú) has by far the most dramatic scenery of Xinjiang's alpine lakes. It's an ideal spot for hiking and trekking. Give yourself a day to acclimate if you're coming from Kashgar; the lake is at 3600m, high enough that some experience mild headaches and shortness of breath upon arrival. The area immediately around the lake is pretty dusty and drab, but many friendly Kyrgyz yurt dwellers happily invite you in for a cup of tea and sell neat Kyrgyz-style hats of camel hair (about Y20). Regulations forbid locals from hosting foreigners and the local PSB has been known to raid suspected yurts. Tentless backpackers must resort to the **"Karakul Resort" ❶** next to the highway. The cinderblock building offers rooms, but more appealing are their nice (if overpriced) yurts, with great views and warm bedding. Ask for one away from the parking lot and be sure to close the door when you leave, or a local goat might wander in to investigate and leave you a "gift." (Doubles Y50, with bath Y120. Yurts Y40 per person.) The **"resort" restaurant ❷** has big windows and a panoramic view, and serves up overpriced Chinese food and a Western breakfast.

TASHKURGAN 塔什库尔干 ☎0998

The small, mostly Tajik town of Tashkurgan plays much the same role today as it did 1500 years ago during the Tang Dynasty: the final isolated outpost of Chinese rule before the big, bad Western world. The town is relaxed and slow-paced, unfettered by administrative demands. Women in long, garish red dresses and flowing capes walk hand in hand with curly-haired toddlers, whose strawberry-blonde locks tumble out from beneath embroidered flat caps. In the summer, the moon shines in the royal blue sky over the mountains in the west well past midday. The ancient Stone City and friendly Tajik neighborhood can captivate the imagination for hours on end. Travelers going to or coming from Pakistan will have to spend the night in Tashkurgan, but even if a border crossing isn't in your future, the town is a great place to kick back and take in the unparalleled mountain scenery.

🔳🚻 ORIENTATION AND PRACTICAL INFORMATION.

The Karakorum Highway runs south along the western edge of town. Most travelers will never need to leave **Tashkurgan Road** (塔什库尔干路), which runs east from the highway. Here you'll find the bus station, Stone City, hotels, and restaurants. The **Mushitage Road** (慕士塔格路) runs parallel to Tashkurgan Rd. to the south. **Hongqilafu Road** (红其拉甫路) is the only major cross street. The **Tashkurgan Bus Station** (tǎshíkù'ěrgān chángtú qìchēzhàn; 塔什库尔干长途汽车站) is on the west end of Tashkurgan Rd., near the highway. Buses run to **Kashgar** (8hr.; 2 buses at 9:30am; local Y36, Pakistan bus Y62) and **Sost, Pakistan** (8hr., 9:30am, Y225). No banks exchange traveler's checks or offer credit card advances. The **Traffic Hotel** can exchange US dollars and Pakistani rupees. If you opted for a dorm room in the budget hotels but absolutely must take a shower, there's a communal **shower**, 6 Hongqilafu Lu, immediately on the right after the Tashkurgan Rd. turn-off. The **PSB** is at 5 Mushitage Rd., at Hongqilafu Rd. **Qinqing Phone Bar** (qīnqíng huàbā; 亲情话吧) provides international dialing services for Y3-6 per hr. Walking east from the Traffic Hotel, turn left on Hongqilafu Rd.; the phone bar is a 2min. walk on the left. The **post office** and **China Telecom** are diagonally across the roundabout from the PSB. (IDD service. Open daily 10am-2pm and 5-8pm Beijing time.)

🚹🏠 ACCOMMODATIONS AND FOOD.

Both of the foreigner-friendly budget hotels in town are good values and near the bus station. **Traffic Hotel ❶** (jiāotōng bīnguǎn; 交通宾馆), 50 Tashkurgan Rd.

THE HIDDEN DEA[L]

MARMET AND MARMOT

Marmet, a 20-year-old Kyrgyz jeep driver, lives with his family in the tiny village of Subaxcun on the edge of Karakul Lake. For jus[t] Y100, he will drive you to the foo[t] of Mt. Muztagata and back. Se[t]ting off around 10am, the drive crosses extremely rough terrain and mountain streams, passes thousands of wildflowers, and arrives 2hr. later at a Kyrgyz yur[t] camp. From here, a climb up [a] mountain path leads to Muzta[-]gata's first base camp, at 4000m[.] On the hike up, a series of bu[r]rows jut up along the mountain[.] Marmots nosily pop up thei[r] heads, then disappear just as quickly. They're difficult to spo[t] with coats matching the rocky sur[-]face. They'll also startle you wit[h] extremely loud, high-pitched whis[-]tles, perhaps warning their mar[-]mot buddies, or just singing [a] little song.

It's important to climb the mountain at a slow pace, espe[-]cially if you just arrived at Karaku[l] Lake the previous day, and res[t] every 5min. At the base camp the hardcore climbers may we[l]come you into their tents for [a] cup of tea. Back at the yurts, Ky[r]gyz families will also invite you in[.] Marmet will drive you back to hi[s] house at 4pm, where an even be[t]ter view of Karakul Lake and the mountains await. You can sta[y] the night in his house, full of tap[-]estries from Turpan and Pakistan[.]

Find Marmet by asking the locals playing pool near the Kra[-]kul Resort.

(☎342 1192), has a super-friendly staff. Doubles are newly renovated, with warm, colorful comforters. Cheaper dorms are equally bright, but have hard beds, concrete floors, exposed pipes, and common baths without showers. (4-bed dorms 1st fl. Y10, 3rd fl. Y20; doubles Y50, with bath Y100.) **Ice Mountain Hotel ❶** (bīngshān bīnguǎn; 冰山宾馆), 77 Tashkurgan Rd. (☎342 2668), is just down the street from the bus station, on the left. A bit older and more casual than the Traffic, this joint is still pretty nice. (3- to 4-bed dorms Y15-20; slightly small doubles with bath Y30 per person, fancier doubles Y100.)

Tajik specialties include *kalie* (喀列), a stir-fried shredded mutton dish, and *alkez* (阿尔孜克), golden, deep-fried cakes of dough. Muslim restaurants cluster on Tashkurgan Rd. and Hongqilafu Rd. **Alramr,** on Hongqilafu Rd. near the Mushitage Rd. intersection, is a charismatic little Uighur joint that fills up with Tajik, Pakistani, and Uighur locals in the evening. The usual *laghman* (Y3) and lamb kebabs (Y1) are on the menu, but also try the roasted lamb kidney (yāozi; 腰子 ; Y35), peppered and served with thinly sliced onions in oil. The best choice for Chinese and Western food is the Traffic Hotel restaurant, left of the main reception.

◨ SIGHTS. The **Stone City** (shítóu chéng; 石头城) is perched behind the Pamir Hotel at the far eastern side of Tashkurgan Rd. More a large, mud-brick fort, it was first built around AD 502-557, but the better-preserved inner castle dates from the Qing Dynasty (AD 1644-1911). Slightly elevated from the town below, the fort presents an excellent vantage point for the yurt-dotted grasslands, hemmed in on all sides by looming mountain ranges. As there's no real entrance, you're on your own finding the steep crumbling path that leads up to the wall. With no admission fee or other travelers in sight, you may feel like you're the first to discover these forlorn ruins. The eerie stillness is broken only by the fluttering of crows, swooping about the cliffs below, or the occasional lizard, sneaking out from beneath a rock. A Tajik residential area sits below the fort. If you continue to the end of Tashkurgan Rd. and around to the left, a street runs north past the far side of the Stone City. Mud-stone houses line the left side of the street, while cows, sheep, ducks, goats, and children muck about in the hot, swampy flatlands on the right.

The town now boasts a new **Tajik Culture and Arts Center** on the Mushitage Rd. and Hongilafu Rd. intersection roundabout, across from the PSB. The complex houses a basement museum, in the form of two locked rooms that will be opened for visitors personally. The first room displays stone relics and tiny figurines unearthed in the Stone City. The second room contains a 1000-year-old baby skeleton and the 3500-year-old corpse of a 25-year-old woman, both unearthed near Tashkurgan. Among the display of grave contents, there's even a 3500-year-old walnut! After the museum, a guide leads visitors up to the **Tajik Folklore Exhibition Hall** on the first floor, a long room filled with photographs of Tajik rituals and customs. Twice per week the center's performance hall hosts an evening of Tajik song and dance. (Performances at 7:30pm, unfixed weekly schedule, Y10. Museum captions in English and Chinese. Museum and exhibition hall Y20, students Y15.)

BEYOND YECHENG

From **Yecheng** (叶城), the road splits: one way links Kashgar and Hotan via **Shache,** the other is an illegal overland route to **Ali** (阿里) in western Tibet (near Kailash). Drivers will approach foreigners in Yecheng and offer to take them to Ali (3-5 days, Y300). Neither the PSB nor *Let's Go* approves of this method— nonetheless, be sure to take food and warm clothes for the long trip. From Ali to Lhasa, the roads are poor and the trip takes at least a week. This requires hitching a ride in a truck, also not recommended by *Let's Go*. Furthermore, temperatures are often below freezing, and many of the mountain passes are over 5000m. After reaching the Tibetan border, some travelers report being fined Y300 but still being allowed to continue into Tibet. As always, regulations, enforcement, and penalties are subject to change. Late summer is not a good time to go, as melting snow can wash away mountain roads.

BORDER CROSSING INTO PAKISTAN: KHUNJERAB PASS.
The Chinese border post is at the southern edge of Tashkurgan; the Pakistani border post is at Sost, 220km away. The actual border is at the Khunjerab Pass, 126km from Tashkurgan. When going over the 4900m-high pass, many travelers experience mild cases of altitude sickness, including headaches and nausea. Travelers coming from Pakistan should bring enough cash to get them to Kashgar; traveler's checks and credit cards are not accepted in Tashkurgan. You can exchange Chinese, Pakistani, and US currency at both border checkpoints (travelers report slightly better rates at the Pakistani post) and at the Traffic Hotel in Tashkurgan. You'll need to buy a new ticket for transport from Tashkurgan to Kashgar (Y62). In the other direction, 1 ticket is good all the way from Kashgar to Sost. Heading to Pakistan, you may need to spend the night in Sost. From here, there are frequent connections to Gilgit, where buses run to Islamabad.

HOTAN 和田 ☎0903

One of the most isolated cities in all of China, Hotan is connected only to Kashgar and to Korla via the new Taklimakan Desert Highway. Enlivened by the Karakash (Black Jade) and Yorungkash (White Jade) Rivers, this town has long been a spiritual and commercial center on the Southern Silk Road, recalled by the ruins of cities and Buddhist temples forgotten in the arid desert. Hotan's flourishing silk and carpet industry is a vivid reminder of the city's rich history. An incredible variety of patterns and colors adorns every market stall and drapes from the backs of veiled Uighur women, adding to the authentic air of this remote desert oasis. Like most desert towns, though, Hotan has more than its fair share of dust. Even a short stroll down one of the main streets leaves travelers caked with grit and in need of a shower. The locals take it all in stride—street magicians regularly ply their tricks on alley corners for hours on end, dazzling crowds well into the hundreds.

TRANSPORTATION AND PRACTICAL INFORMATION

Beijing Lu (北京路) runs from **Wulumuqi Lu** (乌鲁木齐路) in the west to the **White Jade River** (báiyù hé; 白玉河), 5km east of town. In the town center, Beijing Lu intersects **Hetian Lu** (和田路) to the east and **Ta'naiyi Lu** (塔乃依路) to the west, while passing over the north side of **People's Square** (rénmín guǎngchǎng; 人民广场) in between these two streets. **Youyi Lu** (友谊路) runs south from Beijing Lu in between People's Sq. and Hetian Lu. The long-distance bus station is on **Highway 315**, which runs along the north edge of town and becomes **Aiyitika'er Lu** (艾依提卡尔路) after passing a small park that leads east to the bazaar.

Flights: Hotan Airport (hétián fēijīchǎng; 和田飞机场), a Y15-20 taxi ride south of the city. **CAAC Ticket Office,** 3 Wulumuqi Nan Lu (☎251 2178), a 2min. walk south of Beijing Lu on the left. Open daily 9:30am-1pm and 4-7pm. To **Ürümqi** (daily 10:50am, or 2 per day at 2:10 and 11pm; Y560).

Buses: Hotan Long-Distance Bus Station (hétián chángtú qìchē zhàn; 和田长途汽车 站 ;☎203 2700, ext. 8874), on the highway, in the north part of town. Exit to the right, walk 5min. to the 1st intersection, and turn right onto Beijing Lu; it's a 10min. walk to the city center. Open daily 7:30am-10pm. To: **Kashgar** (12hr.; every 2hr.; hard seat Y58-79, sleeper Y73-81); **Qiemo** (48hr., 10am, Y118-131); **Turpan** (20hr., 8pm, Y180-198); **Ürümqi** (24hr.; 1, 8pm; Y200-220) via **Korla** (15hr., Y144-155) and the **Desert Highway** (the best desert scenery can be seen from the 1pm bus); **Yecheng** (8hr.; every 2hr., or any Kashgar bus; Y31); **Yining** (at least 40hr., 1pm, Y187). **Eastern Bus Station** (dōng jiāo qìchē zhàn; 东郊汽车站), on Aiyitika'er Lu, 5min. east of the Hotan Bazaar. Open daily 8am-8pm.

Local Transportation: All points of interest in the city are within a 15min. walk. **Taxis** are unmetered and cost a flat Y5 to destinations within the city center. **Pedicabs** from the bazaar to city center Y3.

Travel Agency: Xinjiang Hotel Grand Desert Travel Service (xīnjiāng hétián dàmò lǚxíngshè; 新疆和田大漠旅行社 ; ☎ 251 6849), 84 Tuowan Kege Gezi Xiang (托万柯格革孜巷), off Hemo Lu. Abdul Kerim (☎ 139 9965 6660), the general manager, speaks fluent English and arranges 1-day tours around Hotan's silk, carpet, and wooden handicrafts factories, and to the Melikawat ruins (transport Y200, English-speaking guide Y100). 1-day tour to the Rewak Buddhist Temple ruins (2hr. land cruiser ride Y450, 2hr. walk free, entrance fee Y450). 2-day trip to Keriya ancient city (3hr. in land cruiser, half-day camel ride; Y1000).

Bank of China: 75 Wulumuqi Nan Lu, a few min. walk south of Beijing Lu on the right. Exchanges traveler's checks. Credit card advances. Open M-F summer 9:30am-1:30pm and 4-8pm; winter 10am-2pm and 3:30-7pm.

Bookstore: Xinhua Bookstore (☎ 202 2490), on Beijing Lu between Hetian Lu and Youyi Lu. City maps on 2nd fl. Open daily 9:30am-9pm.

PSB: 22 Beijing Lu (☎ 203 5525), between Youyi Lu and Ta'naiyi Lu. Open M-F 9:30am-8pm.

Internet Access: Generations Internet Cafe (shìdài wǎngbā; 世代网吧). Walking away from People's Sq. from the Hotan Guesthouse, it's the 3rd door on the right. Y2 per hr.

Post and Telecommunications: On Beijing Lu (☎ 202 1885), across the street from the bookstore. EMS, IDD service (no calling card calls). Open daily 9:30am-8:30pm.

Postal Code: 848000.

ACCOMMODATIONS

All three accommodations listed are conveniently located in the city center within walking distance of the bus station and the old city.

Yurong Hotel (yùróng bīnguǎn; 玉融宾馆), 28 Beijing Lu (☎ 202 5242), at Ta'naiyi Lu. Brand-new hotel, clean and well-ventilated. Coral blue curtains give the rooms a cool and pleasant hue. Doubles have TV, phone, A/C, and bath with Western toilet. 24hr. hot water. 2-bed dorms Y30; 3-bed Y35; doubles Y140; luxury suites Y260. ❶

Yiyuan Hotel (yíyuàn bīnguǎn; 怡苑宾馆 ; ☎ 202 5631), on Ta'naiyi Lu, just north of the Yurong Hotel. Slightly cramped triples and quads. Green carpets a tad worse for wear. 24hr. hot water. Jade jewelry store left of reception. Doubles Y50, with bath Y100, with A/C and bath Y120; triples with A/C and bath Y150; quads with shared bath Y120. ❶

Hotan Guesthouse (hétián yíngbīnguǎn; 和田迎宾馆 ; ☎ 202 2824), on Ta'naiyi Lu. From the bus station, turn left onto the highway and make a sharp left on Yanaiyi Lu, the 1st major cross street. The hotel is a 10min. walk ahead on the left, just before the Yiyuan and Yurong. Set in a pleasant poplar-tree courtyard. Doubles have sparkling bath, spring water dispenser, big screen TV, and crisp white sheets. Singles Y228; doubles Y150, newer doubles Y268. ❷

⬛ FOOD

The best Uighur food is found in the east of town, in the **bazaar** area. Most restaurants downtown are Chinese, with a number of tasty cheapies, such as the **Friend Restaurant ❶** (péngyǒu jiǔjiā; 朋友酒家), on Beijing Lu. Walk toward Wulumuqi Lu from People's Sq.; the restaurant is 2min. on the left. The price here is based on size rather than dish—a small rabbit costs only Y3. Try the smoked pork with green chilis (báijiāo chǎo làròu; 白椒炒腊肉 ; Y18), which is not at all spicy but very oily and tasty. (☎ 203 6955. Chinese dishes Y3-50.) A few doors down, continuing toward Wulumuqi Lu, the tiny **Langwan Restaurant ❶** (làngwǎn cāntīng; 浪宛餐厅) serves delicious chicken, pork, and vegetable dishes for under Y10. The classic twice-cooked pork with noodles (huíguō ròu miàn; 回锅肉面 ; Y8) is wonderful.

⬛ SIGHTS

Hotan's Silk Road-era ruins offer little for the casual observer. Most relics have been carted off to museums, and today these ancient structures are merely eroded mounds of rubble in a sea of sand dunes. If you cross the Taklimakan Desert between Korla and Ürümqi via the Desert Highway, these sights aren't hard to miss. Check with a travel agency if you're interested in the ruins; you'll have to hire a vehicle (Y200-400, guide Y100 per day). A trip to the closest ruin, **Melikawat**, can also be included in a standard one-day Hotan tour. There are a number of grape vineyards and fruit orchards nearby, but visiting the silk, jade, and carpet factories is more interesting, as each opens a window onto the skill, coordination, and sheer volume of labor that goes into the production of Hotan's specialty items.

⬛**HOTAN BAZAAR** (hétiān dà bāzhá; 和田大巴扎). Many disappointed by the Kashgar market's touristy feel enjoy this market much more: it is almost as large but less enclosed, has fewer tourists, and is by far more chaotic and free-spirited. During the week, hundreds of permanent shops line the covered alleyways selling silk, clothing, melons, whole roast chickens, eggs roasted in their shells over hot ashes, the famous Uighur rice dish (zhuāfàn; 抓饭), cold noodles, and enormous *naan*. One of the more unusual items on sale are hand-made, ornate, steel grand-entrance gates. There's even a whole street dedicated to bicycle wheels. The **carpet bazaar** is inside the main gate, to the left. Examine carpets carefully before buying; quality varies greatly. The sellers here are notoriously tough hagglers, with some bargain showdowns lasting 30-40min. Few carpets should cost more than Y1200, but those with 800 to 1200 knots per inch will cost much more than ordinary silk carpets (0.5m×1m about Y200, 1.5m×3m about Y800). For full effect, visit on Sundays. (*Walk north on Hetian Lu from the post office; turn right on Aiyitika'er Lu after the small park. Walk 10min. down the dirt road; the market branches off this main street.*)

⬛**HOTAN CARPET FACTORY** (hétián dìtǎn chǎng; 和田地毯厂). Check out the amazing process of carpet-weaving, which often involves complex symmetrical patterns and cutting and tying hundreds of thousands of pieces of yarn or silk into a massive foundation grid. Hotan's carpet industry is said to date back over 2000 years. More recently, in 1992, the factory wove a carpet for Beijing's Great Hall of the People (p. 143). A large shop features the factory's creations, including custom-made oddities. Most carpets are wool, but lightweight silk rugs (favored by travelers) are also available. Small (0.5m×0.5m) wool carpets start at about Y100, with 1m×1m going for Y400. Prices are better and bargainable at the bazaar, but non-experts might find it safer to shop here, where high quality is guaranteed. (*Turn* *right onto Hwy. 315 at the north of Ta'naiyi Lu and take eastbound bus #10 or 4 past the bazaar; switch to bus #3 and get off at the factory, the last stop. Open daily 9:30am-6pm; avoid weekends and midday rest hours 1-4pm, when factory is empty of workers.)*

WHITE JADE RIVER (bái yù hé; 白玉河). This river, known as the **Yorungkash,** is the area's primary source for white jade. In the late afternoon, locals rake through piles of stones at the river's edge in search of precious stones. Although real jade is scarce, the incredible beauty and variety of stones scattered about the banks is reason enough to visit. On hot afternoons, you can also take a refreshing swim in the fast current. *(On Hwy. 315. Take eastbound bus #10 to the river.)*

SILK FACTORY (sīchóu chǎng; 丝绸厂). The most impressive part of this factory is a huge room where cocoons are boiled in long troughs and almost invisible strands of silk are wrapped around thousands of spinning reels. Hundreds of electric looms crank out a ceaseless flow of silk sheets ready to be dyed in the silk-weaving room. It may be difficult to wander around on your own, as the security guards are a suspicious lot. If you arrive in the late morning or afternoon, head to the second floor of the office building opposite the main gate to arrange a tour. *(From the bus stop on Hetian Lu just south of Aiyitika'er Lu, take bus #1 to the last stop; the factory, with a white tile gate and tan office building, is about 200m back toward town on the right.)* About 1.5km south of the silk factory, the **Hotan Winery** (hétiān zhìjiǔ chǎng; 和田 制酒厂) produces specialty pomegranate and rice wines. Bottles are sold at factory prices (Y20-120). The security guard at the gate will call to arrange a guide.

▣ NIGHTLIFE

Locals congregate in People's Sq. until late evening. Lovers stroll and kids marvel at luminous, inflatable cacti. Street magicians attract an enthusiastic crowd.

Cowboy Disco Bar (niúzǎi díbā; 牛仔迪吧 ; ☎139 9943 5530), on Beijing Lu to the right of the hospital. A 4-piece Uighur band plays recording-quality music over an unfortunately lousy sound system. The lanterns and UV lighting create a warm and fun atmosphere. No cover. Beer Y5. Open 10pm-2am.

Space Nightclub (X kōngjiān; X 空间), 75 Wulumuqi Nan Lu (☎205 9230), in the basement of the Bank of China. Pumping Han Chinese disco. Tom and Jerry chase each other over a TV screen. Graffiti-sprayed pillars on the dance floor, CDs hanging from the ceiling, and red-and-green glowing tables make up the decor. Cover Y5, girls free. Beer Y20. Open 9pm-3am, but it only really gets going at midnight.

Loulan Disco (lóulán wǔtīng; 楼兰舞厅 ; Mardan ☎135 6549 1117), at the corner of Beijing Lu at Wulumuqi Lu. Uighurs dance to traditional Uighur beats, waltzes, and even calypso tunes, all performed by a vocalist and keyboardist. Friendly waiter speaks Mandarin. Just before 11pm (Xinjiang time), the dance floor takes off to 90s Western techno. Beer Y5 for 650ml bottle. Closes 1am Xinjiang time (3am Beijing time).

Hollywood Disco (hǎoláiwù díbā; 好莱坞迪吧 ; ☎202 5708), on Hetian Lu. Uighurs go all out on the dance floor to electro. Clean toilets. Beer Y5. Cover Y10, women free.

SOUTHERN SILK ROAD: BEYOND HOTAN

Beyond Hotan, the towns may appear progressively more dusty and drab, but the journey, which circumnavigates the Taklimakan Desert, passes through some of the most untouched and isolated Uighur towns in all of Xinjiang. The route provides direct access to Golmud and Tibet and puts travelers close to Dunhuang. The bus ride to **Qiemo** (且末) involves at least two days of rough travel along poor roads and generally includes a stop in **Minfeng** (民丰) along the way. Tour operators will take travelers to see a fish lake in Minfeng. Once in Qiemo, travelers can visit the market stalls and the ancient city 30km away either independently or through a travel agency. From Qiemo, take the bus to **Ruoqiang** (若羌). In theory, the area around Ruoqiang is rich in historical and natural treasures; unfortunately, little remains of the ancient ruins at **Milan** (mǐlán; 米兰) and **Loulan** (lóulán; 楼兰), and reaching either is expensive. Both areas lie near Lop Nur, the dry salt lake bed where China used to conduct nuclear weapons tests. Between 1964 and 1996, China conducted 45 tests at Lop Nur, but activity has since stopped, and in the last three years, water has been fed back into the area to replenish the lake. Also nearby is the **Altun Mountain Nature Reserve** (ā ěr jīnshān zìrán bǎohùqū; 阿尔金山 自然保护区), China's largest preserve and home to diverse species like blackneck cranes, Tibetan antelope, wild yaks, camels, and donkeys. Perhaps puzzled by the presence of so much wildlife, the government has set up an International Hunting Ground within the reserve. The reserve, which lies on the Xinjiang-Tibet border in a closed area (make sure you have a permit), is likely to be difficult and costly to reach, as no roads connect it to other towns.

QINGHAI 青海

An enormous salt lake and an acclaimed herbal fungus are two of Qinghai's few claims to fame, although this frontier province is slated for discovery once the government completes the region's railroad and highway constructions. Historically part of Eastern Tibet, Qinghai province, comprised of parts of the Tibetan regions of Kham and Amdo, occupies the northern half of the Tibetan Plateau and is home to many Hui, Tibetans, Mongols, and Kazakhs. However, most of the province is uninhabitable due to severe winds and freezing winter temperatures. With a history as harsh as its climate, since 1717 the Qinghai region has seen a massive influx of Han Chinese, who now make up a majority of the population. In 1928, it was made a province of China, though it continued to be ruled by Hui warlords. Later, the PLA easily drove out the local strongmen and solidified control over the region. Qinghai quickly became a prime spot for penal colonies, most of which were closed in the 1980s due to high operating costs.

In the eyes of travelers, Qaidam Basin in the northwest offers little more than desert and the occasional salt marsh, but the landscape is also a place of stark and magnificent beauty. The vast herds tended by Amdowa nomads, sketched onto the backdrop of Qinghai Lake, are a fascinating living portrait of Tibetan life. Three of China's mightiest rivers—the Yellow, Yangzi, and the Lancang (Mekong)—arise from the towering Bayan Har mountain range and the southern Tanggula Mountains. The combination of high altitude (3600m), majestic glaciers, and thundering gorges attracts daredevils, nature documentary crews, and local tour groups, but transportation is difficult and conditions uncompromising.

XINING 西宁   ☎0971

Guarding the overland route to Tibet at 2200m above sea level, Xining occupies a strategic position on the edge of the Tibetan Plateau. During the Song Dynasty, the city earned its current name, "Western Peace." Though Xining may seem like another dull provincial capital, it has a diverse population of Han, Hui, Tibetans, and even a handful of Chinese Christians. A venture to Kumbum Monastery and Qinghai Lake is another reminder of the city's position on the fringe of Han China.

▭ TRANSPORTATION

Flights: Xining Airport (xīníng jīchǎng; 西宁机场), 30km east of the city. Buses (35min., Y16) run from the **CAAC ticket office**, 34 Bayi Lu (☎813 3333), accessible by local bus #28. Open daily 8am-6:30pm. To: **Beijing** (daily, Y1450); **Chengdu** (daily, Y990); **Golmud** (Tu, F; Y840); **Guangzhou** (daily, Y1630); **Lhasa** (W, Su; Y1610); **Qingdao** (Tu, F; Y1880); **Shanghai** (daily, Y1240); **Shenzhen** (daily, Y2010); **Ürümqi** (M, Y1130); **Xi'an** (daily, Y650).

Trains: Xining Train Station (xīníng huǒchē zhàn; 西宁火车站 ; ☎814 9790), on Qilian Lu. To: **Beijing** (25½hr., daily, Y430); **Golmud** (14-20hr., 3 per day, Y44-126); **Lanzhou** (3hr., 5 per day, Y33-50); **Qingdao** (34½hr., every other day, Y297); **Shanghai** (33hr., daily, Y467); **Yinchuan** (14hr., daily).

Buses: Xining Long-Distance Bus Station (xīníng qìchē zhàn; 西宁汽车站 ; ☎814 9611), on Jianguo Lu, across the river from the train station. Open daily 6am-6pm. To: **Golmud** (18hr., daily, sleeper Y130); **Heimahe** (6hr., 9 per day 7:30am-5pm, Y27) via **Qinghai Lake**; **Lanzhou** (5hr., every 25min. 7am-5pm, Y27); **Linxia** (8hr., 4 per day, Y34); **Yushu** (24hr., 4 per day, Y109-156); **Zhangye** (12hr., 3 per day, Y43).

Local Transportation: Buses cost Y1. Bus #1 runs from the station area to the Great Mosque, Da Shizi, and Xi Men; #2 goes east from the station area; #11 travels to Changjiang Lu, near the North Temple.

Taxis: Base fare Y6 for the 1st 3km, subsequently Y1.1 per km.

▟ ◪ ORIENTATION AND PRACTICAL INFORMATION

The city is centered around **Da Shizi** (大十字; "Big Cross") and **Xi Men** (西门; "West Gate"), about a 5min. walk apart. The city's main road begins at Xi Men as **Xi Dajie** (西大街) and runs east through town, becoming **Dong Dajie** (东大街), **Dongguan Dajie** (东关大街), **Dazhong Jie** (大众街), and **Bayi Lu** (八一路), which exits the city. **Jianguo Lu** (建国路) runs south from the train and bus stations to **Dazhong Jie.**

Travel Agencies: Qinghai Spring and Autumn Travel Service (qīnghǎi chūnqiū lǚxíng shè; 青海春秋旅行社 ; ☎817 4957), 2nd fl., the Post Hotel. English-speaking staff. Trips to Qinghai Lake and Bird Island. Open 24hr. **Nationality Travel Service** (mínzú lǚxíng shè; 民族旅行社 ; ☎823 2748 or 822 5247), in the back of the Nationality Hotel. English-speaking staff. Decent deals on Bird Island trips. Open daily 24hr. **Traffic Travel Service** (jiāotōng lǚxíng shè; 交通旅行社; ☎813 3928), based out of the Long-Distance Bus Station. Bird Island tours about Y90. Open 24hr. **Splendor Travel Service** (yìcǎi lǚxíng shè; 异彩旅行社 ; ☎814 2008), in the Chezhan Hotel, left of the train station, is the only agency with English-speaking guides. Bird Island tour around Y260.

Bank of China: 218 Dongguan Dajie (☎822 7193), 7min. walk east of Da Shizi. Exchanges traveler's checks and issues credit card advances. Open M-F 8:30am-noon and 2:30-5:30pm, Sa-Su 9:30am-4:30pm.

Bookstore: Foreign Language Bookstore (wàiwén shūdiàn; 外文书店), 7 Xiguan Dajie, 10min. walk west of Xi Men, on the left. Open daily 9:30am-6pm.

Hospital: People's Hospital of Qinghai (qīnghǎi shěng rénmín yīyuàn; 青海省人民医院), 143 Gonghe Lu (☎817 7911 or 817 7981), near the train and bus stations.

PSB: 35 Bei Dajie (☎824 8190), 5min. walk north of Da Shizi. Friendly and knowledgeable. Visa extensions available daily 8:30am-noon and 2:30-6pm. Open 24hr.

Internet Access: An **Internet cafe** (wǎngbā; 网吧), on Weiming Xiang, left of the Railway Hotel. On the 2nd fl., a few doors in, on the right. Y3 per hr. Open daily 8am until the last person leaves. Another Internet cafe is just down Qilian Lu from Jianghai Hotel.

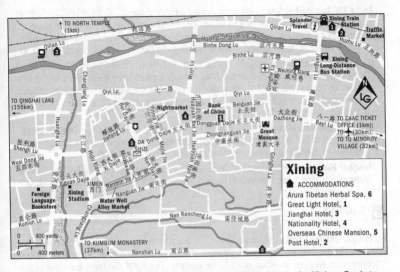

Xining

🏠 ACCOMMODATIONS

Arura Tibetan Herbal Spa, 6
Great Light Hotel, 1
Jianghai Hotel, 3
Nationality Hotel, 4
Overseas Chinese Mansion, 5
Post Hotel, 2

Post Office: Near Da Shizi (☎824 7584), diagonally opposite the Xinhua Bookstore. EMS, Poste Restante, and IDD on the 2nd fl. Open daily 8:30am-6pm.

Postal Code: 810000.

🏠🏠 ACCOMMODATIONS AND FOOD

Xining is a market town of magnificent variety. The **Traffic Market** along Huzhu Lu, east of the train station, is the largest in Xining, followed by **Da Shizi Market** on Nan Dajie. The best place to feast is at the giant **nightmarket** on Yinma Jie, near Da Shizi. You can buy all types of food here, especially "small eats" (xiǎochī; 小吃). Xining's most famous xiǎochī are the savory beef noodles (niúròu miàn; 牛肉面) and the often garlicky chopped noodles (miàn piàn; 面片), both Y3-6. The **Water Well Alley Market** (shuǐjǐng xiàng shìchǎng; 水井巷市场), opposite Huju Xiang and east of Xi Men, sells mostly fresh and dried fruit, vegetables, nuts, and candy, but some places also cook up Xining's famous **shāguō** (沙锅), a delicious concoction of meat, vegetables, and tofu, all slowly simmered together in a clay pot (Y5-9). Don't miss the mouth-watering bowls of sugar-topped yogurt (suānnǎi; 酸奶; Y1). If you're looking for a protein fix after all those noodles, head to the alley off Jianguo Lu, directly across from the bus station, for a string of Tibetan restaurants serving yak meat in all varieties. Try the shamdrey (meat and rice, Y5) and look for yogurt made from yak milk in the summer.

Post Hotel (yóuzhèng bīnguǎn; 邮政宾馆), 138 Huzhu Xi Lu (☎813 3133, ext. 8000 or 8100), east of the train station. You might get a bit winded after climbing 6 flights of stairs to get to your room, but this is still a pretty good deal. The rooms are spartan but clean, with aging showers and baths. Hot water 7am-noon and 4pm-midnight. 4-bed dorms Y14; singles with bath Y40; doubles Y36, with bath Y80 (or Y40 per bed). ❶

Great Light Hotel (hóng guāng fàndiàn; 宏光饭店), ☎711 6968), 100m from the train station's East Port. This takeoff on the Post Hotel has clean rooms, hot water noon-10pm (24hr. in standard rooms), and an extremely helpful English translator Niu Xiaojun (牛晓军), who will most likely find you before you find him. 5- to 6-bed dorms with bath Y15; 3-bed dorms Y20; 2-bed dorms Y25-30; singles Y30-45. ❶

NORTHWEST

Arura Tibetan Herbal Spa (jīnhé zàngyī yàoyù bǎojiàn zhōngxīn; 金河藏医药浴保健中心), 97 Nanshan Dong Lu (☎814 0585, ext. 6688). Attached to the Tibetan Hospital, Arura may be Xining's best deal. A bit removed from town center. Beautiful new rooms with the cleanest, most luxurious baths in Xining. Singles Y128-158; doubles Y180. ❷

Nationality Hotel (mínzú bīnguǎn; 民族宾馆), 1 Huayuan Bei Jie (☎822 5951), at Dong Dajie, 3min. walk east of Da Shizi. Mini-balconies have great views of Xining's sprawl. Spacious rooms. 24hr. hot water, but no public showers for rooms without bath. Reservations recommended. Deposit Y20. Singles with bath Y110; doubles Y130-150; triples with bath Y180. ❷

Overseas Chinese Mansion (huáqiáo dàshà; 华侨大厦), 30 Bei Dajie (☎823 1888). 2min. north of Da Shizi. Dim lighting, lace curtains, and red velvet chairs lend an air of elegance to these small, centrally located rooms. Doubles Y140. ❷

Jianghai Hotel (jiānghǎi bīnguǎn; 江海宾馆), 53 Qilian Lu (☎772 5462). Simple, clean rooms in a quiet, convenient location. No public showers. 2-bed dorms Y40. ❶

👁 SIGHTS

KUMBUM MONASTERY (tǎ'ěr sì; 塔尔寺). Kumbum and Labrang Monastery (p. 762) are the two most important Tibetan Buddhist monasteries outside the Tibet Autonomous Region, in what used to be eastern Tibet. Of the two, Labrang is the larger and more impressive. Kumbum literally means the "100,000 images of the Buddha" in Tibetan. Built in 1560 on the birthplace of Tsong Khapa, who founded the Gelug School of Tibetan Buddhism (p. 836), the monastery is currently home to 600 monks who study *Sutra*, Tantra, and Tibetan medicine. Many of the embroideries, frescoes, and butter sculptures were destroyed in the Cultural Revolution, but enough artwork remains to overwhelm the traveler.

Tours are available, but unfortunately not in English, although the more important buildings generally have explanatory plaques in English. The numbers written on the buildings themselves are completely different than the set of numbers used for the map legend on the admission ticket. Using the map legend numeration, upon entering you will see on your right the **Eight Stupas** (#2), representing the life story of Sakyamuni, the Buddha of the Present. Farther up the road, on the right, the giant **Assembly Hall** (#20) is large enough to hold all the monks at one time. Behind this, the beautiful **Golden Roof Pavilion** (#18) features a giant bodhi tree in the courtyard. At the end of the road, on the right, is Kumbum's most unique attraction, the **Hall of Butter Sculpture** (#27). Each year, the monks mix, mold, and paint a series of intricate scultpures out of yak butter as part of New Year's festivities. (*27km southeast of Xining. Buses go from the left side of the Xining Gymnasium, west of Xi Men, to the tiny village of Huangzhong. The ride lasts 45min. and costs Y4, departing every 30min. 7am-6pm. Unmetered taxis also make the trip, leaving from the same spot for Y5 per person. The monastery is a 3min. walk up the main road. Open daily 8:30am-6pm. Y35.*)

OTHER SIGHTS. Built in 1380, the **Great Mosque** (qīngzhēn dà sì; 清真大寺) is on Dongguan Dajie, a 10-15min. walk east of Da Shizi. Non-Muslims can only peek into the Great Prayer Hall through bars, but the experience may be enlivened by visiting during prayer service. (*Prayer service daily 5:15am, 1:15, 5:30, 8:45, and 9:45pm; largest service F 1:15pm. Open daily 8am-noon and 2:30-6pm. Y5.*) The **North Temple** (běi shān sì; 北山寺) supplies fresh air and rolling hills at the end of a good 1hr. hike to the northwest of Xining along Changjiang Lu. Bus #1 and a ride up the ever-present cable car also works. (*Open daily sunrise-sunset. Y6.*)

🗲 DAYTRIPS FROM XINING

QINGHAI LAKE 青海湖

*155km west of Xining. Tours arranged through a travel agency are more reliable and hassle-free. (12-13hr., departing at 6:30am, Y100-150 depending on volume). Long-distance buses go several times daily from Xining to **Heimahe** (4hr.), a small lakeside settlement on the south shore roughly 1hr. from Bird Island. No public buses go to the island itself; travelers have been known to hike or thumb a ride the rest of the way. Return buses can be very crowded and you may end up without a seat. If you want to see the lake, you can visit Heimahe, or just take a Heimahe-bound bus and get off somewhere along the water. Flag down returning buses anywhere along the route. The Xining-Golmud railway line runs along the north shore of the lake. Admission to Bird Island Y58, Sun Moon Mountain Y10.*

Qinghai means "green sea" in Chinese; in Mongolian its name *Koko Nor* means "blue ocean;" and in Tibetan *Tso Ngonpo* means "turquoise sea." Whatever the name and whatever its hue, China's largest lake sprawls across the Tibetan Plateau at an elevation of 3250m, surrounded by rolling grasslands dotted with vast herds of sheep and yak, along with tents of nomadic herders. In addition to its seemingly unending horizon, the lake is a summer nesting ground for thousands of migratory birds. From April to early July, flocks of gulls, terns, geese, swans, and cranes arrive on **Bird Island** (niǎo dǎo; 鸟岛), a peninsula on the south side of the lake, to mate before heading to the plains of India for the winter. From a tourist's vantage point, Bird Island appears to be more of a "bird rock," and even avid bird-lovers may return disgruntled by the tour buses, the long drive, and the overpriced admission. Tours may stop on nearby Egg Island, where you can buy fungus-infested caterpillar (chóngcǎo; 虫草), a classic of Chinese traditional medicine.

The road to Qinghai Lake offers expansive views of plateau and open stretches of sky. Unfortunately, tour buses often don't allow visitors to linger for as long as may be hoped at the lake, which is a brilliant shade of blue and quite breathtaking. Most tours do, however, make a pleasant first stop at **Sun and Moon Mountain** (rìyuèshān; 日月山), a beautiful mountain pass separating the grasslands from the plateau. There is typically a lunch stop; then it's off to see birds. All in all, you must be an ornithologist and not mind long drives for the trip to be worthwhile.

TU MINORITY VILLAGE

In Huzhu Tu Autonomous County, 32km from Xining. Buses (1-1¼hr., every 15min., Y6) run from the long-distance bus station to Huzhu (互助); ask to be let off at Weiyuanzhen Old Village (wēiyuǎnzhèn gǔchéngcūn; 威远镇古城村). Niu Xiaojun, the helpful English translator at the Great Light Hotel in Xining (p. 821), can help tourists plan trips.

The tiny Tu minority developed its own language, as well as a form of Buddhism with Tibetan and Chinese influences. Numbering 70,000 in total, almost all Tu live in Huzhu county, where they settled after being forced out of Mongol regions. Weiyuanzhen (pop. 700), is 90% Tu. Around the village, visitors can see traditional mud-brick courtyard houses and rural life up close. Three or so tourist centers wait to pounce on visitors, generally charging about Y100 per person for a small-group program, consisting of a 1hr. dance performance followed by a huge traditional feast. More modest programs are available, as is bargaining. The dance, performed by village girls dressed in traditional seven-colored costumes, is elaborate—but be warned that simply entering the complex, let alone watching the dances or toasting the banquet, may require guests to down multiple shots of barley wine. Before you leave, be sure to check out the tiny Buddhist **Bo'er Temple** (bó'ěr sì; 伯尔寺), on the hill overlooking the village, for a glimpse of Tu life from another angle. (Open during daylight hours. Free.) If you have some time to kill, take a passing bus or motorbike (Y2) into the town of Huzhu, where you can visit China's largest **barley wine factory** (hùzhù qīngkē jiǔ chǎng; 互助青稞酒厂). But don't make a trip from Xining just to see this Tibetan specialty. (Free. Bring a cup to sample the wine.) You can hail returning buses to Xining from any point.

GOLMUD 格尔木 ☎0979

Long famed for its ugliness, Golmud is being given a "new face" as part of China's "Develop the West" campaign, though that new face largely consists of paved streets and large, strange art installations at major intersections. The city sits isolated on the edge of vast tracts of salt flats and arid desert, with hot summers and frigid winters. Visitors come only to arrange permits and transportation to Lhasa, as virtually all overland traffic into Tibet goes through Golmud. Once the Golmud-Lhasa train opens in 2007, the constant stream of goods, travelers, and traders into this coal-mining, oil-drilling industrial giant will likely increase. Most of the Han Chinese locals migrated here from Sichuan, Gansu, and eastern Qinghai to scrape out a living along one of China's last frontiers.

🚍❓ TRANSPORTATION AND PRACTICAL INFORMATION

Golmud is arranged in a small grid. The bus and train stations are in the south, connected to the north of the city by **Jiangyuan Lu** (江源路). One block west of Jiangyuan Lu, **Kunlun Lu** (昆仑路) hosts eateries and hotels. The bank, post office, and PSB are on **Chaidamu Lu** (柴达木路), linking Kunlun Lu and Jiangyuan Lu.

The bus ride into the city from Xining is full of magnificent scenery ranging from terraced barley fields to salt flats to lunar landscapes. In contrast, the bus ride from Golmud to Lhasa is cramped and bumpy, often taking one to two full days on poor roads with numerous breakdowns. Although the price is not significantly lower than flying from Xining to Lhasa, the bus ride offers fascinating glimpses into the differences between western China and the Himalayan culture of Tibet.

Trains: Though road quality is improving, traveling by train is safer, more reliable, and faster. **Qinghai Train Station** (qīnghǎi huǒchē zhàn; 青海火车站), on Jiangyuan Lu, in the south part of town. Open daily 7:20am-10pm. To: **Chengdu** (42hr., daily, Y120-257); **Lanzhou** (18hr., daily, Y78-156); **Xining** (12½-20hr., 3 per day, Y44-131).

Buses: Qinghai Bus Station (qīnghǎi qìchē zhàn; 青海汽车站), directly across from the train station. Open daily 7:30am-10pm. To: **Dunhuang** (11hr., 2 per day, Y90) and **Lhasa** (at least 30hr., daily, Y200). Officially, you need a Y50 permit, available from the PSB, to travel to Dunhuang; some travelers have reported being able to buy tickets regardless. The **Tibet Bus Station** (xīzàng qìchē zhàn; 西藏汽车站) in northwest Golmud has 1 bus to **Lhasa** (at least 30hr., 3:30pm, Y200). However, buses to Lhasa are only available to Chinese; foreigners must go through CITS.

Travel Agencies: CITS (☎841 2764), on the 2nd fl. of the Golmud Hotel, is the only travel agency in town. You *must* pay Y1700 for a bus and permit into **Tibet;** fee includes bus (Y1380), permit, and a 4-day "tour" of Lhasa excluding entrance fees. Arranging tours during the weekend is difficult. If you arrive early enough in the day, CITS should be able to put you on a bus that afternoon. Open daily 8:30am-noon and 2:30-6pm.

Bank of China: 19 Chaidamu Lu, at Kunlun Lu, a block south of the Golmud Hotel. Exchanges traveler's checks. Open daily M-F 8:30am-6:30pm, Sa-Su 10am-4pm.

PSB: ☎844 2587. A 3min. walk east of the post office. Does not grant Tibet travel permits. Dunhuang permits Y50. Same-day visa extensions in the little building to the right of the gate. Open daily 8:30am-noon and 2:30-6pm.

Post Office: On Jiangyuan Lu, a 5min. walk east from the Bank of China. EMS at the glass counter and IDD service. Open daily 8am-6pm.

Postal Code: 816000.

ACCOMMODATIONS AND FOOD

Only a few hotels accept foreigners. Most travelers opt for the **Golmud Hotel ❶** (gé'ěrmù bīnguǎn; 格尔木宾馆), 219 Kunlun Lu, up the street from the Bank of China. Its clean dorms are spacious, and CITS is on the second floor. (☎842 4388. 3-bed dorms Y30; singles Y40; doubles with bath Y100.) Make sure you end up at the second building, left of the one with the snazzy fountain out front. Otherwise, the cheapest room you'll find is Y180. If you prefer to stay out of CITS's grip, try the **Wales Hotel ❶** (wēi'ěr shì dàjiǔdiàn; 威尔士大酒店), 26 Jiangyuan Nan Lu. Dorms are cozy and sparklingly clean, with rock-hard beds. The service is friendly, and you'll remain pleasantly odorous from the lack of public showers. (☎841 9208, ext. 8888. Same-day laundry. Dorm rooms Y30-40; triples Y80; standard Y148.)

Along Kunlun Lu, near the Golmud Hotel, many small restaurants offer cheap Sichuanese food (Y3-20 per dish). A **street market,** on the right after exiting the Golmud Hotel, sells fruit, nuts, and sweets, perfect for the long bus ride ahead. Next to the street market, a **supermarket** has dried meat and other packaged foods. You can also stock up at the mini-convenience store in the Golmud Hotel's lobby.

Minority Cultures in Mainland China

The notion of a primordial and homogenous "Han ethnic nationality," bordered by "barbaric ethnic minorities," is often taken for granted by the general public both inside and outside of China. Yet contrary to this widespread, official ideology, the development of the Han ethnic nationality was one of the most pro-active, politically motivated efforts to create a human community in history.

In the early 1910s and 20s, Dr. Sun Yat-sen sought to unify the Chinese against Japanese and other foreign invasions. In particular, Sun had to unify the warlords of the north with the southern merchants. Yet Sun noted a strong bias toward familialism and clanism among the Chinese. They were as difficult to combine as "a sheet of loose sand." Sun himself was southern and spoke Mandarin with a thick accent, and therefore faced traditional northern suspicions. Educated in Japan, Sun borrowed the Japanese term *minzoku*, or ethnic nation, and coined a wholly new phrase in Mandarin—*minzu*, or ethnic nationality. He took the name of the northern Han empire (206 BC to AD 220) for the word *Hanzu*, or the Han ethnic nationality. According to Sun's theories, the Han ethnic nation stood against both "external barbarians" (foreign nations), and "internal barbarians" (ethnic minorities). To counter the Japanese, Sun's philosophy essentially formalized China's internal racial juxtaposition.

When the Chinese Communist Party came to power in 1949, it adopted Sun's theory. The *Hanzu* was the demographic body that theoretically legitimated the government. Moreover, the Han became the "vanguard" of progress for all Chinese ethnic groups. In the 1950s, the Party invited ethnic groups to apply for minority status. They received over 400 requests! A potential nightmare for central planning was mitigated by sending waves of social scientists and linguists all over China to classify these *shaoshu minzu* (ethnic minorities). Many distinctive groups were merged, resulting in an official tally of 55.

These groups were supposedly clustered according to language, geography, and customs. Yet none of these requirements were applied to the Han, who remained a political construction. The Han still speak eight "dialects," which are in reality nearly mutually unintelligible. Most "Han" encounter their own supposed identity through government channels. School matriculation, census forms, and job applications all require self-identification as Han. Many Han are actually

unaware of their status until such time. New media, schools, and public propaganda, however constantly strive to reinforce the idea of China *minzu* family and the dominant Han role there.

Many *shaoshu minzu* also energetically ma tain their ethnic classifications to reap benefits. a sufficiently numerous ethnic group can pro its distinct identity, it can be granted an "autono mous" region or county with limited political an religious privileges. Ethnic minorities are als exempt from the one-child policy and only co pete with other "minorities" in college adm sions. On the other hand, minority identity is vital tool for unified resistance against Chine rule. The Tibetans and Uighurs, for example, c tain many internal, regional differences. Yet th are both oppressed and discriminated again within the Chinese system. Individuals therefo cling to their identities as "ethnic nationals" order to make unified claims for national sov eignty in opposition to the Chinese government

Whereas most ethnic minorities share a l guage and many cultural similarities, the H nationality remains highly contrived, and schism are beginning to arise. In China's southeast, ma ethnic communities within the Han block, su as the Hakka, Fujianese Min, and Swatow, a agitating for greater autonomy and re-associati themselves with the Southern Tang Dynasty (A 618-907). The trend was fueled by their treme dous economic success and their reluctance share their new wealth with Beijing. Some cou ties have avoided paying federal taxes and cr ated trade tariffs across borders with cultura disparate communities. The recent rise in te roads in southern China resulted from the areas striving for greater economic autonomy. the Chinese economy continues to grow, su regional agitation will likely increase as well.

Minzu served Sun Yat-sen as a useful pa digm for resistance against the Japanese. Yet t implicit Han chauvinism quickly turned again ethnic minorities, fueling discriminatory polici and forming barriers to economic entry und CCP rule. Ironically, while the Chinese turned t Japanese concept against their invaders, ethn minorities used *minzu* to rally their own res tance against the Chinese. If tourists, scholars, activists are to understand these evolving all giances within the new China, the "primordi *minzu* must be historically contextualized as politically motivated tool of collective action.

Josh Levin has traveled extensively in China and has spent much time researching minority issues.

༄ TIBET

Closed to foreign eyes until scarcely two decades ago, Tibet has long enchanted Westerners with the promise of a mystical "Shangri-La" high in the Himalayas, untainted by the grime of worldliness. But when Tibet's doors swung open in the mid-1980s, foreign visitors were startled to see Chinese soldiers marching beside ruined monasteries, showing the clear marks of decades of invasion, repression, and transformation. What remains of pre-1959 Tibet, before the Communist government took over, is vanishing. Forests were cut, rivers dammed, and oil drilling and mining projects marred the land. But even more distressing to Tibetans is the feeling—what with government restrictions on cultural and religious practice, the growing Han Chinese immigration, and the changes brought by the modern world—that their civilization may be on its final legs.

Yet for most Tibetans, life remains rich despite the lack of political freedom. Buddhism (p. 835) dominates all aspects of life: even the sweet-talking hawkers in the capital city of Lhasa join the devout pilgrims in walking the sacred circuit around the Jokhang Temple. In recent years, the government has eased some of its religious rules, and Tibetan Buddhist festivities are now carried out in the open. But a shadow continues to loom over life in Tibet.

In this remote corner of the world, the subject of countless dreams and legends, the forces that shape and have shaped this intensely spiritual land have never relented. The climate is harsher, the mountains higher and wilder, the glint of its lakes icier than anywhere else on earth. The heartbreaking historical trauma, fierce natural beauty, and headstrong traditional culture of modern Tibet continue to captivate the imagination of people throughout the world, making this secluded mountain civilization an unexpected international media darling. With increasing numbers of tourists and attention, no one knows what the future has in store for an increasingly earth-bound Tibet. Though it may not be Shangri-La, Tibet is certain to leave deeper impressions than you ever expected.

HIGHLIGHTS OF TIBET

PONDER YOUR REFLECTION in the turquoise waters of **Namtso Lake** (p. 848) or **Yamdroktso Lake** (p. 853).

FIND INNER PEACE at **Lhasa**'s magnificent Potala Palace (p. 843), spiritual Jokhang Temple (p. 844), and Tsurphu Monastery (p. 845).

TRACE THE ROOTS of Tibetan civilization at **Yumbulagang** (p. 852), the site of Tibet's first dynasty, and **Samye Monastery** (p. 850), Tibet's oldest monastery.

WALK THE ROOF OF THE WORLD at the base camp of **Mount Everest** (p. 862), beneath the mighty face of the tallest mountain in the world.

DOCUMENTS AND FORMALITIES

Traveling in Tibet is tightly restricted and monitored by the authorities. To enter Lhasa Prefecture, visitors must obtain a Chinese visa and a Tibet Tourism Bureau (TTB) Permit (see **Travel Permits,** below). To travel anywhere else in Tibet (except Shigatse), you must have an Alien Travel Permit for each of the places you visit.

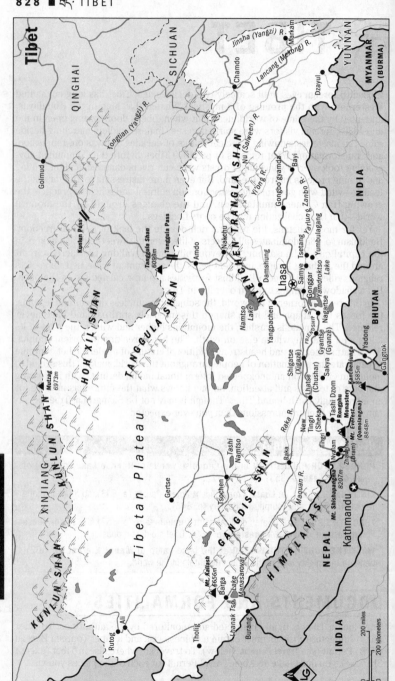

VISAS. When applying for Chinese visas, the application form asks travelers to list their intended destinations in the PRC, but this is not binding and most travelers prefer to omit Tibet and list less politically sensitive destinations. For more information on Chinese visas, see p. 12.

Those who plan to enter Tibet via **Kathmandu** can obtain visas from the Chinese consulate in Kathmandu with two-day processing. Many travelers are herded into tour groups and given group visas. Those who stay in Tibet after their tour must apply for visa extensions at the Chinese affiliate of the Nepalese travel agency; visa extensions are not available in Lhasa unless you have extenuating circumstances (such as a ticket out of China after the visa expiration date). In these cases, the process is a bureaucratic nightmare—and a pricey one at that (Y500-2500). As of August 2004, the Shigatse PSB processes same-day visa extensions.

TRAVEL PERMITS. In addition to high altitude and nearly impassable terrain, individual travelers to Tibet are further burdened by an overwhelming amount of bureaucracy. Before coming into Tibet, visitors must first have the **Tibet Tourism Bureau (TTB) Permit** (pīzhèng; 批证). This can only be obtained through a travel agency and by joining a tour, except in Chengdu, where the bureau issues permits to solo visitors. The TTB grants access only to Lhasa Prefecture, including Namtso Lake, and after the three- to four-day tour, travelers are free to explore the rest of the prefecture on their own.

To travel out of Lhasa, you need to apply for an **Alien Travel Permit** (also called pīzhèng) for each place you plan to visit. Each permit is Y50. Permits are only issued to tour groups, except in **Shigatse**, where the PSB approved permits for independent visitors at the time of writing. Travel agencies arrange for permits, as well as a guide (Y150-200 per day) and a jeep with driver (Y300 per day). Policies and regulations change according to the whims of the local authorities. Ask around for the most current information.

The PSB supposedly conducts frequent sweeps for foreign travelers. Those caught without a permit should resist the temptation to make a scene: there have been documented cases of fines up to US$100 and even deportations, but those who react calmly tend to receive less outrageous penalties. Buses and hotels might have extensive checks, and individual travel, though possible, can be dangerous. Many visitors, however, report that all the talk about permit checks is just inflated hype; checkpoints can be easily avoided by getting off your bus and skirting around, and many establishments are lax about permits.

GETTING TO TIBET

The three main gateways into Tibet are Chengdu (p. 689) in Sichuan province, Xining (p. 819) or Golmud (p. 824) in Qinghai province, and Kathmandu in Nepal. Travel to Tibet from Zhongdian (p. 682) in Yunnan province is also possible. For more information, see the **Transportation** and/or **Practical Information** sections for the respective cities.

FROM SICHUAN PROVINCE. Chengdu is the most popular gateway into Tibet, especially since it's the only jump-off point that allows travelers to obtain the TTB Permit without joining a Lhasa tour. The flight (3-5 per day, Y1500) from Chengdu to Lhasa's **Gonggar Airport** is 2hr. Visitors should get the TTB permit before buying the plane ticket. Many travel agencies in Chengdu offer packaged deals (Y2500), usually including a three-day tour, TTB Permit, a one-way air ticket, transportation from Gonggar Airport to Lhasa, and several nights' accommodations. After three days in Lhasa, the tour group dissolves and travelers go their separate ways. Currently, overland routes on the Sichuan-Tibet highway are closed to foreigners.

FROM QINGHAI PROVINCE. The **Xining-Lhasa** air route (Y1610), opened in 1999, is not as cheap as it used to be, as travelers are now required to buy tour days within Lhasa. The Xining **CITS**, on Qiyi Lu, a few doors down from Xining Hotel, offers four-day tours (around Y1200) that include accommodations, transportation from the airport, and a guide. The air ticket is separate. (☎845 5326 or 368 3810. Open 9am-10pm.) The **Tibet Tourism Bureau of Xining Agency** (xīzàng zìzhìqū lǚyóujú zhù xīníng bànshìchù; 西藏自治区旅游局驻西宁办事处), Xining Hotel, Building No. 2, Rm. 2106 (☎0971 845 8701, ext. 2106), has slightly more expensive tours (Y1440) but the same general deal.

The cheapest, and in some ways the most interesting, route into Tibet is to take the train from Xining to **Golmud** (14hr., Y121-126) before embarking on a grueling 1116km **bus** journey (24-50hr.) on the Qinghai-Tibet Hwy. Standard procedure is for individual travelers to buy a tour package (Y1700) that includes a one-way bus ticket, a four-day tour in Lhasa, guide fees, and accommodations, but not meals or entrance tickets. Foreigners can only obtain permits and bus tickets through the **CITS** in the Golmud Hotel (gé'ěrmù bīnguǎn; 格尔木宾馆), 219 Kunlun Lu, 2nd fl. (☎0979 841 2764). This overland route passes through altitudes above 5000m, and travelers often report suffering from altitude sickness (see below). Bus breakdowns are also frequent.

FROM YUNNAN PROVINCE. The route from Zhongdian is steadily gaining popularity among backpackers. The usual travel restrictions apply. Weekly flights to Lhasa cost Y1380. Travelers must first obtain the TTB and join a tour. The **Long Life Tibetan Travel Service** (p. 683) arranges travel to Tibet by land (Y5000, includes driver and TTB permit) and by air (Y2450, includes plane ticket and TTB permit).

FROM NEPAL. Tourists who wish to make the overland journey from Lhasa to Kathmandu are also required to join a tour. Solo travelers can arrange a seven- to eight-day tour including a two-day guided tour in Lhasa, accommodations, car and guide fees, and all necessary permits (approx. US$500 per person). "Private" tours can be arranged for two people. However, both individual visas and private tour guides are difficult to obtain. The group visa for at least five people is the most convenient and lowers the cost of the tour, but all members of the group are required to enter and leave China together. If you want to continue traveling in China on your own, make sure you insist on an individual visa.

The seven-day overland trip is typically as follows: Kathmandu, Zhangmu/Nyalam, Tingri, Shigatse, Gyantse, and Lhasa. With 6-7hr. of driving each day (other than Lhasa, where one to two days are penciled in), actual time spent at these cities is usually limited to 1-3 hr. Tours that actually give you time to explore can cost upwards of US$1000 per person and can only be arranged for groups of five or more. Flights between Lhasa and Kathmandu add about US$275 to the cost.

The health risks of the overland route from Kathmandu into Tibet are considerable; the road passes through some very high altitudes before travelers have had sufficient time to acclimate. Anyone bent on adding Nepal to a Tibet itinerary should seriously consider arriving in Lhasa from Chengdu and departing for Kathmandu via the border at Zhangmu, not the other way around.

Citizens of Australia, Canada, Ireland, New Zealand, the UK, and the US need **visas** for stays of four days or more in Nepal. Visas can be obtained at Royal Nepalese Embassies and consulates abroad or upon arrival in the Kathmandu airport. (1st visit single-entry 60-day tourist visa US$30, multiple-entry 60-day visa US$80; subsequent visits within 150 days of the same year 30-day single- or multiple-entry visa US$30.)

HEALTH

Due to Tibet's extremely high altitude, the region poses special health risks. Travelers to Tibet should be particularly wary of Acute Mountain Sickness and giardiasis. Ultra-violet rays are also more intense, increasing the risk of **sunburn**, even in cold weather. Tibetan winters are no joke; travelers should come prepared for **severe cold and snow**, and should be aware that much of the tourist infrastructure shuts down in the winter. **Malaria** is not usually transmitted at altitudes above 2000m. Those taking an anti-malarial drug like mefloquine may want to consider not taking their doses until after the descent; some of the drug's side effects are similar to those of AMS. For more information on **sunburn** and **hypothermia**, see p. 29; for general advice about **health concerns**, see p. 27.

ACUTE MOUNTAIN SICKNESS (AMS). Many parts of the Tibetan Plateau sit more than 4000m above sea level. At this altitude, even the hardiest of travelers feel the effects of decreased air pressure and lower oxygen levels. Acute Mountain Sickness (AMS), also known as altitude sickness, typically appears about 12hr. after arrival and lasts three or four days before the body adjusts. **Rate of ascent** affects the risk, duration, and severity of AMS: risk is greatest at altitudes above 3000m if you ascend more than 300m a day. The most common symptoms of AMS are headache, insomnia, fatigue, shortness of breath, dizziness, and nausea. AMS is aggravated by dehydration, alcohol, and other depressants, and overexertion.

The best way to alleviate mild AMS (headache, vomiting, fatigue) is to stay hydrated, avoid sedatives (including alcohol), and take it easy. Travelers should consider budgeting a few days in Lhasa in order to get used to the altitude. Mild symptoms of AMS can be treated by normal over-the-counter pain relievers; some physicians prescribe **Diamox** (acetazolamide) to stimulate respiration. Moderate AMS (persistent vomiting and severe headache) is sometimes treated with supplemental oxygen and steroids. Those with moderate AMS also suffer from ataxia, or decreased coordination. If you can't walk a straight line, heel to toe, an immediate descent of 300-700m is recommended to ensure that symptoms don't get worse.

Severe AMS is a life-threatening condition. There are two types of severe AMS: **High Altitude Pulmonary Edema** (HAPE) and **High Altitude Cerebral Edema** (HACE). HAPE is caused by fluid build-up in the lungs; symptoms include blue or pale lips and face and gurgling respiration or coughing. HACE is caused by swelling in the brain; symptoms include disorientation, memory loss, ataxia, and hallucination. Severe fatigue and shortness of breath are symptoms of both. Travelers with severe AMS can slip into coma or even die. Those who suspect that they may have it should descend 600-1300m and seek immediate medical assistance.

GIARDIASIS. Commonly called **giardia**, giardiasis is caused by the protozoan parasite *giardia lamblia*. This parasite is present in untreated water, particularly in cold and mountainous regions. Travelers should avoid unboiled tap water and raw food washed with unboiled tap water. Swimming in lakes and streams can also lead to infection. Symptoms of giardiasis include diarrhea, abdominal cramps, and nausea; they usually appear one to two weeks after infection and last for four to six weeks. Giardia is treatable by anti-amoebic drugs such as **Flagyl** (metronizade), which is usually available by prescription only.

TIBET

HISTORY

EARLY HISTORY

According to legend, the Tibetan people descended from the Bodhisattva of Compassion, Avalokiteshvara, who took the form of a monkey demon and proceeded to have "relations" with the Goddess Tara. Fossils and records, however, hold that they are descendents of the **Qiang** people, who are mentioned in Chinese records as early as 200 BC. A Tibetan state didn't emerge until some time around 127 BC, when an Indian king came to Tibet. Twelve Bön priests, believing that he had descended from heaven, named him king. For the next few centuries, Tibet was a fairly uninteresting home to squabbling princedoms and little else.

In the 7th century AD, a boy of 13 named **Songsten Gampo** became king of Tibet. He is widely known as the man who unified Tibet; his empire extended far past the boundaries of modern Tibet, and included parts of Xinjiang, Gansu, Qinghai, Sichuan, and Yunnan. He also married a Tang-Dynasty princess, Wencheng, in exchange for diplomatic ties. This is not to say, of course, that China and Tibet became fast friends. In 783, Tibetans sacked Chang'an (modern-day Xi'an).

In the 9th century, struggles over succession to the throne and religion divided Tibet. Introduced to Tibet in AD 173, Buddhism was steadily gaining followers, but many in Tibet's ruling elite practiced the indigenous religion, Bön. The Bön Dynasty ended when a Buddhist monk assassinated the king. For the next 200 years, political authority languished as religion flourished. Missionaries flooded in from India, monasteries (including the one at **Sakya,** p. 837) were founded, and lamas began to consolidate political power.

RED HAT, YELLOW HAT

Disillusioned with the infighting and mysticism of Tibetan Buddhism under the Sakya lamas, in the early 15th century **Tsong Khapa** founded the Gelug school, emphasizing study and monastic discipline. His followers wore yellow hats to distinguish themselves from the other, red-hatted monks, earning the name "Yellow Hat" school. Gelug's popularity did not inspire affection in the other schools of Tibetan Buddhism, who happened at the time to be allied with Tibet's political rulers. As a result, the next two centuries were consumed by sectarian violence.

The Gelug school had been using reincarnation as a method of succession since the late 15th century, when the founder of Tashilhunpo Monastery (p. 860) prophesied that he would be reincarnated in the form of a young boy. The third in this line, Sonam Gyatso, was granted the title of Dalai Lama by the Mongolian leader Altyn Khan. In Mongolian, *dalai* means "ocean-wide," referring to the scope of the Dalai Lama's knowledge. Interestingly, the succeeding Dalai Lama was discovered to be reincarnated in the grandson of Altyn Khan.

Over time, the Gelug school and the Mongols developed a fairly co-dependent relationship. When the Gelug faced increasing aggression from other schools of Tibetan Buddhism, they went to the Mongols for help. In the mid-17th century, the Mongols, with the help of Gelug monks, gained military control of Tibet and executed the king. The Mongols then gave supreme authority of all Tibet to the Dalai Lama and his chief steward, who went about persecuting religious rivals and consolidating land, resources, and influence. The Mongols decided that they liked their new home, and their leader declared himself king. The Dalai Lama, however, still held the real reins of power.

In 1717, Tibet and the Gelug school were once again in disarray. The 6th Dalai Lama had renounced his monastic vows and taken to writing love poems and carousing with young girls. The Mongolian king, Lhabsang Khan, decided that maybe he'd like to have some real power. He allied with some Tibetan aristocrats, executed the regent, and took control of Tibet. Opting for the tried-and-true strategy, the Gelug school went again to the Mongols for help, but this time they approached a different tribe. It happened that this tribe, the Dzungars, were not on the best of terms with the Qing Dynasty. So when the Dzungars took Lhasa, the Qing reacted quickly to curb Mongolian influence. In 1720 they invaded, kicked out the Mongols, and established an overlordship that would last until the fall of the Qing in 1911. Under Chinese **"suzerainty,"** the Tibetans governed internal affairs on their own and the Dalai Lama maintained peaceful relations with China.

SUZERAINTY AND AUTONOMY

In the mid-1800s, Tibet, like much of China, was closed to Western trade, presenting an irresistible challenge to the British. Their first attempts to enter the region were repelled, but in 1904, the British military marched into Lhasa, slapped indemnities on the Tibetans, and forced the 13th Dalai Lama to flee to Mongolia. Britain and Tibet then signed the Anglo-Tibetan Convention of 1904, which declared Tibet a British protectorate. Realizing the importance of Chinese trade relations, the British changed their minds and drew up the Anglo-Chinese Convention in 1906, reaffirming China's control over Tibet. The Qing promptly turned previously autonomous Tibetan areas into Chinese states and sent several thousand troops to Lhasa, forcing the 13th Dalai Lama once more into exile.

After the Chinese revolution of 1911, the indignant Tibetans (led by the newly returned Dalai Lama) declared independence and expelled Chinese residents. Despite the Republic of China's 1912 declaration that Tibet (along with Mongolia and Xinjiang) was an important part of China, nominally reincorporating it into political China, Tibet enjoyed complete sovereignty over the next 40 years. Meanwhile, the 13th Dalai Lama's attempts at reform and modernization were rejected by the conservative aristocracy, and Tibet remained pious but impoverished. Tibet's neutrality during WWII did not help its low international profile; when Chiang Kai-shek declared Tibet a province of Nationalist China, the victorious Allied powers didn't protest. After the PRC victory in 1949, however, Tibet began to face real problems—Mao had set his sights on it.

UNDER CHINESE RULE (1949-PRESENT)

In October 1950, PLA troops invaded Tibet and routed the Tibetan army. Tibet buckled under military pressure and signed the Seventeen-Point Agreement, acknowledging Chinese sovereignty while effectively retaining cultural and religious autonomy. The CCP collectivized Tibetan areas of western Sichuan and Qinghai, but for the most part left Tibet alone. In the mid-1950s, Tibetan rebels engaged the Chinese in a guerrilla war in southern Tibet. By 1959, the rebels had sparked a mass rebellion. It failed, however, and the Dalai Lama was forced to flee to India (accompanied by relatives, ministers, supporters, CIA-trained rebels, and much of the country's gold reserves). In turn, China renounced the Seventeen-Point Agreement and declared martial law in Tibet.

The CCP moved quickly to consolidate power in Tibet, replacing the traditional ruling class with Beijing-appointed officials and Tibetan Communist cadres. After 1959, the Chinese government pursued the same economic programs in Tibet as it did in the rest of China. The results were disastrous. The standard of living in Tibet fell sharply, and thousands became victims of religious persecution. During the Cultural Revolution, Red Guards demolished monasteries and religious relics, nuns and monks were forced to marry, and thousands were sent to prison camps. Although there are no exact figures, over a million Tibetans died in the turmoil.

TIBET

After the rise of Deng Xiaoping in 1979, liberal officials acknowledged past mistakes in Tibet and urged "ethnic sensitivity." Monasteries were rebuilt, economic activity was normalized, and the region was opened to tightly regulated tourism. Nominal religious practice was permitted as long as religious leaders stayed out of politics. In the 1980s, Tibetans began to demand greater political and religious freedom, supported by the **Tibetan government-in-exile,** based in Dharamsala, India. The 14th Dalai Lama visited the US to further his cause and garner support, while Tibetans in Lhasa continued to keep hope alive. On October 1, 1987, a group of monks staged a demonstration to support the Dalai Lama. The police arrested and beat the monks, sparking full-scale riots. Over the next two years, Lhasa would see three more riots before the Chinese government declared martial law in 1989.

Today, monasteries are tightly monitored, and monks are required to undergo political education and swear allegiance to the Chinese state. As China struggles to bring Tibet to heel, the Tibetan Government-in-Exile in Dharamsala works to rally support for a free Tibet from abroad. The government-in-exile is a democratic, constitutional body ruling over the 131,000 Tibetans currently in exile. In the past decade the Dalai Lama has succeeded in drawing world attention to his homeland, but the pleas of American celebrities have little pull over the Chinese government, which has not backed down from its hard-line policies. The display of Dalai Lama photographs has been forbidden since 1994; in June 2001 a woman was sentenced to six years in prison for watching a video of the Dalai Lama. The situation is still tense—staggering numbers of PSB officers are posted in Lhasa, and the Chinese government is suspicious of everyone, including tourists.

PEOPLE

ETHNIC COMPOSITION. About 6.3 million Tibetans live in China, with 2.1 million in the Tibet Autonomous Region, and 4.2 million in Gansu, Sichuan, Yunnan, and the ethnically Tibetan Qinghai (formerly part of Tibet). Since the 1950s, these regions have seen an influx of Han and Hui Chinese, including merchants, workers and peasants from economically depressed areas, government-sponsored cadres, and military personnel. Most Tibetans support themselves through agriculture, nomadic herding, or commerce.

LANGUAGE. Tibetan is related to Chinese (both are members of the Sino-Tibetan language family), but the two languages are wholly distinct. The Tibetan alphabet, introduced around AD 600, is derived from and similar to Indian writing systems, and is read from left to right. Regional dialects vary widely; the central Tibetan dialect is regarded as the standard. For useful phrases in Tibetan, see p. 878.

FOOD. Tibetan **cuisine,** likewise, would never be mistaken for Chinese. The staple is roasted barley flour *(tsampa)*, mixed with water or tea to form a dough that is the foundation of most Tibetan diets. The yak, a pungent, hairy creature well-suited to high altitudes, is also essential to Tibetan food, which uses yak butter, yak meat, yak milk—basically any yak part or derivation thereof. A slaughtered yak is bound to be a well-utilized one. Regional beverages include yak-butter tea and barley beer, known as *chang*. Wheat, mutton, and pork are also widely consumed; favorite dishes include *tukpa* (noodle soups) and *momo* (fried or steamed dumplings). By virtue of the harsh climate, the Tibetan menu is heavily meat-centric, but Tibetans will do their best to cater to vegetarians, though the results may not be particularly tasty or nutritious. *Momo* and *tukpa* can both be made vegetarian, and yogurt is delicious in the summer.

The cheapest restaurants in Lhasa (p. 842) and—to a lesser extent—along the Friendship Highway (p. 853) are Tibetan establishments with neither English nor Chinese menus. Communication can sometimes be difficult; the following chart lists some of the most popular dishes along with approximate prices.

DISH	TIBETAN NAME	TIBETAN SCRIPT	PRICE
sweet tea	ja ngarmo	ཇ་ ཨ་ངར་མོ་	Y1 per glass; Y4 for a small thermos
home-brewed barley beer	chang	ཆང་	Y2 per liter
yak-butter tea	poja	བོད་ཇ་	Y1 per glass; Y3 for a small thermos
Tibetan noodles with soup	tukpa	ཐུག་པ་	Y3-5 per bowl
fried potatoes	shogo ngopa	ཞོགོག་ངོས་པ་	Y7-10 per plate
rice	dray	འབྲས་	Y1-3 per bowl
fried yak meat	yaksha ngopa	གཡག་ཤ་	Y5-8
meat and rice	shamdray	ཤ་འབྲས་	Y10
yak jerkey	sha kampo	ཤ་	Y3
dumplings	momo	མོག་ མོག་	Y10
yogurt	sho	ཞོ་	Y1-2 per bowl

RELIGION

Few cultures on earth invest as much in religion as the Tibetans do. In Tibet, politics, art, science, and literature all derive from and support spiritual faith. Prior to the Cultural Revolution, many Tibetans based their livelihoods around Buddhist monasteries or nunneries. Fifty years of Chinese intervention and policy, however, have succeeded at times in dampening public religious practice, but attempts at dislodging the core of Tibetans' faith have been repeatedly frustrated.

BÖN

Before Buddhism, there was Bön. According to legend, Bön was founded by Tönpa Shenrab, an enlightened teacher who studied in heaven. Believed to be the first faith of Tibet, Bön was a highly mystical religion that incorporated exorcisms, sacrifice, and demon lore into its mythology. After Buddhism gained popularity in the 8th century AD, most Bön institutions were persecuted. Today's Bön has assimilated itself, and the Dalai Lama considers it to be the fifth school of Tibetan Buddhism. Many of Tibetan Buddhism's minor deities and its tradition of religious oracles were also adopted from Bön. A more authentic Bön can still be found in remote villages across the Tibetan-Himalaya world, and both modern Bön and Tibetan Buddhism retain strong influences from Tibet's earlier, indigenous faith.

᠊ᠡ BUDDHISM

᠊ᠡism integrates what it views as the three systems of Indian Bud-
, the "Lesser Vehicle" of individual practice; **Mahayana,** the "Great
᠊ᡄltruistic practice; and **Vajrayana,** the "Diamond Vehicle." Also known
᠊ᡄic Buddhism, the Diamond Vehicle is responsible for most of Tibetan Bud-
᠊ᡄnism's unique features and offers an explosion of art forms, rituals, and medita-
tions. All of these are presented as techniques through which the practitioner can
attain enlightenment, first by calming the mind and then by saving other beings
from the sorrows of the world.

Tibetan Buddhism is comprised of four **schools.** The oldest, **Nyingma** ("Old Translation") traces itself back to **Guru Rinpoche,** the 8th-century master credited with
converting Tibet's wild spirits to Buddhism, thus removing major obstacles to the
flourishing of the new religion in the Himalayas. To this day, the Nyingma retains
much of the charisma and creativity of its founder. The **Kagyu** ("Instruction Lin-
eage") is comprised of several sub-schools, all of which originated in the teachings
of the 11th-century **Milarepa,** Tibet's great saint. Kagyu practitioners are known for
their great skill in meditation. Founded in the 11th century, the **Sakya** ("Gray
Earth") school enjoyed a period of political power and brought Buddhism to Mongolia. With its gray earth walls, the monastery where Sakya was founded gave the
school its name and also produced some of Tibet's finest scholars, including the
13th-century **Sakya Pandita.** Famous for its strict ethical discipline, the **Gelug** ("System of Virtue") school (p. 832) is the one to which the Dalai Lama adheres. It controlled Tibetan politics from the 17th century until the Chinese takeover and is
Tibet's youngest branch of Buddhism.

Tibet's most beloved saint is **Avalokiteshvara** (in Tibetan, *Chenrezig;* in Chinese,
Guanyin), the *bodhisattva* of compassion and love. Avalokiteshvara (female in
the Chinese conception) and his partner, the goddess **Tara,** are seen as the progen-
itors of the Tibetan race and the special protectors of Tibet. Avalokiteshvara is
born in human form as successive **Dalai Lamas.** *Om mani peme hung* is the most
common prayer of Tibetan pilgrims. The prayer of Avalokiteshvara is a plea for
compassion in the world, accompanied by fingering prayer beads, spinning prayer
wheels, offering butter lamps, and prostrating to or circumambulating holy places.

Tibetan monasteries are headed by teachers called **lamas,** distinct from ordinary monks and nuns. Lamas are either individuals who proved themselves in
this lifetime through outstanding study and meditation, or have been recognized
to be the reincarnation of an earlier lama, through the visions of other masters,
astrological consultations, and other tests. Reincarnated lamas pick up the work
and position of their predecessor, thus lending monasteries a continuity of
vision and direction. The Dalai Lama and the **Panchen Lama** of the Gelug school
and the **Karmapa** of the Kagyu school are three of Tibet's most revered and
beloved reincarnated lamas.

FESTIVALS AND HOLIDAYS

Most Tibetan festivals are local affairs, unique to a village or region and buoyed by
strong community spirit. Exact festival dates vary annually based on the lunar calendar. National festivals are mostly Buddhist holidays, but a few display lingering
traces of Tibet's distant past. Various *tauka* festivals take place around the year,
when *tangkas* (scroll paintings several stories tall), are displayed at various monasteries. *Tauka* festivals occur in early July at Tashi Lhunpo, late July in Ganden,
and mid-August in Drepung and Sera.

TIBET

MONTH	FESTIVAL	DETAILS
mid-Feb.	Ghost-Exorcising Festival	Tibetans carry burning straw into each room of their houses in order to cast out evil spirits.
Feb. 9, 2005	Losar (Tibetan New Year)	The old year is purged on the eve. At daybreak, families visit temples and shrines to light incense and make offerings. Festivities can last 2 weeks.
Feb. 23, 2005	Butter Lamp Festival	Held to celebrate Buddha's victory in a religious debate. Tibetans observe this festival by making and displaying butter lamp sculptures.
Feb. 15-25, 2005	Monlam Chenmo (Great Prayer Festival)	This 2-week traditional festival celebrated the submission of the state to religion; lamas from Lhasa's 3 major temples gather and hold services. The Chinese government has placed significant restrictions on the celebration of this festival.
May 9-23, 2005	Saga Dawa	Saga Dawa takes place in the 4th and holiest month of the Tibetan calendar and celebrates the anniversary of Budda's birth, enlightenment, and death. The festival peaks on the 15th day.
June	Gyantse Horse Racing	Held in Gyantse since 1408, this festival features horse races and archery contests.
Sept. 3-10, 2005	Shoton (Yogurt) Festival	Originally, this was the day on the Tibetan calendar when meditating monks emerged from the monasteries to receive gifts of yogurt (in Tibetan, *sho*). Since the 17th century, however, this festival has also been known as the Tibetan Opera Festival; each year, opera troupes perform in Norbulingka, in Lhasa.
Sept. 3, 2005	Bathing Festival	Tibetans, believing the water is at its purest during this week, bathe in rivers or creeks to stave off illness.
Dec. 26, 2005	Death of Tsong Khapa	Tibetans honor the founder of the Gelug school by lighting yak-butter lamps and saying prayers.

ཨྫ་ LHASA 拉萨 ☎ 0891

Buried within the sprawling and very Chinese "new Lhasa," Tibet's age-old spiritual faith continues to radiate from the region's political and religious center. The Potala Palace surveys the city from high on Marpo Hill, its white walls and golden roofs silhouetted by layers of mountains. Narrow gray and maroon alleys wind their way throughout the city, opening onto courtyards and all leading to the Jokhang Temple, heart of the city and the holiest place in Tibet. These days, the Potala's power has been replaced by that of the Communist party, the Dalai Lama no longer looks out upon his city, and the number of monks in the monasteries is now strictly regulated. Nevertheless, Lhasa has somehow retained its identity as the spiritual keystone of Tibet. Amid the cement-block roads, commercial districts, neon TV towers, and the ever-watchful eyes of the PSB, Lhasa treads precariously into an uncertain future, holding onto the intense devotional energy that has always remained the Tibetan people's core of strength.

▐ TRANSPORTATION

Flights: Lhasa Gonggar Airport (lāsà gònggā jīchǎng; 拉萨贡嘎机场; ☎ 618 2221) is 95km southwest, the greatest distance between a city and its airport in the world. An **airport bus** runs from Gonggar Airport to Lhasa (1½hr., around 3-4 per day, Y30). Buses also run to Gonggar (1½hr.; daily 6am, 1, 5pm; Y30 and Tu, Th, Sa 10am; Y35) from Lhasa. **Land cruisers** (1½hr., Y400-500) connect the city center to the airport. People looking to share a taxi or land cruiser to the airport often post notices on the

TIBET

boards at the Yak, Banak Shol, Pentoc, Kirey, and Snowland Hotels. **CAAC Ticket Office,** 1 Niangre Lu (☎683 3446, after-hours 682 2393), books flights 15 days in advance. Open daily 9am-8:30pm. **China Southwest Airlines** serves Tibet. To: **Beijing** (daily, Y2430); **Chengdu** (3-4 per day, Y1500); **Chongqing** (Tu, Th, Sa; Y1630); **Guangzhou** (M and F, Y2500); **Kunming** (F, Y1960); **Xi'an** (M and F, Y1650); **Xining** (Su and W, Y1600). International flights to **Kathmandu, Nepal** (Tu and Sa, Y2290).

Buses: Lhasa Long-Distance Bus Station (☎634 9193), on the corner of Chingdol Lam and Minzhu Lu (enter on Chingdol Lam), in the southwestern section of Lhasa. Undercover PSB officers check for permits. To: **Chengdu** (4 days, 2 per day, Y500); **Chongqing** (daily, Y560); **Golmud** (daily, Y210); **Gyantse** (3 per month, Y230); **Lanzhou** (daily, Y380); **Nakehu** via **Damxung** (3 per day, Y63-100); **Shigatse** (5hr., 5 per day, Y38-80); **Tsetang** (4hr., many per day, Y40) via **Samye Monastery's** ferry crossing; **Xi'an** (daily, Y480); **Xining** (daily, Y340).

Local Transportation: Minibuses run 7am-9pm. Fare Y2. Minibus #3 runs the length of Linkuo Lu; #301 and 302 run from Ramoche Temple to Drepang Monastery; #503 runs from Ramoche Temple to Sera Monastery.

Taxis: Taxis to anywhere in the city Y10 (north of the Kyichu River, excluding Sera and Drepung monasteries); bargain for destinations beyond city limits. **Tricycles** transport 2 passengers. From the end of Beijing Dong Lu to the Potala Palace (3-4km) Y5.

Bike Rental: The **Snowland** and **Yak Hotels** rent bikes. Y3 per hr. Deposit Y300.

◼◼ ◼◼ ORIENTATION AND PRACTICAL INFORMATION

At 3700m above sea level, Lhasa sits on the lowland northern bank of the **Lhasa** or **Kyichu River.** Lhasa's jurisdiction extends over 29,052km^2 of terrain, but its city center spans a mere 20km^2, which visitors can easily navigate with a map and their own two feet. The city center is bounded to the north by **Lingkor Jang Lam** (**Linkuo Bei Lu;** 林廓北路) and to the south by **Chingdol Lam** (**Jinzhu Lu;** 金珠路). **Beijing Lu** (**Peching Lam;** 北京路), Lhasa's main east-west axis, runs from the Potala Palace in the west past tourist services in the heart of the city, a predominantly Tibetan area that surrounds **Jokhang Temple** and the **Barkhor Market.** Most tourists head to this lively, colorful quarter in search of Tibetan culture, bountiful travel agencies, Western-style restaurants, and cheap accommodations.

TOURIST AND FINANCIAL SERVICES

Tourist Offices: Lhasa Tourism Bureau (lāsàshì lǚyóu jú; 拉萨市旅游局), 33 Jiangsu Lu (☎632 3632, English 634 2884), does not process visas or entry permits, but arbitrates between tourists and travel agencies or hotels when necessary. Open M-F 9am-12:30pm and 3:30-6pm.

Travel Agencies: The **Barkhor Market** area has many agencies, most of which are based in local hotels and can arrange trips, especially short ones. Prices vary more than quality; shop around. Anyone renting a land cruiser should look at the vehicle beforehand.

CITS, 208 Beijing Xi Lu (☎683 6626; fax 683 6315), next to the Lhasa Hotel in the far west of town. Open daily 9am-1pm and 3:30-6:30pm. CITS only helps those who are part of a tour. **Shigatse Travels** (rìkāzé guóji lǚxíngshè; 日喀则国际旅行社 ; ☎633 0489), a subsidiary branch of CITS in the Yak Hotel, can reliably arrange visas, permits, guides, and jeeps to local destinations like Namtso and Samye. They only arrange trips out west or to the Nepalese border for travelers who arrive in Tibet on a Shigatse Travel tour. Open daily 9am-1pm and 3-6:30pm. Both of these CITS branches may charge much more than other travel agencies.

F.I.T. Travel Agency (☎634 4397), next to Pentoc Guesthouse on Zangyiyuan Dong Lu. Open daily 9am-midnight. A 2nd **branch** (☎634 9239) in Snowland Hotel has the same hours. These 2 offices are the most common agents for trips to Namtso, Samye, and destinations along the Friendship Hwy.

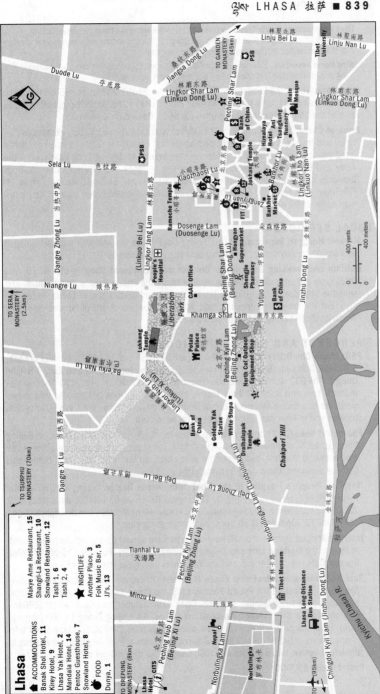

Lhasa

▲ ACCOMMODATIONS
Banak Shol Hotel, **11**
Kirey Hotel, **9**
Lhasa Yak Hotel, **2**
Mandala Hotel, **14**
Pentoc Guesthouse, **7**
Snowland Hotel, **8**

Makye Ame Restaurant, **15**
Shangri-La Restaurant, **10**
Snowland Restaurant, **12**
Tashi 1, **6**
Tashi 2, **4**

✦ FOOD
Dunya, **1**

★ NIGHTLIFE
Another Place, **3**
Folk Music Bar, **5**
JJ's, **13**

TIBET

Tibet International Sports Travel (☎633 1421), in the Himalaya Hotel (xīmǎlāyǎ fàndiàn; 喜马拉雅饭店), 6 Lingkor Shar Lam (Lingkuo Dong Lu), is considerably more expensive and caters to those interested in hard-core, action-packed vacations.

Wind Horse Adventure, 1 Bei Minzu Lu (☎683 3009; www.tibetwindhorse.com), specializes in rafting and trekking trips and offers pricey but high-quality services.

Consulate: Nepal, 13 Luobulinka (Norbulingka) Lu (☎682 2881; fax 683 6890), close to the Lhasa Hotel; take bus #3. 60-day tourist visas Y255. Instant processing. Visas also at the border crossing at Zhangmu (p. 865). Open daily 10am-noon.

Bank of China: The main branch, 28 Lingkor Nub Lam (Linkuo Xi Lu), exchanges currency and traveler's checks. Credit card advances. The **ATM** is finicky; it may be safer to hand your card to the teller for a fee. Another **branch** on Beijing Dong Lu, between the Kirey and Banak Shol hotels, only exchanges currency and traveler's checks. Both branches open summer M-F 9am-1pm and 3:30-6:30pm, Sa-Su 10am-3pm; winter M-F 9:30am-1pm and 3:30-6pm, Sa-Su 10am-5pm. Authorized hotels also exchange foreign currency for a fee.

LOCAL SERVICES

Market: Hongyan Supermarket, on Beijing Dong Lu, is stocked with endless supplies and snacks for any outing. Bring your own bag (or buy one for Y0.6).

Outdoor and Trekking Gear: North Col Outdoor Equipment Shop (☎681 6379, ext. 0891), on the left side of the square that faces the Potala Palace. Rents, buys, and sells the best-quality gear (Ozark, Mt. Hardward, and North Face) in Lhasa. Prices are high, but still lower than prices abroad. Much cheaper knock-offs of famous brands fill shops on Beijing Dong Lu and in the Barkhor area.

EMERGENCY AND COMMUNICATIONS

PSB: Lhasa City Office, 8 Lingkuo Bei Lu (☎624 8154 or 624 8012). Another **branch,** 1 Barkhor Nub Lam (Bakuo Xi Jie) (☎632 3393). **Division of Entry and Exit,** 4 Beijing Dong Lu (☎632 4528). Open daily summer 9am-12:30pm and 3:30-6pm; winter 9:30am-1pm and 3:30-6:30pm. Issues travel permits. Does not process visa extensions; do this before entering Tibet or through a travel agency. The travel agency that brought you to Tibet can also help get travel permits (p. 14).

Pharmacy: Shengjie Pharmacy (shèngjié yàoshì; 圣洁药市 ; ☎633 0766), on Beijing Dong Lu, 1st fl. of Qujiwei Bldg. (区计委楼), the municipal city planning office, a few blocks toward Barkhor, away from the post office, on the right. Western, Tibetan, and Chinese medicine. Open daily 9am-midnight.

Hospital: People's Hospital of the Tibet Autonomous Region (xīzàng zìzhì qū rénmín yīyuàn; 西藏自治区人民医院), 18 Lingkuo Bei Lu (☎633 2462, emergency 632 2200). Specializes in treating altitude sickness. Many doctors speak English. Open daily 9am-12:30pm and 3:30-6pm. 24hr. emergency care.

Internet Access: Dozens of small Internet cafes have sprung up around the major guesthouses in the **Barkhor Lam** and Beijing Lu areas. Don't pay more than Y5 per hr. **Intelligence Cafe,** next to Pentoc, and the **Yak Hotel** both have Internet for Y5 per hr.

Post and Telecommunications: Lhasa City Post Office, on Beijing Zhong Lu (Peching Kyil Lam), just before the Potala Palace. EMS and Poste Restante. International packages may need to go through customs. Open daily summer 9am-8pm; winter 9:30am-6:30pm. **Lhasa City Telecommunications Office,** 64 Beijing Zhong Lu (Peching Kyil Lam). From the post office, walk a few doors away from the Potala. Many small telephone offices in tourist areas offer IDD service for lower prices. An office a few doors to the left of Pentoc has 6 booths with IDD. Calls to the US Y3.8 per min.

Postal Code: 850000.

ACCOMMODATIONS

Intense competition for foreign business has driven dorm rates down to Y20-30.
Most hotels have roof decks, balconies, and similar rooms; the quality of attached
restaurants is one way to distinguish the six guesthouses that line **Beijing Dong Lu**
(Peching Shar Lam) and **Zangyiyuan Dong Lu,** near the Barkhor Market. A brand-
new **hostel (HI)** has made it to town, located in the southwest on Lingyu Bei Lu, by
the university. During the high season, rooms are difficult to come by, and travelers take what they can get. Unless otherwise stated, all listings have IDD service at
the reception, 24hr. hot water, and luggage storage.

> **TIP** **NO ROOM FOR YOU!** Tour groups commonly take up many of the nicer
> budget hotels in Tibet, like the Yak in Lhasa. If you find a room in such an estab-
> lishment, prepare to be kicked out by a tour group from time to time. Pentoc
> Guesthouse often has its guests playing musical rooms for unclear reasons. Per-
> haps the biggest difficulties come in late July and Aug. when tourism peaks, and
> rooms can be almost impossible to find if not booked in advance. Look for late-
> comers sleeping in the restaurant of your guesthouse.

Lhasa Yak Hotel (lāsà yà bīnguǎn; 拉萨亚宾馆), 100 Beijing Dong Lu (☎632 3496).
Lovely Tibetan decorations and clean rooms facing a pleasant courtyard make the Yak
possibly the best Lhasa has to offer in this price range. Friendly staff. In-house Shigatse
Travel Agency. Restaurant attached. Bikes Y3 per hr. Internet Y5 per hr. 6- to 10-bed
dorms Y30-50; doubles with bath Y200, with breakfast Y260. ●

Pentoc Guesthouse (pánduō lǚguǎn; 攀多旅馆), 5 Zangyiyuan Dong Lu (☎632 6686),
a few doors down from Tashi 1 Restaurant. With outdoor staircases and balconies, this
bright, airy guesthouse run by Christian missionaries is often packed with Western travelers of all ages. Spotless rooms with soft beds, though service could be better. Immaculate communal baths. Laundry Y20 per bag. English movies nightly. 3-bed dorms Y30;
singles Y50; doubles Y80. ●

Banak Shol Hotel (bāxuě bīnguǎn; 八雪宾馆), 43 Beijing Dong Lu (☎632 3829), a
20min. walk up Beijing Dong Lu from Zangyiyuan Dong Lu. The oldest (est. 1985) and
most distant of Lhasa's 6 main guesthouses. Popular with Chinese and Tibetan youth,
this huge hotel has a big courtyard and plain but pleasant rooms. Ladder-like stairs. Toilets on every fl., showers on 1st fl. Free safety deposit. F.I.T. office on 1st fl. 10-bed
dorms Y12; 4- to 5-bed Y25; 2-bed Y60; singles Y30; doubles with bath Y150. ●

Mandala Hotel (mǎnzhāi jiǔdiàn; 满斋酒店), 31 Bakuo Nan Jie (☎632 4783 or 633
8940), on the right side of Barkhor Market when you face the Jokhang Temple. Great
location, but lack of dorms means fewer opportunities for backpackers to exchange
information. Bright, shiny, wood-paneled rooms have A/C, heaters, and TV. On-site restaurant (dishes Y12-25) open 24hr. The nearby Makye Ame Restaurant (see **Food,** p.
842) lures many a guest away. Singles Y180; doubles with bath Y260. ❸

Kirey Hotel (jírì lǚguǎn; 吉日旅馆), 105 Beijing Dong Lu (☎632 3462). Backpackers
and tour groups throng to the Tibetan-style rooms, large courtyard, and mountain views.
Tashi 2 and Shangri-La Restaurants onsite. Spotty toilets and somewhat inaccessible
common showers. Hot water 8am-10pm. Free laundry. Curfew midnight. 9-bed dorms
Y25; 3-bed Y30; doubles Y50, with bath Y130. ●

Snowland Hotel (xuěyù bīnguǎn; 雪域宾馆), 4 Zangyiyuan Dong Lu (☎632 3687), on
the left just before the Barkhor Market. Well-equipped and conveniently located. Clean,
small rooms and thin mattresses. Bike rental Y2 per hr. Hotel restaurant open daily
7am-11pm. F.I.T. Travel Service on 2nd fl. 5- to 10-bed dorms Y25; doubles Y40 per
bed, with bath Y260; triples Y30 per bed. ●

WHICH SIDE OF THE TRACKS?

n June 2001, China began work ɔn a railroad linking Tibet to the ʿest of China—an engineering feat ฺqual in scale to the Three Gorges Ɔam. It's no small task to lay .956km of track across some of he Earth's most forbidding terrain ฺt elevations of 3960-5070m. ʿhis daunting project will cost an ฺstimated US$3 billion. Slated for ฺompletion in July 2007, just in ime for the 2008 Olympics, the Ɔinghai-Tibet Railroad saw its first ɔcomotive in March 2004, carry-ng supplies further down the line.

With 16 trains planned per Ɔay, the Qinghai-Tibet line will ฺurely bring change. Scientists ฺvorry about the environmental mpact of the rail on the fragile ʿighland plateaus, home to the ฺndangered Tibetan antelope. ฺibetans fear that they may be ɔverwhelmed by Han Chinese mmigration, much in the manner ɔf ethnic populations in Inner ฺMongolia and Xinjiang.

Still, most Tibetans, even crit-cs of Beijing policy, do welcome he economic gains the railroad ฺvill bring, especially given that ʿibet has long lagged behind in Ɔhina's economic boom. But, like ฺo many developments facing ฺnodern Tibet, the issue is not so ฺnuch the railroad itself, but the ฺquestions it poses to both Bejing ฺnd Tibet: who should be direct-ng the region's economic devel-ɔpment? And who should be ɔenefiting?

▣ FOOD

The "Land of Yaks" extends onto your dinner plate, but after you catch a whiff of your food, it may just stay there. Adventurous travelers can try a variety of **yak** dishes and products in Lhasa, including yak *momo* (dumplings), stewed yak, stir-fried yak, bar-becued yak, and of course, the wildly popular Tibetan equivalent to coffee, yak-butter tea. Used in numerous dishes, *tsampa* (barley flour) is a staple of the local diet, and *tsampa* beer is a must on festive occasions. The universal staple, wide-cut french fries (Y1 for a small bag) are also available.

Due to the recent mass influx of foreigners into Lhasa, dozens of restaurants offering Tibetan, Indian, and Western dishes have sprung up in and around **Barkhor Market.** The food is tasty, but prices are fairly high; it can easily become a habit to drop Y20-40 per meal while lingering in Lhasa. For cheap and authen-tic **Tibetan** food, head into the small streets and alleys in the Tibetan neighborhoods around Barkhor. Chi-nese food here is quite expensive, but prices are more palatable as you move away from the tourist areas around Barkhor. Steer to the **nightmarket** on Dosenge Lam, between Beijing Lu and Lingkor Lam, for filling Muslim kebabs and a wide assortment of tempura-style vegetables, both Y1 per stick. (Open daily 7:30-11:30pm.) On Lingkor Lam, between Dosenge Lam and Niangre Lu, there are at least five **supermarkets,** a great place to stock up on bread, dried meat, and peanut butter for trekking. Most are open 9am-7:30pm.

▨ **Tashi 1** (☎ 633 7303), on the corner of Zangyiyuan Dong Lu at Beijing Dong Lu. Wildly popular with backpackers. The very filling yak burger comes with fries and veggies (Y18). Their burrito-style *bobi* (Y10-13), cheesecake (Y6), and fried apple *momo* (Y12) are highly recom-mended. Open daily summer 7am-11:30pm; winter 8:30am-11pm. The less popular but more intimate **Tashi 2,** in the Kirey Hotel, has the same menu, with big-ger portions. Open Mar.-Oct. daily 7am-11pm. ❶

Makye Ame Restaurant (☎ 632 4455), on the 2nd fl. of the yellow building in the southeast corner of the Barkhor Market, behind the Jokhang Temple. This bohemian eatery takes its name from one of the sixth Dalai Lama's favorite poems. Dainty portions and high prices don't keep budget travelers from the extensive menu of international foods and the chance to kick back on the rooftop patio and to gaze down at the foot traffic circling the Jokhang. Dishes Y15-40. Open daily 9am-midnight. ❷

Dunya (☎ 633 3374), attached to the Yak Hotel. Boasting a full bar complete with min-eral-water ice cubes and homemade cow cheese, Dunya is a haven for the yak-weary traveler. Standard, well-prepared international dishes Y15-40. Drinks Y30-90. ❷

Naga (☎ 632 7509), a few doors down from Pentoc Guesthouse. With delectable French cuisine, fabulous chocolate mousse (Y12), a full bar, and a cat for company, Naga is a sophisticated way to pass any evening. Open 8am until last customer leaves. ❷

Shangri-La Restaurant, in the Kirey Hotel. Full-out Tibetan decor right down to carpeted seats. Cheap Tibetan dishes Y8-25. Every night 7-8:30pm, there is a Tibetan dance show and a 25-course buffet (Y50). Caters mostly to tour groups. Hours variable. ❷

Snowland Restaurant (xuěyù cāntīng; 雪域餐厅), next to the Snowland Hotel. A posh, peaceful dining area packed with Westerners. Delicious Western, Tibetan, and Indian dishes Y20-40. The lasagna is highly recommended. Open daily 7am-11pm. ❷

SIGHTS

Lhasa, meaning "land of the gods," is widely considered the holiest place in Tibet. Centers of pilgrimage for generations of Tibetans from all corners, Lhasa's many monasteries and temples scatter inside the city limits and in the surrounding val-leys. With such heartfelt religious devotion and colorful architecture, the monas-teries are sure to entrance even the non-believer.

> **TIP FEET AND FINGERS IN.** It is impolite to point the soles of your feet toward others or religious objects. Should you spend the night in a temple, arrange your bed so that your feet do not point toward the main shrine. Also avoiding gesturing at respected objects and persons with your index finger. Use your palm facing up instead.

๙ัๆ POTALA PALACE 布达拉宫

New arrivals to Tibet should not visit until after the initial effects of altitude sickness have passed. The best time to go is late morning; by midday, tourists leave for lunch. The ticket office is at the western end of Beijing Dong Lu; open M-F 9am-12:30pm and 3:30-5:30pm, Sa-Su 10am-noon and 3:30-5pm. Pilgrims are allowed in 12:30-3:30pm. Admission Y100; extra fee for pictures. Relics Museum and the Roof of Gold Y10 each.

The Potala Palace (bùdálā gōng; 布达拉宫) dominates Lhasa's landscape. Visible from almost any spot in the city, the Dalai Lama's former residence is an enduring symbol of what Tibet once was. King Songsten Gampo, the same ruler who built the Jokhang, chose the Potala's Marpo Ri (Red Hill) as the site for his palace in the 7th century. Today, his "likeness" (the statue with two heads) stands in **Dharm-raja's Cave.** When the Great Fifth Dalai Lama, Lobsang Gyatso, united Tibet in the 17th century, he formally recognized the Dalai Lama's dual role as the religious and political leader of the nation by rebuilding and dividing the palace into the **White Palace** (for overseeing political matters) and the **Red Palace** (for dealing with religious issues). More recently, during the Cultural Revolution, Premier Zhou Enlai used his personal unit of the PLA to protect the Potala from rioting Red Guards, saving the palace from the destruction that befell so many of Tibet's other religious sites. Although the Dalai Lama's court no longer inhabits the Potala's 1000 rooms, the palace still possesses a somber and awe-inspiring grandeur.

RED PALACE. The remains of past Dalai Lamas rest in the western part of this pal-ace in jewel-encrusted gold **stupas.** The 12.6m *stupa* of Lobsang Gyatso, the Fifth Dalai Lama, is gilded with 3721kg of gold foil, 10,000 pearls, and precious stones.

TIBET

The only Dalai Lama not entombed in the Potala Palace is the Sixth, who most likely died in prison at the hands of Mongolian conquerors. This section of the palace also houses the Dalai Lama's audience hall, **Dharmraja's Cave,** Songsten Gampo's personal retreat, which he later expanded into a palace, and some marvelous Buddha and *bodhisattva* statues. Palace treasures include the **Wheel of Time,** an exquisite 200,000-pearl mandala made of coral, turquoise, and gold thread (p. 836). The **Kalachakra Mandala,** on the east side of the third floor, is a model of the palace paradise of Kalachakra (Dukhor). There are also **sand mandalas,** two-dimensional depictions of the three-dimensional Kalachakra Mandala.

WHITE PALACE. The White Palace was the personal residence of the Dalai Lamas. The 14th Dalai Lama's chambers, including his study, meeting rooms, and meditation chambers, are open to visitors. The balcony from which the Dalai Lama made infrequent contact with the Tibetan people overlooks the palace square. All the Dalai Lamas were crowned in the **Great Eastern Assembly Hall.**

ཇོ་ཁང་ JOKHANG TEMPLE 大昭寺

Open daily 8am-midnight. Y70 for non-Tibetans.

The Jokhang Temple (dàzhāo sì), also called the Tsuklakang, is the center of Lhasa and the spiritual heart of Tibet. Jokhang presents the traveler with the intricate artwork and intense devotion that characterizes Tibetan Buddhism, all permeated by the scent of yak butter lamps offered by pilgrims year after year. One of the most important and lively temples in Tibet, the Jokhang should not be missed.

A rich mosaic of myth surrounds the 7th-century temple. Tibetans see their land as a demoness who was subdued by King Songsten Gampo. Her key body parts were then pinned down by Buddhist temples, the locations determined through divination and astrological calculations by Songsten Gampo's Chinese bride, Princess Wencheng. Jokhang was built on Lake Wothang, thought to be the heart of the demon, and takes its name from the **Jowo Rinpoche,** the statue of Sakyamuni (the Buddha) as a 12-year-old boy, which was brought by Princess Wencheng as part of her dowry. Believed to be one of only three consecrated by Sakyamuni himself, the statue now resides at the back of Jokhang's great prayer hall. Other notable statues in the temple include various representations of **Maitreya** and the 1000-arm figure of **Avalokiteshvara,** which King Songsten Gampo and his wives are said to have dissolved into at the time of their deaths.

The Jokhang fuses Nepali, Indian, Buddhist, and Tang Dynasty architectural elements, but most visitors are ultimately captivated by the mystical spirit of this active place of worship. Butter lamps illuminate corridors decorated with murals depicting tales from the temple's past, and the hum of devotees outside echoes off the walls. Three traditional circumambulatory paths *(kora)* center around the Jokhang. The longest is the **Lingkor,** which includes most of Lhasa and has now mostly been paved over as Lingkor Lam. The mid-length path is the **Barkhor,** Lhasa's famous market. The most fervent and energetic of the three, the **Nangkor** is inside the temple itself and draws both travelers and worshippers into its hypnotic revolutions. Every night at 7:30pm, monks congregate in the main assembly hall to chant. After the chanting, climb up to the top to catch the sunset, or come any time for a breathtaking panorama of the city.

བར་སྐོར་ BARKHOR MARKET 八角市场

The market usually begins in the wee hours of the morning, but doesn't really get going until 10am. It shuts down at about 7:30pm. Single women take note that after 6:30pm, only packs of young men remain to roam the markets.

TAILORING TO TOURISTS. Tailor shops in the Barkhor Market area, along Beijing Dong Lu (Peching Shar Lam), and the streets of most Tibetan cities make Tibetan **chuba**, traditional dress for both men and women. A *chuba* costs anywhere between Y130-400, more if you want a fur trim. If you don't see a fabric you like at the tailor shop, check out the stalls in Barkhor Market for rolls of wools, cloth, silks, and skins. Ask your tailor for an estimate to make sure you buy the proper amount, as the fabric is usually the bulk of the *chuba* cost. Chinese tailors tend to offer faster and cheaper work, often ready for next-day pickup. Tibetan tailors are generally pricier, but they often stock higher-quality Indian fabrics. Expensive tailors can take up to three days per order, but try to negotiate if your schedule does not permit the wait.

The area around Jokhang Temple, Barkhor Market (bājiǎo shìchǎng; 八角市场), also known as **Tromsikang Market,** has flourished without becoming excessively commercialized. The scent of burning incense mingles with the odor of yak butter, while monks interrupt their daily circumambulatory routine around the Jokhang to bargain for prayer beads. The market is a good place to buy Tibetan trinkets, with myriad stalls displaying everything from *katas* (ceremonial scarves; hādá; 哈达) and prayer wheels to lamb skulls and photographs of religious figures. The entire Barkhor circuit proceeds in a clockwise direction, encircling the Jokhang and branching off into various side streets. Be sure to walk with the flow of traffic. Inspect the goods carefully, but don't touch if you're not going to buy. Bargaining can usually bring the price down 40-50% from the original quote, but be respectful in your haggling and have fun. Beware of fakes: turquoise, coral, and "antique" artwork are highly suspicious items and should not be purchased unless you are a competent judge or simply happy with the price. Check out the **Thanka Mandala Gallery and Workshop,** just to the left when facing the Makye Ame Restaurant, where you can see *thanka* painters at work and learn about the intricate layering process that goes into the making of traditional Buddhist scroll paintings.

WHEN IN TIBET... When walking around a holy site, be it a temple, monastery or mountain, always walk **clockwise.** Walking counter-clockwise at a religious site is a major taboo. You stick out like a sore thumb when everyone is going in the same direction except for clueless tourists fighting the flow of traffic. Tibetans generally wear many layers of **clothing** even in the summer. Visitors, including men, should avoid showing shoulders, stomachs, and legs.

ཚུར་ཕུ་དགོན་ TSURPHU MONASTERY

2½hr. from Lhasa. There is no public transportation to Tsurphu Monastery. Rent a land cruiser or minibus. Admission Y20.

Tsurphu Monastery is the traditional residence of the Karmapa Lama, leader of the Kagyu school, behind only the Dalai Lama and Panchen Lama in status. The current Karmapa now lives in India after a dramatic escape in 1999. Founded by Dusum Khenpa, the first Karmapa in the 12th century, the Tsurphu is a major pilgrimage destination in central Tibet.

A meandering valley filled with wildflowers leads to the monastery, which consists of three main temples. If the doors are locked, find a monk to let you in. There are also numerous side chapels to explore, hidden among the monks' residences. For a view of the valley, walk up to the *stupas*. The **kora** can be walked in 2hr. Start up the road, past the monastery, and turn right at the remains of the Karmapa's summer palace. Continue past the sky burial site on your right and follow the path up the ridge to circle back above the monastery. Up here are numerous retreat hermitages still in use by nuns. Don't miss the slab across a rock crevice (at the outcropping marked by prayer flags), where the daringly devout make three prostrations to purify negative karma. After passing above the monastery, watch for the trail down.

DRALHALUPUK TEMPLE AND CHAKPORI HILL

Across from the left corner of the Potala, on the other side of Beijing Zhong Lu (Peching Kyil Lam). A road runs along the side of Chakpori Hill; the entrance is near the white stupa at the site of the old West Gate to the city. Follow the road until you see stairs leading up to two temples on the right, about halfway up the hill. Open daily 9:30am-7pm. Y15.

Dralhalupuk Temple served as a cave temple and private retreat for King Songsten Gampo. Although many of the 1000-year-old rock carvings were damaged during the Cultural Revolution, extensive renovation has restored some of them to their original splendor. Over 60 *bodhisattva* carvings decorate the cliffside temple. A second temple, a few meters above Dralhalupuk, was a meditation cave for Bhrikuti, King Songsten Gampo's Nepali queen. Chakpori Hill originally housed Tibet's medical college, before it was razed during the Cultural Revolution. Try your luck at finding a path to the top of Chakpori Hill, a famously impossible task.

ནོར་བུ་གྲིང་ཁ་ NORBULINGKA 罗布林卡

On Norbulingka Lho Lam, a 10min. walk south of the Lhasa Hotel. Take bus #2 (Y2). Open M-Sa 9:30am-noon and 3:30-6pm, Su 10am-12:30pm and 4-5:30pm. Through ticket Y60; entrance Y3, each gate Y10, hall and palace Y7 each.

The Norbulingka's (luóbùlínkǎ; 罗布林卡) once beautifully manicured grounds now look a bit tired. The complex consists of three main palaces that house a total of 370 rooms. This "Jeweled Garden" served as the summer residence for several Dalai Lamas. The 14th Dalai Lama built the **Daktonmiju Palace** in 1956, but he only lived here for two summers before fleeing to India in 1959. Two gigantic paintings of a lion and tiger greet visitors, and on the second floor an elaborate mural traces Tibetan history from the Avalokiteshvara (p. 832) to the 14th Dalai Lama, sitting with Chairman Mao. His Holiness's private living quarters display a radio sent as a housewarming gift by the Prime Minister of India and a richly decorated, solid gold throne. **Gesang Palace,** the oldest of the three palaces, was the main summer residence of the 7th to 12th Dalai Lamas. Various *tangkas* (painted scrolls) and Eight Medicine Buddhas adorn the walls of the main assembly hall. The two-story **Jianse Palace,** the home of the 13th Dalai Lama, closes to the public periodically.

ར་མོ་ཆེ་གཙུག་ལག་ཁང་ RAMOCHE TEMPLE 小昭寺

500m north of the Jokhang Temple, on Ramoche Lam (Xiaozhaosi Lu), off Peching Shar Lam. Open daily 8am-5pm. Y20.

As the partner temple to the Jokhang, Ramoche Temple (xiǎozhāo sì) isn't as grand, but still greatly loved. Countless pilgrims and 115 monks circumambulate the 4000m² complex, which houses the Upper Tantric College. Ramoche Temple was built in the 7th century, when Princess Wencheng of the Tang court married King Songsten Gampo of Tibet. On her journey to Tibet, the princess brought with her the gold statue of the Sakyamuni Buddha (now in the Jokhang Temple) as part of her dowry. When Princess Wencheng's carriage wheels got stuck in the mud and her attendants could not budge the statue from its position at Lhasa's north gate, four pillars were placed around the statue and a brocade draped over it to protect it from harm. Deciding that the gods intended the statue to stay there, she then requested the building of the Ramoche, combining the styles of Tibet and her native Tang. The statue was later transferred to Jokhang for safekeeping, and the Jokhang's **Jowo** (the Buddha as an eight-year-old boy), brought by Songsten Gampo's Nepali bride, was moved to Ramoche. The Jowo you see in the Jokhang today is *another* Jowo, also brought by Wencheng.

སེ་ར་དགོན་ SERA MONASTERY 色拉寺

At the foot of Phurpa Chokri Mtn., 3km northeast of Lhasa. Take bus #5 (Y2) from Beijing Lu (Peching Lam). Alternatively, bike or walk: from Beijing Lu, follow Sera Lam (Sela Lu) north until it ends; go west on Beijing Lu and turn right just before the Post and Telecom complex on Niangre Lu; follow Niangre Lu for 2-3km; a small road before the General Military Hospital leads to the monastery. Open daily 9am-5pm. Y55, students Y35.

Sera was established in 1419 by Sakya Yeshe, a disciple of the prodigious lama Tsong Khapa, who founded Ganden Monastery, the first and most important of the Gelugpa institutions. In its heyday, Sera was home to over 5000 monks, but under government restrictions, its numbers have dwindled to 500. The spirit remains as strong as ever, however, and the debates held daily in the **Sera Je Tratsang** courtyard (3-5pm) present an opportunity to observe theological discourse as it has been practiced since the 14th-century Gelugpa renaissance. Monks argue loudly over interpretations of the Buddha's teaching. Movement of the left hand represents the relief of suffering, of the right, the destruction of evils; participants slap their hands together to build confidence while making a point. Consistently successful debaters can rise in rank.

Sera's three colleges are **Sera Me,** the novice school; **Sera Je,** which originally taught wandering monks; and **Ngagpa,** the tantric college. The traditional pilgrimage circuit through Sera begins to the left of the main road and bisects the monastic compound, passing Sera Me, Ngagpa, Sera Je, and Hamdong across the main road before reaching Sera's largest building and administrative center, the **Tsokchen.** This large assembly hall has an image of Sakya Yeshe and a very famous statue of the protector Tamdrin. After completing this 3hr. circuit, pilgrims often climb the ridge behind Sera to Tsong Khapa's Hermitage (1-5hr.).

འབྲས་སྤུངས་དགོན་ DREPUNG MONASTERY 哲蚌寺

About 10km from Lhasa. Take bus #301 or 302 (Y2) from Beijing Dong Lu (Peching Shar Lam) to the end of the route. Open daily 9am-5pm. Y55, students Y35.

Nicknamed "rice pile" because of its white, heap-like appearance, Drepung (zhébàng sì; 哲蚌寺) is the largest monastery in Tibet, covering over 20,000m² and housing 600 monks. This gargantuan monastery was built in 1416 by Jamygang Choje, fourth disciple of Tsong Khapa (p. 836), after a dream in which he envisioned the site. Until the Fifth Dalai Lama moved the court to the Potala Palace, Drepung's **Ganden Palace** served as the seat of the Dalai Lamas.

The *kora* through Drepung begins at the Ganden Palace, the first building to the left of the main road, and passes a large prayer wheel spinning in a stream. Walk uphill to the Ngagpa College, or "Tratsang," which specializes in tantric Buddhist studies. To the right, three other colleges focus on logic, medicine, and general studies. From the Ngagpa, cross a small path east to the **Tshomchen,** Drepung's most important and imposing structure. Its assembly hall holds a chapel dedicated to **Manjushri,** the great *bodhisattva* of wisdom. The discovery of a rock bearing Manjushri's likeness supposedly determined the exact site of Drepung, and the revered rock serves as one of the chapel's three walls. A pair of golden deer (representing the disciples of the historical Buddha) holding a wheel (representing Sakyamuni and his success) perches on the roof.

TIBET

དགའ་ལྡན་དགོན་ GANDEN MONASTERY 甘丹寺

From Lhasa, 45km east along the main road, on the south bank of the Lhasa (Kyichu) River. Pilgrim buses depart from Lhasa's Jokhang Temple parking lot (2-2½hr.; departs 6:30-7am, returns 2pm; round-trip Y16, one-way Y9). Non-Tibetans Y35, students Y25.

Straddling the high, grassy ridge of Gokpo Ri, Ganden Monastery overlooks the Kyichu river valley, about 1500m below. From the top, visitors look out upon rocky peaks, terraced farmlands, and the monastery's 15 major buildings sprawling down the mountainside. The foremost monastery of the Gelug school, Ganden, was also the most heavily damaged during the Cultural Revolution, with its top third almost entirely in ruins. Nonetheless, the monastery offers intriguing spaces to explore, and its **lingkor** (circumambulatory circuit) is hands-down the most impressive feature of the complex. Beginning with a dense thicket of prayer flags, which creates a small passageway through the rocks above the parking lot, the *lingkor* descends about 20m down the opposite side of the ridge, passing a dozen or so small shrines wedged into the rocks and strewn with prayer flags. A well-defined path skirts the ridge, revealing breathtaking views of the valley. Just before you complete the circuit to the east side of the monastery, it is possible to descend a small path to a **sky burial** site still in use today, but note that it is illegal to visit sky burial sites. If a burial is taking place, retreat to a respectful distance in the cliffs above. You can **trek** from Ganden to Samye, crossing four major passes in four to five strenuous days. Check message boards at guesthouses in Lhasa for trekking partners and up-to-date information.

🎭 ENTERTAINMENT

With most travelers worn out at the end of the day after hours of hiking and temple-visiting, the most popular evening activity tends to be chatting or playing cards around a table over a few beers. In the Barkhor Market area, there are dozens of **pool halls** and outdoor tables of various qualities (Y1-2 per game). Make sure to ask for 15 balls, as most Tibetans play with six. **Beijing Lu** (Peching Lam) offers a number of hang-out spots popular with backpackers and locals alike. Down the little alley just to the right of Dunya, the very cosmopolitan **Another Place** (☎ 627 3795) has the largest DVD collection in town, plenty of alcohol, and a bunny and a dog to boot. The **Folk Music Bar,** 5 Peching Shar Lam (☎ 632 8671), across and down from the Bank of China, has mellow live performances and a full bar.

If you're up for a night out, join the locals at one of many **nangma**, a true Tibetan-style nightclub with modern takes on traditional dances alternating with karaoke numbers, usually in front of a Potala backdrop. *Nangma* ignite the trail from Chengdu all the way to the Nepalese border, and there's generally no cover. Hostesses eagerly refill glasses, while the crowds throb to the music. Ask around for the latest hot spot. Or try **JJ's,** on the right of the plaza in front of the Potala. (☎ 139 0891 0832. Arrive before 10pm for a seat; show repeats at 2am. Open until 4am.)

གནམ་མཚོ་ NAMTSO LAKE 纳木错

At 4627m above sea level, Namtso (nàmù cuò) is the highest lake in the world. Like its name "Sky Lake" implies, Namtso is a shard of brilliant blue heaven fallen to earth. Bordered to the south by the **Nyanchen Thanglha** mountain range and surrounded by desolate grassy plains, this vast lake, China's second largest (70km long, 30km wide), lies in one of Tibet's coldest and most unpredictable climate zones. Even in the summer, frequent storms and high winds sweep down from the mountains and drench the area with rain and hail, leaving visitors dazzled by misty rainbows and the sight of thousands of prayer flags fluttering against silver gray skies. Countless rock cairns, *lapsi* flag pyramids, and *mani* prayer stones demarcate sacred spaces, lending a sense of Tibet's strong spiritual culture to Namtso's astounding natural beauty.

> **TIP** Be aware that because of its altitude, Namtso is quite cold at night, even during the summer. Bring an extra layer of clothing, especially if you plan on camping. Many people experience varying degrees of altitude sickness (see **Health**, p. 831). Watch your travel companions carefully.

One of Tibet's holiest pilgrimages, circling the entire lake takes 14 to 18 days and is extremely difficult. For those short on time, there are also some shorter hikes, just as lovely as the full circuit. One of the best **dayhikes** around the Tashi Dorje monastery area circumambulates the two main hills, which form a peninsula jutting out into the lake. The route encounters several small temples built into the cliffs and about 30 major caves, most of which were once used as meditation hermitages and are filled with Buddhist carvings. Namtso has strong connections to Gum Rinpoche, and most of the temples belong to the Kagyu school. Hiking to the top of the two cliff formations reveals an amazing diversity of plant and animal life, as well as a fragrant spectrum of wildflowers, sage, and juniper. At the top, inspiring, expansive views of the lake await.

No additional **Alien Travel Permit** is necessary to travel to Namtso Lake from Lhasa. There is no public transportation to the lake. Most people hire a **land cruiser** to take them directly to Tashi Dorje Monastery (3-day, 2-night tour Y1500-2000 per car; 2-day, 1-night about Y1000). Cars seat five passengers comfortably, but you may be able to arrange a sixth or seventh person to sit in back with the luggage to lower prices a bit more. Check the notice boards at hotels (see **Accommodations**, p. 841). The trip between Lhasa and the Tashi Dorje Monastery, depending on road conditions, can take anywhere from 4 to 12hr., so you may want to plan on spending only one day at the lake. Extra days cost Y150-200 per car.

Alternatively, those interested in a good hike can take the Naqu-bound bus (Y20) from the Lhasa Bus Station, get off at Damshung, and **trek** the remaining 40km. Foreigners may have difficulty obtaining Damshung tickets from the **Lhasa Bus Station**. From Damshung, look for the main road that crosses a bridge just west of a strip of restaurants and the Damshung Binguan. North of this bridge, a dirt road runs north to the Namtso Ticket Office (7km) and to the 5500m **Lhachen La Pass** (25km), following a rushing stream up the mountain past several nomad camps. Some travelers choose to hitchhike this portion of the journey, but it takes a full day to trek from the pass to the monastery, making hitching rather difficult. *Let's Go* does not recommend hitchhiking. **Admission** to the grasslands is Y40.

Spending the night by Namtso is highly recommended. Bring your own **tent,** or find accommodations near the **Tashi Dorje Monastery** (3- to 4-bed dorms around Y20-40). The **Shepherd Child Guesthouse ❶** has dorms in Tibetan-style tents, yurts with electricity, and the closest access to the only pit toilet around. For a more comfortable stay, try the new **hotel ❶** by the *stupa*, with its stunning murals, warm rooms (Y40-60), and nightly dancing. Two small **restaurants ❷** next to the guesthouses, both labeled "canteen," serve overpriced Chinese and Tibetan food (noodles Y10; fried rice Y15). Try to bring your own food instead. Many groups stop at **Yangpachen Hot Springs** to warm up on their way back from Namtso. Bathing suits are available for purchase at the hot springs. (Bathing Y40.)

ᠵᠠᠪᠠᠯᠤᠪᠠᠰᠤ ᠳᠪᠣᠨ SAMYE MONASTERY 桑木耶寺

Buses between Lhasa and Tsetang pass the pier for boats to Samye Monastery (3hr., 3 per day, Y25-30). Required **travel permits** are granted only to groups traveling in a car with a guide; you may only be allowed to arrange a **tour** with the agency that brought you to Lhasa (3-day tour about Y2500). There is a checkpoint at the **ferry** crossing. Permits are not checked on the return ferry trip. Entrance fee to ferry crossing Y10. Boat to south shore (45min.; Y3, foreigners usually charged Y10). After arriving at the island, a truck or tractor transports tourists to Samye (30min., Y5-10). Samye's branch temple in Lhasa, Tengyeling (follow the alleys on either side of the Pentoc around to the back of the guesthouse) runs a daily **monastery bus** to Samye, departing at 6:30am from in front of the Jokhang (5hr., get there at 6am, Y35). Bus returns to Lhasa at 7:30am the next day via Trandruk Monastery and Yumbulagang Palace. Another bus may leave Samye at 2pm to Lhasa, but schedules are flexible; ask ahead. From Ganden Monastery, you can **hike** to Samye over 2 mountain passes (4-5 days); travelers report hiring a guide and yaks at Hepu, a town 2-3hr. from Ganden on foot. The manager at Outlook Outdoor Equipment Store in Lhasa (see p. 840) can give you up-to-date info and a good map of the trek. A safer bet is **camping** at one of the beautiful spots southwest or northeast of the monastery. Monastery open daily 8am-6pm. Admission Y30.

With its sparkling golden roof, Samye Monastery (sāngmùyē sì) stands in the midst of sand dunes and rocky ridges covered with small shrubs and fragrant herbs. Thought to be Tibet's first monastery, Samye was built in the 8th century by King Trisong Detsen of the Yarlung Dynasty, who invited the Indian scholar Shantirakshita (Khenpo Bodhisattva) to Tibet to build a monastery. But Shantirakshita proved too kind and gentle a soul for wild Tibet, and each night, malevolent spirits ruined all the construction done during the day. Shantirakshita suggested inviting another Indian master, Guru Rinpoche, who upon arrival, bound the wild spirits under oath and commanded them to help.

Samye is known for its unique layout, mirroring Buddhist and Indian conceptions of the universe. The monastery was built according to the design of a **mandala**, with a circular bounding wall and cardinal orientation of the structures around a central sacred space. The main temple, or *utse*, signifies **Mount Sumeru**, the great mythical mountain said to be the center of the universe in Tibetan and Indian cosmology. Four small temples called *ling*, representing the four continents, surround the *utse*. Each *ling* is straddled by two smaller ones, representing the eight sub-continents. There is also a **moon chapel**, where a giant Sakyamuni statue stares into the heavens, and a now-destroyed **sun chapel**.

The three floors of Samye's *utse* are said to have been constructed according to Tibetan (first floor), Chinese (middle), and Indian (top floor) designs. Be sure to check out the murals decorating the internal **kora** (circumambulatory passageway) around the central chapel devoted to Sakyamuni. The second floor houses the monks' living quarters as well as a few small chapels. The impressive top level is comprised of a large, open chapel devoted to Vairocana. The mandala design on the ceiling is situated at the very center of the entire Samye compound. A small ladder in the rear climbs to a strange, unfurnished attic-like level.

The **Monastery Guesthouse ❶** provides basic facilities for Y15-50 per bed. The **Monastery Restaurant ❶** is cheap and convenient. (Fried rice Y5. Noodles Y6. Yak and vegetables Y10. Small thermos of sweet tea Y4.) There are also several restaurants and another guesthouse outside the east gate.

▶️ DAYTRIPS FROM SAMYE: CHIMPU HERMITAGE

A 13km, 4hr. hike *from Samye Monastery. Exit the monastery's north gate and follow the main road east. As soon as you cross the river, turn left (north) onto a gravel road heading up the valley toward a high ridge. On a clear day, you should be able to see the white dots of Chimpu's temples on the deepest ridge overlooking the valley. The gravel road soon becomes a dirt road, which winds through dozens of switchbacks as it climbs up the valley. Cutting straight up the valley instead of following the road is quicker; follow the main river flowing down from the Chimpu area and you should have no problem finding your way. After approx. 2½hr. of hiking from Samye, you'll pass a series of ruins on the left; continue ascending until you arrive at the main Chimpu temple (30min.). A* truck *or tractor (around 6am) goes from Samye to the end of the dirt road to Chimpu; a hike from here to Chimpu Guesthouse is 30min. A truck returns mid-afternoon. Check with your guide or the Samye Monastery Restaurant manager for departure and return times (Y10-15 round-trip).*

One of Tibet's most active and holiest hermitage centers, Chimpu is a collection of several dozen high caves and small temples built into a ridge overlooking the Samye Valley. Over 100 practitioners live in this mountain area, where crystal-clear streams and winding dirt paths crisscross fields of wildflowers and fragrant herbs. At the temple, there is a guesthouse (Y10 per bed). A snack shop sells instant noodles and bottled water. From here, the *kora* heads up the mountain on the left (western) path, making a lovely dayhike. It passes the **Zangdhok Pelri,** Guru Rinpoche's retreat cave, before reaching the **Drakmar Keutsang,** Chimpu's principle meditation cave, which is behind a temple and houses a shrine. The path then descends to the east and returns to the Chimpu Guesthouse. More cave hermitages and many great camp sites are above Drakmar Keutsang, near the ridge. Staying the night in a tent or cave is highly recommended.

ह्रेम्' TSETANG 泽当 ☎0893

Although Tsetang, 185km southeast of Lhasa, is Tibet's third-largest city, most visitors pass through quickly on their way from Lhasa to the ancient sites of Chongye and Yumbulagang in the Yarlung Valley. The town has little more than a few exorbitantly priced hotels—try to avoid spending the night here.

🛈 🖿 PRACTICAL INFORMATION AND ACCOMMODATIONS

Travel permits (Y50 per person) are required for Tsetang. Individual travelers are rarely given permits; it is best to travel in a group with a guide. Lhasa travel agencies will arrange for land cruiser rentals and all necessary permits to Tsetang, Samye, and Yumbulagang (Y2500-3000 for 3 days).

Naidong Lu (乃东路), Tsetang's main road, leads out of Tsetang toward Tranduk Monastery and Yumbulagang Palace. In the **Shannan Prefecture PSB** (☎782 0359), on Naidong Lu near the edge of town, suspicious officers are on duty 24hr. every day. **People's Hospital** is on Gesang Lu. (☎782 0365. Open daily 24hr.) Several **Internet** cafes line Naidong Lu. The telecom office, on Gesang Lu, has IDD service. The **post office** is on Naidong Lu, opposite the Shannan Prefecture Government building. (Open daily 9am-7pm.) **Postal Code**: 856000.

According to strict government regulations, only three hotels in Tsetang are allowed to take foreigners. The cheapest of the three is the **Postal Hotel** ❸ (yóuzhèng gōngyù; 邮政公寓), 10 Naidong Lu, which has economy doubles for Y188 and nicer rooms for Y280. (☎7812 1888. 24hr. hot water.) The **Regional Guesthouse** ❸ (shānnán dìqū zhāodàisuǒ; 山南地区招待所), on Naidong Lu, has doubles with phone, private bath, and showers spouting 24hr. hot water. (☎782 7984. Doubles Y200.) The **Tsetang Hotel** ❺ (zédāng fàndiàn; 泽当饭店), also on Naidong Lu, provides somewhat luxurious but ludicrously priced rooms. (☎782 1899. 24hr. hot water and bath. Singles and doubles in the east bldg. Y380; "luxury" doubles in main bldg. Y550.) There are several cheap restaurants scattered around town.

▣ DAYTRIPS FROM TSETANG

ཡུམ་བུ་བླ་སྒང YUMBULAGANG PALACE 雍布拉康

15km south of Tsetang, past Tranduk Monastery, on the left as you come from Tsetang. A separate Alien Travel Permit is not needed for Yumbulagang (but is for Tsetang). From Tsetung, visitors can hike or take a taxi (Y80) or pedicab (Y40). Open daily 9am-5pm. Y30.

Yumbulagang (yōngbùlākāng) is awe-inspiring, even from a distance. A thin but imposing tower juts out of the mountain like a sword stuck in stone. The magnificent palace was built more than 2000 years ago as a castle for King Nyatre Tsanpo, the first ruler of the Yarlung Dynasty. Legend has it that he was born in India and abandoned by his parents, who thought he was a demon because of his webbed fingers and other unusual features. Eventually Nyatre Tsanpo came to Tibet, and when some shepherds asked where he was from, he pointed to the sky, not knowing Tibetan. Thinking him a god, they made him king.

After the Red Guard's rampaging during the Cultural Revolution, only a fragmented stump of the palace remained. The present structure was built in 1982, when the original was turned into the temple seen today. Perhaps inspired by the shape of the mountain, Yumbulagang means "palace on the hind of a female deer." The first floor of the palace contains statues of Sakyamuni and important Yarlung monarchs. The second has more bronze statues, including one of Tsong Khapa, and murals of Nyatre Tsanpo and Yumbulagang. The roof offers a picturesque panorama of the Yarlungzanbo (Brahmaputra) River Valley, with burnt umber mountains and mud houses in one direction and verdant fields in the other. For a good view of Yumbulagang, go around the back, climb over a low stone wall, and walk up the slope to the flag pyramid *(lapsi)* at the crest of the first ridge.

ཁྲ་འབྲུག་གོན TRANDRUK MONASTERY 昌珠寺

5km southwest of Tsetang, on the way to Yumbulagang. A separate Alien Travel Permit is not needed for Tranduk (but is for Tsetang). Easily accessible on foot or by taxi (Y50). Open daily 7am-7pm. Admission for foreigners Y25.

One of Tibet's oldest monasteries, Tranduk Monastery (chāngzhū sì) was built in the 7th century by King Songsten Gampo. The king was persuaded by his Chinese wife to build Tranduk and other temples at critical geomantic points on the Tibetan Plateau, in accordance with the powerful demoness whose body the Tibetans believe forms their land. The temples acted as a sort of earthly acupuncture, pinning the demoness down and allowing Buddhism to spread. The monastery was designed as a miniature version of Lhasa's Jokhang temple, and the king and queen used it as their winter palace. Like the Jokhang, Tranduk has an interior *kora* lined with prayer wheels, and a central **dukhang** (assembly hall) with breathtaking murals on the back wall. Tranduk houses a famous statue of Tara *(Drolma)*, from whose throat another image of Tara slowly emerged over time. Upstairs, the monastery's main attraction is a rare pearl **tangka** of Avalokiteshvara, colored in shades of silver, turquoise, and coral. There is also a chapel dedicated to protector deities that women may be asked not to enter.

FRIENDSHIP HIGHWAY

The week-long journey from Lhasa to Nepal over the 920km Friendship Hwy. strings together some of Tibet's most impressive attractions: the turquoise Yamdroktso Lake, gleaming glaciers near Gyantse, the Panchen Lama's seat of Shigatse, the rustic monastery at Sakya, the world's highest temple at Rongphu, Everest Base Camp, the Himalayan town of Tingri, and the subtropical border post of Zhangmu. Most areas of the highway are very well traveled, and road conditions are decent. **Travel permits** are required to stop at any of the sights listed above. Fortunately, the friendly **Shigatse PSB** (p. 859) has jurisdiction over the stretch of the Friendship Hwy. extending from Gyantse (possibly also Yamdroktso Lake) all the way through the border towns and Mt. Everest to Nepal, making travel relatively easier for those not wanting to be part of a tour. Unlike most PSBs in Tibet, Shigatse issues permits to independent travelers. The only time limit to the permit is the expiration date of your visa to China—otherwise, they will theoretically grant however many days you ask for.

TIP

TWO FOR THE ROAD. If you're seeking traveling companions for a land cruiser expedition down the Friendship Hwy., check the notices on the boards of any of Lhasa's backpacker guesthouses, or post one of your own.

A good idea is to base yourself in Lhasa and Shigatse, which don't require permits, and explore from there. From Shigatse, it is possible to go to Sakya and Lhatse without hiring a car; these cities are farther west toward Nepal, from which trekking into the countryside are options. Be aware that those traveling on their own may miss out on certain sights, such as Samye and the Everest Base Camp. Otherwise, travelers can hire a **land cruiser** (Y6000-8000 per vehicle for a 6- to 8-day trip, not including the Y450 entrance fee to Everest Base Camp). *Let's Go* does not recommend attempting the highway without a permit: travel restrictions, PSB checkpoints, and heavy fines have all increased. Keep in mind that regulations may change quickly; be sure to call ahead to ask about the latest situation. The Shigatse PSB speaks English.

YAMDROKTSO LAKE 羊卓雍湖

100km southwest of Lhasa along the Friendship Hwy. southern branch. 50km from Nagartse, the Khambala Pass (4900m) provides an incredible view of the lake. No public buses travel to the area; Yamdroktso is usually visited by land cruiser en route to Gyantse and Shigatse from Lhasa. Some travelers have succeeded in taking public transportation to Gyantse and then hitchhiking to Yamdroktso. An Alien Travel Permit is required.

Yamdroktso is one of Tibet's largest and holiest lakes, covering an area of more than 600km^2 at an altitude of 4500m. The name Yamdroktso (yángzhuō yōng hú; "Scorpion Lake") derives from the unique curves and curls of the lake's outline. Ringed by distant snow-capped mountains, the colorful salt waters of the lake are bright sapphire at some times and an exquisite aquamarine at others. Fish swim in its depths, and its islands shelter ducks and greenery. A hydroelectric power plant slowly draining the lake has diminished the vibrancy of the waters, but Yamdroktso still remains beautiful for now.

SPORTS UTILITY VEHICLES

These gas-guzzling, road-hogging beasts that annoy the living daylights out of so many drivers on Western roads are a lifesaver for travelers in rural Tibet. Due to rugged terrain and frequent mudslides, most sights are inaccessible by public transportation; only 4-wheel-drive jeeps can conquer washed-out highways, tackle Himalayan inclines, and ford glacier streams. As visitors in Tibet spend most of their money on transportation, it's worthwhile to be informed.

1. Hire only imported vehicles—the newer the model, the better. Check out the car (and the driver) the night before your trip, especially for longer journeys. If the jeep breaks down frequently along the way, demand that the driver change jeeps in the next town; companies usually keep vehicles in several towns.

2. Some travelers choose to pick up stragglers along the way. Standard practice is for the stragglers to pay the traveler, who gives a share to the driver. *Let's Go* does not recommend picking up hitchhikers.

3. Plan your itinerary to allow plenty of travel time during daylight hours at reasonable speeds. **Accidents are frequent,** usually the result of daredevil drivers or impatient passengers.

4. Arrange with your tour manager beforehand that if days are wasted due to bad roads, accidents, problems with the guide or driver, etc., the days will be reimbursed or your tour extended.

Most travelers base themselves in the town of **Nagartse** (làngkǎzé; 浪卡子), 2km west of the lake, and hike or drive to the nearby mountains. One of the best views of the lake and encircling snowcaps is from the summit of a small mountain, northwest of Nagartse. The mountain divides the northern branch of Yamdroktso Lake from Lake Dumo Tso to the south. From Nagartse, walk west out of town on a dirt tractor road. After 3km, you'll reach the base of the mountain. Walk counterclockwise for 7km until you reach the partially ruined **Samding Monastery,** upon a low ridge facing the valley. Or hike to the summit (4900m, 2hr.) for a view of the lake.

Nagartse has two main roads perpendicular to each other. The main strip, lined with cheap hotels and small restaurants, runs north-south. None of the hotels has bath or shower, but there is a **public shower** (Y5). Several decent Chinese restaurants are also on this street. The **post office** at the end of the street has IDD service.

RALUNG MONASTERY

About 60km from Gyantse. Ralung Monastery is on the way from Yamdroktso to Gyantse; a red sign on the left indicates the direction. Travel down the track for about 10km. Beware the ferocious sheep dogs; wait for the monks to tie them up before entering. Open 24hr.; ask the monks to let you in. Y15.

At the foot of a range of snow-crowned mountains (7191m), Ralung is surrounded by vast empty grasslands and fields of yellow flowers. One of the most isolated monasteries in central Tibet, this once-sprawling complex housed a famous *chorten* and over 500 monks. During the Cultural Revolution, dynamite leveled most of the temples, leaving saddening, albeit gorgeous, ruins scattered across the hillside. A new monastery is undergoing slow reconstruction and houses a few interesting rooms that may not be worth the Y15 admission fee for those on a tight budget. Several hours can easily be spent exploring the ruins uphill from the new monastery. The ruins of the *chorten* are clearly visible across a small stream.

GYANTSE 江孜 ☎0892

Apart from a small cluster of Han Chinese restaurants and shops around the main crossroads, Gyantse—more than any other Tibetan city of similar size—retains a distinctly Tibetan character, which not even the chaos of construction and the socialist-paved town square can mar. Strategically located at the intersection of several important trade routes connecting Nepal and Bhutan with Central and Eastern Tibet, Gyantse has had a long history of militant conflict, hinted at by the Dzong Fort and the Palkhor Chode Monastery's cliff-top walls. Fanning out between these two military relics, thousands of traditional Tibetan houses are woven together by an entrancing network of winding alleys and sunny courtyards. Visitors share the city's dirt and cobblestone streets with packs of wandering dogs and meanderings cows, the storefronts of mellow tea houses, and scattered outdoor pool tables. Every June, Gyantse's surrounding fertile farmlands come alive for the traditional horseracing festivals.

⚡ ☐ ORIENTATION AND PRACTICAL INFORMATION

As of August 2004, Gyantse is undergoing heavy construction, and the majority of street numbers, and perhaps the street names, are due to change. Currently, the crossroads serve as the heart of the town. Travelers arriving from Yamdroktso enter Gyantse from the east on **Weiguo Lu** (卫国路), which becomes **Baiju/Palchoi Lu** (白居路) west of the crossroads. As the name indicates, Baiju/Palchoi Lu leads to Palkhor Chode Monastery. **Yingxiong Lu** (英雄路) runs north-south through the crossroads, passing the entrance to Dzong Fort and leading to Shigatse north from the crossroads. There is no long-distance bus station in Gyantse; **taxis** (Y200) and **minibuses** (Y25) depart for Shigatse from the crossroads.

An **Alien Travel Permit** is required for Gyantse and its sights. The **Shigatse PSB** (p. 859) issues permits for Gyantse; as they are more helpful and issue permits to travelers not in tours, it may be best to travel first to Shigatse and head to Gyantse from there. As the permit situation constantly changes, call them first to make sure that they will issue Gyantse permits. The **Gyantse County PSB** (24hr. ☎817 2032) is rather gruff, and was on Weiguo Lu prior to construction. The **Gyantse Hospital** (jiāngzī yīyuàn; 江孜医院), on Yingxiong Bei Lu, has someone on call 24hr. (☎817 2003. Open daily 9:30am-12:30pm and 4:30-6pm.) **Postal Code:** 857400.

HORSING AROUND

Each June, the town of Gyantse floods with visitors, both Tibetan and foreign, for a week of wild horseracing and easy revelry. Many horse festivals dot the calendar in the summer with Litang in Sichuan, Jyekundo in Qinghai, and Nakchu in Tibet being other prominent tourist draws. Gyantse's festival, held annually since 1408, is by far the most easily accessible to visitors. Tibet's best riders traditionally hail from Eastern Tibet or nomadic backgrounds, and accordingly, the most famous horse festivals take place in the east, making Central Tibetan Gyantse all the more unique.

Although horseracing is the main attraction, there are also plenty of other track events and ballgames. Traditional Tibetan sports include archery, boulder lifting, and wrestling. Competitions are fierce, but generally in the spirit of fun. Complementing athletic contests are traditional public dancing, singing, and barter trading.

Gyantse's festival lasts about a week long. As dates change each year, check in Lhasa and book your room immediately. Vacancy is rare during the festival—but you can always do as the Tibetans and bring a tent to camp.

ACCOMMODATIONS AND FOOD

Budget options cluster at the crossroads. **Public showers** (Y5) are on Yingxiong Lu, across from the sign for the nonexistent Canda Hotel. **Wutse Hotel** ❶ (wūzī fàndiàn; 乌孜饭店) is on the right on Yingxiong Lu, 100m from the crossroads. Sterile dorms have tile floors and TV. Doubles have absolutely beautiful private showers. (☎817 2999. 24hr. hot water. 4-bed dorms Y40; doubles Y250-300.) **Gyantse Foodstuff Storage Hotel** ❶ (jiāngzī guójiā liángshì chǔbèi zhāodàisuǒ; 江孜国家粮食储备招待所) sits just east of the crossroads, a few steps toward the monastery. Look for the red-and-blue "Hotel" sign. The clean, carpeted rooms clash with the not-so-clean public toilets. (☎817 2873. 3-bed dorms Y30; doubles with bath Y45.)

Gyantse's cheapest eats can be found in any small Chinese or Tibetan restaurant that doesn't have an English menu. Many such places line Yingxiong Lu past the Wutse Hotel; a few small Tibetan spots lie along Palchoi Lu, just west of the crossroads. For Y25-45, you can treat yourself to Western or sub-par Indian food in one of the foreigner-oriented restaurants around the crossroads.

Wutse Restaurant (wūzī cāntīng; 乌孜餐厅 ; ☎817 2880), in the Wutse Hotel. Wutse Restaurant has Gyantse's cheapest menu and a cozy Tibetan feel. A wide selection of Western, Chinese, Tibetan, Nepali, and Indian foods. The deep-dish cheese pizza (Y20) is delicious but not filling. Try their stacked plate of fries (Y6). Open 24hr. ❷

Village Garden (zhuāngyuán cāntīng; 庄园餐厅 ; ☎136 7802 0792), on Yingxong Lu, across and a bit down from Wutse Hotel. Serving possibly the freshest Chinese food in town, the proprietor will likely ask you to contribute a blurb to her book of rave reviews from previous customers. Open 8am-10 or 11pm. ❶

Yak Restaurant (☎133 2252 2888), a few doors down from Village Garden. Standard Western fare with slightly better prices than Tashi and a delightful 2nd fl. location. Open daily 7am until the last customer leaves. ❷

Tashi Restaurant (☎817 2793), on Yingxiong Lu, just before Wutse Hotel. Most foreigners eat here despite inflated prices, perhaps because of the Western music and atmosphere. Entrees Y15-45. Pastas Y25-30. Open daily 8am until last customer leaves. ❷

SIGHTS

དཔལ་འཁོར་ཆོས་སྡེ PALKHOR CHODE MONASTERY

From Gyantse's main crossroads, walk 10min. northwest on Palchoi (Baiju) Lu. Open daily 9am-1:30pm and 3-6pm. Y30. Y10 to take photographs inside the stupa.

Founded in 1418 by Rapten Kunzang and the first Panchen Lama, the Palkhor Chode Monastery, also known as Palchoi Monastery, was traditionally home to the Gelug, Sakya, and Bönpa schools of Tibetan Buddhism. The artwork is well preserved, and even the amateur eye can sense a shift in style from the art of Lhasa's large monasteries. Once occupied by the Dalai Lama, the throne in the main assembly hall now holds a photograph of the 10th Panchen Lama. In the central chapel, **Sakyamuni** (Buddha of the present) is flanked by **Dipamkara** (Buddha of the past) on the left and **Maitreya** (Buddha of the future) on the right, and surrounded by the ministers and messengers responsible for bringing his knowledge to mankind. Upstairs, the main chapel houses an intricate bronze **mandala** capped by a crystal orb. The solitary figure clothed in blue is **Vajrapani**, the *bodhisattva* of energy and power. Statues depicting lamas, teachers, and famous ascetics of the Sakyapa school line the walls surrounding the mandala. Peek into other chapels for some wonderful wood carvings.

TIBET

■ **Palkhor Chode Kumbum** (qiānfó tǎ; 千佛塔) surpasses the monastery in age and fame. The 32m-high, 800-year-old pagoda is one of the world's most famous *stupas*, with 108 doors, 77 chapels, and supposedly 100,000 images of Buddhist deities (the name "Kumbum" means 100,000 images). The cardinally oriented chapels on the first four floors each represent the particular realm of a deity, with a focal sculpture and murals covering the cave-like space. The fifth and top floors house four Buddhas facing north (green), south (red), east (blue), and west (yellow).

■ པ་ལྷ་གཞིས་ཀ་ PALA MANOR HOUSE 帕拉庄园

About 3km from Gyantse's city center. Walk down Yingxiong Nan Lu and turn right after the big "A" structure. A sign indicating the direction of the house is on the left, past the cement factory; the entrance is about 1km down a dirt road. Chinese and Tibetan explanations only. Open daily 8am-8pm. Y15.

Pala Manor House (in Tibetan *Palha Shika*, in Chinese pàlā zhuāngyuán) once belonged to a wealthy aristocrat and reveals a fascinating glimpse into daily life in pre-1959 Tibet. Rebuilt in 1937, the original Pala Manor House, in Gyanka village, about 1km from Gyantse, was destroyed during the British invasion of Tibet. Reputedly the best-preserved manor house in all of Tibet, Pala Manor escaped the ravages of the Cultural Revolution by serving as the PLA's regional headquarters. This three-story house is the perfect antidote to a monastery overdose. A number of the rooms remain furnished, and the dining room even boasts wax figures to inspire the imagination.

The third floor once served as nobleman's private living quarters and now contains a winter solarium and a private prayer hall. During important religious days and festivals, lamas were invited here to pray and meditate. The second floor holds the manor's eclectic assortment of historical and religious items, including turn-of-the-century *tangkas*, old Tibetan stamps (of which only 13 remain in the world), the master's alcohol collection, and his wife's jewelry collection. Across the street you can visit the quarters of the serfs, who were "liberated" in 1959.

གྱལ་རྩེ་རྫོང་ DZONG FORT

From Gyantse's main crossroads, walk south for 3min. on Yingxiong Nan Lu; turn left down a small alleyway marked by a sign in English. It's a 15min. walk up a paved slope to the fort entrance. Open daily 8am-8pm. Y30.

Flanked by crumbling auburn walls, this imposing and handsome citadel overlooks the Palkhor Chode Monastery to the south and unfurls views of the dense Gyantse neighborhoods and the surrounding green and yellow farmlands. Built in AD 967 by the grandson of Tibet's last religious king, Dzong Fort was expanded and used by various regimes and dynasties (the Sakya, Pagdru, and Ganden Podrang in particular) to defend Gyantse from separatist groups. At the crossroads linking Lhasa with Shigatse and the border at Yadong, the fortress was considered impregnable until the British adventurer Younghusband marched into this crucial juncture in 1904, destroying the Tibetan troops. The **Anti-British Imperialist Museum** remembers the bloody aftermath with exhibits describing the British incursion in highly propagandistic and entertaining terms. Next door, a few spooky wax figures recall the Tibetan government's use of the Dzong. Despite the superb aerial view of Gyantse, the fort itself is rather uninteresting and best seen from the city below, given the hefty admissions.

TIBET

གཞིས་ཀ་རྩེ SHIGATSE 日喀则 ☎ 0892

Tibet's second-largest city, Shigatse, is most famous as the seat of the Panchen Lama, traditionally regarded by Tibetans with as much affection and respect as the Dalai Lama. No visit to Shigatse is complete without visiting Tashilhunpo Monastery, home of all the Panchen Lamas since the fourth, including the Chinese-government-chosen 11th (the Dalai Lama's original six-year-old candidate and his family disappeared in 1995). While Han Chinese businesses and modern architecture dominate much of Shigatse, pockets of traditional Tibetan neighborhoods cluster in the north, with lively markets and countless Tibetan-style tea houses. The Chinese neighborhoods provide a wide selection of dining options and most of the services of a city. All in all, cheap, comfortable hotels and the stately Tashilhunpo make Shigatse a must-stop along the Friendship Highway.

■? TRANSPORTATION AND PRACTICAL INFORMATION

An Alien Travel Permit is not necessary for Shigatse. The **Shigatse PSB** has historically been one of the most lenient and helpful offices for foreigners in Tibet. The friendly people there will patiently answer all your questions, even if you ask them five times to repeat something—it's best to call them from Lhasa before setting out for up-to-date information and advice. Before applying for a permit, travelers must first go to **FIT** (see **Travel Agency**) to have FIT sign a form; this is less strict than it sounds, as one of FIT's main tasks is to help travelers obtain permits. The Shigatse PSB is one of the few PSBs that issues permits to independent travelers, and the duration of the permit is entirely dependent upon your visa and how long you wish to stay. Keep in mind that the permit situation is in constant flux.

Buses: Passengers Transportation Co. (☎882 6070), on Shanghai Lu, just south of Zhufeng Dong Lu. Open daily 9:30am-9pm. There are 2 roads from Lhasa to Shigatse: the scenic dirt road passes through Yamdroktso and Gyantse; the new paved highway winds along Yarlung Tsangpo River. Buses run only along the new one, which is 2-3hr. faster. All buses leave Shigatse at 8am; buses to Lhasa and other destinations may have additional morning departure times on demand. Travel time depends on road conditions. To: **Gyantse** (1½hr., Y20-30); **Lhasa** (8-10hr., Y38); **Lhatse** (Y30-40); **Sakya** (5hr., Y32-42); **Tingri** (Y52-65); **Yadong** (Y50). Numerous **minibuses** to **Lhasa** (Y38).

Local Transportation: A bus runs from the main crossroads past the Tashilhunpo gates and ends near the bus station (Y0.5-1). **Tricycle** and **motorcycle** rides cost about Y5 to destinations within the city. **Taxis** are easy to come by, even after dark (Y10).

Travel Agency: FIT Travel Section (lǚyóu bùmén; 旅游部门 ; ☎883 8068) and **FIT Independent Travelers Center** (sǎnkè zhōngxīn; 散客中心 ; ☎883 8065, 24hr. 898 858) on Zhufeng Lu, at the entrance to Gyangen Carpet Factory. The only show in town. Skip the Travel Section and head right to the Independent Travelers Center, whose amiable English-speakers are a pleasant change from the package-tour fixation elsewhere. Helps obtain travel permits and visa extensions and arranges vehicles and guides for the Friendship Hwy. English- and Chinese-speaking guides both Y150 per day.

Bank of China: 7 Shanghai Lu. Exchanges traveler's checks. Open M-F 9am-noon and 3:30-6:30pm, Sa-Su 10am-5pm.

Markets: There are 2 major flea markets in the northwest part of the city. The **Antique Market,** on Bangjia Gonglu opposite the Tenzin Hotel, sells mostly bead necklaces and other handicrafts. The market across the road sells mainly clothing and essentials.

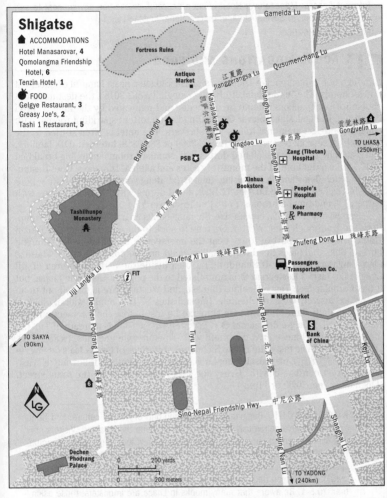

Shigatse

🏠 ACCOMMODATIONS
Hotel Manasarovar, 4
Qomolangma Friendship
  Hotel, 6
Tenzin Hotel, 1

🍎 FOOD
Gelgye Restaurant, 3
Greasy Joe's, 2
Tashi 1 Restaurant, 5

Gameida Lu

Fortress Ruins

Qusumenchang Lu

Antique
Market

江夏路
Jianggerangsa Lu

Shanghai Lu

Bangjia Gonglu

Kaisakakang Lu
凯萨尔拉康路

贡觉林路
Gongjuelin Lu

TO LHASA
(250km)

Qingdao Lu
青岛路

Shanghai Zhong Lu 上海中路

PSB ✚

Zang (Tibetan)
Hospital

Xinhua
Bookstore

People's
Hospital

Keer
℞ Pharmacy

Tashilhunpo
Monastery

Zhufeng Dong Lu 珠峰东路

Jiji Langka Lu

Zhufeng Xi Lu 珠峰西路

ℹ️ FIT

Passengers
Transportation Co.

Dechen Podrang Lu

Beijing Bei Lu 北京北路

■ Nightmarket

TO SAKYA
(90km)

Tiyu Lu

$ Bank
of China

Keti Lu

N
LG

中尼公路

Sino-Nepal Friendship Hwy.

Beijing Nan Lu

Shanghai Lu

Dechen
Phodrang
Palace

0   200 yards
0   200 meters

TO YADONG
(240km)

PSB: 4 Jiji Langka Lu (24hr. ☎ 882 2241), on the pedestrian section of the street. The **Foreign Affairs Office** (☎ 882 2240; vice-section chief Li Xin 24hr. 139 0892 1226), to the right of the main entrance, is the place to obtain permits (see above for procedure). Visa extensions processed with an approval form signed by FIT; UK citizens Y160, US citizens Y420. Foreign affairs office open daily 9:30am-12:30pm and 3:30-6:30pm.

Hospitals: People's Hospital of Shigatse Prefecture (dìqū rénmín yīyuàn; 地区人民医院), 5 Shanghai Zhong Lu (emergency ☎ 882 2650). Ambulance service. Open daily 9am-12:30pm and 4-6:30pm. **Zang (Tibetan) Hospital** (zàng yīyuàn; 藏医院), 3 Shanghai Zhong Lu (☎ 882 2654). Tibetan and Western medicine. Open M-Sa 9am-12:30pm and 4-6:30pm. Emergency ward open until 9pm.

Pharmacy: Keer Pharmacy (☎ 882 3101), Shanghai Zhong Lu, south of the People's Hospital. Open daily 9am-9pm.

Internet Access: Manasarovar Hotel offers a peaceful, smoke-free environment to surf the net. Y15 per hr. Several cheaper places along Qingdao Lu.

Postal Code: 857000.

ACCOMMODATIONS AND FOOD

Although not as backpacker-friendly as Lhasa, Shigatse has a handful of excellent budget hotels. The **Tenzin Hotel,** 10 Banjia Gonglu (☎882 2018), the destination of choice for backpackers, should be re-opened and renovated by the time you roll into town. ☒ **Hotel Manasarovar ❶,** 20 Qingdao Lu, offers sparkling rooms, with equally spotless communal toilets and showers. The hotel is often stuffed to the gills in high season; reserve early. (☎883 9999 or 883 6888. Internet, IDD, laundry, and 2 attached restaurants. 3-bed dorms Y30; standard rooms including breakfast Y240.) Take a right out of the monastery gates and a left at Himalaya Tibet Restaurant to reach **Qomolangma Friendship Hotel ❶** (zhūfēng yǒuyì bīnguǎn; 珠峰友谊宾馆), 14 Dechen Podrang Lu. (☎882 1929. 4-bed dorms with TV Y30; doubles with carpet, TV, and tiny bathrooms Y140. Public shower Y5.)

As can be expected of a city its size, Shigatse cooks up a wide variety of scrumptious food, although most Westerners tend to stick to the eateries near the Tenzin Hotel. The Chinese part of town, near the intersection of Shandong Lu, Zhufeng Lu, and Shanghai Lu, is lined with small *xiǎochī* and hotpot restaurants. There is also a **nightmarket** just off Shandong Lu. Just inside the pedestrian area of Jiji Langka Lu, **Tashi 1 Restaurant ❶** is not related to the popular Tashi 1 in Lhasa, but it has a similar feel. Tasty Tibetan, Chinese, and Western fare is dished out to an almost exclusively Western clientele. (Most dishes Y7-15. Chunky walnut chicken Y20. Open daily 6am-11:30pm.) On Qingdao Lu just before the intersection with Kaisalakang Lu, **Gelgye Restaurant ❷** (སྐྱེ་རྒན་པ་བཟའ་ཁང་།་') is a breath of Tibetan air in a mainly Chinese city, complete with Tibetan-style couches. (☎882 6568. Dishes Y10-20.) The tasty and cheap Sichuanese offerings of **Greasy Joe's** (zhēngxīn fàndiàn; 正鑫饭店), on Kaisalakang Lu, has earned it a faithful following of Westerners. Don't confuse it with "Gresy Joe's," a few doors up on the same street. (Open daily 9am-10:30 or 11pm.)

> **⚡ TIP**
>
> **KUCHI KUCHI.** Begging is an engrained part of Tibetan culture, and Tibetans usually give generously to monks, pilgrims, and the disabled. Visitors may feel overwhelmed by persistent requests for money, food, and pens, accompanied by "thumbs up" ☒ motions and *kuchi kuchi*—Tibetan gestures and words for "please." You can duck away politely or say *"mao zi mindu"* ("I don't have any *máo*"). Should you decide to give, 1 *máo* (Y0.1) is adequate. Don't give more than Y0.5-1. Be aware that many monks in Lhasa are imposters; those asking for donations for monastery projects should have a red stamp on their letters.

👁 SIGHTS

བཀྲ་ཤིས་ལྷུན་པོ་དགོན་ **TASHILHUNPO MONASTERY** (zhāshílún bù sì; 扎什伦布寺). Built in 1447 by the first Dalai Lama, Tashilhunpo Monastery is to the Panchen Lama as the Potala is to the Dalai Lama. Proceeding clockwise in the traditional *kora* circuit, one encounters the westernmost **Jamkhang Chenmo,** a tall red building built in 1914 by the Ninth Panchen Lama, housing a 26m-tall statue of the Maitreya Buddha. Continuing along a stone path eastward, the next building is the **Labrang Gyaltsen Thonpo,** the palace of the Panchen Lamas; it's usually closed to visitors.

Farther east along the main path on your left is the **Kudhung Lhakhang,** built in 1662 out of 547kg of gold and 75kg of silver. It contains the impressive 11m *chorten* tomb of the Fourth Panchen Lama. The final, easternmost building in the *kora,* the **Kesang Lhakhang** is Tashilhunpo's largest building complex, at the center of a stone-paved courtyard decorated with painted murals. This courtyard is used for all important monastic dances, debates, and festivals, as well as daily teachings. Up the stairs behind the balcony is a large **dukhang** assembly hall, where in the late afternoon visitors can often immerse themselves in a sea of chanting monks. *(Open M-Sa 9am-12:30pm and 4-6pm. Y45.)*

ᶘᶘᶘ SAKYA 萨迦 ☎ 0824

The town of Sakya, 150km west of Shigatse, is in the middle of a construction spree, but it remains to be seen whether there are people who will move into the new buildings. In the town center, a fortress-like monastery, rising above a dense network of traditional mud-wall housing, reminds residents of Sakya's glorious dynastic past during the 13th and 14th centuries. Meanwhile, the town's character-istic blue-, red-, and white-striped patterns, a sacred configuration of colors from the early Vinaya Buddhist sect, hints at Sakya's solemn present. Travelers rarely stay long in Sakya, one of the first cities travelers encounter when heading west to Nepal, but this quiet monastic town merits what time you can afford.

⯃⯄ TRANSPORTATION AND PRACTICAL INFORMATION. An **Alien Travel Permit** is required, best obtained in Shigatse (p. 858). The Sakya PSB is known for its strict enforcement, though some travelers get by without stopping at the checkpoint at the town entrance. The enormous **Sakya Monastery** is the town center, and a handful of hotels, shops, and eateries cluster east of its walls. Shigatse-bound **buses** (Y32) depart throughout the day from Gesang Lu at Baogang Lu. **Minibuses** go to Lhatse (every other day, Y10) and Shigatse (Y40). The **post** and **telecom offices** are down Baogang Lu. (IDD service. Open daily summer 9am-1pm and 4-7pm; winter 10am-1pm and 3-6:30pm.) **Postal Code:** 857800.

⯃⯄ ACCOMMODATIONS AND FOOD. Sakya has very limited accommoda-tions. Many travelers choose to stay in nearby **Lhatse** (30km west of the Sakya turn-off), where creature comforts are more plentiful but surroundings are less pleasant. The **Sakya Hotel ❶,** 1 Kaisang Xi Lu, just outside the Sakya Monastery's northeast corner, is part of the Yak Management chain, but don't expect too much. Rooms are spare but reasonably clean—something that can't be said of the common toilets. (☎ 824 2555. Dorms Y30-50; doubles Y180.) Signs for the **Grain Bureau Guesthouse ❶** are all over town but don't mark its actual location. From Gesang Lu, turn onto Baogang Lu; it's on the left of the first block, through a gate. (☎ 824 2643. Public showers outside. Dorms Y20; doubles Y80.) If you decide to bed in Lhatse, the **Lhatse Hotel ❶** has crowded dorms and carpeted Tibetan-style rooms with TV. Ask for a room facing the inner courtyard for a quieter night's sleep. (☎ 832 2208. Showers Y5. Dorms Y20-40; doubles Y90.)

Several restaurants with names involving "Sakya," "monastery," and "Tibetan" all serve similarly overpriced Chinese and Tibetan food. Don't pay more than Y10 for rice, potatoes, and meat, or Y5 for a small thermos of sweet tea. The **Sakya Monastery Restaurant** is a bit dark inside, but the Chinese and Tibetan fare is decent.

◼ SIGHTS. ᶘᶘ ᶘᶘᶘ **Sakya Monastery** (sàjiā sì; 萨迦寺), completed in 1268, is home to the Sakya school of Tibetan Buddhism (p. 836). The monastery is divided into two parts. The northern complex across the river is mostly ruins, with two small, but fascinating active temples. The southern, castle-like complex is nestled within the town. Originally containing 108 structures, the northern complex was laid out according to variations in terrain rather than the strict geometry and cardinal relationships seen in the southern complex. Climbing the monastery walls and walking along the top ridge leads to incredible views of the monastery and surrounding valley. Be careful: there are no side railings. The ground-floor entrance is via the east wall, which leads to the central courtyard.

To the left is the **Purkhang Chapel,** which houses the 700-year-old figure of Sakyamuni, 7000 glass-encased *bodhisattvas*, and other relics. The central figure is Manjushri, the Bodhisattva of Wisdom, and Sakyamuni sits a few paces to the left. The temple across from the chapel holds the *stupas* of 11 Sakya abbots, a dusty *mandala*, and hundreds of ancient books. Directly opposite the main entrance is the cavernous **assembly hall,** where the familiar Sakyamuni is flanked by a symmetrical arrangement of statues. The remains of Kon Konchog Gyelpo, the founder of Sakya Monastery, are preserved inside the enormous central Buddha. The remarkable assortment of figures on display includes Manjushri, Maitreya, and Kunga Nyingpo (the center figure of the trio to the right of Sakyamuni), a famous abbot of Sakya. The pillars themselves are single tree trunks, brought from India. Bring a flashlight to see the mesmerizing murals on the walls. *(Open daily 8am-5pm; closed for a 1hr. lunch break. Y35; fee for taking photos inside monastery Y20.)*

ཇོ་མོ་གླང་མ། MT. EVEREST 珠穆郎玛峰 ☎0892

The approach to Mt. Everest via **Pangla Pass** is one of the most beautiful and stunning routes in the world. After hours of zigzagging across the plateau, the majestic Himalayas unfold in full force, with four of the world's six highest peaks in the world—**Cho Oyu** (8201m), **Malaku** (8463m), **Lhotse** (8516m), and of course, **Qomolangma** (8848.13m; Mt. Everest)—looming before the awestruck traveler. The most magnificent view of the "Third Pole of the World," however, is from Rongphu Monastery. On the rare clear day, lucky visitors can clamber up to the Everest Base Camp and watch the sun's rays illuminating the icy mountain.

🛈🏠 PRACTICAL INFORMATION AND ACCOMMODATIONS

From Lhatse, the Friendship Hwy. continues for 3hr., past **Shegar** (New Tingri) to the 65km **Everest access road.** After the turn-off, the bumpy and windy road swerves up for 1½hr., passing **Pangla Pass** (5220m), before descending to the village of **Tashi Dzom.** Most visitors stop here for food or lodgings. After crossing a large valley and several villages, the road ends up at **Rongphu Monastery.** The **base camp** is a few kilometers up the Rongphu glacier bed.

An **Alien Travel Permit** is required for Rongphu Monastery and Everest Base Camp (EBC). There is a checkpoint at the beginning of the access road. At the time of writing, the Shigatse PSB issued EBC permits to individual travelers, with the help of the Shigatse FIT, who can also arrange transportation. EBC permits are easily obtained in **Lhasa** if you book a car and guide. There is a Y65 per person **admission** fee to enter the Everest region, as well as a hefty Y405 vehicle fee (some travel agencies include this fee in land cruiser packages), collected at **New Tingri (Shekar),** about 5km from the turn-off. After the turn-off, there is another checkpoint.

Tashi Dzom, 2hr. away, has cheaper and often warmer rooms than those at Rongphu, making this town a good place to spend the night before heading back to the Friendship Hwy. Several guesthouses along the main road in Tashi Dzom offer very similar rooms for Y25 per night, as well as overpriced Tibetan food (Y10-15). **Rongphu** itself offers three choices for accommodations. **Camping** on the monastery grounds costs Y10-15. The **guesthouse** next to the monastery has dorm rooms

(Y25 per bed) and a lodge where visitors can warm up by the stove, eat noodles (Y10) or fried rice (Y10), and drink sweet tea (Y5-8). Farther down, the new **Zhufeng Scenic Viewing Point** (zhūfēng guān jǐng tái; 珠峰观景台 ; ☎858 4535) has doubles decorated with colorful paintings for Y200 a night. Basic lodgings (Y15) and a pit toilet are available at the **base camp** itself, but you'll have to arrive with enough daylight left for the pony ride up to the camp.

🔵 SIGHTS

For centuries, the sight of Mt. Everest has taken many a breath away. From 5000m above sea level, the grandeur of the mighty peak may not be apparent at first glance, and you may be rather underwhelmed by the roadside scenery that looks similar to anywhere else in Tibet. But the shimmering beauty of the pyramidal north face and the triumphant glow of being at Mt. Everest makes the trek more than magnificent. The best time to view the mountain is the early morning, when the chance of a cloudless sky is highest, and the rising sun's rays glint off the perpetually snow-encrusted adamantine peak. April and October are the clearest months. During the summer, clouds can enshroud the Himalayas for up to a week, and only the lucky will catch a glimpse of the summit.

The **Everest Base Camp** (zhūfēng dàběnyíng; 珠峰大本营) itself does not have much of note, other than an unbeatable photo-op in front of the "Mt. Qomolangma Base Camp" marker. Tiny **Rongphu Monastery** (róngbù sì; 绒布寺), at 4980m, 2hr. farther up the Everest access road from Tashi Dzom, is the world's highest monastery. It has friendly nuns and monks and chapels with exquisitely detailed murals, but the highlight is its incredible view of the surrounding mountains.

For the intrepid, a hike from Rongphu Monastery to Everest Base Camp takes about 2hr. **Horse carts** make the trip throughout the day (up 90min., down 30-60min.; round-trip Y30 per person). One word of caution: do not attempt to hike to the EBC if you have just arrived in Tibet via Kathmandu. Acute Mountain Sickness (p. 831) can strike without warning and debilitate even the fittest trekker. Spend a few days getting acclimated before setting out on any long hikes. Also note that several **PSB** tents set up at the base camp, waiting to hand out US$200 fines to anyone who tries to continue up the path to Camp 1. If you are planning to hike in the area, avoid problems with the PSB by heading east up a canyon to the Qianjing Glacier rather than toward Camp 1.

ক্ষ্ণ· TINGRI 定日   ☎0892

The small village of Tingri is little more than a few houses along the Friendship Hwy. Foreigners need an **Alien Travel Permit** (although only an individual one) to get there. Tingri is where most travelers spend either their last or first night in Tibet, depending on the direction of travel. There is little to do in the town except admire the snowy mountains of the Himalayan Range, a gorgeous backdrop to the vast plains and open skies of Tingri.

Himalaya Hotel ❶ (xǐmǎlāyǎ lǚguǎn; 喜马拉雅旅馆) on the Friendship Hwy. a few hundred meters before the center of town, is the cheapest place around, with communal toilets and future showers. For now, plenty of hot boiled water is available for washing. (2- to 4-bed dorms Y15.) In the town center, the **Amdo Hotel ❶** has a nice shower and the cleanest pit toilets you'll ever see. (Showers Y10, non-guests Y15. 3- to 4-bed dorms Y25-30.) In the eastern end of town, the new **Everest Snow Leopard Guesthouse ❷** is pricier than other options in town, but makes up for it with attractive rooms and spotless showers. (Doubles Y120 and Y160. Discounts up to 40% available.) In the western end, the **Gangjong Amdo Guesthouse ❶** has charming dorms (Y25) and friendly staff.

The eateries along the Friendship Hwy. all rehash the same pricey Chinese and Tibetan menu with a few Western dishes (Y15-20). On the Nepal-bound side of town, the **Amdo Restaurant ❷** is an old favorite (Tibetan dishes Y10-20). The newer **Gangjong Amdo Restaurant ❷** has a skylight and slightly lower prices. If you're looking for more variety, be patient: you'll be in Kathmandu soon.

གཉའ་ལམ NYALAM 聂拉木

The small but modern town of Nyalam, 40km from Zhangmu and the Nepalese border, huddles around a strip of the Friendship Hwy. Coming from Lhasa, Nyalam's green slopes and beautiful trees give a tantalizing hint of the lush and vibrant ecosystem just within reach, as snowy highlands fade into subtropical greenery. Travelers from Kathmandu often spend the night here.

If you have a few free hours, venture to Nyalam's most famous attraction, the **Milarepa Cave,** about 5km east of town, where Tibet's great saint once lived and meditated. His handprints can be seen on the rocks. (Y15.) Those who are more pressed for time can visit the small **Nyalam Temple** and relax on the surrounding grassy hillside, up the main hall behind the town.

A **PSB checkpoint** next to the prison at the northern end of town, will enforce permits. **Snowlands Trekking Equipment Shop,** a few doors down from Tashi Restaurant, provides IDD and **currency exchange. Internet** access is available at Snowlands Guesthouse for Y10 per hr. Nyalam also has some little shops where you can pick up snacks and provisions for the road ahead.

Accommodations are cheap and plentiful. The cheapest of the lot is probably the **Snowlands Guesthouse ❶** (xuěyù lǚguǎn; 雪域旅馆), near the north end of town. (Dorms Y15-20; doubles Y60.) The larger and slightly better **Nyalam Hotel ❶,** at the southern end of town past the basketball courts, has bright, clean cement-floored dorms (Y30) and doubles (Y30-35). Showers are across the lot (Y10). Down the street from Snowlands, the **Nga-dhon Guesthouse ❷** offers Tibetan-style doubles for Y120. The cheapest food is at **Nepali Restaurant ❷,** next to the basketball courts at the town center. They insistently refill plates of lentils, rice, and curry (Y10-15). **Nga-dhon Restaurant** serves breakfast, but you have to request it the night before. Westerners pack the pleasant **Tashi Restaurant,** across the street from Snowlands.

རྒྱལ་མོ ZHANGMU 樟木   ☎0892

The green cliffs sloping above the border town of Zhangmu (zhāng mù) signal that Nepal is near. Many travelers consider this leg of the journey to have some of the most spectacular scenery in either Tibet or Nepal, with waterfalls splashing down thousands of feet, sometimes drenching passing cars in the process. The entire town lies along the Friendship Hwy. as it curves and descends into Nepal. The population, a curious mix of Tibetan, Nepalese, and Chinese, is growing rapidly, thanks to brisk border trade.

An **Alien Travel Permit** is required for Zhangmu—a PSB checkpoint awaits at the entrance to town; **Bank of China** is around the town center. Money changers work the streets of Zhangmu and offer better rates than in Kathmandu. A number of **Internet** cafes and IDD booths are available in the southern end of town, but connections are cut during bad weather. There is a **post office** near the top of town.

The most luxurious rooms are at the **Zhangmu Hotel ❶,** at the base of town near the border post. (☎874 2277. 4-bed dorms Y50.) Across the street, the **Gang-gyen Hotel ❶** has bright and airy dorms with communal toilets and views of the valley below. (☎874 2188. 24hr. hot water. 5-bed dorms Y50.) Uphill from here, on the left, the **Sherpa Guesthouse ❶** is quite clean with friendly staff and views of both the valley and town. (No hot water. Dorms Y30.) The overpriced Chinese-Tibetan **Gang-gyen Restaurant,** next to the Gang-gyen Hotel, is nonetheless popular with the backpacking crowd. (Open daily 8am-10:30pm.)

BORDER CROSSING INTO NEPAL: ZHANGMU. The customs checkpoint for China is at Zhangmu, at the bottom of town. From Zhangmu, most travelers pay for a jeep ride (US$1-2 per person) or walk the remaining 8km to **Kodari** (about 2hr.) and the Friendship Bridge, where the customs checkpoint for Nepal is located. If you have a light pack, you may want to take a small rocky path that descends steeply to the Friendship Bridge, shortcutting the main road's many switchbacks. The trail (2km) takes about 1½hr. from the Zhangmu border; be careful, as it gets very slippery in the rain. Nepali **visas** are available at the border or from the Nepalese consulate in Lhasa (p. 840). (No visa needed for stays of 3 days or less. 1st entry to Nepal 60-day single-entry tourist visa US$30, subsequent entries within 150 days of the same year 30-day visa US$30.) From Kodari, 2 buses depart in the morning for Kathmandu, leaving from the Friendship Bridge when full (150R). A taxi to Kathmandu costs 2500Rs for 4 people. Cheaper minibuses or vans charge 500R per person, jeeps 1000R. Landslides are frequent in the monsoon season, but taxis run between landslides so you won't be stuck for too long. Barring landslides and other delay, the trip from Kodari to Kathmandu takes about 5hr. Set your **clocks** back 2hr. and 15min. when entering. The Nepalese currency is the **rupee (R)**. The **exchange rate** is approximately 9R to 1Y.

TIBET

APPENDIX

GLOSSARY

apsara: Buddhist angel

arhat: one who has attained spiritual enlightenment

bāozi (包子): steamed, stuffed buns

běi (北): north

bīnguǎn (宾馆): hotel

bodhisattva: a devout Buddhist who has attained enlightenment but remained on earth to help others

CAAC: Civil Aviation Administration of China

CCP: Chinese Communist Party

CITS: China International Travel Service

CTS: China Travel Service

CYTS: China Youth Travel Service

dàdào (大道): boulevard

dagoba: a bell-shaped Buddhist commemorative shrine

dàjiē (大街): avenue

dàshà (大厦): mansion, tower

DDD phones: Domestic Direct Dial phones, from which domestic long-distance numbers can be dialed directly

dim sum: see yum cha

dōng (东): east

fàndiàn (饭店): hotel or restaurant

fànguǎn (饭馆): restaurant

fēn (分): the smallest denomination of Chinese currency; 1/100th of a *yuán*

fēng (峰): peak

GMD: Guomindang; the Nationalist People's Party, also called KMT

Guanyin: Bodhisattva of Mercy

gǔlóu (鼓楼): drum tower

gwailo: Cantonese slang term for foreigner

hǎi (海): sea

Han Chinese: China's ethnic majority; comprises 91% of the population

hé (河): river

hú (湖): lake

hútòng (胡同): an alley

IDD phones: International Direct Dial phones, from which international numbers can be dialed directly

jiāng (江): river

jiē (街): street

jiǔdiàn (酒店): a hotel or restaurant

jiǎo (角): 10 *fēn*; also called "*máo*"

karst: limestone formation

kuài: 1 *yuán*.

lama: spiritual leader in Tibetan Buddhism

lǎowài (老外): Mandarin slang term for "foreigner"

lingkor: a Buddhist pilgrimage circuit around select holy sites

loess: fine, yellowish silt

luóhàn (罗汉): an enlightened being similar to an *arhat*

lù (路): road

lǚshè (旅舍): hostel

mahjong: popular Chinese game that resembles gin played with tiles

máo (毛): unit of Chinese currency; one-tenth of a *yuán*

mén (门): gate or door

miàndí (面的): yellow mini-van taxis that are shaped like loaves of bread

nán (南): south

nòng (弄): alley

PLA: People's Liberation Army

PSB (公安局): Public Security Bureau; the police

PRC: People's Republic of China

qiáo (桥): bridge

rénmínbì (人民币): the official name for Chinese currency; literally, "people's money"

sampan: small, motorized boat

SEZ: Special Economic Zone

shan (山): hill or mountain

sì (寺): temple

shuǐ (水): water

stele (shíbēi; 石碑): an upright stone tablet with carvings or inscriptions

stupa: Buddhist monument, which often houses sacred relics

sutra: sacred Buddhist text

tǎ (塔): pagoda

taipan: a 19th-century term for a powerful foreign businessman in Hong Kong

tiān (天): heaven or sky

tratsang: Buddhist college

wài (外): outer, outside

xī (西): west

xiàng (巷): alley

xiǎochī: literally "small eats"; snacks

yuán (元): unit of Chinese currency

yum cha (yǐn chá; 饮茶): Cantonese dumplings, pastries, and small dishes eaten with tea

yurt: circular tent used by Central Asian nomads

zhàn (站): station

zhāodàisuǒ (招待所): hostel

zhōng (中): middle

zhōngguó (中国): China, literally "Middle Kingdom"

PINYIN PRONUNCIATION GUIDE

The most difficult aspect of the Chinese language for foreigners is the **tone system**. Do not let the challenge posed by tones prevent you from trying out a few Chinese phrases; even with no grasp of them, you should be able to make yourself understood. Most letters used in the pinyin system are pronounced just as they are in English. The exceptions are the following:

a	as in f**a**ther	u	"oo" as in b**oo**t
ai	"i" as in **eye**	ü	"u" as in c**u**te or m**u**te
ao	"ow" as in all**ow**	ui	"way" as in a**way**
ang	"on" as in d**awn**	uo	"wo" as in **wa**r
e	"uh" as in d**uh**	un	"en" as in W**en**dy
ei	"ay" as in **way** or s**ay**	c	"ts" as in ca**ts**
i	"ee" as in f**ee**t after most consonants "rih" sound after "ch," "sh," "zh," and "r" "ih" after "c," "s," and "z"	ch	"ch" as in **ch**eat
ia	"ya" as in **ya**hoo	q	"a" as in an airy sound produced by pushing short burst of air while the tongue is pressed against the palate
ie	"ye" as in **ye**s	r	"r" as in **r**ain
iu	"eo" as in L**eo** or "**yo**, watup?"	sh	"sh" as in **sh**op
ong	"oan" as in l**oan**	x	"sh" as in **sh**eet
ou	"o" as in **o**cean	z	"ds" as in rea**ds**
o	"wo" as in m**o**re	zh	"dj" as in **Dj**ibouti; pronounced like "j" but with the tongue rolled back

MANDARIN PHRASEBOOK

NUMBERS	PINYIN	CHINESE	NUMBERS	PINYIN	CHINESE
0	líng	零	9	jiǔ	九
½	yíbàn	一半	10	shí	十
1	yī or yāo	一	11	shíyī	十一
2	èr or liǎng	二 or 两	12	shíèr	十二
3	sān	三	20	èrshí	二十
4	sì	四	21	èrshíyī	二十一
5	wǔ	五	100	yìbǎi	一百
6	liù	六	200	liǎngbǎi	两百
7	qī	七	1000	yìqiān	一千
8	bā	八	10,000	yíwàn	一万

THE BASICS	PINYIN	CHINESE
Hello	nǐhǎo	你好
Goodbye	zài jiàn	再见
How are you?	nǐ hǎo ma?	你好吗
Please	qǐng	请
Thank you	xièxiè	谢谢
You're welcome	bùkèqi/bùxiè	不客气 / 不谢
Help!	jiùmìng!	救命！
I'm sorry	duìbùqǐ	对不起

THE BASICS	PINYIN	CHINESE
It doesn't matter (when asked to make a choice)	dōu kěyǐ/méi guānxī	都可以 / 没关系
It doesn't matter (don't worry about it)	wú suǒwèi	无所为
Forget about it	suàn le ba	算了吧
What's your name?	nǐ jiào shénme míngzi?	你叫什么名字？
My name is...	wǒ jiào...	我叫 ...
I	wǒ	我
you	nǐ (standard)/nín (formal)	你 / 您
he, she, it	tā	他，她，它
plural: we, you, they	add mén to singular: wǒmén, nǐmén, tāmén	我们，你们，他们
to be	shì (invariable)	是
Yes	shì	是
No	bùshì	不是
to have	yǒu (invariable)	有
to not have	méiyǒu	没有
okay	kěyǐ/xíng	可以 / 行
not okay	bùxíng/bùkěyǐ	不行 / 不可以
to want, would like	yào	要
to not want	bùyào	不要
Do you have...?	yǒu méiyǒu...?	有没有 ...?
I want ...	wǒ yào...	我要 ...
I don't speak Chinese	wǒ bù huì shuō zhōngwén	我不会说中文
Do you speak English?	nǐ huì shuō yīngwén ma?	你会说英文吗？
I can't hear you	wǒ tīng bù jiàn	我听不见
Speak more slowly	màn yi diǎr	慢一点儿
Repeat that	chóngfù yibiàn/zài shuō yi cì	重复一便 / 再说一次
I don't understand	wǒ bù míngbài/wǒ bù dǒng	我不明白 / 我不懂
I need help	wǒ xūyào bāngzhù	我需要帮助
You are cheating me	nǐ zài piàn wǒ	你在骗我
What time do you open?	nǐ jǐdiǎn kāi mén/nǐ jǐdiǎn shàng bān?	你几点开门 / 你几点上班？
What time do you close?	nǐ jǐdiǎn guān mén/nǐ jǐdiǎn xià bān?	你几点关门 / 你几点下班？
restroom	cèsuǒ	厕所
man	nán	男
woman	nǚ	女
toilet paper	wèishēng zhǐ	卫生纸
Western toilet	mǎtǒng	马桶
squat toilet	dūnkēng	蹲坑
big	dà	大
small	xiǎo	小

DIRECTIONS	PINYIN	CHINESE
Where is...?	...zài nǎr?/...zài nǎlǐ?	... 在那儿 ?/... 在那里？
How do I get to ...?	qù...zěnme zǒu?	去 ... 怎么走？

DIRECTIONS	PINYIN	CHINESE
I want to go to...	wǒ yào qù...	我要去 ...
How far is...from here?	...yǒu duō yuǎn?	... 有多远？
How long does it take to get to...?	qù...děi huā duōcháng shíjiān?	去 ... 得花多长时间？
north	běi	北
south	nán	南
east	dōng	东
west	xī	西
left	zuǒ	左
right	yòu	右
front, forward /in the front	qián/qiánmiàn	前 / 前面
back, rear/behind	hòu/hòumiàn	后 / 后面
center, middle	zhōng	中
upper, above, ascend	shàng	上
lower, below, descend	xià	下
between...and...	zài...hé...zhījiān	在 ... 和 ... 之间
to enter/entrance	jìn/rùkǒu	进 / 入口
to exit/exit	chū/chūkǒu	出 / 出口
far, distant	yuǎn	远
close, near/nearby	jìn/fùjìn	近 / 附近
next to...	zài...pángbiān	在 ... 旁边

TRANSPORTATION	PINYIN	CHINESE
passenger (adj.)	kèyùn	客运
insurance	bǎoxiǎn	保险
People's Insurance Company of China (PICC)	zhōngguó rénmín bǎoxiǎn gōngsī	中国人民保险公司
I want to take [a plane, train, bus] to...	wǒ yào zuò [fēijī, huǒchē, qìchē] qù...	我要坐 [飞机 , 火车 , 气车] 去 ...
ticket office	shòupiào chù	售票处
ticket	piào	票
I want to reserve a ticket	wǒ xiǎng dìng piào	我想订票
I want to buy a ticket to...	wǒ xiǎng mǎi qù...de piào	我想买去 ... 的票
one-way ticket	dānchéng piào	单程票
round-trip ticket	wǎngfǎn piào	往反票
Can I cancel my ticket?	kěyǐ tuì piào ma?	可以退票吗？
Can I change my ticket?	kěyǐ huàn piào ma?	可以换票吗？
There are no seats (sleepers)	méi yǒu zuòwèi (pùwèi)	没有坐位 (铺位)
commission	shǒuxù fèi	手续费
schedule	shíkèbiǎo	时刻表
What time does it leave?	jǐ diǎn chūfā?	几点出发？
What time does it arrive?	jǐ diǎn dào?	几点到？
How long does it take?	yàohuā duōshǎo shíjiān?	要花多少时间？
Check (verify) ticket	chá piào	查票
waiting room	hòuchē shì	候车室
luggage storage	jìcún chù	寄存处

TRANSPORTATION	PINYIN	CHINESE
airplane	fēijī	飞机
airport	fēijīchǎng	飞机场
CAAC office	zhōngguó mínháng shòupiào chù	中国民航售票处
train	huǒchē	火车
train station	huǒchē zhàn	火车站
hard/soft seat	yìng zuò/ruǎn zuò	硬座 / 软座
hard/soft sleeper	yìng wò/ruǎn wò	硬卧 / 软卧
upper bunk/middle bunk/lower bunk	shàng pù/zhōng pù/xià pù	上铺 / 中铺 / 下铺
platform	zhàntái	站台
long-distance bus	chángtú qìchē	长途汽车
bus station	qìchē zhàn	汽车站
sleeper bus	wòpù chē	卧铺车
boat	chuán	船
docks	mǎtóu	码头
1st, 2nd,...class cabin	yī, èr,...děng cāng	一，二，...等舱
city bus	gōnggòng qìchē	公共汽车
minibus	zhōngbā	中巴
I want to get off (the bus, etc.)	wǒ yào xià chē	我要下车
subway	dìtiě	地铁
taxi	chūzū chē	出组车
mini-van taxi	miàndī	面的
To request a cab, say: get a cab	dǎ ge dì	打个的
Turn on the meter	dǎ biǎo	打表
bicycle	zìxíngchē	自行车
I want to rent a bicycle	wǒ xiǎng zū liàng zìxíngchē	我想租辆自行车

MONEY	PINYIN	CHINESE
money	qián	钱
Chinese currency	rénmínbì	人民币
one (two, three) yuan	yī (èr, sān) kuài	一（二，三）块
1/10th of one yuan	máo	毛
1/100th of one yuan	fēn	分
cash	xiànjīn	现金
US dollars	měi yuán	美元
traveler's checks	lǚxíng zhīpiào	旅行支票
credit card	xìnyòng kǎ	信用卡
Can I use a foreign credit card?	kěyǐ yòng wàiguó de xìnyòng kǎ ma?	可以用外国的信用卡吗？
bank	yínháng	银行
Bank of China	zhōngguó yínháng	中国银行
to change money	huàn qián	换钱
Can I exchange money (traveler's checks) here?	zhèr kěyǐ huàn qián (lǚxíng zhīpiào) ma?	这儿可以换钱（旅行支票）吗？
ATM	zìdòng qǔ kuǎn/zìdòng yínháng	自动取款 / 自动银行

MONEY	PINYIN	CHINESE
price	jiàqián/jiàgé	价钱 / 价格
pay/pay for	fù qián	付钱
spend money	huā qián	花钱
give change	zhǎo qián	找钱
to bargain	jiǎng jiàqián	讲价钱
How much does it cost?	duōshǎo qián?	多少钱？
inexpensive	piányì	便宜
most inexpensive	zuì piányì	最便宜
expensive	guì	贵
too expensive	tài guìle	太贵了
This is fake	zhè shì jiǎ de	这是假的
Can I have a discount/do you give discounts?	kěyǐ piányì yìdiǎn ma/nǐ dǎ bù dǎ zhé?	可以便一点吗 / 你打不打折？
Write a receipt	kāi piào	开票
I want a receipt	wǒ yào fāpiào	我要发票

HEALTH AND EMERGENCY	PINYIN	CHINESE
sick/disease	bìng	病
Western medicine	xī yī	西医
Chinese medicine	zhōng yī	中医
I am sick	wǒ bìng le	我病了
I don't feel well	wǒ bù shūfu	我不舒服
I am injured	wǒ shòushāngle	我受伤了
hurt/pain	téng	疼
My head hurts	wǒ tóu téng	我头疼
My stomach hurts	wǒ dùzi téng	我肚子疼
I'm allergic to...	wǒ duì...guòmǐn	我对 ... 过敏
I feel nauseous	wǒ ě'xīn	我恶心
I've caught a cold	wǒ gǎnmào le	我感冒了
I have a fever	wǒ fāshāo le	我发烧了
AIDS	àizībìng	艾兹病
altitude sickness	gāoshān fǎnyìng	高山反应
diarrhea	lā dùzi	拉肚子
hepatitis	gānyán	肝炎
malaria	nüèjí	疟疾
rabies	kuángquǎnbìng	狂犬病
tetanus	pòshāngfēng	破伤风
hospital	yīyuàn	医院
Where is the hospital?	yīyuàn zài nǎr?	医院在那儿？
doctor	dàifu	大夫
Please use sterilized equipment	qǐng yòng yīcìxìng yíqì	请用一次性仪器
I do not want a blood transfusion	wǒ bù yào shū xuè	我不要输血
shot/injection	zhùshè	注射
Please use my own syringe	qǐng yòng wǒ zìjǐ de zhùshèqì	请用我自己的注射器

HEALTH AND EMERGENCY	PINYIN	CHINESE
pharmacy	yàodiàn/yàofáng	药店 / 药房
medicine	yàopiàn	药片
antibiotic	kàngshēngsù/kàngjūnsù	抗生素 / 抗菌素
aspirin/painkiller	āsīpǐlín	阿斯匹林
condom	bìyùntào	避孕套
contraceptive	bìyùnyào	避孕药
sanitary napkins	wèi shēng jīn	卫生巾
rehydration salts	fùshuǐ yán	复水盐
Fire!	zháo huǒ la!	着火啦 !
police	jǐngchá	警察
Thief (pickpocket)!	xiǎotōu!	小偷 !
My money/passport has been stolen.	yǒurén tōu le wǒ de qián/hùzhào	有人偷了我的钱 / 护照
I've lost my money/passport.	wǒ bǎ wǒ de qián/hùzhào diū le	我把我的钱 / 护照丢了
danger/dangerous	wēixiǎn	危险
Go away!	zǒukāi !	走开 !

ACCOMMODATIONS	PINYIN	CHINESE
hotel	bīnguǎn/fàndiàn/jiǔdiàn/lǚguǎn	宾馆 / 饭店 / 酒店 / 旅馆
hostel	zhāodàisuǒ/lǚshè	招待所 / 旅舍
yurt	ménggǔ bāo	蒙古包
room	fángjiān	房间
dormitory	duōrén fáng/jiān	多人房 / 间
single room	dānrén fáng/jiān	单人房 / 间
double room	shuāngrén fáng/jiān	双人房 / 间
triple room	sānrén fáng/jiān	三人房 / 间
economy room	jīngjì fáng/jiān	经济房 / 间
standard room	biāozhǔn fáng/jiān	标准房 / 间
luxury room	háohuá tàofáng/jiān	豪华套房 / 间
bed	chuángwèi	床位
You must pay for the entire room	nǐ xūyào bāofáng	你需要包房
check-out	tuìfáng	退房
key	yàoshí	钥匙
deposit	yājīn	押金
attendant	fúwùyuán	服务员
Can I look at the room?	wǒ kěyǐ kànkàn fángjiān ma?	我可以看看房间吗 ?
Is it okay for men and women to stay together?	néng nánnǚ tóngjū ma?	能男女同居吗 ?
We are a married couple	wǒmén shì fūqī	我们是夫妻
(24hr.) hot water	(èrshísì xiǎoshí) rèshuǐ	(二十四小时) 热水
When is hot water available?	shénme shíhòu yǒu rèshuǐ?	什么时候有热水 ?
air-conditioning	kōngtiáo	空调
free breakfast	miǎnfèi zǎocān	免费早餐
Please wash these clothes	qǐng bǎ zhè xiē yīfú xǐ hǎo	请把这些衣服洗好

COMMUNICATIONS	PINYIN	CHINESE
post office	yóujú	邮局
letter	xìn	信
envelope	xìnfēng	信封
postcard	míngxìnpiàn	明信片
stamp	yóupiào	邮票
package	bāoguǒ	包裹
Express Mail International Service (EMS)	guójì tèkuài zhuāndì	国际特快专递
airmail	hángkōng xìn	航空信
surface mail	píngyóu	平邮
registered mail	guà hàoxìn	挂号信
Poste Restante	cúnjú hòulǐng	存局候领
telephone office	diànxùn dàlóu	电讯大楼
China Telecom	zhōngguó diànxìn	中国电信
telephone	diànhuà	电话
phone card	diànhuà kǎ	电话卡
long-distance call	chángtú diànhuà	长途电话
international call	guójì chángtú diànhuà	国际长途电话
collect call	duìfāng fùqián diànhuà	对方付钱电话
I want to make a long-distance phone call	wǒ yào dǎ chángtú diànhuà	我要打长途电话
What is the number for...?	...de diànhuà hàomǎ shì shénme?	... 的电话号码是什么？
First dial "0"	xiān bō líng	先拨零
I want to [send/receive] a fax	wǒ yào [fā/shōu] chuánzhēn	我要 [发 / 收] 传真
Internet bar	wǎngbā	网吧
computer	diànnǎo	电脑
I want to get on the Internet	wǒ yào shàng wǎng	我要上网
I want to send an email	wǒ yào fā diànzi yóujiàn	我要电子邮件
How much is it per hour?	yī ge xiǎoshí duōshǎo qián?	一个小时多少钱？

PASSPORT AND VISA	PINYIN	CHINESE
passport	hùzhào	护照
visa	qiānzhèng	签证
I need to extend my visa	wǒ xūyào yánqī wǒ de qiānzhèng	我需要延期我的签证
PSB Division of Exit and Entry	gōng ān jú chūrù jìng guǎnlǐ chù	公安局出入境理处
PSB Foreign Affairs Branch	gōng ān jú wàishì kē	公安局外事科
embassy	dàshǐguǎn	大使馆
consulate	lǐngshìguǎn	领事馆

LEISURE	PINYIN	CHINESE
film	diànyǐng	电影
I want to watch a film	wǒ xiǎng kàn diànyǐng	我想看电影
movie theater	diànyǐng yuàn	电影院

LEISURE	PINYIN	CHINESE
music	yīnyuè	音乐
music concert	yīnyuè huì	音乐会
play (drama)	xìjù	戏剧
sports	tǐyù	体育
stadium	tǐyùchǎng	体育场
to play (a sport)	dǎ	打
soccer	zú qiú	足球
table tennis	pīngpāng qiú	乒乓球
basketball	lán qiú	蓝球
swimming (pool)	yóuyǒng (chí)	游泳（池）
martial arts	wǔshù	武术
tai chi	tàijí quán	太极拳
mahjong	májiàng	麻将
I am here strictly to travel	wǒ shì zhuānmén lái lǚyóu de	我是专门来旅游的
How old are you?	nǐ duō dà/nǐ duō dà niánlíng?	你多大 / 你多大年龄？
I am (20, 30, ...) years old	wǒ (èrshí, sānshí, ...) suì	我（二十，三十，...）岁
What do you do (what is your occupation)?	nǐ shì zuò shénme de?	你是作什么的？
I am a student/I go to school	wǒ shì xuéshēng/wǒ zài shàng xué	我是学生 / 我在上学
I am a teacher/I teach school	wǒ shì lǎoshī/wǒ zài jiāoshū	我是老师 / 我在教书
I work	wǒ gōngzuò	我工作
I am retired	wǒ tuìxiū le	我退休了
I (don't) have any children	wǒ (méi) yǒu háizi	我（没）有孩子
bar	jiǔbā	酒吧
nightclub	jùlèbù	俱乐部
cover	ménpiào	门票
entertainment center	yúlè chǎng	娱乐场
massage	àn mó	按摩
sauna	sāngná	桑拿
karaoke	kǎlā OK	卡拉OK
You are very pretty/handsome	nǐ hěn piàoliàng/hǎokàn	你很漂亮 / 好看
You are truly remarkable	nǐ zhēn liǎo bù qǐ	你真了不起
I love you	wǒ ài nǐ	我爱你
to make love	zuò ài [colloquial: qí mǎ]	作爱 [骑马]
I am not that casual	wǒ bù nàme suíbiàn	我不那么随便

TIME	PINYIN	CHINESE
minutes	fēnzhōng	分钟
hour	xiǎoshí	小时
...o'clock	...diǎn	... 点
What time is now?	xiànzài jǐ diǎn?	现在几点？
morning	zǎochén	早晨
noon	zhōngwǔ	中午
afternoon	xiàwǔ	下午

TIME	PINYIN	CHINESE
week	xīngqī/lǐbài	星期 / 礼拜
Monday	xīngqī yī	星期一
Tuesday	xīngqī èr	星期二
Wednesday	xīngqī sān	星期三
Thursday	xīngqī sì	星期四
Friday	xīngqī wǔ	星期五
Saturday	xīngqī liù	星期六

TIME	PINYIN	CHINESE
evening	bāngwǎn	傍晚
night	wǎnshàng	晚上
midnight	bànyè	半夜
daytime	báitiān	白天
nighttime	wǎnshàng	晚上
now	xiànzài	现在
day	tiān/rì	天 / 日
today	jīn tiān	今天
yesterday	zuó tiān	作天
tomorrow	míngtiān	明天

TIME	PINYIN	CHINESE
Sunday	xīngqī rì/tiān	星起日 / 天
month (moon)	yuè	月
Months are referred to numerically starting with Jan.:		
January	yīyuè	一月
February	èryuè	二月
year	nián	年
last year	qù nián	去年
1978	yī jiǔ qī bā nián	一九七八年
past	yǐqián	以前
future	jiānglái/wèilái	将来 / 未来

FOOD	PINYIN	CHINESE
to eat	chīfàn	吃饭
supermarket	chāoshì	超市
restaurant	cānguǎn	餐馆
street stall	dà pái dàng	大排挡
to go	dàizǒu	带走
delivery	sòng	送
waitstaff/ waitress	fúwùyuán/ xiǎojiě	服务员 / 小姐
how many people are in your party?	nǐ jǐ wèi?	你几位？
menu	càidān	猜单
check/bill	zhàngdān	账单
chopsticks	kuàizi	筷子
napkin	cānjīnzhǐ	餐巾
fork	chāzi	叉子
knife	dāozi	刀子
spoon	sháozi	勺子
bowl	wǎn	碗
plate	pánzi	盘子
Is the food ready yet?	fàn hǎo le ma?	饭好了吗
delicious	hǎochī	好吃
This has no flavor	zhè méi yǒu wèidào	这没有味道
hot (temp.)	rè	热
cold	liáng	凉
Not too much...	bùyào tài duō	不要太多
spicy	là	辣
garlic	dàsuàn	大蒜

FOOD	PINYIN	CHINESE
I am vegetarian	wǒ chī sù	我吃素
I don't eat meat	wǒ bù chī ròu	我不吃肉
I am on a diet	wǒ jiǎnféi	我减肥
buffet	zìzhù cān	自助餐
dim sum/ snacks	diǎnxīn	点心
snacks	xiǎochī	小吃
Muslim	qīngzhēn	清真
fast food	kuài cān	快餐
McDonald's	màidāngláo	麦当劳
hamburger	hànbǎobāo	汉堡包
white rice	mǐfàn	米饭
fried rice	chǎofàn	炒饭
noodles	miàntiáo	面条
Northwest noodles	xīběi lāmiàn	西北拉面
mixed noodles	bàn miàn	拌面
kebab	ròu chuàn	肉串
bean curd/ tofu	dòufǔ	豆腐
soup	tāng	汤
noodle soup	miàn tāng	面汤
beef noodle soup	niúròu miàn	牛肉面
hotpot	shāguō	沙锅
hotpot (Sichuan)	huǒguō	火锅
curry	gālí	咖喱
wontons	húntun	馄饨
dumplings	jiǎozi	饺子

APPENDIX

FOOD	PINYIN	CHINESE
MSG	wèijīng	味精
oil	yóu	油
pepper	làjiāo	辣椒
salt (salty)	yán (xián)	盐（咸）
soy sauce	jiàng yóu	酱油
sugar (sweet)	táng (tián)	糖（甜）
vinegar	cù	醋
vegetables	shūcài	蔬菜
Chinese cabbage	báicài	白菜
corn	yùmǐ	玉米
cucumber	huángguā	黄瓜
green vegetables	qīngcài	青菜
mushrooms	mógū/xiānggū	蘑菇 / 香菇
peas	wāndòu	豌豆
fruit	shuǐguǒ	水果
apple	píngguǒ	苹果
banana	xiāngjiāo	香蕉
grape	pútáo	葡萄
lychee	lìzhī	荔枝
mango	mángguǒ	芒果
peach	táozi	桃子
pineapple	bōluó	菠萝
watermelon	xīguā	西瓜
ice cream	bīngqílín	冰淇淋
milkshake	nǎixī	奶昔
soy milk	dòujiāng	豆浆
yogurt	suānnǎi	酸奶
mooncake	yuè bǐng	月饼
sweet bean paste rolls	dòushā gāo/dòushā bāo	豆沙糕 / 豆沙包
soft drinks	qìshuǐ	汽水
Coke	kěkǒu kělè	可口可乐

FOOD	PINYIN	CHINESE
steamed dumplings	bāozi	包子
Shanghai-style dumplings	xiǎolóng bāo	小笼包
egg	jīdàn	鸡蛋
steamed buns	mántóu	馒头
bread	miànbāo	面包
fried bread sticks	yóutiáo	油条
beef	niúròu	牛肉
chicken	jī	鸡
dog meat	gǒu ròu	狗肉
Beijing duck	běijīng kǎoyā	北京烤鸭
fish	yú	鱼
frog	tiánjī	田鸡
lamb	yángròu	羊肉
pork	zhūròu	猪肉
seafood	hǎixiān	海鲜
shrimp	xiā	虾
snake	shé	蛇
to drink	hē	喝
beverage	yínliào	饮料
water	shuǐ	水
bottle	píng	瓶
cup	bēi	杯
hot water	bái kāi shuǐ	白开水
tea house	chá guǎn/chá fáng	茶馆 / 茶房
cafe	kāfēiguǎn	咖啡馆
tea	chá	茶
eight-treasures tea	bā bǎo chá	八宝茶
milk pearl tea	zhēnzhū nǎi chá	珍珠奶茶
coffee	kāfēi	咖啡
beer	píjiǔ	啤酒
Tsingtao beer	qīngdǎo píjiǔ	青岛啤酒

PLACES	PINYIN	CHINESE
sea	hǎi	海
river	jiāng or hé	江 or 河

PLACES	PINYIN	CHINESE
What country are you from?	nǐ shì nǎguó rén? or nǐ shì nǎlǐ lái de?	你是那国人？or 你是那里来的？
I am a native of (country).	wǒ shì...rén.	我是 ... 人

PLACES	PINYIN	CHINESE
lake	hú	湖
pond	chí	池
stream	xī	溪
waterfall	pùbù	瀑布
island	dǎo	岛
peninsula	bàndǎo	半岛
beach	hǎitān (shātān)	海滩（沙滩）
forest	sēnlín	森林
grasslands	cǎoyuán	草原
desert	shāmò	沙漠
plateau	gāoyuán	高原
mountain	shān	山
glacier	bīngchuān	冰川
cave	dòng	洞
grotto	shíkū	石窟
hot springs	wēnquán	温泉
countryside	nóngcūn	农村
downtown	shì zhōngxīn	市中心
city	chéngshì	城市
county	xiàn	县
square	guǎngchǎng	广场
temple	sì	寺
park	gōngyuán	公园
museum	bówùguǎn	博物馆
road	lù	路
street	jiē	街
boulevard or avenue	dàjiē or dàdào	大街 or 大道

PLACES	PINYIN	CHINESE
Chinese	zhōngguó rén	中国人
foreigner	wàiguó rén	外国人
What country are you going to?	nǐ qù nǎ gè guójiā?	你去那个国家？
border crossing	jièxiàn	界线
Australia	àodàlìyà	澳大利亚
Canada	jiā'nádà	加拿大
France	fǎguó	法国
India	yìndù	印度
Ireland	ài'ěrlán	爱尔兰
Japan	rìběn	日本
Kazakhstan	hāsàkèsītǎn	哈萨克斯坦
Kyrgyzstan	jíěrjísītǎn	吉尔吉斯坦
Laos	lǎowō	老挝
Mongolia	ménggǔ	蒙古
Myanmar	miǎndiàn	缅甸
Nepal	níbóěr	尼泊尔
New Zealand	xīn xīlán	新西兰
North Korea	běi cháoxiǎn	北朝鲜
Pakistan	bājīsītǎn	巴基斯坦
Russia	éluósī	俄罗斯
South Africa	nánfēi	南非
South Korea	hánguó	韩国
Taiwan	táiwān	台湾
Thailand	tàiguó	泰国
UK	yīngguó	英国
US	měiguó	美国
Vietnam	yuènán	越南

WEATHER	PINYIN	CHINESE
weather	tiānqì	天气
How's the weather?	tiānqì zěnme yàng?	天气怎么样？
weather forecast	tiānqì yùbào	天气预报
°C	shèshí wēndù	摄氏温度
clear	tiānqíng	天晴
sun	tàiyáng	太阳
cloudy	duōyún	多云
windy	guāfēng	刮风
hot and humid	mēnrè	闷热
extremely hot	rè sǐ le	热死了

WEATHER	PINYIN	CHINESE
Is it going to rain?	huì xiàyǔ ma?	会下雨吗？
rain	xiàyǔ	下雨
thunderstorms	léizhènyǔ	雷阵雨
hail	bīngbáo	冰雹
typhoon	táifēng	台风
flood	shuǐzāi	水灾
raincoat	yǔyī	雨衣
umbrella	yǔsǎn	雨伞
snow	xiàxuě	下雪
extremely cold	lěng sǐ le	冷死了

CANTONESE PHRASEBOOK

NUMBERS					
0	ling	6	luk	12	sap yi
1	yat	7	chat	20	yi sap
2	yi/leung	8	baat	21	yi sap yat
3	saam	9	gau	100	yat baak
4	sei	10	sap	10,000	yat maan
5	mm	11	sap yat	100,000	sap maan

USEFUL PHRASES			
How are you?	nei hou ma?	Goodbye	bai bai
Thank you	dor je/mm goi	You're welcome	mm sai (mm goi)
I'm sorry	deui mm jyu	yes/no	hai/mm hai
What's your name?	nei giu meh meng?	My name is ...	ngo giu ...
Where is ... ?	... hai bin dou?	I don't understand.	ngo mm ming
I don't speak Cantonese.	ngo mm sik gong gong dung wa	Do you speak English?	nei sik mm sik gong ying man ah?
How much does it cost?	gei dor chin ah?	... dollars	... mun
It's too expensive.	tai gwai la	Can you make it cheaper?	peng di la

TIBETAN PHRASEBOOK

USEFUL PHRASES			
Hello	Tah-shi de-lah	Goodbye (to the person leaving)	Kah-leh phe
How are you?	Keh-rahng ku-su de-bo yin-peh?	Goodbye (to the person staying behind)	Kah-leh shoo
Please have some	shey shey	No thank you	La meh
What's your name?	Keh-rahng gi ming la kah-rey yin?	My name is ...	Ngah...yin.
Go away!	gyu!	Don't do that!	mah che!
I don't speak Tibetan.	Ngah Phö-keh shing-gi-meh	Do you speak English?	Dhey In-jee-keh shing-ken yo-ray-peh?
I don't understand.	Ha-kho-mah-song	Where is ... ?	...kah-bah yo-ray?
How much does it cost?	...gi kong kah-tsö ray?	Please help me.	Ngah la

UIGHUR PHRASEBOOK

USEFUL PHRASES			
Hello, how are you?	yak-shimi-sis	to eat	tam-ak
Okay	yak-shi	invite to eat	tam-ak yang
Goodbye	hara-hosh	lamb kebab	kawap
What are you doing?	azer ne-mar-ish ka-li-sis	My name is...	lagh-man
How much does it cost?	nai-chi po	lamb and vegetable pita pocket	sam-sa
Out of the way!	bosh, bosh!	hami melon	how-hun
Thank you	rah-mat siz-ga	tea	chai

USEFUL CONVERSIONS

DISTANCE CONVERSIONS

Meters	1	15	50	100	200	500	1000
Feet	3.281	50	164	328	656	1640	3280

TEMPERATURE CONVERSIONS

°Celsius	-40	-20	-18	0	15	25	35
°Fahrenheit	-40	-4	0	32	59	77	95

MEASUREMENT CONVERSIONS

1 inch (in.) = 25.4 mm	1 millimeter (mm) = 0.039 in.
1 foot (ft.) = 0.30 m	1 meter (m) = 3.28 ft.
1 yard (yd.) = 0.914m	1 meter (m) = 1.09 yd.
1 mile (mi.) = 1.61km	1 kilometer (km) = 0.62 mi.
1 ounce (oz.) = 28.35g	1 gram (g) = 0.035 oz.
1 pound (lb.) = 0.454kg	1 kilogram (kg) = 2.202 lb.
1 fluid ounce (fl. oz.) = 29.57ml	1 milliliter (ml) = 0.034 fl. oz.
1 gallon (gal.) = 3.785L	1 liter (L) = 0.264 gal.
1 acre (ac.) = 0.405ha	1 hectare (ha) = 2.47 ac.
1 square mile (sq. mi.) = 2.59km^2	1 square kilometer (km^2) = 0.386 sq. mi.

CLIMATE

To convert from °C to °F, multiply by 1.8 and add 32. For a rough approximation, double the Celsius and add 25. To convert from °F to °C, subtract 32 and multiply by 0.55 (approx. 5/9). For a rough approximation, subtract 25 and cut it in half.

Avg. Temp. (low/high)	January		April		July		October	
	°C	°F	°C	°F	°C	°F	°C	°F
Beijing	-10/1	14/34	7/21	45/70	21/31	70/88	6/20	43/68
Chongqing	5/9	41/49	16/23	60/73	24/34	76/93	16/22	61/71
Harbin	-24/-5	-5/14	0/13	32/54	18/26	65/83	0/12	32/53
Hong Kong	13/18	56/64	19/24	67/75	26/31	78/87	23/27	73/81
Lhasa	-10/7	14/44	1/16	33/60	9/23	49/74	1/17	34/62
Shanghai	1/8	33/46	10/19	50/66	23/32	74/90	14/23	57/74
Ürümqi	-22/-11	-7/13	2/16	36/60	14/28	58/82	-1/10	31/50

Avg. Rain (mm)	Jan	Feb	Mar	Apr	May	Jun	July	Aug	Sep	Oct	Nov	Dec
Beijing	4	5	8	17	35	78	196	244	58	16	11	3
Chongqing	15	20	38	99	142	180	142	122	150	112	48	20
Harbin	5	5	15	20	35	90	150	110	40	25	10	5
Hong Kong	33	46	74	137	292	394	381	367	257	114	43	31
Lhasa	0	13	8	5	25	64	122	89	66	13	3	0
Shanghai	48	58	84	94	94	180	147	142	130	71	51	36
Ürümqi	15	8	13	38	28	38	18	25	15	43	41	10

INDEX

A

Abokh Hoja 811
abortion 33
acrobatics 155, 157
Acute Mountain Sickness (AMS) 831
adapters 22
adventure travel 64, 786
    Gobi 798
    Hanas Lake 792
    Muztagata, Mt. 813
    North Korea 260
    Pamirs 809
    Taklimakan 808
AIDS 32
air travel 43
alcohol 24, 450
alien travel permits 14
    in Tibet 829
Altai City (XJ) 789
Altai Prefecture (XJ) 789–793
American Express 18
    Hong Kong 552
    Macau 588
    Shanghai 342
An Lushan Rebellion 75
Analects, the 89, 95, 206, 276
Anhui province (AH) 412–432
Anshun (GZ) 627
Anyang (HEN) 301
architecture 99
arts 95
Asian financial crisis 92
ATM cards 19
Avalokiteshvara 836, 844, 846, 852
    see also Guanyin
avian flu 32

B

Badaling Great Wall (BJG) 167
badminton 100, 266
Bai 597, 668, 674
Bai Juyi 95
Baisha (YN) 678
Bamboo Sea (SC) 726
Bao, Lord 300, 418
Baoguo Monastery (SC) 711
Baoshan (YN) 662
Baotou (IM) 323
bargaining 21
basketball 100
bathrooms 93
batik 672
beaches
    Beidaihe (HEB) 191
    Clearwater Bay (HK) 577
    Coloane Island (MC) 594
    Dalian (LN) 265
    Deep Water and Repulse Bays (HK) 571
    Jingpo Lake (JL) 238
    Lantau Island (HK) 581
    Putuoshan (ZJ) 411
    Qingdao (SD) 214
    Sanya (HND) 538
    Silver (GX) 622
    Stanley (HK) 571
    Weihai (SD) 221
    Yantai (SD) 218
beer 1, 3, 353
    Tàihú shuǐ 379
    Tsingtao 191, 207, 213
beggars 94

Beidaihe (HEB) 189
Beihai (GX) 619
Beihai Park 145
Beijing (BJG) 119–166
    accommodations 132–137
    buses 128
    daytrips 161–166
    entertainment 155
    food 137–142
    galleries 156
    intercity transportation 120–127
    local transportation 128
    nightlife 159–161
    orientation 127
    practical information 130–132
    shopping 157
    sights 142–155
Beijing and the North Coast 119–222
Beijing duck 139
Beijing opera 97, 155
Big Buddha (SC) 705
Bird Island (QH) 823
Bishkek, Kyrgyzstan 42, 808
Bön 832, 835
border crossings 41
    Hong Kong 524
    Kazakhstan 41, 789
    Kyrgyzstan 42
    Laos 41, 662
    Macau 518
    Mongolia 42, 789
    Myanmar 41, 668
    Nepal 42, 830, 865
    North Korea 42, 258
    Pakistan 42, 815
    Vietnam 41, 652
Bosten Lake (XJ) 804
Buck, Pearl 383
Buddha's Light 706

Buddhism 90
  Tibetan 760, 836
Bulangshan (YN) 661
Bulong 651
Bund, the (SH) 348
bungee jumping 165, 266
Burqin (XJ) 791

C

calligraphy 97
calling card 51
camping
  Changbaishan (JL) 251
  Chimpu (TBT) 851
  Lugu Lake (YN) 682
  Mt. Everest 862
  Namtso (TBT) 849
  Samye (TBT) 850
  Singing Sands (GS) 780
  Tengger Desert 749
  Tianchi (XJ) 788
  Weizhou (GX) 622
Canton. See Guangzhou
Cantonese 87, 88, 542, 878
Canto-pop 97, 543
Cao Xueqin 150
caves
  Four Caves and Gorges
    (GZ) 640
  Jiuxiang (YN) 651
  Longgong (GX) 630
  White Rock Cliff (GS) 763
  Yangshuo (GX) 615
  Yiling (GX) 604
  Zhangjiajie (HUN) 458
  Zhijin (GZ) 631
cell phones. See mobile
  phones
Centers for Disease Control
  (CDC) 28
Central China 267–332
ceramics 98
  institute 115
  Jingdezhen 436

Chang'an (Xi'an) 75, 267
Changbaishan (JL) 249–253
Changchun (JL) 240
Changsha (HUN) 447–454
Chaozhou (GD) 527
Chen Kaige 99, 103
Cheng's Three Residences
  (AH) 421
Chengde (HEB) 181
Chengdu (SC) 689–703
Cheung Chau (HK) 583
Chiang Kai-shek 79, 277,
  357
China National Tourist Office
  (CNTO) 12
Chinese characters 88
Chinese Communist Party
  (CCP) 91, 101, 433, 727,
  833
  founding of 79
  museums 351
  pilgrimage sites 281, 439,
    444, 447, 452, 638, 732
Chishui (GZ) 640
Chong'an (GZ) 636
Chongqing (CQ) 727–733
chuba 845
Chungking Mansions 556
Ci Xi, Dowager Empress 78,
  145, 153, 164, 185
Civil Aviation Administration
  of China (CAAC) 43
Coloane Island (MC) 594
Communism 80, 91
Confucianism 89
Confucius 89, 191, 203, 308
  tomb of 205
Confucius Temple (SD) 206
conservation 105
consulates. See embassies
  and consulates
converters 22
cranes 234
credit cards 18
cuisine
  Dai 647, 655

Muslim 70, 646
  Sichuanese 696
  Tibetan 834
Cultural Revolution 762, 846,
  852
  Red Guards 81, 142
currency 17
  Hong Kong 543
  Macau 584
customs 16
customs and etiquette 93

D

Dai 87, 523, 597, 651
Daju (YN) 680
Dalai Lake. See Hulun Lake
Dalai Lama 93, 832, 833,
  836, 844
Dali (YN) 668–674
Dalian (LN) 261–266
Damenglong (YN) 660
Dandong (LN) 258
Danjia 540
Dao De Jing 89
Daoism 89
Datong (SX) 311–316
Dazu (CQ) 734
Dehong (YN) 662–668
Democracy Wall Movement
  82
Deng Xiaoping 80, 81, 82,
  83, 92, 333
dengue fever 30
Deqin (YN) 686
deserts
  Budain Jaran 769
  Gobi 798
  Mu Us 283
  Singing Sands (GS) 782
  Taklimakan 803, 808, 818
  Tengger 748, 750
Dian, Lake 650
dim sum 504, 558
disabled travelers 68

diseases 29
dog meat 243, 249, 629, 633
Dong 87, 523, 597, 618, 631, 634
Dong villages (GZ) 637
dōngběi. See Northeast
Dongshan (JS) 374
Dongsheng (IM) 327
dragons 247, 311, 315, 397, 410, 554, 649, 706, 738
Dream of the Red Chamber 95, 146, 150, 356, 421
drugs 24
Du Fu 95, 697, 737, 768
Dujiangyan Irrigation System (SC) 700
Dunhuang (GS) 777–782
dynasties
 Han 75
 Liao 76
 Ming 76
 Qin 74
 Qing 76
 Shu 690
 Song 76
 Tang 75
 Western Xia 748
dysentery 31

E

earthquakes 24
Eastern Qing Tombs (BJG) 163
Eight Outer Temples (HEB) 185
email 54
embassies and consulates 9–11
 Chengdu 694
 Chongqing 730
 Kunming 644
 Shenyang (LN) 256
Emeishan (SC) 706

emperors
 Chongzhen 145
 Helu of Wu 366, 373
 Huangdi 74, 96, 202, 206
 Kangxi 77, 185, 247
 Pu Yi 78, 244
 Qianlong 77, 147, 162, 164, 165, 185, 371, 387, 388, 811
 Qin Shihuang 75, 166, 199, 219, 276, 277
 Taizong 75, 289, 711, 800
 Taizu 76
 Wu Zetian 75, 274, 278, 290, 295
 Wudi 219, 278, 279, 777
 Xiangfeng 185
 Yongle 76, 144, 163
 Zhen Wu 471
 Zhengde 311
 Zhu Yuanzhang 364
 Zhuang 410
EMS 49
End of the Earth (HND) 539
engineering follies
 Ci Xi's marble boat 153
ethnic composition 85
Everest, Mount 862

F

Falun Gong 92
Federal Express 50
Feilai Monastery (YN) 687
female travelers 67
feng shui 99
Fengdu (CQ) 737
Fengjie (CQ) 737
festivals 101
 Dragon Boat 577, 609
 Gyantse 855
 Harbin Ice Lantern 230
 in Shanghai 353
 Kaili 635
 Luoyang Peony 290
 Miao 635

Mid-Autumn 395
Naadam 321, 332
Ox Soul 617
peach blossom 355
Qingdao Beer 212
Shanghai International Film 352
Tibetan 836
Water Splashing 660
film 99
 recommended 103
 Shanghai International Film Festival 352
floods 24
food and drink 94
Forbidden City 144
foreign concessions
 Qingdao (SD) 207
 Shamian Island (GZ) 506
 Shanghai (SH) 350
 Tianjin (TJ) 174
 Wuhan (HUB) 459
 Xiamen (FJ) 491
Foshan (GD) 508
Four Heavenly Kings 97
Friendship Highway (TBT) 853–865
Fuhu Monastery (SC) 711
Fujian province (FJ) 477–498
Fuzhou (FJ) 477

G

Gang of Four 82
Gangu (GS) 769
Ganlanba. See Menghan
Gansu province (GS) 752–782
Gate of Heavenly Peace. See Tian'anmen Gate
gay and lesbian travelers 67
Gejia 636
Gelug school 832
Genghis Khan 76

mausoleum 329
Gezhou Dam (HUB) 468
giardiasis (giardia) 831
glaciers
 Hailuogou (SC) 714
 July 1st (GS) 776
 Mingyong (YN) 687
 Qianjing (TBT) 863
goats 164, 505, 812
Golden Mile 562
Golmud (QH) 824
Grand Canal 75, 333, 366,
 369
grasslands
 Ganjia (GS) 763
 Hohhot (IM) 322
 Hulun Buir (IM) 332
 Namtso Lake (TBT) 849
 Sangke (GS) 763
 Tagong (SC) 716
Great Leap Forward 80, 442
Great Wall 73, 75, 166
 Badaling (BJG) 167
 Huanghuacheng (BJG) 168
 Jiaoshan (HEB) 189
 Jiayuguan (GS) 775
 Mutianyu (BJG) 167
 Shanhaiguan (HEB) 188
 Simatai (BJG) 168
 Tiger Mountain (JL) 261
 Yulin (SAX) 284
grottoes
 33rd Heaven (GS) 771
 Bingling Temple (GS) 757
 Kizil (XJ) 806
 Kizilgaha (XJ) 807
 Kumtura (XJ) 807
 Longmen (HEN) 295
 Maijishan (GS) 768
 Mogao (GS) 781
 Simsem (XJ) 807
 Xumishan (NX) 751
 Yungang (SX) 315
GSM 53
Guan Yu 294
Guangdong province (GD)
 498–533

Guangxi Zhuang
 Autonomous Region (GX)
 597–622
Guangzhou (GD) 498–508
Guanyin 410, 411, 497
Guilin (GX) 605–610
Guiyang (GZ) 623
Guizhou province (GZ) 623–
 640
Gulangyu Island (FJ) 496
Guomindang (GMD) 79, 83,
 731
Guyuan (NX) 751
Gyantse (TBT) 855

H

Haikou (HND) 533
Hailar (IM) 332
Hainan Island (HND) 533–
 541
Hakka 540
halal 70
Hanas Lake (XJ) 792
Hangzhou (ZJ) 390–398
Hani 651
Hankou. See Wuhan
Hanyang. See Wuhan
Harbin (HLJ) 224–232
hard sleeper 46
health 27–34
 environmental hazards 29
 immunizations 27
heat exhaustion 29
Hebei province (HEB) 176–
 191
Hefei (AH) 412
Heilongjiang province (HLJ)
 223–240
Hekou (YN) 652
Henan province (HEN) 285–
 303
Hengshan (HUN) 453
Hengshan (SX) 316

hepatitis 31, 32
Heshun (YN) 665
high altitude 29, 831, 849
hiking
 Four Maidens Mountains
 703
 Gunzhong (NX) 748
 Immortal's Cliffs (GS) 768
 Jiuzhaigou (SC) 719
 Namtso Lake (TBT) 849
 Wolong (SC) 702
 Zhangjiajie 457
Himalayas 73, 862
history 74–84
HIV 32
Hohhot (IM) 316–323
Hong Kong (HK) 542–583
 accommodations 556,
 566, 575, 580
 beaches 571, 577, 581,
 583
 Central 568
 Cheung Chau 583
 consulates and visas 551
 entertainment 554
 food 558, 567, 576, 580,
 582
 HKTB 551, 562, 575, 581
 Hong Kong Island (HK)
 564–575
 intercity transportation 546
 Kowloon 554–564
 Lamma Island 582
 Lantau Island 579–582
 local transportation 548
 money 543
 New Territories 575–579
 nightlife 564, 572
 orientation 548
 practical information 551–
 554
 Sai Kung 576
 shopping 562, 572
 sights 561, 568, 576
 Tsim Sha Tsui 561
Hongcun (AH) 422
horseracing 577, 594
Hostelling International (HI)

57
hostels 57
hot springs
Gonggashan (SC) 714
Huangshan (AH) 424
Huaqing (SAX) 277
Longsheng (GX) 618
Sea of Heat (YN) 665
Yangpachen (TBT) 849
Hotan (XJ) 815
hotels 56
hotpot 139
Hu Jintao 84, 91
Huang Fei Hong 509
Huangguoshu Waterfalls (GZ)
629
Huanghuacheng Great Wall
(BJG) 168
Huanglong (SC) 722
Huangshan (AH) 424–429
Huashan (SAX) 279
Huayan Monastery (SX) 314
Hubei province (HUB) 459–
475
Hui 86, 533, 741, 759, 783
Hunan province (HUN)
447–459
Hurka 240
hútòng 147
hypothermia 29

I

IC cards 52
immunizations 27
Imperial Summer Villa (HEB)
184
**Inner Mongolia
Autonomous Region (IM)**
316–332
insurance 27
International Driving Permit
(IDP) 48
International Student Identity
Card (ISIC) 15

international trains 126
Trans-Siberian 39
Vietnam 127, 600
Internet 54
IP cards 52
Islam 747

J

Jade Dragon Snow Mountain
(YN) 679
Japanese encephalitis 30
Japanese occupation 254
Jet Li 561
Ji'nan (SD) 191
Jiang Zemin 83, 91, 385,
524
Jiangsu province (JS) 357–
389
Jiangxi province (JX) 432–
447
Jiayuguan (GS) 772–777
Jilin City (JL) 244
Jilin province (JL) 240–253
Jingdezhen (JX) 436
Jinggangshan (JX) 444
Jinghong (YN) 653
Jingpo Lake (HLJ) 237
Jinsha River 679
Jinuo 651
Jiuhuashan (AH) 429
Jiuxiang Caves (YN) 651
Jiuzhaigou (SC) 716
Journey to the West 95, 801
Jurchens 76

K

Kaili (GZ) 631–638
Kaili Minority Villages (GZ)
634
Kanas Lake. See Hanas Lake
Kangding (SC) 714

Karakorum Highway 42, 808,
812–815
Karakul Lake 812
karaoke 101
by the sea 212
See also every street corner
in China
Karmapa Lama 836
karst 609
Kashgar (XJ) 807
Kazakh 86, 783, 791
Khitans 76
Khunjerab Pass (XJ) 812
Kirin. See Jilin
Kongtongshan (GS) 765
Koreans 86, 247
Korla (XJ) 802
kosher 70
Kowloon (HK) 554–564
kuài. See currency
Kublai Khan 76
Kumbum Monastery (QH)
822
kung fu 289
Kunming (YN) 641–651
Kuqa (XJ) 804
Kyrgyz 86, 812
Kyrgyzstan
Bishkek 808

L

Labrang Monastery (GS) 762
Lahu 651
lakes
Bita (YN) 685
Bosten (XJ) 804
Dian (YN) 650
East (HUB) 465
East (ZJ) 401
Erhai (YN) 673
Hanas (XJ) 792
Jingpo (HLJ) 237
Karakul (XJ) 812
Long (SC) 719

Lugu (YN) 681
Mugecuo (SC) 716
Namtso (TBT) 848
Napa (YN) 685
Qinghai (QH) 823
Sayram (XJ) 796
Shouxi (JS) 388
Songjiang (JL) 246
Taihu (JS) 379
Tianchi (XJ) 788
West (ZJ) 395
Yamdroktso (TBT) 853
Yansai (HEB) 189
lamas 836
Lamma Island (HK) 582
Lan Kwai Fong (HK) 573
land cruisers 854
Langde (GZ) 634
Langmusi (SC) 723
languages
Cantonese 542
Chinese 87
Tibetan 834
Uighur 878
Lantau Island (HK) 579–582
Lanzhou (GS) 752–759
Last Emperor, The 244
Leishan (GZ) 635
Leshan (SC) 703
Lhasa (TBT) 837–848
Li Bai 95, 316, 737
Li people 87, 533, 540
Li River 611, 614
Li Yuan 75, 274, 304
Liaoning province (LN) 254–266
Lijiang (YN) 674–679
Linxia (GS) 759
literature 95
Little Red Book 81
Liu Bei 384, 738
Long March 79, 444, 638
Luding 713
Zunyi Conference 639
Longji Titian (GX) 619
Longmen Grottoes 295

Longsheng (GX) 616
Lu Xun 96, 398, 400
museums 152
residences 402
tomb 351
Lugu Lake (YN) 681
Luobulinka. See Norbulingka
Luoyang (HEN) 290
Lushan (JX) 439

M

Macau (MC) 583–596
accommodations 589
casinos 595
Coloane Island 594
food 591
intercity transportation 584
local transportation 586
money 584
nightlife 596
orientation 586
Taipa Island 594
visas and customs 584
mahjong 100
mail 49
Maitreya 751, 759
malaria 29
Manchu 86
Manzhouli (IM) 329
Mao Zedong 78, 142, 352, 446, 846
founding of PRC 143
mausoleum 143
mountains 238
residences 447
máotái 623
Marco Polo 76
Marco Polo Bridge 79, 165
markets
antique 175, 769
Barkhor (TBT) 844
flea 157
Fuli (GX) 614
Hong Kong Island (HK) 572

Hotan (XJ) 817
Kaili (GZ) 635
Kashgar (XJ) 811
Kowloon (HK) 563
marble 673
pearl 158
Qingping (GD) 506
Ruili (YN) 667
silk 158
Stanley (HK) 571
Xishuangbanna (YN) 659
Yangshuo (GX) 614
martial arts
Shaolin Monastery 289
study of 116
Wudang 471
MasterCard 18
May Fourth Movement 78, 142
medical care 33
Meilixueshan (YN) 687
Meizhou (GD) 529
Mencius 89, 207
Menghai (YN) 659
Menghan (YN) 658
Menghun (YN) 659
Mengla (YN) 662
Miao 87, 533, 540, 597, 631, 634
minority nationalities 86
minority travelers 69
mobile phones 53
Mogao Grottoes (GS) 781
money 17
Mongol 322
Mongols 86, 778
Monkey Island (HND) 539
monkeys 73, 352, 455, 604
malicious 710
photogenic 609
royal 380, 801
safety, and 62
staring 618
mosques
Crane (JS) 389
Emin Minaret (XJ) 800
Hohhot (IM) 321

Id Kah (XJ) 812
Kunming (YN) 648
Kuqa (XJ) 807
Nanguan (GS) 760
Nanguan (NX) 747
Niujie (BJG) 151
Qingjing (FJ) 490
Songjiang (SH) 355
Xi'an (SAX) 274
Mosuo 681
mountains
Cangshan (YN) 673
Cangyanshan (HEB) 180
Changbaishan (JL) 249
Danxiashan (GD) 516
Dinghushan (GD) 514
Drum (FJ) 482
Emeishan (SC) 706
Everest 862
Four Maidens (SC) 702
Friendship Peak 792
Gonggashan (SC) 714
Great Statue (GS) 769
Haba (YN) 679
Hengshan (HUN) 453
Hengshan (SX) 316
Huangshan (AH) 424
Huashan (SAX) 279
Jade Dragon (YN) 679
Jiuhuashan (AH) 429
Kongtong (GS) 765
Laoshan (SD) 215
Lushan (JX) 439
Mao Zedong (HLJ) 238
Meilixueshan (YN) 687
Paomashan 716
Phoenix (LN) 261
Purple Gold Mountain (JS) 363
Qilian 771
Qingchengshan (SC) 701
Songshan (HEN) 288
Taishan (SD) 200
Tanggula 819
Wudangshan (HUB) 471
Wutaishan (SX) 309
Wuyishan (FJ) 483
Yuelushan (HUN) 451
Moxi (SC) 712

Mudanjiang (HLJ) 236
Mulao 636
music 96
Mutianyu Great Wall (BJG) 167

N

Namtso Lake (TBT) 848
Nanchang (JX) 433
Nanchang Uprising 444
nangma 848
Nanjing (JS) 357–366
Nanning (GX) 600
Nanzhao Kingdom 668, 674
National People's Congress 91
nature reserves
Altun Mountain (XJ) 819
Shennongjia 468
Wolong (SC) 702
Wudalianchi 234
Zhalong (HLJ) 234
Zhangjiajie (HUN)
Naxi 87, 597, 674
music 677
1911 Revolution 459
Ningxia Hui Autonomous Region (NX) 741–751
Nixon, Richard 81
Norbulingka (TBT) 846
North Korea 42, 258
border 260
Northeast 223–266
Northwest 741–825
Nyalam (TBT) 864

O

octopus card 548
Olympics 84, 93, 100, 583
one-child policy 85
Opium War 77

outdoors 60
equipment 62, 694

P

painting 98
Pakistan
Sost 808
Palkhor Chode Monastery 856
Panchen Lama 836, 858, 860
pandas 73, 152
Breeding & Research Center 698
Red Panda Center 702
Research Center, Wolong 702
passports 12
Peking Man 166
Penglai (SD) 219
People's Liberation Army (PLA) 79, 833
ping pong 100
Ping'an Village (GX) 619
Pingliang (GS) 764
Pingyao (SX) 308
pinyin 89
see also appendix
poets
Bai Juyi 95
Du Fu 95, 697, 737, 768
Li Bai 95, 316, 737
Su Dongpo 95, 537
Xue Tao 699
Zhang Ji 373
police. See PSB
population growth 85
Poste Restante 50
Potala Palace (TBT) 843
Preface to the Orchid Pavilion 402
Public Security Bureau (PSB) 14, 24
Puning Temple (HEB) 185

INDEX

Puppet Emperor's Palace (JL) 244
pǔtōnghuà 87
Putuoshan (ZJ) 406
Putuozongcheng Temple (HEB) 186
Puxian, *bodhisattva* 711

Q

Qapqal (XJ) 796
Qiang 778
Qianlong, Emperor 77, 147, 164, 165, 185, 387, 388
Qiaotou (YN) 680
Qin Shihuang, Emperor 166, 199, 219
Qing Imperial Palace (LN) 257
Qingchengshan (SC) 701
Qingdao (SD) 207–216
Qingdao Beer Brewery 213
Qinghai Lake (QH) 823
Qinghai province (QH) 819–825
Qiqihar (HLJ) 232
Qomolangma. See Everest, Mount
Quanzhou (FJ) 487
Qufu (SD) 203
Qutang Gorge. See Three Gorges

R

rabies 32
Red Army 79
Red Cross 28
Red Guards. See Cultural Revolution
religion 89
rénmínbì. See currency
rivers

Ertix 789
Jinsha 679
Kelan 789
Li 611, 614
Mekong (YN) 687
Nine-Bend 486
Pearl 506
Shamu 637
Tarim 803
Wuyang 637
Yalu 258, 260
Yangzi 73, 359, 365, 679
Yellow 73
Zuo 604
rocks that look like
buddhas 165
buffalos 650
dragons 189, 486
elephants 609
lions 370
toads 186
tortoises 187
Romance of the Three Kingdoms 95, 294, 380, 384, 738
Ruili (YN) 666
ruins
Gaochang (XJ) 800
Jiaohe (XJ) 800
Silk Road 817
St. Paul (MC) 592
Subashi (XJ) 807

S

safety 25
wilderness 62
Sakya (TBT) 861
Sakyamuni 846, 856
Samye Monastery (TBT) 850
Sanlitun (BJG) 159
Sanya (HND) 537
SARS 32, 84, 546
Sayram Lake (XJ) 796
scorpions 430
sculpture 98, 99

Seven Star Crags (GD) 514
sexually transmitted diseases (STD) 32
Shaanxi province (SAX) 267–285
Shamian Island (GD) 506
Shandong province (SD) 191–222
Shanghai (SH) 333–357
accommodations 343
daytrips 354
entertainment 352
festivals 353
food 345
intercity transportation 335
local transportation 340
Nanjing Lu 349
nightlife 353
orientation 340
practical information 341
sights 348–352
Shanghai and the Yangzi Delta 333–411
Shanhaiguan (HEB) 187
Shantou (GD) 524
Shanxi province (SX) 303–316
Shao Hao 206
Shaoguan (GD) 514
Shaolin Monastery (HEN) 101, 117, 289
Shaoshan (HUN) 452
Shaoxing (ZJ) 398
Shapotou (NX) 750
Shelley St. (HK) 568
Shennongjia (HUB) 468
Shenyang (LN) 254–258
Shenzhen (GD) 520–524
Shibing (GZ) 637
Shigatse (TBT) 858
Shijiazhuang (HEB) 177
Shuangliang (YN) 674
Sichuan and Chongqing 689–740
Sichuan province (SC) 689–727

Siddhartha Gautama 90
Silk Road 75, 741, 772, 804, 807
  southern 818
SIM cards 54
Simatai Great Wall (BJG) 168
Singing Sands
  Dunhuang (GS) 782
Singing Sands Gorge (IM) 326
sky burial 848
snake meat 485, 504
snake wine 450
soccer 100
soft seat 46
solo travelers 67
Song Qingling 146, 351
Songpan (SC) 720
Songshan (HEN) 288
Songtsen Gampo 844, 847
Songzanlin Monastery (YN) 685
Sost, Pakistan 808
South Coast 476–541
Southwest 597–687
Special Economic Zone (SEZ) 92, 476
spelunking 763
spitting 93
staring 93
Stone Forest (YN) 650
student IDs 16
study abroad 112
  language schools 115
  martial arts 116
Su Dongpo 95, 537
Suifenhe (HLJ) 239
Summer Palace (BJG) 152
Sun Yat-sen 78, 357
  former residence 350, 511
  mausoleum 364
superlatives
  first Buddhist monastery in China 294
  highest lake in the world 848

highest mountain in the world 862
largest bronze temple in China 647
largest monastery in Tibet 847
largest salt lake in China 823
largest seated outdoor Buddha in the world 581
largest single-family cemetary in China 205
largest wooden statue in the world 185
longest covered escalator in the world 568
longest river in China 73
longest road and rail suspension bridge in the world 578
longest tobogganing lane in the world 231
lowest glacier in the world 687
tallest bungee jumping tower in the world 266
tallest TV tower in Asia 349
Suzhou (JS) 366–375

T

tai chi 101
Tai'an (SD) 196
Taihu, Lake 379
Taihuai Village (SX) 310
Taipa Island (MC) 594
Taiping Rebellion 77, 623
Taishan (SD) 200
Taiwan 79, 83, 94, 477
Taiyuan (SX) 304–309
Tajik 86, 813
Taklimakan Desert 803
Tanggu (TJ) 176
Tangkou (AH) 422
Tartar 86
Tashilhunpo Monastery (TBT)

860
Tashkurgan (XJ) 42, 813
tea 95
  Chinese Tea Museum 398
  eight-treasures 755
  gardens, Chengdu 697
  kung fu 528
  Longjing 397
  research center (FJ) 486
  silver needle 455
  teahouses (BJG) 157
teaching English 110
telephones 51
Temple of Heaven 148
temples
  Ancestral (GD) 509
  Azure Clouds (BJG) 162
  Azure Clouds (SD) 202
  Bamboo (YN) 648
  Big Buddha (GS) 770
  Bingling (GS) 757
  Bo'er (QH) 823
  Cold Mountain (JS) 373
  Confucius (JL) 246
  Dai (SD) 199
  Daming (JS) 388
  Dralhalupuk (TBT) 846
  Elephant-bathing (SC) 712
  Famen (SAX) 278
  Fayu (ZJ) 410
  Fuxi (GS) 768
  Gao (NX) 750
  Golden (YN) 647
  Golden Summit Huazang (SC) 712
  Great Bell (BJG) 155
  Great Buddha (HEB) 180
  Guangji (BJG) 152
  Haibao Pagoda (NX) 747
  Huiji (ZJ) 410
  Jade Springs (GS) 768
  Jietai (BJG) 165
  Jinshan (JS) 384
  Jokhang (TBT) 844
  Kaiyuan (FJ) 491
  Lama (BJG) 147
  Langmusi (SC) 724
  Linggu (JS) 364

Lingguang (GD) 532
Lingyun (SC) 705
Manfeilong Bamboo (YN) 660
Manjing (YN) 657
Matisi (GS) 771
Mengcius (SD) 207
Menghan Chunman (YN) 658
Nanguo (GS) 768
Nanputou (FJ) 497
Nantai (SX) 311
Puji (ZJ) 410
Pule (HEB) 186
Puning (HEB) 185
Putuozongcheng (HEB) 186
Ramoche (TBT) 846
Ruili (YN) 667
Shangqing (SC) 701
Sleeping Buddha (BJG) 162
Subashi (XJ) 807
Tanzhe (BJG) 165
Ten Thousand Buddhas (HK) 577
Tiantan (BJG) 148
White Horse (HEN) 294
White Pagoda (BJG) 152
Wong Tai Sin (HK) 562
Wudangzhao (IM) 327
Wuyou (SC) 706
Xilai (GS) 771
Xilituzhao (IM) 320
Xumifushou 186
Tengchong (YN) 664
Tengger Desert 748
Terracotta Warriors (SAX) 276
terrorism 23
theater 97
Thomas Cook 18
Three Gorges 734–740
dam construction 740
Three Kingdoms 418
Tian Tan Buddha (HK) 581
Tian'anmen Square 142
Democracy Movement 92
Tianchi Lake (XJ) 788
Tianjin (TJ) 169–176

Tianshui (GS) 765
Tiantan 148
Tibet Autonomous Region (TBT) 827–865
food 834
getting there 829
health 831
history 832
languages 834
people 834
religion 835
Tibet Tourism Bureau (TTB) Permit 14, 829
visas and permits 827
tiered pricing 19
Tiger Leaping Gorge (YN) 679
Tingri (TBT) 863
tombs
Abokh Hoja (XJ) 811
Ci Xi 164
Eastern Qing (BJG) 163
Hai Rui (HND) 536
Han Tomb Museum 389
Lord Bao (AH) 418
Mahao Cave (SC) 706
Maoling (SAX) 278
Ming (BJG) 163
Ming Filial (JS) 364
Nie Er 651
Nurhaci (LN) 258
Prince Yi De (SAX) 278
Puhaddin 389
Qian (SAX) 278
Qianlong 164
Qin Shihuang (SAX) 277
Wang Jian 699
Wang Zhaojun (IM) 322
Wei and Jin (GS) 776
Western Xia (NX) 748
Yue Fei (ZJ) 397
Yusup Khass Hajip (XJ) 811
tones 867
Tongli (JS) 375
Tongzha. See Wuzhishan.
transportation
air 43
land cruisers 854
trains 45

Trans-Siberian Railroad 39
Trans-Mongolian Railroad 127
travel agencies 34
traveler's checks 18
trekking
Ailao Terraces (YN) 656
Damenglong (YN) 661
Gonggashan (SC) 716
Hanas Lake 792
horse 721
Lugu Lake (YN) 682
Tiger Leaping Gorge (YN) 679
Xishuangbanna (YN) 653
Tsetang (TBT) 851
Tsingtao. See Qingdao
Tsong Khapa 832, 837, 847
Tsurphu Monastery (TBT) 845
Tu villages QH) 823
Tunxi (AH) 419
Turpan (XJ) 796, 801
Turpan Depression 796
Tuwa 793
typhoid fever 31
typhoons 25

U

Uighur 86, 778, 783
universities 113
Beijing 114, 137
Chinese University of Hong Kong 577
Fudan 115, 340
Hebei Teachers' University 179
Jiangnan 378
Jingdezhen Ceramics 115
Nanjing 360
Qiongzhou (HND) 541
Shandong University 221
Shenyang 115
Tianjin 172
Wuhan 115
Xiamen (FJ) 497

Yunnan 646, 648
Zhejiang 115, 393
Ürümqi (XJ) 783–789
Uzbek 86

V

vegetarians 69
Victoria Peak (HK) 568
Visa 18
visas 12
  Kazakhstan 789
  Mongolian 39
  Russian 40
visual arts 97
volcanoes
  Tengchong (YN) 665
  Weizhou (GX) 622
  Wudalianchi (HLJ) 234
volunteering 105

W

Wade-Giles 89
Wang Shuo 96
Wang Xizhi 398, 401, 402
Wannian Monastery (SC) 711
Wase (YN) 673
Water Banquet 293
waterfalls
  Changbaishan (JL) 251
  Diaoshuilou (HLJ) 238
  Guanputai (GZ) 630
  Huangguoshu (GZ) 629
  Mandian (YN) 657
Wei, Kingdom of 418
Weihai (SD) 219
Weizhou Island (GX) 622
Wen Jiabao 91
West Lake (ZJ) 395
Western Union 19
White Emperor City (CQ) 738
white-water rafting 457

wilderness 62
wildlife 73
Wolong Nature Reserve 702
Wong Kar-wai 100, 103, 556, 561
work permits 14
The World of Suzie Wong 574
Wu Gorge. See Three Gorges
Wu Zetian 75, 274, 278, 290, 295
Wuchang. See Wuhan
Wudalianchi (HLJ) 234
Wudang Boxing 475
Wudangshan (HUB) 116, 471
Wuhan (HUB) 459–465
Wulingyuan. See Zhangjiajie
Wuming (GX) 604
wushu 101
Wutaishan (SX) 309
Wuxi (JS) 375
Wuyishan (FJ) 483–487
Wuzhishan (HND) 540

X

Xi'an (SAX) 269–279
Xiaguan (YN) 668
Xiahe (GS) 760
Xiamen (FJ) 491–498
Xiangfan (HUB) 470
Xibo 793, 796
Xidi (AH) 422
Xijiang (GZ) 636
Xiling Gorge. See Three Gorges
Xincun (HND) 539
Xining (QH) 819
Xinjiang Uighur Autonomous Region (XJ) 782–819
Xishan (JS) 374
Xishuangbanna (YN) 651–662
Xizhou (YN) 674
Xu Beihong 147
Xuan Zang 274, 800
Xue Tao 699

Y

Yabuli (HLJ) 231
yaks 74, 718
Yamdroktso Lake (TBT) 853
Yan'an (SAX) 281
Yangshuo (GX) 611–616
Yangzhou (JS) 385
Yangzi Basin 412–475
Yangzi River 73, 359, 679
Yanji (JL) 247
Yantai (SD) 216
Yao 87, 619, 651
Yao Ming 100
Yecheng (XJ) 814
Yellow River 73
Yi 87
Yibin (SC) 725
Yichang (HUB) 465
Yinchuan (NX) 744, 747
Yining (XJ) 793
Yixian (AH) 421
yuan. See currency
Yue Fei 397
Yueyang (HUN) 454
Yulin (SAX) 283
Yumbulagang Palace (TBT) 852
Yungang Grottoes (SX) 315
Yunnan province (YN) 640–687
yurts 316, 322, 332, 792, 812, 849

Z

Zhang Liao 418

Zhang Yimou 99, 103, 308
Zhangjiajie (HUN) 456
Zhangmu (TBT) 864
Zhangye (GS) 769
Zhaoqing (GD) 512
Zhejiang Province (ZJ)
 389–411
Zheng Chenggong 496
Zhengzhou (HEN) 285–290

Zhenjiang (JS) 381
Zhenyuan (GZ) 637
Zhijin Caves (GX) 631
Zhongdian (YN) 682
Zhongshan (GD) 510–512
Zhongwei (NX) 748
Zhou Enlai 79, 402, 433,
 639, 781, 843
 former residence 350
 memorial hall 175

Zhoukoudian (BJG) 166
Zhu De 639
Zhuang 87, 619
Zhuge Liang 738
Zhuhai (GD) 517
Zöigê (SC) 723
Zoucheng (SD) 207
Zunyi (GZ) 638
Zuo River Scenic Area 604

MAP INDEX

Baotou 324
Beijing 122–123
  Metro 130
Beijing and the North Coast 121
Central Beijing 124–125
Central China 268
Central Macau 587
Central Nanjing 361
Central Shanghai 338–339
Central Wuxi 377
Changchun 242
Changsha 448
Chengde 183
Chengdu 692–693
Chongqing 729
Dali 670
Dalian 263
Datong 312
Dunhuang 777
Emeishan 708
Fuzhou 479
Guangzhou 500–501
Guilin 607
Guiyang 625
Haikou 535
Hangzhou 390
Harbin 227
Hefei 416
Hohhot 318
Hong Kong 544–545

Huangshan 426
Ji'nan 194
Jiayuguan 773
Jilin City 247
Kaifeng 297
Kashgar 809
Kowloon 555
Kunming 642–643
Lake Taihu 380
Lanzhou 753
Lhasa 839
Luoyang 291
Lushan 440
Macau Overview 585
Meizhou 531
Nanchang 435
Nanjing Overview 358
Nanning 601
Near Beijing 161
Near Xi'an 275
Ningbo 403
Northern Hong Kong Island 565
The Northeast 224
The Northwest 742–743
People's Republic of China xii–xiii
Putuoshan 407
Qingdao 208–209
Quanzhou 489
Qufu 204
Shanghai and Environs 336

Shanghai and the Yangzi Delta 334
Shaoxing 399
Shenyang 255
Shenzhen 521
Shigatse 859
Shijiazhuang 178
Sichuan 691
The South Coast 477
The Southwest 598–599
Suzhou 367
Tai'an and Taishan 197
Taiyuan 305
Tianjin 171
Tibet 828
Tiger Leaping Gorge 680
Turpan 797
Ürümqi 784
Wudangshan 473
Wuhan 461
Xi'an 270
Xiamen 492
Xining 821
Xishuangbanna 652
Yangshuo 611
Yangzhou 387
The Yangzi Basin 414–415
The Yangzi River and the Three Gorges 734–735
Yinchuan 744
Yining 795
Zhengzhou 287

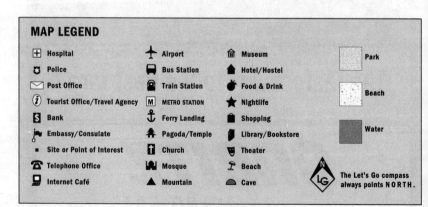

MAP LEGEND

✚ Hospital	✈ Airport	🏛 Museum	Park
🚓 Police	🚌 Bus Station	🛏 Hotel/Hostel	
✉ Post Office	🚂 Train Station	🍎 Food & Drink	Beach
(i) Tourist Office/Travel Agency	Ⓜ METRO STATION	★ Nightlife	
💲 Bank	⚓ Ferry Landing	🛍 Shopping	Water
⚑ Embassy/Consulate	🏯 Pagoda/Temple	📚 Library/Bookstore	
▪ Site or Point of Interest	🏛 Church	🎭 Theater	
☎ Telephone Office	🕌 Mosque	☂ Beach	Ⓝ The Let's Go compass always points NORTH.
💻 Internet Café	▲ Mountain	🕳 Cave	